D0221512

ACCOUNTING

A BUSINESS PERSPECTIVE

The Irwin Series in Undergraduate Accounting

Barr and Morris
Short Audit Case
Seventh Edition

Bernstein
Financial Statement Analysis: Theory, Application and Interpretation
Fifth Edition

Bernstein and Maksy
Cases in Financial Statement Reporting and Analysis
Second Edition

Boatsman, Griffin, Vickrey, and Williams
Advanced Accounting
Seventh Edition

Boockholdt
Accounting Information Systems
Third Edition

Brownlee, Ferris, and Haskins
Corporate Financial Reporting: Text and Cases
Second Edition

Dalton
1994 Individual Tax Return
Ninth Edition

Dalton
1994 Corporate Tax Return
Ninth Edition

Danos and Imhoff
Introduction to Financial Accounting
Second Edition

Dyckman, Dukes, and Davis
Intermediate Accounting
Third Edition

Edwards, Hermanson, and Maher
Principles of Financial and Managerial Accounting
Revised Edition

Engler
Managerial Accounting
Third Edition

Engler, Bernstein, and Lambert
Advanced Accounting
Third Edition

Engstrom and Hay
Essentials of Governmental Accounting for Public Administrators

Epstein and Spalding
The Accountant's Guide to Legal Liability and Ethics

FASB 1994-1995 Editions
Current Text: General Standards
Current Text: Industry Standards
Original Pronouncements Volume I
Original Pronouncements Volume II
Financial Accounting Concepts

Ferris
Financial Accounting and Corporate Reporting: A Casebook
Third Edition

Garrison and Noreen
Managerial Accounting
Seventh Edition

Hay and Engstrom
Essentials of Accounting for Governmental Accounting and Not-for-Profit Organizations
Third Edition

Hay and Wilson
Accounting for Governmental and Nonprofit Entities
Tenth Edition

Hendriksen and Van Breda
Accounting Theory
Fifth Edition

Hermanson and Edwards
Financial Accounting: A Business Perspective
Sixth Edition

Hermanson, Edwards, and Maher
Accounting: A Business Perspective
Sixth Edition

Hermanson, Strawser, and Strawser
Auditing Theory and Practice
Sixth Edition

Hermanson, Walker, Plunkett, and Turner
Computerized Accounting with Peachtree Complete® Accounting,
Version 6.0

Hoyle
Advanced Accounting
Fourth Edition

Jesser
Integrated Accounting Computer Applications

Koerber
College Accounting
Revised Edition

Larson and Miller
Financial Accounting
Sixth Edition

Larson and Miller
Fundamental Accounting Principles
Thirteenth Edition

Larson, Spoede, and Miller
Fundamentals of Financial and Managerial Accounting

Maher and Deakin
Cost Accounting
Fourth Edition

Marshall
A Survey of Accounting: What the Numbers Mean
Second Edition

Miller, Redding, and Bahnson
The FASB: The People, the Process and the Politics
Third Edition

Mueller, Gernon, and Meek
Accountin: An International Perspectie
Third Ediion

Pany and Whittington
Auditing

Pratt and Kulsrud
Corporate Partnership, Estate and Gift Taxaion, 1996 Edition

Pratt and Kulsrud
Federal axation, 1996 Edition

Pratt a Kulsrud
Individl Taxation, 1996 Edition

Raybu
Cost Aounting: Using a Cost Managnent Approach
Fifth ition

Robe on
Auditi
Seven Edition

Schrar
Accoting for the Small Business
Seco Edition

Schr der and Zlatkovich
A Sey of Accounting

Sho
Fun nentals of Financial Ac nting
Se h Edition

Sm and Wiggins
Re gs and Problems in Ac nting Information Systems

W ington and Pany
Pr ples of Auditing
E nth Edition

Y and Terry
C uter Accounting for Windows

ACCOUNTING

SIXTH EDITION

A BUSINESS PERSPECTIVE

ROGER H. HERMANSON, PH.D., CPA
Regents Professor of Accounting
Ernst & Young–J.W. Hollaway Memorial Professor
School of Accountancy
Georgia State University

JAMES DON EDWARDS, PH.D., CPA
J.M. Tull Professor of Accounting
J.M. Tull School of Accounting
University of Georgia

MICHAEL W. MAHER, PH.D., CPA
Graduate School of Management
University of California at Davis

IRWIN

Chicago • Bogota • Boston • Buenos Aires • Caracas
London • Madrid • Mexico City • Sydney • Toronto

Senior sponsoring editor: *Mark Pfaltzgraff*
Marketing manager: *Heather Woods*
Project editor: *Karen Smith*
Production manager: *Bette K. Ittersagen*
Designer: *Michael Warrell*
Part photos: *Arcata Graphics*
Cover art: *Al Held/VAGA, New York, 1994*
Art studio: *Arcata Graphics*
Art coordinator: *Heather Burbridge*
Compositor: *Bi-Comp, Incorporated*
Typeface: *10/12 Times Roman*
Printer: *Von Hoffmann Press, Inc.*

Library of Congress Cataloging-in-Publication Data

Hermanson, Roger H.
Accounting : a business perspective / Roger H. Hermanson, James Don Edwards, Michael W. Maher. — 6th ed.
p. cm. — (The Irwin series in undergraduate accounting)
Includes index.
Rev. ed of: Accounting principles. 5th ed. c1992.
ISBN 0-256-13195-3. — ISBN 0-256-16304-9 (annotated instructor's ed.)
1. Accounting. I. Edwards, James Don. II. Maher, Michael. III. Hermanson, Roger H. Accounting principles. IV. Title. V. Series.
HF5635.H54 1995
657—dc20 94-20946

Printed in the United States of America
1 2 3 4 5 6 7 8 9 0 VH 1 0 9 8 7 6 5 4

About the Authors

Professor Roger H. Hermanson, Ph.D., CPA
Regents Professor of Accounting and Ernst & Young–J. W. Hollaway Memorial Professor at Georgia State University. He received his doctorate at Michigan State University in 1963 and is a CPA in Georgia. Professor Hermanson taught and later served as chairperson of the Division of Accounting at the University of Maryland. He has authored or coauthored numerous articles for professional and scholarly journals and has coauthored numerous editions of several textbooks, including *Accounting Principles*, *Financial Accounting*, *Survey of Financial and Managerial Accounting*, *Auditing Theory and Practice*, *Principles of Financial and Managerial Accounting*, and *Computerized Accounting with Peachtree Complete III*. He also has served on the editorial boards of the *Journal of Accounting Education*, *New Accountant*, *Accounting Horizons*, and *Management Accounting*. Professor Hermanson is coeditor of the Trends in Accounting Education column for *Management Accounting*. He has held the office of vice president of the American Accounting Association and served on its executive committee. He is also a member of the Institute of Management Accountants, the American Institute of Certified Public Accountants, and the Financial Executives Institute.

Professor Hermanson has been awarded two excellence in teaching awards, a doctoral fellow's award, and a Distinguished Alumni Professor award; and he was selected as the Outstanding Faculty Member for 1985 by the Federation of Schools of Accountancy. He has served as a consultant to many companies and organizations. In 1990, Professor Hermanson was named Accounting Educator of the Year by the Georgia Society of CPAs.

Professor James Don Edwards, Ph.D., CPA
J. M. Tull Professor of Accounting in the Terry College of Business at the University of Georgia. He is a graduate of Louisiana State University and has been inducted into the Louisiana State University Alumni Federation's Hall of Distinction. He received his M.B.A. from the University of Denver and his Ph.D. from the University of Texas and is a CPA in Texas and Georgia. He has served as a professor and chairman of the Department of Accounting and Financial Administration at Michigan State University, a professor and dean of the Graduate School of Business Administration at the University of Minnesota, and a Visiting Scholar at Oxford University in Oxford, England.

Professor Edwards is a past president of the American Accounting Association and a past national vice president and executive committee member of the Institute of Management Accountants. He has served on the board of directors of the American Institute of Certified Public Accountants and as chairman of the Georgia State Board of Accountancy. He was an original trustee of the Financial Accounting Foundation, the parent organization of the FASB, and a member of the Public Review Board of Arthur Andersen & Co.

He has published in *The Accounting Review*, *The Journal of Accountancy*, *The Journal of Accounting Research*, *Management Accounting*, and *The Harvard Business History Review*. He is also the author of *History of Public Accounting in the United States*. He has served on various American Institute of Certified Public Accountants committees and boards, including the Objectives of Financial Statements Committee, Standards of Professional Conduct Committee, and the CPA Board of Examiners. He was the managing editor of the centennial issue of *The Journal of Accountancy*.

In 1974, Beta Alpha Psi, the National Accounting Fraternity, selected Professor Edwards for its first annual Outstanding Accountant of the Year award. This selection is made from industry, government, and educational leaders. In 1975, he was selected by the American Accounting Association as its Outstanding Educator.

He has served the AICPA as president of the Benevolent Fund, chairman of the Awards Committee, member of the Professional Ethics Executive Committee and Program for World Congress of Accountants. He is on the Education Standards Committee of the International Federation of Accountants and the Committee on Planning for the Institute of Management Accountants. He was the director of the Seminar for Management Accountants–Financial Reporting for the American Accounting Association. He is also a member of the Financial Executives Institute.

He received the 1993 AICPA Gold Medal Award, the highest award given by the Institute. A Doctor Honoris Causa (Honorary Doctorate) from the University of Paris was awarded to him in 1994. He is the first accountant to receive this distinction in France. The Academy of Accounting Historians awarded him the 1994 Hourglass Award which is the highest international honor in the field of Accounting History.

Professor Michael W. Maher, Ph.D., CPA
Professor of management at the University of California at Davis. He is a graduate of Gonzaga University (B.B.A.) and the University of Washington (M.B.A., Ph.D.). Before going to the University of California at Davis, he taught at the University of Michigan and the University of Chicago. He also worked on the audit staff at Arthur Andersen & Co., and was a self-employed financial consultant for small businesses while attending graduate school.

Professor Maher is the coauthor of two leading textbooks, *Cost Accounting* and *Managerial Accounting*. He has coauthored several additional books and monographs, including *Internal Controls in U.S. Corporations* (Financial Executives Research Foundation, 1980); and *Management Incentive Compensation Plans* (National Association of Accountants, 1986). His articles have appeared in *Management Accounting*, *The Journal of Accountancy*, *The Accounting Review*, *The Journal of Accounting Research*, *Financial Executive*, and *The Wall Street Journal*, among others.

For his research on internal controls, Professor Maher has been awarded the AICPA Gold Medal Notable Contribution to Literature Award and the American Accounting Association Competitive Manuscript Award. He has also been awarded the American Tax Association Manuscript Award, twice awarded the Outstanding Teacher of the Year award, and received a special award for outstanding service from the students of the Graduate School of Management, University of California at Davis. In 1989, Gonzaga University honored Maher with its Outstanding Alumni Merit Award.

PREFACE

Philosophy and Purpose

Imagine that you have graduated from college without taking an accounting course. You are employed by a company as a sales person, and you eventually become the sales manager of a territory. While attending a sales managers' meeting, financial results are reviewed by the Vice President of Sales and terms such as gross margin percentage, cash flows from operating activities, and LIFO inventory methods are being discussed. The Vice President eventually asks you to discuss these topics as they relate to your territory. You try to do so, but it is obvious to everyone in the meeting that you do not know what you are talking about.

Accounting principles courses teach you the "language of business" so you understand terms and concepts used in business decisions. If you understand how accounting information is prepared, you will be in an even stronger position when faced with a management decision based on accounting information.

We wrote this text to give you an understanding of how to use accounting information to analyze business performance and make business decisions. The text takes a business perspective. We use the annual reports of real companies to illustrate many of the accounting concepts. You are familiar with many of the companies we use, such as The Coca-Cola Company, The Home Depot, and Colgate-Palmolive Company.

Gaining an understanding of accounting terminology and concepts, however, is not enough to ensure your success. You also need to be able to analyze various business situations, work effectively as a member of a team, and communicate your ideas clearly. This text was developed to help you develop these skills.

Curriculum Concerns

Significant changes have been recommended for accounting education. Some parties have expressed concern that recent accounting graduates do not possess the necessary set of skills to succeed in an accounting career. The typical accounting graduate seems unable to successfully deal with complex and unstructured "real world" accounting problems and generally lacks communication and interpersonal skills. One recommendation is the greater use of active learning techniques in a reenergized classroom environment. The traditional lecture and structured problem solving method approach would be supplemented or replaced with a more informal classroom setting dealing with cases, simulations, and group projects. Both inside and outside the classroom, there would be two-way communication between (1) professor and student and (2) student and student. Study groups would be formed so that students could tutor other students. The purposes of these recommendations include enhancing students' critical thinking skills, written and oral communication skills, and interpersonal skills.

One of the most important benefits you can obtain from a college education is that you "learn how to learn." The concept that you gain all of your learning in school and then spend the rest of your life applying that knowledge is not valid. Change is occurring at an increasingly rapid pace. You will probably hold many different jobs during your career, and you will probably work for many different companies. Much of the information you learn in college will be obsolete in just a few years. Therefore, you will be expected to engage in life-long learning. Memorizing is much less important than learning how to think critically.

With this changing environment in mind, we have developed a text that will lend itself to developing the skills that will lead to success in your future career in business. The section at the end of each chapter titled, "Beyond the Numbers—Critical Thinking," provides the opportunity for you to address unstructured case situations, the analysis of real companies' financial statements, ethics cases, and team projects. For many of these items, you will use written and oral communication skills in presenting your results.

Objectives and Overall Approach of the Sixth Edition

Since the Fifth Edition was published, the Accounting Education Change Commission (AECC) has made specific recommendations regarding teaching materials and methods used in the first-year accounting course. As a result, significant changes are taking place in that course at many universities. The AECC states:

> The first course in accounting can significantly benefit those who enter business, government, and other organizations, where decision-makers use accounting information. These individuals will be better prepared for their responsibilities if they understand the role of accounting information in decision-making by managers, investors, government regulators, and others. All organizations have accountability responsibilities to their constituents, and accounting, properly used, is a powerful tool in creating information to improve the decisions that affect those constituents.[1]

In making the transition from primarily a preparer's focus to a balanced preparer's and user's focus, we elimi-

[1] Accounting Education Change Commission, *Position Statement No. Two*, "The First Course in Accounting" (Torrance, CA, June 1992), pp. 1–2.

nated chapters on special journals and partnerships and appendixes on (1) payroll and taxes and (2) inflation accounting. We also eliminated the following topics: the net price method for purchases of merchandise, the alternative closing method for a merchandising company, the voucher system, the direct write-off method for receivables, discounting notes receivable, recording capital stock issuances by subscription, and long-term bond investments. The coverage of certain other topics was shortened considerably or relegated to a chapter appendix. For instance, the work sheet for a merchandising company was placed in a chapter appendix.

We have, however, retained a solid coverage of accounting that will serve business students well regardless of the majors they select. Those who choose not to major in accounting, which is a majority of those taking this course, will become better users of accounting information because they will know something about the preparation of that information.

Revision Approach and Organization

Changes were made in every chapter, but several chapters deserve special mention. The chart below describes these specific changes.

Business Emphasis

Without actual business experience, business students sometimes lack a frame of reference in attempting to apply

Sixth Edition	Fifth Edition	Specific Changes
Chapter 1	Chapter 1	We now introduce the statement of cash flows in Chapter 1 along with the other three financial statements to give students a complete picture of the financial information that is the product of accounting. We provide a complete explanation and example of the statement of cash flows based on the Colgate-Palmolive Company in Chapter 16.
Chapter 2	Chapter 2	—
Chapter 3	Chapter 3	—
Chapter 4	Chapter 4	We incorporated some discussion of the evolution of accounting systems, from manual to computerized, into this chapter. That material was covered in Chapter 7 of the Fifth Edition.
Chapter 5	Chapter 12	The accounting theory material was moved forward to give students a theoretical foundation earlier in the text. The chapter now includes the information needs of investors and creditors as identified by the AICPA Special Committee on Financial Reporting (also known as the Jenkins Committee). This report and the committee's subsequent recommendations are important because they identify the kinds of information that investors and creditors need for decision making and are likely to have a significant influence on future FASB statements.
Chapter 6	Chapter 5	The work sheet for a merchandising firm was deemphasized and moved to a chapter appendix. The alternative closing procedure was eliminated to reduce the coverage of bookkeeping. The net price method was eliminated on the advice of reviewers that it is rarely used in business.
—	Chapter 7	We eliminated former Chapter 7, "Accounting Systems and Special Journals," on the advice of reviewers that this material is too mechanical and no longer relevant since manual "special journals" are increasingly giving way to modules in accounting software packages. Chapter 4 now includes some discussion of the evolution of accounting systems.
Chapter 7	Chapter 6	—
Chapter 8	Chapter 8	We eliminated the voucher system from this chapter. After deleting the chapter on special journals, it seemed natural to delete this material as well.
Chapter 9	Chapter 9	We deleted coverage of the direct write-off method for receivables and the discounting of notes receivable to further reduce the emphasis on preparing accounting information.
Chapter 10	Chapter 10	—
Chapter 11	Chapter 11	—
—	Chapter 13	After surveying professors at approximately 100 schools, we decided to eliminate "Partnership Accounting" since the corporate approach is now used throughout the text. Accounting majors will learn about partnership accounting in advanced accounting courses. An appendix to Chapter 1 contains a brief summary of the differences in the owners' (or stockholders') equity section of the balance sheet for the three forms of organization (single proprietorship, partnership, and corporation).

Sixth Edition	Fifth Edition	Specific Changes
Chapter 12	Chapter 14	The issuance of capital stock by subscription was eliminated because it is very procedural and not essential to the concept of issuing capital stock.
Chapter 13	Chapter 15	—
Chapter 14	Chapter 17	Since large international companies almost always prepare consolidated financial statements, we moved the coverage of international accounting from the theory chapter to Chapter 14, "Stock Investments—Cost, Equity, Consolidations; International Accounting." Covering those two closely related topics in the same chapter seemed to be logical.
Chapter 15	Chapter 16	The investment in bonds section was deleted to simplify the coverage in this chapter.
Chapter 16	Chapter 19	The statement of cash flows chapter is now covered before "Analysis and Interpretation of Financial Statements" (Chapter 17) because some of the techniques now shown in the analysis chapter rely on information in the statement of cash flows chapter. Chapter 16 has been completely reworked to focus on management's interpretation and analysis of this document rather than its preparation to help business students understand how to use this statement for making decisions. Again, the intent is to first present the basics of how this information is prepared, but then quickly shift the emphasis to understanding and using that information to make business decisions. The Colgate-Palmolive Company's statement of cash flows for 1993 serves as the basis for the analysis. In addition, many of the problems in the chapter are based on the statements of cash flows of other real companies.
Chapter 17	Chapter 18	This chapter centers on the 1993 annual report of the Colgate-Palmolive Company. New acetate inserts illustrate horizontal and vertical analyses using the Colgate-Palmolive Company's 1993 financial statements. In addition, many of the problems in this chapter are based on the financial statements of other companies. Business majors can use these techniques in analyzing companies throughout their careers. The analytical techniques learned in this chapter are useful to managers, creditors, and investors.
Chapter 18	Chapter 20 Chapter 21	This chapter provides an overview of managerial accounting and illustrates product costing in a job costing environment. To make the chapter less procedural, we removed some procedural discussions of documents, periodic inventory procedure, and the appendix on a work sheet for a manufacturing company. We moved material comparing variable and absorption costing from Chapter 24 in the fifth edition to an appendix to Chapter 18 so instructors could cover those product costing topics with the product costing chapters.
Chapter 19	Chapter 22	We added a section on spoilage and quality management to this chapter to demonstrate why managers interested in improving quality should be informed about the cost of spoilage.
Chapter 20	—	This new chapter was created to bring the text coverage of managerial accounting up to "the cutting edge." Activity-based management, activity-based costing, just-in-time production systems, and other quality techniques, including non-financial performance measures, are discussed in this chapter in terms of their implications for the improvement of quality. The chapter shows why managers need relevant accounting information to be competitive in the production environment.
Chapter 21	Chapter 23	—
Chapter 22	Chapter 24	We added a discussion on contribution margin financial statements and another section on the application of differential analysis to decisions to improve quality.
Chapter 23	Chapter 25	—
Chapter 24	Chapter 26	—
Chapter 25	Chapter 27	—
Chapter 26	Chapter 28	—

accounting concepts to business transactions. In this edition we sought to involve the business student more in real world business applications as we introduced and explained the subject matter.

- Each part opens with "**A Manager's Perspective,**" which features interviews with managers at The Coca-Cola Company. These opening vignettes provide insight into how managers in various areas in business (marketing, HR, finance, manufacturing, etc.) use accounting information to make decisions.
- "**An Accounting Perspective: Business Insight**" boxes throughout the text provide examples of how companies featured in text examples use accounting information every day.
- "**Accounting Perspective: Uses of Technology**" boxes throughout the text demonstrate how technology has affected the way accounting information is prepared, manipulated, and accessed.
- Some chapters contain "**A Broader Perspective**." These situations, taken from annual reports of real companies and from articles in current business periodicals such as *Accounting Today*, *New Accountant*, and *Management Accounting*, relate to subject matter discussed in that chapter or present other useful information. These real world examples demonstrate the business relevance of accounting.
- New real world questions were added to most chapters. New real world business decision cases were added to some chapters.
- The Annual Report Booklet included with this text contains significant portions of the 1993 annual reports of The Coca-Cola Company, John H. Harland Company, The Limited, Inc., and the Maytag Corporation. Many of the real world questions and business decision cases are based on these annual reports.
- Numerous illustrations adapted from *Accounting Trends & Techniques* show the frequency of use in business of various accounting techniques. Placed throughout the text, these illustrations give students real world data to consider while learning about different accounting techniques.
- Throughout the text we have included numerous references to the annual reports of over 75 companies. In fact, Chapter 17 and most of Chapter 16 are based on the 1993 annual report of the Colgate-Palmolive Company.
- Each of the first 16 chapters contains a new section entitled, "Analyzing and Using the Financial Results." This section discusses and illustrates a ratio or other analysis technique that pertains to the content of the chapter. For instance, this section in Chapter 4 discusses the current ratio as it relates to a classified balance sheet.
- Most of the chapters contain end-of-chapter questions, exercises, or business decision cases that require the student to refer to the Annual Reports Booklet and answer certain questions. As stated earlier, this booklet is included with the text and contains the significant portions of the 1993 annual reports of four companies: The Coca-Cola Company, Maytag Corporation, The Limited, Inc., and John H. Harland Company.
- Each chapter contains a new section entitled, "Beyond the Numbers—Critical Thinking." This section contains business decision cases, annual report analysis problems, writing assignments based on the Ethical Perspective and Broader Perspective boxes, and group projects.

Pedagogy

Students often come into accounting principles courses feeling anxious about learning the subject matter. Recognizing this apprehension, we studied ways to make learning easier and came up with some helpful ideas on how to make this edition work even better for students.

- Improvements in the text's organization reflect feedback from adopters, suggestions by reviewers, and a serious study of the learning process itself by the authors and editors. New subject matter is introduced only after the stage has been set by transitional paragraphs between topic headings. These paragraphs provide students with the reasons for proceeding to the new material and explain the progression of topics within the chapter.
- The Introduction contains a section entitled "How to Study the Chapters in This Text," which should be very helpful to students.
- Each chapter has an "Understanding the Learning Objectives" section. These "summaries" enable the student to determine how well the Learning Objectives were accomplished. We were the first authors (1974) to ever include Learning Objectives in an accounting text. These objectives have been included at the beginning of the chapter, as marginal notes within the chapter, at the end of the chapter, and in supplements such as the Test Bank, Instructors' Resource Guide, Computerized Test Bank, and Study Guide. The objectives are also indicated for each exercise and problem.
- Demonstration problems and solutions are included for each chapter, and a different one appears for each chapter in the Study Guide. These demonstration problems help students to assess their own progress by showing them how problems that focus on the topic(s) covered in the chapter are worked before students do assigned homework problems.
- Key terms are printed in another color for emphasis. End-of-chapter glossaries contain the definition and the page number where the new term was first introduced and defined. Students can easily turn back to the original discussion and study the term's significance in context with the chapter material. A "New Terms Index"—an alphabetical list of all key terms in the text with page numbers—is included at the end of the text.
- Each chapter includes a "Self-Test" consisting of true-false and multiple-choice questions. The answers and explanations appear at the end of the chapter. These self-tests are designed to determine

whether the student has learned the essential information in each chapter.

- In the margin beside each exercise and problem, we have included a description of the requirements and the related Learning Objective(s). These descriptions let students know what they are expected to do in the problem.
- Throughout the text we use examples taken from everyday life to relate an accounting concept being introduced or discussed to students' experiences.

End-of-Chapter Materials

Describing teaching methods, the AECC stated, "Teachers . . . should place a priority on their interaction with students and on interaction among students. Students' involvement should be promoted by methods such as cases, simulations, and group projects. . . ."[2] A new section entitled "**Beyond the Numbers—Critical Thinking**" at the end of every chapter is designed to implement these recommendations. **Business Decision Cases** require critical thinking in complex situations often based on real companies. The **Annual Report Analysis** section requires analyzing annual reports and interpreting the results in writing. The **Ethics Cases** require students to respond in writing to situations they are likely to encounter in their careers. These cases do not necessarily have one right answer. The **Group Projects** for each chapter teach students how to work effectively in teams, a skill that was stressed by the AECC and is becoming increasingly necessary for success in business.

A team approach can also be introduced in the classroom using the regular exercises and problems in the text. Teams can be assigned the task of presenting their solutions to exercises or problems to the rest of the class. Using this team approach in class can help reenergize the classroom by creating an active, informal environment in which students learn from each other. (Two additional group projects are described in the Instructor's Resource Guide. These projects are designed to be used throughout the semester or quarter.)

We have included a vast amount of other resource material for each chapter *within* the text from which the instructor may draw: (1) one of the largest selections of end-of-chapter questions, exercises, and problems available; (2) several comprehensive review problems that allow students to review all major concepts covered to that point; and (3) from one to three business decision cases per chapter. Other key features regarding end-of-chapter material follow.

- A uniform chart of accounts appears on the inside covers of the text. This uniform chart of accounts is used consistently throughout the first 11 chapters. The use of general ledger applications software with this edition necessitated the creation of a uniform chart of accounts. We believe students will benefit from using the same chart of accounts for all homework problems in those chapters.
- A comprehensive review problem at the end of Chapter 4 serves as a mini practice set to test all material covered to that point. Another comprehensive problem at the end of Chapter 19 reviews the material covered in Chapters 18 and 19. Two comprehensive budgeting problems are also included as business decision cases at the end of the budgeting chapter (Chapter 23).
- All end-of-chapter problem material (questions, exercises, problems, business decision cases, other "Beyond the Numbers" items, and comprehensive review problems) has been thoroughly revised. Each exercise and problem is identified with the learning objective(s) to which it relates.
- All end-of-chapter exercises and problems have been traced back to the chapters to ensure that nothing is asked of a student that does not appear in the book. This feature was a strength of the previous edition, ensuring that instructors could confidently assign problems without having to check for applicability. Also, we took notes while teaching from the text and clarified problem and exercise instructions that seemed confusing to our students.
- Many of the problems, comprehensive review problems, and business decision cases in the text can be solved using newly developed software. Those problems that can be solved using *General Ledger Applications Software* (*GLAS*), developed by Jack E. Terry of ComSource Associates, are identified in the margin with the symbol below.

This software package can also be used to solve the first two manual practice sets.

Many other exercises, problems, and business decision cases can be solved using *Spreadsheet Applications Template Software* (*SPATS*) developed by Jack Terry. The exercises and problems solvable with *SPATS* are identified in the margin of the text with the following symbol:

Supplements for the Instructor

A complete package of supplemental teaching aids contains all you need to efficiently and effectively teach the course.

Annotated Instructor's Edition This special instructor's edition of the sixth edition contains annotations in the margins to help instructors plan their lessons and teach the materials. There are four types of marginal annotations: (1) the *teaching notes* contain suggestions varying from simple examples that can be used in class to illustrate key concepts to alternative methods of presenting ideas; (2) the references to *transparencies* throughout the chapters indi-

[2] *Ibid*, p. 2.

cate that a *transparency* master is available to illustrate a particular topic; (3) the *reinforcing problems* indicate which exercises, problems, and cases reinforce coverage of a particular topic; and (4) the *check figure* annotations appear by exercises and problems and provide key answers. We hope you will find the annotated instructor's edition helpful.

Instructor's Resource Guide, Chapters 1–13 and Chapters 14–26 This guide contains sample syllabi for both semester- and quarter-based courses. Revised for this edition, each chapter contains: (1) a summary of major concepts; (2) learning objectives from the text; (3) space for the instructor's own notes; (4) an outline of the chapter with an indication of when each exercise can be worked; and (5) detailed lecture notes that also refer to specific end-of-chapter exercise and problem materials illustrating these concepts. Also included are (6) a summary of the estimated time, learning objective(s), level of difficulty, and content of each exercise and problem that is useful in deciding which items to cover in class or to assign as homework; and (7) teaching transparencies masters. The Instructor's Resource Guide for Chapter 17 contains a case study based on Hasbro, Inc. This company is the world's leading manufacturer and marketer of toys, games, puzzles, and infant care products. You may want to assign this case as a special project to individuals or to teams. The results of the analysis, with recommendations, could then be presented to the class.

Solutions Manual, Chapters 1–13 and Chapters 14–26 The solutions manual contains suggested discussion points for each ethics case as well as detailed answers to questions, exercises, two series of problems, business decision cases, other "Beyond the Numbers" items, and comprehensive review problems.

Solutions Transparencies Acetate transparencies of solutions to all exercises and *all* problems with increased clarity are available free to adopters. These transparencies, while useful in many situations, are especially helpful when covering problems in large classroom settings.

Financial/Managerial Accounting Teaching Transparencies An expanded set of approximately 150 teaching transparency acetates is available free to adopters. This set is in addition to the approximately 225 teaching transparency masters in the Instructor's Resource Guide.

Test Bank, Chapters 1–13 and Chapters 14–26 The test bank, *expanded and revised significantly in this edition*, contains approximately 4,500 questions and problems to choose from in preparing examinations. This test bank contains true-false questions, multiple-choice questions, short problems, and questions based on real companies for each chapter. Questions and problems are *classified by the learning objective* to which they relate.

Computest 4 This improved microcomputer version of the Test Bank allows editing of questions; provides up to 99 different versions of each test; and allows question selection based on type of question, level of difficulty, or learning objective. Computest 4 is available on 5.25″ and 3.5″ disks.

Teletest Teletest is an in-house testing service that will prepare your exams within 72 working hours after you phone the publisher.

Videos The Irwin Financial Accounting Video Library covers special topics such as the accounting cycle, merchandising, ethics, and international accounting. The Managerial/Cost Accounting Video Library covers topics such as computer-integrated manufacturing, service, and just-in-time inventory systems. The subject matter lends itself well to a visual approach in the classroom. A video guide is also provided.

The following items are intended for student use at the option of the instructor.

General Ledger Applications Software (GLAS) Many problems, business decision cases, and comprehensive review problems in the text can be solved using this software. GLAS is available on 5.25″ and 3.5″ disks and can be ordered with the text or as a separate item.

Spreadsheet Applications Template Software (SPATS) Many additional exercises, problems, and business decision cases can be solved using SPATS. It contains innovatively designed templates based on Lotus® 1-2-3® and includes a very effective tutorial for Lotus® 1-2-3®. SPATS is available on 5.25″ and 3.5″ disks. SPATS can be ordered with the text or as a separate item.

Peachtree® Complete III™ This leading business accounting software is available for site license by contacting your Irwin representative. The version you will receive is the actual "full-featured" commercial software being sold to many U.S. companies.

Computerized Tutorials, Chapters 1–13 and Chapters 14–26 These software packages by Leland Mansuetti of Sierra College include true-false and multiple-choice questions with explanations for both correct and incorrect answers. Upon adoption, these computerized tutorials are available to instructors for classroom or laboratory use. Tutorials are available on 5.25″ and 3.5″ disks and can be ordered with the text or as a separate item.

Supplements for the Student

In addition to the text, the package of support items for the student includes the following:

Study Guides, Chapters 1–13 and Chapters 14–26 Included for each chapter are learning objectives, a reference outline, a chapter review, and an additional demonstration problem and solution. If students use the study guide throughout the course, their knowledge of accounting will be enhanced significantly. The study guide is a valuable learning tool in that it includes matching, true-false, and multiple-choice questions, completion questions, and exercises. Solutions to all exercises and questions are also included.

Working Papers, Chapters 1–13 and Chapters 14–26 Two sets of working papers are available for completing assigned exercises, problems, business decision cases, other "Beyond the Numbers" items, and comprehensive review problems. In many instances, the working papers are partially filled in to reduce the "pencil pushing" required to solve the problems, yet the working papers are not so complete as to reduce the learning impact.

Check Figures A list of check figures gives key amounts for the problems, business decision cases, other "Beyond the Numbers" items, and comprehensive review problems in the text. Check figures are available in bulk, free to adopters.

Manual Practice Sets Four manual practice sets are available.

- *Dominion Lighting Company* illustrates special journals and includes a work sheet for a retailing company. This practice set can be used anytime after Chapter 9.
- *Aspen Mountain Camping Equipment Company* illustrates the use of business papers for a retailing company. It can be used anytime after Chapter 9.
- *Rocky Mountain Clothes Company, Inc.*, illustrates special journals and includes a work sheet for a retailing company. It can be used anytime after Chapter 9. This practice set is also available on our General Ledger Applications Software (GLAS).
- *Shelborne Manufacturing, Inc.*, by Leland Mansuetti and Keith Weidkamp, both of Sierra College, illustrates a job costing and process costing business simulation for a custom fencing business. This practice set can be used anytime after Chapter 19.

Computer Supplements The following computer supplements are available on 5.25″ and 3.5″ disks:

- *Granite Bay Jet Ski, Level One*, Second Edition, by Leland Manusetti and Keith Weidkamp, both of Sierra College, is a computerized simulation that can be used with any Principles of Accounting text using a single proprietorship approach. Level One is intended for use after coverage of the accounting cycle and accounting for cash (Chapter 8).
- *Granite Bay Jet Ski, Inc., Level Two*, Second Edition, by Leland Mansuetti and Keith Weidkamp, both of Sierra College, adds a corporate dimension to the business presented in Level One. It is intended for use after coverage of (1) plant assets and (2) current and long-term liabilities (Chapter 15).
- *Ramblewood Manufacturing, Inc.*, also by Leland Mansuetti and Keith Weidkamp, introduces students to job costing for a company that specializes in customized fencing. This full corporation simulation is intended for use after coverage of job costing (Chapter 18).

We are indebted to many individuals for reviewing the manuscript of this edition. In addition to those listed on the acknowledgments pages, we are especially indebted to colleagues and students at our respective universities for their helpful suggestions. Our families also provided needed support and showed great patience during the revision process.

Roger H. Hermanson
James Don Edwards
Michael W. Maher

Acknowledgments

The development of the sixth edition of *Accounting: A Business Perspective* was an evolving and challenging process. Significant changes are taking place in the first course in accounting in schools across the country, and the authors and publisher worked hard throughout the development of this text to stay on top of those changes. The sixth edition is the product of extensive market research including interviews with adopters and nonadopters and comprehensive reviews by faculty. In particular, we are grateful to the following individuals for their valuable contributions and suggestions.

Survey Participants

Diane Adcox
University of North Florida-Jacksonville

Sue Atkinson
Tarleton State University

Ed Bader
Holy Family College

Keith Baker
Oglethorpe University

C. Richard Baker
Fordham University

Audrie Beck
The American University

Joe Bentley
Bunker Hill Community College

Robert Bricker
Case Western Reserve

William Brosi
Delhi College

Doug Brown
Eastern Montana College

Stuart Brown
Bristol Community College

Janice Buddinseck
Wagner College

Kurt Buerger
Anglo State University

Bruce Cassel
Dutchess Community College

Stan Chu
Borough of Manhattan Community College

Bruce Collier
University of Texas-El Paso

Rosalind Cranor
Virginia Polytech Institute

James Crockett
University of Southern Mississippi

Lee Daugherty
Lorain County Community College

Mary Davis
University of Maryland

Frances Engel
Niagra University

J. Michael Erwin
University of Tennessee

Ali Fekrat
Georgetown University

Bill Felty
Lindenwood College

Clyde J. Galbraith
West Chester University

Susan D. Garr
Wayne State University

John Gercio
Loyola College

Martin Ginsberg
Rockland Community College

Earl Godfrey
Gardner-Webb College

Thomas Grant
Kutztown University

Paul W. Greenough
Assumption College

Roy Gross
Dutchess Community College

Vincent D.R. Guide
Clemson University

Paul Hajja
Rivier College

Joh Haney
Lansing Community College

Thomas D. Harris
Indiana State University

Dennis Hart
Manchester Community College

Mary Hatch
Thomas College

Margaret Hicks
Howard University

Patricia H. Holmes
Des Moines Area Community College

Anita Hope
Tarrant County Junior College

Andrew Jackson
Central State University

Donald W. Johnson, Sr.
Siena College
Glenn L. Johnson
Washington State University
Richard W. Jones
Lamar University
Ed Kerr
Bunker Hill Community College
David Kleinerman
Roosevelt University
Nathan J. Kranowski
Radford University
Michael Kulper
Santa Barbara Community College
Michael R. Lane
Nassau Community College
Judy Laux
Colorado College
Linda Lessing
SUNY-Farmingdale
Bruce McClane
Hartnell College
Melvin T. McClure
University of Maine
T.J. McCoy
Middlesex Community College
J. Harrison McCraw
West Georgia College
James E. McKinney
Valdosta State
B.J. Michalek
La Roche College
Andrew Miller
Hudson Valley Community College
Cheryl E. Mitchum
Virginia State University
Susan Moncada
Indiana State University
Susan Mulhern
Rivier College
Lee H. Nicholas
University of Northern Iowa
Kristine N. Palmer
Longwood College
Lynn M. Paluska
Nassau Community College
Seong Park
University of Tennessee-Chattanooga
Vikki Passikoff
Dutchess Community College
Barb Pauer
W. Wisconsin Tech Institute
Doug Pfeister
Lansing Community College
Sharyll A. Plato
University of Central Oklahoma
Patricia P. Polk
University of Southern Mississippi
Harry Purcell
Ulster Community College
T.J. Regan
Middlesex County College
Ruthie G. Reynolds
Howard University
E. Barry Rice
Loyola College in Maryland
Cheryl Rumler
Monroe County Community College
Francis Sake
Mercer County Community College
Jackie Sanders
Mercer County Community College
Alex J. Sannella
Rutgers University
Thomas Sears
Hartwich College
Sarah H. Smith
Cedarville College
John Snyder
Mohawk Valley Community College
Leonard E. Stokes
Siena College
Janice Stoudemire
Midlands Technical College-Airport Campus
Marty Stub
DeVry Institute-Chicago
Barbara Sturdevant
Delhi College
William N. Sullivan
Assumption College
Norman A. Sunderman
Angelo State University
Janice M. Swanson
Southern Oregon State College
Norman Swanson
Greenville College
Audrey G. Taylor
Wayne State University
Kayla Tessler
Oklahoma City Community College
Julia Tiernan
Merrimack College
John Vaccaro
Bunker Hill Community College
Al Veragraziano
Santa Barbara Community College
David Wagaman
Kutztown University
Karen Walton
John Carroll University
Linda Wanacott
Portland Community College

Jim Weglin
North Seattle Community College
David P. Weiner
University of San Francisco
L.K. Williams
Morehead State University
Marge Zolldi
Husson College

Reviewers

Wayne G. Bremser
Villanova University
Fred Dial
Stephen F. Austin State University
Larry Falcetto
Emporia State University
Katherine Beal Frazier
North Carolina State University
Al L. Hartgraves
Emory University
Emel Kahya
Rutgers University
Emogene W. King
Tyler Junior College
Charles Konkol
University of Wisconsin-Milwaukee
William Lawler
Tomball College
Keith R. Leeseberg
Manatee Junior College-Bradenton
Susan Moncada
Indiana State University
Lee H. Nicholas
University of Northern Iowa
Douglas R. Pfister
Lansing Community College
Patricia P. Polk
University of Southern Mississippi
Richard Rand
Tennessee Technical University
Ruthie G. Reynolds
Howard University
Marilyn Rholl
Lane Community College
William Richardson
University of Phoenix
Douglas Sharp
Wichita State University
Janet Stoudemire
Midlands Technical College-Airport Campus
Marilyn Young
Tulsa Junior College-Southeast

Annotations Authors

Diane Adcox
Instructor of Accounting
University of North Florida-Jacksonville
C. Sue Cook
Tulsa Junior College
Alan B. Cryzewski
Indiana State University
Patricia H. Holmes, CPA (Coordinator)
Des Moines Area Community College
Donald W. Johnson, Sr.
Siena College
Linda Lessing
SUNY at Farmingdale
Cheryl E. Mitchem (Coordinator)
Virginia State University
Lee H. Nicholas
University of Northern Iowa
Lynn Mazzola Paluska
Nassau Community College
Benjamin Shlaes, CPA (Coordinator)
Des Moines Area Community College
Margaret Skinner
SUNY at New Paltz
Leonard F. Stokes III, CPA
Siena College
Kathy J. Tam, CPA
Tulsa Junior College

Contents in Brief

Contents

PART IV

SOURCES OF EQUITY CAPITAL FOR MANAGEMENT'S USE IN PRODUCING REVENUES 430

CHAPTER 12
STOCKHOLDERS' EQUITY: CLASSES OF CAPITAL STOCK 433

CHAPTER 13
CORPORATIONS: PAID-IN CAPITAL, RETAINED EARNINGS, DIVIDENDS, AND TREASURY STOCK 464

Chapter 14 Stock Investments: Cost, Equity, Consolidations; International Accounting 500

Chapter 15 Long-Term Financing: Bonds 543

PART V

ANALYSIS OF FINANCIAL STATEMENTS: USING THE STATEMENT OF CASH FLOWS 576

CHAPTER 16
ANALYSIS USING THE STATEMENT OF CASH FLOWS 579

CHAPTER 17
ANALYSIS AND INTERPRETATION OF FINANCIAL STATEMENTS 620

PART VI

PRODUCT COSTING 672

CHAPTER 18
MANAGERIAL ACCOUNTING CONCEPTS/JOB COSTING 675

Chapter 19
Process Cost Systems 707

Chapter 20
Using Accounting for Quality and Cost Management 734

Part VII
Using Cost Information for Decision-Making 764

Chapter 21
Cost-Volume-Profit Analysis 767

ACCOUNTING

A BUSINESS PERSPECTIVE

Introduction

The Accounting Environment

You have embarked on the challenging and rewarding study of accounting—an old and time-honored discipline. History indicates that all developed societies require certain accounting records. Record-keeping in an accounting sense is thought to have begun about 4000 B.C.

The record-keeping, control, and verification problems of the ancient world had many characteristics similar to those we encounter today. For example, ancient governments also kept records of receipts and disbursements and used procedures to check on the honesty and reliability of employees.

A study of the evolution of accounting suggests that accounting processes have developed primarily in response to business needs. Also, economic progress has affected the development of accounting processes. History shows that the higher the level of civilization, the more elaborate the accounting methods.

The emergence of double-entry bookkeeping was a crucial event in accounting history. In 1494, a Franciscan monk, Luca Pacioli, described the double-entry Method of Venice system in his text called *Summa de Arithmetica, Geometric, Proportion et Proportionalite* (Everything about Arithmetic, Geometry, and Proportion). Many consider Pacioli's *Summa* to be a reworked version of a manuscript that circulated among teachers and pupils of the Venetian school of commerce and arithmetic.

Since Pacioli's days, the roles of accountants and professional accounting organizations have expanded in business and society. As professionals, accountants have a responsibility for placing public service above their commitment to personal economic gain. Complementing their obligation to society, accountants have analytical and evaluative skills needed in the solution of ever-growing world problems. The special abilities of accountants, their independence, and their high ethical standards permit them to make significant and unique contributions to business and areas of public interest.

You probably will find that of all the business knowledge you have acquired or will learn, the study of accounting will be the most useful. Your financial and economic decisions as a student and consumer involve accounting information.

Learning Objectives

After studying this Introduction, you should be able to:

1. Define accounting.
2. Describe the functions performed by accountants.
3. Describe employment opportunities in accounting.
4. Differentiate between financial and managerial accounting.
5. Identify several organizations that have a role in the development of financial accounting standards.

When you file income tax returns, accounting information helps determine your taxes payable. Understanding the discipline of accounting also can influence many of your future professional decisions. You cannot escape the effects of accounting information on your personal and professional life.

Every profit-seeking business organization that has economic resources, such as money, machinery, and buildings, uses accounting information. For this reason, accounting is called the *language of business*. Accounting also serves as the language providing financial information about not-for-profit organizations such as governments, churches, charities, fraternities, and hospitals. However, this text concentrates on accounting for business firms.

The accounting system of a profit-seeking business is an information system designed to provide relevant financial information on the resources of a business and the effects of their use. Information is relevant if it has some impact on a decision that must be made. Companies present this relevant information in their financial statements. In preparing these statements, accountants consider the users of the information, such as owners and creditors, and decisions they make that require financial information.

As a background for studying accounting, this Introduction defines accounting and lists the functions accountants perform. In addition to surveying employment opportunities in accounting, it differentiates between financial and managerial accounting. Because accounting information must conform to certain standards, we discuss several prominent organizations contributing to these standards. As you continue your study of accounting in this text, accounting—the language of business—also will become your language. You will realize that you are constantly exposed to accounting information in your everyday life.

Accounting Defined

Objective 1
Define accounting

The American Accounting Association—one of the accounting organizations discussed later in this Introduction—defines **accounting** as "*the process of identifying, measuring, and communicating economic information to permit informed judgments and decisions by the users of the information.*"[1] This information is primarily financial—stated in money terms. Accounting, then, is a measurement and communication process used to report on the activities of profit-seeking business organizations and not-for-profit organizations. As a measurement and communication process for business, accounting supplies information that permits informed judgments and decisions by users of the data.

The accounting process provides financial data for a broad range of individuals whose objectives in studying the data vary widely. Bank officials, for example, may study a company's financial statements to evaluate the company's ability to repay a loan. Prospective investors may compare accounting data from several companies to decide which company represents the best investment. Accounting also supplies management with significant financial data useful for decision making.

Reliable information is necessary before decision makers can make a sound decision involving the allocation of scarce resources. Accounting information is valuable because decision makers can use it to evaluate the financial consequences of various alternatives. Accountants eliminate the need for a crystal ball to estimate the future. They can reduce uncertainty by using professional judgment to quantify the future financial impact of taking action or delaying action.

Although accounting information plays a significant role in reducing uncertainty within the organization, it also provides financial data for persons outside the company. This information tells how management has discharged its responsi-

[1] American Accounting Association, *A Statement of Basic Accounting Theory* (Evanston, Ill., 1966), p. 1.

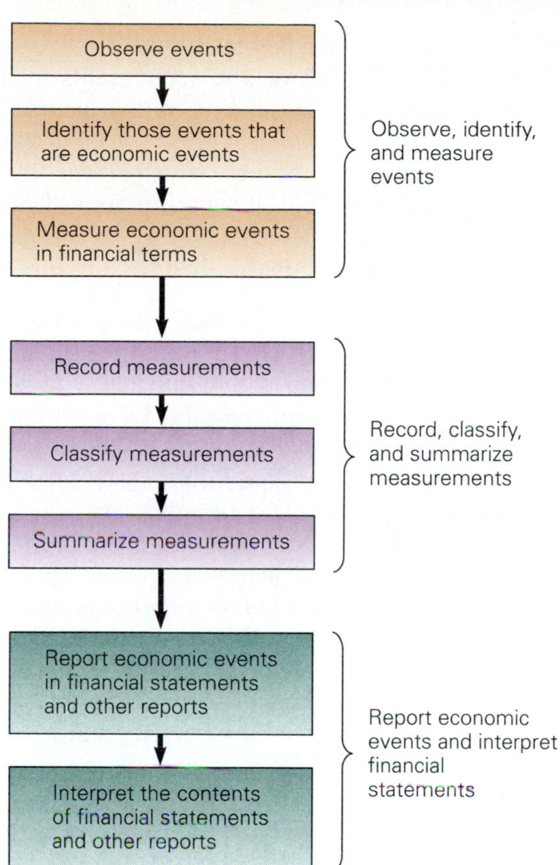

Illustration 0.1
Functions Performed by Accountants

bility for protecting and managing the company's resources. Stockholders have the right to know how a company is managing its investments. In fulfilling this obligation, accountants prepare financial statements such as an income statement, a statement of retained earnings, a balance sheet, and a statement of cash flows. In addition, they prepare tax returns for federal and state governments, as well as fulfill other governmental filing requirements.

Accounting is often confused with bookkeeping. Bookkeeping is a mechanical process that records the routine economic activities of a business. Accounting includes bookkeeping but goes well beyond it in scope. Accountants analyze and interpret financial information, prepare financial statements, conduct audits, design accounting systems, prepare special business and financial studies, prepare forecasts and budgets, and provide tax services.

Objective 2
Describe the functions performed by accountants

Specifically the accounting process consists of the following groups of functions (Illustration 0.1):

1. Accountants *observe* many events (or activities) and *identify* and *measure* in financial terms (dollars) those events considered evidence of economic activity. (Often, these three functions are collectively referred to as *analyze*.) The purchase and sale of goods and services are economic events.
2. Next, the economic events are *recorded, classified* into meaningful groups, and *summarized*.
3. Accountants *report* on economic events (or business activity) by preparing financial statements and special reports. Often accountants *interpret* these statements and reports for various groups such as management, investors, and creditors. Interpretation may involve determining how the business is performing compared to prior years and other similar businesses.

Employment Opportunities in Accounting

Objective 3
Describe employment opportunities in accounting

During the last half-century, accounting has gained the same professional status as the medical and legal professions. Today, the accountants in the United States number well over a million. In addition, several million people hold accounting-related positions. Typically, accountants provide services in various branches of accounting. These include public accounting, management (industrial) accounting, governmental or other not-for-profit accounting, and higher education. According to Bureau of Labor statistics, the demand for accountants will increase by 40% by the year 2000. This increase is greater than for any other profession. You may want to consider accounting as a career.

Public Accounting

Public accounting firms offer professional accounting and related services for a fee to companies, other organizations, and individuals. An accountant may become a **Certified Public Accountant (CPA)** by passing an examination prepared and graded by the American Institute of Certified Public Accountants (AICPA). As of May 1994, the CPA examination became a two-day exam given each May and November. The sections include business law and professional responsibilities, auditing, accounting and reporting, and financial accounting and reporting. The examination contains multiple-choice questions, other objective question formats, and essays or problems. Those who grade the exams consider effective writing skills an important factor when evaluating the essay questions. In addition to passing the exam, CPA candidates must meet other requirements, which include obtaining a state license. These requirements vary by state. A number of states require a CPA candidate to have completed specific accounting courses and earned a certain number of college credits (five years of study in many states); worked a certain number of years in public accounting, industry, or government; and lived in that state a certain length of time before taking the CPA examination. As of the year 2000, five years of course work will be required to become a member of the AICPA.

After a candidate passes the CPA examination, some states (called one-tier states) insist that the candidate meet all requirements before the state grants the CPA certificate and license to practice. Other states (called two-tier states) issue the CPA certificate immediately after the candidate passes the exam. However, these states issue the license to practice only after all other requirements have been met. CPAs who want to renew their licenses to practice must stay current through continuing professional education programs and must prove that they have done so. No one can claim to be a CPA and offer the services normally provided by a CPA unless that person holds an active license to practice.

The public accounting profession in the United States consists of the Big-Six international CPA firms, several national firms, many regional firms, and numerous local firms. The Big-Six firms include Arthur Andersen & Co; Coopers & Lybrand; Deloitte & Touche; Ernst & Young; KPMG Peat Marwick; and Price Waterhouse & Co. At all levels, these public accounting firms provide auditing, tax, and management advisory (or consulting) services. In recent years, teams of auditors, tax experts, and consultants have begun specializing in a particular industry (such as health care) and working together to serve the CPA firm's clients in that industry.

Auditing A business seeking a loan or attempting to have its securities traded on a stock exchange usually must provide financial statements to support its request. Users of a company's financial statements are more confident that the company is presenting its statements fairly when a CPA has audited the statements. For this reason, companies hire CPA firms to conduct examinations **(independent audits)** of their accounting and related records. **Independent auditors** of the CPA firm check some of the company's records by contacting external sources. For example, the accountant may contact a bank to verify the cash balances of the client. After completing a company audit, independent auditors give an **independent auditor's opinion or report.** (For an example of an auditor's opinion, see The Coca-Cola Company annual report in the separate annual report booklet you received with this text.) This report states whether the company's financial statements fairly (equitably) report the economic performance and financial condition of the business. As you will learn in the next section, auditors within a business also conduct audits, which are not independent audits.

Tax Services CPAs often provide expert advice on tax planning and preparing federal, state, and local tax returns. The objective in preparing tax returns is to use legal means to minimize the taxes paid. Almost every major business decision has a tax impact. Tax planning helps clients know the tax effects of each financial decision.

Management Advisory (or Consulting) Services Management advisory services comprise the fastest growing service area for most large and many smaller CPA firms. Management frequently identifies projects for which it decides to retain the services of a CPA. For example, management may seek help in selecting new computer hardware and software. Also, the auditing services provided by CPAs often result in suggestions on how clients can improve their operations. For example, CPAs might suggest improvements in the design and installation of an accounting system, the electronic processing of accounting data, inventory control, budgeting, or financial planning. In addition, a relatively fast-growing service area provided by CPAs is financial planning, often for the executives of audit clients.

Management (or Industrial) Accounting

In contrast to public accountants who provide accounting services for many clients, **management accountants** provide accounting services for a single business. Some companies employ only one management accountant, while others employ a large number. In a company with several management accountants, the person in charge of the accounting activity is often the **controller** or **chief financial officer.**

Management accountants may or may not be CPAs. If management accountants pass an examination prepared and graded by the Institute of Certified Management Accountants (ICMA) and meet certain other requirements, they become **Certified Management Accountants (CMAs).** The ICMA is an affiliate of the Institute of Management Accountants, an organization primarily consisting of management accountants employed in private industry.

Many management accountants specialize in one particular area of accounting. For example, some may specialize in measuring and controlling costs, others in budgeting—the development of plans for future operations, and still others in financial accounting and reporting. Many management accountants become specialists in the design and installation of computerized accounting systems. Other management accountants are **internal auditors** who conduct **internal audits.** They ensure that the company's divisions and departments follow the policies and procedures of management. This last group of management accountants may earn the designation of **Certified Internal Auditor (CIA).** The Institute of Internal Auditors (IIA) grants the CIA certificate to accountants after they have successfully completed the IIA examination and met certain other requirements.

A career in management accounting can be very challenging and rewarding. In recent years, management accountants have realized that to justify their positions they must add value to their organizations through their activities. Management accountants assist managers in implementing **total quality management (TQM).** This technique stresses constantly improving services, products, and the processes that produce them; empowering each member of the organization to make informed decisions; and exceeding customer expectations regarding quality. One tool that management accountants use to help accomplish these goals is

activity based costing (ABC). Activity based costing identifies the cost of producing a product or performing a service so the inefficiencies can be reduced or eliminated. Later chapters describe this tool in greater detail.

Governmental and Other Not-for-Profit Accounting

Many accountants, including CPAs, work in **governmental and other not-for-profit accounting.** They have essentially the same educational background and training as accountants in public accounting and management accounting.

Governmental agencies at the federal, state, and local levels employ governmental accountants. Often the duties of these accountants relate to tax revenues and expenditures. For example, Internal Revenue Service employees use their accounting backgrounds in reviewing tax returns and investigating tax fraud. Government agencies that regulate business activity, such as a state public service commission that regulates public utilities (e.g., telephone company, electric company, etc.), usually employ governmental accountants. These agencies often employ governmental accountants who can review and evaluate the utilities' financial statements and rate increase requests. Also, FBI agents trained as accountants find their accounting backgrounds useful in investigating criminals involved in illegal business activities, such as drugs or gambling.

Not-for-profit organizations—churches, charities, fraternities, and universities—need accountants to record and account for funds received and disbursed. Even though these agencies do not have a profit motive, they should operate efficiently and use resources effectively.

Higher Education

Approximately 10,000 accountants are employed in higher education. The activities of these **academic accountants** include teaching accounting courses, conducting scholarly and applied research and publishing the results, and performing service for the institution and the community. Faculty positions exist in two-year colleges, four-year colleges, and universities with graduate programs. A significant shortage of accounting faculty will probably develop due to the anticipated retirement in the late 1990s of many current faculty members. Starting salaries will continue to rise significantly because of the shortage. You may want to talk with some of your professors about the advantages and disadvantages of pursuing an accounting career in higher education.

Financial Accounting versus Managerial Accounting

Objective 4
Differentiate between financial and managerial accounting

An accounting information system provides data to help decision makers both outside and inside the business. Decision makers outside the business are affected in some way by the performance of the business. Decision makers inside the business are responsible for the performance of the business. For this reason, accounting is divided into two categories: financial accounting for those outside and managerial accounting for those inside.

Financial Accounting

Financial accounting information appears in financial statements that are intended primarily for external use (although management also uses them for certain internal decisions). Stockholders and creditors are two of the outside parties who need financial accounting information. These outside parties decide on matters pertaining to the entire company, such as whether to increase or decrease their investment in a company or to extend credit to a company. Consequently, financial accounting information relates to the company as a whole, while managerial accounting focuses on the parts or segments of the company.

Management accountants in a company prepare the financial statements. Thus, management accountants must be knowledgeable concerning financial accounting and reporting. The financial statements are the representations of management, not the CPA firm that performs the audit.

The external users of accounting information fall into six groups; each has different interests in the company and wants answers to unique questions. The groups and some of their possible questions are:

1. **Owners and prospective owners.** Has the company earned satisfactory income on its total investment? Should an investment be made in this company? Should the present investment be increased, decreased, or retained at the same level? Can the company install costly pollution control equipment and still be profitable?
2. **Creditors and lenders.** Should a loan be granted to the company? Will the company be able to pay its debts as they become due?
3. **Employees and their unions.** Does the company have the ability to pay increased wages? Is the company financially able to provide long-term employment for its workforce?
4. **Customers.** Does the company offer useful products at fair prices? Will the company survive long enough to honor its product warranties?
5. **Governmental units.** Is the company, such as a local public utility, charging a fair rate for its services?
6. **General public.** Is the company providing useful products and gainful employment for citizens without causing serious environmental problems?

General-purpose financial statements provide much of the information needed by external users of financial accounting. These **financial statements** are formal reports providing information on a company's financial position, cash inflows and outflows, and the results of operations. Many companies publish these statements in annual reports. (See The Coca-Cola Company annual report in the separate annual report booklet.) The **annual report** also contains the independent auditor's opinion as to the fairness of the financial statements, as well as information about the company's activities, products, and plans.

Financial accounting information is historical in nature, reporting on what has happened in the past. To facilitate comparisons between companies, this information must conform to certain accounting standards or principles called **generally accepted accounting principles (GAAP).** These generally accepted accounting principles for businesses or governmental organizations have developed through accounting practice or been established by an authoritative organization. We describe several of these authoritative organizations in the next major section of the chapter.

Managerial Accounting

Managerial accounting information is for internal use and provides special information for the managers of a company. The information managers use may range from broad, long-range planning data to detailed explanations of why actual costs varied from cost estimates. Managerial accounting information should:

1. Relate to the part of the company for which the manager is responsible. For example, a production manager wants information on costs of production but not on advertising.
2. Involve planning for the future. For instance, a budget would show financial plans for the coming year.
3. Meet two tests: the accounting information must be useful (relevant) and must not cost more to gather and process than it is worth.

Managerial accounting generates information that managers can use to make sound decisions. The four major types of internal management decisions are:

1. **Financial decisions**—deciding what amounts of capital (funds) are needed to run the business and whether to secure these funds from owners (stockholders) or creditors. In this sense, *capital* means money used by the com-

pany to purchase resources such as machinery and buildings and to pay expenses of conducting the business.

2. **Resource allocation decisions**—deciding how the total capital of a company is to be invested, such as the amount to be invested in machinery.
3. **Production decisions**—deciding what products are to be produced, by what means, and when.
4. **Marketing decisions**—setting selling prices and advertising budgets; determining the location of a company's markets and how to reach them.

Later chapters discuss managerial accounting in depth.

Development of Financial Accounting Standards

Objective 5
Identify several organizations that have a role in the development of financial accounting standards

Several organizations are influential in the establishment of generally accepted accounting principles (GAAP) for businesses or governmental organizations. These are the American Institute of Certified Public Accountants, the Financial Accounting Standards Board, the Governmental Accounting Standards Board, the Securities and Exchange Commission, the American Accounting Association, the Financial Executives Institute, and the Institute of Management Accountants. Each organization has contributed in a different way to the development of GAAP.

American Institute of Certified Public Accountants (AICPA)

The **American Institute of Certified Public Accountants (AICPA)** is a professional organization of CPAs. Many of these CPAs are in public accounting practice. Until recent years, the AICPA was the dominant organization in the development of accounting standards. In a 20-year period ending in 1959, the AICPA Committee on Accounting Procedure issued 51 *Accounting Research Bulletins* recommending certain principles or practices. From 1959 through 1973, the committee's successor, the **Accounting Principles Board (APB),** issued 31 numbered *Opinions* that CPAs generally are required to follow. Through its monthly magazine, the *Journal of Accountancy,* its research division, and its other divisions and committees, the AICPA continues to influence the development of accounting standards and practices. Two of its committees—the Accounting Standards Committee and the Auditing Standards Committee—are particularly influential in providing input to the Financial Accounting Standards Board (the current rule-making body) and to the Securities and Exchange Commission and other regulatory agencies.

Financial Accounting Standards Board (FASB)

In 1973, an independent, seven-member, full-time **Financial Accounting Standards Board (FASB)** replaced the Accounting Principles Board. The FASB has issued numerous *Statements of Financial Accounting Standards*. The old *Accounting Research Bulletins* and *Accounting Principles Board Opinions* are still effective unless specifically superceded by a Financial Accounting Standards Board Statement. The FASB is the *private sector* organization now responsible for the development of new financial accounting standards.

The Emerging Issues Task Force of the FASB interprets official pronouncements for general application by accounting practitioners. The conclusions of this task force must also be followed in filings with the Securities and Exchange Commission.

Governmental Accounting Standards Board (GASB)

In 1984, the **Governmental Accounting Standards Board (GASB)** was established with a full-time chairperson and four part-time members. The GASB issues statements on accounting and financial reporting in the governmental area. This organization is the *private sector* organization now responsible for the development of new governmental accounting concepts and standards. The GASB also has the authority to issue interpretations of these standards.

Securities and Exchange Commission (SEC)

Created under the Securities and Exchange Act of 1934, the **Securities and Exchange Commission (SEC)** is a government agency that administers important acts dealing with the interstate sale of securities (stocks and bonds). The SEC has the authority to prescribe accounting and reporting practices for companies under its jurisdiction. This includes virtually every major U.S. business corporation. Instead of exercising this power, the SEC has adopted a policy of working closely with the accounting profession, especially the FASB, in the development of accounting standards. The SEC indicates to the FASB the accounting topics it believes the FASB should address.

American Accounting Association (AAA)

Consisting largely of accounting educators, the **American Accounting Association (AAA)** has sought to encourage research and study at a theoretical level into the concepts, standards, and principles of accounting. One of its quarterly magazines, *The Accounting Review,* carries many articles reporting on scholarly accounting research. Another quarterly journal, *Accounting Horizons,* reports on more practical matters directly related to accounting practice. A third journal, *Issues in Accounting Education,* contains articles relating to accounting education matters. Students may join the AAA as associate members by contacting the American Accounting Association, 5717 Bessie Drive, Sarasota, Florida 34233.

Financial Executives Institute (FEI)

The **Financial Executives Institute** is an organization established in 1931 whose members are primarily financial policy-making executives. Many of its members are chief financial officers (CFOs) of very large corporations. The role of the CFO has evolved in recent years from number cruncher to strategic planner. These CFOs played a major role in restructuring American businesses in the early 1990s. Slightly more than 13,000 financial officers, representing approximately 7,000 companies in the United States and Canada, are members of the FEI. Through its Committee on Corporate Reporting (CCR) and other means, the FEI is very effective in representing the views of the private financial sector to the FASB and to the Securities and Exchange Commission and other regulatory agencies.

Institute of Management Accountants (IMA)

The **Institute of Management Accountants** (formerly the National Association of Accountants) is an organization with approximately 70,000 members, consisting of management accountants in private industry, CPAs, and academics. The primary focus of the organization is on the use of management accounting information for internal decision making. However, management accountants prepare the financial statements for external users. Thus, through its Management Accounting Practices (MAP) Committee and other means, the IMA provides input on financial accounting standards to the Financial Accounting Standards Board and to the Securities and Exchange Commission and other regulatory agencies.

Other Organizations

Many other organizations such as the Financial Analysts Federation (comprised of investment advisors and investors), the Securities Industry Associates (comprised of investment bankers), and CPA firms have committees or task forces that respond to Exposure Drafts of proposed FASB Statements. Their reactions are in the form of written statements sent to the FASB and testimony given at FASB hearings. Many individuals also make their reactions known to the FASB.

Ethical Behavior of Accountants

Several accounting organizations have codes of ethics governing the behavior of their members. For instance, both the American Institute of Certified Public Accountants and the Institute of Management Accountants have formulated such codes. Many business firms have also developed codes of ethics for their employees to follow.

Ethical behavior involves more than merely making sure you are not violating a code of ethics. Most of us sense what is right and wrong. Yet get-rich-quick opportunities can tempt many of us. Almost any day, newspaper headlines reveal public officials and business leaders who did not do the right thing. Greed won out over their sense of right and wrong. These individuals followed slogans such as: "Get yours while the getting is good"; "Do unto others before they do unto you"; and "You have done wrong only if you get caught." More appropriate slogans might be: "If it seems too good to be true, it usually is"; "There are no free lunches"; and the golden rule, "Do unto others as you would have them do unto you."

An accountant's most valuable asset is an honest reputation. Those who take the *high road* of ethical behavior receive praise and honor; they are sought out for their advice and services. They also like themselves and what they represent. Occasionally, accountants do take the *low road* and suffer the consequences. They sometimes find their names mentioned in *The Wall Street Journal* in an unfavorable light, and former friends and colleagues look down on them. Some of these individuals are removed from the profession. Fortunately, the accounting profession has many leaders who have taken the high road, gained the respect of friends and colleagues, and become role models for all of us to follow.

Many chapters in the text include an ethics case entitled, "An Ethical Perspective." We know you will benefit from thinking about the *situational ethics* in these cases. Often you will not have much difficulty in determining "right and wrong." Instead of making the cases "close calls," we have attempted to include situations business students might actually encounter in their careers.

Critical Thinking and Communication Skills

Accountants in practice and business executives have generally been dissatisfied with accounting graduates' ability to think critically and to communicate their ideas effectively. The Accounting Education Change Commission has recommended that changes be made in the education of accountants to remove these complaints.

To address these concerns, we have included a section at the end of each chapter entitled, "Beyond the Numbers." In that section, you are required to work relatively unstructured business decision cases, analyze real-world annual report data, write about situations involving ethics, and participate in group projects. Most of the other end-of-chapter materials also involve analysis and written communication of ideas.

In some of the cases, analyses, ethics situations, and group projects, you are asked to write a memorandum regarding the situation. In writing such a memorandum, identify your role (auditor, consultant), the audience (management, stockholders, and creditors), and the task (the specific assignment). Present your ideas clearly and concisely.

The purpose of the group projects is to assist you in learning to listen to and work with others. These skills are important in succeeding in the business world. Team players listen to the views of others and work cohesively with them to achieve group goals.

How to Study the Chapters in This Text

In studying each chapter:

1. Begin by reading the Learning Objectives at the beginning of each chapter.
2. Read "Understanding the Learning Objectives" at the end of the chapter for a preview of the chapter content.
3. Read the chapter content. Notice that the Learning Objectives appear in the margins at the appropriate places in the chapter. Each exercise at the

end of the chapters identifies the learning objective(s) to which it pertains. If you learn best by reading about a concept and then working a short exercise that illustrates that concept, work the exercises as you read the chapter. Use the forms in the Working Papers supplement for working these exercises.

4. Reread "Understanding the Learning Objectives" to determine if you have achieved each objective.
5. Study the New Terms to see if you understand each term. If you do not understand a certain term, refer to the page indicated to read about the term in its original context.
6. Take the Self-Test and then check your answers with those at the end of the chapter.
7. Work the Demonstration Problem to further reinforce your understanding of the chapter content. Then, compare your solution to the correct solution that follows immediately.
8. Look over the questions at the end of the chapter and think out an answer to each one. If you cannot answer a particular question, refer back into the chapter for the needed information.
9. Work at least some of the exercises at the end of the chapter.
10. Work any of the Problems assigned by your instructor, using the forms in the Working Papers supplement.
11. Study the items in the "Beyond the Numbers—Critical Thinking" section at the end of each chapter to relate what you have learned to real world situations.
12. Work the Study Guide for the chapter. The Study Guide is a supplement that contains (for each chapter) Learning Objectives; Reference Outline; Chapter Review; Demonstration Problem and Solution (different than in the text); Matching, Completion, True-False, and Multiple-Choice Questions; and Solutions to all Questions and Exercises in the Study Guide.

If you perform each of these steps for each chapter, you should do well in the course. A free computerized Tutorial is also available that you can use to further test your understanding. Ask your instructor about its availability at your school. Remember that a knowledge of accounting will serve you well regardless of the career you pursue.

I

Accounting: The Language of Business

Part Outline

A Manager's Perspective

Ogden Tabb
Deputy Director of Advertising
The Coca-Cola Company

Learning how the numbers fit together in the financial statement and understanding what those numbers mean is crucial. Students can either learn it now in their accounting principles course, or they're going to have to learn it later on the job.

As Deputy Director of Advertising I manage the advertising budget for the production of television, radio, and print advertising for all global brands including Coke, Diet Coke, Sprite, and Fanta. I have little involvement in the creative process;

my job is to produce the ads with an underlying responsibility for the finances. My objective is to get the most for our advertising production dollar.

I began my career at The Coca-Cola Company in the accounting department, and I still rely heavily on that discipline to cover the financial aspects of advertising production.

Estimates for each project are submitted by the ad agencies. These estimates are carefully reviewed on a line-by-line basis by our inhouse staff of executive producers. We know how much we should be paying for each element in the production process.

The lowest estimate is not always necessarily the best one, however, because of the intangibles that exist in advertising. Advertising is only one piece in the marketing mix that drives sales, so it's really hard to quantify what advertising does—we just know we have to do it.

My budget for each brand is based on how much the company plans to spend on media advertising. A general rule is to spend no more than 10% of that amount on production.

The bottom line is that we want great advertising with highest production values at a fair price.

1

ACCOUNTING AND ITS USE IN BUSINESS DECISIONS

The Introduction to this text provided a background for your study of accounting. Now you are ready to learn about the forms of business organizations and the types of business activities they perform. This chapter presents the financial statements used by businesses. These financial statements show the results of decisions made by management. Creditors, investors, and managers use these statements in evaluating management's past decisions and as a basis for making future decisions.

In this chapter, you also study the accounting process (or accounting cycle) that accountants use to prepare those financial statements. This accounting process uses financial data such as the records of sales made to customers and purchases made from suppliers. In a systematic manner, accountants analyze, record, classify, summarize, and finally report these data in the financial statements of businesses. As you study this chapter, you will begin to understand the unique, systematic nature of accounting—the language of business.

LEARNING OBJECTIVES

After studying this chapter, you should be able to:

1. Identify and describe the three basic forms of business organizations.
2. Distinguish among the three types of activities performed by business organizations.
3. Describe the content and purposes of the income statement, statement of retained earnings, balance sheet, and statement of cash flows.
4. State the basic accounting equation and describe its relationship to the balance sheet.

(*continued*)

FORMS OF BUSINESS ORGANIZATIONS

Accountants frequently refer to a business organization as an *accounting entity* or a *business entity*. A business entity is any business organization, such as a hardware store or grocery store, that exists as an economic unit. For accounting purposes, each business organization or **entity** has an existence separate from its owner(s), creditors, employees, customers, and other businesses.[1] This separate existence of the business organization is known as the **business entity concept**

[1] When first studying any discipline, students encounter new terms. Usually these terms are set in boldface color and defined at their first occurrence. The boldface color terms are also listed and defined at the end of each chapter (see pages 35–36 in this chapter). After the definition of the term in the term list, a page number in parentheses indicates where the term is discussed in the chapter.

(concluded)

5. Using the underlying assumptions or concepts, analyze business transactions and determine their effects on items in the financial statements.
6. Prepare an income statement, a statement of retained earnings, and a balance sheet.
7. Analyze and use the financial results—the equity ratio.

Thus, in the accounting records of the business entity, the activities of each business should be kept separate from the activities of other businesses and from the personal financial activities of the owner(s).

Assume, for example, that you own two businesses, a physical fitness center and a horse stable. According to the business entity concept, you would consider each business as an independent business unit. Thus, you would normally keep separate accounting records for each business. Now assume your physical fitness center is unprofitable because you are not charging enough for the use of your exercise equipment. You can determine this fact because you are treating your physical fitness center and horse stable as two separate business entities. You must also keep your personal financial activities separate from your two businesses. Therefore, you cannot include the car you drive only for personal use as a business activity of your physical fitness center or your horse stable. However, the use of your truck to pick up feed for your horse stable is a business activity of your horse stable.

As you will see shortly, the business entity concept applies to the three forms of businesses—single proprietorships, partnerships, and corporations. Thus, for accounting purposes, all three business forms are separate from other business entities and from their owner(s). Although corporations are also legally separate from their owners, this is not true for single proprietorships and partnerships. We use the corporate approach in this text and include only a brief discussion of single proprietorships and partnerships.

Single Proprietorship

Objective 1
Identify and describe the three basic forms of business organizations.[2]

A **single proprietorship** is an unincorporated business owned by an individual and often managed by that same person. Single proprietors include physicians, lawyers, electricians, and other people in business for themselves. Many small service businesses and retail establishments are also single proprietorships. No legal formalities are necessary to organize such businesses, and usually business operations can begin with only a limited investment.

In a single proprietorship, the owner is solely responsible for all debts of the business. For accounting purposes, however, the business is a separate entity from the owner. Thus, single proprietors must keep the financial activities of the business, such as the receipt of fees from selling services to the public, separate from their personal financial activities. For example, owners of single proprietorships should not enter the cost of personal houses or car payments in the financial records of their businesses.

Partnership

A **partnership** is an unincorporated business owned by two or more persons associated as partners. Often the same persons who own the business also manage the business. Many small retail establishments and professional practices, such as dentists, physicians, attorneys, and many CPA firms, are partnerships.

A partnership begins with a verbal or written agreement. A written agreement is preferable because it provides a permanent record of the terms of the partnership. These terms include the initial investment of each partner, the duties of each partner, the means of dividing profits or losses between the partners each year, and the settlement after the death or withdrawal of a partner. Each partner may be held liable for all the debts of the partnership and for the actions of each partner within the scope of the business. However, as with the single proprietorship, for accounting purposes, the partnership is a separate business entity.

---

[2] After reading a portion of text material that covers a certain learning objective, some students immediately want to work an exercise that illustrates that material. The exercises at the end of each chapter are labeled with the learning objective to which they pertain. For instance, turn to pages 37–39 to see which learning objective(s) each exercise covers in Chapter 1.

Corporation

A **corporation** is a business incorporated under the laws of a state and owned by a few stockholders or thousands of stockholders. Almost all large businesses and many small businesses are incorporated.

The corporation is unique in that it is a separate legal business entity. The owners of the corporation are **stockholders or shareholders.** They buy shares of stock, which are units of ownership, in the corporation. Should the corporation fail, the owners would only lose the amount they paid for their stock. The corporate form of business protects the personal assets of the owners from the creditors of the corporation.[3]

Stockholders do not directly manage the corporation. They elect a board of directors to represent their interests. The board of directors selects the officers of the corporation, such as the president and vice presidents, who manage the corporation for the stockholders.

Accounting is necessary for all three forms of business organizations, and each company must follow generally accepted accounting principles (GAAP). Since corporations have such an important impact on our economy, we use them in this text to illustrate basic accounting principles and concepts.

An Accounting Perspective

Business Insight Although corporations constitute about 17% of all business organizations, they account for almost 90% of all sales volume. Single proprietorships constitute about 75% of all business organizations but account for less than 10% of sales volume.

Types of Activities Performed by Business Organizations

Objective 2
Distinguish among the three types of activities performed by business organizations.

The forms of business entities discussed in the previous section are classified according to the type of ownership of the business entity. Business entities can also be grouped by the type of business activities they perform—service companies, merchandising companies, and manufacturing companies. Any of these activities can be performed by companies using any of the three forms of business organizations.

1. **Service companies** perform services for a fee. This group includes accounting firms, law firms, and dry cleaning establishments. The early chapters of this text describe accounting for service companies.
2. **Merchandising companies** purchase goods that are ready for sale and then sell them to customers. Merchandising companies include auto dealerships, clothing stores, and supermarkets. We begin the description of accounting for merchandising companies in Chapter 6.
3. **Manufacturing companies** buy materials, convert them into products, and then sell the products to other companies or to the final consumers. Manufacturing companies include steel mills, auto manufacturers, and clothing manufacturers. We begin our coverage of manufacturing accounting in Chapter 18.

All of these companies produce financial statements as the final end product of their accounting process. These financial statements provide relevant financial information both to those inside the company—management—and to those outside the company—creditors, stockholders, and other interested parties. The next section introduces four common financial statements—the income statement, the statement of retained earnings, the balance sheet, and the statement of cash flows.

---

[3] When individuals seek a bank loan to finance the formation of a small corporation, the bank often requires those individuals to sign documents making them personally responsible for repaying the loan if the corporation cannot pay. In this instance, the individuals can lose their original investments plus the amount of the loan they are obligated to repay.

Financial Statements of Business Organizations

Objective 3
Describe the content and purposes of the income statement, statement of retained earnings, balance sheet, and statement of cash flows.

Business entities may have many objectives and goals. For example, one of your objectives in owning a physical fitness center may be to improve *your* physical fitness. However, the two primary objectives of every business are profitability and solvency. **Profitability** is the ability to generate income. **Solvency** is the ability to pay debts as they become due. Unless a business can produce satisfactory income and pay its debts as they become due, the business cannot survive to realize its other objectives.

The financial statement that reflects a company's profitability is the **income statement.** The **statement of retained earnings** shows the change in retained earnings between the beginning and end of a period (e.g., a month or a year). The **balance sheet** reflects a company's solvency. The **statement of cash flows** shows the cash inflows and outflows for a company over a period of time. The headings and elements of each statement are similar from company to company. You have probably noticed this similarity in the financial statements of actual companies in the annual report booklet.

The Income Statement

The **income statement,** sometimes called an earnings statement, reports the profitability of a business organization for a *stated period of time*. In accounting, we measure profitability for a period, such as a month or year, by comparing the revenues generated with the expenses incurred to produce these revenues. **Revenues** are the inflows of assets (such as cash) resulting from the sale of products or the rendering of services to customers. We measure revenues by the prices agreed on in the exchanges in which a business delivers goods or renders services. **Expenses** are the costs incurred to produce revenues. Expenses are measured by the assets surrendered or consumed in serving customers. If the revenues of a period exceed the expenses of the same period, **net income** results. Thus,

$$\text{Net income} = \text{Revenues} - \text{Expenses}$$

Net income is often called the *earnings* of the company. When expenses exceed revenues, the business has a **net loss,** and it has operated unprofitably.

In Illustration 1.1, Part A shows the income statement of Metro Courier, Inc., for July 1997. This California corporation performs courier delivery services of documents and packages in San Diego.

Metro's income statement for the month ended July 31, 1997, shows that the revenues (or delivery fees) generated by serving customers for July totaled $5,700. Expenses for the month amounted to $3,600. As a result of these business activities, Metro's net income for July was $2,100. To determine its net income, the company subtracts its expenses of $3,600 from its revenues of $5,700. Even though corporations are taxable entities, we ignore corporate income taxes at this point.

The Statement of Retained Earnings

One purpose of the *statement of retained earnings* is to connect the income statement and the balance sheet. The **statement of retained earnings** explains the changes in retained earnings between two balance sheet dates. These changes usually consist of the addition of net income (or deduction of net loss) and the deduction of dividends.

Dividends are the means by which a corporation rewards its stockholders (owners) for providing it with investment funds. A **dividend** is a payment (usually of cash) to the owners of the business; it is a distribution of income to owners rather than an expense of doing business. Because dividends are not an expense, they do not appear on the income statement.

The effect of a dividend is to reduce cash and retained earnings by the amount paid out. Then, the company no longer retains a portion of the income earnings but passes it on to the stockholders. Earning dividends is, of course, one of the primary reasons people invest in corporations.

ILLUSTRATION 1.1

A. Income Statement

METRO COURIER, INC.
Income Statement
For the Month Ended July 31, 1997

Revenues:		
Service revenue		$5,700
Expenses:		
Salaries expense	$2,600	
Rent expense	400	
Gas and oil expense	600	
Total expenses		3,600
Net income		$2,100

B. Statement of Retained Earnings

METRO COURIER, INC.
Statement of Retained Earnings
For the Month Ended July 31, 1997

Retained earnings, July 1	$-0-
Add: Net income for July	2,100
Retained earnings, July 31	$2,100

C. Balance Sheet

METRO COURIER, INC.
Balance Sheet
July 31, 1997

Assets		Liabilities and Stockholders' Equity*	
Cash	$15,500	Liabilities:	
Accounts receivable	700	Accounts payable	$ 600
Trucks	20,000	Notes payable	6,000
Office equipment	2,500	Total liabilities	$ 6,600
		Stockholders' equity:	
		Capital stock	$30,000
		Retained earnings	2,100
		Total stockholders' equity	$32,100
Total assets	$38,700	Total liabilities and stockholders' equity	$38,700

* The liabilities and stockholders' equity portion of the balance sheet may be shown directly beneath the assets instead of to the right of them, as shown here. When liabilities and stockholders' equity are placed under the assets, the balance sheet is in the *vertical format* or *report form*. The vertical format is as acceptable as the *horizontal format* (or account form) used above.

The statement of retained earnings for Metro Courier, Inc., for July 1997 is relatively simple (see Part B of Illustration 1.1). Organized on June 1, Metro did not earn any revenues or incur any expenses during June. So Metro's beginning retained earnings balance on July 1 is zero. Metro then adds its $2,100 net income for July. Since Metro paid no dividends in July, the $2,100 would be the ending balance.

Next, Metro carries this $2,100 ending balance in retained earnings to the balance sheet (Part C). If there had been a net loss, it would have deducted the loss from the beginning balance on the statement of retained earnings. For instance, if during the next month (August) there is a net loss of $500, the loss would be deducted from the beginning balance in retained earnings of $2,100. The retained earnings balance at the end of August would be $1,600.

Dividends could also have affected the Retained Earnings balance. To give a more realistic illustration, assume that (1) Metro Courier, Inc.'s net income for August was actually $1,500 (revenues of $5,600 less expenses of $4,100) and (2) the company declared and paid dividends of $1,000. Then, Metro's statement of retained earnings for August would be:

METRO COURIER, INC.
Statement of Retained Earnings
For the Month Ended August 31, 1997

Retained earnings, August 1	$2,100
Add: Net income for August	1,500
Total	$3,600
Less: Dividends	1,000
Retained earnings, August 31	$2,600

The Balance Sheet

The **balance sheet,** sometimes called the *statement of financial position,* lists the company's assets, liabilities, and stockholders' equity (including dollar amounts) as of a specific moment in time. That specific moment is the close of business on the date of the balance sheet. Notice how the heading of the balance sheet differs from the headings on the income statement and statement of retained earnings. A balance sheet is like a photograph; it captures the financial position of a company at a particular *point* in time. The other two statements are for a *period* of time. As you study about the assets, liabilities, and stockholders' equity contained in a balance sheet, you will understand why this financial statement provides information about the solvency of the business.

Assets are things of value owned by the business. They are also called the *resources* of the business. Examples include cash, machines, and buildings. Assets have value because a business can use or exchange them to produce the services or products of the business. In Part C of Illustration 1.1, the assets of Metro Courier, Inc., amount to $38,700. Metro's assets consist of cash, **accounts receivable** (amounts due from customers for services previously rendered), trucks, and office equipment.

Liabilities are the debts owed by a business. Typically, a business must pay its debts by certain dates. A business incurs many of its liabilities by purchasing items on credit. Metro's liabilities consist of **accounts payable** (amounts owed to suppliers for previous purchases) and **notes payable** (written promises to pay a specific sum of money) totaling $6,600.[4]

Metro Courier, Inc., is a corporation. The owners' interest in a corporation is referred to as **stockholders' equity.** Metro's stockholders' equity consists of (1) $30,000 paid for shares of capital stock and (2) retained earnings of $2,100. **Capital stock** shows the amount of the owners' investment in the corporation. **Retained earnings** generally consists of the accumulated net income of the corporation minus dividends distributed to stockholders. We discuss these items later in the text. At this point, simply note that the balance sheet heading includes the name of the organization and the title and date of the statement. Notice also that the dollar amount of the total assets is equal to the claims on (or interest in) those assets. The balance sheet shows these claims under the heading "Liabilities and Stockholders' Equity."

The Statement of Cash Flows

Management is interested in the cash inflows to the company and the cash outflows from the company because these determine the company's liquidity—its ability to pay its bills when due. The **statement of cash flows** shows the cash inflows and cash outflows from operating, investing, and financing activities. *Operating activities* generally include the cash effects of transactions and other events that enter into the determination of net income. *Investing activities* gener-

[4] Most notes bear interest, but in this chapter we assume that all notes bear no interest. Interest is an amount paid by the borrower to the lender (in addition to the amount of the loan) for use of the money over time.

ally include business transactions involving the acquisition or disposal of long-term assets such as land, buildings, and equipment. *Financing activities* generally include the cash effects of transactions and other events involving creditors and owners (stockholders).

Chapter 16 describes the statement of cash flows in detail. Our purpose here is to merely introduce this important financial statement. Normally, a firm prepares a statement of cash flows for the same time period as the income statement. The following statement, however, shows the cash inflows and outflows for Metro Courier, Inc., since it was formed on June 1, 1997. Thus, this cash flow statement is for two months.

METRO COURIER, INC.
Statement of Cash Flows
For the Two-Month Period Ended July 31, 1997

Cash flows from operating activities:		
Net income	$ 2,100	
Adjustments to reconcile net income to net cash provided by operating activities:		
Increase in accounts receivable	(700)	
Increase in accounts payable	600	
Net cash provided by operating activities		$ 2,000
Cash flows from investing activities:		
Purchase of trucks	$(20,000)	
Purchase of office equipment	(2,500)	
Net cash used by investing activities		(22,500)
Cash flows from financing activities:		
Proceeds from notes payable	$ 6,000	
Proceeds from sale of capital stock	30,000	
Net cash provided by financing activities		36,000
Net increase in cash		$ 15,500

At this point in the course, you need to understand what a statement of cash flows is rather than how to prepare it. We do not ask you to prepare such a statement until you have studied Chapter 16.

The income statement, statement of retained earnings, balance sheet, and the statement of cash flows of Metro Courier, Inc., are the result of management's past decisions. They are the end products of the accounting process, which we explain in the next section. These financial statements give a picture of the solvency and profitability of the company. The accounting process details how this picture was made. Management and other interested parties use these statements to make future decisions. Management is the first to know the financial results; then, it publishes the financial statements to inform other users.

The Financial Accounting Process

In this section, we explain the accounting equation—the framework for the entire accounting process. Then, we show you how to recognize a business transaction and describe underlying assumptions that accountants use to record business transactions. Next, you learn how to analyze and record business transactions.

The Accounting Equation

Objective 4
State the basic accounting equation and describe its relationship to the balance sheet.

In the balance sheet presented in Illustration 1.1 (Part C), the total assets of Metro Courier, Inc., were equal to its total liabilities and stockholders' equity. This equality shows that the assets of a business are equal to its equities; that is,

$$\text{Assets} = \text{Equities}$$

Assets were defined earlier as the things of value owned by the business, or the economic resources of the business. **Equities** are all claims to, or interests in, assets. For example, assume that you purchased a new company automobile for

$15,000 by investing $10,000 in your own corporation and borrowing $5,000 in the name of the corporation from a bank. Your equity in the automobile is $10,000, and the bank's equity is $5,000. You can further describe the $5,000 as a liability because the corporation owes the bank $5,000. Also, you can describe your $10,000 equity as stockholders' equity or interest in the asset. Since the owners in a corporation are stockholders, the basic **accounting equation** becomes:

Assets (A) = Liabilities (L) + Stockholders' Equity (SE)

From Metro's balance sheet in Illustration 1.1 (Part C), we can enter in the amount of its assets, liabilities, and stockholders' equity:

A	=	L	+	SE
$38,700	=	$6,600	+	$32,100

Remember that someone must provide assets or resources—either a creditor or a stockholder. Therefore, this equation must always be in balance.

You can also look at the right side of this equation in another manner. The liabilities and stockholders' equity show the sources of an existing group of assets. Thus, liabilities are not only claims against assets but also sources of assets.

Either creditors or owners provide all the assets in a corporation. The higher the proportion of assets provided by owners, the more solvent the company. However, companies can sometimes improve their profitability by borrowing from creditors and using the funds effectively. As a business engages in economic activity, the dollar amounts and composition of its assets, liabilities, and stockholders' equity change. *However, the equality of the basic accounting equation always holds.*

Analysis of Transactions

Objective 5
Using the underlying assumptions or concepts, analyze business transactions and determine their effects on items in the financial statements.

An accounting **transaction** is a business activity or event that causes a measurable change in the accounting equation, Assets = Liabilities + Stockholders' Equity. An exchange of cash for merchandise is a transaction. The exchange takes place at an agreed price that provides an objective measure of economic activity. For example, the objective measure of the exchange may be $5,000. These two factors—evidence and measurement—make possible the recording of a transaction. Merely placing an order for goods is not a recordable transaction because no exchange has taken place.

A *source document* usually supports the evidence of the transaction. A **source document** is any written or printed evidence of a business transaction that describes the essential facts of that transaction. Examples of source documents are receipts for cash paid or received, checks written or received, bills sent to customers for services performed or bills received from suppliers for items purchased, cash register tapes, sales tickets, and notes given or received. We handle source documents constantly in our everyday life. Each source document initiates the process of recording a transaction.

Underlying Assumptions or Concepts In recording business transactions, accountants rely on certain underlying assumptions or concepts. Both preparers and users of financial statements must understand these assumptions:

1. **Business entity concept** (or accounting entity concept). Data gathered in an accounting system relate to a specific business unit or **entity.** The business entity concept assumes that each business has an existence separate from its owners, creditors, employees, customers, other interested parties, and other businesses.
2. **Money measurement concept.** Economic activity is initially recorded and reported in a common monetary unit of measure—the dollar in the United States. This form of measurement is known as *money measurement*.
3. **Exchange-price (or cost) concept (principle).** Most of the amounts in an accounting system are the objective money prices determined in the ex-

change process. As a result, we record most assets at their acquisition cost. **Cost** is the sacrifice made or the resources given up, measured in money terms, to acquire some desired thing, such as a new truck (asset).

4. **Going-concern (continuity) concept.** Unless strong evidence exists to the contrary, accountants assume that the business entity will continue operations into the indefinite future. Accountants call this assumption the *going-concern or continuity* concept. Assuming that the entity will continue indefinitely allows accountants to value long-term assets, such as land, at cost on the balance sheet since they are to be used rather than sold. Market values of these assets would be relevant only if they were for sale. For instance, accountants would still record land purchased in 1988 at its cost of $100,000 on the December 31, 1997, balance sheet even though its market value has risen to $300,000.
5. **Periodicity (time periods) concept.** According to the *periodicity (time periods)* concept or assumption, an entity's life can be meaningfully subdivided into time periods (such as months or years) to report the results of its economic activities.

Now that you understand business transactions and the five basic accounting assumptions, you are ready to follow some business transactions step by step. To begin, we divide Metro's transactions into two groups: (1) transactions affecting only the balance sheet in June, and (2) transactions affecting the income statement and/or the balance sheet in July. Note that we could also classify these transactions as operating, investing, or financing activities, as shown in the statement of cash flows on page 21.

TRANSACTIONS AFFECTING ONLY THE BALANCE SHEET Since each transaction affecting a business entity must be recorded in the accounting records, analyzing a transaction before actually recording it is an important part of financial accounting. An error in transaction analysis results in incorrect financial statements.

To illustrate the analysis of transactions and their effects on the basic accounting equation, the activities of Metro Courier, Inc., that led to the statements in Illustration 1.1 follow. The first set of transactions (for June), 1a, 2a, and so on, are repeated in the summary of transactions, Illustration 1.2 (Part A) on page 25. The second set of transactions (for July) (1b–6b) are repeated in Illustration 1.3 (Part A) on page 29.

1a. Owners Invested Cash When Metro Courier, Inc., was organized as a corporation on June 1, 1997, the company issued shares of capital stock for $30,000 cash to Ron Chaney, his wife, and their son. This transaction increased assets (cash) of Metro by $30,000 and increased equities (the capital stock element of stockholders' equity) by $30,000. Consequently, the transaction yields the following basic accounting equation:

		Assets				=	Liabilities		+	Stockholders' Equity
Transaction	Explanation	Cash	Accounts Receivable	Trucks	Office Equipment		Accounts Payable	Notes Payable		Capital Stock
	Beginning balances	$ –0–	$ –0–	$ –0–	$ –0–	=	$ –0–	$ –0–	+	$ –0–
1a	Stockholders invested cash	+30,000								+30,000
	Balances after transaction	$30,000				=				$30,000
		↑ Increased by $30,000								↑ Increased by $30,000

2a. Borrowed Money The company borrowed $6,000 from Chaney's father. Chaney signed the note for the company. The note bore no interest and the company promised to repay (recorded as a *note payable*) the amount borrowed within one year. After including the effects of this transaction, the basic equation is:

		Assets				=	Liabilities		+	Stockholders' Equity
Trans-action	Explanation	Cash	Accounts Receiv-able	Trucks	Office Equip-ment		Accounts Payable	Notes Payable		Capital Stock
	Balances before transaction	$30,000				=				$30,000
2a	Borrowed money	+6,000						+6,000		
	Balances after transaction	$36,000				=		$6,000	+	$30,000
		Increased by $6,000						*Increased by $6,000*		

3a. Purchased Trucks and Office Equipment for Cash Metro paid $2,000 cash for two used delivery trucks and $1,000 for office equipment. Trucks and office equipment are assets because the company uses them to earn revenues in the future. Note that this transaction does not change the total amount of assets in the basic equation but only changes the composition of the assets. This transaction decreased cash and increased trucks and office equipment (assets) by the total amount of the cash decrease. Metro received two assets and gave up one asset of equal value. Total assets are still $36,000. The accounting equation now is:

		Assets				=	Liabilities		+	Stockholders' Equity
Trans-action	Explanation	Cash	Accounts Receiv-able	Trucks	Office Equip-ment		Accounts Payable	Notes Payable		Capital Stock
	Balances before transaction . . .	$36,000				=		$6,000	+	$30,000
3a	Purchased equipment for cash . .	−21,500		+20,000	+1,500					
	Balances after transaction	$14,500		$20,000	$1,500	=		$6,000	+	$30,000
		Decreased by $21,500		*Increased by $20,000*	*Increased by $1,500*					

4a. Purchased Office Equipment on Account (for Credit) Metro purchased an additional $1,000 of office equipment on account, agreeing to pay within 10 days after receiving the bill. (To purchase an item *on account* means to buy it on credit.) This transaction increased assets (office equipment) and liabilities (accounts payable) by $1,000. As stated earlier, accounts payable are amounts owed to suppliers for items purchased on credit. Now you can see the $1,000 increase in the assets and liabilities as follows:

		Assets				=	Liabilities		+	Stockholders' Equity
Trans-action	Explanation	Cash	Accounts Receiv-able	Trucks	Office Equip-ment		Accounts Payable	Notes Payable		Capital Stock
	Balances before transaction . . .	$14,500		$20,000	$1,500	=		$6,000	+	$30,000
4a	Purchased office equipment on account				+1,000		+1,000			
	Balances after transaction	$14,500		$20,000	$2,500	=	$1,000	$6,000	+	$30,000
					Increased by $1,000		*Increased by $1,000*			

5a. Paid an Account Payable Eight days after receiving the bill, Metro paid $1,000 for the office equipment purchased on account (transaction 4a). This trans-

ILLUSTRATION 1.2

A. Summary of Transactions

METRO COURIER, INC.
Summary of Transactions
Month of June 1997

		Assets				=	Liabilities		+	Stockholders' Equity
Trans-action	**Explanation**	**Cash**	**Accounts Receiv-able**	**Trucks**	**Office Equip-ment**		**Accounts Payable**	**Notes Payable**		**Capital Stock**
	Beginning balances	$ –0–	$ –0–	$ –0–	$ –0–	=	$ –0–	$ –0–		$ –0–
1a	Stockholders invested cash	+30,000								+30,000
		$30,000				=				$30,000
2a	Borrowed money	+6,000						+6,000		
		$36,000				=		$6,000	+	$30,000
3a	Purchased trucks and office equipment for cash	−21,500		+20,000	+1,500					
		$14,500		$20,000	$1,500	=		$6,000	+	$30,000
4a	Purchased office equipment on account				+1,000		+1,000			
		$14,500		$20,000	$2,500	=	$1,000	$6,000	+	$30,000
5a	Paid an account payable	−1,000					−1,000			
	End-of-month balances	$13,500	$ –0–	$20,000	$2,500	=	$ –0–	$6,000	+	$30,000

B. Balance Sheet

METRO COURIER, INC.
Balance Sheet
June 30, 1997

Assets		**Liabilities and Stockholders' Equity**		
Cash	$13,500	Liabilities:		
Trucks	20,000	Notes payable	$6,000	
Office Equipment	2,500	Total liabilities		$ 6,000
		Stockholders' equity:		
		Capital Stock		30,000
Total assets	$36,000	Total liabilities and stockholders' equity		$36,000

action reduced cash by $1,000 and reduced accounts payable by $1,000. Thus, the assets and liabilities both are reduced by $1,000, and the equation again balances as follows:

		Assets				=	Liabilities		+	Stockholders' Equity
Trans-action	**Explanation**	**Cash**	**Accounts Receiv-able**	**Trucks**	**Office Equip-ment**		**Accounts Payable**	**Notes Payable**		**Capital Stock**
	Balances before transaction	$14,500		$20,000	$2,500	=	$1,000	$6,000	+	$30,000
5a	Paid an account payable	−1,000					−1,000			
	End-of-month balances	$13,500	$ –0–	$20,000	$2,500	=	$ –0–	$6,000	+	$30,000
		Decreased by $1,000					*Decreased by $1,000*			

Illustration 1.2, Part A, is a *summary of transactions* prepared in accounting equation form for June. A **summary of transactions** is a teaching tool used to show the effects of transactions on the accounting equation. Note that the stockholders' equity has remained at $30,000. This amount changes as the business begins to earn revenues or incur expenses. You can see how the totals at the bottom of Part A of Illustration 1.2 tie into the balance sheet shown in Part B. The date on the balance sheet is June 30, 1997. These totals become the beginning balances for July 1997.

Thus far, all transactions have consisted of exchanges or acquisitions of assets either by borrowing or by owner investment. We used this procedure to help you focus on the accounting equation as it relates to the balance sheet. However, people do not form a business only to hold present assets. They form businesses so their assets can generate greater amounts of assets. Thus, a business increases its assets by providing goods or services to customers. The results of these activities appear in the income statement. The section that follows shows more of Metro's transactions as it began earning revenues and incurring expenses.

Transactions Affecting the Income Statement and/or Balance Sheet To survive, a business must be profitable. This means that the revenues earned by providing goods and services to customers must exceed the expenses incurred.

In July 1997, Metro Courier, Inc., began selling services and incurring expenses. The explanations of transactions that follow allow you to participate in this process and learn the necessary accounting procedures.

1b. Earned Service Revenue and Received Cash As its first transaction in July, Metro performed delivery services for customers and received $4,800 cash. This transaction increased an asset (cash) by $4,800. Stockholders' equity (retained earnings) also increased by $4,800, and the accounting equation was in balance.

The $4,800 is a revenue earned by the business and, as such, increases stockholders' equity (in the form of retained earnings) because stockholders prosper when the business earns profits. Likewise, the stockholders would sustain any losses, which would reduce retained earnings.

Revenues increase the amount of retained earnings and expenses and dividends decrease them. (In this first chapter, we show all of these items as immediately affecting retained earnings. In later chapters, the revenues, expenses, and dividends are accounted for separately from retained earnings during the accounting period and are transferred to retained earnings only at the end of the accounting period as part of the "closing process" described in Chapter 4.) The effects of this $4,800 transaction on the financial status of Metro are:

		Assets				=	Liabilities		+	Stockholders' Equity	
Transaction	Explanation	Cash	Accounts Receivable	Trucks	Office Equipment		Accounts Payable	Notes Payable		Capital Stock	Retained Earnings
	Beginning balances (Illustration 1.2)	$13,500	$ -0-	$20,000	$2,500	=	$ -0-	$6,000	+	$30,000	$ -0-
1b	Earned service revenue and received cash	+4,800									+4,800 (service revenue)
	Balances after transaction	$18,300		$20,000	$2,500	=		$6,000	+	$30,000	$4,800

Cash: *Increased by $4,800*

Retained Earnings: *Increased by $4,800*

Metro would record the increase in stockholders' equity brought about by the revenue transaction as a separate item, "Retained earnings." This does not increase capital stock because the Capital Stock account increases only when the company issues shares of stock. The expectation is that revenue transactions will exceed expenses and yield net income. If net income is not distributed to stockholders, it is in fact retained. Later chapters show that because of complexities in handling large numbers of transactions, revenues and expenses affect retained earnings only at the end of an accounting period. The preceding procedure is a shortcut used to explain why the accounting equation remains in balance.

2b. Service Revenue Earned on Account (for Credit) Metro performed courier delivery services for a customer who agreed to pay $900 at a later date. The company granted credit rather than requiring the customer to pay cash immediately. This is called earning revenue *on account*. The transaction consists of exchanging services for the customer's promise to pay later. This transaction is similar to the preceding transaction in that stockholders' equity (retained earnings) increases because the company has earned revenues. However, the transaction differs because the company has not received cash. Instead, the company has received another asset, an *account receivable*. As noted earlier, an account receivable is the amount due from a customer for goods or services already provided. The company has a legal right to collect from the customer in the future. Accounting recognizes such claims as assets. The accounting equation, including this $900 item, is as follows:

		Assets				=	Liabilities		+	Stockholders' Equity	
Transaction	Explanation	Cash	Accounts Receivable	Trucks	Office Equipment		Accounts Payable	Notes Payable		Capital Stock	Retained Earnings
	Balances before transaction	$18,300		$20,000	$2,500	=		$6,000	+	$30,000	$4,800
2b	Earned service revenue on account		+900								+900 (service revenue)
	Balances after transaction	$18,300	$900	$20,000	$2,500	=		$6,000	+	$30,000	$5,700
			Increased by $900								*Increased by $900*

3b. Collected Cash on Accounts Receivable Metro collected $200 on account from the customer in transaction 2b. The customer will pay the remaining $700 later. This transaction affects only the balance sheet and consists of giving up a claim on a customer in exchange for cash. The transaction increases cash by $200 and decreases accounts receivable by $200. Note that this transaction consists solely of a change in the composition of the assets. When the company performed the services, it recorded the revenue. Therefore, the company does not record the revenue again when collecting the cash.

		Assets				=	Liabilities		+	Stockholders' Equity	
Transaction	Explanation	Cash	Accounts Receivable	Trucks	Office Equipment		Accounts Payable	Notes Payable		Capital Stock	Retained Earnings
	Balances before transaction . .	$18,300	$900	$20,000	$2,500	=		$6,000	+	$30,000	$5,700
3b	Collected cash on account . . .	+200	−200								
	Balances after transaction . . .	$18,500	$700	$20,000	$2,500	=		$6,000	+	$30,000	$5,700
		Increased by $200	*Decreased by $200*								

4b. Paid Salaries Metro paid employees $2,600 in salaries. This transaction is an exchange of cash for employee services. Typically, companies pay employees for their services after they perform their work. Salaries (or wages) are costs companies incur to produce revenues, and companies consider them an expense. Thus, the accountant treats the transaction as a decrease in an asset (cash) and a decrease in stockholders' equity (retained earnings) because the company has incurred an expense. Expense transactions reduce net income. Since net income becomes a part of the retained earnings balance, expense transactions reduce the retained earnings.

		Assets				=	Liabilities	+	Stockholers' Equity	
Trans-action	Explanation	Cash	Accounts Receiv-able	Trucks	Office Equip-ment		Accounts Payable	Notes Payable	Capital Stock	Re-tained Earn-ings
	Balances before transaction . . .	$18,500	$700	$20,000	$2,500	=		$6,000	+ $30,000	$5,700
4b	Paid salaries. . . .	−2,600								−2,600 (salaries expense)
	Balances after transaction . . .	$15,900	$700	$20,000	$2,500	=		$6,000	+ $30,000	$3,100
		Decreased by $2,600								Decreased by $2,600

5b. Paid Rent In July, Metro paid $400 cash for office space rental. This transaction causes a decrease in cash of $400 and a decrease in retained earnings of $400 because of the incurrence of rent expense.

Transaction 5b has the following effects on the amounts in the accounting equation:

		Assets				=	Liabilities	+	Stockholders' Equity	
Trans-action	Explanation	Cash	Accounts Receiv-able	Trucks	Office Equip-ment		Accounts Payable	Notes Payable	Capital Stock	Re-tained Earn-ings
	Balances before transaction. . . .	$15,900	$700	$20,000	$2,500	=		$6,000	+ $30,000	$3,100
5b	Paid rent	−400								−400 (rent expense)
	Balances after transaction. . . .	$15,500	$700	$20,000	$2,500	=		$6,000	+ $30,000	$2,700
		Decreased by $400								Decreased by $400

6b. Received Bill for Gas and Oil Used At the end of the month, Metro received a $600 bill for gas and oil consumed during the month. This transaction involves an increase in accounts payable (a liability) because Metro has not yet paid the bill and a decrease in retained earnings because Metro has incurred an expense. Metro's accounting equation now reads:

		Assets				=	Liabilities	+	Stockholders' Equity	
Trans-action	Explanation	Cash	Accounts Receiv-able	Trucks	Office Equip-ment		Accounts Payable	Notes Payable	Capital Stock	Re-tained Earn-ings
	Balances before transaction . . .	$15,500	$700	$20,000	$2,500	=		$6,000	+ $30,000	$2,700
6b	Received bill for gas and oil used . . .						+600			−600 (gas and oil expense)
	End-of-month balances	$15,500	$700	$20,000	$2,500	=	$600	$6,000	+ $30,000	$2,100
							Increased by $600			Decreased by $600

Illustration 1.3

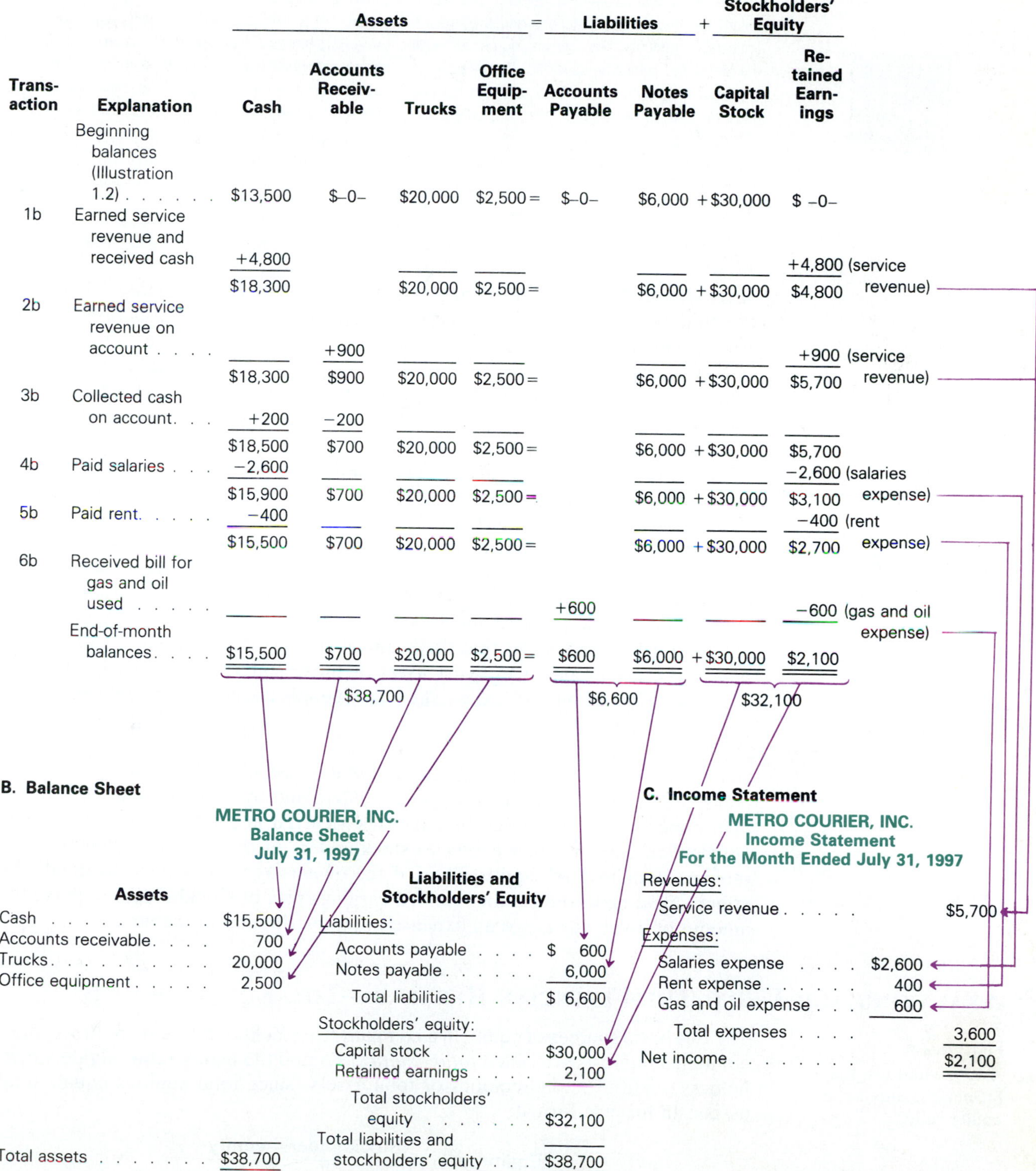

A. Summary of Transactions

METRO COURIER, INC.
Summary of Transactions
Month of July 1997

		Assets				= Liabilities		+ Stockholders' Equity		
Trans-action	Explanation	Cash	Accounts Receiv-able	Trucks	Office Equip-ment	Accounts Payable	Notes Payable	Capital Stock	Re-tained Earn-ings	
	Beginning balances (Illustration 1.2)	$13,500	$-0-	$20,000	$2,500 =	$-0-	$6,000	+ $30,000	$ -0-	
1b	Earned service revenue and received cash	+4,800							+4,800	(service revenue)
		$18,300		$20,000	$2,500 =		$6,000	+ $30,000	$4,800	
2b	Earned service revenue on account		+900						+900	(service revenue)
		$18,300	$900	$20,000	$2,500 =		$6,000	+ $30,000	$5,700	
3b	Collected cash on account	+200	−200							
		$18,500	$700	$20,000	$2,500 =		$6,000	+ $30,000	$5,700	
4b	Paid salaries	−2,600							−2,600	(salaries expense)
		$15,900	$700	$20,000	$2,500 =		$6,000	+ $30,000	$3,100	
5b	Paid rent	−400							−400	(rent expense)
		$15,500	$700	$20,000	$2,500 =		$6,000	+ $30,000	$2,700	
6b	Received bill for gas and oil used					+600			−600	(gas and oil expense)
	End-of-month balances	$15,500	$700	$20,000	$2,500 =	$600	$6,000	+ $30,000	$2,100	
		$38,700				$6,600		$32,100		

B. Balance Sheet

METRO COURIER, INC.
Balance Sheet
July 31, 1997

Assets		Liabilities and Stockholders' Equity	
Cash	$15,500	Liabilities:	
Accounts receivable	700	Accounts payable	$ 600
Trucks	20,000	Notes payable	6,000
Office equipment	2,500	Total liabilities	$ 6,600
		Stockholders' equity:	
		Capital stock	$30,000
		Retained earnings	2,100
		Total stockholders' equity	$32,100
Total assets	$38,700	Total liabilities and stockholders' equity	$38,700

C. Income Statement

METRO COURIER, INC.
Income Statement
For the Month Ended July 31, 1997

Revenues:		
Service revenue		$5,700
Expenses:		
Salaries expense	$2,600	
Rent expense	400	
Gas and oil expense	600	
Total expenses		3,600
Net income		$2,100

AN ETHICAL PERSPECTIVE

State University

James Bender was taking an accounting course at State University. Also, he was helping companies find accounting systems that would fit their information needs. He advised one of his clients to acquire a software computer package that could record the business transactions and prepare the financial statements. The licensing agreement with the software company specified that the basic charge for one site was $4,000 and that $1,000 must be paid for each additional site where the software was used.

James was pleased that his recommendation to acquire the software was followed. However, he was upset that management wanted him to install the software at eight other sites in the company and did not intend to pay the extra $8,000 due the software company. A member of management stated, "The software company will never know the difference and, besides, everyone else seems to be pirating software. If they do find out, we will pay the extra fee at that time. Our expenses are high enough without paying these unnecessary costs." James believed he might lose this client if he did not do as management instructed.

SUMMARY OF BALANCE SHEET AND INCOME STATEMENT TRANSACTIONS Part A of Illustration 1.3 summarizes the effects of all the preceding transactions on the assets, liabilities, and stockholders' equity of Metro Courier, Inc., in July. The beginning balances are the ending balances in Part A of Illustration 1.2. The summary shows subtotals after each transaction; these subtotals are optional and may be omitted. Note how the accounting equation remains in balance after each transaction and at the end of the month.

Objective 6
Prepare an income statement, a statement of retained earnings, and a balance sheet.

The ending balances in each of the columns in Part A of Illustration 1.3 are the dollar amounts in Part B and those reported earlier in the balance sheet in Part C of Illustration 1.1. The itemized data in the Retained Earnings column are the revenue and expense items in Part C of Illustration 1.3 and those reported earlier in the income statement in Part A of Illustration 1.1. The beginning balance in the Retained Earnings column ($–0–) plus net income for the month ($2,100) is equal to the ending balance in retained earnings ($2,100) shown earlier in Part B of Illustration 1.1. Remember that the financial statements are not an end in themselves, but are prepared to assist users of those statements to make informed decisions. Throughout the text we show how people use accounting information in decision making.

DIVIDENDS PAID TO OWNERS (STOCKHOLDERS) Stockholders' equity is (1) increased by capital contributed by stockholders and by revenues earned through operations and (2) decreased by expenses incurred in producing revenues. The payment of cash or other assets to stockholders in the form of dividends also reduces stockholders' equity. Thus, if the owners receive a cash dividend, the effect would be to reduce the retained earnings part of stockholders' equity; the amount of dividends is not an expense but a distribution of income.

ANALYZING AND USING THE FINANCIAL RESULTS—THE EQUITY RATIO

Objective 7
Analyze and use the financial results—the equity ratio.

The two basic sources of equity in a company are stockholders and creditors; their combined interests are called *total equities*. To find the **equity ratio,** divide stockholders' equity by total equities or total assets, since total equities equals total assets. In formula format:

$$\text{Equity ratio} = \frac{\text{Stockholders' equity}}{\text{Total equities}}$$

The higher the proportion of equities (or assets) supplied by the owners, the more solvent the company. However, a high portion of debt may indicate higher profitability because quite often the interest rate on debt is lower than the rate of earnings realized from using the proceeds of the debt.

An example illustrates this concept: Suppose that a company with $100,000 in assets could have raised the funds to acquire those assets in these two ways:

Case 1

Assets	$100,000	Liabilities	$20,000
		Stockholders' equity	80,000

Case 2

Assets	$100,000	Liabilities	$80,000
		Stockholders' equity	20,000

When a company suffers operating losses, its assets shrink. In Case 1, the assets would have to shrink by 80% before the liabilities would equal the assets. In Case 2, the assets would have to shrink only 20% before the liabilities would equal the assets. When the liabilities exceed the assets, the company is said to be insolvent. Therefore, creditors are safer in Case 1.

However, if funds borrowed at 10% are used to produce earnings at a 20% rate, Case 2 is preferable in terms of profitability. Therefore, owners are better off in Case 2 if the borrowed funds can earn more than they cost.

Next, we examine the 1992 equity ratios of some actual companies:

Name of Company	Stockholders' Equity ($ millions)	Total Equities ($ millions)	Equity Ratio
Johnson & Johnson	$ 5,171	$ 11,884	43.5%
GTE Corporation	10,076	42,144	23.9
3M Corporation	6,599	11,955	55.2
CBS, Inc.	447	3,175	14.1
General Electric Company	23,459	192,876	12.2

Johnson & Johnson, the world's largest manufacturer of health care products, sells products in more than 150 countries.

GTE is the largest U.S.-based local telephone company and the second largest U.S. cellular service provider.

3M Corporation, one of the world's leading manufacturing companies, produces abrasives, automotive fasteners, specialty films and chemicals, tapes (Scotch tape), electrical/electronic connectors, and imaging and medical products.

CBS, Inc., one of the three major television networks, offers successful programs such as "60 Minutes," "Murphy Brown," "Murder, She Wrote," and "Northern Exposure."

General Electric Company, one of the most successful U.S. companies, sells products and services to industries such as aerospace, appliances, industrial and power systems, medical systems, and plastics.

As you can see from the preceding data, the equity ratios of actual companies vary widely. Companies such as Johnson & Johnson and 3M Corporation employ a higher proportion of stockholders' equity (a lower proportion of debt) than the others in an effort to have stronger balance sheets (more solvency). The other companies employ a greater proportion of debt, possibly in an attempt to increase profitability. Every company must strike a balance between solvency and profitability to ensure long-run survival. The correct balance between proportions of stockholder and creditor equities depends on the industry, general business conditions, and management philosophy.

Chapter 1 has introduced two important components of the accounting process—the accounting equation and the business transaction. In Chapter 2, you learn about debits and credits and how accountants use them in recording transactions. Understanding how data are accumulated, classified, and reported in financial statements helps you understand how to use financial statement data in making decisions.

An Accounting Perspective

Uses of Technology When you apply for your first job after graduation, prospective employers will expect you to know how to use a microcomputer to perform many tasks. Therefore, before you graduate you should be able to use word processing, spreadsheet, and database software. In many universities, you can learn these skills in courses taken for credit. If your school does not offer credit courses, take noncredit courses or attend a training center.

Understanding the Learning Objectives

Objective 1
Identify and describe the three basic forms of business organizations.

- A single proprietorship is an unincorporated business owned by an individual and often managed by that individual.
- A partnership is an unincorporated business owned by two or more persons associated as partners and is often managed by them.
- A corporation is a business incorporated under the laws of a state and owned by a few stockholders or by thousands of stockholders.

Objective 2
Distinguish among the three types of activities performed by business organizations.

- Service companies perform services for a fee.
- Merchandising companies purchase goods that are ready for sale and then sell them to customers.
- Manufacturing companies buy materials, convert them into products, and then sell the products to other companies or to final customers.

Objective 3
Describe the content and purposes of the income statement, statement of retained earnings, balance sheet, and statement of cash flows.

- The income statement reports the revenues and expenses of a company and shows the profitability of that business organization for a stated period of time.
- The statement of retained earnings shows the change in retained earnings between the beginning of the period (e.g., a month) and its end.
- The balance sheet lists the assets, liabilities, and stockholders' equity (including dollar amounts) of a business organization at a specific moment in time.
- The statement of cash flows shows the cash inflows and cash outflows for a company for a stated period of time.

Objective 4
State the basic accounting equation and describe its relationship to the balance sheet.

- The accounting equation is Assets = Liabilities + Stockholders' Equity.
- The left side of the equation represents the left side of the balance sheet and shows things of value owned by the business.
- The right side of the equation represents the right side of the balance sheet and shows who provided the funds to acquire the things of value (assets).

Objective 5
Using the underlying assumptions or concepts, analyze business transactions and determine their effects on items in the financial statements.

- Some transactions affect only balance sheet items: assets (such as cash, accounts receivable, and equipment), liabilities (such as accounts payable and notes payable), and stockholders' equity (capital stock). Other transactions affect both balance sheet items and income statement items (revenues, expenses, and eventually retained earnings).
- Illustrations 1.2 (Part A) and 1.3 (Part A) show the effects of business transactions on the accounting equation.

Objective 6
Prepare an income statement, a statement of retained earnings, and a balance sheet.

- The income statement appears in Illustrations 1.1 (Part A) and 1.3 (Part C).
- The statement of retained earnings appears in Illustration 1.1 (Part B).
- The balance sheet appears in Illustrations 1.1 (Part C) and 1.3 (Part B).

Objective 7
Analyze and use the financial results—the equity ratio.

- The equity ratio is the stockholders' equity divided by total equities (or total assets).
- The equity ratio shows the percentage that assets would have to shrink before a company would become insolvent (liabilities exceed assets).

A Comparison of Corporate Accounting with Accounting for a Single Proprietorship and a Partnership

Appendix

Some textbook authors use a single proprietorship and a partnership form of business ownership to illustrate accounting concepts and practices. In a survey of users and nonusers of our text, we learned that the majority preferred the corporate approach because most students will probably work for or invest in corporations. Also, many small businesses operate as corporations because of the investors' desire for limited liability.

This appendix briefly describes the differences in accounting for these three forms of business ownership. The major difference is in the stockholders' equity or owner's equity section of the balance sheet.

As you learned in this chapter, the stockholders' equity section of the balance sheet for a corporation consists of capital stock and retained earnings. The owner's equity section of the balance sheet for a single proprietorship consists only of the owner's capital account. The owner's equity section of a partnership is similar to that of a single proprietorship except that it shows a capital account and its balance for each partner.

Corporation		**Single Proprietorship**		**Partnership**	
Stockholders' equity:		Owner's equity:		Partners' capital:	
Capital stock . .	$100,000	John Smith, Capital	$150,000	John Smith, Capital	$ 75,000
Retained earnings . . .	50,000			Sam Jones, Capital	75,000
Total	$150,000		$150,000		$150,000

The stockholders' equity section of a corporate balance sheet can become more complex as you will see later in the text. However, the items in the owner's equity section of the balance sheets of a single proprietorship and a partnership always remain as just shown. In a single proprietorship, the owner's capital balance consists of the owner's investments in the business, plus cumulative net income since the beginning of the business, less any amounts withdrawn by the owner. Thus, all of the amounts in the various stockholders' equity accounts for a corporation are in the owner's capital account in a single proprietorship. In a partnership, each partner's capital account balance consists of that partner's investments in the business, plus that partner's cumulative share of net income since that partner became a partner, less any amounts withdrawn by that partner.

The Dividends account in a corporation is similar to an owner's drawing account in a single proprietorship. These accounts both show amounts taken out of the business by the owners. In a partnership, each partner has a drawing account. Accountants treat asset, liability, revenue, and expense accounts similarly in all three forms of organization.

Demonstration Problem

On June 1, 1997, Green Hills Riding Stable, Incorporated, was organized. The following transactions occurred during June:

June 1 Shares of capital stock were issued for $10,000 cash.
4 A horse stable and riding equipment were rented (and paid for) for the month at a cost of $1,200.
8 Horse feed for the month was purchased on credit, $800.
15 Boarding fees of $3,000 for June were charged to those owning horses boarded at the stable. (This amount is due on July 10.)
20 Miscellaneous expenses of $600 were paid.
29 Land was purchased from a savings and loan association by borrowing $40,000 on a note from that association. The loan is due to be repaid in five years. Interest payments are due at the end of each month beginning July 31.
30 Salaries of $700 for the month were paid.
30 Riding and lesson fees were billed to customers in the amount of $2,800. (They are due on July 10.)

Required

a. Prepare a summary of the preceding transactions. Use columns headed Cash, Accounts Receivable, Land, Accounts Payable, Notes Payable, Capital Stock, and

Retained Earnings. Determine balances after each transaction to show that the basic equation is in balance.

b. Prepare an income statement for June 1997.

c. Prepare a statement of retained earnings for June 1997.

d. Prepare a balance sheet as of June 30, 1997.

Solution to Demonstration Problem

a.

GREEN HILLS RIDING STABLE, INCORPORATED
Summary of Transactions
Month of June 1997

		Assets			=	Liabilities		+	Stockholders' Equity	
Date	**Explanation**	**Cash**	**Accounts Receivable**	**Land**		**Accounts Payable**	**Notes Payable**		**Capital Stock**	**Retained Earnings**
June 1	Capital stock issued	$10,000			=				$10,000	
4	Rent expense	−1,200								$−1,200
		$ 8,800			=				$10,000	$−1,200
8	Feed expense					$+800				$ −800
		$ 8,800			=	$ 800		+	$10,000	$−2,000
15	Boarding fees		$+3,000							$+3,000
		$ 8,800	$ 3,000		=	$ 800		+	$10,000	$ 1,000
20	Miscellaneous expenses	−600								−600
		$ 8,200	$ 3,000		=	$ 800		+	$10,000	$ 400
29	Purchased land by borrowing			$+40,000			$+40,000			
		$ 8,200	$ 3,000	$ 40,000	=	$ 800	$ 40,000	+	$10,000	$ 400
30	Salaries paid	−700								−700
		$ 7,500	$ 3,000	$ 40,000	=	$ 800	$ 40,000	+	$10,000	$ −300
30	Riding and lesson fees billed		+2,800							+2,800
		$ 7,500	$ 5,800	$ 40,000		$ 800	$ 40,000		$10,000	$ 2,500

b.

GREEN HILLS RIDING STABLE, INCORPORATED
Income Statement
For the Month Ended June 30, 1997

Revenues:		
Horse boarding fees revenue	$3,000	
Riding and lesson fees revenue	2,800	
Total revenues		$5,800
Expenses:		
Rent expense	$1,200	
Feed expense	800	
Salaries expense	700	
Miscellaneous expense	600	
Total expenses		3,300
Net income		$2,500

c.

GREEN HILLS RIDING STABLE, INCORPORATED
Statement of Retained Earnings
For the Month Ended June 30, 1997

Retained earnings, June 1	$–0–
Add: Net income for June	2,500
Total	$2,500
Less: Dividends	–0–
Retained earnings, June 30	$2,500

d.

GREEN HILLS RIDING STABLE, INCORPORATED
Balance Sheet
June 30, 1997

Assets		
Cash		$ 7,500
Accounts receivable		5,800
Land		40,000
Total assets		$53,300
Liabilities and Stockholders' Equity		
Liabilities:		
Accounts payable		$ 800
Notes payable		40,000
Total liabilities		$40,800
Stockholders' equity:		
Capital stock	$10,000	
Retained earnings	2,500	
Total stockholders' equity		12,500
Total liabilities and stockholders' equity		$53,300

NEW TERMS

Accounting equation Assets = Equities; or Assets = Liabilities + Stockholders' Equity. *22*

Accounts payable Amounts owed to suppliers for goods or services purchased on credit. *20*

Accounts receivable Amounts due from customers for services already provided. *20*

Assets Things of value owned by the business. Examples include cash, machines, and buildings. To their owners, assets possess service potential or utility that can be measured and expressed in money terms. *20*

Balance sheet Financial statement that lists a company's assets, liabilities, and stockholders' equity (including dollar amounts) as of a specific moment in time. Also called a *statement of financial position*. *18, 20*

Business entity concept The separate existence of the business organization. *15, 22*

Capital stock The title given to an equity account showing the investment in a business corporation by its stockholders. *20*

Continuity See Going concern.

Corporation Business incorporated under the laws of one of the states and owned by a few stockholders or by thousands of stockholders. *17*

Cost Sacrifice made or the resources given up, measured in money terms, to acquire some desired thing, such as a new truck (asset). *23*

Dividend Payment (usually of cash) to the owners of the business; it is a distribution of income to owners rather than an expense of doing business. *18*

Entity A unit that is deemed to have an existence separate and apart from its owners, creditors, employees, customers, other interested parties, and other businesses, and for which accounting records are maintained. *15,22*

Equities Broadly speaking, all claims to, or interests in, assets; includes liabilities and stockholders' equity. *21*

Equity ratio A ratio found by dividing stockholders' equity by total equities (or total assets). *30*

Exchange-price (or cost) concept (principle) The objective money prices determined in the exchange process are used to record most assets. *22*

Expenses Costs incurred to produce revenues, measured by the assets surrendered or consumed in serving customers. *18*

Going concern (continuity) concept The assumption by the accountant that unless strong evidence exists to the contrary, a business entity will continue operations into the indefinite future. *23*

Income statement Financial statement that shows the revenues and expenses and reports the profitability of a business organization for a stated period of time. Sometimes called an *earnings statement*. *18*

Liabilities Debts owed by a business—or creditors' equity. Examples: notes payable, accounts payable. *20*

Manufacturing companies Companies that buy materials, convert them into products, and then sell the products to other companies or to final customers. *17*

Merchandising companies Companies that purchase goods ready for sale and sell them to customers. *17*

Money measurement concept Recording and reporting economic activity in a common monetary unit of measure such as the dollar. *22*

Net income Amount by which the revenues of a period exceed the expenses of the same period. *18*

Net loss Amount by which the expenses of a period exceed the revenues of the same period. *18*

Notes payable Amounts owed to parties who loan the company money after the owner signs a written agreement (a note) for the company to repay each loan. *20*

Partnership An unincorporated business owned by two or more persons associated as partners. *16*

Periodicity (time periods) concept An assumption that an entity's life can be meaningfully subdivided into time periods (such as months or years) for purposes of reporting its economic activities. *23*

Profitability Ability to generate income. The income statement reflects a company's profitability. *18*

Retained earnings Accumulated net income less dividend distributions to stockholders. *20*

Revenues Inflows of assets (such as cash) resulting from the sale of products or the rendering of services to customers. *18*

Service companies Companies (such as accounting firms, law firms, or dry cleaning establishments) that perform services for a fee. *17*

Single proprietorship An unincorporated business owned by an individual and often managed by that individual. *16*

Solvency Ability to pay debts as they become due. The balance sheet reflects a company's solvency. *18*

Source document Any written or printed evidence of a business transaction that describes the essential facts of that transaction, such as receipts for cash paid or received. *22*

Statement of cash flows Shows cash inflows and outflows for a company over a period of time. *18, 20*

Statement of retained earnings Statement used to explain the changes in retained earnings that occurred between two balance sheet dates. *18*

Stockholders' equity The owners' interest in a corporation. *20*

Stockholders or shareholders Owners of a corporation; they buy shares of stock, which are units of ownership, in the corporation. *17*

Summary of transactions Teaching tool used in Chapter 1 to show the effects of transactions on the accounting equation. *25*

Transaction A business activity or event that causes a measurable change in the items in the accounting equation, Assets = Liabilities + Stockholders' Equity. *22*

Self-Test

True-False

Indicate whether each of the following statements is true or false.

1. The three forms of business organizations are single proprietorship, partnership, and trust.
2. The three types of business activity are service, merchandising, and manufacturing.
3. The income statement shows the profitability of the company and is dated as of a particular date, such as December 31, 1997.
4. The statement of retained earnings shows both the net income for the period and the beginning and ending balances of retained earnings.
5. The balance sheet contains the same major headings as appear in the accounting equation.

Multiple-Choice

Select the best answer for each of the following questions.

1. The ending balance in retained earnings is shown in the:
   - **a.** Income statement.
   - **b.** Statement of retained earnings.
   - **c.** Balance sheet.
   - **d.** Both **(b)** and **(c)**.
2. Which of the following is *not* a correct form of the accounting equation?
   - **a.** Assets = Equities.
   - **b.** Assets = Liabilities + Stockholders' Equity.
   - **c.** Assets − Liabilities = Stockholders' Equity.
   - **d.** Assets + Stockholders' Equity = Liabilities.
3. Which of the following is *not* one of the five underlying assumptions or concepts mentioned in the chapter?
   - **a.** Exchange-price concept.
   - **b.** Inflation accounting concept.
   - **c.** Business entity concept.
   - **d.** Going-concern concept.
4. When the stockholders invest cash in the business, what is the effect?
   - **a.** Liabilities increase and stockholders' equity increases.
   - **b.** Both assets and liabilities increase.
   - **c.** Both assets and stockholders' equity increase.
   - **d.** None of the above.
5. When services are performed on account, what is the effect?
   - **a.** Both cash and retained earnings decrease.
   - **b.** Both cash and retained earnings increase.
   - **c.** Both accounts receivable and retained earnings increase.
   - **d.** Accounts payable increases and retained earnings decreases.

Now turn to page 46 to check your answers.

QUESTIONS

1. Accounting has often been called the language of business. In what respects would you agree with this description? How might you argue that this description is deficient?
2. Define asset, liability, and stockholders' equity.
3. How do liabilities and stockholders' equity differ? How are they similar?
4. How do accounts payable and notes payable differ? How are they similar?
5. Define revenues. How are revenues measured?
6. Define expenses. How are expenses measured?
7. What is a balance sheet? On what aspect of a business does the balance sheet provide information?
8. What is an income statement? On what aspect of a business does this statement provide information?
9. What information does the statement of retained earnings provide?
10. Identify the three types of activities shown in a statement of cash flows.
11. What is a transaction? What use does the accountant make of transactions? Why?
12. What is the accounting equation? Why must it always balance?
13. Give an example from your personal life that illustrates your use of accounting information in reaching a decision.
14. You have been elected to the governing board of your church. At the first meeting you attend, mention is made of building a new church. What accounting information would the board need in deciding whether or not to go ahead?
15. A company purchased equipment for $1,000 cash. The vendor stated that the equipment was worth $1,200. At what amount should the equipment be recorded?
16. What is meant by money measurement?
17. Of what significance is the exchange-price (or cost) concept? How is the cost to acquire an asset determined?
18. What effect does the going-concern (continuity) concept have on the amounts at which long-term assets are carried on the balance sheet?
19. Of what importance is the periodicity (time periods) concept to the preparation of financial statements?
20. Describe a transaction that would:
    - **a.** Increase both an asset and capital stock.
    - **b.** Increase both an asset and a liability.
    - **c.** Increase one asset and decrease another asset.
    - **d.** Decrease both a liability and an asset.
    - **e.** Increase both an asset and retained earnings.
    - **f.** Decrease both an asset and retained earnings.
    - **g.** Increase a liability and decrease retained earnings.
    - **h.** Decrease both an asset and retained earnings.
21. Identify the causes of increases and decreases in stockholders' equity.

MAYTAG

22. **Real World Question** Refer to the 1993 financial statements of Maytag Corporation in the separate annual report booklet that came with your text. What were the net income or loss amounts in the latest three years? Discuss the meaning of the changes after reading management's discussion and analysis of financial condition and results of operations.

HARLAND

23. **Real World Question** Referring to the financial statements of John H. Harland Company in the separate annual report booklet, has net income improved over the period reported? Has the solvency of the company improved from 1992 to 1993? Discuss.

EXERCISES

Exercise 1–1
Matching (L.O. 1, 2)

Match the descriptions in Column B with the appropriate terms in Column A.

Column A	Column B
1. Corporation.	**a.** An unincorporated business owned by an individual.
2. Merchandising company.	**b.** The form of organization used by most large businesses.
3. Partnership.	**c.** Buys raw materials and converts them into finished products.
4. Manufacturing company.	**d.** Buys goods in their finished form and sells them to customers in that same form.
5. Service company.	**e.** An unincorporated business with more than one owner.
6. Single proprietorship.	**f.** Performs services for a fee.

Exercise 1–2
Compute net income and revenue (L.O. 3)

Assume that retained earnings increased by $7,200 from June 30, 1997, to June 30, 1998. A cash dividend of $600 was declared and paid during the year.

a. Compute the net income for the year.

b. Assume expenses for the year were $18,000. Compute the revenue for the year.

Exercise 1–3
Compute retained earnings (L.O. 3, 4)

On December 31, 1997, Sanchez Company had assets of $130,000, liabilities of $97,500, and capital stock of $30,000. During 1998, Sanchez earned revenues of $45,000 and incurred expenses of $33,750. Dividends declared and paid amounted to $3,000.

a. Compute the company's retained earnings on December 31, 1997.

b. Compute the company's retained earnings on December 31, 1998.

Exercise 1–4
Compute retained earnings and total assets at beginning of year (L.O. 3, 4)

At the start of the year, a company had liabilities of $100,000 and capital stock of $300,000. At the end of the year, retained earnings amounted to $270,000. Net income for the year was $90,000, and $30,000 of dividends were declared and paid. Compute retained earnings and total assets at the beginning of the year.

Exercise 1–5
Analyze transactions (L.O. 4, 5)

For each of the following events, determine if it has an effect on the specific items (such as cash) in the accounting equation. For the events that do have an effect, present an analysis of the transaction showing its two sides or dual nature.

a. Purchased equipment for cash, $6,000.

b. Purchased a truck for $60,000, signed a note (with no interest) promising payment in 10 days.

c. Paid $1,200 for the current month's utilities.

d. Paid for the truck purchased in (**b**).

e. Employed Mary Childers as a salesperson at $1,000 per month. She is to start work next week.

f. Signed an agreement with a bank in which the bank agreed to lend the company up to $150,000 any time within the next two years.

Exercise 1–6
Indicate effect of transactions on items in the accounting equation (L.O. 4, 5)

Bently Company, engaged in a courier service business, completed the following selected transactions during July 1997:

a. Purchased office equipment on account.

b. Paid an account payable.

c. Earned service revenue on account.

d. Borrowed money by signing a note at the bank.

e. Paid salaries for month to employees.

f. Received cash on account from a charge customer.

g. Received gas and oil bill for month.

h. Purchased delivery truck for cash.

i. Declared and paid a cash dividend.

Using a tabular form similar to Illustration 1.3 (Part A), indicate the effect of each transaction on the accounting equation using (+) for increase and (−) for decrease. No dollar amounts are needed, and you need not fill in the Explanation column.

Exercise 1–7
Determine effect of transactions on stockholders' equity (L.O. 5)

Indicate the amount of change (if any) in the stockholders' equity balance based on each of the following transactions:

a. The stockholders invested $60,000 cash in the business by purchasing capital stock.

b. Land costing $10,000 was purchased by paying cash.

c. The company performed services for a customer who agreed to pay $16,000 in one month.

d. Paid salaries for the month, $14,400.

e. Paid $5,000 on an account payable.

Exercise 1–8
Analyze transactions (L.O. 5)

Give examples of transactions that would have the following effects on the items in a firm's financial statements:

a. Increase cash; decrease some other asset.

b. Decrease cash; increase some other asset.

c. Increase an asset; increase a liability.

d. Decrease retained earnings; decrease an asset.

e. Increase an asset other than cash; increase retained earnings.

f. Decrease an asset; decrease a liability.

Exercise 1–9
Identify transactions that decrease retained earnings (L.O. 5)

Which of the following transactions results in a decrease in retained earnings? Why?

a. Employees were paid $30,000 for services received during the month.
b. $175,000 was paid to acquire land.
c. Paid an $18,000 note payable. No interest was involved.
d. Paid a $200 account payable.

Exercise 1–10
Prepare income statement (L.O. 6)

Assume that the following items were included in the Retained Earnings column in the summary of transactions for Clark Company for July 1997:

Salaries expense	$120,000
Service revenue	260,000
Gas and oil expense	27,000
Rent expense	48,000
Dividends paid	40,000

Prepare an income statement for July 1997.

Exercise 1–11
Prepare statement of retained earnings (L.O. 6)

Given the following facts, prepare a statement of retained earnings for Cancun Company, a tanning salon, for August 1997:

Balance in retained earnings at end of July, $168,000.
Dividends paid in August, $63,600.
Net income for August, $72,000.

Exercise 1–12
Prepare balance sheet (L.O. 6)

The column totals of a summary of transactions for Allen Printer Repair, Inc., as of December 31, 1997, were as follows:

Accounts payable	$ 40,000
Accounts receivable	70,000
Capital stock	100,000
Cash	40,000
Land	80,000
Building	50,000
Equipment	30,000
Notes payable	20,000
Retained earnings	?

Prepare a balance sheet. We have purposely listed the accounts out of order.

Exercise 1–13
Calculate the equity ratios for General Motors Corporation and comment (L.O. 7)

General Motors Corporation is the world's largest full-line vehicle manufacturer with nameplates including Chevrolet, Pontiac, Oldsmobile, Buick, Cadillac, GMC Truck, and Saturn. GM also manufactures auto components for every major automobile manufacturer and provides financing and insurance to customers and dealers. Subsidiaries of GM are involved in automotive electronics, telecommunications and space, and applying information technologies. Given the following data for the General Motors Corporation, calculate the equity ratios for 1992 and 1991. Then comment on the situation.

	1992	1991
Stockholders' equity	$ 6,225,600,000	$ 27,327,600,000
Total equities	$191,012,800,000	$184,325,500,000

PROBLEMS

Problem 1–1
Prepare summary of transactions (L.O. 4, 5)

Jamestown Personal Finance Company, which provides financial advisory services, engaged in the following transactions during May 1997:

May 1 Received $200,000 cash for shares of capital stock issued when company was organized.
2 The company borrowed $40,000 from the bank on a note.
7 The company bought $182,400 of computer equipment for cash.
11 Cash received for services performed to date was $15,200.
14 Services performed for a customer who agreed to pay within a month were $10,000.
15 Employee wages were paid, $13,200.
19 The company paid $14,000 on the note to the bank.
31 Interest paid to the bank for May was $140. (Interest is an expense, which reduces retained earnings.)

May 31 The customer of May 14 paid $3,200 of the amount owed to the company.
31 An order was received from a customer for services to be rendered next week, which will be billed at $12,000.

Required Prepare a summary of transactions (see Part A of Illustration 1.3). Use money columns headed Cash, Accounts Receivable, Equipment, Notes Payable, Capital Stock, and Retained Earnings. Determine balances after each transaction to show that the accounting equation balances.

Problem 1–2
Prepare summary of transactions and balance sheet (L.O. 4–6)

Mow-It Lawn Care Service, Inc., a company that takes care of lawns and shrubbery of personal residences, engaged in the following transactions in April 1997:

Apr. 1 The company was organized and received $200,000 cash from the owners in exchange for capital stock issued.
4 The company bought equipment for cash, $101,760.
9 The company bought additional mowing equipment that cost $9,120 and agreed to pay for it in 30 days.
15 Cash received for services performed to date was $3,840.
16 Amount due from a customer for services performed totaled $5,280.
30 Of the receivable (see April 16), $3,072 was collected in cash.
30 Miscellaneous operating expenses of $6,240 were paid during the month.
30 An order was placed for miscellaneous equipment costing $28,800.

Required

a. Prepare a summary of transactions (see Part A of Illustration 1.3). Use money columns headed Cash, Accounts Receivable, Equipment, Accounts Payable, Capital Stock, and Retained Earnings. Determine balances after each transaction to show that the basic accounting equation balances.

b. Prepare a balance sheet as of April 30.

Problem 1–3
Prepare income statement, statement of retained earnings, and balance sheet (L.O. 6)

Analysis of the transactions of the Midnight Drive-In Theater for June 1997 disclosed the following:

Ticket revenue	$160,000
Equipment rent expense	50,000
Film rent expense	53,400
Concession revenue	29,600
Advertising expense	18,600
Salaries expense	40,000
Utilities expense	14,100
Cash dividends	12,000

Balance sheet figures at June 30 include the following:

Cash	$240,000
Land	48,000
Accounts payable	87,600
Capital stock	114,000
Retained earnings as of June 1, 1997	84,900

Required

a. Prepare an income statement for June 1997.

b. Prepare a statement of retained earnings for June 1997.

c. Prepare a balance sheet as of June 30, 1997.

d. How solvent does this company appear to be?

Problem 1–4
Prepare income statement, statement of retained earnings, and balance sheet (L.O. 4–6)

Baseball, Inc., was formed by a group of parents to meet a need for a place for kids to play baseball. At the beginning of its second year of operations, its balance sheet appeared as follows:

BASEBALL, INC.
Balance Sheet
April 30, 1997

Assets

Cash	$ 86,000
Accounts receivable	80,000
Land	600,000
Total assets	$766,000

Liabilities and Stockholders' Equity

Liabilities:		
Accounts payable.		$ 94,000
Stockholders' equity:		
Capital stock	$400,000	
Retained earnings	272,000	672,000
Total liabilities and stockholders' equity . .		$766,000

The summarized transactions for May 1997 are as follows:

- **a.** Issued additional capital stock for cash, $200,000.
- **b.** Collected $80,000 on accounts receivable.
- **c.** Paid $64,000 on accounts payable.
- **d.** Received membership fees from parents (nonrefundable): in cash, $260,000; and on account, $120,000.
- **e.** Incurred operating expenses: for cash, $60,000; and on account, $160,000.
- **f.** Paid dividends of $16,000.
- **g.** Purchased more land for cash, $96,000.
- **h.** Placed an order for new equipment expected to cost $120,000.

Required

- **a.** Prepare a summary of transactions (see Part A of Illustration 1.3) using column headings as given in the balance sheet. Determine balances after each transaction.
- **b.** Prepare an income statement for May 1997.
- **c.** Prepare a statement of retained earnings for May 1997.
- **d.** Prepare a balance sheet as of May 31, 1997.

Problem 1–5
State causes of balance sheet changes (L.O. 3, 6)

The balance sheets for May 31, 1997, and April 30, 1997, and the income statement for May of the Duffers' Golf Driving Range follow. (Common practice is to show the most recent period first.)

DUFFERS' GOLF DRIVING RANGE
Comparative Balance Sheets

	May 31, 1997	April 30, 1997
Assets		
Cash	$ 56,400	$ 46,800
Land	213,200	194,000
Total assets	$269,600	$240,800
Liabilities and Stockholders' Equity		
Accounts payable.	$ 68,000	$ 77,600
Capital stock.	144,000	144,000
Retained earnings	57,600	19,200
Total liabilities and stockholders' equity	$269,600	$240,800

DUFFERS' GOLF DRIVING RANGE
Income Statement
For the Month Ended May 31, 1997

Revenues:		
Service revenue		$164,000
Expenses:		
Salaries expense	$116,000	
Equipment rental expense.	9,600	125,600
Net income		$ 38,400

All revenues earned are on account.

Required

State the probable cause(s) of the change in each of the balance sheet accounts from April 30 to May 31, 1997.

Alternate Problems

Problem 1–1A
Prepare summary of transactions (L.O. 4, 5)

Like-New Auto Paint Company had the temporary free use of an old building and completed the following transactions in September 1997:

Sept. 1 The company was organized and received $80,000 cash from the issuance of capital stock.
5 The company bought painting and sanding equipment for cash at a cost of $25,000.
7 The company painted the auto fleet of a customer who agreed to pay $8,000 in one week. The customer furnished the special paint.
14 The company received the $8,000 from the transaction of September 7.
20 Additional sanding equipment that cost $2,800 was acquired today; payment was postponed until September 28.
28 $2,400 was paid on the liability incurred on September 20.
30 Employee salaries for the month, $2,200, were paid.
30 Placed an order for additional painting equipment advertised at $20,000.

Required Prepare a summary of transactions (see Part A of Illustration 1.3) for the company for these transactions. Use money columns headed Cash, Accounts Receivable, Equipment, Accounts Payable, Capital Stock, and Retained Earnings. Determine balances after each transaction to show that the basic accounting equation balances.

Problem 1–2A
Prepare summary of transactions and balance sheet (L.O. 4–6)

Reliable Home Repair Company completed the following transactions in June 1997:

June 1 The company was organized and received $100,000 cash from the issuance of capital stock.
4 The company paid $48,000 cash for a truck.
7 The company borrowed $10,000 from its bank on a note.
9 Cash received for repair services performed was $4,500.
12 Expenses of operating the business so far this month were paid in cash, $3,400.
18 Repair services performed for a customer who agreed to pay within a month amounted to $5,400.
25 The company paid $4,065 on its loan from the bank, including $4,050 of principal and $15 of interest. (The principal is the amount of the loan. Interest is an expense, which reduces retained earnings.)
30 Miscellaneous expenses incurred in operating the business from June 13 to date were $3,825 and were paid in cash.
30 An order (contract) was received from a customer for repair services to be performed tomorrow, which will be billed at $3,000.

Required

a. Prepare a summary of transactions (see Part A of Illustration 1.3). Include money columns for Cash, Accounts Receivable, Trucks, Notes Payable, Capital Stock, and Retained Earnings. Determine balances after each transaction to show that the basic accounting equation balances.

b. Prepare a balance sheet as of June 30, 1997.

Problem 1–3A
Prepare income statement (L.O. 6)

Following are summarized transaction data for Executive Apartments, Inc., for the year ending June 30, 1997. The company owns and operates an apartment building.

Rent revenue from building owned	$120,000
Building repairs	2,870
Building cleaning, labor cost	3,185
Property taxes on the building	4,000
Insurance on the building	1,225
Commissions paid to rental agent	5,000
Legal and accounting fees (for preparation of tenant leases)	1,260
Utilities expense	8,225
Cost of new awnings (installed on June 30, will last 10 years)	5,000

Of the $120,000 rent revenue, $5,000 was not collected in cash until July 5, 1997.

Required Prepare an income statement for the year ended June 30, 1997.

Problem 1–4A
Prepare summary of transactions, income statement, statement of retained earnings, and balance sheet (L.O. 4–6)

The following data are for Discount Parking Corporation:

DISCOUNT PARKING CORPORATION
Balance Sheet
September 30, 1997

Assets	
Cash	$244,000
Accounts receivable	18,000
Total assets	$262,000
Liabilities and Stockholders' Equity	
Accounts payable	$ 94,000
Capital stock	132,000
Retained earnings	36,000
Total liabilities and stockholders' equity	$262,000

The summarized transactions for October 1997 are as follows:

Oct. 1 The accounts payable owed as of September 30 ($94,000) were paid.
1 The company paid rent for the premises for October, $19,200.
7 The company received cash of $4,200 for parking by daily customers during the week.
10 The company collected $14,400 of the accounts receivable in the balance sheet at September 30.
14 Cash receipts for the week from daily customers were $6,600.
15 Parking revenue earned but not yet collected from fleet customers was $6,000.
16 The company paid salaries of $2,400 for the period October 1–15.
19 The company paid advertising expenses of $1,200 for October.
21 Cash receipts for the week from daily customers were $7,200.
24 The company incurred miscellaneous expenses of $840. Payment will be due November 10.
31 Cash receipts for the last 10 days of the month from daily customers were $8,400.
31 The company paid salaries of $3,000 for the period October 16–31.
31 Billings to monthly customers totaled $21,600 for October.
31 Paid cash dividends of $24,000.

Required

a. Prepare a summary of transactions (see Part A of Illustration 1.3) using column headings as given in the preceding balance sheet. Determine balances after each transaction.

b. Prepare an income statement for October 1997.

c. Prepare a statement of retained earnings for October 1997.

d. Prepare a balance sheet as of October 31, 1997.

Problem 1–5A
State causes of balance sheet changes (L.O. 3, 6)

The following balance sheets for June 30, 1997, and May 31, 1997, and the income statement for June are for Camping Trailer Storage, Inc. (Common practice is to show the most recent period first.)

CAMPING TRAILER STORAGE, INC.
Comparative Balance Sheets

	June 30, 1997	**May 31, 1997**
Assets		
Cash	$ 42,000	$60,000
Accounts receivable	24,000	-0-
Land	36,000	36,000
Total assets	$102,000	$96,000
Liabilities and Stockholders' Equity		
Liabilities	$ 18,000	$24,000
Capital stock	60,000	60,000
Retained earnings	24,000	12,000
Total liabilities and stockholders' equity	$102,000	$96,000

CAMPING TRAILER STORAGE, INC.
Income Statement
For the Month Ended June 30, 1997

Revenues:		
Service revenue		$90,000
Expenses:		
Salaries expense	$48,000	
Supplies bought and used	24,000	72,000
Net income		$18,000

A cash dividend of $6,000 was declared and paid in June.

Required State the probable causes of the changes in each of the balance sheet accounts from May 31 to June 30, 1997.

Beyond the Numbers—Critical Thinking

Business Decision Case 1–1
Identify information needed to make decision
(L.O. 3)

Upon graduation from high school, Jim Crane went to work for a builder of houses and small apartment buildings. During the next six years, Crane earned a reputation as an excellent employee—hardworking, dedicated, and dependable—in the light construction industry. He could handle almost any job requiring carpentry, electrical, or plumbing skills.

Crane then decided to go into business for himself under the name Jim's Fix-It Shop, Inc. He invested cash, some power tools, and a used truck in his business. He completed many repair and remodeling jobs for homeowners and apartment owners. The demand for his services was so large that he had more work than he could handle. He operated out of his garage, which he had converted into a shop, adding several new pieces of power woodworking equipment.

Now, two years after going into business for himself, Crane must decide whether to continue in his own business or to accept a position as construction supervisor for a home builder. He has been offered an annual salary of $50,000 and a package of fringe benefits (medical and hospitalization insurance, pension contribution, vacation and sick pay, and life insurance) worth approximately $8,000 per year. The offer is attractive to Crane. But he dislikes giving up his business since he has thoroughly enjoyed being his own boss, even though it has led to an average workweek well in excess of the standard 40 hours.

Required Suppose Crane comes to you for assistance in gathering the information needed to help him make a decision. He brings along the accounting records that have been maintained for his business by an experienced accountant. Using logic and your own life experiences, indicate the nature of the information Jim needs if he is to make an informed decision. Pay particular attention to the information likely to be found in his business accounting records. Does the accounting information available enter directly into the decision? Write a memorandum to Jim describing the information he will need to make an informed decision. The memo's headings should include Date, To, From, and Subject. (See the format in Group Project 1–5 below.)

Annual Report Analysis 1–2
Comment on solvency of The Coca-Cola Company
(L.O. 7)

Refer to The Coca-Cola Company annual report in the separate annual report booklet that came with your text. Then turn to the section entitled "Selected Financial Data." Recall that in this chapter we showed that the equity ratio is calculated by dividing stockholders' equity by total equities (or total assets). Another format for analyzing solvency is to divide total debt by total equities. This latter calculation tells the proportion of assets financed by debt rather than the proportion of assets financed by stockholders' equity. These two ratios are complements and must add to 100%. Thus, if 25% of assets were financed by debt, 75% were financed by stockholders' equity.

Under "Selected Financial Data" (pages 52–53 of the annual report), The Coca-Cola Company shows "Total-debt-to-total-capital," which is the same as total debt to total equities. These percentages are for 1983 through 1993. Also shown are the "Total debt" amounts for the same period. Study these amounts and comment on the solvency of the company. What does the trend indicate about management's decisions regarding debt?

Annual Report Analysis 1–3
Answer questions about Ralston Purina's annual report

The Ralston Purina Company was founded in 1894. The company manufactures pet foods; bakery products; dry cell battery products; breakfast cereals; cookies, crackers, and snack foods; dietary soy protein, fiber food ingredients, polymer products; and feeds for livestock and poultry. Included in its 1992 Annual Report were the following items:

Responsibility for Financial Statements

The preparation and integrity of the financial statements of Ralston Purina Company are the responsibility of its management. These statements have been prepared in conformance with generally accepted accounting principles and in the opinion of management fairly present the Company's financial position, results of operations and cash flows.

The Company maintains accounting and internal control systems which it believes are adequate to provide reasonable assurance that assets are safeguarded against loss from unauthorized use or disposition and that the financial records are reliable for preparing financial statements. The selection and training of qualified personnel, the establishment and communication of accounting and administrative policies and procedures, and an extensive program of internal audits are important elements of these control systems.

The report of Price Waterhouse, independent accountants, on their audits of the accompanying financial statements is shown below. This report states that the audits were made in accordance with generally accepted auditing standards. These standards include a study and evaluation of internal control for the purpose of establishing a basis for reliance thereon relative to the scope of their audits of the financial statements.

The Board of Directors, through its Audit Committee consisting solely of nonmanagement directors, meets periodically with management, internal audit and the independent accountants to discuss audit and financial reporting matters. To assure independence, Price Waterhouse has direct access to the Audit Committee.

Report of Independent Accountants

To the Shareholders and Board of Directors of Ralston Purina Company

In our opinion, the accompanying consolidated balance sheet and the related consolidated statements of earnings, of shareholders' equity and of cash flows present fairly, in all material respects, the financial position of Ralston Purina Company and its subsidiaries at September 30, 1992 and 1991, and the results of their operations and their cash flows for each of the three years in the period ended September 30, 1992, in conformity with generally accepted accounting principles. These financial statements are the responsibility of the Company's management; our responsibility is to express an opinion on these financial statements based on our audits. We conducted our audits of these statements in accordance with generally accepted auditing standards which require that we plan and perform the audit to obtain reasonable assurance about whether the financial statements are free of material misstatement. An audit includes examining, on a test basis, evidence supporting the amounts and disclosures in the financial statements, assessing the accounting principles used and signficant estimates made by management, and evaluating the overall financial statement presentation. We believe that our audits provide a reasonable basis for the opinion expressed above.

Price Waterhouse

St. Louis, Missouri
November 2, 1992

Required

Write answers to the following questions:

1. Who is responsible for preparing the financial statements?
2. Of what importance is the internal audit?
3. What is the role of the audit committee?
4. What is the responsibility of the external independent auditor?
5. Does the independent auditor have absolute assurance that the financial statements are free of material misstatement?
6. To what extent does the independent auditor examine evidence?

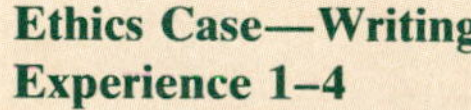
Ethics Case—Writing Experience 1–4

Refer to "An Ethical Perspective" on page 30. Write a short essay discussing the alternatives James Bender could pursue and the likely outcomes of those alternatives. Which of the alternatives you have discussed would you recommend?

Group Project 1–5
Interview with a business person

In teams of two or three students, interview in person or by speaker phone, a businessperson in your community. Ask how that person uses accounting information in making business decisions and obtain specific examples. Each team should write a memorandum to the instructor summarizing the results of the interview. Information contained in the memo should include:

Date:
To:
From:
Subject:

Content of the memo must include the name and title of the person interviewed, name of the company, date of the interview, examples of the use of accounting information for decision making, and any other pertinent information.

Answers to Self-Test

True-False

1. **False.** Corporation, not trust, is the third form.
2. **True.** The accounting for all three of these is covered in this text.
3. **False.** The income statement is dated using a period of time, such as "For the Year Ended December 31, 1997."
4. **True.** In addition, the statement of retained earnings shows dividends declared.
5. **True.** Both show assets, liabilities, and stockholders' equity.

Multiple-Choice

1. **d.** The ending balance in retained earnings is shown in both the statement of retained earnings and in the balance sheet.
2. **d.** This form of the equation would not balance.
3. **b.** The inflation accounting concept was not one of the ones discussed. The other two were the money measurement concept and the periodicity concept.
4. **c.** When the stockholders invest cash, assets and stockholders' equity increase.
5. **c.** The performance of services on account increases both accounts receivable and retained earnings.

Processing Information for Decisions and Establishing Accounting Policy

A Manager's Perspective

Eric Thompson
Financial Manager, Marketing
The Coca-Cola Company

As the Financial Manager for the Marketing department, I coordinate and monitor the budget for that group. My job is to ensure they have enough money available to accomplish their goals. I do this primarily by comparing requests to amounts requested in previous years. Managers request money based on individual projects and their projected costs, and I evaluate each one to assess whether a request is warranted.

The budget is also used as a benchmark to evaluate the department's overall performance. Each department reports a "rolling estimate" every month, which reviews what they have spent to date and helps managers determine whether they are under or over the budget. Managers prefer to use this figure because the rolling estimate allows time to make corrections and changes. If they were to wait until the actual numbers were available, it would be too late to make adjustments.

I also prepare an annual profit-and-loss statement for each brand. The marketing department uses the profit margin to determine how much to spend on marketing efforts for each product. This also helps the department assess prices for products by analyzing the cost of producing them.

Before deciding to undertake a major new investment such as launching a new product or investing in a new plant, we use discounted cash flow analysis to determine the feasibility of such an expenditure.

Marketing managers must understand the basics of financial information. Too many managers assume the more products you sell, the more value you are creating, and this isn't always true. The more they understand concepts like discounted cash flow analysis, the better they will be as marketeers. Otherwise, they could actually be losing money for the company.

2

Recording Business Transactions

In Chapter 1, we illustrated the income statement, statement of retained earnings, balance sheet, and statement of cash flows. These statements are the end products of the financial accounting process, which is based on the accounting equation. The financial accounting process quantifies past management decisions. The results of these decisions are communicated to users—management, creditors, and investors—and serve as a basis for making future decisions.

The raw data of accounting are the business transactions. We recorded the transactions in Chapter 1 as increases or decreases in the assets, liabilities, and stockholders' equity items of the accounting equation. This procedure showed you how various transactions affected the accounting equation. When working through these sample transactions, you probably suspected that listing all transactions as increases or decreases in the transactions summary columns would be too cumbersome in practice. Most businesses, even small ones, enter into many transactions every day. Chapter 2 teaches you how to actually record business transactions in the accounting process.

To explain the dual procedure of recording business transactions with debits and credits, we introduce you to some new tools: the T-account, the journal, and the ledger. You can follow a company through its various business transactions using these tools. Like accountants, you can use a trial balance to check the equality of your recorded debits and credits. This is the double-entry accounting system that the Franciscan monk, Luca Pacioli, described centuries ago. Understanding this system enables you to better understand the content of financial statements so you can use the information provided to make informed business decisions.

Learning Objectives

After studying this chapter, you should be able to:

1. Use the account as the basic classifying and storage unit for accounting information.
2. Express the effects of business transactions in terms of debits and credits to different types of accounts.
3. List the steps in the accounting cycle.
4. Record the effects of business transactions in a journal.
5. Post journal entries to the accounts in the ledger.

(continued)

The Account and Rules of Debit and Credit

A business may engage in thousands of transactions during a year. An accountant classifies and summarizes the data in these transactions to create useful information.

(concluded)

6. Prepare a trial balance to test the equality of debits and credits in the journalizing and posting process.
7. Analyze and use the financial results—horizontal and vertical analyses.

Steps in Recording Business Transactions

Look at Illustration 2.1 to see the steps in recording and posting the effects of a business transaction. Note that source documents provide the evidence that a business transaction occurred. These source documents include bills received from suppliers for goods or services received, bills sent to customers for goods sold or services performed, and cash register tapes. The information in the source document serves as the basis for preparing a journal entry. Then a firm posts (transfers) that information to accounts in the ledger.

You can see from Illustration 2.1 that after you prepare the journal entry, you post it to the accounts in the ledger. However, before you can record the journal entry, you must understand the rules of debit and credit. To teach you these rules, we begin by studying the nature of an account.

The Account

Objective 1
Use the account as the basic classifying and storage unit for accounting information.

Fortunately, most business transactions are repetitive. This makes the task of accountants somewhat easier because they can classify the transactions into groups having common characteristics. For example, a company may have thousands of receipts or payments of cash during a year. As a result, a part of every cash transaction can be recorded and summarized in a single place called an *account*.

An **account** is a part of the accounting system used to classify and summarize the increases, decreases, and balances of each asset, liability, stockholders' equity item, dividend, revenue, and expense. Firms set up accounts for each different business element, such as cash, accounts receivable, and accounts payable. Every business has a Cash account in its accounting system because knowledge of the amount of cash on hand is useful information.

Accountants may differ on the account title (or name) they give the same item. For example, one accountant might name an account Notes Payable and another might call it Loans Payable. Both account titles refer to the amounts borrowed by the company. The account title should be logical to help the accountant group similar transactions into the same account. Once you give an account a title, you must use that same title throughout the accounting records.

The number of accounts in a company's accounting system depends on the information needs of those interested in the business. The main requirement is that each account provides information useful in making decisions. Thus, one account may be set up for all cash rather than having a separate account for each form of cash (coins on hand, currency on hand, and deposits in banks). The amount of cash is useful information; the form of cash often is not.

The T-Account

To illustrate recording the increases and decreases in an account, texts use the **T-account,** which looks like a capital letter T. The name of the account, such as cash, appears across the top of the T. We record increases on one side of the vertical line of the T and decreases on the other side. A T-account appears as follows:

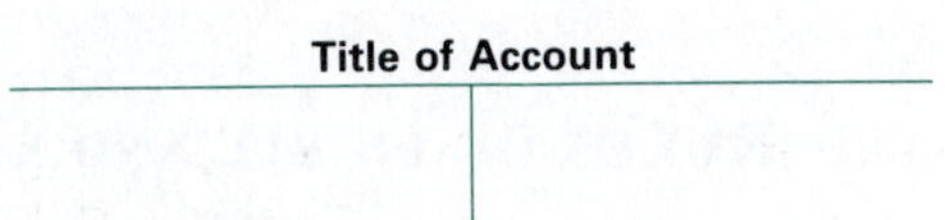

In Chapter 1, you saw that each business transaction affects at least two items. For example, if you—an owner—invest cash in your business, the compa-

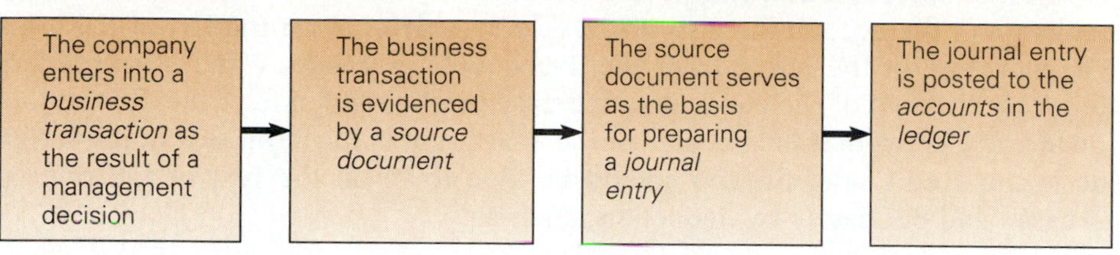
The company enters into a *business transaction* as the result of a management decision
The business transaction is evidenced by a *source document*
The source document serves as the basis for preparing a *journal entry*
The journal entry is posted to the *accounts* in the *ledger*

Illustration 2.1
The Steps in Recording and Posting the Effects of a Business Transaction

An Accounting Perspective

Business Insight Have you ever considered starting your own business? If so, you'll need to understand accounting to successfully run your business. To know how well your business is doing, you must understand and analyze financial statements. Accounting information also tells you why you are performing as reported. If you are in business to sell or develop a certain product or perform a specific service, you cannot operate profitably or consider expanding unless you base your business decisions on accounting information.

ny's assets increase and its stockholders' equity increases. This result was illustrated in the summary of transactions in Illustration 1.3. In the following sections, we use debits and credits and the double-entry procedure to record the increases and decreases caused by business transactions.

Debits and Credits

Objective 2
Express the effects of business transactions in terms of debits and credits to different types of accounts.

Accountants use the term **debit** instead of saying, "Place an entry on the left side of the T-account." They use the term **credit** for "Place an entry on the right side of the T-account." Debit (abbreviated Dr.) simply means left side; credit (abbreviated Cr.) means right side.[1] Thus, for all accounts a debit entry is an entry on the left side, while a credit entry is an entry on the right side.

Any Account	
Left, or debit, side	Right, or credit, side

Double-Entry Procedure

After recognizing a business event as a business transaction, we analyze it to determine its increase or decrease effects on the assets, liabilities, stockholders' equity items, dividends, revenues, or expenses of the business. Then we translate these increase or decrease effects into debits and credits.

In each business transaction we record, the total dollar amount of debits must equal the total dollar amount of credits. When we debit one account (or accounts) for $100, we must credit another account (or accounts) for a total of $100. The accounting requirement that each transaction be recorded by an entry that has equal debits and credits is called **double-entry procedure,** or *duality*. This double-entry procedure keeps the accounting equation in balance.

The dual recording process produces two sets of accounts—those with debit balances and those with credit balances. The totals of these two groups of accounts must be equal. Then, some assurance exists that the arithmetic part of the transaction recording process has been properly carried out. Now, let us actually record business transactions in T-accounts using debits and credits.

Recording Changes in Assets, Liabilities, and Stockholders' Equity While recording business transactions, remember that the foundation of the accounting process is the following basic accounting equation:

Assets = Liabilities + Stockholders' Equity

[1] The abbreviations "Dr." and "Cr." are based on the Latin words "*debere*" and "*credere*." A synonym for *debit* an account is *charge* an account.

Recording transactions into the T-accounts is easier when you focus on the equal sign in the accounting equation. Assets, which are on the left of the equal sign, increase on the left side of the T-accounts. Liabilities and stockholders' equity, to the right of the equal sign, increase on the right side of the T-accounts. You already know that the left side of the T-account is the debit side and the right side is the credit side. So you should be able to fill in the rest of the rules of increases and decreases by deduction, such as:

Assets		=	**Liabilities**		+	**Stockholders' Equity**	
Debit for increases	Credit for decreases		Debit for decreases	Credit for increases		Debit for decreases	Credit for increases

To summarize:

1. Assets *increase* by debits (left side) of the T-account and *decrease* by credits (right side) of the T-account.
2. Liabilities and stockholders' equity *decrease* by debits (left side) of the T-account and *increase* by credits (right side) of the T-account.

Applying these two rules keeps the accounting equation in balance. Now we apply the debit and credit rules for assets, liabilities, and stockholders' equity to business transactions.

Assume a corporation issues shares of its capital stock for $10,000 in transaction 1. (Note the figure in parentheses is the number of the transaction and ties the two sides of the transaction together.) The company records the receipt of $10,000 as follows:

(Dr.)	**Cash**		*(Cr.)*
(1)	10,000		

(Dr.)	**Capital Stock**		*(Cr.)*
		(1)	10,000

This transaction increases the asset, cash, which is recorded on the left side of the Cash account. Then, the transaction increases stockholders' equity, which is recorded on the right side of the Capital Stock account.

Assume the company borrowed $5,000 from a bank on a note (transaction 2). A **note** is an unconditional written promise to pay to another party (the bank) the amount owed either when demanded or at a specified date, usually with interest at a specified rate. The firm records this transaction as follows:

(Dr.)	**Cash**		*(Cr.)*
(1)	10,000		
(2)	5,000		

(Dr.)	**Notes Payable**		*(Cr.)*
		(2)	5,000

Observe that liabilities, Notes Payable, increase with an entry on the right (credit) side of the account.

Recording Changes in Revenues and Expenses In Chapter 1, we recorded the revenues and expenses directly in the Retained Earnings account. However, this is not done in practice because of the volume of revenue and expense transactions. Instead, businesses treat the expense accounts as if they were subclassifications of the debit side of the Retained Earnings account, and the revenue accounts as if they were subclassifications of the credit side. Since they need the amounts of revenues and expenses to prepare the income statement, firms keep a separate account for each revenue and expense. The recording rules for revenues and expenses are:

- Record increases in revenues on the right (credit) side of the T-account and decreases on the left (debit) side. The reasoning behind this rule is that revenues increase retained earnings, and increases in retained earnings are recorded on the right side.

- Record increases in expenses on the left (debit) side of the T-account and decreases on the right (credit) side. The reasoning behind this rule is that expenses decrease retained earnings, and decreases in retained earnings are recorded on the left side.

To illustrate these rules, assume the same company received $1,000 cash from a customer for services rendered (transaction 3). The Cash account, an asset, increases on the left (debit) side of the T-account; and the Service Revenue account, an increase in retained earnings, increases on the right (credit) side.

(Dr.)	Cash		(Cr.)
(1)	10,000		
(2)	5,000		
(3)	1,000		

(Dr.)	Service Revenue		(Cr.)
		(3)	1,000

Now assume this company paid $600 in salaries to employees (transaction 4). The Cash account, an asset, decreases on the right (credit) side of the T-account; and the Salaries Expense account, a decrease in retained earnings, increases on the left (debit) side.[2]

(Dr.)	Cash		(Cr.)
(1)	10,000	(4)	600
(2)	5,000		
(3)	1,000		

(Dr.)	Salaries Expense		(Cr.)
(4)	600		

Recording Changes in Dividends Since dividends decrease retained earnings, increases appear on the left side of the Dividends account and decreases on the right side. Thus, the firm records payment of a $2,000 cash dividend (transaction 5) as follows:

(Dr.)	Cash		(Cr.)
(1)	10,000	(4)	600
(2)	5,000	(5)	2,000
(3)	1,000		

(Dr.)	Dividends[3]		(Cr.)
(5)	2,000		

At the end of the accounting period, the accountant transfers any balances in the expense, revenue, and Dividends accounts to the Retained Earnings account. This transfer occurs only after the information in the expense and revenue accounts has been used to prepare the income statement. We discuss and illustrate this step in Chapter 4.

Determining the Balance of an Account

To determine the balance of any T-account, total the debits to the account, total the credits to the account, and subtract the smaller sum from the larger. If the sum of the debits exceeds the sum of the credits, the account has a **debit balance.** For example, the following Cash account uses information from the preceding transactions. The account has a debit balance of $13,400, computed as total debits of $16,000 less total credits of $2,600.

(Dr.)	Cash		(Cr.)
(1)	10,000	(4)	600
(2)	5,000	(5)	2,000
(3)	1,000		
	16,000		2,600
Dr. bal.	13,400		

[2] Certain deductions are normally taken out of employees' pay for social security taxes, federal and state withholding, and so on. Those deductions are ignored here.

[3] As we illustrate later in the text, some companies debit dividends directly to the Retained Earnings account rather than to a Dividends account.

If, on the other hand, the sum of the credits exceeds the sum of the debits, the account has a **credit balance.** For instance, assume that a company has an Accounts Payable account with a total of $10,000 in debits and $13,000 in credits. The account has a credit balance of $3,000, as shown in the following T-account:

(Dr.)	**Accounts Payable**		*(Cr.)*
	10,000		7,000
			6,000
	10,000		13,000
		Cr. bal.	3,000

Normal Balances Since debits increase asset, expense, and Dividend accounts, they normally have debit (or left-side) balances. Conversely, because credits increase liability, capital stock, retained earnings, and revenue accounts, they normally have credit (or right-side) balances.

The following chart shows the normal balances of the seven accounts we have used:

Types of Accounts	Normal Balances	
	Debit	**Credit**
Assets	X	
Liabilities		X
Stockholders' equity:		
Capital stock		X
Retained earnings		X
Dividends	X	
Expenses	X	
Revenues		X

Rules of Debit and Credit Summarized

At this point, you should memorize the six rules of debit and credit. Later, as you proceed in your study of accounting, the rules will become automatic. Then, you will no longer ask yourself, "Is this increase a debit or credit?"

Asset accounts increase on the debit side, while liability and stockholders' equity accounts increase on the credit side. When the account balances are totaled, they conform to the following independent equations:

Assets = Liabilities + Stockholders' Equity

Debits = Credits

The arrangement of these two formulas gives the first three rules of debit and credit:

1. Increases in asset accounts are debits; decreases are credits.
2. Decreases in liability accounts are debits; increases are credits.
3. Decreases in stockholders' equity accounts are debits; increases are credits.

The debit and credit rules for expense and Dividends accounts and for revenue accounts follow logically if you remember that expenses and dividends are decreases in stockholders' equity and revenues are increases in stockholders' equity. Since stockholders' equity accounts decrease on the debit side, expense and Dividend accounts increase on the debit side. Since stockholders' equity accounts increase on the credit side, revenue accounts increase on the credit side. The last three debit and credit rules are:

4. Decreases in revenue accounts are debits; increases are credits.
5. Increases in expense accounts are debits; decreases are credits.
6. Increases in Dividends accounts are debits; decreases are credits.

ILLUSTRATION 2.2 Rules of Debit and Credit **Transparency**

Assets = Liabilities + Stockholders' Equity

Asset Accounts		=	**Liability Accounts**		+	**Stockholders' Equity Account(s) (Capital Stock and Retained Earnings)**	
Debit*	Credit		Debit	Credit*		Debit	Credit*
+ Debit for increase	− Credit for decrease		− Debit for decrease	+ Credit for increase		− Debit for decrease	+ Credit for increase

Expense Accounts and Dividends Account		**Revenue Accounts**	
Debit*	Credit	Debit	Credit*
+ Debit for increase	− Credit for decrease	− Debit for decrease	+ Credit for increase

Debits	**Credits**
1. Increase assets.	1. Decrease assets.
2. Decrease liabilities.	2. Increase liabilities.
3. Decrease stockholders' equity.	3. Increase stockholders' equity.
4. Decrease revenues.	4. Increase revenues.
5. Increase expenses.	5. Decrease expenses.
6. Increase dividends.	6. Decrease dividends.

* Normal balance.

In Illustration 2.2, we depict these six rules of debit and credit. Note first the treatment of expense and Dividends accounts as if they were subclassifications of the debit side of the Retained Earnings account. Second, note the treatment of the revenue accounts as if they were subclassifications of the credit side of the Retained Earnings account. Next, we discuss the accounting cycle and indicate where steps in the accounting cycle are discussed in Chapters 2 through 4.

THE ACCOUNTING CYCLE

Objective 3
List the steps in the accounting cycle.

The **accounting cycle** is a series of steps performed during the accounting period (some throughout the period and some at the end) to analyze, record, classify, summarize, and report useful financial information for the purpose of preparing financial statements. Before you can visualize the eight steps in the accounting cycle, you must be able to recognize a business transaction. **Business transactions** are measurable events that affect the financial condition of a business. For example, assume that the owner of a business spilled a pot of coffee in her office or broke her leg while skiing. These two events may briefly interrupt the operation of the business. However, they are not measurable in terms that affect the solvency and profitability of the business.

Business transactions can be the exchange of goods for cash between the business and an external party, such as the sale of a book, or they can involve paying salaries to employees. These events have one fundamental criterion: They must have caused a measurable change in the amounts in the accounting equation, Assets = Liabilities + Stockholders' Equity. The evidence that a business event has occurred is a source document such as a sales ticket, check, and so on. Source documents are important because they are the ultimate proof of business transactions.

After you have determined that an event is a measurable business transaction and have adequate proof of this transaction, mentally analyze the transaction's effects on the accounting equation. You learned how to do this in Chapter 1. This chapter and Chapters 3 and 4 describe other steps in the accounting cycle. The eight steps in the accounting cycle and the chapters that discuss them are:

Illustration 2.3 Steps in the Accounting Cycle

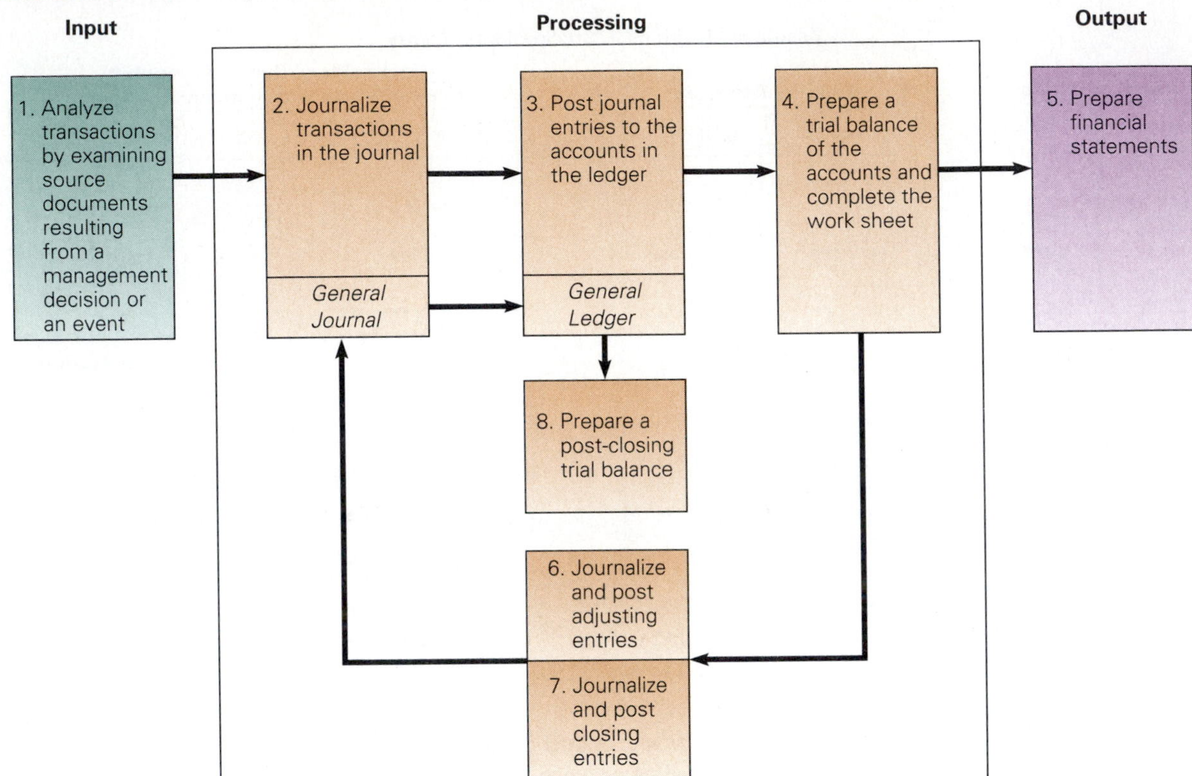

Performed throughout the accounting period

1. Analyze transactions by examining source documents (Chapters 1 and 2).
2. Journalize transactions in the journal (Chapter 2).
3. Post journal entries to the accounts in the ledger (Chapter 2).

Performed only at end of the accounting period

4. Prepare a trial balance of the accounts (Chapter 2) and complete the work sheet (Chapter 4). (This step includes adjusting entries from Chapter 3.)
5. Prepare financial statements (Chapter 4).
6. Journalize and post adjusting entries (Chapters 3 and 4).
7. Journalize and post closing entries (Chapter 4).
8. Prepare a post-closing trial balance (Chapter 4).

This listing serves as a preview of what you will study in Chapters 2–4. Notice that firms perform the last five steps at the end of the accounting period. Step 5 precedes steps 6 and 7 because management needs the financial statements at the earliest possible date. After the statements have been delivered to management, the adjusting and closing entries can be journalized and posted. In Illustration 2.3, we diagram the eight steps in the accounting cycle.

You can perform many of these steps on a computer with an accounting software package. However, you must understand a manual accounting system and all of the steps in the accounting cycle to understand what the computer is doing. This understanding removes the mystery of what the computer is doing when it takes in raw data and produces financial statements.

The Journal

Objective 4
Record the effects of business transactions in a journal.

In explaining the rules of debit and credit, we recorded transactions directly in the accounts. Each ledger (general ledger) account shows only the increases and decreases in that account. Thus, all the effects of a single business transaction would not appear in any one account. For example, the Cash account contains only data on changes in cash and does not show how the cash was generated or

ILLUSTRATION 2.4 General Journal

MICROTRAIN COMPANY
General Journal

Page 1

Date		Account Titles and Explanation	Post. Ref.	Debit	Credit
1997					
Nov.	28	Cash	100	50000	
		Capital Stock	300		50000
		Stockholders invested $50,000 cash in the business.			

how it was spent. To have a permanent record of an entire transaction, the accountant uses a book or record known as a *journal*.

A **journal** is a chronological (arranged in order of time) record of business transactions. A *journal entry* is the recording of a business transaction in the journal. A **journal entry** shows all the effects of a business transaction as expressed in debit(s) and credit(s) and may include an explanation of the transaction. *A transaction is entered in a journal before it is entered in ledger accounts.* Because each transaction is initially recorded in a journal rather than directly in the ledger, a journal is called a *book of original entry*.

The General Journal

A business usually has more than one journal. Chapter 4 briefly describes several special journals. In this chapter, we use the basic form of journal, the general journal. As shown in Illustration 2.4, a general journal contains the following columns:

1. **Date column.** The first column on each journal page is for the date. For the first journal entry on a page, this column contains the year, month, and day (number). For all other journal entries on a page, this column contains only the day of the month, until the month changes.
2. **Account Titles and Explanation column.** The first line of an entry shows the account debited. The second line shows the account credited. Notice that we indent the credit account title to the right. For instance, in Illustration 2.4 we show the debit to the Cash account and then the credit to the Capital Stock account. Any necessary explanation of a transaction appears on the line(s) below the credit entry and is indented halfway between the accounts debited and credited. A journal entry explanation should be concise and yet complete enough to describe fully the transaction and prove the entry's accuracy. When a journal entry is self-explanatory, we omit the explanation.
3. **Posting Reference column.** This column shows the account number of the debited or credited account. For instance, in Illustration 2.4, the number 100 in the first entry means that the Cash account number is 100. No number appears in this column until the information has been posted to the appropriate ledger account. We discuss posting later in the chapter.
4. **Debit column.** In the debit column, the amount of the debit is on the same line as the title of the account debited.
5. **Credit column.** In the credit column, the amount of the credit is on the same line as the title of the account credited.

An Accounting Perspective

Uses of Technology Preparing journal entries in a computerized system is different than in a manual system. The computer normally asks for the number of the account to be debited. After you type the account number, the computer shows the account title in its proper position. The cursor then moves to the debit column and waits for you to enter the amount of the debit. Then it asks if there are more debits. If not, the computer prompts you for the account number of the credit. After you type the account number, the computer supplies the account name of the credit and enters the same amount debited as the credit. When there is more than one credit, you can override the amount and enter the correct amount. Then you would enter the other credit in the same way. If your debits and credits are not equal, the computer warns you and makes you correct the error. You can supply an explanation for the entry from a standard list or type it in. As you enter the journal entries, the computer automatically posts them to the ledger accounts. At any time, you can have the computer print a trial balance.

Functions and Advantages of a Journal

A summary of the functions and advantages of using a journal follows:

The journal—

1. Records transactions in chronological order.
2. Shows the analysis of each transaction in debits and credits.
3. Supplies an explanation of each transaction when necessary.
4. Serves as a source for future reference to accounting transactions.
5. Eliminates the need for lengthy explanations from the accounts.
6. Makes possible posting to the ledger at convenient times.
7. Assists in maintaining the ledger in balance because the debit(s) must always equal the credit(s) in each journal entry.
8. Aids in tracing errors when the ledger is not in balance.

The Ledger

A **ledger** (general ledger) is the complete collection of all the accounts of a company. The ledger may be in loose-leaf form, in a bound volume, or in computer memory.

Accounts fall into two general groups: (1) *balance sheet accounts* (assets, liabilities, and stockholders' equity) and (2) *income statement accounts* (revenues and expenses). The terms *real accounts* and *permanent accounts* also refer to balance sheet accounts. Balance sheet accounts are **real accounts** because they are not subclassifications or subdivisions of any other account. They are **permanent accounts** because their balances are not transferred (or closed) to any other account at the end of the accounting period. Income statement accounts and the Dividends account are **nominal accounts** because they are merely subclassifications of the stockholders' equity accounts. *Nominal* literally means "in name only." Nominal accounts are also called **temporary accounts** because they temporarily contain revenue, expense, and dividend information that is transferred (or closed) to the Retained Earnings account at the end of the accounting period.

The **chart of accounts** is a complete listing of the titles and numbers of all the accounts in the ledger. The chart of accounts can be compared to a table of contents. The groups of accounts usually appear in this order: assets, liabilities, stockholders' equity, dividends, revenues, and expenses.

Individual accounts are in sequence in the ledger. Each account typically has an identification number and a title to help locate accounts when recording data. For example, a company might number asset accounts, 100–199; liability accounts, 200–299; stockholders' equity accounts and Dividends account, 300–399; revenue accounts, 400–499; and expense accounts, 500–599. We use this numbering system in this text. The uniform chart of accounts used in the first 11 chapters appears on the inside cover of the text. Companies may use other numbering systems. For instance, sometimes a company numbers its accounts in sequence starting with 1, 2, and so on. The important idea is that companies use some numbering system.

Now that you understand how to record debits and credits in an account and how all accounts together form a ledger, you are ready to study the accounting process in operation.

The Accounting Process in Operation

MicroTrain Company is a small corporation that provides on-site microcomputer software training using the clients' equipment. The company offers beginning through advanced training with convenient scheduling. A small fleet of trucks transports personnel and teaching supplies to the clients' sites. The company rents a building and is responsible for paying the utilities.

We illustrate the capital stock transaction that occurred to form the company (in November) and the first month of operations (December). The accounting process used by this company is similar to that of any small company. The ledger accounts used by MicroTrain Company are:

	Acct. No.	Account Title	Description
Assets	100	Cash	Bank deposits and cash on hand.
	103	Accounts Receivable	Amounts owed to the company by customers.
	107	Supplies on Hand	Items such as paper, envelopes, writing materials, and other materials used in performing training services for customers or in doing administrative and clerical office work.
	108	Prepaid Insurance	Insurance policy premiums paid in advance of the periods for which the insurance coverage applies.
	112	Prepaid Rent	Rent paid in advance of the periods for which the rent payment applies.
	150	Trucks	Trucks used to transport personnel and training supplies to clients' locations.
Liabilities	200	Accounts Payable	Amounts owed to creditors for items purchased from them.
	216	Unearned Service Fees	Amounts received from customers before the training services have been performed for them.
Stockholders' equity	300	Capital Stock	The stockholders' investment in the business.
	310	Retained Earnings	The earnings retained in the business.
Dividends	320	Dividends	The amount of dividends declared to stockholders.
Revenues	400	Service Revenue	Amounts earned by performing training services for customers.
Expenses	505	Advertising Expense	The cost of advertising incurred in the current period.
	506	Gas and Oil Expense	The cost of gas and oil used in trucks in the current period.
	507	Salaries Expense	The amount of salaries incurred in the current period.
	511	Utilities Expense	The cost of utilities incurred in the current period.

Notice the gaps left between account numbers (100, 103, 107, etc.). These gaps allow the firm to later add new accounts between the existing accounts.

The Recording of Transactions and Their Effects on the Accounts

To begin, a transaction must be *journalized*. **Journalizing** is the process of entering the effects of a transaction in a journal. Then, the information is transferred, or posted, to the proper accounts in the ledger. **Posting** is the process of recording in the ledger accounts the information contained in the journal. We explain posting in more detail later in the chapter.

In the following example, notice that each business transaction affects two or more accounts in the ledger. Also note that the transaction date in both the general journal and the general ledger accounts is the same. In the ledger accounts, the date used is the date that the transaction was recorded in the general journal, even if the entry is not posted until several days later. Our example shows the journal entries posted to T-accounts. In practice, firms post journal entries to three-column ledger accounts, as we show later in the chapter.

Accountants use the *accrual basis of accounting*. Under the **accrual basis of accounting,** they recognize revenues when the company makes a sale or performs a service, regardless of when the company receives the cash. They recognize expenses as incurred, whether or not the company has paid out cash. Chapter 3 discusses the accrual basis of accounting in more detail.

In the following MicroTrain Company example, transaction 1 increases (debits) Cash and increases (credits) Capital Stock by $50,000. First, MicroTrain records the transaction in the general journal; second, it posts the entry to the accounts in the general ledger.

Transaction 1: Nov. 28, 1997 Stockholders invested $50,000 and formed MicroTrain Company.

General Journal

Date		Account Titles and Explanation	Post. Ref.	Debit	Credit
1997					
Nov.	28	Cash	100	50000	
		Capital Stock	300		50000
		Stockholders invested $50,000 cash in the business.			

General Ledger

(Dr.)	Cash	Acct. No. 100	(Cr.)
1997 Nov. 28	50,000		

(Dr.)	Capital Stock	Acct. No. 300	(Cr.)
		1997 Nov. 28	50,000

No other transactions occurred in November. The company prepares financial statements at the end of each month. Illustration 2.5 shows the company's balance sheet at November 30, 1997.

The balance sheet reflects ledger account balances as of the close of business on November 30, 1997. These closing balances are the beginning balances on December 1, 1997. The ledger accounts show these closing balances as beginning balances (Beg. bal.).

Now assume that in December 1997, MicroTrain Company engaged in the following transactions. We show the proper recording of each transaction in the journal and then in the ledger accounts (in T-account form), and describe the effects of each transaction.

ILLUSTRATION 2.5
Balance Sheet

MICROTRAIN COMPANY
Balance Sheet
November 30, 1997

Assets		**Liabilities and Stockholders' Equity**	
Cash	$50,000	Stockholders' equity:	
		Capital stock	$50,000
Total assets	$50,000	Total liabilities and stockholders' equity	$50,000

Transaction 2: Dec. 1 Paid cash for four small trucks, $40,000.

General Journal

Date		Account Titles and Explanation	Post. Ref.	Debit	Credit
1997 Dec.	1	Trucks	150	40000	
		Cash	100		40000
		To record the purchase of four trucks.			

General Ledger

(Dr.)		Trucks		Acct. No. 150	(Cr.)
1997 **Dec. 1**		**40,000**			

(Dr.)		Cash		Acct. No. 100	(Cr.)
1997 Dec. 1	Beg. bal.	50,000	1997 **Dec. 1**		**40,000**

Effects of Transaction

One asset, trucks, increases (debited); and another asset, cash, decreases (credited) by $40,000.

Transaction 3: Dec. 1 Paid $2,400 cash for insurance on the trucks to cover a one-year period from this date.

General Journal

Date		Account Titles and Explanation	Post. Ref.	Debit	Credit
1997 Dec.	1	Prepaid Insurance	108	2400	
		Cash	100		2400
		Purchased truck insurance to cover a one-year period.			

General Ledger

(Dr.)		Prepaid Insurance		Acct. No. 108	(Cr.)
1997 **Dec. 1**		**2,400**			

(Dr.)		Cash		Acct. No. 100	(Cr.)
1997 Dec. 1	Beg. bal.	50,000	1997 Dec. 1		40,000
			1		**2,400**

Effects of Transaction

An asset, prepaid insurance, increases (debited); and an asset, cash, decreases (credited) by $2,400. The debit is to Prepaid Insurance rather than Insurance Expense because the policy covers more than the current accounting period of December (insurance policies are usually paid one year in advance). As you see in Chapter 3, prepaid items are expensed as they are used. If this insurance policy was only written for December, the entire $2,400 debit would have been to Insurance Expense.

Transaction 4: Dec. 1 Rented a building and paid $1,200 to cover a three-month period from this date.

General Journal

Date		Account Titles and Explanation	Post. Ref.	Debit	Credit
1997 Dec.	1	Prepaid Rent	112	1200	
		Cash	100		1200
		Paid three months' rent on a building.			

General Ledger

(Dr.)		Prepaid Rent		Acct. No. 112 (Cr.)
1997 **Dec. 1**		**1,200**		

(Dr.)		Cash		Acct. No. 100 (Cr.)
1997 Dec. 1	Beg. bal.	50,000	1997 Dec. 1	40,000
			1	2,400
			1	**1,200**

Effects of Transaction

An asset, prepaid rent, increases (debited); and another asset, cash, decreases (credited) by $1,200. The debit is to Prepaid Rent rather than Rent Expense because the payment covers more than the current month. If the payment had just been for December, the debit would have been to Rent Expense.

Transaction 5: Dec. 4 Purchased $1,400 of training supplies on account to be used over the next several months.

General Journal

Date		Account Titles and Explanation	Post. Ref.	Debit	Credit
1997 Dec.	4	Supplies on Hand	107	1400	
		Accounts Payable	200		1400
		To record the purchase of training supplies for future use.			

General Ledger

(Dr.)		Supplies on Hand		Acct. No. 107 (Cr.)
1997 **Dec. 4**		**1,400**		

(Dr.)		Accounts Payable		Acct. No. 200 (Cr.)
			1997 **Dec. 4**	**1,400**

Effects of Transaction

An asset, supplies on hand, increases (debited); and a liability, accounts payable, increases (credited) by $1,400. The debit is to Supplies on Hand rather than Supplies Expense because the supplies are to be used over several accounting periods.

In each of the three preceding entries, we debited an asset rather than an expense. The reason is that the expenditure applies to (or benefits) more than just the current accounting period. Whenever a company will not fully use up an item such as insurance, rent, or supplies in the period when purchased, it usually debits an asset. In practice, however, sometimes the expense is initially debited in these situations.

Companies sometimes buy items that they fully use up within the current accounting period. For example, during the first part of the month a company may buy supplies that it intends to consume fully during that month. If the company fully consumes the supplies during the period of purchase, the best practice is to debit Supplies Expense at the time of purchase rather than Supplies on Hand. This same advice applies to insurance and rent. If a company purchases insurance that it fully consumes during the current period, the company should debit Insurance Expense at the time of purchase rather than Prepaid Insurance. Also, if a company pays rent that applies only to the current period, Rent Expense should be debited at the time of purchase rather than Prepaid Rent. As illustrated in Chapter 3, following this advice simplifies the procedures at the end of the accounting period.

Transaction 6: Dec. 7 Received $4,500 from a customer in payment for future training services.

General Journal

Date		Account Titles and Explanation	Post. Ref.	Debit	Credit
1997 Dec.	7	Cash	100	4500	
		Unearned Service Fees	216		4500
		To record the receipt of cash from a customer in payment			
		for future training services.			

General Ledger

(Dr.)		Cash	Acct. No. 100		(Cr.)
1997			1997		
Dec. 1	Beg. bal.	50,000	Dec. 1		40,000
7		**4,500**	1		2,400
			1		1,200

(Dr.)	Unearned Service Fees	Acct. No. 216	(Cr.)
		1997	
		Dec. 7	**4,500**

Effects of Transaction

An asset, cash, increases (debited); and a liability, unearned service revenue, increases (credited) by $4,500. The credit is to Unearned Service Fees rather than Service Revenue because the $4,500 applies to more than just the current accounting period. Unearned Service Fees is a liability because, if the services are never performed, the $4,500 will have to be refunded. If the payment had been for services to be provided in December, the credit would have been to Service Revenue.

Transaction 7: Dec. 15 Performed training services for a customer for cash, $5,000.

General Journal

Date		Account Titles and Explanation	Post. Ref.	Debit	Credit
1997 Dec.	15	Cash	100	5000	
		Service Revenue	400		5000
		To record the receipt of cash for performing training			
		services for a customer.			

General Ledger

(Dr.)		Cash	Acct. No. 100		(Cr.)
1997			1997		
Dec. 1	Beg. bal.	50,000	Dec. 1		40,000
7		4,500	1		2,400
15		**5,000**	1		1,200

(Dr.)	Service Revenue	Acct. No. 400	(Cr.)
		1997	
		Dec. 15	**5,000**

Effects of Transaction

An asset, cash, increases (debited); and a revenue, service revenue, increases (credited) by $5,000.

Transaction 8: Dec. 17 Paid the $1,400 account payable resulting from the transaction of December 4.

General Journal

Date		Account Titles and Explanation	Post. Ref.	Debit	Credit
1997 Dec.	17	Accounts Payable	200	1400	
		Cash	100		1400
		Paid the account payable arising from the purchase of			
		supplies on December 4.			

General Ledger

Accounts Payable — Acct. No. 200

(Dr.)			(Cr.)
1997		1997	
Dec. 17	**1,400**	Dec. 4	1,400

Cash — Acct. No. 100

(Dr.)				(Cr.)
1997			1997	
Dec. 1	Beg. bal.	50,000	Dec. 1	40,000
7		4,500	1	2,400
15		5,000	1	1,200
			17	**1,400**

Effects of Transaction

A liability, accounts payable, decreases (debited); and an asset, cash, decreases (credited) by $1,400.

Transaction 9: Dec. 20 Billed a customer for training services performed, $5,700.

General Journal

Date		Account Titles and Explanation	Post. Ref.	Debit	Credit
1997 Dec.	20	Accounts Receivable	103	5700	
		Service Revenue	400		5700
		To record the performance of training services on account			
		for which a customer was billed.			

General Ledger

Accounts Receivable — Acct. No. 103

(Dr.)			(Cr.)
1997			
Dec. 20	**5,700**		

Service Revenue — Acct. No. 400

(Dr.)			(Cr.)
		1997	
		Dec. 15	5,000
		20	**5,700**

Effects of Transaction

An asset, accounts receivable, increases (debited); and a revenue, service revenue, increases (credited) by $5,700.

Transaction 10: Dec. 24 Received a bill for advertising that appeared in a local newspaper in December, $50.

General Journal

Date		Account Titles and Explanation	Post. Ref.	Debit	Credit
1997 Dec.	24	Advertising Expense	505	50	
		Accounts Payable	200		50
		Received a bill for advertising for the month of December			

General Ledger

(Dr.)		Advertising Expense	Acct. No. 505 (Cr.)
1997 **Dec. 24**	**50**		

(Dr.)		Accounts Payable	Acct. No. 200 (Cr.)
1997 Dec. 17	1,400	1997 Dec. 4	1,400
		24	**50**

Effects of Transaction

An expense, advertising expense, increases (debited); and a liability, accounts payable, increases (credited) by $50. The reason for debiting an expense rather than an asset is because all the cost pertains to the current accounting period, the month of December. Otherwise, Prepaid Advertising (an asset) would have been debited.

Transaction 11: Dec. 26 Received $500 on accounts receivable from a customer.

General Journal

Date		Account Titles and Explanation	Post. Ref.	Debit	Credit
1997 Dec.	26	Cash	100	500	
		Accounts Receivable	103		500
		Received $500 from a customer on accounts receivable.			

General Ledger

(Dr.)			Cash		Acct. No. 100 (Cr.)
1997			1997		
Dec. 1	Beg. bal.	50,000	Dec. 1		40,000
7		4,500	1		2,400
15		5,000	1		1,200
26		**500**	17		1,400

(Dr.)		Accounts Receivable	Acct. No. 103 (Cr.)
1997 Dec. 20	5,700	1997 **Dec. 26**	**500**

Effects of Transaction

One asset, cash, increases (debited); and another asset, accounts receivable, decreases (credited) by $500.

Transaction 12: Dec. 28 Paid salaries of $3,600 to training personnel for the first four weeks of December. (Payroll and other deductions are to be ignored since they have not yet been discussed.)

General Journal

Date		Account Titles and Explanation	Post. Ref.	Debit	Credit
1997 Dec.	28	Salaries Expense	507	3600	
		Cash	100		3600
		Paid training personnel salaries for the first four weeks of December.			

General Ledger

(Dr.) **Salaries Expense** Acct. No. 507 (Cr.)

Debit		Credit	
1997 **Dec. 28**	**3,600**		

(Dr.) **Cash** Acct. No. 100 (Cr.)

Date		Debit	Date	Credit
1997 Dec. 1	Beg. bal.	50,000	1997 Dec. 1	40,000
7		4,500	1	2,400
15		5,000	1	1,200
26		500	17	1,400
			28	**3,600**

Effects of Transaction

An expense, salaries expense, increases (debited); and an asset, cash, decreases (credited) by $3,600.

Transaction 13: Dec. 29 Received and paid the utilities bill for December, $150.

General Journal

Date		Account Titles and Explanation	Post. Ref.	Debit	Credit
1997 Dec.	29	Utilities Expense	511	150	
		Cash	100		150
		Paid the utilities bill for December.			

General Ledger

(Dr.) **Utilities Expense** Acct. No. 511 (Cr.)

Debit		Credit	
1997 **Dec. 29**	**150**		

(Dr.) **Cash** Acct. No. 100 (Cr.)

Date		Debit	Date	Credit
1997 Dec. 1	Beg. bal.	50,000	1997 Dec. 1	40,000
7		4,500	1	2,400
15		5,000	1	1,200
26		500	17	1,400
			28	3,600
			29	**150**

Effects of Transaction

An expense, utilities expense, increases (debited); and an asset, cash, decreases (credited) by $150.

Transaction 14: Dec. 30 Received a bill for gas and oil used in the trucks for December, $680.

General Journal

Date		Account Titles and Explanation	Post. Ref.	Debit	Credit
1997					
Dec.	30	Gas and Oil Expense	506	680	
		Accounts Payable	200		680
		Received a bill for gas and oil used in the trucks for December.			

General Ledger

(Dr.)	Gas and Oil Expense		Acct. No. 506 (Cr.)
1997			
Dec. 30	**680**		

(Dr.)	Accounts Payable		Acct. No. 200 (Cr.)
1997		1997	
Dec. 17	1,400	Dec. 4	1,400
		24	50
		30	**680**

Effects of Transaction

An expense, gas and oil expense, increases (debited); and a liability, accounts payable, increases (credited) by $680.

Transaction 15: Dec. 31 A dividend of $3,000 was paid to stockholders.

General Journal

Date		Account Titles and Explanation	Post. Ref.	Debit	Credit
1997					
Dec.	31	Dividends	320	3000	
		Cash	100		3000
		Dividends were paid to stockholders.			

General Ledger

(Dr.)	Dividends		Acct. No. 320 (Cr.)
1997			
Dec. 31	**3,000**		

(Dr.)		Cash		Acct. No. 100 (Cr.)
1997			1997	
Dec. 1	Beg. bal.	50,000	Dec. 1	40,000
7		4,500	1	2,400
15		5,000	1	1,200
26		500	17	1,400
			28	3,600
			29	150
			31	**3,000**

Effects of Transaction

The Dividends account increases (debited); and an asset, cash, decreases (credited) by $3,000.

Transaction 15 concludes the analysis of the MicroTrain Company transactions. The next section discusses and illustrates posting to three-column ledger accounts and cross-indexing.

The Use of Three-Column Ledger Accounts

Posting to Three-Column Ledger Accounts

Objective 5
Post journal entries to the accounts in the ledger.

A journal entry is like a set of instructions. The carrying out of these instructions is known as posting. As stated earlier, **posting** is recording in the ledger accounts the information contained in the journal. A journal entry directs the entry of a certain dollar amount as a debit in a specific ledger account and directs the entry of a certain dollar amount as a credit in a specific ledger account. Earlier, we posted the journal entries for MicroTrain Company to T-accounts. In practice, however, companies post these journal entries to three-column ledger accounts.

Using a new example, Jenks Company, we illustrate posting to three-column ledger accounts. Later, we show you how to post the MicroTrain Company journal entries to three-column ledger accounts.

In Illustration 2.6, the first journal entry for the Jenks Company directs that $10,000 be posted in the ledger as a debit to the Cash account and as a credit to the Capital Stock account. We post the debit in the general ledger Cash account by using the following procedure: Enter in the Cash account the date, a short explanation, the journal designation (''G'' for general journal) and the journal page number from which the debit is posted, and the $10,000 in the Debit column. Then, enter the number of the account to which the debit is posted in the Posting Reference column of the general journal. Post the credit in a similar manner but as a credit to Account No. 300. The arrows in Illustration 2.6 show how these amounts were posted to the correct accounts.

Illustration 2.6 shows the three-column ledger account. In contrast to the two-sided T-account format shown so far, the three-column format has columns for debit, credit, and balance. The three-column form has the advantage of showing the balance of the account after each item has been posted. In addition, in this chapter, we indicate whether each balance is a debit or a credit. In later chapters and in practice, the nature of the balance is usually not indicated since it is understood. Also, notice that we give an explanation for each item in the ledger accounts. Often accountants omit these explanations because each item can be traced back to the general journal for the explanation.

Posting is always from the journal to the ledger accounts. Postings can be made (1) at the time the transaction is journalized; (2) at the end of the day, week, or month; or (3) as each journal page is filled. The choice is a matter of personal taste. When posting the general journal, the date used in the ledger accounts is the date the transaction was recorded in the journal, not the date the journal entry was posted to the ledger accounts.

Cross-Indexing (Referencing)

Frequently, accountants must check and trace the origin of their transactions, so they provide *cross-indexing*. **Cross-indexing** is the placing of (1) the account number of the ledger account in the general journal and (2) the general journal page number in the ledger account. As shown in Illustration 2.6, the account number of the ledger account to which the posting was made is in the Posting Reference column of the general journal. Note the arrow from Account No. 100 in the ledger to the 100 in the Posting Reference column beside the first debit in the general journal. Accountants place the number of the general journal page from which the entry was posted in the Posting Reference column of the ledger account. Note the arrow from page 1 in the general journal to G1 in the Posting Reference column of the Cash account in the general ledger. The notation ''G1'' means general journal, page 1. The date of the transaction also appears in the general ledger. Note the arrows from the date in the general journal to the dates in the general ledger.

Cross-indexing aids the tracing of any recorded transaction, either from general journal to general ledger or from general ledger to general journal. Normally, they place cross-reference numbers in the Posting Reference column of the general journal when the entry is posted. If this practice is followed, the cross-reference numbers indicate that the entry has been posted.

ILLUSTRATION 2.6 General Journal and General Ledger; Posting and Cross-Indexing

JENKS COMPANY
General Journal

Page 1

Date		Account Titles and Explanation	Post. Ref.	Debit	Credit
1997 Jan.	1	Cash	100	10000	
		Capital Stock	300		10000
		Stockholders invested $10,000 cash in the business.			
	5	Cash	100	5000	
		Notes Payable	201		5000
		Borrowed $5,000 from the bank on a note.			

General Ledger

Cash *Account No. 100*

Date		Explanation	Post. Ref.	Debit	Credit	Balance
1997 Jan.	1	Stockholder investment	G1	10000		10000 Dr.
	5	Bank loan	G1	5000		15000 Dr.

Notes Payable *Account No. 201*

Date		Explanation	Post. Ref.	Debit	Credit	Balance
1997 Jan.	5	Borrowed cash	G1		5000	5000 Cr.

Capital Stock *Account No. 300*

Date		Explanation	Post. Ref.	Debit	Credit	Balance
1997 Jan.	1	Cash from stockholders	G1		10000	10000 Cr.

To understand the posting and cross-indexing process, trace the entries from the general journal to the general ledger. The ledger accounts need not contain explanations of all the entries, since any needed explanations can be obtained from the general journal.

Posting and Cross-Indexing—An Illustration

Look at Illustration 2.7 to see how all the November and December transactions of MicroTrain Company presented on pages 62–69 would be journalized. As shown in Illustration 2.7, you skip a line between journal entries to show where one journal entry ends and another begins. This procedure is standard practice among accountants. Note that no dollar signs appear in journals or ledgers. When

Illustration 2.7 General Journal (after posting)

MICROTRAIN COMPANY
General Journal

Page 1

Date		Account Titles and Explanation	Post. Ref.	Debit	Credit
1997 Nov.	28	Cash	100*	50000	
		Capital Stock	300		50000
		Stockholders invested $50,000 cash in the business.			
Dec.	1	Trucks	150	40000	
		Cash	100		40000
		To record the purchase of four trucks.			
	1	Prepaid Insurance	108	2400	
		Cash	100		2400
		Purchased truck insurance to cover a one-year period.			
	1	Prepaid Rent	112	1200	
		Cash	100		1200
		Paid three months' rent on a building.			
	4	Supplies on Hand	107	1400	
		Accounts Payable	200		1400
		To record the purchase of training supplies for future use.			
	7	Cash	100	4500	
		Unearned Service Fees	216		4500
		To record the receipt of cash from a customer in payment for			
		future training services.			
	15	Cash	100	5000	
		Service Revenue	400		5000
		To record the receipt of cash for performing training services			
		for a customer.			
	17	Accounts Payable	200	1400	
		Cash	100		1400
		Paid the account payable arising from the purchase of supplies			
		on December 4.			

* These posting references would be entered only after each amount has been posted.

amounts are in even dollar amounts, accountants leave the cents column blank or use zeros or a dash. When they use lined accounting work papers, commas or decimal points are not needed to record an amount. When they use unlined paper, they add both commas and decimal points.

Next, observe Illustration 2.8, the three-column general ledger accounts of MicroTrain Company after the journal entries have been posted. Each ledger account would appear on a separate page in the ledger. Trace the postings from the general journal to the general ledger to make sure you know how to post journal entries.

Compound Journal Entries

All the journal entries illustrated so far have involved one debit and one credit; these journal entries are called **simple journal entries.** Many business transactions, however, affect more than two accounts. The journal entry for these transactions

ILLUSTRATION 2.7 (concluded)

General Journal *Page 2*

Date		Account Titles and Explanation	Post. Ref.	Debit	Credit
1997					
Dec.	20	Accounts Receivable	103	5700	
		Service Revenue	400		5700
		To record the performance of training services on account for			
		which a customer was billed.			
	24	Advertising Expense	505	50	
		Accounts Payable	200		50
		Received a bill for advertising for the month of December.			
	26	Cash	100	500	
		Accounts Receivable	103		500
		Received $500 from a customer on accounts receivable.			
	28	Salaries Expense	507	3600	
		Cash	100		3600
		Paid training personnel salaries for the first four weeks of December.			
	29	Utilities Expense	511	150	
		Cash	100		150
		Paid the utilities bill for December.			
	30	Gas and Oil Expense	506	680	
		Accounts Payable	200		680
		Received a bill for gas and oil used in the trucks for December.			
	31	Dividends	320	3000	
		Cash	100		3000
		Dividends were paid to stockholders.			

involves more than one debit and/or credit. Such journal entries are called **compound journal entries.**

As an illustration of a compound journal entry, assume that on January 2, 1998, MicroTrain Company purchased $8,000 of training equipment from Wilson Company. MicroTrain paid $2,000 cash with the balance due on March 3, 1998. The general journal entry for MicroTrain Company is:

			Debit	Credit
1998				
Jan.	2	Equipment	8,000	
		Cash		2,000
		Accounts Payable		6,000
		Training equipment purchased from Wilson Company.		

Note that the firm credits two accounts, Cash and Accounts Payable, in this one entry. However, the dollar totals of the debits and credits are equal.

ILLUSTRATION 2.8 General Ledger—Extended Illustration

MICROTRAIN COMPANY
General Ledger

Page 1

Cash *Account No. 100*

Date		Explanation	Post. Ref.	Debit	Credit	Balance
1997 Dec.	1	Beginning balance*				50000 Dr.
	1	Trucks	G1		40000	10000 Dr.
	1	Prepaid insurance	G1		2400	7600 Dr.
	1	Prepaid rent	G1		1200	6400 Dr.
	7	Unearned service fees	G1	4500		10900 Dr.
	15	Service revenue	G1	5000		15900 Dr.
	17	Paid account payable	G1		1400	14500 Dr.
	26	Collected account receivable	G2	500		15000 Dr.
	28	Salaries	G2		3600	11400 Dr.
	29	Utilities	G2		150	11250 Dr.
	31	Dividends	G2		3000	8250 Dr.

Accounts Receivable *Account No. 103*

Date		Explanation	Post. Ref.	Debit	Credit	Balance
1997 Dec.	20	Service revenue	G2	5700		5700 Dr.
	26	Collections	G2		500	5200 Dr.

Supplies on Hand *Account No. 107*

Date		Explanation	Post. Ref.	Debit	Credit	Balance
1997 Dec.	4	Purchased on account	G1	1400		1400 Dr.

Prepaid Insurance *Account No. 108*

Date		Explanation	Post. Ref.	Debit	Credit	Balance
1997 Dec.	1	One-year policy on trucks	G1	2400		2400 Dr.

* Beginning balances result from carrying forward a balance from a preceding page for this account. The Cash account, for example, is likely to use page after page over a period since so many transactions involve cash. This particular beginning balance came from the stockholders' investments in November. Often no explanation is included in the Explanation column since explanations may be found in the general journal or are not relevant.

ILLUSTRATION 2.8 (continued)

General Ledger *Page 2*

Prepaid Rent *Account No. 112*

Date		Explanation	Post. Ref.	Debit	Credit	Balance
1997 Dec.	1	Three-month payment	G1	1200		1200 Dr.

Trucks *Account No. 150*

Date		Explanation	Post. Ref.	Debit	Credit	Balance
1997 Dec.	1	Paid cash	G1	40000		40000 Dr.

Accounts Payable *Account No. 200*

Date		Explanation	Post. Ref.	Debit	Credit	Balance
1997 Dec.	4	Supplies	G1		1400	1400 Cr.
	17	Paid for supplies	G1	1400		-0-
	24	Advertising	G2		50	50 Cr.
	30	Gas and oil	G2		680	730 Cr.

Unearned Service Fees *Account No. 216*

Date		Explanation	Post. Ref.	Debit	Credit	Balance
1997 Dec.	7	Received cash	G1		4500	4500 Cr.

Capital Stock *Account No. 300*

Date		Explanation	Post. Ref.	Debit	Credit	Balance
1997 Dec.	1	Beginning balance				50000 Cr.

Illustration 2.8 (concluded)

General Ledger *Page 3*

Dividends *Account No. 320*

Date		Explanation	Post. Ref.	Debit	Credit	Balance
1997 Dec.	31	Cash	G2	3000		3000 Dr.

Service Revenue *Account No. 400*

Date		Explanation	Post. Ref.	Debit	Credit	Balance
1997 Dec.	15	Cash	G1		5000	5000 Cr.
	20	On account	G2		5700	10700 Cr.

Advertising Expense *Account No. 505*

Date		Explanation	Post. Ref.	Debit	Credit	Balance
1997 Dec.	24	On account	G2	50		50 Dr.

Gas and Oil Expense *Account No. 506*

Date		Explanation	Post. Ref.	Debit	Credit	Balance
1997 Dec.	30	On account	G2	680		680 Dr.

Salaries Expense *Account No. 507*

Date		Explanation	Post. Ref.	Debit	Credit	Balance
1997 Dec.	28	Cash paid	G2	3600		3600 Dr.

Utilities Expense *Account No. 511*

Date		Explanation	Post. Ref.	Debit	Credit	Balance
1997 Dec.	29	Cash paid	G2	150		150 Dr.

ILLUSTRATION 2.9
Trial Balance

MICROTRAIN COMPANY
Trial Balance
December 31, 1997

Acct. No.	Account Title	Debits	Credits
100	Cash	$ 8,250	
103	Accounts Receivable	5,200	
107	Supplies on Hand	1,400	
108	Prepaid Insurance	2,400	
112	Prepaid Rent	1,200	
150	Trucks	40,000	
200	Accounts Payable		$ 730
216	Unearned Service Fees		4,500
300	Capital Stock		50,000
320	Dividends	3,000	
400	Service Revenue		10,700
505	Advertising Expense	50	
506	Gas and Oil Expense	680	
507	Salaries Expense	3,600	
511	Utilities Expense	150	
		$65,930	$65,930

The Trial Balance

Objective 6
Prepare a trial balance to test the equality of debits and credits in the journalizing and posting process.

Periodically, accountants use a *trial balance* to test the equality of their debits and credits. A **trial balance** is a listing of the ledger accounts and their debit or credit balances to determine that debits equal credits in the recording process. The accounts appear in this order: assets, liabilities, stockholders' equity, dividends, revenues, and expenses. Within the assets category, the most liquid (closest to becoming cash) asset appears first and the least liquid appears last. Within the liabilities, those liabilities with the shortest maturities appear first. Study Illustration 2.9, the trial balance for MicroTrain Company. Note the listing of the account numbers and account titles on the left, the column for debit balances, the column for credit balances, and the equality of the two totals.

When the trial balance does not balance, try retotaling the two columns. If this step does not locate the error, divide the difference in the totals by 2 and then by 9. If the difference is divisible by 2, you may have transferred a debit-balanced account to the trial balance as a credit, or a credit-balanced account as a debit. When the difference is divisible by 2, look for an amount in the trial balance that is equal to one half of the difference. Thus, if the difference is $800, look for an account with a balance of $400 and see if it is in the wrong column.

If the difference is divisible by 9, you may have made a transposition error in transferring a balance to the trial balance or a slide error. A transposition error occurs when two digits are reversed in an amount (e.g., writing 753 as 573 or 110 as 101). A slide error occurs when you place a decimal point incorrectly (e.g., $1,500 recorded as $15.00). Thus, when a difference is divisible by 9, compare the trial balance amounts with the general ledger account balances to see if you made a transposition or slide error in transferring the amounts.

If you still cannot find the error, it may be due to one of the following causes:

1. Failing to post part of a journal entry.
2. Posting a debit as a credit, or vice versa.
3. Incorrectly determining the balance of an account.
4. Recording the balance of an account incorrectly in the trial balance.
5. Omitting an account from the trial balance.
6. Making a transposition or slide error in the accounts or the journal.

Usually, you should work backward through the steps taken to prepare the trial balance. Assuming you have already retotaled the columns and traced the

An Ethical Perspective

Financial Deals, Inc.

Larry Fisher was captain of the football team at Prestige University. Later, he earned a masters degree in business administration with a concentration in accounting.

Upon graduation, Larry accepted a position with Financial Deals, Inc., in the accounting and finance division. At first, things were going smoothly. He was tall, good looking, and had an outgoing personality. The president of the company took a liking to him. However, Larry was somewhat bothered when the president started asking him to do some things that were slightly unethical. When he protested mildly, the president said, "Come on, son, this is the way the business world works. You have great potential if you don't let things like this get in your way."

As time went on, Larry was asked to do things that were more unethical, and finally he was performing illegal acts. When he resisted, the president appealed to his loyalty and asked him to be a team player. The president also promised Larry great wealth sometime in the future. Finally, when he was told to falsify some financial statements by making improper adjusting entries and to sign some documents containing material errors, the president supported his request by stating, "You are in too deep now to refuse to cooperate. If I go down, you are going with me." Through various company schemes, Larry had convinced some friends and relatives to invest about $10 million. Most of this would be lost if the various company schemes were revealed.

Larry could not sleep at night and began each day with a pain in his stomach and by becoming physically ill. He was under great strain and believed that he could lose his mind. He also heard that the president had a shady past and could become violent in retaliating against his enemies. If Larry blows the whistle, he believes he will go to prison for his part in the schemes. (Note: This scenario is based on an actual situation with some facts changed to protect the guilty.)

amounts appearing in the trial balance back to the general ledger account balances, use the following steps: Verify the balance of each general ledger account, verify postings to the general ledger, verify general journal entries, and then review the transactions and possibly the source documents.

The equality of the two totals in the trial balance does not necessarily mean that the accounting process has been error-free. Serious errors may have been made, such as failure to record a transaction, or posting a debit or credit to the wrong account. For instance, if a transaction involving payment of a $100 account payable is never recorded, the trial balance totals still balance, but at an amount that is $100 too high. Both cash and accounts payable would be overstated by $100.

You can prepare a trial balance at any time—at the end of a day, a week, a month, a quarter, or a year. Typically, you would prepare a trial balance before preparing the financial statements. Dollar signs may be used but are not required.

Analyzing and Using the Financial Results—Horizontal and Vertical Analyses

Objective 7
Analyze and use the financial results—horizontal and vertical analyses.

The calculation of dollar and/or percentage changes from one year to the next in an item on financial statements is **horizontal analysis.** For instance, in the following data taken from the 1992 annual report of E. J. du Pont de Nemours & Company, the amount of cash and cash equivalents increased by $1.206 billion from December 31, 1991, to December 31, 1992. This amount represented a 258% increase. To find the amount of the increase, subtract the 1991 amount from the 1992 amount. To find the percentage change, divide the increase by the 1991 amount.

Knowing the dollar amount and percentage of change in an amount is much more meaningful than merely knowing the amount at one point in time. By analyzing the data, we can see that accounts and notes receivable, inventories, and prepaid expenses all declined in 1992. Their decline at least partially explains the increase in cash and cash equivalents. We can also see that the company invested in property, plant, and equipment, and in affiliated companies. Other assets remained about the same. Any terms in DuPont's list of assets that you may not understand are explained in later chapters. At this point, all we want you to understand is the nature of horizontal and vertical analyses.

Vertical analysis shows the percentage that each item in a financial statement is of some significant total such as total assets or sales. For instance, in the DuPont data we can see that cash and cash equivalents were 1.3% of total assets as of December 31, 1991, and had risen to 4.3% of total assets by December 31, 1992. Total current assets (cash plus other amounts that will become cash or be used up within one year) remained about 31% of total assets, although the relative composition of current assets changed. Property, plant, and equipment; investments; and other assets remained at fairly constant percentages of total assets.

Management performs horizontal and vertical analyses along with other forms of analysis to help evaluate the wisdom of its past decisions and to plan for the future. Other data would have to be examined before decisions could be made regarding the assets shown. For instance, if you discovered the liabilities that would have to be paid within a short time by DuPont were more than $10 billion, you might conclude that the company is short of cash even though cash and cash equivalents increased substantially during 1992. We illustrate horizontal and vertical analyses to a much greater extent later in the text.

			Increase or (Decrease) 1992 over 1991		Percent of Total Assets December 31	
December 31 ($ millions)	**1992**	**1991**	**Dollars**	**Percent**	**1991**	**1991**
Assets						
Current Assets						
Cash and cash equivalents	$ 1,674	$ 468	$1,206	258%	4.3%	1.3%
Accounts and notes receivable	5,238	5,546	(308)	(6)	13.5	15.2
Inventories	4,401	4,428	(27)	(1)	11.3	12.1
Prepaid expenses	345	432	(87)	(20)	0.9	1.2
Deferred income taxes	570	442	128	29	1.5	1.2
Total current assets	$12,228	$11,316	$ 912	8	31.5%	31.0%
Property, Plant, and Equipment (net)	21,882	20,610	1,272	6	56.3	56.4
Investment in Affiliates	1,746	1,580	166	11	4.5	4.3
Other Assets	3,014	3,053	(39)	(1)	7.7	8.3
Total	$38,870	$36,559	$2,311	6	100.0%	100.0%

DuPont
DuPont, one of the 10 largest U.S. companies, is a global company with markets that include aerospace, apparel, chemicals, health care, and transportation.

AN ACCOUNTING PERSPECTIVE

BUSINESS INSIGHT Many companies have been restructuring their organizations and reducing the number of employees to cut expenses. General Motors, AT&T, IBM, and numerous other companies have taken this action. One could question whether companies place as much value on their employees as in the past. In previous years it was common to see the following statement in the annual reports of companies: "Our employees are our most valuable asset." Companies are not permitted to show employees as assets on their balance sheets. Do you think they should be allowed to do so?

Sometimes companies include horizontal and vertical analyses in reports to stockholders. In its 1993 first quarter report to stockholders, Kimberly-Clark Corporation included the following analysis regarding amounts on its income statement:

Kimberly-Clark
Kimberly-Clark Corporation manufactures and markets Kleenex, Huggies, health care products, newsprint and other papers, aircraft services, commercial air transportation, and other products and services.

		Percent Change	Percent of Sales	
($ millions)	**1993**	**vs. 1992**	**1993**	**1992**
Three Months Ended March 31				
Net sales	$1,702.0	−2.2%	100.0%	100.0%
Gross profit	602.7	−6.1	35.4	36.9
Operating profit	196.0	−5.1	11.5	11.9
Income before income taxes	174.7	−6.1	10.3	10.7
Income before equity interests	108.3	−6.8	6.4	6.7
Net income	124.8	−5.5	7.3	7.6
Net income per share	.78	−4.9		

Although the company did not show the dollar amount of changes, the amounts could be calculated from the information given. The company's management attributed the declines to "weak markets for certain consumer and industrial products in North America and Europe and accompanying pricing pressures resulted in declines in sales and profits."

What you have learned in this chapter is basic to your study of accounting. The entire process of accounting is based on the double-entry concept. Chapter 3 explains that adjustments usually bring the accounts to their proper balances before accurate financial statements are prepared.

Understanding The Learning Objectives

Objective 1
Use the account as the basic classifying and storage unit for accounting information.

- An account is a storage unit used to classify and summarize money measurements of business activities of a similar nature.
- A firm sets up an account whenever it needs to provide useful information about a particular business item to some party having a valid interest in the business.

Objective 2
Express the effects of business transactions in terms of debits and credits to different types of accounts.

- A T-account resembles the letter T.
- Debits are entries on the left side of a T-account.
- Credits are entries on the right side of a T-account.
- Debits increase asset, expense, and Dividends accounts.
- Credits increase liability, stockholders' equity, and revenue accounts.

Objective 3
List the steps in the accounting cycle.

- Analyze transactions by examining source documents.
- Journalize transactions in the journal.
- Post journal entries to the accounts in the ledger.
- Prepare a trial balance of the accounts and complete the work sheet.
- Prepare financial statements.
- Journalize and post adjusting entries.
- Journalize and post closing entries.
- Prepare a post-closing trial balance.

Objective 4
Record the effects of business transactions in a journal.

- A journal contains a chronological record of the transactions of a business.
- An example of a general journal is shown in Illustration 2.7.
- Journalizing is the process of entering a transaction in a journal.

Objective 5
Post journal entries to the accounts in the ledger.

- Posting is the process of transferring information recorded in the journal to the proper places in the ledger.
- Cross-indexing is the placing of (1) the account number of the ledger account in the general journal and (2) the general journal page number in the ledger account.
- An example of cross-indexing appears in Illustration 2.6.

Objective 6
Prepare a trial balance to test the equality of debits and credits in the journalizing and posting process.

- A trial balance is a listing of the ledger accounts and their debit or credit balances.
- If the trial balance does not balance, an accountant works backward to discover the error.
- A trial balance is shown in Illustration 2.9.

- Horizontal analysis involves calculating the dollar and/or percentage changes in an item from one year to the next.
- Vertical analysis shows the percentage that each item in a financial statement is of some significant total.

Objective 7
Analyze and use the financial results—horizontal and vertical analyses.

DEMONSTRATION PROBLEM

Green Hills Riding Stable, Incorporated, had the following balance sheet on June 30, 1997:

GREEN HILLS RIDING STABLE, INCORPORATED
Balance Sheet
June 30, 1997

Assets		
Cash		$ 7,500
Accounts receivable		5,400
Land		40,000
Total assets		$52,900
Liabilities and Stockholders' Equity		
Liabilities:		
Accounts payable		$ 800
Notes payable		40,000
Total liabilities		$40,800
Stockholders' equity:		
Capital stock	$10,000	
Retained earnings	2,100	
Total stockholders' equity		12,100
Total liabilities and stockholders' equity		$52,900

Transactions for July 1997 were as follows:

July 1 Additional shares of capital stock were issued for $25,000 cash.
1 Paid for a prefabricated building constructed on the land at a cost of $24,000.
8 Paid the accounts payable of $800.
10 Collected the accounts receivable of $5,400.
12 Horse feed to be used in July was purchased on credit for $1,100.
15 Boarding fees for July were charged to customers in the amount of $4,500. (This amount is due on August 10.)
24 Miscellaneous expenses of $800 for July were paid.
31 Paid interest expense on the notes payable of $200.
31 Salaries of $1,400 for the month were paid.
31 Riding and lesson fees for July were billed to customers in the amount of $3,600. (They are due on August 10.)
31 Paid a $1,000 dividend to the stockholders.

Required

a. Prepare the journal entries to record the transactions for July 1997.

b. Post the journal entries to the ledger accounts after entering the beginning balances in those accounts. Insert cross-indexing references in the journal and ledger. Use the following chart of accounts:

100	Cash	320	Dividends
103	Accounts Receivable	402	Horse Boarding Fees Revenue
130	Land	404	Riding and Lesson Fees Revenue
140	Buildings	507	Salaries Expense
200	Accounts Payable	513	Feed Expense
201	Notes Payable	540	Interest Expense
300	Capital Stock	568	Miscellaneous Expense
310	Retained Earnings		

c. Prepare a trial balance.

Solution to Demonstration Problem

a.

GREEN HILLS RIDING STABLE, INCORPORATED
General Journal

Page 1

Date		Account Titles and Explanation	Post. Ref.	Debit	Credit
1997 July	1	Cash	100	25000	
		Capital Stock	300		25000
		Additional capital stock issued.			
	1	Buildings	140	24000	
		Cash	100		24000
		Paid for building.			
	8	Accounts Payable	200	800	
		Cash	100		800
		Paid accounts payable.			
	10	Cash	100	5400	
		Accounts Receivable	103		5400
		Collected accounts receivable.			
	12	Feed Expense	513	1100	
		Accounts Payable	200		1100
		Purchased feed on credit.			
	15	Accounts Receivable	103	4500	
		Horse Boarding Fees Revenue	402		4500
		Billed boarding fees for July.			
	24	Miscellaneous Expense	568	800	
		Cash	100		800
		Paid miscellaneous expense for July.			
	31	Interest Expense	540	200	
		Cash	100		200
		Paid interest.			
	31	Salaries Expense	507	1400	
		Cash	100		1400
		Paid salaries for July.			
	31	Accounts Receivable	103	3600	
		Riding and Lesson Fees Revenue	404		3600
		Billed riding and lesson fees for July.			
	31	Dividends	320	1000	
		Cash	100		1000
		Paid a dividend to stockholders.			

b.

GREEN HILLS RIDING STABLE, INCORPORATED
General Ledger

Cash *Account No. 100*

Date		Explanation	Post. Ref.	Debit	Credit	Balance
1997 June	30	Balance				7500 Dr.
July	1	Stockholders' investment	G1	25000		32500 Dr.
	1	Buildings	G1		24000	8500 Dr.
	8	Accounts payable	G1		800	7700 Dr.
	10	Accounts receivable	G1	5400		13100 Dr.
	24	Miscellaneous expense	G1		800	12300 Dr.
	31	Interest expense	G1		200	12100 Dr.
	31	Salaries expense	G1		1400	10700 Dr.
	31	Dividends	G1		1000	9700 Dr.

Accounts Receivable *Account No. 103*

Date		Explanation	Post. Ref.	Debit	Credit	Balance
1997 June	30	Balance				5400 Dr.
July	10	Cash	G1		5400	–0–
	15	Horse boarding fees	G1	4500		4500 Dr.
	31	Riding and lesson fees	G1	3600		8100 Dr.

Land *Account No. 130*

Date		Explanation	Post. Ref.	Debit	Credit	Balance
1997 June	30	Balance				40000 Dr.

Buildings *Account No. 140*

Date		Explanation	Post. Ref.	Debit	Credit	Balance
1997 July	1	Cash	G1	24000		24000 Dr.

Accounts Payable *Account No. 200*

Date		Explanation	Post. Ref.	Debit	Credit	Balance
1997 June	30	Balance				800 Cr.
July	8	Cash	G1	800		–0–
	12	Feed expense	G1		1100	1100 Cr.

General Ledger (continued)

Notes Payable

Account No. 201

Date		Explanation	Post. Ref.	Debit	Credit	Balance
1997 June	30	Balance				40000 Cr.

Capital Stock

Account No. 300

Date		Explanation	Post. Ref.	Debit	Credit	Balance
1997 June	30	Balance				10000 Cr.
July	1	Cash	G1		25000	35000 Cr.

Retained Earnings

Account No. 310

Date		Explanation	Post. Ref.	Debit	Credit	Balance
1997 June	30	Balance				2100 Cr.

Dividends

Account No. 320

Date		Explanation	Post. Ref.	Debit	Credit	Balance
1997 July	31	Cash	G1	1000		1000 Dr.

Horse Boarding Fees Revenue

Account No. 402

Date		Explanation	Post. Ref.	Debit	Credit	Balance
1997 July	15	Accounts receivable	G1		4500	4500 Cr.

Riding and Lesson Fees Revenue

Account No. 404

Date		Explanation	Post. Ref.	Debit	Credit	Balance
1997 July	31	Accounts receivable	G1		3600	3600 Cr.

General Ledger (concluded)

Salaries Expense

Account No. 507

Date		Explanation	Post. Ref.	Debit	Credit	Balance
1997 July	31	Cash	G1	1400		1400 Dr.

Feed Expense

Account No. 513

Date		Explanation	Post. Ref.	Debit	Credit	Balance
1997 July	12	Accounts payable	G1	1100		1100 Dr.

Interest Expense

Account No. 540

Date		Explanation	Post. Ref.	Debit	Credit	Balance
1997 July	31	Cash	G1	200		200 Dr.

Miscellaneous Expense

Account No. 568

Date		Explanation	Post. Ref.	Debit	Credit	Balance
1997 July	24	Cash	G1	800		800 Dr.

c.

GREEN HILLS RIDING STABLE, INCORPORATED
Trial Balance
July 31, 1997

Acct. No.	Account Title	Debits	Credits
100	Cash	$ 9,700	
103	Accounts Receivable	8,100	
130	Land	40,000	
140	Buildings	24,000	
200	Accounts Payable		$ 1,100
201	Notes Payable		40,000
300	Capital Stock		35,000
310	Retained Earnings		2,100
320	Dividends	1,000	
402	Horse Boarding Fees Revenue		4,500
404	Riding and Lesson Fees Revenue		3,600
507	Salaries Expense	1,400	
513	Feed Expense	1,100	
540	Interest Expense	200	
568	Miscellaneous Expense	800	
		$86,300	$86,300

New Terms

Account A part of the accounting system used to classify and summarize the increases, decreases, and balances of each asset, liability, stockholders' equity item, dividend, revenue, and expense. The three-column account is normally used. It contains columns for debit, credit, and balance. *52*

Accounting cycle A series of steps performed during the accounting period (some throughout the period and some at the end) to analyze, record, classify, summarize, and report useful financial information for the purpose of preparing financial statements. *57*

Accrual basis of accounting Recognizes revenues when sales are made or services are performed, regardless of when cash is received. Recognizes expenses as incurred, whether or not cash has been paid out. *62*

Business transactions Measurable events that affect the financial condition of a business. *57*

Chart of accounts The complete listing of the account titles and account numbers of all of the accounts in the ledger; somewhat comparable to a table of contents. *60*

Compound journal entry A journal entry with more than one debit and/or credit. *73*

Credit The right side of any account; when used as a verb, to enter a dollar amount on the right side of an account; credits increase liability, stockholders' equity, and revenue accounts and decrease asset, expense, and Dividends accounts. *53*

Credit balance The balance in an account when the sum of the credits to the account exceeds the sum of the debits to that account. *56*

Cross-indexing The placing of (1) the account number of the ledger account in the general journal and (2) the general journal page number in the ledger account. *70*

Debit The left side of any account; when used as a verb, to enter a dollar amount on the left side of an account; debits increase asset, expense, and Dividends accounts and decrease liability, stockholders' equity, and revenue accounts. *53*

Debit balance The balance in an account when the sum of the debits to the account exceeds the sum of the credits to that account. *55*

Double-entry procedure The accounting requirement that each transaction must be recorded by an entry that has equal debits and credits. *53*

Horizontal analysis The calculation of dollar and/or percentage changes in an item on the financial statements from one year to the next. *78*

Journal A chronological (arranged in order of time) record of business transactions; the simplest form of journal is the two-column general journal. *59*

Journal entry Shows all of the effects of a business transaction as expressed in debit(s) and credit(s) and may include an explanation of the transaction. *59*

Journalizing A step in the accounting recording process that consists of entering the effects of a transaction in a journal. *61*

Ledger The complete collection of all of the accounts of a company; often referred to as the *general ledger*. *60*

Note An unconditional written promise to pay to another party the amount owed either when demanded or at a certain specified date. *54*

Permanent accounts (real accounts) Balance sheet accounts; their balances are not transferred (or closed) to any other account at the end of the accounting period. *60*

Posting Recording in the ledger accounts the information contained in the journal. *61, 70*

Simple journal entry An entry with one debit and one credit. *72*

T-account An account resembling the letter T, which is used for illustrative purposes only. Debits are entered on the left side of the account, and credits are entered on the right side of the account. *52*

Temporary accounts (nominal accounts) They temporarily contain the revenue, expense, and dividend information that is transferred (or closed) to a stockholders' equity account (Retained Earnings) at the end of the accounting period. *60*

Trial balance A listing of the ledger accounts and their debit or credit balances to determine that debits equal credits in the recording process. *77*

Vertical analysis Shows the percentage that each item in a financial statement is of some significant total such as total assets or sales. *79*

Self-Test

True-False

Indicate whether each of the following statements is true or false.

1. All of the steps in the accounting cycle are performed only at the end of the accounting period.
2. A transaction must be journalized in the journal before it can be posted to the ledger accounts.
3. The left side of any account is the credit side.
4. Revenues, liabilities, and Capital Stock accounts are increased by debits.
5. The Dividends account is increased by debits.
6. If the trial balance has equal debit and credit totals, it cannot contain any errors.

Multiple-Choice

Select the best answer for each of the following questions.

1. When the stockholders invest cash in the business:
   - **a.** Capital Stock is debited and Cash is credited.
   - **b.** Cash is debited and Dividends is credited.
   - **c.** Cash is debited and Capital Stock is credited.
   - **d.** None of the above.
2. Assume that cash is paid for insurance to cover a three-year period. The recommended debit and credit are:
   - **a.** Debit Insurance Expense, credit Cash.
   - **b.** Debit Prepaid Insurance, credit Cash.
   - **c.** Debit Cash, credit Insurance Expense.
   - **d.** Debit Cash, credit Prepaid Insurance.
3. A company received cash from a customer in payment for future delivery services. The correct debit and credit are:
   - **a.** Debit Cash, credit Unearned Delivery Fees.
   - **b.** Debit Cash, credit Delivery Fee Revenue.
   - **c.** Debit Accounts Receivable, credit Delivery Fee Revenue.
   - **d.** None of the above.
4. A company performed delivery services for a customer for cash. The correct debit and credit are:
   - **a.** Debit Cash, credit Unearned Delivery Fees.
   - **b.** Debit Cash, credit Delivery Fee Revenue.
   - **c.** Debit Accounts Receivable, credit Delivery Fee Revenue.
   - **d.** None of the above.
5. A cash dividend of $500 was declared and paid to stockholders. The correct journal entry is:

		Debit	Credit
a.	Capital Stock	500	
	Cash		500
b.	Cash	500	
	Dividends		500
c.	Dividends	500	
	Cash		500
d.	Cash	500	
	Capital Stock		500

Now turn to page 97 to check your answers.

Questions

1. Describe the steps in recording and posting the effects of a business transaction.
2. Give some examples of source documents.
3. Define an account. What are the two basic forms (styles) of accounts illustrated in the chapter?
4. What is meant by the term *double-entry procedure,* or duality?
5. Describe how you would determine the balance of a T-account.
6. Define debit and credit. Name the types of accounts that are:
   - **a.** Increased by a debit.
   - **b.** Decreased by a debit.
   - **c.** Increased by a credit.
   - **d.** Decreased by a credit.

   Do you think this system makes sense? Can you conceive of other possible methods for recording changes in accounts?
7. Which of the steps in the accounting cycle are performed throughout the accounting period?
8. Which of the steps in the accounting cycle are performed only at the end of the accounting period?
9. Why are expense and revenue accounts used when all revenues and expenses could be shown directly in the Retained Earnings account?
10. What is the purpose of the Dividends account and how is it increased?
11. Are the following possibilities conceivable in an entry involving only one debit and one credit? Why?
    - **a.** Increase a liability and increase an expense.
    - **b.** Increase an asset and decrease a liability.
    - **c.** Increase a revenue and decrease an expense.
    - **d.** Decrease an asset and increase another asset.
    - **e.** Decrease an asset and increase a liability.
    - **f.** Decrease a revenue and decrease an asset.
    - **g.** Decrease a liability and increase a revenue.
12. Describe the nature and purposes of the general journal. What does journalizing mean? Give an example of a compound entry in the general journal.
13. Describe a ledger and a chart of accounts. How do these two compare with a book and its table of contents?
14. Describe the act of posting. What difficulties could arise if no cross-indexing existed between the general journal and the ledger accounts?
15. Which of the following cash payments would involve the immediate recording of an expense? Why?
    - **a.** Paid vendors for office supplies previously purchased on account.
    - **b.** Paid an automobile dealer for a new company auto.
    - **c.** Paid the current month's rent.
    - **d.** Paid salaries for the last half of the current month.
16. What types of accounts appear in the unadjusted trial balance? What are the purposes of this trial balance?
17. You have found that the total of the Debits column of the trial balance of Burns Company is $200,000, while the total of the Credits column is $180,000. What are some possible causes of this difference? If the difference between the columns is divisible by 9, what types of errors are possible?

18. Store equipment was purchased for $2,000. Instead of debiting the Store Equipment account, the debit was made to Delivery Equipment. Of what help will the trial balance be in locating this error? Why?

19. A student remembered that the side toward the window in the classroom was the debit side of an account. The student took an examination in a room where the windows were on the other side of the room and became confused and consistently reversed debits and credits. Would the student's trial balance have equal debit and credit totals? If there were no existing balances in any of the accounts to begin with, would the error prevent the student from preparing correct financial statements? Why?

EXERCISES

Exercise 2–1
Indicate rules of debit and credit (L.O. 1, 2)

A diagram of the various types of accounts follows. Show where pluses (+) or minuses (−) should be inserted to indicate the effect debits and credits have on each account.

Asset Accounts		=	Liability Accounts		+	Stockholders' Equity Accounts	
Debit	Credit		Debit	Credit		Debit	Credit

Expense Accounts and Dividends Accounts		Revenue Accounts	
Debit	Credit	Debit	Credit

Exercise 2–2
Prepare journal entries (L.O. 4)

Prepare the journal entry required for each of the following transactions:

a. Cash was received for services performed for customers, $2,400.

b. Services were performed for customers on account, $3,600.

Exercise 2–3
Prepare journal entries (L.O. 4)

Prepare the journal entry required for each of the following transactions:

a. Capital stock was issued for $60,000.

b. Purchased machinery for cash, $30,000.

Exercise 2–4
Prepare journal entries (L.O. 4)

Prepare the journal entry required for each of the following transactions:

a. Capital stock was issued for $50,000 cash.

b. A $30,000 loan was arranged with a bank. The bank increased the company's checking account by $30,000 after management of the company signed a written promise to return the $30,000 in 30 days.

c. Cash was received for services performed for customers, $800.

d. Services were performed for customers on account, $1,200.

Exercise 2–5
Show entries using journal entries and T-accounts (L.O. 4, 5)

For each of the following unrelated transactions, give the journal entry to record the transaction. Then show how the journal entry would be posted to T-accounts. You need not include explanations or account numbers.

a. Capital stock was issued for $200,000 cash.

b. Salaries for a period were paid to employees, $24,000.

c. Services were performed for customers on account, $40,000.

Exercise 2–6
Explain sets of debits and credits (L.O. 1–5)

Explain each of the sets of debits and credits in these accounts for Tuxedos, Inc., a company that rents wedding clothing and accessories. There are 10 transactions to be explained. Each set is designated by the small letters to the left of the amount. For example, the first transaction is the issuance of capital stock for cash and is denoted by the letter *(a)*.

Cash			
(a)	300,000	*(b)*	150,000
(d)	1,800	*(e)*	1,000
		(f)	600
		(g)	2,000
		(i)	30,000
Bal.	118,200		

Dividends		
(e)	1,000	

Accounts Receivable

	Debit		Credit
(c)	1,800	*(d)*	1,800
(j)	12,000		
Bal.	12,000		

Service Revenue

	Debit		Credit
		(c)	1,800
		(j)	12,000
		Bal.	13,800

Supplies on Hand

	Debit		Credit
(b)	150,000		
(i)	30,000		
Bal.	180,000		

Rent Expense

	Debit		Credit
(f)	600		

Accounts Payable

	Debit		Credit
		(h)	800

Delivery Expense

	Debit		Credit
(h)	800		

Capital Stock

	Debit		Credit
		(a)	300,000

Salaries Expense

	Debit		Credit
(g)	2,000		

Exercise 2–7
Prepare trial balance (L.O. 6)

Assume the ledger accounts given in Exercise 2–6 are those of Tuxedos, Inc., as they appear at December 31, 1997. Prepare the trial balance as of that date.

Exercise 2–8
Prepare journal entries (L.O. 4)

Prepare journal entries to record each of the following transactions for Ruiz Company. Use the letter of the transaction in place of the date. Include an explanation for each entry.

a. Capital stock was issued for cash, $384,000.
b. Purchased trucks by signing a note bearing no interest, $210,000.
c. Earned service revenue on account, $4,800.
d. Collected the account receivable resulting from transaction **(c)**, $4,800.
e. Paid the note payable for the trucks purchased, $210,000.
f. Paid utilities for the month in the amount of $1,800.
g. Paid salaries for the month in the amount of $7,500.
h. Incurred supplies expenses on account in the amount of $1,920, but did not yet pay for them.
i. Purchased another truck for cash, $48,000.
j. Performed delivery services on account, $24,000.

Exercise 2–9
Post journal entries to T-accounts (L.O. 5)

Using the data in Exercise 2–8, post the entries to T-accounts. Write the letter of the transaction in the account before the dollar amount. Determine a balance for each account.

Exercise 2–10
Prepare trial balance (L.O. 6)

Using your answer for Exercise 2–9, prepare a trial balance. Assume the date of the trial balance is March 31, 1997.

Exercise 2–11
Determine trial balance errors (L.O. 6)

John Adams owns and manages a bowling center called Strike Lanes. He also maintains his own accounting records and was about to prepare financial statements for the year 1997. When he prepared the trial balance from the ledger accounts, the total of the debits column was $335,000, and the total of the credits column was $325,000. What are the possible reasons why the totals of the debits and credits are out of balance? How would you normally proceed to find an error if the two trial balance columns do not agree?

Exercise 2–12
Perform horizontal and vertical analyses on Bristol-Myers Squibb's assets and comment (L.O. 7)

Bristol-Myers Squibb Company manufactures and sells pharmaceuticals, consumer products, nutritionals, and medical devices. Some of its brand names include Clairol, Excedrin, Bufferin, Ban, and Corgard. The following data are for Bristol-Myers Squibb Company and its consolidated subsidiaries. Perform horizontal and vertical analyses, treating total assets as a significant total for the vertical analysis. Comment on the results.

($ millions)	December 31 1992	1991
Assets		
Current Assets		
Cash and cash equivalents	$ 2,137	$1,435
Time deposits	165	81
Marketable securities	83	67
Receivables, net of allowances	1,984	1,971
Inventories	1,490	1,451
Prepaid expenses	762	562
Total current assets	$ 6,621	$5,567
Property, Plant, and Equipment—net	3,141	2,936
Other Assets	889	743
Excess of cost over net tangible assets received in business acquisitions	153	170
Total assets	$10,804	$9,416

PROBLEMS

Problem 2–1
Prepare journal entries (L.O. 4)

The transactions of Speedy Package Delivery Company for March 1997 follow:

Mar. 1 The company was organized and issued capital stock for $200,000 cash.
2 Paid $7,000 as the rent for March on a completely furnished building.
5 Paid cash for delivery trucks, $180,000.
6 Paid $4,000 as the rent for March on two forklift trucks.
9 Paid $2,200 for supplies received and used in March.
12 Performed delivery services for customers who promised to pay $85,000 at a later date.
20 Collected cash of $48,000 from customers on account (see March 12 entry).
21 Received a bill for $1,200 for advertising in the local newspaper in March.
27 Paid cash for gas and oil consumed in March, $450.
31 Paid $6,500 salaries to employees for March.
31 Received an order for services at $80,000. The services will be performed in April.
31 Paid cash dividend, $10,000.

Required Prepare the journal entries required to record these transactions in the general journal of the company.

Problem 2–2
Record transactions in journal, post to T-accounts, and prepare trial balance (L.O. 4–6)

Discount Laundry Company had the following transactions in August 1997:

Aug. 1 Issued capital stock for cash, $100,000.
3 Borrowed $40,000 from the bank on a note.
4 Purchased cleaning equipment for $25,000 cash.
6 Performed services for customers who promised to pay later, $16,000.
7 Paid this month's rent on a building, $2,800.
10 Collections were made for the services performed on August 6, $3,200.
14 Supplies were purchased on account for use this month, $3,000.
17 A bill for $400 was received for utilities for this month.
25 Laundry services were performed for customers who paid immediately, $22,000.
31 Paid employee salaries, $6,000.
31 Paid cash dividend, $2,000.

Required

a. Prepare journal entries for these transactions.

b. Post the journal entries to T-accounts. Enter the account number in the Posting Reference column of the journal as you post each amount. Use the following account numbers:

Acct. No.	Account Title
100	Cash
103	Accounts Receivable
170	Equipment
200	Accounts Payable
201	Notes Payable
300	Capital Stock
320	Dividends
400	Service Revenue
507	Salaries Expense
511	Utilities Expense
515	Rent Expense
518	Supplies Expense

c. Prepare a trial balance as of August 31, 1997.

Problem 2–3
Prepare ledger accounts, journalize transactions, post to three-column ledger accounts, and prepare trial balance (L.O. 4–6)

Superior Janitorial, Inc., a company providing janitorial services, was organized July 1, 1997. The following account numbers and titles constitute the chart of accounts for the company:

Acct. No.	Account Title
100	Cash
103	Accounts Receivable
150	Trucks
160	Office Furniture
170	Equipment
200	Accounts Payable
201	Notes Payable
300	Capital Stock
310	Retained Earnings
320	Dividends
400	Service Revenue
506	Gas and Oil Expense
507	Salaries Expense
511	Utilities Expense
512	Insurance Expense
515	Rent Expense
518	Supplies Expense

Transactions

July 1 The company issued $400,000 of capital stock for cash.
5 Office space was rented for July, and $5,760 was paid for the rental.
8 Desks and chairs were purchased for the office on account, $28,800.
10 Equipment was purchased for $50,000; a note was given, to be paid in 30 days.
15 Purchased trucks for $150,000, paying $120,000 cash and giving a 60-day note to the dealer for $30,000.
18 Paid for supplies received and already used, $2,880.
23 Received $17,280 cash as service revenue.
27 Insurance expense for July was paid, $4,500.
30 Paid for gasoline and oil used by the truck in July, $576.
31 Billed customers for janitorial services rendered, $40,320.
31 Paid salaries for July, $51,840.
31 Paid utilities bills for July, $5,280.
31 Paid cash dividends, $9,600.

Required

a. Prepare general ledger accounts for all of these accounts except Retained Earnings. The Retained Earnings account has a beginning balance of zero and maintains this balance throughout the period.

b. Journalize the transactions given for July 1997 in the general journal.

c. Post the journal entries to three-column ledger accounts.

d. Prepare a trial balance as of July 31, 1997.

Problem 2–4
Prepare journal entries, post to three-column ledger accounts, and prepare trial balance (L.O. 4–6)

Green Lawn, Inc., is a lawn care company. Thus, the company earns its revenue from sending its trucks to customers' residences and certain commercial establishments to care for lawns and shrubbery. Green Lawn's trial balance at the end of the first 11 months of the year follows:

GREEN LAWN, INC.
Trial Balance
November 30, 1997

Acct. No.	Account Title	Debits	Credits
100	Cash	$ 73,740	
103	Accounts Receivable	88,600	
150	Trucks	102,900	
160	Office Furniture	8,400	
200	Accounts Payable		$ 33,600
300	Capital Stock		30,000
310	Retained Earnings, January 1, 1997		40,540
400	Service Revenue		371,010
505	Advertising Expense	18,300	
506	Gas and Oil Expense	21,900	
507	Salaries Expense	65,850	
511	Utilities Expense	2,310	
515	Rent Expense	15,000	
518	Supplies Expense	75,600	
531	Entertainment Expense	2,550	
		$475,150	$475,150

Transactions

Dec. 2 Paid rent for December, $3,000.
5 Paid the accounts payable of $33,600.
8 Paid advertising for December, $1,500.
10 Purchased a new office desk on account, $1,050.
13 Purchased $240 of supplies on account for use in December.
15 Collected cash from customers on account, $75,000.
20 Paid for customer entertainment, $450.
24 Collected an additional $6,000 from customers on account.
26 Paid for gasoline used in the trucks in December, $270.
28 Billed customers for services rendered, $79,500.
30 Paid for more December supplies, $12,000.
31 Paid December salaries, $15,300.
31 Paid a $4,000 cash dividend. (The Dividends account is No. 320.)

Required

a. Open three-column general ledger accounts for each of the accounts in the trial balance under the date of December 1, 1997. Place the word *Balance* in the explanation space of each account. Also open an account for Dividends, No. 320.

b. Prepare entries in the general journal for the preceding transactions for December 1997.

c. Post the journal entries to three-column general ledger accounts.

d. Prepare a trial balance as of December 31, 1997.

Problem 2–5
Prepare corrected trial balance (L.O. 6)

Michael Miller prepared the following trial balance from the ledger of the Kline TV Repair Company. The trial balance did not balance.

KLINE TV REPAIR COMPANY
Trial Balance
December 31, 1997

Acct. No.	Account Title	Debits	Credits
100	Cash	$ 59,200	
103	Accounts Receivable	60,800	
160	Office Furniture	120,000	
172	Office Equipment	48,000	
200	Accounts Payable		$ 22,400
300	Capital Stock		180,000
310	Retained Earnings		80,000
320	Dividends	28,800	
400	Service Revenue		360,000
507	Salaries Expense	280,000	
515	Rent Expense	40,000	
568	Miscellaneous Expense	7,200	
		$644,000	$642,400

The difference in totals in the trial balance caused Miller to carefully examine the company's accounting records. In searching back through the accounting records, Miller found that the following errors had been made:

1. One entire entry that included an $8,000 debit to Cash and an $8,000 credit to Accounts Receivable was never posted.
2. In computing the balance of the Accounts Payable account, a credit of $3,200 was omitted from the computation.
3. In preparing the trial balance, the Retained Earnings account balance was shown as $80,000. The ledger account has the balance as its correct amount of $83,200.
4. One debit of $2,400 to the Dividends account was posted as a credit to that account.
5. Office equipment of $12,000 was debited to Office Furniture when purchased.

Required

Prepare a corrected trial balance for the Kline TV Repair Company as of December 31, 1997. Also, write a description of the effect(s) of each error.

Alternate Problems

Problem 2–1A
Prepare journal entries (L.O. 4)

Merit Laundry Company, Inc., entered into the following transactions in August 1997:

Aug. 1 Received cash for capital stock issued to owners, $300,000.
3 Paid rent for August on a building and laundry equipment rented, $6,000.
6 Performed laundry services for $8,000 cash.
8 Secured an order from a customer for laundry services of $9,000. The services are to be performed next month.
13 Performed laundry services for $8,500 on account to various customers.
15 Received and paid a bill for $430 for supplies used in operations.
23 Cash collected from customers on account, $4,800.
31 Paid $2,400 salaries to employees for August.
31 Received the electric and gas bill for August, $920, but did not pay it at this time.
31 Paid cash dividend, $1,000.

Required

Prepare journal entries for these transactions in the general journal.

Problem 2–2A
Record transactions in journal, post to T-accounts, and prepare trial balance (L.O. 4–6)

The transactions listed below are those of On-Site Computer Repair, Inc., for April 1997:

Apr. 1 Cash of $480,000 was received for capital stock issued to the owners.
3 Rent was paid for April, $3,500.
6 Trucks were purchased for $56,000 cash.
7 Office equipment was purchased on account from Wagner Company for $76,800.
14 Salaries for first two weeks were paid, $12,000.
15 $32,000 was received for services performed.
18 An invoice was received from Roger's Gas Station for $400 for gas and oil used during April.

Apr. 23 A note was arranged with the bank for $80,000. The cash was received, and a note promising to return the $80,000 on May 30, 1997, was signed.
29 Purchased trucks for $73,600 by signing a note.
30 Salaries for the remainder of April were paid, $14,400.

Required

a. Prepare journal entries for these transactions.

b. Post the journal entries to T-accounts. Enter the account number in the Posting Reference column of the journal as you post each amount. Use the following account numbers:

Acct. No.	Account Title
100	Cash
150	Trucks
172	Office Equipment
200	Accounts Payable
201	Notes Payable
300	Capital Stock
400	Service Revenue
506	Gas and Oil Expense
507	Salaries Expense
515	Rent Expense

c. Prepare a trial balance as of April 30, 1997.

Problem 2–3A
Prepare ledger accounts, journalize transactions, post to three-column ledger accounts, and prepare trial balance (L.O. 4–6)

Quick Pick Up & Delivery, Inc., was organized January 1, 1997. Its chart of accounts is as follows:

Acct. No.	Account Title
100	Cash
103	Accounts Receivable
150	Trucks
160	Office Furniture
172	Office Equipment
200	Accounts Payable
201	Notes Payable
300	Capital Stock
310	Retained Earnings
400	Service Revenue
506	Gas and Oil Expense
507	Salaries Expense
511	Utilities Expense
512	Insurance Expense
515	Rent Expense
530	Repairs Expense

Transactions

Jan. 1 The company received $660,000 cash and $240,000 of office furniture in exchange for $900,000 of capital stock.
2 Paid garage rent for January, $6,000.
4 Purchased microcomputers on account, $13,200.
6 Purchased delivery trucks for $280,000; payment was made by giving cash of $150,000 and a 30-day note for the remainder.
12 Purchased insurance for January on the delivery trucks. The cost of the policy, $800, was paid in cash.
15 Received and paid January utilities bills, $960.
15 Paid salaries for first half of January, $3,600.
17 Cash received for delivery services to date amounted to $1,800.
20 Received bill for gasoline purchased and used in January, $180.
23 Purchased delivery trucks for cash, $108,000.
25 Cash sales of delivery services were $2,880.
27 Purchased a copy machine on account, $3,600.
31 Paid salaries for last half of January, $4,800.
31 Sales of delivery services on account amounted to $11,400.
31 Paid for repairs to a delivery truck, $1,120.

Required

a. Prepare general ledger accounts for all these accounts except Retained Earnings. The Retained Earnings account has a beginning balance of zero and maintains this balance throughout the period.
b. Journalize the transactions given for January 1997 in the general journal.
c. Post the journal entries to three-column ledger accounts.
d. Prepare a trial balance as of January 31, 1997.

Problem 2–4A
Prepare journal entries, post to three-column ledger accounts, and prepare trial balance (L.O. 4–6)

The trial balance of New York Tennis Center, Inc., at the end of the first 11 months of its fiscal year follows:

NEW YORK TENNIS CENTER, INC.
Trial Balance
November 30, 1997

Acct. No.	Account Title	Debits	Credits
100	Cash	$ 91,180	
103	Accounts Receivable	81,750	
130	Land	60,000	
200	Accounts Payable		$ 18,750
201	Notes Payable		15,000
300	Capital Stock		70,000
310	Retained Earnings, January 1, 1997		53,700
413	Membership and Lesson Revenue		202,500
505	Advertising Expense	21,000	
507	Salaries Expense	66,000	
511	Utilities Expense	2,100	
515	Rent Expense	33,000	
518	Supplies Expense	2,250	
530	Repairs Expense	1,500	
531	Entertainment Expense	870	
540	Interest Expense	300	
		$359,950	$359,950

Transactions

Dec. 1 Paid building rent for December, $4,000.
2 Paid vendors on account, $18,000.
5 Purchased land for cash, $10,000.
7 Sold memberships on account for December, $27,000.
10 Paid the note payable of $15,000, plus interest of $150.
13 Cash collections from customers on account, $36,000.
19 Received a bill for repairs, $225.
24 Paid the December utilities bill, $180.
28 Received a bill for December advertising, $1,650.
29 Paid the equipment repair bill received on the 19th, $225.
30 Gave tennis lessons for cash, $4,500.
30 Paid salaries, $6,000.
30 Sales of memberships on account since December 7, $18,000 (for the month of December).
30 Costs paid in entertaining customers in December, $350.
30 Paid dividends of $1,500. (The Dividends account is No. 320.)

Required

a. Open three-column general ledger accounts for each of the accounts in the trial balance. Place the word *Balance* in the explanation space and enter the date December 1, 1997, on this same line. Also open an account for Dividends, No. 320.
b. Prepare entries in the general journal for the transactions during December 1997.
c. Post the journal entries to three-column ledger accounts.
d. Prepare a trial balance as of December 31, 1997.

Problem 2–5A
Prepare corrected trial balance (L.O. 6)

Bill Baxter prepared a trial balance for Fun Party Rentals, Inc., a company that rents tables, chairs, and other party supplies. The trial balance did not balance. The trial balance he prepared was as follows:

FUN PARTY RENTALS, INC.
Trial Balance
December 31, 1997

Acct. No.	Account Title	Debits	Credits
100	Cash	$ 64,000	
103	Accounts Receivable	50,800	
170	Equipment	160,000	
200	Accounts Payable		$ 24,000
300	Capital Stock		130,000
310	Retained Earnings		44,000
320	Dividends	16,000	
400	Service Revenue		432,000
505	Advertising Expense	1,200	
507	Salaries Expense	176,000	
511	Utilities Expense	44,800	
515	Rent Expense	64,000	
		$576,800	$630,000

In trying to find out why the trial balance did not balance, Baxter discovered the following errors:

1. Cash was understated (too low) by $12,000 because of an error in addition in determining the balance of that account in the ledger.
2. A credit of $4,800 to Accounts Receivable in the journal was not posted to the ledger account at all.
3. A debit of $16,000 for a semiannual dividend was posted as a credit to the Capital Stock account.
4. The balance of $12,000 in the Advertising Expense account was entered as $1,200 in the trial balance.
5. Miscellaneous Expense (Account No. 568), with a balance of $3,200, was omitted from the trial balance.

Required Prepare a corrected trial balance as of December 31, 1997. Also, write a description of the effect(s) of each error.

BEYOND THE NUMBERS—CRITICAL THINKING

Business Decision Case 2–1
Prepare journal entries, post to T-accounts, and judge profitability (L.O. 4, 5)

Jim Johnson lost his job as a carpenter with a contractor when a recession hit the construction industry. Johnson had been making $50,000 per year. He decided to form his own company, Johnson Corporation, and do home repairs.

The following is a summary of the transactions of the business during the first three months of operations in 1997:

Jan. 15	Stockholders invested $20,000 in the business.
Feb. 25	Received payment of $4,400 for remodeling a basement into a recreation room. The homeowner purchased all of the building materials.
Mar. 5	Paid cash for an advertisement that appeared in the local newspaper, $150.
Apr. 10	Received $8,000 for converting a room over a garage into an office for a college professor. The professor purchased all of the materials for the job.
11	Paid gas and oil expenses for automobile, $900.
12	Miscellaneous business expenses were paid, $450.
15	Paid dividends of $2,000.

Required

a. Prepare journal entries for these transactions.
b. Post the journal entries to T-accounts.
c. How profitable is this new venture? Should Johnson stay in this business?

Annual Report Analysis 2–2
Perform horizontal and vertical analyses and comment (L.O. 7)

Refer to the balance sheets of John H. Harland Company in the separate annual report booklet. Perform horizontal and vertical analyses of the assets section of the balance sheets for December 31, 1992, and 1993. Horizontal analysis involves showing the dollar amount and percentage increase or decrease of 1993 amounts over 1992 amounts. Vertical analysis involves showing the percentage of total assets that each asset represents as of December

31, 1991, and December 31, 1992. Write comments on any important changes between the two years that are evidence of decisions made by management.

Annual Report Analysis 2–3

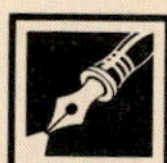

In The Home Depot's 1992 Annual Report, the following passages appear:

The primary key to our success is our 39,000 employees who wear those orange aprons you see in our stores.

Few great achievements—in business or in any aspect of life—are reached and sustained without the support and involvement of large numbers of people committed to shared values and goals they deem worthy. Indeed, one need look no further than the business section of the morning newspaper to read of how yet another "blue chip" American business, entrenched in and isolated by its own bureaucracy, has lost the support of its employees and customers. . .

Frankly, the biggest difference between The Home Depot and our competitors is not the products on our shelves, it's our people and their ability to forge strong bonds of loyalty and trust with our customers. . .

. . . Contrary to conventional management wisdom, those at the top of organization charts are not the source of all wisdom. Many of our best ideas come from the people who work on the sales floor. We encourage our employees to challenge senior management directives if they feel strongly enough about their dissenting opinions. . .

. . . We want our people to be themselves and to be bold enough to apply their talents as individuals. Certainly, people can often perceive great risk acting this way. Thus, we go to great lengths to empower our employees to be mavericks, to express differences of opinion without fear of being fired or demoted. . . We do everything we can to make people feel challenged and inspired at work instead of being threatened and made to feel insecure. An organization can, after all, accomplish more when people work together instead of against each other.

Required

Write answers to the following questions:

a. Do you think The Home Depot management regards its employees more as expenses or assets? Explain.

b. What does The Home Depot regard as its most valuable asset? Explain your answer.

c. Is The Home Depot permitted to list its human resources as assets on its balance sheet? Why or why not?

d. Could its philosophy regarding its employees be the major factor in its outstanding financial performance? Explain.

Ethics Case—Writing Experience 2–4

Refer to "An Ethical Perspective" on page 78. Write out the answers to the following questions:

a. What motivated Larry to go along with unethical and illegal actions? Explain.

b. What are Larry's options now? List each possibility.

c. What would you do if you were Larry? Describe in detail.

d. What do you think the real Larry did? Describe in detail.

Group Project 2–5
Interview a new staff member at a CPA firm

In teams of two or three students, interview in person or by speakerphone a new staff member who has worked for a CPA firm for only one or two years. Seek information on the advantages and disadvantages of working for a CPA firm. Also, inquire about the nature of the work and the training programs offered by the firm for new employees. As a team, write a memorandum to the instructor summarizing the results of the interview. The heading of the memorandum should contain the date, to whom it is written, from whom, and the subject matter.

Answers to Self-Test

True-False

1. **False.** Only the last five steps are performed at the end of the period. The first three steps are performed throughout the accounting period.
2. **True.** The journal is the book of original entry. Any amounts appearing in a ledger account must have been posted from the journal.
3. **False.** The left side of any account is the *debit* side.
4. **False.** These accounts are all increased by credits.
5. **True.** Since dividends reduce stockholders' equity, the Dividends account is increased by debits.
6. **False.** An entire journal entry may not have been posted, or a debit or credit might have been posted to the wrong account.

MULTIPLE-CHOICE

1. **c.** An asset, Cash, is increased by a debit, and the Capital Stock account is increased by a credit.
2. **b.** Since the insurance covers more than the current accounting period, an asset is debited instead of an expense. The credit is to Cash.
3. **a.** The receipt of cash before services are performed creates a liability, Unearned Delivery Fees. To increase a liability, it is credited. Cash is debited to increase its balance.
4. **b.** Cash is increased by the debit, and Delivery Service Revenue is increased by the credit.
5. **c.** Dividends is increased by the debit, and Cash is decreased by the credit.

3

Adjustments for Financial Reporting

Chapters 1 and 2 introduced the accounting process of analyzing, classifying, and summarizing business transactions into accounts. You learned how these transactions are entered into the journal and posted to the ledger accounts. You also know how to use the trial balance to test the equality of debits and credits in the journalizing and posting process. The purpose of the accounting process is to produce accurate financial statements so they may be used for making sound business decisions. At this point in your study of accounting, you are concentrating on three financial statements—the income statement, the statement of retained earnings, and the balance sheet. Detailed coverage of the statement of cash flows appears in Chapter 16.

When you began to analyze business transactions in Chapter 1, you saw that the evidence of the transaction is usually a source document. It is any written or printed evidence that describes the essential facts of a business transaction. Examples are receipts for cash paid or received, checks written or received, bills sent to customers, or bills received from suppliers. The giving, receiving, or creating of source documents triggered the journal entries made in Chapter 2.

The journal entries we discuss in this chapter are *adjusting entries*. The arrival of the end of the accounting period triggers adjusting entries. Accountants use adjusting entries to bring accounts to their proper balances before preparing financial statements. In this chapter, you learn the difference between the cash basis and accrual basis of accounting. Then you learn about the classes and types of adjusting entries and how to prepare them.

Learning Objectives

After studying this chapter, you should be able to:

1. Describe the basic characteristics of the cash basis and the accrual basis of accounting.
2. Identify the reasons why adjusting entries must be made.
3. Identify the classes and types of adjusting entries.
4. Prepare adjusting entries.
5. Determine the effects of failing to prepare adjusting entries.
6. Analyze and use the financial results—trend percentages.

Cash versus Accrual Basis Accounting

Some relatively small businesses and professionals such as physicians and lawyers may account for their revenues and expenses on a cash basis. The **cash basis of accounting** recognizes revenues when cash is received and recognizes expenses when cash is paid out. For example, under the cash basis, a company would treat services rendered to clients in 1997 for which the company collected cash in 1998

Illustration 3.1
Cash Basis and Accrual Basis of Accounting Compared

	Cash Basis	Accrual Basis
Revenues are recognized	As cash is received	As earned (goods are delivered or services are performed)
Expenses are recognized	As cash is paid	As incurred to produce revenues

Objective 1
Describe the basic characteristics of the cash basis and the accrual basis of accounting.

as 1998 revenues. Similarly, under the cash basis, a company would treat expenses incurred in 1997 for which the company disbursed cash in 1998 as 1998 expenses. Under the "pure" cash basis, even the purchase of a building would be debited to an expense. However, under the "modified" cash basis, the purchase of long-lived assets (such as a building) would be debited to an asset and depreciated (gradually charged to expense) over its useful life. Normally the "modified" cash basis is used by those few individuals and small businesses that use the cash basis.

Since the cash basis of accounting does not match expenses incurred and revenues earned, it is generally considered theoretically unacceptable. The cash basis is acceptable in practice only under those circumstances when it approximates the results that a company could obtain under the accrual basis of accounting. Companies using the cash basis do not have to prepare any adjusting entries unless they discover they have made a mistake in preparing an entry during the accounting period. Under certain circumstances, companies may use the cash basis for income tax purposes.

Throughout the text we use the accrual basis of accounting, which matches expenses incurred and revenues earned, because most companies use the accrual basis. The **accrual basis of accounting** recognizes revenues when sales are made or services are performed, regardless of when cash is received. Expenses are recognized as incurred, whether or not cash has been paid out. For instance, assume a company performs services for a customer on account. Although the company has received no cash, the revenue is recorded at the time the company performs the service. Later, when the company receives the cash, no revenue is recorded because the company has already recorded the revenue. Under the accrual basis, adjusting entries are needed to bring the accounts up to date for unrecorded economic activity that has taken place. In Illustration 3.1, we show when revenues and expenses are recognized under the cash basis and under the accrual basis.

The Need for Adjusting Entries

Objective 2
Identify the reasons why adjusting entries must be made.

The income statement of a business reports all revenues earned and all expenses incurred to generate those revenues during a given period. An income statement that does not report all revenues and expenses is incomplete, inaccurate, and possibly misleading. Similarly, a balance sheet that does not report all of an entity's assets, liabilities, and stockholders' equity at a specific time may be misleading. Each adjusting entry has a dual purpose: (1) to make the income statement report the proper revenue or expense and (2) to make the balance sheet report the proper asset or liability. Thus, every adjusting entry affects at least one income statement account and one balance sheet account.

Since those interested in the activities of a business need timely information, companies must prepare financial statements periodically. To prepare such statements, the accountant divides an entity's life into time periods. These time periods are usually equal in length and are called *accounting periods*. An **accounting**

ILLUSTRATION 3.2
Summary—Fiscal Year Endings by Month

	1992	1991	1990	1989
January	21	21	22	22
February	14	14	15	15
March	15	12	14	16
April	7	7	7	8
May	16	16	16	15
June	60	62	62	57
July	15	16	16	16
August	18	18	17	16
September	33	31	33	37
October	22	21	21	20
November	18	18	17	17
Subtotal	239	236	240	239
December	361	364	360	361
Total Companies	600	600	600	600

Source: American Institute of Certified Public Accountants, *Accounting Trends & Techniques* (New York: AICPA, 1993), p. 29.

period may be one month, one quarter, or one year. An **accounting year,** or fiscal year, is an accounting period of one year. A **fiscal year** is any 12 consecutive months. The fiscal year may or may not coincide with the **calendar year,** which ends on December 31. As we show in Illustration 3.2, more than half of the companies surveyed have fiscal years that coincide with the calendar year. Companies in certain industries often have a fiscal year that differs from the calendar year. For instance many retail stores end their fiscal year on January 31 to avoid closing their books during their peak sales period. Other companies select a fiscal year ending at a time when inventories and business activity are lowest.

Periodic reporting and the matching principle necessitate the preparation of *adjusting entries*. **Adjusting entries** are journal entries made at the end of an accounting period or at any time financial statements are to be prepared to bring about a proper *matching* of revenues and expenses. The **matching principle** requires that expenses incurred in producing revenues be deducted from the revenues they generated during the accounting period. The matching principle is one of the underlying principles of accounting. This matching of expenses and revenues is necessary for the income statement to present an accurate picture of the profitability of a business. Adjusting entries reflect unrecorded economic activity that has taken place but has not yet been recorded. Why has the company not recorded this activity by the end of the period? One reason is that it is more convenient and economical to wait until the end of the period to record the activity. A second reason is that no source document concerning that activity has yet come to the accountant's attention.

Adjusting entries bring the amounts in the general ledger accounts to their proper balances before the company prepares its financial statements. That is, adjusting entries convert the amounts that are actually in the general ledger accounts to the amounts that should be in the general ledger accounts for proper financial reporting. To make this conversion, the accountants analyze the accounts to determine which need adjustment. For example, assume a company purchased a three-year insurance policy costing $600 at the beginning of the year and debited $600 to Prepaid Insurance. At year-end, the company should remove $200 of the cost from the asset and record it as an expense. Failure to do so misstates assets and net income on the financial statements.

Companies continuously receive benefits from many assets such as prepaid expenses (e.g., prepaid insurance and prepaid rent). Thus, an entry could be made daily to record the expense incurred. Typically, firms do not make the entry until financial statements are to be prepared. Therefore, if monthly financial statements are prepared, monthly adjusting entries are required. By custom, and in some

Illustration 3.3
Two Classes and Four Types of Adjusting Entries

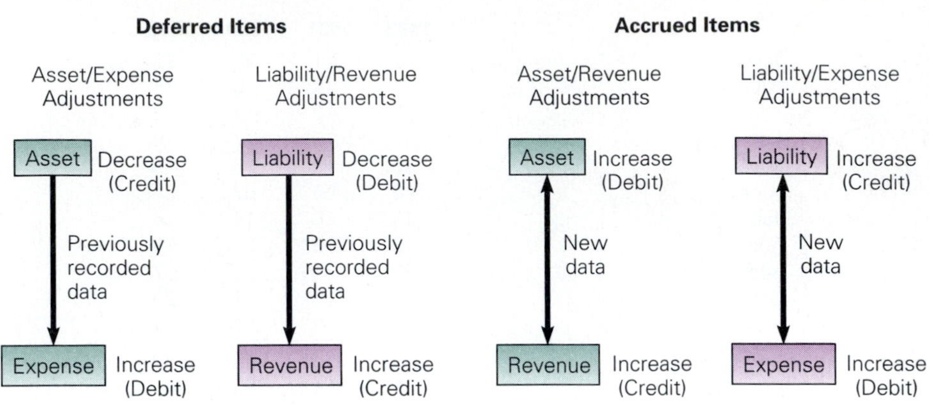

instances by law, businesses report to their owners at least annually. Accordingly, adjusting entries are required at least once a year. Remember, however, that the entry transferring an amount from an asset account to an expense account should transfer only the asset cost that has expired.

An Accounting Perspective

Uses of Technology Eventually, computers will probably enter adjusting entries continuously on a real-time basis so that up-to-date financial statements can be printed without prior notice at any time. Computers will be fed the facts concerning activities that would normally result in adjusting entries and instructed to seek any necessary information from their own databases or those of other computers to continually adjust the accounts.

Classes and Types of Adjusting Entries

Objective 3
Identify the classes and types of adjusting entries.

Adjusting entries fall into two broad classes: deferred (meaning to postpone or delay) items and accrued (meaning to grow or accumulate) items. **Deferred items** consist of adjusting entries involving data previously recorded in accounts. These entries involve the transfer of data already recorded in asset and liability accounts to expense and revenue accounts, respectively. **Accrued items** consist of adjusting entries relating to activity on which no data have been previously recorded in the accounts. These entries involve the initial, or first, recording of assets and liabilities and the related revenues and expenses (see Illustration 3.3).

Deferred items consist of two types of adjusting entries: asset/expense adjustments and liability/revenue adjustments. For example, prepaid insurance and prepaid rent are assets until they are used up; then they become expenses. Also, unearned revenue is a liability until the company renders the service; then the unearned revenue becomes earned revenue.

Accrued items consist of two types of adjusting entries: asset/revenue adjustments and liability/expense adjustments. For example, assume a company performs a service for a customer but has not yet billed the customer. The accountant records this transaction as an asset in the form of a receivable and as revenue because the company has earned a revenue. Also, assume a company owes its employees salaries not yet paid. The accountant records this transaction as a liability and an expense because the company has incurred an expense.

In this chapter, we illustrate each of the four types of adjusting entries: asset/expense, liability/revenue, asset/revenue, and liability/expense. Look at Illustra-

ILLUSTRATION 3.4
Trial Balance

MICROTRAIN COMPANY
Trial Balance
December 31, 1997

Acct. No.	Account Title	Debits	Credits
100	Cash	$ 8,250	
103	Accounts Receivable	5,200	
107	Supplies on Hand	1,400	
108	Prepaid Insurance	2,400	
112	Prepaid Rent	1,200	
150	Trucks	40,000	
200	Accounts Payable		$ 730
216	Unearned Service Fees		4,500
300	Capital Stock		50,000
320	Dividends	3,000	
400	Service Revenue		10,700
505	Advertising Expense	50	
506	Gas and Oil Expense	680	
507	Salaries Expense	3,600	
511	Utilities Expense	150	
		$65,930	$65,930

tion 3.4, the trial balance of the MicroTrain Company at December 31, 1997. As you can see, MicroTrain must adjust several accounts before it can prepare accurate financial statements. The adjustments for these accounts involve data already recorded in the company's accounts.

In making adjustments for MicroTrain Company, we must add several accounts to the company's chart of accounts shown in Chapter 2 on page 61. These new accounts are:

Type of Account	Acct. No.	Account Title	Description
Asset	121	Interest Receivable	The amount of interest earned but not yet received.
Contra asset*	151	Accumulated Depreciation—Trucks	The total depreciation expense taken on trucks since the acquisition date. The balance of this account is deducted from that of Trucks on the balance sheet.
Liability	206	Salaries Payable	The amount of salaries earned by employees but not yet paid by the company.
Revenue	418	Interest Revenue	The amount of interest earned in the current period.
Expenses	512	Insurance Expense	The cost of insurance incurred in the current period.
	515	Rent Expense	The cost of rent incurred in the current period.
	518	Supplies Expense	The cost of supplies used in the current period.
	521	Depreciation Expense—Trucks	The portion of the cost of the trucks assigned to expense during the current period.

* Accountants deduct the balance of a contra asset from the balance of the related asset account on the balance sheet. We explain the reasons for using a contra asset account later in the chapter.

Now you are ready to follow as MicroTrain Company makes its adjustments for deferred items. If you find the process confusing, review the beginning of this chapter so you clearly understand the purpose of adjusting entries.

Adjustments for Deferred Items

Objective 4
Prepare adjusting entries.

This section discusses the two types of adjustments for deferred items: asset/expense adjustments and liability/revenue adjustments. In the asset/expense group, you learn how to prepare adjusting entries for prepaid expenses and depreciation. In the liability/revenue group, you learn how to prepare adjusting entries for unearned revenues.

Asset/Expense Adjustments—Prepaid Expenses and Depreciation

MicroTrain Company must make several asset/expense adjustments for prepaid expenses. A **prepaid expense** is an asset awaiting assignment to expense, such as prepaid insurance, prepaid rent, and supplies on hand. Note that the nature of these three adjustments is the same.

Prepaid Insurance When a company pays an insurance policy premium in advance, the purchase creates the asset, *prepaid insurance*. This advance payment is an asset because the company will receive insurance coverage in the future. With the passage of time, however, the asset gradually expires. The portion that has expired becomes an expense. To illustrate this point, recall that in Chapter 2, MicroTrain Company purchased for cash an insurance policy on its trucks for the period December 1, 1997, to November 30, 1998. The journal entry made on December 1, 1997, to record the purchase of the policy was:

1997				
Dec.	1	Prepaid Insurance	2,400	
		Cash		2,400
		Purchased truck insurance to cover a one-year period.		

The two accounts relating to insurance are Prepaid Insurance (an asset) and Insurance Expense (an expense). After posting this entry, the Prepaid Insurance account has a $2,400 debit balance on December 1, 1997. The Insurance Expense account has a zero balance on December 1, 1997, because no time has elapsed to use any of the policy's benefits.

(Dr.)	**Prepaid Insurance**	*(Cr.)*
1997 Dec. 1 Bal.	2,400	

(Dr.)	**Insurance Expense**	*(Cr.)*
1997 Dec. 1 Bal.	–0–	

By December 31, 1997, one month of the year covered by the policy has expired. Therefore, part of the **service potential** (or benefit obtained from the asset) has expired. The asset now provides less future services or benefits than when the company acquired it. We recognize this reduction by treating the cost of the services received from the asset as an expense. For the MicroTrain Company example, the service received was one month of insurance coverage. Since the policy provides the same services for every month of its one-year life, we assign an equal amount ($200) of cost to each month. Thus, MicroTrain charges 1/12 of the annual premium to Insurance Expense on December 31, 1997. The adjusting journal entry is:

Adjustment 1—Insurance

1997				
Dec.	31	Insurance Expense	200	
		Prepaid Insurance		200
		To record insurance expense for December.		

After posting these two journal entries, the accounts in T-account format appear as follows:

(Dr.)	Prepaid Insurance		(Cr.)	
1997 Dec. 1 Purchased on account	2,400	1997 Dec. 31 Adjustment 1	200	Decreased by $200
Bal. after adjustment	2,200			

	(Dr.)	Insurance Expense		(Cr.)
Increased by $200	1997 Dec. 31 Adjustment 1	200		

In practice, accountants do not use T-accounts. Instead, they use three-column ledger accounts that have the advantage of showing a balance after each transaction. After posting the preceding two entries, the three-column ledger accounts appear as follows:

Prepaid Insurance *Account No. 108*

Date		Explanation	Post. Ref.	Debit	Credit	Balance
1997 Dec.	1	Purchased on account	G1	2400		2400 Dr.
	31	Adjustment	G3*		200	2200 Dr.

Insurance Expense *Account No. 512*

Date		Explanation	Post. Ref.	Debit	Credit	Balance
1997 Dec.	31	Adjustment	G3*	200		200 Dr.

* Assumed journal page number.

Before this adjusting entry was made, the entire $2,400 insurance payment made on December 1, 1997, was a prepaid expense for 12 months of protection. So on December 31, 1997, one month of protection had passed, and an adjusting entry transferred $200 of the $2,400 ($2,400/12 = $200) to Insurance Expense. On the income statement for the year ended December 31, 1997, MicroTrain reports one month of insurance expense, $200, as one of the expenses it incurred in generating that year's revenues. It reports the remaining amount of the prepaid expense, $2,200, as an asset on the balance sheet. The $2,200 prepaid expense represents 11 months of insurance protection that remains as a future benefit.

Prepaid Rent Prepaid rent is another example of the gradual consumption of a previously recorded asset. Assume a company pays rent in advance to cover more than one accounting period. On the date it pays the rent, the company debits the prepayment to the Prepaid Rent account (an asset account). The company has not yet received benefits resulting from this expenditure. Thus, the expenditure creates an asset.

We measure rent expense similarly to insurance expense. Generally, the rental contract specifies the amount of rent per unit of time. If the prepayment covers a three-month rental, we charge one third of this rental to each month. Notice that the amount charged is the same each month even though some months have more days than other months.

For example, MicroTrain Company paid $1,200 rent in advance on December 1, 1997, to cover a three-month period beginning on that date. The journal entry would be:

1997				
Dec.	1	Prepaid Rent	1,200	
		Cash		1,200
		Paid three months' rent on a building.		

The two accounts relating to rent are Prepaid Rent (an asset) and Rent Expense. After this entry is posted, the Prepaid Rent account has a $1,200 balance and the Rent Expense account has a zero balance because no part of the rent period has yet elapsed.

(Dr.)	**Prepaid Rent**	*(Cr.)*
1997 Dec. 1 Bal. Cash paid 1,200		

(Dr.)	**Rent Expense**	*(Cr.)*
1997 Dec. 1 Bal. –0–		

On December 31, 1997, MicroTrain must prepare an adjusting entry. Since one third of the period covered by the prepaid rent has elapsed, it charges one third of the $1,200 of prepaid rent to expense. The required adjusting entry is:

Adjustment 2—Rent

1997				
Dec.	31	Rent Expense	400	
		Prepaid Rent		400
		To record rent expense for December.		

After posting this adjusting entry, the T-accounts appear as follows:

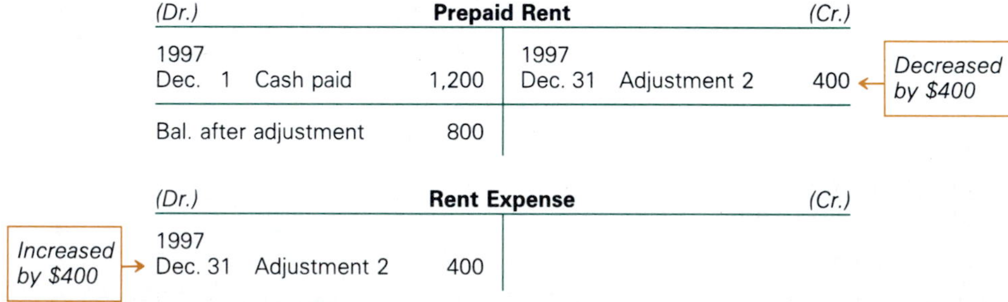

The $400 rent expense appears in the income statement for the year ended December 31, 1997. MicroTrain reports the remaining $800 of prepaid rent as an asset in the balance sheet on December 31, 1997. Thus, the adjusting entries have accomplished their purpose of maintaining the accuracy of the financial statements.

Supplies on Hand Almost every business uses supplies in its operations. It may classify supplies simply as supplies (to include all types of supplies), or more specifically as office supplies (paper, stationery, floppy diskettes, pencils), selling supplies (gummed tape, string, paper bags, cartons, wrapping paper), or training supplies (transparencies, training manuals). Frequently, companies buy supplies in bulk. These supplies are an asset until the company uses them. This asset may be called *supplies on hand* or *supplies inventory*. Even though these terms indicate a prepaid expense, the firm does not use *prepaid* in the asset's title.

On December 4, 1997, MicroTrain Company purchased supplies for $1,400 and recorded the transaction as follows:

1997				
Dec.	4	Supplies on Hand	1,400	
		Cash		1,400
		To record the purchase of supplies for future use.		

MicroTrain's two accounts relating to supplies are Supplies on Hand (an asset) and Supplies Expense. After this entry is posted, the Supplies on Hand account shows a debit balance of $1,400 and the Supplies Expense account has a zero balance as shown in the following T-accounts:

(Dr.)	**Supplies on Hand**	*(Cr.)*
1997 Dec. 4 Bal. Cash paid 1,400		

(Dr.)	**Supplies Expense**	*(Cr.)*
1997 Dec. 4 Bal. –0–		

An actual physical inventory (a count of the supplies on hand) at the end of the month showed only $900 of supplies on hand. Thus, the company must have used $500 of supplies in December. An adjusting journal entry brings the two accounts pertaining to supplies to their proper balances. The adjusting entry recognizes the reduction in the asset (Supplies on Hand) and the recording of an expense (Supplies Expense) by transferring $500 from the asset to the expense. According to the physical inventory, the asset balance should be $900 and the expense balance, $500. So MicroTrain makes the following adjusting entry:

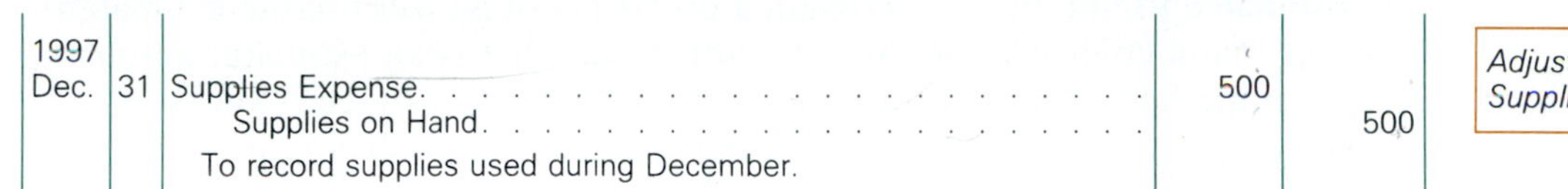

1997				
Dec.	31	Supplies Expense	500	
		Supplies on Hand		500
		To record supplies used during December.		

Adjustment 3—Supplies

After posting this adjusting entry, the T-accounts appear as follows:

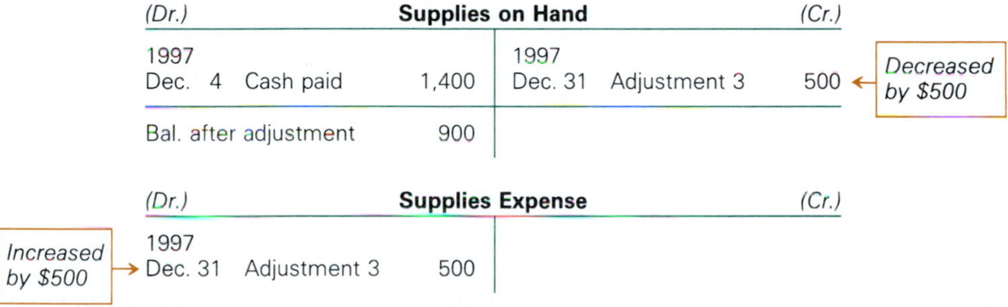

(Dr.)		**Supplies on Hand**		*(Cr.)*
1997 Dec. 4 Cash paid	1,400		1997 Dec. 31 Adjustment 3	500
Bal. after adjustment	900			

(Dr.)	**Supplies Expense**	*(Cr.)*
1997 Dec. 31 Adjustment 3 500		

Increased by $500

The entry to record the use of supplies could be made when the supplies are issued from the storeroom. However, such careful accounting for small items each time they are issued is usually too costly a procedure.

Accountants make adjusting entries for supplies on hand, like for any other prepaid expense, before preparing financial statements. Supplies expense appears in the income statement. Supplies on hand is an asset in the balance sheet.

Sometimes companies buy assets relating to insurance, rent, and supplies knowing that they will use them up before the end of the current accounting period (usually one month or one year). If so, an expense account is usually debited at the time of purchase rather than debiting an asset account. This procedure avoids having to make an adjusting entry at the end of the accounting period. Sometimes, too, a company debits an expense even though the asset will benefit more than the current period. Then, at the end of the accounting period, the firm's adjusting entry transfers some of the cost from the expense to the asset. For instance, assume that on January 1, a company paid $1,200 rent to cover a three-year period and debited the $1,200 to Rent Expense. At the end of the year, it transfers $800 from Rent Expense to Prepaid Rent. To simplify our approach, we will consistently debit the asset when the asset will benefit more than the current accounting period.

DEPRECIATION Just as prepaid insurance and prepaid rent indicate a gradual using up of a previously recorded asset, so does depreciation. However, the overall time involved in using up a depreciable asset (such as a building) is much longer and less definite than for prepaid expenses. Also, a prepaid expense generally involves a fairly small amount of money. Depreciable assets, however, usually involve larger sums of money.

A **depreciable asset** is a manufactured asset such as a building, machine, vehicle, or piece of equipment that provides service to a business. In time, these assets lose their utility because of (1) wear and tear from use or (2) obsolescence due to technological change. Since companies gradually use up these assets over time, they record depreciation expense on them. **Depreciation expense** is the amount of asset cost assigned as an expense to a particular period. The process of recording depreciation expense is called **depreciation accounting.** The three factors involved in computing depreciation expense are:

1. **Asset cost.** The **asset cost** is the amount that a company paid to purchase the depreciable asset.
2. **Estimated salvage value.** The **estimated salvage value (scrap value)** is the amount that the company can probably sell the asset for at the end of its estimated useful life.
3. **Estimated useful life.** The **estimated useful life** of an asset is the estimated time that a company can use the asset. Useful life is an estimate, not an exact measurement, that a company must make in advance. However, sometimes the useful life is determined by company policy (e.g., keep a fleet of automobiles for three years).

Accountants use different methods for recording depreciation. The method illustrated here is the *straight-line method.* We discuss other depreciation methods in Chapter 10. Straight-line depreciation assigns the same amount of depreciation expense to each accounting period over the life of the asset. The **depreciation formula (straight-line)** to compute straight-line depreciation for a one-year period is:

$$\text{Annual depreciation} = \frac{\text{Asset cost} - \text{Estimated salvage value}}{\text{Estimated years of useful life}}$$

To illustrate the use of this formula, recall that on December 1, MicroTrain Company purchased four small trucks at a cost of $40,000. The journal entry was:

1997				
Dec.	1	Trucks	40,000	
		Cash		40,000
		To record the purchase of four trucks.		

The estimated salvage value for each truck was $1,000, so MicroTrain estimated the total salvage value for all four trucks at $4,000. The company estimated the useful life of each truck to be four years. Using the straight-line depreciation formula, MicroTrain calculated the annual depreciation on the trucks as follows:

$$\text{Annual depreciation} = \frac{\$40{,}000 - \$4{,}000}{4 \text{ years}} = \$9{,}000$$

The amount of depreciation expense for one month would be 1/12 of the annual amount. Thus, depreciation expense for December is $9,000 ÷ 12 = $750.

The difference between an asset's cost and its estimated salvage value is an asset's **depreciable amount.** To satisfy the matching principle, the firm must allocate the depreciable amount as an expense to the various periods in the asset's useful life. It does this by debiting the amount of depreciation for a period to a depreciation expense account and crediting the amount to an accumulated depreciation account. MicroTrain's depreciation on its delivery trucks for December is $750. The company records the depreciation as follows:

			Dr.	Cr.
1997				
Dec.	31	Depreciation Expense—Trucks	750	
		Accumulated Depreciation—Trucks		750
		To record depreciation expense for December.		

Adjustment 4—Depreciation

After posting the adjusting entry, the T-accounts appear as follows:

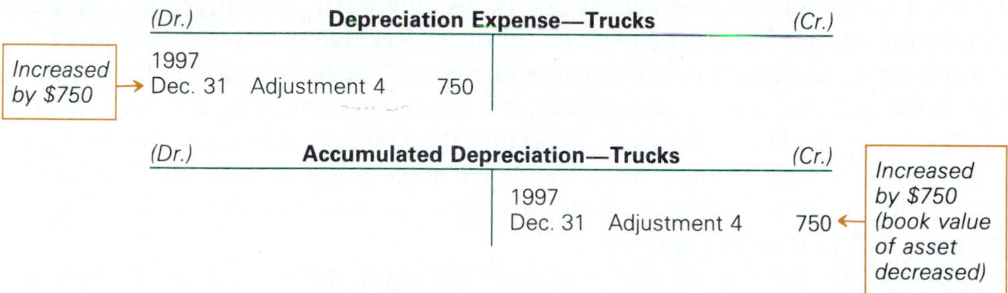

(Dr.)
Depreciation Expense—Trucks
(Cr.)
Increased by $750
1997
Dec. 31 Adjustment 4 750
(Dr.)
Accumulated Depreciation—Trucks
(Cr.)
1997
Dec. 31 Adjustment 4 750
Increased by $750 (book value of asset decreased)

MicroTrain reports depreciation expense in its income statement. And, it reports accumulated depreciation in the balance sheet as a deduction from the related asset.

The **accumulated depreciation account** is a contra asset account that shows the total of all depreciation recorded on the asset *from the date of acquisition up through the balance sheet date*. A **contra asset account** is a deduction from the asset to which it relates in the balance sheet. The purpose of a contra asset account is to reduce the original cost of the asset down its remaining undepreciated cost or book value. The *undepreciated cost of the asset* is the debit balance in the asset account (original cost) minus the credit balance in the accumulated depreciation contra account. Accountants also refer to an asset's cost less accumulated depreciation as the **book value** (or net book value) of the asset. Thus, book value is the cost not yet allocated to an expense. In the previous example, the book value of the equipment after the first month is:

Cost	$40,000
Less: Accumulated depreciation	750
Book value (or cost not yet allocated as an expense)	$39,250

MicroTrain credits the depreciation amount to an accumulated depreciation account, which is a contra asset, rather than directly to the asset account. Companies use contra accounts when they want to show statement readers the original amount of the account to which the contra account relates. For instance, for the asset Trucks, it is useful to know both the original cost of the asset and the total accumulated depreciation amount recorded on the asset. Therefore, the asset account shows the original cost. The contra account, Accumulated Depreciation—Trucks, shows the total amount of recorded depreciation from the date of acquisition. By having both original cost and the accumulated depreciation amounts, a user can estimate the approximate percentage of the benefits embodied in the asset that the company has consumed. For instance, assume the accumulated depreciation amount is about three-fourths the cost of the asset. Then, the benefits would be approximately three-fourths consumed, and the company may have to replace the asset soon.

Thus, to provide more complete balance sheet information to users of financial statements, companies show both the original acquisition cost and accumulated depreciation. In the preceding example for adjustment 4, the balance sheet at December 31, 1997, would show the asset and contra asset as follows:

Assets

Trucks	$40,000
Less: Accumulated depreciation	750
	$39,250

As you may expect, the accumulated depreciation account balance increases each period by the amount of depreciation expense recorded until the remaining book value of the asset equals the estimated salvage value.

Liability/Revenue Adjustments—Unearned Revenues

A liability/revenue adjustment involving unearned revenues covers situations in which a customer has transferred assets, usually cash, to the selling company before the receipt of merchandise or services. Receiving assets before they are earned creates a liability called **unearned revenue.** The firm debits such receipts to the asset account, Cash, and credits a liability account. The liability account credited may be Unearned Fees, Revenue Received in Advance, Advances by Customers, or some similar title. The seller must either provide the services or return the customer's money. By performing the services, the company earns revenue and cancels the liability.

Companies receive advance payments for many items, such as training services, delivery services, tickets, and magazine or newspaper subscriptions. Although we illustrate and discuss only advanced receipt of training fees, firms treat the other items similarly.

Unearned Service Fees On December 7, MicroTrain Company received $4,500 from a customer in payment for future training services. The firm recorded the following journal entry:

1997				
Dec.	7	Cash	4,500	
		Unearned Service Fees		4,500
		To record the receipt of cash from a customer in payment for future training services.		

The two T-accounts relating to training fees are Unearned Service Fees (a liability) and Service Revenue. These accounts appear as follows on December 31, 1997 (before adjustment):

(Dr.)	Unearned Service Fees	(Cr.)
	1997 Dec. 7 Cash received in advance	4,500

(Dr.)	Service Revenue	(Cr.)
	1997 Bal. before adjustment	10,700*

* The $10,700 balance came from transactions discussed in Chapter 2.

The balance in the Unearned Service Fees liability account established when MicroTrain received the cash will be converted into revenue as the company performs the training services. Before MicroTrain prepares its financial statements, it must make an adjusting entry to transfer the amount of the services performed by the company from a liability account to a revenue account. If we assume that MicroTrain earned one third of the $4,500 in the Unearned Service Fees account by December 31, then the company transfers $1,500 to the Service Revenue account as follows:

Adjustment 5—Revenue earned

1997				
Dec.	31	Unearned Service Fees	1,500	
		Service Revenue		1,500
		To transfer a portion of training fees from the liability account to the revenue account.		

After posting the adjusting entry, the T-accounts would appear as follows:

Unearned Service Fees

(Dr.)			(Cr.)	
1997			1997	
Dec. 31	Adjustment 5	1,500	Dec. 7 Cash received in advance	4,500
			Bal. after adjustment	3,000

Decreased by $1,500 (Adjustment 5 debit)

Service Revenue

(Dr.)	(Cr.)	
	1997	
	Bal. before adjustment	10,700
	Dec. 31 Adjustment 5	1,500
	Bal. after adjustment	12,200

Increased by $1,500 (Adjustment 5 credit)

MicroTrain reports the service revenue in its income statement for 1997. The company reports the $3,000 balance in the Unearned Service Fees account as a liability in the balance sheet. In 1998, the company will likely earn the $3,000 and transfer it to a revenue account.

If MicroTrain does not perform the training services, the company would have to refund the money to the training service customers. For instance, assume that MicroTrain could not perform the remaining $3,000 of training services and would have to refund the money. Then, the company would make the following entry:

Unearned Service Fees	3,000	
Cash		3,000
To record the refund of unearned training fees.		

Thus, the company must either perform the training services or refund the fees. This fact should strengthen your understanding that unearned service fees and similar items are liabilities.

Accountants make the adjusting entries for deferred items for data already recorded in a company's asset and liability accounts. They also make adjusting entries for accrued items, which we discuss in the next section, for business data not yet recorded in the accounting records.

Adjustments for Accrued Items

Accrued items require two types of adjusting entries: asset/revenue adjustments and liability/expense adjustments. The first group—asset/revenue adjustments—involves accrued assets; the second group—liability/expense adjustments—involves accrued liabilities.

Asset/Revenue Adjustments—Accrued Assets

Accrued assets are assets, such as interest receivable or accounts receivable, that have not been recorded by the end of an accounting period. These assets represent rights to receive future payments that are not due at the balance sheet date. To present an accurate picture of the affairs of the business on the balance sheet, firms recognize these rights at the end of an accounting period by preparing an adjusting entry to correct the account balances. To indicate the dual nature of these adjustments, they record a related revenue in addition to the asset. We also call these adjustments **accrued revenues** because the revenues must be recorded.

Interest Revenue Savings accounts literally earn interest moment by moment. Rarely is payment of the interest made on the last day of the accounting period. Thus, the accounting records normally do not show the interest revenue earned (but not yet received), which affects the total assets owned by the investor, unless the company makes an adjusting entry. The adjusting entry at the end of the accounting period debits a receivable account (an asset) and credits a revenue account to record the interest earned and the asset owned.

For example, assume MicroTrain Company has some money in a savings account. On December 31, 1997, the money on deposit has earned one month's interest of $600, although the company has not received the interest. An entry must show the amount of interest earned by December 31, 1997, as well as the amount of the asset, interest receivable (the right to receive this interest). The entry to record the accrual of revenue is:

Adjustment 6—Interest revenue accrued

1997				
Dec.	31	Interest Receivable	600	
		Interest Revenue		600
		To record one month's interest revenue.		

The T-accounts relating to interest would appear as follows:

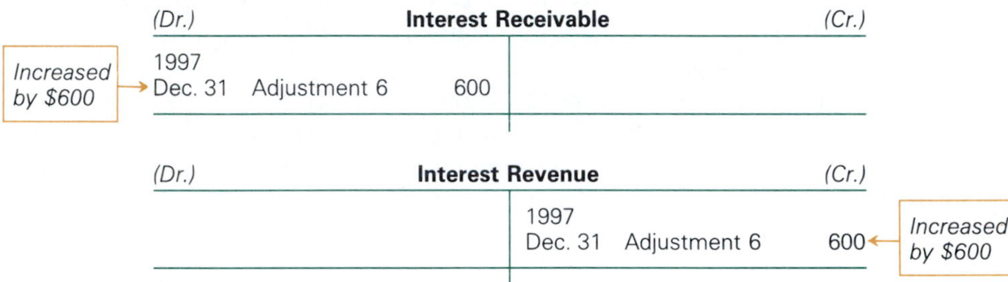

(Dr.) Interest Receivable (Cr.)
Increased by $600
1997
Dec. 31 Adjustment 6 600
(Dr.) Interest Revenue (Cr.)
1997
Dec. 31 Adjustment 6 600
Increased by $600

MicroTrain reports the $600 debit balance in Interest Receivable as an asset in the December 31, 1997, balance sheet. This asset accumulates gradually with the passage of time. The $600 credit balance in Interest Revenue is the interest earned during the month. Recall that in recording revenue under accrual basis accounting, it does not matter whether the company collects the actual cash during the year or not. It reports the interest revenue earned during the accounting period in the income statement.

Unbilled Training Fees A company may perform services for customers in one accounting period while it bills for the services in a different accounting period.

MicroTrain Company performed $1,000 of training services on account for a client at the end of December. Since it takes time to do the paper work, MicroTrain will bill the client for the services in January. The necessary adjusting journal entry at December 31, 1997, is:

Adjustment 7—Unbilled revenues

1997				
Dec.	31	Accounts Receivable (or Service Fees Receivable)	1,000	
		Service Revenue		1,000
		To record unbilled training services performed in December.		

After posting the adjusting entry, the T-accounts appear as follows:

Increased by $1,000

(Dr.) Accounts Receivable		(Cr.)
1997		
Previous bal.	5,200*	
Dec. 31 Adjustment 7	1,000	
Bal. after adjustment	6,200	

* This previous balance came from transactions discussed in Chapter 2.

(Dr.)	Service Revenue	(Cr.)
	1997	
	Bal. before adjustment	10,700
	Dec. 31 Adjustment 5—previously unearned revenue	1,500
	31 Adjustment 7	1,000 ← Increased by $1,000
	Bal. after both adjustments	13,200

The service revenue appears in the income statement; the asset, accounts receivable, appears in the balance sheet.

Liability/Expense Adjustments—Accrued Liabilities

Accrued liabilities are liabilities not yet recorded at the end of an accounting period. They represent obligations to make payments not legally due at the balance sheet date, such as employee salaries. At the end of the accounting period, the company recognizes these obligations by preparing an adjusting entry including both a liability and an expense. For this reason, we also call these obligations **accrued expenses.**

Salaries The recording of the payment of employee salaries usually involves a debit to an expense account and a credit to Cash. Unless a company pays salaries on the last day of the accounting period for a pay period ending on that date, it must make an adjusting entry to record any salaries incurred but not yet paid.

MicroTrain Company paid $3,600 of salaries on Friday, December 28, 1997, to cover the first four weeks of December. The entry made at that time was:

1997				
Dec.	28	Salaries Expense	3,600	
		Cash		3,600
		Paid training employee salaries for the first four weeks of December.		

Assuming that the last day of December 1997 falls on a Monday, this expense account does not show salaries earned by employees for the last day of the month. Nor does the account show the employer's obligation to pay these salaries. The T-accounts pertaining to salaries appear as follows before adjustment:

(Dr.)	Salaries Expense	(Cr.)
1997		
Dec. 28	3,600	

(Dr.)	Salaries Payable	(Cr.)
	1997	
	Dec. 28 Bal.	-0-

If salaries are $3,600 for four weeks, they are $900 per week. For a five-day workweek, daily salaries are $180. MicroTrain makes the following adjusting entry on December 31 to accrue salaries for one day:

1997				
Dec.	31	Salaries Expense	180	
		Salaries Payable		180
		To accrue one day's salaries that were earned but are unpaid.		

Adjustment 8—Accrued salaries

A Broader Perspective

Retirement Benefits

A very significant example of a liability/expense adjustment became prominent in 1990. Many companies pay for retired employees' medical benefits. Until recently, companies waited until they actually paid the benefits before recognizing an expense. Thus, they debited an expense and credited Cash when they paid the benefits. However, a rule passed by the Financial Accounting Standards Board in December 1990 requires that companies prepare an adjusting entry to account for the unfunded and unrecognized postretirement obligation and the related expense on the accrual basis.* The adjusting entry results in a debit to an expense and a credit to a liability.

Making this adjusting entry significantly reduced the reported earnings of many large companies by about 33% in 1992. The total net worth of approximately 60 of the largest U.S. companies shrunk by about $100 billion in 1992 as a result of this change. For instance, the net worth of General Motors Corporation declined by roughly 80% in 1992 as the result of recording this $20.72 billion expense on the accrual basis. Some companies have already reduced their retirees' medical benefits to minimize the future impact on earnings. Many more companies are expected to reduce theirs in the future.

Typical of the disclosure made in annual reports regarding postretirement benefits is the following taken from the 1992 annual report of Waste Management, Inc. This company provides comprehensive environmental, waste management, and related services to industry, government, and consumers.

> The Company and its principal subsidiaries adopted Statement of Financial Accounting Standards No. 106, "Employers' Accounting for Postretirement Benefits Other Than Pensions" ("FAS 106") on the immediate recognition basis, effective as of January 1, 1992. This new Standard requires that the expected cost of future benefits be charged to expense during the years in which the employees render service. Previously, the Company recognized these costs, which relate primarily to health care costs and were not material, on a cash basis.
>
> The cumulative effect of this accounting change was to decrease income for 1992 by $77,837,000 ($36,579,000, or $.07 per share, after tax and minority interest), representing the amount of the unfunded obligation measured as of January 1, 1992.

* Financial Accounting Standards Board, *Statement of Financial Accounting Standards No. 106,* "Employers' Accounting for Postretirement Benefits Other Than Pensions" (Norwalk, Conn., 1990).

After adjustment, the two T-accounts involved appear as follows:

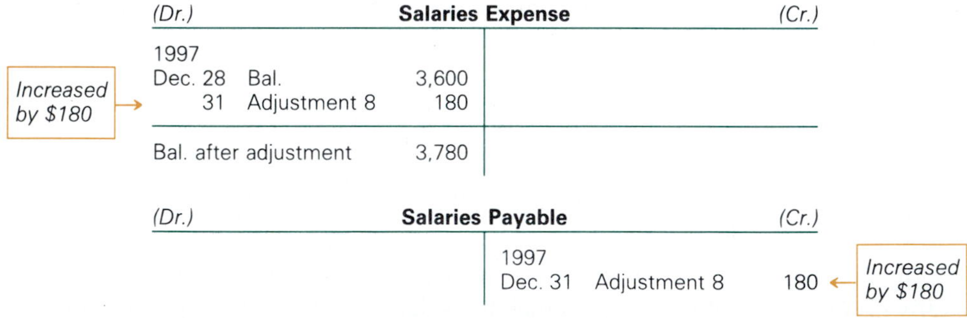

(Dr.)		Salaries Expense			(Cr.)
1997					
Dec. 28	Bal.	3,600			
31	Adjustment 8	180			
Bal. after adjustment		3,780			

(Dr.)			Salaries Payable		(Cr.)
			1997		
			Dec. 31	Adjustment 8	180

The debit in the adjusting journal entry brings the month's salaries expense up to its correct $3,780 amount for income statement purposes. The credit to Salaries Payable records the $180 salary liability to employees. The balance sheet shows salaries payable as a liability.

Another example of a liability/expense adjustment is when a company incurs interest on a note payable. The debit would be to Interest Expense, and the credit would be to Interest Payable. We discuss this adjustment in Chapter 9.

Effects of Failing to Prepare Adjusting Entries

Objective 5
Determine the effects of failing to prepare adjusting entries.

Failure to prepare proper adjusting entries causes net income and the balance sheet to be in error. You can see the effect of failing to record each of the major types of adjusting entries on net income and balance sheet items in Illustration 3.5.

Using MicroTrain Company as an example, this chapter has discussed and illustrated many of the typical entries that companies must make at the end of an accounting period. Later chapters explain other examples of adjusting entries.

Illustration 3.5
Effects of Failure to Recognize Adjustments

	Failure to Recognize	Effect on Net Income	Effect on Balance Sheet Items
1.	Consumption of the benefits of an asset (prepaid expense)	Overstates net income	Overstates assets Overstates retained earnings
2.	Earning of previously unearned revenues	Understates net income	Overstates liabilities Understates retained earnings
3.	Accrual of assets	Understates net income	Understates assets Understates retained earnings
4.	Accrual of liabilities	Overstates net income	Understates liabilities Overstates retained earnings

Analyzing and Using the Financial Results—Trend Percentages

Objective 6
Analyze and use the financial results—trend percentages.

Rather than looking only at the dollar amount of an item, it is sometimes more informative to express all the dollar amounts as a percentage of one of the amounts in the base year. You can calculate **trend percentages** by dividing the amount for each year for an item, such as net income or net sales, by the amount of that item for the base year:

$$\text{Trend percentage} = \frac{\text{Current year amount}}{\text{Base year amount}}$$

Wal-Mart
Wal-Mart Stores, Inc., is a mass consumer goods merchandiser with about 1,900 Wal-Mart stores and 250 Sam's Club stores throughout the nation.

To illustrate, Wal-Mart Stores, Inc., and its subsidiaries reported the following net income for the years ended January 31, 1984, through 1993. The last column expresses these dollar amounts as a percentage of the 1984 amount. For instance, we would calculate the 138% for 1985 as:

$$\left[\left(\frac{\$270{,}767{,}000}{\$196{,}244{,}000}\right) \times 100\right]$$

	Dollar Amount of Net Income	Percentage of 1984 Net Income
1984	$ 196,244,000	100%
1985	270,767,000	138
1986	327,473,000	167
1987	450,086,000	229
1988	627,643,000	320
1989	837,221,000	427
1990	1,075,900,000	548
1991	1,291,024,000	658
1992	1,608,476,000	820
1993	1,994,794,000	1,016

Examining the trend percentages, we can see that Wal-Mart's net income has increased steadily over the 10-year period. The 1993 net income is more than 10 times as much as the 1984 amount. This is the kind of performance that management and stockholders seek. Sam Walton started and built this company; when he died in 1993, he was one of the world's richest individuals. Walton spent considerable time at his stores talking with employees and customers. Wal-Mart currently is considered to be one of the greatest success stories in American business.

In the first three chapters of this text, you have learned most of the steps of the accounting process. Chapter 4 shows the final steps in the accounting cycle.

An Accounting Perspective

Business Insight The following quote is from the chairman's letter in the 1992 annual report of Wal-Mart Stores, Inc.

> When we began our "Buy American" efforts in 1985, . . . we did it because we believed it was the right thing to do, right for American manufacturers, right for American workers, and right for Wal-Mart. We still believe it is right! As a result of our efforts, hundreds and hundreds of items previously manufactured overseas are now made in the USA by American workers.

Understanding the Learning Objectives

Objective 1
Describe the basic characteristics of the cash basis and the accrual basis of accounting.

- The cash basis of accounting recognizes revenues when cash is received and recognizes expenses when cash is paid out.
- The accrual basis of accounting recognizes revenues when sales are made or services are performed, regardless of when cash is received; expenses are recognized as incurred, whether or not cash has been paid out.
- The accrual basis is more generally accepted than the cash basis because it provides a better matching of revenues and expenses.

Objective 2
Identify the reasons why adjusting entries must be made.

- Adjusting entries convert the amounts that are actually in the accounts to the amounts that should be in the accounts for proper periodic financial reporting.
- Adjusting entries reflect unrecorded economic activity that has taken place but has not yet been recorded.

Objective 3
Identify the classes and types of adjusting entries.

- Deferred items consist of adjusting entries involving data previously recorded in accounts. Adjusting entries in this class normally involve moving data from asset and liability accounts to expense and revenue accounts. The two types of adjustments within this deferred items class are asset/expense adjustments and liability/revenue adjustments.
- Accrued items consist of adjusting entries relating to activity on which no data have been previously recorded in the accounts. These entries involve the initial recording of assets and liabilities and the related revenues and expenses. The two types of adjustments within this accrued items class are asset/revenue adjustments and liability/expense adjustments.

Objective 4
Prepare adjusting entries.

- This chapter illustrates entries for deferred items and accrued items.

Objective 5
Determine the effects of failing to prepare adjusting entries.

- Failure to prepare adjusting entries causes net income and the balance sheet to be in error.

Objective 6
Analyze and use the financial results—trend percentages.

- For a particular item such as sales or net income select a base year and express all dollar amounts in other years as a percentage of the base year dollar amount.

Demonstration Problem

Among other items, the trial balance of Korman Company for December 31, 1997, includes the following account balances:

	Debits	Credits
Supplies on Hand	$ 6,000	
Prepaid Rent.	25,200	
Buildings	200,000	
Accumulated Depreciation—Buildings		$33,250
Salaries Expense	124,000	
Unearned Delivery Fees.		4,000

Additional data

1. Some of the supplies represented by the $6,000 balance of the Supplies on Hand account have been consumed. An inventory count of the supplies actually on hand at December 31 totaled $2,400.
2. On May 1 of the current year, a rental payment of $25,200 was made for 12 months' rent; it was debited to Prepaid Rent.
3. The annual depreciation for the buildings is based on the cost shown in the Buildings account less an estimated salvage value of $10,000. The estimated useful lives of the buildings are 40 years each.
4. The salaries expense of $124,000 does not include $6,000 of unpaid salaries earned since the last payday.
5. The company has earned one fourth of the unearned delivery fees by December 31.
6. Delivery services of $600 were performed for a customer, but a bill has not yet been sent.

Required

a. Prepare the adjusting journal entries for December 31, assuming adjusting entries are prepared only at year-end.

b. Based on the adjusted balance shown in the Accumulated Depreciation—Buildings account, how many years has Korman Company owned the building?

Solution to Demonstration Problem

a.

KORMAN COMPANY
General Journal

Date		Account Titles and Explanation	Post. Ref.	Debit	Credit
1997					
Dec.	31	Supplies Expense		3600	
		Supplies on Hand			3600
		To record supplies expense ($6,000 − $2,400).			
	31	Rent Expense		16800	
		Prepaid Rent			16800
		To record rent expense ($25,200 × 8/12).			
	31	Depreciation Expense—Buildings		4750	
		Accumulated Depreciation—Buildings			4750
		To record depreciation [($200,000 − $10,000) ÷ 40 years].			
	31	Salaries Expense		6000	
		Salaries Payable			6000
		To record accrued salaries.			
	31	Unearned Delivery Fees		1000	
		Service Revenue			1000
		To record delivery fees earned.			
	31	Accounts Receivable		600	
		Service Revenue			600
		To record delivery fees earned.			

b. Eight years; computed as:

$$\frac{\text{Total accumulated depreciation}}{\text{Annual depreciation expense}} = \frac{\$33,250 + \$4,750}{\$4,750} = 8$$

New Terms

Accounting period A time period normally of one month, one quarter, or one year into which an entity's life is arbitrarily divided for financial reporting purposes. *100*

Accounting year An accounting period of one year. The accounting year may or may not coincide with the calendar year. *101*

Accrual basis of accounting Recognizes revenues when sales are made or services are performed, regardless of when cash is received. Recognizes expenses as incurred, whether or not cash has been paid out. *100*

Accrued assets and liabilities Assets and liabilities that exist at the end of an accounting period but have not yet been recorded; they represent rights to receive, or obligations to make, payments that are not legally due at the balance sheet date. Examples are accrued fees receivable and salaries payable. *111, 113*

Accrued items See Accrued assets and liabilities.

Accrued revenues and expenses Other names for accrued assets and liabilities. *111, 113*

Accumulated depreciation account A contra asset account that shows the total of all depreciation recorded on the asset up through the balance sheet date. *109*

Adjusting entries Journal entries made at the end of an accounting period to bring about a proper matching of revenues and expenses; they reflect economic activity that has taken place but has not yet been recorded. Adjusting entries are made to bring the accounts to their proper balances before financial statements are prepared. *101*

Book value For depreciable assets, book value equals cost less accumulated depreciation. *109*

Calendar year The normal year, which ends on December 31. *101*

Cash basis of accounting Recognizes revenues when cash is received and recognizes expenses when cash is paid out. *99*

Contra asset account An account shown as a deduction from the asset to which it relates in the balance sheet; used to reduce the original cost of the asset down to its remaining undepreciated cost or book value. *109*

Deferred items Adjusting entries involving data previously recorded in the accounts. Data are transferred from asset and liability accounts to expense and revenue accounts. Examples are prepaid expenses, depreciation, and unearned revenues. *102*

Depreciable amount The difference between an asset's cost and its estimated salvage value. *108*

Depreciable asset A manufactured asset such as a building, machine, vehicle, or equipment on which depreciation expense is recorded. *108*

Depreciation accounting The process of recording depreciation expense. *108*

Depreciation expense The amount of asset cost assigned as an expense to a particular time period. *108*

Depreciation formula (straight-line):

$$\text{Annual depreciation} = \frac{\text{Asset cost} - \text{Estimated salvage value}}{\text{Estimated years of useful life}}$$ *108*

Estimated salvage value (scrap value) The amount that the company can probably sell the asset for at the end of its estimated useful life. *108*

Estimated useful life The estimated time periods that a company can make use of the asset. *108*

Fiscal year An accounting year of any 12 consecutive months that may or may not coincide with the calendar year. For example, a company may have an accounting or fiscal year that runs from April 1 of one year to March 31 of the next. *101*

Matching principle An accounting principle requiring that expenses incurred in producing revenues be deducted from the revenues they generated during the accounting period. *101*

Prepaid expense An asset awaiting assignment to expense. An example is prepaid insurance. Assets such as cash and accounts receivable are not prepaid expenses. *104*

Service potential The benefits that can be obtained from assets. The future services that assets can render make assets "things of value" to a business. *104*

Trend percentages Calculated by dividing the amount of an item for each year by the amount of that item for the base year. *115*

Unearned revenue Assets received from customers before services are performed for them. Since the revenue has not been earned, it is a liability, often called *revenue received in advance* or *advances by customers*. *110*

Self-Test

True-False

Indicate whether each of the following statements is true or false.

1. Every adjusting entry affects at least one income statement account and one balance sheet account.
2. All calendar years are also fiscal years, but not all fiscal years are calendar years.
3. The accumulated depreciation account is an asset account that shows the amount of depreciation for the current year only.
4. The Unearned Delivery Fees account is a revenue account.
5. If all of the adjusting entries are not made, the financial statements are incorrect.

Multiple-Choice

Select the best answer for each of the following questions.

1. An insurance policy premium of $1,200 was paid on September 1, 1997, to cover a one-year period from that date. An asset was debited on that date. Adjusting entries are prepared once a year, at year-end. The necessary adjusting entry at the company's year-end, December 31, 1997, is:

		Debit	Credit
a.	Prepaid Insurance	400	
	Insurance Expense		400
b.	Insurance Expense	800	
	Prepaid Insurance		800
c.	Prepaid Insurance	800	
	Insurance Expense		800
d.	Insurance Expense	400	
	Prepaid Insurance		400

2. The Supplies on Hand account has a balance of $1,500 at year-end. The actual amount of supplies on hand at the end of the period was $400. The necessary adjusting entry is:

		Debit	Credit
a.	Supplies Expense	1,100	
	Supplies on Hand		1,100
b.	Supplies Expense	400	
	Supplies on Hand		400
c.	Supplies on Hand	1,100	
	Supplies Expense		1,100
d.	Supplies on Hand	400	
	Supplies Expense		400

3. A company purchased a truck for $20,000 on January 1, 1997. The truck has an estimated salvage value of $5,000 and is expected to last five years. Adjusting entries are prepared only at year-end. The necessary adjusting entry at December 31, 1997, the company's year-end, is:

		Debit	Credit
a.	Depreciation Expense—Trucks	4,000	
	Accumulated Depreciation—Trucks		4,000
b.	Depreciation Expense—Trucks	3,000	
	Trucks		3,000
c.	Depreciation Expense—Trucks	3,000	
	Accumulated Depreciation—Trucks		3,000
d.	Accumulated Depreciation—Trucks	3,000	
	Depreciation Expense—Trucks		3,000

4. A company received cash of $24,000 on October 1, 1997, as subscriptions for a one-year period from that date. A liability account was credited when the cash was received. The magazine is to be published by the company and delivered to subscribers each month. The company prepares adjusting entries at the end of each month because it prepares financial statements each month. The adjusting entry the company would make at the end of each of the next 12 months would be:

		Debit	Credit
a.	Unearned Subscription Fees. .	6,000	
	Subscription Fee Revenue		6,000
b.	Unearned Subscription Fees. .	2,000	
	Subscription Fee Revenue		2,000
c.	Unearned Subscription Fees. .	18,000	
	Subscription Fee Revenue		18,000
d.	Subscription Fee Revenue . .	2,000	
	Unearned Subscription Fees		2,000

5. When a company earns interest on a note receivable or on a bank account, the debit and credit are as follows:

	Debit	Credit
a.	Accounts Receivable	Interest Revenue
b.	Interest Receivable	Interest Revenue
c.	Interest Revenue	Accounts Receivable
d.	Interest Revenue	Interest Receivable

6. If $3,000 has been earned by a company's workers since the last payday in an accounting period, the necessary adjusting entry would be:
   - **a.** Debit an expense and credit a liability.
   - **b.** Debit an expense and credit an asset.
   - **c.** Debit a liability and credit an asset.
   - **d.** Debit a liability and credit an expense.

Now turn to page 129 to check your answers.

Questions

1. Which events during an accounting period trigger the recording of normal journal entries? Which event triggers the making of adjusting entries?
2. Describe the difference between the cash basis and accrual basis of accounting.
3. Why are adjusting entries necessary? Why not treat every cash disbursement as an expense and every cash receipt as a revenue when the cash changes hands?
4. "Adjusting entries would not be necessary if the 'pure' cash basis of accounting were followed (assuming no mistakes were made in recording cash transactions as they occurred). Under the cash basis, receipts that are of a revenue nature are considered revenue when received, and expenditures that are of an expense nature are considered expenses when paid. It is the use of the accrual basis of accounting, where an effort is made to match expenses incurred against the revenues they create, that makes adjusting entries necessary." Do you agree with this statement? Why?
5. Why don't accountants keep all the accounts at their proper balances continuously throughout the period so that adjusting entries would not have to be made before financial statements are prepared?
6. What is the fundamental difference between deferred items and accrued items?
7. Identify the types of adjusting entries included in each of the two major classes of adjusting entries.
8. Give an example of a journal entry for each of the following:
   a. Equal growth of an expense and a liability.
   b. Earning of revenue that was previously recorded as unearned revenue.
   c. Equal growth of an asset and a revenue.
   d. Increase in an expense and decrease in an asset.
9. A fellow student makes the following statement: "You can easily tell whether a company is using the cash or accrual basis of accounting. When an amount is paid for future rent or insurance services, a firm that is using the cash basis debits an expense account while a firm that is using the accrual basis debits an asset account." Is the student correct?
10. You notice that the Supplies on Hand account has a debit balance of $2,700 at the end of the accounting period. How would you determine the extent to which this account needs adjustment?
11. Some assets are converted into expenses as they expire and some liabilities become revenues as they are earned. Give examples of asset and liability accounts for which this statement is true. Give examples of asset and liability accounts to which the statement does not apply.
12. Give the depreciation formula to compute straight-line depreciation for a one-year period.
13. What does the term *accrued liability* mean?
14. What is meant by the term *service potential?*
15. When assets are received before they are earned, what type of an account is credited? As the amounts are earned, what type of account is credited?
16. What does the word *accrued* mean? Is there a conceptual difference between interest payable and accrued interest payable?
17. Matching expenses incurred with revenues earned is more difficult than matching expenses paid with revenues received. Do you think the effort is worthwhile?
18. Refer to "A Broader Perspective" on page 114. What type of adjusting entry is involved? How do you think the managements of some companies might react to having to record postretirement benefits in this way?

The Coca-Cola Company

19. **Real World Question** Refer to the financial statements of The Coca-Cola Company in its annual report in the annual report booklet. Approximately what percentage of the depreciable assets under property, plant, and equipment has been depreciated as of December 31, 1993?

MAYTAG

20. **Real World Question** Refer to the financial statements of Maytag Corporation in the annual report booklet. What percentage of depreciable property, plant, and equipment has been depreciated as of December 31, 1993? (Construction in progress is not a depreciable asset.)

Exercises

Exercise 3–1
Answer multiple-choice questions (L.O. 1)

Select the correct response for each of the following multiple-choice questions:

1. The cash basis of accounting:
   a. Recognizes revenues when sales are made or services are rendered.
   b. Recognizes expenses as incurred.
   c. Is typically used by some relatively small businesses and professional persons.
   d. Recognizes revenues when cash is received and recognizes expenses when incurred.
2. The accrual basis of accounting:
   a. Recognizes revenues only when cash is received.
   b. Is used by almost all companies.

c. Recognizes expenses only when cash is paid out.
d. Recognizes revenues when sales are made or services are performed and recognizes expenses only when cash is paid out.

Exercise 3–2
Answer multiple-choice questions (L.O. 2)

Select the correct response for each of the following multiple-choice questions:

1. The least common accounting period among the following is:
   a. One month.
   b. Two months.
   c. Three months.
   d. Twelve months.
2. The need for adjusting entries is based on:
   a. The matching principle.
   b. Source documents.
   c. The cash basis of accounting.
   d. Activity that has already been recorded in the proper accounts.

Exercise 3–3
Answer multiple-choice questions (L.O. 3)

Select the correct response for each of the following multiple-choice questions:

1. Which of the following types of adjustments belongs to the deferred items class?
   a. Asset/revenue adjustments.
   b. Liability/expense adjustments.
   c. Asset/expense adjustments.
   d. Asset/liability adjustments.
2. Which of the following types of adjustments belongs to the accrued items class?
   a. Asset/expense adjustments.
   b. Liability/revenue adjustments.
   c. Asset/liability adjustments.
   d. Liability/expense adjustments.

Exercise 3–4
Prepare and post adjusting entry for insurance (L.O. 4)

a. A one-year insurance policy was purchased on August 1 for $1,200, and the following entry was made at that time:

Prepaid Insurance	1,200	
Cash		1,200

What adjusting entry is necessary at December 31, the end of the accounting year?

b. Show how the T-accounts for Prepaid Insurance and Insurance Expense would appear after the entries are posted.

Exercise 3–5
Prepare adjusting entry for rent (L.O. 4)

Assume that rent of $24,000 was paid on September 1, 1997, to cover a one-year period from that date. Prepaid Rent was debited. If financial statements are prepared only on December 31 of each year, what adjusting entry is necessary on December 31, 1997, to bring the accounts involved to their proper balances?

Exercise 3–6
Determine date and entry for rent paid (L.O. 4)

At December 31, 1997, an adjusting entry was made as follows:

Rent Expense	3,000	
Prepaid Rent		3,000

You know that the gross amount of rent paid was $9,000, which was to cover a one-year period. Determine:

a. The opening date of the year to which the $9,000 of rent applies.
b. The entry that was made on the date the rent was paid.

Exercise 3–7
Prepare entries for purchase of supplies and adjustment at year-end (L.O. 4)

Supplies were purchased for cash on May 2, 1997, for $7,500. Show how this purchase would be recorded. Then show the adjusting entry that would be necessary, assuming that $2,500 of the supplies remained at the end of the year.

Exercise 3–8
Prepare adjusting entry for depreciation (L.O. 4)

Assume that a company acquired a building on January 1, 1997, at a cost of $2,000,000. The building has an estimated useful life of 40 years and an estimated salvage value of $400,000. What adjusting entry is needed on December 31, 1997, to record the depreciation for the entire year 1997?

Exercise 3–9
Prepare entries for receipt of subscription fees and adjustment at year-end (L.O. 4)

On September 1, 1997, Professional Bowler Journal, Inc. received a total of $240,000 as payment in advance for one-year subscriptions to a monthly magazine. A liability account was credited to record this cash receipt. By the end of the year, one third of the magazines paid for in advance had been delivered. Give the entries to record the receipt of the subscription fees and to adjust the accounts at December 31, assuming annual financial statements are prepared at year-end.

Exercise 3–10
Prepare entries for receipt of ticket fees, adjustment for earning revenue, and refund of fees (L.O. 4)

On April 15, 1997, Harris Theater sold $180,000 in tickets for the summer musicals to be performed (one per month) during June, July, and August. On July 15, 1997, Harris Theater discovered that the group that was to perform the July and August musicals could not do so. It was too late to find another group qualified to perform the musicals. A decision was made to refund the remaining unearned ticket revenue to its ticket holders, and this was done on July 20. Show the appropriate journal entries to be made on April 15, June 30, and July 20. Harris has a June 30th year-end.

Exercise 3–11
Prepare adjusting entry for accrued legal services (L.O. 4)

Guilty & Innocent, a law firm, performed legal services in late December 1997 for clients. The $24,000 of services would be billed to the clients in January 1998. Give the adjusting entry that is necessary on December 31, 1997, if financial statements are prepared at the end of each month.

Exercise 3–12
Prepare adjusting entry for accrued interest (L.O. 4)

A firm borrowed $20,000 on November 1. By December 31, $200 of interest had been incurred. Prepare the adjusting entry required on December 31.

Exercise 3–13
Prepare adjusting entry for accrued salaries (L.O. 4)

Mailing Services, Inc., incurs salaries at the rate of $1,500 per day. The last payday in January is Friday, January 27. Salaries for Monday and Tuesday of the next week have not been recorded or paid as of January 31. Financial statements are prepared monthly. Give the necessary adjusting entry on January 31.

Exercise 3–14
Determine effect on net income from failing to record adjusting entries (L.O. 5)

State the effect that each of the following independent situations would have on the amount of annual net income reported for 1997 and 1998.

a. No adjustment was made for accrued salaries of $6,000 as of December 31, 1997.

b. The collection of $4,000 for services yet unperformed as of December 31, 1997, was credited to a revenue account and not adjusted. The services are performed in 1998.

Exercise 3–15
Show the effects of failing to recognize indicated adjustments (L.O. 5)

In the following table, indicate the effects of failing to recognize each of the indicated adjustments by writing "O" for overstated and "U" for understated.

		Effect on Balance Sheet Items		
Failure to Recognize	**Effect on Net Income**	**Assets**	**Liabilities**	**Stockholders' Equity**
1. Depreciation on a building				
2. Consumption of supplies on hand				
3. The earning of ticket revenue received in advance				
4. The earning of interest on a bank account				
5. Salaries incurred but unpaid				

Exercise 3–16
Calculate the trend percentages for net income (loss) for Chevron Corporation and comment (L.O. 6)

The following data regarding net income are for the Chevron Corporation for the period 1982–92. Chevron Corporation is one of the world's largest oil and natural gas companies.

	Net Income ($ millions)		Net Income ($ millions)
1982	$1,377	1988	$1,768
1983	1,590	1989	251
1984	1,534	1990	2,157
1985	1,547	1991	1,293
1986	(1,411)	1992	1,569
1987	1,250		

Using 1982 as the base year, calculate the trend percentages, and comment on the results.

Problems

Problem 3–1
Prepare adjusting entries (L.O. 4)

Among other items, the trial balance of Blockblaster, Inc., a movie rental company, at December 31 of the current year includes the following account balances:

	Debits
Prepaid Insurance	$12,000
Prepaid Rent	14,400
Supplies on Hand	2,800

Examination of the records shows that adjustments should be made for the following items:

a. Of the prepaid insurance in the trial balance, $5,000 is for coverage during the months after December 31 of the current year.
b. The balance in the Prepaid Rent account is for a 12-month period that started October 1 of the current year.
c. $150 of interest has been earned but not received.
d. Supplies used during the year amount to $1,800.

Required

Prepare the annual year-end adjusting journal entries at December 31.

Problem 3–2
Prepare adjusting entries and post to ledger accounts (L.O. 4)

Triathlon Magazine, Inc., has the following account balances, among others, in its trial balance at December 31 of the current year:

	Debits	Credits
Supplies on Hand	$ 3,720	
Prepaid Rent	7,200	
Unearned Subscription Fees		$ 13,500
Subscriptions Revenue		261,000
Salaries Expense	123,000	

Additional data

1. The inventory of supplies on hand at December 31 amounts to $270.
2. The balance in the Prepaid Rent account is for a one-year period starting October 1 of the current year.
3. One third of the $13,500 balance in Unearned Subscription Fees has been earned.
4. Since the last payday, the employees of the company have earned additional salaries in the amount of $5,430.

Required

a. Prepare the year-end adjusting journal entries at December 31. Assume you used page 22 of the general journal to record the journal entries.
b. Open ledger accounts for each of the accounts involved, enter the balances as shown in the trial balance, post the adjusting journal entries, and calculate year-end balances.

Problem 3–3
Prepare adjusting entries (L.O. 4)

Luxury Apartments, Inc., adjusts and closes its books each December 31. Assume the accounts for all prior years have been properly adjusted and closed. Following are some of the company's account balances prior to adjustment on December 31, 1997:

LUXURY APARTMENTS, INC.
Partial Trial Balance
December 31, 1997

	Debits	Credits
Prepaid Insurance	$ 7,500	
Supplies on Hand	8,000	
Buildings	255,000	
Accumulated Depreciation—Buildings		$ 96,000
Unearned Rent		2,700
Salaries Expense	69,000	
Rental Revenue		277,500

Additional data

1. The Prepaid Insurance account balance represents the remaining cost of a four-year insurance policy dated June 30, 1995, having a total premium of $12,000.
2. The physical inventory of the office supply stockroom indicates that the supplies on hand cost $2,000.
3. The building was originally acquired on January 1, 1981, at which time management estimated that the building would last 40 years and have a salvage value of $15,000.
4. Salaries earned since the last payday but unpaid at December 31 amount to $4,000.
5. Interest earned but not collected on a savings account during the year amounts to $300.
6. The Unearned Rent account arose through the prepayment of rent by a tenant in the building for 12 months beginning October 1, 1997.

Required Prepare the annual year-end adjusting entries indicated by the additional data.

Problem 3–4
Calculate correct net income (L.O. 5)

The reported net income amounts for Marathon Magazine, Inc., for calendar years 1997 and 1998 were $100,000 and $122,000, respectively. No annual adjusting entries were made at either year-end for any of the following transactions:

1. A fire insurance policy to cover a three-year period from the date of payment was purchased on March 1, 1997, for $3,600. The Prepaid Insurance account was debited at the date of purchase.
2. Subscriptions for magazines in the amount of $72,000 to cover an 18-month period from May 1, 1997, were received on April 15, 1997. The Unearned Subscription Fees account was credited when the payments were received.
3. A building costing $180,000 and having an estimated useful life of 50 years and a salvage value of $30,000 was purchased and put into service on January 1, 1997.
4. On January 12, 1998, salaries of $9,600 were paid to employees. The account debited was Salaries Expense. One third of the amount paid was earned by employees in December of 1997.

Required Calculate the correct net income for 1997 and 1998. In your answer, start with the reported net income. Then show the effects of each correction (adjustment), using a plus or a minus to indicate whether reported income should be increased or decreased as a result of the correction. When the corrections are added to or deducted from the reported net income amounts, the result should be the correct net income amounts. The answer format should appear as follows:

Explanation of Corrections	1997	1998
Reported net income	$100,000	$122,000
To correct error in accounting for:		
a. Fire insurance policy premium:		
Correct expense in 1997	−1,000	
Correct expense in 1998		−1,200

Problem 3–5
Prepare journal entries under cash basis and accrual basis (L.O. 1, 4)

Astronomy Publishing Company began operations on December 1, 1997. The company's bookkeeper intended to use the cash basis of accounting. Consequently, the bookkeeper recorded all cash receipts and disbursements for items relating to operations in revenue and expense accounts. No adjusting entries were made prior to preparing the financial statements for December.

Transactions

Dec. 1 Issued capital stock for $200,000 cash.
3 Received $144,000 for magazine subscriptions to run for two years from this date. The magazine is published monthly on the 23rd.
4 Paid for advertising to be run in a national periodical for six months (starting this month). The cost was $54,000.
7 Purchased for cash an insurance policy to cover a two-year period beginning December 15, $24,000.
12 Paid the annual rent on the building, $72,000, effective through November 30, 1998.
15 Received $216,000 cash for two-year subscriptions starting with the December issue.
15 Salaries for the period December 1–15 amounted to $48,000. Beginning as of this date, salaries will be paid on the 5th and 20th of each month for the preceding two-week period.
20 Salaries for the period December 1–15 were paid.
23 Supplies purchased for cash, $21,600. (Only $1,800 of these were subsequently used in 1997.)
27 Printing costs applicable equally to the next six issues beginning with the December issue were paid in cash, $144,000.
31 Cash sales of the December issue, $84,000.
31 Unpaid salaries for the period December 16–31 amounted to $22,000.
31 Sales on account of December issue, $14,000.

Required

a. Prepare journal entries for the transactions as the bookkeeper prepared them.

b. Prepare journal entries as they would have been prepared under the accrual basis. Where the entry is the same as under the cash basis, merely indicate "same." Where possible, record the original transaction so that no adjusting entry would be necessary at the end of the month. Ignore explanations.

ALTERNATE PROBLEMS

Problem 3–1A
Prepare adjusting entries (L.O. 4)

The trial balance of South Pacific Vacation Tours, Inc., at December 31 of the current year includes, among other items, the following account balances:

	Debits	Credits
Prepaid Insurance	$ 12,000	
Prepaid Rent	24,000	
Buildings	188,000	
Accumulated Depreciation—Buildings		$31,600
Salaries Expense	200,000	

Additional data

1. The balance in the Prepaid Insurance account is the advance premium for one year from September 1 of the current year.
2. The buildings are expected to last 25 years, with an expected salvage value of $30,000.
3. Salaries incurred but not paid as of December 31 amount to $8,400.
4. The balance in Prepaid Rent is for a one-year period that started March 1 of the current year.

Required

Prepare the annual year-end adjusting journal entries at December 31.

Problem 3–2A
Prepare adjusting entries and post to ledger accounts (L.O. 4)

Among the account balances shown in the trial balance of Mail Station, Inc., at December 31 of the current year are the following:

	Debits	Credits
Supplies on Hand	$ 18,000	
Prepaid Insurance	6,000	
Buildings	168,000	
Accumulated Depreciation—Buildings		$39,000

Additional data

1. The inventory of supplies on hand at December 31 amounts to $3,000.
2. The balance in the Prepaid Insurance account is for a two-year policy taken out June 1 of the current year.

3. Depreciation for the buildings is based on the cost shown in the Buildings account, less salvage value estimated at $18,000. When acquired, the lives of the buildings were estimated at 50 years each.

Required

a. Prepare the year-end adjusting journal entries at December 31. Assume you used page 27 of the general journal to record the journal entries.

b. Open ledger accounts for each of the accounts involved, enter the balances as shown in the trial balance, post the adjusting journal entries, and calculate year-end balances.

Problem 3–3A
Prepare adjusting entries (L.O. 4)

Camping Equipment Rental Company occupies rented quarters on the main street of the city. To get this location, the company rented a store larger than needed and subleased (rented) a portion of the area to Max's Restaurant. The partial trial balance of Camping Equipment Rental Company as of December 31, 1997, is as follows:

CAMPING EQUIPMENT RENTAL COMPANY
Partial Trial Balance
December 31, 1997

	Debits	Credits
Cash	$200,000	
Prepaid Insurance	11,400	
Supplies on Hand	20,000	
Camping Equipment	176,000	
Accumulated Depreciation—Camping Equipment		$ 19,200
Notes Payable		40,000
Equipment Rental Revenue		1,500,000
Sublease Rental Revenue		8,800
Building Rent Expense	14,400	
Salaries Expense	196,000	

Additional data

a. Salaries of employees amount to $600 per day and were last paid through Wednesday, December 27. December 31 is a Sunday. The store is closed Sundays.

b. An analysis of the Camping Equipment account disclosed:

Balance, January 1, 1997	$128,000
Addition, July 1, 1997	48,000
Balance, December 31, 1997, per trial balance	$176,000

The company estimates that all equipment will last 20 years from the date they were acquired and that the salvage value will be zero.

c. The store carries one combined insurance policy, which is taken out once a year effective August 1. The premium on the policy now in force amounts to $7,200 per year.

d. Unused supplies on hand at December 31, 1997, have a cost of $11,400.

e. December's rent from Max's Restaurant has not yet been received, $800.

f. Interest accrued on the note payable is $1,000.

Required Prepare the annual year-end entries required by the preceding statement of facts.

Problem 3–4A
Calculate correct net income (L.O. 5)

The reported net income amounts for Reliable Waste Control Company were 1997, $100,000; and 1998, $130,000. *No* annual adjusting entries were made at either year-end for any of these transactions:

a. A building was rented on April 1, 1997. Cash of $14,400 was paid on that date to cover a two-year period. Prepaid Rent was debited.

b. The balance in the Office Supplies on Hand account on December 31, 1997, was $6,000. An inventory of the supplies on December 31, 1997, revealed that only $3,500 were actually on hand at that date. No new supplies were purchased during 1998. At December 31, 1998, an inventory of the supplies revealed that $800 were on hand.

c. A building costing $1,200,000 and having an estimated useful life of 40 years and a salvage value of $240,000 was put into service on January 1, 1997.

d. Services were performed for customers in December 1997. The $24,000 bill for these services was not sent until January 1998. The only transaction that was recorded was a debit to Cash and a credit to Service Revenue when payment was received in January.

Required

Calculate the correct net income for 1997 and 1998. In your answer, start with the reported net income amounts. Then show the effects of each correction (adjustment) using a plus or a minus to indicate whether reported income should be increased or decreased as a result of the correction. When the corrections are added to or deducted from the reported net income amounts, the result should be the correct net income amounts. The answer format should be as follows:

Explanation of Corrections	1997	1998
Reported net income	$100,000	$130,000
To correct error in accounting for:		
a. Prepaid rent:		
Correct expense in 1997.	−5,400	
Correct expense in 1998.		−7,200

Problem 3–5A
Prepare journal entries under cash basis and accrual basis (L.O. 1, 4)

On June 1, 1997, Richard Ryan opened a swimming pool cleaning and maintenance service, Ryan Pool Company. He vaguely recalled the process of making journal entries and establishing ledger accounts from a high school bookkeeping course he had taken some years ago. At the end of June, he prepared an income statement for the month of June, but he had the feeling that he had not proceeded correctly. He contacted his brother, John, a recent college graduate with a major in accounting, for assistance. John immediately noted that his brother had kept his records on a cash basis.

Transactions

June 1 Received cash of $27,000 from various customers in exchange for service agreements to clean and maintain their pools for June, July, August, and September.
5 Paid rent for automotive and cleaning equipment to be used during the period June through September, $6,000. The payment covered the entire period.
8 Purchased a two-year liability insurance policy effective June 1 for $12,000 cash.
10 Received an advance of $7,500 from a Florida building contractor in exchange for an agreement to help service pools in his housing development during October through May.
16 Paid salaries for the first half of June, $8,400.
17 Paid $900 for advertising to be run in a local newspaper for two weeks in June and four weeks in July.
19 Paid the rent of $24,000 under a four-month lease on a building rented and occupied on June 1.
26 Purchased $5,400 of supplies for cash. (Only $900 of these supplies were used in June.)
29 Billed various customers for services rendered, $18,000.
30 Unpaid employee services received in the last half of June amounted to $12,600.
30 Received a bill for $600 for gas and oil used in June.

Required

a. Prepare the entries for the transactions as Richard must have recorded them under the cash basis of accounting.

b. Prepare journal entries as they would have been prepared under the accrual basis. Where the entry is the same as under the cash basis, merely indicate "same." Where possible, record the original transaction so that no adjusting entry would be necessary at the end of the month. Ignore explanations.

Beyond the Numbers—Critical Thinking

Business Decision Case 3–1
Explain why adjusting entries are made and which accounts need adjustment (L.O. 2, 4)

You have just been hired by Executive Employment Agency, Inc., to help prepare adjusting entries at the end of an accounting period. It becomes obvious to you that management does not seem to have much of an understanding about the necessity for adjusting entries or which accounts might possibly need adjustment. The first step you take is to prepare the following unadjusted trial balance from the general ledger. Only those ledger accounts that had end-of-year balances are included in the trial balance.

	Debits	Credits
Cash	$ 60,000	
Accounts Receivable	28,000	
Supplies on Hand	3,000	
Prepaid Insurance	2,700	
Office Equipment	120,000	
Accumulated Depreciation—Office Equipment		$ 45,000
Buildings	360,000	
Accumulated Depreciation—Buildings		105,000
Accounts Payable		9,000
Loan Payable (Bank)		15,000
Unearned Commission Fees		30,000
Capital Stock		160,000
Retained Earnings		69,300
Commissions Revenue		270,000
Advertising Expense	6,000	
Salaries Expense	112,500	
Utilities Expense	7,500	
Miscellaneous Expense	3,600	
	$703,300	$703,300

Required

a. Explain to management why adjusting entries in general are made.

b. Explain to management why some of the specific accounts appearing in the trial balance may need adjustment and what the nature of each adjustment might be (do not worry about specific dollar amounts).

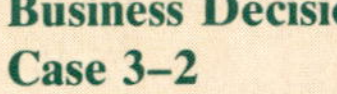

Business Decision Case 3–2

Prepare an appraisal and an approximate income statement (L.O. 1, 4)

A friend of yours, Jack Billings, is quite excited over the opportunity he has to purchase the land and several miscellaneous assets of Allen Bowling Lanes Company for $400,000. Billings tells you that Mr. and Mrs. Allen (the sole stockholders in the company) are moving due to Mr. Allen's ill health. The annual rent on the building and equipment is $54,000.

Allen reports that the business earned a profit of $90,000 in 1997 (last year). Billings believes an annual profit of $90,000 on an investment of $400,000 is a really good deal. But, before completing the deal, he asks you to look it over. You agree and discover the following:

1. Allen has computed his annual profit for 1997 as the sum of his cash dividends plus the increase in the Cash account: Dividends of $60,000 + Increase in Cash account of $30,000 = $90,000 profit.

2. As buyer of the business, Billings will take over responsibility for repayment of a $300,000 loan (plus interest) on the land. The land was acquired at a cost of $624,000 seven years ago.

3. An analysis of the Cash account shows the following for 1997:

Rental revenues received		$465,000
Cash paid out in 1997 for—		
Salaries paid to employees in 1997	$270,000	
Utilities paid for 1997	18,000	
Advertising expenses paid	15,000	
Supplies purchased and used in 1997	24,000	
Interest paid on loan	18,000	
Loan principal paid	30,000	
Cash dividends	60,000	435,000
Increase in cash balance for the year		$ 30,000

4. You also find that the annual rent of $54,000, a December utility bill of $4,000, and an advertising bill of $6,000 have not been paid.

Required

a. Prepare a written report for Billings giving your appraisal of Allen Bowling Lanes Company as an investment. Comment on Allen's method of computing the annual profit of the business.

b. Include in your report an approximate income statement for 1997.

Annual Report Analysis 3–3
Develop trend percentages for The Coca-Cola Company's net income and comment (L.O. 6)

Turn to the "Selected Financial Data" section of The Coca-Cola Company's annual report in the annual report booklet. Prepare trend percentages for the net income amounts using 1983 as the base year. Comment on the trend of performance.

Group Project 3–4
Library project concerning annual reports (L.O. 6)

In teams of two or three students, go to the library to locate one company's annual report for the most recent year. (The university may have received the annual reports of companies either in published form, in microfiche form, or in computer readable format.) Identify the name of the company and the major products or services offered, as well as gross revenues, major expenses, and the trend of profits over the last three years. Calculate trend percentages for revenues, expenses, and profits using the oldest year as the base year. Each team should write a memorandum to management summarizing the data and commenting on the trend percentages. The heading of the memorandum should contain the date, to whom it is written, from whom, and the subject matter.

Answers to Self-Test

True-False

1. **True.** Every adjusting entry involves either moving previously recorded data from an asset account to an expense account or from a liability account to a revenue account (or in the opposite direction) or simultaneously entering new data in an asset account and a revenue account or in a liability account and an expense account.
2. **True.** A fiscal year is *any* 12 consecutive months, so all calendar years are also fiscal years. A calendar year, however, must end on December 31, so it does not include fiscal years that end on any date other than December 31 (such as June 30).
3. **False.** The accumulated depreciation account is a *contra asset* that shows the total of all depreciation recorded on an asset from its acquisition date up through the balance sheet date.
4. **False.** The Unearned Delivery Fees account is a liability. As the fees are earned, the amount in that account is transferred to a revenue account.
5. **True.** If an adjusting entry is overlooked and not made, at least one income statement account and one balance sheet account will be incorrect.

Multiple-Choice

1. **d.** One third of the benefits have expired. Therefore, $400 must be moved from the asset (credit) to an expense (debit).
2. **a.** $1,100 of the supplies have been used, so that amount must be moved from the asset (credit) to an expense (debit).
3. **c.** The amount of annual depreciation is determined as ($20,000 − $5,000) divided by 5 = $3,000. The debit is to Depreciation Expense—Trucks, and the credit is to Accumulated Depreciation—Trucks, a contra asset account.
4. **b.** Each month $2,000 would be transferred from the liability account (debit), Unearned Subscription Fees, to a revenue account (credit).
5. **b.** An asset, Interest Receivable, is debited, and Interest Revenue is credited.
6. **a.** The debit would be to Salaries Expense, and the credit would be to Salaries Payable.

4

Completing the Accounting Cycle

This chapter explains two new steps in the **accounting cycle**—the preparation of the work sheet and closing entries. In addition, we briefly discuss the evolution of accounting systems and present a classified balance sheet. This balance sheet format more closely resembles actual company balance sheets, such as those in the annual report booklet. After completing this chapter, you will understand how accounting begins with source documents that are evidence of a business entity's transactions and ends with financial statements that show the solvency and profitability of the entity.

Learning Objectives

After studying this chapter, you should be able to:

1. Summarize the steps in the accounting cycle.
2. Prepare a work sheet for a service company.
3. Prepare an income statement, statement of retained earnings, and balance sheet using information contained in the work sheet.
4. Prepare adjusting and closing entries using information contained in the work sheet.
5. Prepare a post-closing trial balance.

(continued)

The Accounting Cycle Summarized

In Chapter 1, you learned that when an event is a measureable business transaction, you need adequate proof of this transaction. Then, you analyze the transaction's effects on the accounting equation, Assets = Liabilities + Stockholders' Equity. In Chapters 2 and 3, you performed other steps in the accounting cycle. Chapter 2 presented the eight steps in the accounting cycle as a preview of the content of chapters 2 through 4. As a review, study the diagram of the eight steps in the accounting cycle in Illustration 4.1 (page 133). Remember that the first three steps occur during the accounting period and the last five occur at the end. The next section explains how to use the work sheet to facilitate the completion of the accounting cycle.

The Work Sheet

The **work sheet** is a columnar sheet of paper or a computer spreadsheet on which accountants summarize information needed to make the adjusting and closing entries and to prepare the financial statements. Usually, they save these work sheets to document the end-of-period entries. A work sheet is only an accounting tool and not part of the formal accounting records. Therefore, work sheets may

(concluded)

6. Describe the evolution of accounting systems.
7. Prepare a classified balance sheet.
8. Analyze and use the financial results—the current ratio.

vary in format; some are prepared in pencil so that errors can be corrected easily. Other work sheets are prepared on personal computers with spreadsheet software. Accountants prepare work sheets each time financial statements are needed—monthly, quarterly, or at the end of the accounting year.

This chapter illustrates a 12-column work sheet that includes sets of columns for an unadjusted trial balance, adjustments, adjusted trial balance, income statement, statement of retained earnings, and balance sheet. Each set has a debit and a credit column. (See Illustration 4.2 on page 134.)

Accountants use these initial steps in preparing the work sheet. The following sections describe the detailed steps for completing the work sheet.

Objective 1
Summarize the steps in the accounting cycle.

Objective 2
Prepare a work sheet for a service company.

1. Enter the titles and balances of ledger accounts in the Trial Balance columns.
2. Enter adjustments in the Adjustments columns.
3. Enter adjusted account balances in the Adjusted Trial Balance columns.
4. Extend adjusted balances of revenue and expense accounts from the Adjusted Trial Balance columns to the Income Statement columns.
5. Extend any balances in the Retained Earnings and Dividends accounts to the Statement of Retained Earnings columns.
6. Extend adjusted balances of asset, liability, and capital stock accounts from the Adjusted Trial Balance columns to the Balance Sheet columns.

The Trial Balance Columns

Instead of preparing a separate trial balance as we did in Chapter 2, accountants use the Trial Balance columns on a work sheet. Look at Illustration 4.2 and note that the numbers and titles of the ledger accounts of MicroTrain Company are on the left portion of the work sheet. Usually, only those accounts with balances as of the end of the accounting period are listed. (Some firms do list the entire chart of accounts, even those with zero balances.) Assume you are MicroTrain's accountant. You list the Retained Earnings account in the trial balance even though it has a zero balance (1) to show its relative position among the accounts and (2) to indicate that December 1997 is the first month of operations for this company. Next, you enter the balances of the ledger accounts in the Trial Balance columns. The accounts are in the order in which they appear in the general ledger: assets, liabilities, stockholders' equity, dividends, revenues, and expenses. Then, total the columns. If the debit and credit column totals are not equal, an error exists that must be corrected before you proceed with the work sheet.

The Adjustments Columns

As you learned in Chapter 3, adjustments bring the accounts to their proper balances before accountants prepare the income statement, statement of retained earnings, and balance sheet. You enter these adjustments in the Adjustments columns of the work sheet. Also, you cross-reference the debits and credits of the entries by placing a key number or letter to the left of the amounts. This key number facilitates the actual journalizing of the adjusting entries later because you do not have to rethink the adjustments to record them. For example, the number *(1)* identifies the adjustment debiting Insurance Expense and crediting Prepaid Insurance. Note in the Account Titles column that the Insurance Expense account title is below the trial balance totals because the Insurance Expense account did not have a balance before the adjustment and, therefore, did not appear in the trial balance.

Work sheet preparers often provide brief explanations at the bottom for the keyed entries as in Illustration 4.2. Although these explanations are optional, they provide valuable information for those who review the work sheet later.

The adjustments (which were discussed and illustrated in Chapter 3) for MicroTrain Company are:

ILLUSTRATION 4.1
Steps in the Accounting Cycle

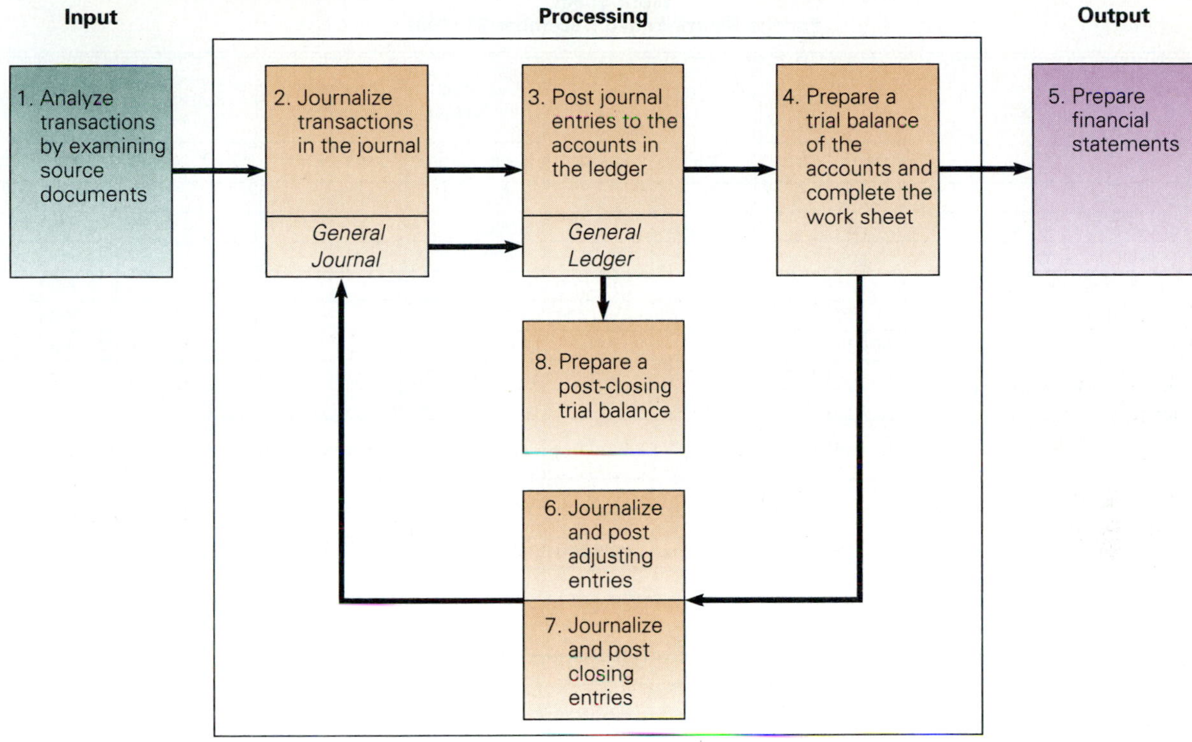

- Entry *(1)* records the expiration of $200 of prepaid insurance in December.
- Entry *(2)* records the expiration of $400 of prepaid rent in December.
- Entry *(3)* records the using up of $500 of supplies during the month.
- Entry *(4)* records $750 depreciation expense on the trucks for the month. MicroTrain acquired the trucks at the beginning of December.
- Entry *(5)* records the earning of $1,500 of the $4,500 in the Unearned Service Fees account.
- Entry *(6)* records $600 of interest earned in December.
- Entry *(7)* records $1,000 of unbilled training services performed in December.
- Entry *(8)* records the $180 accrual of salaries expense at the end of the month.

Often it is difficult to discover all the adjusting entries that should be made. The following steps are helpful:

1. Examine adjusting entries made at the end of the preceding accounting period. The same types of entries often are necessary period after period.
2. Examine the account titles in the trial balance. For example, if the company has an account titled Trucks, an entry must be made for depreciation.
3. Examine various business documents (such as bills for services received or rendered) to discover other assets, liabilities, revenues, and expenses that have not yet been recorded.
4. Ask the manager or other personnel specific questions regarding adjustments that may be necessary. For example, "Were any services performed during the month that have not yet been billed?"

ILLUSTRATION 4.2 Completed Work Sheet

MICROTRAIN COMPANY
Work Sheet
For the Month Ended December 31, 1997

Acct. No.	Account Titles	Trial Balance		Adjustments		Adjusted Trial Balance		Income Statement		Statement of Retained Earnings		Balance Sheet	
		Debit	Credit	Debit	Credit	Debit	Credit	Debit	Credit	Debit	Credit	Debit	Credit
100	Cash	8,250				8,250						8,250	
103	Accounts Receivable	5,200		(7) 1,000		6,200						6,200	
107	Supplies on Hand	1,400			(3) 500	900						900	
108	Prepaid Insurance	2,400			(1) 200	2,200						2,200	
112	Prepaid Rent	1,200			(2) 400	800						800	
150	Trucks	40,000				40,000						40,000	
200	Accounts Payable		730				730						730
216	Unearned Service Fees		4,500	(5) 1,500			3,000						3,000
300	Capital Stock		50,000				50,000						50,000
310	Retained Earnings, 12/1/97		–0–				–0–				–0–		
320	Dividends	3,000				3,000				3,000			
400	Service				(5) 1,500								
	Revenue		10,700		(7) 1,000		13,200		13,200				
505	Advertising Expense	50				50		50					
506	Gas and Oil Expense	680				680		680					
507	Salaries Expense	3,600		(8) 180		3,780		3,780					
511	Utilities Expense	150				150		150					
		65,930	65,930										
512	Insurance Expense			(1) 200		200		200					
515	Rent Expense			(2) 400		400		400					
518	Supplies Expense			(3) 500		500		500					
521	Depreciation Expense—												
	Trucks			(4) 750		750		750					
151	Accumulated Depreciation—												
	Trucks				(4) 750		750						750
121	Interest Receivable			(6) 600		600						600	
418	Interest Revenue				(6) 600		600		600				
206	Salaries Payable				(8) 180		180						180
				5,130	5,130	68,460	68,460	6,510	13,800				
	Net Income							7,290			7,290		
								13,800	13,800	3,000	7,290		
	Retained Earnings, 12/31/97									4,290			4,290
										7,290	7,290	58,950	58,950

Adjustments explanations:

(1) To record insurance expense for December.
(2) To record rent expense for December.
(3) To record supplies expense for December.
(4) To record depreciation expense for December.
(5) To transfer fees for services provided in December from the liability account to the revenue account.
(6) To record one month's interest revenue.
(7) To record unbilled training services performed in December.
(8) To accrue one day's salaries that were earned but are unpaid.

After all the adjusting entries are entered in the Adjustments columns, total the two columns. The totals of these two columns should be equal when all debits and credits are entered properly.

The Adjusted Trial Balance Columns

After MicroTrain's adjustments, compute the adjusted balance of each account and enter these in the Adjusted Trial Balance columns. For example, Supplies on Hand (Account No. 107) had an unadjusted balance of $1,400. Adjusting entry *(3)* credited the account for $500, leaving a debit balance of $900. This amount is a debit in the Adjusted Trial Balance columns.

Next, extend all accounts having balances to the Adjusted Trial Balance columns. Note carefully how the rules of debit and credit apply in determining whether an adjustment increases or decreases the account balance. For example, Salaries Expense (Account No. 507) has a $3,600 debit balance in the Trial Balance columns. A $180 debit adjustment increases this account, which has a $3,780 debit balance in the Adjusted Trial Balance columns.

Some account balances remain the same because no adjustments have affected them. For example, the balance in Accounts Payable (Account No. 200) does not change and is simply extended to the Adjusted Trial Balance columns.

Now, total the Adjusted Trial Balance debit and credit columns. The totals must be equal before taking the next step in completing the work sheet. When the Trial Balance and Adjustments columns both balance but the Adjusted Trial Balance columns do not, the most probable cause is a math error or an error in extension. The Adjusted Trial Balance columns make the next step of sorting the amounts to the Income Statement, the Statement of Retained Earnings, and the Balance Sheet columns much easier.

The Income Statement Columns

Begin by extending all of MicroTrain's revenue and expense account balances in the Adjusted Trial Balance columns to the Income Statement columns. Since revenues carry credit balances, extend them to the credit column. After extending expenses to the debit column, subtotal each column. MicroTrain's total expenses are $6,510 and total revenues are $13,800. Thus, net income for the period is $7,290 ($13,800 − $6,510). Enter this $7,290 income in the debit column to make the two column totals balance. You would record a net loss in the opposite manner; expenses (debits) would have been larger than revenues (credits) so a net loss would be entered in the credit column to make the columns balance.

The Statement of Retained Earnings Columns

Next, complete the Statement of Retained Earnings columns. Enter the $7,290 net income amount for December in the credit Statement of Retained Earnings column. Thus, this net income amount is the balancing figure for the Income Statement columns and is also in the credit Statement of Retained Earnings column. Net income appears in the Statement of Retained Earnings credit column because it causes an increase in Retained Earnings. Add the $7,290 net income to the beginning retained earnings balance of $–0–, and deduct the dividends of $3,000. As a result, the ending balance of the Retained Earnings account is $4,290.

The Balance Sheet Columns

Now extend the assets, liabilities, and capital stock accounts in the Adjusted Trial Balance columns to the Balance Sheet columns. Extend asset amounts as debits and liability and capital stock amounts as credits.

Note that the ending retained earnings amount determined in the Statement of Retained Earnings columns appears again as a credit in the Balance Sheet columns. The ending retained earnings amount is a debit in the Statement of Retained Earnings columns to balance the Statement of Retained Earnings columns. The ending retained earnings is a credit in the Balance Sheet columns because it increases stockholders' equity, and increases in stockholders' equity are credits. (Retained earnings would have a debit ending balance only if losses and dividends exceed earnings.) With the inclusion of the ending retained earnings amount, the Balance Sheet columns balance.

Locating Errors

When the Balance Sheet column totals do not agree on the first attempt, work backward through the process used in preparing the work sheet. Specifically, take the following steps until you discover the error:

ILLUSTRATION 4.3
Income Statement

MICROTRAIN COMPANY
Income Statement
For the Month Ended December 31, 1997

Revenues:		
Service revenue		$13,200
Interest revenue		600
Total revenue		$13,800
Expenses:		
Advertising expense	$ 50	
Gas and oil expense	680	
Salaries expense	3,780	
Utilities expense	150	
Insurance expense	200	
Rent expense	400	
Supplies expense	500	
Depreciation expense—trucks	750	
Total expenses		6,510
Net income		$ 7,290

1. Retotal the two Balance Sheet columns to see if you made an error in addition. If the column totals do not agree, check to see if you did not extend a balance sheet item or if you made an incorrect extension from the Adjusted Trial Balance columns.
2. Retotal the Statement of Retained Earnings columns and determine whether you entered the correct amount of retained earnings in the appropriate Statement of Retained Earnings and Balance Sheet columns.
3. Retotal the Income Statement columns and determine whether you entered the correct amount of net income or net loss for the period in the appropriate Income Statement and Statement of Retained Earnings columns.

AN ACCOUNTING PERSPECTIVE

USES OF TECHNOLOGY Electronic spreadsheets have numerous applications in accounting. An electronic spreadsheet is simply a large blank page that contains rows and columns on the computer screen. The blocks created by the intersection of the rows and columns are cells; each cell can hold one or more words, a number, or the product of a mathematical formula. Spreadsheets are ideal for creating large work sheets, trial balances, and other schedules, and for performing large volumes of calculations such as depreciation calculations. Some of the most popular spreadsheet programs are Lotus 1-2-3®, Microsoft Excel®, QuattroPro®, and AppleWorks®.

PREPARING FINANCIAL STATEMENTS FROM THE WORK SHEET

Objective 3
Prepare an income statement, statement of retained earnings, and balance sheet using information contained in the work sheet.

When the work sheet is completed, all the necessary information to prepare the income statement, statement of retained earnings, and balance sheet is readily available. Now, you need only recast the information into the appropriate financial statement format.

Income Statement

The information you need to prepare the income statement in Illustration 4.3 is in the work sheet's Income Statement columns in Illustration 4.2.

Statement of Retained Earnings

The information you need to prepare the statement of retained earnings is taken from the Statement of Retained Earnings columns in the work sheet. Look at Illustration 4.4, MicroTrain Company's statement of retained earnings for the

ILLUSTRATION 4.4
Statement of Retained Earnings

MICROTRAIN COMPANY
Statement of Retained Earnings
For the Month Ended December 31, 1997

Retained earnings, December 1, 1997	$ -0-
Net income for December	7,290
Total	$7,290
Less: Dividends	3,000
Retained earnings, December 31, 1997	$4,290

ILLUSTRATION 4.5
Balance Sheet

MICROTRAIN COMPANY
Balance Sheet
December 31, 1997

Assets

Cash		$ 8,250
Accounts receivable		6,200
Supplies on hand		900
Prepaid insurance		2,200
Prepaid rent		800
Interest receivable		600
Trucks	$40,000	
Less: Accumulated depreciation	750	39,250
Total assets		$58,200

Liabilities and Stockholders' Equity

Liabilities:		
Accounts payable		$ 730
Unearned service fees		3,000
Salaries payable		180
Total liabilities		$ 3,910
Stockholders' equity:		
Capital stock	$50,000	
Retained earnings	4,290	
Total stockholders' equity		54,290
Total liabilities and stockholders' equity		$58,200

month ended December 31, 1997. To prepare this statement, use the beginning Retained Earnings account balance (Account No. 310), add the net income (or deduct the net loss), and then subtract the Dividends (Account No. 320). Carry the ending Retained Earnings balance forward to the balance sheet. Remember that the statement of retained earnings helps to relate income statement information to balance sheet information. It does this by indicating how net income on the income statement relates to retained earnings on the balance sheet.

Balance Sheet

The information needed to prepare a balance sheet comes from the Balance Sheet columns of MicroTrain's work sheet (Illustration 4.2). As stated earlier, the correct amount for the ending retained earnings appears on the statement of retained earnings. See the completed balance sheet for MicroTrain in Illustration 4.5.

JOURNALIZING ADJUSTING ENTRIES

Objective 4
Prepare adjusting and closing entries using information contained in the work sheet.

After completing MicroTrain's financial statements from the work sheet, you should enter the adjusting entries in the general journal and post them to the appropriate ledger accounts. You would prepare these adjusting entries as you learned in Chapter 3, except that the work sheet is now your source for making the entries. The preparation of a work sheet does not eliminate the need to prepare and post adjusting entries because the work sheet is only an informal accounting tool and is not part of the formal accounting records.

The numerical notations in the Adjustments columns and the adjustments explanations at the bottom of the work sheet identify each adjusting entry. The Adjustments columns show each entry with its appropriate debit and credit. MicroTrain's adjusting entries as they would appear in the general journal after posting are:

MICROTRAIN COMPANY
General Journal

Page 3

Date		Account Titles and Explanation	Post. Ref.	Debit	Credit
1997		**Adjusting Entries**			
Dec.	31	Insurance Expense	512	200	
		Prepaid Insurance	108		200
		To record insurance expense for December.			
	31	Rent Expense	515	400	
		Prepaid Rent	112		400
		To record rent expense for December.			
	31	Supplies Expense	518	500	
		Supplies on Hand	107		500
		To record supplies used during December.			
	31	Depreciation Expense—Trucks	521	750	
		Accumulated Depreciation—Trucks	151		750
		To record depreciation expense for December.			
	31	Unearned Service Fees	216	1500	
		Service Revenue	400		1500
		To transfer a portion of training fees from the liability account to			
		the revenue account.			
	31	Interest Receivable	121	600	
		Interest Revenue	418		600
		To record one month's interest revenue.			
	31	Accounts Receivable	103	1000	
		Service Revenue	400		1000
		To record unbilled training services performed in December.			
	31	Salaries Expense	507	180	
		Salaries Payable	206		180
		To accrue one day's salaries that were earned but are unpaid.			

The Closing Process

In Chapter 2, you learned that revenue, expense, and Dividends accounts are nominal (temporary) accounts that are merely subclassifications of a real (permanent) account, Retained Earnings. And you learned that we prepare financial statements for certain accounting periods. The **closing process** transfers (1) the balances in the revenue and expense accounts to a clearing account called *Income Summary* and then to Retained Earnings, and (2) the balance in the Dividends account to the Retained Earnings account. The closing process reduces revenue, expense, and Dividends account balances to zero so they are ready to receive data for the next accounting period. Accountants may perform the closing process monthly or annually.

The **Income Summary account** is a clearing account used only at the end of an accounting period to summarize revenues and expenses for the period. After transferring all revenue and expense account balances to Income Summary, the balance in the Income Summary account represents the net income or net loss for the period. Closing or transferring the balance in the Income Summary account to the Retained Earnings account results in a zero balance in Income Summary.

Also closed at the end of the accounting period is the Dividends account containing the dividends declared by the board of directors to the stockholders. We close the Dividends account directly to the Retained Earnings account and not to Income Summary because dividends have no effect on income or loss for the period.

In accounting, we often refer to the process of closing as closing the books. Remember that only revenue, expense, and Dividend accounts are closed—not asset, liability, Capital Stock, or Retained Earnings accounts. The four basic steps in the closing process are:

1. **Closing the revenue accounts**—transferring the balances in the revenue accounts to a clearing account called Income Summary.
2. **Closing the expense accounts**—transferring the balances in the expense accounts to a clearing account called Income Summary.
3. **Closing the Income Summary account**—transferring the balance of the Income Summary account to the Retained Earnings account.
4. **Closing the Dividends account**—transferring the balance of the Dividends account to the Retained Earnings account.

Step 1: Closing the Revenue Accounts

Revenues appear in the Income Statement credit column of the work sheet. The two revenue accounts in the Income Statement credit column for MicroTrain Company are service revenue of $13,200 and interest revenue of $600 (Illustration 4.2). Because revenue accounts have credit balances, you must debit them for an amount equal to their balance to bring them to a zero balance. When you debit Service Revenue and Interest Revenue, credit Income Summary (Account No. 600). Enter the account numbers in the Posting Reference column when the journal entry has been posted to the ledger. Do this for all other closing journal entries.

MICROTRAIN COMPANY
General Journal

Page 4

Date		Account Titles and Explanation	Post. Ref.	Debit	Credit
1997		**Closing Entries**			
Dec.	31	Service Revenue	400	13200	
		Interest Revenue	418	600	
		Income Summary	600		13800
		To close the revenue accounts in the Income Statement credit			
		column to Income Summary.			

After the closing entries have been posted, the Service Revenue and Interest Revenue accounts (in T-account format) of MicroTrain appear as follows. Note that the accounts now have zero balances.

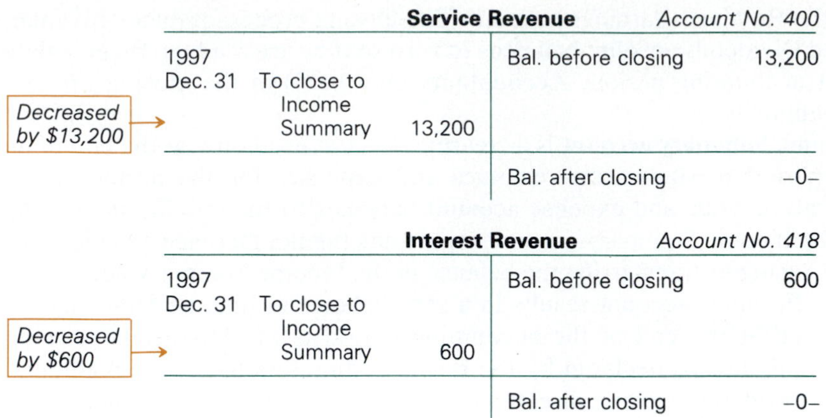

Service Revenue *Account No. 400*

1997			Bal. before closing	13,200
Dec. 31	To close to Income Summary	13,200		
			Bal. after closing	–0–

Decreased by $13,200 →

Interest Revenue *Account No. 418*

1997			Bal. before closing	600
Dec. 31	To close to Income Summary	600		
			Bal. after closing	–0–

Decreased by $600 →

As a result of the previous entry, you would credit the Income Summary account for $13,800. We show the Income Summary account in Step 3.

Step 2: Closing the Expense Accounts

Expenses appear in the Income Statement debit column of the work sheet. MicroTrain Company has eight expenses in the Income Statement debit column. As shown by the column subtotal, these expenses add up to $6,510. Since expense accounts have debit balances, credit each account to bring it to a zero balance. Then, make the debit in the closing entry to the Income Summary account for $6,510. Thus, to close the expense accounts, MicroTrain makes the following entry:

MICROTRAIN COMPANY
General Journal

Page 4

Date		Account Titles and Explanation	Post. Ref.	Debit	Credit
1997					
Dec.	31	Income Summary	600	6510	
		Advertising Expense	505		50
		Gas and Oil Expense	506		680
		Salaries Expense	507		3780
		Utilities Expense	511		150
		Insurance Expense	512		200
		Rent Expense	515		400
		Supplies Expense	518		500
		Depreciation Expense—Trucks	521		750
		To close the expense accounts appearing in the Income Statement			
		debit column to Income Summary.			

The debit of $6,510 to the Income Summary account agrees with the Income Statement debit column subtotal in the work sheet. This comparison with the work sheet serves as a check that all revenue and expense items have been listed and closed. If the debit in the preceding entry was made for a different amount than the column subtotal, the company would have an error in the closing entry for expenses.

After they have been closed, MicroTrain's expense accounts appear as follows. Note that each account has a zero balance after closing.

Advertising Expense *Account No. 505*

Bal. before closing	50	1997 Dec. 31 To close to Income Summary	50 ← *Decreased by $50*
Bal. after closing	-0-		

Gas and Oil Expense *Account No. 506*

Bal. before closing	680	1997 Dec. 31 To close to Income Summary	680 ← *Decreased by $680*
Bal. after closing	-0-		

Salaries Expense *Account No. 507*

Bal. before closing	3,780	1997 Dec. 31 To close to Income Summary	3,780 ← *Decreased by $3,780*
Bal. after closing	-0-		

Utilities Expense *Account No. 511*

Bal. before closing	150	1997 Dec. 31 To close to Income Summary	150 ← *Decreased by $150*
Bal. after closing	-0-		

Insurance Expense *Account No. 512*

Bal. before closing	200	1997 Dec. 31 To close to Income Summary	200 ← *Decreased by $200*
Bal. after closing	-0-		

Rent Expense *Account No. 515*

Bal. before closing	400	1997 Dec. 31 To close to Income Summary	400 ← *Decreased by $400*
Bal. after closing	-0-		

Supplies Expense *Account No. 518*

Bal. before closing	500	1997 Dec. 31 To close to Income Summary	500 ← *Decreased by $500*
Bal. after closing	-0-		

Depreciation Expense—Trucks *Account No. 521*

Bal. before closing	750	1997 Dec. 31 To close to Income Summary	750 ← *Decreased by $750*
Bal. after closing	-0-		

The expense accounts could be closed before the revenue accounts; the end result is the same.

Step 3: Closing the Income Summary Account

As the result of closing the revenues and expenses of MicroTrain, the total revenues and expenses have been transferred to the Income Summary account.

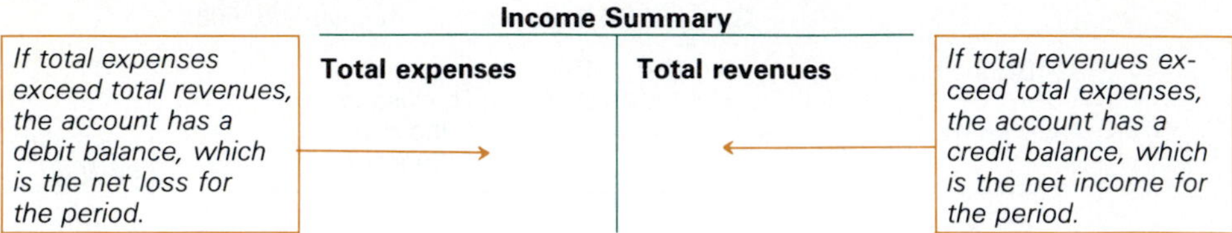

MicroTrain's Income Summary account now has a credit balance of $7,290, the company's net income for December.

Income Summary

1997			1997		
Dec. 31	From closing the expense accounts	6,510	Dec. 31	From closing the revenue accounts	13,800
				Bal. before closing this account (net income)	7,290

Next, close MicroTrain's Income Summary account to its Retained Earnings account. The journal entry to do this is:

MICROTRAIN COMPANY
General Journal

Page 4

Date		Account Titles and Explanation	Post. Ref.	Debit	Credit
1997					
Dec.	31	Income Summary	600	7290	
		Retained Earnings	310		7290
		To close the Income Summary account to the Retained Earnings account.			

After its Income Summary account is closed, the company's Income Summary and Retained Earnings accounts appear as follows:

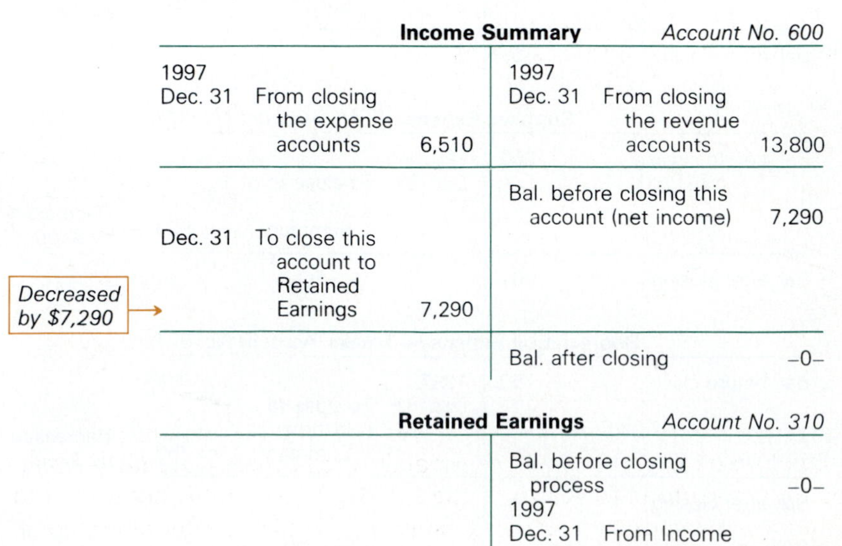

A Broader Perspective

Skills for the Long Haul

The decision has been made: You [Tracy] have opted to start your career by joining an international accounting firm. But you can't help wondering if you have the right skills both for short- and long-term success in public accounting. . . .

Most students understand that accounting knowledge, organizational ability and interpersonal skills are critical to success in public accounting. But it is important for the beginner to realize that different skills are emphasized at different points in a public accountant's career. . . .

Let's examine the duties and skills needed at each level—Staff Accountant (years 1–2), Senior Accountant (years 3–4), Manager/Senior Manager (years 5–11) and Partner (years 11+).

Staff accountant—Enthusiastic learner

Let's travel with Tracy as she begins her career at the staff level. At the outset, she works directly under a senior accountant on each of her audits and is responsible for completing audits and administrative tasks assigned to her. Her duties include documenting workpapers, interacting with client accounting staff, clerical tasks and discussing questions that arise with her senior. Tracy will work on different audit engagements during her first year and learn the firm's audit approach. She will be introduced to various industries and accounting systems.

The two most important traits to be demonstrated at the staff level are (1) a positive attitude and (2) the ability to learn quickly while adapting to unfamiliar situations. . . .

Senior accountant—Organizer and teacher

As a senior accountant, Tracy will be responsible for the day-to-day management of several audit engagements during the year. She will plan the audits, oversee the performance of interim audit testing and direct year-end field work. She will also perform much of the final wrap-up work, such as preparing checklists, writing the management letter and reviewing or drafting the financial statements. Throughout this process, Tracy will spend a substantial amount of time instructing and supervising staff accountants.

The two most critical skills needed at the senior level are (1) the ability to organize and control an audit and (2) the ability to teach staff accountants how to audit. . . .

Manager/senior manager—General manager and salesperson

Upon promotion to manager, Tracy will begin the transformation from auditor to executive. She will manage several audits at one time and become active in billing clients as well as negotiating audit fees. She will handle many important client meetings and closing conferences. Tracy will also become more involved in the firm's administrative tasks. . . . Finally, outside of her client service and administrative duties, Tracy will be evaluated to a large extent on her community involvement and ability to assist the partners in generating new business for the firm.

The two skills most emphasized at the manager level are (1) general management ability and (2) sales and communication skills. . . .

Partner—Leader and expert

As a partner in the firm, Tracy will have many broad responsibilities. She will engage in high-level client service activities, business development, recruiting, strategic planning, office administration and counseling. Besides serving as the engagement partner on several audits, she will have ultimate responsibility for the quality of service provided to each of her clients. Although a certain industry or administrative function will become her specialty, she will often be called upon to perform a wide variety of audit and administrative duties when other partners have scheduling conflicts. She will be expected to serve as a positive example to those who work for her and will train others in her areas of expertise.

At the partnership level, what's looked for is leadership ability plus the ability to become an expert in a specific industry or administrative function. . . .

In the meantime

Those planning on a public accounting career should do more than just learn accounting. To develop the needed skills, a broad education background in business and nonbusiness courses is required plus participation in extracurricular activities that promote leadership and communication skills. It is never too early to start building the skills for long-term success.

Source: Dana R. Hermanson and Heather M. Hermanson, *New Accountant*, January 1990, pp. 24–26, © 1990, New DuBois Corporation.

Step 4: Closing the Dividends Account

The last closing entry closes MicroTrain's Dividends account. This account has a debit balance before closing. To close the account, credit the Dividends account and debit the Retained Earnings account. The Dividends account is not closed to the Income Summary because it is not an expense and does not enter into income determination. The journal entry to close MicroTrain's Dividends account is:

MICROTRAIN COMPANY
General Journal

Page 4

Date		Account Titles and Explanation	Post. Ref.	Debit	Credit
1997 Dec.	31	Retained Earnings	310	3000	
		Dividends	320		3000
		To close the Dividends account to the Retained Earnings account.			

After this closing entry is posted, the company's Dividends and Retained Earnings accounts appear as follows:

Dividends *Account No. 320*

Bal. before closing	3,000	1997 Dec. 31 To close to Retained Earnings	3,000 ← *Decreased by $3,000*
Bal. after closing	–0–		

Retained Earnings *Account No. 310*

1997		Bal. before closing process	–0–
Decreased by $3,000 → Dec. 31 From Dividends	3,000	1997 Dec. 31 From Income Summary	7,290
		Bal. after closing process is complete	4,290

Post-Closing Trial Balance

Objective 5
Prepare a post-closing trial balance.

Reinforcing Problem
E4–13 Identify accounts in the post-closing trial balance.

After you have completed the closing, the only accounts in the general ledger that have not been closed are the permanent balance sheet accounts. Because these accounts contain the opening balances for the coming accounting period, debit balance totals must equal credit balance totals. The preparation of a post-closing trial balance serves as a check on the accuracy of the closing process and ensures that the books are in balance at the start of the new accounting period. The post-closing trial balance differs from the adjusted trial balance in only two important respects: (1) it excludes all temporary accounts since they have been closed; and (2) it updates the Retained Earnings account to its proper ending balance.

A **post-closing trial balance** is a trial balance taken after the closing entries have been posted. The only accounts that should be open are assets, liabilities, capital stock, and Retained Earnings accounts. List all the account balances in the debit and credit columns and total them to make sure debits and credits are equal.

Look at Illustration 4.6, a post-closing trial balance for MicroTrain Company as of December 31, 1997. The amounts in the post-closing trial balance are from the ledger after the closing entries have been posted.

The next section briefly describes the evolution of accounting systems from the one-journal, one-ledger manual system you have been studying to computerized systems. Then, we discuss the role of an accounting system.

Accounting Systems: From Manual to Computerized

Objective 6
Describe the evolution of accounting systems.

The manual accounting system with only one general journal and one general ledger has been in use for hundreds of years and is still used by some very small companies. Gradually, some manual systems evolved to include multiple journals and ledgers for increased efficiency. For instance, a manual system with multiple journals and ledgers often includes (1) a sales journal to record all credit sales, (2)

MICROTRAIN COMPANY
Post-Closing Trial Balance
December 31, 1997

Acct. No.	Account Title	Debits	Credits
100	Cash	$ 8,250	
103	Accounts Receivable	6,200	
107	Supplies on Hand	900	
108	Prepaid Insurance	2,200	
112	Prepaid Rent	800	
121	Interest Receivable	600	
150	Trucks	40,000	
151	Accumulated Depreciation—Trucks		$ 750
200	Accounts Payable		730
206	Salaries Payable		180
216	Unearned Service Fees		3,000
300	Capital Stock		50,000
310	Retained Earnings		4,290
		$58,950	$58,950

ILLUSTRATION 4.6
Post-Closing Trial Balance

a purchases journal to record all credit purchases, (3) a cash receipts journal to record all cash receipts, and (4) a cash disbursements journal to record all cash payments. Still recorded in the general journal are adjusting and closing entries and any other entries that do not fit in one of the special journals. Besides the general ledger, such a system normally has subsidiary ledgers for accounts receivable and accounts payable showing how much each customer owes and how much is owed to each supplier. The general ledger shows the total amount of accounts receivable and accounts payable, but the details in the subsidiary ledgers allow companies to send bills to customers and pay bills to suppliers.

AN ACCOUNTING PERSPECTIVE

BUSINESS INSIGHT Imagine a company with an Accounts Receivable account and an Accounts Payable account in its general ledger and no Accounts Receivable subsidiary ledger or Accounts Payable subsidiary ledger. How would this company know to whom to send bills and in what amounts? Also, how would employees know for which suppliers to write checks and in what amounts? Such subsidiary records are necessary either on paper or in a computer file.

Another innovation in manual systems was the "one write" or pegboard system. By creating one document and aligning other records under it on a pegboard, companies could record transactions more efficiently. These systems permit the writing of a check and the simultaneous recording of the check in the cash disbursements journal. Even though some of these systems are still in use today, computers make them obsolete.

During the 1950s, companies also used bookkeeping machines to supplement manual systems. These machines recorded recurring transactions such as sales on account. They posted transactions to the general ledger and subsidiary ledger accounts and computed new balances. With the development of computers, bookkeeping machines became obsolete. They were quite expensive, and computers easily outperformed them. In the mid-1950s, large companies began using mainframe computers. Early accounting applications were in payroll, accounts receivable, accounts payable, and inventory. Within a few years, programs existed for all phases of accounting, including manufacturing operations and the total integration of other accounting programs with the general ledger. Until the 1980s, small- and medium-sized companies either continued with a manual system, rented time on another company's computer, or hired a service bureau to perform at least some accounting functions.

ILLUSTRATION 4.7 The Role of an Accounting System

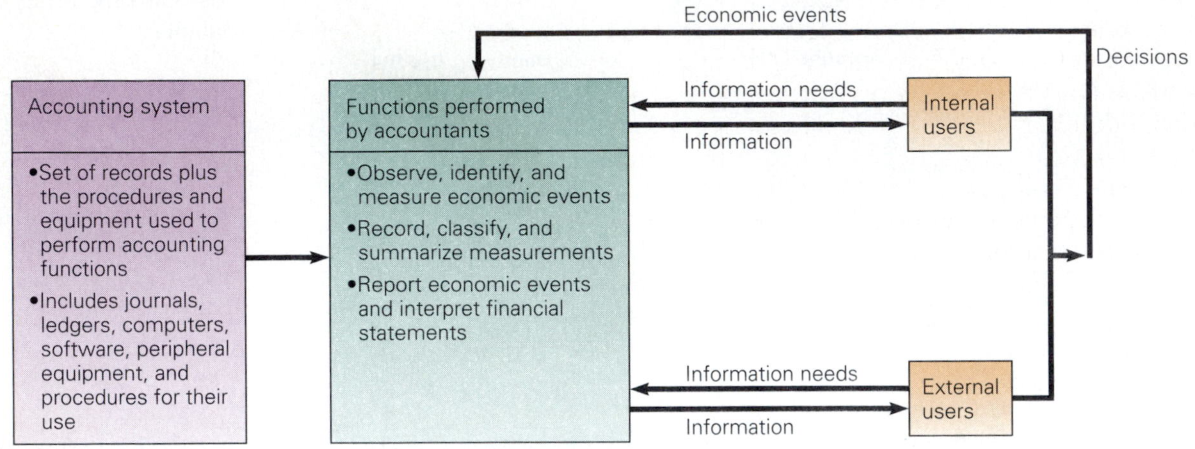

The development of the microcomputer in 1975 and its widespread use a decade later drastically changed the accounting systems of small- and medium-sized businesses. Accounting software packages for these computers and the power of the microcomputers quickly increased. Soon small- and medium-sized businesses could maintain all accounting functions on a microcomputer. By the 1990s, the cost of microcomputers and accounting software packages had decreased significantly, accounting software packages had become more user-friendly, and computer literacy had increased so much that many very small businesses converted from manual to computerized systems. However, some small business owners still use manual systems because they are familiar and meet their needs, and the persons keeping the records may not be computer literate.

Your knowledge of the basic manual accounting system described in these first four chapters enables you to better understand a computerized accounting system. The computer automatically performs some of the steps in the accounting cycle, such as posting journal entries to the ledger accounts, closing the books, and preparing the financial statements. However, if you understand all of the steps in the accounting cycle, you will better understand how to use the resulting data in decision making.

AN ACCOUNTING PERSPECTIVE

USES OF TECHNOLOGY Numerous microcomputer accounting systems are currently available; prices range from about $100 to $2,500. Some of the most popular are Peachtree Complete Accounting®, MAS Master Accounting®, Acc Pac Plus®, and Dac Easy Accounting®. Using these programs, small- to medium-sized businesses can greatly reduce the clerical work performed by their accounting staffs. Although employees must journalize transactions during the accounting period and make adjusting entries, computerized systems automatically prepare postings, closing entries, and financial statements.

The Role of an Accounting System

As we show in Illustration 4.7, an **accounting system** is a set of records and the procedures and equipment used to perform the accounting functions. Manual systems consist of journals and ledgers on paper. Computerized accounting systems consist of accounting software, computer files, computers, and related peripheral equipment such as printers.

Regardless of the system, the functions of accountants include: (1) observing, identifying, and measuring economic events; (2) recording, classifying, and summarizing measurements; and (3) reporting economic events and interpreting financial statements. Both internal and external users tell accountants their information needs. The accounting system enables a company's accounting staff to supply relevant accounting information to meet those needs. As internal and external users make decisions that become economic events, the cycle of information, decisions, and economic events begins again.

The primary focus of the first four chapters has been on how you can use an accounting system to prepare financial statements. However, we also discussed how to use that information in making decisions. Later chapters also show how to prepare information and how that information helps users to make informed decisions. We have not eliminated the preparation aspects because we believe that the most informed users are ones who also understand how the information was prepared. These users understand not only the limitations of the information but also its relevance for decision making.

The next section discusses and illustrates the classified balance sheet, which aids in the analysis of the financial position of companies. One example of this analysis is the current ratio and its use in analyzing the short-term debt-paying ability of a company.

An Accounting Perspective

Uses of Technology Accounting software packages are typically menu driven and organized into modules such as general ledger, accounts payable, accounts receivable, invoicing, inventory, payroll, fixed assets, job cost, and purchase order. For instance, general journal entries are made in the general ledger module, and this module contains all of the company's accounts. The accounts payable module records all transactions involving credit purchases from suppliers and payments made to those suppliers. The accounts receivable module records all sales on credit to various customers and amounts received from customers.

A Classified Balance Sheet

Objective 7
Prepare a classified balance sheet.

The balance sheets we presented so far have been unclassified balance sheets. As shown in Illustration 4.5, an **unclassified balance sheet** has three major categories: assets, liabilities, and stockholders' equity. A **classified balance sheet** contains the same three major categories and subdivides them to provide useful information for interpretation and analysis by users of financial statements.

Illustration 4.8 on page 148, shows a classified balance sheet for The Home Depot, Inc., and subsidiaries.[1] Note that The Home Depot classified balance sheet is in a vertical format (assets appearing above liabilities and stockholders' equity) rather than the horizontal format (assets on the left and liabilities and stockholders' equity on the right). The two formats are equally acceptable.

The Home Depot classified balance sheet subdivides two of its three major categories. The Home Depot subdivides its assets into current assets, property and equipment, long-term investments, intangible assets (cost in excess of the fair value of net assets acquired), and other assets. The company subdivides its liabilities into current liabilities and long-term liabilities (including deferred income taxes). Stockholders' equity is the same in a classified balance sheet as in an unclassified balance sheet. Later chapters describe further subdivisions of the stockholders' equity section.

We discuss the individual items in the classified balance sheet later in the text. Our only purpose here is to briefly describe the items that can be listed under each category. Some of these items are not in The Home Depot's balance sheet.

Current Assets

Current assets are cash and other assets that a business can convert to cash or uses up in a relatively short period—one year or one operating cycle, whichever is

[1] Founded in 1978, The Home Depot is America's largest home improvement retailer and ranks among the nation's 30 largest retailers. The company has more than 200 full-service warehouse stores. Their primary customers are do-it-yourselfers.

ILLUSTRATION 4.8
A Classified Balance Sheet

THE HOME DEPOT, INC. AND SUBSIDIARIES
Consolidated Balance Sheets
January 31, 1993
(amounts in thousands, except share data)

Assets

Current Assets:	
Cash and cash equivalents	$ 121,744
Short-term investments, including current maturities of long-term investments	292,451
Accounts receivable, net	177,502
Merchandise inventories	939,824
Other current assets	30,452
Total current asstes	$1,561,973
Property and Equipment, at cost:	
Land	$ 514,468
Buildings	619,909
Furniture, fixtures, and equipment	344,139
Leasehold improvements	212,196
Construction in progress	101,064
	$1,791,776
Less: Accumulated depreciation and amortization	(183,792)
Net property and equipment	$1,607,984
Long-Term investments	694,276
Cost in Excess of the Fair Value of Net Assets Acquired, net of accumulated amortization of $5,155 at January 31, 1993	20,136
Other	47,421
Total assets	$3,931,790

Liabilities and Stockholders' Equity

Current Liabilities:	
Accounts payable	$ 420,318
Accrued salaries and related expenses	127,133
Sales taxes payable	46,320
Other accrued expenses	135,478
Income taxes payable	23,868
Current installments of long-term debt	1,828
Total current liabilities	$ 754,945
Long-Term Debt, excluding current installments	843,672
Other Long-Term Liabilities	12,968
Deferred Income Taxes	16,124
Total liabilities	$1,627,709
Stockholders' Equity:	
Common stock, par value $.05. Authorized: 1,000,000,000 shares; issued and outstanding—443,585,000 shares at January 31, 1993 and 422,224,000 shares at February 2, 1992	$ 22,179
Paid-in capital	1,339,821
Retained earnings	993,517
	$2,355,517
Less: Notes receivable from employee stock ownership plan	(51,436)
Total stockholders' equity	$2,304,081
Total liabilities and stockholders' equity	$3,931,790

longer. An **operating cycle** is the time it takes to start with cash, buy necessary items to produce revenues (such as materials, supplies, labor, and/or finished goods), sell services or goods, and receive cash by collecting the resulting receivables. Companies in service industries and merchandising industries generally have operating cycles shorter than one year. Companies in some manufacturing industries, such as distilling and lumber, have operating cycles longer than one year. However, since most operating cycles are shorter than one year, the one year period is usually used in identifying current assets and current liabilities.

Common current assets in a service business include cash, marketable securities, accounts receivable, notes receivable, interest receivable, and prepaid expenses. Note that on a balance sheet current assets are in order of how easily they are convertible to cash, from most liquid to least liquid.

Cash includes deposits in banks available for current operations at the balance sheet date plus cash on hand consisting of currency, undeposited checks, drafts, and money orders. Cash is the first current asset to appear on a balance sheet. The term *cash* normally includes cash equivalents.

Cash equivalents are highly liquid, short-term investments acquired with temporarily idle cash and easily convertible into a known cash amount. Examples are Treasury bills, short-term notes maturing within 90 days, certificates of deposit, and money market funds.

Marketable securities are temporary investments such as short-term ownership of stocks and bonds of other companies. Such investments do not qualify as cash equivalents. These investments earn additional money on cash that the business does not need at present but will probably need within one year.

Accounts receivable (also called *trade accounts receivable*) are amounts owed to a business by customers. An account receivable arises when a company performs a service or sells merchandise on credit. Customers normally provide no written evidence of indebtedness on sales invoices or delivery tickets except their signatures. Notice the term *net* in the balance sheet of The Home Depot (Illustration 4.8). This term indicates the possibility that the company may not collect some of its accounts receivable. In the balance sheet, the accounts receivable amount is the sum of the individual accounts receivable from customers shown in a subsidiary ledger or file.

Merchandise inventories are goods held for sale. Chapter 6 begins our discussion of merchandise inventories.

A **note** is an unconditional written promise to pay another party the amount owed either when demanded or at a certain specified date, usually with interest (a charge made for use of the money) at a specified rate. A *note receivable* appears on the balance sheet of the company to which the note is given. A note receivable arises (1) when a company makes a sale and receives a note from the customer, (2) when a customer gives a note for an amount due on an account receivable, or (3) when a company loans money and receives a note in return. Chapter 9 discusses notes at length.

Other current assets might include interest receivable and prepaid expenses. **Interest receivable** arises when a company has earned but not collected interest by the balance sheet date. Usually, the amount is not due until later. **Prepaid expenses** include rent, insurance, and supplies that have been paid for but from which all the benefits have not yet been realized (or consumed). If prepaid expenses had not been paid for in advance, they would require the future disbursement of cash. Furthermore, prepaid expenses are considered assets because they have service potential.

Long-Term Assets

Long-term assets are assets that a business has on hand or uses for a relatively long time. Examples include plant, property, and equipment; long-term investments; and intangible assets.

Property, Plant, and Equipment **Property, plant, and equipment** are assets with useful lives of more than one year; a company acquires them for use in the business rather than for resale. (These assets are called property and equipment in The Home Depot's balance sheet.) The terms *plant assets* or *fixed assets* are also used for property, plant, and equipment. To agree with the order in the heading, balance sheets generally list property first, plant next, and equipment last. These items are *fixed assets* because the company uses them for long-term purposes. We describe several types of property, plant, and equipment next.

Land is ground the company uses for business operations; this includes ground on which the company locates its business buildings and that is used for outside storage space or parking. Land owned for investment is not a plant asset because it is a long-term investment.

Buildings are structures the company uses to carry on its business. Again, the buildings that a company owns as investments are not plant assets.

Office furniture includes file cabinets, desks, chairs, and shelves.

Office equipment includes computers, copiers, FAX machines, and phone answering machines.

Leasehold improvements are any physical alterations made by the lessee to the leased property when these benefits are expected to last beyond the current accounting period. An example is when the lessee builds room partitions in a leased building. (The lessee is the one obtaining the rights to possess and use the property.)

Construction in progress represents the partially completed stores or other buildings that a company such as The Home Depot plans to occupy when completed.

Accumulated depreciation is a contra asset account to depreciable assets such as buildings, machinery, and equipment. This account shows the total depreciation taken for the depreciable assets. On the balance sheet, companies often deduct the accumulated depreciation (as a contra asset) from its related asset.

Long-Term Investments A **long-term investment** usually consists of securities of another company held with the intention of (1) obtaining control of another company, (2) securing a permanent source of income for the investor, or (3) establishing friendly business relations. The long-term investment classification in the balance sheet does not include those securities purchased for short-term purposes. For most businesses, long-term investments may be stocks or bonds of other corporations. Occasionally, long-term investments include funds accumulated for specific purposes, rental properties, and plant sites for future use.

Intangible Assets **Intangible assets** consist of the noncurrent, nonmonetary, nonphysical assets of a business. Companies must charge the costs of intangible assets to expense over the period benefited up to a maximum of 40 years. Among the intangible assets are rights granted by governmental bodies, such as patents and copyrights. Other intangible assets include leaseholds and goodwill.

A **patent** is a right granted by the federal government; it gives the owner of an invention the authority to manufacture a product or to use a process for a specified time.

A **copyright** granted by the federal government gives the owner the exclusive privilege of publishing written material for a specified time.

Leaseholds are rights to use rented properties, usually for several years.

Goodwill is an intangible value attached to a business evidenced by the ability to earn larger net income per dollar of investment than that earned by competitors in the same industry. The ability to produce superior profits is a valuable resource of a business. Normally, companies record goodwill only at the time of purchase and then only at the price paid for it. The Home Depot has labeled its goodwill "cost in excess of the fair value of net assets acquired."

Accumulated amortization is a contra asset account to intangible assets. This account shows the total amortization taken on the intangible assets.

Current Liabilities

Current liabilities are debts due within one year or one operating cycle, whichever is longer. The payment of current liabilities normally requires the use of current assets. Balance sheets list current liabilities in the order they must be paid; the sooner a liability must be paid, the earlier it is listed. Examples of current liabilities follow.

Accounts payable are amounts owed to suppliers for goods or services purchased on credit. Accounts payable are generally due in 30 or 60 days and do not bear interest. In the balance sheet, the accounts payable amount is the sum of the individual accounts payable to suppliers shown in a subsidiary ledger or file.

Notes payable are unconditional written promises by the company to pay a specific sum of money at a certain future date. The notes may arise from borrowing money from a bank, from the purchase of assets, or from the giving of a note in settlement of an account payable. Generally, only notes payable due in one year or less are included as current liabilities.

Salaries payable are amounts owed to employees for services rendered. The company has not paid these salaries by the balance sheet date because they are not due until later.

Sales taxes payable are the taxes a company has collected from customers but not yet remitted to the taxing authority, usually the state.

Other accrued expenses might include taxes withheld from employees, income taxes payable, and interest payable. **Taxes withheld from employees** include federal income taxes, state income taxes, and social security taxes withheld from employees' paychecks. The company plans to pay these amounts to the proper governmental agencies within a short period. **Income taxes payable** are the taxes paid to the state and federal governments by a corporation on its income. **Interest payable** is interest that the company has accumulated on notes or bonds but has not paid by the balance sheet date because it is not due until later.

Dividends payable, or amounts the company has declared payable to stockholders, represent a distribution of income. Since the corporation has not paid these declared dividends by the balance sheet date, they are a liability.

Unearned revenues (revenues received in advance) result when a company receives payment for goods or services before earning the revenue, such as payments for subscriptions to a magazine. These unearned revenues represent a liability to perform the agreed services or other contractual requirements or to return the assets received.

Companies report any current installment on long-term debt due within one year under current liabilities. The remaining portion continues to be reported as a long-term liability.

Long-Term Liabilities

Long-term liabilities are debts such as a mortgage payable and bonds payable that are not due for more than one year. Companies should show maturity dates in the balance sheet for all long-term liabilities. Normally, the liabilities with the earliest due dates are listed first.

Notes payable with maturity dates at least one year beyond the balance sheet date are long-term liabilities.

Bonds payable are long-term liabilities and are evidenced by formal printed certificates sometimes secured by liens (claims) on property, such as mortgages. Maturity dates should appear on the balance sheet for all major long-term liabilities.

The deferred income taxes on The Home Depot's balance sheet result from a difference between income tax expense in the accounting records and the income tax payable on the company's tax return.

Stockholders' Equity

Stockholders' equity shows the owners' interest in the business. This interest is equal to the amount contributed plus the income left in the business.

The items under stockholders' equity in The Home Depot's balance sheet are paid-in capital (including common stock) and retained earnings. **Paid-in capital** shows the capital paid into the company as the owners' investment. **Retained earnings** shows the cumulative income of the company less the amounts distributed to the owners in the form of dividends.

The next section shows how two categories on the classified balance sheet relate to each other. Together they reveal a company's short-term debt-paying ability.

Analyzing and Using the Financial Results—The Current Ratio

Objective 8
Analyze and use the financial results—the current ratio.

The current ratio indicates the short-term debt-paying ability of a company. To find the **current ratio,** we divide current assets by current liabilities. For instance, Illustration 4.8 shows that The Home Depot's current assets as of January 31, 1993, were \$1,561,973,000 and its current liabilities were \$754,945,000. Thus, its current ratio was:

$$\text{Current ratio} = \frac{\text{Current assets}}{\text{Current liabilities}} = \frac{\$1{,}561{,}973{,}000}{\$754{,}945{,}000} = 2.07:1$$

The current ratio of 2.07 : 1 for The Home Depot means that it has more than twice as many current assets as current liabilities. Because current liabilities are normally paid with current assets, the company appears to be able to pay its short-term obligations easily.

In evaluating a company's short-term debt-paying ability, you should also examine the quality of the current assets. If they include large amounts of uncollectable accounts receivable and/or obsolete and unsalable inventory, even a 2 : 1 current ratio may be inadequate to allow the company to pay its current liabilities. The Home Depot undoubtedly does not have such a problem.

The current assets, current liabilities, and current ratios of some other companies as of the end of 1992 were:

Company	Current Assets	Current Liabilities	Current Ratio
Chevron Corporation*	\$ 8,772,000,000	\$9,835,000,000	.89 : 1
Wal-Mart Stores, Inc.*	10,197,590,000	6,754,286,000	1.51 : 1
3M Corporation*	6,209,000,000	3,241,000,000	1.92 : 1
Rite Aid Corporation	1,013,144,000	289,949,000	3.49 : 1
GTE Corporation*	6,296,000,000	7,511,000,000	.84 : 1
Sprint Corporation	1,444,100,000	2,506,700,000	.58 : 1

* We described these companies earlier in the text.

Rite Aid
Rite Aid Corporation is the nation's largest drugstore chain, operating about 2,500 stores in 22 eastern states. These stores offer professional pharmacy services, traditional drugstore merchandise, and the industry's largest private label program in a small, convenient shopping format.

Sprint
Sprint Corporation is a diversified telecommunications company providing global voice, data, and videoconferencing services and related products.

As you can see from these comparisons, the current ratios vary a great deal. An old rule of thumb is that the current ratio should be at least 2 : 1. However, what constitutes an adequate current ratio depends on the cash generating ability of the company and the nature of the industry in which the company operates. For instance, companies in the airline industry are able to generate huge amounts of cash on a daily basis and may be able to pay their current liabilities even if their current ratio is less than 1 : 1. Comparing a company's current ratio with other companies in the same industry makes sense because all of these companies face about the same economic conditions. A company with the lowest current ratio in its industry may be unable to pay its short-term obligations on a timely basis. A company with the highest current ratio in its industry may have on hand too many current assets, such as cash and marketable securities, which could be invested in more productive assets.

The next chapter describes the assumptions, concepts, and principles that comprise the accounting theory underlying financial accounting. Thus, accounting theory dictates the standards and procedures applied to the reporting of financial information in the financial statements.

Understanding the Learning Objectives

Objective 1
Summarize the steps in the accounting cycle.

- Analyze transactions by examining source documents.
- Journalize transactions in the journal.
- Post journal entries to the accounts in the ledger.
- Prepare a trial balance of the accounts and complete the work sheet.
- Prepare financial statements.
- Journalize and post adjusting entries.
- Journalize and post closing entries.
- Prepare a post-closing trial balance.

Objective 2
Prepare a work sheet for a service company.

- The work sheet is a columnar sheet of paper on which accountants summarize information needed to make the adjusting and closing entries and to prepare the financial statements.
- Work sheets may vary in format. The work sheet illustrated in the chapter has 12 columns—two each for trial balance, adjustments, adjusted trial balance, income statement, statement of retained earnings, and balance sheet.

Objective 3
Prepare an income statement, statement of retained earnings, and balance sheet using information contained in the work sheet.

- The information needed to prepare the income statement is in the Income Statement columns of the work sheet. Net income for the period is the amount needed to balance the two Income Statement columns in the work sheet.
- The information needed to prepare the statement of retained earnings is in the Statement of Retained Earnings columns of the work sheet. The ending Retained Earnings balance is carried forward to the balance sheet.
- The information needed to prepare the balance sheet is in the Balance Sheet columns of the work sheet.

Objective 4
Prepare adjusting and closing entries using information contained in the work sheet.

- As explained in Chapter 3, adjusting entries are necessary to bring the accounts to their proper balances before preparing the financial statements.
- Closing entries are necessary to reduce the balances of revenue, expense, and Dividends accounts to zero so they are ready to receive data for the next accounting period.
- Revenue accounts are closed by debiting them and crediting the Income Summary account.
- Expense accounts are closed by crediting them and debiting the Income Summary account.
- The balance in the Income Summary account represents the net income or net loss for the period.
- To close the Income Summary account, the balance is transferred to the Retained Earnings account.
- To close the Dividends account, the balance is transferred to the Retained Earnings account.

Objective 5
Prepare a post-closing trial balance.

- Only the balance sheet accounts have balances and appear on the post-closing trial balance.
- All revenue, expense, and Dividends accounts have zero balances and are not included in the post-closing trial balance.

Objective 6
Describe the evolution of accounting systems.

- Manual systems and computerized systems perform the same accounting functions.
- The ease of accounting with a microcomputer has encouraged even small companies to convert to computerized systems.

Objective 7
Prepare a classified balance sheet.

- A classified balance sheet subdivides the major categories on the balance sheet. For instance, a classified balance sheet subdivides assets into current assets; long-term investments; property, plant, and equipment; and intangible assets. It subdivides liabilities into current liabilities and long-term liabilities. Later chapters show more accounts in the stockholders' equity section, but the subdivisions remain basically the same.

Objective 8
Analyze and use the financial results—the current ratio.

- The current ratio gives some indication of the short-term debt-paying ability of a company.
- To find the current ratio, divide current assets by current liabilities.

Demonstration Problem

This problem involves using a work sheet for Green Hills Riding Stable, Incorporated, for the month ended July 31, 1997, and performing the closing process. The trial balance for Green Hills Riding Stable, Incorporated, as of July 31, 1997, was as follows:

GREEN HILLS RIDING STABLE, INCORPORATED
Trial Balance
July 31, 1997

Acct. No.	Account Title	Debits	Credits
100	Cash	$10,700	
103	Accounts Receivable	8,100	
130	Land	40,000	
140	Buildings	24,000	
200	Accounts Payable		$ 1,100
201	Notes Payable		40,000
300	Capital Stock		35,000
310	Retained Earnings, July 1, 1997		3,100
320	Dividends	1,000	
402	Horse Boarding Fees Revenue		4,500
404	Riding and Lesson Fees Revenue		3,600
507	Salaries Expense	1,400	
513	Feed Expense	1,100	
540	Interest Expense	200	
568	Miscellaneous Expense	800	
		$87,300	$87,300

Additional data Depreciation expense for the month is $200. Accrued salaries on July 31 are $300.

Required

a. Prepare a 12-column work sheet for the month ended July 31, 1997.

b. Journalize the adjusting entries.

c. Journalize the closing entries.

Solution to Demonstration Problem

a. See the work sheet on page 155.

GREEN HILLS RIDING STABLE, INCORPORATED
Work Sheet
For the Month Ended July 31, 1997

Acct. No.	Account Titles	Trial Balance		Adjustments		Adjusted Trial Balance		Income Statement		Statement of Retained Earnings		Balance Sheet	
		Debit	Credit	Debit	Credit	Debit	Credit	Debit	Credit	Debit	Credit	Debit	Credit
100	Cash	10,700				10,700						10,700	
103	Accounts Receivable	8,100				8,100						8,100	
130	Land	40,000				40,000						40,000	
140	Buildings	24,000				24,000						24,000	
200	Accounts Payable		1,100				1,100						1,100
201	Notes Payable		40,000				40,000						40,000
300	Capital Stock		35,000				35,000						35,000
310	Retained Earnings, July 1, 1997		3,100				3,100				3,100		
320	Dividends	1,000				1,000				1,000			
402	Horse Boarding Fees Revenue		4,500				4,500		4,500				
404	Riding and Lesson Fees Revenue		3,600				3,600		3,600				
507	Salaries Expense	1,400		*(2)* 300		1,700		1,700					
513	Feed Expense	1,100				1,100		1,100					
540	Interest Expense	200				200		200					
568	Miscellaneous Expense	800				800		800					
		87,300	87,300										
520	Depreciation Expense—Buildings			*(1)* 200		200		200					
141	Accumulated Depreciation—Buildings				*(1)* 200		200						200
206	Salaries Payable				*(2)* 300		300						300
				500	500	87,800	87,800						
								4,000	8,100				
	Net Income							4,100			4,100		
								8,100	8,100	1,000	7,200	82,800	76,600
	Retained Earnings, July 31, 1997									6,200			6,200
										7,200	7,200	82,800	82,800

Adjustments:
(1) To record depreciation of building for July.
(2) To record accrued salaries of $300.

b.

GREEN HILLS RIDING STABLE, INCORPORATED
General Journal

Page 4

Date		Account Titles and Explanation	Post. Ref.	Debit	Credit
1997		**Adjusting Entries**			
July	31	Depreciation Expense—Buildings	520	200	
		Accumulated Depreciation—Buildings	141		200
		To record depreciation expense.			
	31	Salaries Expense	507	300	
		Salaries Payable	206		300
		To record accrued salaries.			

c.

GREEN HILLS RIDING STABLE, INCORPORATED
General Journal

Page 4

Date		Account Titles and Explanation	Post. Ref.	Debit	Credit
1997		**Closing Entries**			
July	31	Horse Boarding Fees Revenue	402	4500	
		Riding and Lesson Fees Revenue	404	3600	
		Income Summary	600		8100
		To close revenue accounts.			
	31	Income Summary	600	4000	
		Salaries Expense	507		1700
		Feed Expense	513		1100
		Interest Expense	540		200
		Miscellaneous Expense	568		800
		Depreciation Expense—Buildings	520		200
		To close expense accounts.			
	31	Income Summary	600	4100	
		Retained Earnings	310		4100
		To close Income Summary account.			
	31	Retained Earnings	310	1000	
		Dividends	320		1000
		To close Dividends account.			

NEW TERMS*

Accounting cycle Series of steps performed during the accounting period to analyze, record, classify, summarize, and report useful financial information for the purpose of preparing financial statements. The steps include analyzing transactions, journalizing transactions, posting journal entries, taking a trial balance and completing the work sheet, preparing financial statements, journalizing and posting adjusting entries, journalizing and posting closing entries, and taking a post-closing trial balance. *131*

Accounting system A set of records and the procedures and equipment used to perform accounting functions. *146*

Accounts payable Amounts owed to suppliers for goods or services purchased on credit. *151*

Accounts receivable Amounts due from customers for services performed or merchandise sold on credit. *149*

Accumulated amortization A contra account to intangible assets. *150*

* Some of these terms have been defined in earlier chapters but are included here for your convenience.

Bonds payable Written promises to pay a definite sum at a certain date as evidenced by formal printed certificates that are sometimes secured by liens on property, such as mortgages. *151*

Buildings Structures used to carry on the business. *150*

Cash Includes deposits in banks available for current operations at the balance sheet date plus cash on hand consisting of currency, undeposited checks, drafts, and money orders. *149*

Cash equivalents Highly liquid, short-term investments acquired with temporarily idle cash. *149*

Classified balance sheet Subdivides the three major balance sheet categories (assets, liabilities, and stockholders' equity) to provide more information for users of financial statements. Assets may be divided into current assets; long-term investments; property, plant, and equipment; and intangible assets. Liabilities may be divided into current liabilities and long-term liabilities. *147*

Closing process The act of transferring the balances in the revenue and expense accounts to a clearing account called *Income Summary* and then to the Retained Earnings account. The balance in the Dividends account is also transferred to the Retained Earnings account. *138*

Construction in progress Represents the partially completed stores or other buildings that a company plans to occupy when completed. *150*

Copyright Grants the owner the exclusive privilege of publication of written material for a specific time. *150*

Current assets Cash and other assets that a business can convert into cash or use up in one year or one operating cycle, whichever is longer. *147*

Current liabilities Debts due within one year or one operating cycle, whichever is longer. The payment of current liabilities normally requires the use of current assets. *150*

Current ratio Calculated by dividing current assets by current liabilities. *152*

Dividends payable Amounts declared payable to stockholders and that represent a distribution of income. *151*

Goodwill An intangible value attached to a business evidenced by the ability to earn larger net income per dollar of investment than that earned by competitors in the same industry. *150*

Income Summary account A clearing account used only at the end of an accounting period to summarize revenues and expenses for the period. *139*

Income taxes payable Are the taxes payable to the state and federal governments by a corporation based on its income. *151*

Intangible assets Noncurrent, nonmonetary, nonphysical assets of a business. *150*

Interest payable Interest that has accumulated on debts, such as notes or bonds. This accrued interest has not been paid at the balance sheet date because it is not due until later. *151*

Interest receivable Arises when interest has been earned but not collected at the balance sheet date. *149*

Land Ground the company uses for business operations. Land could include ground on which the company locates its business buildings and that used for outside storage space or a parking lot. *150*

Leasehold improvements Are any physical alterations made by the lessee to the leased property when these benefits are expected to last beyond the current accounting period. *150*

Leaseholds Rights to use rented properties. *150*

Long-term assets Assets that are on hand or used by a business for a relatively long time. Examples include long-term investments; property, plant, and equipment; and intangible assets. *149*

Long-term investment Usually securities of another company held with the intention of *(1)* obtaining control of another company, *(2)* securing a permanent source of income for the investor, or *(3)* establishing friendly business relations. *150*

Long-term liabilities Debts such as a mortgage payable and bonds payable that are not due for more than one year. *151*

Marketable securities Temporary investments that a company makes to earn a return on idle cash. *149*

Merchandise inventory Goods held for sale. *149*

Note An unconditional written promise to pay to another party the amount owed either when demanded or at a certain date. *149*

Notes payable Unconditional written promises by a company to pay a specific sum of money at a certain future date. *151*

Office equipment Includes computers, copiers, FAX machines, and phone answering machines. *150*

Operating cycle The time it takes to start with cash, buy necessary items to produce revenues (such as materials, supplies, labor, and/or inventories), sell services or goods, and receive cash by collecting the resulting receivables. *148*

Paid-in capital Shows the capital paid into the company as the owners' investment. *151*

Patent A right granted by the federal government authorizing the owner of an invention to manufacture a product or to use a process for a specific time. *150*

Post-closing trial balance A trial balance taken after the closing entries have been posted. *144*

Prepaid expenses Assets awaiting assignment to expense. Items such as rent, insurance, and supplies that have been paid for but from which all of the benefits have not yet been realized (or consumed). Prepaid expenses are classified as current assets. *149*

Property, plant, and equipment Assets with useful lives of more than one year that a company acquired for use in a business rather than for resale; also called *plant assets* or *fixed assets*. *149*

Retained earnings Shows the cumulative income of the company less the amounts distributed to the owners in the form of dividends. *151*

Salaries payable Amounts owed to employees for services rendered. *151*

Sales taxes payable Are taxes a company has collected from customers but has not remitted to the taxing authority, usually the state. *151*

Stockholders' equity Shows the owners' interest (equity) in the business. *151*

Taxes withheld from employees Items such as federal income taxes, state income taxes, and social security taxes withheld from employees' paychecks. *151*

Unclassified balance sheet A balance sheet showing only three major categories: assets, liabilities, and stockholders' equity. *147*

Unearned revenues (revenues received in advance) Result when payment is received for goods or services before revenue has been earned. *151*

Work sheet A columnar sheet of paper on which accountants have summarized information needed to make the adjusting and closing entries and to prepare the financial statements. *131*

Self-Test

True-False

Indicate whether each of the following statements is true or false.

1. At the end of the accounting period, three trial balances are prepared.
2. The amounts in the Adjustments columns are always added to the amounts in the Trial Balance columns to determine the amounts in the Adjusted Trial Balance columns.
3. If a net loss occurs, it appears in the Income Statement credit column and Statement of Retained Earnings debit column.
4. After the closing process is complete, no balance can exist in any revenue, expense, Dividends, or Income Summary account.
5. The post-closing trial balance may contain revenue and expense accounts.
6. All accounting systems currently in use are computerized.

Multiple-Choice

Select the best answer for each of the following questions.

1. Which of the following accounts is *least* likely to be adjusted on the work sheet?
   - **a.** Supplies on Hand.
   - **b.** Land.
   - **c.** Prepaid Rent.
   - **d.** Unearned Delivery Fees.
2. If the Balance Sheet columns do not balance, the error is most likely to exist in the:
   - **a.** General journal.
   - **b.** General ledger.
   - **c.** Last six columns of the work sheet.
   - **d.** First six columns of the work sheet.
3. Net income for a period appears in all but which one of the following?
   - **a.** Income Statement debit column of the work sheet.
   - **b.** Statement of Retained Earnings credit column of the work sheet.
   - **c.** Statement of retained earnings.
   - **d.** Balance sheet.
4. Which of the following statements is *false* regarding the closing process?
   - **a.** The Dividends account is closed to Income Summary.
   - **b.** The closing of expense accounts results in a debit to Income Summary.
   - **c.** The closing of revenues results in a credit to Income Summary.
   - **d.** The Income Summary account is closed to the Retained Earnings account.
5. Which of the following statements is *true* regarding the classified balance sheet?
   - **a.** Current assets include cash, accounts receivable, and equipment.
   - **b.** Plant, property, and equipment is one category of long-term assets.
   - **c.** Current liabilities include accounts payable, salaries payable, and notes receivable.
   - **d.** Stockholders' equity is subdivided into current and long-term categories.

Now turn to page 170 to check your answers.

Questions

1. At which stage of the accounting cycle is a work sheet usually prepared?
2. Why are the financial statements prepared before the adjusting and closing entries are journalized and posted?
3. Describe the purposes for which the work sheet is prepared.
4. You have taken over a set of accounting books for a small business as a part-time job. At the end of the first accounting period, you have partially completed the work sheet by entering the proper ledger accounts and balances in the Trial Balance columns. You turn to the manager and ask, "Where is the list of additional information I can use in entering the

adjusting entries?" The manager indicates there is no such list. (In all the text problems you have done, you have always been given this information.) How would you obtain the information for this real-life situation? What are the consequences of not making all of the required adjustments at the end of the accounting period?

5. How are the amounts in the Adjusted Trial Balance columns of a work sheet determined?
6. The work sheet for Bridges Company shows net income of $40,000. The following four adjustments were ignored:
   1. Subscriptions Fees earned, $1,200.
   2. Depreciation of equipment, $4,000.
   3. Depreciation of building, $10,000.
   4. Salaries accrued, $3,000.

   What is the correct net income?
7. After the Adjusted Trial Balance columns of a work sheet have been totaled, which account balances are extended to the Income Statement columns, which account balances are extended to the Statement of Retained Earnings columns, and which account balances are extended to the Balance Sheet columns?
8. How is the statement of retained earnings prepared?
9. What is the purpose of closing entries? What accounts are not affected by closing entries?
10. A company has net income of $5,000 for the year. In which columns of the work sheet would net income appear?
11. Is it possible to prepare monthly financial statements without journalizing and posting adjusting and closing entries? How?
12. What is the purpose of a post-closing trial balance?
13. Describe some of the ways in which the manual accounting system has evolved.
14. When did computerized accounting systems come into use?
15. Define an accounting system.
16. How is a classified balance sheet different than an unclassified balance sheet?
17. **Real World Question** Refer to "A Broader Perspective" on page 143 to answer the following true-false questions:
   a. The same skills are needed at each level in a CPA firm.
   b. The two most important traits at the staff accountant level are a positive attitude and the ability to learn quickly while adapting to unfamiliar situations.
   c. The senior accountant needs management skills in addition to technical skills.
   d. Partners become increasingly involved in technical matters and have less and less interaction with people.
18. **Real World Question** Referring to the annual report booklet, identify the classifications (or categories) of assets used by The Coca-Cola Company, Maytag Corporation, The Limited, Inc., and John H. Harland Company in their respective balance sheets.
19. **Real World Question** Referring to the annual report booklet, identify the classifications (or categories) of liabilities used by The Coca-Cola Company, Maytag Corporation, The Limited, Inc., and John H. Harland Company in their respective balance sheets.

EXERCISES

Exercise 4–1
Identify the steps in the accounting cycle (L.O. 1)

List the steps in the accounting cycle. Would the system still work if any of the steps were performed out of order?

Exercise 4–2
Determine where items would appear in the work sheet (L.O. 2)

Three of the major column headings on a work sheet are Trial Balance, Income Statement, and Balance Sheet. Determine under which major column heading each of the following items would appear and whether it would be a debit or credit. (For example, Cash would appear on the debit side of the Trial Balance Sheet columns.)

		Trial Balance		Income Statement		Balance Sheet	
	Account Titles	Debit	Credit	Debit	Credit	Debit	Credit
a.	Accounts Receivable						
b.	Accounts Payable						
c.	Interest Revenue						
d.	Advertising Expense						
e.	Capital Stock						
f.	Service revenue						
g.	Net income for the month						

Exercise 4–3
Determine where items would appear in the work sheet (L.O. 2)

Assume a beginning balance in Retained Earnings of $84,000 and net income for the year of $36,000. Illustrate how these would appear in the Statement of Retained Earnings columns and Balance Sheet columns in the work sheet.

Exercise 4–4
Determine where items would appear in the work sheet (L.O. 2)

In Exercise 4–3, if there were a debit balance of $216,000 in the Retained Earnings account as of the beginning of the year and a net loss of $192,000 for the year, show how these would be treated in the work sheet.

Exercise 4–5
Find cause of Balance Sheet columns not in balance (L.O. 2)

Damon Davis was preparing the work sheet for Drano Plumbing Company. He calculated the net income to be $50,000. When he totaled the Balance Sheet columns, the column totals were debit, $300,000; and credit, $400,000. What was the probable cause of this difference? If this was not the cause, what should he do to find the error?

Exercise 4–6
Prepare a work sheet (L.O. 2)

The Trial Balance of the FAX Repair Company at December 31, 1997, contains the following account balances listed in alphabetical order to increase your skill in sorting amounts to the proper work sheet columns.

FAX REPAIR COMPANY
Trial Balance Account Balances
December 31, 1997

Accounts Payable	$ 41,000
Accounts Receivable	92,000
Accumulated Depreciation—Buildings	25,000
Accumulated Depreciation—Equipment	9,000
Buildings	140,000
Capital Stock	65,000
Cash	50,000
Equipment	36,000
Prepaid Insurance	3,600
Retained Earnings, January 1, 1997	4,800
Salaries Expense	96,000
Service Revenue	280,000
Supplies on Hand	4,000
Utilities Expense	3,200

Using these account balances and the following additional information, prepare a work sheet for FAX Repair Company. Arrange the accounts in their approximate usual order.

Additional data

1. Supplies on hand at December 31, 1997, have a cost of $2,400.
2. The balance in the Prepaid Insurance account represents the cost of a two-year insurance policy covering the period from January 1, 1997, through December 31, 1998.
3. The estimated lives of depreciable assets are buildings, 40 years, and equipment, 20 years. No salvage values are anticipated.

Exercise 4–7
Prepare statement of retained earnings (L.O. 3)

Rextex Corporation had a January 1, 1997, balance in its Retained Earnings account of $80,000. For the year 1997, net income was $50,000 and dividends declared and paid were $24,000. Prepare a statement of retained earnings for the year ended December 31, 1997.

Exercise 4–8
Prepare adjusting entries and determine correct net income (L.O. 4)

Santiago Company reported net income of $100,000 for the current year. Examination of the work sheet and supporting data indicates that the following items were ignored:

1. Accrued salaries were $6,000 at December 31.
2. Depreciation on equipment acquired on July 1 amounted to $8,000.

Based on this information, *(a)* what adjusting journal entries should have been made at December 31, and *(b)* what is the correct net income?

Exercise 4–9
Prepare adjusting and closing entries (L.O. 4)

Refer to the work sheet prepared in Exercise 4–6. Prepare the adjusting and closing journal entries.

Exercise 4–10
Post to Income Summary account from Income Statement column totals (L.O. 4)

The Income Statement column totals on a work sheet prepared at December 31, 1997, are debit, $600,000; and credit, $900,000. In T-account format, show how the postings to the Income Summary account would appear as a result of the closing process. Identify what each posting represents.

Exercise 4–11
Show how closing entries would be posted to T-accounts (L.O. 4)

After adjustment, these selected account balances of Sleepy Campground are:

	Debits	Credits
Retained Earnings		$640,000
Rental Revenue		960,000
Salaries Expense	$336,000	
Depreciation Expense—Buildings	64,000	
Utilities Expense	208,000	
Dividends	32,000	

In T-account format, show how journal entries to close the books for the period would be posted. (You do not need to show the closing journal entries.) Enter these balances in the accounts before doing so. Key the postings from the first closing entry with the number (1), the second with the number (2), and so on.

Exercise 4–12
Prepare closing entries (L.O. 4)

The following account balances appeared in the Income Statement columns of the work sheet prepared for Lee & Wong Company for the year ended December 31, 1997:

Account Titles	Income Statement	
	Debit	Credit
Service Revenue		340,000
Advertising Expense	1,350	
Salaries Expense	130,000	
Utilities Expense	2,250	
Insurance Expense	900	
Rent Expense	6,750	
Supplies Expense	2,250	
Depreciation Expense—Equipment	4,500	
Interest Expense	562	
Interest Revenue		1,125
	148,562	341,125
Net Income	192,563	
	341,125	341,125

Prepare the closing journal entries.

Exercise 4–13
Identify accounts in the post-closing trial balance (L.O. 5)

Which of the following accounts are likely to appear in the post-closing trial balance for the Blake Company?

1. Accounts Receivable.
2. Cash.
3. Service Revenue.
4. Buildings.
5. Salaries Expense.
6. Capital Stock.
7. Dividends.
8. Accounts Payable.
9. Income Summary.
10. Unearned Subscription Fees.

Exercise 4–14
Categorize items for classified balance sheet (L.O. 7)

Using the legend at the right, determine the category (number) into which you would place each of these items.

	Item	Legend
________	**a.** Land.	**1.** Current assets.
________	**b.** Marketable securities.	**2.** Long-term investments.
________	**c.** Notes payable, due in three years.	**3.** Property, plant, and equipment.
________	**d.** Taxes withheld from employees.	**4.** Intangible assets.
________	**e.** Patents.	**5.** Current liabilities.
________	**f.** Retained earnings.	**6.** Long-term liabilities.
________	**g.** Unearned subscription fees.	**7.** Stockholders' equity.
________	**h.** Bonds of another corporation (a 20-year investment).	
________	**i.** Notes payable, due in six months.	
________	**j.** Accumulated depreciation.	

Exercise 4–15
Calculate current ratios for Ralston Purina Company and subsidiaries and comment (L.O. 8)

The following data are from the 1992 annual report of the Ralston Purina Company and its subsidiaries. This company manufactures pet foods, bakery goods, dry cell batteries, breakfast cereals, baby foods, snack foods, polymers, and livestock and poultry feed. The dollar amounts are in millions.

	September 30	
	1992	**1991**
Current assets	$1,780.3	$1,675.5
Current liabilities	1,745.3	1,193.9

Calculate the current ratios for the two years. Comment on whether the trend is favorable or unfavorable.

PROBLEMS

Problem 4–1
Prepare closing entries (L.O. 4)

The following adjusted trial balance is for Kelly Appliance Repair Company:

KELLY APPLIANCE REPAIR COMPANY
Adjusted Trial Balance
June 30, 1997

	Debits	Credits
Cash	$ 33,000	
Accounts Receivable	42,000	
Trucks	110,000	
Accumulated Depreciation—Trucks		$ 30,000
Accounts Payable		10,800
Notes Payable		20,000
Capital Stock		50,000
Retained Earnings, July 1, 1996		5,500
Dividends	10,000	
Service Revenue		200,000
Rent Expense	12,000	
Advertising Expense	5,000	
Salaries Expense	90,000	
Supplies Expense	1,500	
Insurance Expense	1,200	
Depreciation Expense—Trucks	10,000	
Interest Expense	1,000	
Miscellaneous Expense	600	
	$316,300	$316,300

Required Prepare the closing journal entries at the end of the fiscal year, June 30, 1997.

Problem 4–2
Prepare income statement, statement of retained earnings, classified balance sheet, closing entries, and post-closing trial balance (L.O. 3–5, 7)

The adjusted trial balance for Modern Architects, Inc., follows.

MODERN ARCHITECTS, INC.
Adjusted Trial Balance
December 31, 1997

	Debits	Credits
Cash	$ 50,000	
Accounts Receivable	20,000	
Interest Receivable	200	
Notes Receivable	4,000	
Prepaid Insurance	960	
Prepaid Rent	2,400	
Supplies on Hand	600	
Equipment	60,000	
Accumulated Depreciation—Equipment		$ 12,500
Buildings	140,000	
Accumulated Depreciation—Buildings		15,000
Land	56,240	
Accounts Payable		60,000
Notes Payable		10,000
Interest Payable		750
Salaries Payable		7,000
Capital Stock		100,000
Retained Earnings, January 1, 1997		20,200
Dividends	40,000	
Service Revenue		320,000
Insurance Expense	1,920	
Rent Expense	9,600	
Advertising Expense	1,200	
Depreciation Expense—Equipment	2,500	
Depreciation Expense—Buildings	3,000	
Supplies Expense	2,280	
Salaries Expense	150,000	
Interest Expense	750	
Interest Revenue		200
	$545,650	$545,650

Required

a. Prepare an income statement.

b. Prepare a statement of retained earnings.

c. Prepare a classified balance sheet.

d. Prepare the closing journal entries.

e. Show the post-closing trial balance assuming you had posted the closing entries to the general ledger.

Problem 4–3
Prepare work sheet, adjusting entries, and closing entries (L.O. 2, 4)

The following trial balance and additional data are for Quick Sale Realty Company:

QUICK SALE REALTY COMPANY
Trial Balance
December 31, 1997

	Debits	Credits
Cash	$ 32,800	
Accounts Receivable	117,120	
Prepaid Rent	46,080	
Equipment	173,760	
Accumulated Depreciation—Equipment		$ 21,120
Accounts Payable		62,400
Capital Stock		96,000
Retained Earnings, January 1, 1997		49,920
Dividends	46,080	
Commissions Revenue		623,200
Salaries Expense	321,600	
Travel Expense	96,480	
Miscellaneous Expense	18,720	
	$852,640	$852,640

Additional data

1. The prepaid rent is for the period July 1, 1997, to June 30, 1998.
2. The equipment has an expected life of 10 years with no salvage value.
3. Accrued salaries are $11,520.
4. Travel expenses accrued but unreimbursed to sales staff at December 31 were $17,280.

Required

a. Prepare a 12-column work sheet for the year ended December 31, 1997. You need not include account numbers or explanations of adjustments.
b. Prepare adjusting journal entries.
c. Prepare closing journal entries.

Problem 4–4
Prepare work sheet and closing entries (L.O. 2, 4)

The following trial balance and additional data are for European Tours, Inc.:

EUROPEAN TOURS, INC.
Trial Balance
December 31, 1997

	Debits	Credits
Cash	$109,050	
Accounts Receivable	153,750	
Prepaid Insurance	4,350	
Prepaid Advertising	18,000	
Notes Receivable	11,250	
Land	90,000	
Buildings	165,000	
Accumulated Depreciation—Buildings		$ 49,500
Office Equipment	83,400	
Accumulated Depreciation—Office Equipment		16,680
Accounts Payable		56,850
Notes Payable		75,000
Capital Stock		240,000
Retained Earnings, January 1, 1997		47,820
Dividends	30,000	
Service Revenue		388,350
Salaries Expense	96,000	
Travel Expense	111,000	
Interest Revenue		600
Interest Expense	3,000	
	$874,800	$874,800

The company consistently followed the policy of initially debiting all prepaid items to asset accounts.

Additional data

1. The buildings have an expected life of 50 years with no salvage value.
2. The office equipment has an expected life of 10 years with no salvage valuc.
3. Accrued interest on notes receivable is $450.
4. Accrued interest on the notes payable is $1,000.
5. Accrued salaries are $2,100.
6. Expired prepaid insurance is $3,750.
7. Expired prepaid advertising is $16,500.

Required

a. Prepare a 12-column work sheet for the year ended December 31, 1997. You need not include account numbers. Briefly explain the entries in the Adjustments columns at the bottom of the work sheet, as was done in Illustration 4.2.
b. Prepare the required closing entries.

Problem 4–5
Prepare work sheet, income statement, statement of retained earnings, classified balance sheet, and adjusting and closing entries (L.O. 2–5, 7)

The following trial balance and additional data are for California Time-Share Property Management Company:

CALIFORNIA TIME-SHARE PROPERTY MANAGEMENT COMPANY
Trial Balance
December 31, 1997

	Debits	Credits
Cash	$404,000	
Prepaid Rent	28,800	
Prepaid Insurance	7,680	
Supplies on Hand	2,400	
Office Equipment	24,000	
Accumulated Depreciation—Office Equipment		$ 5,760
Automobiles	64,000	
Accumulated Depreciation—Automobiles		16,000
Accounts Payable		2,880
Unearned Management Fees		12,480
Capital Stock		360,000
Retained Earnings, January 1, 1997		120,640
Dividends	28,000	
Commissions Revenue		240,000
Management Fee Revenue		19,200
Salaries Expense	199,840	
Advertising Expense	2,400	
Gas and Oil Expense	14,240	
Miscellaneous Expense	1,600	
	$776,960	$776,960

Additional data

1. Insurance expense for the year, $3,840.
2. Rent expense for the year, $19,200.
3. Depreciation expense: office equipment, $2,880; and automobiles, $12,800.
4. Salaries earned but unpaid at December 31, $26,640.
5. Supplies on hand at December 31, $1,000.
6. The unearned management fees were received and recorded on November 1, 1997. The advance payment covered six months' management of an apartment building.

Required

a. Prepare a 12-column work sheet for the year ended December 31, 1997. You need not include account numbers or explanations of adjustments.
b. Prepare an income statement.
c. Prepare a statement of retained earnings.
d. Prepare a classified balance sheet.
e. Prepare adjusting and closing entries.

ALTERNATE PROBLEMS

Problem 4–1A
Prepare closing entries
(L.O. 4)

The following adjusted trial balance is for Vacation Home Realty Company:

VACATION HOME REALTY COMPANY
Adjusted Trial Balance
June 30, 1997

	Debits	Credits
Cash	$ 88,000	
Accounts Receivable	40,000	
Office Equipment	35,000	
Accumulated Depreciation—Office Equipment		$ 14,000
Automobiles	40,000	
Accumulated Depreciation—Automobiles		20,000
Accounts Payable		63,000
Capital Stock		75,000
Retained Earnings, July 1, 1996		54,700
Dividends	5,000	
Commissions Revenue		160,000
Salaries Expense	25,000	
Commissions Expense	120,000	
Gas and Oil Expense	4,000	
Rent Expense	14,800	
Supplies Expense	1,400	
Utilities Expense	2,000	
Depreciation Expense—Office Equipment	3,500	
Depreciation Expense—Automobiles	8,000	
	$386,700	$386,700

Required Prepare the closing journal entries at the end of the fiscal year, June 30, 1997.

Problem 4–2A
Prepare income statement, statement of retained earnings, classified balance sheet, closing entries, and post-closing trial balance
(L.O. 3–5, 7)

The adjusted trial balance for Batten Insurance Consultants, Inc., follows:

BATTEN INSURANCE CONSULTANTS, INC.
Adjusted Trial Balance
December 31, 1997

	Debits	Credits
Cash	$117,200	
Accounts Receivable	68,000	
Interest Receivable	400	
Notes Receivable	20,000	
Prepaid Insurance	2,400	
Supplies on Hand	1,800	
Land	32,000	
Buildings	190,000	
Accumulated Depreciation—Buildings		$ 40,000
Office Equipment	28,000	
Accumulated Depreciation—Office Equipment		8,000
Accounts Payable		48,000
Salaries Payable		8,500
Interest Payable		900
Notes Payable (due 1998)		64,000
Capital Stock		120,000
Retained Earnings, January 1, 1997		42,800
Dividends	40,000	
Commissions Revenue		392,520
Advertising Expense	14,000	
Commissions Expense	75,440	
Travel Expense	12,880	
Depreciation Expense—Buildings	8,500	
Salaries Expense	98,400	
Depreciation Expense—Office Equipment	2,800	
Supplies Expense	3,800	
Insurance Expense	3,600	
Repairs Expense	1,900	
Utilities Expense	3,400	
Interest Expense	1,800	
Interest Revenue		1,600
	$726,320	$726,320

Required

a. Prepare an income statement for the year ended December 31, 1997.
b. Prepare a statement of retained earnings.
c. Prepare a classified balance sheet.
d. Prepare the closing journal entries.
e. Show the post-closing trial balance assuming you had posted the closing entries to the general ledger.

Problem 4–3A
Prepare work sheet, adjusting entries, and closing entries (L.O. 2, 4)

The following trial balance and additional data are for Garcia Data Processing Company:

GARCIA DATA PROCESSING COMPANY
Trial Balance
December 31, 1997

	Debits	Credits
Cash	$ 56,000	
Accounts Receivable	98,000	
Prepaid Rent	7,200	
Prepaid Insurance	2,400	
Equipment	80,000	
Accumulated Depreciation—Equipment		$ 40,000
Accounts Payable		30,000
Capital Stock		100,000
Retained Earnings, January 1, 1997		65,600
Dividends	24,000	
Service Revenue		350,000
Commissions Expense	270,000	
Travel Expense	36,000	
Miscellaneous Expense	12,000	
	$585,600	$585,600

Additional data

1. The prepaid rent is for the period January 1, 1997, to December 31, 1998.
2. The equipment is expected to last 10 years with no salvage value.
3. The prepaid insurance was for the period April 1, 1997, to March 31, 1998.
4. Accrued commissions payable total $3,000 at December 31.

Required

a. Prepare a 12-column work sheet for the year ended December 31, 1997. You need not include account numbers or explanations of adjustments.
b. Prepare the adjusting journal entries.
c. Prepare the closing journal entries.

Problem 4–4A
Prepare work sheet and closing entries (L.O. 2, 4)

The following trial balance and additional data are for Gentle-Care Pet Hospital, Inc.:

GENTLE-CARE PET HOSPITAL, INC.
Trial Balance
December 31, 1997

	Debits	Credits
Cash	$ 26,490	
Accounts Receivable	54,390	
Supplies on Hand	900	
Prepaid Fire Insurance	1,800	
Prepaid Rent	21,600	
Equipment	125,000	
Accumulated Depreciation—Equipment		$ 25,000
Accounts Payable		29,550
Notes Payable		9,000
Capital Stock		150,000
Retained Earnings, January 1, 1997		20,685
Service Revenue		179,010
Interest Expense	225	
Salaries Expense	142,200	
Advertising Expense	29,250	
Supplies Expense	2,135	
Miscellaneous Expense	3,705	
Legal and Accounting Expense	3,750	
Utilities Expense	1,800	
	$413,245	$413,245

The company consistently followed the policy of initially debiting all prepaid items to asset accounts.

Additional data

1. Prepaid fire insurance is $600 as of the end of the year.
2. Supplies on hand are $638 as of the end of the year.
3. Prepaid rent is $2,625 as of the end of the year.
4. The equipment is expected to last 10 years with no salvage value.
5. Accrued salaries are $2,625.

Required

a. Prepare a 12-column work sheet for the year ended December 31, 1997. You need not include account numbers. Briefly explain the entries in the Adjustments columns at the bottom of the work sheet, as was done in Illustration 4.2.
b. Prepare the December 31, 1997, closing entries.

Problem 4–5A
Prepare work sheet, income statement, statement of retained earnings, classified balance sheet, and adjusting and closing entries (L.O. 2–5, 7)

The following trial balance and additional data are for Boswell Interior Decorators, Inc.:

BOSWELL INTERIOR DECORATORS, INC.
Trial Balance
December 31, 1997

	Debits	Credits
Cash	$ 55,400	
Accounts Receivable	81,600	
Supplies on Hand	4,000	
Prepaid Rent	12,240	
Prepaid Advertising	2,880	
Prepaid Insurance	4,400	
Office Equipment	7,600	
Accumulated Depreciation—Office Equipment		$ 2,760
Office Furniture	29,200	
Accumulated Depreciation—Office Furniture		8,280
Accounts Payable		25,200
Notes Payable (due 1998)		4,000
Capital Stock		100,000
Retained Earnings, January 1, 1997		22,400
Dividends	42,520	
Service Revenue		220,000
Salaries Expense	98,800	
Utilities Expense	20,000	
Miscellaneous Expense	24,000	
	$382,640	$382,640

Additional data

1. Supplies on hand at December 31, 1997, are $1,000.
2. Rent expense for 1997 is $10,000.
3. Advertising expense for 1997 is $2,304.
4. Insurance expense for 1997 is $2,400.
5. Depreciation expense is office equipment, $912, and office furniture, $3,000.
6. Accrued interest on notes payable is $150.
7. Accrued salaries are $4,200.

Required

a. Prepare a 12-column work sheet for the year ended December 31, 1997. You need not include account numbers or explanations of adjustments.
b. Prepare an income statement.
c. Prepare a statement of retained earnings.
d. Prepare a classified balance sheet.
e. Prepare adjusting and closing entries.

Beyond the Numbers—Critical Thinking

Business Decision Case 4–1
Prepare report on profitability of business (L.O. 3)

Susan and Danny Vance met while both were employed in the interior trim and upholstery department of an auto manufacturer. After their marriage, they decided to earn some extra income by doing small jobs involving canvas, vinyl, and upholstered products. Their work was considered excellent, and at the urging of their customers, they decided to go into business for themselves, operating out of the basement of the house they owned. To do

this, they invested $120,000 cash in their business. They spent $10,500 for a sewing machine (expected life, 10 years) and $12,000 for other miscellaneous tools and equipment (expected life, 5 years). They undertook only custom work, with the customers purchasing the required materials, to avoid stocking any inventory other than supplies. Generally, they required an advance deposit on all jobs.

The business seemed successful from the start, as the Vances received orders from many customers. But they felt something was wrong. They worked hard and charged competitive prices. Yet there seemed to be barely enough cash available from the business to cover immediate personal needs. Summarized, the checkbook of the business for 1997, their second year of operations, showed:

Balance, January 1, 1997		$ 89,200
Cash received from customers:		
For work done in 1996	$ 36,000	
For work done in 1997	200,000	
For work to be done in 1998	48,000	284,000
		$373,200
Cash paid out:		
Two-year insurance policy dated January 1, 1997	$ 19,200	
Utilities	48,000	
Supplies	104,000	
Other expenses	72,000	
Taxes, including sales taxes	26,400	
Dividends	40,000	309,600
Balance, December 31, 1997		$ 63,600

Considering how much they worked, the Vances were concerned that the cash balance decreased by $25,600 even though they only received dividends of $40,000. Their combined income from the auto manufacturer had been $45,000. They were seriously considering giving up their business and going back to work for the auto manufacturer. They turned to you for advice. You discovered the following:

1. Of the supplies purchased in 1997, $24,000 were used on jobs billed to customers in 1997; no supplies were used for any other work.
2. Work completed in 1997 and billed to customers for which cash had not yet been received by year-end amounted to $50,000.

Required

Prepare a written report for the Vances, responding to their belief that their business is not sufficiently profitable. (Hint: Prepare an income statement for 1997 and include it in your report.)

Annual Report Analysis 4–2
Calculate current ratios for four real companies (L.O. 8)

Using the annual report booklet, calculate the current ratios for the two years shown for The Coca-Cola Company, The Limited, Inc., Maytag Corporation, and John H. Harland Company. Write a summary of the results of your calculations. Also, look at some of the other data provided by the companies in preparing your comments. For instance, look at the net income for the last three years.

Broader Perspective—Writing Experience 4–3

Read the "A Broader Perspective" on page 143. Write a description of a career in public accounting at each level within the firm. Discuss the skills needed and how you could develop these skills.

Group Project 4–4
Interview a management accountant

In teams of two or three students, interview a management accountant in person or by speaker phone. Management accountants may have the title of chief financial officer (CFO), controller, or some other accounting title within a company. Seek information on the advantages and disadvantages of working as a management accountant. Also inquire about the nature of the work and any training programs offered by the company. As a team, write a memorandum to the instructor summarizing the results of the interview. The heading of the memorandum should contain the date, to whom it is written, from whom, and the subject matter.

Answers to Self-Test

True-False

1. **True.** The three trial balances are the unadjusted trial balance, the adjusted trial balance, and the post-closing trial balance. The first two trial balances appear on the work sheet.
2. **False.** If a debit-balance account (such as Prepaid Rent) is credited in the adjustment, the amount in the Adjustments columns is deducted from the amount in the Trial Balance columns to determine the amount for that item in the Adjusted Trial Balance columns.
3. **True.** The net loss appears in the Income Statement credit column to balance the Income Statement columns. Then the loss appears in the Statement of Retained Earnings debit column because it reduces Retained Earnings.
4. **True.** All of these accounts are closed, or reduced to zero balances, as a result of the closing process.
5. **False.** All revenue and expense accounts have zero balances after closing.
6. **False.** Some manual accounting systems are still in use.

Multiple-Choice

1. **b.** The other accounts are very likely to be adjusted. The Land account would be adjusted only if an error has been made involving that account.
2. **c.** The Adjusted Trial Balance columns should balance before items are spread to the Income Statement, Statement of Retained Earnings, and Balance Sheet columns. Therefore, if the Balance Sheet columns do not balance, the error is likely to exist in the last six columns of the work sheet.
3. **d.** The net income for the period does not appear in the balance sheet. It does appear in all of the other places listed.
4. **a.** The Dividends account is closed to the Retained Earnings account rather than to the Income Summary account.
5. **b.** Plant, property, and equipment is one of the long-term asset categories. Response **a** should not include equipment. Response **c** should not include notes receivable. Stockholders' equity is not subdivided into current and long-term categories.

Comprehensive Review Problem

Problem covers all steps in the accounting cycle covered in Chapters 1–4. Open ledger accounts and enter beginning balances. Journalize transactions and post to ledger accounts. Prepare work sheet, income statement, statement of retained earnings, classified balance sheet, adjusting and closing entries, and post-closing trial balance.

Sanchez Delivery Service Company has the following chart of accounts:

Acct. No.	Account Title	Acct. No.	Account Title
100	Cash	310	Retained Earnings
103	Accounts Receivable	320	Dividends
107	Supplies on Hand	400	Service Revenue
108	Prepaid Insurance	507	Salaries Expense
112	Prepaid Rent	511	Utilities Expense
140	Buildings	512	Insurance Expense
141	Accumulated Depreciation—Buildings	515	Rent Expense
150	Trucks	518	Supplies Expense
151	Accumulated Depreciation—Trucks	520	Depreciation Expense—Buildings
200	Accounts Payable	521	Depreciation Expense—Trucks
206	Salaries Payable	568	Miscellaneous Expense
300	Capital Stock	600	Income Summary

The post-closing trial balance as of May 31, 1997, was as follows:

SANCHEZ DELIVERY SERVICE COMPANY
Post-Closing Trial Balance
May 31, 1997

Acct. No.	Account Title	Debits	Credits
100	Cash	$ 60,000	
103	Accounts Receivable	30,000	
107	Supplies on Hand	14,000	
108	Prepaid Insurance	4,800	
112	Prepaid Rent	12,000	
140	Buildings	320,000	
141	Accumulated Depreciation—Buildings		$ 36,000
150	Trucks	80,000	
151	Accumulated Depreciation—Trucks		30,000
200	Accounts Payable		24,000
300	Capital Stock		300,000
310	Retained Earnings		130,800
		$520,800	$520,800

The transactions for June 1997 were as follows:

June 1 Performed delivery services for customers on account, $60,000.
3 Paid dividends, $10,000.
4 Purchased a $20,000 truck on account.
7 Collected $22,000 of the accounts receivable.
8 Paid $16,000 of the accounts payable.
11 Purchased $4,000 of supplies on account. The asset account for supplies was debited.
17 Performed delivery services for cash, $32,000.
20 Paid the utilities bills for June, $1,200.
23 Paid miscellaneous expenses for June, $600.
28 Paid salaries of $28,000 for June.

Additional data

1. Depreciation expense on the buildings for June is $800.
2. Depreciation expense on the trucks for June is $400.
3. Accrued salaries at June 30 are $4,000.
4. A physical count showed $12,000 of supplies on hand on June 30.
5. The prepaid insurance balance of $4,800 applies to a two-year period beginning June 1, 1997.
6. The prepaid rent of $12,000 applies to a one-year period beginning June 1, 1997.
7. Performed $12,000 of delivery services for customers as of June 30 that will not be billed to those customers until July.

Required

a. Open three-column ledger accounts for the accounts listed in the chart of accounts.
b. Enter the May 31, 1997, account balances in the accounts.
c. Journalize the transactions for June 1997.
d. Post the June journal entries and include cross-references (assume all journal entries appear on page 10 of the journal).
e. Prepare a 12-column work sheet as of June 30, 1997.
f. Prepare an income statement, a statement of retained earnings, and a classified balance sheet.
g. Prepare and post the adjusting entries (assume they appear on page 11 of the general journal).
h. Prepare and post the closing entries (assume they appear on page 12 of the general journal).
i. Prepare a post-closing trial balance.

5

ACCOUNTING THEORY UNDERLYING FINANCIAL ACCOUNTING

Chapter 1 briefly introduced the body of theory underlying accounting procedures. In this chapter, we discuss accounting theory in greater depth. Now that you have learned some accounting procedures, you are better able to relate these theoretical concepts to accounting practice. **Accounting theory** is "a set of basic concepts and assumptions and related principles that explain and guide the accountant's actions in identifying, measuring, and communicating economic information."[1]

To some people, the word *theory* implies something abstract and out of reach. Understanding the theory behind the accounting process, however, helps one make decisions in diverse accounting situations. Accounting theory provides a logical framework for accounting practice.

The first part of the chapter describes underlying accounting assumptions or concepts, the measurement process, major principles, and modifying conventions or constraints. Accounting theory has developed over the years and is contained in authoritative accounting literature and textbooks. The next part of the chapter describes the development of the Financial Accounting Standards Board's conceptual framework for accounting. This framework builds on accounting theory developed over time and serves as a basis for formulating accounting standards in the future. Presenting the traditional body of theory first and the conceptual framework second gives you a sense of the historical development of accounting theory. Despite some overlap between the two parts of the chapter, remember that FASB's conceptual framework builds on traditional theory rather than replacing it. The final part of the chapter discusses (1) the information needs of investors and creditors as identified by a committee of the American Institute of Certified Public Accountants and (2) significant accounting policies contained in annual reports issued by companies.

LEARNING OBJECTIVES

After studying this chapter, you should be able to:

1. Identify and discuss the underlying assumptions or concepts of accounting.
2. Identify and discuss the major principles of accounting.
3. Identify and discuss the modifying conventions (or constraints) of accounting.
4. Describe the conceptual framework project of the Financial Accounting Standards Board.

(*continued*)

---

[1] American Accounting Association, *A Statement of Basic Accounting Theory* (Sarasota, Fla., 1966), pp. 1–2.

(continued)

5. Describe the information needs of investors and creditors.
6. Discuss the nature of a company's summary of significant accounting policies in its annual report.

Traditional Accounting Theory

Traditional accounting theory consists of underlying assumptions, rules of measurement, major principles, and modifying conventions (or constraints). The following sections describe these aspects of accounting theory that greatly influence accounting practice.

Underlying Assumptions or Concepts

The major underlying assumptions or concepts of accounting are (1) business entity, (2) going concern (continuity), (3) money measurement, (4) stable dollar, and (5) periodicity. This section discusses the effects of these assumptions on the accounting process.

Business Entity

Objective 1
Identify and discuss the underlying assumptions or concepts of accounting.

Data gathered in an accounting system must relate to a specific business unit or entity. The **business entity concept** assumes that each business has an existence separate from its owners, creditors, employees, customers, interested parties, and other businesses. For each business (such as a horse stable or a fitness center), the business, not the business owner, is the accounting entity. Therefore, financial statements are identified as belonging to a particular business entity. The content of these financial statements reports only on the activities, resources, and obligations of that entity.

A business entity may be made up of several different legal entities. For instance, a large business (such as General Motors Corporation) may consist of several separate corporations, each of which is a separate legal entity. For reporting purposes, however, the corporations may be considered as one business entity because they have a common ownership. Chapter 14 illustrates this concept.

Going Concern (Continuity)

When accountants record business transactions for an entity, they assume it is a going concern. The **going-concern (continuity) assumption** states that an entity will continue to operate indefinitely unless strong evidence exists that the entity will terminate. The termination of an entity occurs when a company ceases business operations and sells its assets. The process of termination is called **liquidation.** If liquidation appears likely, the going-concern assumption is no longer valid.

Accountants often cite the going-concern assumption to justify using historical costs rather than market values in measuring assets. Market values are of little or no significance to an entity using its assets rather than selling them. On the other hand, if an entity is liquidating, it should use liquidation values to report assets.

The going-concern assumption permits the accountant to record certain items as assets. For example, printed advertising matter may promote a special sale next month. This advertising material may have little, if any, value to anyone but its owner. However, since management expects to continue operating long enough to benefit from the advertising, the accountant classifies the expenditure as an asset, prepaid advertising, and not an expense.

Money Measurement

The economic activity of a business is normally recorded and reported in money terms. **Money measurement** is the use of a monetary unit such as the dollar instead of physical or other units of measurement. Using a particular monetary unit provides accountants with a common unit of measurement to report economic activity. Without a monetary unit, it would be impossible to add such items as buildings, equipment, and inventory on a balance sheet.

Financial statements identify their unit of measure (the dollar in the United States) so the statement user can make valid comparisons of amounts. For example, it would be difficult to compare relative asset amounts or profitability of a company reporting in U.S. dollars with a company reporting in Japanese yen.

Stable Dollar

In the United States, accountants make another assumption regarding money measurement—the stable dollar assumption. Under the **stable dollar assumption,** the dollar is accepted as a reasonably stable unit of measurement. Thus, accountants make no adjustments for the changing value of the dollar in the primary financial statements.

Using the stable dollar assumption creates a difficulty in depreciation accounting. Assume, for example, that a company acquired a building in 1967 and computed the 30-year straight-line depreciation on the building without adjusting for any changes in the value of the dollar. Thus, the depreciation deducted in 1997 is the same as the depreciation deducted in 1967. The company makes no adjustments for the difference between the values of the 1967 dollar and the 1997 dollar. Both dollars are treated as equal monetary units of measurement despite substantial price inflation over the 30-year period. Accountants and business executives have expressed concern over this inflation problem, especially during periods of high inflation.

Periodicity (Time Periods)

According to the **periodicity (time periods) assumption,** accountants divide an entity's life into months or years to report its economic activities. Then, accountants attempt to prepare accurate reports on the entity's activities for these periods. Although these time-period reports provide useful and timely financial information for investors and creditors, they may be inaccurate for some of these time periods because accountants must estimate depreciation expense and certain other adjusting entries.

Accounting reports cover relatively short periods. These time periods are usually of equal length so that statement users can make valid comparisons of a company's performance from period to period. The length of the accounting period must be stated in the financial statements. For instance, so far, the income statements in this text were for either one month or one year. Companies that publish their financial statements, such as publicly held corporations, generally prepare monthly statements for internal management and publish financial statements quarterly and annually for external statement users.

Accrual Basis and Periodicity Chapter 3 demonstrated that financial statements more accurately reflect the financial status and operations of a company when prepared under the accrual basis rather than the cash basis of accounting. Under the cash basis, we record revenues when cash is received and expenses when cash is paid. Under the accrual basis, however, we record revenues when services are rendered or products are sold and expenses when incurred.

The periodicity assumption requires preparing adjusting entries under the accrual basis. Without the periodicity assumption, a business would have only one time period running from its inception to its termination. Then, the concepts of cash basis and accrual basis accounting would be irrelevant because all revenues and all expenses would be recorded in that one time period and would not have to be assigned to artificially short periods of one year or less.

Approximation and Judgment because of Periodicity To provide periodic financial information, accountants must often estimate expected uncollectible accounts (see Chapter 9) and the useful lives of depreciable assets. Uncertainty about future events prevents precise measurement and makes estimates necessary in accounting. Fortunately, these estimates are often reasonably accurate.

Other Basic Concepts

Other basic accounting concepts that affect accounting for entities are (1) general-purpose financial statements, (2) substance over form, (3) consistency, (4) double-entry, and (5) articulation. We discuss these basic accounting concepts next.

General-Purpose Financial Statements

Accountants prepare general-purpose financial statements at regular intervals to meet many of the information needs of external parties and top-level internal managers. In contrast, accountants can gather special-purpose financial information for a specific decision, usually on a one-time basis. For example, management may need specific information to decide whether to purchase a new computer. Since special-purpose financial information must be specific, this information is best obtained from the detailed accounting records rather than from the financial statements.

Substance over Form

In some business transactions, the economic substance of the transaction conflicts with its legal form. For example, a contract that is legally a lease may, in fact, be equivalent to a purchase. A company may have a three-year contract to lease (rent) an automobile at a stated monthly rental fee. At the end of the lease period, the company receives title to the auto after paying a nominal sum (say, $1). The economic substance of this transaction is a purchase rather than a lease of the auto. Thus, under the substance-over-form concept, the auto is an asset on the balance sheet and is depreciated instead of showing rent expense on the income statement. Accountants record a transaction's *economic substance* rather than its *legal form*.

Consistency

Consistency generally requires that a company use the same accounting principles and reporting practices through time. This concept prohibits indiscriminate switching of accounting principles or methods, such as changing inventory methods every year. However, consistency does not prohibit a change in accounting principles if the information needs of financial statement users are better served by the change. When a company makes a change in accounting principles, it must make the following disclosures in the financial statements: (1) nature of the change; (2) reasons for the change; (3) effect of the change on current net income, if significant; and (4) cumulative effect of the change on past income.

Double Entry

Chapter 2 introduced the basic accounting concept of the double-entry method of recording transactions. Under the double-entry approach, every transaction has a two-sided effect on each party engaging in the transaction. Thus, to record a transaction, each party debits at least one account and credits at least one account. The total debits equal the total credits in each journal entry.

Articulation

When learning how to prepare work sheets in Chapter 4, you learned that financial statements are fundamentally related and *articulate* (interact) with each other. For example, we carry the amount of net income from the income statement to the statement of retained earnings. Then we carry the ending balance on the statement of retained earnings to the balance sheet to bring total assets and total equities into balance.

In Illustration 5.1 we summarize the underlying assumptions or concepts. The next section discusses the measurement process used in accounting.

Measurement in Accounting

Earlier, we defined accounting as "the process of identifying, measuring, and communicating economic information to permit informed judgments and decisions by the users of the information."[2] In this section, we focus on the *measurement* process of accounting.

[2] Ibid., p. 1.

ILLUSTRATION 5.1 The Underlying Assumptions or Concepts

Assumption or Concept	Description	Importance
Business entity	Each business has an existence separate from its owners, creditors, employees, customers, other interested parties, and other businesses.	Defines the scope of the business such as a horse stable or physical fitness center. Identifies which transactions should be recorded on the company's books.
Going concern (continuity)	An entity will continue to operate indefinitely unless strong evidence exists that the entity will terminate.	Allows a company to continue carrying plant assets at their historical costs in spite of a change in their market values.
Money measurement	Each business uses a monetary unit of measurement, such as the dollar, instead of physical or other units of measurement.	Provides accountants with a common unit of measure to report economic activity. This concept permits us to add and subtract items on the financial statements.
Stable dollar	The dollar is accepted as a reasonably stable unit of measure.	Permits us to make no adjustments in the financial statements for the changing value of the dollar. This assumption works fairly well in the United States because of our relatively low rate of inflation.
Periodicity (time periods)	An entity's life can be subdivided into months or years to report its economic activities.	Permits us to prepare financial statements that cover periods shorter than the entire life of a business. Thus, we know how well a business is performing before it terminates its operations. The need for adjusting entries arises because of this concept and the use of accrual accounting.
General-purpose financial statements	One set of financial statements serves the needs of all users.	Allows companies to prepare only one set of financial statements instead of a separate set for each potential type of user of those statements. The financial statements should be free of bias so they do not favor the interests of any one type of user.
Substance over form	Accountants should record the economic substance of a transaction rather than its legal form.	Encourages the accountant to record the true nature of a transaction rather than its apparent nature. This approach is the accounting equivalent of "tell it like it is." An apparent lease transaction that has all the characteristics of a purchase should be recorded as a purchase.
Consistency	Generally requires that a company use the same accounting principles and reporting practices every accounting period.	Prevents a company from changing accounting methods whenever it likes to present a better picture or to manipulate income. The inventory and depreciation chapters (Chapters 7 and 10) both mention the importance of this concept.
Double entry	Every transaction has a two-sided effect on each company or party engaging in the transaction.	Uses a system of checks and balances to help identify whether or not errors have been made in recording transactions. When the debits do not equal the credits, this inequality immediately signals us to stop and find the error.
Articulation	Financial statements are fundamentally related and articulate (interact) with each other.	Changes in account balances during an accounting period are reflected in financial statements that are related to one another. For instance, earning revenue increases net income on the income statement, retained earnings on the statement of retained earnings, and assets and retained earnings on the balance sheet. The statement of retained earnings ties the income statement and balance sheet together.

Accountants measure a business entity's assets, liabilities, and stockholders' equity and any changes that occur in them. By assigning the effects of these changes to particular time periods (periodicity), they can find the net income or net loss of the accounting entity for those periods.

Measuring Assets and Liabilities

Accountants measure the various assets of a business in different ways. They measure cash at its specified amount. Chapter 9 explains how they measure claims to cash, such as accounts receivable, at their expected cash inflows, taking into consideration possible uncollectibles. They measure inventories, prepaid expenses, plant assets, and intangibles at their historical costs (actual amounts paid). After the acquisition date, they carry some items, such as inventory, at the lower-of-cost-or-market value. After the acquisition date, they carry plant assets and intangibles at original cost less accumulated depreciation or amortization. They measure liabilities at the amount of cash that will be paid or the value of services that will be performed to satisfy the liabilities.

Measuring Changes in Assets and Liabilities

Accountants can easily measure some changes in assets and liabilities, such as the acquisition of an asset on credit and the payment of a liability. Other changes in assets and liabilities, such as those recorded in adjusting entries, are more difficult to measure because they often involve estimates and/or calculations. The accountant must determine when a change has taken place and the amount of the change. These decisions involve matching revenues and expenses and are guided by the principles discussed next.

The Major Principles

Objective 2
Identify and discuss the major principles of accounting.

Generally accepted accounting principles (GAAP) set forth standards or methods for presenting financial accounting information. A standardized presentation format enables users to compare the financial information of different companies more easily. Generally accepted accounting principles have been either developed through accounting practice or established by authoritative organizations. Organizations that have contributed to the development of the principles are the American Institute of Certified Public Accountants (AICPA), the Financial Accounting Standards Board (FASB), the Securities and Exchange Commission (SEC), the American Accounting Association (AAA), the Financial Executives Institute (FEI), and the Institute of Management Accounting (IMA). This section explains the following major principles:

1. Exchange-price (or cost) principle.
2. Matching principle.
3. Revenue recognition principle.
4. Expense recognition principle.
5. Gain and loss recognition principle.
6. Full disclosure principle.

Exchange-Price (or Cost) Principle

Whenever resources are transferred between two parties, such as buying merchandise on account, the accountant must follow the *exchange-price (or cost) principle* in presenting that information. The **exchange-price (or cost) principle** requires an accountant to record transfers of resources at prices agreed on by the parties to the exchange at the time of exchange. This principle sets forth (1) what goes into the accounting system—transaction data; (2) when it is recorded—at the time of exchange; and (3) the amounts—exchange prices—at which assets, liabilities, stockholders' equity, revenues, and expenses are recorded.

As applied to most assets, this principle is often called the **cost principle.** It dictates that purchased or self-constructed assets are initially recorded at historical cost. **Historical cost** is the amount paid, or the fair market value of the liability incurred or other resources surrendered, to acquire an asset and place it in a condition and position for its intended use. For instance, when the cost of a plant asset (such as a machine) is recorded, its cost includes the net purchase price plus any costs of reconditioning, testing, transporting, and placing the asset in the location for its intended use. Accountants prefer the term *exchange-price principle* to cost principle because it seems inappropriate to refer to liabilities, stockholders' equity, and such assets as cash and accounts receivable as being measured in terms of cost.

Matching Principle

Using the **matching principle,** we determine the net income of a period by associating or relating revenues earned with expenses incurred to generate those revenues. The logic underlying this principle is that whenever economic resources are used, someone wants to know what was accomplished and at what cost. Every evaluation of economic activity involves matching benefit with sacrifice. We discuss and illustrate the application of the matching principle later in this chapter.

An Accounting Perspective

Business Insight In some European countries, the financial statements contain *secret reserves.* These secret reserves arise from a company not reporting all of its profits when it has a very good year. The justification is that the stockholders vote on the amount of dividends they receive each year; if all profits were reported, the stockholders might vote to pay the entire amount out as dividends. By holding back some profits, not only are the creditors more protected but the company is also more solvent and has more resources to invest in productive assets.

Revenue Recognition Principle

Revenue is not difficult to define or measure; it is the inflow of assets from the sale of goods and services to customers, measured by the cash expected to be received from customers. However, the crucial question for the accountant is when to record a revenue. Under the **revenue recognition principle,** revenues should be earned and realized before they are recognized (recorded).

Earning of Revenue All economic activities undertaken by a company to create revenues are part of the earning process. Many activities may have preceded the actual receipt of cash from a customer, including (1) placing advertisements, (2) calling on the customer several times, (3) submitting samples, (4) acquiring or manufacturing goods, and (5) selling and delivering goods. For these activities, the company incurs costs. Although revenue was actually being earned by these activities, accountants do not recognize revenue until the time of sale because of the requirement that revenue be *substantially* earned before it is recognized (recorded). This requirement is the **earning principle.**

Realization of Revenue Under the **realization principle,** the accountant does not recognize (record) revenue until the seller acquires the right to receive payment from the buyer. The seller acquires this right from the buyer at the time of sale for merchandise transactions or when services have been performed in service transactions. Legally, a sale of merchandise occurs when title to the goods passes to the buyer. The time at which title passes normally depends on the shipping terms—FOB shipping point or FOB destination (as we discuss in Chapter 6). As a practical matter, accountants generally record revenue when goods are delivered.

The advantages of recognizing revenue at the time of sale are (1) the actual transaction—delivery of goods—is an observable event; (2) revenue is easily measured; (3) risk of loss due to price decline or destruction of the goods has passed to the buyer; (4) revenue has been earned, or substantially so; and (5) because the revenue has been earned, expenses and net income can be determined. As discussed later, the disadvantage of recognizing revenue at the time of sale is that the revenue might not be recorded in the period during which most of the activity creating it occurred.

Exceptions to the Realization Principle The following examples are instances when practical considerations may cause accountants to vary the point of revenue recognition from the time of sale. These examples illustrate the effect that the business environment has on the development of accounting principles and standards.

Cash Collection as Point of Revenue Recognition Some small companies record revenues and expenses at the time of cash collection and payment, which may not occur at the time of sale. This procedure is the **cash basis** of accounting. The cash basis is acceptable primarily in service enterprises that do not have substantial credit transactions or inventories, such as business entities of doctors or dentists.

Installment Basis of Revenue Recognition When collecting the selling price of goods sold in monthly or annual installments and considerable doubt exists as to collectibility, the company may use the installment basis of accounting. Companies make these sales in spite of the doubtful collectibility of the account because their margin of profit is high and the goods can be repossessed if the payments are not received. Under the **installment basis,** the percentage of total gross margin (selling price of a good minus its cost) recognized in a period is equal to the percentage of total cash from a sale that is received in that period. Thus, the gross margin recognized in a period is equal to the cash received times the gross margin percentage (gross margin divided by selling price). The formula to recognize gross profit on cash collections made on installment sales of a certain year is:

Cash collections	×	Gross margin percentage	=	Gross margin recognized

To be more precise, we expand the descriptions in the formula as follows:

Cash collections this year resulting from installment sales made in a certain year	×	Gross margin percentage for the year of sale	=	Gross margin recognized this year on cash collections this year from installment sales made in a certain year

To illustrate, assume a company sold a stereo set. The facts of the sale are:

Date of Sale	Selling Price	Cost	Gross Margin (Selling price − Cost)	Gross Margin Percentage (Gross margin ÷ Selling price)
October 1, 1997	$500	$300	($500 − $300) = $200	($200 ÷ $500) = 40%

The buyer makes 10 equal monthly installment payments of $50 to pay for the set (10 × $50 = $500). If the company receives three monthly payments in 1997, the total amount of cash received in 1997 is $150 (3 × $50). The gross margin to recognize in 1997 is:

1997 cash collections from 1997 installment sales	×	Gross margin percentage on 1997 installment sales	=	1997 gross margin recognized on 1997 cash collections from 1997 installment sales
$150	×	**40%**	=	**$60**

The company collects the other installments when due so it receives a total of $350 in 1998 from 1997 installment sales. The gross margin to recognize in 1998 on these cash collections is as follows:

1998 cash collections from 1997 installment sales	×	Gross margin percentage on 1997 installment sales	=	1998 gross margin recognized on 1998 cash collections from 1997 installment sales
$350	×	**40%**	=	**$140**

In summary, the total receipts and gross margin recognized in the two years are as follows:

Year	Total Amount of Cash Received	Gross Margin Recognized
1997	$150 (30%)	$ 60 (30%)
1998	350 (70%)	140 (70%)
Total	$500 100%	$200 100%

An accountant may use the installment basis of revenue recognition for tax purposes only in very limited circumstances. Because the installment basis delays revenue recognition beyond the time of sale, it is acceptable for accounting purposes only when considerable doubt exists as to collectibility of the installments.

Revenue Recognition on Long-Term Construction Projects Companies recognize revenue from a long-term construction project under two different methods: (1) the completed-contract method or (2) the percentage-of-completion method. The **completed-contract method** does not recognize any revenue until the project is completed. In that period, they recognize all revenue even though the contract may have required three years to complete. Thus, the completed-contract method recognizes revenues at the time of sale, as is true for most sales transactions. Companies carry costs incurred on the project forward in an inventory account (Construction in Process) and charge them to expense in the period in which the revenue is recognized.

Some accountants argue that waiting so long to recognize any revenue is unreasonable. They believe that because revenue-producing activities have been performed during each year of construction, revenue should be recognized in each year of construction even if estimates are needed. The **percentage-of-completion method** recognizes revenue based on the estimated stage of completion of a long-term project. To measure the stage of completion, firms compare actual costs incurred in a period with the total estimated costs to be incurred on the project.

To illustrate, assume that a company has a contract to build a dam for $44 million. The estimated construction cost is $40 million. You calculate the estimated gross margin as follows:

Sales Price of Dam	Estimated Costs to Construct Dam	Estimated Gross Margin (Sales price − Estimated costs)
$44 million	$40 million	($44 million − $40 million) = $4 million

The firm recognizes the $4 million gross margin in the financial statements by recording the assigned revenue for the year and then deducting actual costs incurred that year. The formula to recognize revenue is:

$$\left(\frac{\text{Actual construction costs incurred during the period}}{} \div \text{Total estimated construction costs for the entire project}\right) \times \text{Total sales price} = \text{Revenue recognized for period}$$

Suppose that by the end of the first year (1997), the company had incurred actual construction costs of $30 million. These costs are 75% of the total estimated construction costs ($30 million ÷ $40 million = 75%). Under the percentage-of-completion method, the firm would use the 75% figure to assign revenue to the first year. In 1998, it incurs another $6 million of construction costs. In 1999, it

ILLUSTRATION 5.2
Methods of Accounting for Long-Term Contracts

	Number of Companies			
	1992	1991	1990	1989
Percentage-of-completion	94	92	91	92
Units-of-delivery	35	36	34	33
Completed contract	5	8	9	6
Not determinable	1	2	4	2

Source: American Institute of Certified Public Accountants, *Accounting Trends & Techniques* (New York: AICPA, 1993), p. 367.

incurs the final $4 million of construction costs. The amount of revenue to assign to each year is as follows:

Year	Ratio of Actual Construction Costs to Total Estimated Construction Costs	×	Agreed Price of Dam	=	Amount of Revenue to Recognize (Assign)
1997 . . .	($30 million ÷ $40 million) = 75%				
	75%	×	$44 million	=	$33 million
1998 . . .	($6 million ÷ $40 million) = 15%				
	15%	×	$44 million	=	$6.6 million
1999 . . .	($4 million ÷ $40 million) = 10%				
	10%	×	$44 million	=	$4.4 million

The amount of gross margin to recognize in each year is as follows:

Year	Assigned Revenues	–	Actual Construction Costs	=	Recognized Gross Margin
1997.	$33.0 million	–	$30.0 million	=	$3.0 million
1998.	6.6	–	6.0	=	0.6
1999.	4.4	–	4.0	=	0.4
Total.	$44.0 million	–	$40.0 million	=	$4.0 million

This company would deduct other costs incurred in the accounting period, such as general and administrative expenses, from gross margin to determine net income. For instance, assuming general and administrative expenses were $100,000 in 1997, net income would be ($3,000,000 – $100,000) = $2,900,000.

In Illustration 5.2, you can see which methods of accounting for long-term contracts are used most often in the financial statements of 600 companies. The percentage-of-completion method is the most widely used. (Units of delivery is a form of the percentage-of-completion method.)

REVENUE RECOGNITION AT COMPLETION OF PRODUCTION Businesses that recognize revenue at the time of completion of production or extraction use the **production basis**. The production basis is an acceptable procedure when accounting for many farm products (wheat, corn, and soybeans) and for certain precious metals (gold). Accountants justify recognizing revenue before the sale of these products because (1) the products are homogeneous in nature, (2) they can usually be sold at their market prices, and (3) unit production costs for these products are often difficult to determine.

To recognize revenue on completion of production or extraction, they debit inventory (an asset) and credit a revenue account for the expected selling price of the goods. Then they treat all costs incurred in the period as expenses. For example, assume that a firm mined 1,000 ounces of gold at a time when gold sold for $400 per ounce. The entry to record the extraction of 1,000 ounces of gold would be:

	Debit	Credit
Inventory of Gold	400,000	
Revenue from Extraction of Gold		400,000
To record extraction of 1,000 ounces of gold. Selling price is $400 per ounce.		

Later, if the company sells the gold at $400 per ounce, it debits Cash and credits Inventory of Gold for $400,000 as follows:

Cash	400,000	
Inventory of Gold		400,000
To record sale of 1,000 ounces of gold at $400 per ounce.		

If expenses in producing the gold amounted to $300,000, net income on the gold mined would be $100,000.

Expense Recognition Principle

Expense recognition is closely related to, and sometimes discussed as part of, the revenue recognition principle. The **expense recognition principle** states that expenses should be recognized (recorded) as they are incurred to produce revenues. An expense is the outflow or using up of assets in the generation of revenue. Firms voluntarily incur expense to produce revenue. For instance, a television set delivered by a dealer to a customer in exchange for cash is an asset consumed to produce revenue; its cost becomes an expense. Similarly, the cost of services such as labor are voluntarily incurred to produce revenue.

The Measurement of Expense Accountants measure most assets used in operating a business by their historical costs. Therefore, they measure a depreciation expense resulting from the consumption of those assets by the historical costs of those assets. They measure other expenses, such as wages that are paid for currently, at their current costs.

The Timing of Expense Recognition The matching principle implies that a relationship exists between expenses and revenues. For certain expenses, such as costs of acquiring or producing the products sold, you can easily see this relationship. However, when a direct relationship cannot be seen, we charge the costs of assets with limited lives to expense in the periods benefited on a systematic and rational allocation basis. Depreciation of plant assets is an example.

Product costs are costs incurred in the acquisition or manufacture of goods. As you will see in the next chapter, included as product costs for purchased goods are invoice, freight, and insurance-in-transit costs. For manufacturing companies, product costs include all costs of materials, labor, and factory operations necessary to produce the goods. Product costs attach to the goods purchased or produced and remain in inventory accounts as long as the goods are on hand. We charge product costs to expense when the goods are sold. The result is a precise matching of cost of goods sold expense to its related revenue.

Period costs are costs not traceable to specific products and expensed in the period incurred. Selling and administrative costs are period costs.

An Accounting Perspective

Business Insight In the third quarter of 1993, U.S. corporate profits surged 24% because of cost-cutting efforts. This sharp increase overshadowed an 11% increase in the second quarter. The availability and use of accounting information undoubtedly assisted management in making these cost reductions.

Source: *The Wall Street Journal,* November 1, 1993, p. A1.

Gain and Loss Recognition Principle

The **gain and loss recognition principle** states that we record gains only when realized, but losses when they first become evident. Thus, we recognize losses at an earlier point than gains. This principle is related to the conservatism concept.

Gains typically result from the sale of long-term assets for more than their book value. Firms should not recognize gains until they are realized through sale or exchange. Recognizing potential gains before they are actually realized is generally forbidden in accounting.

ILLUSTRATION 5.3 The Major Principles

Principle	Description	Importance
Exchange-price (or cost)	Requires transfers of resources to be recorded at prices agreed on by the parties to the exchange at the time of the exchange.	Tells the accountant to record a transfer of resources at an objectively determinable amount at the time of the exchange. Also, self-constructed assets are recorded at their actual cost rather than at some estimate of what they would have cost if they had been purchased.
Matching	Net income of a period is determined by associating or relating revenues earned in a period with expenses incurred to generate those revenues.	Identifies how to calculate net income under the accrual concept of income. In Chapter 3 we illustrated the matching principle; all chapters reinforce the importance of this fundamental principle.
Revenue recognition	Revenues should be earned and realized before they are recognized (recorded).	Informs accountant that revenues generally should be recognized when services are performed or goods are sold. Exceptions are made for installment sales, long-term construction projects, certain farm products, and precious metals.
Expense recognition	Expenses should be recognized (recorded) as they are incurred to produce revenues.	Indicates that expenses are to be recorded as soon as they are incurred rather than waiting until some future time.
Gain and loss recognition	Gains may be recorded only when realized, but losses should be recorded when they first become evident.	Tells the accountant to be conservative when recognizing gains and losses. Gains can only be recognized when they have been realized through sale or exchange. Losses should be recognized as soon as they become evident. Thus, potential losses can be recorded, but only gains that have actually been realized can be recorded.
Full disclosure	Information important enough to influence the decisions of an informed user of the financial statements should be disclosed.	Requires the accountant to disclose everything that is important. A good rule to follow is—if in doubt, disclose. Another good rule is—if you are not consistent, disclose all the facts and the effect on income.

Losses consume assets, as do expenses. However, unlike expenses, they do not produce revenues. Losses are usually *involuntary,* such as the loss suffered from destruction by fire on an uninsured building. A loss on the sale of a building may be voluntary when management decides to sell the building even though incurring a loss.

Full Disclosure Principle

The **full disclosure principle** states that information important enough to influence the decisions of an informed user of the financial statements should be disclosed. Depending on its nature, companies should disclose this information either in the financial statements, in notes to the financial statements, or in supplemental statements. For instance, the annual report booklet illustrates how The Coca-Cola Company discloses information in notes to its financial statements. In judging whether or not to disclose information, it is better to err on the side of too much disclosure rather than too little. Many lawsuits against CPAs and their clients have resulted from inadequate or misleading disclosure of the underlying facts.

We summarize the major principles and describe the importance of each in Illustration 5.3.

AN ACCOUNTING PERSPECTIVE

BUSINESS INSIGHT The accounting model involves reporting revenues earned and expenses incurred by the company. Some have argued that social benefits and social costs created by the company should also be reported. Suppose, for instance, that a company is dumping toxic waste into a river and this action causes cancer among the citizens downstream. Should this cost be reported when preparing financial statements showing the performance of the company? What do you think?

Modifying Conventions (or Constraints)

Objective 3
Identify and discuss the modifying conventions (or constraints) of accounting.

In certain instances, companies do not strictly apply accounting principles because of modifying conventions (or constraints). **Modifying conventions** are customs emerging from accounting practice that alter the results obtained from a strict application of accounting principles. Three modifying conventions are cost-benefit, materiality, and conservatism.

Cost-Benefit The **cost-benefit consideration** involves deciding whether the benefits of including optional information in financial statements exceed the costs of providing the information. Users tend to think information is cost free since they incur none of the costs of providing the information. Preparers realize that providing information is costly. The benefits of using information should exceed the costs of providing it. The measurement of benefits is nebulous and inexact, which makes application of this modifying convention difficult in practice.

Materiality **Materiality** is a modifying convention that allows accountants to deal with immaterial (unimportant) items in an expedient but theoretically incorrect manner. The fundamental question accountants must ask in judging the materiality of an item is whether a knowledgeable user's decisions would be different if the information were presented in the theoretically correct manner. If not, the item is immaterial and may be reported in a theoretically incorrect but expedient manner. For instance, because inexpensive items such as calculators often do not make a difference in a statement user's decision to invest in the company, they are *immaterial* (unimportant) and may be expensed when purchased. However, because expensive items such as mainframe computers usually do make a difference in such a decision, they are *material* (important) and should be recorded as assets and depreciated. Accountants should record all material items in a theoretically correct manner. They may record immaterial items in a theoretically incorrect manner simply because it is more convenient and less expensive to do so. For example, they may debit the cost of a wastebasket to an expense account rather than an asset account even though the wastebasket has an expected useful life of 30 years. It simply is not worth the cost of recording depreciation expense on such a small item over its life.

The FASB defines materiality as "the magnitude of an omission or misstatement of accounting information that, in the light of surrounding circumstances, makes it probable that the judgment of a reasonable person relying on the information would have been changed or influenced by the omission or misstatement."[3] The term *magnitude* in this definition suggests that the materiality of an item may be assessed by looking at its relative size. A $10,000 error in an expense in a company with earnings of $30,000 is material. The same error in a company earning $30,000,000 may not be material.

Materiality involves more than the relative dollar amounts. Often the nature of the item makes it material. For example, it may be quite significant to know that a company is paying bribes or making illegal political contributions, even if the dollar amounts of such items are relatively small.

Conservatism **Conservatism** means being cautious or prudent and making sure that net assets and net income are not overstated. Such overstatements can mislead potential investors in the company and creditors making loans to the company. We apply conservatism when the lower-of-cost-or-market rule is used for inventory (see Chapter 7). Accountants must realize a fine line exists between conservative and incorrect accounting.

---

[3] FASB, *Statement of Financial Accounting Concepts No. 2,* "Qualitative Characteristics of Accounting Information" (Stamford, Conn., 1980), p. xv. Copyright © by the Financial Accounting Standards Board, High Ridge Park, Stamford, Connecticut 06905, U.S.A. Quoted (or excerpted) with permission. Copies of the complete documents are available from the FASB.

ILLUSTRATION 5.4 Modifying Conventions

Modifying Convention	Description	Importance
Cost-benefit	Optional information should be included in financial statements only if the benefits of providing it exceed its costs.	Lets the accountant know that information that is not required should be made available only if its benefits exceed its costs. An example may be companies going to the expense of providing information on the effects of inflation when the inflation rate is low and/or users do not seem to benefit significantly from the information.
Materiality	Only items that would affect a knowledgeable user's decision are material (important) and must be reported in a theoretically correct way.	Allows accountants to treat immaterial (relatively small dollar amount) information in a theoretically incorrect but expedient manner. For instance, a wastebasket can be expensed rather than capitalized and depreciated even though it may last for 30 years.
Conservatism	Transactions should be recorded so that net assets and net income are not overstated.	Warns accountants that net assets and net income are not to be overstated. "Anticipate (and record) all possible losses and do not anticipate (or record) any possible gains" is common advice under this constraint. Also, conservative application of the matching principle involves making sure that adjustments for expenses for such items as uncollectible accounts, warranties, and depreciation are adequate.

See Illustration 5.4 for a summary of the modifying conventions and their importance.

The remainder of this chapter discusses the conceptual framework project of the Financial Accounting Standards Board. The FASB designed the conceptual framework project to resolve some disagreements about the proper theoretical foundation for accounting. We present only the portions of the project relevant to this text.

THE FINANCIAL ACCOUNTING STANDARDS BOARD'S CONCEPTUAL FRAMEWORK PROJECT

Objective 4
Describe the conceptual framework project of the Financial Accounting Standards Board.

Experts have debated the exact nature of the basic concepts and related principles composing accounting theory for years. The debate continues today despite numerous references to generally accepted accounting principles (GAAP). To date, all attempts to present a concise statement of GAAP have received only limited acceptance.

Due to this limited success, many accountants suggest that the starting point in reaching a concise statement of GAAP is to seek agreement on the objectives of financial accounting and reporting. The belief is that if a person (1) carefully studies the environment, (2) knows what objectives are sought, (3) can identify certain qualitative traits of accounting information, and (4) can define the basic elements of financial statements, that person can discover the principles and standards leading to the stated objectives. The FASB completed the first three goals by publishing "Objectives of Financial Reporting by Business Enterprises" and "Qualitative Characteristics of Accounting Information."[4] Addressing the

[4] FASB, *Statement of Financial Accounting Concepts No. 1,* "Objectives of Financial Reporting by Business Enterprises" (Stamford, Conn., 1978); and *Statement of Financial Accounting Concepts No. 2,* "Qualitative Characteristics of Accounting Information" (Stamford, Conn., 1980). Copyright © by the Financial Accounting Standards Board, High Ridge Park, Stamford, Connecticut 06905, U.S.A. Quoted (or excerpted) with permission. Copies of the complete documents are available from the FASB.

fourth goal are concepts statements entitled "Elements of Financial Statements of Business Enterprises" and "Elements of Financial Statements."[5]

Objectives of Financial Reporting

Financial reporting objectives are the broad overriding goals sought by accountants engaging in financial reporting. According to the FASB, the first objective of financial reporting is to:

> provide information that is useful to present and potential investors and creditors and other users in making rational investment, credit, and similar decisions. The information should be comprehensible to those who have a reasonable understanding of business and economic activities and are willing to study the information with reasonable diligence.[6]

Interpreted broadly, the term *other users* includes employees, security analysts, brokers, and lawyers. Financial reporting should provide information to all who are willing to learn to use it properly.

The second objective of financial reporting is to:

> provide information to help present and potential investors and creditors and other users in assessing the amounts, timing, and uncertainty of prospective cash receipts from dividends [owner withdrawals] or interest and the proceeds from the sale, redemption, or maturity of securities or loans. Since investors' and creditors' cash flows are related to enterprise cash flows, financial reporting should provide information to help investors, creditors, and others assess the amounts, timing, and uncertainty of prospective net cash inflows to the related enterprise.[7]

This objective ties the cash flows of investors (owners) and creditors to the cash flows of the enterprise, a tie-in that appears entirely logical. Enterprise cash inflows are the source of cash for dividends, interest, and the redemption of maturing debt.

Third, financial reporting should:

> provide information about the economic resources of an enterprise, the claims to those resources (obligations of the enterprise to transfer resources to other entities and owners' equity), and the effects of transactions, events, and circumstances that change its resources and claims to those resources.[8]

We can draw some conclusions from these three objectives and from a study of the environment in which financial reporting is carried out. For example, financial reporting should:

1. Provide information about an enterprise's past performance because such information is a basis for predicting future enterprise performance.
2. Focus on earnings and its components, despite the emphasis in the objectives on cash flows. (Earnings computed under the accrual basis generally provide a better indicator of ability to generate favorable cash flows than do statements prepared under the cash basis.)

On the other hand, financial reporting does not seek to:

---

[5] FASB, *Statement of Financial Accounting Concepts No. 3,* "Elements of Financial Statements of Business Enterprises" (Stamford, Conn., 1980); and *Statement of Financial Accounting Concepts No. 6,* "Elements of Financial Statements" (Stamford, Conn., 1985). Copyright © by the Financial Accounting Standards Board, High Ridge Park, Stamford, Connecticut 06905, U.S.A. Quoted (or excerpted) with permission. Copies of the complete documents are available from the FASB.

[6] FASB, *Statement of Financial Accounting Concepts No. 1,* p. viii.

[7] Ibid.

[8] Ibid.

1. Measure the value of an enterprise but to provide information useful in determining its value.
2. Evaluate management's performance, predict earnings, assess risk, or estimate earning power but to provide information to persons who wish to make these evaluations.

These conclusions are some of those reached in *Statement of Financial Accounting Concepts No. 1*. As the Board stated, these statements "are intended to establish the objectives and concepts that the Financial Accounting Standards Board will use in developing standards of financial accounting and reporting."[9] How successful the Board will be in the approach adopted remains to be seen.

Qualitative Characteristics

Accounting information should possess **qualitative characteristics** to be useful in decision making. This criterion is difficult to apply. The usefulness of accounting information in a given instance depends not only on information characteristics but also on the capabilities of the decision makers and their professional advisers. Accountants cannot specify who the decision makers are, their characteristics, the decisions to be made, or the methods chosen to make the decisions. Therefore, they direct their attention to the characteristics of accounting information. Note the FASB's graphic summarization of the qualities accountants consider in Illustration 5.5.[10]

Relevance

To have **relevance,** information must be pertinent to or affect a decision. The information must make a difference to someone who does not already have it. Relevant information makes a difference in a decision either by affecting users' predictions of outcomes of past, present, or future events or by confirming or correcting expectations. Note that information need not be a prediction to be useful in developing, confirming, or altering expectations. Expectations are commonly based on the present or past. For example, any attempt to predict future earnings of a company would quite likely start with a review of present and past earnings. Although information that merely confirms prior expectations may be less useful, it is still relevant because it reduces uncertainty.

Critics have alleged that certain types of accounting information lack relevance. For example, some argue that a cost of $1 million paid for a tract of land 40 years ago and reported in the current balance sheet at that amount is irrelevant (except for possible tax implications) to users for decision making today. Such criticism has encouraged research into the types of information relevant to users. Some suggest using a different valuation basis, such as current cost, in reporting such assets.

Predictive Value and Feedback Value Since actions taken now can affect only future events, information is obviously relevant when it possesses **predictive value,** or improves users' abilities to predict outcomes of events. Information that reveals the relative success of users in predicting outcomes possesses **feedback value.** Feedback reports on past activities and can make a difference in decision making by (1) reducing uncertainty in a situation, (2) refuting or confirming prior expectations, and (3) providing a basis for further predictions. For example, a report on the first quarter's earnings of a company reduces the uncertainty surrounding the amount of such earnings, confirms or refutes the predicted amount of such earnings, and provides a possible basis on which to predict earnings for the full year. Remember that although accounting information may possess predictive

---

[9] Ibid., p. i.

[10] FASB, *Statement of Financial Accounting Concepts No. 2*, p. 15.

ILLUSTRATION 5.5 A Hierarchy of Accounting Qualities

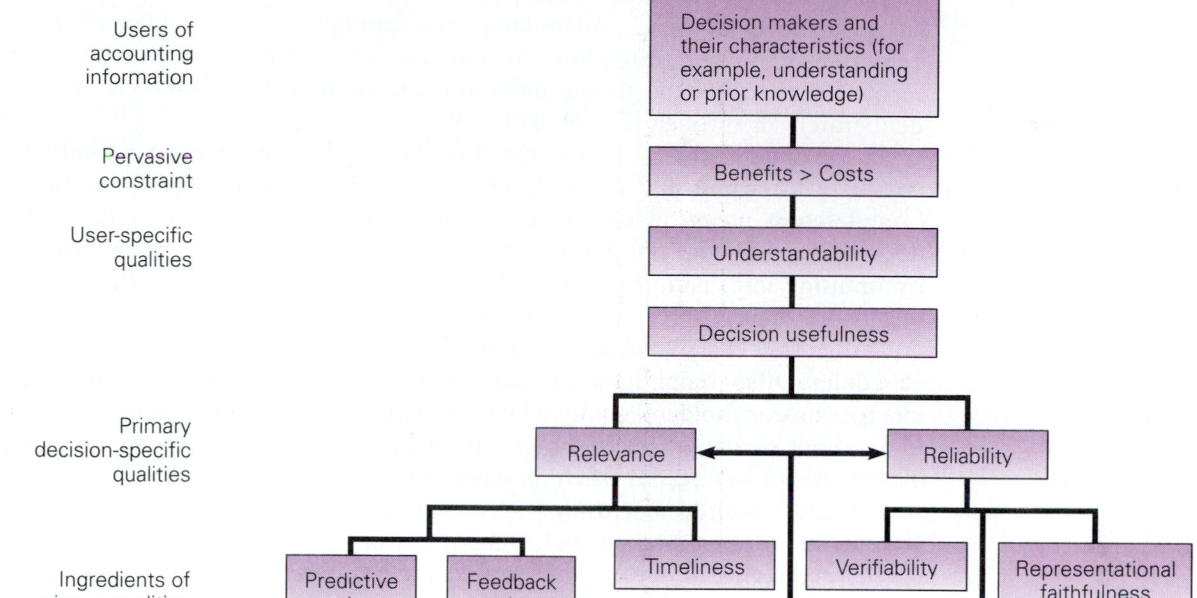

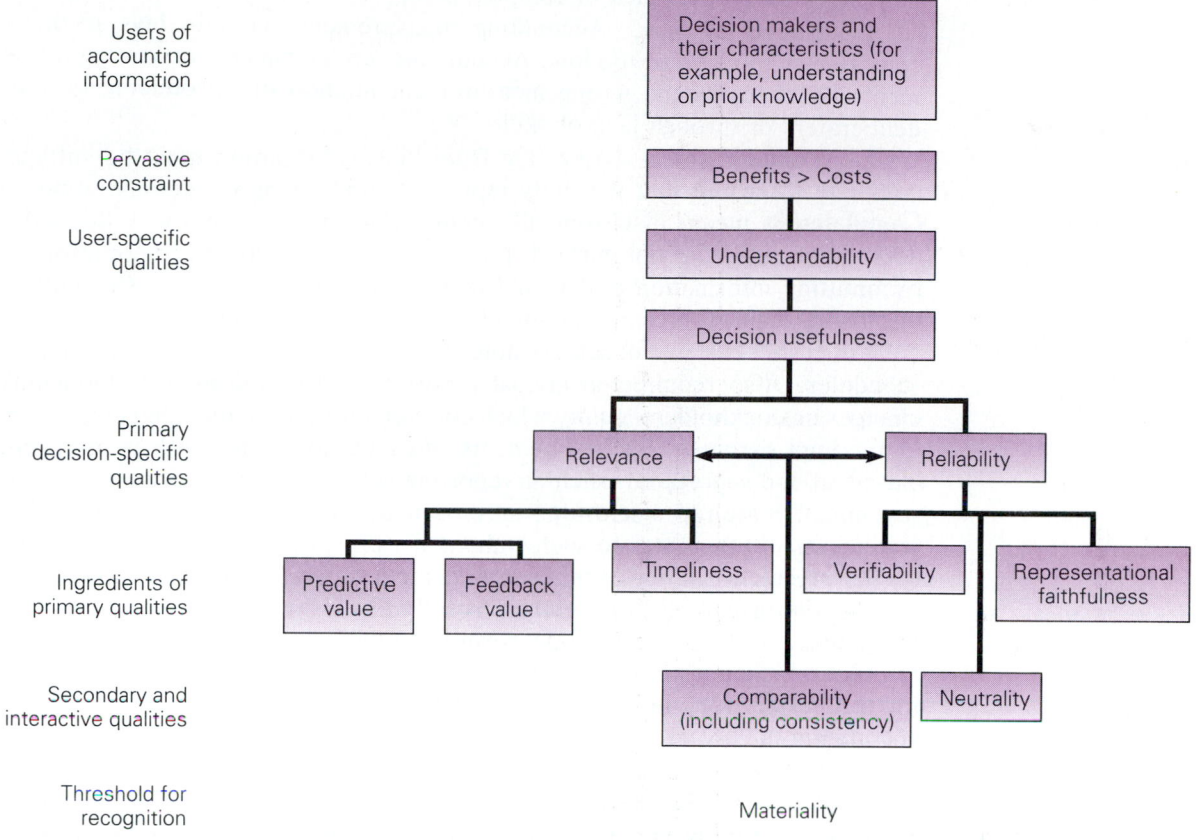

value, it does not consist of predictions. Making predictions is a function performed by the decision maker, not the accountant.

TIMELINESS **Timeliness** requires accountants to provide accounting information at a time when it may be considered in reaching a decision. Utility of information decreases with age—to know what the net income for 1997 was in early 1998 is much more useful than receiving this information a year later. If information is to be of any value in decision making, it must be available before the decision is made. If not, the information is of little value. In determining what constitutes timely information, accountants consider the other qualitative characteristics and the cost of gathering information. For example, a timely estimate for uncollectible accounts may be more valuable than a later, verified actual amount. Timeliness alone cannot make information relevant, but potentially relevant information can be rendered irrelevant by a lack of timeliness.

Reliability

In addition to being relevant, information must be reliable to be useful. Information has **reliability** when it faithfully depicts for users what it purports to represent. Thus, accounting information is reliable if users can depend on it to reflect the underlying economic activities of the organization. The reliability of information depends on its representational faithfulness, verifiability, and neutrality. The information must also be complete and free of bias.

REPRESENTATIONAL FAITHFULNESS To gain insight into this quality, consider a map. When it shows roads and bridges where roads and bridges actually exist, a map possesses representational faithfulness. A correspondence exists between what is on the map and what is present physically. Similarly, **representational**

faithfulness exists when accounting statements on economic activity correspond to the actual underlying activity. Where there is no correspondence, the cause may be (1) bias or (2) lack of completeness.

1. **Effects of bias.** Accounting measurements contain **bias** if they are consistently too high or too low. Accountants create bias in accounting measurements by choosing the wrong measurement method or introducing bias either deliberately or through lack of skill.

2. **Completeness.** To be free from bias, information must be sufficiently complete to ensure that it validly represents underlying events and conditions. **Completeness** means disclosing all significant information in a way that aids understanding and does not mislead. Firms can reduce the relevance of information by omitting information that would make a difference to users. Currently, full disclosure requires presentation of a balance sheet, an income statement, a statement of cash flows, and necessary notes to the financial statements and supporting schedules. Also required in annual reports of corporations are statements of changes in stockholders' equity which contain information included in a statement of retained earnings. Such statements must be complete, with items properly classified and segregated (such as reporting sales revenue separately from other revenues). Required disclosures may be made in (1) the body of the financial statements, (2) the notes to such statements, (3) special communications, and/or (4) the president's letter or other management reports in the annual report.

Another aspect of completeness is fully disclosing all changes in accounting principles and their effects.[11] Disclosure should include unusual activities (loans to officers), changes in expectations (losses on inventory), depreciation expense for the period, long-term obligations entered into that are not recorded by the accountant (a 20-year lease on a building), new arrangements with certain groups (pension and profit-sharing plans for employees), and significant events that occur after the date of the statements (loss of a major customer). Firms must also disclose accounting policies (major principles and their manner of application) followed in preparing the financial statements.[12] Because of its emphasis on disclosure, we often call this aspect of reliability the *full disclosure principle*.

Verifiability Financial information has **verifiability** when independent measurers can substantially duplicate it by using the same measurement methods. Verifiability eliminates measurer bias, rather than measurement method bias. The requirement that financial information be based on objective evidence arises from the demonstrated needs of users for reliable, unbiased financial information. Unbiased information is especially necessary when parties with opposing interests (credit seekers and credit grantors) rely on the same information. If the information is verifiable, this enhances the reliability of information.

Financial information is never free of subjective opinion and judgment; it always possesses varying degrees of verifiability. Canceled checks and invoices support some measurements. Accountants can never verify other measurements, such as periodic depreciation charges, because of their very nature. Thus, financial information in many instances is verifiable only in that it represents a consensus of what other accountants would report if they followed the same procedures.

Neutrality **Neutrality** means that the accounting information should be free of measurement method bias. The primary concern should be relevance and reliability of the information that results from application of the principle, not the effect that the principle may have on a particular interest. Nonneutral accounting information favors one set of interested parties over others. For example, a particular

---

[11] APB, *APB Opinion No. 20,* "Accounting Changes" (New York: AICPA, July 1971).

[12] APB, *APB Opinion No. 22,* "Disclosure of Accounting Policies" (New York: AICPA, April 1972).

form of measurement might favor stockholders over creditors, or vice versa. "To be neutral, accounting information must report economic activity as faithfully as possible, without coloring the image it communicates for the purpose of influencing behavior in *some particular direction*."[13] Accounting standards are not like tax regulations that deliberately foster or restrain certain types of activity. Verifiability seeks to eliminate measurer bias; neutrality seeks to eliminate measurement method bias.

Comparability (and Consistency)

When **comparability** exists, reported differences and similarities in financial information are real and not the result of differing accounting treatments. Comparable information reveals relative strengths and weaknesses in a single company through time and between two or more companies at the same time.

Consistency requires that a company use the same accounting principles and reporting practices through time. Consistency leads to comparability of financial information for a single company through time. Comparability between companies is more difficult because they may account for the same activities in different ways. For example, Company B may use one method of depreciation, while Company C accounts for an identical asset in similar circumstances using another method. A high degree of intercompany comparability in accounting information does not exist unless accountants are required to account for the same activities in the same manner across companies and through time.

Pervasive Constraint and Threshold for Recognition

As we show in Illustration 5.5, accountants must consider one pervasive constraint and one threshold for recognition in providing useful information. First, the benefits secured from the information must be greater than the costs of providing that information. Second, only material items need be disclosed and accounted for strictly in accordance with generally accepted accounting principles (GAAP). We discussed cost-benefit and materiality earlier in the chapter.

The Basic Elements of Financial Statements

Thus far we have discussed objectives of financial reporting and qualitative characteristics of accounting information. A third important task in developing a conceptual framework for any discipline is identifying and defining its basic elements. The FASB identified and defined the basic elements of financial statements in *Concepts Statement No. 3*. Later, *Concepts Statement No. 6* revised some of the definitions. We defined most of the terms earlier in this text in a less technical way; the more technical definitions follow. (These items are not repeated in this chapter's New Terms.)

Assets are probable future economic benefits obtained or controlled by a particular entity as a result of past transactions or events.

Liabilities are probable future sacrifices of economic benefits arising from present obligations of a particular entity to transfer assets or provide services to other entities in the future as a result of past transactions or events.

Equity or net assets is the residual interest in the assets of an entity that remains after deducting its liabilities. In a business enterprise, the equity is the ownership interest. In a not-for-profit organization, which has no ownership interest in the same sense as a business enterprise, net assets is divided into three classes based on the presence or absence of donor-imposed restrictions—permanently restricted, temporarily restricted, and unrestricted net assets.

Comprehensive income is the change in equity of a business enterprise during a period from transactions and other events and circumstances from nonowner sources. It

[13] FASB, *Statement of Financial Accounting Concepts No. 2*, par. 100.

includes all changes in equity during a period except those resulting from investments by owners and distributions to owners.

Revenues are inflows or other enhancements of assets of any entity or settlements of its liabilities (or a combination of both) from delivering or producing goods, rendering services, or other activities that constitute the entity's ongoing major or central operations.

Expenses are outflows or other using up of assets or incurrences of liabilities (or a combination of both) from delivering or producing goods, rendering services, or carrying out other activities that constitute the entity's ongoing major or central operations.

Gains are increases in equity (net assets) from peripheral or incidental transactions of an entity and from all other transactions and other events and circumstances affecting the entity except those that result from revenues or investments by owners.

Losses are decreases in equity (net assets) from peripheral or incidental transactions of an entity and from all other transactions and other events and circumstances affecting the entity except those that result from expenses or distributions to owners.

Investments by owners are increases in equity of a particular business enterprise resulting from transfers to it from other entities of something valuable to obtain or increase ownership interests (or equity) in it. Assets are most commonly received as investments by owners, but that which is received may also include services or satisfaction or conversion of liabilities of the enterprise.

Distributions to owners are decreases in equity of a particular business enterprise resulting from transferring assets, rendering services, or incurring liabilities by the enterprise to owners. Distributions to owners decrease ownership interest (or equity) in an enterprise.[14]

An Accounting Perspective

Business Insight Accountants record expenditures on physical resources such as land, buildings, and equipment that benefit future periods as assets. However, they expense expenditures on human resources for hiring and training that benefit future periods. Also, when a computer is dropped and destroyed, accountants record a loss. However, when the president of the company dies, they record no loss. Should the accounting model be changed regarding the accounting for human resources?

Note the requirement that assets and liabilities be based on past transactions normally rules out the recording of contracts that are mutual promises to do something, such as entering into an employment contract with an officer. For a similar reason, the accountant refuses to record an asset and a liability when a contract is signed whereby the entity agrees to purchase a certain amount of a product over a future period.

Recognition and Measurement in Financial Statements

In December 1984, the FASB issued *Statement of Financial Accounting Concepts No. 5,* "Recognition and Measurement in Financial Statements of Business Enterprises," describing recognition criteria and providing guidance for the timing and nature of information included in financial statements.[15] The recognition criteria established in the *Statement* are fairly consistent with those used in current practice. The *Statement* indicates, however, that when information more useful than

---

[14] FASB, *Statement of Financial Accounting Concepts No. 6.*

[15] FASB, *Statement of Financial Accounting Concepts No. 5,* "Recognition and Measurement in Financial Statements of Business Enterprises" (Stamford, Conn., 1984). Copyright © by the Financial Accounting Standards Board, High Ridge Park, Stamford, Connecticut 06905, U.S.A. Copies of the complete document are available from the FASB. (In case you are wondering why we do not mention *Statement of Financial Accounting Concepts No. 4,* it pertains to accounting for not-for-profit organizations and is, therefore, not relevant to this text.)

AN ETHICAL PERSPECTIVE

Maplehurst Company

Maplehurst Company manufactures large spinning machines for the textile industry. The company had purchased $100,000 of small hand tools to use in its business. The company's accountant recorded the tools in an asset account and was going to write them off over 20 years. Management wanted to write these tools off as an expense of this year because revenues this year had been abnormally high and were expected to be lower in the future. Management's goal was to smooth out income rather than showing sharp increases and decreases. When told by the accountant that $100,000 was a material item that must be accounted for in a theoretically correct manner, management decided to consider the tools as consisting of 10 groups, each having a cost of $10,000. Since amounts under $20,000 are considered immaterial for this company, all of the tools could then be charged to expense this year.

The accountant is concerned about this treatment. She doubts that she could successfully defend management's position if the auditors challenge the expensing of these items.

currently reported information is available at a reasonable cost, it should be included in financial statements.

THE INFORMATION NEEDS OF INVESTORS AND CREDITORS

Objective 5
Describe the information needs of investors and creditors.

In 1991 the Board of Directors of the American Institute of Certified Public Accountants (AICPA) appointed The AICPA Special Committee on Financial Reporting to address increasing concerns about the relevance and usefulness of financial reporting. The committee's specific charge was "to recommend (1) the nature and extent of information that should be made available to others by management and (2) the extent to which auditors should report on the various elements of that information." Before making recommendations, the committee decided to research and identify the information needs of investors and creditors. In November 1993 the committee issued a report, *The Information Needs of Investors and Creditors*.[16] As of this writing (early 1994), the committee had not made any recommendations for changes that are responsive to its research on users' needs. The committee's recommendations were scheduled for June 1994.

The committee is not a standard-setting body. However, its ultimate recommendations are likely to affect financial accounting theory and practice in the future by influencing the output of the Financial Accounting Standards Board.

The committee examined the published research of others and the types of information included in financial analysts' reports. It also held meetings with portfolio managers, analysts, bankers, certain knowledgeable committees of financial accounting policy organizations, and investors and creditors.

The committee's findings regarding user needs (quoted from the report) were as follows:

> **Value information:** Users oppose replacing the current historical cost-based accounting model with a fair value accounting model. However, they view fair value information as useful for particular types of assets and liabilities and in certain types of industries.
>
> **Disaggregated information:** Both investors and creditors place a high value on segment reporting and believe that current disaggregated disclosures generally do not provide adequate information to help them predict an entity's future earnings and cash flows. They also want segment information on a quarterly basis.

[16] The AICPA Special Committee on Financial Reporting, *The Information Needs of Investors and Creditors*, "A Report on the AICPA Special Committee's Study of the Information Needs of Today's Users of Financial Reporting," November 1993, Copyright © 1993 by American Institute of Certified Public Accountants, Inc., New York, NY (16 pp.).

Core earnings: Users want information about the portion of a company's reported earnings that is stable or recurring and that provides a basis for estimating sustainable earnings.

Estimates, assumptions, and off-balance-sheet risks: Users want companies to disclose information about the estimates and assumptions used to determine material asset and liability amounts. They also want more qualitative and quantitative information about the risks associated with financial instruments and off-balance-sheet financing arrangements.

Nonfinancial business information: Users need to understand the relationship between the events and activities of a company and how those events and activities are reported in its financial statements. Nonfinancial business information serves the critical function of helping users understand that relationship as they evaluate a company's operations.

Forward-looking information: Investors and creditors need forward-looking information on which to base their own projections. But they do not expect management to provide projections or forecasts. They also want more information about operating opportunities and risks that are relatively near-term and relatively certain and quantifiable.

Consistency and comparability: Information about a company that is consistent over time is valued more highly than information that is comparable between two or more companies—but both are significant.

Credibility: Credibility of reporting is a serious problem. Investors, creditors and their advisors believe that the reports of many companies reflect the natural tendency of management to report information in the best possible light and to avoid reporting poor company performance.

The role of auditing: Users believe audited information has value because auditors provide independent assurance of the reliability of amounts reported and accompanying disclosures. They would like auditors to provide additional qualitative commentary in their reporting.[17]

The committee's recommendations will be responsive to the users' needs as identified by the committee's research. The Financial Accounting Standards Board will be aware of the recommendations and will probably be influenced by them in future deliberations.

Summary of Significant Accounting Policies

Objective 6
Discuss the nature of a company's summary of significant accounting policies in its annual report.

As part of their annual reports, companies include summaries of significant accounting policies. These policies assist users in interpreting the financial statements. To a large extent, accounting theory determines the nature of these policies. Companies must follow generally accepted accounting principles in preparing their financial statements.

The accounting policies of 3M Corporation, one of the world's leading manufacturers, as contained in its 1992 annual report follow. After each, the chapter of this text where we discuss that particular policy is in parentheses. The only policies not covered in this text are the fifth and seventh. While a few of the items have already been covered, the remainder offer a preview of the concepts explained in later chapters.

Accounting Policies

Consolidation: All significant subsidiaries are consolidated. Unconsolidated subsidiaries and affiliates are included on the equity basis. Certain Balance Sheet amounts for 1991 have been reclassified to conform to the 1992 presentation. (Chapter 14)

Cash and cash equivalents: Cash and cash equivalents consist of cash and temporary investments with maturities of three months or less when purchased. (Chapter 8)

---

[17] Ibid., pp. 4, 5.

Other securities: Other securities consist of marketable securities and interest-bearing bank deposits with varied maturity dates. These securities are employed in the company's banking, captive insurance and cash management operations. The securities are stated at cost, which approximates fair value. (Chapter 14)

Inventories: Inventories are stated at lower of cost or market, with cost generally determined on a first-in, first-out basis. (Chapter 7)

Investments: Investments primarily include assets from captive insurance and banking operations and from venture capital investments. These investments are stated at cost, which approximates fair value.

Other assets: Other assets include goodwill, patents, other intangibles, deferred taxes, and other noncurrent assets. Goodwill is generally amortized on a straight-line basis over 10 years. Other intangible items are amortized on a straight-line basis over their estimated economic lives. (Chapter 11)

Deferred income taxes: Deferred income taxes arise from differences in basis for tax and financial-reporting purposes.

Revenue recognition: Revenue is recognized upon shipment of goods to customers and upon performance of services. (Chapter 5)

Depreciation: Depreciation of property, plant and equipment is generally computed on a straight-line basis over the estimated useful lives of these assets. (Chapters 3 and 10)

Research and development: Research and development costs are charged to operations as incurred and totaled $1.007 billion in 1992, $914 million in 1991 and $865 million in 1990. (Chapter 5)

Foreign currency translation: Local currencies are generally considered the functional currencies outside the United States, except in countries with highly inflationary economies. Assets and liabilities are translated at year-end exchange rates for operations in local currency environments. Income and expense items are translated at average rates of exchange prevailing during the year. Translation adjustments are recorded as a component of stockholders' equity.

For operations in countries with highly inflationary economies, certain financial statement amounts are translated at historical exchange rates, with all other assets and liabilities translated at year-end exchange rates. These translation adjustments are reflected in the results of operations. They increased net income by $10 million in 1992, and reduced net income by $6 million in 1991 and $31 million in 1990. (Appendix to Chapter 14)

As you proceed through the remaining chapters, you can see the accounting theories introduced in this chapter being applied. In Chapter 6, for instance, we discuss why sales revenue is recognized and recorded only after goods have been delivered to the customer. So far, we have used service companies to illustrate accounting techniques. Chapter 6 introduces merchandising operations. Merchandising companies, such as clothing stores, buy goods in their finished form and sell them to customers.

Understanding the Learning Objectives

Objective 1
Identify and discuss the underlying assumptions or concepts of accounting.

- The major underlying assumptions or concepts of accounting are (1) business entity, (2) going concern (continuity), (3) money measurement, (4) stable dollar, and (5) periodicity.
- Other basic accounting concepts that affect the accounting for entities are (1) general-purpose financial statements, (2) substance over form, (3) consistency, (4) double entry, and (5) articulation.

Objective 2
Identify and discuss the major principles of accounting.

- The major principles include exchange-price (or cost), matching, revenue recognition, expense recognition, gain and loss recognition, and full disclosure. Major exceptions to the realization principle include cash collection as point of revenue recognition, installment basis of revenue recognition, the percentage-of-completion method of recognizing revenue on long-term construction projects, and revenue recognition at completion of production.

Objective 3
Identify and discuss the modifying conventions (or constraints) of accounting.

- Modifying conventions include cost-benefit, materiality, and conservatism.

Objective 4
Describe the conceptual framework project of the Financial Accounting Standards Board.

- The FASB has defined the objectives of financial reporting, qualitative characteristics of accounting information, and elements of financial statements.
- Financial reporting objectives are the broad overriding goals sought by accountants engaging in financial reporting.
- Qualitative characteristics are those that accounting information should possess to be useful in decision making. The two primary qualitative characteristics are relevance and reliability. Another qualitative characteristic is comparability.
- Pervasive constraints include cost-benefit analysis and materiality.
- The FASB has identified and defined the basic elements of financial statements.
- The FASB has also described revenue recognition criteria and provided guidance as to the timing and nature of information to be included in financial statements.

Objective 5
Describe the information needs of investors and creditors.

- A committee of the American Institute of Certified Public Accountants was assigned to address increasing concerns about the relevance and usefulness of financial reporting.
- As of this writing (early 1994) the committee had researched and identified the information needs of investors and creditors.
- The committee's final recommendations were scheduled for June 1994.

Objective 6
Discuss the nature and content of a company's summary of significant accounting policies in its annual report.

- These policies aid users in interpreting the financial statements.
- To a large extent, accounting theory determines the nature of those policies.

Demonstration Problem

For each of the following transactions or circumstances and the entries made, state which, if any, of the assumptions, concepts, principles, or modifying conventions of accounting have been violated. For each violation, give the entry to correct the improper accounting assuming the books have not been closed.

During the year, Dorsey Company did the following:

1. Had its buildings appraised. They were found to have a market value of $410,000, although their book value was only $380,000. The accountant debited the Buildings and Accumulated Depreciation—Buildings accounts for $15,000 each and credited Paid-in Capital—From Appreciation. No separate mention was made of this action in the financial statements.
2. Purchased new electric pencil sharpeners for its offices at a total cost of $60. These pencil sharpeners were recorded as assets and are being depreciated over five years.
3. Produced agricultural products at a cost of $26,000. These costs were charged to expense when the products were harvested. The products were set up in inventory at their net market value of $35,000, and the Farm Revenues Earned account was credited for $35,000.

Solution to Demonstration Problem

1. The realization principle and the modifying convention of conservatism may have been violated. Such write-ups simply are not looked on with favor in accounting. To correct the situation, the entry made needs to be reversed:

Paid-in Capital—From Appreciation	30,000	
Buildings		15,000
Accumulated Depreciation—Buildings		15,000

2. Theoretically, no violations occurred, but the cost of compiling insignificant information could be considered a violation of acceptable accounting practice. As a practical matter, the $60 could have been expensed on materiality grounds.
3. No violations occurred. The procedures followed are considered acceptable for farm products that are interchangeable and readily marketable. No correcting entry is needed, provided due allowance has been made for the costs to be incurred in delivering the products to the market.

New Terms

Accounting theory "A set of basic concepts and assumptions and related principles that explain and guide the accountant's actions in identifying, measuring, and communicating economic information." *173*

Bias Exists when accounting measurements are consistently too high or too low. *190*

Business entity concept The specific unit for which accounting information is gathered. Business entities have a separate existence from owners, creditors, employees, customers, other interested parties, and other businesses. *174*

Comparability A qualitative characteristic of accounting information; when information is comparable, it reveals differences and similarities that are real and are not the result of differing accounting treatments. *191*

Completed-contract method A method of recognizing revenue on long-term projects under which no revenue is recognized until the period in which the project is completed; similar to recognizing revenue upon the completion of a sale. *181*

Completeness A qualitative characteristic of accounting information; requires disclosure of all significant information in a way that aids understanding and does not mislead; sometimes called the *full disclosure principle*. *190*

Conservatism Being cautious or prudent and making sure that net assets and net income are not overstated. *185*

Consistency Requires a company to use the same accounting principles and reporting practices through time. *176, 191*

Cost-benefit consideration Determining whether benefits of including information in financial statements exceed costs. *185*

Cost principle See Exchange-price principle.

Earning principle The requirement that revenue be substantially earned before it is recognized (recorded). *179*

Exchange-price (or cost) principle Transfers of resources are recorded at prices agreed on by the parties at the time of the exchange. *178*

Expense recognition principle Expenses should be recognized as they are incurred to produce revenues. *183*

Feedback value A qualitative characteristic that information has when it reveals the relative success of users in predicting outcomes. *188*

Financial reporting objectives The broad overriding goals sought by accountants engaging in financial reporting. *187*

Full disclosure principle Information important enough to influence the decisions of an informed user of the financial statements should be disclosed. *184*

Gain and loss recognition principle Gains may be recorded only when realized, but losses should be recorded when they first become evident. *183*

Gains Typically result from the sale of long-term assets for more than their book value. *183*

Going-concern (continuity) assumption The assumption that an entity will continue to operate indefinitely unless strong evidence exists that the entity will terminate. *174*

Historical cost The amount paid, or the fair market value of a liability incurred or other resources surrendered, to acquire an asset and place it in a condition and position for its intended use. *179*

Installment basis A revenue recognition procedure in which the percentage of total gross margin recognized in a period on an installment sale is equal to the percentage of total cash from the sale that is received in that period. *180*

Liquidation Terminating a business by ceasing business operations and selling off its assets. *174*

Losses Asset expirations that are usually involuntary and do not create revenues. *184*

Matching principle The principle that net income of a period is determined by associating or relating revenues earned in a period with expenses incurred to generate those revenues. *179*

Materiality A modifying convention that allows the accountant to deal with immaterial (unimportant) items in an expedient but theoretically incorrect manner; also a qualitative characteristic specifying that financial accounting report only information significant enough to influence decisions or evaluations. *185*

Modifying conventions Customs emerging from accounting practice that alter the results obtained from a strict application of accounting principles; conservatism is an example. *185*

Money measurement Use of a monetary unit of measurement, such as the dollar, instead of physical or other units of measurement—feet, inches, grams, and so on. *174*

Neutrality A qualitative characteristic that requires accounting information to be free of measurement method bias. *190*

Percentage-of-completion method A method of recognizing revenue based on the estimated stage of completion of a long-term project. The stage of completion is measured by comparing actual costs incurred in a period with total estimated costs to be incurred in all periods. *181*

Period costs Costs that cannot be traced to specific products and are expensed in the period incurred. *183*

Periodicity (time periods) assumption An assumption of the accountant that an entity's life can be divided into time periods for reporting its economic activities. *175*

Predictive value A qualitative characteristic that information has when it improves users' abilities to predict outcomes of events. *188*

Product costs Costs incurred in the acquisition or manufacture of goods. Product costs are accounted for as if they were attached to the goods, with the result that they are charged to expense when the goods are sold. *183*

Production basis A method of revenue recognition used in limited circumstances that recognizes revenue at the time of completion of production or extraction. *182*

Qualitative characteristics Characteristics that accounting information should possess to be useful in decision making. *188*

Realization principle A principle that directs that revenue is recognized only after the seller acquires the right to receive payment from the buyer. *179*

Relevance A qualitative characteristic requiring that information be pertinent to or affect a decision. *188*

Reliability A qualitative characteristic requiring that information faithfully depict for users what it purports to represent. *189*

Representational faithfulness A qualitative characteristic requiring that accounting statements on economic activity correspond to the actual underlying activity. *189*

Revenue recognition principle The principle that revenues should be earned and realized before they are recognized (recorded). *179*

Stable dollar assumption An assumption that the dollar is a reasonably stable unit of measurement. *175*

Timeliness A qualitative characteristic requiring that accounting information be provided at a time when it may be considered before making a decision. *189*

Verifiability A qualitative characteristic of accounting information; information is verifiable when it can be substantially duplicated by independent measurers using the same measurement methods. *190*

SELF-TEST

TRUE-FALSE

Indicate whether each of the following statements is true or false.

1. The business entity concept assumes that each business has an existence separate from all parties except its owners.
2. When the substance of a transaction differs from its legal form, the accountant should record the economic substance.
3. The matching principle is fundamental to the accrual basis of accounting.
4. Exceptions to the realization principle include the installment basis of revenue recognition for sales revenue and the completed-contract method for long-term construction projects.
5. Immaterial items do not have to be recorded at all.
6. The conceptual framework project resulted in identifying two primary qualitative characteristics that accounting information should possess—relevance and reliability.

MULTIPLE-CHOICE

Select the best answer for each of the following questions.

1. The underlying assumptions of accounting include all the following except:
   - **a.** Business entity.
   - **b.** Going concern.
   - **c.** Matching.
   - **d.** Money measurement and periodicity.
2. The concept that requires all companies to use the same accounting practices and reporting practices through time is:
   - **a.** Substance over form.
   - **b.** Consistency.
   - **c.** Articulation.
   - **d.** None of the above.
3. Which of the following statements is false regarding the revenue recognition principle?
   - **a.** Revenue must be substantially earned before it is recognized.
   - **b.** The accountant usually recognizes revenue before the seller acquires the right to receive payment from the buyer.
   - **c.** Some small companies use the cash basis of accounting.
   - **d.** Under the installment basis, the gross margin recognized in a period is equal to the amount of cash received from installment sales times the gross margin percentage for the year of sale.

4. Assume the following facts regarding the construction of a bridge:

Construction costs this period	$ 3,000,000
Total estimated construction costs . . .	10,000,000
Total sales price	15,000,000

The revenue that should be recognized this period is:
   a. $3,000,000.
   b. $4,500,000.
   c. $5,000,000.
   d. $6,500,000.

5. Modifying conventions include all of the following except:
   a. Periodicity.
   b. Cost-benefit.
   c. Materiality.
   d. Conservatism.

6. Which of the following is not part of the conceptual framework project?
   a. Objectives of financial reporting.
   b. Quantitative characteristics.
   c. Qualitative characteristics.
   d. Basic elements of financial statements.

Now turn to page 207 to check your answers.

Questions

1. Name the assumptions underlying generally accepted accounting principles. Comment on the validity of the stable unit of measurement assumption during periods of high inflation.
2. Why does the accountant use the business entity concept?
3. When is the going-concern assumption not to be used?
4. What is meant by the term *accrual basis of accounting?* What is its alternative?
5. What does it mean to say that accountants record substance rather than form?
6. If a company changes an accounting principle because the change better meets the information needs of users, what disclosures must be made?
7. What is the exchange-price (or cost) principle? What is the significance of adhering to this principle?
8. What two requirements generally must be met before recognizing revenue in a period?
9. Under what circumstances, if any, is the receipt of cash an acceptable time to recognize revenue?
10. What two methods may be used in recognizing revenues on long-term construction contracts?
11. Define expense. What principles guide the recognition of expense?
12. How does an expense differ from a loss?
13. What is the full disclosure principle?
14. What role does cost-benefit play in financial reporting?
15. What is meant by the accounting term *conservatism?* How does it affect the amounts reported in the financial statements?
16. Does materiality relate only to the relative size of dollar amounts?
17. Identify the three major parts of the conceptual framework project.
18. What are the two primary qualitative characteristics?
19. **Real World Question** A recent annual report of the American Ship Building Company stated:

    Revenues, costs, and profits applicable to construction and conversion contracts are included in the consolidated statements of operations using the . . . percentage-of-completion accounting method. . . . The completed contract method was used for income tax reporting in the years this method was allowed.

    Why might the management of a company want to use two different methods for accounting and tax purposes?
20. **Real World Question** A recent annual report of Chevron Corporation stated:

    Environmental expenditures that relate to current or future revenues are expensed or capitalized as appropriate. Expenditures that relate to an existing condition caused by past operations, and do not contribute to current or future revenue generation, are expensed.

    Which principle of accounting is being followed by this policy?
21. The AICPA Special Committee on Financial Reporting issued a report that identified the information needs of investors and creditors. Based on the needs contained in that report, what recommendations would you expect the committee to include in its final report?
22. What is the purpose of including a "Summary of Significant Accounting Policies" in a company's annual report?

EXERCISES

Exercise 5–1
Match theory terms with definitions (L.O. 1–3)

Match the items in Column A with the proper descriptions in Column B.

Column A

1. Going concern (continuity).
2. Consistency.
3. Disclosure.
4. Periodicity.
5. Conservatism.
6. Stable dollar.
7. Matching.
8. Materiality.
9. Exchange-price.
10. Business entity.

Column B

a. An assumption relied on in the preparation of the primary financial statements that would be unreasonable when the inflation rate is high.
b. Concerned with relative dollar amounts.
c. The usual basis for the recording of assets.
d. Required if the accounting treatment differs from that previously used for a particular item.
e. An assumption that would be unreasonable to use in reporting on a firm that had become insolvent.
f. None of these.
g. Requires a company to use the same accounting procedures and practices through time.
h. An assumption that the life of an entity can be subdivided into time periods for reporting purposes.
i. Discourages undue optimism in measuring and reporting net assets and net income.
j. Requires separation of personal from business activities in the recording and reporting processes.

Exercise 5–2
Compute net income under accrual basis and under installment basis (L.O. 2)

Parker Clothing Company sells its products on an installment sales basis. Data for 1997 and 1998 follow:

	1997	1998
Installment sales	$400,000	$480,000
Cost of goods sold on installment sales	280,000	360,000
Other expenses	60,000	80,000
Cash collected from 1997 sales	240,000	120,000
Cash collected from 1998 sales		320,000

a. Compute the net income for 1998, assuming use of the accrual (sales) basis of revenue recognition.
b. Compute the net income for 1998, assuming use of the installment basis of recognizing gross margin.

Exercise 5–3
Recognize revenue under percentage-of-completion method (L.O. 2)

A company has a contract to build a ship at a price of $600 million and an estimated cost of $400 million. In 1997, costs of $100 million were incurred. Under the percentage-of-completion method, how much revenue would be recognized in 1997? Revenue, $150.0 million

Exercise 5–4
Compute the effect on financial statements of incorrectly expensing an asset (L.O. 2)

A company follows a practice of expensing the premium on its fire insurance policy when the policy is paid. In 1997, the company charged to expense the $6,000 premium paid on a three-year policy covering the period July 1, 1997, to June 30, 2000. In 1994, a premium of $5,400 was charged to expense on the same policy for the period July 1, 1994, to June 30, 1997.

a. State the principle of accounting that was violated by this practice.
b. Compute the effects of this violation on the financial statements for the calendar year 1997.
c. State the basis on which the company's practice might be justified.

Exercise 5–5
Compute gross margin under GAAP and then as production is completed (L.O. 2)

Maryland Patio Umbrella Company produces umbrellas at a cost of $60 per unit that it sells for $90. The company has been very successful and sells all of the units it can produce. During 1997, the company manufactured 50,000 units, but (because of a transportation strike) sold and delivered only 40,000 units.

a. Compute the gross margin for 1997 following the realization principle. The cost of the units sold should be entitled "cost of goods sold" and treated as an expense.
b. Compute the gross margin for 1997, assuming the realization principle is ignored and revenue is recognized as production is completed.

Exercise 5–6
Match accounting qualities with proper descriptions (L.O. 4)

Match the descriptions in Column B with the accounting qualities in Column A. Use some descriptions more than once.

Column A: Accounting Qualities

1. Relevance.
2. Feedback value.
3. Decision makers.
4. Representational faithfulness.
5. Reliability.
6. Comparability.
7. Benefits exceed costs.
8. Predictive value.
9. Timeliness.
10. Decision usefulness.
11. Verifiability.
12. Understandability.
13. Neutrality.
14. Materiality.

Column B: Descriptions

a. Users of accounting information.
b. Pervasive constraint.
c. User-specific qualities.
d. Primary decision-specific qualities.
e. Ingredients of primary qualities.
f. Secondary and interactive qualities.
g. Threshold for recognition.

PROBLEMS

Problem 5–1
Answer multiple-choice questions regarding accounting theory (L.O. 1–3)

Select the best answer to each of the following questions:

1. The assumption that each business has an existence separate from its owners, creditors, employees, customers, other interested parties, and other businesses is the:
   a. Going-concern assumption.
   b. Business entity concept.
   c. Separate entity concept.
   d. Corporation concept.
2. Companies should use liquidation values to report assets if which of the following conditions exists?
   a. There are changes in the value of the dollar.
   b. The periodicity assumption is applied.
   c. The company is not a going concern and will be dissolved.
   d. The accrual basis of accounting is not used.
3. Assume that a company has paid for advertising and that the ad has already appeared. The company chose to report the item as prepaid advertising and includes it among the assets on the balance sheet. Previously, the company had always expensed expenditures such as this. This practice is a violation of:
   a. Generally accepted accounting principles.
   b. The matching concept.
   c. The consistency concept.
   d. All of the above.
4. Recording revenue only after the seller has obtained the right to receive payment from the buyer for merchandise sold or services performed is called the:
   a. Earning principle.
   b. Installment basis.
   c. Realization principle.
   d. Completed-contract method.
5. Assume that 2,000 ounces of gold were mined at a time when gold sold for $500 an ounce. The cost to extract the gold was $300 per ounce. Revenue was recognized under the production basis. The gold has not yet been sold. The entry to record the extraction of the gold would include:
   a. A debit to Inventory of Gold for $600,000.
   b. A credit to Revenue from Extraction of Gold of $1,000,000.
   c. A debit to Cash of $1,000,000.
   d. A credit to Inventory of Gold of $1,000,000.

Problem 5–2
Compute income assuming revenues are recognized at time of sale and then assuming installment method is used (L.O. 2)

Martinez Video, Inc., sells video recorders under terms calling for a small down payment and monthly payments spread over three years. Following are data for the first three years of the company's operations:

	1995	1996	1997
Gross margin rate	30%	40%	50%
Cash collected in 1997:			
From sales in	$216,000		
From sales in		$288,000	
From sales in			$450,000

Total sales for 1997 were $1,200,000, while general and selling expenses amounted to $400,000.

Required

a. Compute net income for 1997, assuming revenues are recognized at the time of sale.

b. Compute net income for 1997, using the installment method of accounting for sales and gross margin.

Problem 5–3
Compute income under completed-contract and percentage-of-completion methods (L.O. 2)

The following data relate to Quality Construction Company's long-term construction projects for the year 1997:

	Completed Projects	Incomplete Projects
Contract price	$20,000,000	$100,000,000
Costs incurred prior to 1997	3,700,000	16,000,000
Costs incurred in 1997	11,100,000	32,000,000
Estimated costs to be incurred in future years	–0–	32,000,000

General and administrative expenses incurred in 1997 amounted to $3 million, none of which is to be considered a construction cost.

Required

a. Compute net income for 1997 under the completed-contract method.

b. Compute net income for 1997 under the percentage-of-completion method.

Problem 5–4
Match principles, assumptions, or concepts with certain accounting procedures followed (L.O. 1–3)

For each of the following numbered items, state the letter or letters of the principle(s), assumption(s), or concept(s) used to justify the accounting procedure followed. The accounting procedures are all correct.

a—Business entity.
b—Conservatism.
c—Earning principle of revenue recognition.
d—Going concern (continuity).
e—Exchange-price principle.
f—Matching principle.
g—Period cost (or principle of immediate recognition of expense).
h—Realization principle.
i—Stable dollar assumption.

1. The estimated liability for federal income taxes was increased by $14,000 over the amount reported on the tax return to cover possible differences found by the Internal Revenue Service in determining the income taxes payable.
2. A truck purchased in January was reported at 80% of its cost even though its market value at year-end was only 70% of its cost.
3. The collection of $50,000 of cash for services to be performed next year was reported as a current liability.
4. The president's salary was treated as an expense of the year even though he spent most of his time planning the next two years' activities.
5. No entry was made to record the company's receipt of an offer of $600,000 for land carried in its accounts at $435,000.
6. A supply of printed stationery, checks, and invoices with a cost of $8,800 was treated as a current asset at year-end even though it had no value to others.

7. A tract of land acquired for $196,000 was recorded at that price even though it was appraised at $230,000, and the company would have been willing to pay that amount.
8. The company paid and charged to expense the $5,400 paid to Craig Nelson for rent of a truck owned by him. Craig Nelson is the sole stockholder of the company.

Problem 5–5
Answer matching question regarding the conceptual framework project
(L.O. 4)

Match the descriptions in Column B with the proper terms in Column A.

Column A	Column B
1. Financial reporting objectives.	a. Information is free of measurement method bias.
2. Qualitative characteristics.	b. The benefits exceed the costs.
3. Relevance.	c. Relatively large items must be accounted for in a theoretically correct way.
4. Predictive value.	d. The information can be substantially duplicated by independent measurers using the same measurement methods.
5. Feedback value.	e. When information improves users' ability to predict outcomes of events.
6. Timeliness.	f. Broad overriding goals sought by accountants engaging in financial reporting.
7. Reliability.	g. When information is pertinent or bears on a decision.
8. Representational faithfulness.	h. The characteristics that accounting information should possess to be useful in decision making.
9. Verifiability.	i. Information that reveals the relative success of users in predicting outcomes.
10. Neutrality.	j. When accounting statements on economic activity correspond to the actual underlying activity.
11. Comparability.	k. When information is provided soon enough that it may be considered in decision making.
12. Consistency.	l. When information faithfully depicts for users what it purports to represent.
13. Cost-benefit.	m. Requires a company to use the same accounting principles and reporting practices through time.
14. Materiality.	n. When reported differences and similarities in information are real and not the result of differing accounting treatments.

ALTERNATE PROBLEMS

Problem 5–1A
Answer multiple-choice questions regarding accounting theory
(L.O. 1–3)

Select the best answer to each of the following questions:

1. A set of basic concepts and assumptions and related principles that explain and guide the accountant's actions in identifying, measuring, and communicating economic information is called:
   - **a.** Accounting theory.
   - **b.** Accounting rules.
   - **c.** Accrual basis.
   - **d.** Matching concept.
2. Which of the following statements is false?
   - **a.** Several separate legal entities properly may be considered to be one accounting entity.
   - **b.** The stable dollar assumption is used only when the dollar is absolutely stable.
   - **c.** Publicly held corporations generally prepare monthly financial statements for internal management and publish quarterly and annual financial statements for users outside the company.
   - **d.** Without the periodicity assumption, a business would have only one time period running from the inception of the business to its termination.
3. Which of the following statements is true?
   - **a.** When the substance of a transaction conflicts with the legal form of the transaction, the accountant should be guided by the legal form in recording the transaction.
   - **b.** The consistency concept prohibits a change in accounting principle even when such a change would better meet the information needs of financial statement users.
   - **c.** Under the double-entry approach, each transaction must be recorded with one debit and one credit of equal dollar amounts.

   - **d.** Special-purpose financial information for a specific decision, such as whether or not to purchase a new machine, is best obtained from the detailed accounting records rather than from the financial statements.

4. Which of the following statements is true?
   - **a.** All assets are carried indefinitely at their original costs in the financial statements.
   - **b.** Liabilities are measured in the cash to be paid or the value of services to be performed to satisfy the liabilities.
   - **c.** Accounting principles are derived by merely summarizing accounting practices used to date.
   - **d.** Accountants can easily measure all changes in assets and liabilities since they never involve estimates or calculations.
5. Which of the following statements is false?
   - **a.** The exchange-price principle is also called the cost principle.
   - **b.** The matching principle is closely related to the revenue recognition principle and the expense recognition principle.
   - **c.** The installment sales method recognizes revenue sooner than it would normally be recognized.
   - **d.** The percentage-of-completion method recognizes revenue sooner than the completed-contract method.

Problem 5–2A
Compute net income assuming revenues are recognized at time of sale and then assuming the installment basis is used
(L.O. 2)

Arizona Real Estate Sales Company sells lots in its development in Dry Creek Canyon under terms calling for small cash down payments with monthly installment payments spread over a few years. Following are data on the company's operations for its first three years:

	1995	1996	1997
Gross margin rate	45%	48%	50%
Cash collected in 1997 from sales of lots made in.	$640,000	$800,000	$960,000

The total selling price of the lots sold in 1997 was $3,200,000, while general and administrative expenses (which are not included in the costs used to determine gross margin) were $800,000.

Required

a. Compute net income for 1997 assuming revenue is recognized on the sale of a lot.

b. Compute net income for 1997 assuming use of the installment basis of accounting for sales and gross margin.

Problem 5–3A
Compute net income under completed-contract and percentage-of-completion methods
(L.O. 2)

The following contract prices and costs relate to all of Tampa Construction Company's long-term construction projects (in millions of dollars):

		Costs Incurred		
	Contract Price	Prior to 1997	In 1997	Costs to Be Incurred in Future Years
On projects completed in 1997 . . .	$ 46	$ 4	$36	$-0-
On incomplete projects.	144	24	48	48

General and administrative expenses for 1997 amounted to $1,800,000. Assume that the general and administrative expenses are not to be treated as a part of the construction cost.

Required

a. Compute net income for 1997 using the completed-contract method.

b. Compute net income for 1997 using the percentage-of-completion method.

Problem 5–4A
Indicate agreement or disagreement with accounting practices followed and comment
(L.O. 1–3)

In each of these circumstances, the accounting practices may be questioned. Indicate whether you agree or disagree with the accounting practice employed and state the assumptions, concepts, or principles that justify your position.

1. The salaries paid to the top officers of the company were charged to expense in the period in which they were incurred even though the officers spent over half of their time planning next year's activities.
2. No entry was made to record the belief that the market value of the land owned (carried in the accounts at $500,000) had increased.

3. The acquisition of a tract of land was recorded at the price paid for it of $500,000, even though the company would have been willing to pay $600,000.
4. A truck acquired at the beginning of the year was reported at year-end at 80% of its acquisition price even though its market value then was only 65% of its original acquisition price.

Problem 5–5A
Answer multiple-choice questions regarding the conceptual framework project (L.O. 4)

Select the best answer to each of the following questions:

1. In the conceptual framework project, how many financial reporting objectives were identified by the FASB?
   a. One.
   b. Two.
   c. Three.
   d. Four.
2. The two primary qualitative characteristics are:
   a. Predictive value and feedback value.
   b. Timeliness and verifiability.
   c. Comparability and neutrality.
   d. Relevance and reliability.
3. A pervasive constraint of accounting information is that:
   a. Benefits must exceed costs.
   b. The information must be timely.
   c. The information must be neutral.
   d. The information must be verifiable.
4. To be reliable, information must (identify the *incorrect* quality):
   a. Be verifiable.
   b. Be timely.
   c. Have representational faithfulness.
   d. Be neutral.
5. The *basic elements* of financial statements consist of:
   a. Terms and their definitions.
   b. The objectives of financial reporting.
   c. The qualitative characteristics.
   d. The new income statement format.

BEYOND THE NUMBERS—CRITICAL THINKING

Business Decision Case 5–1
Evaluate correctness of accounting practices and give reasons for conclusions (L.O. 1–3)

Jim Casey recently received his accounting degree from State University and went to work for a Big-Six CPA firm. After he had been with the firm for about six months, he was sent to the Essex Clothing Company to work on the audit. He was not very confident of his knowledge at this early point in his career. He noticed, however, that some of the company's transactions and events were recorded in a way that might be in violation of accounting theory and generally accepted accounting principles.

Required

Study each of the following facts to see if the auditors should challenge the financial accounting practices used or the intentions of management. Write your decisions and the reasoning behind your conclusions.

This problem can serve as an opportunity to apply accounting theory to situations with which you are not yet familiar and as a preview of future chapters. Some of the following situations relate to material you have already covered, and some situations relate to material to be covered in future chapters. After each item, we have given an indication of the chapter in which that item is discussed. You may research future chapters to find the correct answer. Alternatively, you could use your present knowledge of accounting theory to determine whether or not Casey should challenge each of the financial accounting practices used. Realize, however, that some generally accepted accounting practices were based on compromise and seem to differ with accounting theory as described in this chapter.

1. One of the senior members of management stated the company planned to replace all of the furniture next year. He said that the cash in the Accumulated Depreciation account woul l be used to pay for the furniture. (Ch. 3)

2. The company held the books open at the end of 1997 so they could record some early 1998 sales as 1997 revenue. The justification for this practice was that 1997 was not a good year for profits. (Ch. 3, 5, 6)
3. The company's buildings were appraised for insurance purposes. The appraised values were $10,000,000 higher than the book value. The accountant debited Buildings and credited Paid-in Capital from Appreciation for the difference. (Ch. 5)
4. The company recorded purchases of merchandise at the list price rather than the gross selling (invoice) price. (Ch. 6)
5. Goods shipped to the company from a supplier, FOB destination, were debited to Purchases. The goods were not included in ending inventory because the goods had not yet arrived. (Ch. 5, 6)
6. The company counted some items twice in taking the physical inventory at the end of the year. The person taking the inventory said he had forgotten to include some items in last year's physical inventory, and counting some items twice would make up for the items missed last year so that net income this year would be about correct. (Ch. 7)
7. The company switched from FIFO to LIFO in accounting for inventories. The preceding year it had switched from the weighted-average method to FIFO. The reason given for the most recent change was that federal income taxes would be lower. No indication of this switch was to appear in the financial statements. (Ch. 5, 7)
8. Since things were pretty hectic at year-end, the accountant made no effort to reconcile the bank account. His reason was that the bank probably had not made any errors. The bank balance was lower than the book balance, so the accountant debited Miscellaneous Expense and credited Cash for the difference. (Ch. 8)
9. When a customer failed to pay the amount due, the accountant debited Allowance for Uncollectible Accounts and credited Accounts Receivable. The amount of accounts written off in this manner was huge. (Ch. 9)
10. A completely depreciated machine was still being used. The accountant left the asset and its related accumulated depreciation on the books, stopped recording depreciation on the machine, and did not go back and correct earlier years' net income and reduce accumulated depreciation. (Ch. 10)
11. The accountant stated that even though research and development costs incurred to develop a new product would benefit future periods, these costs must be expensed as incurred. This year $200,000 of these costs were charged to expense. (Ch. 11)
12. An old truck was traded for a new truck. Since the trade-in value of the old truck was higher than its book value, a gain was recorded on the transaction. (Ch. 11)
13. The company paid for a franchise giving it the exclusive right to operate in a given geographical area for 60 years. The accountant is amortizing the asset over 60 years. (Ch. 11)
14. The company leases a building and has a nonrenewable lease that expires in 15 years. The company made some improvements to the building. Since the improvements will last 30 years, they are being written off over 30 years. (Ch. 11)

Annual Report Analysis 5–2
List "Summary of Significant Accounting Policies" for four real companies (L.O. 6)

Refer to the "Summary of Significant Accounting Policies" in the annual reports of The Coca-Cola Company, Maytag Corporation, The Limited, Inc., and John H. Harland Company in the annual report booklet. For each company, list the policies discussed. Then place a check (✔) by the topics common to at least two of the companies. For each of the common policies, explain in writing what the company is trying to communicate.

Ethics—A Writing Experience 5–3
Answer questions regarding ethics case

Refer to the item "An Ethical Perspective" on page 193. Write out the answers to the following questions:

Is management being ethical in this situation? Explain.

Is the accountant correct in believing that management's position could not be successfully defended? Explain.

What would you do if you were the accountant? Describe in detail.

Group Project 5–4
Library project concerning annual reports

In teams of two or three students, go to the library to locate one company's annual report for the most recent year. (The university may have received the annual reports of companies in either published form, microfiche form, or a computer readable format.) Examine the "Summary of Accounting Policies," which is part of the "Notes to Financial Statements" section immediately following the financial statements. As a team, write a memorandum to the instructor detailing the significant accounting policies of the company. The heading of the memorandum should contain the date, to whom it is written, from whom, and the subject matter.

Answers to Self-Test

True-False

1. **False.** The business entity concept assumes that each business has an existence separate from its owners, creditors, employees, customers, other interested parties, and other businesses.
2. **True.** Accountants should be guided by the economic substance of a transaction rather than its legal form.
3. **True.** The accrual basis of accounting seeks to match effort and accomplishment by matching expenses against the revenues they created.
4. **False.** Exceptions include the installment basis of revenue recognition for sales and the percentage-of-completion method for long-term construction projects.
5. **False.** Immaterial items do have to be recorded, but they can be recorded in a theoretically incorrect way (e.g., expensing a wastebasket that will last many years).
6. **True.** Relevance and reliability are the two primary characteristics.

Multiple-Choice

1. **c.** The matching concept is one of the major principles of accounting rather than an assumption.
2. **d.** If you answered **(b)**, note that the consistency concept requires that a given company (not all companies) use the same accounting principles and reporting practices through time.
3. **b.** Usually, the accountant does not recognize revenue until the seller acquires the right to receive payment from the buyer.
4. **b.** $3,000,000/$10,000,000 × $15,000,000 = $4,500,000.
5. **a.** Periodicity is an underlying assumption rather than a modifying convention.
6. **b.** The category, quantitative characteristics, is not part of the conceptual framework project.

6

MERCHANDISING TRANSACTIONS

INTRODUCTION TO INVENTORIES AND CLASSIFIED INCOME STATEMENT

LEARNING OBJECTIVES

After studying this chapter, you should be able to:

1. Record journal entries for sales transactions involving merchandise.
2. Describe briefly cost of goods sold and the distinction between perpetual and periodic inventory procedures.
3. Record journal entries for purchase transactions involving merchandise.
4. Describe the freight terms and record transportation costs.
5. Determine cost of goods sold.

(continued)

Your study of accounting began with service companies as examples because they are the least complicated type of business. You are now ready to apply the accounting process to a more complex business—a merchandising company. Although the fundamental accounting concepts for service businesses apply to merchandising businesses, they require some additional accounts and techniques to record sales and purchases.

The normal flow of goods from manufacturer to final customer is as follows:

Merchandising Companies

Manufacturer → Wholesaler → Retailer → Final customer

Manufacturers produce goods from raw materials and normally sell them to wholesalers. After performing certain functions, such as packaging or labeling, **wholesalers** sell the goods to retailers. **Retailers** sell the goods to final customers. The two middle boxes in the diagram represent merchandising companies. These companies buy goods in finished form for resale.

This chapter compares the income statement of a service company with that of a merchandising company. Then, we describe how to record merchandise-related transactions. Finally, we explain the work sheet and the closing process for a merchandising company.

TWO INCOME STATEMENTS COMPARED—SERVICE COMPANY AND MERCHANDISING COMPANY

In Illustration 6.1 we compare the main divisions of an income statement for a service company with those for a merchandising company. To determine profitability or net income, a service company deducts total expenses incurred from

ILLUSTRATION 6.1 Condensed Income Statements of a Service Company and a Merchandising Company Compared

SERVICE COMPANY Income Statement For the Year Ended December 31, 1997		MERCHANDISING COMPANY Income Statement For the Year Ended December 31, 1997	
Service revenues	$13,200	Sales revenues	$262,000
		Cost of goods sold	159,000
		Gross margin	$103,000
Expenses	6,510	Expenses	74,900
Net income	$ 6,690	Net income	$ 28,100

revenues earned. A merchandising company is a more complex business and, therefore, has a more complex income statement.

As shown in Illustration 6.1, merchandising companies must deduct from revenues the cost of the goods they sell to customers. Then, they deduct other expenses. The income statement of a merchandising company has three main divisions: (1) sales revenues, which result from the sale of goods by the company; (2) cost of goods sold, which is an expense that indicates how much the company paid for the goods sold; and (3) expenses, which are the company's other expenses in running the business.

In the next two sections we discuss the first two main divisions of the income statement of a merchandising company. The third division (expenses) is similar to expenses for a service company, which we illustrated in preceding chapters. As you study these sections, keep in mind how the divisions of the merchandising income statement are related to each other and produce the final figure—net income or net loss—which indicates the profitability of the company.

(concluded)

6. Prepare a classified income statement.
7. Analyze and use the financial results—gross margin percentage.
8. Prepare a work sheet and closing entries for a merchandising company (Appendix).

SALES REVENUES

Objective 1
Record journal entries for sales transactions involving merchandise.

The sale of goods occurs between two parties. The seller of the goods transfers them to the buyer in exchange for cash or a promise to pay at a later date. This exchange is a relatively simple business transaction. Sellers make sales to create revenues; this inflow of assets results from selling goods to customers.

In Illustration 6.1, we show a condensed income statement to emphasize its major divisions. Next, we describe the more complete income statement actually prepared by accountants. The merchandising company that we use to illustrate the income statement is Hanlon Retail Food Store. This section explains how to record sales revenues, including the effect of trade discounts. Then, we explain how to record two deductions from sales revenues—sales discounts and sales returns and allowances (Illustration 6.2). The amount that remains is **net sales.** The formula, then, for determining net sales is:

Net sales = Gross sales − (Sales discounts + Sales returns and allowances)

Recording Gross Sales

In a sales transaction, the seller transfers the legal ownership (title) of the goods to the buyer. Usually, the physical delivery of the goods occurs at the same time as the sale of the goods. A business document called an *invoice* (a *sales invoice* for the seller and a *purchase invoice* for the buyer) becomes the basis for recording the sale.

An **invoice** is a document prepared by the seller of merchandise and sent to the buyer. The invoice contains the details of a sale, such as the number of units sold, unit price, total price billed, terms of sale, and manner of shipment. A retail company prepares the invoice at the point of sale. A wholesale company, which supplies goods to retailers, prepares the invoice after the shipping department notifies the accounting department that it has shipped the goods to the retailer. See Illustration 6.3, an invoice prepared by a wholesale company for goods sold to a retail company.

ILLUSTRATION 6.2
Partial Income Statement of Merchandising Company

HANLON RETAIL FOOD STORE
Partial Income Statement
For the Year Ended December 31, 1997

Operating revenues:		
Gross sales		$282,000
Less: Sales discounts	$ 5,000	
Sales returns and allowances	15,000	20,000
Net sales		$262,000

ILLUSTRATION 6.3
Invoice

BRYAN WHOLESALE CO.
476 Mason Street
Detroit, Michigan 48823

Invoice No.: 1258
Date: Dec. 19, 1997

Customer's Order No.: 218
Sold to: Baier Company
Address: 2255 Hannon Street
Big Rapids, Michigan 48106
Terms: Net 30, FOB Destination

Date Shipped: Dec. 19, 1997
Shipped by: Nagel Trucking Co.

Description	*Item Number*	*Quantity*	*Price per Unit*	*Total Amount*
True-tone stereo radios	Model No. 5868-24393	200	$100	$20,000
		Total		$20,000

Using the invoice as the source document, a wholesale company records the revenue from the sale at the time of the sale for the following reasons:

1. The seller has passed *legal title* of the goods to the buyer, and the goods are now the responsibility and property of the buyer.
2. The seller has established the selling price of the goods.
3. The seller has completed its obligation.
4. The seller has exchanged the goods for another asset, such as cash or accounts receivable.
5. The seller can determine the costs incurred in selling the goods.

Each time a company makes a sale, the company earns revenue. This revenue increases a revenue account called *Sales*. Recall from Chapter 2 that credits increase revenues. Therefore, the firm credits the Sales account for the amount of the sale.

Usually sales are for cash or on account. When a sale is for cash, the company credits the Sales account and debits Cash. When a sale is on account, it credits the Sales account and debits Accounts Receivable. For example, it records a $20,000 sale for cash as follows:

Cash	20,000	
Sales		20,000
To record the sale of merchandise for cash.		

This entry records a $20,000 sale on account:

Accounts Receivable	20,000	
Sales		20,000
To record the sale of merchandise on account.		

Usually, a seller quotes the gross selling price, also called the invoice price, of goods to the buyer; sometimes a seller quotes a list price of goods along with available trade discounts. In this latter situation, the buyer must calculate the gross selling price. The list price less all trade discounts is the **gross selling price.** Merchandising companies that sell goods use the gross selling price as the credit to sales.

An Accounting Perspective

Uses of Technology A database management system stores related data—such as monthly sales data (salespersons, customers, products, and sales amounts)—independent of the application. Once you have defined this information to the database management system, you can use commands to answer such questions as: Which products have been sold to which customers? What are the amounts of sales by individual salespersons? You could also print a customer list sorted by ZIP code, the alphabet, or salesperson. Leading programs include dBase®, rBase®, PC-File®, PFS®: Professional File®, and Hypercard®.

Determining Gross Selling Price when Companies Offer Trade Discounts

A **trade discount** is a percentage deduction, or discount, from the specified list price or catalog price of merchandise. Companies use trade discounts to:

1. Reduce the cost of catalog publication. A seller can use a catalog for a longer time by printing list prices in the catalog and giving separate discount sheets to salespersons whenever prices change.
2. Grant quantity discounts.
3. Allow quotation of different prices to various customers, such as retailers and wholesalers.

The seller's invoice may show trade discounts. However, sellers do not record trade discounts in their accounting records because the discounts are used only to calculate the gross selling price. Nor do trade discounts appear on the books of the purchaser. To illustrate, assume an invoice contains the following data:

List price, 200 swimsuits at $24.	$4,800
Less: Trade discount, 30%	1,440
Gross selling price (invoice price)	$3,360

The seller records a sale of $3,360. The purchaser records a purchase of $3,360. Thus, neither the seller nor the purchaser enters list prices and trade discounts on their books.

Sometimes the list price of a product is subject to several trade discounts; this series of discounts is a **chain discount.** Chain discounts exist, for example, when a wholesaler receives two trade discounts for services performed, such as packaging and distributing. When more than one discount is given, the buyer applies each discount to the declining balance successively. If a product has a list price of $100 and is subject to trade discounts of 20% and 10%, the gross selling price (invoice price) would be $100 – 0.2($100) = $80; $80 – 0.1($80) = $72, computed as follows:

List price	$100
Less 20%	– 20
	$ 80
Less 10%	– 8
Gross selling price (invoice price)	$ 72

You could obtain the same results by multiplying the list price by the complements of the trade discounts allowed. The complement of 20% is 80% because 20% + 80% = 100%. The complement of 10% is 90% because 10% + 90% = 100%. Thus, the gross selling price is $100 × 0.8 × 0.9 = $72.

Recording Deductions from Gross Sales

Two common deductions from gross sales are (1) sales discounts and (2) sales returns and allowances. Sellers record these deductions in contra revenue accounts to the Sales account. Contra accounts have normal balances that are opposite the balance of the account they reduce. For example, since the Sales account normally has a credit balance, the Sales Discounts account and Sales Returns and Allowances account have debit balances. We explain the methods of recording these contra revenue accounts next.

Sales Discounts Whenever a company sells goods on account, it clearly specifies terms of payment on the invoice. For example, the invoice in Illustration 6.3 states the terms of payment as "net 30."

Net 30 is sometimes written as "n/30." Either way, this term means that the buyer may not take a discount and must pay the entire amount of the invoice ($20,000) on or before 30 days after December 19, 1997 (invoice date)—or January 18, 1998. In Illustration 6.3, if the terms had read "n/10/EOM" (EOM means end of month), the buyer could not take a discount, and the invoice would be due on the 10th day of the month following the month of sale—or January 10, 1998. Credit terms vary from industry to industry.

In some industries, credit terms include a *cash discount* of 1% to 3% to induce early payment of an amount due. A **cash discount** is a deduction from the invoice price that can be taken only if the invoice is paid within a specified time. A cash discount differs from a trade discount in that a cash discount is a deduction from the gross selling price for the prompt payment of an invoice. Whereas a trade discount is a deduction from the list price to determine the gross selling price (or invoice price). Sellers call a cash discount a **sales discount** and buyers call it a **purchase discount**.

Companies often state cash discount terms as follows:

- **2/10, n/30**—means a buyer who pays within 10 days following the invoice date may deduct a discount of 2% of the invoice price. If payment is not made within the discount period, the entire invoice price is due 30 days from the invoice date.
- **2/EOM, n/60**—means a buyer who pays by the end of the month of purchase may deduct a 2% discount from the invoice price. If payment is not made within the discount period, the entire invoice price is due 60 days from the invoice date.
- **2/10/EOM, n/60**—means a buyer who pays by the 10th of the month following the month of purchase may deduct a 2% discount from the invoice price. If payment is not made within the discount period, the entire invoice price is due 60 days from the invoice date.

Sellers cannot record the sales discount before they receive payment since they do not know when the buyer will pay the invoice. A cash discount taken by the buyer reduces the cash that the seller actually collects from the sale of the goods, so the seller must indicate this fact in its accounting records. The following entries show how to record a sale and a subsequent sales discount.

Assume that on July 12, a business sold merchandise for $2,000 on account; terms are 2/10, n/30. On July 21 (nine days after invoice date), the business received a $1,960 check in payment of the account. The required journal entries for the seller are:

			Debit	Credit
July	12	Accounts Receivable	2,000	
		Sales		2,000
		To record sale on account; terms 2/10, n/30.		
	21	Cash	1,960	
		Sales Discounts	40	
		Accounts Receivable		2,000
		To record collection on account, less discount.		

The **Sales Discounts account** is a contra revenue account to the Sales account. In the income statement, the seller deducts this contra revenue account from gross sales. Sellers use the Sales Discounts account (rather than directly reducing the Sales account) so management can examine the sales discounts figure to evaluate the company's sales discount policy. Note that the Sales Discounts account is not an expense incurred in generating revenue. Rather, the purpose of the account is to reduce recorded revenue to the amount actually realized from the sale.

Sales Returns and Allowances Merchandising companies usually allow customers to return goods that are defective or unsatisfactory for a variety of reasons, such as wrong color, wrong size, wrong style, wrong amounts, or inferior quality. In fact, when their policy is satisfaction guaranteed, some companies allow customers to return goods simply because they do not like the merchandise. A **sales return** is merchandise returned by a buyer. Sellers and buyers regard a sales return as a cancellation of a sale. Alternatively, some customers keep unsatisfactory goods, and the seller gives them an allowance off the original price. A **sales allowance** is a deduction from the original invoiced sales price granted when the customer keeps the merchandise but is dissatisfied for any of a number of reasons, including inferior quality, damage, or deterioration in transit. When a seller agrees to the sales return or sales allowance, the seller sends the buyer a credit memorandum indicating a reduction (crediting) of the buyer's account receivable. A credit memorandum is a document that provides space for the name and address of the concerned parties and contains the preprinted words, "WE CREDIT YOUR ACCOUNT," followed by a space for the reason for the credit and the amount to be credited. A credit memorandum becomes the basis for recording a sales return or a sales allowance.

In theory, sellers could record both sales returns and sales allowances as debits to the Sales account because they cancel part of the recorded selling price. However, because the amount of sales returns and sales allowances is useful information to management, it should be shown separately. The amount of returns and allowances in relation to goods sold can indicate the quality of the goods (high-return percentage, low quality) or of pressure applied by salespersons (high-return percentage, high-pressure sales). Thus, sellers record sales returns and sales allowances in a separate *Sales Returns and Allowances account*. The **Sales Returns and Allowances account** is a contra revenue account (to Sales) that records the selling price of merchandise returned by buyers or reductions in selling prices granted. (Some companies use separate accounts for sales returns and for sales allowances, but this text does not.)

Following are two examples illustrating the recording of sales returns in the Sales Returns and Allowances account:

1. Assume that a customer returns $300 of goods sold on account. If payment has not yet been received, the required entry is:

Sales Returns and Allowances	300	
Accounts Receivable		300
To record a sales return from a customer.		

2. Assume that the customer has already paid the account and the seller gives the customer a cash refund. Now, the credit is to Cash rather than to Accounts Receivable. If the customer has taken a 2% discount when paying the account, the company would return to the customer the sales price less the sales discount amount. For example, if a customer returns goods that sold for $300, on which a 2% discount was taken, the following entry would be made:

Sales Returns and Allowances	300	
Cash		294
Sales Discounts		6
To record a sales return from a customer who had taken a discount and was sent a cash refund.		

ILLUSTRATION 6.4
Partial Income Statement*

HANLON RETAIL FOOD STORE
Partial Income Statement
For the Year Ended December 31, 1997

Operating revenues:		
Gross sales		$282,000
Less: Sales discounts	$ 5,000	
Sales returns and allowances	15,000	20,000
Net sales		$262,000

* This illustration is the same as Illustration 6.2, repeated here for your convenience.

The debit to the Sales Returns and Allowances account is for the full selling price of the purchase. The credit of $6 reduces the balance of the Sales Discounts account.

Next, we illustrate the recording of a sales allowance in the Sales Returns and Allowances account. Assume that a company grants a $400 allowance to a customer for damage resulting from improperly packed merchandise. If the customer has not yet paid the account, the required entry would be:

	Debit	Credit
Sales Returns and Allowances	400	
Accounts Receivable		400
To record sales allowance granted for damaged merchandise.		

If the customer has already paid the account, the credit is to Cash instead of Accounts Receivable. If the customer took a 2% discount when paying the account, the company would refund only the net amount ($392). Sales Discounts would be credited for $8. The entry would be:

	Debit	Credit
Sales Returns and Allowances	400	
Cash		392
Sales Discounts		8
To record sales allowance when a customer has paid and taken a 2% discount.		

Reporting Net Sales in the Income Statement

Illustration 6.4 shows how a company could report sales, sales discounts, and sales returns and allowances in the income statement. More often, the income statement in a company's annual report begins with "Net sales" because sales details are not important to external financial statement users.

AN ACCOUNTING PERSPECTIVE

BUSINESS INSIGHT When examining a company's sales cycle, management and users of financial data should be aware of any seasonal changes that may affect its reported sales. Baroid Corporation provides specialized products and services to the oil and gas industry. Baroid includes the following paragraph describing seasonality in its Form 10-K.

Seasonality

Operations in the U.S. historically have been seasonal with a low point in the second quarter of each year, generally due to poorer weather conditions and drilling budgeting cycles, and a peak reached in the fourth quarter of each year as oil and gas operators endeavor to complete planned programs by year end. However, in 1991 no such surge in U.S. drilling activity occurred in the third and fourth quarters. U.S. drilling activity actually dropped to then-record lows. Drilling in the U.S. continued to decline in the first two quarters of 1992. Not until October did the current rig count exceed that of the prior year. The late surge in 1992 drilling was attributed to a combination of the historic seasonal trend and certain tax incentives that expired December 31, 1992. In general, other than with respect to Sub Sea, the international operations are not seasonal.

A substantial majority of Sub Sea's revenues are generated in the period from May through September of each year, the period of relatively favorable oceanic weather conditions in the North Sea and the Gulf of Mexico.

Someone thinking about investing in this company in April might conclude that Baroid's subsidiary, Sub Sea, will soon be generating a lot of revenue for the company.

ILLUSTRATION 6.5
Determination of Cost of Goods Sold for Hanlon Retail Food Store

Cost of goods sold:			
Merchandise inventory, January 1, 1997			$ 24,000
Purchases		$167,000	
Less: Purchase discounts	$3,000		
Purchase returns and allowances	8,000	11,000	
Net purchases		$156,000	
Add: Transportation-in		10,000	
Net cost of purchases			166,000
Cost of goods available for sale			$190,000
Less: Merchandise inventory, December 31, 1997			31,000
Cost of goods sold			$159,000

COST OF GOODS SOLD

Objective 2
Describe briefly cost of goods sold and the distinction between perpetual and periodic inventory procedures.

The second main division of an income statement for a merchandising business is cost of goods sold. **Cost of goods sold** is the cost to the seller of the goods sold to customers. For a merchandising company, the cost of goods sold can be relatively large. All merchandising companies have a quantity of goods on hand called *merchandise inventory* to sell to customers. **Merchandise inventory** (or *inventory*) is the quantity of goods available for sale at any given time. Cost of goods sold is determined by computing the cost of (1) the beginning inventory, (2) the net cost of goods purchased, and (3) the ending inventory.

Look at the cost of goods sold section of Hanlon Retail Food Store's income statement in Illustration 6.5. The merchandise inventory on January 1, 1997, was $24,000. The net cost of purchases for the year was $166,000. Thus, Hanlon had $190,000 of merchandise available for sale during 1997. On December 31, 1997, the merchandise inventory was $31,000, meaning that this amount was left unsold. Subtracting the unsold inventory (the ending inventory), $31,000, from the amount Hanlon had available for sale during the year, $190,000, gives the cost of goods sold for the year of $159,000. Understanding this relationship shown on Hanlon Retail Food Store's partial income statement gives you the necessary background to determine the cost of goods sold as presented in this section.

Two Procedures for Accounting for Inventories

To determine the cost of goods sold, accountants must have accurate merchandise inventory figures. Accountants use two basic methods for determining the amount of merchandise inventory—perpetual inventory procedure and periodic inventory procedure. We mention perpetual inventory procedure only briefly here as periodic inventory procedure is used extensively in this chapter. In the next chapter, we emphasize perpetual inventory procedure and further compare it with periodic inventory procedure.

When discussing inventory, we need to clarify whether we are referring to the physical goods on hand or the Merchandise Inventory account, which is the financial representation of the physical goods on hand. The difference between perpetual and periodic inventory procedures is the frequency with which the Merchandise Inventory account is updated to reflect what is physically on hand. Under **perpetual inventory procedure,** the Merchandise Inventory account is continuously updated to reflect items on hand. For example, your supermarket uses a scanner to ring up your purchases. When your box of Rice Krispies crosses the scanner, the Merchandise Inventory account shows that one less box of Rice Krispies is on hand.

Under **periodic inventory procedure,** the Merchandise Inventory account is updated periodically after a physical count has been made. Usually, the physical count takes place immediately before the preparation of financial statements.

PERPETUAL INVENTORY PROCEDURE Companies use perpetual inventory procedure in a variety of business settings. Historically, companies that sold merchandise with a high individual unit value, such as automobiles, furniture, and appliances, used perpetual inventory procedure. Today, computerized cash registers, scanners, and accounting software programs automatically keep track of inflows and outflows of each inventory item. Computerization makes it economical for many retail stores to use perpetual inventory procedure for goods of low unit value, such as groceries.

Under perpetual inventory procedure, the Merchandise Inventory account provides close control by showing the cost of the goods that are supposed to be on hand at any particular time. Companies debit the Merchandise Inventory account for each purchase and credit it for each sale so that the current balance is shown in the account at all times. Usually, firms also maintain detailed unit records showing the quantities of each type of goods that should be on hand. At the end of the accounting period, company personnel take a physical inventory by actually counting the units of inventory on hand. Then they compare this physical count with the records showing the units that should be on hand. Chapter 7 describes perpetual inventory procedure in more detail.

Periodic Inventory Procedure Merchandising companies selling low unit value merchandise (such as nuts and bolts, nails, Christmas cards, or pencils) that have not computerized their inventory systems often find that the extra costs of record-keeping under perpetual inventory procedure more than outweigh the benefits. These merchandising companies often use periodic inventory procedure.

Under periodic inventory procedure, companies do not use the Merchandise Inventory account to record each purchase and sale of merchandise. Instead, a company corrects the balance in the Merchandise Inventory account as the result of a physical inventory count at the end of the accounting period. Also, the company usually does not maintain other records showing the exact number of units that should be on hand. Although periodic inventory procedure reduces record-keeping considerably, it also reduces control over inventory items.

Companies using periodic inventory procedure make no entries to the Merchandise Inventory account nor do they maintain unit records during the accounting period. Thus, these companies have no up-to-date balance against which to compare the physical inventory count at the end of the period. Also, these companies make no attempt to determine the cost of goods sold at the time of each sale. Instead, they calculate the cost of all the goods sold during the accounting period at the *end* of the period. To determine the cost of goods sold, a company must know:

1. Beginning inventory (cost of goods on hand at the beginning of the period).
2. Net cost of purchases during the period.
3. Ending inventory (cost of unsold goods at the end of the period).

The company would show this information as follows:

Beginning inventory	$ 34,000
Add: Net cost of purchases during the period	140,000
Cost of goods available for sale during the period	$174,000
Deduct: Ending inventory	20,000
Cost of goods sold during the period	$154,000

In this schedule, notice that the company began the accounting period with $34,000 of merchandise and purchased an additional $140,000, making a total of $174,000 of goods that could have been sold during the period. Then, a physical inventory showed that $20,000 remained unsold, which implies that $154,000 was the cost of goods sold during the period. Of course, the $154,000 is not necessarily the precise amount of goods sold because no actual record was made of the dollar amount of goods sold. Periodic inventory procedure basically assumes that everything not on hand at the end of the period has been sold. This method disregards problems such as theft or breakage because the Merchandise Inventory account contains no up-to-date balance at the end of the accounting period against which to compare the physical count.

Because this chapter emphasizes periodic inventory, an in-depth discussion of the accounts and journal entries used under periodic inventory procedure follows.

Purchases of Merchandise

Objective 3
Record journal entries for purchase transactions involving merchandise.

Under periodic inventory procedure, a merchandising company uses the **Purchases account** to record the cost of merchandise bought for resale during the current accounting period. The Purchases account, which is increased by debits, appears with the income statement accounts in the chart of accounts.

To illustrate entries affecting the Purchases account, assume that Hanlon Retail Food Store made two purchases of merchandise from Smith Wholesale Company. Hanlon purchased $30,000 of merchandise on credit (on account) on May 4 and on May 21 purchased $20,000 of merchandise for cash. The required journal entries for Hanlon are:

May	4	Purchases	30,000	
		Accounts Payable		30,000
		To record purchase of merchandise on account.		
	21	Purchases	20,000	
		Cash		20,000
		To record purchase of merchandise for cash.		

Deductions from Purchases

The buyer deducts purchase discounts and purchase returns and allowances from purchases to arrive at net purchases. The accountant records these items in contra accounts to the Purchases account.

Purchase Discounts Often companies purchase merchandise under credit terms that permit them to deduct a stated cash discount if they pay invoices within a specifed time. Assume that credit terms for Hanlon's May 4 purchase are 2/10, n/30. If Hanlon pays for the merchandise by May 14, the store may take a 2% discount. Thus, Hanlon must pay only $29,400 to settle the $30,000 account payable. The entry to record the payment of the invoice on May 14 is:

May	14	Accounts Payable	30,000	
		Cash		29,400
		Purchase Discounts		600
		To record payment on account within discount period.		

The buyer records the purchase discount only when the invoice is paid within the discount period and the discount is taken. The **Purchase Discounts account** is a contra account to Purchases that reduces the recorded invoice price of the goods purchased to the price actually paid. Hanlon reports purchase discounts in the income statement as a deduction from purchases.

Companies base purchase discounts on the invoice price of goods. If an invoice shows purchase returns or allowances, they must be deducted from the invoice price before calculating purchase discounts. For example, in the previous transaction, the invoice price of goods purchased was $30,000. If Hanlon returned $2,000 of the goods, the seller calculates the purchase discount on $28,000.

Interest Rate Implied in Cash Discounts To decide whether you should take advantage of discounts by using your cash or borrowing, make this simple analysis. Assume that you must pay $10,000 within 30 days or $9,800 within 10 days to settle a $10,000 invoice with terms of 2/10, n/30. By advancing payment 20 days from the final due date, you can secure a discount of $200. The interest expense incurred to borrow $9,800 at 12% per year for 20 days is $65.33. You would save $134.67 ($200 − $65.33) by borrowing the money and paying the invoice within the discount period.

In terms of an annual rate of interest, the 2% rate of discount for 20 days is equivalent to a 36% annual rate: (360 ÷ 20) × 2%. The formula is:

$$\text{Equivalent annual rate of interest} = \frac{\text{The number of days in a year (assumed to be 360)}}{\text{The number of days from the end of the discount period until the final due date}} \times \text{The percentage rate of discount}$$

You can convert all cash discount terms to their approximate annual interest rate equivalents by use of this formula. Thus, a company could afford to pay up to 36% [(360 ÷ 20) × 2%] on borrowed funds to take advantage of discount terms of 2/10, n/30. The company could pay 18% on terms of 1/10, n/30.

Purchase Returns and Allowances A purchase return occurs when a buyer returns merchandise to a seller. When a buyer receives a reduction in the price of goods shipped, a purchase allowance results. Then, the buyer commonly uses a debit memorandum to notify the seller that the account payable with the seller is being reduced (Accounts Payable is debited). A debit memorandum is similar to a credit memorandum except for the preprinted words, "WE DEBIT YOUR ACCOUNT." The buyer may use a copy of a debit memorandum to record the returns or allowances or may wait for confirmation, usually a credit memorandum, from the seller.

Both returns and allowances reduce the buyer's debt to the seller and decrease the cost of the goods purchased. The buyer may want to know the amount of returns and allowances as the first step in controlling the costs incurred in returning unsatisfactory merchandise or negotiating purchase allowances. For this reason, buyers record purchase returns and allowances in a separate **Purchase Returns and Allowances account.** If Hanlon returned $350 of merchandise to Smith Wholesale before paying for the goods, it would make this journal entry:

Accounts Payable	350	
Purchase Returns and Allowances		350
To record return of damaged merchandise to supplier.		

The entry would have been the same to record a $350 allowance. Only the explanation would change.

If Hanlon had already paid the account, the debit would be to Cash instead of Accounts Payable, since Hanlon would receive a refund of cash. If the company took a discount at the time it paid the account, only the net amount would be refunded. For instance, if a 2% discount had been taken, Hanlon's journal entry for the return would be:

Cash	343	
Purchase Discounts	7	
Purchase Returns and Allowances		350
To record return of damaged merchandise to supplier and record receipt of cash.		

Purchase Returns and Allowances is a contra account to the Purchases account, and the income statement shows it as a deduction from purchases. When both purchase discounts and purchase returns and allowances are deducted from purchases, the result is **net purchases.**

Transportation Costs

Transportation costs are an important part of cost of goods sold. To understand how to account for transportation costs, you must know the meaning of the following terms:

Objective 4
Describe the freight terms and record transportation costs.

- **FOB shipping point:** The term **FOB shipping point** means "free on board at shipping point." The buyer incurs all transportation costs after the merchandise has been loaded on a railroad car or truck at the point of shipment. Thus, the buyer is responsible for ultimately paying the freight charges.
- **FOB destination:** The term **FOB destination** means "free on board at destination." The seller ships the goods to their destination without charge to the buyer. Thus, the seller is ultimately responsible for paying the freight charges.
- **Passage of title:** **Passage of title** is a term that indicates the transfer of the legal ownership of goods. Title to the goods normally passes from seller to buyer at the FOB point. Thus, when goods are shipped FOB shipping point, title usually passes to the buyer at the shipping point. When goods are shipped FOB destination, title usually passes at the destination.
- **Freight prepaid:** When the *seller* must initially pay the freight at the time of shipment, companies use the term **freight prepaid.**
- **Freight collect:** When the *buyer* must initially pay the freight bill on the arrival of the goods, companies use the term **freight collect.**

To illustrate the use of these terms, assume that a company ships goods FOB shipping point, freight collect. Title passes at the shipping point. The buyer is responsible for paying the $100 freight costs and does so. The seller makes no entry for freight charges; the entry on the *buyer's books* is:

Transportation-In (or Freight-In)	100	
Cash		100
To record payment of freight bill on goods purchased.		

The **Transportation-In account** records the inward freight costs of acquiring merchandise. Transportation-In is an adjunct account in that it is added to net purchases to arrive at **net cost of purchases.** An **adjunct account** is closely related to another account (Purchases, in this instance), and its balance is added to the balance of the related account in the financial statements. Recall that a contra account is just the opposite of an adjunct account. Buyers deduct a contra account, such as accumulated depreciation, from the related account in the financial statements.

When shipping goods FOB destination, freight prepaid, the seller is responsible for and pays the freight bill. Because the seller cannot bill a separate freight cost to the buyer, the buyer shows no entry for freight on its books. The seller, however, has undoubtedly considered the freight cost in setting selling prices. The following entry is required on the *seller's books:*

Delivery Expense (or Transportation-Out Expense)	100	
Cash		100
To record freight cost on goods sold.		

When the terms are FOB destination, the seller records the freight costs as **delivery expense;** this selling expense appears on the income statement with other selling expenses.

FOB terms are especially important at the end of an accounting period. Goods in transit then belong to either the seller or the buyer, and one of these parties must include these goods in its ending inventory. Goods shipped FOB destination belong to the seller while in transit, and the seller includes these goods in its ending inventory. Goods shipped FOB shipping point belong to the buyer while in transit, and the buyer records these goods as a purchase and includes them in its ending inventory. For example, assume that a seller ships goods on December 30, 1996, and they arrive at their destination on January 5, 1997. If terms are FOB destination, the seller includes the goods in its December 31, 1996, inventory, and neither seller nor buyer records the exchange transaction until January 5, 1997. If

ILLUSTRATION 6.6
Summary of Shipping Terms

Shipping point: Detroit — Destination: San Diego

Goods travel from shipping point to destination

If shipping terms are:

FOB shipping point—Buyer incurs the freight charges

FOB destination—Seller incurs the freight charges

Freight prepaid—Seller initially pays the freight charges

Freight collect—Buyer initially pays the freight charges

If the freight terms are combined as follows:

FOB shipping point, freight collect—Buyer both incurs and initially pays the freight charges. The proper party paid the freight. The buyer debits Transportation-In and credits Cash.

FOB destination, freight prepaid—Seller both incurs and initially pays the freight charges. The proper party paid the freight. The seller debits Delivery Expense and credits Cash.

FOB shipping point, freight prepaid—Buyer incurs the freight charges, and seller initially pays the freight charges. Buyer must reimburse seller for freight charges. The seller debits Accounts Receivable and credits Cash upon paying the freight. The buyer debits Transportation-In and credits Accounts Payable when informed of the freight charges.

FOB destination, freight collect—Seller incurs freight charges, and buyer initially pays freight charges. Buyer deducts freight charges from amount owed to seller. The buyer debits Accounts Payable and credits Cash when paying the freight. The seller debits Delivery Expense and credits Accounts Receivable when informed of the freight charges.

terms are FOB shipping point, the buyer includes the goods in its December 31, 1996, inventory, and both parties record the exchange transaction as of December 30, 1996.

Sometimes the seller prepays the freight as a convenience to the buyer, even though the buyer is ultimately responsible for it. The buyer merely reimburses the seller for the freight paid. For example, assume that Wood Company sold merchandise to Loud Company with terms of FOB shipping point, freight prepaid. The freight charges were $100. The following entries are necessary on the books of the buyer and the seller:

Buyer—Loud Company			**Seller—Wood Company**		
Transportation-In	100		Accounts Receivable	100	
Accounts Payable . . .		100	Cash		100

Such entries are necessary because Wood initially paid the freight charges when not required to do so. Therefore, Loud Company must reimburse Wood for the charges. If the buyer pays freight for the seller (e.g., FOB destination, freight collect), the buyer merely deducts the freight paid from the amount owed to the seller. The following entries are necessary on the books of the buyer and the seller:

Buyer—Loud Company			**Seller—Wood Company**		
Accounts Payable	100		Delivery Expense	100	
Cash		100	Accounts Receivable . .		100

Purchase discounts may be taken only on the purchase price of goods. Therefore, a buyer who owes the seller for freight charges cannot take a discount on the freight charges owed, even if the buyer makes payment within the discount period. We summarize our discussion of freight terms and the resulting journal entries to record the freight charges in Illustration 6.6.

Merchandise Inventories

Merchandise inventory is the cost of goods on hand and available for sale at any given time. To determine the cost of goods sold in any accounting period, management needs inventory information. Management must know its cost of goods on hand at the start of the period (beginning inventory), the net cost of purchases during the period, and the cost of goods on hand at the close of the period (ending inventory). Since the ending inventory of the preceding period is the beginning

ILLUSTRATION 6.7
Determination of Cost of Goods Sold for Hanlon Retail Food Store*

Cost of goods sold:			
Merchandise inventory, January 1, 1997			$ 24,000
Purchases		$167,000	
Less: Purchase discounts	$3,000		
Purchase returns and allowances	8,000	11,000	
Net purchases		$156,000	
Add: Transportation-in		10,000	
Net cost of purchases			166,000
Cost of goods available for sale			$190,000
Less: Merchandise inventory, December 31, 1997			31,000
Cost of goods sold			$159,000

* This illustration is the same as Illustration 6.5, repeated here for your convenience.

inventory for the current period, management already knows the cost of the beginning inventory. Companies record purchases, purchase discounts, purchase returns and allowances, and transportation-in throughout the period. Therefore, management needs to determine only the cost of the ending inventory at the end of the period in order to calculate cost of goods sold.

TAKING A PHYSICAL INVENTORY Under periodic inventory procedure, company personnel determine ending inventory cost by taking a *physical inventory*. Taking a **physical inventory** consists of counting physical units of each type of merchandise on hand. To calculate inventory cost, they multiply the number of each kind of merchandise by its unit cost. Then, they combine the total costs of the various kinds of merchandise to provide the total ending inventory cost.

In taking a physical inventory, company personnel must be careful to count all goods owned, regardless of where they are located, and include them in the inventory. Thus, companies should include goods shipped to potential customers on approval in their inventories. Similarly, companies should not record **consigned goods** (goods delivered to another party who attempts to sell them for a commission) as sold goods. These goods remain the property of the owner (consignor) until sold by the consignee and must be included in the owner's inventory.

Merchandise in transit is merchandise in the hands of a freight company on the date of a physical inventory. As stated above, buyers must record merchandise in transit at the end of the accounting period as a purchase if the goods were shipped FOB shipping point and they have received title to the merchandise. In general, the goods belong to the party who ultimately bears the transportation charges.

Determining Cost of Goods Sold

Objective 5
Determine cost of goods sold.

When accounting personnel know the beginning and ending inventories and the various items making up the net cost of purchases, they can determine the cost of goods sold. To illustrate, assume the following account balances for Hanlon Retail Food Store as of December 31, 1997:

Merchandise Inventory, January 1, 1997	$ 24,000 Dr.
Purchases	167,000 Dr.
Purchase Discounts	3,000 Cr.
Purchase Returns and Allowances	8,000 Cr.
Transportation-In	10,000 Dr.

By taking a physical inventory, Hanlon determined the December 31, 1997, merchandise inventory to be $31,000. Hanlon then calculated its cost of goods sold as shown in Illustration 6.7. This computation appears in a section of the income statement directly below the calculation of net sales.

In Illustration 6.7, Hanlon's beginning inventory ($24,000) plus net cost of purchases ($166,000) is equal to **cost of goods available for sale** ($190,000). The firm deducts the ending inventory cost ($31,000) from cost of goods available for sale to arrive at cost of goods sold ($159,000).

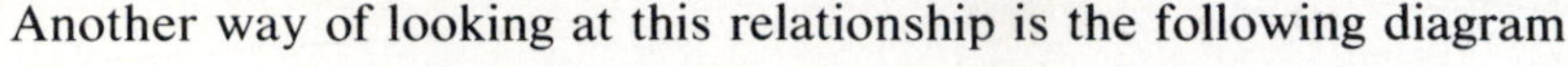

Another way of looking at this relationship is the following diagram:

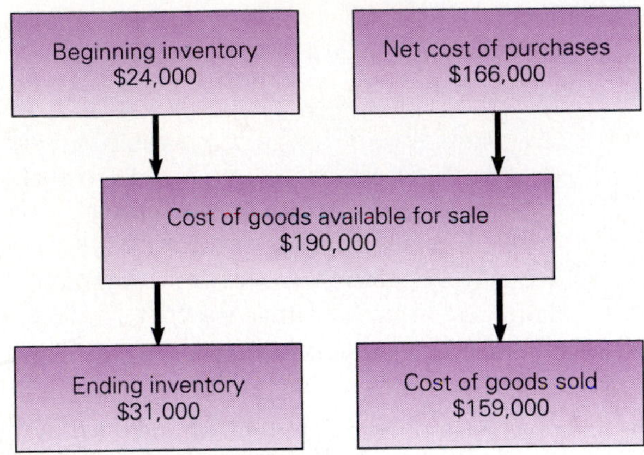

Beginning inventory and net cost of purchases combine to form cost of goods available for sale. Hanlon divides the cost of goods available for sale into ending inventory (which is the cost of goods not sold) and cost of goods sold.

To continue the calculation appearing in Illustration 6.7, net cost of purchases ($166,000) is equal to purchases ($167,000), *less* purchase discounts ($3,000) and purchase returns and allowances ($8,000), *plus* transportation-in ($10,000).

As shown in Illustration 6.7, ending inventory cost (merchandise inventory) appears in the income statement as a deduction from cost of goods available for sale to compute cost of goods sold. Ending inventory cost (merchandise inventory) is also a current asset in the end-of-period balance sheet.

Lack of Control under Periodic Inventory Procedure

Companies use periodic inventory procedure because of its simplicity and relatively low cost. However, periodic inventory procedure provides little control over inventory. Firms assume any items not included in the physical count of inventory at the end of the period have been sold. Thus, they mistakenly assume items that have been stolen have been sold and include their cost in cost of goods sold.

To illustrate, suppose that the cost of goods available for sale was $200,000 and ending inventory was $60,000. These figures suggest that the cost of goods sold was $140,000. Now suppose that $2,000 of goods were actually shoplifted during the year. If such goods had not been stolen, the ending inventory would have been $62,000 and the cost of goods sold only $138,000. Thus, the $140,000 cost of goods sold calculated under periodic inventory procedure includes both the cost of the merchandise delivered to customers and the cost of merchandise stolen.

Classified Income Statement

Objective 6
Prepare a classified income statement.

In preceding chapters, we illustrated the unclassified (or single-step) income statement. An **unclassified income statement** has only two categories—revenues and expenses. In contrast, a **classified income statement** divides both revenues and expenses into operating and nonoperating items. The statement also separates operating expenses into selling and administrative expenses. A classified income statement is also called a multiple-step income statement.

In Illustration 6.8, we present a classified income statement for Hanlon Retail Food Store. This statement uses the previously presented data on sales (Illustration 6.4) and cost of goods sold (Illustration 6.7), together with additional assumed data on operating expenses and other expenses and revenues. Note in Illustration 6.8 that a classified income statement has the following four major sections:

1. Operating revenues.
2. Cost of goods sold.
3. Operating expenses.
4. Nonoperating revenues and expenses (other revenues and other expenses).

The classified income statement shows important relationships that help in analyzing how well the company is performing. For example, by deducting cost of goods sold from operating revenues, you can determine by what amount sales revenues exceed the cost of items being sold. If this margin, called gross margin, is lower than desired, a company may need to increase its selling prices and/or decrease its cost of goods sold. The classified income statement subdivides operating expenses into selling and administrative expenses. Thus, statement users can see how much expense is incurred in selling the product and how much in administering the business. Statement users can also make comparisons with other years' data for the same business and with other businesses. Nonoperating revenues and expenses appear at the bottom of the income statement because they are less significant in assessing the profitability of the business.

An Accounting Perspective

Business Insight Management chooses whether to use a classified or unclassified income statement to present a company's financial data. This choice may be based either on how their competitors present their data or on the costs associated with assembling the data.

Baldor Motors and Drives included an unclassified income statement in its 1991 annual report, while Engelhard Corporation issued a classified income statement in its annual report for the same year. The classified income statement provides more information for users.

Next, we explain the major headings of the classified income statement in Illustration 6.8. The terms in some of these headings are already familiar to you. Although future illustrations of classified income statements may vary somewhat in form, we retain the basic organization.

1. **Operating revenues** are the revenues generated by the major activities of the business—usually the sale of products or services or both.

2. **Cost of goods sold** is the major expense in merchandising companies. Note the cost of goods sold section of the classified income statement in Illustration 6.8. This chapter has already discussed the items used in calculating cost of goods sold. Merchandisers usually highlight the amount by which sales revenues exceed the cost of goods sold in the top part of the income statement. The excess of net sales over cost of goods sold is the **gross margin or gross profit.** To express gross margin as a percentage rate, we divide gross margin by net sales. In Illustration 6.8, the gross margin rate is approximately 39.3% ($103,000/$262,000). The gross margin rate indicates that out of each sales dollar, approximately 39 cents is available to cover other expenses and produce income. Business owners watch the gross margin rate closely since a small percentage fluctuation can cause a large dollar change in net income. Also, a downward trend in the gross margin rate may indicate a problem, such as theft of merchandise. For instance, one Southeastern sporting goods company, SportsTown, Inc., suffered significant gross margin deterioration in fiscal year 1994 from increased shoplifting and employee theft.

3. **Operating expenses** for a merchandising company are those expenses, other than cost of goods sold, incurred in the normal business functions of a company. Usually, operating expenses are either selling expenses or administrative expenses. **Selling expenses** are expenses a company incurs in selling and marketing efforts. Examples include salaries and commissions of salespersons, expenses for salespersons' travel, delivery, advertising, rent (or depreciation, if owned) and utilities on a sales building, sales supplies used, and depreciation on delivery trucks used in sales. **Administrative expenses** are expenses a company

ILLUSTRATION 6.8 Classified Income Statement for a Merchandising Company

HANLON RETAIL FOOD STORE
Income Statement
For the Year Ended December 31, 1997

Operating revenues:				
Gross sales				$282,000
Less: Sales discounts			$ 5,000	
Sales returns and allowances			15,000	20,000
Net sales				$262,000
Cost of goods sold:				
Merchandise inventory, January 1, 1997			$ 24,000	
Purchases		$167,000		
Less: Purchase discounts	$3,000			
Purchase returns and allowances	8,000	11,000		
Net purchases		$156,000		
Add: Transportation-in		10,000		
Net cost of purchases			166,000	
Cost of goods available for sale			$190,000	
Less: Merchandise inventory, December 31, 1997			31,000	
Cost of goods sold				159,000
Gross margin				$103,000
Operating expenses:				
Miscellaneous selling expenses:				
Sales salaries and commissions expense		$ 26,000		
Salespersons' travel expense		3,000		
Delivery expense		2,000		
Advertising expense		4,000		
Rent expense—store building		2,500		
Supplies expense		1,000		
Utilities expense		1,800		
Depreciation expense—store equipment		700		
Other selling expense		400	$ 41,400	
Miscellaneous administrative expenses:				
Salaries expense, executive		$ 29,000		
Rent expense—administrative building		1,600		
Insurance expense		1,500		
Supplies expense		800		
Depreciation expense—office equipment		1,100		
Other administrative expenses		300	34,300	
Total operating expenses				75,700
Income from operations				$ 27,300
Nonoperating revenues and expenses:				
Nonoperating revenues:				
Interest revenue				1,400
				$ 28,700
Nonoperating expenses:				
Interest expense				600
Net income				$ 28,100

incurs in the overall management of a business. Examples include administrative salaries, rent (or depreciation, if owned) and utilities on an administrative building, insurance expense, administrative supplies used, and depreciation on office equipment.

Certain operating expenses may be shared by the selling and administrative functions. For example, a company might incur rent, taxes, and insurance on a building for both sales and administrative purposes. Expenses covering both the selling and administrative functions must be analyzed and prorated between the two functions on the income statement. For instance, if $1,000 of depreciation expense relates 60% to selling and 40% to administrative based on the square footage or number of employees, the income statement would show $600 as a selling expense and $400 as an administrative expense.

4. Nonoperating revenues (other revenues) and **nonoperating expenses (other expenses)** are revenues and expenses not related to the sale of products or services regularly offered for sale by a business. An example of a nonoperating revenue is interest that a business earns on notes receivable. An example of a nonoperating expense is interest incurred on money borrowed by the company.

Important Relationships in the Income Statement

To summarize the more important relationships in the income statement of a merchandising firm in equation form:

1. **Net sales** = Gross sales − (Sales discounts + Sales returns and allowances).
2. **Net purchases** = Purchases − (Purchase discounts + Purchase returns and allowances).
3. **Net cost of purchases** = Net purchases + Transportation-in.
4. **Cost of goods sold** = Beginning inventory + Net cost of purchases − Ending inventory.
5. **Gross margin** = Net sales − Cost of goods sold.
6. **Income from operations** = Gross margin − Operating (selling and administrative) expenses.
7. **Net income** = Income from operations + Nonoperating revenues − Nonoperating expenses.

Each of these relationships is important because of the way it relates to an overall measure of business profitability. For example, a company may produce a high gross margin on sales. However, because of large sales commissions and delivery expenses, the owner may realize only a very small percentage of the gross margin as profit. The classifications in the income statement allow a user to focus on the whole picture as well as on how net income was derived (statement relationships).

Analyzing and Using the Financial Results—Gross Margin Percentage

Objective 7
Analyze and use the financial results—gross margin percentage.

As discussed on page 223, you can calculate the **gross margin percentage** by using the following formula:

$$\text{Gross Margin Percentage} = \frac{\text{Gross Margin}}{\text{Net Sales}}$$

To demonstrate the use of this ratio, consider the following information from the 1992 Annual Report of Sterling Chemicals:

	Year Ended September 30		
	1992	1991	1990
Revenues	$430,529	$542,664	$506,046
Cost of goods sold	402,794	472,407	399,643
Gross profit	$ 27,735	$ 70,257	$106,403
Gross profit (margin) percentage	$\frac{\$27,735}{\$430,529} = 6.44\%$	$\frac{\$70,257}{\$542,664} = 12.95\%$	$\frac{\$106,403}{\$506,046} = 21.03\%$

Sterling Chemicals
Sterling Chemicals produces seven commodity petrochemical products and manufactures chemicals used in the pulp paper industry

Sterling's downward trend in gross margin percentage could indicate a problem, such as theft of merchandise. Alternatively, maybe severe competition has reduced selling prices.

An Ethical Perspective

World Auto Parts Corporation

John Bentley is the chief financial officer for World Auto Parts Corporation. The company buys approximately $500 million of auto parts each year from small suppliers all over the world and resells them to auto repair shops in the United States.

Most of the suppliers have cash discount terms of 2/10, n/30. John has instructed his personnel to pay invoices on the 30th day after the invoice date but to take the 2% discount even though they are not entitled to do so. Whenever a supplier complains, John instructs his purchasing agent to find another supplier who will go along with this practice. When some of his own employees questioned the practice, John responded as follows:

> This practice really does no harm. These small suppliers are much better off to go along and have our business than to not go along and lose it. For most of them, we are their largest customer. Besides, if they are willing to sell to others at a 2% discount, why should they not be willing to sell to us at that same discount even though we pay a little later? The benefit to our company is very significant. Last year our profits were $100 million. A total of $10 million of the profits was attributable to this practice. Do you really want me to change this practice and give up 10% of our profits?

An Accounting Perspective

Business Insight Sara Lee Corporation is a global manufacturer and marketer of high-quality, brand-name food and clothing products. Management often watches gross margin percentage to see if trends can be explained. Take, for example, Sara Lee Corporation's 1992 Annual Report. Under Financial Review, Sara Lee's management discusses the gross profit margin as follows:

> The gross profit margin was 37.3% in 1992 compared to 34.8% in 1991, and 33.2% in 1990. The improvement in 1992 is attributable to a mix of sales more heavily weighted toward Packaged Consumer Products, which has higher margins than food products; the disposition of certain low margin meat and foodservice businesses; lower raw material costs in the Packaged Foods business; and operating efficiencies resulting from capital expenditures and business restructuring. The improvement in 1991 margins is related to operating efficiencies resulting from capital expenditures and the disposition of lower-margin businesses.

You should now understand the distinction between accounting for a service company and a merchandising company. The next chapter continues the discussion of merchandise inventory carried by merchandising companies.

Understanding the Learning Objectives

Objective 1
Record journal entries for sales transactions involving merchandise.

- In a sales transaction, the seller transfers the legal ownership (title) of the goods to the buyer.
- An invoice is a document, prepared by the seller of merchandise and sent to the buyer, that contains the details of a sale, such as the number of units sold, unit price, total price, terms of sale, and manner of shipment.
- Usually sales are for cash or on account. When a sale is for cash, the debit is to Cash and the credit is to Sales. When a sale is on account, the debit is to Accounts Receivable and the credit is to Sales.
- When companies offer trade discounts, the gross selling price (gross invoice price) at which the sale is recorded is equal to the list price minus any trade discounts.
- Two common deductions from gross sales are (1) sales discounts and (2) sales returns and allowances. These deductions are recorded in contra revenue accounts to the Sales account. Both the Sales Discounts account and the Sales Returns and Allowances account normally have debit balances. Net sales = Sales − (Sales discounts + Sales returns and allowances).
- Sales discounts arise when the seller offers the buyer a cash discount of 1% to 3% to induce early payment of an amount due.
- Sales returns result from merchandise being returned by a buyer because the goods are considered unsatisfactory or have been damaged. A sales allowance is a deduction from the original invoiced sales price granted to a customer when the customer keeps the merchandise but is dissatisfied.

Objective 2
Describe briefly cost of goods sold and the distinction between perpetual and periodic inventory procedures.

- Cost of goods sold = Beginning inventory + Net cost of purchases − Ending inventory. Net cost of purchases = Purchases − (Purchase discounts + Purchase returns and allowances) + Transportation-in.
- Two methods of accounting for inventory are perpetual inventory procedure and periodic inventory procedure. Under perpetual inventory procedure, the inventory account is continuously updated during the accounting period. Under periodic inventory procedure, the inventory account is updated only periodically—after a physical count has been made.

Objective 3
Record journal entries for purchase transactions involving merchandise.

- Purchases of merchandise are recorded by debiting Purchases and crediting Cash (for cash purchases) or crediting Accounts Payable (for purchases on account).
- Two common deductions from purchases are (1) purchase discounts and (2) purchase returns and allowances. In the general ledger, both of these items normally carry credit balances. From the buyer's side of the transactions, cash discounts are purchase discounts, and merchandise returns and allowances are purchase returns and allowances.

Objective 4
Describe the freight terms and record transportation costs.

- FOB shipping point means free on board at shipping point—the buyer incurs the freight.
- FOB destination means free on board at destination—the seller incurs the freight.
- Passage of title is a term indicating the transfer of the legal ownership of goods.
- Freight prepaid is when the seller must initially pay the freight at the time of shipment.
- Freight collect is when the buyer must initially pay the freight on the arrival of the goods.

Objective 5
Determine cost of goods sold.

- Expansion and application of the relationship introduced in Learning Objective 2. Beginning inventory + Net cost of purchases = Cost of goods available for sale. Cost of goods available for sale − Ending inventory = Cost of goods sold.

Objective 6
Prepare a classified income statement.

- A classified income statement has four major sections—operating revenues, cost of goods sold, operating expenses, and nonoperating revenues and expenses.
- Operating revenues are the revenues generated by the major activities of the business—usually the sale of products or services or both.
- Cost of goods sold is the major expense in merchandising companies.
- Operating expenses for a merchandising company are those expenses other than cost of goods sold incurred in the normal business functions of a company. Usually, operating expenses are classified as either selling expenses or administrative expenses.
- Nonoperating revenues and expenses are revenues and expenses not related to the sale of products or services regularly offered for sale by a business.

Objective 7
Analyze and use the financial results—gross margin percentage.

- Gross margin percentage = Gross margin/Net sales.
- The gross margin rate indicates the amount of sales dollars available to cover expenses and produce income.

Objective 8
Prepare a work sheet and closing entries for a merchandising company (Appendix).

- Except for the merchandise-related accounts, the work sheet for a merchandising company is the same as for a service company.
- Any revenue accounts and contra purchases accounts in the Adjusted Trial Balance credit column of the work sheet are carried to the Income Statement credit column.
- Beginning inventory, contra revenue accounts, Purchases, Transportation-In, and expense accounts in the Adjusted Trial Balance debit column are carried to the Income Statement debit column.
- Ending merchandise inventory is entered in the Income Statement credit column and in the Balance Sheet debit column.
- Closing entries may be prepared directly from the work sheet. The first journal entry debits all items appearing in the Income Statement credit column and credits

Income Summary. The second entry credits all items appearing in the Income Statement debit column and debits Income Summary. The third entry debits Income Summary and credits the Retained Earnings account (assuming positive net income). The fourth entry debits the Retained Earnings account and credits the Dividends account.

APPENDIX THE WORK SHEET FOR A MERCHANDISING COMPANY

Objective 8
Prepare a work sheet and closing entries for a merchandising company.

Illustration 6.9 shows a work sheet for a merchandising company. Lyons Company is a small sporting goods firm. The illustration for Lyons Company focuses on merchandise-related accounts. Thus, we do not show the fixed assets (land, building, and equipment). Except for the merchandise-related accounts, the work sheet for a merchandising company is the same as for a service company. Recall that use of a work sheet assists in the preparation of the adjusting and closing entries. The work sheet also contains all the information needed for the preparation of the financial statements.

To further simplify this illustration, assume Lyons needs no adjusting entries at month-end. The trial balance is from the ledger accounts at December 31, 1997. The $7,000 merchandise inventory in the trial balance is the beginning inventory. The sales and sales-related accounts and the purchases and purchases-related accounts summarize the merchandising activity for December 1997.

Completing the Work Sheet

Lyons carries any revenue accounts (Sales) and contra purchases accounts (Purchase Discounts, Purchase Returns and Allowances) in the Adjusted Trial Balance credit columns of the work sheet to the Income Statement credit column. It carries beginning inventory, contra revenue accounts (Sales Discounts, Sales Returns and Allowances), Purchases, Transportation-In, and expense accounts (Selling Expenses, Administrative Expenses) in the Adjusted Trial Balance debit column to the Income Statement debit column.

Assume that ending inventory is $8,000. Lyons enters this amount in the Income Statement credit column because it is deducted from cost of goods available for sale (beginning inventory plus net cost of purchases) in determining cost of goods sold. It also enters the ending inventory in the Balance Sheet debit column to establish the proper balance in the Merchandise Inventory account. The beginning and ending inventories are on the Income Statement because Lyons uses both to calculate cost of goods sold in the income statement. Net income of $5,843 for the period balances the Income Statement columns. The firm carries the net income to the Statement of Retained Earnings credit column. Retained earnings of $18,843 balances the Statement of Retained Earnings columns. Lyons Company carries the retained earnings to the Balance Sheet credit column.

Lyons carries all other asset account balances (Cash, Accounts Receivable, and ending Merchandise Inventory) to the Balance Sheet debit column. It also carries the liability (Accounts Payable) and Capital Stock account balances to the Balance Sheet credit column. The balance sheet columns total to $29,543.

Financial Statements for a Merchandising Company

Once the work sheet has been completed, Lyons prepares the financial statements. After entering any adjusting and closing entries in the journal, the firm posts them to the ledger. This process clears the records for the next accounting period. Finally, it prepares a post-closing trial balance.

INCOME STATEMENT Illustration 6.10 shows the income statement Lyons prepared from its work sheet in Illustration 6.9. The focus in this income statement is on determining the cost of goods sold.

STATEMENT OF RETAINED EARNINGS The statement of retained earnings, as you recall, is a financial statement that summarizes the transactions affecting the Retained Earnings account balance. In Illustration 6.11, the statement of retained earnings shows an increase in equity resulting from net income and a decrease in equity resulting from dividends.

ILLUSTRATION 6.9 Work Sheet for a Merchandising Company

LYONS COMPANY
Work Sheet
For the Month Ended December 31, 1997

Acct. No.	Account Titles	Trial Balance		Adjustments		Adjusted Trial Balance		Income Statement		Statement of Retained Earnings		Balance Sheet	
		Debit	Credit	Debit	Credit	Debit	Credit	Debit	Credit	Debit	Credit	Debit	Credit
100	Cash	19,663				19,663						19,663	
103	Accounts Receivable	1,880				1,880						1,880	
105	Merchandise Inventory,												
	December 1	7,000				7,000		7,000	8,000			8,000	
200	Accounts Payable		700				700						700
300	Capital Stock		10,000				10,000						10,000
310	Retained Earnings, December 1		15,000				15,000				15,000		
320	Dividends	2,000				2,000				2,000			
410	Sales		14,600				14,600		14,600				
411	Sales Discounts	44				44		44					
412	Sales Returns and Allowances	20				20		20					
500	Purchases	6,000				6,000		6,000					
501	Purchase Discounts		82				82		82				
502	Purchase Returns and Allowances		100				100		100				
503	Transportation-In	75				75		75					
557	Miscellaneous Selling Expenses	2,650				2,650		2,650					
567	Miscellaneous Administrative												
	Expenses	1,150				1,150		1,150					
		40,482	40,482			40,482	40,482	16,939	22,782				
	Net Income							5,843			5,843		
								22,782	22,782	2,000	20,843	29,543	10,700
	Retained Earnings, December 31									18,843			18,843
										20,843	20,843	29,543	29,543

ILLUSTRATION 6.10
Income Statement for a Merchandising Company

LYONS COMPANY
Income Statement
For the Month Ended December 31, 1997

Operating revenues:				
Gross sales				$14,600
Less: Sales discounts			$ 44	
Sales returns and allowances			20	64
Net sales				$14,536
Cost of goods sold:				
Merchandise inventory, December 1, 1997			$ 7,000	
Purchases		$6,000		
Less: Purchase discounts	$ 82			
Purchase returns and allowances	100	182		
Net purchases		$5,818		
Add: Transportation-in		75		
Net cost of purchases			5,893	
Cost of goods available for sale			$12,893	
Less: Merchandise inventory, December 31, 1997			8,000	
Cost of goods sold				4,893
Gross margin				$ 9,643
Operating expenses:				
Miscellaneous selling expenses			$ 2,650	
Miscellaneous administrative expenses			1,150	
Total operating expenses				3,800
Net income				$ 5,843

ILLUSTRATION 6.11
Statement of Retained Earnings

LYONS COMPANY
Statement of Retained Earnings
For the Month Ended December 31, 1997

Retained earnings, December 1, 1997	$15,000
Add: Net income for the month	5,843
Total	$20,843
Deduct: Dividends	2,000
Retained earnings, December 31, 1997	$18,843

ILLUSTRATION 6.12
Balance Sheet for a Merchandising Company

LYONS COMPANY
Balance Sheet
December 31, 1997

Assets

Current assets:		
Cash		$19,663
Accounts receivable		1,880
Merchandise inventory		8,000
Total assets		$29,543

Liabilities and Stockholders' Equity

Current liabilities:		
Accounts payable		$ 700
Stockholders' equity:		
Capital stock	$10,000	
Retained earnings	18,843	
Total stockholders' equity		28,843
Total liabilities and stockholders' equity		$29,543

Balance Sheet The balance sheet, Illustration 6.12, contains the assets, liabilities, and stockholders' equity items taken from the work sheet. Note the $8,000 ending inventory is a current asset. The Retained Earnings account balance comes from the statement of retained earnings.

Closing Entries

Recall from Chapter 4 that the closing process normally takes place after the accountant has prepared the financial statements for the period. The closing process closes revenue and expense accounts by transferring their balances to a clearing account called Income Summary and then to Retained Earnings. The closing process reduces the revenue and expense account balances to zero so that information for each accounting period may be accumulated separately.

Lyons's accountant would prepare closing entries directly from the work sheet in Illustration 6.9 using the same procedure presented in Chapter 4. The closing entries for Lyons Company follow.

The first journal entry *debits* all items appearing in the Income Statement credit column of the work sheet and *credits* Income Summary for the total of the column, $22,782.

1997				
Dec.	31	Merchandise Inventory (ending)	8,000	
		Sales	14,600	
		Purchase Discounts	82	
		Purchase Returns and Allowances	100	
		Income Summary		22,782
		To close accounts with a credit balance in the Income Statement columns and to establish ending merchandise inventory.		

1st entry

The second entry *credits* all items appearing in the Income Statement debit column and *debits* Income Summary for the total of that column, $16,939.[1]

Dec.	31	Income Summary	16,939	
		Merchandise Inventory (beginning)		7,000
		Sales Discounts		44
		Sales Returns and Allowances		20
		Purchases		6,000
		Transportation-In		75
		Miscellaneous Selling Expenses		2,650
		Miscellaneous Administrative Expenses		1,150
		To close accounts with a debit balance in the Income Statement columns.		

2nd entry

The third entry closes the credit balance in the Income Summary account of $5,843 to the Retained Earnings account.

Dec.	31	Income Summary	5,843	
		Retained Earnings		5,843
		To close the Income Summary account to the Retained Earnings account.		

3rd entry

The fourth entry closes the Dividends account balance of $2,000 to the Retained Earnings account by debiting Retained Earnings and crediting Dividends.

Dec.	31	Retained Earnings	2,000	
		Dividends		2,000
		To close the Dividends account to the Retained Earnings account.		

4th entry

Note how the first three closing entries tie into the totals in the Income Statement columns of the work sheet in Illustration 6.9. In the first closing journal entry, the credit to the Income Summary account is equal to the total of the Income Statement credit column. In the second entry, the debit to the Income Summary account is equal to the subtotal of

[1] You may close debit balanced accounts (in the Income Statement) before credit balanced accounts. This practice does not affect the balance of the Income Summary account or the amount of net income.

the Income Statement debit column. The difference between the totals of the two Income Statement columns ($5,843) represents net income and is the amount of the third closing entry.

Demonstration Problem

The following transactions occurred between Companies C and D in June of 1997:

June 10 Company C purchased merchandise from Company D for $80,000; terms 2/10/EOM, n/60, FOB destination, freight prepaid.

11 Company D paid freight of $1,200.

14 Company C received an allowance of $4,000 from the gross selling price because of damaged goods.

23 Company C returned $8,000 of goods purchased because they were not the quality ordered.

30 Company D received payment in full from Company C.

Required

a. Journalize the transactions for Company C.

b. Journalize the transactions for Company D.

Solution to Demonstration Problem

a.

General Journal

Date		Account Titles and Explanation	Post. Ref.	Debit	Credit
		Company C			
1997					
June	10	Purchases		80000	
		Accounts Payable			80000
		Purchased merchandise from Company D; terms 2/10/EOM, n/60.			
	14	Accounts Payable		4000	
		Purchase Returns and Allowances			4000
		Received an allowance from Company D for damaged goods.			
	23	Accounts Payable		8000	
		Purchase Returns and Allowances			8000
		Returned merchandise to Company D because of improper quality.			
	30	Accounts Payable ($80,000 − $4,000 − $8,000)		68000	
		Purchase Discounts ($68,000 × 0.02)			1360
		Cash ($68,000 − $1,360)			66640
		Paid the amount due to Company D.			

b.

General Journal

Date		Account Titles and Explanation	Post. Ref.	Debit	Credit
		Company D			
1997 June	10	Accounts Receivable		80000	
		Sales			80000
		Sold merchandise to Company C; terms 2/10/EOM, n/60.			
	11	Delivery Expense		1200	
		Cash			1200
		Paid freight on sale of merchandise shipped FOB destination, freight prepaid.			
	14	Sales Returns and Allowances		4000	
		Accounts Receivable			4000
		Granted an allowance to Company C for damaged goods.			
	23	Sales Returns and Allowances		8000	
		Accounts Receivable			8000
		Merchandise returned from Company C due to improper quality.			
	30	Cash ($68,000 − $1,360)		66640	
		Sales Discounts ($68,000 × 0.02)		1360	
		Accounts Receivable ($80,000 − $4,000 − $8,000)			68000
		Received the amount due from Company C.			

NEW TERMS

Adjunct account Closely related to another account; its balance is added to the balance of the related account in the financial statements. *219*

Administrative expenses Expenses a company incurs in the overall management of a business. *223*

Cash discount A deduction from the invoice price that can be taken only if the invoice is paid within a specified time. To the seller, it is a sales discount; to the buyer, it is a purchase discount. *212*

Chain discount Occurs when the list price of a product is subject to a series of trade discounts. *211*

Classified income statement Divides both revenues and expenses into operating and nonoperating items. The statement also separates operating expenses into selling and administrative expenses. Also called the multiple-step income statement. *222*

Consigned goods Goods delivered to another party who attempts to sell the goods for the owner at a commission. *221*

Cost of goods available for sale Equal to beginning inventory plus net cost of purchases. *221*

Cost of goods sold Shows the cost to the seller of the goods sold to customers; under periodic inventory procedure, cost of goods sold is computed as Beginning inventory + Net cost of purchases − Ending inventory. *215, 225*

Delivery expense A selling expense recorded by the seller for freight costs incurred when terms are FOB destination. *219*

FOB destination Means free on board at destination; goods are shipped to their destination without charge to the buyer; the seller is responsible for paying the freight charges. *219*

FOB shipping point Means free on board at shipping point; buyer incurs all transportation costs after the merchandise is loaded on a railroad car or truck at the point of shipment. *219*

Freight collect Terms that require the buyer to pay the freight bill on arrival of the goods. *219*

Freight prepaid Terms that indicate the seller has paid the freight bill at the time of shipment. *219*

Gross margin or gross profit Net sales − Cost of goods sold; identifies the number of dollars available to cover expenses other than cost of goods sold. *223, 225*

Gross margin percentage Gross margin divided by net sales. *225*

Gross selling price (also called the invoice price) The list price less all trade discounts. *211*

Income from operations Gross margin − Operating (selling and administrative) expenses. *225*

Invoice A document prepared by the seller of merchandise and sent to the buyer. It contains the details of a sale, such as the number of units sold, unit price, total price billed, terms of sale, and manner of shipment. It is a purchase invoice from the buyer's point of view and a sales invoice from the seller's point of view. *209*

Manufacturers Companies that produce goods from raw materials and normally sell them to wholesalers. *208*

Merchandise in transit Merchandise in the hands of a freight company on the date of a physical inventory. *221*

Merchandise inventory The quantity of goods available for sale at any given time. *215, 220*

Net cost of purchases Net purchases + Transportation-in. *219, 225*

Net income Income from operations + Nonoperating revenues − Nonoperating expenses. *225*

Net purchases Purchases − (Purchase discounts + Purchase returns and allowances). *218, 220*

Net sales Gross sales − (Sales discounts + Sales returns and allowances). *209, 225*

Nonoperating expenses (other expenses) Expenses incurred by a business that are not related to the acquisition and sale of the products or services regularly offered for sale. *225*

Nonoperating revenues (other revenues) Revenues not related to the sale of products or services regularly offered for sale by a business. *225*

Operating expenses Those expenses other than cost of goods sold incurred in the normal business functions of a company. *223*

Operating revenues Those revenues generated by the major activities of a business. *223*

Passage of title A legal term used to indicate transfer of legal ownership of goods. *219*

Periodic inventory procedure A method of accounting for merchandise acquired for sale to customers wherein the cost of merchandise sold and the cost of merchandise on hand are determined only at the end of the accounting period by taking a physical inventory. *215*

Perpetual inventory procedure A method of accounting for merchandise acquired for sale to customers wherein the Merchandise Inventory account is continuously updated to reflect items on hand; this account is debited for each purchase and credited for each sale so that the current balance is shown in the account at all times. *215*

Physical inventory Consists of counting physical units of each type of merchandise on hand. *221*

Purchase discount See Cash discount.

Purchase Discounts account A contra account to Purchases that reduces the recorded gross invoice cost of the purchase to the price actually paid. *217*

Purchase Returns and Allowances account An account used under periodic inventory procedure to record the cost of merchandise returned to a seller and to record reductions in selling prices granted by a seller because merchandise was not satisfactory to a buyer; viewed as a reduction in the recorded cost of purchases. *218*

Purchases account An account used under periodic inventory procedure to record the cost of goods or merchandise bought for resale during the current accounting period. *217*

Retailers Companies that sell goods to final consumers. *208*

Sales allowance A deduction from original invoiced sales price granted to a customer when the customer keeps the merchandise but is dissatisfied for any of a number of reasons, including inferior quality, damage, or deterioration in transit. *213*

Sales discount See Cash discount.

Sales Discounts account A contra revenue account to Sales; it is shown as a deduction from gross sales in the income statement. *213*

Sales return From the seller's point of view, merchandise returned by a buyer for any of a variety of reasons; to the buyer, a purchase return. *213*

Sales Returns and Allowances account A contra revenue account to Sales used to record the selling price of merchandise returned by buyers or reductions in selling prices granted. *213*

Selling expenses Expenses a company incurs in selling and marketing efforts. *223*

Trade discount A percentage deduction, or discount, from the specified list price or catalog price of merchandise to arrive at the gross invoice price; granted to particular categories of customers (e.g., retailers and wholesalers). Also see Chain discount. *211*

Transportation-In account An account used under periodic inventory procedure to record inward freight costs incurred in the acquisition of merchandise; a part of cost of goods sold. *219*

Unclassified income statement Shows only major categories for revenues and expenses. Also called the single-step income statement. *222*

Wholesalers Companies that normally sell goods to other companies (retailers) for resale. *208*

SELF-TEST

TRUE-FALSE

Indicate whether each of the following statements is true or false.

1. To compute net sales, sales discounts are added to, and sales returns and allowances are deducted from, gross sales.

2. Under perpetual inventory procedure, the Merchandise Inventory account is debited for each purchase and credited for each sale.

3. Purchase discounts and purchase returns and allowances are recorded in contra accounts to the Purchases account.
4. In taking a physical inventory, consigned goods are usually not included in the ending inventory, but merchandise in transit is included.
5. A classified income statement consists of only two categories of items, revenues and expenses.

Multiple-Choice

Select the best answer for each of the following questions.

1. A seller sold merchandise which has a list price of $4,000 on account, giving a trade discount of 20%. The entry on the books of the seller is:

a.	Accounts Receivable	3,200	
	Trade Discounts	800	
	Sales		4,000
b.	Accounts Receivable	4,000	
	Sales		4,000
c.	Accounts Receivable	3,200	
	Sales Discounts	800	
	Sales		4,000
d.	Accounts Receivable	3,200	
	Sales		3,200

   e. None of the above.

2. Y Company began the accounting period with $60,000 of merchandise, and net cost of purchases was $240,000. A physical inventory showed $72,000 of merchandise unsold at the end of the period. The cost of goods sold of Y Company for the period is:
   a. $300,000.
   b. $228,000.
   c. $252,000.
   d. $168,000.
   e. None of the above.

3. A business purchased merchandise for $12,000 on account; terms are 2/10, n/30. If $2,000 of the merchandise was returned and the remaining amount due was paid within the discount period, the purchase discount would be:
   a. $240.
   b. $200.
   c. $1,200.
   d. $1,000.
   e. $3,600.

4. A classified income statement consists of all of the following major sections except for:
   a. Operating revenues.
   b. Cost of goods sold.
   c. Operating expenses.
   d. Nonoperating revenues and expenses.
   e. Current assets.

5. (Appendix) Closing entries for merchandise-related accounts include all of the following except for:
   a. A credit to Sales Discounts.
   b. A credit to Merchandise Inventory for the cost of ending inventory.
   c. A debit to Purchase Discounts.
   d. A credit to Transportation-In.
   e. A debit to Sales.

Now turn to page 244 to check your answers.

Questions

1. Which account titles are likely to appear in a merchandising company's ledger that do not appear in the ledger of a service enterprise?
2. What entry is made to record a sale of merchandise on account under periodic inventory procedure?
3. Describe trade discounts and chain discounts.
4. Sales discounts and sales returns and allowances are deducted from sales on the income statement to arrive at net sales. Why not deduct these directly from the Sales account by debiting Sales each time a sales discount, return, or allowance occurs?
5. What are the two basic procedures for accounting for inventory? How do these two procedures differ?
6. What useful purpose does the Purchases account serve?
7. What do the letters FOB stand for? When terms are *FOB destination,* who incurs the cost of freight?
8. What type of an expense is delivery expense? Where is this expense reported in the income statement?
9. Periodic inventory procedure is said to afford little control over inventory. Explain why.
10. How does the accountant arrive at the total dollar amount of the inventory after taking a physical inventory?
11. How is cost of goods sold determined under periodic inventory procedure?
12. If the cost of goods available for sale and the cost of the ending inventory are known, what other amount appearing on the income statement can be calculated?
13. What are the major sections in a classified income statement for a merchandising company, and in what order do these sections appear?
14. What is gross margin? Why might management be interested in the percentage of gross margin to net sales?
15. (Appendix) After closing entries are posted to the ledger, which types of accounts have balances? Why?

MAYTAG

16. **Real World Question** Based on the financial statements of Maytag Corporation contained in the annual report booklet, what were the 1993 selling, general, and administrative expenses? For each of the three years shown, what percentage of net sales were these expenses? Is the trend favorable or unfavorable?

THE LIMITED, INC.

17. **Real World Question** Based on the financial statements of The Limited, Inc., contained in the annual report booklet, what were the 1993 cost of goods sold, occupancy, and buying costs? For each of the three years shown, what percentage of net sales were these expenses? Is the trend favorable or unfavorable?

HARLAND

18. **Real World Question** Based on the financial statements of John H. Harland Company contained in the annual report booklet, what was the 1993 income from operations? For each of the three years shown, what percentage of net sales was income from operations? Is the trend favorable or unfavorable?

Exercises

Exercise 6–1
Apply rules of debit and credit for merchandise-related accounts (L.O. 1, 3)

In the following table, indicate how to increase or decrease (debit or credit) each account, and indicate its normal balance (debit or credit).

Title of Account	Increased by (debit or credit)	Decreased by (debit or credit)	Normal Balance (debit or credit)
Merchandise Inventory			
Sales			
Sales Returns and Allowances			
Sales Discounts			
Accounts Receivable			
Purchases			
Purchase Returns and Allowances			
Purchase Discounts			
Accounts Payable			
Transportation-In			

Exercise 6–2
Prepare entries for merchandise purchase/sale, return, and allowance on both buyer's and seller's books (L.O. 1, 3)

a. Copper Company purchased $56,000 of merchandise from Fulton Company on account. Before paying its account, Copper Company returned damaged merchandise with an invoice price of $11,680. Assuming use of periodic inventory procedure, prepare entries on both companies' books to record both the purchase/sale and the return.

b. Show how any of the required entries would change assuming that Fulton Company granted an allowance of $3,360 on the damaged goods instead of giving permission to return the merchandise.

Exercise 6–3
Determine end of discount period and prepare an entry to record payment (L.O. 1, 3)

What is the last payment date on which the cash discount can be taken on goods sold on March 5 for $102,400; terms 3/10/EOM, n/60? Assume that the bill is paid on this date and prepare the correct entries on both the buyer's and seller's books to record the payment.

Exercise 6–4
Calculate effect of trade and cash discounts on payment (L.O. 1, 3)

You have purchased merchandise with a list price of $36,000. Because you are a wholesaler, you are granted trade discounts of 30%, 20%, and 10%. The cash discount terms are 2/EOM, n/60. How much will you remit if you pay the invoice by the end of the month of purchase? How much will you remit if you do not pay the invoice until the following month?

Exercise 6–5
Calculate gross selling price and final payment (L.O. 1, 3)

Jenkins Company sold merchandise with a list price of $30,000 on July 1, 1997. For each of the following independent assumptions, calculate (1) the gross selling price used to record the sale and (2) the amount that the buyer would have to remit when paying the invoice.

	Trade Discount Granted	Credit Terms	Date Paid
a.	30%, 20%	2/10, n/30	July 10
b.	40%, 10%	2/EOM, n/60	August 10
c.	30%, 10%, 5%	3/10/EOM, n/60	August 10
d.	40%	1/10, n/30	July 12

Exercise 6–6
Determine cash discount available and amount of cash paid (L.O. 1, 3, 4)

Murray Company purchased goods at a gross selling price of $2,400 on August 1, 1997. Discount terms of 2/10, n/30 were available. For each of the following independent situations, determine (1) the cash discount available on the final payment and (2) the amount paid if payment is made within the discount period.

	Transportation Terms	Freight Paid (by)	Purchase Allowance Granted
a.	FOB shipping point	$240 (buyer)	$480
b.	FOB destination	120 (seller)	240
c.	FOB shipping point	180 (seller)	720
d.	FOB destination	192 (buyer)	120

Exercise 6–7
Prepare entries for purchase, transportation-in, purchase discounts, and payment (L.O. 3, 4)

Lewis Company purchased goods for $42,000 on June 14, 1997, under the following terms: 3/10, n/30; FOB shipping point, freight collect. The bill for the freight was paid on June 15, $1,200.

a. Assume that the invoice was paid on June 24, and prepare all entries required on Lewis Company's books.

b. Assume that the invoice was paid on July 11. Prepare the entry to record the payment made on that date.

Exercise 6–8
Determine cost of goods sold (L.O. 2, 3, 5)

Crabtree Company uses the periodic inventory procedure. Determine the cost of goods sold for the company assuming purchases during the period were $40,000, transportation-in was $300, purchase returns and allowances were $1,000, beginning inventory was $25,000, purchase discounts were $2,000, and ending inventory was $13,000.

Exercise 6–9
Supply missing amounts in the income statement (L.O. 1–4, 6)

In each case, use the following information to calculate the missing information:

	Case 1	Case 2	Case 3
Gross sales	$640,000	$?	$?
Sales discounts	?	25,600	19,200
Sales returns and allowances	19,200	44,800	32,000
Net sales	608,000	1,209,600	?
Merchandise inventory, January 1	256,000	?	384,000
Purchases	384,000	768,000	?
Purchase discounts	7,680	13,440	12,800
Purchase returns and allowances	24,320	31,360	32,000
Net purchases	352,000	?	672,000
Transportation-in	25,600	38,400	32,000
Net cost of purchases	377,600	761,600	?
Cost of goods available for sale	?	1,081,600	1,088,000
Merchandise inventory, December 31	?	384,000	448,000
Cost of goods sold	320,000	?	640,000
Gross margin	?	512,000	320,000

Exercise 6–10
Supply missing terms in formulas showing income statement relationships (L.O. 6)

In each of the following equations supply the missing term(s):

a. Net sales = Gross sales − (__________ __________ + Sales returns and allowances).

b. Cost of goods sold = Beginning inventory + Net cost of purchases − __________ __________.

c. Gross margin = __________ __________ − Cost of goods sold.

d. Income from operations = __________ __________ − Operating expenses.

e. Net income = Income from operations + __________ __________ − __________ __________.

Exercise 6–11
Prepare a partial work sheet using merchandise-related accounts (based on Appendix) (L.O. 8)

Given the balances in this partial trial balance, indicate how the balances would be treated in the work sheet. The ending inventory is $96. (The amounts are unusually small for ease in rewriting the numbers.)

Account Titles	Trial Balance		Adjustments		Adjusted Trial Balance		Income Statement		Balance Sheet	
	Debit	Credit	Debit	Credit	Debit	Credit	Debit	Credit	Debit	Credit
Merchandise Inventory	120									
Sales		840								
Sales Discounts	18									
Sales Returns and Allowances	48									
Purchases	600									
Purchase Discounts		12								
Purchase Returns and Allowances		24								
Transportation-In	36									

Exercise 6–12
Prepare and post closing entries using T-accounts (based on Appendix)
(L.O. 8)

Using the data in Exercise 6–11 prepare closing entries for the preceding accounts. Do not close the Income Summary account.

PROBLEMS

Problem 6–1
Journalize merchandise transactions for two different companies
(L.O. 1, 3, 4)

a. Grant Sporting Goods Company engaged in the following transactions in April 1997:

Apr. 1 Sold merchandise on account for $144,000; terms 2/10, n/30, FOB shipping point, freight collect.

5 $21,600 of the goods sold on account on April 1 were returned for a full credit. Payment for these goods had not yet been received.

8 A sales allowance of $2,880 was granted on the merchandise sold on April 1 because the merchandise was damaged in shipment.

10 Payment was received for the net amount due from the sale of April 1.

b. Rydell Stereo Company engaged in the following transactions in July 1997:

July 2 Purchased stereo merchandise on account at a cost of $21,600; terms 2/10, n/30, FOB destination, freight prepaid.

15 Sold merchandise for $32,400, terms 2/10, n/30, FOB destination, freight prepaid.

16 Paid freight costs on the merchandise sold, $1,080.

20 Rydell Stereo Company was granted an allowance of $1,440 on the purchase of July 2 because of damaged merchandise.

31 Paid the amount due on the purchase of July 2.

Required Prepare journal entries to record the transactions.

Problem 6–2
Journalize merchandise transactions on both buyer's and seller's books
(L.O. 1, 3, 4)

Venus Musical Instrument Company and Jaguar Company engaged in the following transactions with each other during July 1997:

July 2 Venus Musical Instrument Company purchased merchandise on account with a list price of $48,000 from Jaguar Company. The terms were 3/EOM, n/60, FOB shipping point, freight collect. Trade discounts of 15%, 10%, and 5% were granted by Jaguar Company.

5 The buyer paid the freight bill on the purchase of July 2, $1,104.

6 The buyer returned damaged merchandise with an invoice price of $2,790 to the seller and received full credit.

On the last day of the discount period, the buyer paid the seller for the merchandise.

Required Prepare all the necessary journal entries for the buyer and the seller.

Problem 6–3
Prepare and post journal entries, and prepare a trial balance and classified income statement (L.O. 1–6)

The following data for June 1997 are for Dean Company's first month of operations:

June 1 Dean Company was organized, and the stockholders invested $504,000 cash, $168,000 of merchandise inventory, and a $144,000 plot of land in exchange for capital stock.
4 Merchandise was purchased for cash, $216,000; FOB shipping point, freight collect.
9 Cash of $5,040 was paid to a trucking company for delivery of the merchandise purchased June 4.
13 The company sold merchandise on account, $144,000; terms 2/10, n/30.
15 The company sold merchandise on account, $115,200; terms 2/10, n/30.
16 Of the merchandise sold June 13, $15,840 was returned for credit.
20 Salaries for services received were paid as follows: to office employees, $15,840; to salespersons, $41,760.
22 The company collected the amount due on the remaining $128,160 of accounts receivable arising from the sale of June 13.
24 The company purchased merchandise on account at a cost of $172,800; terms 2/10, n/30, FOB shipping point, freight collect.
26 The company returned $28,800 of the merchandise purchased June 24 to the vendor for credit.
27 A trucking company was paid $3,600 for delivery to Dean Company of the goods purchased June 24.
29 The company sold merchandise on account, $192,000; terms 2/10, n/30.
30 Sold merchandise for cash, $86,400.
30 Payment was received for the sale of June 15.
30 Paid store rent for June, $21,600.
30 Paid the amount due on the purchase of June 24.

Additional data

The inventory on hand at the close of business June 30 was $336,000 at cost.

Required

a. Prepare journal entries for the transactions.
b. Post the journal entries to the proper ledger accounts. Use the account numbers in the chart of accounts on the inside covers of the text. Assume that all postings are from page 20 of the general journal.
c. Prepare a trial balance as of June 30, 1997.
d. Prepare a classified income statement for the month ended June 30, 1997. No adjusting entries are needed.

Problem 6–4 ✓
Prepare and post journal entries, prepare trial balance, classified income statement, and classified balance sheet (L.O. 1–6)

Carlos Western Wear Company, a wholesaler of western wear clothing, sells to retailers. The company entered into the following transactions in May 1997:

May 1 Carlos Western Wear Company was organized as a corporation. The stockholders purchased stock at par for the following assets in the business: $462,000 cash, $168,000 merchandise, and $105,000 land.
1 Paid rent on administrative offices for May, $25,200.
5 The company purchased merchandise from Carlyle Company on account, $189,000; terms 2/10, n/30. Freight terms were FOB shipping point, freight collect.
8 Cash of $8,400 was paid to a trucking company for delivery of the merchandise purchased May 5.
14 The company sold merchandise on account, $315,000; terms 2/10, n/30.
15 Paid Carlyle Company the amount due on the purchase of May 5.
16 Of the merchandise sold May 14, $13,860 was returned for credit.
19 Salaries for services received were paid for May as follows: office employees, $16,800; salespersons, $33,600.
24 The company collected the amount due on $126,000 of the accounts receivable arising from the sale of May 14.
25 The company purchased merchandise on account from Stock Company, $151,200; terms 2/10, n/30. Freight terms were FOB shipping point, freight collect.
27 Of the merchandise purchased May 25, $25,200 was returned to the vendor.
28 A trucking company was paid $2,100 for delivery to Carlos Western Wear Company of the goods purchased May 25.

May 29 The company sold merchandise on open account, $15,120; terms 2/10, n/30.
30 Cash sales were $74,088.
30 Cash of $100,800 was received from the sale of May 14.
31 Paid Stock Company for the merchandise purchased on May 25, taking into consideration the merchandise returned on May 27.

Additional data The inventory on hand at the close of business on May 31 is $299,040.

Required From the data given for Carlos Western Wear Company:

a. Prepare journal entries for the transactions.

b. Post the journal entries to the proper ledger accounts. Use the account numbers in the chart of accounts on the inside covers of the text. Assume that all postings are from page 15 of the general journal. (There were no adjusting journal entries.)

c. Prepare a trial balance.

d. Prepare a classified income statement for the month ended May 31, 1997.

e. Prepare a classified balance sheet as of May 31, 1997.

Problem 6–5
Prepare work sheet, classified income statement, statement of retained earnings, classified balance sheet, and closing entries (based on Appendix) (L.O. 5–8)

(Appendix) The following data are for Lee Lumber Company:

LEE LUMBER COMPANY
Trial Balance
December 31, 1997

Acct. No.	Account Title	Debits	Credits
100	Cash	$ 70,640	
103	Accounts Receivable	159,520	
105	Merchandise Inventory	285,200	
107	Supplies on Hand	5,360	
108	Prepaid Insurance	4,800	
112	Prepaid Rent	57,600	
170	Equipment	88,000	
171	Accumulated Depreciation—Equipment		$ 17,600
200	Accounts Payable		102,800
300	Capital Stock		200,000
310	Retained Earnings, 1/1/97		219,640
410	Sales		1,122,360
412	Sales Returns and Allowances	5,160	
418	Interest Revenue		1,000
500	Purchases	500,840	
502	Purchase Returns and Allowances		4,040
503	Transportation-In	7,840	
505	Advertising Expense	78,000	
508	Sales Salaries Expense	138,400	
509	Office Salaries Expense	80,800	
510	Officers' Salaries Expense	160,000	
511	Utilities Expense	4,800	
536	Legal and Accounting Expense	10,000	
540	Interest Expense	600	
567	Miscellaneous Administrative Expense	9,880	
		$1,667,440	$1,667,440

Additional data

1. A total of $3,400 of the prepaid insurance has expired.
2. An inventory of supplies showed that $1,700 are still on hand.
3. Prepaid rent expired during the year is $50,600.
4. Depreciation expense on store equipment is $8,800.
5. Accrued sales salaries are $4,000.
6. Accrued office salaries are $3,000.
7. Merchandise inventory on hand is $350,000.

Required Prepare the following:

a. A work sheet for the year ended December 31, 1997. Refer to the chart of accounts on the inside covers of the text for any other account numbers you need.

b. A classified income statement. The only selling expenses are sales salaries, advertising, supplies, and depreciation—equipment.

c. A statement of retained earnings.

d. A classified balance sheet.

e. The December 31, 1997, closing entries.

ALTERNATIVE PROBLEMS

Problem 6–1A
Journalize merchandise transactions for two different companies
(L.O. 1, 3, 4)

a. Baker Carpet Company engaged in the following transactions in August 1997:

Aug. 2 Sold merchandise on account for $150,000; terms 2/10, n/30, FOB shipping point, freight collect.
18 Received payment for the sale of August 2.
20 A total of $5,000 of the merchandise sold on August 2 was returned, and a full refund was made because it was the wrong merchandise.
28 An allowance of $8,000 was granted on the sale of August 2 because some merchandise was found to be damaged; $8,000 cash was returned to the customer.

b. Harper Furniture Company engaged in the following transactions in August 1997:

Aug. 4 Purchased merchandise on account at a cost of $70,000; terms 2/10, n/30, FOB shipping point, freight collect.
6 Paid freight of $1,000 on the purchase of August 4.
10 Sold goods for $50,000; terms 2/10, n/30.
12 Returned $12,000 of the merchandise purchased on August 4.
14 Paid the amount due on the purchase of August 4.

Required

Prepare journal entries for the transactions.

Problem 6–2A
Journalize merchandise transactions on both buyer's and seller's books
(L.O. 1, 3, 4)

Alvarez Auto Parts Company and Fork Company engaged in the following transactions with each other during August 1997:

Aug. 15 Alvarez Auto Parts Company purchased merchandise on account with a list price of $192,000 from Fork Company. Trade discounts of 20% and 10% were allowed. Terms were 2/10, n/30, FOB destination, freight prepaid.
16 The seller paid the freight charges, $2,400.
17 The buyer requested an allowance of $4,512 against the amount due because the goods were damaged in transit.
20 The seller granted the allowance requested on August 17.

The buyer paid the amount due on the last day of the discount period.

Required

Record all of the entries required on the books of both the buyer and the seller.

Problem 6–3A
Prepare and post journal entries, and prepare trial balance and classified income statement
(L.O. 1–6)

Gerhardt Company engaged in the following transactions in June 1997, the company's first month of operations:

June 1 Stockholders invested $192,000 cash and $72,000 of merchandise inventory in the business in exchange for capital stock.
3 Merchandise was purchased on account, $96,000; terms 2/10, n/30, FOB shipping point, freight collect.
4 Paid freight on the June 3 purchase, $2,640.
7 Merchandise was purchased on account, $48,000; terms 2/10, n/30, FOB destination, freight prepaid.
10 Sold merchandise on account, $115,200; terms 2/10, n/30, FOB shipping point, freight collect.
11 Returned $14,400 of the merchandise purchased on June 3.
12 Paid the amount due on the purchase of June 3.
13 Sold merchandise on account, $120,000; terms 2/10, n/30, FOB destination, freight prepaid.
14 Paid freight on sale of June 13, $7,200.
20 Paid the amount due on the purchase of June 7.
21 $24,000 of the goods sold on June 13 were returned for credit.
22 Received the amount due on sale of June 13.
25 Received the amount due on sale of June 10.
29 Paid rent for the administration building for June, $9,600.

June 30 Paid sales salaries of $28,800 for June.
30 Purchased merchandise on account, $24,000; terms 2/10, n/30, FOB destination, freight prepaid.

Additional data The inventory on hand on June 30 was $144,000.

Required

a. Prepare journal entries for the transactions.

b. Post the journal entries to the proper ledger accounts. Use the account numbers in the chart of accounts on the inside covers of the text. Assume that all postings are from page 10 of the general journal.

c. Prepare a trial balance as of June 30, 1997.

d. Prepare a classified income statement for the month ended June 30, 1997. No adjusting entries are needed.

Problem 6–4A
Prepare and post journal entries; prepare trial balance and classified income statement
(L.O. 1–6)

Organized on May 1, 1997, Wyley Cabinet Company engaged in the following transactions:

May 1 The stockholders invested $900,000 in this new business by purchasing capital stock.
1 Purchased merchandise on account from Stringer Company, $46,800; terms n/60, FOB shipping point, freight collect.
3 Sold merchandise for cash, $28,800.
6 Paid transportation charges on May 1 purchase, $1,440 cash.
7 Returned $3,600 of merchandise to Stringer Company due to improper size.
10 Requested and received an allowance of $1,800 from Stringer Company for improper quality of certain items.
14 Sold merchandise on account to Embry Company, $18,000; terms 2/20, n/30, FOB shipping point, freight collect.
16 Issued cash refund for return of merchandise relating to sale made on May 3, $180.
18 Purchased merchandise on account from Black Company invoiced at $28,800; terms 2/15, n/30, FOB shipping point, freight collect.
18 Received a bill for freight charges of $900 from Lucille Trucking Company on the purchase from Black Company.
19 Embry Company returned $360 of merchandise purchased on May 14.
24 Returned $2,880 of defective merchandise to Black Company. Received full credit.
28 Embry Company remitted balance due on sale of May 14.
31 Paid Black Company for the purchase of May 18 after adjusting for transaction of May 24.
31 Paid miscellaneous selling expenses of $7,200.
31 Paid miscellaneous administrative expenses of $10,800.

Additional data The May 31st inventory is $57,600.

Required From the data for Wyley Cabinet Company:

a. Journalize the transactions. Round all amounts to the nearest dollar.

b. Post the entries to the proper ledger accounts. Use the account numbers appearing in the chart of accounts on the inside covers of the text. Assume all postings are from page 5 of the general journal. (There were no adjusting journal entries.)

c. Prepare a trial balance.

d. Prepare a classified income statement for the month ended May 31, 1997.

Problem 6–5A
Prepare a work sheet, classified income statement, statement of retained earnings, classified balance sheet, and closing entries (based on Appendix) (L.O. 5–8)

The following data are for Bauer Lamp Company:

BAUER LAMP COMPANY
Trial Balance
December 31, 1997

Acct. No.	Account Title	Debits	Credits
100	Cash	$ 114,400	
103	Accounts Receivable	96,600	
105	Merchandise Inventory, January 1, 1997	83,200	
108	Prepaid Insurance	5,800	
130	Land	120,000	
140	Buildings	220,000	
141	Accumulated Depreciation—Buildings		$ 66,000
174	Store Fixtures	111,200	
175	Accumulated Depreciation—Store Fixtures		22,240
200	Accounts Payable		75,800
300	Capital Stock		200,000
310	Retained Earnings, 1/1/97		240,360
410	Sales		1,103,000
411	Sales Discounts	7,400	
412	Sales Returns and Allowances	4,000	
418	Interest Revenue		800
500	Purchases	625,800	
501	Purchase Discounts		5,200
502	Purchase Returns and Allowances		2,800
503	Transportation-In	14,600	
505	Advertising Expense	24,000	
508	Sales Salaries Expense	128,000	
509	Office Salaries Expense	148,000	
519	Delivery Expense	9,200	
540	Interest Expense	4,000	
		$1,716,200	$1,716,200

Additional data

1. Depreciation expense on the store building is $4,400.
2. Depreciation expense on the store fixtures is $11,120.
3. Accrued sales salaries are $2,800.
4. Insurance expired in 1997 is $5,000.
5. Cost of merchandise inventory on hand December 31, 1997, is $111,000.

Required

Prepare the following:

a. A work sheet for the year ended December 31, 1997. Refer to the chart of accounts on the inside covers of the text for any other account numbers you need.
b. A classified income statement. The only administrative expenses are office salaries and insurance. The building depreciation is on the store building.
c. A statement of retained earnings.
d. A classified balance sheet.
e. The required closing entries.

BEYOND THE NUMBERS—CRITICAL THINKING

Business Decision Case 6–1
Prepare income statements and evaluate feasibility (L.O. 5, 6)

Millie's Shirts, Inc., has an opportunity to purchase 40,000 shirts with the logo of the 1996 Olympics in January 1994. Millie, who is not currently in business, is considering buying these shirts and then renting a display cart from which to sell these shirts (called a kiosk) in an Atlanta shopping mall. Based on the following information and estimates, Millie needs to decide if the business would be profitable:

1. Cost of the 40,000 shirts, all of which must be purchased in January 1994, is $440,000.
2. Millie thinks it would take two years to sell all of the shirts. She estimates her sales at 25,000 shirts in 1994 and 15,000 shirts in 1995.
3. Rent of the kiosk would be $1,500 per month in 1994 and $1,600 per month in 1995.

4. Millie can buy some counters on which to display the merchandise for $4,000. She could sell the counters for $500 at the end of the second year.
5. Millie estimates the cost to decorate her kiosk would be $2,500.
6. Millie would hire employees and pay them $1 per shirt sold.
7. Millie plans to sell the shirts for $17 each.
8. Millie and her husband purchased $100,000 of capital stock in the business. Therefore, she plans to borrow $400,000 from their family banker. Interest expense on this loan will be $52,000 in 1994 and $6,500 in 1995. Millie plans to repay $300,000 on January 2, 1995, and the remaining $100,000 on July 1, 1995.
9. Millie needs to rent some storage space because all 40,000 shirts cannot be stored at the kiosk. Storage space costs $2,500 per year.

Required

a. Prepare estimated income statements for 1994 and 1995 for Millie's business. Does it appear that the business will be profitable?
b. Will Millie have the cash available to pay the bank loan as she planned?

Business Decision Case 6–2
Analyze the importance of the gross margin percentage (L.O. 7)

Vulcan Materials Company is the nation's foremost producer of construction aggregates and a leading chemical manufacturer, producing a diversified line of chlorinated solvents and other industrial chemicals.

Using the following information from Vulcan Materials Company's 1992 annual report, calculate the gross margin percentage and write an explanation of what the results mean.

($ millions)	1992	1991	1990
Net sales	$1,078.0	$1,007.5	$1,105.3
Cost of goods sold	828.9	795.4	813.9
Gross profit on sales	$ 249.1	$ 212.1	$ 291.4

Annual Report Analysis 6–3
Classify income statement items and calculate gross margin percentages (L.O. 6, 7)

Refer to the consolidated statements of income of The Coca-Cola Company in the annual reports booklet. Identify the 1993 net operating revenues; cost of goods sold; gross profit; selling, administrative, and general expenses; and operating income. Do the results of 1993 compare favorably with those of 1992? Also calculate the gross profit (margin) percentages and comment.

Ethics Case—Writing Experience 6–4
Respond to questions regarding ethics case

Based on the ethics case related to World Auto Parts Corporation on page 226, respond in writing to the following questions:

a. Do you agree that the total impact of this practice could be as much as $10 million?
b. Are the small suppliers probably better off going along with the practice?
c. Is this practice ethical?

Group Project 6–5
Library project concerning annual reports—gross margin percentages (L.O. 7)

In teams of two or three students, go to the library to locate one merchandising company's annual report for the most recent year. Calculate the company's gross margin percentage for each of the most recent three years. As a team, write a memorandum to the instructor showing your calculations and commenting on the results. The heading of the memorandum should contain the date, to whom it is written, from whom, and the subject matter.

Answers to Self-Test

True-False

1. **False.** Sales discounts, as well as sales returns and allowances, are deducted from gross sales.
2. **True.** Under perpetual inventory procedure, the Merchandise Inventory account is debited for each purchase and credited for each sale.
3. **True.** Purchase discounts and purchase returns and allowances are contra accounts to the Purchases account. The balances of those accounts are deducted from purchases to arrive at net purchases.
4. **False.** Both consigned goods and goods in transit are included in the ending inventory.
5. **False.** An unclassified income statement, not a classified income statement, has only two categories of items.

Multiple-Choice

1. **d.** Trade discounts are not recorded on the books of either a buyer or a seller. In other words, the invoice price of sales (purchases) is recorded:

$$\$4{,}000 \times 0.8 = \$3{,}200$$

2. **b.** The cost of goods sold is computed as follows:

Beginning inventory	$ 60,000
Net cost of purchases	240,000
Cost of goods available for sale	$300,000
Ending inventory	72,000
Cost of goods sold	$228,000

3. **b.** Purchase discounts are based on invoice prices less purchase returns and allowances, if any.

Purchase discount =
$$(\$12{,}000 - \$2{,}000) \times 0.02 = \$200$$

4. **e.** All of the sections mentioned in **(a–d)** appear in a classified income statement. Current assets appear on a classified balance sheet.
5. **b.** Merchandise Inventory is debited for the cost of ending inventory.

7

Measuring and Reporting Inventories

Learning Objectives

After studying this chapter, you should be able to:

1. Explain and calculate the effects of inventory errors on certain financial statement items.
2. Indicate which costs are properly included in inventory.
3. Calculate cost of ending inventory and cost of goods sold under the four major inventory costing methods using perpetual and periodic inventory procedures.
4. Explain the advantages and disadvantages of the four major inventory costing methods.

(continued)

Have you ever taken advantage of a pre-inventory sale at your favorite retail store? Many stores offer bargain prices to reduce the merchandise on hand and to minimize the time and expense of taking the inventory. A smaller inventory also enhances the probability of taking an accurate inventory since the store has less merchandise to count. From Chapter 6 you know that companies use inventory amounts to determine the cost of goods sold; this major expense affects a merchandising company's net income. In this chapter, you learn how important inventories are in preparing an accurate income statement, statement of retained earnings, and balance sheet.

This chapter discusses merchandise inventory carried by merchandising retailers and wholesalers. A later chapter discusses other types of inventory carried by manufacturers. **Merchandise inventory** is the quantity of goods held by a merchandising company for resale to customers. Merchandising companies determine the quantity of inventory items by a physical count.

The merchandise inventory figure used by accountants depends on the quantity of inventory items and the cost of the items. This chapter discusses four accepted methods of costing the items: (1) specific identification; (2) first-in, first-out (FIFO); (3) last-in, first-out (LIFO); and (4) weighted-average. Each method has advantages and disadvantages.

This chapter stresses the importance of having accurate inventory figures and the serious consequences of using inaccurate inventory figures. This explains why your favorite retail store closes early to take inventory or why its employees work late to take inventory. When you finish this chapter, you should understand how taking inventory connects with the cost of goods sold figure on the store's income statement, the retained earnings amount on the statement of retained earnings, and both the inventory figure and the retained earnings amount on the store's balance sheet.

INVENTORIES AND COST OF GOODS SOLD

(*concluded*)

5. Record merchandise transactions under perpetual inventory procedure.

6. Apply net realizable value and the lower-of-cost-or-market method to inventory.

7. Estimate cost of ending inventory using the gross margin and retail inventory methods.

8. Analyze and use the financial results—inventory turnover ratio.

Inventory is often the largest and most important asset owned by a merchandising business. The inventory of some companies, like car dealerships or jewelry stores, may cost several times more than any other asset the company owns. As an asset, the inventory figure has a direct impact on reporting the solvency of the company in the balance sheet. As a factor in determining cost of goods sold, the inventory figure has a direct impact on the profitability of the company's operations as reported in the income statement. Thus, the importance of the inventory figure should not be underestimated.

Importance of Proper Inventory Valuation

Objective 1
Explain and calculate the effects of inventory errors on certain financial statement items.

A merchandising company can prepare accurate income statements, statements of retained earnings, and balance sheets only if its inventory is correctly valued. On the income statement, a company using periodic inventory procedure takes a physical inventory to determine the cost of goods sold. Since the cost of goods sold figure affects the company's net income, it also affects the balance of retained earnings on the statement of retained earnings. On the balance sheet, incorrect inventory amounts affect both the reported ending inventory and retained earnings. Inventories appear on the balance sheet under the heading "Current Assets," which reports current assets in a descending order of liquidity. Because inventories are consumed or converted into cash within a year or one operating cycle, whichever is longer, inventories usually follow cash and receivables on the balance sheet.

Recall that under periodic inventory procedure we determine the cost of goods sold figure by adding the beginning inventory to the net cost of purchases and deducting the ending inventory. In each accounting period, the appropriate expenses must be matched with the revenues of that period to determine the net income. Applied to inventory, matching involves determining (1) how much of the cost of goods available for sale during the period should be deducted from current revenues and (2) how much should be allocated to goods on hand and thus carried forward as an asset (merchandise inventory) in the balance sheet to be matched against future revenues. Because we determine the cost of goods sold by deducting the ending inventory from the cost of goods available for sale, a highly significant relationship exists: *Net income for an accounting period depends directly on the valuation of ending inventory.* This relationship involves three items:

First, a merchandising company must be sure that it has properly valued its ending inventory. If the ending inventory is overstated, cost of goods sold is understated, resulting in an overstatement of gross margin and net income. Also, overstatement of ending inventory causes current assets, total assets, and retained earnings to be overstated. Thus, any change in the calculation of ending inventory is reflected, dollar for dollar (ignoring any income tax effects), in net income, current assets, total assets, and retained earnings.

Second, when a company misstates its ending inventory in the current year, the company carries forward that misstatement into the next year. This misstatement occurs because the ending inventory amount of the current year is the beginning inventory amount for the next year.

Third, an error in one period's ending inventory automatically causes an error in net income in the opposite direction in the next period. After two years, however, the error washes out, and assets and retained earnings are properly stated.

Illustrations 7.1 and 7.2 prove that net income for an accounting period depends directly on the valuation of the inventory. Allen Company's income statements and the statements of retained earnings for years 1996 and 1997 show this relationship.

In Illustration 7.1, the correctly stated ending inventory for the year 1996 is $35,000. As a result, Allen has a gross margin of $135,000 and net income of

ILLUSTRATION 7.1
Effects of an Overstated Ending Inventory

ALLEN COMPANY
For Year Ended December 31, 1996

	Ending Inventory Correctly Stated		Ending Inventory Overstated by $5,000	
Income Statement				
Sales		$400,000		$400,000
Cost of goods available for sale	$300,000		$300,000	
Ending inventory	35,000		40,000	
Cost of goods sold		265,000		260,000
Gross margin		$135,000		$140,000
Other expenses		85,000		85,000
Net income		$ 50,000		$ 55,000
Statement of Retained Earnings				
Beginning retained earnings		$120,000		$120,000
Net income		50,000		55,000
Ending retained earnings		$170,000		$175,000

ILLUSTRATION 7.2
Effects of an Overstated Beginning Inventory

ALLEN COMPANY
For Year Ended December 31, 1997

	Beginning Inventory Correctly Stated		Beginning Inventory Overstated by $5,000	
Income Statement				
Sales		$425,000		$425,000
Beginning inventory	$ 35,000		$ 40,000	
Purchases	290,000		290,000	
Cost of goods available for sale	$325,000		$330,000	
Ending inventory	45,000		45,000	
Cost of goods sold		280,000		285,000
Gross margin		$145,000		$140,000
Other expenses		53,500		53,500
Net income		$ 91,500		$ 86,500
Statement of Retained Earnings				
Beginning retained earnings		$170,000		$175,000
Net income		91,500		86,500
Ending retained earnings		$261,500		$261,500

$50,000. The statement of retained earnings shows a beginning retained earnings of $120,000 and an ending retained earnings of $170,000. When the ending inventory is overstated by $5,000, as shown on the right in Illustration 7.1, the gross margin is $140,000, and net income is $55,000. The statement of retained earnings then has an ending retained earnings of $175,000. The ending inventory overstatement of $5,000 causes a $5,000 overstatement of net income and a $5,000 overstatement of retained earnings. The balance sheet would show both an overstated inventory and an overstated retained earnings. Due to the error in ending inventory, both the stockholders and creditors may overestimate the profitability of the business.

Illustration 7.2 is a continuation of Illustration 7.1 and contains Allen's operating results for the year ended December 31, 1997. Note that the ending inventory in Illustration 7.1 now becomes the beginning inventory of Illustration 7.2. However, Allen's inventory at December 31, 1997, is now an accurate inventory of $45,000. As a result, the gross margin in the income statement with the beginning inventory correctly stated is $145,000, and Allen Company has net income of $91,500 and an ending retained earnings of $261,500. In the income statement columns at the right, in which the beginning inventory is overstated by $5,000, the gross margin is $140,000 and net income is $86,500, with the ending retained earnings also at $261,500.

Thus, in contrast to an overstated ending inventory, resulting in an overstatement of net income, an overstated beginning inventory results in an understatement of net income. If the beginning inventory is overstated, then cost of goods available for sale and cost of goods sold also are overstated. Consequently, gross margin and net income are understated. Note, however, that when net income in the second year is closed to retained earnings, the retained earnings account is stated at its proper amount. The overstatement of net income in the first year is offset by the understatement of net income in the second year. For the two years combined the net income is correct. At the end of the second year, the balance sheet contains the correct amounts for both inventory and retained earnings. To summarize the effects of errors of inventory valuation:

	Ending Inventory		**Beginning Inventory**	
	Understated	**Overstated**	**Understated**	**Overstated**
Cost of goods sold	Overstated	Understated	Understated	Overstated
Net income.	Understated	Overstated	Overstated	Understated

Determining Inventory Cost

To place the proper valuation on inventory, a business must answer the question: Which costs should be included in inventory cost? Then, when the business purchases identical goods at different costs, it must answer the question: Which cost should be assigned to the items sold? In this section, you learn how accountants answer these questions.

Objective 2
Indicate which costs are properly included in inventory.

The costs included in inventory depend on two variables: quantity and price. To arrive at a current inventory figure, companies must begin with an accurate physical count of inventory items. They multiply the quantity of inventory by the unit cost to compute the cost of ending inventory. This section discusses the taking of a physical inventory and the methods of costing the physical inventory under both perpetual and periodic inventory procedures. The remainder of the chapter discusses departures from the cost basis of inventory measurement.

Taking a Physical Inventory

As briefly described in Chapter 6, to take a physical inventory, a company must count, weigh, measure, or estimate the physical quantities of the goods on hand. For example, a clothing store may count its suits; a hardware store may weigh bolts, washers, and nails; a gasoline company may measure gasoline in storage tanks; and a lumberyard may estimate quantities of lumber, coal, or other bulky materials. Throughout the taking of a physical inventory, the goal should be accuracy.

Taking a physical inventory may disrupt the normal operations of a business. Thus, the count should be administered as quickly and as efficiently as possible. The actual taking of the inventory is not an accounting function; however, accountants often plan and coordinate the count. Proper forms are required to record accurate counts and determine totals. Identification names or symbols must be chosen, and those persons who count, weigh, or measure the inventory items must know these symbols.

Taking a physical inventory often involves using inventory tags, such as that in Illustration 7.3. These tags are consecutively numbered for control purposes. A tag usually consists of a stub and a detachable duplicate section. The duplicate section facilitates checking discrepancies. The format of the tags can vary. How-

ILLUSTRATION 7.3
Inventory Tag

Inventory Tag
JMA Corp.

Inventory Tag No. _281_ Date ________
Description ________________________
____
Location ________________________
Quantity Counted ________
Counted by ________
Checked by ________

Duplicate Inventory Tag

Inventory Tag No. _281_ Date ________
Description ________________________
____
Location ________________________
Quantity Counted ________
Counted by ________
Checked by ________

ever, the tag usually provides space for (1) a detailed description and identification of inventory items by product, class, and model; (2) location of items; (3) quantity of items on hand; and (4) initials of the counters and checkers.

The descriptive information and count may be entered on one copy of the tag by one team of counters. Another team of counters may record its count on the duplicate copy of the tag. Discrepancies between counts of the same items by different teams are reconciled by supervisors, and the correct counts are assembled on intermediate inventory sheets. Only when the inventory counts are completed and checked does management send the final sheets to the accounting department for pricing and extensions (quantity × price). The tabulated result is the dollar amount of the physical inventory. Later in the chapter we explain the different methods accountants use to cost inventory.

Costs Included in Inventory Cost

Usually, inventory cost includes all the necessary outlays to obtain the goods, get the goods ready to sell, and have the goods in the desired location for sale to customers. Thus, inventory cost includes:

1. Seller's invoice price less any purchase discount.
2. Cost of the buyer's insurance to cover the goods while in transit.
3. Transportation charges when borne by the buyer.
4. Handling costs, such as the cost of pressing clothes wrinkled during shipment.

In theory, the cost of each unit of inventory should include its net invoice price plus its share of other costs incurred in shipment. The 1986 Tax Reform Act requires companies to assign these costs to inventory for tax purposes. For accounting purposes, these cost assignments are recommended but not required.

Practical difficulties arise in allocating some of these costs to inventory items. Assume, for example, that the freight bill on a shipment of clothes does not separate out the cost of shipping one shirt. Also, assume that the company wants to include the freight cost as part of the inventory cost of the shirt. Then, the freight cost would have to be *allocated* to each unit because it cannot be measured directly. In practice, allocations of freight, insurance, and handling costs to the individual units of inventory purchased are often not worth the additional cost. Consequently, in the past many companies have not assigned the costs of freight,

Illustration 7.4
Frequency of Use of Inventory Methods

	Companies			
	1992	**1991**	**1990**	**1989**
Methods				
First-in, first-out (fifo)	415	421	411	401
Last-in, first-out (lifo)	358	361	366	366
Average cost	193	200	195	200
Other	45	50	44	48
Use of LIFO				
All inventories	23	23	20	26
50% or more of inventories	189	186	186	191
Less than 50% of inventories	91	95	92	99
Not determinable	55	57	68	50
Companies using LIFO	358	361	366	366

Source: American Institute of Certified Public Accountants, *Accounting Trends & Techniques* (New York: AICPA, 1993), p. 145.

insurance, and handling to inventory. Instead, they have expensed these costs as incurred. When companies omit these costs from both beginning and ending inventories, they minimize the effect of expensing these costs on net income. The required allocation for tax purposes has probably resulted in many companies using the same inventory amounts in their financial statements.

Even if a company derives a cost for each unit in inventory, the inventory valuation problem is not solved. Management must consider two other aspects of the problem:

Hi-Fi Buys, Inc.
Hi-Fi Buys is a well-known retailer of electronic products, including home stereo systems, televisions, VCRs, and cameras.

1. If goods were purchased at varying unit costs, how should the cost of goods available for sale be allocated between the units sold and those that remain in inventory? For example, assume Hi-Fi Buys, Inc., purchased two identical VCRs for resale. One cost $250 and the other, $200. If one recorder was sold during the period, should Hi-Fi Buys assign it a cost of $250, $200, or an average cost of $225?
2. Does the fact that current replacement costs are less than the costs of some units in inventory have any bearing on the amount at which inventory should be carried? Using the same example, if Hi-Fi Buys can currently buy all VCRs for $200, is it reasonable to carry some units in inventory at $250 rather than $200?

We answer these questions in the next section.

Inventory Valuation under Changing Prices

Generally companies should account for inventories at historical cost; that is, the cost at which the items were purchased. However, this rule does not indicate how to assign costs to ending inventory and to cost of goods sold when the goods have been purchased at different unit costs. For example, suppose a retailer has three shirts on hand. One unit cost $20; another, $22; and a third, $24. If the retailer sells two shirts for $30 each, what is the cost of the two shirts sold?

Methods of Determining Inventory Cost

Accountants developed these four inventory costing methods to solve costing problems: (1) specific identification; (2) first-in, first-out (FIFO); (3) last-in, first-out (LIFO); and (4) weighted-average. Look at Illustration 7.4 to see how often 600 companies used these methods for the years 1992–1989. Obviously, some companies use one method for certain inventory items and another method for other inventory items.

Before explaining the inventory costing methods, we briefly introduce perpetual inventory procedure and compare periodic and perpetual inventory procedures.

Perpetual Inventory Procedure

Objective 3
Calculate cost of ending inventory and cost of goods sold under the four major inventory costing methods using perpetual and periodic inventory procedures (applies to each method separately).

In Chapter 6, the emphasis was on periodic inventory procedure. Under periodic inventory procedure, firms debit the Purchases account when goods are acquired; they use other accounts, such as Purchase Discounts, Purchase Returns and Allowances, and Transportation-In, for purchase-related transactions. Companies determine cost of goods sold only at the end of the period as the difference between cost of goods available for sale and ending inventory. They keep no records of the cost of items as they are sold, and have no information on possible inventory shortages. They assume any goods not in ending inventory have been sold.

The availability of inventory management software packages is causing more and more businesses to change from periodic to perpetual inventory procedure. Under perpetual inventory procedure, companies have no Purchases and purchase-related accounts. Instead, they make all entries involving merchandise purchased for sale to customers directly in the Merchandise Inventory account. Thus, they debit or credit Merchandise Inventory in place of debiting or crediting Purchases, Purchase Discounts, Purchase Returns and Allowances, and Transportation-In. At the time of each sale, firms make two entries: the first debits Accounts Receivable or Cash and credits Sales at the retail selling price. The second debits Cost of Goods Sold and credits Merchandise Inventory at cost. Therefore, at the end of the period the Merchandise Inventory account shows the cost of the inventory that should be on hand. Comparison of this amount with the cost obtained by taking and pricing a physical inventory reveals inventory shortages. Thus, perpetual inventory procedure is an important element in providing internal control over goods in inventory.

Perpetual Inventory Records Even though companies could apply perpetual inventory procedure manually, tracking units and dollars in and out of inventory is much easier using a computer. Both manual and computer processing maintain a record for each item in inventory. Look at Illustration 7.5, an inventory record for Entertainment World, a firm that sells many different brands of television sets. This inventory record shows the information on one particular brand and model of television set carried in inventory. Other information on the record includes (1) the maximum and minimum number of units the company wishes to stock at any time, (2) when and how many units were acquired and at what cost, and (3) when and how many units were sold and what cost was assigned to cost of goods sold. The number of units on hand and their cost are readily available also. Entertainment World assumes that the first units acquired are the first units sold. This assumption is the first-in, first-out (FIFO) method of inventory costing; we will discuss it later.

An Accounting Perspective

Uses of Technology Keeping track of inventories under a perpetual inventory system is much more cost-effective with computers. Under a manual system, the cost of an up-to-date inventory for stores with high turnover would outweigh the benefit. Most retail stores use scanning devices to read the inventory numbers of products purchased at the cash register. These scanning tags not only provide accurate sales prices but also record the merchandise sold so that the total cost of the store's inventory is always up to date.

Comparing Journal Entries under Periodic and Perpetual Inventory Procedures

The following comparison reveals several differences between accounting for inventories under periodic and perpetual procedures. We explain these differences by using data from Illustration 7.5 and making additional assumptions. Later, we discuss other journal entries under perpetual inventory procedure.

These entries record the purchase on July 5 under each of the methods:

Periodic Procedure			Perpetual Procedure		
Purchases	3,000		Merchandise Inventory	3,000	
Accounts Payable		3,000	Accounts Payable		3,000

ILLUSTRATION 7.5
Perpetual Inventory Record (FIFO method)

Item TV-96874 Maximum 26
Location Minimum 6

1996 Date	Purchased Units	Purchased Unit Cost	Purchased Total Cost	Sold Units	Sold Unit Cost	Sold Total Cost	Balance Units	Balance Unit Cost	Balance Total
Beg. inv.							8	$300	$2,400
July 5	10	$300	$3,000				18	300	5,400
7				12	$300	$3,600	6	300	1,800
12	10	315	3,150				6	300	1,800
							10	315	3,150
22				6	300	1,800			
				2	315	630	8	315	2,520
24	8	320	2,560				8	315	2,520
							8	320	2,560

Assuming the merchandise sold on July 7 was priced at $4,800, these entries record the sale:

Periodic Procedure

Accounts Receivable	4,800	
Sales		4,800

Perpetual Procedure

Accounts Receivable	4,800	
Sales		4,800
Cost of Goods Sold	3,600	
Merchandise Inventory .		3,600

Several other transactions not included in Illustration 7.5 could occur:

1. Assume that two of the units purchased on July 5 were returned to the supplier because they were defective. The entries would be:

Periodic Procedure

Accounts Payable	600	
Purchase Returns and Allowances		600

Perpetual Procedure

Accounts Payable	600	
Merchandise Inventory		600

2. Assume that the supplier instead granted an allowance of $600 to the company because of the defective merchandise. The entries would be:

Periodic Procedure

Accounts Payable	600	
Purchase Returns and Allowances		600

Perpetual Procedure

Accounts Payable	600	
Merchandise Inventory		600

3. Assume that the company incurred and paid freight charges of $100 on the purchase of July 5. The entries would be:

Periodic Procedure

Transportation-In	100	
Cash		100

Perpetual Procedure

Merchandise Inventory . .	100	
Cash		100

In these entries, notice that under perpetual inventory procedure the Merchandise Inventory account records purchases, purchase returns and allowances,

ILLUSTRATION 7.6 Beginning Inventory, Purchases, and Sales

Beginning Inventory and Purchases				Sales			
Date	Units	Unit Cost	Total Cost	Date	Units	Price	Total
Beginning inventory	10	$8.00	$ 80	March 10	10	$12.00	$120
March 2	10	8.50	85	July 14	20	12.00	240
May 28	20	8.40	168	September 7	10	14.00	140
August 12	10	9.00	90	November 22	20	14.00	280
October 12	20	8.80	176				
December 21	10	9.10	91				
	80		$690		60		$780

Ending inventory = 20 units, determined by taking a physical inventory.

purchase discounts, and transportation-in. Also, when goods are sold, the seller debits (increases) Cost of Goods Sold and credits or reduces Merchandise Inventory.

At the end of the accounting period, under perpetual inventory procedure, the only merchandise-related expense account to be closed is Cost of Goods Sold. The Purchases, Purchase Returns and Allowances, Purchase Discounts, and Transportation-In accounts do not even exist.

An Extended Illustration of Four Inventory Methods under Perpetual and Periodic Inventory Procedures

Using the data for purchases, sales, and beginning inventory in Illustration 7.6, next we explain the four inventory costing methods. Except for the specific identification method, we present each method using perpetual inventory procedure and periodic inventory procedure. Total goods available for sale consist of 80 units with a total cost of $690. A physical inventory determined that 20 units are on hand at the end of the period. Sales revenue for the 60 units sold was $780. The questions to be answered are: What is the cost of the 20 units in inventory? What is the cost of the 60 units sold?

SPECIFIC IDENTIFICATION The **specific identification** method of inventory costing attaches the actual cost to an identifiable unit of product. Firms find this method easy to apply when purchasing and selling large inventory items (such as autos). Under the specific identification method, the firm must identify each unit in inventory, unless it is unique, with a serial number plate or identification tag.

To illustrate, assume that the company in Illustration 7.6 can identify the 20 units on hand at year-end as 10 units from the August 12 purchase and 10 units from the December 21 purchase. The company computes the ending inventory as shown in Illustration 7.7; it subtracts the $181 ending inventory cost from the $690 cost of goods available for sale to obtain the $509 cost of goods sold. Note that you can also determine the cost of goods sold for the year by recording the cost of each unit sold. The $509 cost of goods sold is an expense on the income statement, and the $181 ending inventory is a current asset on the balance sheet.

The specific identification costing method attaches cost to an identifiable unit of inventory. This method does not involve any assumptions about the flow of the costs as in the other inventory costing methods. Conceptually, the method matches the cost to the physical flow of the inventory and eliminates the emphasis on the timing of the cost determination. Therefore, periodic and perpetual inventory procedures produce the same results for the specific identification method.

Objective 4
Explain the advantages and disadvantages of the four major inventory costing methods (applies to each method separately).

Advantages and Disadvantages of Specific Identification Companies that use the specific identification method of inventory costing state their cost of goods sold and ending inventory at the actual cost of specific units sold and on hand. Some accountants argue that this method provides the most precise matching of costs

ILLUSTRATION 7.7
Determining Ending Inventory under Specific Identification

	Units	Unit Cost	Total Cost
Ending inventory composed of purchases made on:			
August 12	10	$9.00	$ 90
December 21	10	9.10	91
Ending inventory	20		$181
Cost of goods sold composed of:			
Beginning inventory	10	8.00	$ 80
Purchases made on:			
March 2	10	8.50	85
May 28	20	8.40	168
October 12	20	8.80	176
			$509
Cost of goods available for sale			$690
Ending inventory			181
Cost of goods sold			$509

and revenues and is, therefore, the most theoretically sound method. This statement is true for some one-of-a-kind items, such as autos or real estate. For these items, use of any other method would seem illogical.

One disadvantage of the specific identification method is that it permits the manipulation of income. For example, assume that a company bought three identical units of a given product at different prices. One unit cost $2,000, the second cost $2,100, and the third cost $2,200. The company sold one unit for $2,800. The units are alike, so the customer does not care which of the identical units the company ships. However, the gross margin on the sale could be either $800, $700, or $600, depending on which unit the company ships.

FIFO (FIRST-IN, FIRST-OUT) Some companies use a method based on a cost flow assumption rather than specific identification. The **FIFO (first-in, first-out)** method of inventory costing assumes that the costs of the first goods purchased are those charged to cost of goods sold when the company actually sells goods. This method assumes the first goods purchased are the first goods sold. In some companies, the first units in (bought) must be the first units out (sold) to avoid large losses from spoilage. Such items as fresh dairy products, fruits, and vegetables should be sold on a FIFO basis. In these cases, an assumed first-in, first-out flow corresponds with the actual physical flow of goods.

Because a company using FIFO assumes the older units are sold first and the newer units are still on hand, the ending inventory consists of the most recent purchases. Under perpetual inventory procedure, the ending balance in the Merchandise Inventory account reflects these most recent purchases as a result of making the required entries during the period. Also, the firm has already recorded the cost of goods sold in the Cost of Goods Sold account. When using periodic inventory procedure, to determine the cost of the ending inventory at the end of the period under FIFO, you would begin by listing the cost of the most recent purchase. If the ending inventory contains more units than acquired in the most recent purchase, it also includes units from the next-to-the-latest purchase at the unit cost incurred, and so on. You would list these units from the latest purchases until that number agrees with the units in the ending inventory.

Illustration 7.8 shows how to determine the cost of ending inventory under FIFO using perpetual inventory procedure. This illustration uses the same format as the earlier perpetual inventory record. The company keeps a record of the balance in the inventory account as it makes purchases and sells items from inventory. Notice in Illustration 7.8 that each time a sale occurs, the company

ILLUSTRATION 7.8 Determining FIFO Cost of Ending Inventory under Perpetual Inventory Procedure

	Purchased			Sold			Balance		
Date	Units	Unit Cost	Total Cost	Units	Unit Cost	Total Cost	Units	Unit Cost	Total
Beg. inv.							10	$8.00	$ 80
Mar. 2	10	$8.50	$ 85				10	8.00	80
							10	8.50	85
Mar. 10				10	$8.00	$80	10	8.50	85
May 28	20	8.40	168				10	8.50	85
							20	8.40	168
July 14				10	8.50	85			
				10	8.40	84	10	8.40	84
Aug. 12	10	9.00	90				10	8.40	84
							10	9.00	90
Sept. 7				10	8.40	84	10	9.00	90
Oct. 12	20	8.80	176				10	9.00	90
							20	8.80	176
Nov. 22				10	9.00	90			
				10	8.80	88	10	8.80	88
Dec. 21	10	9.10	91				10	8.80	88
							10	9.10	91
						Total cost of ending inventory =			$179

Sales are assumed to be from the oldest units on hand.

Total of $179 would agree with balance already existing in Merchandise Inventory account.

assumes the items sold are the oldest on hand. Thus, after each transaction, it can readily determine the balance in the Merchandise Inventory account from the perpetual inventory record. The balance after the December 21 purchase represents the 20 units from the most recent purchases. The total cost of ending inventory is $179, which the company reports as a current asset on the balance sheet. During the accounting period, as sales occurred the firm would have debited a total of $511 to Cost of Goods Sold. Adding this $511 to the ending inventory of $179 accounts for the $690 cost of goods available for sale.

In Illustration 7.9, you can see how to determine the cost of ending inventory under FIFO using periodic inventory procedure. The company assumes that the 20 units in inventory consist of 10 units purchased December 21 and 10 units purchased October 12. As with the perpetual inventory procedure, the total cost of ending inventory is $179, and the cost of goods sold is $511. **Under FIFO, using either perpetual or periodic inventory procedures results in the same total costs for ending inventory and cost of goods sold.**

We show the relationship between the cost of goods sold and the cost of ending inventory under FIFO using periodic inventory procedure in Illustration 7.10. The 80 units in cost of goods available for sale consists of the beginning inventory and all of the purchases during the period. Under FIFO, the ending inventory of 20 units consists of the most recent purchases—10 units of December 21 purchase and 10 units of October 12 purchase—costing $179. We assume the beginning inventory and other earlier purchases have been sold during the period, representing the cost of goods sold of $511.

Advantages and Disadvantages of FIFO The FIFO method has four major advantages: (1) it is easy to apply, (2) the assumed flow of costs corresponds with the normal physical flow of goods, (3) no manipulation of income is possible, and (4)

ILLUSTRATION 7.9 Determining FIFO Cost of Ending Inventory under Periodic Inventory Procedure

	Units	Unit Cost	Total Cost
Ending inventory composed of purchases made on:			
December 21	10	$9.10	$ 91
October 12	10	8.80	88
Ending inventory	20		$179
Cost of goods sold composed of:			
Beginning inventory	10	8.00	$ 80
Purchases made on:			
March 2	10	8.50	85
May 28	20	8.40	168
August 12	10	9.00	90
October 12	10	8.80	88
			$511
Cost of goods available for sale			$690
Ending inventory			179 ← *Used to establish the ending balance in the Merchandise Inventory account*
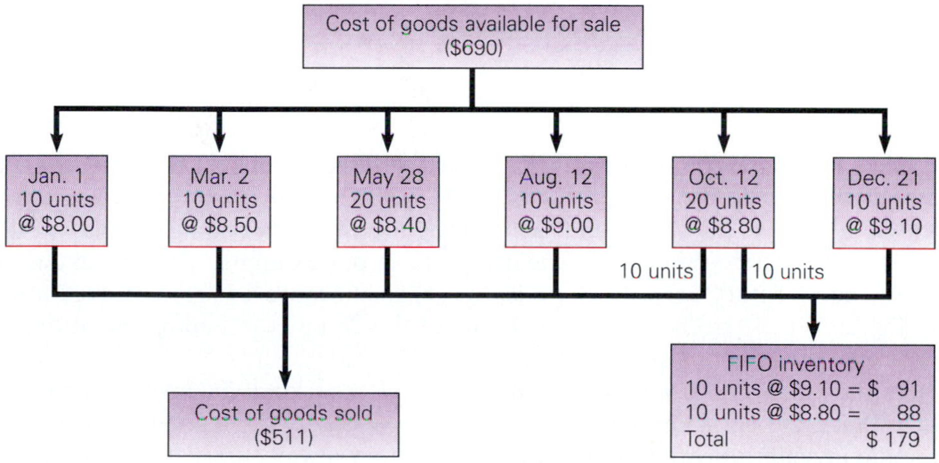 Cost of goods sold			$511

ILLUSTRATION 7.10 FIFO Flow of Costs

the balance sheet amount for inventory is likely to approximate the current market value. All the advantages of FIFO occur because when a company sells goods, the first costs it removes from inventory are the oldest unit costs. A company cannot manipulate income by choosing which unit to ship because the cost of a unit sold is not determined by a serial number. Instead, the cost attached to the unit sold is always the oldest cost. Under FIFO, purchases at the end of the period have no effect on cost of goods sold or net income.

The disadvantages of FIFO include (1) the recognition of paper profits and (2) a heavier tax burden if used for tax purposes in periods of inflation. We discuss these disadvantages later as advantages of LIFO.

LIFO (Last-In, First-Out) The **LIFO (last-in, first-out)** method of inventory costing assumes that the costs of the most recent purchases are the first costs charged to cost of goods sold when the company actually sells the goods. The results can differ under perpetual and periodic inventory procedure.

Look at Illustration 7.11 to see the LIFO method using perpetual inventory procedure. Under this procedure, the inventory composition and balance are

ILLUSTRATION 7.11 Determining LIFO Cost of Ending Inventory under Perpetual Inventory Procedure

	Purchased			Sold			Balance		
Date	**Units**	**Unit Cost**	**Total Cost**	**Units**	**Unit Cost**	**Total Cost**	**Units**	**Unit Cost**	**Total**
Beg. inv.							10	$8.00	$ 80
Mar. 2	10	$8.50	$ 85				10	8.00	80
							10	8.50	85
Mar. 10				10	$8.50	$ 85	10	8.00	80
May 28	20	8.40	168				10	8.00	80
							20	8.40	168
July 14				20	8.40	168	10	8.00	80
Aug. 12	10	9.00	90				10	8.00	80
							10	9.00	90
Sept. 7				10	9.00	90	10	8.00	80
Oct. 12	20	8.80	176				10	8.00	80
							20	8.80	176
Nov. 22				20	8.80	176	10	8.00	80
Dec. 21	10	9.10	91				10	8.00	80
							10	9.10	91
							Total cost of ending inventory =		$171

Sales are assumed to be from the most recent purchases.

Balance of $171 would agree with balance already existing in the Merchandise Inventory account.

updated with each purchase and sale. Notice in Illustration 7.11 that each time a sale occurs, the items sold are assumed to be the most recent ones acquired. Despite numerous purchases and sales during the year, the ending inventory still includes the 10 units from beginning inventory in our example. The remainder of the ending inventory consists of the last purchase because no sale occurred after the December 21 purchase. The total cost of the 20 units in ending inventory is $171; the cost of goods sold is $519.

In Illustration 7.12, we show the use of LIFO under periodic inventory procedure. Since the company charges the latest costs to cost of goods sold under periodic inventory procedure, the ending inventory always consists of the oldest costs. Therefore, when determining the cost of inventory under periodic inventory procedure, the company lists the oldest units and their costs. The first units listed are those in beginning inventory, then the first purchase, and so on, until the number listed agrees with the units in ending inventory. Thus, ending inventory in Illustration 7.12 consists of the 10 units from beginning inventory and the 10 units purchased on March 2. The total cost of these 20 units, $165, is the ending inventory cost; the cost of goods sold is $525.

Applying LIFO on a perpetual basis during the accounting period, as shown in Illustration 7.11, results in different ending inventory and cost of goods sold figures than applying LIFO only at year-end using periodic inventory procedure. (Compare Illustrations 7.11 and 7.12 to verify that ending inventory and cost of goods sold are different under the two procedures.) For this reason, if LIFO is applied on a perpetual basis during the period, special adjustments are sometimes necessary at year-end to take full advantage of using LIFO for tax purposes. Complicated applications of LIFO perpetual inventory procedures that require such adjustments are beyond the scope of this text.

Look at Illustrations 7.13 and 7.14, the flow of inventory costs under LIFO using both the perpetual and periodic inventory procedures. Note that ending inventory and cost of goods sold are different under the two procedures.

ILLUSTRATION 7.12
Determining LIFO Cost of Ending Inventory under Periodic Inventory Procedure

	Units	Unit Cost	Total Cost
Ending inventory composed of:			
Beginning inventory	10	$8.00	$ 80
March 2 purchase	10	8.50	85
Ending inventory	20		$165
Cost of goods sold composed of purchases made on:			
December 21	10	9.10	$ 91
October 12	20	8.80	176
August 12	10	9.00	90
May 28	20	8.40	168
			$525
Cost of goods available for sale			$690
Ending inventory			165
Cost of goods sold			$525

ILLUSTRATION 7.13
LIFO Flow of Costs under Perpetual Inventory Procedure

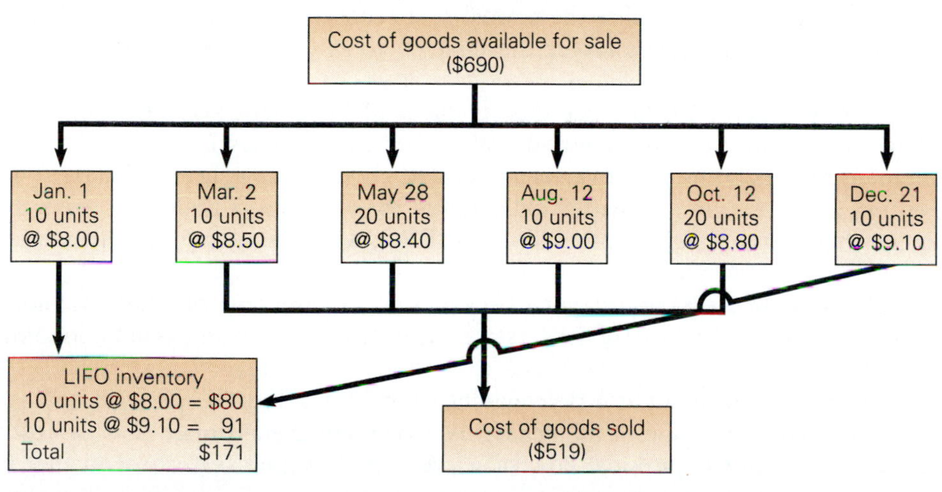

ILLUSTRATION 7.14
LIFO Flow of Costs under Periodic Inventory Procedure

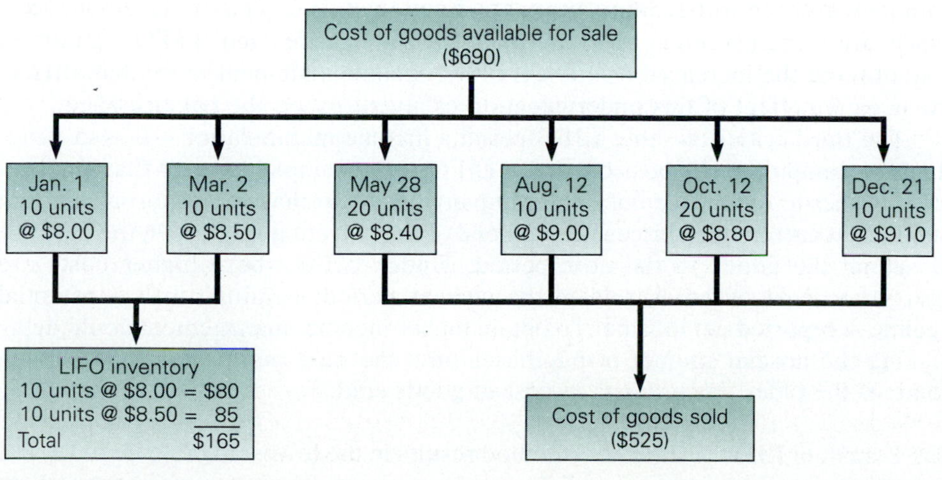

Advantages and Disadvantages of LIFO The advantages of the LIFO method are based on the fact that prices have risen almost constantly for decades. LIFO supporters claim this upward trend in prices leads to *inventory, or paper, profits* if the FIFO method is used. **Inventory, or paper, profits** are equal to the current replacement cost of a unit of inventory at the time of sale minus the unit's historical cost.

For example, assume a company has three units of a product on hand, each purchased at a different cost: $12, $15, and $20 (the most recent cost). The sales price of the unit normally rises because the unit's replacement cost is rising. Assume that the company sells one unit for $30. FIFO gross margin would be $18 ($30 − $12), while LIFO would show a gross margin of $10 ($30 − $20). LIFO supporters would say that the extra $8 gross margin shown under FIFO represents inventory (paper) profit; it is merely the additional amount that the company must spend over cost of goods sold to purchase another unit of inventory ($8 + $12 = $20). Thus, the profit is not real; it exists only on paper. The company cannot distribute the $8 to owners, but must retain it to continue handling that particular product. LIFO shows the actual profits that the company can distribute to the owners while still replenishing inventory.

During periods of inflation, LIFO shows the largest cost of goods sold of any of the costing methods because the newest costs charged to cost of goods sold are also the highest costs. The larger the cost of goods sold, the smaller the net income.

Those who favor LIFO argue that its use leads to a better matching of costs and revenues than the other methods. When a company uses LIFO, the income statement reports both sales revenue and cost of goods sold in current dollars. The resulting gross margin is a better indicator of management's ability to generate income than gross margin computed using FIFO, which may include substantial inventory (paper) profits.

Supporters of FIFO argue that LIFO (1) matches the cost of goods not sold against revenues, (2) grossly understates inventory, and (3) permits income manipulation.

The first criticism—that LIFO matches the cost of goods not sold against revenues—is an extension of the debate over whether the assumed flow of costs should agree with the physical flow of goods. LIFO supporters contend that it makes more sense to match current costs against current revenues than to worry about matching costs for the physical flow of goods.

The second criticism—that LIFO grossly understates inventory—is valid. A company may report LIFO inventory at a fraction of its current replacement cost, especially if the historical costs are from several decades ago. LIFO supporters contend that the increased usefulness of the income statement more than offsets the negative effect of this undervaluation of inventory on the balance sheet.

The third criticism—that LIFO permits income manipulation—is also valid. Income manipulation is possible under LIFO. For example, assume that management wishes to reduce income. The company could purchase an abnormal amount of goods at current high prices near the end of the current period, with the purpose of selling the goods in the next period. Under LIFO, these higher costs are charged to cost of goods sold in the current period, resulting in a substantial decline in reported net income. To obtain higher income, management could delay making the normal amount of purchases until the next period and thus include some of the older, lower costs in cost of goods sold.

Tax Benefit of LIFO The LIFO method results in the lowest taxable income, and thus the lowest income taxes, when prices are rising. The Internal Revenue Service allows companies to use LIFO for tax purposes only if they use LIFO for financial reporting purposes. Companies may also report an alternative inventory amount in the notes to their financial statements for comparison purposes. Be-

ILLUSTRATION 7.15 Determining Ending Inventory under Weighted-Average Method Using Perpetual Inventory Procedure

	Purchased			Sold			Balance		
Date	Units	Unit Cost	Total Cost	Units	Unit Cost	Total Cost	Units	Unit Cost	Total
Beg. inv.							10	$8.00	$ 80.00
Mar. 2	10	$8.50	$ 85				20	8.25[a]	165.00
Mar. 10				10	$8.25	$ 82.50	10	8.25	82.50
May 28	20	8.40	168				30	8.35[b]	250.50
July 14				20	8.35	167.00	10	8.35	83.50
Aug. 12	10	9.00	90				20	8.675[c]	173.50
Sept. 7				10	8.675	86.75	10	8.675	86.75
Oct. 12	20	8.80	176				30	8.758[d]	262.75
Nov. 22				20	8.758	175.17*	10	8.758	87.58
Dec. 21	10	9.10	91				20	$8.929[e]	$178.58

[a] $165.00/20 = $8.25. [b] $250.50/30 = $8.35. [c] $173.50/20 = $8.675. [d] $262.75/30 = $8.758. [e] $178.58/20 = $8.929. * Rounding difference.

A new unit cost is calculated after each purchase.

The unit cost of sales is the most recently calculated unit cost.

Balance of $178.58 would agree with balance already existing in the Merchandise Inventory account.

cause of high inflation during the 1970s, many companies switched from FIFO to LIFO for tax advantages.

WEIGHTED-AVERAGE The **weighted-average method** of inventory costing is a means of costing ending inventory using a weighted-average unit cost. Companies most often use the weighted-average method to determine a cost for units that are basically the same, such as identical games in a toy store or identical electrical tools in a hardware store. Since the units are alike, firms can assign the same unit cost to them.

Under perpetual inventory procedure, firms compute a new weighted-average unit cost after each purchase by dividing total cost of goods available for sale by total units available for sale. The unit cost is a moving weighted-average because it changes after each purchase. In Illustration 7.15, you can see how to compute the moving weighted-average using perpetual inventory procedure. The new weighted-average unit cost computed after each purchase is the unit cost for inventory items sold until a new purchase is made. The unit cost of the 20 units in ending inventory is $8.929 for a total inventory cost of $178.58. Cost of goods sold under this procedure is $690 minus the $178.58, or $511.42.

Under periodic inventory procedure, a company determines the average cost at the end of the accounting period by dividing the total units purchased plus those in beginning inventory into total cost of goods available for sale. The ending inventory is carried at this per unit cost. To see how a company uses the weighted-average method to determine inventory costs using periodic inventory procedure, look at Illustration 7.16. Note that we compute weighted-average cost per unit by dividing the cost of units available for sale, $690, by the total number of units available for sale, 80. Thus, the weighted-average cost per unit is $8.625, meaning that each unit sold or remaining in inventory is valued at $8.625.

ILLUSTRATION 7.16
Determining Ending Inventory under Weighted-Average Method Using Periodic Inventory Procedure

	Units	Unit Cost	Total Cost
Beginning inventory	10	$8.00	$ 80.00
Purchases			
March 2	10	8.50	85.00
May 28	20	8.40	168.00
August 12	10	9.00	90.00
October 12	20	8.80	176.00
December 21	10	9.10	91.00
Total	80		$690.00
Weighted-average unit cost is $690 ÷ 80, or $8.625.			
Ending inventory then is $8.625 × 20			172.50
Cost of goods sold: $8.625 × 60			$517.50

Advantages and Disadvantages of Weighted-Average When a company uses the weighted-average method and prices are rising, its cost of goods sold is less than that obtained under LIFO, but more than that obtained under FIFO. Inventory is not as badly understated as under LIFO, but it is not as up to date as under FIFO. Weighted-average costing takes a middle-of-the-road approach. A company can manipulate income under the weighted-average costing method by buying or failing to buy goods near year-end. However, the averaging process reduces the effects of buying or not buying.

Differences in Costing Methods Summarized

The four inventory costing methods—specific identification, FIFO, LIFO, and weighted-average—involve assumptions about how costs flow through a business. In some instances, assumed cost flows may correspond with the actual physical flow of goods. For example, fresh meats and dairy products must flow in a FIFO manner to avoid spoilage losses. In contrast, firms use lumber or coal stacked in a pile in a LIFO manner because the newest units purchased are unloaded on top of the pile and sold first. Gasoline held in a tank is a good example of an inventory that has an average physical flow. As the tank is refilled, the new gasoline mixes with the old. Thus, any amount used is a blend of the old gas with the new.

Although physical flows are sometimes cited as support for an inventory method, accountants now recognize that an inventory method's assumed cost flows need not necessarily correspond with the actual physical flow of the goods. In fact, good reasons exist for simply ignoring physical flows and choosing an inventory method based on more significant criteria.

In Illustrations 7.17 and 7.18, we use data from Illustration 7.6 to show the cost of goods sold, inventory cost, and gross margin for each of the four basic costing methods using perpetual and periodic inventory procedures. The differences for the four methods occur because the company paid different prices for goods purchased. No differences would occur if purchase prices were constant. Since a company's purchase prices are seldom constant, inventory costing method affects cost of goods sold, inventory cost, gross margin, and net income. Therefore, companies must disclose on their financial statements which inventory costing methods were used.

WHICH IS THE CORRECT METHOD? All four methods of inventory costing are acceptable; no single method is the only correct method. Different methods are attractive under different conditions.

If a company wants to match sales revenue with current cost of goods sold, it would use LIFO. If a company seeks to reduce its income taxes in a period of

ILLUSTRATION 7.17
Effects of Different Inventory Costing Methods Using Perpetual Inventory Procedure

	Specific Identification	FIFO	LIFO	Weighted-Average
Sales	$780.00	$780.00	$780.00	$780.00
Cost of goods sold:				
Beginning inventory	$ 80.00	$ 80.00	$ 80.00	$ 80.00
Purchases	610.00	610.00	610.00	610.00
Cost of goods available for sale	$690.00	$690.00	$690.00	$690.00
Ending inventory	181.00	179.00	171.00	178.58
Cost of goods sold	$509.00	$511.00	$519.00	$511.42
Gross margin	$271.00	$269.00	$261.00	$268.58

ILLUSTRATION 7.18
Effects of Different Inventory Costing Methods Using Periodic Inventory Procedure

	Specific Identification	FIFO	LIFO	Weighted-Average
Sales	$780.00	$780.00	$780.00	$780.00
Cost of goods sold:				
Beginning inventory	$ 80.00	$ 80.00	$ 80.00	$ 80.00
Purchases	610.00	610.00	610.00	610.00
Cost of goods available for sale	$690.00	$690.00	$690.00	$690.00
Ending inventory	181.00	179.00	165.00	172.50
Cost of goods sold	$509.00	$511.00	$525.00	$517.50
Gross margin	$271.00	$269.00	$255.00	$262.50

rising prices, it would also use LIFO. On the other hand, LIFO often charges against revenues the cost of goods not actually sold. Also, LIFO may allow the company to manipulate net income by changing the timing of additional purchases.

The FIFO and specific identification methods result in a more precise matching of historical cost with revenue. However, FIFO can give rise to paper profits, while specific identification can give rise to income manipulation. The weighted-average method also allows manipulation of income. Only under FIFO is the manipulation of net income not possible.

AN ACCOUNTING PERSPECTIVE

BUSINESS INSIGHT Management decides which inventory costing method or methods (LIFO, FIFO, etc.) to use. Also, management must determine which method is the most meaningful and useful in representing economic results. Then, it must use the method selected consistently.

The principal business of Goodyear Tire and Rubber Company is developing, manufacturing, distributing, marketing, and selling tires for most applications throughout the world. Note in the following footnote from Goodyear's financial statements that it, like other companies, uses several costing methods within the same enterprise:

Note 1 [In part]: Accounting Policies Inventory Pricing
Inventories are stated at the lower of cost or market. Cost is determined using the last-in, first-out (LIFO) method for a significant portion of domestic inventories and the first-in, first-out (FIFO) method or average cost method for other inventories.

Changing Inventory Methods

Generally, companies use the inventory method that best fits their individual circumstances. However, this freedom of choice does not include changing inventory methods every year or so, especially if the goal is to report higher income. Continuous switching of methods violates the accounting principle of *consistency*, which requires using the same accounting methods from period to period in preparing financial statements. Consistency of methods in preparing financial statements enables financial statement users to compare statements of a company from period to period and determine trends.

An Accounting Perspective

Business Insight Sometimes, companies change inventory methods in spite of the principle of consistency. Improved financial reporting is the only justification for a change in inventory method. A company that changes its inventory method must make a full disclosure of the change. Usually, the company makes a full disclosure in a footnote to the financial statements. The footnote consists of a complete description of the change, the reasons why the change was made, and, if possible, the effect of the change on net income.

J. M. Tull Industries, Inc., sells a diverse range of metals (aluminum, brass, copper, steel, stainless steel, and nickel alloys) for severe corrosion conditions and high-temperature applications. For example, when J. M. Tull changed from lower of average cost or market to LIFO, the following footnote appeared in its annual report:

Note B. Change in accounting method for inventory
Effective with the year ending December 31, 1975, the company changed its method of determining inventory cost from the lower of average cost or market method to the last-in, first-out (LIFO) method for substantially all inventory. This change was made because management believes LIFO more clearly reflects income by providing a closer matching of current cost against current revenue.

Journal Entries under Perpetual Inventory Procedure

Objective 5
Record merchandise transactions under perpetual inventory procedure.

Now we illustrate in more detail the journal entries made when using perpetual inventory procedure. Data from Illustration 7.8 serve as the basis for some of the entries.

You would debit the Merchandise Inventory account to record the increases in the asset due to purchase costs and transportation-in costs. And you would credit Merchandise Inventory to record the decreases in the asset brought about by purchase returns and allowances, purchase discounts, and cost of goods sold to customers. The balance in the account is the cost of the inventory that should be on hand at any date. This entry records the purchase of 10 units on March 2 in Illustration 7.8:

Mar.	2	Merchandise Inventory	85	
		Accounts Payable		85
		To record purchase of 10 units at $8.50 on account.		

You would also record the 10 units sold on the perpetual inventory record in Illustration 7.8 on page 256. The perpetual inventory procedure requires two journal entries for each sale. One entry is at selling price—a debit to Accounts Receivable (or Cash) and a credit to Sales. The other entry is at cost—a debit to Cost of Goods Sold and a credit to Merchandise Inventory. Assuming that the 10 units sold on March 10 in Illustration 7.8 had a retail price of $13 each, you would record the following entries:

Mar.	10	Accounts Receivable	130	
		Sales		130
		To record 10 units sold at $13 each on account.		
	10	Cost of Goods Sold	80	
		Merchandise Inventory		80
		To record cost of $8 on each of the 10 units sold.		

When a company sells merchandise to customers, it transfers the cost of the merchandise from an asset account (Merchandise Inventory) to an expense account (Cost of Goods Sold). The company makes this transfer because the sale reduces the asset, and the cost of the goods sold is one of the expenses of making the sale. Thus, the Cost of Goods Sold account accumulates the cost of all the merchandise that the company sells during a period.

A sales return also requires two entries, one at selling price and one at cost. Assume that a customer returned merchandise that cost $20 and originally sold for $32. The entry to reduce the accounts receivable and to record the sales return of $32 is:

Mar.	17	Sales Returns and Allowances	32	
		Accounts Receivable		32
		To record the reduction in amount owed by a customer upon return of goods.		

The entry that increases the Merchandise Inventory account and decreases the Cost of Goods Sold account by $20 is as follows:

Mar.	17	Merchandise Inventory	20	
		Cost of Goods Sold		20
		To record replacement of goods returned to inventory.		

Sales returns affect both revenues and cost of goods sold because the goods charged to cost of goods sold are actually returned to the seller. In contrast, sales allowances granted to customers affect only revenues because the customers do not have to return goods. Thus, if the company had granted a sales allowance of $32 on March 17, only the first entry would be required.

The balance of the Merchandise Inventory account is the cost of the inventory that should be on hand. This fact is a major reason some companies choose to use perpetual inventory procedure. The cost of inventory that should be on hand is readily available. Periodically, usually at year-end, a physical inventory determines the accuracy of the account balance. Management may investigate any major discrepancies between the balance in the account and the cost based on the physical count. It thereby achieves greater control over inventory. When a shortage is discovered, an adjusting entry is required. Assuming a $15 shortage (at cost) is discovered, the entry is:

Dec.	31	Loss from Inventory Shortage	15	
		Merchandise Inventory		15
		To record inventory shortage		

Assume that the Cost of Goods Sold account had a balance of $200,000 by year-end when it is closed to Income Summary. There are no other purchase-related accounts to be closed. The entry to close the Cost of Goods Sold account is:

Dec.	31	Income Summary.	200,000	
		Cost of Goods Sold		200,000
		To close Cost of Goods Sold account to Income Summary at the end of the year.		

Departures from Cost Basis of Inventory Measurement

Generally, companies should use historical cost to value inventories and cost of goods sold. However, some circumstances justify departures from historical cost. One of these circumstances is when the utility or value of inventory items is less than their cost. A decline in the selling price of the goods or their replacement cost may indicate such a loss of utility. This section explains how accountants handle some of these departures from the cost basis of inventory measurement.

Net Realizable Value

Objective 6
Apply net realizable value and the lower-of-cost-or-market method to inventory.

Companies should not carry goods in inventory at more than their net realizable value. **Net realizable value** is the estimated selling price of an item less the estimated costs that the company incurs in preparing the item for sale and selling it. Damaged, obsolete, or shopworn goods often have a net realizable value lower than their historical cost and must be written down to their net realizable value. However, goods do not have to be damaged, obsolete, or shopworn for this situation to occur. Technological changes and increased competition have caused significant reductions in selling prices for such products as computers, VCRs, calculators, and microwave ovens.

Illustration 7.19
Application of Lower-of-Cost-or-Market Method

Item	Quantity	Unit Cost	Unit Market	Total Cost	Total Market	LCM on Item-by-Item Basis
1	100 units	$10	$9.00	$1,000	$ 900	$ 900
2	200 units	8	8.75	1,600	1,750	1,600
3	500 units	5	5.00	2,500	2,500	2,500
				$5,100	$5,150	$5,000

To illustrate a necessary write-down in the cost of inventory, assume that an automobile dealer has a demonstrator on hand. The dealer acquired the auto at a cost of $18,000. The auto had an original selling price of $19,600. Since the dealer used the auto as a demonstrator and the new models are coming in, the auto now has an estimated selling price of only $18,100. However, the dealer can get the $18,100 only if the demonstrator receives some scheduled maintenance, including a tune-up and some paint damage repairs. This work and the sales commission cost $300. The net realizable value of the demonstrator, then, is $17,800 (selling price of $18,100 less costs of $300). For inventory purposes, the required journal entry is:

	Debit	Credit
Loss Due to Decline in Market Value of Inventory	200	
Merchandise Inventory		200
To write down inventory to net realizable value ($18,000 − $17,800).		

This entry treats the $200 inventory decline as a loss in the period in which the decline in utility occurred. Such an entry is necessary only when the net realizable value is less than cost. If net realizable value declines but still exceeds cost, the dealer would continue to carry the item at cost.

Lower-of-Cost-or-Market Method

The **lower-of-cost-or-market (LCM) method** is an inventory costing method that values inventory at the lower of its historical cost or its current market (replacement) cost. The term *cost* refers to historical cost of inventory as determined under the specific identification, FIFO, LIFO, or weighted-average inventory method. *Market* generally refers to a merchandise item's replacement cost in the quantity usually purchased. The basic assumption of the LCM method is that if the purchase price of an item has fallen, its selling price also has fallen or will fall. The LCM method has long been accepted in accounting.

Under LCM, inventory items are written down to market value when the market value is less than the cost of the items. For example, assume that the market value of the inventory is $39,600 and its cost is $40,000. Then, the company would record a $400 loss because the inventory has lost some of its revenue-generating ability. The company must recognize the loss in the period the loss occurred. On the other hand, if ending inventory has a market value of $45,000 and a cost of $40,000, the company would not recognize this increase in value. To do so would recognize revenue before the time of sale.

LCM Applied A company may apply LCM to each inventory item (such as Trivial Pursuit), each inventory class (such as games), or total inventory. To see how the company would apply the method to individual items and total inventory, look at Illustration 7.19.

If LCM is applied on an item-by-item basis, ending inventory would be $5,000. The company would deduct the $5,000 ending inventory from cost of goods available for sale on the income statement and report this inventory in the current assets section of the balance sheet. Under the class method, a company applies LCM to the total cost and total market for each class of items compared. One class might be games; another might be toys. Then, the company values each class at the lower of its cost or market amount. If LCM is applied on a total inventory basis, ending inventory would be $5,100, since total cost of $5,100 is lower than total market of $5,150.

An annual report of Du Pont contains an actual example of applying LCM. The report states that "substantially all inventories are valued at cost as determined by the last-in, first-out (LIFO) method; in the aggregate, such valuations are not in excess of market." The term *in the aggregate* means that Du Pont applied LCM to total inventory.

An Accounting Perspective

Business Insight CSS Industries, Inc., a diversified holding company, manufactures and sells decorative paper and other products. CSS's footnote in its Summary of Significant Accounting Policies illustrates that companies often disclose LCM in their notes to financial statements.

Inventories are stated primarily at the lower of first-in, first-out (FIFO) cost or market. The remaining portion of the inventory is valued at cost using the last-in, first-out method. Had all inventories been valued at the lower of FIFO cost or market, inventories would have been greater by $1,567,000 and $1,444,000 at December 31, 1991 and 1990, respectively.[1]

[1] Annual Report textual copy: 1993 CSS Industries, Inc.

Estimating Inventory

Objective 7
Estimate cost of ending inventory using the gross margin and retail inventory methods.

A company using periodic inventory procedure may estimate its inventory for any of the following reasons:

1. To obtain an inventory cost for use in monthly or quarterly financial statements without taking a physical inventory. The effort of taking a physical inventory can be very expensive and disrupts normal business operations; once a year is often enough.
2. To compare with physical inventories to determine whether shortages exist.
3. To determine the amount recoverable from an insurance company when fire has destroyed inventory or the inventory has been stolen.

Next, we introduce two recognized methods of estimating the cost of ending inventory when a company has not taken a physical inventory—the gross margin method and the retail inventory method.

Gross Margin Method The steps in calculating ending inventory under the gross margin method are:

1. Estimate gross margin (based on net sales) using the same gross margin rate experienced in prior accounting periods.
2. Determine estimated cost of goods sold by deducting estimated gross margin from net sales.
3. Determine estimated ending inventory by deducting estimated cost of goods sold from cost of goods available for sale.

Thus, the **gross margin method** estimates ending inventory by deducting estimated cost of goods sold from cost of goods available for sale.

The gross margin method assumes that a fairly stable relationship exists between gross margin and net sales. In other words, gross margin has been a fairly constant percentage of net sales, and this relationship has continued into the current period. If this percentage relationship has changed, the gross margin method does not yield satisfactory results.

To illustrate the gross margin method of computing inventory, assume that for several years Field Company has maintained a 30% gross margin on net sales. The following data for 1996 are available: The January 1 inventory was $40,000; net cost of purchases of merchandise was $480,000; and net sales of merchandise were $700,000. As shown in Illustration 7.20, Field can estimate the inventory for December 31, 1996, by deducting the estimated cost of goods sold from the actual cost of goods available for sale.

ILLUSTRATION 7.20
Inventory Estimation Using Gross Margin Method

Merchandise inventory, January 1, 1996		$ 40,000
Net cost of purchases		480,000
Cost of goods available for sale		$520,000
Less estimated cost of goods sold:		
Net sales	$700,000	
Gross margin (30% of $700,000)	210,000	
Estimated cost of goods sold		490,000
Estimated inventory, December 31, 1996		$ 30,000

An alternative format for calculating estimated ending inventory uses the standard income statement format and solves for the one unknown (ending inventory):

Net sales		$700,000
Less cost of goods sold:		
Merchandise inventory, January 1, 1996	$ 40,000	
Net cost of purchases	480,000	
Cost of goods available for sale	$520,000	
Less estimated inventory, December 31, 1996	?	
Estimated cost of goods sold		490,000 (70% of net sales)
Estimated gross margin		$210,000 (30% of net sales)

We know that:

$$\text{Cost of goods available for sale} - \text{Ending inventory} = \text{Cost of goods sold}$$

Therefore (let X = Ending inventory):

$$\$520,000 - X = \$490,000$$
$$X = \$30,000$$

The gross margin method is not precise enough to be used for year-end financial statements. At year-end, a physical inventory must be taken and valued by either the specific identification, FIFO, LIFO, or weighted-average methods.

RETAIL INVENTORY METHOD Retail stores frequently use the retail inventory method to estimate ending inventory at times other than year-end. Taking a physical inventory during an accounting period (such as monthly or quarterly) is too time consuming and significantly interferes with business operations. The **retail inventory method** estimates the cost of the ending inventory by applying a cost/retail price ratio to ending inventory stated at retail prices. The advantage of this method is that companies can estimate ending inventory (at cost) without taking a physical inventory. Thus, the use of this estimate permits the preparation of interim financial statements (monthly or quarterly) without taking a physical inventory. The steps for finding the ending inventory by the retail inventory method are:

1. Total the beginning inventory and the net amount of goods purchased during the period at both cost and retail prices.
2. Divide the cost of goods available for sale by the retail price of the goods available for sale to find the cost/retail price ratio.
3. Deduct the retail sales from the retail price of the goods available for sale to determine ending inventory at retail.
4. Multiply the cost/retail price ratio or percentage by the ending inventory at retail prices to reduce it to the ending inventory at cost.

ILLUSTRATION 7.21
Inventory Estimation

	Cost	Retail
Merchandise inventory, January 1, 1997	$ 22,000	$ 40,000
Purchases	182,000	303,000
Purchase returns	(2,000)	(3,000)
Purchase allowances	(3,000)	
Transportation-in	5,000	
Goods available for sale	$204,000	$340,000
Cost/retail price ratio: $204,000/$340,000 = 60%		
Sales		280,000
Ending inventory at retail prices		$ 60,000
Times cost/retail price ratio		×60%
Ending inventory at cost, March 31, 1997	$ 36,000	

In Illustration 7.21, we show the retail inventory method. In the illustration, the cost ($22,000) and retail ($40,000) amounts for beginning inventory are available from the preceding period's computation. The amounts for the first quarter purchases, purchase returns, purchase allowances, and transportation-in came from the accounting records. The amounts for purchase allowances and transportation-in appear only in the cost column. The first quarter sales amount ($280,000) is from the Sales account and stated at retail (sales) prices. The difference between what was available for sale at retail prices and what was sold at retail prices (which is sales) equals what should be on hand (March 31 inventory of $60,000) expressed in retail prices. The retail price of the March 31 inventory needs to be converted into cost for use in the financial statements. We do this by multiplying it times the cost/retail price ratio. In the example, the cost/retail price ratio is 60%, which means that on the average, 60 cents of each sales dollar is cost of goods sold. To find the March 31, 1997, inventory at cost ($36,000), we multiplied the ending inventory at retail ($60,000) by 60%.

Once the March 31 inventory has been estimated at cost ($36,000), we deduct the cost of the inventory from cost of goods available for sale ($204,000) to determine cost of goods sold ($168,000). We can also find the cost of goods sold by multiplying the cost/retail price ratio of 60% by sales of $280,000.

For the next quarterly period, the $36,000 and $60,000 amounts would appear on the schedule as beginning inventory at cost and retail, respectively. We would include other quarterly data regarding purchases, purchase returns, purchase allowances, and transportation-in to determine goods available for sale at cost and at retail. From these amounts, we could compute a new cost/retail price ratio for the second quarter.

At the end of each year, merchandisers usually take a physical inventory at retail prices. Since the retail prices are on the individual items (while the cost is not), taking an inventory at retail prices is more convenient than taking an inventory at cost. Accountants can then compare the results of the physical inventory to the calculation of inventory at retail under the retail inventory method for the fourth quarter to determine whether a shortage exists.

Both the gross margin and the retail methods can help you detect inventory shortages. To illustrate how you can determine inventory shortages using the retail method, assume that a physical inventory taken on December 31, 1997, showed only $62,000 of retail-priced goods in the store. Assume that use of the retail method for the fourth quarter showed that $66,000 of goods should be on hand, thus indicating a $4,000 inventory shortage at retail. After converting the $4,000 to $2,400 of cost ($4,000 × 0.60) you would report this as a "Loss from inventory shortage" in the income statement. Knowledge of such shortages may lead management to reduce or prevent them, by increasing security or improving the training of employees.

An Ethical Perspective

Dorsey Hardware

Terry Dorsey started Dorsey Hardware, a small hardware store, two years ago and has struggled to make it successful. The first year of operations resulted in a substantial loss; in the second year, there was a small net income. His initial cash investment was almost depleted because he had to withdraw money for living expenses. The current year of operations looked much better. His customer base was growing and seemed to be loyal. To increase sales, however, Terry had to invest his remaining funds and the proceeds of a $40,000 bank loan into doubling the size of his inventory and purchasing some new display shelves and a new truck.

At the end of the third year, Terry's accountant asked him for his ending inventory figure and later told him that initial estimates indicated that net income (and taxable income) for the year would be approximately $80,000. Terry was delighted until he learned that the federal income taxes on that income would be about $17,250. He told the accountant that he did not have enough cash to pay the taxes and could not even borrow it, since he already had an outstanding loan at the bank.

Terry asked the accountant for a copy of the income statement figures so he could see if any items had been overlooked that might reduce his net income. He noticed that ending inventory of $160,000 had been deducted from cost of goods available for sale of $640,000 to arrive at cost of goods sold of $480,000. Net sales of $720,000 and expenses of $160,000 could not be changed. But Terry hit on a scheme to reduce his net income. The next day he told his accountant that he had made an error in determining ending inventory and that its correct amount was $120,000. This lower inventory amount would increase cost of goods sold by $40,000 and reduce net income by that same amount. The resulting income taxes would be about $6,000, which was just about what Terry had paid in estimated taxes.

To justify his action in his own mind, Terry used the following arguments: (1) federal taxes are too high, and the federal government seems to be taxing the little guy out of existence; (2) no harm is really done because, when the business becomes more profitable, I will use correct inventory amounts, and this loan from the government will be paid back; (3) since I am the only one who knows the correct ending inventory I will not get caught; and (4) I'll bet a lot of other people do this same thing.

Analyzing and Using Financial Results—Inventory Turnover Ratio

Objective 8
Analyze and use the financial results—inventory turnover ratio.

An important ratio for managers, investors, and creditors to consider when analyzing a company's inventory is the inventory turnover ratio. This ratio tests whether a company is generating a sufficient volume of business based on its inventory. To calculate the **inventory turnover ratio:**

$$\text{Inventory Turnover Ratio} = \frac{\text{Cost of Goods Sold}}{\text{Average Inventory}}$$

Inventory turnover measures the efficiency of the firm in managing and selling inventory: thus, it gauges the liquidity of the firm's inventory. A high inventory turnover is generally a sign of efficient inventory management and profit for the firm; the faster inventory sells, the less time funds are tied up in inventory. A relatively low turnover could be the result of a company carrying too much inventory or stocking inventory that is obsolete, slow-moving, or inferior.

In assessing inventory turnover, analysts also consider the type of industry. When making comparisons among firms, they check the cost-flow assumption used to value inventory and cost of products sold.

Procter & Gamble
Procter & Gamble markets a broad range of laundry, cleaning, paper, beauty care, health care, food, and beverage products around the world.

The Procter & Gamble Company (P&G) and its subsidiaries reported the following financial data for 1992 (in millions):

Cost of goods sold	$17,324
Beginning inventory	3,190
Ending inventory	3,311

P&G's inventory turnover is:

$$\$17{,}324/[(\$3{,}190 + \$3{,}311)/2] = 5.33\%$$

You should now understand the importance of taking an accurate physical inventory and knowing how to value this inventory. In the next chapter, you will learn the general principles of internal control and how to control cash. Cash is one of a company's most important and mobile assets.

UNDERSTANDING THE LEARNING OBJECTIVES

Objective 1
Explain and calculate the effects of inventory errors on certain financial statement items.

- Net income for an accounting period depends directly on the valuation of ending inventory.
- If ending inventory is overstated, cost of goods sold is understated, resulting in an overstatement of gross margin, net income, and retained earnings.
- When ending inventory is misstated in the current year, companies carry that misstatement forward into the next year.
- An error in the net income of one year caused by misstated ending inventory automatically causes an error in net income in the opposite direction in the next period because of the misstated beginning inventory.

Objective 2
Indicate which costs are properly included in inventory.

- Inventory cost includes all necessary outlays to obtain the goods, get the goods ready to sell, and have the goods in the desired location for sale to customers.
- Inventory cost includes:
  a. Seller's gross selling price less purchase discount.
  b. Cost of insurance on the goods while in transit.
  c. Transportation charges when borne by the buyer.
  d. Handling costs, such as the cost of pressing clothes wrinkled during shipment.

Objective 3
Calculate cost of ending inventory and cost of goods sold under the four major inventory costing methods using perpetual and periodic inventory procedures.

- **Specific identification:** Attaches actual cost of each unit of product to units in ending inventory and cost of goods sold. Specific identification creates precise matching in determining net income.
- **FIFO (first-in, first-out):** Ending inventory consists of the most recent purchases. FIFO assumes that the costs of the first goods purchased are those charged to cost of goods sold when goods are sold. During periods of rising prices, FIFO creates higher net income since the costs charged to cost of goods sold are lower.
- **LIFO (last-in, first-out):** Ending inventory consists of the oldest costs. LIFO assumes that the costs of the most recent purchases are the first costs charged to cost of goods sold. Net income is usually lower under LIFO since the costs charged to cost of goods sold are higher due to inflation. The ending inventory may differ between perpetual and periodic inventory procedures.
- **Weighted-average:** Ending inventory is priced using a weighted-average unit cost. Under perpetual inventory procedure, a new weighted-average is determined after each purchase. Under periodic procedure, the average is determined at the end of the accounting period by dividing the total number of units purchased plus those in beginning inventory into total cost of goods available for sale. In determining cost of goods sold, this average unit cost is applied to each item. Under the weighted-average method, in a period of rising prices net income is usually higher than income under LIFO and lower than income under FIFO.

Objective 4
Explain the advantages and disadvantages of the four major inventory costing methods.

- **Specific identification:** *Advantages:* (1) States cost of goods sold and ending inventory at the actual cost of specific units sold and on hand, and (2) provides the most precise matching of costs and revenues. *Disadvantage:* Income manipulation is possible.
- **FIFO:** *Advantages:* (1) FIFO is easy to apply, (2) the assumed flow of costs often corresponds with the normal physical flow of goods, (3) no manipulation of income is possible, and (4) the balance sheet amount for inventory is likely to approximate the current market value. *Disadvantages:* (1) Recognizes paper profits, and (2) tax burden is heavier if used for tax purposes when prices are rising.
- **LIFO:** *Advantages:* (1) LIFO reports both sales revenue and cost of goods sold in current dollars, and (2) lower income taxes result if used for tax purposes when prices are rising. *Disadvantages:* (1) Often matches the cost of goods *not* sold against revenues, (2) grossly understates inventory, and (3) permits income manipulation.
- **Weighted-average:** *Advantages:* Due to the averaging process, the effects of year-end buying or not buying are lessened. *Disadvantage:* Manipulation of income is possible.

Objective 5
Record merchandise transactions under perpetual inventory procedure.

- Perpetual inventory procedure requires an entry to Merchandise Inventory whenever goods are purchased, returned, sold, or otherwise adjusted, so that inventory records reflect actual units on hand at all times. Thus, an entry is required to record cost of goods sold for each sale.

Objective 6
Apply net realizable value and the lower-of-cost-or-market method to inventory.

- Companies should not carry goods in inventory at more than their net realizable value. Net realizable value is the estimated selling price of an item less the estimated costs incurred in preparing the item for sale and selling it.
- Inventory items are written down to market value when the market value is less than the cost of the items. If market value is greater than cost, the increase in value is not recognized. LCM may be applied to each inventory item, each inventory class, or total inventory.

Objective 7
Estimate cost of ending inventory using the gross margin and retail inventory methods.

- The steps in calculating ending inventory under the gross margin method are:
  - **a.** Estimate gross margin (based on net sales) using the same gross margin rate experienced in prior accounting periods.
  - **b.** Determine estimated cost of goods sold by deducting estimated gross margin from net sales.
  - **c.** Determine estimated ending inventory by deducting estimated cost of goods sold from cost of goods available for sale.
- The retail inventory method estimates the cost of the ending inventory by applying a cost/retail price ratio to ending inventory stated at retail prices. To find the cost/retail price ratio, divide the cost of goods available for sale by the retail price of the goods available for sale.

Objective 8
Analyze and use the financial results—inventory turnover ratio.

- $\text{Inventory Turnover Ratio} = \dfrac{\text{Cost of Goods Sold}}{\text{Average Inventory}}$
- Inventory turnover measures the efficiency of the firm in managing and selling inventory. It gauges the liquidity of the firm's inventory.

Demonstration Problem 7–A

Following are data related to Adler Company's beginning inventory, purchases, and sales for the year 1997:

Beginning Inventory and Purchases	Units		Unit Cost
Beginning inventory	6,250	@	$3.00
March 15	5,000	@	3.12
May 10	8,750	@	3.30
August 12	6,250	@	3.48
November 20	3,750	@	3.72
	30,000		

Sales	Units
February 3	5,250
May 4	4,500
September 16	8,000
October 9	7,250
	25,000

Required

a. Compute the ending inventory under each of the following methods:

1. Specific identification (assume ending inventory is taken equally from the August 12 and November 20 purchases).
2. FIFO: (*a*) Assume use of perpetual inventory procedure.
   (*b*) Assume use of periodic inventory procedure.
3. LIFO: (*a*) Assume use of perpetual inventory procedure.
   (*b*) Assume use of periodic inventory procedure.
4. Weighted-average: (*a*) Assume use of perpetual inventory procedure.
   (*b*) Assume use of periodic inventory procedure.
   (Carry unit cost to four decimal places and round total cost to nearest dollar.)

b. Give the journal entries to record the individual purchases and sales (Cost of Goods Sold entry only) under the LIFO method and perpetual procedure.

Solution to Demonstration Problem 7–A

a. The ending inventory is 5,000 units, calculated as follows:

	Units
Beginning inventory	6,250
Purchases	23,750
Goods available	30,000
Sales	25,000
Ending inventory	5,000

1. Ending inventory under specific identification:

Purchased	Units	Unit Cost	Total Cost
November 20	2,500	$3.72	$ 9,300
August 12	2,500	3.48	8,700
			$18,000

2. Ending inventory under FIFO:

(a) Perpetual:

	Purchased			Sold			Balance		
Date	Units	Unit Cost	Total Cost	Units	Unit Cost	Total Cost	Units	Unit Cost	Total Cost
Beg. inv.							6,250	$3.00	$18,750
Feb. 3				5,250	$3.00	$15,750	1,000	3.00	3,000
Mar. 15	5,000	$3.12	$15,600				1,000	3.00	3,000
							5,000	3.12	15,600
May 4				1,000	3.00	3,000			
				3,500	3.12	10,920	1,500	3.12	4,680
May 10	8,750	3.30	28,875				1,500	3.12	4,680
							8,750	3.30	28,875
Aug. 12	6,250	3.48	21,750				1,500	3.12	4,680
							8,750	3.30	28,875
							6,250	3.48	21,750
Sept. 16				1,500	3.12	4,680			
				6,500	3.30	21,450	2,250	3.30	7,425
							6,250	3.48	21,750
Oct. 9				2,250	3.30	7,425			
				5,000	3.48	17,400	1,250	3.48	4,350
Nov. 20	3,750	3.72	13,950				1,250	3.48	4,350
							3,750	3.72	13,950

Ending inventory = (1,250 × $3.48) + (3,750 × $3.72) = $18,300

(b) Periodic:

Purchased	Units	Unit Cost	Total Cost
November 20	3,750	$3.72	$13,950
August 12	1,250	3.48	4,350
	5,000		$18,300*

* Note that the cost of ending inventory is the same as under perpetual.

3. Ending inventory under LIFO:
(a) Perpetual:

	Purchased			Sold			Balance		
Date	**Units**	**Unit Cost**	**Total Cost**	**Units**	**Unit Cost**	**Total Cost**	**Units**	**Unit Cost**	**Total Cost**
Beg. inv.							6,250	$3.00	$18,750
Feb. 3				5,250	$3.00	$15,750	1,000	3.00	3,000
Mar. 15	5,000	$3.12	$15,600				1,000	3.00	3,000
							5,000	3.12	15,600
May 4				4,500	3.12	14,040	1,000	3.00	3,000
							500	3.12	1,560
May 10	8,750	3.30	28,875				1,000	3.00	3,000
							500	3.12	1,560
							8,750	3.30	28,875
Aug. 12	6,250	3.48	21,750				1,000	3.00	3,000
							500	3.12	1,560
							8,750	3.30	28,875
							6,250	3.48	21,750
Sept. 16				6,250	3.48	21,750			
				1,750	3.30	5,775	1,000	3.00	3,000
							500	3.12	1,560
							7,000	3.30	23,100
Oct. 9				7,000	3.30	23,100			
				250	3.12	780	1,000	3.00	3,000
							250	3.12	780
Nov. 20	3,750	3.72	13,950				1,000	3.00	3,000
							250	3.12	780
							3,750	3.72	13,950

Ending inventory = (1,000 × $3.00) + (250 × $3.12) + (3,750 × $3.72) = $17,730

(b) Periodic:

	Units	Unit Cost	Total Cost
Merchandise inventory, January 1	5,000	$3.00	$15,000

4. Ending inventory under weighted-average:
(a) Perpetual:

	Purchased			Sold			Balance		
Date	**Units**	**Unit Cost**	**Total Cost**	**Units**	**Unit Cost**	**Total Cost**	**Units**	**Unit Cost**	**Total Cost**
Beg. inv.							6,250	$3.0000	$18,750
Feb. 3				5,250	$3.00	$15,750	1,000	3.0000	3,000
Mar. 15	5,000	$3.12	$15,600				6,000	3.1000[a]	18,600
May 4				4,500	3.10	13,950	1,500	3.1000	4,650
May 10	8,750	3.30	28,875				10,250	3.2707[b]	33,525
Aug. 12	6,250	3.48	21,750				16,500	3.3500[c]	55,275
Sept. 16				8,000	3.3500	26,800	8,500	3.3500	28,475*
Oct. 9				7,250	3.3500	24,288	1,250	3.3500	4,187*
Nov. 20	3,750	3.72	13,950				5,000	3.6274[d]	18,137

Ending inventory = (5,000 × $3.6274) = $18,137

[a] $\frac{\$18,600}{6,000} = \$3.1000.$ [b] $\frac{\$33,525}{10,250} = \$3.2707.$ [c] $\frac{\$55,275}{16,500} = \$3.3500.$ [d] $\frac{\$18,137}{5,000} = \$3.6274.$

* Rounding difference.

(b) Periodic:

Purchased	Units	Unit Cost	Total Cost
Merchandise inventory, January 1	6,250	$3.00	$18,750
March 15	5,000	3.12	15,600
May 10	8,750	3.30	28,875
August 12	6,250	3.48	21,750
November 20	3,750	3.72	13,950
	30,000		$98,925

Weighted-average unit cost = $98,925 ÷ 30,000 = $3.2975
Ending inventory cost = $3.2975 × 5,000 = $16,488*

* Rounding difference.

b. Journal entries under LIFO perpetual:

			Debit	Credit
Feb.	3	Cost of Goods Sold	15,750	
		Merchandise Inventory		15,750
		To record cost of $3 on 5,250 units sold.		
Mar.	15	Merchandise Inventory	15,600	
		Accounts Payable		15,600
		To record purchase of 5,000 units at $3.12 on account.		
May	4	Cost of Goods Sold	14,040	
		Merchandise Inventory		14,040
		To record cost of $3.12 on 4,500 units sold.		
	10	Merchandise Inventory	28,875	
		Accounts Payable		28,875
		To record purchase of 8,750 units at $3.30 on account.		
Aug.	12	Merchandise Inventory	21,750	
		Accounts Payable		21,750
		To record purchase of 6,250 units at $3.48 on account.		
Sept.	16	Cost of Goods Sold	27,525	
		Merchandise Inventory		27,525
		To record costs of $3.48 and $3.30 on 6,250 units and 1,750 units sold, respectively.		
Oct.	9	Cost of Goods Sold	23,880	
		Merchandise Inventory		23,880
		To record costs of $3.30 and $3.12 on 7,000 units and 250 units sold, respectively.		
Nov.	20	Merchandise Inventory	13,950	
		Accounts Payable		13,950
		To record purchase of 3,750 units at $3.72 on account.		

Demonstration Problem 7–B

a. Joel Company reported annual net income as follows:

1994	$27,200
1995	28,400
1996	24,000

Analysis of the inventories shows that certain clerical errors were made with the following results:

	Incorrect Inventory Amount	Correct Inventory Amount
December 31, 1994	$4,800	$5,680
December 31, 1995	5,600	4,680

Required

What is the corrected net income for 1994, 1995, and 1996?

b. The records of Little Corporation show the following account balances on the day a fire destroyed the company's inventory:

Merchandise inventory, January 1	$ 40,000
Net cost of purchases (to date)	200,000
Sales (to date)	300,000
Average rate of gross margin for the past five years	30% of net sales

Required Compute an estimated value of the ending inventory using the gross margin method.

c. The records of Draper Company show the following account balances at year-end:

	Cost	Retail
Merchandise inventory, January 1	$17,600	$ 25,000
Purchases	68,000	100,000
Transportation-in	1,900	
Sales		101,000

Required Compute the estimated ending inventory at cost using the retail inventory method.

Solution to Demonstration Problem 7–B

a. Corrected net income:

	1994	1995	1996	Total
Net income as reported	$27,200	$28,400	$24,000	$79,600
Adjustments:				
(1)	880			
(2)		(880)		
		(920)		
(3)			920	
Corrected net income	$28,080	$26,600	$24,920	$79,600

(1) Ending inventory understated ($5,680 − $4,800 = $880).
(2) Beginning inventory understated ($5,680 − $4,800 = $880).
Ending inventory overstated ($5,600 − $4,680 = $920).
(3) Beginning inventory overstated ($5,600 − $4,680 = $920).

b. Computation of inventory:

Merchandise inventory, January 1		$ 40,000
Net cost of purchases		200,000
Cost of goods available for sale		$240,000
Less estimated cost of goods sold:		
Net sales	$300,000	
Gross margin ($300,000 × 0.30)	90,000	
Estimated cost of goods sold		210,000
Inventory at cost, estimated by gross margin method		$ 30,000

c. Computation of inventory:

	Cost	Retail
Merchandise inventory, January 1	$17,600	$ 25,000
Purchases	68,000	100,000
Transportation-in	1,900	—
Goods available for sale	$87,500	$125,000
Cost/retail price ratio: $87,500/$125,000 = 70%		
Sales		101,000
Ending inventory at retail price		$ 24,000
Times cost/retail price ratio		× 70%
Ending inventory at cost, December 31	$16,800	

New Terms

FIFO (first-in, first-out) A method of costing inventory that assumes the costs of the first goods purchased are those charged to cost of goods sold when the company actually sells goods. *255*

Gross margin method A procedure for estimating inventory cost in which estimated cost of goods sold (determined using an estimated gross margin) is deducted from the cost of goods available for sale to determine estimated ending inventory. The estimated gross margin is calculated using gross margin rates (in relation to net sales) of prior periods. *267*

Inventory, or paper, profits Equal to the current replacement cost to purchase a unit of inventory at time of sale minus the unit's historical cost. *260*

Inventory turnover ratio Cost of Goods Sold ÷ Average inventory. *270*

LIFO (last-in, first-out) A method of costing inventory that assumes the costs of the most recent purchases are the first costs charged to cost of goods sold when the company actually sells the goods. *257*

Lower-of-cost-or-market (LCM) method An inventory costing method that values inventory at the lower of its historical cost or its current market (replacement) cost. *266*

Merchandise inventory The quantity of goods held by a merchandising company for resale to customers. *246*

Net realizable value Estimated selling price of an item less the estimated costs incurred in preparing the item for sale and selling it. *265*

Retail inventory method A procedure for estimating the cost of the ending inventory by applying a cost/retail price ratio to ending inventory stated at retail prices. *268*

Specific identification An inventory costing method that attaches the actual cost to an identifiable unit of product. *254*

Weighted-average method A method of costing ending inventory using a weighted-average unit cost. Under perpetual inventory procedure, a new weighted-average is calculated after each purchase. Under periodic procedure, the weighted-average is determined by dividing the total number of units purchased plus those in beginning inventory into total cost of goods available for sale. Units in the ending inventory are carried at this per unit cost. *261*

Self-Test

True-False

Indicate whether each of the following statements is true or false.

1. Overstated ending inventory results in an overstatement of cost of goods sold and an understatement of gross margin and net income.
2. In a period of rising prices, FIFO results in the lowest cost of goods sold.
3. Under LCM, inventory is written down to market value when the market value is less than the cost, and inventory is written up to market value when the market value is greater than the cost.
4. Under the gross margin method, an estimate must be made of gross margin to determine estimated cost of goods sold and estimated ending inventory.
5. To use the retail inventory method, both cost and retail prices must be known for the goods available for sale.
6. Under perpetual procedure, cost of goods sold is determined as a result of the closing entries made at the end of the period.

Multiple-Choice

Select the best answer for each of the following questions.

On July 1, 1997, Claxton Company began the accounting period with inventory of 3,000 units at $30 each. During the period, the company purchased an additional 5,000 units at $36 each and sold 4,600 units. Assume the use of periodic inventory procedure for Questions 1–6.

1. Cost of ending inventory using FIFO is:
   - **a.** $104,400.
   - **b.** $122,400.
   - **c.** $120,000.
   - **d.** $147,600.
   - **e.** None of the above.
2. Cost of goods sold using FIFO is:
   - **a.** $165,600.
   - **b.** $150,000.
   - **c.** $147,600.
   - **d.** $122,400.
   - **e.** None of the above.
3. Cost of ending inventory using LIFO is:
   - **a.** $104,400.
   - **b.** $114,750.
   - **c.** $156,000.
   - **d.** $122,400.
   - **e.** None of the above.
4. Cost of goods sold using LIFO is:
   - **a.** $155,250.
   - **b.** $114,000.
   - **c.** $147,600.
   - **d.** $165,600.
   - **e.** None of the above.

5. Cost of ending inventory using weighted-average is:
   - **a.** $114,750.
   - **b.** $157,600.
   - **c.** $122,400.
   - **d.** $109,650.
   - **e.** None of the above.
6. Cost of goods sold using weighted-average is:
   - **a.** $147,200.
   - **b.** $160,350.
   - **c.** $155,250.
   - **d.** $114,000.
   - **e.** None of the above.
7. During a period of rising prices, which inventory method might be expected to give the highest net income?
   - **a.** Weighted-average.
   - **b.** FIFO.
   - **c.** LIFO.
   - **d.** Specific identification.
   - **e.** Cannot determine.

Now turn to page 290 to check your answers.

Questions

1. Why is proper inventory valuation so important?
2. Why does an understated ending inventory understate net income for the period by the same amount?
3. Why does an error in ending inventory affect two accounting periods?
4. What is the meaning of taking a physical inventory?
5. What is the accountant's responsibility regarding taking a physical inventory?
6. Which cost elements are included in inventory? What practical problems arise by including the costs of such elements?
7. Which accounts that are used under periodic inventory procedure are not used under perpetual inventory procedure?
8. What entries are necessary under perpetual inventory procedure when goods are sold?
9. Why is there closer control over inventory under perpetual inventory procedure than under periodic inventory procedure?
10. Why is perpetual inventory procedure being used increasingly in business?
11. What is the cost flow assumption? What is meant by the physical flow of goods? Does a relationship between cost flows and the physical flow of goods exist, or should such a relationship exist?
12. Indicate how a company can manipulate its net income if it uses LIFO. Is the same opportunity available under FIFO? Why or why not?
13. What are the main advantages of using FIFO and LIFO?
14. Which inventory method is the correct one? Can a company change inventory methods?
15. Why are ending inventory and cost of goods sold the same under FIFO perpetual and FIFO periodic?
16. Would you agree with the following statement? Reducing the amount of taxes payable currently is a valid objective of business management and, since LIFO results in such a reduction, all businesses should use LIFO.
17. What is net realizable value, and how is it used?
18. Why is it acceptable accounting practice to recognize a loss by writing down an item in inventory to market, but unacceptable to recognize a gain by writing up an inventory item?
19. Under what conditions would the gross margin method of computing an estimated inventory yield approximately correct amounts?
20. What are the main reasons for estimating ending inventory?
21. Should a company rely exclusively on the gross margin method to determine the ending inventory and cost of goods sold for the end-of-year financial statements?
22. How can the retail method be used to estimate inventory?

MAYTAG

23. **Real World Question** Based on the notes to the financial statements of Maytag Corporation contained in the annual report booklet, what inventory methods were used?

THE LIMITED, INC.

24. **Real World Question** Based on the notes to the financial statements of The Limited, Inc., contained in the annual report booklet, what inventory methods were used?

HARLAND

25. **Real World Question** Based on the notes to the financial statements of John H. Harland Company contained in the annual report booklet, what inventory methods were used?

Exercises

Exercise 7–1
Determine effects of inventory errors (L.O. 1)

Betty Company reported annual net income as follows:

1995	$242,240
1996	243,840
1997	204,992

Analysis of its inventories revealed the following incorrect inventory amounts and these correct amounts:

	Incorrect Inventory Amount	Correct Inventory Amount
December 31, 1995	$38,400	$44,800
December 31, 1996	43,200	38.800

Compute the annual net income for each of the three years assuming the correct inventories had been used.

Exercise 7–2
Compute the impact on net income under specific identification (L.O. 3, 4)

Plant Truck Company manufactures trucks and identifies each truck with a unique serial plate. On December 31, a customer ordered 5 trucks from the company, which currently has 20 trucks in its inventory. Ten of these trucks cost $20,000 each, and the other 10 cost $25,000 each. If Plant wished to minimize its net income, which trucks would it ship? By how much could Plant reduce net income by selecting units from one group versus the other group?

Exercise 7–3
Compute ending inventory using FIFO perpetual inventory procedure (L.O. 3)

Wintel Company inventory records show:

	Units	Unit Cost	Total Cost
Beginning inventory . . .	3,000	$38.00	$114,000
Purchases:			
February 14	900	39.00	35,100
March 18	2,400	40.00	96,000
July 21	1,800	40.30	72,540
September 27	1,800	40.60	73,080
November 27.	600	41.00	24,600
Sales:			
April 15	2,800		
August 20	2,000		
October 3	1,500		

The December 31 inventory was 4,200 units. Wintel Company uses perpetual inventory procedure. Present a schedule showing the measurement of the ending inventory using the FIFO method.

Exercise 7–4
Compute ending inventory under LIFO perpetual inventory procedure (L.O. 3)

Using the data in Exercise 7–3 for Wintel Company, present a schedule showing the measurement of the ending inventory using the LIFO method.

Exercise 7–5
Compute ending inventory under weighted-average perpetual inventory procedure (L.O. 3)

Delk Company had a beginning inventory of 80 units at $12 (total = $960) and the following inventory transactions during 1996:

1. January 8, sold 20 units.
2. January 11, purchased 40 units at $15.00.
3. January 15, purchased 40 units at $16.00.
4. January 22, sold 40 units.

Using the preceding information, price the ending inventory at its weighted-average cost, assuming perpetual inventory procedure.

Exercise 7–6
Compute cost of ending inventory using FIFO, LIFO, and weighted-average under periodic inventory procedure (L.O. 3)

Denny Company made the following purchases of Product A in its first year of operations:

	Units		Unit Cost
January 2	1,400	@	$7.40
March 31.	1,200	@	7.00
July 5	2,400	@	7.60
November 1	1,800	@	8.00

The ending inventory that year consisted of 2,400 units. Denny uses periodic inventory procedure.

a. Compute the cost of the ending inventory using each of the following methods: (1) FIFO, (2) LIFO, and (3) weighted-average.

b. Which method would yield the highest amount of gross margin? Explain why it does.

Exercise 7–7
Prepare journal entries for inventory under FIFO perpetual inventory procedure (L.O. 3, 5)

The following are selected transactions and other data of the Sherman Company:

1. Purchased 20 units @ $360 per unit on account on September 18, 1997.
2. Sold 6 units on account for $576 per unit on September 20, 1997.
3. Discovered a shortage of $2,640 at year-end after a physical inventory.

Prepare journal entries for these transactions using FIFO perpetual inventory procedure. Assume the beginning inventory consists of 20 units @ $336 per unit.

Exercise 7–8
Prepare journal entries under FIFO perpetual inventory procedure (L.O. 3, 5)

Following are selected transactions of Proctor Company:

1. Purchased 100 units of merchandise at $240 each; terms 2/10, n/30.
2. Paid the invoice in transaction 1 within the discount period.
3. Sold 80 units at $384 each for cash.
4. Purchased 100 units at $360; terms 2/10, n/30.
5. Paid the invoice in transaction 4 within the discount period.
6. Sold 60 units at $552 each for cash.

Prepare journal entries for the six preceding items. Assume Proctor uses FIFO perpetual inventory procedure.

Exercise 7–9
Prepare journal entries affecting inventory using LIFO perpetual inventory procedure (L.O. 3, 5)

Jacob Company had the following transactions during February:

1. Purchased 270 units at $130 on account.
2. Sold 216 units at $180 on account.
3. Purchased 340 units at $150 on account.
4. Sold 245 units at $190 on account.
5. Sold 135 units at $200 on account.

The beginning inventory consisted of 135 units purchased at a cost of $110.

Prepare the journal entries relating to inventory for these five transactions, assuming Jacob accounts for inventory using perpetual inventory procedure and the LIFO inventory method. Do not record the entry for sales.

Exercise 7–10
Prepare journal entries affecting inventory using weighted-average periodic inventory procedure (L.O. 3)

Following are inventory data for 1996 for Marley Company:

1. January 1 inventory on hand, 400 units @ $28.80.
2. January sales were 80 units.
3. February sales totaled 120 units.
4. March 1, purchased 200 units @ $30.24.
5. Sales for March through August were 160 units.
6. September 1, purchased 40 units @ $33.12.
7. September through December sales were 180 units.

A physical inventory on December 31, 1996, showed 100 units on hand. Determine the cost of the ending inventory using the weighted-average method under periodic inventory procedure.

Exercise 7–11
Compute inventory (paper) profit under FIFO (L.O. 3, 4)

A company purchased 1,000 units of a product at $24.00 and 2,000 units at $26.40. It sold all of these units at $36.00 each at a time when the current cost to replace the units sold was $27.60. Compute the amount of gross margin under FIFO that LIFO supporters would call inventory, or paper, profits.

Exercise 7–12
Indicate whether FIFO or LIFO would yield the higher net income (L.O. 3, 4)

Clayman Company's inventory was 12,000 units with a cost of $160 each on January 1, 1996. During 1996, numerous units were purchased and sold. Also during 1996, the purchase price of this product fell steadily until at year-end it was $120. The inventory at year-end was 18,000 units. State which method of inventory measurement, LIFO or FIFO, would have resulted in higher reported net income, and explain briefly.

Exercise 7–13
Using net realizable value, compute carrying cost of inventory item (L.O. 6)

Levich Motor Company owns a truck that it has used as a demonstrator for eight months. The truck has a list or sticker price of $75,000 and cost Levich $65,000. At the end of the fiscal year, the truck is on hand and has an expected selling price of $70,000. Costs expected to be incurred to sell the truck include tune-up and maintenance costs of $2,000, advertising of $500, and a commission of 5% of selling price to the employee selling the truck. Compute the amount at which the truck should be carried in inventory.

Exercise 7–14
Determine the proper carrying value of damaged (L.O. 6)

Lyon Sound Systems used one sound system as a floor model. It cost $3,600 and had an original selling price of $4,800. After six months, the sound system was damaged and replaced by a newer model. The sound system had an estimated selling price of $2,880, but when the company performed $480 in repairs, it could be sold for $3,840. Prepare the journal entry, if any, that must be made on Lyon's books to record the decline in market value.

Exercise 7–15
Compute value of ending inventory using LCM applied on an item-by-item basis (L.O. 6)

Your assistant has compiled the following data:

Item	Quantity (units)	Unit Cost	Unit Market	Total Cost	Total Market
A	300	$57.60	$55.20	$17,280	$16,560
B	300	28.80	33.60	8.640	10,080
C	900	21.60	21.60	19,440	19,440
D	500	12.00	13.20	6,000	6,600

Calculate the dollar amount of the ending inventory using the LCM method, applied on an item-by-item basis, and the amount of the decline from cost to lower-of-cost-or-market.

Exercise 7–16
Compute value of total inventory using LCM (L.O. 6)

Use the data in Exercise 7–15 to compute the cost of the ending inventory using the LCM method applied to the total inventory.

Exercise 7–17
Estimate ending inventory using gross margin method (L.O. 7)

Large Company takes a physical inventory at the end of each calendar-year accounting period to establish the ending inventory amount for financial statement purposes. Its financial statements for the past few years indicate an average gross margin on net sales of 25%. On July 18, a fire destroyed the entire store building and its contents. The records in a fireproof vault were intact. Through July 17, these records show:

Merchandise inventory, January 1	$ 1,344,000
Merchandise purchases	18,816,000
Purchase returns	268,800
Transportation-in	1,008,000
Sales	28,672,000
Sales returns.	1,344,000

The company was fully covered by insurance and asks you to determine the amount of its claim for loss of merchandise.

Exercise 7–18
Estimate ending inventory using gross margin method (L.O. 7)

Rymon Company takes a physical inventory at the end of each calendar-year accounting period. Its financial statements for the past few years indicate an average gross margin on net sales of 30%.

On June 12, a fire destroyed the entire store building and the inventory. The records in a fireproof vault were intact. Through June 11, these records show:

Merchandise inventory, January 1	$ 120,000
Merchandise purchases	3,000,000
Purchase returns	36,000
Transportation-in	204,000
Sales	3,720,000

The company was fully covered by insurance and asks you to determine the amount of its claim for loss of merchandise.

Exercise 7–19
Estimate ending inventory using retail inventory method (L.O. 7)

Jessica Company, Inc., records show the following account balances for the year ending December 31, 1996:

	Cost	Retail
Beginning inventory	$82,000	$115,000
Purchases	50,000	75,000
Transportation-in	1,000	
Sales		105,000

Using these data, compute the estimated cost of ending inventory using the retail method of inventory valuation.

PROBLEMS

Problem 7–1
Compute corrected net income given inventory errors (L.O. 1)

Cable Company reported net income of $716,100 for 1996, $742,800 for 1997, and $651,600 for 1998, using the incorrect inventory amounts shown for December 31, 1996, and 1997. Recently, Cable corrected the inventory amounts for those dates. Cable used the correct December 31, 1998, inventory amount in calculating 1998 net income.

	Incorrect	Correct
December 31, 1996	$145,200	$170,400
December 31, 1997	168,000	140,400

Required

Prepare a schedule that shows: *(a)* the reported net income for each year, *(b)* the amount of correction needed for each year, and *(c)* the correct net income for each year.

Problem 7–2
Compute corrected net income given inventory errors; indicate balance sheet errors and comment (L.O. 1)

An examination of the financial records of Michelle Company on December 31, 1996, disclosed the following with regard to merchandise inventory for 1996 and prior years:

1. December 31, 1992, inventory was correct.
2. December 31, 1993, inventory was overstated $200,000.
3. December 31, 1994, inventory was overstated $100,000.
4. December 31, 1995, inventory was understated $220,000.
5. December 31, 1996, inventory was correct.

The reported net income for each year was:

1993	$384,000
1994	544,000
1995	670,000
1996	846,000

Required

a. Prepare a schedule of corrected net income for each of the four years—1993–96.
b. What error(s) would have been included in each December 31 balance sheet? Assume each year's error is independent of the other years' errors.
c. Comment on the implications of your corrected net income as contrasted with reported net income.

Problem 7–3
Maximize and minimize gross margin using specific identification (L.O. 3, 4)

Brent Company sells minicomputers and uses the specific identification method to account for its inventory. On November 30, 1996, the company had 23 Orange III minicomputers on hand that were acquired on the following dates and at these stated costs:

	Units		Unit Cost
July 3	5	@	$10,240
September 10	10	@	9,600
November 29	8	@	11,200

Brent sold 18 Orange III computers at $14,720 each in December. There were no purchases of this model in December.

Required

a. Compute the gross margin on December sales of Orange III computers assuming the company shipped those units that would maximize reported gross margin.

b. Repeat part **a** assuming the company shipped those units that would minimize reported gross margin for December.

c. In view of your answers to parts **a** and **b**, what would be your reaction to an assertion that the specific identification method should not be considered an acceptable method for costing inventory?

Problem 7–4
Prepare journal entries for purchases and sales using FIFO perpetual inventory procedure (L.O. 3, 5)

The inventory records of Button Company show the following:

Mar. 1 Beginning inventory consists of 10 units costing $40 per unit.
3 Sold 5 units at $94 per unit.
10 Purchased 16 units at $48 per unit.
12 Sold 8 units at $96 per unit.
20 Sold 7 units at $96 per unit.
25 Purchased 16 units at $50 per unit.
31 Sold 8 units at $96 per unit.

Assume all purchases and sales are made on credit.

Required

Using FIFO perpetual inventory procedure, prepare the appropriate journal entries for March.

Problem 7–5
Compute ending inventory under FIFO, LIFO, and weighted-average using perpetual and periodic inventory procedures (L.O. 3)

The following purchases and sales for Noble Company are for April 1996. There was no inventory on April 1.

Purchases			Sales	
	Units	Unit Cost		Units
April 3	3,200 @	$33.00	April 6	1,500
April 10	1,600 @	34.00	April 12	1,400
April 22	2,000 @	35.00	April 25	2,300
April 28	1,800 @	36.00		

Required

a. Compute the ending inventory as of April 30, 1996, using perpetual inventory procedure, under each of the following methods: (1) FIFO, (2) LIFO, and (3) weighted-average (carry unit cost to four decimal places and round total cost to nearest dollar).

b. Repeat **a** using periodic inventory procedure.

Problem 7–6
Prepare journal entries for purchases and sales using LIFO perpetual and periodic inventory procedures (L.O. 5)

Refer to the data in Problem 7–5.

Required

a. Using LIFO perpetual inventory procedure, prepare the journal entries for the purchases and sales (Cost of Goods Sold entry only).

b. Repeat **a** using LIFO periodic inventory procedure, including closing entries. (Note: You may want to refer to the Appendix in Chapter 6 for this part.)

Problem 7–7
Compute ending inventory and cost of goods sold under FIFO, LIFO, and weighted-average using perpetual and periodic inventory procedures (L.O. 3)

The following data relate to the beginning inventory, purchases, and sales of Daryl Company for the year 1997:

	Units	Unit Cost
Merchandise inventory,		
January 1	1,400 @	$5.04
Purchases:		
February 2	1,000 @	4.80
April 5	2,000 @	3.60
June 15	1,200 @	3.00
September 30	1,400 @	2.88
November 28.	1,800 @	4.20
Sales:		
March 10	900	
May 15	1,800	
July 6	800	
August 23	600	
December 22.	2,500	

Required

a. Assuming use of perpetual inventory procedure, compute the ending inventory and cost of goods sold under each of the following methods: (1) FIFO, (2) LIFO, and (3) weighted-average (carry unit cost to four decimal places and round total cost to nearest dollar).

b. Repeat **a** assuming use of periodic inventory procedure.

Problem 7–8
Compute gross margin using LIFO and FIFO illustrating effects of end-of-year purchases (L.O. 3, 4)

Rachel Company accounts for a product it sells using LIFO periodic inventory procedure. Product data for the year ended December 31, 1996, follow. Merchandise inventory on January 1 was 6,000 units at $28.80 each.

Purchases			Sales		
	Units	Unit Cost		Units	Unit Cost
January 5	12,000 @	$36.00	January 10	8,000 @	$57.60
March 31.	36,000 @	43.20	April 2	30,000 @	64.80
August 12	24,000 @	54.00	August 22	32,000 @	72.00
December 26.	12,000 @	57.60	December 24.	6,000 @	79.20

Required

a. Compute the gross margin earned on sales of this product for 1996.

b. Repeat part **a** assuming that the December 26 purchase was made in January of 1997.

c. Recompute the gross margin assuming that 20,000 rather than 12,000 units were purchased on December 26 at the same cost per unit.

d. Solve parts **a, b,** and **c** using the FIFO method.

Problem 7–9
Compute ending inventory using LCM (L.O. 6)

The accountant for Clark Company prepared the following schedule of the company's inventory at December 31, 1996, and used the LCM method applied to total inventory in determining cost of goods sold:

Item	Quantity	Unit Cost	Unit Market
Q	8,400	$7.20	$7.20
R	4,800	6.00	5.76
S	10,800	4.80	4.56
T	9,600	4.20	4.32

Required

a. State whether this approach is an acceptable method of inventory measurement and show the calculations used to determine the amounts.

b. Compute the amount of the ending inventory using the LCM method on an item-by-item basis.

c. State the effect on net income in 1996 if the method in **b** was used rather than the method referred to in **a**.

Problem 7–10
Prepare quarterly and six-month income statements using the gross margin method (L.O. 6)

As part of a loan agreement with a local bank, Fulton Company must present quarterly and cumulative income statements for the year 1996. The company uses periodic inventory procedure and marks its merchandise to sell at a price yielding a gross margin of 30%. Selected data for the first six months of 1996 are as follows:

	First Quarter	Second Quarter
Sales	$248,000	$256,000
Purchases	160,000	184,000
Purchase returns and allowances	9,600	11,200
Purchase discounts	3,200	3,520
Sales returns and allowances	8,000	4,800
Transportation-in	8,000	8,320
Miscellaneous selling expenses	25,600	24,000
Miscellaneous administrative expenses	9,600	8,000

The cost of the physical inventory taken December 31, 1995, was $30,400.

Required

a. Indicate how income statements can be prepared without taking a physical inventory at the end of each of the first two quarters of 1996.

b. Prepare income statements for the first quarter, the second quarter, and the first six months of 1996.

Problem 7–11
Estimate ending inventory using retail inventory method (L.O. 7)

Patton Company records show the following information for 1997:

	Cost	Retail
Sales	—	$700,800
Purchases	$540,000	840,000
Transportation-in	52,560	—
Merchandise inventory, January 1	24,000	34,800
Purchase returns	30,240	37,200

Required

Compute the estimated year-end inventory balance at cost using the retail method of estimating inventory.

Alternate Problems

Problem 7–1A
Compute corrected net income given inventory errors (L.O. 1)

Aiken Company reported net income of $624,000 for 1996, $648,000 for 1997, and $696,000 for 1998, using the incorrect inventory amounts shown for December 31, 1996, and 1997. Recently Aiken corrected these inventory amounts. Aiken used the correct December 31, 1998, inventory amount in calculating 1998 net income.

	Incorrect	Correct
December 31, 1996	$192,000	$216,000
December 31, 1997	182,400	168,000

Required

Prepare a schedule that shows: *(a)* the reported net income for each year, *(b)* the amount of correction needed for each year, and *(c)* the correct net income for each year.

Problem 7–2A
Compute corrected net income given inventory errors; indicate balance sheet errors and comment (L.O. 1)

An examination of the financial records of Brooks Company on December 31, 1996, disclosed the following with regard to merchandise inventory for 1996 and prior years:

1. December 31, 1992, inventory was correct.
2. December 31, 1993, inventory was understated $50,000.
3. December 31, 1994, inventory was overstated $35,000.
4. December 31, 1995, inventory was understated $30,000.
5. December 31, 1996, inventory was correct.

The reported net income for each year was:

1993	$292,500
1994	355,000
1995	382,500
1996	350,000

Required

a. Prepare a schedule of corrected net income for each of the four years—1993–96.

b. What errors would have been included in each December 31 balance sheet? Assume each year's error is independent of the other years' errors.

c. Comment on the implications of the corrected net income as contrasted with reported net income.

Problem 7–3A
Maximize and minimize gross margin using specific identification
(L.O. 3, 4)

Jimmy Surf Company sells the Ultra-Light model wind surfer and uses the specific identification method to account for its inventory. The Ultra-Lights are identical except for identifying serial numbers. On August 1, 1996, the company had three Ultra-Lights that cost $28,000 each in its inventory. During the month, the company purchased the following:

	Units	Unit Cost
August 3	5	@ $26,000
August 17	6	@ 29,000
August 28	6	@ 30,000

Jimmy Surf Company sold 13 Ultra-Lights in August at $40,000 each.

Required

a. Compute the gross margin earned by the company in August if it shipped the units that would maximize gross margin.

b. Repeat part **a** assuming the company shipped the units that would minimize gross margin.

c. Do you think Jimmy Surf Company should be permitted to use the specific identification method of accounting for Ultra-Lights in view of the manipulation possible as shown by your calculations in **a** and **b**?

Problem 7–4A
Compute cost of goods sold using FIFO for both perpetual and periodic inventory procedures
(L.O. 3, 5)

The inventory records of Gable Company show the following:

Jan.	1	Beginning inventory consists of 12 units costing $48 per unit.
	5	Purchased 15 units @ $49.92 per unit.
	10	Sold 9 units @ $108 per unit.
	12	Sold 7 units @ $108 per unit.
	20	Purchased 20 units @ $50.16 per unit.
	22	Purchased 5 units @ $48 per unit.
	30	Sold 20 units @ $110.40 per unit.

Assume all purchases and sales are made on account.

Required

a. Using FIFO perpetual inventory procedure, compute cost of goods sold for January.

b. Using FIFO perpetual inventory procedure, prepare the journal entries for January.

c. Compute the cost of goods sold under FIFO periodic inventory procedure. Is there a difference between the amount computed using the two different procedures?

Problem 7–5A
Compute ending inventory under FIFO, LIFO, and weighted-average using perpetual and periodic inventory procedures
(L.O. 3)

Following are data for Steele Company for the year 1996:

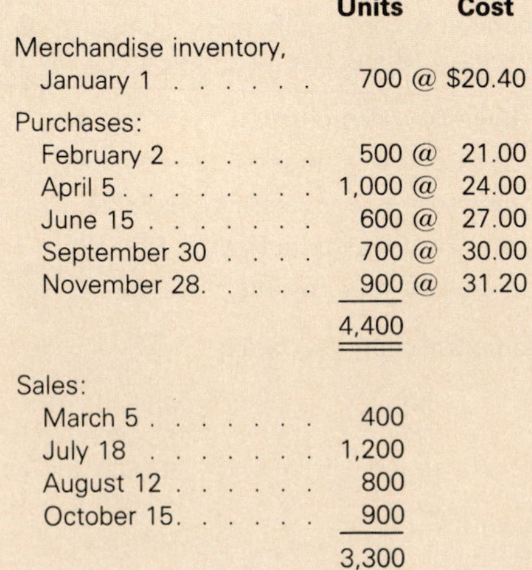

	Units	Unit Cost
Merchandise inventory,		
January 1	700 @	$20.40
Purchases:		
February 2	500 @	21.00
April 5	1,000 @	24.00
June 15	600 @	27.00
September 30	700 @	30.00
November 28.	900 @	31.20
	4,400	
Sales:		
March 5	400	
July 18	1,200	
August 12	800	
October 15.	900	
	3,300	

Required

a. Compute the ending inventory as of December 31, 1996, assuming use of perpetual inventory procedure, under each of the following methods: (1) FIFO, (2) LIFO, and (3) weighted-average (carry unit cost to four decimal places and round total cost to nearest dollar).

b. Compute the ending inventory as of December 31, 1996, assuming use of periodic inventory procedure, under each of the following methods: (1) FIFO, (2) LIFO, and (3) weighted-average.

Problem 7–6A
Record journal entries for purchases and sales under FIFO perpetual and periodic inventory procedures (L.O. 5)

Refer to the data in Problem 7–5A.

Required

a. Give the journal entries to record the purchases and sales (Cost of Goods Sold entry only) for the year under FIFO perpetual.

b. Give the journal entries to record the purchases for the year and necessary year-end entries to charge Income Summary with the cost of goods sold for the year under FIFO periodic. (Note: You may want to refer to the Appendix in Chapter 6 for this part.)

Problem 7–7A
Compute ending inventory and cost of goods sold under FIFO, LIFO, and weighted-average using perpetual and periodic inventory procedures (L.O. 3)

Following are data related to a product of Leonard Company for the year 1997:

	Units	Unit Cost
Merchandise inventory,		
January 1	2,100 @	$12.60
Purchases:		
March 10	1,500 @	12.00
May 24	3,000 @	11.20
July 15	1,800 @	10.50
September 20	2,100 @	9.00
December 1	2,700 @	10.00
Sales:		
April 5	1,400	
June 13	2,900	
October 9	2,300	
November 21.	1,700	

Required

a. Assuming use of perpetual inventory procedure, compute the ending inventory and cost of goods sold under each of the following methods: (1) FIFO, (2) LIFO, and (3) weighted-average (carry unit cost to four decimal places and round total cost to nearest dollar).

b. Assuming use of periodic inventory procedure, compute the ending inventory and cost of goods sold under each of the following methods: (1) FIFO, (2), LIFO, and (3) weighted-average (carry unit cost to four decimal places and round total cost to nearest dollar).

Problem 7–8A
Compute gross margin using FIFO and LIFO illustrating effects of end-of-year purchases (L.O. 3, 4)

Smith Company accounts for its inventory using the LIFO method under periodic inventory procedure. Data on purchases, sales, and inventory for the year ended December 31, 1996, are:

	Units	Unit Cost
Merchandise inventory,		
January 1	4,000 @	$40
Purchases:		
January 7	10,000 @	48
July 7	20,000 @	56
December 21	12,000 @	64

During 1996, 32,000 units were sold for $2,560,000, leaving an inventory on December 31, 1996, of 14,000 units.

Required

a. Compute the gross margin earned on sales during 1996.

b. Compute the change in gross margin that would have resulted if the purchase of December 21 had been delayed until January 6, 1997.

c. Recompute the gross margin assuming that 18,000 units rather than 12,000 units were purchased on December 21 at the same cost per unit.

d. Solve parts **a, b,** and **c** using the FIFO method.

Problem 7–9A
Compute ending inventory using (L.O. 6)

Data on the ending inventory of Evans Company on December 31, 1996, are:

Item	Quantity	Unit Cost	Unit Market
1	8,400	$3.20	$3.12
2	16,800	2.88	3.04
3	5,600	2.80	2.88
4	14,000	3.84	3.60
5	11,200	3.60	3.68
6	2,800	3.04	2.88

Required

a. Compute the ending inventory applying the LCM method to the total inventory.

b. Determine the ending inventory by applying the LCM method on an item-by-item basis.

Problem 7–10A
Estimate inventory using gross margin method (L.O. 7)

The sales and cost of goods sold for Phelps Company for the past five years were as follows:

Year	Sales (net)	Cost of Goods Sold
1991	$ 9,984,960	$6,240,600
1992	10,794,240	6,746,400
1993	12,346,560	7,716,600
1994	11,926,080	7,272,000
1995	12,747,840	7,920,000

The following information is for the seven months ended July 31, 1996:

Sales	$7,748,000
Purchases	4,588,800
Purchase returns	28,800
Sales returns.	173,760
Merchandise inventory, January 1, 1996	948,000

To secure a loan, Phelps Company has been asked to present current financial statements. However, the company does not wish to take a complete physical inventory as of July 31, 1996.

Required

a. Indicate how financial statements can be prepared without taking a complete physical inventory.

b. From the data given, compute the estimated inventory as of July 31, 1996.

Problem 7–11A
Estimate ending inventory using retail inventory method (L.O. 7)

Pecan Company's records contained the following inventory information for 1995:

	Cost	Retail
Sales	—	$ 840,000
Purchases	$792,000	1,164,000
Purchase returns	16,800	24,000
Transportation-in	21,600	—
Merchandise inventory, January 1.	43,200	60,000

Required

Compute the estimated year-end inventory balance at cost using the retail method of inventory valuation.

BEYOND THE NUMBERS—CRITICAL THINKING

Business Decision Case 7–1
Prepare income statement using LIFO and FIFO. Determine inventory turnover (L.O. 3, 4, 8)

Two sisters, Mary Ann Kozak and Linda Franz, were interested in starting part-time business activities to supplement their family incomes. Both heard a presentation by the manufacturer of an exercise device and decided to become a distributor of this exerciser. Kozak's sales territory is Cobb County, and Franz's sales territory is Gwinett County. Each owns her own business.

To induce Kozak and Franz to become distributors, the manufacturer made price concessions on the first 1,000 units that each sister purchased. The manufacturer sold the first 200 units at $15 each, the next 300 at $18 per unit, and the next 500 at $19 per unit. After that, Kozak and Franz had to pay $20 per unit.

During the first year, each sister bought 1,200 units; coincidentally, both sold exactly 950 units for $27 each. Kozak had $2,600 of selling expenses; Franz incurred $1,700 of selling expenses. (Kozak's expenses were considerably higher because on December 28 she distributed 4,000 sales brochures to households in her territory at a cost of $800. The brochures stressed that people would want to take off the extra pounds gained during the holiday season; also, these exercisers were inexpensive and could be used at home.)

At the end of the year, both sisters had to determine their net incomes. Kozak received a B in the accounting course she took at State University. She remembered the FIFO inventory method and plans to use it. Franz knows nothing about inventory costing methods. However, her husband is acquainted with the LIFO inventory method used at the company where he works. He will help her compute the cost of the ending inventory and the cost of goods using LIFO.

Required

a. Prepare income statements for Kozak and Franz.
b. Which sister's business has performed better? Explain why.
c. Determine the inventory turnovers for both sisters.

Business Decision Case 7–2
Determine insurance settlement using gross margin method (L.O. 7)

Donna Green owns and operates a sporting goods store. On February 2, 1996, the store suffered extensive fire damage, and all of the inventory was destroyed. Green uses periodic inventory procedure and has the following information in her accounting records, which were undamaged:

Merchandise inventory,	
January 1	$ 80,000
Purchases:	
January 8	32,000
January 20	48,000
January 30	64,000
Net sales:	
During January	240,000
February 1 and 2	16,000

Green's gross margin rate on net sales has been 40% for the past three years. Her insurance company offered to pay $56,000 to settle this inventory loss unless Green can show that she suffered a greater loss. She has asked you, her CPA, to help her in determining her loss.

Required

Answer these questions: Based on your analysis, should Green settle for $56,000? If not, how can she show that she suffered a greater loss? What is your estimate of her loss?

Annual Report Analysis 7–3
Determine lower-of-cost-or-market (L.O. 6)

Refer to the financial statements of The Coca-Cola Company in the annual report booklet. Note that the company states its inventories at LCM. Determine the current cost of inventories for 1993 and 1992 and state whether they are being carried at cost or market value.

Ethics Case—Writing Experience 7–4

Respond in writing to the following questions based on the ethics case concerning Terry Dorsey on page 270:

a. Do you believe that Terry's scheme will work?
b. What would you do if you were Terry's accountant?
c. Comment on each of Terry's points of justification.

Group Project 7–5
Inventory control and measurement—interview with manager of merchandising company

In teams of two or three students, interview the manager of a merchandising company (in person or by speakerphone). Inquire about inventory control methods, inventory costing methods, and any other information about the company's inventory procedures. As a team, write a memorandum to your instructor summarizing the results of the interview. The heading of the memorandum should include the date, to whom it is written, from whom, and the subject matter.

Answers to Self-Test

True-False

1. **False.** Overstated ending inventory results in an understatement of cost of goods sold and an overstatement of gross margin and net income.
2. **True.** The cost of goods sold consists of the earliest purchases at the lowest costs in a period of rising prices.
3. **False.** Under LCM, inventory is adjusted to market value only when the market (replacement) value is less than the cost.
4. **True.** The first step in the gross margin method is to estimate gross margin using the gross margin rate experienced in the past.
5. **True.** The cost/retail ratio is computed by dividing the cost of goods available for sale by the retail price of the goods available for sale.
6. **False.** Under perpetual procedure, the Cost of Goods Sold account is updated as sales occur.

Multiple-Choice

1. **b.** The cost of ending inventory using FIFO consists of the most recent purchase:

   Cost of ending inventory = 3,400 × $36
   = $122,400

2. **c.** The cost of goods sold using FIFO is:

   Cost of goods available for sale = (3,000 × $30) + (5,000 × $36)
   = $270,000

   Cost of goods sold = $270,000 − $122,400
   = $147,600

3. **a.** The cost of ending inventory using LIFO is:

   (3,000 × $30) + (400 × $36) = $104,400

4. **d.** The cost of goods sold using LIFO is:

   $270,000 − $104,400 = $165,600

5. **a.** The cost of ending inventory using weighted-average cost is computed:

   Unit cost = $270,000 ÷ 8,000 = $33.75

   Cost of ending inventory = 3,400 × $33.75
   = $114,750

6. **c.** The cost of goods sold using weighted-average cost is:

   $270,000 − $114,750 = $155,250

7. **b.** During a period of rising prices, FIFO results in the lowest cost of goods sold, thus the highest net income.

III

Management's Perspectives in Accounting for Resources

Part Outline

A Manager's Perspective

Ann Stapinski

Staffing, Processing Project Leader

Human Resources

The Coca-Cola Company

I am responsible for staffing at The Coca-Cola Company, and I also handle special projects pertaining to general human resources activities. I have to understand basic financial information because I am often a job candidate's first impression of the company. Good candidates ask about the

company's financials and information in the annual report during the hiring process, and I need to be able to respond well to those queries in order to attract bright people to the company.

Human resources managers (or generalists) often work with managers from various other departments within the corporation to help resolve individual management issues, so they must understand the nature of each manager's business in order to be a helpful resource.

At the department level, we rely on a budget in human resources to make decisions about head count, capital purchases, general expenditures, and merit increases.

Another important function in human resources is compensation planning. We evaluate current salary structures and expected economic changes to forecast salary increases and incentive pay expenses.

In every profession, accounting—budget structures and so forth—serves as a framework for evaluating business results. If you don't understand how the numbers fit together, you won't be able to understand general business principles or make sound decisions.

8

Control of Cash

In a small corporation the president might make all the important decisions and will usually maintain a close watch over the affairs of the business. However, as the business grows and the need arises for additional employees, officers, and managers, the president begins to lose absolute control. Realizing that precautions are necessary to protect the company's interests, the company establishes an internal control structure at this point.

The **internal control structure** of a company consists of "the policies and procedures established to provide reasonable assurance that specific entity objectives will be achieved."[1] The three elements of an internal control structure are the control environment, the accounting system, and the control procedures.

The **control environment** reflects the overall attitude, awareness, and actions of the board of directors, management, and stockholders. The **accounting system** consists of the methods and records that identify, assemble, analyze, classify, record, and report an entity's transactions to provide complete, accurate, and timely financial information. The **control procedures** of a company are additional policies and procedures that management establishes to provide reasonable assurance that the company achieves its specific objectives. These control procedures may pertain to proper authorization, segregation of duties, design and use of adequate documents and records, adequate safeguards over access to assets, and independent checks on performance.

Internal control not only prevents theft and fraud but also serves many purposes: (1) Companies must implement policies requiring compliance with federal law; (2) personnel must perform their assigned duties to promote efficiency of operations; and (3) correct accounting records must supply accurate and reliable information in the accounting reports.

Learning Objectives

After studying this chapter, you should be able to:

1. Describe the necessity for and features of internal control.
2. Define cash and list the objectives sought by management in handling a company's cash.
3. Identify procedures for controlling cash receipts and disbursements.
4. Prepare a bank reconciliation and make necessary journal entries based on that schedule.

(continued)

---

[1] AICPA, *Statement on Auditing Standards No. 55*, "Consideration of the Internal Control Structure in a Financial Statement Audit" (New York, 1988), p. 4. The sixth edition of this text adopts the terminology (internal control structure) of the AICPA. Previous editions have referred to the "internal control system."

(concluded)

5. Explain why a company uses a petty cash fund, describe its operations, and make the necessary journal entries.
6. Analyze and use the financial results—quick ratio.

This chapter discusses the internal control structure that a company establishes to protect its assets and promote the accuracy of its accounting records. You will learn how to establish internal control through control of cash receipts and cash disbursements, proper use of the bank checking account, preparation of the bank reconciliation, and protection of petty cash funds. The internal control structure is enhanced by hiring competent and trustworthy employees, a fact you will appreciate if you become a business owner.

Internal Control

Objective 1
Describe the necessity for and features of internal control.

An effective **internal control structure** includes a company's plan of organization and all the procedures and actions it takes to:

1. Protect its assets against theft and waste.
2. Ensure compliance with company policies and federal law.
3. Evaluate the performance of all personnel to promote efficient operations.
4. Ensure accurate and reliable operating data and accounting reports.

As you study the basic procedures and actions of an effective internal control structure, remember that even small companies can benefit from using some internal control measures. Preventing theft and waste is only a part of internal control.

In general terms, the purpose of internal control is to ensure the efficient operations of a business, thus enabling the business to effectively reach its goals. Since additional control procedures are necessary in a computer environment, a discussion of these controls concludes this section on internal control.

An Accounting Perspective

Business Insight When performing an audit, one of an outside auditor's first duties is to examine the internal control structure of the corporation. To understand the internal control structure, an auditor focuses mainly on management's attitude and awareness concerning controls and the accounting system's processing of transactions. To increase understanding, the auditor inspects documents in the accounting system, discusses external influences on the company with management, reads accounting manuals, and observes the happenings in the company. This understanding of the company's control environment helps the auditor to plan the audit and to determine the nature, timing, and extent of tests of account balances.

Protection of Assets

Companies protect their assets by (1) segregating employee duties, (2) assigning specific duties to each employee, (3) rotating employee job assignments, and (4) using mechanical devices.

Segregation of Employee Duties **Segregation of duties** requires that someone other than the employee responsible for safeguarding an asset must maintain the accounting records for that asset. Also, employees share responsibility for related transactions so that one employee's work serves as a check on the work of other employees.

When a company segregates the duties of employees, it minimizes the probability of an employee being able to steal assets and cover up the theft. For example, an employee could not steal cash from a company and have the theft go undetected unless someone changes the cash records to cover the shortage. To change the records, the employee stealing the cash must also maintain the cash records or be in collusion with the employee who maintains the cash records.

Assignment of Specific Duties to Each Employee When the responsibility for a particular work function is assigned to one employee, that employee is accountable for specific tasks. Should a problem occur, the company can quickly identify the responsible employee.

When a company gives each employee specific duties, it can trace lost documents or determine how a particular transaction was recorded. Also, the employee responsible for a given task can provide information about that task. Being responsible for specific duties gives people a sense of pride and importance that usually makes them want to perform to the best of their ability.

Rotation of Employee Job Assignments Some companies rotate job assignments to discourage employees from engaging in long-term schemes to steal from them. Employees realize that if they steal from the company, the next employees assigned to their positions may discover the theft.

Frequently, companies have the policy that all employees must take an annual vacation. This policy also discourages theft because many dishonest schemes collapse when the employee does not attend to the scheme on a daily basis.

Use of Mechanical Devices Companies use several mechanical devices to help protect their assets. Check protectors (machines that perforate the check amount into the check), cash registers, and time clocks make it extremely difficult for employees to alter certain company documents and records.

Compliance with Company Policies and Federal Law

Internal control policies are effective only when employees follow them. To ensure that they carry out its internal control policies, a company must hire competent and trustworthy employees. Thus, the execution of effective internal control begins with the time and effort a company expends in hiring employees. Once the company hires the employees, it must train those employees and clearly communicate to them company policies, such as obtaining proper authorization before making a cash disbursement. Frequently, written job descriptions establish the responsibilities and duties of employees. The initial training of employees should include a clear explanation of their duties and how to perform them.

In publicly held corporations, the company's internal control structure must satisfy the requirements of federal law. In December 1977, Congress enacted the Foreign Corrupt Practices Act (FCPA). This law requires a publicly held corporation to devise and maintain an effective internal control structure and to keep accurate accounting records. This law came about partly because company accounting records covered up bribes and kickbacks made to foreign governments or government officials. The FCPA made this specific type of bribery illegal.

Evaluation of Personnel Performance

To evaluate how well employees are doing their jobs, many companies use an internal auditing staff. **Internal auditing** consists of investigating and evaluating employees' compliance with the company's policies and procedures. Companies employ **internal auditors** to perform these audits. Once trained in company policies and internal auditing duties, internal auditors periodically test the effectiveness of controls and procedures throughout the company.

Internal auditors encourage operating efficiency throughout the company and are constantly alert for breakdowns in the company's internal control structure. In addition, internal auditors make recommendations for the improvement of the company's internal control structure. All companies and nonprofit organizations can benefit from internal auditing. However, internal auditing is especially necessary in large organizations because the owners (stockholders) cannot be involved personally with all aspects of the business.

Accuracy of Accounting Records

Companies should maintain complete and accurate accounting records. The best method to ensure such accounting records is to hire and train competent and honest individuals. Periodically, supervisors evaluate an employee's performance to make sure the employee is following company policies. Inaccurate or inadequate accounting records serve as an invitation to theft by dishonest employees because theft can be concealed more easily.

ILLUSTRATION 8.1
Purchase Requisition

PURCHASE REQUISITION **No.** *2416*

BRYAN WHOLESALE COMPANY

From: *Automotive Supplies Department* **Date:** *November 20, 1997*
To: *Purchasing Department* **Suggested supplier:** *Wilkes Radio Company*

Please purchase the following items:

Description	Item Number	Quantity	Estimated Price
True-tone stereo radios	*Model No. 5868-24393*	*200*	*$50 per unit*

Reason for request:
Customer order
Baier Company

To be filled in by purchasing department:
Date ordered *11/21/97*
Purchase order number *N-145*
Approved *R.S.T.*

One or more business documents support most accounting transactions. These source documents are an integral part of the internal control structure. For optimal control, source documents should be serially numbered. (Transaction documentation and related aspects of internal control are presented throughout the text.)

Since source documents serve as documentation of business transactions, from time to time firms check the validity of these documents. For example, to review a merchandise transaction, they check the documents used to record the transaction against the proper accounting records. When the accounting department records a merchandise transaction, it should receive copies of the following four documents:

1. **Purchase requisition.** A **purchase requisition** (Illustration 8.1) is a written request from an employee inside the company to the purchasing department to purchase certain items.
2. **Purchase order.** A **purchase order** (Illustration 8.2) is a document sent from the purchasing department to a supplier requesting that merchandise or other items be shipped to the purchaser.
3. **Invoice.** An **invoice** (Illustration 8.3) is the statement sent by the supplier to the purchaser requesting payment for the merchandise shipped.
4. **Receiving report.** A **receiving report** is a document prepared by the receiving department showing the descriptions and quantities of all items received from a supplier in a particular shipment. A copy of the purchase order can serve as a receiving report if the quantity ordered is omitted. Then, because receiving department personnel do not know what quantity to expect, they will count the quantity received more accurately.

These four documents together serve as authorization to pay for merchandise and should be checked against the accounting records. Without these documents, a company might fail to pay a legitimate invoice, pay fictitious invoices, or pay an invoice more than once. Companies can accomplish proper internal control only by periodically checking the source documents of business transactions with the accounting records of those transactions. In Illustration 8.4, we show the flow of documents and goods in a merchandise transaction.

Unfortunately, even though a company implements all of these features in its internal control structure, theft may still occur. If employees are dishonest, they can usually figure out a way to steal from a company, thus circumventing even the

ILLUSTRATION 8.2
Purchase Order

PURCHASE ORDER No. *N-145*

BRYAN WHOLESALE COMPANY
476 Mason Street
Detroit, Michigan 48823

To: *Wilkes Radio Company*
2515 West Peachtree Street
Atlanta, Georgia 30303
Ship to: *Above address*

Date: *November 21, 1997*
Ship by: *December 20, 1997*
FOB terms requested: *Destination*
Discount terms requested: *2/10, n/30*

Please send the following items:

Description	Item Number	Quantity	Price per Unit	Total Amount
True-tone stereo radios	*5868-24393*	*200*	*$50*	*$10,000*

Ordered by: *Jane Knight*

Please include order number on all invoices and shipments.

ILLUSTRATION 8.3
Invoice

INVOICE **Invoice No.:** *1574*
Date: *Dec. 15, 1997*

WILKES RADIO COMPANY
2515 West Peachtree Street
Atlanta, Georgia 30303

Customer's Order No.: *N-145*
Sold to: *Bryan Wholesale Co.*
Address: *476 Mason Street*
Detroit, Michigan 48823
Terms: *2/10, n/30, FOB destination*

Date shipped: *Dec. 15, 1997*
Shipped by: *Nagel Trucking Co.*

Description	Item Number	Quantity	Price per Unit	Total Amount
True-tone stereo radios	*Model No. 5868-24393*	*200*	*$50*	*$10,000*
		Total		*$10,000*

most effective internal control structure. Therefore, companies should carry adequate casualty insurance on assets. This insurance reimburses the company for loss of a nonmonetary asset such as specialized equipment. Companies should also have **fidelity bonds** on employees handling cash and other negotiable instruments. These bonds ensure that a company is reimbursed for losses due to theft of cash and other monetary assets. With both casualty insurance on assets and fidelity bonds on employees, a company can recover at least a portion of any loss that occurs.

Components of Internal Control

According to the Committee of Sponsoring Organizations of the Treadway Commission, there are five components of an internal control structure. When these components are linked to the organization's operations, they can quickly respond to shifting conditions. The components are:

ILLUSTRATION 8.4
Flow of Documents and Goods in a Merchandising Transaction

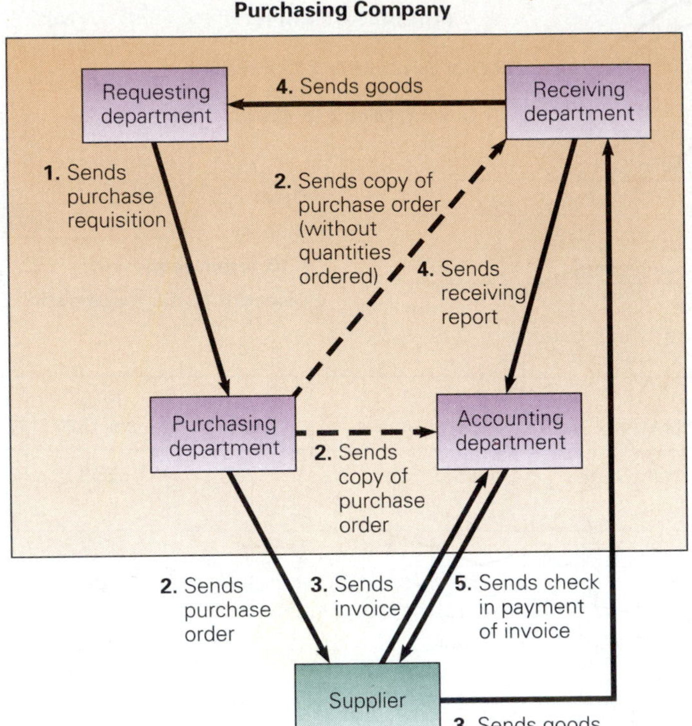

Steps

1. Requesting department sends purchase requisition to purchasing department.
2. Purchasing department sends purchase order to supplier, with copies going to the receiving department (without quantities ordered) and the accounting department.
3. Supplier sends goods to receiving department, where goods received are checked against purchase order, and sends invoice to accounting department.
4. Receiving department sends goods to requesting department and sends receiving report to accounting department.
5. Accounting department checks receiving report against purchase order and invoice and sends check in payment of invoice to the supplier.

1. **Control environment.** The control environment is the basis for all other elements of the internal control structure. The control environment includes many factors such as ethical values, management's philosophy, the integrity of the employees of the corporation, and the guidance provided by management or the board of directors.
2. **Risk assessment.** After the entity sets objectives, the risks (such as theft and waste of assets) from external and internal sources must be assessed. Examining the risks associated with each objective allows management to develop the means to control these risks.
3. **Control activities.** To address the risks associated with each objective, management establishes control activities. These activities include procedures that employees must follow. Examples include procedures to protect the assets through segregation of employee duties and the other means we discussed earlier.

4. **Information and communication.** Information relevant to decision making must be collected and reported in a timely manner. The events that yield these data may come from internal or external sources. Communication throughout the entity is important to achieve management's goals. Employees must understand what is expected of them and how their responsibilities relate to the work of others. Communication with external parties such as suppliers and shareholders is also important.
5. **Monitoring.** After the internal control structure is in place, the firm should monitor its effectiveness so that it can make changes before serious problems arise. In testing components of the internal control structure, companies base their thoroughness on the risk assigned to those components.

Responsibility for Internal Control

Internal control is the general responsibility of all members in an organization. However, the following three groups have specific responsibilities regarding the internal control structure.

Management holds ultimate responsibility for establishing and maintaining an effective internal control structure. Through leadership and example, management demonstrates ethical behavior and integrity within the company.

The *board of directors* provides guidance to management. Because board members have a working knowledge of the functions of the company, they help shield the company from managers who try to override some control procedures for dishonest purposes. Often, an efficient board that has access to the company's internal auditors can discover such fraud.

Auditors within the organization evaluate the effectiveness of the internal control structure and determine whether company policies and procedures are being followed. All employees are part of a communications network that enables an internal control structure to work effectively.

Internal Control in a Computer Environment

Computerized financial records require the same internal control principles of separation of duties and control over access as a manual accounting system. The exact control steps depend on whether a company is using mainframe computers and minicomputers or microcomputers.

Large corporations might use all three types of computers in their accounting environments. The size and complexity of mainframe computers and minicomputers require specially trained persons to keep these systems operating. While systems specialists operate the computer system itself, programmers develop the programs that direct the computer to perform specific tasks. In a mainframe or minicomputer environment, internal control should include the following:

- Control computer access by placing the computer in an easily secured room, and allow only persons authorized to operate the computer to enter the room.
- Restrict the access of systems specialists (who operate the computer) to software programs and the access of programmers to the computer. This policy prevents the running of unauthorized, altered programs.
- Run some programs, such as ones used to print monthly accounts receivable statements to send to credit customers, only during an authorized time period. If programs and data are stored on magnetic tape, store the tapes under lock and key and under the control of a tape librarian. The librarian should be independent of the computer systems and programming functions.

Many smaller companies use microcomputers instead of a mainframe or a minicomputer. Also, large companies might supply certain employees with microcomputers. The use of microcomputers changes the control environment somewhat. Small companies generally do not employ systems specialists and programmers. Instead, these companies use off-the-shelf programs such as accounting, spreadsheet, database management, and word processing packages. The data created by use of these programs are valuable (e.g., the company's accounting records) and often sensitive. Thus, controls are also important. In a microcomputer environment, the following controls can be useful:

- Keep each microcomputer locked when not in use, and give keys only to persons authorized to use that computer.
- Require computer users to have tight control over their diskettes on which programs and data are stored. Just as one person maintains custody over a certain set of records in a manual system, in a computer system one person maintains custody over diskettes containing certain information (such as the accounts receivable subsidiary ledger). Lock up these diskettes at night, and make backup copies that are retained in a different secured location.
- Require passwords (kept secret) to gain entry into data files maintained on the hard disk.
- In situations where a local area network (LAN) links the microcomputers into one system, permit only certain computers and persons in the network to have access to some data files (the accounting records, for example).

Computerized accounting systems do not lessen the need for internal control. In fact, access to a computer by an unauthorized person could result in significant theft in less time than with a manual system.

Controlling Cash

Objective 2
Define cash and list the objectives sought by management in handling a company's cash.

Since cash is the most liquid of all assets, a business cannot survive and prosper if it does not have adequate control over its cash. In accounting, **cash** includes coins; currency; undeposited negotiable instruments such as checks, bank drafts, and money orders; amounts in checking and savings accounts; and demand certificates of deposit. A **certificate of deposit (CD)** is an interest-bearing deposit that can be withdrawn from a bank at will (demand CD) or at a fixed maturity date (time CD). Cash only includes demand CDs that may be withdrawn at any time without prior notice or penalty. Cash does not include postage stamps, IOUs, time CDs, or notes receivable.

In its general ledger, a company usually maintains two cash accounts—Cash and Petty Cash. On the company's balance sheet, it combines the balances of these two accounts into one amount reported as Cash.

An Accounting Perspective

Business Insight Users of financial data must look to footnotes to see the real meaning behind the numbers. Meredith Corporation publishes a variety of magazines and books, owns television stations, and operates two cable television systems. In Meredith Corporation's 1993 annual report, for example, the company defines cash and cash equivalents in this footnote:

> For purposes of reporting cash flows, all cash and short-term investments with original maturities of three months or less are considered cash and cash equivalents, since they are readily convertible into cash.

The footnote provides more insight to the number on the financial statement.

Since many business transactions involve cash, it is a vital factor in the operation of a business. Of all the company's assets, cash is the most easily mishandled either through theft or carelessness. To control and manage its cash, a company should:

1. Account for all cash transactions accurately so that correct information is available regarding cash flows and balances.
2. Make certain that enough cash is available to pay bills as they come due.

3. Avoid holding too much idle cash because excess cash could be invested to generate income, such as interest.
4. Prevent loss of cash due to theft or fraud.

The need to control cash is clearly evident and has many aspects. Without the proper timing of cash flows and the protection of idle cash, a business cannot survive. This section discusses cash receipts and cash disbursements. Later in the chapter, we explain the importance of preparing a bank reconciliation for each bank checking account and controlling the petty cash fund.

Controlling Cash Receipts

Objective 3
Identify procedures for controlling cash receipts and disbursements.

When a merchandising company sells its merchandise, it may receive cash immediately or several days or weeks later. A clerk receives the cash immediately *over the counter*, records it, and places it in a cash register. The presence of the customer as the sale is *rung up* usually ensures that the cashier enters the correct amount of the sale in the cash register. At the end of each day, stores reconcile the cash in each cash register with the cash register tape or computer printout for that register. Payments received later are almost always in the form of checks. Stores prepare a record of the checks received as soon as they are received. Some merchandising companies receive all their cash receipts on a delayed basis as payments on accounts receivable. (See the cash receipts cycle for merchandise transactions in Illustration 8.5).

Although businesses vary their specific procedures for controlling cash receipts, they usually observe the following principles:

1. Prepare a record of all cash receipts as soon as cash is received. Most thefts of cash occur before a record is made of the receipt. Once a record is made, it is easier to trace a theft.
2. Deposit all cash receipts as soon as feasible, preferably on the day they are received or on the next business day. Undeposited cash is more susceptible to misappropriation.
3. Arrange duties so that the employee who handles cash receipts does not record the receipts in the accounting records. This control feature follows the general principle of *segregation of duties* given earlier in the chapter, as does item 4.
4. Arrange duties so that the employee who receives the cash does not disburse the cash. This control measure is possible in all but the smallest companies.

Controlling Cash Disbursements

Companies also need controls over cash disbursements. Since a company spends most of its cash by check, many of the internal controls for cash disbursements deal with checks and authorizations for cash payments. The basic principle of segregation of duties also applies in controlling cash disbursements. Following are some basic control procedures for cash disbursements:

- Make all disbursements by check or from petty cash. Obtain proper approval for all disbursements and create a permanent record of each disbursement. Many retail stores make refunds for returned merchandise from the cash register. When this practice is followed, clerks should have refund tickets approved by a supervisor before refunding cash.
- Require all checks to be serially numbered and limit access to checks to employees authorized to write checks.
- Require two signatures on each check so that one person cannot withdraw funds from the bank account.
- Arrange duties so that the employee who authorizes payment of a bill does not sign checks. Otherwise, the checks could be written to friends in payment of fictitious invoices.

ILLUSTRATION 8.5
Cash Receipts Cycle for Merchandise Transactions

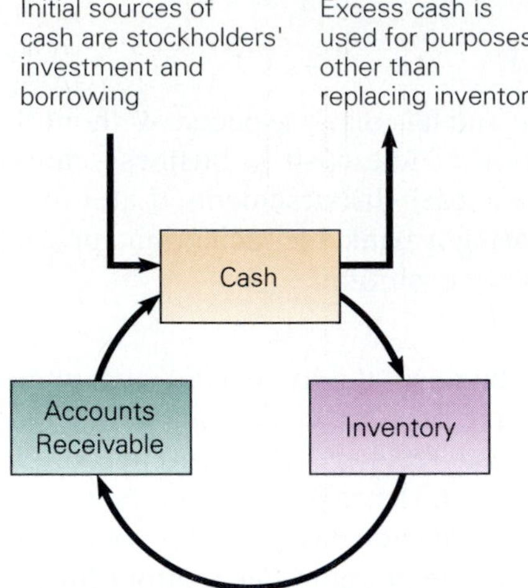

Cash initially comes into the business from stockholders' investment and borrowing. Cash is then invested in inventory and other assets. When inventory is sold, cash may be received immediately, or receipt may be delayed and involve accounts receivable. The inventory generally is sold at more than cost so the company can make a profit. Each time the cycle is completed, the amount of cash grows and may be used for purposes other than replacing inventory.

ILLUSTRATION 8.6
Internal Control Considerations Regarding Cash

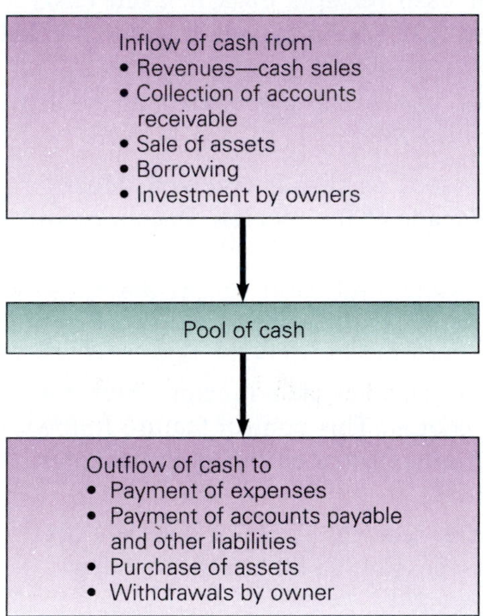

Inflow of cash from
• Revenues—cash sales
• Collection of accounts receivable
• Sale of assets
• Borrowing
• Investment by owners
Pool of cash
Outflow of cash to
• Payment of expenses
• Payment of accounts payable and other liabilities
• Purchase of assets
• Withdrawals by owner

Internal control considerations

1. Are all cash receipts being properly recorded and actually going into the company's pool of cash, or are individuals siphoning off some of these receipts for their own use?
2. Is the pool of cash protected from theft? Is the cash on hand managed so as to produce income for the company and yet be available when needed to make legitimate disbursements?
3. Is there close control over cash disbursements to ensure that only legitimate disbursements are made in the proper amounts and on a timely basis?

- Require approved documents to support all checks issued.
- Instruct the employee authorizing cash disbursements to make certain that payment is for a legitimate purpose and is made out for the exact amount and to the proper party.
- Stamp the supporting documents *paid* when liabilities are paid and indicate the date and number of the check issued. These procedures lessen the chance of paying the same debt more than once.
- Arrange duties so that those employees who sign checks neither have access to canceled checks nor prepare the bank reconciliation. This policy makes it more difficult for an employee to conceal a theft.
- Have an employee who has no other cash duties prepare the bank reconciliation each month, so that errors and shortages can be discovered quickly.
- Void all checks incorrectly prepared. Mark these checks *void* and retain them to prevent unauthorized use.

Illustration 8.6 shows an overview of some of the internal control considerations relating to cash.

ILLUSTRATION 8.7
Deposit Ticket

CURRENCY	150	—
COIN	45	50
CHECKS (LIST CHECKS SINGLY) Williams	100	—
Sloans	200	—
TOTAL FROM OTHER SIDE		
SUB-TOTAL	495	50
TOTAL ITEMS / LESS CASH RECEIVED		
TOTAL DEPOSIT	495	50

NAME M. MILLER COMPANY

ACCT. NO. 10-03-38-3

DATE July 7 19 97

CHECKS AND OTHER ITEMS ARE RECEIVED FOR DEPOSIT SUBJECT TO THE TERMS AND CONDITIONS OF THIS FINANCIAL INSTITUTION'S ACCOUNT AGREEMENT. DEPOSITS MAY NOT BE AVAILABLE FOR IMMEDIATE WITHDRAWAL.

SIGN HERE ONLY IF CASH RECEIVED FROM DEPOSIT

64-376/611

DEPOSIT TICKET

PLEASE ITEMIZE ADDITIONAL CHECKS ON REVERSE SIDE

GEORGIA NATIONAL BANK
ATHENS, GA 30601

⑆061103768⑆

© HARLAND 1989

Most companies use checking accounts to handle their cash transactions. The company deposits its cash receipts in a bank checking account and writes checks to pay its bills. The bank sends the company a statement each month. The company checks this statement against its records to determine if it must make any corrections or adjustments in either the company's balance or the bank's balance. You learn how to do this bank reconciliation later. In the next section, we discuss the bank checking account. If you have a personal checking account, some of this information will be familiar to you.

THE BANK CHECKING ACCOUNT

Banks earn income by providing a variety of services to individuals, businesses, and other entities such as churches or libraries. One of these services is the checking account. A **checking account** is a money balance maintained in the bank; it is subject to withdrawal by the depositor, or owner of the money, on demand. To provide depositors with an accurate record of depositor funds received and disbursed, a bank uses the business documents discussed in this section.[2]

Signature Card

A bank requires a new depositor to complete a **signature card,** which provides the signatures of persons authorized to sign checks drawn on an account. The bank retains the card and uses it to identify signatures on checks it pays. The bank does not compare every check with this signature card. Usually, it makes a comparison only when the depositor disputes the validity of a check paid by the bank or when someone presents a check for an unusually large sum for payment.

Deposit Ticket

When depositors make a bank deposit, they prepare a deposit ticket or slip. A **deposit ticket** is a form that shows the date and the items that make up the deposit (Illustration 8.7). Often, the ticket is preprinted to show the depositor's name, address, and account number. A depositor enters the items comprising the deposit—cash and a list of checks—on the ticket when making the deposit. The depositor receives a receipt showing the date of deposit and the amount deposited.

Check

A **check** is a written order to a bank to pay a specific sum of money to the party designated as the payee by the party issuing the check. Thus, every check transac-

[2] Due to relaxed federal regulations, institutions other than banks—such as savings and loan associations and credit unions—now offer checking account services. All of these institutions function somewhat similarly; but, for simplicity's sake, we discuss only banks here.

ILLUSTRATION 8.8
Check with Attached Remittance Advice

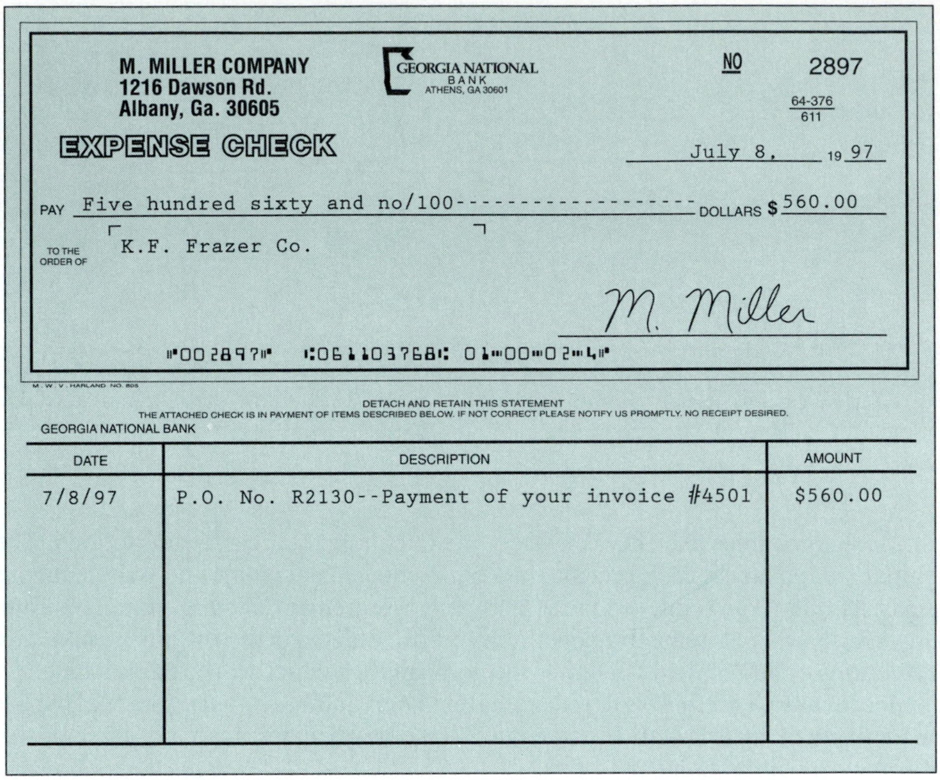

M. MILLER COMPANY
1216 Dawson Rd.
Albany, Ga. 30605

GEORGIA NATIONAL BANK
ATHENS, GA 30601

NO 2897

64-376
611

EXPENSE CHECK

July 8, 19 97

PAY Five hundred sixty and no/100------------------ DOLLARS $560.00

TO THE ORDER OF K.F. Frazer Co.

M. Miller

⑈002897⑈ ⑆061103768⑆ 01⑈00⑈02⑈4⑈

M. W. V. HARLAND NO. 806

DETACH AND RETAIN THIS STATEMENT
THE ATTACHED CHECK IS IN PAYMENT OF ITEMS DESCRIBED BELOW. IF NOT CORRECT PLEASE NOTIFY US PROMPTLY. NO RECEIPT DESIRED.
GEORGIA NATIONAL BANK

DATE	DESCRIPTION	AMOUNT
7/8/97	P.O. No. R2130--Payment of your invoice #4501	$560.00

tion involves three parties: the *bank*, the **payee** (party to whom the check is made payable), and the **drawer** (depositor). Most depositors use serially numbered checks preprinted with information about the depositor, such as name, address, and telephone number. Often a business check has an attached remittance advice. A **remittance advice** informs the payee why the drawer (or maker) of the check is making this payment. Before cashing or depositing it, the payee detaches the remittance advice from the check (Illustration 8.8).

Bank Statement

A **bank statement** is a statement issued (usually monthly) by a bank describing the activities in a depositor's checking account during the period. Illustration 8.9 shows a bank statement that includes the following data:

1. Deposits made to the checking account during the period.
2. Checks paid out of the depositor's checking account by the bank during the period. These checks have *cleared* the bank and are *canceled*.
3. Other deductions from the checking account for service charges, NSF (not sufficient funds) checks, safe-deposit box rent, and check printing fees. Banks assess **service charges** on the depositor to cover the cost of handling the checking account, such as check clearing charges. An **NSF (Not Sufficient Funds) check** is a customer's check returned from the customer's bank to the depositor's bank because the funds in the customer's checking account balance were insufficient to cover the check. The depositor's bank deducts the amount of the returned check from the depositor's checking account. Since the customer still owes the depositor money, the depositor restores the amount of the NSF check to the account receivable for that customer in the company's books.
4. Other additions to the checking account from proceeds of a note collected by the bank for the depositor and interest earned on the account.

ILLUSTRATION 8.9
Bank Statement

THE
GEORGIA
NATIONAL
BANK

P. O. BOX 1684
ATHENS, GEORGIA 30603

FDIC

CHECKING STATEMENT

DIRECT INQUIRIES TO THE ABOVE ADDRESS OR CALL (404) 548-5511

R. L. LEE COMPANY
1021 ROY LANE
ATHENS, GA 30603

01 45 65 2

ACCOUNT NUMBER	STATEMENT DATE	
01-45-65-2	5/31/97	21 ENCLOSURES

BEGINNING BALANCE	ADDITIONS	SUBTRACTIONS	ENDING BALANCE
$2,248.00	$12,358.00	$11,354.00	$3,252.00

SUBTRACT 22 ITEMS

CHECKS	AMOUNT	DATE PAID	CHECKS	AMOUNT	DATE PAID	CHECKS	AMOUNT	DATE PAID
9515*	351.00	5/3	9531	1,250.00	5/8	9537	111.00	5/22
9519*	154.00	5/3	9532	800.00	5/15	9538	2,071.00	5/23
9527	208.00	5/7	9533	925.00	5/15	9539	413.00	5/25
9528	467.00	5/7	9534	417.00	5/18	9540	1,093.00	5/25
9529	125.00	5/7	9535	230.00	5/17	9541	1,005.00	5/25
9530	411.00	5/8	9536	169.00	5/21	9542	818.00	5/29
						9543	211.00	5/29

NSF CHECK	102.00	5/30
SERVICE CHARGE	8.00	5/31
SAFE DEPOSIT BOX RENT	15.00	5/31

*PRECEDING CHECK(S) NOT PAID DURING THIS PERIOD

ADD 23 ITEMS

AMOUNT	DATE	AMOUNT	DATE	AMOUNT	DATE
624.00	5/1	514.00	5/10	333.00	5/22
776.00	5/2	401.00	5/11	407.00	5/23
526.00	5/3	702.00	5/14	371.00	5/24
474.00	5/4	303.00	5/15	331.00	5/25
631.00	5/7	471.00	5/16	507.00	5/28
608.00	5/8	653.00	5/17	601.00	5/29
1,225.00**	5/8	414.00	5/18	400.00	5/30
667.00	5/9	419.00	5/21		

**NOTE COLLECTED FROM A CUSTOMER

ENDING BALANCE FOR EACH DAY YOUR ACCOUNT HAD ACTIVITY

BALANCE	DATE	BALANCE	DATE	BALANCE	DATE
2,248.00	4/30	5,327.00	5/10	6,371.00	5/22
2,872.00	5/1	5,728.00	5/11	4,707.00	5/23
3,648.00	5/2	6,430.00	5/14	5,078.00	5/24
3,669.00	5/3	5,008.00	5/15	2,898.00	5/25
4,143.00	5/4	5,479.00	5/16	3,405.00	5/28
3,974.00	5/7	5,902.00	5/17	2,977.00	5/29
4,146.00	5/8	5,899.00	5/18	3,275.00	5/30
4,813.00	5/9	6,149.00	5/21	3,252.00	5/31

In addition to the data in the bank statement in Illustration 8.9, bank statements also can show nonroutine deposits made to the depositor's checking account. Such deposits are made by a third party. For example, the bank may have received a wire transfer of funds for the depositor.

A **wire transfer of funds** is an interbank transfer of funds by telephone. Companies that operate in many widely scattered locations and have checking accounts with several different local banks often use interbank transfers of funds. These companies may set up special procedures to avoid accumulating too much idle cash in local bank accounts. One such procedure involves the use of special-instruction bank accounts. For example, a company may set up **transfer bank accounts** so local banks automatically transfer to a central bank (by wire or bank draft) all amounts on deposit in excess of a stated amount. In this way, transfers move funds not needed for local operations quickly to headquarters, where the company can use the funds or invest them.

ILLUSTRATION 8.10
Debit Memorandum (top) and Credit Memorandum (bottom)

GENERAL LEDGER **DEBIT** ACCT. TITLE
R. L. Lee Company
1021 Roy Lane
Athens, GA 30603
Acct. No. 01 45 65 2
DATE May 31, 1997

DESCRIPTION	AMOUNT	
Safe Deposit Box Rental		
CONTRA ENTRY		
DRAWN BY CWT CENTER APPROVED BY MRC TOTAL	15	00

BANKERS SYSTEMS, INC., ST. CLOUD, MN 56301

⑆037600800⑆

GENERAL LEDGER **CREDIT** ACCT. TITLE
R. L. Lee Company
1021 Roy Lane
Athens, GA 30603
Acct. No. 01 45 65 2
DATE 5/8/97

DESCRIPTION	AMOUNT	
Collection of note for the Lee Company from X Company		
CONTRA ENTRY		
DRAWN BY CWT CENTER APPROVED BY MRC TOTAL	1,225	00

BANKERS SYSTEMS, INC., ST. CLOUD, MN 56301

⑆037600208⑆

Frequently, the bank returns canceled checks and original deposit tickets with the bank statement. Since it is expensive to sort, handle, and mail these items, some banks no longer return them to depositors. These banks usually store the documents on microfilm, with photocopies available if needed. Most depositors need only a detailed bank statement, as shown in Illustration 8.9, and not the original documents to show what transactions occurred during a given period.

When banks debit or credit a depositor's checking account, they prepare debit and credit memoranda (memos). Banks may also return these memos with the bank statement. A **debit memo** is a form used by a bank to explain a deduction from the depositor's account; a **credit memo** explains an addition to the depositor's account. The terms *debit memo* and *credit memo* may seem reversed, but remember that the depositor's checking account is a liability—an account payable—of the bank. So, when the bank seeks to reduce a depositor's balance, it prepares a debit memo. To increase the balance, it prepares a credit memo. Illustration 8.10 contains examples of debit and credit memos. Some banks no longer mail these documents to the depositor and rely instead on explanations in the bank statements.

Information that the depositor did not know before receiving the bank statement (items 3 and 4 on page 306) requires new journal entries on the company's books. After the entries have been made to record the new information, the balance in the Cash account is the actual cash available to the company. When the depositor has already received notice of NSF checks and other bank charges or credits, the needed journal entries may have been made earlier. In this chapter, we assume no entries have been made for these items unless stated otherwise.

When a company receives its bank statement, it must reconcile the balance shown by the bank with the cash balance in the company's books. If you have a personal checking account, you also should reconcile your bank statement with your checkbook. You can use the reconciliation form on the back of the bank

Illustration 8.11
Bank Reconciliation

R. L. LEE COMPANY Bank Reconciliation May 31, 1997		
① Balance per bank statement, May 31, 1997		$3,252
② Add: Deposit in transit		452
		$3,704
③ Less: Outstanding checks:		
No. 9544	$322	
No. 9545	168	
No. 9546	223	713
Adjusted balance, May 31, 1997		$2,991
① Balance per ledger, May 31, 1997		$1,891
④ Add: Note collected (including interest of $25)		1,225
		$3,116
⑤ Less: NSF check (R. Johnson)	$102	
⑥ Safe-deposit box rent	15	
⑥ Service charges	8	125
Adjusted balance, May 31, 1997		$2,991

statement to list your checks that have not yet been paid by the bank and your deposits not yet shown on the bank statement. Some small businesses use this form. Others prepare a separate bank reconciliation, which we discuss in the next section.

Bank Reconciliation

A **bank reconciliation,** often called a *bank reconciliation statement* or *schedule,* is a schedule the company (depositor) prepares to *reconcile,* or explain, the difference between the cash balance on the bank statement and the cash balance on the company's books. The company prepares a bank reconciliation to determine its actual cash balance and prepare the entry(ies) to correct the cash balance in the ledger.

Objective 4
Prepare a bank reconciliation and make necessary journal entries based on that schedule.

An Accounting Perspective

Business Insight Within the internal control structure, segregation of duties is an important way to prevent fraud. One place to segregate duties is between the cash disbursement cycle and bank reconciliations. To prevent collusion among employees, the person who reconciles the bank account should not be involved in the cash disbursement cycle. Also, the bank should mail the statement directly to the person who reconciles the bank account each month. Sending the statement directly limits the number of employees who would have an opportunity to tamper with the statement.

Look at Illustration 8.11; the bank reconciliation has two main sections. The top section begins with the balance on the bank statement. The bottom section begins with the balance on the company's books. After the company makes adjustments to both the *bank* and *book* balances, both adjusted balances should be the same. The steps in preparing a bank reconciliation are as follows:

Deposits. Compare the deposits listed on the bank statement with the deposits on the company's books. To make this comparison, place check marks in the bank statement and in the company's books by the deposits that agree. Then determine the deposits in transit. A **deposit in transit** is typically a day's cash receipts recorded in the depositor's books in one period but recorded as a deposit by the bank in the succeeding period. The most common deposit in transit is the cash receipts deposited on the last business day of the month. Normally, deposits in transit occur only near the end of the period covered by the bank statement. For example, a deposit made in a bank's night depository on May 31 would be recorded by the company on May 31 and by the bank on June 1. Thus, the deposit does not appear on a bank statement for the month ended May 31. Also check the deposits in transit listed in last month's bank reconciliation against the bank statement. Immediately investigate any deposit made during the month but missing from the bank statement (unless it involves a deposit made at the end of the period).

Paid checks. If canceled checks are returned with the bank statement, compare them to the statement to be sure both amounts agree. Then, sort the checks in numerical order. Next, determine which checks are outstanding. **Outstanding checks** are those issued by a depositor but not paid by the bank on which they are drawn. The party receiving the check may not have deposited it immediately. Once deposited, checks may take several days to clear the banking system, although this process has been expedited in recent years. Determine the outstanding checks by comparing the check numbers that have cleared the bank with the check numbers issued by the company. Use check marks in the company's record of checks issued to identify those checks returned by the bank. Checks issued that have not yet been returned by the bank are the outstanding checks. If the bank does not return checks but only lists the cleared checks on the bank statement, determine the outstanding checks by comparing this list with the company's record of checks issued.

Sometimes checks written long ago are still outstanding. Checks outstanding as of the beginning of the month appear on the prior month's bank reconciliation. Most of these have cleared during the current month; list those that have not cleared as still outstanding on the current month's reconciliation.

Bank debit and credit memos. Verify all debit and credit memos on the bank statement. Debit memos reflect deductions for such items as service charges, NSF checks, safe-deposit box rent, and notes paid by the bank for the depositor. Credit memos reflect additions for such items as notes collected for the depositor by the bank and wire transfers of funds from another bank in which the company sends funds to the home office bank. Check the bank debit and credit memos with the depositor's books to see if they have already been recorded. Make journal entries for any items not already recorded in the company's books.

Errors. List any errors. A common error by depositors is recording a check in the accounting records at an amount that differs from the actual amount. For example, a $47 check may be recorded as $74. Although the check clears the bank at the amount written on the check ($47), the depositor frequently does not catch the error until reviewing the bank statement or canceled checks.

Deposits in transit, outstanding checks, and bank service charges usually account for the difference between the company's Cash account balance and the bank balance. (These same items can cause a difference between your personal checkbook balance and the balance on your bank statement.) Remember that all items shown on the bank reconciliation as adjustments of the book (ledger) balance require journal entries to adjust the Cash account (items 4, 5, and 6 in Illustration 8.11 and in the following example). Items appearing as adjustments to the balance per bank statement do not require entries by the depositor (items 2 and 3). Of course, you should call any bank errors to the bank's attention.

To illustrate the preparation of the bank reconciliation in Illustration 8.11, assume the following (these items are keyed to numbers in that illustration):

1. On May 31, 1997, R. L. Lee Company showed a balance in its Cash account of $1,891. On June 2, Lee received its bank statement for the month ended May 31, which showed an ending balance of $3,252.

2. A matching of debits to the Cash account on the books with deposits on the bank statement showed that the $452 receipts of May 31 were included in Cash but not included as a deposit on the bank statement. This deposit was in the bank's night deposit chute on May 31.
3. A comparison of checks issued with checks that had cleared the bank showed three checks outstanding:

No. 9544	$322
No. 9545	168
No. 9546	223
Total	$713

4. Included with the bank statement was a credit memo for $1,225 (principal of $1,200 + interest of $25) for collection of a note owed to Lee by Shipley Company.
5. Included with the bank statement was a $102 debit memo for an NSF check written by R. Johnson and deposited by Lee.
6. Charges made to Lee's account include $15 for safe-deposit box rent and $8 for service charges.

After reconciling the book and bank balances as shown in Illustration 8.11, Lee Company finds that its actual cash balance is $2,991. The following entries record information from the bank reconciliation:

		Debit	Credit
④	Cash	1,225	
	Notes Receivable—Shipley Company		1,200
	Interest Revenue		25
	To record note collected from Shipley Company.		
⑤	Accounts Receivable—R. Johnson*	102	
	Cash		102
	To charge NSF check back to customer, R. Johnson.		
⑥	Bank Service Charge Expense (or Miscellaneous Expense)	23	
	Cash		23
	To record bank service charges.		

* This debit would be posted to the Accounts Receivable control account in the general ledger and to R. Johnson's account in the accounts receivable subsidiary ledger.

The income statement for the period ending May 31, 1997, would include the $23 bank service charge as an expense and the $25 interest as revenue. The May 31 balance sheet would show $2,991 cash, the actual cash balance.

You could combine the preceding three entries into one compound entry as follows:

	Debit	Credit
Cash	1,100	
Bank Service Charge Expense	23	
Accounts Receivable—R. Johnson	102	
Notes Receivable		1,200
Interest Revenue		25
To correct the accounts for needed changes identified in the bank reconciliaton.		

The bank routinely handles the deposit in transit and any outstanding checks already recorded in the depositor's books. Since these items appear on the bank balance side of the reconciliation, they require no entry in the company's books. The bank processes these items in the subsequent period.

When a company maintains more than one checking account, it must reconcile each account separately with the balance on the bank statement for that account. The depositor should also check carefully to see that the bank did not combine the transactions of the two accounts.

Certified and Cashier's Checks

To make sure a check cannot *bounce* and become an NSF check, a payee may demand a certified or cashier's check from the maker. Both certified checks and cashier's checks are liabilities of the issuing bank rather than the depositor. As a result, payees usually accept these checks without question.

- A **certified check** is a check written, or drawn, by a depositor and taken to the depositor's bank for certification. The bank stamps *certified* across the face of the check and inserts the name of the bank and the date; a bank official signs the certification. The bank certifies a check only when the depositor's balance is large enough to cover the check. The bank deducts the amount of the check from the depositor's account at the time it certifies the check.
- A **cashier's check** is a check made out to either the depositor or a third party and written, or drawn, by a bank after deducting that amount from the depositor's account or receiving cash from the depositor.

In this section, you learned that all cash receipts should be deposited in the bank and all cash disbursements should be made by check. However, the next section explains the convenience of having small amounts of cash (petty cash) available for minor expenditures.

An Accounting Perspective

Uses of Technology Some companies now offer to deposit employees' paychecks directly into their bank accounts. This process of transferring money by telephone, computer, or wire is called *electronic fund transferring.* Often companies prefer this method because it limits the number of employees involved in the payroll process. Manipulation and fraud can still occur whenever firms do not separate duties; however, limiting access to the payroll function may eliminate some of the risk associated with internal control weaknesses.

Petty Cash Funds

Objective 5
Explain why a company uses a petty cash fund, describe its operations, and make the necessary journal entries.

At times, every business finds it convenient to have small amounts of cash available for immediate payment of items such as delivery charges, postage stamps, taxi fares, supper money for employees working overtime, and other small items. To permit these cash disbursements and still maintain adequate control over cash, companies frequently establish a **petty cash fund** of a round figure such as $100 or $500.

Usually one individual, called the *petty cash custodian* or *cashier,* is responsible for the control of the petty cash fund and documenting the disbursements made from the fund. By assigning the responsibility for the fund to one individual, the company has internal control over the cash in the fund.

Establishing the Fund

A business establishes a petty cash fund by writing a check for, say, $100. It is payable to the petty cash custodian. The petty cash fund should be large enough to make disbursements for a reasonable period, such as a month. The following entry records this transaction as follows:

	Debit	Credit
Petty Cash	100	
Cash		100
To establish a petty cash fund.		

After the check is cashed, the petty cash custodian normally places the money in a small box that can be locked. The fund is now ready to be disbursed as needed.

Operating the Fund

One of the conveniences of the petty cash fund is that payments from the fund require no journal entries at the time of payment. Thus, using a petty cash fund

PETTY CASH VOUCHER NO. 359

To Local Cartage, Inc. Date June 29, 1997

EXPLANATION	ACCT. NO.	AMOUNT	
Freight on parts	27	12	57

APPROVED BY A.E.S. RECEIVED PAYMENT Ken Black

Illustration 8.12
Petty Cash Voucher

avoids the need for making many entries for small amounts. Only when the fund is reimbursed, or when the end of the accounting period arrives, does the firm make an entry in the journal.

When disbursing cash from the fund, the petty cash custodian prepares a petty cash voucher, which should be signed by the person receiving the funds. A **petty cash voucher** (Illustration 8.12) is a document or form that shows the amount of and reason for a petty cash disbursement. The custodian should prepare a voucher for each disbursement and staple any invoices for expenditures to the petty cash voucher. At all times, the employee responsible for petty cash is accountable for having cash and petty cash vouchers equal to the total amount of the fund.

Replenishing the Fund

Companies replenish the petty cash fund at the end of the accounting period, or sooner if it becomes low. The reason for replenishing the fund at the end of the accounting period is that no record of the fund expenditures is in the accounts until the check is written and a journal entry is made. (Sometimes we refer to this fund as an *imprest* fund since it is replenished when it becomes low.) The petty cash custodian presents the vouchers to the employee having authority to order that the fund be reimbursed. After the vouchers are examined, if all is in order, that employee draws a check to restore the fund to its original amount.

To determine which accounts to debit, an employee summarizes the petty cash vouchers according to the reasons for expenditure. Next, that person stamps or defaces the petty cash vouchers to prevent reuse. The journal entry to record replenishing the fund would debit the various accounts indicated by the summary and credit Cash.

For example, assume the $100 petty cash fund currently has a money balance of $7.40. A summary of the vouchers shows payments of $22.75 for transportation-in, $50.80 for stamps, and $19.05 for an advance to an employee; these payments total $92.60. After the vouchers have been examined and approved, an employee draws a check for $92.60 which, when cashed, restores the cash in the fund to its $100 balance. The journal entry to record replenishment is:

Transportation-In	22.75	
Postage Expense	50.80	
Receivable from Employees (or Advances to Employees)	19.05	
Cash		92.60
To replenish petty cash fund.		

Note that the entry to record replenishing the fund does not credit the Petty Cash account. We make entries to the Petty Cash account only when the fund is established, when the end of the accounting period arrives and the fund is not replenished, or when the size of the fund is changed.

At the end of an accounting period, the firm records any petty cash disbursements for which the fund has not yet been replenished. Since the fund has not been replenished, the credit would be to Petty Cash rather than Cash. Failure to make an entry at the end of an accounting period would cause errors in both the income statement and balance sheet. The easiest way to record these disbursements is to replenish the fund.

After a time, if the petty cash custodian finds that the petty cash fund is larger than needed, the excess petty cash should be deposited in the company's checking account. The required entry to record a decrease in the fund debits Cash and credits Petty Cash for the amount returned and deposited. On the other hand, a petty cash fund may be too small, requiring replenishment every few days. The entry to record an increase in the fund debits Petty Cash and credits Cash for the amount of the increase.

To illustrate, the entry to *decrease* the petty cash fund by $50 would be:

Cash	50	
Petty Cash		50
To decrease the size of the petty cash fund by $50.		

The entry to *increase* the petty cash fund by $600 would be:

Petty Cash	600	
Cash		600
To increase the size of the petty cash fund by $600.		

Cash Short and Over

Sometimes, the petty cash custodian makes errors in making change from the fund. These errors cause the cash in the fund to be more or less than the amount of the fund less the total vouchers. When the fund is restored to its original amount, the credit to Cash is for the difference between the established amount and the actual cash in the fund. We would debit all vouchered items. Any discrepancy should be debited or credited to an account called *Cash Short and Over*. The Cash Short and Over account is an expense or a revenue, depending on whether it has a debit or credit balance.

To illustrate, assume in the preceding example that the balance in the fund was only $6.10 instead of $7.40. Restoring the fund to $100 requires a check for $93.90. Since the petty cash vouchers total only $92.60, the fund is short $1.30. The entry for replenishment is:

Transportation-In	22.75	
Postage Expense	50.80	
Receivable from Employees	19.05	
Cash Short and Over	1.30	
Cash		93.90
To replenish petty cash fund.		

Entries in the Cash Short and Over account also result from other change-making activities. For example, assume that a clerk accidentally shortchanges a customer $1 and that total cash sales for the day are $740.50. At the end of the day, actual cash is $1 over the sum of the sales tickets or the total of the cash register tape. The journal entry to record the day's cash sales is:

Cash	741.50	
Sales		740.50
Cash Short and Over		1.00
To record cash sales for the day.		

Analyzing and Using the Financial Results—The Quick Ratio

Objective 6
Analyze and use the financial results—quick ratio.

The **quick ratio** measures a company's short-term debt-paying ability. It is the ratio of quick assets (cash, marketable securities, and net receivables) to current liabilities. When computing quick assets, we do not include inventories and prepaid expenses because they might not be readily convertible into cash. A rule of thumb is that the ratio of quick assets to current liabilities should be 1 : 1 or higher. However, a lower quick ratio is satisfactory in companies that generate a steady

AN ETHICAL PERSPECTIVE

City Club Restaurant

The City Club Restaurant is a member-owned entity in Carson City. For 20 years, John Blue has managed the restaurant and received only minimal salary increases. He believes he is grossly underpaid in view of the significant inflation that has occurred. A few years ago he began supplementing his income by placing phony "peanut" invoices in the petty cash box, writing a petty cash voucher for the amount of each invoice, withdrawing cash equal to the amount of each invoice for his personal use, and later approving the vouchers for reimbursement. Through this mechanism, John increased his income by about $12,000 per year, an amount that he considered fair. No one else knows what is happening, and the manager feels fully justified in supplementing his income in this way.

flow of cash in their operations. Short-term creditors are interested in this ratio since it relates the pool of cash and immediate cash inflows to immediate cash outflows. The formula for the quick ratio is:

$$\text{Quick ratio} = \frac{\text{Quick assets}}{\text{Current liabilities}}$$

Based on the following information, we can determine that The Gillette Company and its subsidiaries' 1992 and 1991 quick ratios are .79 and.77, respectively:

The Gillette Company
The Gillette Company is the world leader in blades and razors, holds a major position in North America in sales of toiletries, and is among the world's top sellers of writing instruments.

	1992	1991
Cash	$ 35,300	$ 52,800
Short-term investments	4,500	3,900
Net receivables	1,186,100	1,083,900
Current liabilities	1,560,800	1,484,600
	$\frac{\$1,225,900}{\$1,560,800} = .79$	$\frac{\$1,140,600}{\$1,484,600} = .77$

Note: All amounts are in $ thousands.

Now that you have learned how to control a company's most liquid asset, cash, in the next chapter you are ready to study receivables and payables. As you realize, the backbone of our economy is credit. In all probability, the next automobile you plan to buy will be financed. Companies are anxious to offer credit to worthy customers and prospective customers. The many offers of credit we receive from various businesses are evidence of the importance companies place on credit as a method of stimulating sales and expanding their business.

UNDERSTANDING THE LEARNING OBJECTIVES

Objective 1
Describe the necessity for and features of internal control.

- The internal control structure of a company includes its plan of organization and all the procedures and actions taken by the company to protect its assets against theft and waste, ensure compliance with company policies and federal law, evaluate the performance of all personnel in the company to promote efficiency of operations, and ensure accurate and reliable operating data and accounting records.
- The purpose of internal control is to ensure the efficient operation of a business.

Objective 2
Define cash and list the objectives sought by management in handling a company's cash.

- Cash includes coins; currency; undeposited negotiable instruments such as checks, bank drafts, and money orders; amounts in checking and saving accounts; and demand certificates of deposit.
- To protect their cash, companies should account for all cash transactions accurately, make certain enough cash is available to pay bills as they come due, avoid holding too much idle cash, and prevent loss of cash due to theft or fraud.

Objective 3
Identify procedures for controlling cash receipts and disbursements.

- Procedures for controlling cash receipts include such basic principles as recording all cash receipts as soon as cash is received; depositing all cash receipts on the day they are received or on the next business day; and preventing the employee who handles cash receipts from also recording the receipts in the accounting records or from disbursing cash.
- Procedures for controlling cash disbursements include, among others, making all disbursements by check or from petty cash, using checks that are serially numbered, requiring two signatures on each check, and having a different person authorize payment of a bill than the persons allowed to sign checks.

Objective 4
Prepare a bank reconciliation and make necessary journal entries based on that schedule.

- A bank reconciliation is prepared to *reconcile,* or explain, the difference between the cash balance on the bank statement and the cash balance on the company's books and to make the required entry(ies) to correct the cash balance in the ledger.
- A bank reconciliation is shown in Illustration 8.11.
- Journal entries are needed for all items that appear in the bank reconciliation as adjustments to the balance per ledger to arrive at the adjusted cash balance.

Objective 5
Explain why a company uses a petty cash fund, describe its operations, and make the necessary journal entries.

- Companies establish a petty cash fund to permit minor cash disbursements and still maintain adequate control over cash.
- When the cash in the petty cash fund becomes low, the fund should be replenished. A journal entry is necessary to record the replenishment.

Objective 6
Analyze and use the financial results—quick ratio.

- Quick ratio equals cash, marketable securities, and net receivables divided by current liabilities.
- The quick ratio measures a company's short-term debt-paying ability.

Demonstration Problem 8–A

You are the manager of a restaurant that has an ice cream parlor as a separate unit. Your accountant comes in once a year to prepare financial statements and the tax return. In the current year, you have a feeling that even though business seems good, net income is going to be lower. You ask the accountant to prepare condensed statements on a monthly basis. All sales are priced to yield an estimated gross margin of 40%. You, your accountant, and several of the accountant's assistants take physical inventories at the end of each of the following four months. The resulting sales, cost of goods sold, and gross margins are:

	March		April		May		June	
	Restaurant	Ice Cream Parlor	Restaurant	Ice Cream Parlor	Restaurant	Ice Cream Parlor	Restaurant	Ice Cream Parlor
Sales	$36,300	$53,000	$39,050	$42,750	$38,100	$39,000	$41,250	$35,500
Cost of goods sold	23,275	31,500	23,800	31,000	22,975	30,750	25,500	31,125
Gross margin	$13,025	$21,500	$15,250	$11,750	$15,125	$ 8,250	$15,750	$ 4,375

Required What would you suspect after analyzing these reports? What sales control procedures would you recommend to correct the situation? All of the points in this problem were not specifically covered in the chapter, although the principles were. Use logic, common sense, and knowledge gained elsewhere in coming up with some of the control procedures.

Solution to Demonstration Problem 8–A

The gross margin percentages are as follows:

	March	April	May	June
Restaurant	35.88%	39.05%	39.70%	38.18%
Ice cream parlor	40.57	27.49	21.15	12.32

Either cash or inventory is being stolen or given away in the ice cream parlor. Employees or outsiders may be pocketing cash. Or the employees may be giving extra-large ice cream cones to friends, or eating the ice cream themselves. Several things could be done to improve the sales control procedures:

1. The manager could hire an investigator to come in and watch the employees in action. If cash is being pocketed, the employees could be fired.
2. The prices of ice cream cones could be changed to odd amounts so that employees would not be as able to make change without going to the cash register. Also, the No Sale lever could be removed from the cash register.
3. The customers could be encouraged to ask for their cash register receipts by having a monthly drawing (for some prize) by cash register receipt number.
4. The cash register should be placed in a prominent position so that each customer could see the amount recorded for each sale. No customer is going to be willing to pay 65 cents when the employee rings up 50 cents.
5. The cash register tapes should be inaccessible to the employees. The manager (and possibly assistant manager) should have the only keys to the cash registers.
6. Mention to the employees that you have an effective internal control structure. The employees do not have to know what the structure is.
7. Pay the employees a competitive wage.
8. Require that all sales be rung up immediately after the sale.
9. The manager or assistant manager should reconcile the cash register tapes at the end of each day.

Demonstration Problem 8–B

The following data pertain to Carr Company:

1. Balance per bank statement, dated March 31, 1997, is $4,450.
2. Balance of the Cash account on the company's books as of March 31, 1997, is $4,459.
3. The $1,300 deposit of March 31 was not on the bank statement.
4. Of the checks recorded as cash disbursements in March, some checks, totaling $1,050, have not yet cleared the bank.
5. Service and collection charges for the month were $10.
6. The bank erroneously charged the Carr Company account for the $200 check of another company. The check was included with the canceled checks returned with the bank statement.
7. The bank credited the company's account with the $1,000 proceeds of a non-interest-bearing note that it collected for the company.
8. A customer's $75 check marked NSF was returned with the bank statement.
9. As directed, the bank paid and charged to the company's account a $507.50 non-interest-bearing note of Carr Company. This payment has not been recorded by the company.
10. An examination of the cash receipts and the deposit tickets revealed that the bookkeeper erroneously recorded a customer's check of $148.50 as $135.00.
11. The bank credited the company's checking account for $20 interest earned.

Required

a. Prepare a bank reconciliation as of March 31, 1997.
b. Prepare the necessary journal entry or entries to adjust the Cash account.

Solution to Demonstration Problem 8–B

a.

CARR COMPANY
Bank Reconciliation
March 31, 1997

Balance per bank statement, March 31, 1997		$4,450.00
Add: Deposit in transit	$1,300.00	
Check charged in error	200.00	1,500.00
		$5,950.00
Less: Outstanding checks		1,050.00
Adjusted balance, March 31, 1997		$4,900.00
Balance per ledger, March 31, 1997		$4,459.00
Add: Note collected	$1,000.00	
Interest earned on checking account	20.00	
Error in recording customer's check	13.50	1,033.50
		$5,492.50
Less: Service and collection charges	$ 10.00	
NSF check	75.00	
Carr Company note charged against account	507.50	592.50
Adjusted balance, March 31, 1997		$4,900.00

b.

1997				
Mar.	31	Cash	441.00	
		Bank Service Charge Expense	10.00	
		Accounts Receivable	75.00	
		Notes Payable	507.50	
		Notes Receivable		1,000.00
		Interest Revenue		20.00
		Accounts Receivable		13.50
		To record adjustments to Cash account.		

Alternatively:

1997				
Mar.	31	Cash	1,033.50	
		Notes Receivable		1,000.00
		Interest Revenue		20.00
		Accounts Receivable		13.50
		To record additions to Cash account.		
		Bank Service Charge Expense	10.00	
		Accounts Receivable	75.00	
		Notes Payable	507.50	
		Cash		592.50
		To record deductions from Cash account.		

New Terms

Accounting system Methods and records established to identify, assemble, analyze, classify, record, and report an entity's transactions to provide complete, accurate, and timely financial information. *295*

Bank reconciliation A schedule the company (depositor) prepares to *reconcile*, or explain, the difference between the cash balance on the bank statement and the cash balance on the company's books; often called a *bank reconciliation statement* or *schedule*. *309*

Bank statement A statement issued (usually monthly) by a bank describing the activities in a depositor's checking account during the period. *306*

Cash Includes coins; currency; certain undeposited negotiable instruments such as checks, bank drafts, and money orders; amounts in checking and savings accounts; and demand certificates of deposit. *302*

Cashier's check A check made out to either the depositor or a third party and written, or drawn, by a bank after deducting the amount of the check from the depositor's account or receiving cash from the depositor. *312*

Certificate of deposit (CD) An interest-bearing deposit that can be withdrawn from a bank at will (demand CD) or at a fixed maturity date (time CD). *302*

Certified check A check written, or drawn, by a depositor and taken to the depositor's bank for certification. The check is deducted from the depositor's balance immediately and becomes a liability of the bank. Thus, it usually is accepted without question. *312*

Check A written order to a bank to pay a specific sum of money to the party designated as the payee by the party issuing the check. *305*

Checking account A money balance maintained in a bank that is subject to withdrawal by the depositor, or owner of the money, on demand. *305*

Control environment Reflects the overall attitude, awareness, and actions of the board of directors, management, and stockholders. *295*

Control procedures Policies and procedures in addition to the control environment and the accounting system that management has established to provide reasonable assurance that the company will achieve its specific objectives. *295*

Credit memo A form used by a bank to explain an addition to the depositor's account. *308*

Debit memo A form used by a bank to explain a deduction from the depositor's account. *308*

Deposit in transit Typically, a day's cash receipts recorded in the depositor's books in one period but recorded as a deposit by the bank in the succeeding period. *309*

Deposit ticket A form that shows the date and the items that make up the deposit. *305*

Drawer The party (depositor) writing a check. *306*

Fidelity bonds Ensure that a company is reimbursed for losses due to theft of cash and other monetary assets. *299*

Internal auditing Consists of investigating and evaluating employees' compliance with the company's policies and procedures. Internal auditing is performed by company personnel. *297*

Internal auditors Auditors employed by the company to perform internal audits. These auditors are trained in company policies and in internal auditing duties such as testing effectiveness of controls and procedures involving cash receipts and cash disbursements. *297*

Internal control structure Policies and procedures established to provide reasonable assurance that specific entity objectives will be achieved. *295, 296*

Invoice Statement sent by the supplier to the purchaser requesting payment for the merchandise shipped. *298*

NSF (Not Sufficient Funds) check A customer's check returned from the customer's bank to the depositor's bank because the funds in the customer's checking account balance were insufficient to cover the check. *306*

Outstanding checks Checks issued by a depositor that have not yet been paid by the bank on which they are drawn. *310*

Payee The party to whom a check is made payable. *306*

Petty cash fund A nominal sum of money established as a separate fund from which minor cash disbursements for valid business purposes are made. The cash in the fund plus the vouchers covering disbursements should always equal the balance at which the fund was established and at which it is carried in the Petty Cash account. *312*

Petty cash voucher A document or form that shows the amount of, and reason for, a petty cash disbursement. *313*

Purchase order A document sent from the purchasing department to a supplier requesting that merchandise or other items be shipped to the purchaser. *298*

Purchase requisition A written request from an employee inside the company to the purchasing department to purchase certain items. *298*

Quick ratio The ratio of quick assets (cash, marketable securities, and net receivables) to current liabilities. The quick ratio measures a company's short-term debt-paying ability. *314*

Receiving report A document prepared by the receiving department showing the descriptions and quantities of all items received from a supplier in a particular shipment. *298*

Remittance advice Informs the payee why the drawer (or maker) of the check is making this payment. *306*

Segregation of duties Having one employee responsible for safeguarding an asset and a second employee responsible for maintaining the accounting records for that asset. *296*

Service charges Charges assessed by the bank on the depositor to cover the cost of handling the checking account. *306*

Signature card Provides the signatures of persons authorized to sign checks drawn on an account. *305*

Transfer bank accounts Bank accounts set up so that local banks automatically transfer to a central bank (by wire or written bank draft) all amounts on deposit in excess of a stated amount. *307*

Wire transfer of funds Interbank transfer of funds by telephone. *307*

Self-Test

True-False

Indicate whether each of the following statements is true or false.

1. Cash includes coin, currency, postdated checks, money orders, and money on deposit with banks.
2. To effectively manage its cash, a company should make certain that enough cash is available to pay bills as they come due.
3. The cash balance on the bank statement is usually equal to the cash balance in the depositor's books.
4. A deposit in transit requires an entry in the depositor's books after the bank reconciliation is prepared.
5. For control purposes, a company should issue checks for every payment, regardless of its amount.

Multiple-Choice

Select the best answer for each of the following questions.

1. The objectives of the internal control structure of a company include all of the following except:
   - **a.** Compliance with company policies and federal law.
   - **b.** Protection of its assets.
   - **c.** Increase in accuracy and reliability of accounting data.
   - **d.** Guarantee of a certain level of profit.
   - **e.** Evaluation of personnel performance to promote efficiency of operations.

Use the following information to answer Questions 2–4:

Balance per bank statement	$1,951.20
Balance per ledger	1,869.60
Deposits in transit	271.20
Outstanding checks	427.80
NSF check	61.20
Service charges	13.80

2. The adjusted cash balance is:
   - **a.** $1,794.60.
   - **b.** $1,719.60.
   - **c.** $1,638.00.
   - **d.** $1,713.00.
   - **e.** $1,876.20.
3. In a bank reconciliation, deposits in transit should be:
   - **a.** Deducted from the balance per books.
   - **b.** Deducted from the balance per bank statement.
   - **c.** Added to the balance per ledger.
   - **d.** Added to the balance per bank statement.
   - **e.** Disregarded in the bank reconciliation.
4. After the bank reconciliation is prepared, the entry to record bank service charges would have a credit to:
   - **a.** Bank Service Charge Expense.
   - **b.** Cash.
   - **c.** Petty Cash.
   - **d.** Cash Short and Over.
   - **e.** None of the above.
5. The entry to replenish the petty cash fund for disbursements made for stamps includes:
   - **a.** A credit to Petty Cash.
   - **b.** A credit to Postage Expense.
   - **c.** A debit to Accounts Payable.
   - **d.** A credit to Cash.
   - **e.** None of the above.

Now turn to page 328 to check your answers.

Questions

1. Why should a company establish an internal control structure?
2. Why are mechanical devices used in an internal control structure?
3. Identify some features that could strengthen an internal control structure.
4. Name several control documents used in merchandise transactions.
5. What are the four objectives sought in effective cash management?
6. List four essential features of internal control over cash receipts.
7. The bookkeeper of a given company was stealing cash received from customers in payment of their accounts. To conceal the theft, the bookkeeper made out false credit memos indicating returns and allowances made by or granted to customers. What feature of internal control would have prevented the thefts?
8. List six essential features of internal control over cash disbursements.
9. What types of items cause the balance per ledger and the balance per bank statement to disagree?
10. "The difference between a company's Cash account balance and the balance on its bank statement is usually a matter of timing." Do you agree or disagree? Why?
11. Explain how transfer bank accounts can help bring about effective cash management.
12. Describe the operation of a petty cash fund and its advantages. Indicate how control is maintained over petty cash transactions.
13. When are entries made to the Petty Cash account?

The Coca-Cola Company

14. **Real World Question** From the consolidated balance sheet of The Coca-Cola Company in the annual report booklet, identify the total 1993 cash and marketable securities. Explain the definition of cash equivalents and marketable securities in accordance with footnote 1—Accounting Policies.

MAYTAG

15. **Real World Question** Based on the financial statements of Maytag Corporation contained in the annual report booklet, what was the 1993 ending cash and cash equivalents balance? What percentage of current assets does the amount of cash and cash equivalents represent for each of the two years shown?

THE LIMITED, INC.

16. **Real World Question** Based on the financial statements of The Limited, Inc., in the annual report booklet, what was the 1993 ending cash and cash equivalents balance? What percentage of current assets does the amount of cash and cash equivalents represent for each of the two years shown?

HARLAND

17. **Real World Question** Based on the financial statements of John H. Harland Company contained in the annual report booklet, what was the 1993 ending short-term investments balance? How does this compare with the preceding year?

EXERCISES

Exercise 8–1
Answer true-false questions about internal control (L.O. 1)

State whether each of the following statements about internal control is *true* or *false:*

a. Those employees responsible for safeguarding an asset should maintain the accounting records for that asset.
b. Complete, accurate, and up-to-date accounting records should be maintained.
c. Whenever possible, responsibilities should be assigned and duties subdivided in such a way that only one employee is responsible for a given function.
d. Employees should be assigned to one job and should remain in that job so that skill levels will be as high as possible.
e. The use of check protectors, cash registers, and time clocks is recommended.
f. An internal auditing function should not be implemented because it leads the employees to believe that management does not trust them.
g. One of the best protections against theft is to hire honest, competent employees.
h. A foolproof internal control structure can be devised if management puts forth the effort.

Exercise 8–2
Answer multiple-choice question about internal control (L.O. 1)

Concerning internal control, which one of the following statements is correct? Explain.

a. Broadly speaking, an internal control structure is only necessary in large organizations.
b. The purposes of internal control are to check the accuracy of accounting data, safeguard assets against theft, promote efficiency of operations, and ensure that management's policies are being followed.
c. Once an internal control structure has been established, it should be effective as long as the formal organization remains unchanged.
d. An example of internal control is having one employee count the day's cash receipts and compare the total with the total of the cash register tapes.

Exercise 8–3
Determine available cash balance from bank statement and Cash account data (L.O. 4)

The bank statement for Monroe Company at the end of August showed a balance of $25,725. Checks outstanding totaled $7,875, and deposits in transit were $11,981.25. If these amounts are the only pertinent data available to you, what was the adjusted balance of cash at the end of August?

Exercise 8–4
Prepare bank reconciliation and specify cash available (L.O. 4)

From the following data, prepare a bank reconciliation and determine the correct available cash balance for Weeks Company as of October 31, 1997.

Balance per bank statement, October 31, 1997	$13,974
Ledger account balance, October 31, 1997	8,088
Proceeds of a note collected by bank not yet entered in ledger (includes $500 of interest)	6,000
Bank service charges not yet entered by Weeks Company	18
Deposit in transit	1,680
Outstanding checks:	
No. 327	654
No. 328	288
No. 329	390
No. 331	252

Exercise 8–5
Record necessary journal entry or entries to correct cash balance (L.O. 4)

The following is a bank reconciliation for Conrad Company as of August 31, 1997.

Balance per bank statement, August 31, 1997		$3,735
Add: Deposit in transit		2,838
		$6,573
Less: Outstanding checks		3,012
Adjusted balance, August 31, 1997		$3,561
Balance per ledger, August 31, 1997		$3,624
Add: Error correction		27*
		$3,651
Less: NSF check	$75	
Service charges	15	90
Adjusted balance, August 31, 1997		$3,561

* The error occurred when the bookkeeper debited Accounts Payable and credited Cash for $46.50, instead of the correct amount, $19.50.

Prepare the journal entry or entries needed to adjust or correct the Cash account.

Exercise 8–6
Determine checks outstanding (L.O. 4)

On March 1 of the current year, Sherman Company had outstanding checks of $15,000. During March, the company issued an additional $57,000 of checks. As of March 31, the bank statement showed $48,000 of checks had cleared the bank during the month. What is the amount of outstanding checks on March 31?

Exercise 8–7
Determine deposits in transit (L.O. 4)

Mason Company's bank statement as of August 31, 1997, shows total deposits into the company's account of $15,402 and a total of 14 separate deposits. On July 31, deposits of $810 and $630 were in transit. The total cash receipts for August were $19,752, and the company's records show 13 deposits made in August. What is the amount of deposits in transit at August 31?

Exercise 8–8
Prepare a bank reconciliation and necessary journal entry or entries (L.O. 4)

Spring Company deposits all cash receipts intact each day and makes all payments by check. On October 31, after all posting was completed, its Cash account had a debit balance of $4,325. The bank statement for the month ended on October 31 showed a balance of $3,988. Other data are:

1. Outstanding checks total $425.
2. October 31 cash receipts of $838 were placed in the bank's night depository and do not appear on the bank statement.
3. Bank service charges for October are $14.
4. Check No. 772 for store supplies on hand was entered at $405, but paid by the bank at its actual amount of $315.

Prepare a bank reconciliation for Spring Company as of October 31. Also prepare any necessary journal entry or entries.

Exercise 8–9
Record reimbursement of petty cash fund (L.O. 5)

On August 31, 1997, Cheon Company's petty cash fund contained coins and currency of $130, an IOU from an employee of $15, and vouchers showing expenditures of $60 for postage, $26 for taxi fare, and $69 to entertain a customer. The Petty Cash account shows a balance of $300. The fund is replenished on August 31 because financial statements are to be prepared. What journal entry is required on August 31?

Exercise 8–10
Record reimbursement of petty cash fund (L.O. 5)

Use the data in Exercise 8–9. What entry would have been required if the amount of coin and currency had been $123.60? Which of the accounts debited would not appear in the income statement?

Exercise 8–11
Prepare journal entries regarding petty cash (L.O. 5)

Silver Company has a $450 petty cash fund. The following transactions occurred in December:

Dec. 2 The petty cash fund was increased to $675.
8 Petty Cash Voucher No. 318 for $12.10 delivery expense was prepared and paid. The fund was not replenished at this time.
20 The company decided that the fund was too large and reduced it to $560.

Prepare any necessary journal entries for these transactions.

PROBLEMS

Problem 8–1
Prepare bank reconciliation with necessary journal entry or entries (L.O. 4)

The following June 30, 1997, bank reconciliation pertains to Carter Company:

		Cash Account	Bank Statement
Balance, June 30		$19,143.36	$18,644.31
Add: Deposit not credited by bank			942.60
Total			$19,586.91
Less: Outstanding checks:			
No. 724	$ 18.45		
No. 886	15.00		
No. 896	143.55		
No. 897	187.65		
No. 898	78.90		443.55
Adjusted cash balance, June 30		$19,143.36	$19,143.36

Carter's July bank statement follows:

Balance, July 1		$18,644.31	
Deposits during July		5,441.94	$24,086.25
Canceled checks returned:			
No. 724	$ 18.45		
No. 896	143.55		
No. 897	187.65		
No. 898	78.90		
No. 899	18.86		
No. 900	1,349.55		
No. 902	946.92		
No. 904	44.01	$ 2,787.89	
NSF check of Starr Company		139.98	2,927.87
Bank statement balance, July 31			$21,158.38

The cash receipts deposited in July, including receipts of July 31, amounted to $5,178.30. Carter wrote these checks in July:

No. 899	$ 18.86
No. 900	1,349.55
No. 901	27.75
No. 902	946.92
No. 903	59.70
No. 904	44.01
No. 905	1,093.50
No. 906	15.00

The cash balance per the ledger on July 31, 1997, was $20,766.37.

Required

Prepare a bank reconciliation as of July 31, 1997, and any necessary journal entry or entries to correct the accounts.

Problem 8–2
Prepare bank reconciliation with necessary journal entry or entries (L.O. 4)

The following information pertains to Williams Company as of May 31, 1997:

1. Balance per bank statement as of May 31, 1997, was $49,410.
2. Balance per Williams Company's Cash account at May 31, 1997, was $50,904.
3. A late deposit on May 31 did not appear on the bank statement, $4,275.
4. Outstanding checks as of May 31 totaled $7,614.
5. During May, the bank credited Williams Company with the proceeds, $6,795, of a note which it had collected for the company. Interest revenue was $45 of the total.
6. Bank service and collection charges for May amounted to $18.
7. Comparison of the canceled checks with the check register revealed that one check in the amount as $1,458 had been recorded in the books as $1,539. The check had been issued in payment of an account payable.
8. A review of the deposit slips with the bank statement showed that a deposit for $2,250 of a company with a similar account number had been credited to the Williams Company account in error.

9. A $270 check received from a customer, R. Petty, was returned with the bank statement marked NSF.
10. During May, the bank paid a $13,500 note of Williams Company plus interest of $135 and charged it to the company's account per instructions received. Williams Company had not recorded the payment of this note.
11. An examination of the cash receipts and the deposit tickets revealed that the bookkeeper erroneously recorded a check from a customer, C. Parker, of $1,458 as $1,944.
12. The bank statement showed a credit to the company's account for interest earned on the account balance in May of $450.

Required

a. Prepare a bank reconciliation as of May 31, 1997.
b. Prepare the journal entry or entries necessary to adjust the accounts as of May 31, 1997.

Problem 8–3
Prepare journal entries to record establishment and reimbursement of petty cash fund (L.O. 5)

The following transactions pertain to the petty cash fund of Pennington Company during 1997:

Nov. 2 A $900 check is drawn, cashed, and the cash placed in the care of the assistant office manager to be used as a petty cash fund.

Dec. 17 The fund is replenished. An analysis of the fund shows:

Coins and currency	$294.81
Petty cash vouchers for:	
Delivery expenses	346.95
Transportation-in	222.24
Postage stamps purchased	30.00

31 The end of the accounting period falls on this date. The fund was not replenished. The fund's contents on this date consist of:

Coins and currency	$704.10
Petty cash vouchers for:	
Delivery expenses	63.30
Postage stamps purchased	72.60
Employee's IOU	60.00

Required

Present journal entries to record these transactions. Use the Cash Short and Over account for any shortage or overage in the fund.

Problem 8–4
Prepare journal entries to record establishment, reimbursement, and increase of petty cash fund (L.O. 5)

The following transactions relate to the petty cash fund of Davis Wrecking Company in 1997:

Apr. 1 The petty cash fund is set up with a $350 cash balance.

19 Because the money in the fund is down to $70.20, the fund is replenished. Petty cash vouchers are as follows:

Flowers for hospitalized employee (miscellaneous expense)	$ 84.38
Postage stamps	135.00
Office supplies	46.71

30 The cash in the fund is $193.07. The fund is replenished to include petty cash payments in this period's financial statements. The petty cash vouchers are for the following:

Transportation-in	$64.12
Office supplies	92.81

May 1 The petty cash fund balance is increased to $400.

Required

Prepare the journal entries to record these transactions.

ALTERNATIVE PROBLEMS

Problem 8–1A
Prepare bank reconciliation with necessary journal entry or entries (L.O. 4)

The following data pertain to Land Company:

1. Balance per the bank statement dated June 30, 1997, is $30,570.
2. Balance of the Cash in Bank account on the company books as of June 30, 1997, is $8,985.
3. Outstanding checks as of June 30, 1997, total $14,966.
4. Bank deposit of June 30 for $2,355 was not included in the deposits per the bank statement.
5. The bank had collected proceeds of a note, $22,612 (of which $112 was interest), that it credited to the Land Company account. The bank charged the company a collection fee of $15 on the note.
6. The bank erroneously charged the Land Company account for a $10,500 debit memo of another company that has a similar name.
7. Bank service charges for June, exclusive of the collection fee, amounted to $75.
8. Among the canceled checks was one for $518 given in payment of an account. The bookkeeper had recorded the check at $720 in the company records.
9. A check of Crosby, a customer, for $3,115, deposited on June 20, was returned by the bank marked NSF. No entry has been made to reflect the returned check on the company records.
10. A check for $1,335 of Malcolm, a customer, which had been deposited in the bank, was erroneously recorded by the bookkeeper as $1,470. The check had been received as a payment on the customer's account receivable.

Required

Prepare a bank reconciliation as of June 30, 1997, and any necessary journal entry or entries to correct the accounts.

Problem 8–2A
Prepare bank reconciliation with necessary journal entry or entries (L.O. 4)

The bank statement of Bailey Company's checking account with the First National Bank shows:

Balance, June 30, 1997		$166,118
Deposits		245,700
		$411,818
Less: Checks deducted	$243,001	
Service charges.	67	243,068
Balance, July 31, 1997		$168,750

The following additional data are available:

1. Balance per ledger account as of July 31 was $128,209.
2. A credit memo included with the bank statement indicated the collection of a note by the bank for Bailey Company. Proceeds were $13,500, of which $375 was interest.
3. An NSF check in the amount of $6,210 was returned by the bank and included in the total of checks deducted on the bank statement.
4. Deposits in transit as of July 31 totaled $33,750.
5. Checks outstanding as of July 31 were $55,350.
6. The bank added the $29,025 deposit of another company to Bailey's account in error.
7. The bank deducted one of Bailey's checks as $20,250 instead of the correct amount of $2,025.
8. Deposit of July 21 was recorded by the company as $4,299.75 and by the bank at the actual amount of $4,542.75. The receipts for the day were from collections on account.
9. The deposits amount shown on the bank statement includes $675 of interest earned by Bailey on its checking account with the bank.

Required

a. Prepare a bank reconciliation as of July 31, 1997, for Bailey Company.
b. Prepare any journal entry or entries needed at July 31, 1997.

Problem 8–3A
Prepare journal entries to record establishment and reimbursement of petty cash fund (L.O. 5)

Transactions involving the petty cash fund of Solar Company during 1997 are as follows:

Mar. 1 Established a petty cash fund of $375, which will be under the control of the assistant office manager.

31 Fund was replenished on this date. Prior to replenishment, the fund consisted of the following:

Coins and currency	$245.75
Petty cash vouchers indicating disbursements for:	
Postage stamps	41.00
Supper money for office employees working overtime	18.00
Office supplies	16.35
Window washing service	30.00
Flowers for wedding of employee	7.50
Flowers for hospitalized employee	7.50
Employee's IOU	7.50

Required Present journal entries for these transactions. Use the Cash Short and Over account for any shortage or overage in the fund.

Problem 8–4A
Prepare journal entries to record establishment, reimbursement, and increase of petty cash fund (L.O. 5)

Sadie Company has decided to use a petty cash fund. Transactions involving this fund in 1997 follow:

June 4 Set up a petty cash fund of $225.

22 When the fund had a cash amount of $31.35, the custodian of the fund was reimbursed for expenditures made, including:

Transportation-in	$82.50
Postage	27.00
Office supplies	81.75

30 The fund was reimbursed to include petty cash items in the financial statements prepared for the fiscal year ending on this date. The fund had the following cash and vouchers before reimbursement:

Coins and currency	$174.00
Petty cash vouchers for:	
Employee's IOU	15.00
Postage	27.00
Office supplies	11.10

July 1 The petty cash fund balance is increased to $300.

Required Prepare journal entries for all of these transactions.

Beyond the Numbers—Critical Thinking

Business Decision Case 8–1
Discuss steps to prevent theft (L.O. 1, 3)

During the 1992 Persian Gulf War (Desert Storm), a managerial accountant was called back to active duty with the U.S. Army. An acquaintance of the accountant forged papers and assumed the identity of the accountant. He obtained a position in a small company as the only accountant. Eventually he took over from the manager the functions of approving bills for payment, preparing and signing checks, and almost all other financial duties. On one weekend, he traveled to some neighboring cities and mailed invoices made out to the company for which he worked. On Monday morning, he returned to work and began receiving, approving, and paying the invoices he had prepared. The following weekend he returned to the neighboring cities and cashed and deposited the checks in bank accounts under his own name. After continuing this practice for several months, he withdrew all of the funds and never was heard from again.

Required Prepare a written list of the steps you would have taken to prevent this theft. Remember that this small company had limited financial resources.

Business Decision Case 8–2
List procedures that would have prevented theft of cash (L.O. 1, 3)

John Burnette was set up in business by his father, who purchased the business of an elderly acquaintance wishing to retire. One of the few changes in personnel made by Burnette was to install a college classmate as the office manager-bookkeeper-cashier-sales manager. During the course of the year, Burnette borrowed money from the bank with his father as cosigner. Although his business seemed profitable, there was a shortage of cash.

The company's investments in inventories and receivables grew substantially. Finally, after a year had elapsed, Burnette's father employed you, a certified public accountant, to audit the records of his business. You reported that the office manager-bookkeeper-cashier-sales manager had been misappropriating funds and had been using a variety of schemes to cover his actions. More specifically, he had:

1. Pocketed cash receipts from sales and understated the cash register readings at the end of the day or altered the copies of the sales tickets retained.
2. Stolen checks mailed to the company in payment of accounts receivable, credited the proper accounts, and then debited fictitious receivables to keep the records in balance.
3. Issued checks to fictitious suppliers and deposited them in accounts bearing these names with himself as signer of checks drawn on these accounts; the books were kept in balance by debiting the Purchases account.
4. Stolen petty cash funds by drawing false vouchers purporting to cover a variety of expenses incurred.
5. Prepared false sales returns vouchers indicating the return of cash sales to cover further thefts of cash receipts.

Required

For each item in the preceding list, describe in writing at least one feature of good internal control that would have prevented the losses due to dishonesty.

Business Decision Case 8–3*

Describe method used to steal cash; determine amount stolen; prepare correct bank reconciliation; and describe internal control procedures that would have prevented such theft (L.O. 1, 3, 4)

The outstanding checks of Warner Company at November 30, 1997, were:

No. 229	$1,000
No. 263	1,089
No. 3678	679
No. 3679	804
No. 3680	1,400

During December, Warner issued checks numbered 3681–3720; and all of these checks cleared the bank except 3719 and 3720 for $963 and $726, respectively. Checks 3678, 3679, and 3680 also cleared the bank.

The bank statement on December 31 showed a balance of $23,944. Service charges amounted to $20, and two checks were returned by the bank, one marked NSF in the amount of $114 and the other marked "No account" in the amount of $2,000.

Brian Askew recently retired as the office manager-cashier-bookkeeper for Warner Company and was replaced by Fred Hannah. Hannah noted the absence of an internal control structure but was momentarily deterred from embezzling for lack of a scheme of concealment. Finally, he hit upon several schemes. The $2,000 check marked "No account" by the bank is the product of one scheme. Hannah took cash receipts and replaced them with a check drawn on a nonexistent account to make it appear that a customer had given the company a worthless check.

The other scheme was more subtle. Hannah pocketed cash receipts in an amount equal to two unlisted outstanding checks and prepared the following bank reconciliation:

Balance per bank statement, December 31, 1997		$23,944.00
Add: Deposit in transit		2,837.80
		$26,781.80
Less: Outstanding checks:		
No. 3719	$963.00	
No. 3720	726.00	1,689.00
Adjusted balance		$25,092.80
Balance, Cash account December 31, 1997		$27,226.80
Less: Worthless check	$2,000.00	
NSF check	114.00	
Service charges	20.00	2,134.00
Adjusted balance, December 31, 1997		$25,092.80

* Note: This challenging problem was not specifically illustrated in the chapter, but it can be worked by applying the principles discussed in the chapter.

Required

a. State the nature of the second scheme hit on by Hannah. How much in total does it appear he has stolen by use of the two schemes together?
b. Prepare a correct bank reconciliation as of December 31, 1997.
c. After your analysis in (**a**) and (**b**), describe several procedures that would have defeated Fred Hannah's attempts to misappropriate funds and conceal these actions.

Annual Report Analysis 8–4
Discuss internal control elements (L.O. 1)

In General Electric Company's 1991 annual report, under Management's Discussion of Financial Responsibility, the chairman of the board and the senior vice president of finance stated:

To safeguard Company assets, it is important to have a sound but dynamic system of internal financial controls and procedures that balances benefits and costs. One of the key elements of internal financial controls has been the Company's success in recruiting, selecting, training and developing professional financial managers. Their responsibilities include implementing and overseeing the financial control system, reporting on management's stewardship of the assets entrusted to it by share owners, and performing accurate and proper maintenance of its accounts.

Required

What is your opinion of the chairman's statement? To which basic elements of the internal control structure does the chairman refer?

Annual Report Analysis 8–5
Calculate the quick ratio (L.O. 6)

Determine the 1993 and 1992 quick ratios for the John H. Harland Company based on its annual report in the annual report booklet. Comment on the results.

Ethics Case—Writing Experience 8–6
Respond regarding the ethics case

After reading the ethics case on page 315, discuss the ethical situation at the City Club Restaurant. Describe the steps the owners could take to end John Blue's wage supplement scheme.

Group Project 8–7
Describe internal controls for petty cash

In teams of two to three students, read this case and discuss the operation of the petty cash fund from an internal control point of view. As a team, write a brief memorandum to management indicating the current weaknesses and suggesting how the internal control structure can be improved. The heading of the memorandum should contain the date, to whom it is written, from whom, and the subject matter.

Olivia Sadler recently acquired an importing business from a friend. The business employs 10 salesclerks and four office employees. Sadler established a petty cash fund of $125. All of the employees are allowed to make disbursements from the fund. Vouchers are not used, and no one keeps a record of the disbursements. The petty cash is kept in a large shoe box in the office.

Answers to Self-Test

True-False

1. **False.** Postdated checks are not included as cash.
2. **True.** A company should make sure that enough cash is available to pay bills as they come due.
3. **False.** The cash balance on a bank statement is not usually the same as the cash balance in the depositor's books because of deposits in transit, outstanding checks, and bank service charges.
4. **False.** A deposit in transit is one of the items that has been correctly recorded as a debit to the Cash account of the depositor and will be recorded as a deposit by the bank after the bank employees open the night deposit chute.
5. **False.** For convenience, a company may use a petty cash fund for small amounts of cash payments such as delivery charges or postage stamps.

Multiple-Choice

1. **d.** An effective internal control structure does not necessarily guarantee a certain level of profits.

2. **a.**

Balance per bank statement	$1,951.20
Add: Deposits in transit	271.20
Less: Outstanding checks	(427.80)
Adjusted balance	$1,794.60
Balance per ledger	$1,869.60
Less: NSF check	(61.20)
Service charges	(13.80)
Adjusted balance	$1,794.60

3. **d.** Deposits in transit have been recorded in the company's accounting records but have not yet been recorded in the bank's records.

4. **b.** The entry to record bank service charges on the books is:

Bank Service Charge Expense	13.80	
Cash		13.80

5. **d.** The entry to replenish the petty cash fund has a credit to Cash, not Petty Cash.

Postage Expense	xxx	
Cash		xxx

9

Receivables and Payables

Learning Objectives

After studying this chapter, you should be able to:

1. Account for uncollectible accounts receivable under the allowance method.
2. Record credit card sales and collections.
3. Define liabilities, current liabilities, and long-term liabilities.
4. Define and account for clearly determinable, estimated, and contingent liabilities.
5. Account for notes receivable and payable, including calculation of interest.

(continued)

Much of the growth of business in recent years is due to the immense expansion of credit. Managers of companies have learned that by granting customers the privilege of *charging* their purchases, sales and profits increase. Using credit is not only a convenient way to make purchases but also the only way many people can own high-priced items such as automobiles.

This chapter, discusses receivables and payables. For a company, a **receivable** is any sum of money due to be paid to that company from any party for any reason. Similarly, a **payable** describes any sum of money to be paid by that company to any party for any reason.

Primarily, receivables arise from the sale of goods and services. The two types of receivables are accounts receivable, which companies offer for short-term credit with no interest charge; and notes receivable, which companies sometimes extend for both short- and long-term credit with an interest charge. We pay particular attention to accounting for uncollectible accounts receivable.

Like their customers, companies use credit, which they show as accounts payable or notes payable. Accounts payable normally result from the purchase of goods or services and do not carry an interest charge. Short-term notes payable carry an interest charge and may arise from the same transactions as accounts payable, but they can also result from borrowing money from a bank or other institution. Chapter 4 identified accounts payable and short-term notes payable as current liabilities. A company also incurs other current liabilities, including payables such as sales tax payable, estimated product warranty payable, and certain liabilities that are contingent on the occurrence of future events. Long-term notes payable usually result from borrowing money from a bank or other institution to finance the acquisition of plant assets. As you study this chapter and learn how important credit is to our economy, you will realize that credit in some form will probably always be with us.

ACCOUNTS RECEIVABLE

(*concluded*)

6. Account for borrowing money using an interest-bearing note versus a noninterest-bearing note.

7. Analyze and use the financial results—accounts receivable turnover and the number of days' sales in accounts receivable.

In Chapter 3, you learned that most companies use the accrual basis of accounting since it better reflects the actual results of the operations of a business. Under the accrual basis, a merchandising company that extends credit records revenue when it makes a sale because at this time it has earned and realized the revenue. The company has earned the revenue because it has completed the seller's part of the sales contract by delivering the goods. The company has realized the revenue because it has received the customer's promise to pay in exchange for the goods. This promise to pay by the customer is an account receivable to the seller. Accounts receivable are amounts that customers owe a company for goods sold and services rendered on account. Frequently, these receivables resulting from credit sales of goods and services are called **trade receivables.**

When a company sells goods on account, customers do not sign formal, written promises to pay, but they agree to abide by the company's customary credit terms. However, customers may sign a sales invoice to acknowledge purchase of goods. Payment terms for sales on account typically run from 30 to 60 days. Companies usually do not charge interest on amounts owed, except on some past-due amounts.

Because customers do not always keep their promises to pay, companies must provide for these uncollectible accounts in their records. Companies use two methods for handling uncollectible accounts. The allowance method provides in advance for uncollectible accounts. The direct write-off method recognizes bad accounts as an expense at the point when judged to be uncollectible and is the required method for federal income tax purposes. However, since the allowance method represents the accrual basis of accounting and is the accepted method to record uncollectible accounts for financial accounting purposes, we only discuss and illustrate the allowance method in this text.

The Allowance Method for Recording Uncollectible Accounts

Objective 1
Account for uncollectible accounts receivable under the allowance method.

Even though companies carefully screen credit customers, they cannot eliminate all uncollectible accounts. Companies expect some of their accounts to become uncollectible, but they do not know which ones. The matching principle requires deducting expenses incurred in producing revenues from those revenues during the accounting period. The allowance method of recording uncollectible accounts adheres to this principle by recognizing the uncollectible accounts expense in advance of identifying *specific accounts* as being uncollectible. The required entry has some similarity to the depreciation entry in Chapter 3 because it debits an expense and credits an allowance (contra asset). The purpose of the entry is to make the income statement fairly present the proper expense and the balance sheet fairly present the asset. **Uncollectible accounts expense** (also called *doubtful accounts expense* or **bad debts expense**) is an operating expense that a business incurs when it sells on credit. We classify uncollectible accounts expense as a selling expense because it results from credit sales. Other accountants might classify it as an administrative expense because the credit department has an important role in setting credit terms.

To adhere to the matching principle, companies must match the uncollectible accounts expense against the revenues it generates. Thus, an uncollectible account arising from a sale made in 1997 is a 1997 expense even though this treatment requires the use of estimates. Estimates are necessary because the company cannot determine until 1998 or later which 1997 customer accounts will become uncollectible.

RECORDING THE UNCOLLECTIBLE ACCOUNTS ADJUSTMENT A company that estimates uncollectible accounts makes an adjusting entry at the end of each accounting period. It debits Uncollectible Accounts Expense, thus recording the operating expense in the proper period. The credit is to an account called *Allowance for Uncollectible Accounts.*

As a contra account to the Accounts Receivable account, the **Allowance for Uncollectible Accounts** (also called *Allowance for Doubtful Accounts* or *Allowance for Bad Debts*) reduces accounts receivable to their net realizable value. **Net realizable value** is the amount the company expects to collect from accounts receivable. When the firm makes the uncollectible accounts adjusting entry, it does not know which specific accounts will become uncollectible. Thus, the company cannot enter credits in either the Accounts Receivable control account or the customers' accounts receivable subsidiary ledger accounts. If only one or the other were credited, the Accounts Receivable control account balance would not agree with the total of the balances in the accounts receivable subsidiary ledger. Without crediting the Accounts Receivable control account, the allowance account lets the company show that some of its accounts receivable are probably uncollectible.

To illustrate the adjusting entry for uncollectible accounts, assume a company has $100,000 of accounts receivable and estimates its uncollectible accounts expense for a given year at $4,000. The required year-end adjusting entry is:

Dec.	31	Uncollectible Accounts Expense	4,000	
		Allowance for Uncollectible Accounts		4,000
		To record estimated uncollectible accounts.		

The debit to Uncollectible Accounts Expense brings about a matching of expenses and revenues on the income statement; uncollectible accounts expense is matched against the revenues of the accounting period. The credit to Allowance for Uncollectible Accounts reduces accounts receivable to their net realizable value on the balance sheet. When the books are closed, the firm closes Uncollectible Accounts Expense to Income Summary. It reports the allowance on the balance sheet as a deduction from accounts receivable as follows:

BRICE COMPANY
Balance Sheet
December 31, 1997
Assets

Current assets:		
Cash		$21,200
Accounts receivable	$100,000	
Less: Allowance for uncollectible accounts	4,000	96,000

Estimating Uncollectible Accounts Accountants use two basic methods to estimate uncollectible accounts for a period. The first method—percentage-of-sales method—focuses on the income statement and the relationship of uncollectible accounts to sales. The second method—percentage-of-receivables method—focuses on the balance sheet and the relationship of the allowance for uncollectible accounts to accounts receivable. Either of these estimation methods is acceptable, and over time their results are similar. However, some accountants claim the percentage-of-sales method does a better job of matching expenses with revenues.

Percentage-of-Sales Method The **percentage-of-sales method** estimates uncollectible accounts from the credit sales of a given period. In theory, the method is based on a percentage of prior years' actual uncollectible accounts to prior years' credit sales. When cash sales are small or make up a fairly constant percentage of total sales, firms base the calculation on total net sales. Since at least one of these conditions is usually met, companies commonly use total net sales rather than credit sales. The formula to determine the amount of the entry is:

$$\text{Amount of journal entry for uncollectible accounts} = \text{Net sales (total or credit)} \times \text{Percentage estimated as uncollectible}$$

To illustrate, assume that Rankin Company's uncollectible accounts from 1995 sales were 1.1% of total net sales. A similar calculation for 1996 showed an uncollectible account percentage of 0.9%. The average for the two years is 1% [(1.1 + 0.9) ÷ 2]. Rankin does not expect 1997 to differ from the previous two years. Total net sales for 1997 were $500,000; receivables at year-end were $100,000; and the Allowance for Uncollectible Accounts had a zero balance. Rankin would make the following adjusting entry for 1997:

Dec.	31	Uncollectible Accounts Expense	5,000	
		Allowance for Uncollectible Accounts		5,000
		To record estimated uncollectible accounts ($500,000 × 0.01).		

Using T-accounts, Rankin would show:

Uncollectible Accounts Expense

Debit		Credit	
Dec. 31 Adjustment	5,000		

Allowance for Uncollectible Accounts

Debit		Credit	
		Bal. before adjustment	-0-
		Dec. 31 Adjustment	5,000
		Bal. after adjustment	5,000

Rankin reports Uncollectible Accounts Expense on the income statement. It reports the accounts receivable less the allowance among current assets in the balance sheet as follows:

Accounts receivable	$100,000	
Less: Allowance for uncollectible accounts	5,000	$95,000

Or Rankin's balance sheet could show:

Accounts receivable (less estimated uncollectible accounts, $5,000).	$95,000

On the income statement, Rankin would match the uncollectible accounts expense against sales revenues in the period. We would classify this expense as a selling expense since it is a normal consequence of selling on credit.

The Allowance for Uncollectible Accounts account usually has either a debit or credit balance before the year-end adjustment. Under the percentage-of-sales method, the company ignores any existing balance in the allowance when calculating the amount of the year-end adjustment (except that the allowance account must have a credit balance after adjustment).

For example, assume Rankin's allowance account had a $300 credit balance before adjustment. The adjusting entry would still be for $5,000. However, the balance sheet would show $100,000 accounts receivable less a $5,300 allowance for uncollectible accounts, resulting in net receivables of $94,700. On the income statement, Uncollectible Accounts Expense would still be 1% of total net sales, or $5,000.

In applying the percentage-of-sales method, companies annually review the percentage of uncollectible accounts that resulted from the previous year's sales. If the percentage rate is still valid, the company makes no change. However, if the situation has changed significantly, the company increases or decreases the percentage rate to reflect the changed condition. For example, in periods of recession and high unemployment, a firm may increase the percentage rate to reflect the customers' decreased ability to pay. However, if the company adopts a more stringent credit policy, it may have to decrease the percentage rate because the company would expect fewer uncollectible accounts.

Percentage-of-Receivables Method The **percentage-of-receivables method** estimates uncollectible accounts by determining the desired size of the Allowance for Uncollectible Accounts. Rankin would multiply the ending balance in Accounts Receivable by a rate (or rates) based on its uncollectible accounts experience. In the percentage-of-receivables method, the company may use either an overall rate or a different rate for each age category of receivables.

To calculate the amount of the entry for uncollectible accounts under the percentage-of-receivables method using an overall rate, Rankin would use:

$$\text{Amount of entry for uncollectible accounts} = \left(\text{Accounts Receivable ending balance} \times \text{Percentage estimated as uncollectible}\right) - \text{Existing credit balance in Allowance for Uncollectible Accounts or} + \text{Existing debit balance in Allowance for Uncollectible Accounts}$$

Using the same information as before, Rankin makes an estimate of uncollectible accounts at the end of 1997. The balance of accounts receivable is $100,000, and the allowance account has no balance. If Rankin estimates that 6% of the receivables will be uncollectible, the adjusting entry would be:

Dec.	31	Uncollectible Accounts Expense	6,000	
		Allowance for Uncollectible Accounts		6,000
		To record estimated uncollectible accounts ($100,000 × 0.06).		

Using T-accounts, Rankin would show:

Uncollectible Accounts Expense

Debit		Credit	
Dec. 31 Adjustment	6,000		

Allowance for Uncollectible Accounts

Debit		Credit	
		Bal. before adjustment	-0-
		Dec. 31 Adjustment	6,000
		Bal. after adjustment	6,000

If Rankin had a $300 credit balance in the allowance account before adjustment, the entry would be the same, except that the amount would be $5,700. The difference in amounts arises because management wants the allowance account to contain a credit balance equal to 6% of the outstanding receivables when presenting the two accounts on the balance sheet. The calculation of the necessary adjustment is [($100,000 × 0.06) − $300] = $5,700. Thus, under the percentage-of-receivables method, firms consider any existing balance in the allowance account when adjusting for uncollectible accounts. Using T-accounts, Rankin would show:

Uncollectible Accounts Expense

Debit		Credit	
Dec. 31 Adjustment	5,700		

Allowance for Uncollectible Accounts

Debit		Credit	
		Bal. before adjustment	300
		Dec. 31 Adjustment	5,700
		Bal. after adjustment	6,000

As another example, suppose that Rankin had a $300 debit balance in the allowance account before adjustment. Then, a credit of $6,300 would be necessary to get the balance to the required $6,000 credit balance. The calculation of the necessary adjustment is [($100,000 × 0.06) + $300] = $6,300. Using T-accounts, Rankin would show:

ILLUSTRATION 9.1
Accounts Receivable Aging Schedule

Balance in the Accounts Receivable account in the general ledger

Desired credit balance in the Allowance for Uncollectible Accounts

DARCY COMPANY
Accounts Receivable Aging Schedule
December 31, 1997

Customer	Accounts Receivable Balance	Not Yet Due	Days Past Due			
			1–30	31–60	61–90	Over 90
X	$ 5,000					$ 5,000
Y	14,000		$ 12,000	$2,000		
Z	400				$200	200
All others	808,600	$560,000	240,000	2,000	600	6,000
	$828,000	$560,000	$252,000	$4,000	$800	$11,200
Percentage estimated as uncollectible		1%	5%	10%	25%	50%
Estimated amount uncollectible	$ 24,400	$ 5,600	$ 12,600	$ 400	$200	$ 5,600

Uncollectible Accounts Expense

Debit		Credit	
Dec. 31 Adjustment	6,300		

Allowance for Uncollectible Accounts

Debit		Credit	
Bal. before adjustment	300	Dec. 31 Adjustment	6,300
		Bal. after adjustment	6,000

No matter what the preadjustment allowance account balance is, when using the percentage-of-receivables method, Rankin adjusts the Allowance for Uncollectible Accounts so that it has a credit balance of $6,000—equal to 6% of its $100,000 in Accounts Receivable. The desired $6,000 ending credit balance in the Allowance for Uncollectible Accounts serves as a "target" in making the adjustment.

So far, we have used one uncollectibility rate for all accounts receivable, regardless of their age. However, some companies use a different percentage for each age category of accounts receivable. When accountants decide to use a different rate for each age category of receivables, they prepare an aging schedule. An **aging schedule** classifies accounts receivable according to how long they have been outstanding and uses a different uncollectibility percentage rate for each age category. Companies base these percentages on experience. In Illustration 9.1, the aging schedule shows that the older the receivable, the less likely the company is to collect it.

Classifying accounts receivable according to age often gives the company a better basis for estimating the total amount of uncollectible accounts. For example, based on experience, a company can expect only 1% of the accounts not yet due (sales made less than 30 days before the end of the accounting period) to be uncollectible. At the other extreme, a company can expect 50% of all accounts over 90 days past due to be uncollectible. For each age category, the firm multiplies the accounts receivable by the percentage estimated as uncollectible to find the estimated amount uncollectible. The sum of the estimated amounts for all categories yields the total estimated amount uncollectible and is the desired credit balance (the target) in the Allowance for Uncollectible Accounts.

Since the aging schedule approach is an alternative under the percentage-of-receivables method, the balance in the allowance account before adjustment affects the year-end adjusting entry amount recorded for uncollectible accounts. For example, the schedule in Illustration 9.1 shows that $24,400 is needed as the ending credit balance in the allowance account. If the allowance account has a $5,000 credit balance before adjustment, the adjustment would be for $19,400.

The information in an aging schedule also is useful to management for other purposes. Analysis of collection patterns of accounts receivable may suggest the need for changes in credit policies or for added financing. For example, if the age of many customer balances has increased to 61–90 days past-due, collection efforts may have to be strengthened. Or, the company may have to find other sources of cash to pay its debts within the discount period. Preparation of an aging schedule may also help identify certain accounts that should be written off as uncollectible.

An Accounting Perspective

Business Insight According to the Fair Debt Collection Practices Act, collection agencies can call persons only between 8 A.M. and 9 P.M., and cannot use foul language. Agencies can call employers only if the employers allow such calls. And, they can threaten to sue only if they really intend to do so.

Write-Off of Receivables As time passes and a firm considers a specific customer's account to be uncollectible, it writes that account off. It debits the Allowance for Uncollectible Accounts. The credit is to the Accounts Receivable control account in the general ledger and to the customer's account in the accounts receivable subsidiary ledger. For example, assume Smith's $750 account has been determined to be uncollectible. The entry to write off this account is:

Allowance for Uncollectible Accounts	750	
Accounts Receivable—Smith		750
To write off Smith's account as uncollectible.		

The credit balance in Allowance for Uncollectible Accounts before making this entry represented potential uncollectible accounts not yet specifically identified. Debiting the allowance account and crediting Accounts Receivable shows that the firm has identified Smith's account as uncollectible. Notice that the debit in the entry to write-off an account receivable does not involve recording an expense. The company recognized the uncollectible accounts expense in the same accounting period as the sale. If Smith's $750 uncollectible account were recorded in Uncollectible Accounts Expense again, it would be counted as an expense twice.

A write-off does not affect the net realizable value of accounts receivable. For example, suppose that Amos Company has total accounts receivable of $50,000 and an allowance of $3,000 before the previous entry; the net realizable value of the accounts receivable is $47,000. After posting that entry, accounts receivable are $49,250, and the allowance is $2,250; net realizable value is still $47,000, as shown here:

	Before Write-Off	Entry for Write-Off	After Write-Off
Accounts receivable	$50,000 Dr.	$750 Cr.	$49,250 Dr.
Allowance for uncollectible accounts	3,000 Cr.	750 Dr.	2,250 Cr.
Net realizable value	$47,000		$47,000

You might wonder how the allowance account can develop a debit balance before adjustment. To explain this, assume that Jenkins Company began business on January 1, 1996, and decided to use the allowance method and make the adjusting entry for uncollectible accounts only at year-end. Thus, the allowance account would not have any balance at the beginning of 1996. If the company wrote off any uncollectible accounts during 1996, it would debit Allowance for Uncollectible Accounts and cause a debit balance in that account. At the end of

A Broader Perspective

GECS Allowance for Losses on Financing Receivables

GECS allowance for losses on financing receivables represented 2.63% of total financing receivables at year-end 1992 and 1991. The allowance for small-balance receivables is determined principally on the basis of actual experience during the preceding three years. Further allowances are provided to reflect management's judgment of additional loss potential. For other receivables, principally the larger loans and leases, the allowance for losses is determined primarily on the basis of management's judgment of net loss potential, including specific allowances for known troubled accounts. The table below shows the activity in the allowance for losses on financing receivables during each of the last three years.

(In millions)	1992	1991	1990
Balance at January 1 . . .	$1,508	$1,360	$1,127
Provisions charged to operations	1,056	1,102	688
Net transfers related to companies acquired or sold.	52	135	230
Amounts written off—net .	(1,009)	(1,089)	(685)
Balance at December 31 . .	$1,607	$1,508	$1,360

All accounts or portions thereof deemed to be uncollectible or to require an excessive collection cost are written off to the allowance for losses. Small-balance accounts are progressively written down (from 10% when more than three months delinquent to 100% when 9-12 months delinquent) to record the balances at estimated realizable value. If at any time during that period an account is judged to be uncollectible, such as in the case of a bankruptcy, the uncollectible balance is written off. Large-balance accounts are reviewed at least quarterly, and those accounts that are more than three months delinquent are written down, if necessary, to record the balances at estimated realizable value. Amounts written off in 1992 were approximately 1.58% of average financing receivables outstanding during the year, compared with 1.87% and 1.37% of average financing receivables outstanding during 1991 and 1990, respectively.

Source: General Electric Company, *1992 Annual Report*, p. 49.

1996, the company would debit Uncollectible Accounts Expense and credit Allowance for Uncollectible Accounts. This adjusting entry would cause the allowance account to have a credit balance. During 1997, the company would again begin debiting the allowance account for any write-offs of uncollectible accounts. Even if the adjustment at the end of 1996 was adequate to cover all accounts receivable existing at that time that would later become uncollectible, some accounts receivable from 1997 sales may be written off before the end of 1997. If so, the allowance account would again develop a debit balance before the end-of-year 1997 adjustment.

Uncollectible Accounts Recovered Sometimes companies collect accounts previously considered to be uncollectible after the accounts have been written off. A company usually learns that an account has been written off erroneously when it receives payment. Then, the company reverses the original write-off entry and reinstates the account by debiting Accounts Receivable and crediting Allowance for Uncollectible Accounts for the amount received. It posts the debit to both the general ledger account and to the customer's accounts receivable subsidiary ledger account. The firm also records the amount received as a debit to Cash and a credit to Accounts Receivable. And, it posts the credit to both the general ledger and to the customer's accounts receivable subsidiary ledger account.

To illustrate, assume that on May 17 a company received a $750 check from Smith in payment of the account previously written off. The two required journal entries are:

May	17	Accounts Receivable—Smith	750	
		Allowance for Uncollectible Accounts		750
		To reverse original write-off of Smith's account.		
	17	Cash.	750	
		Accounts Receivable—Smith		750
		To record collection of account.		

The debit and credit to Accounts Receivable—Smith on the same date is to show in Smith's subsidiary ledger account that he did eventually pay the amount due. As a result, the company may decide to sell to him in the future.

When a company collects part of a previously written off account, the usual procedure is to reinstate only that portion actually collected, unless evidence indicates the amount will be collected in full. If a company expects full payment, it reinstates the entire amount of the account.

Because of the problems companies have with uncollectible accounts when they offer customers credit, many now allow customers to use bank or external credit cards. This policy relieves the company of the headaches of collecting overdue accounts.

Credit Cards

Objective 2
Record credit card sales and collections.

Credit cards are either nonbank (American Express and Diners Club) or bank (VISA and MasterCard) charge cards that customers use to purchase goods and services. For some businesses, uncollectible account losses and other costs of extending credit are a burden. By paying a service charge of 2% to 8%, businesses pass these costs on to banks and agencies issuing national credit cards. The banks and credit card agencies then absorb the uncollectible accounts and costs of extending credit and maintaining records.

Usually, banks and agencies issue credit cards to approved credit applicants for an annual fee. When a business agrees to honor these credit cards, it also agrees to pay the percentage fee charged by the bank or credit agency.

When making a credit card sale, the seller checks to see if the customer's card has been canceled and requests approval if the sale exceeds a prescribed amount, such as $50. This procedure allows the seller to avoid accepting lost, stolen, or canceled cards. Also, this policy protects the credit agency from sales causing customers to exceed their established credit limits.

The seller's accounting procedures for credit card sales differ depending on whether the business accepts a nonbank or a bank credit card. To illustrate the entries for the use of *nonbank* credit cards (such as American Express or Diners Club), assume that a restaurant has Diners Club invoices amounting to $1,400 at the end of a day. The Diners Club charges the restaurant a 5% service charge. The restaurant uses the **Credit Card Expense account** to record the credit card agency's service charge and makes the following entry:

Accounts Receivable—Diners Club	1,330	
Credit Card Expense	70	
Sales		1,400
To record credit card sales.		

The restaurant mails the invoices to Diners Club. Sometime later, the restaurant receives payment from Diners Club and makes the following entry:

Cash	1,330	
Accounts Receivable—Diners Club		1,330
To record remittance from Diners Club.		

To illustrate the accounting entries for the use of *bank* credit cards (such as VISA or MasterCard), assume that a retailer has made sales of $1,000 for which VISA cards were accepted and the service charge is $50 (which is 5% of sales). VISA sales are treated as cash sales because the receipt of cash is certain. The retailer deposits the credit card sales invoices in its VISA checking account at a bank just as it deposits checks in its regular checking account. The entry to record this deposit is:

Cash	950	
Credit Card Expense	50	
Sales		1,000
To record VISA credit card sales.		

AN ACCOUNTING PERSPECTIVE

BUSINESS INSIGHT Recent innovations in credit cards include picture IDs on cards to reduce theft, credits toward purchases of new automobiles (Ford Citibank and General Motors cards), credit toward free trips on airlines, and cash rebates on all purchases. Discover Card remits 1% of all charges back to credit card holders at the end of the year. Also some credit card companies have reduced interest rates on unpaid balances and have eliminated the annual fee.

Just as every company must have current assets such as cash and accounts receivable to operate, every company incurs current liabilities in conducting its operations. Corporations (IBM and General Motors), partnerships (CPA firms), and single proprietorships (corner grocery stores) all have one thing in common—they have liabilities. The next section discusses some of the current liabilities companies incur.

CURRENT LIABILITIES

Objective 3
Define liabilities, current liabilities, and long-term liabilities.

Liabilities result from some past transaction and are obligations to pay cash, provide services, or deliver goods at some future time. This definition includes each of the liabilities discussed in previous chapters and the new liabilities presented in this chapter. The balance sheet divides liabilities into current liabilities and long-term liabilities. **Current liabilities** are obligations that (1) are payable within one year or one operating cycle, whichever is longer, or (2) will be paid out of current assets or create other current liabilities. **Long-term liabilities** are obligations that do not qualify as current liabilities. This chapter focuses on current liabilities and Chapter 15 describes long-term liabilities.

Note the definition of a current liability uses the term *operating cycle*. An **operating cycle** (or cash cycle) is the time it takes to begin with cash, buy necessary items to produce revenues (such as materials, supplies, labor, and/or finished goods), sell goods or services, and receive cash by collecting the resulting receivables. For most companies, this period is no longer than a few months. Service companies generally have the shortest operating cycle, since they have no cash tied up in inventory. Manufacturing companies generally have the longest cycle because their cash is tied up in inventory accounts and in accounts receivable before coming back. Even for manufacturing companies, the cycle is generally less than one year. Thus, as a practical matter, current liabilities are due in one year or less, and long-term liabilities are due after one year from the balance sheet date.

The operating cycles for various businesses follow:

Type of Business	Operating Cycle
Service company selling for cash only	Instantaneous
Service company selling on credit	Cash → Accounts receivable → Cash
Merchandising company selling for cash	Cash → Inventory → Cash
Merchandising company selling on credit	Cash → Inventory → Accounts receivable → Cash
Manufacturing company selling on credit	Cash → Materials inventory → Work in process inventory → Finished goods inventory → Accounts receivable → Cash

Current liabilities fall into these three groups:

Objective 4
Define and account for clearly determinable, estimated, and contingent liabilities.

1. **Clearly determinable liabilities.** The existence of the liability and its amount are certain. Examples include most of the liabilities discussed previously, such as accounts payable, notes payable, interest payable, unearned delivery fees, and wages payable. Sales tax payable, federal excise tax payable, current portions of long-term debt, and payroll liabilities are other examples.
2. **Estimated liabilities.** The existence of the liability is certain, but its amount only can be *estimated*. An example is estimated product warranty payable.

3. **Contingent liabilities.** The existence of the liability is uncertain and usually the amount is uncertain because contingent liabilities depend (or are *contingent*) on some future event occurring or not occurring. Examples include liabilities arising from lawsuits, discounted notes receivable, income tax disputes, penalties that may be assessed because of some past action, and failure of another party to pay a debt that a company has guaranteed.

The following table summarizes the characteristics of current liabilities:

Type of Liability	Is the Existence Certain?	Is the Amount Certain?
Clearly determinable liabilities	Yes	Yes
Estimated liabilities	Yes	No
Contingent liabilities	No	No

Clearly Determinable Liabilities

Clearly determinable liabilities have clearly determinable amounts. In this section, we describe liabilities not previously discussed that are clearly determinable—sales tax payable, federal excise tax payable, current portions of long-term debt, and payroll liabilities. Later in this chapter, we discuss clearly determinable liabilities such as notes payable.

Sales Tax Payable Many states have a state sales tax on items purchased by consumers. The company selling the product is responsible for collecting the sales tax from customers. When the company collects the taxes, the debit is to Cash and the credit is to Sales Tax Payable. Periodically, the company pays the sales taxes collected to the state. At that time, the debit is to Sales Tax Payable and the credit is to Cash.

To illustrate, assume that a company sells merchandise in a state that has a 6% sales tax. If it sells goods with a sales price of $1,000 on credit, the company makes this entry:

Accounts Receivable	1,060	
Sales		1,000
Sales Tax Payable		60
To record sales and sales tax payable.		

Now assume that sales for the entire period are $100,000 and that $6,000 is in the Sales Tax Payable account when the company remits the funds to the state taxing agency. The following entry shows the payment to the state:

Sales Tax Payable	6,000	
Cash		6,000
To record the payment to the state for sales taxes collected from customers.		

An alternative method of recording sales taxes payable is to include these taxes in the credit to Sales. For instance, the previous company could record sales as follows:

Accounts Receivable	1,060	
Sales		1,060

When recording sales taxes in the same account as sales revenue, the firm must separate the sales tax from sales revenue at the end of the accounting period. To make this separation, it adds the sales tax rate to 100% and divides this percentage into recorded sales revenue. For instance, assume that total recorded sales revenues for an accounting period are $10,600, and the sales tax rate is 6%. To find the sales revenue, use the following formula:

$$\text{Sales} = \frac{\text{Amount recorded in Sales account}}{100\% + \text{Sales tax rate}}$$

$$= \frac{\$10{,}600}{106\%} = \$10{,}000$$

The sales revenue is $10,000 for the period. Sales tax is equal to the recorded sales revenue of $10,600 less actual sales revenue of $10,000, or $600.

Federal Excise Tax Payable Consumers pay federal excise tax on some goods, such as alcoholic beverages, tobacco, gasoline, cosmetics, tires, luxury automobiles, boats, airplanes, cameras, radios, television sets, and jewelry. The 1990 federal budget compromise increased the tax on many of these items. The entries a company makes when selling these goods are similar to those made for sales taxes payable. For example, assume that the Dixon Jewelry Store sells a diamond ring to a young couple for $2,000. The sale is subject to a 6% sales tax and a 10% federal excise tax. The entry to record the sale is:

Accounts Receivable	2,320	
Sales		2,000
Sales Tax Payable		120
Federal Excise Tax Payable		200
To record the sale of a diamond ring.		

The company records the remittance of the taxes to the federal taxing agency by debiting Federal Excise Tax Payable and crediting Cash.

Current Portions of Long-Term Debt Accountants move any portion of long-term debt that becomes due within the next year to the current liability section of the balance sheet. For instance, assume a company signed a series of 10 individual notes payable for $10,000 each; beginning in the 6th year, one comes due each year through the 15th year. Beginning in the 5th year, an accountant would move a $10,000 note from the long-term liability category to the current liability category on the balance sheet. The current portion would then be paid within one year.

An Accounting Perspective

Uses of Technology Many companies use service bureaus to process their payrolls because these bureaus keep up to date on rates, bases, and changes in the laws affecting payroll. Companies can either send their data by modem or have the service bureaus pick up time sheets and other data. Managers instruct service bureaus either to print the payroll checks or to transfer data by modem back to the company, so it can print the checks.

Payroll Liabilities In most business organizations, accounting for payroll is particularly important because (1) payrolls often are the largest expense that a company incurs, (2) both federal and state governments require maintaining detailed payroll records, and (3) companies must file regular payroll reports with state and federal governments and remit amounts withheld or otherwise due. Payroll liabilities include taxes and other amounts withheld from employees' paychecks and taxes paid by employers.

Employers normally withhold amounts from employees' paychecks for federal income taxes; state income taxes; FICA (social security) taxes; and other items such as union dues, medical insurance premiums, life insurance premiums, pension plans, and pledges to charities. Assume that a company had a payroll of $35,000 for the month of April 1997. The company withheld the following amounts from the employees' pay: federal income taxes, $4,100; state income taxes, $360; FICA taxes, $2,678; and medical insurance premiums, $940. This entry records the payroll:

1997				
April	30	Salaries Expense	35,000	
		Employees' Federal Income Taxes Payable		4,100
		Employees' State Income Taxes Payable		360
		FICA Taxes Payable		2,678
		Employees' Medical Insurance Premiums Payable		940
		Salaries Payable		26,922
		To record the payroll for the month ending April 30.		

All accounts credited in the entry are current liabilities and will be reported on the balance sheet if not paid prior to the preparation of financial statements. When these liabilities are paid, the employer debits each one and credits Cash.

Employers normally record payroll taxes at the same time as the payroll to which they relate. Assume the payroll taxes an employer pays for April are FICA taxes, $2,678; state unemployment taxes, $1,890; and federal unemployment taxes, $280. The entry to record these payroll taxes would be:

1997				
April	30	Payroll Taxes Expense	4,848	
		FICA Taxes Payable		2,678
		State Unemployment Taxes Payable		1,890
		Federal Unemployment Taxes Payable		280
		To record employer's payroll taxes.		

These amounts are in addition to the amounts withheld from employees' paychecks. The credit to FICA Taxes Payable is equal to the amount withheld from the employees' paychecks. The company can credit both its own and the employees' FICA taxes to the same liability account, since both are payable at the same time to the same agency. When these liabilities are paid, the employer debits each of the liability accounts and credits Cash.

An Accounting Perspective

Uses of Technology. One of the basic components in accounting software packages is the payroll module. As long as companies update this module each time rates, bases, or laws change, they can calculate withholdings, print payroll checks, and complete reporting forms for taxing agencies. In addition to calculating the employer's payroll taxes, this software maintains all accounting payroll records.

Estimated Liabilities

Managers of companies that have estimated liabilities know these liabilities exist but can only estimate the amount. The primary accounting problem is to estimate a reasonable liability as of the balance sheet date. An example of an estimated liability is product warranty payable.

Estimated Product Warranty Payable When companies sell products such as computers, often they must guarantee against defects by placing a warranty on their products. When defects occur, the company is obligated to reimburse the customer or repair the product. For many products, companies can predict the number of defects based on experience. To provide for a proper matching of revenues and expenses, the accountant estimates the warranty expense resulting from an accounting period's sales. The debit is to Product Warranty Expense and the credit to Estimated Product Warranty Payable.

To illustrate, assume that a company sells personal computers and warrants all parts for one year. The average price per computer is $1,500, and the company sells 1,000 computers in 1997. The company expects 10% of the computers to develop defective parts within one year. By the end of 1997, customers have returned 40 computers sold that year for repairs, and the repairs on those 40 computers have been recorded. The estimated average cost of warranty repairs per defective computer is $150. To arrive at a reasonable estimate of product warranty expense, the accountant makes the following calculation:

Number of computers sold	1,000
Percent estimated to develop defects	× 10%
Total estimated defective computers	100
Deduct computers returned as defective to date	40
Estimated additional number to become defective during warranty period	60
Estimated average warranty repair cost per computer	×$ 150
Estimated product warranty payable	$9,000

The entry made at the end of the accounting period is:

Product Warranty Expense	9,000	
Estimated Product Warranty Payable		9,000
To record estimated product warranty expense.		

When a customer returns one of the computers purchased in 1997 for repair work in 1998 (during the warranty period), the company debits the cost of the repairs to Estimated Product Warranty Payable. For instance, assume that Evan Holman returns his computer for repairs within the warranty period. The repair cost includes parts, $40, and labor, $160. The company makes the following entry:

Estimated Product Warranty Payable	200	
Repair Parts Inventory		40
Wages Payable		160
To record replacement of parts under warranty.		

An Accounting Perspective

Business Insight Another estimated liability that is quite common relates to clean-up costs for industrial pollution. One company had the following note in its recent financial statements:

In the past, the Company treated hazardous waste at its chemical facilities. Testing of the ground waters in the areas of the treatment impoundments at these facilities disclosed the presence of certain contaminants. In compliance with environmental regulations, the Company developed a plan that will prevent further contamination, provide for remedial action to remove the present contaminants, and establish a monitoring program to monitor ground water conditions in the future. A similar plan has been developed for a site previously used as a metal pickling facility. Estimated future costs of $2,860,000 have been accrued in the accompanying financial statements . . . to complete the procedures required under these plans.

Contingent Liabilities

When liabilities are contingent, the company usually is not sure that the liability exists and is uncertain about the amount. *FASB Statement No. 5* defines a contingency as "an existing condition, situation, or set of circumstances involving uncertainty as to possible gain or loss to an enterprise that will ultimately be resolved when one or more future events occur or fail to occur."[1]

According to *FASB Statement No. 5*, if the liability is probable and the amount can be reasonably estimated, companies should record contingent liabilities in the accounts. However, since most contingent liabilities may not occur and the amount often cannot be reasonably estimated, the accountant usually does not record them in the accounts. Instead, firms typically disclose these contingent liabilities in notes to their financial statements.

Many contingent liabilities arise as the result of lawsuits. In fact, 366 of the 600 companies contacted in the AICPA's annual survey of accounting practices reported contingent liabilities resulting from litigation.[2]

The following two examples from annual reports are typical of the disclosures made in notes to the financial statements. Be aware that just because a suit is brought, the company being sued is not necessarily guilty. One company included the following note in its annual report to describe its contingent liability regarding various lawsuits against the company:

Contingent Liabilities:

Various lawsuits and claims, including those involving ordinary routine litigation incidental to its business, to which the Company is a party, are pending, or have been asserted, against the Company. In addition, the Company was advised in 1985 that the United States Environmental Protection Agency had determined the existence of PCBs in a river and

[1] FASB, *Statement of Financial Accounting Standards No. 5*, "Accounting for Contingencies" (Stamford, Conn., 1975). Copyright © by Financial Accounting Standards Board, High Ridge Park, Stamford, Connecticut 06905, USA.

[2] AICPA, *Accounting Trends & Techniques* (New York, 1993), p. 57.

harbor near Sheboygan, Wisconsin, and that the Company, as well as others, allegedly contributed to that contamination. It is not presently possible to determine with certainty what corrective action, if any, will be required, what portion of any costs thereof will be attributable to the Company, or whether all or any portion of such costs will be covered by insurance or will be recoverable from others. Although the outcome of these matters cannot be predicted with certainty, and some of them may be disposed of unfavorably to the Company, management has no reason to believe that their disposition will have a materially adverse effect on the consolidated financial position of the Company.

Another company dismissed an employee and included the following note to disclose the contingent liability resulting from the ensuing litigation:

Contingencies:

In May 1988, a jury awarded $5.2 million to a former employee of the Company for an alleged breach of contract and wrongful termination of employment. The Company has appealed the judgment on the basis of errors in the judge's instructions to the jury and insufficiency of evidence to support the amount of the jury's award. The Company is vigorously pursuing the appeal.

The Company and its subsidiaries are also involved in various other litigation arising in the ordinary course of business.

Since it presently is not possible to determine the outcome of these matters, no provision has been made in the financial statements for their ultimate resolution. The resolution of the appeal of the jury award could have a significant effect on the Company's earnings in the year that a determination is made; however, in management's opinion, the final resolution of all legal matters will not have a material adverse effect on the Company's financial position.

Contingent liabilities may also arise from discounted notes receivable, income tax disputes, penalties that may be assessed because of some past action, and failure of another party to pay a debt that a company has guaranteed.

The remainder of this chapter discusses notes receivable and notes payable. Business transactions often involve one party giving another party a note.

Notes Receivable and Notes Payable

Objective 5
Account for notes receivable and payable, including calculation of interest.

A note (also called a **promissory note**) is an unconditional written promise by a borrower **(maker)** to pay a definite sum of money to the lender **(payee)** on demand or on a specific date. On the balance sheet of the lender (payee), a note is a receivable; on the balance sheet of the borrower (maker), a note is a payable. Since the note is usually negotiable, the payee may transfer it to another party, who then receives payment from the maker. Look at the promissory note in Illustration 9.2.

A customer may give a note to a business for an amount due on an account receivable or for the sale of a large item such as a refrigerator. Also, a business may give a note to a supplier in exchange for merchandise to sell or to a bank or an individual for a loan. Thus, a company may have notes receivable or notes payable arising from transactions with customers, suppliers, banks, or individuals.

Companies usually do not establish a subsidiary ledger for notes. Instead, they maintain a file of the actual notes receivable and copies of notes payable.

Interest Calculation

Most promissory notes have an explicit interest charge. **Interest** is the fee charged for use of money over a period. To the maker of the note, or borrower, interest is an expense; to the payee of the note, or lender, interest is a revenue. A borrower incurs interest expense; a lender earns interest revenue. For convenience, bankers sometimes calculate interest on a 360-day year; we calculate it on that basis in this text. (Some companies use a 365-day year.)

The basic formula for computing interest is:

$$\text{Interest} = \text{Principal} \times \text{Rate} \times \text{Time, or } I = P \times R \times T$$

ILLUSTRATION 9.2 Promissory Note

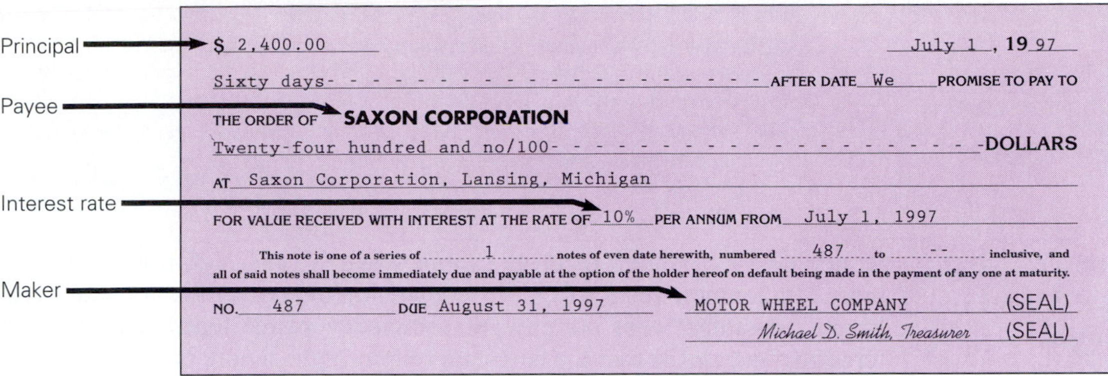

Principal
Payee
Interest rate
Maker
$ 2,400.00
July 1, 19 97
Sixty days- AFTER DATE We PROMISE TO PAY TO
THE ORDER OF SAXON CORPORATION
Twenty-four hundred and no/100- -DOLLARS
AT Saxon Corporation, Lansing, Michigan
FOR VALUE RECEIVED WITH INTEREST AT THE RATE OF 10% PER ANNUM FROM July 1, 1997
This note is one of a series of 1 notes of even date herewith, numbered 487 to -- inclusive, and all of said notes shall become immediately due and payable at the option of the holder hereof on default being made in the payment of any one at maturity.
NO. 487 DUE August 31, 1997
MOTOR WHEEL COMPANY (SEAL)
Michael D. Smith, Treasurer (SEAL)

Principal is the face value of the note. The **rate** is the stated interest rate on the note; interest rates are generally stated on an annual basis. **Time,** which is the amount of time the note is to run, can be either days or months.

To show how to calculate interest, assume a company borrowed $20,000 from a bank. The note has a principal (face value) of $20,000, an annual interest rate of 10%, and a life of 90 days. The interest calculation is:

$$\text{Interest} = \$20,000 \times 0.10 \times 90/360$$
$$\text{Interest} = \$500$$

Note that in this calculation we expressed the time period as a fraction of a 360-day year because the interest rate is an annual rate.

Determination of Maturity Date

The **maturity date** is the date on which a note becomes due and must be paid. Sometimes notes require monthly installments (or payments) but usually all of the principal and interest must be paid at the same time as in Illustration 9.2. The wording in the note expresses the maturity date and determines when the note is to be paid. A note falling due on a Sunday or a holiday is due on the next business day. Examples of the maturity date wording are:

1. *On demand.* "On demand, I promise to pay . . ." When the maturity date is on demand, it is at the option of the holder and cannot be computed. The holder is the payee, or another person who legally acquired the note from the payee.
2. *On a stated date.* "On July 18, 1997, I promise to pay . . ." When the maturity date is designated, computing the maturity date is not necessary.
3. *At the end of a stated period.*
   a. "One year after date, I promise to pay . . ." When the maturity is expressed in years, the note matures on the same day of the same month as the date of the note in the year of maturity.
   b. "Four months after date, I promise to pay . . ." When the maturity is expressed in months, the note matures on the same date in the month of maturity. For example, one month from July 18, 1997, is August 18, 1997, and two months from July 18, 1997, is September 18, 1997. If a note is issued on the last day of a month and the month of maturity has fewer days than the month of issuance, the note matures on the last day of the month of maturity. A one-month note dated January 31, 1997, matures on February 28, 1997.
   c. "Ninety days after date, I promise to pay . . ." When the maturity is expressed in days, the exact number of days must be counted. The first day (date of origin) is omitted, and the last day (maturity date) is in-

cluded in the count. For example, a 90-day note dated October 19, 1997, matures on January 17, 1998, as shown here:

Life of note (days)		90 days
Days remaining in October not counting date of origin of note:		
Days to count in October (31 − 19)	12	
Total days in November	30	
Total days in December	31	73
Maturity date in January		17 days

Accounting for Notes in Normal Business Transactions

Sometimes a company receives a note when it sells high-priced merchandise; more often, a note results from the conversion of an overdue account receivable. When a customer does not pay an account receivable that is due, the company (creditor) may insist that the customer (debtor) give a note in place of the account receivable. This action allows the customer more time to pay the balance due, and the company earns interest on the balance until paid. Also, the company may be able to sell the note to a bank or other financial institution.

To illustrate the conversion of an account receivable to a note, assume that Price Company (maker) had purchased $18,000 of merchandise on August 1 from Cooper Company (payee) on account. The normal credit period has elapsed, and Price cannot pay the invoice. Cooper agrees to accept Price's $18,000, 15%, 90-day note dated September 1 to settle Price's open account. Assuming Price paid the note at maturity and both Cooper and Price have a December 31 year-end, the entries on the books of the payee and the maker are:

Cooper Company, Payee

Aug.	1	Accounts Receivable—Price Company	18,000	
		Sales		18,000
		To record sale of merchandise on account.		
Sept.	1	Notes Receivable	18,000	
		Accounts Receivable—Price Company		18,000
		To record exchange of note from Price Company for open account.		
Nov.	30	Cash	18,675	
		Notes Receivable		18,000
		Interest Revenue ($18,000 × 0.15 × 90/360)		675
		To record receipt of Price Company note principal and interest.		

Price Company, Maker

Aug.	1	Purchases	18,000	
		Accounts Payable—Cooper Company		18,000
		To record purchase of merchandise on account.		
Sept.	1	Accounts Payable—Cooper Company	18,000	
		Notes Payable		18,000
		To record exchange of note to Cooper Company for open account.		
Nov.	30	Notes Payable	18,000	
		Interest Expense ($18,000 × 0.15 × 90/360)	675	
		Cash		18,675
		To record payment of note principal and interest.		

The $18,675 paid by Price to Cooper is called the *maturity value of the note*. **Maturity value** is the amount that the maker must pay on a note on its maturity date; typically, it includes principal and accrued interest, if any.

Sometimes the maker of a note does not pay the note when it becomes due. The next section describes how to record a note not paid at maturity.

Dishonored Notes

A **dishonored note** is a note that the maker failed to pay at maturity. Since the note has matured, the holder or payee removes the note from Notes Receivable and records the amount due in Accounts Receivable (or Dishonored Notes Receivable).

At the maturity date of a note, the maker should pay the principal plus interest. If the interest has not been accrued in the accounting records, the maker of a dishonored note should record interest expense for the life of the note by debiting Interest Expense and crediting Interest Payable. The payee should record the interest earned and remove the note from its Notes Receivable account. Thus, the payee of the note should debit Accounts Receivable for the maturity value of the note and credit Notes Receivable for the note's face value and Interest Revenue for the interest. After these entries have been posted, the full liability on the note—principal plus interest—is included in the records of both parties. Interest continues to accrue on the note until it is paid, replaced by a new note, or written off as uncollectible. To illustrate, assume that Price did not pay the note at maturity. The entries on each party's books are:

Cooper Company, Payee

Nov.	30	Accounts Receivable—Price Company	18,675	
		Notes Receivable		18,000
		Interest Revenue		675
		To record dishonor of Price Company note.		

Price Company, Maker

Nov.	30	Interest Expense	675	
		Interest Payable		675
		To record interest on note payable.		

When unable to pay a note at maturity, sometimes the maker pays the interest on the original note or includes the interest in the face value of a new note that replaces the old note. Both parties account for the new note in the same manner as the old note. However, if it later becomes clear that the maker of a dishonored note will never pay, the payee writes off the account with a debit to Uncollectible Accounts Expense (or to an account with a title such as Loss on Dishonored Notes) and a credit to Accounts Receivable. The debit should be to the Allowance for Uncollectible Accounts if the payee made an annual provision for uncollectible notes receivable.

Renewal of Notes

Assume that Price Company pays the interest at the maturity date and issues a new 15%, 90-day note for $18,000. The entries on both sets of books would be:

Cooper Company, Payee			Price Company, Maker		
Cash	675		Interest Expense	675	
Interest Revenue		675	Cash		675
To record the receipt of interest on Price Company note.			To record the payment of interest on note to Cooper Company.		
(Optional entry)			(Optional entry)		
Notes Receivable	18,000		Notes Payable	18,000	
Notes Receivable		18,000	Notes Payable		18,000
To replace old 15%, 90-day note from Price Company with new 15%, 90-day note.			To replace old 15%, 90-day note to Cooper Company with new 15%, 90-day note.		

Although the second entry on each set of books has no effect on the existing account balances, it indicates that the old note was renewed (or replaced). Both parties substitute the new note, or a copy, for the old note in a file of notes.

Now assume that Price Company does not pay the interest at the maturity date but instead includes the interest in the face value of the new note. The entries on both sets of books would be:

Cooper Company, Payee			**Price Company, Maker**		
Notes Receivable	18,675		Interest Expense	675	
Interest Revenue		675	Notes Payable	18,000	
Notes Receivable		18,000	Notes Payable		18,675
To record the replacement of the old Price Company $18,000, 15%, 90-day note with a new $18,675, 15%, 90-day note.			To record the replacement of the old $18,000, 15%, 90-day note to Cooper Company with a new $18,675, 15%, 90-day note.		

Accruing Interest

On an interest-bearing note, even though interest accrues, or accumulates, on a day-to-day basis, usually both parties record it only at the note's maturity date. If the note is outstanding at the end of an accounting period, however, the time period of the interest overlaps the end of the accounting period and requires an adjusting entry at the end of the accounting period. Both the payee and maker of the note must make an adjusting entry to record the accrued interest and report the proper assets and revenues for the payee and the proper liabilities and expenses for the maker. Failure to record accrued interest understates the payee's assets and revenues by the amount of the interest earned but not collected and understates the maker's expenses and liabilities by the interest expense incurred but not yet paid.

Payee's Books To illustrate how to record accrued interest on the payee's books, assume that the payee, Cooper Company, has a fiscal year ending on October 31 instead of December 31. On October 31, Cooper would make the following adjusting entry relating to the Price Company note:

Oct.	31	Interest Receivable	450	
		Interest Revenue ($18,000 × 0.15 × 60⁄360)		450
		To record interest earned on Price Company note for the period September 1 through October 31.		

The **Interest Receivable account** shows the interest earned but not yet collected. Interest receivable is a current asset in the balance sheet because the interest will be collected in 30 days. The interest revenue appears in the income statement. When Price pays the note on November 30, Cooper makes the following entry to record the collection of the note's principal and interest:

Nov.	30	Cash	18,675	
		Notes Receivable		18,000
		Interest Receivable		450
		Interest Revenue		225
		To record collection of Price Company note and interest.		

Note that the entry credits the Interest Receivable account for the $450 interest accrued from September 1 through October 31, which was debited to the account in the previous entry, and credits Interest Revenue for the $225 interest earned in November.

Maker's Books Assume Price Company's accounting year also ends on October 31 instead of December 31. Price's accounting records would be incomplete unless the company makes an adjusting entry to record the liability owed for the accrued interest on the note it gave to Cooper Company. The required entry is:

Oct.	31	Interest Expense ($18,000 × 0.15 × 60⁄360)	450	
		Interest Payable		450
		To record accrued interest on note to Cooper Company for the period September 1 through October 31.		

The **Interest Payable account,** which shows the interest expense incurred but not yet paid, is a current liability in the balance sheet because the interest will be paid in 30 days. Interest expense appears in the income statement. When the note is paid, Price makes the following entry:

Nov.	30	Notes Payable	18,000	
		Interest Payable	450	
		Interest Expense	225	
		Cash		18,675
		To record payment of principal and interest on note to Cooper Company.		

In this illustration, Cooper's financial position made it possible for the company to *carry* the Price note to the maturity date. Alternatively, Cooper could have sold, or discounted, the note to receive the proceeds before the maturity date. This topic is reserved for a more advanced text.

Short-Term Financing through Notes Payable

Objective 6
Account for borrowing money using an interest-bearing note versus a noninterest-bearing note.

A company sometimes needs short-term financing. This situation may occur when (1) the company's cash receipts are delayed because of lenient credit terms granted customers, or (2) the company needs cash to finance the buildup of seasonal inventories, such as before Christmas. To secure short-term financing, companies issue interest-bearing or noninterest-bearing notes.

Interest-Bearing Notes To receive short-term financing, a company may issue an interest-bearing note to a bank. An interest-bearing note specifies the interest rate charged on the principal borrowed. The company receives from the bank the principal borrowed; when the note matures, the company pays the bank the principal plus the interest.

Accounting for an interest-bearing note is simple. For example, assume the company's accounting year ends on December 31. Needham Company issued a $10,000, 90-day, 9% note on December 1, 1996. The following entries would record the loan, the accrual of interest on December 31, 1996, and its payment on March 1, 1997:

1996				
Dec.	1	Cash	10,000	
		Notes Payable		10,000
		To record 90-day bank loan.		
	31	Interest Expense	75	
		Interest Payable		75
		To record accrued interest on a note payable at year-end ($10,000 × 0.09 × 30/360).		
1997				
Mar.	1	Notes Payable	10,000	
		Interest Expense ($10,000 × 0.09 × 60/360)	150	
		Interest Payable	75	
		Cash		10,225
		To record principal and interest paid on bank loan.		

Noninterest-Bearing Notes (Discounting Notes Payable) A company may also issue a noninterest-bearing note to receive short-term financing from a bank. A noninterest-bearing note does not have a stated interest rate applied to the face value of the note. Instead, the note is drawn for a maturity amount less a bank discount; the borrower receives the proceeds. A **bank discount** is the difference between the maturity value of the note and the cash proceeds given to the borrower. The **cash proceeds,** are equal to the maturity amount of a note less the bank discount. This entire process is called **discounting a note payable.** The purpose of this process is to introduce interest into what appears to be a noninterest-bearing note. The meaning of *discounting* here is to deduct interest in advance.

Because interest is related to time, the bank discount is not interest on the date the loan is made; however, it becomes interest expense to the company and interest revenue to the bank as time passes. To illustrate, assume that on December 1, 1996, Needham Company presented its $10,000, 90-day, noninterest-bearing note to the bank, which discounted the note at 9%. The discount is $225 ($\$10,000 \times 0.09 \times 90/360$), and the proceeds to Needham are $9,775. The entry required on the date of the note's issue is:

1996				
Dec.	1	Cash	9,775	
		Discount on Notes Payable	225	
		Notes Payable		10,000
		Issued 90-day note to bank.		

Needham credits Notes Payable for the face value of the note. **Discount on Notes Payable** is a contra account used to reduce Notes Payable from face value to the net amount of the debt. The balance in the Discount on Notes Payable account appears on the balance sheet as a deduction from the balance in the Notes Payable account.

Over time, the discount becomes interest expense. If Needham paid the note before the end of the fiscal year, it would charge the entire $225 discount to Interest Expense and credit Discount on Notes Payable. However, if Needham's fiscal year ended on December 31, an adjusting entry would be required as follows:

1996				
Dec.	31	Interest Expense	75	
		Discount on Notes Payable		75
		To record accrued interest on a note payable at year-end.		

This entry records the interest expense incurred by Needham for the 30 days the note has been outstanding. The expense can be calculated as $\$10,000 \times 0.09 \times 30/360$, or $30/90 \times \$225$. Notice that for entries involving discounted notes payable, no separate Interest Payable account is needed. The Notes Payable account already contains the total liability that will be paid at maturity, $10,000. From the date the proceeds are given to the borrower to the maturity date, the liability grows by reducing the balance in the Discount on Notes Payable contra account. Thus, the current liability section of the December 31, 1996, balance sheet would show:

Current liabilities:		
Notes payable	$10,000	
Less: Discount on notes payable	150	$9,850

When the note is paid at maturity, the entry is:

1997				
Mar.	1	Notes Payable	10,000	
		Interest Expense	150	
		Cash		10,000
		Discount on Notes Payable		150
		To record note payment and interest expense.		

The T-accounts for Discount on Notes Payable and for Interest Expense appear as follows:

ILLUSTRATION 9.3 Comparison between Interest-Bearing Notes and Noninterest-Bearing Notes

Interest-Bearing Notes

Date		Account	Debit	Credit
1996 Dec.	1	Cash	10,000	
		Notes Payable		10,000
		To record 90-day bank loan.		
	31	Interest Expense	75	
		Interest Payable		75
		To record accrued interest on a note payable at year-end.		
1997 Mar.	1	Notes Payable	10,000	
		Interest Expense	150	
		Interest Payable	75	
		Cash		10,225
		To record note principal and interest payment.		

Noninterest-Bearing Notes

Date		Account	Debit	Credit
1996 Dec.	1	Cash	9,775	
		Discount on Notes Payable	225	
		Notes Payable		10,000
		To record 90-day bank loan.		
	31	Interest Expense	75	
		Discount on Notes Payable		75
		To record accrued interest on a note payable at year-end.		
1997 Mar.	1	Notes Payable	10,000	
		Interest Expense	150	
		Cash		10,000
		Discount on Notes Payable		150
		To record note payment and interest expense.		

Discount on Notes Payable

Debit		Credit	
1996 Dec. 1	225	1996 Dec. 31	75
Dec. 31 Balance	150	1997 Mar. 1	150

Interest Expense

Debit		Credit	
1996 Dec. 31	75	1996 Dec. 31 To close	75
1997 Mar. 1	150		

In Illustration 9.3, we compare the journal entries for interest-bearing notes and noninterest-bearing notes used by Needham Company.

ANALYZING AND USING THE FINANCIAL RESULTS—ACCOUNTS RECEIVABLE TURNOVER AND NUMBER OF DAYS' SALES IN ACCOUNTS RECEIVABLE

Objective 7
Analyze and use the financial results—accounts receivable turnover and the number of days' sales in accounts receivable.

Accounts receivable turnover is the number of times per year that the average amount of accounts receivable is collected. To calculate this ratio divide net credit sales, or net sales, by the average net accounts receivable (accounts receivable after deducting the allowance for uncollectible accounts):

$$\text{Accounts receivable turnover} = \frac{\text{Net credit sales (or net sales)}}{\text{Average net accounts receivable}}$$

Ideally, average net accounts receivable should represent weekly or monthly averages; often, however, beginning and end-of-year averages are the only amounts available to users outside the company. Although analysts should use net credit sales, frequently net credit sales are not known to those outside the company. Instead, they use net sales in the numerator.

Generally, the faster firms collect accounts receivable, the better. A company with a high accounts receivable turnover ties up a smaller proportion of its funds in accounts receivable than a company with a low turnover. Both the company's credit terms and collection policies affect turnover. For instance, a company with credit terms of 2/10, n/30 would expect a higher turnover than a company with terms of n/60. Also, a company that aggressively pursues overdue accounts receivable has a higher turnover of accounts receivable than one that does not.

Using their 1992 annual reports, we calculated these accounts receivable turnovers for the following companies:

Borden, Inc., is a worldwide producer of foods, nonfood consumer products, and packaging and industrial products.

Scott Paper Company is the world's leading manufacturer and marketer of sanitary tissue paper products.

Kimberly-Clark manufactures and markets a wide range of paper and lumber products for personal, business, and industrial uses.

Allergan Company is a global provider of specialty therapeutic products, including skin care and eye care products.

American Home Products Corporation is a leader in researching, developing, manufacturing, and marketing health care products worldwide and quality food brands in the U.S. and Canada.

		Accounts Receivable	
Company	**Net Sales**	**Average Net**	**Turnover**
Borden, Inc.	$7,142,600,000	$ 927,450,000	7.70
Scott Paper Company	4,886,200,000	658,500,000	7.42
Kimberly-Clark Corporation	7,091,100,000	733,100,000	9.67
Allergan Company	897,700,000	156,550,000	5.73
American Home Products Corporation	7,873,687,000	1,137,352,000	6.92

We calculate the **number of days' sales in accounts receivable** (also called the *average collection period for accounts receivable*) as follows:

$$\text{Number of days' sales in accounts receivable} = \frac{\text{Number of days in year (365)}}{\text{Accounts receivable turnover}}$$

This ratio measures the average liquidity of accounts receivable and gives an indication of their quality. The faster a firm collects receivables, the more liquid (the closer to being cash) they are and the higher their quality. The longer accounts receivable remain outstanding, the greater the probability they never will be collected. As the time period increases, so does the probability that customers will declare bankruptcy or go out of business.

Based on 365 days, we calculated the number of days' sales for each of these companies in 1992:

	Accounts Receivable	
Company	**Turnover**	**Number of Days' sales in**
Borden, Inc.	7.70	47.4
Scott Paper Company	7.42	49.2
Kimberly-Clark Corporation	9.67	37.7
Allergan Company	5.73	63.7
American Home Products Corporation	6.92	52.7

These companies have collection period ranging from 37.7 to 63.7 days. Undoubtedly, the recession of the early 90s was a factor in slowing the collection period of many companies. Assuming credit terms of 2/10, n/30, one would expect the average collection period to be under 30 days. If customers do not pay within 10 days and take the discount offered, they incur an annual interest rate of 36.5% on these funds. (They lose a 2% discount and get to use the funds another 20 days, which is equivalent to an annual rate of 36.5%.) Possibly, some of these five companies had more lenient discount terms such as 2/20, n/60 or 2/10/EOM, n/60.

Having studied receivables and payables in this chapter, you will study plant assets in the next chapter. These long-term assets include land and depreciable assets such as buildings, machinery, and equipment.

Understanding the Learning Objectives

Objective 1
Account for uncollectible accounts receivable under the allowance method.

- Companies use two methods to account for uncollectible accounts receivable: the allowance method, which provides in advance for uncollectible accounts; and the direct write-off method, which recognizes uncollectible accounts as an expense when judged uncollectible. The allowance method is the preferred method and is the only method discussed and illustrated in this text.
- The two basic methods for estimating uncollectible accounts under the allowance method are the percentage-of-sales method and the percentage-of-receivables method.

- The percentage-of-sales method focuses attention on the income statement and the relationship of uncollectible accounts to sales. The debit to Uncollectible Accounts Expense is a certain percent of credit sales or total net sales.
- The percentage-of-receivables method focuses attention on the balance sheet and the relationship of the allowance for uncollectible accounts to accounts receivable. The credit to the Allowance for Uncollectible Accounts is the amount necessary to bring that account up to a certain percentage of the Accounts Receivable balance. Either one overall percentage or an aging schedule may be used.

Objective 2
Record credit card sales and collections.

- Credit cards are charge cards used by customers to charge purchases of goods and services. These cards are of two types—nonbank credit cards (such as American Express) and bank credit cards (such as VISA).
- The sale is recorded at the gross amount of the sale, and the cash or receivable is recorded at the net amount the company will receive.

Objective 3
Define liabilities, current liabilities, and long-term liabilities.

- Liabilities result from some past transaction and are obligations to pay cash, provide services, or deliver goods at some time in the future.
- Current liabilities are obligations that (1) are payable within one year or one operating cycle, whichever is longer, or (2) will be paid out of current assets or create other current liabilities.
- Long-term liabilities are obligations that do not qualify as current liabilities.

Objective 4
Define and account for clearly determinable, estimated, and contingent liabilities.

- Clearly determinable liabilities are those for which the existence of the liability and its amount are certain. An example is accounts payable.
- Estimated liabilities are those for which the existence of the liability is certain, but its amount can only be estimated. An example is estimated product warranty payable.
- Contingent liabilities are those for which the existence, and usually the amount, are uncertain because these liabilities depend (or are contingent) on some future event occurring or not occurring. An example is a liability arising from a lawsuit.

Objective 5
Account for notes receivable and payable, including calculation of interest.

- A promissory note is an unconditional written promise by a borrower (maker) to pay the lender (payee) or someone else who legally acquired the note a certain sum of money on demand or at a definite time.
- Interest is the fee charged for the use of money through time. Interest = Principal × Rate of interest × Time.

Objective 6
Account for borrowing money using an interest-bearing note versus a noninterest-bearing note.

- Companies sometimes need short-term financing. Short-term financing may be secured by issuing interest-bearing notes or by issuing noninterest-bearing notes.
- An interest-bearing note specifies the interest rate that will be charged on the principal borrowed.
- A noninterest-bearing note does not have a stated interest rate applied to the face value of the note.

Objective 7
Analyze and use the financial results—accounts receivable turnover and the number of days' sales in accounts receivable.

- Calculate accounts receivable turnover by dividing net credit sales, or net sales, by average net accounts receivable.
- Calculate the number of days' sales in accounts receivable (or average collection period) by dividing the number of days in the year by the accounts receivable turnover.
- Together, these ratios show the liquidity of accounts receivable and give some indication of their quality. Generally, the higher the accounts receivable turnover, the better; and the shorter the average collection period, the better.

Demonstration Problem 9–A

a. Prepare the journal entries for the following transactions:

1. As of the end of 1997, Post Company estimates its uncollectible accounts expense to be 1% of sales. Sales in 1997 were $1,125,000.
2. On January 15, 1998, the company decided that the account for John Nunn in the amount of $750 was uncollectible.
3. On February 12, 1998, John Nunn's check for $750 arrived.

b. Prepare the journal entries in the records of Lyle Company for the following:
   1. On June 15, 1997, Lyle Company received a $22,500, 90-day, 12% note dated June 15, 1997, from Stone Company in payment of its account.
   2. Assume that Stone Company did not pay the note at maturity. Lyle Company decided that the note was uncollectible.

Solution to Demonstration Problem 9–A

a.

1.	1997 Dec.	31	Uncollectible Accounts Expense	11,250	
			Allowance for Uncollectible Accounts		11,250
			To record estimated uncollectible accounts for the year.		
2.	1998 Jan.	15	Allowance for Uncollectible Accounts	750	
			Accounts Receivable—John Nunn		750
			To write off the account of John Nunn as uncollectible.		
3.	Feb.	12	Accounts Receivable—John Nunn	750	
			Allowance for Uncollectible Accounts		750
			To correct the write-off of John Nunn's account on January 15.		
		12	Cash	750	
			Accounts Receivable—John Nunn		750
			To record the collection of John Nunn's account receivable.		

b.

1.	1997 June	15	Notes Receivable	22,500	
			Accounts Receivable—Stone Company		22,500
			To record receipt of a note from Stone Company.		
2.	Sept.	13	Accounts Receivable—Stone Company	23,175	
			Notes Receivable		22,500
			Interest Revenue		675
			To record the default of the Stone Company note of $22,500. Interest revenue was $675.		
		13	Allowance for Uncollectible Accounts*	23,175	
			Accounts Receivable—Stone Company		23,175
			To write off the Stone Company note as uncollectible.		

*This debit assumes that Notes Receivable were taken into consideration when an allowance was established. If not, the debit should be to Loss from Dishonored Notes Receivable.

Demonstration Problem 9–B

a. Prepare the entries on the books of Cromwell Company assuming the company borrowed $10,000 at 7% from First National Bank and signed a 60-day noninterest-bearing note payable on December 1, 1996, accrued interest on December 31, 1996, and paid the debt on the maturity date.

b. Prepare the entries on the books of Cromwell Company assuming it purchased equipment from Jones Company for $5,000 and signed a 30-day, 9% interest-bearing note payable on February 24, 1997. Cromwell paid the note on its maturity date.

SOLUTION TO DEMONSTRATION PROBLEM 9–B

a.

Date		Account	Debit	Credit
1996				
Dec.	1	Cash	9,883.33	
		Bank Discount ($10,000 × 0.07 × 60⁄360)	116.67	
		Notes Payable		10,000.00
	31	Interest Expense	58.33	
		Bank Discount		58.33
		($10,000 × 0.07 × 30⁄360)		
1997				
Jan.	30	Notes Payable	10,000.00	
		Interest Expense	58.33	
		Bank Discount		58.33
		Cash		10,000.00

b.

Date		Account	Debit	Credit
1997				
Feb.	24	Purchases	5,000.00	
		Notes Payable		5,000.00
Mar.	26	Notes Payable	5,000.00	
		Interest Expense	37.50	
		Cash		5,037.50
		($5,000 × 0.09 × 30⁄360) = $37.50		

NEW TERMS

Accounts receivable turnover Net credit sales (or net sales) divided by average net accounts receivable. *351*

Aging schedule A means of classifying accounts receivable according to their age; used to determine the necessary balance in an Allowance for Uncollectible Accounts. A different uncollectibility percentage rate is used for each age category. *335*

Allowance for Uncollectible Accounts A contra-asset account to the Accounts Receivable account; it reduces accounts receivable to their net realizable value. Also called *Allowance for Doubtful Accounts* or *Allowance for Bad Debts*. *332*

Bad debts expense See Uncollectible accounts expense.

Bank discount The difference between the maturity value of a note and the actual amount—the note's proceeds—given to the borrower. *349*

Cash proceeds The maturity amount of a note less the bank discount. *349*

Clearly determinable liabilities Liabilities for which both their existence and amount are certain. Examples include accounts payable, notes payable, interest payable, unearned delivery fees, wages payable, sales tax payable, federal excise tax payable, current portions of long-term debt, and various payroll liabilities. *339*

Contingent liabilities Liabilities for which their existence is uncertain. Their amount is also usually uncertain. Both their existence and amount depend on some future event occurring or not occurring. Examples include liabilities arising from lawsuits, discounted notes receivable, income tax disputes, penalties that may be assessed because of some past action, and failure of another party to pay a debt that a company has guaranteed. *340*

Credit Card Expense account Used to record credit card agency's service charges for services rendered in processing credit card sales. *338*

Credit cards Nonbank charge cards (American Express and Diners Club) and bank charge cards (VISA and MasterCard) that customers use to charge their purchases of goods and services. *338*

Current liabilities Obligations that (1) are payable within one year or one operating cycle, whichever is longer, or (2) will be paid out of current assets or result in the creation of other current liabilities. *339*

Discount on Notes Payable A contra account used to reduce Notes Payable from face value to the net amount of the debt. *350*

Discounting a note payable The act of borrowing on a noninterest-bearing note drawn for a maturity amount, from which a bank discount is deducted, and the proceeds are given to the borrower. *349*

Dishonored note A note that the maker failed to pay at maturity. *346*

Estimated liabilities Liabilities for which their existence is certain, but their amount can only be estimated. An example is estimated product warranty payable. *339*

Interest The fee charged for use of money over a period of time ($I = P \times R \times T$). *344*

Interest Payable account An account showing the interest expense incurred but not yet paid; reported as a current liability in the balance sheet. *349*

Interest Receivable account An account showing the interest earned but not yet collected; reported as a current asset in the balance sheet. *348*

Liabilities Obligations that result from some past transaction and are obligations to pay cash, perform services, or deliver goods at some time in the future. *339*

Long-term liabilities Obligations that do not qualify as current liabilities. *339*

Maker (of a note) The party who prepares a note and is responsible for paying the note at maturity. *344*

Maturity date The date on which a note becomes due and must be paid. *345*

Maturity value The amount that the maker must pay on the note on its maturity date. *346*

Net realizable value The amount the company expects to collect from accounts receivable. *332*

Number of days' sales in accounts receivable The number of days in a year (365) divided by the accounts receivable turnover. *352*

Operating cycle The time it takes to start with cash, buy necessary items to produce revenues (such as materials, supplies, labor, and/or finished goods), sell goods or services, and receive cash by collecting the resulting receivables. *339*

Payable Any sum of money due to be paid by a company to any party for any reason. *330*

Payee (of a note) The party who receives a note and will be paid cash at maturity. *344*

Percentage-of-receivables method A method for determining the desired size of the Allowance for Uncollectible Accounts by basing the calculation on the Accounts Receivable balance at the end of the period. *334*

Percentage-of-sales method A method of estimating the uncollectible accounts from the sales of a given period's total net credit sales or net sales. *332*

Principal (of a note) The face value of a note. *345*

Promissory note An unconditional written promise by a borrower (maker) to pay a definite sum of money to the lender (payee) on demand or at a specific date. *344*

Rate (of a note) The stated interest rate on the note. *345*

Receivable Any sum of money due to be paid to a company from any party for any reason. *330*

Time (of a note) The amount of time the note is to run; can be expressed in days, months, or years. *345*

Trade receivables Amounts customers owe a company for goods sold or services rendered on account. Also called *accounts receivable* or *trade accounts receivable*. *331*

Uncollectible accounts expense An operating expense that a business incurs when it sells on credit; also called *doubtful accounts expense* or *bad debts expense*. *331*

Self Test

True-False

Indicate whether each of the following statements is true or false.

1. The percentage-of-sales method estimates the uncollectible accounts from the ending balance in Accounts Receivable.
2. Under the allowance method, uncollectible accounts expense is recognized when a specific customer's account is written off.
3. Bank credit card sales are treated as cash sales because the receipt of cash is certain.
4. Liabilities result from some future transaction.
5. Current liabilities are classified as clearly determinable, estimated, and contingent.
6. A dishonored note is removed from Notes Receivable, and the total amount due is recorded in Accounts Receivable.
7. When an interest-bearing note is given to a bank when taking out a loan, the difference between the cash proceeds and the maturity amount is debited to Discount on Notes Payable.

Multiple-Choice

Select the best answer for each of the following questions.

1. Which of the following statements is false?
   - **a.** Any existing balance in the Allowance for Uncollectible Accounts is ignored in calculating the uncollectible accounts expense under the percentage-of-sales method except that the allowance account must have a credit balance after adjustment.
   - **b.** The percentage-of-receivables method may use either an overall rate or a different rate for each age category.
   - **c.** The Allowance for Uncollectible Accounts reduces accounts receivable to their net realizable value.
   - **d.** A write-off of an account reduces the net amount shown for accounts receivable on the balance sheet.
   - **e.** None of the above.
2. Hunt Company estimates uncollectible accounts using the percentage-of-receivables method and expects that 5% of outstanding receivables will be uncollectible for 1997. The balance in Accounts Receivable is $200,000, and the allowance account has a $3,000 credit balance before adjustment at year-end. The uncollectible accounts expense for 1997 will be:

a. $7,000.
b. $10,000.
c. $13,000.
d. $9,850.
e. None of the above.

3. Which type of company typically has the longest operating cycle?
   a. Service company.
   b. Merchandising company.
   c. Manufacturing company.
   d. All equal.
4. Maxwell Company records its sales taxes in the same account as sales revenues. The sales tax rate is 6%. At the end of the current period, the Sales account has a balance of $265,000. The amount of sales tax payable is:
   a. $12,000.
   b. $15,000.
   c. $15,900.
   d. $18,000.
5. Dawson Company sells fax machines. During 1997, the company sold 2,000 fax machines. The company estimates that 5% of the machines require repairs under warranty. To date, 30 machines have been repaired. The estimated average cost of warranty repairs per defective fax machine is $200. The required amount of the adjusting entry to record estimated product warranty payable is:
   a. $400,000.
   b. $6,000.
   c. $14,000.
   d. $–0–.
6. To compute interest on a promissory note, all of the following elements must be known except:
   a. The face value of the note.
   b. The stated interest rate.
   c. The name of the payee.
   d. The life of the note.
   e. None of the above.
7. Keats Company issued its own $10,000, 90-day, noninterest-bearing note to a bank. If the note is discounted at 10%, the proceeds to Keats are:
   a. $10,000.
   b. $9,000.
   c. $9,750.
   d. $10,250.
   e. None of the above.

Now turn to page 363 to check your answers.

Questions

1. In view of the difficulty in estimating future events, would you recommend that accountants wait until collections are made from customers before recording sales revenue? Should they wait until known accounts prove to be uncollectible before charging an expense account?
2. The credit manager of a company has established a policy of seeking to completely eliminate all losses from uncollectible accounts. Is this policy a desirable objective for a company? Explain.
3. What are the two major purposes of establishing an allowance for uncollectible accounts?
4. In view of the fact that it is impossible to estimate the exact amount of uncollectible accounts receivable for any one year in advance, what exactly does the Allowance for Uncollectible Accounts account contain after a number of years?
5. What must be considered before adjusting the allowance for uncollectible accounts under the percentage-of-receivables method?
6. How might information in an aging schedule prove useful to management for purposes other than estimating the size of the required allowance for uncollectible accounts?
7. For a company using the allowance method of accounting for uncollectible accounts, which of the following directly affects its reported net income: (1) the establishment of the allowance, (2) the writing off of a specific account, or (3) the recovery of an account previously written off as uncollectible?
8. Why might a retailer agree to sell by credit card when such a substantial discount is taken by the credit card agency in paying the retailer?
9. Define liabilities, current liabilities, and long-term liabilities.
10. What is an operating cycle? Which type of company is likely to have the shortest operating cycle, and which is likely to have the longest operating cycle? Why?
11. Describe the differences between clearly determinable, estimated, and contingent liabilities. Give one or more examples of each type.
12. In what instances might a company acquire notes receivable?
13. How is the maturity value of a note calculated?
14. What is a dishonored note receivable and how is it reported in the balance sheet?
15. Under what circumstances does the account Discount on Notes Payable arise? How is it reported in the financial statements? Explain why.
16. **Real World Question** Refer to "A Broader Perspective" on page 337. What factors are taken into account by the General Electric Company in determining the adjusting entry to establish the desired balance in the Allowance for Uncollectible Accounts?
17. **Real World Question** Refer to "A Broader Perspective" on page 337. Explain how the General Electric Company writes off uncollectible accounts.
18. **Real World Question** Refer to the annual reports of The Coca-Cola Company and Maytag Corporation in the annual report booklet. Determine the percentage of accounts receivable on December 31, 1993, that each of the companies estimates will be uncollectible (round to the nearest whole percent).

Exercises

Exercise 9–1
Prepare journal entries to record uncollectible accounts expense (L.O. 1)

The accounts of Rogers Company as of December 31, 1997, show Accounts Receivable, $170,000; Allowance for Uncollectible Accounts, $950 (credit balance); Sales, $985,000; and Sales Returns and Allowances, $12,000. Prepare journal entries to adjust for possible uncollectible accounts under each of the following assumptions:

a. Uncollectible accounts are estimated at 1% of net sales.

b. The allowance is to be increased to 3% of accounts receivable.

Exercise 9–2
Use aging schedule to estimate Allowance for Uncollectible Accounts (L.O. 1)

Compute the required balance of the Allowance for Uncollectible Accounts for the following receivables:

Accounts Receivable	Age (months)	Probability of Collection
$165,000.	Less than 1	95%
90,000.	1–3	85
39,000.	3–6	75
12,000.	6–9	35
2,250.	9–12	10

Exercise 9–3
Record write-off and subsequent recovery of account (L.O. 1)

On April 1, 1996, Kester Company, which uses the allowance method of accounting for uncollectible accounts, wrote off Bob Dyer's $200 account. On December 14, 1996, the company received a check in that amount from Dyer marked "in full payment of account." Prepare the necessary entries.

Exercise 9–4
Record use of nonbank and bank credit cards (L.O. 2)

Furniture Mart, Inc., sold $120,000 of furniture in May to customers who used their Carte Blanche credit cards. Such sales are subject to a 3% discount by Carte Blanche (a nonbank credit card),

a. Prepare journal entries to record the sales and the subsequent receipt of cash from the credit card company.

b. Do the same as requirement **a,** but assume the credit cards used were VISA cards (a bank credit card).

Exercise 9–5
Determine sales revenue and sales tax payable (L.O. 4)

Discount Toys, Inc., sells merchandise in a state that has a 5% sales tax. Rather than record sales taxes collected in a separate account, the company records both the sales revenue and the sales taxes in the Sales account. At the end of the first quarter of operations, when it is time to remit the sales taxes to the state taxing agency, the company has $493,500 in the Sales account. Determine the correct amount of sales revenue and the amount of sales tax payable.

Exercise 9–6
Answer questions regarding note in financial statements (L.O. 3, 4)

Assume the following note appeared in the annual report of a company:

> In 1994, two small retail customers filed separate suits against the company alleging misrepresentation, breach of contract, conspiracy to violate federal laws, and state antitrust violations arising out of their purchase of retail grocery stores through the company from a third party. Damages sought range up to $10 million in each suit for actual and treble damages and punitive damages of $2 million in one suit and $10 million in the other. The company is vigorously defending the actions and management believes there will be no adverse financial effect.

What kind of liability is being reported? Why is it classified this way? Do you think it is possible to calculate a dollar amount for this obligation? How much would the company have to pay if it lost the suit and had to pay the full amount?

Exercise 9–7
Determine maturity dates on several notes (L.O. 5)

Determine the maturity date for each of the following notes:

Issue Date	Life
January 13, 1997	30 days
January 31, 1997	90 days
June 4, 1997	1 year
December 2, 1997	1 month

Exercise 9–8
Prepare entries for a note (L.O. 5)

Candler, Inc., gave a $60,000, 120-day, 12% note to Daley, Inc., in exchange for merchandise. Candler uses periodic inventory procedure. Prepare journal entries to record the issuance of the note and the entries needed at maturity for both parties, assuming payment is made.

Exercise 9–9
Prepare entries when maker defaults (L.O. 5)

Based on the facts in the previous exercise, prepare the entries that Candler, Inc., and Daley, Inc., would make at the maturity date, assuming Candler defaults.

Exercise 9–10
Prepare entries for noninterest-bearing note and interest-bearing note (L.O. 6)

Bob Kelley is negotiating a bank loan for his company, Kelley, Inc., of $8,000 for 90 days. The bank's current interest rate is 10%. Prepare Kelley's entries to record the loan under each of the following assumptions:

a. Kelley signs a note for $8,000. Interest is deducted in calculating the proceeds turned over to him.

b. Kelley signs a note for $8,000 and receives that amount. Interest is to be paid at maturity.

Exercise 9–11
Prepare entries at maturity date (L.O. 6)

Based on the previous exercise, prepare the entry or entries that would be made at maturity date for each alternative, assuming the loan is paid before the end of the accounting period.

Exercise 9–12
Calculate the accounts receivable turnover and the number of days' sales in accounts receivable for Baker Hughes Incorporated (L.O. 7)

Baker Hughes Incorporated provides products and services to the petroleum and continuous process industries. Its fiscal year ends on September 30. The following amounts were included in its 1993 Annual Report:

Net sales	$2,701,697,000
Net Accounts Receivable, 9/30/93	$ 619,953,000
Net Accounts Receivable, 9/30/92	$ 632,726,000

Calculate the accounts receivable turnover and the number of days' sales in accounts receivable. Use net sales instead of net credit sales in the calculation. Comment on the results.

PROBLEMS

Problem 9–1
Write off uncollectible account, record expense under alternative methods of estimation (L.O. 1)

As of December 31, 1996, Birmingham Company's accounts prior to adjustment show:

Accounts receivable	$ 21,000
Allowance for uncollectible accounts (credit balance)	750
Sales	225,000

Birmingham Company estimates uncollectible accounts at 1% of sales.

On February 23, 1997, the account of Dan Hall in the amount of $300 was considered uncollectible and written off. On August 12, 1997, Hall remitted $200 and indicated that he intends to pay the balance due as soon as possible. By December 31, 1997, no further remittance had been received from Hall and no further remittance was expected.

Required

a. Prepare journal entries to record all of these transactions and adjusting entries.

b. Give the entry necessary as of December 31, 1997, if Birmingham Company estimated its uncollectible accounts at 8% of outstanding receivables rather than at 1% of sales.

Problem 9–2
Record use of bank and nonbank credit cards (L.O. 2)

At the close of business, Joe's Restaurant had credit card sales of $14,000. Of this amount, $6,000 were VISA (bank credit card) sales invoices, which can be deposited in a bank for immediate credit, less a discount of 3%. The balance of $8,000 consisted of American Express (nonbank credit card) charges, subject to a 5% service charge. These invoices were mailed to American Express. Shortly thereafter, a check was received.

Required

Prepare journal entries for all these transactions.

Problem 9–3
Prepare journal entries for sales and excise taxes (L.O. 4)

Lopez Company sells merchandise in a state that has a 5% sales tax. On January 2, 1997, Lopez sold goods with a sales price of $80,000 on credit. Sales taxes collected are recorded in a separate account. Assume that sales for the entire month were $700,000. On January 31, 1997, the company remitted the sales taxes collected to the state taxing agency.

Required

a. Prepare the general journal entries to record the January 2 sales revenue. Also prepare the entry to show the remittance of the taxes on January 31.

b. Now assume that the merchandise sold on January 2 also is subject to federal excise taxes of 12%. The federal excise taxes collected are remitted to the proper agency on January 31. Show the entries on January 2 and January 31.

Problem 9–4
Prepare journal entries for product warranty (L.O. 4)

Honest Ed's Auto Company sells used cars and warrants all parts for one year. The average price per car is $10,000, and the company sold 800 in 1996. The company expects 30% of the cars to develop defective parts within one year of sale. The estimated average cost of warranty repairs per defective car is $600. By the end of the year, 80 cars sold that year had been returned and repaired under warranty. On January 4, 1997, a customer returned a car purchased in 1996 for repairs under warranty. The repairs were made on January 8. The cost of the repairs included parts, $400, and labor, $210.

Required

a. Calculate the amount of the estimated product warranty payable.

b. Prepare the entry to record the estimated product warranty payable on December 31, 1996.

c. Prepare the entry to record the repairs made on January 8, 1997.

Problem 9–5
Prepare entries to record a number of note transactions, adjusting entries for interest, and entries for payment of notes (L.O. 5)

Bemus Point Boat Company is in the power boat manufacturing business. As of September 1, the balance in its Notes Receivable account is $192,000. The balance in Dishonored Notes Receivable is $60,660. A schedule of the notes (including the dishonored note) is as follows:

Face Amount	Maker	Date of Note	Life	Interest Rate	Comments
$120,000	C. Glass Co.	6/1/96	120 days	12%	
72,000	A. Lamp Co.	6/15/96	90	8	
84,000	C. Wall Co.	7/1/96	90	10	
60,000	N. Case Co.	7/1/96	60	6	Dishonored, interest, $600; protest fee, $60.
$336,000					

Following are Bemus Point Boat Company's transactions for September:

Sept. 10 Received $36,660 from N. Case Company as full settlement of the amount due from it. The company does not charge losses on notes to the Allowance for Uncollectible Accounts account.

? The A. Lamp Company note was collected when due.

? The C. Glass Company note was not paid at maturity.

? C. Wall Company paid its note at maturity.

30 Received a new 60-day, 12% note from C. Glass Company for the total balance due on the dishonored note. The note was dated as of the maturity date of the dishonored note. Bemus Point Company accepted the note in good faith.

Required Prepare dated journal entries for these transactions.

Problem 9–6
Account for discounted note payable (L.O. 6)

Discount Office Equipment, Inc., discounted its own $60,000, noninterest-bearing, 180-day note on November 16, 1996, at Niagara County Bank at a discount rate of 12%.

Required Prepare dated journal entries for:

a. The original discounting on November 16.

b. The adjustment required at the end of the company's calendar-year accounting period.

c. Payment at maturity.

ALTERNATE PROBLEMS

Problem 9–1A
Write off uncollectible account, record expense under alternative methods of estimation (L.O. 1)

The following selected accounts are for Kennestone, Inc., a name brand shoe wholesale store, as of December 31, 1996. Prior to closing the accounts and making allowance for uncollectible accounts entries, the $4,500 account of Morgan Company is to be written off (this was a credit sale of February 12, 1996).

Accounts receivable	$ 360,000
Allowance for uncollectible accounts (credit)	6,000
Sales	1,680,000
Sales returns and allowances	30,000

Required

a. Prepare journal entries to record all of these transactions and the uncollectible accounts expense for the period. Assume the estimated expense is 2% of net sales.

b. Give the entry to record the estimated expense for the period if the allowance account is to be adjusted to 5% of outstanding receivables instead of as in **a.**

Problem 9–2A
Record use of bank and nonbank credit cards (L.O. 2)

The cash register at Pete's Restaurant at the close of business showed cash sales of $5,400 and credit card sales of $10,000 ($6,000 VISA and $4,000 American Express). The VISA (bank credit card) invoices were discounted 5% when they were deposited. The American Express (nonbank credit card) charges were mailed to the company and were subject to a 5% service charge. A few days later, Pete received a check for the net amount of the American Express credit card charges.

Required

Prepare journal entries for all of these transactions.

Problem 9–3A
Prepare journal entries for sales and excise taxes (L.O. 4)

Quality Hardware, Inc. sells merchandise in a state that has a 6% sales tax. On July 1, 1997, it sold goods with a sales price of $30,000 on credit. Sales taxes collected are recorded in a separate account. Assume that sales for the entire month were $400,000. On July 31, 1997, the company remitted the sales taxes collected to the state taxing agency.

Required

a. Prepare the general journal entries to record the July 1 sales revenue and sales tax payable. Also prepare the entry to show the remittance of the taxes on July 31.

b. Now assume that the merchandise sold also is subject to federal excise taxes of 10% in addition to the 6% sales tax. Quality remitted the federal excise taxes collected to the proper agency on July 31. Show the entries on July 1 and July 31.

Problem 9–4A
Prepare journal entries for product warranty (L.O. 4)

Speed Wheels, Inc., sells racing bicycles and warrants all parts for one year. The average price per bicycle is $450, and the company sold 4,000 in 1996. The company expects 20% of the bicycles to develop defective parts within one year of sale. The estimated average cost of warranty repairs per defective bicycle is $30. By the end of the year, 500 bicycles sold that year had been returned and repaired under warranty. On January 2, 1997, a customer returned a bicycle purchased in 1996 for repairs under warranty. The repairs were made on January 3. The cost of the repairs included parts, $25, and labor, $15.

Required

a. Calculate the amount of the estimated product warranty payable.

b. Prepare the entry to record the estimated product warranty payable on December 31, 1996.

c. Prepare the entry to record the repairs made on January 3, 1997.

Problem 9–5A
Prepare entries to record a number of note transactions, discounting of a note payable, adjusting entries for interest, and payment of notes (L.O. 5, 6)

Hayes Commercial Properties, Inc., has an accounting period of one year, ending on July 31. On July 1, 1996, the balances of certain ledger accounts are Notes Receivable, $654,000; and Notes Payable, $900,000. A schedule of the notes receivable is as follows:

Face Amount	Maker	Date of Note	Life	Interest Rate
$270,000	Parker Co.	5/15/96	60 days	12%
120,000	Dot Co.	5/31/96	60	12
264,000	Fixx Co.	6/15/96	30	10
$654,000				

The note payable is a 60-day bank loan dated May 20, 1996. Notes Payable—Discount was debited for the discount of $6,000. Following are the company's transactions during July:

July 1 Hayes Commercial Properties, Inc., discounted its own $180,000, 60-day, noninterest-bearing note at Key Bank. The discount rate is 10%, and the note was dated today.

3 Received a 20-day, 12% note, dated today, from Sox Company in settlement of an account receivable of $36,000.

6 Purchased merchandise from Link Company, $288,000, and issued a 60-day, 12% note, dated today, for the purchase.

July 8 Sold merchandise to Fan Company, $360,000. A 30-day, 12% note, dated today, is received to cover the sale.

14 Received payment on the Parker Company note dated June 15, 1996.

15 Fixx Company sent a $120,000, 30-day, 12% note, dated today, and a check to cover the part of the old note not covered by the new note, *plus* all interest expense incurred on the prior note.

19 The note payable dated May 20, 1996, was paid in full.

23 Sox Company dishonored its note of July 3 and sent a check for the interest on the dishonored note and a new 30-day, 12% note dated July 23, 1996.

30 The Dot Company note dated May 31, 1996, was paid with interest in full.

Required Prepare dated journal entries for these transactions and necessary July 31 adjusting entries.

Problem 9–6A
Account for discounted note payable (L.O. 6)

On November 1, 1996, Gulf Coast Property Management, Inc., discounted its own $75,000, 180-day, noninterest-bearing note at its bank at 18%. The note was paid on its maturity date. The company uses a calendar-year accounting period.

Required Prepare dated journal entries to record *(a)* the discounting of the note, *(b)* the year-end adjustment, and *(c)* the payment of the note.

Beyond the Numbers—Critical Thinking

Business Decision Case 9–1
Compare costs of maintaining own accounts receivable with costs of allowing the use of credit cards; identify other factors to consider (L.O. 1, 3)

Susan Ivancevich owns a hardware store; she sells items for cash and on account. During 1996, which seemed to be a typical year, some of her company's operating data and other data were as follows:

Sales:	
For cash	$1,200,000
On credit	2,400,000
Cost of obtaining credit reports on customers	3,600
Cost incurred in paying a part-time bookkeeper to keep the accounts receivable subsidiary ledger up to date	12,000
Cost associated with preparing and mailing invoices to customers and other collection activities	18,000
Uncollectible accounts expense	45,000
Average outstanding accounts receivable balance (on which Ivancevich estimates she could have earned 10% if it had been invested in other assets)	180,000

A national credit card agency has tried to convince Ivancevich that instead of carrying her own accounts receivable, she should accept only the agency's credit card for sales on credit. The agency would pay her two days after she submits sales charges, deducting 6% from the amount and paying her 94%.

Required

a. Using the data given, prepare an analysis showing whether or not Ivancevich would benefit from switching to the credit card method of selling on credit.

b. What other factors should she take into consideration?

Business Decision Case 9–2
Evaluate alternative means of making sales (L.O. 3, 4)

John Adams operates a large fruit and vegetable stand on the outskirts of a city. In a typical year he sells $800,000 of goods to regular customers. His sales are 40% for cash and 60% on credit. He carries all of the credit himself. Only after a customer has a $300 unpaid balance on which no payments have been made for two months does he refuse that customer credit for future purchases. His income before taxes is approximately $95,000. The total of uncollectible accounts for a given year is about 10% of credit sales, or $48,000.

You are one of Adams' regular customers. He knows that you are taking a college course in accounting and has asked you to tell him your opinion of several alternatives recommended to him to reduce or eliminate the $48,000 per year uncollectible accounts expense. The alternatives are as follows:

1. Do not sell on credit.
2. Sell on credit by national credit card only.
3. Allow customers to charge only until their account balances reach $50.
4. Allow a bill collector to go after uncollectible accounts and keep half of the amount collected.

Required

Write a report for Adams about the advisability of following any of these alternatives.

Annual Report Analysis 9–3
Calculate accounts receivable turnover and the number of days' sales in accounts receivable for four real companies and comment on the results (L.O. 7)

Refer to the annual reports of The Coca-Cola Company, Maytag Corporation, The Limited, Inc., and John H. Harland Company in the annual report booklet. For the most recent year shown, calculate accounts receivable turnover and the number of days' sales in accounts receivable for each company and prepare a written comment on the results.

Group Project 9–4
Write paper on a specific topic

In groups of two or three students, write a two-page, double-spaced paper on one of the following topics:

Which is better—the percentage-of-sales method or the percentage-of-receivables method?

Why not eliminate bad debts by selling only for cash?

Why allow customers to use credit cards when credit card expense is so high?

Should banks be required to use 365 days instead of 360 days in interest calculations?

Present your analysis in a convincing manner, without spelling or grammatical errors. This paper should be the result of several drafts and neatly prepared using word processing software. If a computer is not available, type this paper. Include a cover page with the title and authors' names.

Answers to Self Test

True-False

1. **False.** The percentage-of-sales method estimates the uncollectible accounts from the net credit sales or net sales of a given period.
2. **False.** Uncollectible accounts expense is recognized at the end of the accounting period in an adjusting entry.
3. **True.** The retailer deposits the credit card invoices directly in a special checking account.
4. **False.** Liabilities result from a past transaction.
5. **True.** Current liabilities are classified into those three categories.
6. **True.** The note has passed its maturity date and should be removed from the Notes Receivable account. The maturity value plus any protest fee should be debited to Accounts Receivable.
7. **False.** Discount on Notes Payable is recorded when a noninterest-bearing note is issued.

Multiple-Choice

1. **d.** A write-off of an account receivable results in a debit to Allowance for Uncollectible Accounts and a credit to Accounts Receivable for the same amount. The net amount (accounts receivable minus allowance for uncollectible accounts) does not change.
2. **a.** The uncollectible accounts expense for 1997 is computed as follows:

Allowance balance after adjustment ($200,000 × 0.05)	$10,000
Balance before adjustment	(3,000)
Uncollectible accounts expense	$ 7,000

3. **c.** Manufacturing companies tend to have the longest operating cycle. They must invest cash in raw materials, convert these raw materials into work in process and then finished goods, sell the items on account, and then collect the accounts receivable.
4. **b.** $265,000 divided by 1.06 = $250,000; $265,000 − $250,000 = $15,000.
5. **c.** 2,000 × 5% = 100 machines expected to be defective. 100 − 30 already returned = 70 more expected to be returned. 70 × $200 = $14,000 estimated product warranty payable.
6. **c.** The name of the payee is not needed to compute interest expense on a promissory note.
7. **c.** The proceeds from a bank are computed as follows:

$$\text{Discount amount} = \$10{,}000 \times 0.10 \times 90/360 = \$250$$

$$\text{Proceeds} = \$10{,}000 - \$250 = \$9{,}750$$

10

Property, Plant, and Equipment

Learning Objectives

After studying this chapter, you should be able to:

1. List the characteristics of plant assets and identify the costs of acquiring plant assets.
2. List the four major factors affecting depreciation expense.
3. Describe the various methods of calculating depreciation expense.
4. Distinguish between capital and revenue expenditures for plant assets.

(continued)

On a classified balance sheet, the asset section contains: (1) current assets; (2) property, plant, and equipment; and (3) other categories such as intangible assets and long-term investments. Previous chapters discussed current assets. This chapter begins a discussion of property, plant, and equipment that is concluded in Chapter 11. Property, plant, and equipment are often called **plant and equipment** or simply *plant assets*. Plant assets are long-lived assets because they are expected to last for more than one year. Long-lived assets consist of tangible assets and intangible assets. **Tangible assets** have physical characteristics that we can see and touch; they include plant assets such as buildings and furniture, and natural resources such as gas and oil. *Intangible assets* have no physical characteristics that we can see and touch but represent exclusive privileges and rights to their owners.

Nature of Plant Assets

To be classified as a *plant asset,* an asset must: (1) be tangible, that is, capable of being seen and touched; (2) have a useful service life of more than one year; and (3) be used in business operations rather than held for resale. Common plant assets are buildings, machines, tools, and office equipment. On the balance sheet, these assets appear under the heading ''Property, plant, and equipment.''

Plant assets include all long-lived tangible assets used to generate the principal revenues of the business. Inventory is a tangible asset but not a plant asset because inventory is usually not long-lived and it is held for sale rather than for use. What represents a plant asset to one company may be inventory to another. For example, a business such as a retail appliance store may classify a delivery truck as a plant asset because the truck is used to deliver merchandise. A business such as a truck dealership would classify the same delivery truck as inventory because the truck is held for sale. Also, land held for speculation or not yet put into service is a long-term investment rather than a plant asset because the land is

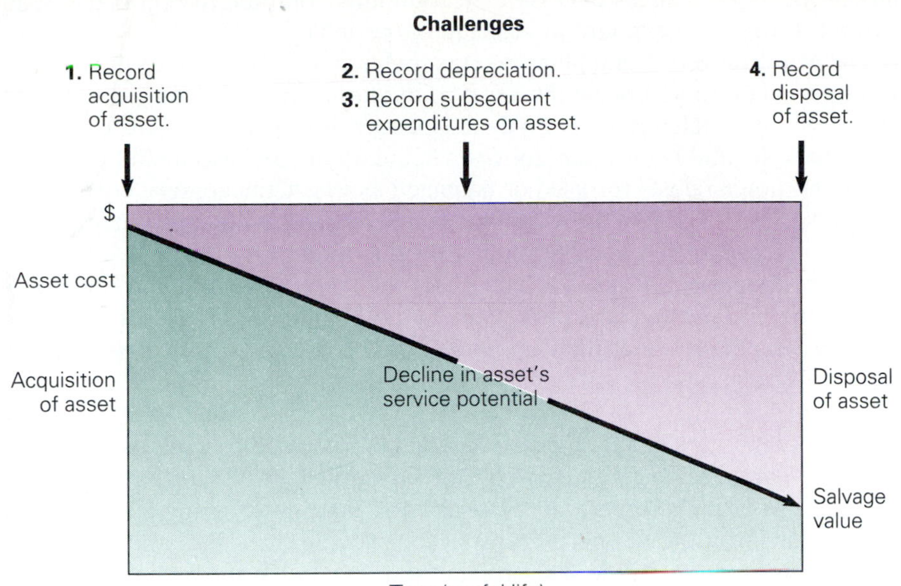

ILLUSTRATION 10.1
Recording the Life History of a Depreciable Asset

not being used by the business. However, standby equipment used only in peak or emergency periods is a plant asset because it is used in the operations of the business.

(concluded)

5. Describe the subsidiary records used to control plant assets.
6. Analyze and use the financial results—rate of return on operating assets.

Accountants view plant assets as a collection of *service potentials* that are consumed over a long time. For example, over several years, a delivery truck may provide 100,000 miles of delivery services to an appliance business. A new building may provide 40 years of shelter, while a machine may perform a particular operation on 400,000 parts. In each instance, purchase of the plant asset actually represents the advance payment or prepayment for expected services. Plant asset costs are a form of prepaid expense. As with short-term prepayments, the accountant must allocate the cost of these services to the accounting periods benefited.

Accounting for plant assets involves the following four steps:

1. Record the acquisition cost of the asset.
2. Record the allocation of the asset's original cost to periods of its useful life through depreciation.
3. Record subsequent expenditures on the asset.
4. Account for the disposal of the asset.

Objective 1
List the characteristics of plant assets and identify the costs of acquiring plant assets.

In Illustration 10.1, note how the asset's life begins with its procurement and the recording of its acquisition cost, which is usually in the form of a dollar purchase. Then, as the asset provides services through time, accountants record the asset's depreciation and any subsequent expenditures related to the asset. Finally, accountants record the disposal of the asset. We discuss the first three steps in this chapter and the disposal of an asset in Chapter 11. The last section in this chapter explains how accountants use subsidiary ledgers to control assets.

Remember that in recording the life history of an asset, accountants match expenses related to the asset with the revenues generated by it. Because measuring the periodic expense of plant assets affects net income, accounting for property, plant, and equipment is important to financial statement users.

Initial Recording of Plant Assets

When a company acquires a plant asset, accountants record the asset at the cost of acquisition (historical cost). This cost is objective, verifiable, and the best measure of an asset's fair market value at the time of purchase. Even if the market value of the asset changes over time, accountants continue to report the acquisition cost in the asset account in subsequent periods.

The **acquisition cost** of a plant asset is the amount of cash or cash equivalents given up to acquire and place the asset in operating condition at its proper location. Thus, cost includes all normal, reasonable, and necessary expenditures to obtain the asset and get it ready for use. Acquisition cost also includes the repair and reconditioning costs for used or damaged assets. Unnecessary costs (such as traffic tickets or fines) that must be paid as a result of hauling machinery to a new plant are not part of the acquisition cost of the asset.

The next sections discuss which costs are capitalized (debited to an asset account) for: (1) land and land improvements; (2) buildings; (3) group purchases of assets; (4) machinery and other equipment; (5) self-constructed assets; (6) noncash acquisitions; and (7) gifts of plant assets.

Land and Land Improvements

The cost of land includes its purchase price and other costs such as option cost, real estate commissions, title search and title transfer fees, and title insurance premiums. Also included are an existing mortgage note or unpaid taxes (back taxes) assumed by the purchaser; costs of surveying, clearing, and grading; and local assessments for sidewalks, streets, sewers, and water mains. Sometimes land purchased as a building site contains an unusable building that must be removed. Then, the accountant debits the entire purchase price to Land, including the cost of removing the building less any cash received from the sale of salvaged items while the land is being readied for use.

To illustrate, assume that Spivey Company purchased an old farm on the outskirts of San Diego, California, as a factory site. The company paid $225,000 for the property. In addition, the company agreed to pay unpaid property taxes from previous periods (called *back taxes*) of $12,000. Attorneys' fees and other legal costs relating to the purchase of the farm totaled $1,800. Spivey demolished (razed) the farm buildings at a cost of $18,000. The company salvaged some of the structural pieces of the building and sold them for $3,000. Because the firm was constructing a new building at the site, the city assessed Spivey Company $9,000 for water mains, sewers, and street paving. Spivey computed the cost of the land as follows:

	Land
Cost of factory site	$225,000
Back taxes	12,000
Attorneys' fees and other legal costs	1,800
Demolition	18,000
Sale of salvaged parts	(3,000)
City assessment	9,000
	$262,800

Accountants assigned all costs relating to the farm purchase and razing of the old buildings to the Land account because the old buildings purchased with the land were not usable. The real goal was to purchase the land, but the land was not available without the buildings.

Land is considered to have an unlimited life and is therefore not depreciable. However, **land improvements,** including driveways, temporary landscaping, parking lots, fences, lighting systems, and sprinkler systems, are attachments to the land. They have limited lives and therefore are depreciable. Owners record depreciable land improvements in a separate account called Land Improvements. They record the cost of permanent landscaping, including leveling and grading, in the Land account.

Buildings

When a business buys a building, its cost includes the purchase price, repair and remodeling costs, unpaid taxes assumed by the purchaser, legal costs, and real estate commissions paid.

Determining the cost of constructing a new building is often more difficult. Usually this cost includes architect's fees; building permits; payments to contractors; and the cost of digging the foundation. Also included are labor and materials to build the building; salaries of officers supervising the construction; and insurance, taxes, and interest during the construction period. Any miscellaneous amounts earned from the building during construction reduce the cost of the building. For example, an owner who could rent out a small completed portion during construction of the remainder of the building, would credit the rental proceeds to the Buildings account rather than to a revenue account.

Group Purchases of Assets

Sometimes a company buys land and other assets for a lump sum. When land and buildings purchased together are to be used, the firm divides the total cost and establishes separate ledger accounts for land and for buildings. This division of cost establishes the proper balances in the appropriate accounts. This is especially important later because the depreciation recorded on the buildings affects reported income, while no depreciation is taken on the land.

Returning to our example of Spivey Company, suppose one of the farm buildings was going to be remodeled for use by the company. Then, Spivey would determine what portion of the purchase price of the farm, back taxes, and legal fees ($225,000 + $12,000 + $1,800 = $238,800) it could assign to the buildings and what portion to the land. (The net cost of demolition would not be incurred, and the city assessment would be incurred at a later time.) Spivey would assign the $238,800 to the land and the buildings on the basis of their appraised values. For example, assume that the land was appraised at $162,000 and the buildings at $108,000. Spivey would determine the cost assignable to each of these plant assets as follows:

Asset	Appraised Value	Percent of Total Value
Land	$162,000	60% (162/270)
Buildings . . .	108,000	40 (108/270)
	$270,000	100% (270/270)

	Percent of Total Value	×	Purchase Price	=	Cost Assigned
Land	60%	×	$238,800*	=	$143,280
Buildings.	40	×	238,800	=	95,520
					$238,800

* The purchase price is the sum of the cash price, back taxes, and legal fees.

The journal entry to record the purchase of the land and buildings would be:

Land	143,280	
Buildings	95,520	
Cash		238,800
To record purchase of land and buildings.		

When the city eventually assessed the charges for the water mains, sewers, and street paving, the company would still debit these costs to the Land account as in the previous example.

Machinery and Other Equipment

Often companies purchase machinery or other equipment such as delivery or office equipment. Its cost includes the seller's *net* invoice price (whether the discount is taken or not), transportation charges incurred, insurance in transit, cost of installation, costs of accessories, and testing and break-in costs. Also included are other costs needed to put the machine or equipment in operating condition in its intended location. The cost of machinery does not include removing and disposing of a replaced, old machine that has been used in operations.

Such costs are part of the gain or loss on disposal of the old machine, as discussed in Chapter 11.

To illustrate, assume that Clark Company purchased new equipment to replace equipment that it has used for five years. The company paid a net purchase price of $150,000, brokerage fees of $5,000, legal fees of $2,000, and freight and insurance in transit of $3,000. In addition, the company paid $1,500 to remove old equipment and $2,000 to install new equipment. Clark would compute the cost of new equipment as follows:

Net purchase price	$150,000
Brokerage fees	5,000
Legal fees	2,000
Freight and insurance in transit	3,000
Installation costs	2,000
Total cost	$162,000

Self-Constructed Assets

If a company builds a plant asset for its own use, the cost includes all materials and labor directly traceable to construction of the asset. Also included in the cost of the asset are interest costs related to the asset and amounts paid for utilities (such as heat, light, and power) and for supplies used during construction. To determine how much of these indirect costs to capitalize, the company compares utility and supply costs during the construction period with those costs in a period when no construction occurred. The firm records the increase as part of the asset's cost. For example, assume a company normally incurred a $600 utility bill for June. This year, the company constructed a machine during June, and the utility bill was $975. Thus, it records the $375 increase as part of the machine's cost.

To illustrate further, assume that Tanner Company needed a new die-casting machine and received a quote from Smith Company for $23,000, plus $1,000 freight costs. Tanner decided to build the machine rather than buy it. The company incurred the following costs to build the machine: materials, $4,000; labor, $13,000; and indirect services of heat, power, and supplies, $3,000. Tanner would record the machine at its cost of $20,000 ($4,000 + $13,000 + $3,000) rather than $24,000, the purchase price of the machine. The $20,000 is the cost of the resources given up to construct the machine. Also, recording the machine at $24,000 would require Tanner to recognize a gain on construction of the assets. Accountants do not subscribe to the idea that a business can earn revenue (or realize a gain), and therefore net income, by dealing with itself.

You can apply the general guidelines we have just discussed to other plant assets, such as furniture and fixtures. The accounting methods are the same.

Noncash Acquisitions

When a plant asset is purchased for cash, its acquisition cost is simply the agreed on cash price. However, when a business acquires plant assets in exchange for other noncash assets (shares of stock, a customer's note, or a tract of land) or as gifts, it is more difficult to establish a cash price. This section discusses three possible asset valuation bases.

FAIR MARKET VALUE **Fair market value** is the price received for an item sold in the normal course of business (not at a forced liquidation sale). Accountants record noncash exchange transactions at fair market value.

The general rule on noncash exchanges is to value the noncash asset received at its fair market value or the fair market value of what was given up, whichever is more clearly evident. The reason for not using the book value of the old asset to value the new asset is that the asset being given up is often carried in the accounting records at historical cost or book value. Neither amount may adequately represent the actual fair market value of either asset. Therefore, if the fair market value of one asset is clearly evident, a firm should record this amount for the new asset at the time of the exchange.

Appraised Value Sometimes, neither of the items exchanged has a clearly determinable fair market value. Then, accountants record exchanges of items at their appraised values as determined by a professional appraiser. An **appraised value** is an expert's opinion of an item's fair market price if the item were sold. Appraisals are used often to value works of art, rare books, and antiques.

Book Value The **book value** of an asset is its recorded cost less accumulated depreciation. An old asset's book value is usually not a valid indication of the new asset's fair market value. If a better basis is not available, however, a firm could use the book value of the old asset.

Gifts of Plant Assets

Occasionally, a company receives an asset without giving up anything for it. For example, to attract industry to an area and provide jobs for local residents, a city may give a company a tract of land on which to build a factory. Although such a gift costs the recipient company nothing, it usually records the asset (land) at its fair market value. Accountants record gifts of plant assets at fair market value to provide information on all assets owned by the company. Omitting some assets may make information provided misleading. They would credit assets received as gifts to a stockholders' equity account titled Paid-in Capital—Donations.

Depreciation of Plant Assets

Companies record depreciation on all plant assets except land. Since the amount of depreciation may be relatively large, depreciation expense is often a significant factor in determining net income. For this reason, most financial statement users are interested in the amount of, and the methods used to compute, a company's depreciation expense.

Depreciation is the amount of plant asset cost allocated to each accounting period benefiting from the plant asset's use. Depreciation is a *process of allocation*, not valuation. Eventually, all assets except land wear out or become so inadequate or outmoded that they are sold or discarded; therefore, firms must record depreciation on every plant asset except land. They record depreciation even when the market value of a plant asset temporarily rises above its original cost because eventually the asset is no longer useful to its current owner.

Major causes of depreciation are (1) physical deterioration, (2) inadequacy for future needs, and (3) obsolescence. **Physical deterioration** results from the use of the asset—wear and tear—and the action of the elements. For example, an automobile may have to be replaced after a time because its body rusted out. The **inadequacy** of a plant asset is its inability to produce enough products or provide enough services to meet current demands. For example, an airline cannot provide air service for 125 passengers using a plane that seats 90. The **obsolescence** of an asset is its decline in usefulness brought about by inventions and technological progress. For example, the development of the xerographic process of reproducing printed matter rendered almost all previous methods of duplication obsolete.

The use of a plant asset in business operations transforms a plant asset cost into an operating expense. Depreciation, then, is an operating expense resulting from the use of a depreciable plant asset. Because depreciation expense does not require a current cash outlay, it is often called a *noncash expense*. The purchaser gave up cash in the period when the asset was acquired, not during the periods when depreciation expense is recorded.

ILLUSTRATION 10.2
Factors Affecting Depreciation

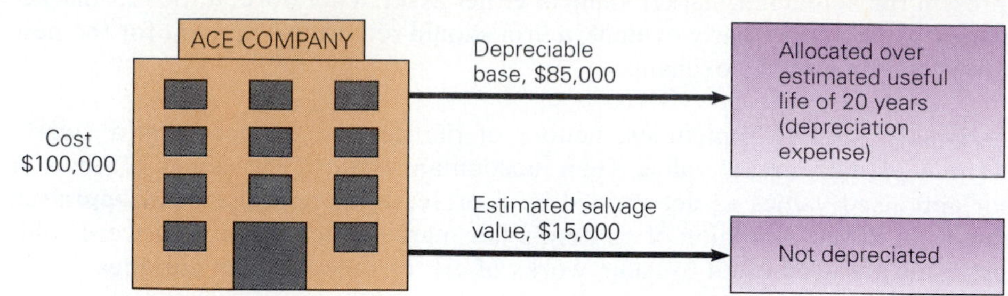

Factors Affecting Depreciation

Objective 2
List the four major factors affecting depreciation expense.

To compute depreciation expense, accountants consider four major factors:

1. Cost of the asset.
2. Estimated salvage value of the asset. **Salvage value** (or *scrap value*) is the amount of money the company expects to recover, less disposal costs, on the date a plant asset is scrapped, sold, or traded in.
3. Estimated useful life of the asset. **Useful life** refers to the time the company owning the asset intends to use it; useful life is not necessarily the same as either economic life or physical life. The economic life of a car may be 7 years and its physical life may be 10 years, but if a company has a policy of trading cars every 3 years, the useful life for depreciation purposes is 3 years. Various firms express useful life in years, months, working hours, or units of production. Obsolescence also affects useful life. For example, a machine capable of producing units for 20 years, may be expected to be obsolete in 6 years. Thus, its estimated useful life is 6 years—not 20. Another example, on TV you may have seen a demolition crew setting off explosives in a huge building and wondering why the owners decided to destroy what looked like a perfectly good building. The building was destroyed because it had reached the end of its economic life. The land on which the building stood could be put to better use, possibly by constructing a new building.
4. Depreciation method used in depreciating the asset. We describe the four common depreciation methods in the next section.

In Illustration 10.2, note the relationship among these factors. Assume Ace Company purchased an office building for $100,000. The building has an estimated salvage value of $15,000 and a useful life of 20 years. The depreciable cost of the building is $85,000 (cost less estimated salvage value). Ace would allocate this depreciable base over the useful life of the building using the proper depreciation method under the circumstances.

Depreciation Methods

Objective 3
Describe the various methods of calculating depreciation expense.

Today, companies can use many different methods to calculate depreciation on assets.[1] This section discusses and illustrates the most common methods—straight-line, units-of-production, and two accelerated depreciation methods (sum-of-the-years'-digits and double-declining-balance).

As is true for inventory methods, normally a company is free to adopt the most appropriate depreciation method for its business operations. According to accounting theory, companies should use a depreciation method that reflects most closely their underlying economic circumstances. Thus, companies should adopt the depreciation method that allocates plant asset cost to accounting periods according to the benefits received from the use of the asset. Illustration 10.3 shows the frequency of use of these methods for 600 companies. You can see that most companies use the straight-line method for financial reporting purposes.

[1] Because depreciation expense is an estimate, calculations may be rounded to the nearest dollar.

ILLUSTRATION 10.3
Depreciation Methods Used

Method	Number of Companies			
	1992	1991	1990	1989
Straight-line	564	558	560	562
Declining-balance	26	28	38	40
Sum-of-the-years'-digits	12	8	11	16
Accelerated method—not specified	62	70	69	69
Units-of-production	47	50	50	50
Other	5	7	8	8

Source: American Institute of Certified Public Accountants, *Accounting Trends & Techniques* (New York: AICPA, 1993), p. 341.

Note that some companies use one method for certain assets and another method for other assets. In practice, measuring the benefits from the use of a plant asset is impractical and often not possible. As a result, a depreciation method must meet only one standard: the depreciation method **must** allocate plant asset cost to accounting periods in a systematic and rational manner. The following four methods meet this requirement.

AN ACCOUNTING PERSPECTIVE

BUSINESS INSIGHT Regardless of the method or methods of depreciation chosen, companies must disclose their depreciation methods in the footnotes to their financial statements. They include this information in the first footnote, which summarizes significant accounting policies.

The disclosure is generally straightforward: Sears, Roebuck & Co. operates department stores, paint and hardware stores, auto supply stores, and eyewear stores. Its annual report states simply that "depreciation is provided principally by the straight-line method." Companies may use different depreciation methods for different assets. General Electric Company is a highly diversified multinational corporation that develops, manufactures, and markets aerospace products, major appliances, industrial products, and high-performance engineered plastics. It uses an accelerated method for most of its property, plant, and equipment; however, it depreciates some assets on a straight-line basis, while the company's mining properties are depreciated under the units-of-production method.

In the illustrations of the four depreciation methods that follow, we assume the following: On January 1, 1997, a company purchased a machine for $54,000 with an estimated useful life of 10 years, or 50,000 units of output, and an estimated salvage value of $4,000.

STRAIGHT-LINE METHOD **Straight-line depreciation** has been the most widely used depreciation method in the United States for many years because, as you saw in Chapter 3, it is easily applied. To apply the straight-line method, a firm charges an equal amount of plant asset cost to each accounting period. The formula for calculating depreciation under the straight-line method is:

$$\text{Depreciation per period} = \frac{\text{Asset cost} - \text{Estimated salvage value}}{\text{Number of accounting periods in estimated useful life}}$$

Using our example of a machine purchased for $54,000, the depreciation is:

$$\frac{\$54{,}000 - \$4{,}000}{10 \text{ years}} = \$5{,}000 \text{ per year}$$

In Illustration 10.4, we present a schedule of annual depreciation entries, cumulative balances in the accumulated depreciation account, and the book (or carrying) values of the $54,000 machine.

Using the straight-line method for assets is appropriate where (1) time rather than obsolescence is the major factor limiting the asset's life and (2) the asset

ILLUSTRATION 10.4
Straight-Line Depreciation Schedule

End of Year	Depreciation Expense Dr.; Accumulated Depreciation Cr.	Total Accumulated Depreciation	Book Value
			$54,000
1	$ 5,000	$ 5,000	49,000
2	5,000	10,000	44,000
3	5,000	15,000	39,000
4	5,000	20,000	34,000
5	5,000	25,000	29,000
6	5,000	30,000	24,000
7	5,000	35,000	19,000
8	5,000	40,000	14,000
9	5,000	45,000	9,000
10	5,000	50,000	4,000*
	$50,000		

* Estimated salvage value.

produces relatively constant amounts of periodic services. Assets that possess these features include items such as pipelines, fencing, and storage tanks.

UNITS-OF-PRODUCTION (OUTPUT) METHOD The **units-of-production depreciation** method assigns an equal amount of depreciation to each unit of product manufactured or service rendered by an asset. Since this method of depreciation is based on physical output, firms apply it in situations where usage rather than obsolescence leads to the demise of the asset. Under this method, you would compute the depreciation charge per unit of output. Then, multiply this figure by the number of units of goods or services produced during the accounting period to find the period's depreciation expense. The formula is:

$$\text{Depreciation per unit} = \frac{\text{Asset cost} - \text{Estimated salvage value}}{\text{Estimated total units of production (or service) during useful life of asset}}$$

$$\text{Depreciation per period} = \text{Depreciation per unit} \times \text{Number of units of goods or services produced}$$

You would determine the depreciation charge for the $54,000 machine as:

$$\frac{\$54,000 - \$4,000}{50,000 \text{ units}} = \$1 \text{ per unit}$$

If the machine produced 1,000 units in 1997 and 2,500 units in 1998, depreciation expense for those years would be $1,000 and $2,500, respectively.

ACCELERATED DEPRECIATION METHODS **Accelerated depreciation methods** record higher amounts of depreciation during the early years of an asset's life and lower amounts in the asset's later years. A business might choose an accelerated depreciation method for the following reasons:

1. The value of the benefits received from the asset decline with age (for example, office buildings).
2. The asset is a high-technology asset subject to rapid obsolescence (for example, computers).
3. Repairs increase substantially in the asset's later years; under this method, the depreciation and repairs together remain fairly constant over the asset's life (for example, automobiles).

The two most common accelerated methods of depreciation are the *sum-of-the-years'-digits (SOYD)* method and the *double-declining-balance (DDB)* method.

Illustration 10.5
Sum-of-the-Years'-Digits Depreciation Schedule

End of Year		Depreciation Expense Dr.; Accumulated Depreciation Cr.	Total Accumulated Depreciation	Book Value
				$54,000
1.	$50,000* × 10/55	$ 9,091	$ 9,091	44,909
2.	$50,000 × 9/55	8,182	17,273	36,727
3.	$50,000 × 8/55	7,273	24,546	29,454
4.	$50,000 × 7/55	6,364	30,910	23,090
5.	$50,000 × 6/55	5,455	36,365	17,635
6.	$50,000 × 5/55	4,545	40,910	13,090
7.	$50,000 × 4/55	3,636	44,546	9,454
8.	$50,000 × 3/55	2,727	47,273	6,727
9.	$50,000 × 2/55	1,818	49,091	4,909
10.	$50,000 × 1/55	909	50,000	4,000
		$50,000		

* $54,000 cost − $4,000 salvage value.

Sum-of-the-Years'-Digits Method The **sum-of-the-years'-digits (SOYD)** method adds the consecutive digits for each year of an asset's estimated life together and uses that as the denominator of a fraction. The numerator is the years of useful life remaining at the *beginning* of the accounting period. To compute that period's depreciation expense, you would multiply this fraction by the the asset cost less the estimated salvage value. The formula is:

$$\text{Depreciation per period} = \frac{\text{Number of years of useful life remaining at beginning of accounting period}}{\text{SOYD}} \times \left(\text{Asset cost} - \text{Estimated salvage value}\right)$$

The years are totaled to find SOYD. For an asset with a 10-year useful life, SOYD = 10 + 9 + 8 + 7 + 6 + 5 + 4 + 3 + 2 + 1 = 55. Alternatively, rather than adding the digits for all years together, you can use this formula to find the SOYD for any given number of periods:

$$\text{SOYD} = \frac{n(n+1)}{2}$$

where n is the number of periods in the asset's useful life. Thus, SOYD for an asset with a 10-year useful life is:

$$\text{SOYD} = \frac{10(10+1)}{2} = 55$$

To apply the SOYD method to the $54,000 machine, you would determine that at the beginning of year 1 (1997), the machine has 10 years of useful life remaining. Then, using the formula, compute the first year's depreciation as 10/55 times $50,000 (the $54,000 cost less the $4,000 salvage value). The depreciation for the first year is $9,091 (see Illustration 10.5). Note that the fraction gets smaller every year, resulting in a declining depreciation charge for each successive year.

Double-Declining-Balance Method To apply the **double-declining-balance (DDB)** method of computing periodic depreciation charges you begin by calculating the straight-line depreciation rate. To do this, divide 100% by the number of years of useful life of the asset. Then, multiply this rate by 2. Next, apply the resulting double-declining rate to the declining book value of the asset. Ignore salvage value in making the calculations. At the point where book value is equal to the salvage value, no more depreciation is taken. The formula for DDB depreciation is:

ILLUSTRATION 10.6
Double-Declining-Balance (DDB) Depreciation Schedule

End of Year	Depreciation Expense Dr.; Accumulated Depreciation Cr.	Total Accumulated Depreciation	Book Value
			$54,000
1. (20% of $54,000)	$10,800	$10,800	43,200
2. (20% of $43,200)	8,640	19,440	34,560
3. (20% of $34,560)	6,912	26,352	27,648
4. (20% of $27,648)	5,530	31,882	22,118
5. (20% of $22,118)	4,424	36,306	17,694
6. (20% of $17,694)	3,539	39,845	14,155
7. (20% of $14,155)	2,831	42,676	11,324
8. (20% of $11,324)	2,265	44,941	9,059
9. (20% of $9,059).	1,812	46,753	7,247
10. (20% of $7,247).	1,449*	48,202	5,798

* This amount could be $3,247 to reduce the book value to the estimated salvage value of $4,000. Then, accumulated depreciation would be $50,000.

$$\text{Depreciation per period} = \left(2 \times \text{Straight-line rate}\right) \times \left(\text{Asset cost} - \text{Accumulated depreciation}\right)$$

Look at the calculations for the $54,000 machine using the DDB method in Illustration 10.6. The straight-line rate is 10% (100%/10 years), which, when doubled, yields a DDB rate of 20%. (Expressed as fractions, the straight-line rate is $\frac{1}{10}$, and the DDB rate is $\frac{2}{10}$.) Since at the beginning of year 1 no accumulated depreciation has been recorded, cost is the basis of the calculation. In each of the following years, book value is the basis of the calculation at the beginning of the year.

In the 10th year, you could increase depreciation to $3,247 if the asset is to be retired and its salvage value is still $4,000. This higher depreciation amount for the last year ($3,247) would reduce the book value of $7,247 down to the salvage value of $4,000. If an asset is continued in service, depreciation should only be recorded until the asset's book value equals its estimated salvage value.

For a summary of the four depreciation methods, see Illustration 10.7.

In Illustration 10.8, we compare three of the depreciation methods just discussed—straight-line, sum-of-the-years'-digits, and double-declining-balance—using the same example of a machine purchased on January 1, 1997, for $54,000. The machine has an estimated useful life of 10 years and an estimated salvage value of $4,000.

Partial-Year Depreciation

So far we have assumed that the assets were put into service at the beginning of an accounting period and ignored the fact that often assets are put into service *during* an accounting period. When assets are acquired during an accounting period, the first recording of depreciation is for a partial year. Normally, firms calculate the depreciation for the partial year to the nearest full month the asset was in service. For example, they treat an asset purchased on or before the 15th day of the month as if it were purchased on the 1st day of the month. And, they treat an asset purchased after the 15th of the month as if it were acquired on the 1st day of the following month.

To illustrate how to calculate partial-year depreciation for each of the four depreciation methods we use a machine purchased for $7,600 on September 1, 1997, with an estimated salvage value of $400, an estimated useful life of five years, and an estimated total units of production of 25,000 units.

STRAIGHT-LINE METHOD Partial-year depreciation calculations for the straight-line depreciation method are relatively easy. Begin by finding the 12-month charge by the normal computation explained earlier. Then, multiply this annual amount by the fraction of the year for which the asset was in use. For example, for the

ILLUSTRATION 10.7 Summary of Depreciation Methods

Method	Base	Calculation
Straight-line	Asset cost − Estimated salvage value	Base ÷ Number of accounting periods in estimated useful life
Units-of-production	Asset cost − Estimated salvage value	(Base ÷ Estimated total units of production) × Units produced this period
Sum-of-the-years'-digits	Asset cost − Estimated salvage value	Base × (Number of years of useful life remaining at beginning of accounting period / SOYD)
Double-declining-balance	Asset cost − Accumulated depreciation	Base × (2 × Straight-line rate)

ILLUSTRATION 10.8 Comparison of Straight-Line, Sum-of-the-Years'-Digits, and Double-Declining-Balance Depreciation Methods

Straight-Line Method

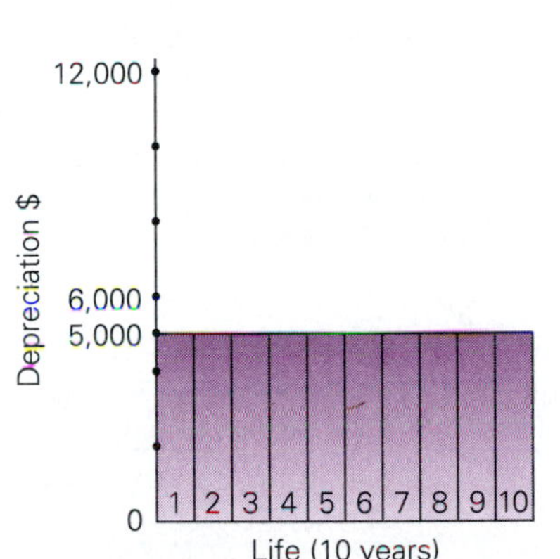

Sum-of-the-Years'-Digits Method

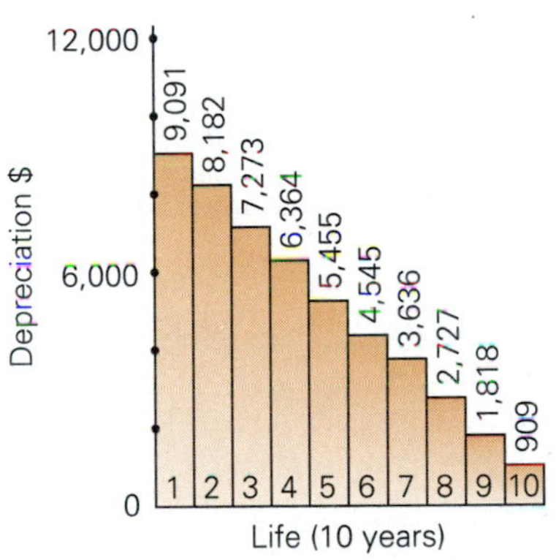

Double-Declining-Balance Method

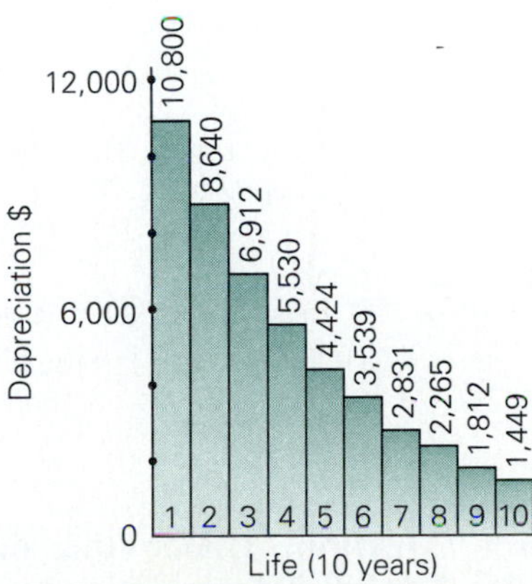

$7,600 machine purchased September 1, 1997 (estimated salvage value, $400; and estimated useful life, five years), the annual straight-line depreciation is [($7,600 − $400)/5 years] = $1,440. The machine would operate for four months prior to the end of the accounting year, December 31, or one-third of a year. The 1997 depreciation is ($1,440 × 1/3) = $480.

Units-of-Production Method The units-of-production method requires no unusual computations to record depreciation for a partial year. To compute the partial-year depreciation, multiply the depreciation charge per unit by the units produced. The charge for a partial year would be less than for a full year because fewer units of goods or services are produced.

Sum-of-the-Years'-Digits Method Under the SOYD method, computing partial-year depreciation is more complex. Problems occur because the 12 months for which depreciation is computed using the SOYD fraction do not correspond with the 12 months for which the financial statements are being prepared. For example, the depreciation recorded in 1997 on the $7,600 asset is for the last four months of 1997, which is the first one-third of the first year of the asset's life. You would compute the depreciation for the four months of 1997 as ($7,600 − $400) × 5/15 × 1/3; thus, depreciation is $800. In 1998, the depreciation recorded is $2,240, computed as follows:

For the first two-thirds of the year:	($7,200 × 5/15 × 2/3) =	$1,600
For the last one-third of the year:	($7,200 × 4/15 × 1/3) =	640
Total depreciation expense for 1998		$2,240

With the SOYD method, you compute annual depreciation charges in this same way throughout the asset's life:

Year	Depreciation for Each Year of Life of Asset (September 1–August 31)	Depreciation for Each Calendar Year (January 1–December 31)		
		1997:		
		Sept. 1–Dec. 31 ($2,400 × 1/3) =		$ 800
1	$7,200 × 5/15 = $2,400	1998:		
		Jan. 1–Aug. 31 ($2,400 × 2/3) =	$1,600	
		Sept. 1–Dec. 31 ($1,920 × 1/3) =	640	
				2,240
2	$7,200 × 4/15 = 1,920	1999:		
		Jan. 1–Aug. 31 ($1,920 × 2/3) =	$1,280	
		Sept. 1–Dec. 31 ($1,440 × 1/3) =	480	
				1,760
3	$7,200 × 3/15 = 1,440	2000:		
		Jan. 1–Aug. 31 ($1,440 × 2/3) =	$ 960	
		Sept. 1–Dec. 31 ($960 × 1/3) =	320	
				1,280
4	$7,200 × 2/15 = 960	2001:		
		Jan. 1–Aug. 31 ($960 × 2/3) =	$ 640	
		Sept. 1–Dec. 31 ($480 × 1/3) =	160	
				800
5	$7,200 × 1/15 = 480	2002:		
		Jan. 1–Aug. 31 ($480 × 2/3) =		320
	Total depreciation = $7,200	Total depreciation =		$7,200

Double-Declining-Balance Method Under the double-declining-balance method, it is relatively easy to determine depreciation for a partial year and then for subsequent full years. For the partial year, simply multiply the fixed rate times the cost of the asset times the fraction of the partial year. For example, DDB depreciation on the $7,600 asset for 1997 is ($7,600 × 0.4 × 1/3) = $1,013. For subsequent years, compute the depreciation using the regular procedure of multiplying the book value at the beginning of the period by the fixed rate. The 1998 depreciation would be [($7,600 − $1,013) × 0.4] = $2,635.

AN ACCOUNTING PERSPECTIVE

USES OF TECHNOLOGY Most companies report property, plant, and equipment as one amount in the balance sheet in their annual report; however, that account is made up of many items. Computers and accounting software have simplified recordkeeping for all of a company's depreciable assets. When depreciable plant assets are purchased, employees enter the cost, estimated useful life, and estimated salvage value of the assets in the computer. In addition, they enter the method of depreciation that the company decides to use on the assets. After processing this information, the computer calculates the company's depreciation expense and accumulates depreciation for each type of asset and each individual asset (e.g., a machine).

Changes in Estimates

After depreciating an asset down to its estimated salvage value, a firm records no more depreciation on the asset even if continuing to use it. At times, a firm finds the estimated useful life of an asset or its estimated salvage value is incorrect before the asset is depreciated down to its estimated salvage value; then, it computes revised depreciation charges for the remaining useful life. These revised charges do not correct past depreciation taken; they merely compensate for past incorrect charges through changed expense amounts in current and future periods. To compute the new depreciation charge per period, divide the book value less the newly estimated salvage value by the estimated periods of useful life remaining.

For example, assume that a machine cost $30,000, has an estimated salvage value of $3,000, and originally had an estimated useful life of eight years. At the end of the fourth year of the machine's life, the balance in its accumulated depreciation account (assuming use of the straight-line method) was ($30,000 − $3,000) × 4/8 = $13,500. At the beginning of the fifth year, a manager estimates that the asset will last six more years. The newly estimated salvage value is $2,700. To determine the revised depreciation per period:

Original cost	$30,000
Less: Accumulated depreciation at the end of 4th year	13,500
Book value at the beginning of 5th year	$16,500
Less: revised salvage value	2,700
Remaining depreciable base	$13,800
Revised depreciation per period: $13,800/6	$ 2,300

Had this company used the units-of-production method, its revision of the life estimate would have been in units. Thus, to determine depreciation expense, compute a new per-unit depreciation charge by dividing book value less salvage value by the estimated remaining units of production. Multiply this per unit charge by the periodic production to determine depreciation expense.

Using the double-declining-balance method, the book value at the beginning of year 5 would be $9,492.19 (cost of $30,000 less accumulated depreciation of $20,507.81). Depreciation expense for year 5 would be twice the new straight-line rate times book value. The straight-line rate is 100%/6 = 16.67%. So twice the straight-line rate is 33.33%, or 1/3. Thus, 1/3 × $9,492.19 = $3,164.06.

Under the sum-of-the-years'-digits method, you must calculate a new fraction. The sum-of-the-years'-digits is now 6 + 5 + 4 + 3 + 2 + 1 = 21. The fraction for year 5 is 6/21. To compute depreciation under the sum-of-the-years'-digits method:

Book value at the beginning of 5th year	$10,500.00
Revised salvage value	2,700.00
Remaining depreciable base	$ 7,800.00
Depreciation expense for year 5: $7,800 × 6/21	$ 2,228.57

ILLUSTRATION 10.9
Partial Balance Sheet

REED COMPANY
Partial Balance Sheet
June 30, 1997

Property, plant, and equipment:		
Land		$30,000
Buildings	$75,000	
Less: Accumulated depreciation	45,000	30,000
Equipment	$ 9,000	
Less: Accumulated depreciation	1,500	7,500
Total property, plant, and equipment		$67,500

AN ACCOUNTING PERSPECTIVE

BUSINESS INSIGHT On their financial statements, companies often provide one amount for property, plant, and equipment that is net of accumulated depreciation. Nonetheless, notes (footnotes) actually provide the additional information regarding the separate types of assets. Perkin-Elmer Corporation is the world leader in the development, manufacture, and distribution of analytical instrumentation and life science systems used in environmental technology, pharmaceuticals, biotechnology, chemicals, plastics, food, agriculture, and scientific research. For instance, its June 30, 1993, balance sheet showed property, plant, and equipment, net equal to $162,689,000. In Note 1 (slightly modified to clarify), management explained this amount as follows:

Property, Plant and Equipment and Depreciation. Property, plant and equipment are stated at cost and consisted of the following:

(Dollar amounts in millions)	End of Fiscal Year 1993	1992
Land	$ 27.9	$ 29.0
Buildings and leasehold improvements	131.2	135.4
Machinery and equipment	193.7	198.4
Property, plant and equipment, at cost	$352.8	$362.8
Accumulated depreciation and amortization	190.1	183.4
Property, plant and equipment, net	$162.7	$179.4

Major renewals and improvements that significantly add to productive capacity or extend the life of an asset are capitalized. Repairs, maintenance and minor renewals and improvements are expensed when incurred.

Provisions for depreciation of owned property, plant and equipment are based upon the expected useful lives of the assets and computed primarily by the straight-line method. U.S. operations generally use accelerated methods of depreciation for assets acquired prior to 1987 and straight-line depreciation for asset additions in subsequent years. In countries other than the U.S., the straight-line method is generally used.

Depreciation and Financial Reporting

APB Opinion No. 12 requires that companies separately disclose the methods of depreciation they use and the amount of depreciation expense for the period in the body of the income statement or in the notes to the financial statements. Major classes of plant assets and their related accumulated depreciation amounts are reported as shown in Illustration 10.9.

Showing cost less accumulated depreciation in the balance sheet gives statement users a better understanding of the percentages of a company's plant assets that have been used up than reporting only the book value (remaining undepreciated cost) of the assets. For example, reporting buildings of $75,000 less $45,000 of accumulated depreciation, resulting in a net amount of $30,000, is quite different from merely reporting $30,000 of buildings. In the first case, the statement user can see that the assets are about 60% used up. In the latter case, the statement user has no way of knowing whether the assets are new or old.

A MISCONCEPTION Some mistaken financial statement users believe that accumulated depreciation represents cash available for replacing old plant assets with new assets. However, the accumulated depreciation account balance does not represent cash; accumulated depreciation simply shows how much of an asset's cost has been charged to expense. Companies use the plant asset and its contra account, accumulated depreciation, so that data on the total original acquisition

A Broader Perspective

Oxford Industries, Inc.

Oxford Industries, Inc., designs, manufactures, and sells apparel for men, women, and children. The information below is from the its 1991 annual report.

($ in thousands)	May 31 1991	1990
Total current assets	$154,153	$174,933
Property, plant and equipment (Notes A, C, and D)	32,351	32,824
Other assets	710	672
Total assets	$187,214	$208,429

Notes to Consolidated Financial Statements

A (In Part): Summary of Significant Accounting Policies

7. Property, Plant and Equipment—Depreciation and amortization of property, plant and equipment is provided on both straight-line and accelerated methods over the estimated useful lives of the assets as follows:

Buildings and improvements	10–40 years
Machinery and equipment	3–15 years
Office fixtures and equipment	3–10 years
Autos, trucks and airplane	3–6 years
Leasehold improvements	Life of lease

Substantially all fixed assets, except buildings, are depreciated by an accelerated method.

Certain leases in which the Company is lessee are considered to be installment purchases for purposes of accounting presentation, and are included in property, plant and equipment. The related lease obligations, less current installments, are included in long-term debt in the accompanying balance sheets.

C. Property, Plant and Equipment:

Property, plant and equipment, carried at cost, is summarized as follows:

($ in thousands)	May 31, 1991	June 1, 1990
Land	$ 1,583	$ 1,594
Buildings	27,905	27,219
Machinery and equipment	67,225	68,703
Leasehold improvements	4,464	4,693
	101,177	102,209
Less accumulated depreciation and amortization	68,826	69,385
	$ 32,351	$ 32,824

The above includes property under capital leases with costs of approximately $533,000 in 1991 and 1990.

Source: Based on American Institute of Certified Public Accountants, *Accounting Trends & Techniques* (New York: AICPA, 1992), p. 159.

cost and accumulated depreciation are readily available to meet reporting requirements.

Costs or Market Values in the Balance Sheet In the balance sheet, firms report plant assets at original cost less accumulated depreciation. One of the justifications for reporting the remaining undepreciated costs of the asset rather than market values is the going-concern concept. As you recall from Chapter 5, the going-concern concept assumes that the company will remain in business indefinitely, which implies the company will use its plant assets rather than sell them. Generally, analysts do not consider market values relevant for plant assets in primary financial statements, although they may be reported in supplemental statements.

Subsequent Expenditures (Capital and Revenue) on Assets

Objective 4
Distinguish between capital and revenue expenditures for plant assets.

Companies often spend additional funds on plant assets that have been in use for some time. They debit these expenditures to: (1) an asset account; (2) an accumulated depreciation account; or (3) an expense account.

Expenditures debited to an asset account or to an accumulated depr ion account are **capital expenditures.** Capital expenditures increase the book value of plant assets. **Revenue expenditures,** on the other hand, do not qualify as capital expenditures because they help to generate the current period's revenues rather than future periods' revenues. As a result, companies expense these revenue expenditures immediately and report them in the income statement as expenses.

Expenditures Capitalized in Asset Accounts

Betterments or **improvements** to existing plant assets are capital expenditures because they increase the *quality* of services obtained from the asset. Because betterments or improvements add to the service-rendering ability of assets, firms charge them to the asset accounts. For example, installing an air conditioner in an automobile that did not previously have one is a betterment. The debit for such an expenditure is to the asset account, Automobiles.

Expenditures Capitalized as Charges to Accumulated Depreciation

Occasionally, expenditures made on plant assets extend the *quantity* of services *beyond the original estimate* but do not improve the quality of the services. Since these expenditures benefit an increased number of future periods, accountants capitalize rather than expense them. However, since there is no visible, tangible addition to, or improvement in, the quality of services, they charge the expenditures to the accumulated depreciation account, thus reducing the credit balance in that account. Such expenditures cancel a part of the existing accumulated depreciation; firms often call them **extraordinary repairs.**

To illustrate, assume that after operating a press for four years, a company spent $5,000 to recondition the press. The reconditioning increased the machine's life to 14 years instead of the original estimate of 10 years. The journal entry to record the extraordinary repair is:

Accumulated Depreciation—Machinery	5,000	
Cash (or Accounts Payable)		5,000
To record the cost of reconditioning a press.		

Originally, the press cost $40,000, had an estimated useful life of 10 years, and had no estimated salvage value. At the end of the fourth year, the balance in its accumulated depreciation account under the straight-line method is [($40,000 ÷ 10) × 4] = $16,000. After debiting the $5,000 spent to recondition the press to the accumulated depreciation account, the balances in the asset account and its related accumulated depreciation account are as shown in the last column:

	Before Extraordinary Repair	After Extraordinary Repair
Press	$40,000	$40,000
Accumulated depreciation	16,000	11,000
Book value (end of four years)	$24,000	$29,000

In effect, the expenditure increases the carrying amount (book value) of the asset by reducing its contra account, accumulated depreciation. Under the straight-line method, we would divide the new book value of the press, $29,000, equally among the 10 remaining years in amounts of $2,900 per year (assuming that the estimated salvage value is still zero).

As a practical matter, expenditures for major repairs not extending the asset's life are sometimes charged to accumulated depreciation. This avoids distorting net income by expensing these expenditures in the year incurred. Then, firms calculate a revised depreciation expense, and spread the cost of major repairs over a number of years. This treatment is not theoretically correct.

To illustrate, assume the same facts as in the previous example except that the $5,000 expenditure did not extend the life of the asset. Because of the size of this expenditure, the company still charges it to accumulated depreciation. Now, it would spread the $29,000 remaining book value over the remaining six years of the life of the press. Under the straight-line method, annual depreciation would then be ($29,000 ÷ 6) = $4,833.

Expenditures Charged to Expense

Accountants treat as expenses those recurring and/or minor expenditures that neither add to the asset's service-rendering quality nor extend its quantity of services beyond its original estimated useful life. Thus, firms immediately expense

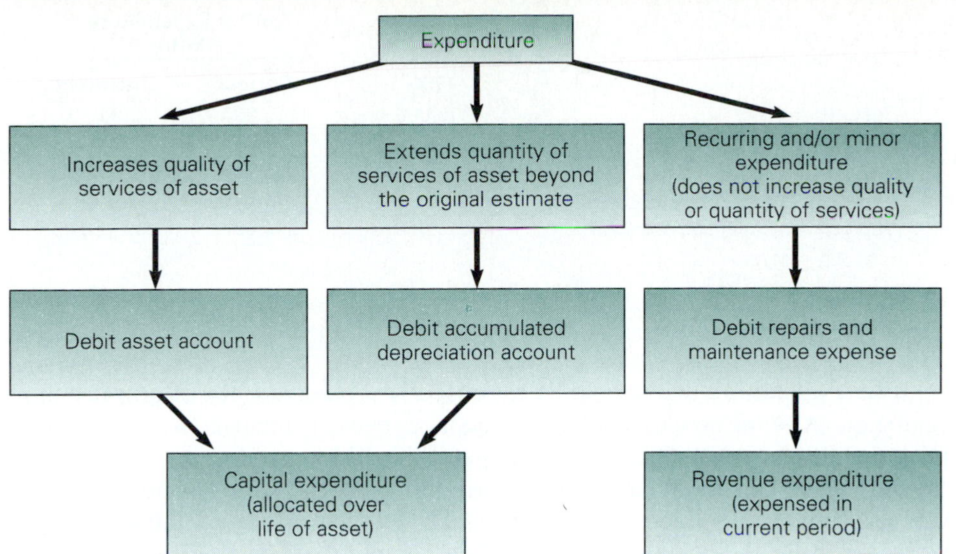

ILLUSTRATION 10.10
Expenditures on Plant Assets after Acquisition

regular maintenance (lubricating a machine) and ordinary repairs (replacing a broken fan belt on an automobile) as revenue expenditures. For example, a company that spends $190 to repair a machine after using it for some time, debits Maintenance Expense or Repairs Expense.

LOW-COST ITEMS Most businesses purchase **low-cost items** that provide years of service, such as paperweights, hammers, wrenches, and drills. Because of the small dollar amounts involved, it is impractical to use the ordinary depreciation methods for such assets, and it is often costly to maintain records of individual items. Also, the effect of low-cost items on the financial statements is not significant. Accordingly, it is more efficient to record the items as expenses when they are purchased. For instance, many companies charge any expenditure less than an arbitrary minimum, say, $100, to expense regardless of its impact on the asset's useful life. This practice of accounting for such low unit cost items as expenses is an example of the modifying convention of materiality that was discussed in Chapter 5. In Illustration 10.10, we summarize expenditures on plant assets after acquisition.

Errors in Classification

In practice, it is difficult to decide whether to debit an expenditure to the asset account or to the accumulated depreciation account. For example, some expenditures seem to affect both the quality and quantity of services. Even if the wrong account were debited for the expenditure, the book value of the plant asset at that point would be the same amount it would have been if the correct account had been debited. However, both the asset and accumulated depreciation accounts would be misstated.

As an example of the effect of misstated asset and accumulated depreciation accounts, assume Watson Company had an asset that had originally cost $15,000 and had been depreciated to a book value of $6,000 at the beginning of 1997. At that time, Watson estimated the equipment had a remaining useful life of two years. The company spent $4,000 in early January 1997 to install a new motor in the equipment. This motor extended the useful life of the asset four years beyond the original estimate. Since the expenditure extended the life, the firm should capitalize it by a debit to the Accumulated Depreciation account. We show the calculations for depreciation expense if the entry was made correctly and if the expenditure had been improperly charged (debited) to the asset account in Illustration 10.11.

ILLUSTRATION 10.11
Expenditure Extending Plant Asset Life

	December 31, 1996	After Expenditure Entry	
		Correct	Incorrect
Cost	$15,000	$15,000	$19,000†
Accumulated depreciation	9,000	5,000*	9,000
Book value	$ 6,000	$10,000	$10,000
Remaining life	2 years	6 years	6 years
Depreciation expense per year	$ 3,000	$ 1,667	$ 1,667

* ($9,000 − $4,000)
† ($15,000 + $4,000)

If an expenditure that should be expensed is capitalized, the effects are more significant. Assume now that $6,000 in repairs expense is incurred for a plant asset that originally cost $40,000 and had a useful life of four years and no estimated salvage value. This asset had been depreciated using the straight-line method for one year and had a book value of $30,000 ($40,000 cost − $10,000 first-year depreciation) at the beginning of 1997. The company capitalized the $6,000 that should have been charged to repairs expense in 1997. The charge for depreciation should have remained at $10,000 for each of the next three years. With the incorrect entry, however, depreciation increases.

Regardless of whether the repair was debited to the asset account or the accumulated depreciation account, the firm would change the depreciation expense amount to $12,000 for each of the next three years [($30,000 book value + $6,000 repairs expense) ÷ 3 more years of useful life]. These errors would cause net income for the year 1997 to be overstated $4,000: (1) repairs expense is understated by $6,000, causing income to be overstated by $6,000; and (2) depreciation expense is overstated by $2,000, causing income to be understated by $2,000. In 1998, the overstatement of depreciation by $2,000 would cause 1998 income to be understated by $2,000.

Note that the $6,000 recording error affects more than just the expense accounts and net income. Plant asset and Retained Earnings accounts on the balance sheet also reflect the impact of this error. To see the effect of incorrectly capitalizing the $6,000 to the asset account rather than correctly expensing it, look at Illustration 10.12.

SUBSIDIARY RECORDS USED TO CONTROL PLANT ASSETS

Objective 5
Describe the subsidiary records used to control plant assets.

Most companies maintain formal records (ranging from handwritten documents to computer tapes) to ensure control over their plant assets. These records include an asset account and a related accumulated depreciation account in the general ledger for *each* major class of depreciable plant assets, such as buildings, factory machinery, office equipment, delivery equipment, and store equipment.

Because the general ledger account has no room for detailed information about each item in a major class of depreciable plant assets, many companies use plant asset subsidiary ledgers. These subsidiary ledgers and detailed records provide more information and allow the company to maintain better control over plant and equipment.

When they are kept for each major class of plant and equipment, a company may have subsidiary ledgers for factory machinery, office equipment, and other classes of depreciable plant assets. Then there may be an additional subsidiary ledger for each type of asset within each category. For example, the subsidiary office equipment ledger may contain accounts for microcomputers, printers, fax machines, copying machines, and so on. Companies also keep a detailed record for each item represented in a subsidiary ledger account. For example, there may be a separate detailed record for each microcomputer represented in the micro-

ILLUSTRATION 10.12
Effect of Revenue Expenditure Treated as Capital Expenditure

	1997	
	Correctly Expensing	**Incorrectly Capitalizing**
Depreciation expense	$10,000	$12,000
Repair expense	6,000	–0–
Net income overstated by $4,000, which affects retained earnings	$16,000	$12,000
Asset cost	$40,000	$46,000
Accumulated depreciation	20,000	22,000
Book value	$20,000	$24,000

	1998	
	Correctly Expensing	**Incorrectly Capitalizing**
Depreciation expense	$10,000	$12,000
Repair expense	–0–	–0–
Net income understated by $2,000, which affects retained earnings	$10,000	$12,000
Asset cost	$40,000	$46,000
Accumulated depreciation	30,000	34,000
Book value	$10,000	$12,000

ILLUSTRATION 10.13
Detailed Record of a Specific Plant Asset

Item IBM 486 SX/33
Id. No. Z-43806
Location Rm. 403, Adm. bldg.
Date acquired Jan. 1, 1994
Cost $3,000
Estimated salvage value $200
Estimated useful life 4 yrs.
Depreciation per year $700
Accumulated depreciation:
12/31/94 $ 700
12/31/95 1,400
12/31/96 ______
12/31/97 ______

Insurance coverage:
United Ins. Co.
Pol. No. 0052-61481-24
Amt. $3,000
Repairs:
6/13/95 $140
______
______
Disposal date ______
Gain or loss ______

computer subsidiary ledger account. Each detailed record should include a description of the asset, identification or serial number, location of the asset, date of acquisition, cost, estimated salvage value, estimated useful life, annual depreciation, accumulated depreciation, insurance coverage, repairs, date of disposal, and gain or loss on final disposal of the asset. Note the detailed record for one particular microcomputer as of December 31, 1995, in Illustration 10.13.

To enhance control over plant and equipment, companies stencil on or attach the identification or serial number to each asset. Periodically, firms must take a physical inventory to determine whether all items in the accounting records actually exist, whether they are located where they should be, and whether they are still being used. A company that does not use detailed records and identification numbers or take physical inventories finds it difficult to determine whether assets have been discarded or stolen.

The general ledger control account balance for each major class of plant and equipment should equal the total of the amounts in the subsidiary ledger accounts for that class of plant assets. Also, the totals in the detailed records for a specific subsidiary ledger account (such as microcomputers) should equal the balance of

Illustration 10.14

Johnson & Johnson
Johnson & Johnson develops, manufactures, and sells toiletries, hygienic products, nonprescription drugs, pharmaceutical products, and professional products such as sutures, surgical instruments, and diagnostic products.

JOHNSON & JOHNSON AND SUBSIDIARIES
Consolidated Balance Sheet
At January 3, 1993 and December 29, 1991 (Dollars in Millions)

Assets	1992	1991
Current assets		
Cash and cash equivalents	$ 745	$ 589
Marketable securities, at cost	133	203
Accounts receivable, trade, less allowances $143 (1991, $136)	1,855	1,763
Inventories	1,742	1,702
Deferred taxes on income	327	238
Prepaid expenses and other receivables	621	438
Total current assets	$5,423	$4,933
Marketable securities, non-current, at cost	355	276
Property, plant and equipment, net	4,115	3,667
Intangible assets, net	716	738
Deferred taxes on income	506	100
Other assets	769	799
Total assets	$11,884	$10,513
Net operating earnings	$ 2,238	$ 2,079

that account. Each time a plant asset is acquired, exchanged, or disposed of, the firm posts an entry to both a general ledger control account and the appropriate subsidiary ledger account. It also updates the detailed record for the items affected.

Analyzing and Using the Financial Results—Rate of Return on Operating Assets

Objective 6
Analyze and use the financial results—rate of return on operating assets.

Analyzing the ratios of income statement and balance sheet items from one year to the next can reveal important trends. Management uses these ratios to measure performance by establishing targets and evaluating results. As an example, look at Illustration 10.14 taken from the 1992 annual report of Johnson & Johnson. Analysts use these figures to calculate the ratios and to explain the importance of this information to management and investors.

To determine the **rate of return on operating assets** for Johnson & Johnson for 1991 and 1992, use the following formula:

$$\text{Rate of return on operating assets} = \frac{\text{Net operating income}}{\text{Operating assets}}$$

1991: $2,079,000,000/$10,513,000,000 = 19.78%

1992: $2,238,000,000/$11,884,000,000 = 18.83%

Net operating income is also called "net operating earnings" or "income before interest and taxes." In calculating Johnson & Johnson's ratio, we have assumed that all assets are operating assets used in producing operating revenues.

This ratio measures the profitability of the company in carrying out its primary business function. For Johnson & Johnson, these figures indicate a slight decrease in the earning power of the company in 1992. Although net operating income increased, operating assets increased more than proportionately. Perhaps future performance will justify the increase in operating assets. However, management may want to examine the numbers behind this ratio more closely to see if a problem in operations may be arising.

In this chapter, you learned how to account for the acquisition of plant assets and depreciation. The next chapter discusses how to record the disposal of plant assets and how to account for natural resources and intangible assets.

UNDERSTANDING THE LEARNING OBJECTIVES

Objective 1
List the characteristics of plant assets and identify the costs of acquiring plant assets.

- To be classified as a plant asset, an asset must: (1) be tangible; (2) have a useful service life of more than one year; and (3) be used in business operations rather than held for resale.
- In accounting for plant assets, accountants must:
  1. Record the acquisition cost of the asset.
  2. Record the allocation of the asset's original cost to periods of its useful life through depreciation.
  3. Record subsequent expenditures on the asset.
  4. Account for the disposal of the asset.

Objective 2
List the four major factors affecting depreciation expense.

- Accountants consider four major factors in computing depreciation: (1) cost of the asset; (2) estimated salvage value of the asset; (3) estimated useful life of the asset, and (4) depreciation method to use in depreciating the asset.

Objective 3
Describe the various methods of calculating depreciation expense.

- **Straight-line method:** Assigns an equal amount of depreciation to each period. The formula for calculating straight-line depreciation is:

$$\text{Depreciation per period} = \frac{\text{Asset cost} - \text{Estimated salvage value}}{\text{Number of accounting periods in estimated useful life}}$$

- **Units-of-production method:** Assigns an equal amount of depreciation to each unit of product manufactured by an asset. The units-of-production depreciation formulas are:

$$\text{Depreciation per unit} = \frac{\text{Asset cost} - \text{Estimated salvage value}}{\text{Estimated total units of production (or service) during useful life of asset}}$$

$$\text{Depreciation per period} = \text{Depreciation per unit} \times \text{Number of units of goods or services produced}$$

- **Sum-of-the-years'-digits (SOYD) method:** SOYD is an accelerated depreciation method. The SOYD depreciation formulas are:

$$\text{Depreciation per period} = \frac{\text{Number of years of useful life remaining at beginning of accounting period}}{\text{SOYD}} \times \left(\text{Asset cost} - \text{Estimated salvage value}\right)$$

$$\text{Sum-of-the-years'-digits (SOYD)} = \frac{n(n+1)}{2}$$

- **Double-declining-balance method:** DDB is an accelerated depreciation method. Salvage value is ignored in making annual calculations. The formula for DDB depreciation is:

$$\text{Depreciation per period} = (2 \times \text{Straight-line rate}) \times \left(\text{Asset cost} - \text{Accumulated depreciation}\right)$$

Objective 4
Distinguish between capital and revenue expenditures for plant assets.

- Capital expenditures are debited to an asset account or an accumulated depreciation account and increase the book value of plant assets. Expenditures that increase the quality of services or extend the quantity of services beyond the original estimate are capital expenditures.
- Revenue expenditures are expensed immediately and reported in the income statement as expenses. Recurring and/or minor expenditures that neither add to the asset's quality of service-rendering abilities nor extend its quantity of services beyond the asset's original estimated useful life are expenses.

Objective 5
Describe the subsidiary records used to control plant assets.

- Plant asset subsidiary ledgers contain detailed information that cannot be maintained in the general ledger account about each item in a major class of depreciable plant assets.

- Control over plant and equipment is enhanced by plant asset subsidiary ledgers and other detailed records. Information in a detailed record may include a description of the asset, identification or serial number, location of the asset, date of acquisition, cost, estimated salvage value, estimated useful life, annual depreciation, accumulated depreciation, insurance coverage, repairs, date of disposal, and gain or loss on final disposal of the asset. A periodic physical inventory should be taken to determine whether items in accounting records actually exist and are still being used at the proper location.

Objective 6
Analyze and use the financial results—rate of return on operating assets.

- To calculate the rate of return on operating assets, divide net operating income by operating assets. This ratio helps management determine how effectively it used assets to produce a profit.

Demonstration Problem 10–A

Cleveland Company purchased a 2-square-mile farm under the following terms: cash paid, $486,000; mortgage note assumed, $240,000; and accrued interest on mortgage note assumed, $6,000. The company paid $55,200 for brokerage and legal services to acquire the property and secure clear title. Cleveland planned to subdivide the property into residential lots and to construct homes on these lots. Clearing and leveling costs of $21,600 were paid. Crops on the land were sold for $14,400. A house on the land, to be moved by the buyer of the house, was sold for $5,040. The other buildings were torn down at a cost of $9,600, and salvaged material was sold for $10,080.

Approximately 6 acres of the land were deeded to the township for roads, and another 10 acres were deeded to the local school district as the site for a future school. After the subdivision was completed, this land would have an approximate value of $7,680 per acre. The company secured a total of 1,200 salable lots from the remaining land.

Required Present a schedule showing in detail the composition of the cost of the 1,200 salable lots.

Solution to Demonstration Problem 10–A

CLEVELAND COMPANY
Schedule of Cost of 1,200 Residential Lots

Costs incurred:		
Cash paid	$486,000	
Mortgage note assumed	240,000	
Interest accrued on mortgage note assumed	6,000	
Broker and legal services	55,200	
Clearing and leveling costs	21,600	
Tearing down costs	9,600	$818,400
Less proceeds from sale of:		
Crops	$ 14,400	
House	5,040	
Salvaged materials	10,080	29,520
Net cost of land to be subdivided into 1,200 lots		$788,880

Demonstration Problem 10–B

Calvin Company acquired and put into use a machine on January 1, 1997, at a total cost of $45,000. The machine was estimated to have a useful life of 10 years and a salvage value of $5,000. It was also estimated that the machine would produce one million units of product during its life. The machine produced 90,000 units in 1997 and 125,000 units in 1998.

Required Compute the amounts of depreciation to be recorded in 1997 and 1998 under each of the following:

a. Straight-line method.

b. Units-of-production method.

c. Sum-of-the-years'-digits method.

d. Double-declining-balance method.
e. Assume 30,000 units were produced in the first quarter of 1999. Compute depreciation for this quarter under each of the four methods.

Solution to Demonstration Problem 10–B

a. Straight-line method:
   1997: ($45,000 − $5,000)/10 = $4,000
   1998: ($45,000 − $5,000)/10 = $4,000

b. Units-of-production method:
   1997: [($45,000 − $5,000)/1,000,000] × 90,000 = $3,600
   1998: [($45,000 − $5,000)/1,000,000] × 125,000 = $5,000

c. Sum-of-the-years'-digits method:
   1997: ($45,000 − $5,000) × 10/55 = $7,272.73
   1998: ($45,000 − $5,000) × 9/55 = $6,545.45

d. Double-declining-balance method:
   1997: $45,000 × 20% = $9,000
   1998: ($45,000 − $9,000) × 20% = $7,200

e. Straight-line: ($45,000 − $5,000)/10 × 1/4 = $1,000
   Units-of-production: (30,000 × $0.04) = $1,200
   Sum-of-the-years'-digits: ($45,000 − $5,000) × 8/55 × 1/4 = $1,454.55
   Double-declining-balance:
   ($45,000 − $9,000 − $7,200) × 0.2 × 1/4 = $1,440

New Terms

Accelerated depreciation methods Record higher amounts of depreciation during the early years of an asset's life and lower amounts in later years. *372*

Acquisition cost Amount of cash and/or cash equivalents given up to acquire a plant asset and place it in operating condition at its proper location. *366*

Appraised value An expert's opinion as to what an item's market price would be if the item were sold. *369*

Betterments (improvements) Capital expenditures that are properly charged to asset accounts because they add to the service-rendering ability of the assets; they increase the quality of services obtained from an asset. *380*

Book value An asset's recorded cost less its accumulated depreciation. *369*

Capital expenditures Expenditures debited to an asset account or to an accumulated depreciation account. *379*

Depreciation The amount of plant asset cost allocated to each accounting period benefiting from the plant asset's use (*369*). The **straight-line-depreciation** method charges an equal amount of plant asset cost to each period (*371*). The **units-of-production depreciation** method assigns an equal amount of depreciation for each unit of product manufactured or service rendered by an asset (*372*). The **sum-of-the-years'-digits (SOYD)** (*373*) and the **double-declining-balance (DDB)** (*373*) methods assign decreasing amounts of depreciation to successive periods of time.

Double-declining-balance depreciation (DDB) See Depreciation.

Extraordinary repairs Expenditures that cancel a part of the existing accumulated depreciation because they increase the quantity of services expected from an asset. *380*

Fair market value The price that would be received for an item being sold in the normal course of business (not at a forced liquidation sale). *368*

Inadequacy The inability of a plant asset to produce enough products or provide enough services to meet current demands. *369*

Land improvements Attachments to land, such as driveways, landscaping, parking lots, fences, lighting systems, and sprinkler systems, that have limited lives and therefore are depreciable. *366*

Low-cost items Items that provide years of service at a relatively low unit cost, such as hammers, paperweights, and drills. *381*

Obsolescence Decline in usefulness of an asset brought about by inventions and technological progress. *369*

Physical deterioration Results from use of the asset—wear and tear—and the action of the elements. *369*

Plant and equipment A shorter title for property, plant, and equipment; also called *plant assets*. Included are land and manufactured or constructed assets such as buildings, machinery, vehicles, and furniture. *364*

Rate of return on operating assets Net operating income/Operating assets. This ratio helps management determine how effectively it used assets to produce a profit. *384*

Revenue expenditures Expenditures (on a plant asset) that are immediately expensed. *379*

Salvage value The amount of money the company expects to recover, less disposal costs, on the date a plant asset is scrapped, sold, or traded in. Also called *scrap value* or *residual value*. *370*

Straight-line-depreciation See Depreciation.

Sum-of-the-years'-digits depreciation (SOYD) See Depreciation.

Tangible assets Assets that we can see and touch such as land, buildings, and equipment. *364*

Units-of-production depreciation See Depreciation.

Useful life Refers to the length of time the company owning the asset intends to use it. *370*

Self-Test

True-False

Indicate whether each of the following statements is true or false.

1. The cost of land includes its purchase price and other related costs, including the cost of removing an old unusable building that is on the land.
2. Depreciation is the process of valuation of an asset to arrive at its market value.
3. The purpose of depreciation accounting is to provide the cash required to replace plant assets.
4. Expenditures made on plant assets that increase the quality of services are debited to the Accumulated Depreciation account.
5. Plant asset subsidiary ledgers are used to increase control over plant assets.

Multiple-Choice

Select the best answer for each of the following questions.

1. On January 1, 1997, Jackson Company purchased equipment for $400,000, and installation and testing costs totaled $40,000. The equipment has an estimated useful life of 10 years and an estimated salvage value of $40,000. If Jackson uses the straight-line depreciation method, the depreciation expense for 1997 is:
   a. $36,000.
   b. $40,000.
   c. $44,000.
   d. $80,000.
   e. $88,000.
2. In Question 1, if the equipment were purchased on July 1, 1997, and Jackson used the double-declining-balance method, the depreciation expense for 1997 would be:
   a. $88,000.
   b. $72,000.
   c. $36,000.
   d. $44,000.
   e. $40,000.
3. In Question 1, if Jackson acquired the asset on January 1, 1997, and uses the sum-of-the-years'-digits method, the depreciation expense for 1997 is:
   a. $72,727.
   b. $80,000.
   c. $65,454.
   d. $7,272.
   e. $8,000.
4. Hatfield Company purchased a computer on January 2, 1997, for $10,000. The computer had an estimated salvage value of $3,000 and an estimated useful life of five years. At the beginning of 1999, the estimated salvage value changed to $1,000, and the computer is expected to have a remaining useful life of two years. Using the straight-line method, the depreciation expense for 1999 is:
   a. $1,400.
   b. $1,750.
   c. $2,250.
   d. $1,800.
   e. $3,100.
5. The result of recording a capital expenditure as a revenue expenditure is an:
   a. Overstatement of current year's expense.
   b. Understatement of current year's expense.
   c. Understatement of subsequent year's net income.
   d. Overstatement of current year's net income.
   e. None of the above.

Now turn to page 396 to check your answers.

QUESTIONS

1. What is the main distinction between inventory and a plant asset?
2. Which of the following items are properly classifiable as plant assets on the balance sheet?
   - **a.** Advertising that will appear in the future to inform the public about new energy-saving programs at a manufacturing plant.
   - **b.** A truck acquired by a manufacturing company to be used to deliver the company's products to wholesalers.
   - **c.** An automobile acquired by an insurance company to be used by one of its salespersons.
   - **d.** Adding machines acquired by an office supply company to be sold to customers.
   - **e.** The cost of constructing and paving a driveway that has an estimated useful life of 10 years.
3. In general terms, what does the cost of a plant asset include?
4. In what way does the purchase of a plant asset resemble the prepayment of an expense?
5. Brown Company purchased an old farm with a vacant building as a factory site for $1,040,000. Brown decided to use the building in its operations. How should Brown allocate the purchase price between the land and the building? How should this purchase be handled if the building is to be torn down?
6. Describe how a company may determine the cost of a self-constructed asset.
7. In any exchange of noncash assets, the accountant's task is to find the most appropriate valuation for the asset received. What is the general rule for determining the most appropriate valuation in such a situation?
8. Why should periodic depreciation be recorded on all plant assets except land?
9. Define the terms *inadequacy* and *obsolescence* as used in accounting for depreciable plant assets.
10. What four factors must be known to compute depreciation on a plant asset? How *objective* is the calculation of depreciation?
11. A friend, Mindy Jacobs, tells you her car depreciated $5,000 last year. Explain whether her concept of depreciation is the same as the accountant's concept.
12. What does the term *accelerated depreciation* mean? Give an example showing how depreciation is accelerated.
13. Provide a theoretical reason to support using an accelerated depreciation method.
14. If a machine has an estimated useful life of nine years, what will be the total digits to use in calculating depreciation under the sum-of-the-years'-digits method? How is this figure used in the depreciation calculation?
15. Nancy Company purchased a machine that originally had an estimated eight years of useful life. At the end of the third year, Nancy determined that the machine would last only three more years. Does this revision affect past depreciation taken?
16. What does the balance in the accumulated depreciation account represent? Does this balance represent cash that can be used to replace the related plant asset when it is completely depreciated?
17. What is the justification for reporting plant assets on the balance sheet at undepreciated cost (book value) rather than market value?
18. Distinguish between *capital expenditures* and *revenue expenditures*.
19. For each of the following, state whether the expenditure made should be charged to an expense, an asset, or an accumulated depreciation account:
   - **a.** Cost of installing air-conditioning equipment in a building that was not air conditioned.
   - **b.** Painting of an owned factory building every other year.
   - **c.** Cost of replacing the roof on a 10-year-old building that was purchased new and has an estimated total life of 40 years. The expenditure did not extend the life of the asset beyond the original estimate.
   - **d.** Cost of repairing an electric motor. The expenditure extended the estimated useful life beyond the original estimate.
20. Indicate which type of account (asset, accumulated depreciation, or expense) would be debited for each of the following expenditures:
   - **a.** Painting an office building at a cost of $1,000. The building is painted every year.
   - **b.** Adding on a new plant wing at a cost of $24,000,000.
   - **c.** Expanding a paved parking lot at a cost of $144,000.
   - **d.** Replacing a stairway with an escalator at a cost of $20,000.
   - **e.** Replacing the transmission in an automobile at a cost of $1,600, thus extending its useful life two years beyond the original estimate.
   - **f.** Replacing a broken fan belt at a cost of $600.
21. How do subsidiary records provide control over a company's plant assets?
22. What advantages can accrue to a company that maintains plant asset subsidiary records?

The Coca-Cola Company

23. **Real World Question** From the consolidated balance sheet of The Coca-Cola Company in the annual report booklet, identify the 1993 gross property, plant, and equipment and the net property, plant, and equipment. What percentage of the depreciable assets have been depreciated? Are the assets almost completely depreciated?

MAYTAG

24. **Real World Question** Based on the financial statements of Maytag Corporation contained in the an-

nual report booklet, what was the 1993 ending balance in the Land account? Did the company acquire any of these assets in 1993?

THE LIMITED, INC.

25. **Real World Question** Based on the financial statements and the notes to those statements of The Limited, Inc., contained in the annual report booklet, what was the 1993 ending net property and equipment balance? Did the company acquire any of these assets in 1993? What depreciation method did the company use?

HARLAND

26. **Real World Question** Based on the financial statements and the notes of John H. Harland Company contained in the annual report booklet, what was the 1993 ending balance of accumulated depreciation and amortization? Did the company acquire any of these assets in 1993? What depreciation methods did the company use?

Exercises

Exercise 10–1
Determine cost of land (L.O. 1)

Griffin Company paid $320,000 cash for a tract of land on which it plans to erect a new warehouse, and paid $4,000 in legal fees related to the purchase. Griffin also agreed to assume responsibility for $12,800 of unpaid taxes on the property. The company incurred a cost of $14,400 to remove an old apartment building from the land. Prepare a schedule showing the cost of the land acquired.

Exercise 10–2
Determine cost of land and building when acquired together (L.O. 1)

Ingles Company paid $840,000 cash for real property consisting of a tract of land and a building. The company intended to remodel and use the old building. To allocate the cost of the property acquired, Ingles had the property appraised. The appraised values were as follows: land, $576,000, and office building, $384,000. The cost of clearing the land was $18,000. The building was remodeled at a cost of $76,800. The cost of a new identical office building was estimated to be $432,000. Prepare a schedule showing the cost of the assets acquired.

Exercise 10–3
Determine cost of a machine (L.O. 1)

Young Company purchased a heavy machine to be used in its factory for $360,000, less a 2% cash discount. The company paid a fine of $1,800 because an employee hauled the machine over city streets without securing the required permits. The machine was installed at a cost of $10,800, and testing costs of $3,600 were incurred to place the machine in operation. Prepare a schedule showing the recorded cost of the machine.

Exercise 10–4
Determine cost of machine in noncash acquisition (L.O. 1)

A machine is acquired in exchange for 50 shares of Martin Corporation capital stock. The stock recently traded at $400 per share. The machine cost $30,000 three years ago. At what amount should the machine be recorded?

Exercise 10–5
Record cost of office equipment, depreciation, and repairs expense (L.O. 1, 3, 4)

Nichols Company purchased some office furniture for $14,880 cash on March 1, 1996. It also paid $240 cash for freight costs incurred. The furniture is being depreciated over four years under the straight-line method, assuming a salvage value of $720. The company employs a calendar-year accounting period. On July 1, 1997, it spent $96 to refinish the furniture. Prepare journal entries for the Nichols Company to record all of the data, including the annual depreciation adjustments through 1997.

Exercise 10–6
Compute annual depreciation for two years under each of four different depreciation methods (L.O. 3)

On January 2, 1996, a new machine was acquired for $900,000. The machine has an estimated salvage value of $100,000 and an estimated useful life of 10 years. The machine is expected to produce a total of 500,000 units of product throughout its useful life. Compute depreciation for 1996 and 1997 using each of the following methods:

a. Straight-line.
b. Units-of-production (assume 30,000 and 60,000 units were produced in 1996 and 1997, respectively).
c. Sum-of-the-years'-digits.
d. Double-declining-balance.

Exercise 10–7
Determine information concerning machinery (L.O. 3)

DeLoach Company finds its records are incomplete concerning a piece of machinery used in its plant. According to the company records, the machinery has an estimated useful life of 10 years and an estimated salvage value of $12,000. It has recorded $6,000 in depreciation each year using the straight-line method. If the Accumulated Depreciation account shows a balance of $36,000, what is the original cost of the machinery and how many years remain to be depreciated?

Exercise 10–8
Compute depreciation under SOYD and DDB methods (L.O. 3)

Christin Company purchased a machine on April 1, 1996, for $72,000. The machine has an estimated useful life of five years with no expected salvage value. The company's accounting year ends on December 31.

Compute the depreciation expense for 1996 and 1997 under (*a*) the sum-of-the-years'-digits method and (*b*) the double-declining-balance method.

Exercise 10–9
Compute DDB depreciation (L.O. 3)

Foster Company purchased a machine for $1,600 and incurred installation costs of $400. The estimated salvage value of the machine is $100. The machine has an estimated useful life of four years. Compute the annual depreciation charges for this machine under the double-declining-balance method.

Exercise 10–10
Compute depreciation before and after revision of expected life and salvage value (L.O. 3)

Frake Company acquired a delivery truck on January 2, 1996, for $53,600. The truck had an estimated salvage value of $2,400 and an estimated useful life of eight years. At the beginning of 1999, a revised estimate shows that the truck has a remaining useful life of six years. The estimated salvage value changed to $800.

Compute the depreciation charge for 1996 and the revised depreciation charge for 1999 using the straight-line method.

Exercise 10–11
Allocate periodic depreciation to building and to expense (L.O. 3)

Assume that the truck described in Exercise 10–10 was used 40% of the time in 1997 to haul materials used in the construction of a building by Frake Company for its own use. (Remember that 1997 is before the revision was made on estimated life.) During the remaining time, Frake used the truck to deliver merchandise to its customers.

Prepare the journal entry to record straight-line depreciation on the truck for 1997.

Exercise 10–12
Compute straight-line depreciation given changes in estimated life and salvage value (L.O. 3)

Hampton Company purchased a computer for $60,000 and placed it in operation on January 2, 1995. Depreciation was recorded for 1995 and 1996 using the straight-line method, a six-year life, and an expected salvage value of $2,400. The introduction of a new model of this computer in 1997 caused the company to revise its estimate of useful life to four years and to reduce the estimated salvage value to zero.

Compute the depreciation expense on the computer for 1997.

Exercise 10–13
Compute straight-line depreciation after major overhaul (L.O. 3, 4)

On January 2, 1996, a company purchased and placed in operation a new machine at a total cost of $30,000. Depreciation was recorded on the machine for 1996 and 1997 under the straight-line method using an estimated useful life of five years and no expected salvage value. Early in 1998, the machine was overhauled at a cost of $10,000. The estimated useful life of the machine was revised upward to a total of seven years.

Compute the depreciation expense on the machine for 1998.

Exercise 10–14
Compute error in net income when installation and freight costs are expensed (L.O. 4)

Ricky Company purchased a machine on January 3, 1996, at a cost of $50,000. It debited freight and installation charges of $10,000 to Repairs Expense. It recorded straight-line depreciation on the machine in 1996 and 1997 using an estimated life of 10 years and no expected salvage value.

Compute the amount of the error in net income for 1996 and 1997, and state whether net income is understated or overstated.

Exercise 10–15
Determine the effect of an error in classification (L.O. 4)

Tucker Company owns a plant asset that originally cost $120,000 in 1993. The asset has been depreciated for three years assuming an eight-year useful life and no salvage value. During 1996, Tucker incorrectly capitalized $60,000 in repairs on the plant asset rather than expensing them. Describe the impact of this error on the asset's cost and Tucker's net income over the next five years.

PROBLEMS

Problem 10–1
Determine cost of machine (L.O. 1)

Martin Company purchased a machine for use in its operations that had an invoice price of $40,000 excluding sales tax. A 4% sales tax was levied on the sale. Terms were net 30. The company estimated the total cost of hauling the machine from the dealer's warehouse to the company's plant at $2,800, which did not include a fine of $800 for failure to secure the necessary permits to use city streets in transporting the machine. In delivering the machine to its plant, a Martin employee damaged the truck used; repairs cost $1,800. The machine was also slightly damaged with repair costs amounting to $800.

Martin incurred installation costs of $16,000 that included the $2,000 cost of shoring up the floor under the machine. Testing costs amounted to $1,200. Safety guards were installed on the machine at a cost of $320, and the machine was placed in operation.

Required Prepare a schedule showing the amount at which the machine should be recorded in Martin's accounts.

Problem 10–2
Determine cost of land and building (L.O. 1)

Walton Company planned to erect a new factory building and a new office building in Atlanta, Georgia. A report on a suitable site showed an appraised value of $180,000 for land and orchard and $120,000 for a building.

After considerable negotiation, the company and the owner reached the following agreement: Walton Company was to pay $216,000 in cash, assume a $90,000 mortgage note on the property, assume the interest of $1,920 accrued on the mortgage note, and assume unpaid property taxes of $13,200. Walton Company paid $18,000 cash for brokerage and legal services in acquiring the property.

Shortly after acquisition of the property, Walton Company sold the fruit on the trees for $2,640, remodeled the building into an office building at a cost of $38,400, and removed the trees from the land at a cost of $9,000. Construction of the factory building was to begin in a week.

Required Prepare schedules showing the proper valuation of the assets acquired by Walton Company.

Problem 10–3
Prepare entry for acquisition of machine, for depreciation under DDB, and for straight-line depreciation assuming a change in estimated life (L.O. 1, 3)

Ruth Company acquired and placed into use a heavy factory machine on October 1, 1996. The machine had an invoice price of $720,000, but the company received a 3% cash discount by paying the bill on the date of acquisition. An employee of Ruth Company hauled the machine down a city street without a permit. As a result, the company had to pay a $3,000 fine. Installation and testing costs totaled $71,600. The machine is estimated to have a $70,000 salvage value and a seven-year useful life. (A fraction should be used for the DDB calculation rather than a percentage.)

Required

a. Prepare the journal entry to record the acquisition of the machine.

b. Prepare the journal entry to record depreciation for 1996 under the double-declining-balance method.

c. Assume Ruth Company used the straight-line depreciation method. At the beginning of 1999, it estimated the machine will last another six years. Prepare the journal entry to record depreciation for 1999. The estimated salvage value would not change.

Problem 10–4
Compute cost of land, land improvements, building, and machinery; prepare entry to correct the accounts (L.O. 1, 4)

Orange Company has the following entries in its Building account:

Debits

Date		Description	Amount
1996			
May	5	Cost of land and building purchased	$200,000
	5	Broker fees incident to purchase of land and building	12,000
1997			
Jan.	3	Contract price of new wing added to south end	84,000
	15	Cost of new machinery, estimated life 10 years	160,000
June	10	Real estate taxes for six months ended 6/30/97	3,600
Aug.	10	Cost of building parking lot for employees in back of building	4,960
Sept.	6	Replacement of windows broken in August	160
Oct.	10	Repairs due to regular usage	2,240

Credits

Date		Description	Amount
1996			
May	24	Transfer to Land account, per allocation of purchase cost authorized in minutes of board of directors	32,000
1997			
Jan.	5	Proceeds from lease of second floor for six months ended 12/31/96	8,000

Orange acquired the original property on May 5, 1996. Orange immediately engaged a contractor to construct a new wing on the south end of the building. While the new wing was being constructed, the company leased the second floor as temporary warehouse space to Kellett Company. During this period (July 1 to December 31, 1996), the company installed new machinery costing $160,000 on the first floor of the building. Regular operations began on January 2, 1997.

Required

a. Compute the correct balance for the Buildings account as of December 31, 1997. The company employs a calendar-year accounting period.

b. Prepare the necessary journal entries to correct the records of Orange Company at December 31, 1997. No depreciation entries are required.

Problem 10–5
Compute depreciation for first year under each of four different depreciation methods (L.O. 3)

Carl Company acquired and placed into use equipment on January 2, 1996, at a cash cost of $1,870,000. Transportation charges amounted to $15,000, and installation and testing costs totaled $110,000.

The equipment was estimated to have a useful life of nine years and a salvage value of $75,000 at the end of its life. It was further estimated that the equipment would be used in the production of 1,920,000 units of product during its life. During 1996, 426,000 units of product were produced.

Required

Compute the depreciation to the nearest dollar for the year ended December 31, 1996, using:

a. Straight-line method.
b. Units-of-production method.
c. Sum-of-the-years'-digits method.
d. Double-declining-balance method (use a fraction rather than a percentage).

Problem 10–6
Compute depreciation for two years using three depreciation methods; partial-year depreciation used first year (L.O. 3)

Froelich Company purchased a machine on October 1, 1996, for $100,000. The machine has an estimated salvage value of $30,000 and an estimated useful life of eight years.

Required

Compute to the nearest dollar the amount of depreciation Froelich should record on the machine for the years ending December 31, 1996, and 1997, under each of the following methods:

a. Straight-line.
b. Sum-of-the-years'-digits.
c. Double-declining-balance.

ALTERNATE PROBLEMS

Problem 10–1A
Determine cost of machine (L.O. 1)

Askew Company purchased a machine that had an invoice price of $200,000 excluding sales tax. Terms were net 30. A 4% sales tax was levied on the sale. The company incurred and paid freight costs of $5,000. Special electrical connections were run to the machine at a cost of $7,000 and a special reinforced base for the machine was built at a cost of $9,000. The machine was dropped and damaged while being mounted on this base. Repairs cost $2,000. Raw materials with a cost of $500 were consumed in testing the machine. Safety guards were installed on the machine at a cost of $700, and the machine was placed in operation. In addition, $250 of costs were incurred in removing an old machine.

Required

Prepare a schedule showing the amount at which the machine should be recorded in Askew Company's account.

Problem 10–2A
Determine cost of land (L.O. 1)

Hornet Company purchased 2 square miles of farmland under the following terms: $968,000 cash; and liability assumed on mortgage note of $320,000 and interest accrued on mortgage note assumed, $12,800. The company paid $67,200 of legal and brokerage fees and also paid $3,200 for a title search on the property.

The company planned to use the land as a site for a new office building and a new factory. Hornet paid clearing and leveling costs of $28,800. It sold crops on the land for $7,360 and sold one of the houses on the property for $19,200. The other buildings were torn down at a cost of $14,400; sale of salvaged materials yielded cash proceeds of $13,600. Approximately 1% of the land acquired was deeded to the county for roads. The cost of excavating a basement for the office building amounted to $9,120.

Required

Prepare a schedule showing the amount at which the land should be carried on Hornet Company's books.

Problem 10–3A
Determine cost of truck; prepare entry for depreciation under DDB and for straight-line depreciation assuming change in estimated life (L.O. 1, 3)

Sanders Company purchased a used panel truck for $14,400 cash. The next day the company's name and business were painted on the truck at a total cost of $744. The truck was then given a minor overhaul at a cost of $96, and new tires were mounted on the truck at a cost of $960, less a trade-in allowance of $120 for the old tires. The truck was placed in service on April 1, 1996, at which time it had an estimated useful life of five years and a salvage value of $1,680.

Required

a. Prepare a schedule showing the cost to be recorded for the truck.

b. Prepare the journal entry to record depreciation at the end of the calendar-year accounting period, December 31, 1996. Use the double-declining-balance method.

c. Assume that the straight-line depreciation method has been used. At the beginning of 1999 it is estimated the truck will last another four years. The estimated salvage value changed to $960. Prepare the entry to record depreciation for 1999.

Problem 10–4A
Compute cost of land, land improvements, building, and machinery; prepare entry to correct the accounts (L.O. 1, 4)

You are the new controller for Lark Company, which began operations on October 1, 1996, after a start-up period that ran from the middle of 1995. While reviewing the accounts, you find an account entitled "Fixed Assets," which contains the following items:

Cash paid to previous owner of land and old building	$ 192,000
Cash given to construction company as partial payment for the new building	72,000
Legal and title search fees	2,400
Real estate commission	14,400
Cost of demolishing old building	16,800
Cost of leveling and grading	9,600
Architect's fee (90% building and 10% improvements)	36,000
Cost of excavating (digging) basement for new building	21,600
Cash paid to construction company for new building	288,000
Repair damage done by vandals	7,200
Sprinkler system for lawn	31,200
Lighting system for parking lot	40,800
Paving of parking lot	60,000
Net invoice price of machinery	1,152,000
Freight cost incurred on machinery	50,400
Installation and testing of machinery	19,200
Medical bill paid for employee injured in installing machinery	3,600
Landscaping (permanent)	38,400
Repair damage to building in installation of machinery	4,800
Special assessment paid to city for water mains and sewer line	45,600
Account balance	$2,106,000

In addition, you discover that cash receipts of $1,200 from selling materials salvaged from the old building were credited to Miscellaneous Revenues in 1996. Digging deeper, you find that the plant manager spent all of his time for the first nine months of 1996 supervising installation of land improvements (10%), building construction (40%), and installation of machinery (50%). The plant manager's nine-month salary of $108,000 was debited to Officers' Salaries Expense.

Required

a. List all items on a form containing columns for Land, Land Improvements, Building, and Machinery. Sort the items into the appropriate columns, omitting those items not properly included as an element of asset cost. Show negative amounts in parentheses. Total your columns.

b. Prepare one compound journal entry to reclassify and adjust the accounts and to eliminate the Fixed Assets account. Do not attempt to record depreciation for the partial year.

Problem 10–5A
Compute depreciation for first year under each of four different depreciation methods (L.O. 3)

Park Company acquired and put into use a machine on January 1, 1996, at a cash cost of $60,000 and immediately spent $2,500 to install it. The machine had an estimated useful life of eight years and an estimated salvage value of $12,500 at the end of this time. It was further estimated that the machine would produce 500,000 units of product during its life. In the first year, the machine produced 100,000 units.

Required

Prepare journal entries to record depreciation to the nearest dollar for 1996, using:

a. Straight-line method.
b. Units-of-production method.
c. Sum-of-the-years'-digits method.
d. Double-declining-balance method.

Problem 10–6A
Compute depreciation for two years using three depreciation methods; partial-year depreciation used first year (L.O. 3)

Williams Company paid $60,000 for a machine on April 1, 1996, and placed it in use on that same date. The machine has an estimated life of 10 years and an estimated salvage value of $10,000.

Required

Compute the amount of depreciation to the nearest dollar the company should record on this asset for the years ending December 31, 1996, and 1997, under each of the following methods:

a. Straight-line.
b. Sum-of-the-years'-digits.
c. Double-declining-balance.

BEYOND THE NUMBERS—CRITICAL THINKING

Business Decision Case 10–1
Compute correct cost of land, buildings, and land improvements; compute depreciation; prepare entry to correct the accounts (L.O. 1, 3)

You are a new staff auditor assigned to audit Davis Company's Buildings account. You determine that Davis Company made the following entries in its Buildings account in 1996:

		Debits	
1996			
Jan.	2	Cost of land and old buildings purchased	$ 720,000
	2	Legal fees incident to purchase	9,600
	2	Fee for title search	1,200
	12	Cost of demolishing old buildings on land	19,200
June	16	Cost of insurance during construction of new building	4,800
July	30	Payment to contractor on completion of new building	1,080,000
Aug.	5	Architect's fees for design of new building	48,000
Sept.	15	City assessment for sewers and sidewalks (considered permanent)	16,800
Oct.	6	Cost of landscaping (considered permanent)	9,600
Nov.	1	Cost of driveways and parking lots	60,000
		Credit	
Jan.	15	Proceeds received upon sale of salvaged materials from old buildings	4,800

In addition to the entries in the account, you obtained the following information in your interview with the accountant in charge of the Buildings account:

1. The company began using the new building on September 1, 1996. The building is estimated to have a 40-year useful life and no salvage value.
2. The company began using the driveways and parking lots on November 1, 1996. The driveways and parking lots have an estimated 10-year useful life and no salvage value.
3. The company uses the straight-line depreciation method to depreciate all of its plant assets.

Using all of this information, do the following:

a. Prepare a schedule that shows the separate cost of land, buildings, and land improvements.
b. Compute the amount of depreciation expense for 1996.

c. Complete the journal entries required to correct the accounts at December 31, 1996. Assume that closing entries have not been made.

d. Write a brief statement describing to management why depreciation must be recorded and how recording depreciation affects net income.

Business Decision Case 10–2
Compute partial-year depreciation under each of four different methods; cite circumstances in which each of the different methods seems most appropriate (L.O. 2, 3)

On October 1, 1997, Grant Company acquired and placed into use new equipment costing $504,000. The equipment has an estimated useful life of five years and an estimaed salvage value of $24,000. Grant estimates that the equipment will produce 2 million units of product during its life. In the last quarter of 1997, the equipment produced 120,000 units of product. As Grant Company's accountant, management has asked you to do the following:

a. Compute the depreciation for the last quarter of 1997, using each of the following methods:

1. Straight-line.
2. Units-of-production.
3. Sum-of-the-years'-digits.
4. Double-declining-balance.

b. Prepare a written report describing the conditions in which each of these four methods would be most appropriate.

Business Decision Case 10–3
Discuss appropriate use of accelerated methods of depreciation (L.O. 3)

The notes to the financial statements of Oxford Industries, Inc., in "A Broader Perspective" on page 379, stated that substantially all fixed assets, except buildings, are depreciated using an accelerated method. Explain why an accelerated method of depreciation is appropriate for all fixed assets except buildings.

Business Decision Case 10–4
Discuss the rate of return on operating assets and calculate the ratio for four actual companies (L.O. 6)

Discuss the meaning of rate of return on operating assets, its elements, and what it means to investors and management.

Calculate the rate of return on operating assets for the four companies in the annual report booklet for the two most recent years. Assume all assets are operating assets. Comment on the results.

Annual Report Analysis 10–5
Determine the number of depreciation methods used. Cite the advantages of each method. (L.O. 3)

The following footnote excerpted from the 1993 annual report of John H. Harland Company describes the company's accounting policies for property, plant, and equipment:

Property, plant, and equipment are carried at cost. Depreciation of buildings is computed primarily by the declining balance method. Depreciation of equipment, furniture and fixtures is calculated by the straight-line or sum-of-the-years'-digits methods. Accelerated methods are used for income tax purposes for all property where it is allowed.

Required

a. How many different depreciation methods are used by John H. Harland Company? Does this practice conform with generally accepted accounting principles?

b. Discuss why management might select each of these methods to depreciate plant assets.

Group Project 10–6
Comment on data in Toro Company's 1993 annual report

Consider the following footnote from The Toro Company's 1993 annual report:

Assets
Total assets as of July 31, 1993 were $419.2 million, down $2.1 million from fiscal 1992. Cash and cash equivalents increased $36.3 million to $61.8 million as a result of the improved cash flow mentioned above. The asset increase was offset by a $26.3 million decrease in net accounts receivable resulting from a change in the company's distribution and terms of sale. In addition, net property, plant and equipment decreased $10.4 million due to the combined effect of the consolidation of operations and the annual accumulation of amortization and depreciation which were offset, in part, by current year capital spending.

Property and Depreciation
Property, plant and equipment are carried at cost. The company provides for depreciation of plant and equipment utilizing the straight-line method over the estimated useful lives of the assets. Buildings, including leasehold improvements and equipment, are generally depreciated over 10 to 45 years and 3 to 7 years, respectively. Tooling costs are generally amortized using the units of production basis. Expenditures for major renewals and betterments which substantially increase the useful lives of existing assets are capitalized, and maintenance and repairs are charged to operating expenses as incurred.

Toro
The Toro Company sells commercial, irrigation, and consumer lawn care and turf care products.

In groups of two or three, identify some accounting policies management must have implemented to yield the above data. In addition, discuss management's probable reasons for calculating depreciation on property, plant, and equipment in the manner they selected.

Answers to Self-Test

True-False

1. **True.** The cost of land includes all normal, reasonable, and necessary expenditures to obtain the land and get it ready for use.
2. **False.** Depreciation is a process of allocation, not valuation, and the book value of an asset has little to do with its market value.
3. **False.** Depreciation accounting does not provide funds required to replace plant assets. Instead, accumulated depreciation simply shows how much of an asset's cost has been charged to expense since the asset was acquired.
4. **False.** Expenditures that improve the quality of services are charged to the asset account.
5. **True.** Plant asset subsidiary ledgers provide detailed information that the general ledger account cannot provide and thus give better control over plant assets.

Multiple-Choice

1. **b**. The depreciation expense for 1997 using the straight-line method is computed as follows:

$$(\$440{,}000 - \$40{,}000)/10 = \$40{,}000$$

2. **d.**

$$\text{Double-declining balance rate} = 2 \times (100\%/10) = 20\%$$

$$\text{Depreciation expense for 1997} = (20\% \times \$440{,}000) \times 6/12 = \$44{,}000$$

3. **a.**

$$\text{SOYD} = \frac{10(10+1)}{2} = 55$$

$$\text{Depreciation expense} = \frac{10}{55} \times (\$440{,}000 - \$40{,}000) = \$72{,}727$$

4. **e.** At the beginning of 1999, the balance of accumulated depreciation is $2,800 (annual depreciation of $1,400 × 2) and book value is $7,200, or ($10,000 − $2,800). The revised annual depreciation expense is $3,100, or [($7,200 − $1,000)/2].
5. **a.** The error in recording a capital expenditure as a revenue expenditure results in an overstatement of current year's expense, as well as an understatement of current year's net income.

11

Plant Asset Disposals, Natural Resources, and Intangible Assets

Learning Objectives

After studying this chapter, you should be able to:

1. Calculate and prepare entries for the sale, retirement, and destruction of plant assets.
2. Describe and record exchanges of dissimilar and similar plant assets.
3. Determine the periodic depletion cost of a natural resource and calculate depreciation of plant assets located on extractive industry property.

(*continued*)

Your study of long-term assets—plant assets, natural resources, and intangible assets—began in Chapter 10, which focused on determining plant asset cost, computing depreciation, and distinguishing between capital and revenue expenditures. This chapter begins by discussing the disposal of plant assets. The next topic is accounting for natural resources such as ores, minerals, oil and gas, and timber. The final topic is accounting for intangible assets such as patents, copyrights, franchises, trademarks and trade names, leases, and goodwill.

Note that accounting for all the long-term assets discussed in these chapters is basically the same. A company that purchases a long-term asset records it at cost. As the company receives benefits from the asset and its future service potential decreases, the accountant transfers the cost from an asset account to an expense account. Finally, the asset is sold, retired, or traded in on a new asset. Because the lives of long-term assets can extend for many years, the methods accountants use in reporting such assets can have a dramatic effect on the financial statements of many accounting periods.

Disposal of Plant Assets

All plant assets except land eventually wear out or become inadequate or obsolete and must be sold, retired, or traded for new assets. When disposing of a plant asset, a company must remove both the asset's cost and accumulated depreciation from the accounts. Overall, then, all plant asset disposals have the following steps in common:

1. Bring the asset's depreciation up to date.
2. Record the disposal by:
   - **a.** Writing off the asset's cost.
   - **b.** Writing off the accumulated depreciation.
   - **c.** Recording any consideration (usually cash) received or paid or to be received or paid.
   - **d.** Recording the gain or loss, if any.

(*concluded*)

4. Prepare entries for the acquisition and amortization of intangible assets.

5. Analyze and use the financial results—total assets turnover.

As you study this section, remember these common procedures accountants use to record the disposal of plant assets. In the paragraphs that follow, we discuss accounting for the (1) sale of plant assets, (2) retirement of plant assets without sale, (3) destruction of plant assets, (4) exchange of plant assets, and (5) cost of dismantling and removing plant assets.

Sale of Plant Assets

Objective 1
Calculate and prepare entries for the sale, retirement, and destruction of plant assets.

Companies frequently dispose of plant assets by selling them. By comparing an asset's book value (cost less accumulated depreciation) with its selling price (or net amount realized if there are selling expenses), the company may show either a gain or loss. If the sales price is greater than the asset's book value, the company shows a gain. If the sales price is less than the asset's book value, the company shows a loss. Of course, when the sales price equals the asset's book value, no gain or loss occurs.

To illustrate accounting for the sale of a plant asset, assume that a company sells equipment costing $45,000 with accumulated depreciation of $14,000 for $35,000. The firm realizes a gain of $4,000:

Equipment cost	$45,000
Accumulated depreciation	14,000
Book value	$31,000
Sales price	35,000
Gain realized	$ 4,000

The journal entry to record the sale is:

	Debit	Credit
Cash	35,000	
Accumulated Depreciation—Equipment	14,000	
Equipment		45,000
Gain on Disposal of Plant Assets		4,000
To record sale of equipment at a price greater than book value.		

If on the other hand, the company sells the equipment for $28,000, it realizes a loss of $3,000 ($31,000 book value − $28,000 sales price). The journal entry to record the sale is:

	Debit	Credit
Cash	28,000	
Accumulated Depreciation—Equipment	14,000	
Loss from Disposal of Plant Assets	3,000	
Equipment		45,000
To record sale of equipment at a price less than book value.		

If a firm sells the equipment for $31,000, no gain or loss occurs. The journal entry to record the sale is:

	Debit	Credit
Cash	31,000	
Accumulated Depreciation—Equipment	14,000	
Equipment		45,000
To record sale of equipment at a price equal to book value.		

Accounting for Depreciation to Date of Disposal When selling or otherwise disposing of a plant asset, a firm must record the depreciation up to the date of sale or disposal. For example, if it sold an asset on April 1 and last recorded depreciation on December 31, the company should record depreciation for three months (January 1–April 1). When depreciation is not recorded for the three months, operating expenses for that period are understated, and the gain on the sale of the asset is understated or the loss overstated.

To illustrate, assume that on August 1, 1998, Ray Company sold a machine for $1,500. When purchased on January 2, 1990, the machine cost $12,000; Ray was depreciating it at the straight-line rate of 10% per year. As of December 31, 1997, after closing entries were made, the machine's accumulated depreciation account had a balance of $9,600. Before determining a gain or loss and before making an entry to record the sale, the firm must make the following entry to record depreciation for the seven months ended July 31, 1998:

			Debit	Credit
July	31	Depreciation Expense—Machinery	700	
		Accumulated Depreciation—Machinery		700
		To record depreciation for seven months ($12,000 × 0.10 × 7/12).		

An accountant would compute the $200 loss on the sale as follows:

Machine cost	$12,000
Accumulated depreciation ($9,600 + $700)	10,300
Book value	$ 1,700
Sales price	1,500
Loss realized	$ 200

The journal entry to record the sale is:

	Debit	Credit
Cash	1,500	
Accumulated Depreciation—Machinery	10,300	
Loss from Disposal of Plant Assets	200	
Machinery		12,000
To record sale of machinery at a price less than book value.		

Retirement of Plant Assets without Sale

When retiring a plant asset from service, a company removes the asset's cost and accumulated depreciation from its plant asset accounts. For example, Hayes Company would make the following journal entry when it retired a fully depreciated machine that cost $15,000 and had no salvage value:

	Debit	Credit
Accumulated Depreciation—Machinery	15,000	
Machinery		15,000
To record the retirement of a fully depreciated machine.		

Occasionally, a company continues to use a plant asset after it has been fully depreciated. In such a case, the firm should not remove the asset's cost and accumulated depreciation from the accounts until the asset is sold, traded, or retired from service. Of course, the company cannot record more depreciation on a fully depreciated asset because total depreciation expense taken on an asset may not exceed its cost.

Sometimes a business retires or discards a plant asset before fully depreciating it. When selling the asset as scrap (even if not immediately), the firm removes its cost and accumulated depreciation from the asset and accumulated depreciation accounts. In addition, the accountant records its estimated salvage value in a Salvaged Materials account and recognizes a gain or loss on disposal. To illustrate, assume that a firm retires a machine with a $10,000 original cost and $7,500 of accumulated depreciation. If the machine's estimated salvage value is $500, the following entry is required:

	Debit	Credit
Salvaged Materials	500	
Accumulated Depreciation—Machinery	7,500	
Loss from Disposal of Plant Assets	2,000	
Machinery		10,000
To record retirement of machinery, which will be sold for scrap at a later time.		

An Accounting Perspective

Business Insight Many debt-ridden companies avoid filing bankruptcy through restructuring. Wang Laboratories, Inc., manufactures and services office computer systems. In an effort to downsize operations, Wang incurred restructuring charges of $138 million for asset write-downs and $36 million for abandonment of facilities in 1992. Wang partially offset these restructuring charges by a $17 million gain on the sale of real estate.

Destruction of Plant Assets

Sometimes accidents, fires, floods, and storms wreck or destroy plant assets, causing companies to incur losses. For example, assume that fire completely destroyed an *uninsured* building costing $40,000 with up-to-date accumulated depreciation of $12,000. The journal entry is:

Fire Loss	28,000	
Accumulated Depreciation—Buildings	12,000	
Buildings		40,000
To record fire loss.		

If the building was *insured*, the company would debit only the amount of the fire loss exceeding the amount to be recovered from the insurance company to the Fire Loss account. To illustrate, assume the company partially insured the building and will recover $22,000 from the insurance company. The journal entry is:

Receivable from Insurance Company	22,000	
Fire Loss	6,000	
Accumulated Depreciation—Buildings	12,000	
Buildings		40,000
To record fire loss and amount recoverable from insurance company.		

Exchanges of Plant Assets (Nonmonetary Assets)

Nonmonetary assets are those whose price may change over time, such as inventories, property, plant, and equipment. In accounting for the exchange of nonmonetary assets, ordinarily firms base the recorded amount on the fair market value of the asset given up or the fair market value of the asset received, whichever is more clearly evident. If a gain or loss results from the exchange, companies always recognize the loss. They may or may not recognize the gain, depending on whether the asset exchanged is similar or dissimilar to the asset received.

Similar assets are those of the same general type, that perform the same function, or that are employed in the same line of business. Examples of the exchange of similar assets include exchanging a building for another building, a delivery truck for another delivery truck, and equipment for other equipment. Conversely, examples of the exchange of dissimilar assets include exchanging a building for land or equipment for inventory.

In general, companies recognize losses on nonmonetary assets regardless of whether the assets are similar or dissimilar. They recognize gains if the assets are dissimilar in nature because the earnings process related to those assets is considered to be completed. With one exception, firms defer gains on the exchange of similar nonmonetary assets. The exception occurs when they receive monetary consideration in addition to the similar asset. Companies recognize a partial gain when they receive cash along with an asset. Because the specific details of monetary consideration are reserved for an intermediate accounting text, assume in the examples given that cash has been paid, not received. Compute both gains and losses on the disposal of nonmonetary assets by comparing the book value of the asset given up with the fair market value of the asset given up.

Objective 2
Describe and record exchanges of dissimilar and similar plant assets.

Exchanges of Dissimilar Plant Assets Sometimes firms trade a machine for a dissimilar plant asset such as a truck. For exchanges of dissimilar plant assets, accountants record the new asset at the fair market value of the asset received or the asset(s) given up, whichever is more clearly evident.[1] When the cash price of the new asset is stated, they use the cash price to record the new asset. If the cash price is not stated, they assume the fair market value of the old asset plus any cash paid is the cash price and use it to record the new asset. Thus, accountants would normally record the asset received at either (1) the stated cash price of the new asset or (2) a known fair market value of the asset given up plus any cash paid.

[1] APB, *APB Opinion No. 29*, "Accounting for Nonmonetary Transactions" (New York: AICPA, May 1973), par. 16.

Debiting accumulated depreciation and crediting the old asset removes the book value of the old asset from the accounts. The firm credits the Cash account for any amount paid. If the amount at which the new asset is recorded exceeds the book value of the old asset plus any cash paid, a company records a gain to balance the journal entry. If the situation is reversed, it records a loss to balance the journal entry.

To illustrate such an exchange, assume a factory exchanges an old machine for a new delivery truck. The machine cost $45,000 and had an up-to-date accumulated depreciation balance of $38,000. The truck had a $55,000 cash price and was acquired by trading in the machine with a fair value of $3,000 and paying $52,000 cash. The journal entry to record the exchange is:

	Debit	Credit
Trucks	55,000	
Accumulated Depreciation—Machinery	38,000	
Loss from Disposal of Plant Assets	4,000	
Machinery		45,000
Cash		52,000
To record loss on exchange of dissimilar plant assets.		

Another way to compute the $4,000 loss on the exchange is to use the book value of the old asset less the fair market value of the old asset. The calculation is as follows:

Machine cost	$45,000
Accumulated depreciation	38,000
Book value	$ 7,000
Fair market value of old asset (trade-in allowance)	3,000
Loss realized	$ 4,000

To illustrate the recognition of a gain from an exchange of dissimilar plant assets, assume that the fair market value of the machine was $9,000 instead of $3,000, and that only $46,000 was paid in cash. The journal entry to record the exchange would be:

	Debit	Credit
Trucks	55,000	
Accumulated Depreciation—Machinery	38,000	
Machinery		45,000
Cash		46,000
Gain on Disposal of Plant Assets		2,000
To record gain on exchange of dissimilar plant assets.		

Another way to compute the gain of $2,000 on the exchange is to use the fair market value of the old asset less the book value of the old asset. The calculation is as follows:

Machine cost	$45,000
Accumulated depreciation	38,000
Book value	$ 7,000
Fair market value of old asset (trade-in allowance)	9,000
Gain realized	$ 2,000

Remember, companies always recognize both gains and losses on exchanges of dissimilar plant assets. They do not recognize gains on exchanges of similar plant assets.

Exchanges of Similar Plant Assets Often firms exchange plant assets such as automobiles, trucks, and office equipment by trading the old asset for a similar new one. When such an exchange occurs, the company receives a trade-in allowance for the old asset, and pays the balance in cash.[2] Usually, the cash price of the

---

[2] Trade-in allowance is sometimes expressed as the difference between *list* price and cash paid, but we choose to define it as the difference between *cash* price and cash paid because this latter definition seems to agree with current practice for exchange transactions.

new asset is stated. If not, accountants assume the cash price is the fair market value of the old asset plus the cash paid.

When similar assets are exchanged, we must modify the general rule that new assets are recorded at the fair market value of what is given up or received. Thus, companies record the new asset at (1) the cash price of the asset received or (2) the book value of the old asset plus the cash paid, whichever is lower. When applying this rule to exchanges of similar assets, firms recognize losses, but not gains.

To illustrate the accounting for exchanges of similar plant assets, assume that a delivery service exchanged $50,000 cash and truck No. 1—which cost $45,000, had $38,000 of up-to-date accumulated depreciation, and had a $5,000 fair market value—for truck No. 2. The new truck has a cash price (fair market value) of $55,000. The delivery service realized a loss of $2,000 on the exchange.

Cost of truck No. 1	$45,000
Accumulated depreciation	38,000
Book value	$ 7,000
Fair market value of old asset (trade-in allowance)	5,000
Loss on exchange of plant assets	$ 2,000

The journal entry to record the exchange is:

	Debit	Credit
Trucks (cost of No. 2)	55,000	
Accumulated Depreciation—Trucks	38,000	
Loss from Disposal of Plant Assets	2,000	
Trucks (cost of No. 1)		45,000
Cash		50,000
To record loss on exchange of similar plant assets.		

Note that firms record exchanges of similar plant assets just like exchanges of dissimilar plant assets when a *loss* occurs from the exchange.

Accounting for any gain resulting from exchanges of similar plant assets is different than accounting for a gain resulting from exchanges of dissimilar plant assets. To illustrate, assume that in the preceding example, the delivery service gave truck No. 1 (now with a fair market value of $9,000) and $46,000 cash in exchange for truck No. 2. The gain on the exchange is $2,000:

Cost of truck No. 1	$45,000
Accumulated depreciation	38,000
Book value	$ 7,000
Fair market value of old asset (trade-in allowance)	9,000
Gain indicated	$ 2,000

The journal entry to record the exchange is:

	Debit	Credit
Trucks (cost of No. 2)	53,000	
Accumulated Depreciation—Trucks	38,000	
Trucks (cost of No. 1)		45,000
Cash		46,000
To record exchange of similar plant assets.		

When a firm exchanges similar assets, it does not recognize a gain. It records the new asset at book value of the old asset ($7,000) plus cash paid ($46,000). The company deducts the gain from the cost of the new asset ($55,000). Thus, the cost basis of the new delivery truck is equal to $55,000 less the $2,000 gain, or $53,000. The delivery service uses this $53,000 cost basis in recording depreciation on the truck and determining any gain or loss on its disposal.

Book value of old truck (No. 1)	$ 7,000	
Cash paid	46,000	
Cost of new truck (No. 2)	$53,000	
Fair market value of new truck (No. 2)	$55,000	(equal)
Less: Gain indicated	2,000	
Cost of new truck (No. 2)	$53,000	

ILLUSTRATION 11.1
Summary of Rules for Recording Exchanges of Plant Assets

	Dissimilar Assets	Similar Assets	
Recognize Gains?	Yes	No	
Recognize Losses?	Yes	Yes	
Record New Asset at:	Cash price of new asset **or** fair market value of old asset plus cash paid	**If loss:** Cash price of new asset **or** fair market value of old asset plus cash paid	**If gain:** Book value of old asset plus cash paid

The justification used by the Accounting Principles Board for not recognizing gains on exchanges of similar plant assets is that "revenue should not be recognized merely because one productive asset is substituted for a similar productive asset but rather should be considered to flow from the production and sale of the goods or services to which the substituted productive asset is committed."[3] In effect, firms would realize the gain on an exchange of similar plant assets in future accounting periods as increased net income resulting from smaller depreciation charges on the newly acquired asset. In the preceding example, annual depreciation expense is less if it is based on the truck's $53,000 cost basis than if it is based on the truck's $55,000 cash price. Thus, future net income per year will be larger.

In Illustration 11.1, we summarize the rules for recording plant asset exchanges.

AN ACCOUNTING PERSPECTIVE

USES OF TECHNOLOGY Although sophisticated computer systems automatically compute the gain or loss on the disposal of assets, such programs depend on human input. If an error was made in inputting the type of disposal or exchange or if the life of the asset was estimated inaccurately, the calculated gain or loss would be incorrect.

Removal Costs

Companies incur removal costs when dismantling and removing old plant assets. They deduct these costs from salvage proceeds to determine the asset's net salvage value. (The removal costs could be greater than the salvage proceeds.) Accountants associate removal costs with the old asset, not the new asset acquired as a replacement.

The next section discusses natural resources. Note the underlying accounting principle of matching the expenses with the revenues earned in that same accounting period.

NATURAL RESOURCES

Resources supplied by nature, such as ore deposits, mineral deposits, oil reserves, gas deposits, and timber stands, are **natural resources** or **wasting assets.** Natural resources represent inventories of raw materials that can be consumed (exhausted) through extraction or removal from their natural setting (e.g., removing oil from the ground).

On the balance sheet, we classify natural resources as a separate group among

[3] *APB Opinion No. 29*, par. 16.

noncurrent assets under headings such as ''Timber stands'' and ''Oil reserves.'' Typically, we record natural resources at their cost of acquisition plus exploration and development costs; on the balance sheet, we report them at total cost less accumulated depletion. (Accumulated depletion is similar to the accumulated depreciation used for plant assets.) When analyzing the financial condition of companies owning natural resources, exercise caution because the historical costs reported for the natural resources may be only a small fraction of their current value.

An Accounting Perspective

Business Insight Union Texas Petroleum Corporation is engaged in oil and gas exploration and production overseas and has petrochemical interests in the United States. Oil and gas reserves cannot be measured exactly. In notes to their financial statements, Union Texas states that the reliability of reserve estimates at any time depends on both the quality and quantity of the technical and economic data, the production performance of the reservoirs, and extensive engineering judgment. Consequently, as additional data become available during the producing life of a reservoir, the company revises its reserve estimates.

Depletion

Depletion is the exhaustion that results from the physical removal of a part of a natural resource. In each accounting period, the depletion recognized is an estimate of the cost of the natural resource that was removed from its natural setting during the period. To record depletion, debit a Depletion account and credit an Accumulated Depletion account, which is a contra account to the natural resource asset account.

By crediting the Accumulated Depletion account instead of the asset account, we continue to report the original cost of the entire natural resource on the financial statements. Thus, statement users can see the percentage of the resource that has been removed. To determine the total cost of the resource available, we combine this depletion cost with other extraction, mining, or removal costs. We can assign this total cost to either the cost of natural resources sold or the inventory of the natural resource still on hand. Thus, we could expense all, some, or none of the depletion and removal costs recognized in an accounting period, depending on the portion sold. If all of the resource is sold, we expense all of the depletion and removal costs. The cost of any portion not yet sold is part of the cost of inventory.

Objective 3
Determine the periodic depletion cost of a natural resource and calculate depreciation of plant assets located on extractive industry property.

Computing Periodic Depletion Cost To compute depletion charges, companies usually use the units-of-production method. They divide total cost by the estimated number of units—tons, barrels, or board feet—that can be economically extracted from the property. This calculation provides a per unit depletion cost. For example, assume that in 1997 a company paid $650,000 for a tract of land containing ore deposits. The company spent $100,000 in exploration costs. The results indicated that approximately 900,000 tons of ore can be removed economically from the land, after which the land will be worth $50,000. The company incurred costs of $200,000 to develop the site, including the cost of running power lines and building roads. Total cost subject to depletion is the net cost assignable to the natural resource plus the exploration and development costs. When the property is purchased, a journal entry assigns the purchase price to the two assets purchased—the natural resource and the land. The entry would be:

	Debit	Credit
Land	50,000	
Ore Deposits	600,000	
Cash		650,000
To record purchase of land and mine.		

After the purchase, an entry debits all costs to develop the site (including exploration) to the natural resource account. The entry would be:

	Debit	Credit
Ore Deposits ($100,000 + $200,000)	300,000	
Cash		300,000
To record costs of exploration and development.		

The formula for finding depletion cost per unit is:

$$\text{Depletion cost per unit} = \frac{\text{Cost of site} - \text{Residual value of land (if owned)} + \text{Costs to develop site}}{\text{Estimated number of units that can be economically extracted}}$$

In some instances, companies buy only the right to extract the natural resource from someone else's land. **When the land is not purchased, its residual value is irrelevant and should be ignored.** If there is an obligation to restore the land to a usable condition, the firm adds these estimated restoration costs to the costs to develop the site.

In the example where the land was purchased, the total costs of the mineral deposits equal the cost of the site ($650,000) minus the residual value of land ($50,000) plus costs to develop the site ($300,000), or a total of $900,000. The unit (per ton) depletion charge is $1 (or $900,000/900,000 tons).

The formula to compute the depletion cost of a period is:

$$\text{Depletion cost of a period} = \text{Depletion cost per unit} \times \text{Number of units extracted during period}$$

In this example, if 100,000 tons are mined in 1997, this entry records the depletion cost of $100,000 ($1 × 100,000) for the period:

	Debit	Credit
Depletion	100,000	
Accumulated Depletion—Ore Deposits[4]		100,000
To record depletion for 1997.		

The Depletion account contains the "in the ground" cost of the ore or natural resource mined. Combined with other extractive costs, this cost determines the total cost of the ore mined. To illustrate, assume that in addition to the $100,000 depletion cost, mining labor costs totaled $320,000, and other mining costs, such as depreciation, property taxes, power, and supplies, totaled $60,000. If 80,000 tons were sold and 20,000 remained on hand at the end of the period, the firm would allocate total cost of $480,000 as follows:

Depletion cost	$100,000
Mining labor costs	320,000
Other mining costs	60,000
Total cost of 100,000 tons mined ($4.80 per ton)	$480,000
Less: Ore inventory (20,000 tons at $4.80)	96,000
Cost of ore sold (80,000 tons at $4.80)	$384,000

Note that the average cost per ton to mine 100,000 tons was $4.80 (or $480,000/100,000). The income statement would show cost of ore sold of $384,000. The mining company does not report depletion separately as an expense because depletion is included in cost of ore sold. The balance sheet would show inventory of ore on hand (a current asset) at $96,000 (or $4.80 × 20,000). Also, it would report the cost less accumulated depletion of the natural resource as follows:

Ore deposits	$900,000	
Less: Accumulated depletion	100,000	$800,000

Another method of calculating depletion cost is the percentage of revenue method. Because firms use this method only for income tax purposes and not for financial statements, we do not discuss it in this text.

[4] Instead of crediting the accumulated depletion account, the Ore Deposits account could have been credited directly. But for reasons indicated earlier, the credit is usually to an accumulated depletion account.

Depreciation of Plant Assets Located on Extractive Industry Property

Companies depreciate plant assets erected on extractive industry property the same as other depreciable assets. If such assets will be abandoned when the natural resource is exhausted, they depreciate these assets over the shorter of the (*a*) physical life of the asset or (*b*) life of the natural resource. In many cases, firms compute periodic depreciation charges using the units-of-production method. Using this method matches the life of the plant asset with the life of the natural resource. This method is recommended where the *physical* life of the plant asset equals or exceeds the resource's life but its *useful* life is limited to the life of the natural resource.

Assume a mining company acquires mining property with a building it plans to use only in the mining operations. Also assume that the firm uses the units-of-production method for computing building depreciation. Relevant facts are:

Building cost	$310,000
Estimated physical life of building	20 years
Estimated salvage value of building (after mine is exhausted)	$ 10,000
Capacity of mine	1,000,000 tons
Expected life of mine	10 years

Because the life of the mine (10 years or 1,000,000 tons) is shorter than the life of the building (20 years), the building should be depreciated over the life of the mine. The basis of the depreciation charge is tons of ore rather than years because the mine's life could be longer or shorter than 10 years, depending on how rapidly the ore is removed.

Suppose that during the first year of operations, workers extracted 150,000 tons of ore. Building depreciation for the first year is $45,000, computed as follows:

$$\text{Depreciation per unit} = \frac{\text{Asset cost} - \text{Estimated salvage value}}{\text{Total tons of ore in mine that can be economically extracted}}$$

$$= \frac{\$310{,}000 - \$10{,}000}{1{,}000{,}000 \text{ tons}} = \$0.30 \text{ per ton}$$

$$\text{Depreciation for year} = \text{Depreciation per unit} \times \text{Units extracted}$$

$$= \$0.30 \text{ per ton} \times 150{,}000 \text{ tons} = \$45{,}000$$

On the income statement, depreciation on the building appears as part of the cost of ore sold and is carried as part of inventory cost for ore not sold during the period. On the balance sheet, accumulated depreciation on the building appears with the related asset account.

Plant assets and natural resources are tangible assets used by a company to produce revenues. A company also may acquire intangible assets to assist in producing revenues.

Intangible Assets

Although they have no physical characteristics, **intangible assets** have value because of the advantages or exclusive privileges and rights they provide to a business. Intangible assets generally arise from two sources: (1) exclusive privileges granted by governmental authority or by legal contract, such as patents, copyrights, franchises, trademarks and trade names, and leases; and (2) superior entrepreneurial capacity or management know-how and customer loyalty, which is called *goodwill*.

All intangible assets are nonphysical, but not all nonphysical assets are intangibles. For example, accounts receivable and prepaid expenses are nonphysical, yet classified as current assets rather than intangible assets. Intangible assets are generally both nonphysical and noncurrent; they appear in a separate long-term section of the balance sheet entitled "Intangible assets."

Acquisition of Intangible Assets

Objective 4
Prepare entries for the acquisition and amortization of intangible assets.

Initially, firms record intangible assets at cost like most other assets. However, computing an intangible asset's acquisition cost differs from computing a plant asset's acquisition cost. Firms may include only outright purchase costs in the acquisition cost of an intangible asset; **the acquisition cost does not include cost of internal development or self-creation of the asset.** If an intangible asset is internally generated in its entirety, none of its costs are capitalized. Therefore, some companies have extremely valuable assets that may not even be recorded in their asset accounts. To explain the reasons for this practice, we discuss the history of accounting for research and development costs next.

Research and development (R&D) costs are costs incurred in a planned search for new knowledge and in translating such knowledge into new products or processes. Prior to 1975, businesses often capitalized research and development costs as intangible assets when future benefits were expected from their incurrence. Due to the difficulty of determining the costs applicable to future benefits, many companies expensed all such costs as incurred. Other companies capitalized those costs that related to proven products and expensed the rest as incurred.

As a result of these varied accounting practices, in 1974 the Financial Accounting Standards Board in *Statement No. 2* ruled that firms must expense all research and development costs when incurred, unless they were directly reimbursable by government agencies and others. Immediate expensing is justified on the grounds that (1) the amount of costs applicable to the future cannot be measured with any high degree of precision; (2) doubt exists as to whether any future benefits will be received; and (3) even if benefits are expected, they cannot be measured. Thus, research and development costs no longer appear as intangible assets on the balance sheet. The Board applies the same line of reasoning to other costs associated with internally generated intangible assets, such as the internal costs of developing a patent.

Amortization of Intangible Assets

Amortization is the systematic write-off of the cost of an intangible asset to expense. A portion of an intangible asset's cost is allocated to each accounting period in the economic (useful) life of the asset. All intangible assets are subject to amortization, which is similar to plant asset depreciation. Generally, we record amortization by debiting Amortization Expense and crediting the intangible asset account. An accumulated amortization account could record amortization. However, the information gained from such accounting would not be significant because normally intangibles do not account for as many total asset dollars as do plant assets.

Intangibles should be amortized over the shorter of (1) their economic life, (2) their legal life, or (3) 40 years. In *APB Opinion No. 17,* the Accounting Principles Board requires an intangible asset acquired after October 31, 1970, to be amortized over a period not to exceed 40 years. Straight-line amortization must be used unless another method of amortization (such as units-of-production) can be shown to be superior. We calculate straight-line amortization in the same way as straight-line depreciation for plant assets.

Patents

A **patent** is a right granted by the federal government. This exclusive right enables the owner to manufacture, sell, lease, or otherwise benefit from an invention for a limited period. The value of a patent lies in its ability to produce revenue. Patents have a legal life of 17 years. Protection for the patent owner begins at the time of patent application and lasts for 17 years from the date the patent is granted.

When purchasing a patent, a company records it in the Patents account at cost. The firm also debits the Patents account for the cost of the first successful defense of the patent in lawsuits (assuming an outside law firm was hired rather than using internal legal staff). Such a lawsuit establishes the validity of the patent and thereby increases its service potential. In addition, the firm debits the cost of any competing patents purchased to ensure the revenue-generating capability of its own patent to the Patents account.

The firm would amortize the cost of a purchased patent over the shorter of 17 years (or remaining legal life) or its estimated useful life. If a patent cost $40,000 and has a useful life of 10 years, the journal entries to record the patent and periodic amortization are:

Patents	40,000	
Cash.		40,000
To record purchase of patent.		
Patent Amortization Expense	4,000	
Patents		4,000
To record patent amortization.		

For a patent that becomes worthless before it is fully amortized, the company expenses the unamortized balance in the Patents account.

As noted earlier, all R&D costs incurred in the internal development of a product, process, or idea that is later patented must be expensed, rather than capitalized. In the previous example, the company amortized the cost of the purchased patent over its useful life of 10 years. If the patent had been the result of an internally generated product or process, the firm would have expensed its cost of $40,000 as incurred, in accordance with *Statement No. 2* of the Financial Accounting Standards Board.

Copyrights

A **copyright** is an exclusive right granted by the federal government giving protection against the illegal reproduction by others of the creator's written works, designs, and literary productions. The copyright period is for the life of the creator plus 50 years. Most publications have a limited life; a creator may charge the cost of the copyright to expense on a straight-line basis over the life of the first edition published or based on projections of the copies to be sold per year.

Franchises

A **franchise** is a contract between two parties granting the franchisee (the purchaser of the franchise) certain rights and privileges ranging from name identification to complete monopoly of service. In many instances, both parties are private businesses. For example, an individual who wishes to open a hamburger restaurant may purchase a McDonald's franchise; the two parties involved are the individual business owner and McDonald's Corporation. This franchise would allow the business owner to use the McDonald's name and golden arch, and would provide the owner with advertising and many other benefits. The legal life of a franchise may be limited by contract.

The parties involved in a franchise arrangement are not always private businesses. A government agency may grant a franchise to a private company. A city may give a franchise to a utility company, giving the utility company the exclusive right to provide service to a particular area.

In addition to providing benefits, a franchise usually places certain restrictions on the franchisee. These restrictions generally are related to rates or prices charged; also they may be in regard to product quality or to the particular supplier from whom supplies and inventory items must be purchased.

If periodic payments to the grantor of the franchise are required, the franchisee debits them to a Franchise Expense account. If a lump-sum payment is made to obtain the franchise, the franchisee records the cost in an asset account entitled Franchise and amortizes it over the shorter of the legal life (if limited by contract), the economic life of the franchise, or 40 years.

An Accounting Perspective

Business Insight Coca-Cola Enterprises, Inc., is the world's largest bottler of products of The Coca-Cola Company. Intangible assets can be quite substantial. On December 31, 1992, the total assets of Coca-Cola Enterprises were $8,085 million, $5,651 million of which consisted of franchise and other noncurrent assets. Accumulated amortization amounted to $577 million.

Trademarks; Trade Names

A **trademark** is a symbol, design, or logo used in conjunction with a particular product or company. A **trade name** is a brand name under which a product is sold or a company does business. Often trademarks and trade names are extremely valuable to a company, but if they have been internally developed, they have no recorded asset cost. However, when a business purchases such items from an external source, it records them at cost and amortizes them over their economic life or 40 years, whichever is shorter.

Leases

A **lease** is a contract to rent property. The property owner is the grantor of the lease and is the *lessor*. The person or company obtaining rights to possess and use the property is the *lessee*. The rights granted under the lease are a **leasehold.** The accounting for a lease depends on whether it is a capital lease or an operating lease.

Capital Leases A **capital lease** transfers to the lessee virtually all rewards and risks that accompany ownership of property. A lease is a capital lease if, among other provisions, it (1) transfers ownership of the leased property to the lessee at the end of the lease term or (2) contains a bargain purchase option that permits the lessee to buy the property at a price significantly below fair market value at the end of the lease term.

A capital lease is a means of financing property acquisitions; it has the same economic impact as a purchase made on an installment plan. Thus, the lessee in a capital lease must record the leased property as an asset and the lease obligation as a liability. Because a capital lease is an asset, the lessee depreciates the leased property over its useful life. The lessee records part of each lease payment as interest expense and the balance as a payment on the lease liability.

The proper accounting for capital leases for both lessees and lessors has been an extremely difficult problem. We leave further discussion of capital leases for an intermediate accounting text.

Operating Leases A lease that does not qualify as a capital lease is an **operating lease.** A one-year lease on an apartment and a week's rental of an automobile are examples of operating leases. Such leases make no attempt to transfer any of the rewards and risks of ownership to the lessee. As a result, there may be no recordable transaction when a lease is signed.

In some situations, the lease may call for an immediate cash payment that must be recorded. Assume that a business signed a lease requiring the immediate payment of the annual rent of $15,000 for each of the first and fifth years of a five-year lease. The lessee would record the payment as follows:

Prepaid Rent	15,000	
Leasehold	15,000	
Cash		30,000
To record first and fifth years' rent on a five-year lease.		

Since the Leasehold account is actually a long-term prepaid rent account for the fifth year's annual rent, it is an intangible asset until the beginning of the fifth year. Then the Leasehold account becomes a current asset and may be transferred into a Prepaid Rent account. Accounting for the balance in the Leasehold account depends on the terms of the lease. In the previous example, the firm would charge the $15,000 in the Leasehold account to expense over the fifth year only. It would charge the balance in Prepaid Rent to expense in the first year. Thus, assuming the lease year and fiscal year coincide, the entry for the first year is:

Rent Expense	15,000	
Prepaid Rent		15,000
To record rent expense.		

The entry in the fifth year is:

Rent Expense	15,000	
Leasehold		15,000
To record rent expense.		

The accounting for the second, third, and fourth years would be the same as for the first year. The lessee records the rent in Prepaid Rent when paid in advance for the year and then expenses it. As stated above, the lessee may transfer the amount in the Leasehold account to Prepaid Rent at the beginning of the fifth year by debiting Prepaid Rent and crediting Leasehold. If this entry was made, the previous entry would have credited Prepaid Rent.

In some cases, when a lease is signed, the lump-sum payment does not cover a specific year's rent. The lessee debits this payment to the Leasehold account and amortizes it over the life of the lease. The straight-line method is required unless another method can be shown to be superior. Assume the $15,000 rent for the fifth year in the example was, instead, a lump-sum payment on the lease in addition to the annual rent payments. An annual adjusting entry to amortize the $15,000 over five years would read:

Rent Expense	3,000	
Leasehold		3,000
To amortize leasehold.		

In this example, the annual rental expense is $18,000: $15,000 annual cash rent plus $3,000 amortization of leasehold ($15,000/5).

The lessee may base periodic rent on current-year sales or usage rather than being a constant amount. For example, if a lease called for rent equal to 5% of current-year sales and sales were $400,000 in 1997, the rent for 1997 would be $20,000. The rent would either be paid or an adjusting entry would be made at the end of the year.

Leasehold Improvements

A **leasehold improvement** is any physical alteration made by the lessee to the leased property in which benefits are expected beyond the current accounting period. Leasehold improvements made by a lessee usually become the property of the lessor after the lease has expired. However, since leasehold improvements are an asset of the lessee during the lease period, the lessee debits them to a Leasehold Improvements account. The lessee then amortizes the leasehold improvements to expense over the period benefited by the improvements. The amortization period for leasehold improvements should be the shorter of the life of the improvements or the life of the lease. If the lease can (and probably will) be renewed at the option of the lessee, the life of the lease should include the option period.

As an illustration, assume that on January 2, 1997, Wolf Company leases a building for 20 years under a nonrenewable lease at an annual rental of $20,000, payable on each December 31. Wolf immediately incurs a cost of $80,000 for improvements to the building, such as interior walls for office separation, ceiling fans, and recessed lighting. The improvements have an estimated life of 30 years. The company should amortize the $80,000 over the 20-year lease period, since that period is shorter than the life of the improvements, and Wolf cannot use the improvements beyond the life of the lease. If only annual financial statements are prepared, the following journal entry properly records the rental expense for the year ended December 31, 1997:

Rent Expense (or Leasehold Improvement Expense)	4,000	
Leasehold Improvements		4,000
To record amortization of leasehold improvement.		

Rent Expense	20,000	
Cash		20,000
To record annual rent.		

Thus, the total cost to rent the building each year equals the $20,000 cash rent plus the amortization of the leasehold improvements.

Although leaseholds are intangible assets, leaseholds and leasehold improvements sometimes appear in the property, plant, and equipment section of the balance sheet.

Goodwill

In accounting, **goodwill** is an intangible value attached to a company resulting mainly from the company's management skill or know-how and a favorable reputation with customers. A company's value may be greater than the total of the fair market value of its tangible and identifiable intangible assets. This greater value means that the company generates an above-average income on each dollar invested in the business. Thus, proof of a company's goodwill is its ability to generate superior earnings or income.

A Goodwill account appears in the accounting records only if goodwill has been purchased. A company cannot purchase goodwill by itself; it must buy an entire business or a part of a business to obtain the accompanying intangible asset, goodwill.

To illustrate, assume that Lenox Company purchased all of Martin Company's assets for $700,000. Lenox also agreed to assume responsibility for a $350,000 mortgage note payable owed by Martin. Goodwill is the difference between the amount paid for the business including the debt assumed ($700,000 + $350,000 = $1,050,000) and the fair market value of the assets purchased. Notice that Lenox would use the fair market value of the assets rather than book value to determine the amount of goodwill. The following computation is for the goodwill purchased by Lenox:

Cash paid		$ 700,000
Mortgage note payable assumed		350,000
Total price paid		$1,050,000
Less fair market values of individually identifiable assets:		
Accounts receivable	$ 95,000	
Merchandise inventory	100,000	
Land	240,000	
Buildings	275,000	
Equipment	200,000	
Patents	65,000	975,000
Goodwill		$ 75,000

The $75,000 is the goodwill Lenox records as an intangible asset; it records all of the other assets at their fair market values, and the liability at the amount due. Specific reasons for a company's goodwill include a good reputation, customer loyalty, superior product design, unrecorded intangible assets (because they were developed internally), and superior human resources. Since these positive factors are not individually quantifiable, when grouped together they constitute *goodwill*. The journal entry to record the purchase is:

Accounts Receivable	95,000	
Merchandise Inventory	100,000	
Land	240,000	
Buildings	275,000	
Equipment	200,000	
Patents	65,000	
Goodwill	75,000	
Cash		700,000
Mortgage Note Payable		350,000
To record the purchase of Martin Company's assets and assumption of mortgage note payable.		

ILLUSTRATION 11.2
Intangible Assets Held by 600 Companies

Assets Being Amortized	Number of Companies 1992	1991	1990	1989
Goodwill recognized in a business combination	383	381	379	367
Patents, patent rights	62	59	62	62
Trademarks, brand names, copyrights	50	48	46	38
Noncompete covenants	21	18	20	11
Licenses, franchises, memberships	17	17	16	19
Other—described	45	42	37	41

Source: American Institute of Certified Public Accountants, *Accounting Trends & Techniques* (New York: AICPA, 1993), p. 177.

As with all other intangibles, Lenox must amortize goodwill. No legal life exists for goodwill, nor can anyone accurately determine the useful life of goodwill. If, for example, the new owner made substantial changes in the method of doing business, goodwill that existed at the purchase date could rapidly disappear. Therefore, current accounting practice requires the amortization of goodwill over a period not to exceed 40 years. This requirement is necessary because the value of purchased goodwill eventually disappears. Even though it generates other goodwill in its place, the organization cannot record internally created goodwill any more than it can any other internally generated intangible assets. The entry to amortize the $75,000 goodwill over a 40-year period is:

Goodwill Amortization Expense	1,875	
Goodwill		1,875
To amortize goodwill ($75,000/40 years).		

Reporting Amortization

In Illustration 11.2, we show how often 600 companies amortized intangible assets for the years 1989–92.

Amortization expense for most intangible assets discussed in this chapter appears among the operating expenses on the income statement. The account titles are all of this type: "Amortization of Goodwill (or Patents, Copyrights, Franchises, Leaseholds) Expense." Often companies report periodic amortization of leaseholds and leasehold improvements as rent expense. The 1993 tax law allows straight-line amortization over 15 years for many intangible assets (including goodwill) if they were acquired after August 10, 1993. Prior to 1993, goodwill could not be amortized for tax purposes, while several other intangible assets could be amortized.

The following intangible asset note and General Electric Company's reporting of amortization appeared in its 1993 annual report:

Note 16: Intangible Assets

	December 31 (in $ millions) 1993	1992
GE		
Goodwill	$ 5,713	$5,873
Other intangibles	753	734
	$ 6,466	$6,607
GEFS		
Goodwill	$ 2,133	1,841
Other intangibles	1,765	1,062
	$ 3,898	$2,903
	$10,364	$9,510

GE's intangible assets are shown net of accumulated amortization of $1,760 million in 1993 and $1,476 million in 1992. GEFS' intangible assets are net of accumulated amortization of $878 million in 1993 and $646 million in 1992.

In Illustration 11.3, we summarize the amortization rules for intangible assets.

ILLUSTRATION 11.3
Rules for Amortization of Intangible Assets

Intangible Asset	Useful Life	Legal Life	Maximum Life (years)
	Amortized over Shorter of		
Patents	?	17 years	40
Copyrights	?	Life of creator plus 50 years	40
Franchises	?	No limit (unless limited by contract)	40
Trademarks; trade names	?	No limit	40
Leasehold improvements	?	Life of lease	40
Goodwill	?	No limit	40

ILLUSTRATION 11.4
Partial Balance Sheet

REED COMPANY
Partial Balance Sheet
June 30, 1997

Property, plant, and equipment:			
Land		$ 30,000	
Buildings	$75,000		
Less: Accumulated depreciation	45,000	30,000	
Equipment	$ 9,000		
Less: Accumulated depreciation	1,500	7,500	
Total property, plant, and equipment			$ 67,500
Natural resources:			
Mineral deposits		$300,000	
Less: Accumulated depletion		100,000	
Total natural resources			$200,000
Intangible assets:			
Patents		$ 10,000	
Goodwill		20,000	
Total intangible assets			$ 30,000

Balance Sheet Presentation

Look at Illustration 11.4, a partial balance sheet for Reed Company. Unlike plant assets or natural resources, intangible assets usually are a net amount in the balance sheet.

ANALYZING AND USING THE FINANCIAL RESULTS—TOTAL ASSETS TURNOVER

Objective 5
Analyze and use the financial results—total assets turnover.

In determining the productivity of assets, management may compare one year's assets turnover ratio to a previous year's. **Total assets turnover** shows the relationship between the dollar volume of sales and the average total assets used in the business. To calculate this ratio:

$$\text{Total assets turnover} = \frac{\text{Net sales}}{\text{Average total assets}}$$

This ratio indicates the efficiency with which a company uses its assets to generate sales. When the ratio is low relative to industry standards or the company's ratio in previous years, it could indicate an overinvestment in assets, a slow year in sales, or both. Thus, if the ratio is relatively low and there was no significant decrease in sales during the current year, management should identify and dispose of any inefficient equipment.

The total assets turnover in 1992 for several actual companies was as follows:

An Ethical Perspective

ABC Corporation

ABC Corporation acquired XYZ Company for $10,000,000 cash. ABC acquired the following assets:

Accounts receivable		$80,000
	Old Book Value	**Fair Market Value**
Merchandise inventory. .	$ 200,000	$ 300,000
Buildings.	3,000,000	4,000,000
Land	1,000,000	3,000,000
Equipment	500,000	700,000

An experienced appraiser with an excellent reputation established the fair market values of the assets. ABC also assumed the liability for paying XYZ's $50,000 of accounts payable.

John Gilbert, ABC's accountant, prepared the following journal entry to record the purchase:

Accounts Receivable	80,000	
Merchandise Inventory . . .	300,000	
Buildings	4,000,000	
Land	3,000,000	
Equipment	700,000	
Goodwill.	1,970,000	
Accounts Payable . . .		50,000
Cash		10,000,000
To record the purchase of XYZ Company.		

In explaining the entry to ABC's president, Gilbert said that the assets had to be recorded at their fair market values. He also stated that the goodwill had to be amortized over a period not to exceed 40 years for accounting purposes, but that the goodwill could not be amortized for tax purposes.

The president reacted with, "It's not fair that we are prohibited from amortizing goodwill for tax purposes when it is a part of the cost of the purchase. Besides, appraisals are very inexact, and maybe some of our other assets are worth more than the one appraiser indicated. I want you to reduce goodwill down to $470,000 and assign the other $1,500,000 to the buildings and equipment. Then, we can benefit from the depreciation on these assets. If I need to find an appraiser who will support the new allocations, I will."

When Gilbert protested, the president stated, "If you are going to have a future with us, you need to be a team player. We just can't afford to lose those tax deductions." Gilbert feared that if he did not go along, he would soon be unemployed.

Company	Net Sales ($ thousands)	Total Assets ($ thousands)—1992 Beginning of Year	End of Year	Average	Turnover
Texas Instruments, Inc. . . (TEXAS INSTRUMENTS)	$ 7,440,000	$ 5,009,000	$ 5,185,000	$ 5,097,000	145.97%
The Home Depot, Inc.. .	7,148,436	2,510,292	3,931,790	3,221,041	221.93%
International Paper Company . . . . . . (INTERNATIONAL PAPER)	13,598,000	14,941,000	16,459,000	15,700,000	86.61%
Quaker Oats Company .	5,576,400	3,060,500	3,039,900	3,050,200	182.82%
The GAP, Inc.	2,960,409	1,147,414	1,379,248	1,263,331	234.33%

Texas Instruments sells and manufactures semiconductors, defense electronics systems, and computer and other electronic products.

The Home Depot is America's largest home improvement retailer for do-it-yourselfers.

International Paper Company is a worldwide, integrated paper and forest products company.

Quaker Oats Company sells packaged food: beverages, cereals, rice, and pasta.

The GAP is a specialty retailer selling casual apparel.

These five companies compete in very different industries. However, they are all manufacturers. To see if each of these companies is performing above standard, management should compare its company's percentage to the industry's standard. In addition, calculating this ratio over approximately five years would help management see any trends indicating problems or confirm successful asset management.

This chapter concludes your study of accounting for long-term assets. In Chapter 12, you learn about classes of capital stock.

Understanding the Learning Objectives

Objective 1
Calculate and prepare entries for the sale, retirement, and destruction of plant assets.

- By comparing an asset's book value (cost less up-to-date accumulated depreciation) with its sales price, the company may show either a gain or a loss. If sales price is greater than book value, the company shows a gain. If sales price is less than book value, the company shows a loss. If sales price equals book value, no gain or loss results.
- When a plant asset is retired from service, the asset's cost and accumulated depreciation must be removed from the plant asset accounts.
- Plant assets are sometimes wrecked in accidents or destroyed by fire, flood, storm, and other causes. If the asset was not insured, the loss is equal to the book value. If the asset was insured, only the amount of the loss exceeding the amount to be recovered from the insurance company would be debited to a loss account.

Objective 2
Describe and record exchanges of dissimilar and similar plant assets.

- In exchanges of dissimilar assets, the firm records the asset received at either (1) the stated cash price of the new asset or (if the cash price is not stated) (2) the known fair market value of the asset given up plus any cash paid.
- In exchanges of similar assets, the firm records the new asset at (1) the cash price of the asset received or (2) the book value of the old asset plus the cash paid, whichever is lower.

Objective 3
Determine the periodic depletion cost of a natural resource and calculate depreciation of plant assets located on extractive industry property.

- Depletion charges usually are computed by the units-of-production method. Total cost is divided by the estimated number of units that are economically extractable from the property. This calculation provides a per unit depletion cost that is multiplied by the units extracted each year to obtain the depletion cost for that year.
- Depreciable assets located on extractive industry property should be depreciated over the shorter of the (1) physical life of the asset or (2) life of the natural resource. The periodic depreciation charges usually are computed using the units-of-production method. Using this method matches the life of the plant asset with the life of the natural resource.

Objective 4
Prepare entries for the acquisition and amortization of intangible assets.

- Only outright purchase costs are included in the acquisition cost of an intangible asset. If an intangible asset is internally generated, its cost is immediately expensed.
- Intangibles should be amortized over the shorter of (1) their economic life, (2) their legal life, or (3) 40 years. Straight-line amortization must be used unless another method can be shown to be superior.

Objective 5
Analyze and use the financial results—total assets turnover.

- $\text{Total assets turnover} = \dfrac{\text{Net sales}}{\text{Average total assets}}$
- This ratio indicates the efficiency with which a company uses its assets to generate sales.

Demonstration Problem 11–A

On January 2, 1994, Darton Company purchased a machine for $36,000 cash. The machine has an estimated useful life of six years and an estimated salvage value of $1,800. Darton uses the straight-line method of depreciation.

Required

a. Compute the book value of the machine as of July 1, 1997.

b. Assume the machine was disposed of on July 1, 1997. Prepare the journal entries to record the disposal of the machine under each of the following unrelated assumptions:

1. The machine was sold for $12,000 cash.
2. The machine was sold for $18,000 cash.
3. The machine and $24,000 cash were exchanged for a new machine that had a cash price of $39,000.
4. The machine was completely destroyed by fire. Darton expects to recover cash of $10,800 from the insurance company.

Solution to Demonstration Problem 11–A

a.

DARTON COMPANY
Schedule to Compute Book Value
July 1, 1997

Cost	$36,000
Less accumulated depreciation:	
$\frac{\$36,000 - \$1,800}{6 \text{ years}} = \$5,700$ per year	
$5,700 × 3½ years = $19,950	19,950
Book value	$16,050

b.

		Debit	Credit
1.	Cash	12,000	
	Accumulated Depreciation—Machinery	19,950	
	Loss from Disposal of Plant Assets	4,050	
	Machinery		36,000
	To record sale of machinery at a loss.		
2.	Cash	18,000	
	Accumulated Depreciation—Machinery	19,950	
	Machinery		36,000
	Gain on Disposal of Plant Assets		1,950
	To record sale of machinery at a gain.		
3.	Machinery (new)	39,000	
	Accumulated Depreciation—Machinery	19,950	
	Loss from Disposal of Plant Assets	1,050	
	Machinery (old)		36,000
	Cash		24,000
	To record exchange of machines.		
4.	Receivable from Insurance Company	10,800	
	Accumulated Depreciation—Machinery	19,950	
	Fire Loss	5,250	
	Machinery		36,000
	To record loss of machinery.		

Demonstration Problem 11–B

Howard Company acquired on January 1, 1997, a tract of property containing timber at a cost of $8,000,000. After the timber is removed, the land will be worth about $3,200,000 and will be sold to another party. Costs of developing the site were $800,000. A building was erected at a cost of $160,000. The building had an estimated physical life of 20 years and will have an estimated salvage value of $80,000 when the timber is gone. It was expected that 50,000,000 board feet of timber can be economically cut. During the first year, 16,000,000 board feet were cut. Howard uses the units-of-production basis to depreciate the building.

Required

Prepare the entries to record:

a. The acquisition of the property.
b. The development costs.
c. Depletion cost for the first year.
d. Depreciation on the building for the first year.

Solution to Demonstration Problem 11–B

		Debit	Credit
a.	Land	3,200,000	
	Timber Stands	4,800,000	
	Cash		8,000,000
	To record purchase of land and timber.		
b.	Timber Stands	800,000	
	Cash		800,000
	To record costs of development of the site.		

		Debit	Credit
c.	Depletion	1,792,000	
	Accumulated Depreciation—Timber Stands		1,792,000
	To record depletion for 1997: ($4,800,000 + $800,000)/50,000,000 = $0.112 per board foot. $0.112 × 16,000,000 = $1,792,000.		
d.	Depreciation Expense—Buildings	25,600	
	Accumulated Depreciation—Buildings		25,600
	To record depreciation expense: $\frac{\$160,000 - \$80,000}{50,000,000 \text{ board feet}} = \$0.0016$ per board foot. $0.0016 × 16,000,000 = $25,600		

Demonstration Problem 11–C

On January 2, 1997, Bedford Company purchased a 10-year sublease on a warehouse for $30,000. Bedford will also pay annual rent of $6,000. Bedford immediately incurred costs of $20,000 for improvements to the warehouse, such as lighting fixtures, replacement of a ceiling, heating system, and loading dock. The improvements have an estimated life of 12 years and no residual value.

Required Prepare the entries to record:

a. The payment for the sublease on a warehouse.
b. The rent payment for the first year.
c. The payment for the improvements.
d. Amortization of the leasehold for the first year.
e. Amortization of the leasehold improvements for the first year.

Solution to Demonstration Problem 11–C

		Debit	Credit
a.	Leasehold	30,000	
	Cash		30,000
	To record purchase of sublease on warehouse.		
b.	Rent Expense	6,000	
	Cash		6,000
	To record annual rent payment.		
c.	Leasehold Improvements	20,000	
	Cash		20,000
	To record payment for leasehold improvements.		
d.	Rent Expense	3,000	
	Leasehold		3,000
	To record leasehold amortization for 1997: Annual amortization $= \frac{\$30,000}{10 \text{ years}} = \$3,000$		
e.	Rent Expense	2,000	
	Leasehold Improvements		2,000
	To amortize leasehold improvements: Annual amortization $= \frac{\$20,000}{10 \text{ years}} = \$2,000$		

New Terms

The term used to describe the systematic write-off of the cost of an intangible asset to expense. *408*

A lease that transfers to the lessee virtually all of the rewards and risks that accompany ownership of property. *410*

Copyright An exclusive right granted by the federal government giving protection against the illegal reproduction by others of the creator's written works, designs, and literary productions. *409*

Depletion The exhaustion of a natural resource; an estimate of the cost of the resource that was removed from its natural setting during the period. *405*

Franchise A contract between two parties granting the franchisee (the purchaser of the franchise) certain rights and privileges ranging from name identification to complete monopoly of service. *409*

Goodwill An intangible value attached to a company resulting mainly from the company's management skill or know-how and a favorable reputation with customers. Evidenced by the ability to generate an above-average rate of income on each dollar invested in the business. *412*

Intangible assets Items that have no physical characteristics but are of value because of the advantages or exclusive privileges and rights they provide to a business. *407*

Lease A contract to rent property. Grantor of the lease is the **lessor;** the party obtaining the rights to possess and use property is the **lessee.** *410*

Leasehold The rights granted under a lease. *410*

Leasehold improvement Any physical alteration made by the lessee to the leased property in which benefits are expected beyond the current accounting period. *411*

Natural resources Resources supplied by nature, such as ore deposits, mineral deposits, oil reserves, gas deposits, and timber stands supplied by nature. *404*

Operating lease A lease that does not qualify as a capital lease. *410*

Patent A right granted by the federal government giving the owner the exclusive right to manufacture, sell, lease, or otherwise benefit from an invention for a limited period. *408*

Research and development (R&D) costs Costs incurred in a planned search for new knowledge and in translating such knowledge into a new product or process. *408*

Total assets turnover Equal to Net sales/Average total assets. This ratio indicates the efficiency with which a company uses its assets to generate sales. *414*

Trademark A symbol, design, or logo used in conjunction with a particular product or company. *410*

Trade name A brand name under which a product is sold or a company does business. *410*

Wasting assets See Natural resources.

SELF-TEST

TRUE-FALSE

Indicate whether each of the following statements is true or false.

1. When a plant asset is still being used after it has been fully depreciated, depreciation can be taken in excess of its cost.
2. In an exchange of dissimilar assets, the new asset is recorded at the fair market value of the asset received or the fair market value of the asset given up plus cash paid, whichever is more clearly evident.
3. In calculating depletion, the residual value of acquired land containing an ore deposit is included in total costs subject to depletion.
4. All recorded intangible assets are subject to amortization.

MULTIPLE-CHOICE

Select the best answer for each of the following questions.

1. When a fully depreciated asset is still in use:
   a. Prior years' depreciation should be adjusted.
   b. The cost should be adjusted to market value.
   c. Part of the depreciation should be reversed.
   d. The cost and accumulated depreciation should remain in the ledger and no more depreciation should be taken.
   e. It should be written off the books.
2. A truck costing $45,000 and having an estimated salvage value of $4,500 and an original life of five years is exchanged for a new truck. The cash price of the new truck is $57,000, and a trade-in allowance of $22,500 is received. The old truck has been depreciated for three years using the straight-line method. The new truck would be recorded at:
   a. $55,200.
   b. $57,000.
   c. $34.500.
   d. $43,200.
   e. None of the above.
3. Land containing a mine having an estimated 1,000,000 tons of economically extractable ore is purchased for $375,000. After the ore deposit is removed, the land will be worth $75,000. If 100,000 tons of ore are mined and sold during the first year, the depletion cost charged to expense for the year is:
   a. $300,000.
   b. $37,500.
   c. $30,000.

d. $375,000.
e. None of the above.

4. Stan Company purchased a patent for $36,000. The patent is expected to have value for 10 years even though its legal life is 17 years. The amortization for the first year is:
a. $36,000.
b. $3,600.
c. $2,118.
d. $3,240.
e. None of the above.

Now turn to page 428 to check your answers.

QUESTIONS

1. When depreciable plant assets are sold for cash, how is the gain or loss measured?
2. A plant asset that cost $27,000 and has a related accumulated depreciation account balance of $27,000 is still being used in business operations. Would it be appropriate to continue recording depreciation on this asset? Explain. When should the asset's cost and accumulated depreciation be removed from the accounting records?
3. A machine and $22,500 cash were exchanged for a delivery truck. How should the cost basis of the delivery truck be measured?
4. A plant asset was exchanged for a new asset of a similar type. How is the cost of the new asset determined?
5. When similar assets are exchanged, a resulting gain is not recognized. Justify this.
6. What is the proper accounting treatment for the costs of removing or dismantling a company's old plant assets?
7. **a.** Distinguish between depreciation, depletion, and amortization. Name two assets that are subject to depreciation, to depletion, and to amortization.
   b. Distinguish between tangible and intangible assets, and classify the assets named in part (**a**) accordingly.
8. A building with an estimated physical life of 40 years was constructed at the site of a coal mine. The coal mine is expected to be completely exhausted within 20 years. Over what length of time should the building be depreciated, assuming the building will be abandoned after all the coal has been extracted?
9. What are the characteristics of intangible assets? Give an example of an asset that has no physical existence but is not classified as an intangible asset.
10. What reasons justify the immediate expensing of most research and development costs?
11. Over what length of time should intangible assets be amortized?
12. Should costs incurred on internally generated intangible assets be capitalized in asset accounts?
13. Describe the typical accounting for a patent.
14. During 1997, Atkins Company incurred $123,000 of research and development costs in its laboratory to develop a patent that was granted on December 29, 1997. Legal fees (outside counsel) and other costs associated with registration of the patent totaled $22,800. What amount should be recorded as a patent on December 29, 1997?
15. What is a capital lease? What features may characterize a capital lease?
16. What is the difference between a leasehold (under an operating lease contract) and a leasehold improvement? Is there any difference in the accounting procedures applicable to each?
17. Smythe Company leased a tract of land for 40 years at an agreed annual rental fee of $18,000. The effective date of the lease was July 1, 1996. During the last six months of 1996, Smythe constructed a building on the land at a cost of $450,000. The building was placed in operation on January 2, 1997, at which time it was estimated to have a physical life of 50 years. Over what period should the building be depreciated? Why?
18. You note that a certain store seems to have a steady stream of regular customers, a favorable location, courteous employees, high-quality merchandise, and a reputation for fairness in dealing with customers, employees, and suppliers. Does it follow automatically that this business should have goodwill recorded as an asset? Explain.

The Coca-Cola Company

19. **Real World Question** From the consolidated balance sheet of The Coca-Cola Company in the annual report booklet, identify the 1993 intangible assets ending balance. What percentage increase does this amount represent over the 1992 ending balance and what percentage did the intangible assets balance represent of the 1992 and 1993 total assets?

MAYTAG

20. **Real World Question** Based on the financial statements of Maytag Corporation contained in the annual report booklet, what was the 1993 allowance for amortization of intangibles? What percentage change does this represent from the preceding year?

EXERCISES

Exercise 11–1
Record sale of equipment; account for removal costs (L.O. 1)

Plant equipment originally costing $16,200, on which $10,800 of up-to-date depreciation has been accumulated, was sold for $4,050.

a. Prepare the journal entry to record the sale.

b. Prepare the entry to record the sale of the equipment if $45 of removal costs were incurred to allow the equipment to be moved.

Exercise 11–2
Update depreciation and record sale of truck (L.O. 1)

On August 31, 1996, Ben Company sold a truck for $6,900 cash. The truck was acquired on January 1, 1993, at a cost of $17,400. Depreciation of $10,800 on the truck has been recorded through December 31, 1995, using the straight-line method, four-year expected useful life, and an expected salvage value of $3,000.

Prepare the journal entries to update the depreciation on the truck on August 31, 1996, and to record the sale of the truck.

Exercise 11–3
Record the destruction of machinery by fire—uninsured and insured asset (L.O. 1)

A machine costing $60,000, on which $45,000 of up-to-date depreciation has been accumulated, was completely destroyed by fire. What journal entry should record the machine's destruction and the resulting fire loss under each of the following unrelated assumptions?

a. The machine was *not* insured.

b. The machine was insured, and it is estimated that $11,250 will be recovered from the insurance company.

Exercise 11–4
Record exchange of automobiles (L.O. 2)

Warren Company owned an automobile acquired on January 1, 1994, at a cash cost of $35,100; at that time, the automobile was estimated to have a useful life of four years and a $2,700 salvage value. Depreciation has been recorded through December 31, 1996, on a straight-line basis. On January 1, 1997, the automobile was traded for a new automobile. The old automobile had a fair market value (trade-in allowance) of $6,750. Cash of $31,050 was paid.

Prepare the journal entry to record the trade-in under generally accepted accounting principles.

Exercise 11–5
Record variety of cases involving sale, retirement, or exchange of equipment (L.O. 1, 2)

Equipment costing $165,000, on which $112,500 of up-to-date accumulated depreciation has been recorded, was disposed of on January 2, 1996. What journal entries are required to record the equipment's disposal under each of the following unrelated assumptions?

a. The equipment was sold for $60,000 cash.

b. The equipment was sold for $43,500 cash.

c. The equipment was retired from service and hauled to the junkyard. No material was salvaged.

d. The equipment was exchanged for similar equipment having a cash price of $225,000. A trade-in allowance of $75,000 from the cash price was received, and the balance was paid in cash.

e. The equipment was exchanged for similar equipment having a cash price of $225,000. A trade-in allowance of $37,500 was received, and the balance was paid in cash.

Exercise 11–6
Compute depletion cost per ton (L.O. 3)

Monroe Mining Company purchased a tract of land containing ore for $630,000. After spending $90,000 in exploration costs, the company determined that 600,000 tons of ore existed on the tract but only 500,000 tons could be economically removed. No other costs were incurred. When the company finishes with the tract, it estimates the land will be worth $180,000. Determine the depletion cost per ton.

Exercise 11–7
Determine depletion cost and expense (L.O. 3)

Griffith Company paid $3,600,000 for the right to extract all of the mineral-bearing ore, estimated at 5 million tons, that can be economically extracted from a certain tract of land. During the first year, Griffith Company extracted 500,000 tons of the ore and sold 400,000 tons. What part of the $3,600,000 should be charged to expense during the first year?

Exercise 11–8
Compute depreciation charge on plant asset used for mining purposes (L.O. 3)

The Violet Mining Company acquired a tract of land for mining purposes and erected a building on-site at a cost of $675,000 and having no salvage value. Though the building has a useful life of 10 years, the mining operations are expected to last only 6 years. The company has determined that 800,000 tons of ore exist on the tract but only 600,000 tons can be economically removed. If 100,000 tons of ore are extracted in the first year of operations, what is the appropriate depreciation charge, using the units-of-production method?

Exercise 11–9
Determine patent cost and periodic amortization (L.O. 4)

Chuck Company purchased a patent on January 1, 1982, at a total cost of $30,600. In January 1993, the company hired an outside law firm and successfully defended the patent in a lawsuit. The legal fees amounted to $6,750. What will be the amount of patent cost amortized in 1996? (The useful life of the patent is the same as its legal life—17 years.)

Exercise 11–10
Record franchise; record accrued franchise fees and franchise amortization (L.O. 4)

Don Jackson paid Hungry Hannah's Hamburgers $54,000 for the right to operate a fast-food restaurant in Thomasville under the Hungry Hannah's name. Jackson also agreed to pay an operating fee of 0.5% of sales for advertising and other services rendered by Hungry Hannah's. Jackson began operations on January 2, 1996. Sales for 1996 amounted to $540,000.

Give the entries to record the payment of the $54,000 and to record expenses incurred relating to the right to use the Hungry Hannah's name.

Exercise 11–11
Record leasehold; record rent accrued and leasehold amortization (L.O. 4)

Thomas Company leased the first three floors in a building under an operating lease contract for a 10-year period beginning January 1, 1996. The company paid $120,000 in cash (not representing a specific period's rent) and agreed to make annual payments equal to 1% of the first $750,000 of sales and 0.5% of all sales over $750,000. Sales for 1996 amounted to $2,250,000. Payment of the annual amount will be made in January 1997.

Prepare journal entries to record the cash payment of January 1, 1996, and the proper expense to be recognized for the use of the space in the leased building for 1996.

Exercise 11–12
Determine amount of goodwill (L.O. 4)

Tate Company purchased all of the assets of Eli Company for $900,000. Tate Company also agreed to assume responsibility for Eli Company's liabilities of $90,000. The fair market value of the assets acquired was $810,000. How much goodwill should be recorded in this transaction?

PROBLEMS

Problem 11–1
Record exchange of automobiles (L.O. 2)

Martin Company traded in an automobile that cost $36,000 and on which $30,000 of up-to-date depreciation has been recorded for a new automobile with a cash price of $69,000. The company received a trade-in allowance (its fair value) for the old automobile of $4,200 and paid the balance in cash.

Required Record the exchange of automobiles.

Problem 11–2
Update depreciation and record six cases of asset disposal (L.O. 1, 2)

On January 2, 1994, Chip Company purchased a delivery truck for $78,750 cash. The truck has an estimated useful life of six years and an estimated salvage value of $6,750. The straight-line method of depreciation is being used.

Required

a. Prepare a schedule showing the computation of the book value of the truck on December 31, 1996.

b. Assume the truck is to be disposed of on July 1, 1997. Prepare the journal entry to record depreciation for the six months ended June 30, 1997.

c. Prepare the journal entries to record the disposal of the truck on July 1, 1997, under each of the following unrelated assumptions:

1. The truck was sold for $26,250 cash.
2. The truck was sold for $48,000 cash.
3. The truck was retired from service, and it is expected that $20,625 will be received from the sale of salvaged materials.
4. The truck and $60,000 cash were exchanged for office equipment that had a cash price of $105,000.
5. The truck and $67,500 cash were exchanged for a new delivery truck that had a cash price of $112,500.
6. The truck was completely destroyed in an accident. Cash of $25,500 is expected to be recovered from the insurance company.

Problem 11–3
Update depreciation and record exchange of plant asset for similar asset (L.O. 2)

Cox Moving Company purchased a new moving van on October 1, 1996. The cash price of the new van was $45,000, and the company received a trade-in allowance of $7,500 for a 1994 model. The balance was paid in cash. The 1994 model had been acquired on January 1, 1994, at a cost of $30,000. Depreciation has been recorded through December 31, 1995, on a straight-line basis, with three years of expected useful life and no expected salvage value.

Required

Prepare journal entries to update the depreciation and to record the exchange of the moving vans.

Problem 11–4
Record leasehold amortization; record depreciation and trade-in (L.O. 2, 4)

On January 1, 1996, Curtis Company had the following balances in some of its accounts:

	Asset	Accumulated Depreciation
Land	$ 624,000	
Leasehold.	780,000	
Buildings	3,425,760	$ 286,650
Equipment	2,995,200	1,389,960
Trucks	449,280	158,790

Additional data

1. The leasehold covers a plot of ground leased on January 1, 1992, for a period of 20 years.
2. Building No. 1 is on the owned land and was completed on July 1, 1995, at a cost of $1,965,600; its life is set at 40 years with no salvage value. Building No. 2 is on the leased land and was completed on July 1, 1992, at a cost of $1,460,160; its life is also set at 40 years with no expected salvage value.
3. The equipment had an expected useful life of eight years with no estimated salvage value.
4. Truck A, purchased on January 1, 1994, at a cost of $149,760, had an expected useful life of 2½ years and a salvage value of $9,360. Truck B, purchased on July 1, 1994, at a cost of $131,040, had an expected life of two years and an estimated salvage value of $21,840. Truck C, purchased on July 1, 1995, at a cost of $168,480, had an expected life of three years and an estimated salvage value of $21,060.

The following transactions occurred in 1996:

Jan.	2	Rent for 1996 on leased land was paid, $87,360.
April	1	Truck B was traded in for truck D. The cash price of the new truck was $149,760. A trade-in allowance of $28,080 was granted from the cash price. The balance was paid in cash. Truck D has an expected life of 2½ years and an estimated salvage value of $9,360.
	1	Truck A was sold for $28,080 cash.

Required

Prepare journal entries to record the 1996 transactions and the necessary December 31, 1996, adjusting entries, assuming a calendar-year accounting period. Use the straight-line depreciation method.

Problem 11–5
Determine depletion for period and depreciation on mining equipment; compute average cost per ton of ore mined (L.O. 3)

On January 2, 1996, Borden Mining Company acquired land with ore deposits at a cash cost of $900,000. Exploration and development costs amounted to $96,000. The residual value of the land is expected to be $180,000. The ore deposits contain an estimated 3 million tons. Present technology will allow the economical extraction of only 85% of the total deposit. Machinery, equipment, and temporary sheds were installed at a cost of $127,500. The assets will have no further value to the company when the ore body is exhausted; they have a physical life of 12 years. In 1996, 100,000 tons of ore were extracted. The company expects the mine to be exhausted in 10 years, with sharp variations in annual production.

Required

a. Compute the depletion charge for 1996. Round to the nearest cent.
b. Compute the depreciation charge for 1996 under the units-of-production method.
c. If all other mining costs, except depletion, amounted to $630,000, what was the average cost per ton mined in 1996? (The depreciation calculated in **b** is included in the $630,000.)

Problem 11–6
Record cost and amortization of patent (L.O. 4)

Larkin Company spent $249,900 to purchase a patent on January 2, 1996. Management assumes that the patent will be useful during its full legal life. In January 1997, the company hired an outside law firm and successfully defended the patent in a lawsuit at a cost of $48,000. Also, in January 1997, the company paid $72,000 to obtain patents that could, if used by competitors, make the earlier Larkin patent useless. The purchased patents will never be used.

Required Give the entries for 1996 and 1997 to record the information relating to the patents.

Problem 11–7
Record amortization expense for a variety of intangible assets (L.O. 4)

Following are selected transactions and other data relating to Kern Company for the year ended December 31,1996.

a. The company rented the second floor of a building for five years on January 2, 1996, and paid the annual rent of $9,000 for the first and fifth years in advance.

b. In 1995, the company incurred legal fees of $27,000 paid to an outside law firm in applying for a patent and paid a fee of $9,000 to a former employee who conceived a device that substantially reduced the cost of manufacturing one of the company's products. The patent on the device has a market value of $270,000 and is expected to be useful for 10 years.

c. In 1995, the company entered into a 10-year operating lease on several floors of a building, paying $18,000 in cash immediately and agreeing to pay $9,000 at the end of each of the 10 years of life in the lease. The company then incurred costs of $36,000 to install partitions, shelving, and fixtures. These items would normally last 25 years.

d. The company spent $10,800 promoting a trademark in a manner that it believed enhanced the value of the trademark considerably. The trademark has an indefinite life.

e. The company incurred costs amounting to $90,000 in 1995 and $117,000 in 1996 for research and development of new products that are expected to enhance the company's revenues for at least five years.

f. The company paid $90,000 to the author of a book that the company published on July 2, 1996. Sales of the book are expected to be made over a two-year period from that date.

Required For each of the situations just described, prepare only the journal entries to record the expense applicable to 1996.

Alternate Problems

Problem 11–1A
Update depreciation and record exchange of automobiles (L.O. 2)

Johnson, Inc., purchased a new 1997 model automobile on December 31, 1997. The cash price of the new automobile was $14,040, from which Johnson received a trade-in allowance of $2,160 for a 1995 model traded in. The 1995 model had been acquired on January 1, 1995, at a cost of $10,350. Depreciation has been recorded on the 1995 model through December 31, 1996, using the straight-line method, an expected four-year useful life, and an expected salvage value of $1,350.

Required

a. Record depreciation expense for 1997.

b. Prepare the journal entries needed to record the exchange of automobiles.

Problem 11–2A
Update depreciation and record six cases of asset disposal (L.O. 1, 2)

On January 1, 1994, Joker Company purchased a truck for $43,200 cash. The truck has an estimated useful life of six years and an expected salvage value of $5,400. Depreciation on the truck was computed using the straight-line method.

Required

a. Prepare a schedule showing the computation of the book value of the truck on December 31, 1996.

b. Prepare the journal entry to record depreciation for the six months ended June 30, 1997.

c. Prepare journal entries to record the disposal of the truck on June 30, 1997, under each of the following unrelated assumptions:
   1. The truck was sold for $3,600 cash.
   2. The truck was sold for $25,200 cash.
   3. The truck was scrapped. Used parts valued at $6,660 were salvaged.

4. The truck (which has a fair market value of $10,800) and $32,400 of cash were exchanged for a used back hoe that did not have a known market value.
5. The truck and $29,700 cash were exchanged for another truck that had a cash price of $51,300.
6. The truck was stolen July 1, and insurance proceeds of $7,560 were expected.

Problem 11–3A
Update depreciation and record exchange of plant asset for similar asset (L.O. 2)

Jackson Company purchased a new Model II computer October 1, 1996. Cash price of the new computer was $49,920; Jackson received a trade-in allowance of $18,600 from the cash price for a Model I computer. The old computer was acquired on January 1, 1994, at a cost of $46,080. Depreciation has been recorded through December 31, 1995, on a straight-line basis, with an estimated useful life of four years and $7,680 expected salvage value.

Required

Prepare the journal entries to record the exchange.

Problem 11–4A
Record leasehold amortization; record depreciation and trade-in (L.O. 2, 4)

On July 1, 1996, Henry Company had the following balances in some of its accounts:

	Asset	Accumulated Depreciation
Land	$ 672,000	
Leasehold.	252,000	
Buildings	3,151,680	$369,768
Equipment	1,370,880	436,800
Trucks	238,560	71,652

Additional data

1. The leasehold covers a plot of ground leased on July 1, 1991, for a period of 25 years under an operating lease.
2. The office building is on the leased land and was completed on July 1, 1992, at a cost of $967,680; its physical life is set at 40 years. The factory building is on the owned land and was completed on July 1, 1991, at a cost of $2,184,000; its life is also set at 40 years with no expected salvage value.
3. The equipment has a 15-year useful life with no expected salvage value.
4. The company owns three trucks—A, B, and C. Truck A, purchased on July 1, 1994, at a cost of $53,760, had an expected useful life of three years and a salvage value of $3,360. Truck B, purchased on January 2, 1995, at a cost of $84,000, had an expected life of four years and an estimated salvage value of $6,720. Truck C, purchased on January 2, 1996, at a cost of $100,800, had an expected life of five years and an estimated salvage value of $10,080.

The following transactions occurred in the fiscal year ended June 30, 1997:

1996
July 1 Rent for July 1, 1996, through June 30, 1997, on leased land was paid, $31,920.
Oct. 1 Truck A was traded in on truck D. Cash price of the new truck was $107,520. Cash of $90,720 was paid. Truck D has an expected life of four years and a salvage value of $5,880.

1997
Feb. 2 Truck B was sold for $47,040 cash.
June 1 Truck C was completely demolished in an accident. The truck was not insured.

Required

Prepare journal entries to record these transactions and the necessary June 30, 1997, adjusting entries. Use the straight-line depreciation method.

Problem 11–5A
Determine depletion for period and depreciation on building and mining equipment; compute average cost per ton of ore mined (L.O. 3)

In December 1995, Hardin Company acquired a mine for $1,350,000. The mine contained an estimated 5 million tons of ore. It was also estimated that the land would have a value of $120,000 when the mine was exhausted and that only 2 million tons of ore could be economically extracted. A building was erected on the property at a cost of $180,000. The building had an estimated useful life of 35 years and no salvage value. Specialized mining equipment was installed at a cost of $247,500. This equipment had an estimated useful life of seven years and an estimated $16,500 salvage value. The company began operating on January 1, 1996, and put all of its assets into use on that date. During the year ended December 31, 1996, 200,000 tons of ore were extracted. The company decided to use the units-of-production method to record depreciation on the building and the straight-line method to record depreciation on the equipment.

Required Prepare journal entries to record the depletion and depreciation charges for the year ended December 31, 1996. Show calculations.

Problem 11–6A
Record cost and amortization of patent (L.O. 4)

Hardy Company purchased a patent for $108,000 on January 2, 1996. The patent was estimated to have a useful life of 10 years. The $108,000 cost was properly charged to an asset account and amortized in 1996. On January 1, 1997, the company incurred legal and court costs of $32,400 in a successful defense of the patent in a lawsuit. The legal work was performed by an outside law firm.

Required

a. Compute the patent amortization expense for 1996 and give the entry to record it.

b. Compute the patent amortization expense for 1997 and give the entry to record it.

Problem 11–7A
Record amortization expense for a variety of intangible assets (L.O. 4)

Selected transactions and other data for Aderholt Company:

a. The company purchased a patent in early January 1993 for $72,000 and began amortizing it over 10 years. In early January 1995, the company hired an outside law firm and successfully defended the patent in an infringement suit at a cost of $19,200.

b. Research and development costs incurred in 1995 of $21,600 were expected to provide benefits over the three succeeding years.

c. On January 2, 1996, the company rented space in a warehouse for five years at an annual fee of $4,800. Rent for the first and last years was paid in advance.

d. A total of $48,000 was spent uniformly throughout 1996 by the company in promoting its lesser known trademark, which is expected to have an indefinite life.

e. In January 1994, the company purchased all of the assets and assumed all of the liabilities of another company, paying $96,000 more than the fair market value of all identifiable assets acquired, less the liabilities assumed. The company expects the benefits for which it paid the $96,000 to last 10 years.

Required For each of these unrelated transactions, prepare journal entries to record only those entries required for 1996. Note any items that do not require an entry in 1996.

BEYOND THE NUMBERS—CRITICAL THINKING

Business Decision Case 11–1
Record exchange of similar assets; adjust accounts for errors in accounting for depreciable assets (L.O. 2)

During your audit examination of the Basket Company's Plant, Property, and Equipment accounts, the following transaction came to your attention. On January 2, 1996, machine A was exchanged for machine B. Basket Company acquired machine A for $90,000 on January 2, 1994. Machine A had an estimated useful life of four years and no salvage value, and the machine was depreciated on the straight-line basis. Machine B had a cash price of $108,000. In addition to machine A, cash of $30,000 was given up in the exchange. Machine B has an estimated useful life of five years and no salvage value, and the machine is being depreciated using the straight-line method. Upon further analysis, you discovered that the company recorded the transaction as an exchange of dissimilar assets instead of an exchange of similar assets. You must now determine the following:

a. What journal entry did the Basket Company make when it recorded the exchange of machines? (Show computations.)

b. What journal entry should the Basket Company have made to record the exchange of machines?

c. Assume the error was discovered on December 31, 1997, before adjusting journal entries have been made. What journal entries should be made to correct the accounting records? (Adjustments of prior years' net income because of errors should be debited or credited to Retained Earnings.) What adjusting journal entry should be made to record depreciation for 1997? (Ignore income taxes.)

d. What effect did the error have on reported net income for 1996? (Ignore income taxes.)

e. How should machine B be reported on the December 31, 1997, balance sheet?

Business Decision Case 11–2
Record purchase of two businesses and explain differences between the two; advise client as to which company should be purchased (L.O. 4)

Currently, many corporations are looking for acquisition opportunities. McArdle, Inc., is trying to decide whether to buy Amite Company or Beauman Company. McArdle, Inc., has hired you as a consultant to analyze the two companies' financial information and to determine the more advantageous acquisition. Your review of the companies' books has revealed that both Amite and Beauman have assets with the following book values and fair market values:

	Book Value	Fair Market Value
Accounts receivable	$150,000	$ 150,000
Inventories	450,000	750,000
Land	375,000	675,000
Buildings	450,000	1,050,000
Equipment	180,000	300,000
Patents	120,000	150,000

Liabilities assumed on the purchase of either company include accounts payable, $300,000, and notes payable, $75,000.

The only difference between the companies is that Amite has net income that is about average for the industry, while Beauman's net income is greatly above average for the industry.

Required

Top-level management at McArdle, Inc., has asked you to respond in writing to the following possible situations:

a. Assume McArdle, Inc., can buy Amite Company for $2,700,000 or Beauman Company for $3,450,000. Prepare the journal entries to record the acquisition of Amite Company and Beauman Company. What accounts for the difference between the purchase price of the two companies?

b. Assume McArdle, Inc, can buy either company for $2,700,000. Write a report for McArdle, Inc., advising which company to buy.

Annual Report Analysis 11–3
Calculate and discuss total assets turnover (L.O. 5)

Eli Lilly & Company is a global research-based corporation that develops, manufactures, and markets pharmaceuticals, medical devices and diagnostic products, and animal health products.

Using the following excerpt from the Eli Lilly 1992 annual report, calculate the firm's total assets turnover for 1991 and 1992. (Amounts are in $ millions.)

	1992	1991	1990
Net sales	$6,167.3	$5,725.7	$5,191.6
Total assets	$8,672.8	$8,298.6	$7,142.8

In a written report, discuss the meaning of the total assets turnover ratio and what the ratio means to management and investors. Use the total assets turnover ratios you computed for Eli Lilly as an example in your report.

Ethics Case 11–4
Answer questions regarding ethics case

Based on the situation described in the ethics case on page 415 regarding ABC Corporation, respond in writing to the following questions.

a. Depending on his actions, what are the possible consequences for John Gilbert in this situation?

b. Assuming that the president cannot find another appraiser to support the new allocations, what would you do if you were Gilbert?

c. If the president can find a reputable appraiser to support these new allocations, what would you do if you were Gilbert?

Group Project 11–5
Make intangible assets presentation

In teams of two or three students, find a recent annual report that includes intangible assets on the balance sheet. Select one member of each team to give an informal presentation discussing intangible asset disclosures on the face of the statements and in the notes to the financial statements. All members should be prepared to discuss intangible asset disclosures from their annual report in detail.

Answers to Self-Test

True-False

1. **False.** No more depreciation can be taken on a fully depreciated plant asset.
2. **True.** The new asset is recorded at the fair market value of the asset received or given up, whichever is more clearly evident.
3. **False.** The residual value of land should be deducted from total costs subject to depletion.
4. **True.** All recorded intangible assets should be amortized over their economic life, their legal life, or 40 years, whichever is shorter.

Multiple-Choice

1. **d.** The cost and accumulated depreciation should not be removed from the accounts until the disposal of the asset.
2. **a.** On the date of exchange, the book value of the old truck is $20,700 ($45,000 minus accumulated depreciation of $24,300). The trade-in allowance of $22,500 indicates a gain on exchange of $1,800. In an exchange of similar assets, a gain is not recognized, but reduces the cost of a new asset. Therefore, the cost of the new truck is $55,200 ($57,000 minus $1,800), and no gain is recognized.
3. **c.** The depletion charge for the first year is:

   Depletion charge per ton = ($375,000 − $75,000)/1,000,000
   = $0.30

   Depletion charge for the year = $0.30 × 100,000
   = $30,000

   Since all of the ore that was extracted was sold, all of the $30,000 is expensed as cost of ore sold.
4. **b.** The patent is amortized over 10 years:

   Annual amortization expense = $36,000/10
   = $3,600

IV

Sources of Equity Capital for Management's Use in Producing Revenues

Part Outline

A Manager's Perspective

Judy Knighten

Senior Sales Development Manager

The Coca-Cola Company

I call on retailers such as grocery stores and convenience stores based in Atlanta that are serviced by multiple Coca-Cola bottlers. Since our bottlers are all independent of The Coca-Cola Company, my primary responsibilities revolve around coordinating sales between the bottlers and the retail accounts.

I work with my accounts and Coca-Cola bottlers to develop marketing programs that will drive sales of Coca-Cola products. Profitability analyses are used to determine the effectiveness of our sales programs.

I also manage a budget and ensure the budget is allocated properly to the bottlers. If I don't understand the accounting functions, I can't effectively work with the finance group to ensure a reasonable budget is allocated for my accounts. Companies are bottom-line oriented these days, so you have to understand how the numbers are determined and what they mean in order to get the resources you need to achieve your objectives.

It's also important to understand how a profit-and-loss statement is used to make decisions, or I could actually end up losing money. For example, if I don't understand the systems my retail accounts are using to account for inventory, I won't be able to put together the most effective plan for them, and I could potentially lose business.

My top three objectives as a sales manager are based on sales in the Atlanta market. In order to be an effective sales manager, I need to understand basic financial information so I can make sound business decisions that will meet my objective of growing sales for both our retail partners and Coca-Cola bottlers.

12

STOCKHOLDERS' EQUITY: CLASSES OF CAPITAL STOCK

In this chapter, you study the corporate form of business organization in greater detail than in preceding chapters. Although corporations are fewer in number than single proprietorships and partnerships, corporations possess the bulk of our business capital and currently supply us with most of our goods and services.

This chapter discusses the advantages and disadvantages of the corporation, how to form and direct a corporation, and some of the unique situations encountered in accounting for and reporting on the different classes of capital stock.

LEARNING OBJECTIVES

After studying this chapter, you should be able to:

1. State the advantages and disadvantages of the corporate form of business.
2. List the values commonly associated with capital stock and give their definitions.
3. List the various kinds of stock and describe the differences between them.
4. Present in proper form the stockholders' equity section of a balance sheet.
5. Account for the issuances of stock for cash and other assets.

(continued)

THE CORPORATION

A **corporation** is an entity recognized by law as possessing an existence separate and distinct from its owners; that is, it is a separate legal entity. Endowed with many of the rights and obligations possessed by a person, a corporation can enter into contracts in its own name; buy, sell, or hold property; borrow money; hire and fire employees; and sue and be sued.

Corporations have a remarkable ability to obtain the huge amounts of capital necessary for large-scale business operations. Corporations acquire their capital by issuing **shares of stock;** these are the units into which corporations divide their ownership. Investors buy shares of stock in a corporation for two basic reasons. First, investors expect the value of their shares to increase over time so that the stock may be sold in the future at a profit. Second, while investors hold stock, they expect the corporation to pay them dividends (usually in cash) in return for using their money. Chapter 13 discusses the various kinds of dividends and their accounting treatment.

Advantages of the Corporate Form of Business

Corporations have many advantages over single proprietorships and partnerships. The major advantages a corporation has over a single proprietorship are the same

(concluded)

6. Determine book values of both preferred and common stock.
7. Analyze and use the financial results—return on average common stockholders' equity.

Objective 1
State the advantages and disadvantages of the corporate form of business.

advantages a partnership has over a single proprietorship. Although corporations have more owners than partnerships, both have a broader base for investment, risk, responsibilities, and talent than do single proprietorships. Since corporations are more comparable to partnerships than to single proprietorships, the following discussion of advantages contrasts the partnership with the corporation.

1. **Easy transfer of ownership.** In a partnership, a partner cannot transfer ownership in the business to another person if the other partners do not want the new person involved in the partnership. In a publicly held (owned by many stockholders) corporation, shares of stock are traded on a stock exchange between unknown parties; one owner usually cannot dictate to whom another owner can or cannot sell shares.
2. **Limited liability.** Each partner in a partnership is personally responsible for all the debts of the business. In a corporation, the stockholders are not personally responsible for its debts; the maximum amount a stockholder can lose is the amount of his or her investment. However, when a small, closely held corporation (owned by only a few stockholders) borrows money, banks and lending institutions often require an officer of the small corporation to sign the loan agreement. Then, the officer has to repay the loan if the corporation does not.
3. **Continuous existence of the entity.** In a partnership, many circumstances, such as the death of a partner, can terminate the business entity. These same circumstances have no effect on a corporation because it is a legal entity, separate and distinct from its owners.
4. **Easy capital generation.** The easy transfer of ownership and the limited liability of stockholders are attractive features to potential investors. Thus, it is relatively easy for a corporation to raise capital by issuing shares of stock to many investors. Corporations with thousands of stockholders are not uncommon.
5. **Professional management.** Generally, the partners in a partnership are also the managers of that business, regardless of whether they have the necessary expertise to manage a business. In a publicly held corporation, most of the owners (stockholders) do not participate in the day-to-day operations and management of the entity. They hire professionals to run the business on a daily basis.
6. **Separation of owners and entity.** Since the corporation is a separate legal entity, the owners do not have the power to bind the corporation to business contracts. This feature eliminates the potential problem of mutual agency that exists between partners in a partnership. In a corporation, one stockholder cannot jeopardize other stockholders through poor decision making.

Disadvantages of the Corporate Form of Business

The corporate form of business has the following disadvantages:

1. **Double taxation.** Because a corporation is a separate legal entity, its net income is subject to double taxation. The corporation pays a tax on its income, and stockholders pay a tax on corporate income received as dividends.
2. **Government regulation.** Because corporations are created by law, they are subject to greater regulation and control than single proprietorships and partnerships.
3. **Entrenched, inefficient management.** A corporation may be burdened with an inefficient management that remains in control by using corporate funds to solicit the needed stockholder votes to back its positions. Stockholders scattered across the country, who individually own only small portions of a corporation's stock, find it difficult to organize and oppose existing management.

4. **Limited ability to raise creditor capital.** The limited liability of stockholders makes a corporation an attractive means for accumulating stockholder capital. At the same time, this limited liability feature restrains the amount of creditor capital a corporation can amass because creditors cannot look to stockholders to pay the debts of a corporation. Thus, beyond a certain point, creditors do not lend some corporations money without the personal guarantee of a stockholder or officer of the corporation to repay the loan if the corporation does not.

Incorporating

Corporations are chartered by the state. Each state has a corporation act that permits the formation of corporations by qualified persons. **Incorporators** are persons seeking to bring a corporation into existence. Most state corporation laws require a minimum of three incorporators, each of whom must be of legal age, and a majority of whom must be citizens of the United States.

The laws of each state view a corporation organized in that state as a **domestic corporation** and a corporation organized in any other state as a **foreign corporation.** If a corporation intends to conduct business solely within one state, it normally seeks incorporation in that state because most state laws are not as severe for domestic corporations as for foreign corporations. Corporations conducting interstate business usually incorporate in the state that has laws most advantageous to the corporation being formed. Important considerations in choosing a state are the powers granted to the corporation, the taxes levied, the defenses permitted against hostile takeover attempts by others, and the reports required by the state.

Articles of Incorporation

Once incorporators agree on the state in which to incorporate, they apply for a corporate charter. A **corporate charter** is a contract between the state and the incorporators, and their successors, granting the corporation its legal existence. The application for the corporation's charter is called the **articles of incorporation.**

After supplying the information requested in the incorporation application form, incorporators file the articles with the proper office in the state of incorporation. Each state requires different information in the articles of incorporation, but most states ask for the following:

1. Name of corporation.
2. Location of principal offices.
3. Purposes of business.
4. Number of shares of stock authorized, class or classes of shares, and voting and dividend rights of each class of shares.
5. Value of assets paid in by the incorporators (the stockholders who organize the corporation).
6. Limitations on authority of the management and owners of the corporation.

On approving the articles, the state office (frequently the secretary of state's office) grants the charter and creates the corporation.

Bylaws

As soon as the corporation obtains the charter, it is authorized to operate its business. The incorporators call the first meeting of the stockholders. Two of the purposes of this meeting are to elect a board of directors and to adopt the bylaws of the corporation.

The **bylaws** are a set of rules or regulations adopted by the board of directors of a corporation to govern the conduct of corporate affairs. The bylaws must be in agreement with the laws of the state and the policies and purposes in the corporate charter. The bylaws contain, along with other information, provisions for: (1) the place, date, and manner of calling the annual stockholders' meeting; (2) the number of directors and the method for electing them; (3) the duties and powers of the directors; and (4) the method for selecting officers of the corporation.

Organization Costs

Organization costs are the costs of organizing a corporation, such as state incorporation fees and legal fees applicable to incorporation. The firm debits these costs to an account called *Organization Costs*. The Organization Costs account is an asset because the costs yield benefits over the life of the corporation; if the fees had not been paid, no corporate entity would exist. Since the account is classified on the balance sheet as an intangible asset, it is amortized over a period not to exceed 40 years. Most organizations write off these costs fairly rapidly because they are small in amount.

As an illustration, assume that De-Leed Corporation pays state incorporation fees of $10,000 and attorney's fees of $5,000 for services rendered related to the acquisition of a charter with the state. The entry to record these costs is:

	Debit	Credit
Organization Costs	15,000	
Cash		15,000
To record costs incurred in organizing corporation.		

Assuming the corporation amortizes the organization costs over a 10-year period, this entry records amortization at the end of the year:

	Debit	Credit
Amortization Expense—Organization Costs	1,500	
Organization Costs		1,500
To record organization costs amortization expense ($15,000/10 years = $1,500).		

Directing the Corporation

Management of the corporation is through the delegation of authority from the stockholders to the directors to the officers, as shown in the organization chart in Illustration 12.1. The stockholders elect the board of directors. The board of directors formulates the broad policies of the company and selects the principal officers, who execute the policies.

STOCKHOLDERS Stockholders do not have the right to participate actively in the management of the business unless they serve as directors and/or officers. However, stockholders do have certain basic rights, including the right to (1) dispose of their shares, (2) buy additional newly issued shares in a proportion equal to the percentage of shares they already own (called the **preemptive right**), (3) share in dividends when declared, (4) share in assets in case of liquidation, and (5) participate in management indirectly by voting at the stockholders' meeting.

The preemptive right allows stockholders to maintain their percentage of ownership in a corporation when additional shares are issued. For example, assume Joe Thornton owns 10% of the outstanding shares of Corporation X. When Corporation X decides to issue 1,000 additional shares of stock, Joe Thornton has the right to buy 100 (10%) of the new shares. Should he decide to do so, he maintains his 10% interest in the corporation. If he does not wish to exercise his preemptive right, the corporation may sell the shares to others.[1]

Normally, companies hold stockholders' meetings annually. At the annual stockholders' meeting, stockholders indirectly share in management by voting on such issues as changing the charter, increasing the number of authorized shares of stock to be issued, approving pension plans, selecting the independent auditor, and other related matters.

At stockholders' meetings, each stockholder is entitled to one vote for each share of voting stock held. Stockholders who do not personally attend the stockholders' meeting may vote by proxy. A **proxy** is a legal document signed by a

[1] Some corporations have eliminated the preemptive right because the preemptive right makes it difficult to issue large blocks of stock to the stockholders of another corporation to acquire that corporation.

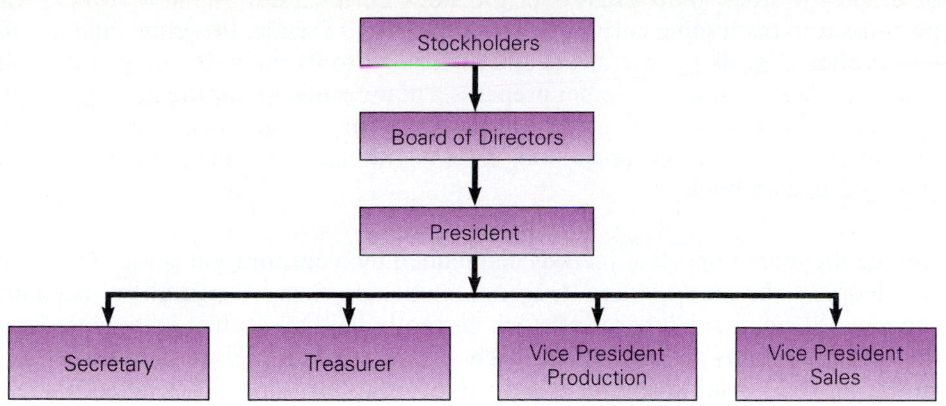

Illustration 12.1
Typical Corporation's Organization Chart

stockholder, giving a designated person the authority to vote the stockholder's shares at a stockholders' meeting.

Board of Directors Elected by the stockholders, the **board of directors** is primarily responsible for formulating policies for the corporation. The board appoints administrative officers and delegates to them the execution of the policies established by the board. The board's more specific duties include: (1) authorizing contracts, (2) declaring dividends, (3) establishing executive salaries, and (4) granting authorization to borrow money. The decisions of the board are recorded in the minutes of its meetings. The minutes are an important source of information to an independent auditor, since they may serve as notice to record transactions (such as a dividend declaration) or to identify certain future transactions (such as a large loan).

Corporate Officers A corporation's bylaws usually specify the titles and duties of the officers of a corporation. The number of officers and their exact titles vary from corporation to corporation, but most have a president, several vice presidents, a secretary, a treasurer, and a controller.

The president is the chief executive officer of the corporation. He or she is empowered by the bylaws to hire all necessary employees except those appointed by the board of directors.

Most corporations have more than one vice president. Each vice president is responsible for one particular corporate operation, such as sales, engineering, or production. The corporate secretary maintains the official records of the company and records the proceedings of meetings of stockholders and directors. The treasurer is accountable for corporate funds and may supervise the accounting function within the company. A controller carries out the accounting function. The controller usually reports to the treasurer of the corporation.

Documents, Books, and Records Relating to Capital Stock

Capital stock consists of transferable units of ownership in a corporation. Each unit of ownership is called a *share of stock.* Typically, traders sell between 100 and 400 million shares of corporate capital stock every business day on stock exchanges, such as the New York Stock Exchange and the American Stock Exchange, and on the over-the-counter market. These sales (or *trades*) seldom involve the corporation issuing the stock as a party to the exchange. Existing stockholders sell their shares to other individual or institutional investors. The physical transfer of the stock certificates follows these trades.

A **stock certificate** is a printed or engraved document serving as evidence that the holder owns a certain number of shares of capital stock. When selling shares of stock, the stockholder signs over the stock certificate to the new owner, who presents it to the issuing corporation. When the old certificate arrives, the issuing corporation cancels the certificate and attaches it to its corresponding stub in the stock certificate book. The issuer prepares a new certificate for the new owner. To determine the number of shares of stock outstanding at any time, the issuer sums the shares shown on the open stubs (stubs without certificates attached) in the stock certificate book.

Stockholders' Ledger

Among the more important records maintained by a corporation is the stockholders' ledger. The **stockholders' ledger** contains a group of subsidiary accounts showing the number of shares of stock currently held by each stockholder. Since the ledger contains an account for **each** stockholder, in a large corporation this ledger may have more than a million individual accounts. Each stockholder's account shows the number of shares currently or previously owned, their certificate numbers, and the dates on which shares were acquired or sold. Entries are made in the number of shares rather than in dollars.

The stockholders' ledger and the stock certificate book contain the same information, but the stockholders' ledger summarizes it alphabetically by stockholder. Since a stockholder may own a dozen or more certificates, each representing a number of shares, this summary enables a corporation to (1) determine the number of shares a stockholder is entitled to vote at a stockholders' meeting and (2) prepare one dividend check per stockholder rather than one per stock certificate.

Many large corporations with actively traded shares turn the task of maintaining reliable stock records over to an outside *stock-transfer agent* and a *stock registrar*. The **stock-transfer agent,** usually a bank or trust company, transfers stock between buyers and sellers for a corporation. The stock-transfer agent cancels the certificates covering shares sold, issues new stock certificates, and makes appropriate entries in the stockholders' ledger. It sends new certificates to the **stock registrar,** typically another bank, that maintains separate records of the shares outstanding. This control system makes it difficult for a corporate employee to issue stock certificates fraudulently and steal the proceeds.

The Minutes Book

The **minutes book,** kept by the secretary of the corporation, is (1) a record book of the actions taken at stockholders' and board of directors' meetings and (2) the written authorization for many actions taken by corporate officers. Remember that all actions taken by the board of directors and the stockholders must be in accordance with the provisions in the corporate charter and the bylaws. The minutes book contains a variety of data, including:

1. A copy of the corporate charter.
2. A copy of the bylaws.
3. Dividends declared by the board of directors.
4. Authorization for the acquisition of major assets.
5. Authorization for borrowing.
6. Authorization for increases or decreases in capital stock.

Par Value and No-Par Capital Stock

Par Value Stock

Objective 2
List the values commonly associated with capital stock and give their definitions.

Many times, companies issue par value stock. **Par value** is an arbitrary amount assigned to each share of a given class of stock and printed on the stock certificate. Par value per share is no indication of the amount for which the stock sells; it is simply the amount per share credited to the capital stock account for each share issued. Also, the total par value of all issued stock constitutes the legal capital of the corporation. The concept of legal capital protects creditors from losses. **Legal capital,** or **stated capital,** is an amount prescribed by law below which a corporation may not reduce stockholders' equity through declaration of dividends or other payments to stockholders. Legal capital does not guarantee that a company can pay its debts, but it does keep a company from compensating owners to the detriment of creditors.

No-Par Stock

In 1912, the state of New York first enacted laws permitting the issuance of **no-par stock (stock without par value).** Many other states have passed similar, but not uniform, legislation.

A corporation might issue no-par stock for two reasons. One reason is to avoid confusion. The use of a par value may confuse some investors because the par value usually does not conform to the market value. Issuing a stock with no par value avoids this source of confusion.

A second reason is related to state laws regarding the original issue price per share. A **discount on capital stock** is the amount by which the shares' par value exceeds their issue price. Thus, if stock with a par value of $100 is issued at $80, the discount is $20. Most states do not permit the original issuance of stock at a discount. Only Maryland, Georgia, and California allow its issuance. The original purchasers of the shares are contingently liable for the discount unless they have transferred (by contract) the discount liability to subsequent holders. If the contingent liability has been transferred, the present stockholders are contingently liable to creditors for the difference between par value and issue price. Although this contingent liability seldom becomes an actual liability, the issuance of no-par stock avoids such a possibility.

No-Par Stock with a Stated Value

The board of directors of a corporation issuing no-par stock may assign a stated value to each share of capital stock. **Stated value** is an arbitrary amount assigned by the board to each share of a given class of no-par stock. The board may set this stated value, like par value, at any amount, although some state statutes specify a minimum amount, such as $5 per share. If not specified by applicable state law, the board may establish stated value either before or after the shares are issued.

Other Values Commonly Associated with Capital Stock

Market Value

Market value is the price of shares of capital stock bought and sold by investors in the market; it is the value of greatest interest to investors. Market price is directly affected by (1) all the factors that influence general economic conditions, (2) investors' expectations concerning the corporation, and (3) the corporation's earnings.

Book Value

Book value per share is the amount per share that each stockholder would receive if the corporation were liquidated without incurring any further expenses and if assets were sold and liabilities liquidated at their recorded amounts. A later section discusses book value per share in greater detail.

Liquidation Value

Liquidation value is the amount a stockholder would receive if a corporation discontinued operations and liquidated by selling its assets, paying its liabilities, and distributing the remaining cash among the stockholders. Since the assets might be sold for more or less than the amounts at which they are recorded in the corporation's accounts, liquidation value may be more or less than book value. If only one class of capital stock is outstanding, each stockholder would receive, per share, the amount obtained by dividing the remaining cash by the number of outstanding shares. If two or more classes of stock are outstanding, liquidation value depends on the rights of the various classes.

Redemption Value

A corporation issues certain capital stock with the stipulation that it has the right to redeem it. **Redemption value** is the price per share at which a corporation may call in (or redeem) its capital stock for retirement.

Capital Stock Authorized and Outstanding

Objective 3
List the various kinds of stock and describe the differences between them.

The corporate charter states the number of shares and the par value, if any, per share of each class of stock that the corporation is permitted to issue. **Capital stock authorized** is the number of shares of stock that a corporation is entitled to issue as designated in its charter.

A corporation might not issue all of its authorized stock immediately; it might hold some stock for future issuance when additional funds are needed. If all authorized stock has been issued and more funds are needed, the state of incorporation must consent to an increase in authorized shares.

The authorization to issue stock does not trigger a journal entry. Instead, companies note the authorization in the capital stock account in the ledger (and often in the general journal) as a reminder of the number of shares authorized. **Capital stock issued** is the number of shares of stock sold and issued to stockholders.

Capital stock outstanding is the number of authorized shares of stock issued and currently held by stockholders. The total ownership of a corporation rests with the holders of the capital stock outstanding. For example, when a corporation authorized to issue 10,000 shares of capital stock has issued only 8,000 shares, the holders of the 8,000 shares own 100% of the corporation.

Each outstanding share of stock of a given class carries rights and privileges identical to any other outstanding share of that class. Shares authorized but not yet issued are referred to as **unissued shares** (the previous example had 2,000 unissued shares). No rights or privileges are attached to these shares until they are issued; they are not entitled to dividends, nor can they be voted at stockholders' meetings.

The number of shares issued and the number of shares outstanding may be different. Issued stock has been issued at some time, while outstanding shares are currently held by stockholders. All outstanding stock is issued stock, but the reverse is not necessarily true. The difference is due to shares returned to the corporation by stockholders; it is called *treasury stock*. Chapter 13 discusses treasury stock.

An Accounting Perspective

Business Insight International Flavors & Fragrances, Inc. creates and manufactures flavors and fragrances used in a wide variety of consumer products. The following illustration is adapted from the company's balance sheet. The stockholders' equity section shows the number of shares of common stock authorized and outstanding:

	1992	1991
Common Stock \$.12½ par value:		
authorized 80,000,000 shares;		
shares issued and outstanding:	\$4,823,385	\$4,783,785
1992: 38,587,080		
1991: 38,270,277		

Classes of Capital Stock

A corporation may issue two basic classes or types of capital stock—common and preferred.

Common Stock

If a corporation issues only one class of stock, this stock is *common stock*. All of the stockholders enjoy equal rights. **Common stock** is usually the **residual equity** in

ILLUSTRATION 12.2
Capital Structures

	1992	1991	1990	1989
Common stock with:				
No preferred stock	450	456	447	438
One class of preferred stock	112	109	118	117
Two classes of preferred stock	31	27	28	36
Three or more classes of preferred stock	7	8	7	9
Total companies	600	600	600	600

Source: American Institute of Certified Public Accountants, *Accounting Trends & Techniques* (New York: AICPA, 1993), p. 246.

the corporation. This term means that all other claims against the corporation rank ahead of the claims of the common stockholder.

Preferred Stock

Preferred stock is a class of capital stock that carries certain features or rights not carried by common stock. Within the basic class of preferred stock, a company may have several specific classes of preferred stock, each with different dividend rates or other features.

Companies issue preferred stock to avoid: (1) using bonds with fixed interest charges that must be paid regardless of the amount of net income; (2) issuing so many additional shares of common stock that earnings per share are less in the current year than in prior years; and (3) diluting the common stockholders' control of the corporation, since preferred stockholders generally have no voting rights.

Unlike common stock, which has no set maximum or minimum dividend, the dividend return on preferred stock is usually stated at an amount per share or as a percentage of par value. Therefore, the firm fixes the dividend per share. Illustration 12.2 shows the various classes and combinations of capital stock outstanding for a sample of 600 companies.

Types of Preferred Stock

When a corporation issues both preferred and common stock, the preferred stock may be:

1. Preferred as to dividends. It may be noncumulative or cumulative.
2. Preferred as to assets in the event of liquidation.
3. Convertible or nonconvertible.
4. Callable.

Stock Preferred as to Dividends

A **dividend** is a distribution of assets (usually cash) that represents a withdrawal of earnings by the owners. Dividends are normally paid in cash.

Stock preferred as to dividends means that the preferred stockholders receive a specified dividend per share before common stockholders receive any dividends. A **dividend on preferred stock** is the amount paid to preferred stockholders as a return for the use of their money. For no-par preferred stock, the dividend is a specific dollar amount per share per year, such as $4.40. For par value preferred stock, the dividend is usually stated as a percentage of the par value, such as 8% of par value; occasionally, it is a specific dollar amount per share. Most preferred stock has a par value.

Usually, stockholders receive dividends on preferred stock quarterly. Such dividends—in full or in part—must be declared by the board of directors before being paid. In some states, corporations can declare preferred stock dividends only if they have retained earnings (income that has been retained in the business) at least equal to the dividend declared.

Noncumulative Preferred Stock **Noncumulative preferred stock** is preferred stock on which the right to receive a dividend expires whenever the dividend is not declared. When noncumulative preferred stock is outstanding, a dividend omitted or not paid in any one year need not be paid in any future year. Because omitted dividends are lost forever, noncumulative preferred stocks are not attractive to investors and are rarely issued.

Cumulative Preferred Stock **Cumulative preferred stock** is preferred stock for which the right to receive a basic dividend, usually each quarter, accumulates if the dividend is not paid. Companies must pay unpaid cumulative preferred dividends before paying any dividends on the common stock. For example, assume a company has cumulative, $10 par value, 10% preferred stock outstanding of $100,000, common stock outstanding of $100,000, and retained earnings of $30,000. It has paid no dividends for two years. The company would pay the preferred stockholders dividends of $20,000 ($10,000 per year times two years) before paying any dividends to the common stockholders.

Dividends in arrears are cumulative unpaid dividends, including the quarterly dividends not declared for the current year. Dividends in arrears never appear as a liability of the corporation because they are not a legal liability until declared by the board of directors. However, since the amount of dividends in arrears may influence the decisions of users of a corporation's financial statements, firms disclose such dividends in a footnote. An appropriate footnote might read: "Dividends in the amount of $20,000, representing two years' dividends on the company's 10%, cumulative preferred stock, were in arrears as of December 31, 1997."

Stock Preferred as to Assets

Most preferred stocks are preferred as to assets in the event of liquidation of the corporation. **Stock preferred as to assets** is preferred stock that receives special treatment in liquidation. Preferred stockholders receive the par value (or a larger stipulated liquidation value) per share before any assets are distributed to common stockholders. A corporation's cumulative preferred dividends in arrears at liquidation are payable even if there are not enough accumulated earnings to cover the dividends. Also, the cumulative dividend for the current year is payable. Stock may be preferred as to assets, dividends, or both.

Convertible Preferred Stock

Convertible preferred stock is preferred stock that is convertible into common stock of the issuing corporation. Many preferred stocks do not carry this special feature; they are nonconvertible. Holders of convertible preferred stock shares may exchange them, at their option, for a certain number of shares of common stock of the same corporation.

Investors find convertible preferred stock attractive for two reasons: First, there is a greater probability that the dividends on the preferred stock will be paid (as compared to dividends on common shares). Second, the conversion privilege may be the source of substantial price appreciation. To illustrate this latter feature, assume that Olsen Company issued 1,000 shares of 6%, $100 par value convertible preferred stock at $100 per share. The stock is convertible at any time into four shares of Olsen $10 par value common stock, which has a current market value of $20 per share. In the next several years, the company reported much higher net income and increased the dividend on the common stock from $1 to $2 per share. Assume that the common stock now sells at $40 per share. The preferred stockholders can: (1) convert each share of preferred stock into four shares of common stock and increase the annual dividend they receive from $6 to $8; (2) sell their preferred stock at a substantial gain, since it sells in the market at approximately $160 per share, the market value of the four shares of common stock into which it is convertible; or (3) continue to hold their preferred shares in the expectation of realizing an even larger gain at a later date.

If all 1,000 shares of $100 par value Olsen Company preferred stock are converted into 4,000 shares of $10 par value common stock, the entry is:

Preferred Stock	100,000	
Common Stock		40,000
Paid-In Capital in Excess of Par Value—Common		60,000
To record the conversion of preferred stock into common stock.		

An Accounting Perspective

Uses of Technology Brokers buy and sell the stocks of corporations in over-the-counter markets or through exchanges, such as the New York Stock Exchange. To maintain the level of trading that occurs every day, they use computers. Computers allow brokers to conduct business with the exchange without having to go to the building in which trading occurs.

On September 14, 1993, *The Wall Street Journal* reported that the volume of stocks traded on Monday, September 13, 1993, was 243,429,640 shares. A separate article entitled "Cyclical Shares Help Market Rally Continue, but with Less Steam" stated: "A handful of economically sensitive stocks kept alive the rally of the previous session, though the market's advance lost some strength." The article also pointed out that 1,057 issues were advancing and 969 declining.

Callable Preferred Stock

Most preferred stocks are callable at the option of the issuing corporation. **Callable preferred stock** means that the corporation can inform nonconvertible preferred stockholders that they must surrender their stock to the company. Also, convertible preferred stockholders must either surrender their stock or convert it to common shares.

Preferred shares are usually callable at par value plus a small premium of 3 or 4% of the par value of the stock. This **call premium** is the difference between the amount at which a corporation calls its preferred stock for redemption and the par value of the stock.

An issuing corporation may force conversion of convertible preferred stock by calling in the preferred stock for redemption. Stockholders who do not want to surrender their stock have to convert it to common shares. When preferred stockholders surrender their stock, the corporation pays these stockholders par value plus the call premium, any dividends in arrears from past years, and a prorated portion of the current period's dividend. If the market value of common shares into which the preferred stock could be converted is higher than the amount the stockholders would receive in redemption, they should convert their preferred shares to common shares. For instance, assume that a stockholder owns 1,000 shares of convertible preferred stock. Each share is callable at $104 per share, convertible to two common shares (currently selling at $62 per share), and entitled to $10 of unpaid dividends. If the issuing corporation calls in its preferred stock, it would give the stockholder either (1) $114,000 [($104 + $10) × 1,000] if the shares are surrendered or (2) common shares worth $124,000 ($62 × 2,000) if the shares are converted. Obviously, the stockholder should convert these preferred shares to common shares.

Why would a corporation call in its preferred stock? Corporations call in preferred stock for many reasons: (1) the outstanding preferred stock may require a 12% annual dividend at a time when the company can secure capital to retire the stock by issuing a new 8% preferred stock; (2) the issuing company may have been sufficiently profitable to retire the preferred stock out of earnings; or (3) the company may wish to force conversion of its convertible preferred stock because the cash dividend on the equivalent common shares is less than the dividend on the preferred shares.

Balance Sheet Presentation of Stock

Objective 4
Present in proper form the stockholders' equity section of a balance sheet.

The stockholders' equity section of a corporation's balance sheet contains two main elements: paid-in capital and retained earnings. **Paid-in capital** is the part of stockholders' equity that normally results from cash or other assets invested by owners. Paid-in capital also results from services performed for the corporation in exchange for capital stock and from certain other transactions discussed in Chapter 13. As stated earlier, **retained earnings** is the part of stockholders' equity resulting from accumulated net income, reduced by dividends and net losses. Net income increases the Retained Earnings account balance and net losses decrease it. In addition, dividends declared to stockholders decrease Retained Earnings. Since Retained Earnings is a stockholders' equity account and represents accumulated net income retained by the company, it normally has a credit balance. We discuss retained earnings in more detail in Chapter 13.

The following illustration shows the proper financial reporting for preferred and common stock. Assume that a corporation is authorized to issue 10,000 shares of $100 par value, 6%, cumulative, convertible preferred stock (five common for one preferred), all of which have been issued and are outstanding; and 200,000 shares of $10 par value common stock, of which 80,000 shares are issued and outstanding. The stockholders' equity section of the balance sheet (assuming $450,000 of retained earnings) is:

Stockholders' equity:		
Paid-in capital:		
Preferred stock—$100 par value, 6%, cumulative, convertible (5 common for 1 preferred); authorized, issued, and outstanding, 10,000 shares	$1,000,000	
Common stock—$10 par value; authorized, 200,000 shares; issued and outstanding, 80,000 shares	800,000	
Total paid-in capital		$1,800,000
Retained earnings		450,000
Total stockholders' equity		$2,250,000

Notice that the balance sheet lists preferred stock before common stock because the preferred stock is preferred as to dividends, assets, or both. The company discloses the conversion rate in a parenthetical note within the description of preferred stock or in a footnote.

An Accounting Perspective

Business Insight Baker Hughes, Inc., provides products and services to the petroleum and other continuous process industries. Its 1992 annual report provided the following presentation of preferred stock in the stockholders' equity section of its balance sheet:

	1992
Preferred stock, $1 par value (authorized and outstanding 4,000,000 shares in 1992 of $3.00 convertible preferred stock; $50 liquidation preference per share)	$4,000,000

Stock Issuances for Cash

Issuance of Par Value Stock for Cash

Objective 5
Account for the issuances of stock for cash and other assets.

Each share of common or preferred capital stock either has a par value or lacks one. The corporation's charter determines the par value printed on the stock certificates issued. Par value may be any amount—1 cent, 10 cents, 16⅔ cents, $1, $5, or $100. Low par values of $10 or less are common in our economy.

As previously mentioned, par value gives no clue as to the stock's market value. Shares with a par value of $5 have traded (sold) in the market for more than $600, and many $100 par value preferred stocks have traded for considerably less than par. Par value is not even a reliable indicator of the price at which shares can be issued. New corporations can issue shares at prices well in excess of par value or for less than par value if state laws permit. Par value gives the accountant a constant amount at which to record capital stock issuances in the capital stock accounts. As stated earlier, the total par value of all issued shares is generally the legal capital of the corporation.

To illustrate the issuance of stock for cash, assume a company issues 10,000 authorized shares of $20 par value common stock at $22 per share. The following entry records the issuance:

Cash	220,000	
Common Stock		200,000
Paid-In Capital in Excess of Par Value—Common		20,000
To record the issuance of 10,000 shares of stock for cash.		

Notice that the credit to the Common Stock account is the par value ($20) times the number of shares issued. The accountant credits the excess over par value ($20,000) to Paid-In Capital in Excess of Par Value; it is part of the paid-in capital contributed by the stockholders. Thus, **paid-in capital in excess of par (or stated) value** represents capital contributed to a corporation in addition to that assigned to the shares issued and recorded in capital stock accounts. The paid-in capital section of the balance sheet appears as follows:

Paid-in capital:	
Common stock—par value, $20; 10,000 shares authorized, issued, and outstanding	$200,000
Paid-in capital in excess of par value—common	20,000
Total paid-in capital	$220,000

Issuance of No-Par, Stated Value Stock for Cash

When it issues no-par stock with a stated value, a company carries the shares in the capital stock account at the stated value. Any amounts received in excess of the stated value per share represent a part of the paid-in capital of the corporation and the company credits them to Paid-In Capital in Excess of Stated Value. The legal capital of a corporation issuing no-par shares with a stated value is usually equal to the total stated value of the shares issued.

To illustrate, assume that the DeWitt Corporation, which is authorized to issue 10,000 shares of common stock without par value, assigns a stated value of $20 per share to its stock. DeWitt issues the 10,000 authorized shares for cash at $22 per share. The entry to record this transaction is:

Cash	220,000	
Common Stock		200,000
Paid-In Capital in Excess of Stated Value—Common		20,000
To record issuance of 10,000 shares for cash.		

The paid-in capital section of the balance sheet appears as follows:

Paid-in capital:	
Common stock—without par value; stated value, $20; 10,000 shares authorized, issued, and outstanding	$200,000
Paid-in capital in excess of stated value—common	20,000
Total paid-in capital	$220,000

DeWitt carries the $20,000 received over and above the stated value of $200,000 permanently as paid-in capital because it is a part of the capital originally contributed by the stockholders. However, the legal capital of the DeWitt Corporation is $200,000.

Issuance of No-Par Stock without a Stated Value for Cash

A corporation that issues no-par stock without a stated value credits the entire amount received to the capital stock account. For instance, consider the DeWitt Corporation's issuance of no-par stock. If no stated value had been assigned, the entry would have been as follows:

Cash	220,000	
Common Stock		220,000
To record the issuance of 10,000 shares for cash.		

Since the company may issue shares at different times and at differing amounts, its credits to the capital stock account are not uniform amounts per share. This contrasts with issuing par value shares or shares with a stated value.

To continue our example, the paid-in capital section of the company's balance sheet would be as follows:

Paid-in capital:	
Common stock—without par or stated value; 10,000 shares authorized, issued, and outstanding	$220,000
Total paid-in capital	$220,000

The actual capital contributed by stockholders is $220,000. In some states, the entire amount received for shares without par or stated value is the amount of legal capital. The legal capital in this example would then be equal to $220,000.

Capital Stock Issued for Property or Services

When issuing capital stock for property or services, companies must determine the dollar amount of the exchange. Accountants generally record the transaction at the fair value of (1) the property or services received or (2) the stock issued, whichever is more clearly evident.

To illustrate, assume that the owners of a tract of land deeded it to a corporation in exchange for 1,000 shares of $12 par value common stock. The firm can only estimate the fair market value of the land. At the time of the exchange, the stock has an established total market value of $14,000. The required entry is:

Land	14,000	
Common Stock		12,000
Paid-In Capital in Excess of Par Value—Common		2,000
To record the receipt of land for capital stock.		

As another example, assume a firm issues 100 shares of common stock with a par value of $40 per share in exchange for legal services received in organizing as a corporation. No shares have been traded recently, so there is no established market value. The attorney previously agreed to a price of $5,000 for these legal services but decided to accept stock in lieu of cash. In this example, the correct entry is:

Organization Costs	5,000	
Common Stock		4,000
Paid-In Capital in Excess of Par Value—Common		1,000
To record the receipt of legal services for capital stock.		

The company should value the services at the price previously agreed on since that value is more clearly evident than the market value of the shares. It should debit an intangible asset account because these services benefit the corporation throughout its entire life. The company credits the amount by which the value of the services received exceeds the par value of the shares issued to a Paid-In Capital in Excess of Par Value—Common account.

Balance Sheet Presentation of Paid-In Capital in Excess of Par (or Stated) Value—Common or Preferred

Accountants credit amounts received in excess of the par or stated value of shares to a Paid-In Capital in Excess of Par (or Stated) Value—Common (or Preferred) account. They carry the amounts received in excess of par or stated value in separate accounts for each class of stock issued. Using the following assumed data, the stockholders' equity section of the balance sheet of a company with both preferred and common stock outstanding would appear as follows:

Stockholders' equity:			
Paid-in capital:			
Preferred stock—$100 par value, 6% cumulative; 1,000 shares authorized, issued, and outstanding	$100,000		
Common stock—without par value, stated value $5; 100,000 shares authorized, 80,000 shares issued and outstanding	400,000	$500,000	
Paid-in capital in excess of par (or stated) value:			
From preferred stock issuances	$ 5,000		
From common stock issuances	20,000	25,000	
Total paid-in capital			$525,000
Retained earnings			200,000
Total stockholders' equity			$725,000

Book Value

Objective 6
Determine book values of both preferred and common stock.

The total book value of a corporation's outstanding shares is equal to its recorded net asset value—that is, assets minus liabilities. Quite simply, the amount of net assets is equal to stockholders' equity. When only common stock is outstanding, companies compute the **book value per share** by dividing total stockholders' equity by the number of common shares outstanding. In calculating book value, they assume that (1) the corporation could be liquidated without incurring any further expenses, (2) the assets could be sold at their recorded amounts, and (3) the liabilities could be satisfied at their recorded amounts. Assume the stockholders' equity of a corporation is as follows:

Stockholders' equity:		
Paid-in capital:		
Common stock—without par value, stated value $10; authorized, 20,000 shares; issued and outstanding, 15,000 shares	$150,000	
Paid-in capital in excess of stated value	10,000	
Total paid-in capital		$160,000
Retained earnings		50,000
Total stockholders' equity		$210,000

To determine the book value per share of the stock:

Total stockholders' equity	$210,000
Total shares outstanding	÷15,000
Book value per share	$ 14

When two or more classes of capital stock are outstanding, the computation of book value per share is more complex. The book value for each share of stock depends on the rights of the preferred stockholders. Preferred stockholders typically are entitled to a specified liquidation value per share, plus cumulative dividends in arrears, since most preferred stocks are preferred as to assets and are cumulative. In each case, the specific provisions in the preferred stock contract govern. To illustrate, assume the Celoron Corporation's stockholders' equity is as follows:

Stockholders' equity:		
Paid-in capital:		
Preferred stock—$100 par value, 6% cumulative; 5,000 shares authorized, issued, and outstanding	$ 500,000	
Common stock—$10 par value, 200,000 shares authorized, issued, and outstanding	2,000,000	
Paid-in capital in excess of par value—preferred	200,000	
Total paid-in capital		$2,700,000
Retained earnings		400,000
Total stockholders' equity		$3,100,000

The preferred stock is 6%, cumulative. It is preferred as to dividends and as to assets in liquidation to the extent of the liquidation value of $100 per share, plus any cumulative dividends on the preferred stock. Dividends for four years (including the current year) are unpaid. You would calculate the book values of each class of stock as follows:

		Total	Per Share
Total stockholders' equity		$3,100,000	
Book value of preferred stock (5,000 shares):			
Liquidation value (5,000 shares × $100)	$500,000		
Dividends (4 years at $30,000)	120,000	620,000	$124.00*
Book value of common stock (200,000 shares)		$2,480,000	12.40†

* $620,000 ÷ 5,000 shares.
† $2,480,000 ÷ 200,000 shares.

Notice that Celeron did not assign the paid-in capital in excess of par value—preferred to the preferred stock in determining the book values. Celeron assigned only the liquidation value and cumulative dividends on the preferred stock to the preferred stock.

Assume now that the features attached to the preferred stock are the same except that the preferred stockholders have the right to receive $103 per share in liquidation. The book values of each class of stock would be:

		Total	Per Share
Total stockholders' equity		$3,100,000	
Book value of preferred stock (5,000 shares):			
Liquidation value (5,000 shares × $103)	$515,000		
Dividends (4 years at $30,000)	120,000	635,000	$127.00
Book value of common stock (200,000 shares)		$2,465,000	12.33

Book value rarely equals market value of a stock because many of the assets have changed in value due to inflation. Thus, the market prices of the shares of many corporations traded regularly are different from their book values.

An Accounting Perspective

Business Insight *The Wall Street Journal* publishes the New York Stock Exchange (NYSE) Composite Transactions each Monday through Friday except when the exchange is closed. For each stock listed on the NYSE, it lists the following data. We use data for the Kellogg Company, which produces ready-to-eat cereals and other food products, as recently reported in *The Wall Street Journal* as an example:

52 Weeks											
Hi	Low	Stock	Sym	Div	Yld %	PE	Vol 100s	Hi	Low	Close	Net Chg
75⅜	49½	Kellogg	K	1.28	2.6	17	4996	50¾	48⅜	49⅜	−½

The first two columns show the high and low price over the preceding 52 weeks plus the current week. The next two columns show the company name (Kellogg) and the NYSE's symbol (K) for that company. The Div column is the annual dividend based on the last quarterly, semiannual, or annual declaration. Yield % is calculated as dividends paid divided by the current market price. The PE ratio is the closing market price divided by the total earnings per share for the most recent four quarters. The Vol 100s column shows the unofficial daily total of shares traded, quoted in hundreds. Thus, 499,600 shares of Kellogg's stock were traded that day. The next two columns show the high and low price for that day. The next to last column shows the closing price for that day. The final column shows the change in the closing price as compared to the closing price of the preceding day.

An Ethical Perspective

Belex Corporation

Joe Morrison is the controller for Belex Corporation. He is involved in a discussion with other members of management concerning how to get rid of some potentially harmful toxic waste materials that are a by-product of the company's manufacturing process.

There are two alternative methods of disposing of the materials. The first alternative is to bury the waste in steel drums on a tract of land adjacent to the factory building. There is currently no legal prohibition against doing this. The cost of disposing of the materials in this way is estimated to be $50,000 per year. The best estimate is that the steel drums would not leak for at least 50 years, but probably would begin leaking after that time. The second alternative is to seal the materials in lead drums that would be disposed of at sea by a waste management company. The cost of this alternative is estimated to be $400,000 per year. The federal government has certified this method as the preferred method of disposal. The best estimate is that the lead drums would never rupture or leak.

Belex Corporation has seen some tough economic times. The company suffered losses until last year, when it showed a profit of $750,000 as a result of a new manufacturing project. So far, the waste materials from that project have been accumulating in two large vats on the company's land. However, these vats are almost full, so soon management must decide how to dispose of the materials.

One group of managers is arguing in favor of the first alternative because it is legally permissible and results in annual profits of about $700,000. They point out that using the second alternative would reduce profits to about $350,000 per year and cut managers' bonuses in half. They also claim that some of their competitors are now using the first alternative, and to use the second alternative would place the company at a serious competitive disadvantage.

Another group of managers argues that the second alternative is the only safe alternative to pursue. They claim that when the steel drums start leaking they will contaminate the ground water and could cause serious health problems. When this contamination occurs, the company will lose public support and may even have to pay for the cleanup. The cost of that cleanup could run into the millions.

Analyzing and Using the Financial Results—Return on Average Common Stockholders' Equity

Objective 7
Analyze and use the financial results—return on average common stockholders' equity.

Stockholders' equity is particularly important to managers, creditors, and investors in determining the return on equity, which is the return on average common stockholders' equity.

The **return on average common stockholders' equity** measures what a given company earned for its common stockholders from all sources as a percentage of the common stockholders' investment. From the common stockholders' point of view, it is an important measure of the income-producing ability of the company. The ratio's formula is:

$$\text{Return on average common stockholders' equity} = \frac{\text{Net income available to common stockholders}}{\text{Average common stockholders' equity}}$$

If preferred stock is outstanding, the numerator is net income minus the annual dividend on preferred stock, and the denominator is the average total book value of common stock. If no preferred stock is outstanding, the numerator is net income, and the denominator is average stockholders' equity.

BellSouth
BellSouth Corporation is America's largest local telephone company. Its services include cellular communication, paging, and publishing.

BellSouth Corporation reported the following information in its 1992 financial statements ($ millions):

	1992
Net income	$ 1,617.7
Stockholders' equity, beginning	13,104.9
Stockholders' equity, ending	13,798.6

The return on average common stockholders' equity for BellSouth is 12%, or $1,617.7/[($13,104.9 + $13,798.6)/2]. Investors view any increase from year to year as favorable and any decrease as unfavorable.

Since the stock market is frequently referred to as an economic indicator, the knowledge you now have on corporate stock issuances should help you relate to stocks traded in the market. Chapter 13 continues the discussion of paid-in capital and also discusses treasury stock, retained earnings, and dividends.

Understanding the Learning Objectives

Objective 1
State the advantages and disadvantages of the corporate form of business.

- Advantages:
  1. Easy transfer of ownership.
  2. Limited liability.
  3. Continuous existence of the entity.
  4. Easy capital generation.
  5. Professional management.
  6. Separation of owners and entity.
- Disadvantages:
  1. Double taxation.
  2. Government regulation.
  3. Entrenched, inefficient management.
  4. Limited ability to raise creditor capital.

Objective 2
List the values commonly associated with capital stock and give their definitions.

- Par value—an arbitrary amount assigned to each share of a given class of stock and printed on the stock certificate.
- Stated value—an arbitrary amount assigned by the board of directors to each share of a given class of no-par stock.
- Market value—the price at which shares of capital stock are bought and sold in the market.
- Book value—the amount per share that each stockholder would receive if the corporation were liquidated without incurring any further expenses and if assets were sold and liabilities liquidated at their recorded amounts.
- Liquidation value—the amount a stockholder would receive if a corporation discontinues operations, pays its liabilities, and distributes the remaining cash among the stockholders.
- Redemption value—the price per share at which a corporation may call in (redeem) its capital stock for retirement.

Objective 3
List the various kinds of stock and describe the differences between them.

- Capital stock authorized—the number of shares of stock that a corporation is entitled to issue as designated in its charter.
- Capital stock issued—the number of shares of stock that have been sold and issued to stockholders.
- Capital stock outstanding—the number of authorized shares of stock that have been issued and that are still currently held by stockholders.
- Two basic classes of capital stock:
  1. Common stock—represents the residual equity.
  2. Preferred stock—may be preferred as to dividends and/or assets. Also may be cumulative and/or callable.

Objective 4
Present in proper form the stockholders' equity section of a balance sheet.

- If the company has paid-in capital in excess of par value:

Stockholders' equity:			
Paid-in capital:			
Preferred stock—$100 par value, 6% cumulative; 1,000 shares authorized, issued, and outstanding	$100,000		
Common stock—without par value, stated value $5; 100,000 shares authorized, 80,000 shares issued and outstanding	400,000	$500,000	
Paid-in capital in excess of par (or stated) value:			
From preferred stock issuances	$ 5,000		
From common stock issuances	20,000	25,000	
Total paid-in capital			$525,000
Retained earnings			200,000
Total stockholders' equity			$725,000

The following examples illustrate the issuance for cash of: (1) stock with a par value, (2) no-par value stock with a stated value, and (3) no-par value stock without a stated value.

Objective 5
Account for the issuances of stock for cash and for other assets.

- Issuance of par value stock for cash—10,000 shares of $20 par value common stock issued for $22 per share.

Cash	220,000	
Common Stock		200,000
Paid-In Capital in Excess of Par Value—Common		20,000

- Issuance of no-par, stated value stock for cash—10,000 shares (no-par value) with $20 per share stated value issued for $22 per share.

Cash	220,000	
Common Stock		200,000
Paid-In Capital in Excess of Stated Value—Common		20,000

- Issuance of no-par stock without a stated value for cash—10,000 shares (no-par value) issued at $22 per share.

Cash	220,000	
Common Stock		220,000

Objective 6
Determine book values of both preferred and common stock.

- *Example:* A corporation has 200,000 shares of common stock and 5,000 shares of preferred stock outstanding. Preferred stock is 6% and cumulative. It is preferred as to dividends and as to assets in liquidation to the extent of the liquidation value of $100 per share, plus any cumulative dividends on the preferred stock. Dividends for three years are unpaid. Total stockholders' equity is $4,100,000. Calculations are as follows:

		Total	Per Share
Total stockholders' equity		$4,100,000	
Book value of preferred stock (5,000 shares):			
Liquidation value (5,000 × $100)	$500,000		
Dividends (3 years at $30,000)	90,000	590,000	$118.00
Book value of common stock (200,000 shares)		$3,510,000	17.55

Objective 7
Analyze and use the financial results—return on average common stockholders' equity.

- The return on average common stockholders' equity equals net income available to common stockholders divided by average common stockholders' equity.
- The return on average common stockholders' equity is an important measure of the income-producing ability of the company.

Demonstration Problem 12–A

Violet Company has paid all required preferred dividends through December 31, 1991. Its outstanding stock consists of 10,000 shares of $125 par value common stock and 4,000 shares of 6%, $125 par value preferred stock. During five successive years, the company's dividend declarations were as follows:

1992	$85,000
1993	52,500
1994	7,500
1995	15,000
1996	67,500

4000 x125 x .06 = 30,000
85-30 = 55,000

Required

Compute the amount of dividends that would have been paid to each class of stock in each of the last five years assuming the preferred stock is:

a. Cumulative.

b. Noncumulative.

Solution to Demonstration Problem 12–A

VIOLET COMPANY

Year	Dividends to	Assumptions a	Assumptions b
1992	Preferred	$30,000*	$30,000
	Common	55,000	55,000
1993	Preferred	30,000	30,000
	Common	22,500	22,500
1994	Preferred	7,500	7,500
	Common	–0–	–0–
1995	Preferred	15,000	15,000
	Common	–0–	–0–
1996	Preferred	67,500†	30,000‡
	Common	–0–	37,500

* 4,000 shares × $125 × 0.06 = $30,000.

† $30,000 + $22,500 preferred dividend missed in 1994 + $15,000 preferred dividend missed in 1995.

‡ Only the basic $30,000 dividend is paid because the stock is noncumulative.

Demonstration Problem 12–B

Terrier Company has been authorized to issue 100,000 shares of $6 par value common stock and 1,000 shares of 14%, cumulative, preferred stock with a par value of $12.

Required

a. Prepare the entries for the following transactions that all took place in June 1996:

1. 50,000 shares of common stock are issued for cash at $24 per share.
2. 750 shares of preferred stock are issued for cash at $18 per share.
3. 1,000 shares of common stock are issued in exchange for legal services received in the incorporation process. The fair market value of the legal services is $9,000.

b. Prepare the paid-in capital section of Terrier's balance sheet as of June 30, 1996.

Solution to Demonstration Problem 12–B

a.

	Account	Debit	Credit
1.	Cash	1,200,000	
	Common Stock		300,000
	Paid-In Capital in Excess of Par Value—Common		900,000
	To record issuance of 50,000 shares at $24 per share.		
2.	Cash	13,500	
	Preferred Stock		9,000
	Paid-In Capital in Excess of Par Value—Preferred		4,500
	To record the issuance of 750 shares for cash, at $18 per share.		
3.	Organization Costs	9,000	
	Common Stock		6,000
	Paid-In Capital in Excess of Par Value—Common		3,000
	To record issuance of 1,000 shares in exchange for legal services.		

b.

TERRIER COMPANY
Partial Balance Sheet
June 30, 1996

Paid-in capital:		
Preferred stock—$12 par value, 14% cumulative; 1,000 shares authorized; issued and outstanding, 750 shares	$ 9,000	
Common stock—$6 par value per share; 100,000 shares authorized; issued and outstanding, 51,000 shares	306,000	$ 315,000
Paid-in capital in excess of par value:		
From preferred stock issuances	$ 4,500	
From common stock issuances	903,000	907,500
Total paid-in capital		$1,222,500

New Terms

Articles of incorporation The application for the corporation's charter. *435*

Board of directors Elected by the stockholders and is primarily responsible for formulating policies for the corporation. The board also authorizes contracts, declares dividends, establishes executive salaries, and grants authorization to borrow money. *437*

Book value per share Stockholders' equity per share; the amount per share each stockholder would receive if the corporation were liquidated without incurring any further expenses and if assets were sold and liabilities liquidated at their recorded amounts. *439, 447*

Bylaws A set of rules or regulations adopted by the board of directors of a corporation to govern the conduct of corporate affairs. The bylaws must be in agreement with the laws of the state and the policies and purposes in the corporate charter. *435*

Callable preferred stock If the stock is nonconvertible, it must be surrendered to the company when the holder is requested to do so. If the stock is convertible, it may be either surrendered or converted into common shares when called. *443*

Call premium (on preferred stock) The difference between the amount at which a corporation calls its preferred stock for redemption and the par value of the stock. *443*

Capital stock Transferable units of ownership in a corporation. *437*

Capital stock authorized The number of shares of stock that a corporation is entitled to issue as designated in its charter. *440*

Capital stock issued The number of shares of stock that have been sold and issued to stockholders. *440*

Capital stock outstanding The number of shares of authorized stock issued and currently held by stockholders. *440*

Common stock Shares of stock representing the residual equity in the corporation. If only one class of stock is issued, it is known as *common stock*. All other claims rank ahead of common stockholders' claims. *440*

Convertible preferred stock Preferred stock that is convertible into common stock of the issuing corporation. *442*

Corporate charter The contract between the state and the incorporators of a corporation, and their successors, granting the corporation its legal existence. *435*

Corporation An entity recognized by law as possessing an existence separate and distinct from its owners; that is, it is a separate legal entity. A corporation is granted many of the rights, and placed under many of the obligations, of a natural person. In any given state, all corporations organized under the laws of that state are **domestic corporations;** all others are **foreign corporations.** *433*

Cumulative preferred stock Preferred stock for which the right to receive a basic dividend accumulates if any dividends have not been paid; unpaid cumulative preferred dividends must be paid before any dividends can be paid on the common stock. *442*

Discount on capital stock The amount by which the par value of shares issued exceeds their issue price. The original issuance of shares at a discount is illegal in most states. *439*

Dividend A distribution of assets (usually cash) that represents a withdrawal of earnings by the owners. *441*

Dividend on preferred stock The amount paid to preferred stockholders as a return for the use of their money; usually a fixed or stated amount expressed in dollars per share or as a percentage of par value per share. *441*

Dividends in arrears Cumulative unpaid dividends, including quarterly dividends not declared for the current year. *442*

Domestic corporation See Corporation.

Foreign corporation See Corporation.

Incorporators Persons seeking to bring a corporation into existence. *435*

Legal capital (stated capital) An amount prescribed by law (often par value or stated value of shares issued) below which a corporation may not reduce stockholders' equity through the declaration of dividends or other payments to stockholders. *438*

Liquidation value The amount a stockholder will receive if a corporation discontinues operations and liquidates by selling its assets, paying its liabilities, and distributing the remaining cash among the stockholders. *439*

Market value The price at which shares of capital stock are bought and sold in the market. *439*

Minutes book The record book in which actions taken at stockholders' and board of directors' meetings are recorded; the written authorization for many actions taken by corporate officers. *438*

Noncumulative preferred stock Preferred stock on which the right to receive a dividend expires if the dividend is not declared. *442*

No-par stock Capital stock without par value, to which a stated value may or may not be assigned. *439*

Organization costs Costs of organizing a corporation, such as incorporation fees and legal fees applicable to incorporation. *436*

Paid-in capital Amount of stockholders' equity that normally results from the cash or other assets invested by owners; it may also result from services provided for shares of stock and certain other transactions. *444*

Paid-in capital in excess of par (or stated) value—common or preferred Capital contributed to a corporation in addition to that assigned to the shares issued and recorded in capital stock accounts. *445*

Par value An arbitrary amount assigned to each share of a given class of stock and printed on the stock certificate. *438*

Preemptive right The right of stockholders to buy additional shares in a proportion equal to the percentage of shares already owned. *436*

Preferred stock Capital stock that carries certain features or rights not carried by common stock. Preferred stock may be preferred as to dividends, as to assets, or as to both dividends and assets. Preferred stock may be callable and/or convertible and may be cumulative or noncumulative. *441*

Proxy A legal document signed by a stockholder, giving another person the authority to vote the stockholder's shares at a stockholders' meeting. *436*

Redemption value The price per share at which a corporation may call in (or redeem) its capital stock for retirement. *440*

Retained earnings The part of stockholders' equity resulting from net income, reduced by dividends and net losses. *444*

Return on average common stockholders' equity A measure of the income-producing ability of the company. It is the ratio of net income available to common stockholders divided by average common stockholders' equity. *449*

Shares of stock Units of ownership in a corporation. *433*

Stated value An arbitrary amount assigned by the board of directors to each share of a given class of no-par stock. *439*

Stock certificate A printed or engraved document serving as evidence that the holder owns a certain number of shares of capital stock. *437*

Stockholders' ledger Contains a group of subsidiary accounts showing the number of shares of stock currently held by each stockholder. *438*

Stock preferred as to assets Means that in liquidation, the preferred stockholders are entitled to receive the par value (or a larger stipulated liquidation value) per share before any assets may be distributed to common stockholders. *442*

Stock preferred as to dividends Means that the preferred stockholders are entitled to receive a specified dividend per share before any dividend on common stock is paid. *441*

Stock registrar Typically, a bank that maintains records of the shares outstanding for a company. *438*

Stock-transfer agent Typically, a bank or trust company employed by a corporation to transfer stock between buyers and sellers. *438*

Stock without par value See No-par stock.

Unissued shares Capital stock authorized but not yet issued. *440*

Self-Test

True-False

Indicate whether each of the following statements is true or false.

1. A person may favor the corporate form of organization for a risky business enterprise primarily because a corporation's shares can be easily transferred.
2. In the event of corporate liquidation, stockholders whose stock is preferred as to assets are entitled to receive the par value of their shares before any amounts are distributed to creditors or common stockholders.
3. The par value of a share of capital stock is no indication of the market value or book value of the share of stock.
4. When 10,000 shares of $20 par value common stock are issued in payment for a parcel of land with a fair market value of $300,000, the Common Stock account is credited for $200,000, and the Paid-In Capital in Excess of Par Value—Common account is credited for $100,000.

Multiple-Choice

Select the best answer for each of the following questions.

1. Which of the following is not an advantage of the corporate form of organization?
   a. Continuous existence of the entity.
   b. Limited liability of stockholders.
   c. Government regulation.
   d. Easy transfer of ownership.
2. An arbitrary amount assigned by the board of directors to each share of a given class of no-par stock is:
   a. Quasi-par value.
   b. Stated value.
   c. Redemption value.
   d. Liquidation value.
3. Preferred stock that has dividends in arrears is:
   a. Noncumulative preferred stock.
   b. Noncumulative and callable preferred stock.
   c. Noncumulative and convertible preferred stock.
   d. Cumulative preferred stock.
4. Wyley Corporation issued 10,000 shares of $20 par value common stock at $50 per share. The amount that would be credited to Paid-In Capital in Excess of Par Value—Common is:
   a. $200,000.
   b. $300,000.
   c. $500,000.
   d. $700,000.
   e. None of the above.
5. You are given the following information: Capital Stock, $80,000 ($80 par); Paid-In Capital in Excess of Par Value—Common, $200,000; and Retained Earnings, $400,000. Assuming only one class of stock, the book value per share is:
   a. $680.
   b. $280.
   c. $80.
   d. $400.
   e. None of the above.

Now turn to page 462 to check your answers.

Questions

1. Cite the major advantages of the corporate form of business organization and indicate why each is considered an advantage.
2. What is meant by the statement that corporate income is subject to double taxation? Cite several other disadvantages of the corporate form of organization.
3. Why is Organization Expense not a good title for the account that records the costs of organizing a corporation? Could you justify leaving the balance of an Organization Costs account intact throughout the life of a corporation?
4. What are the basic rights associated with a share of capital stock if there is only one class of stock outstanding?
5. Explain the purpose or function of: *(a)* the stockholders' ledger, *(b)* the minutes book, *(c)* the stock-transfer agent, and *(d)* the stock registrar.
6. What are the differences between par value stock and stock with no-par value?
7. Corporate capital stock is seldom issued for less than par value. Give two reasons why this statement is true.
8. Explain the terms *liquidation value* and *redemption value*.
9. What are the meanings of the terms *stock preferred as to dividends* and *stock preferred as to assets?*
10. What do the terms *cumulative* and *noncumulative* mean in regard to preferred stock?
11. What are *dividends in arrears*, and how should they be disclosed in the financial statements?
12. A corporation has 1,000 shares of 8%, $200 par value, cumulative, preferred stock outstanding. Dividends on this stock have not been declared for three years. Is the corporation legally liable to its preferred stockholders for these dividends? How should this fact be shown in the balance sheet, if at all?
13. Explain why a corporation might issue a preferred stock that is both convertible into common stock and callable.
14. Explain the nature of the account entitled Paid-In Capital in Excess of Par Value. Under what circumstances is this account credited?
15. Wyley Corporation issued 5,000 shares of $100 par value common stock at $120 per share. What is the legal capital of Wyley Corporation, and why is the amount of legal capital important?
16. What is the general approach of the accountant in determining the dollar amount at which to record the issuance of capital stock for services or property other than cash?
17. What assumptions are made in determining book value?
18. Assuming there is no preferred stock outstanding, how can the book value per share of common stock be determined? Of what significance is the book value per share? What is the relationship of book value per share to market value per share?

MAYTAG

19. **Real World Question** Based on the financial statements of Maytag Corporation contained in the annual report booklet, what was the number of shares of common stock authorized?

THE LIMITED, INC.

20. **Real World Question** Based on the financial statements of The Limited, Inc., contained in the annual report booklet, what was the 1993 ending paid-in capital?

HARLAND

21. **Real World Question** Based on the financial statements of John H. Harland Company contained in the annual report booklet, what was the 1993 ending number of shares of common stock issued?

Exercises

Exercise 12–1
Determine dividends for common and noncumulative preferred stock (L.O. 3)

Bingham Corporation has outstanding 1,000 shares of noncumulative preferred stock and 2,000 shares of common stock. The preferred stock is entitled to an annual dividend of $50 per share before dividends are declared on common stock. What are the total dividends received by each class of stock if Bingham Corporation distributes $140,000 in dividends in 1997?

Exercise 12–2
Determine dividends for common and cumulative preferred stock (L.O. 3)

Carey Corporation has 2,000 shares outstanding of cumulative preferred stock and 6,000 shares of common stock. The preferred stock is entitled to an annual dividend of $18 per share before dividends are declared on common stock. No preferred dividends were paid for last year and the current year. What are the total dividends received by each class of stock if Carey Corporation distributes $108,000 in dividends?

Exercise 12–3
Journalize stock issuance (L.O. 5)

G&R Company issued 10,000 shares of common stock for $560,000 cash. The common stock has a par value of $50 per share. Give the journal entry for the stock issuance.

Exercise 12–4
Prepare entries for stock issuance (L.O. 5)

Mylar Company issued 30,000 shares of $20 par value common stock for $680,000. What is the journal entry for this transaction? What would the journal entry be if the common stock had no-par or stated value?

Exercise 12–5
Journalize stock issuance for property (L.O. 5)

Li & Tu, Inc., needed land for a plant site. It issued 100 shares of $240 par value common stock to the incorporators of their corporation in exchange for land, which cost $28,000 one year ago. Experienced appraisers recently valued the land at $36,000. What journal entry would be appropriate to record the acquisition of the land?

Exercise 12–6
Journalize stock issuance to satisfy liability (L.O. 5)

Bright Corporation owes a trade creditor $30,000 on open account which the corporation does not have sufficient cash to pay. The trade creditor suggests that Bright Corporation issue to him 750 shares of the $24 par value common stock, which is currently selling on the market at $40. Present the entry or entries that should be made on Bright Corporation's books.

Exercise 12–7
Journalize stock issuance for legal services (L.O. 5)

Why would a law firm ever consider accepting stock of a new corporation having a total par value of $160,000 as payment in full of a $240,000 bill for legal services rendered? If such a transaction occurred, give the journal entry the issuing company would make on its books.

Exercise 12–8
Compute the book value and average price of common stock (L.O. 6)

The stockholders' equity section of Winter Company's balance sheet is as follows:

Stockholders' equity:		
Paid-in capital:		
Common stock—without par value, $12 stated value; authorized 100,000 shares; issued and outstanding, 70,000 shares	$840,000	
Paid-in capital in excess of stated value	340,000	
Total paid-in capital		$1,180,000
Retained earnings		80,000
Total stockholders' equity		$1,260,000

Compute the average price at which the 70,000 issued shares of common stock were sold. Compute the book value per share of common stock.

PROBLEMS

Problem 12–1
Determine dividends for common stock and cumulative and noncumulative preferred stock (L.O. 3)

The outstanding capital stock of Jacob Corporation consisted of 3,000 shares of 10% preferred stock, $500 par value, and 30,000 shares of no-par common stock with a stated value of $500. The preferred was issued at $824, the common at $960 per share. On January 1, 1992, the retained earnings of the company were $500,000. During the succeeding five years, net income was as follows:

1992	$1,535,000
1993	1,020,000
1994	96,000
1995	320,000
1996	1,325,000

No dividends were in arrears as of January 1, 1992, and during the five years 1992–96, the board of directors declared dividends in each year equal to net income of the year.

Required

Prepare a schedule showing the dividends declared each year on each class of stock assuming the preferred stock is:

a. Cumulative.

b. Noncumulative.

Problem 12–2
Journalize stock issuances for cash, services (organization costs), and property; prepare resulting balance sheet (L.O. 5)

On December 27, 1995, Carlton Company was authorized to issue 250,000 shares of $24 par value common stock. It then completed the following transactions:

1996

Jan. 14 Issued 45,000 shares of common stock at $30 per share for cash.

29 Gave the promoters of the corporation 25,000 shares of common stock for their

services in organizing the company. The board of directors valued these services at $744,000.

Feb. 19 Exchanged 50,000 shares of common stock for the following assets at the indicated fair market values:

Land	$216,000
Building	528,000
Machinery	720,000

Required

a. Prepare general journal entries to record the transactions.

b. Prepare the balance sheet of the company as of March 1, 1996.

Problem 12–3
Post transactions; prepare balance sheets for par value stock, stated value stock, and no-par or stated value stock (L.O. 2, 4, 5)

In the corporate charter that it received on May 1, 1996, Douglas Company was authorized to issue 15,000 shares of common stock. The company issued 1,000 shares immediately for $164 per share, cash.

On July 2, the company issued 100 shares of stock to a lawyer to satisfy a $16,800 bill for legal services rendered in organizing the corporation.

On July 5, the company issued 1,000 shares to the principal promoter of the corporation in exchange for a patent. Another 200 shares were issued to this same person for costs incurred and services rendered in bringing the corporation into existence. The market value of the stock was $168 per share.

Required

a. Set up T-accounts, and post these transactions. Then prepare a balance sheet for the Douglas Company as of July 5, 1996, assuming the authorized stock has a par value of $150 per share.

b. Repeat part **(a)** for the stockholders' equity accounts, and prepare the stockholders' equity section of the July 5 balance sheet assuming the stock authorized has no par value but has a $60 per share stated value.

c. Repeat part **(a)** for the stockholders' equity accounts assuming the stock authorized has neither par nor stated value. Prepare the stockholders' equity section of the balance sheet.

Problem 12–4
Journalize stock issuances for cash, property, and services; and prepare resulting stockholders' equity section (L.O. 5)

On May 1, 1996, Sellers Company received a charter that authorized it to issue:

1. 4,000 shares of no-par preferred stock to which a stated value of $12 per share is assigned. The stock is entitled to a cumulative dividend of $9.60, convertible into two shares of common stock, callable at $208, and entitled to $200 per share in liquidation.
2. 1,500 shares of $400 par value, $20 cumulative preferred stock, which is callable at $420 and entitled to $412 in liquidation.
3. 60,000 shares of no-par common stock to which a stated value of $40 is assigned.

Transactions

May 1 All of the $9.60 cumulative preferred was issued at $204 per share, cash.

2 All of the $20 cumulative preferred was exchanged for merchandise inventory, land, and buildings valued at $128,000, $160,000, and $425,000, respectively.

3 Cash of $15,000 was paid to reimburse promoters for costs incurred for accounting, legal, and printing services. In addition, 1,000 shares of common stock were issued to the promoters for their services. The value of all of the services (including those paid in cash) was $55,000.

Required

a. Prepare journal entries for these transactions.

b. Assume that retained earnings were $200,000. Prepare the stockholders' equity section of the May 31, 1996, balance sheet.

Problem 12–5
Prepare stockholders' equity section; determine book values of stock; and determine dividends for each class of stock (L.O. 3, 6)

On January 2, 1995, the Queen Company received its charter. It issued all of its authorized 3,000 shares of no-par preferred stock at $208 and all of its 12,000 authorized shares of no-par common stock at $80 per share. The preferred stock has a stated value of $100 per share, is entitled to a basic cumulative dividend of $12 per share, is callable at $212 beginning in 1997, and is entitled to $200 per share plus cumulative dividends in the event of liquidation. The common stock has a stated value of $20 per share.

On December 31, 1996, the end of the second year of operations, retained earnings were $180,000. No dividends have been declared or paid on either class of stock.

Required

a. Prepare the stockholders' equity section of Queen Company's December 31, 1996, balance sheet.

b. Compute the book value of each class of stock.

c. If $84,000 of dividends were declared as of December 31, 1996, compute the amount paid to each class of stock.

Problem 12–6
Compute total market value for common stock; compute book value of common and preferred stock (L.O. 6)

The common stock of Satter Corporation is selling on a stock exchange for $90 per share. The stockholders' equity of the corporation at December 31, 1996, consists of:

Stockholders' equity:		
Paid-in capital:		
Preferred stock—9% cumulative, $120 par value, $120 liquidation value, 3,000 shares authorized, issued, and outstanding	$ 360,000	
Common stock—$72 par value, 30,000 shares authorized, issued, and outstanding	2,160,000	
Total paid-in capital		$2,520,000
Retained earnings		354,600
Total stockholders' equity		$2,874,600

Assume that in liquidation the preferred stock is entitled to par value plus cumulative unpaid dividends.

Required

a. What is the total market value of all of the corporation's common stock?

b. If all dividends have been paid on the preferred stock as of December 31, 1996, what are the book values of the preferred stock and the common stock?

c. If two years' dividends were due on the preferred stock as of December 31, 1996, what are the book values of the preferred stock and common stock?

Problem 12–7
Compute book values of a stockholder's preferred and common stock (L.O. 6)

Maple Corporation has an agreement with each of its 15 preferred and 30 common stockholders that in the event of the death of a stockholder, it will purchase at book value from the stockholder's estate or heirs the shares of Maple Corporation stock held by the deceased at the time of death. The book value is to be computed in accordance with generally accepted accounting principles.

Following is the stockholders' equity section of the Maple Corporation's December 31, 1996, balance sheet.

Stockholders' equity:		
Paid-in capital:		
Preferred stock—without par value, $100 stated value, $30 cumulative; 3,000 shares authorized, issued, and outstanding	$ 300,000	
Common stock—$125.00 par value, 60,000 shares authorized, issued, and outstanding	7,500,000	
Paid-in capital in excess of stated value—preferred	1,680,000	
Paid-in capital in excess of par value—common	60,000	
Total paid-in capital		$ 9,540,000
Retained earnings		3,600,000
Total stockholders' equity		$13,140,000

The preferred stock is cumulative and entitled to $600 per share plus cumulative dividends in liquidation. No dividends have been paid for 1½ years.

A stockholder who owned 100 shares of preferred stock and 1,000 shares of common stock died on December 31, 1996. You have been employed by the stockholder's executor to compute the book value of each class of stock and to determine the price to be paid for the stock held by her late husband.

Required Prepare a schedule showing the computation of the amount to be paid for the deceased stockholder's preferred and common stock.

Alternate Problems

Problem 12–1A
Determine dividends for common stock and cumulative and noncumulative preferred stock (L.O. 3)

On January 1, 1992, the retained earnings of Quinton Company were $216,000. Net income for the succeeding five years was as follows:

1992	$144,000
1993	108,000
1994	2,400
1995	24,000
1996	132,000

The outstanding capital stock of the corporation consisted of 2,000 shares of preferred stock with a par value of $240 per share that pays a dividend of $9.60 per year and 8,000 shares of no-par common stock with a stated value of $120 per share. No dividends were in arrears as of January 1, 1992.

Required

Prepare schedules showing how the net income for these five years was distributed to the two classes of stock if in each of the years the entire current net income was distributed as dividends and the preferred stock was:

a. Cumulative.

b. Noncumulative.

Problem 12–2A
Journalize stock issuances for cash, services (organization costs), and property; prepare resulting balance sheet (L.O. 5)

On January 1, 1996, Balboa Company was authorized to issue 500,000 shares of $5 par value common stock. It then completed the following transactions:

1996

Jan. 14 Issued 90,000 shares of common stock at $24 per share for cash.

29 Gave the promoters of the corporation 50,000 shares of common stock for their services in organizing the company. The board of directors valued these services at $620,000.

Feb. 19 Exchanged 100,000 shares of common stock for the following assets at the indicated fair market values:

Equipment	$180,000
Building	440,000
Land	600,000

Required

a. Prepare general journal entries to record the transactions.

b. Prepare the balance sheet of the company as of March 1, 1996.

Problem 12–3A
Post transactions; prepare balance sheets for par value stock, stated value stock, and no-par or stated value stock (L.O. 2, 4, 5)

On July 3, 1996, Kicker Company was authorized to issue 15,000 shares of common stock; 3,000 shares were issued immediately to the incorporators of the company for cash at $160 per share. On July 5 of that year, an additional 300 shares were issued to the incorporators for services rendered in organizing the company. The board valued these services at $48,000. On July 6, 1996, legal and printing costs of $6,000 were paid. These costs related to securing the corporate charter and the stock certificates.

Required

a. Set up T-accounts, and post these transactions. Then prepare the balance sheet of the Kicker Company as of the close of July 10, 1996, assuming the authorized stock has an $80 par value.

b. Repeat **(a)** for the T-accounts involving stockholders' equity, assuming the stock is no-par stock with a $120 stated value. Prepare the stockholders' equity section of the balance sheet.

c. Repeat **(a)** for the T-accounts involving stockholders' equity, assuming the stock is no-par stock with no stated value. Prepare the stockholders' equity section of the balance sheet.

Problem 12–4A
Journalize stock transactions, including conversions; prepare stockholders' equity section (L.O. 3–5)

Hank Company received its charter on April 1, 1996, authorizing it to issue: (1) 10,000 shares of $400 par value, $32 cumulative, convertible preferred stock; (2) 10,000 shares of $12 cumulative no-par preferred stock having a stated value of $20 per share and a liquidation value of $100 per share; and (3) 100,000 shares of no-par common stock without a stated value.

On April 2, incorporators of the corporation acquired 50,000 shares of the common stock for cash at $80 per share, and 200 shares were issued to an attorney for services rendered in organizing the corporation. On April 3, the company issued all of its authorized

shares of $32 convertible preferred stock for land valued at $1,600,000 and a building valued at $4,800,000. The property was subject to a mortgage of $2,400,000. On April 8, the company issued 5,000 shares of the $12 preferred stock in exchange for a patent valued at $1,040,000. On April 10, the company issued 1,000 shares of common stock for cash at $80 per share.

Required

a. Prepare general journal entries for these transactions.

b. Prepare the stockholders' equity section of the April 30, 1996, balance sheet. Assume retained earnings were $80,000.

c. Assume that each share of the $32 convertible preferred stock is convertible into six shares of common stock and that one-half of the preferred is converted on September 1, 1996. Give the required journal entry.

Problem 12–5A
Prepare stockholders' equity section; determine book values of stock; and determine dividends for each class of stock
(L.O. 3, 6)

Ringling Company issued all of its 5,000 shares of authorized preferred stock on January 1, 1995, at $206 per share. The preferred stock is no-par stock, has a stated value of $10 per share, is entitled to a cumulative basic preference dividend of $12 per share, is callable at $220 beginning in 2000, and is entitled to $200 per share in liquidation plus cumulative dividends. On this same date, Ringling also issued 10,000 authorized shares of no-par common stock with a $20 stated value at $100 per share.

On December 31, 1996, the end of its second year of operations, the company's retained earnings amounted to $320,000. No dividends have been declared or paid on either class of stock since the date of issue.

Required

a. Prepare the stockholders' equity section of Ringling Company's December 31, 1996, balance sheet.

b. Compute the book value in total and per share of each class of stock as of December 31, 1996.

c. If $220,000 of dividends are to be declared as of December 31, 1996, compute the amount payable to each class of stock.

Problem 12–6A
Determine book value for each class of stock
(L.O. 6)

The stockholders' equity sections from three different corporations' balance sheets follow.

1. Stockholders' equity:

Paid-in capital:		
Preferred stock—7% cumulative, $240 par value, 500 shares authorized, issued, and outstanding	$ 120,000	
Common stock—$48 par value, 10,000 shares authorized, issued, and outstanding	480,000	
Total paid-in capital		$ 600,000
Retained earnings		422,400
Total stockholders' equity		$ 1,022,400

(All dividends have been paid.)

2. Stockholders' equity:

Paid-in capital:		
Preferred stock—6% cumulative, $80 par value, 10,000 shares authorized, issued, and outstanding	$ 800,000	
Common stock—$240 par value, 30,000 shares authorized, issued, and outstanding	7,200,000	
Total paid-in capital		$ 8,000,000
Retained earnings		88,000
Total stockholders' equity		$ 8,088,000

(The current year's dividends have not been paid.)

3. Stockholders' equity:

Paid-in capital:		
Preferred stock—7% cumulative, $480 par value, 10,000 shares authorized, issued, and outstanding	$ 4,800,000	
Common stock—$240 par value, 50,000 shares authorized, issued, and outstanding	12,000,000	
Total paid-in capital		$16,800,000
Retained earnings (deficit)		(1,872,000)
Total stockholders' equity		$14,928,000

(Dividends have not been paid for 2 previous years or the current year.)

Required

Compute the book values per share of the preferred and common stock of each corporation assuming that in a liquidation the preferred stock receives par value plus dividends in arrears.

Problem 12–7A
Compute book values of a stockholder's preferred and common stock (L.O. 6)

Packard, Inc., is a corporation in which all of the outstanding preferred and common stock is held by the four Lehman brothers. The brothers have an agreement stating that the remaining brothers will, upon the death of a brother, purchase from the estate his holdings of stock in the company at book value.

The stockholders' equity section of the balance sheet for the company on December 31, 1996, the date of the death of James Lehman, shows:

Stockholders' equity:		
Paid-in capital:		
Preferred stock—6%; $640 par value; $640 liquidation value; 4,000 shares authorized, issued, and outstanding	$2,560,000	
Paid-in capital in excess of par—preferred	128,000	
Common stock—without par value, $32 stated value, 60,000 shares authorized, issued, and outstanding	1,920,000	
Paid-in capital in excess of par—common	1,920,000	
Total paid-in capital		$6,528,000
Retained earnings		256,000
Total stockholders' equity		$6,784,000

No dividends have been paid for the last year on the preferred stock, which is cumulative. At the time of his death, James Lehman held 2,000 shares of preferred stock and 10,000 shares of common stock of the company.

Required

a. Compute the book value of the preferred stock.

b. Compute the book value of the common stock.

c. Compute the amount the remaining brothers must pay to the estate of James Lehman for the preferred and common stock that he held at the time of his death.

BEYOND THE NUMBERS—CRITICAL THINKING

Business Decision Case 12–1
Compute dividends on preferred stock and common stock and determine their relationship to stock prices (L.O. 3)

Blank Company and Dash Company have extremely stable net income amounts of $9,600,000 and $6,400,000, respectively. Both companies distribute all their net income as dividends each year. Blank Company has 100,000 shares of $160 par value, 6% preferred stock, and 500,000 shares of $16 par value common stock outstanding. Dash Company has 50,000 shares of $80 par value, 8% preferred stock, and 400,000 shares of $16 par value common stock outstanding. Both preferred stocks are cumulative.

Required

a. Compute the annual dividend per share of preferred stock and per share of common stock for each company.

b. Based solely on the preceding information, which common stock would you predict to have the higher market price per share? Why?

c. Which company's stock would you buy? Why?

Business Decision Case 12–2
Determine book values and their relationship to investment decisions (L.O. 6)

Jesse Waltrip recently inherited $480,000 cash that he wishes to invest in the common stock of either the Tank Corporation or the Excise Corporation. Both corporations have manufactured the same types of products for five years. The stockholders' equity sections of the two corporations' latest balance sheets follow:

TANK CORPORATION

Stockholders' equity:	
Paid-in capital:	
Common stock—$125.00 par value, 30,000 shares authorized, issued, and outstanding	$3,750,000
Retained earnings	3,450,000
Total stockholders' equity	$7,200,000

EXCISE CORPORATION

Stockholders' equity:		
Paid-in capital:		
Preferred stock—8%, $500 par value, cumulative 4,000 shares authorized, issued, and outstanding	$2,000,000	
Common stock—$125.00 par value, 40,000 shares authorized, issued, and outstanding	5,000,000	
Total paid-in capital		$7,000,000
Retained earnings		560,000
Total stockholders' equity		$7,560,000

The Tank Corporation has paid a cash dividend of $6 per share each year since its creation; its common stock is currently selling for $590 per share. The Excise Corporation's common stock is currently selling for $480 per share. The current year's dividend and three prior years' dividends on the preferred stock are in arrears. The preferred stock has a liquidation value of $600 per share.

Required

a. What is the book value per share of the Tank Corporation common stock and the Excise Corporation common stock? Is book value the major determinant of market value of the stock?

b. Based solely on the previous information, which investment would you recommend to Waltrip? Why?

Annual Report Analysis 12–3
Determine original issuance price of common stock (L.O. 4)
Determine return on average common stockholders' equity (L.O. 7)

Refer to the consolidated balance sheet of The Coca-Cola Company in the annual report booklet. In the shareholders' equity section, determine the price paid per share of common stock upon original issuance. Assume that the capital surplus represents additional paid-in capital from the issuance of common stock.

Determine the return on average common stockholders' equity for each of the companies in the annual report booklet. Explain in writing why this information is important to managers, investors, and creditors.

Ethics Case 12–4
Answer questions regarding the ethics case

Refer to the ethics case concerning Joe Morrison on page 449 to answer the following questions:

a. Which alternative would benefit the company and its management over the next several years?

b. Which alternative would benefit society?

c. If you were Morrison, which side of the argument would you take?

Group Project 12–5
Calculate return on average common stockholders' equity and make investment decision

In teams of two or three students, examine the annual reports of three companies and calculate each company's return on common shareholders' equity for the most recent two years. At least two years are needed to observe any changes. As a team, decide in which of the three companies you would invest. Appoint a spokesperson for the team to explain to the class which company the team would invest in and why.

Answers to Self-Test

True-False

1. **False.** This is not the primary reason a person may prefer the corporate form of business organization in a situation involving considerable risk. The primary reason is that stockholders can lose only the amount of capital they have invested in a corporation.
2. **False.** The claims of the creditors rank ahead of the claims of the stockholders, even those stockholders whose stock is preferred as to assets.
3. **True.** Par value is simply the amount per share that is credited to the Capital Stock account for each share issued and is no indication of the market value or the book value of the stock.
4. **True.** When capital stock is issued for property or services, the transaction is recorded at the fair market value of (1) the property or services received or (2) the stock issued, whichever is more clearly evident.

Multiple-Choice

1. **c.** This feature of corporations is one of the disadvantages of the corporate form of organization.
2. **b.** Stated value is an arbitrary amount assigned by the board of directors to each share of capital stock without a par value.
3. **d.** Dividends in arrears are cumulative unpaid dividends. Only cumulative preferred stock has dividends in arrears.
4. **b.** The amount credited to the Paid-In Capital in Excess of Par Value—Common is computed as follows:

   10,000 shares × ($50 − $20) = $300,000

5. **a.** The book value of common stock is computed as follows:

Total book value of stockholders' equity ($80,000 + $200,000 + $400,000)	$680,000
Total shares	÷1,000
Book value per share	$ 680

13

CORPORATIONS

PAID-IN CAPITAL, RETAINED EARNINGS, DIVIDENDS, AND TREASURY STOCK

LEARNING OBJECTIVES

After studying this chapter, you should be able to:

1. Identify the different sources of paid-in capital and describe how to present them on a balance sheet.
2. Account for a cash dividend, a stock dividend, a stock split, and a retained earnings appropriation.
3. Account for the acquisition and reissuance of treasury stock.
4. Describe the proper accounting treatment of discontinued operations, extraordinary items, and changes in accounting principle.

(continued)

As owners of a corporation, stockholders provide much of the capital for its activities. On the balance sheet, we show the stockholders' capital investment in the corporation as paid-in capital under stockholders' equity. Also included in stockholders' equity is the capital accumulated through the retention of corporate earnings (retained earnings). Paid-in capital is a relatively permanent portion of stockholders' equity; the retained earnings balance is a relatively temporary portion of corporate capital and is the source of stockholders' dividends.

The preceding chapter discussed the paid-in capital obtained by issuing shares of stock for cash, property, or services. This chapter describes additional sources of paid-in capital and items affecting retained earnings.

PAID-IN (OR CONTRIBUTED) CAPITAL

As you have learned in the preceding chapter, **paid-in capital**, or **contributed capital**, refers to all of the contributed capital of a corporation, including the capital carried in the capital stock accounts. The general ledger does not contain an account titled ''Paid-In Capital.'' Instead, paid-in capital is a category, and companies establish a separate account for each source of paid-in capital.

In Illustration 13.1, we summarize several sources of stockholders' equity and list general ledger account titles used to record increases and decreases in capital from each of these sources. Chapter 12 discussed some of these general ledger accounts. This chapter discusses other general ledger accounts that record sources of stockholders' equity.

The stockholders' equity section of a balance sheet shows the different sources of the corporation's paid-in capital because these sources are important information. For example, these additional sources may be from stock dividends, treasury stock transactions, or donations.

ILLUSTRATION 13.1
Sources of Stockholders' Equity

Sources of Stockholders' Equity	Illustrative General Ledger Account Titles
I. Capital paid in (or contributed).	
A. For, or assigned to, shares:	
1. Issued to the extent of par or stated value or the amount received for shares without par or stated value.	Common Stock 5% Preferred Stock
2. To be distributed as a stock dividend.	Stock Dividend Distributable—Common (Preferred)
3. In addition to par or stated value:	
a. In excess of par.	Paid-In Capital in Excess of Par Value—Common (Preferred)
b. In excess of stated value.	Paid-In Capital in Excess of Stated Value—Common (Preferred)
c. Resulting from declaration of stock dividends.	Paid-In Capital—Stock Dividends
d. Resulting from reissue of treasury stock at a price above its acquisition price.	Paid-In Capital—Common (Preferred) Treasury Stock Transactions
B. Donations (gifts), whether from stockholders or from others.	Paid-In Capital—Donations
II. Capital accumulated by retention of earnings (retained earnings).	
A. Appropriated retained earnings.	Appropriation per Loan Agreement
B. Free and unappropriated retained earnings.	Retained Earnings (Unappropriated)

Paid-In Capital—Stock Dividends

When it declares a stock dividend, a corporation distributes additional shares of stock (instead of cash) to its present stockholders. A later section discusses and illustrates how the issuance of a stock dividend results in a credit to a Paid-In Capital—Stock Dividends account.

(*concluded*)

5. Define prior period adjustments and show their proper presentation in the financial statements.
6. Analyze and use the financial results—earnings per share and price-earnings ratio.

Paid-In Capital—Treasury Stock Transactions

Another source of capital is treasury stock transactions. **Treasury stock** is the corporation's own stock, either preferred or common, that it has issued and reacquired. It is legally available for reissuance. By reacquiring shares of its own outstanding capital stock at one price and later reissuing them at a higher price, a corporation can increase its capital by the difference between the two prices. If the reissue price is **less** than acquisition cost, however, corporate capital decreases. We discuss treasury stock transactions at length later in this chapter.

Objective 1
Identify the different sources of paid-in capital and describe how to present them on a balance sheet.

Paid-In Capital—Donations

Occasionally, a corporation receives a gift of assets, such as a $500,000 building. These donated gifts increase stockholders' equity and are called **donated capital.** The entry to record the gift of a $500,000 building is a debit to Buildings and a credit to Paid-In Capital—Donations. Accountants would make this entry in the amount of the $500,000 fair market value of the gift when received.

RETAINED EARNINGS

The **retained earnings** portion of stockholders' equity typically results from accumulated earnings, reduced by net losses and dividends. Like paid-in capital, retained earnings is a source of assets received by a corporation. Paid-in capital is the actual investment by the stockholders; retained earnings is the investment by the stockholders through earnings not yet withdrawn.

The balance in the corporation's Retained Earnings account is the corporation's net income, less net losses, from the date the corporation began to the present, less the sum of dividends paid during this period. Net income increases Retained Earnings, while net losses and dividends decrease Retained Earnings in any given year. Thus, the balance in Retained Earnings represents the corporation's accumulated net income not distributed to stockholders.

When the Retained Earnings account has a debit balance, a **deficit** exists. A company indicates a deficit by listing retained earnings with a negative amount in the stockholders' equity section of the balance sheet. The firm need not change the title of the general ledger account even though it contains a debit balance. The most common credits and debits made to Retained Earnings are for income (or losses) and dividends. Occasionally, accountants make other entries to the Retained Earnings account. We discuss some of these entries later in the chapter.

Paid-In Capital and Retained Earnings on the Balance Sheet

The following stockholders' equity section of a balance sheet presents the various sources of capital in proper form:

Stockholders' equity:		
Paid-in capital:		
Preferred stock—6%, $100 par value; authorized, issued, and outstanding, 4,000 shares	$ 400,000	
Common stock—no-par value, $5 stated value; authorized, issued, and outstanding, 400,000 shares	2,000,000	$2,400,000
Paid-in capital—		
From preferred stock issuances*	$ 40,000	
From donations	10,000	50,000
Total paid-in capital		$2,450,000
Retained earnings		500,000
Total stockholders' equity		$2,950,000

* This label is not the exact account title but is representative of the descriptions used on balance sheets. The exact account title could be used, but shorter descriptions are often shown.

In their highly condensed, published balance sheets, companies often omit the details regarding the sources of the paid-in capital in excess of par or stated value and replace them by a single item, such as:

Paid-in capital in excess of par (or stated) value $50,000

Dividends

Objective 2
Account for a cash dividend, a stock dividend, a stock split, and a retained earnings appropriation.

Dividends are distributions of earnings by a corporation to its stockholders. Usually the corporation pays dividends in cash, but it may distribute additional shares of the corporation's own capital stock as dividends. Occasionally, a company pays dividends in merchandise or other assets. Since dividends are the means whereby the owners of a corporation share in its earnings, accountants charge them against retained earnings.

Before dividends can be paid, the board of directors must declare them so they can be recorded in the corporation's minutes book. Three dividend dates are significant:

1. **Date of declaration.** The date of declaration indicates when the board of directors approved a motion declaring that dividends should be paid. The board action creates the liability for dividends payable (or stock dividends distributable for stock dividends).
2. **Date of record.** The board of directors establishes the date of record; it determines which stockholders receive dividends. The corporation's rec-

ILLUSTRATION 13.2
Types of Dividends

	Number of Companies			
	1992	**1991**	**1990**	**1989**
Cash dividends paid to common stock shareholders:				
Per share amount disclosed in retained earnings statement	290	286	288	301
Per share amount not disclosed in retained earnings statement	162	170	175	174
Total	452	456	463	475
Cash dividends paid to preferred stock shareholders:				
Per share amount disclosed in retained earnings statement	47	52	53	63
Per share amount not disclosed in retained earnings statement	83	86	93	87
Total	130	138	146	150
Dividends paid to pooled companies	1	2	1	—
Stock dividends	10	10	10	10
Dividends in kind	12	7	5	7
Stock purchase rights	2	9	25	54

Source: American Institute of Certified Public Accountants, *Accounting Trends & Techniques* (New York: AICPA, 1993), p. 387.

ords (the stockholders' ledger) determine its stockholders as of the date of record.

3. **Date of payment.** The date of payment indicates when the corporation will pay dividends to the stockholders.

To illustrate how these three dates relate to an actual situation, assume the board of directors of the Allen Corporation declared a cash dividend on May 5, 1997 (date of declaration). The cash dividend declared is $1.25 per share to stockholders of record on July 1, 1997 (date of record), payable on July 10 (date of payment). Because financial transactions occur on both the date of declaration (a liability is incurred) and on the date of payment (cash is paid), journal entries record the transactions on both of these dates. No journal entry is required on the date of record.

Illustration 13.2 shows the frequencies of dividend payments made by a sample of 600 companies for the years 1989–92. Note that cash dividends are far more numerous than stock dividends or dividends in kind (paid in merchandise or other assets).

AN ACCOUNTING PERSPECTIVE

USES OF TECHNOLOGY After original issuance, investors may trade the stock of a company on secondary markets, such as the New York Stock Exchange. The company makes no entry on its books for these outside trades after issuance. Often, a company uses a spreadsheet or database program to note trades between shareholders. These computer programs can print a report on the date of record. This information allows a company that declares a dividend to be certain the money or stock goes to the stockholders who own the stock on the date of record rather than to the stockholders who originally purchased the stock.

Cash Dividends

Cash dividends are cash distributions of accumulated earnings by a corporation to its stockholders. To illustrate the entries for cash dividends, consider the following example. On January 21, 1997, a corporation's board of directors declared a 2% quarterly cash dividend on $100,000 of outstanding preferred stock. This dividend is one fourth of the annual dividend on 1,000 shares of $100 par value, 8% preferred stock. The dividend will be paid on March 1, 1997, to stockholders of record on February 5, 1997. An entry is not needed on the date of record; however, the entries at the declaration and payment dates are as follows:

			Debit	Credit
1997				
Jan.	21	Retained Earnings	2,000	
		Dividends Payable		2,000
		Dividends declared: 2% on $100,000 of outstanding preferred stock, payable March 1, 1997, to stockholders of record on February 5, 1997.		
Mar.	1	Dividends Payable	2,000	
		Cash		2,000
		Paid the dividend declared on January 21, 1997.		

Often a cash dividend is stated as so many dollars per share. For instance, the quarterly dividend could have been stated as $2 per share. When they declare a cash dividend, some companies debit a Dividends account instead of Retained Earnings. (Both methods are acceptable.) The Dividends account is then closed to Retained Earnings at the end of the fiscal year.

Once a cash dividend is declared and notice of the dividend is given to stockholders, a company generally cannot rescind it unless all stockholders agree to such action.[1] Thus, the credit balance in the Dividends Payable account appears as a current liability on the balance sheet.

AN ACCOUNTING PERSPECTIVE

BUSINESS INSIGHT Beckman Company designs, manufactures, sells, and services laboratory systems for biological analysis and investigation into life processes. Often investors believe a company that pays dividends is doing well. Therefore, companies try to maintain a record of paying dividends, as Beckman Company noted in its 1992 annual report:

Dividends

The Company paid cash dividends to stockholders of $0.30 per share in 1992 and $0.28 per share in 1991 and 1990. The Company intends to continue paying cash dividends of at least the current per share amount, subject to future business conditions, requirements of the operations and financial condition of the Company.

In January 1993 the Board of Directors declared a first quarter dividend of $0.09 per share. This dividend is payable March 4, 1993 to stockholders of record on February 12, 1993.

A company that lacks sufficient cash for a cash dividend may declare a stock dividend to satisfy its shareholders. Note that in the long run it may be more beneficial to the company and the shareholders to reinvest the capital in the business rather than paying a cash dividend. If so, the company would be more profitable and the shareholders would be rewarded with a higher stock price in the future.

Stock Dividends

Stock dividends are payable in additional shares of the declaring corporation's capital stock. When declaring stock dividends, companies issue additional shares of the same class of stock as that held by the stockholders.

Corporations usually account for stock dividends by transferring a sum from retained earnings to permanent paid-in capital. The amount transferred for stock dividends depends on the size of the stock dividend. For stock dividends, most states permit corporations to debit Retained Earnings or any paid-in capital accounts other than those representing legal capital. In most circumstances, however, they debit Retained Earnings when a stock dividend is declared.

Stock dividends have no effect on the total amount of stockholders' equity or on net assets. They merely decrease retained earnings and increase paid-in capital by an equal amount. Immediately after the distribution of a stock dividend, each share of similar stock has a lower book value per share. This decrease occurs because more shares are outstanding with no increase in total stockholders' equity.

[1] Stockholders might agree to rescind (cancel) a dividend already declared if the company is in difficult financial circumstances and needs to retain cash to pay bills or acquire assets to continue operations.

Stock dividends do not affect the individual stockholder's percentage of ownership in the corporation. For example, a stockholder who owns 1,000 shares in a corporation having 100,000 shares of stock outstanding, owns 1% of the outstanding shares. After a 10% stock dividend, the stockholder still owns 1% of the outstanding shares—1,100 of the 110,000 outstanding shares.

A corporation might declare a stock dividend for several reasons:

1. Retained earnings may have become large relative to total stockholders' equity, so the corporation may desire a larger permanent capitalization.
2. The market price of the stock may have risen above a desirable trading range. A stock dividend generally reduces the per share market value of the company's stock.
3. The board of directors of a corporation may wish to have more stockholders (who might then buy its products) and eventually increase their number by increasing the number of shares outstanding. Some of the stockholders receiving the stock dividend are likely to sell the shares to other persons.
4. Stock dividends may silence stockholders' demands for cash dividends from a corporation that does not have sufficient cash to pay cash dividends.

The percentage of shares issued determines whether a stock dividend is a small stock dividend or a large stock dividend. Firms use different accounting treatments for each category.

Recording Small Stock Dividends A stock dividend of less than 20 to 25% of the outstanding shares is a small stock dividend and has little effect on the market value (quoted market price) of the shares. Thus, the firm accounts for the dividend at the current market value of the outstanding shares.

Assume a corporation is authorized to issue 20,000 shares of $100 par value common stock, of which 8,000 shares are outstanding. Its board of directors declares a 10% stock dividend (800 shares). The quoted market price of the stock is $125 per share immediately before the stock dividend is announced. Since the distribution is less than 20 to 25% of the outstanding shares, the dividend is accounted for at market value. The entry for the declaration of the stock dividend on August 10, 1997, is:

Aug.	10	Retained Earnings (or Stock Dividends) (800 shares × $125) . . .	100,000	
		Stock Dividend Distributable—Common (800 shares × $100)		80,000
		Paid-In Capital—Stock Dividends (800 shares × $25)		20,000
		To record the declaration of a 10% stock dividend; shares to be distributed on September 20, 1997, to stockholders of record on August 31, 1997.		

This entry records the issuance of the shares:

Sept.	20	Stock Dividend Distributable—Common	80,000	
		Common Stock		80,000
		To record the distribution of 800 shares of common stock as authorized in stock dividend declared on August 10, 1997.		

The **Stock Dividend Distributable—Common account** is a stockholders' equity (paid-in capital) account credited for the par or stated value of the shares distributable when recording the declaration of a stock dividend. Since a stock dividend distributable is not to be paid with assets, it is not a liability. When a balance sheet is prepared between the date the 10% dividend is declared and the date the shares are issued, the proper statement presentation of the effects of the stock dividend is:

Stockholders' equity:		
Paid-in capital:		
Common stock—$100 par value; authorized, 20,000 shares; issued and outstanding, 8,000 shares	$800,000	
Stock dividend distributable on September 20, 1997, 800 shares at par value	80,000	
Total par value of shares issued and to be issued	$880,000	
Paid-in capital from stock dividends	20,000	
Total paid-in capital		$ 900,000
Retained earnings		150,000
Total stockholders' equity		$1,050,000

Suppose, on the other hand, that the common stock in the preceding example is no-par stock and has a stated value of $50 per share. The entry to record the declaration of the stock dividend (when the market value is $125) is:

Account	Debit	Credit
Retained Earnings (800 shares × $125)	100,000	
Stock Dividend Distributable—Common (800 shares × $50)		40,000
Paid-In Capital—Stock Dividends (800 shares × $75)		60,000
To record the declaration of a stock dividend.		

The entry to record the issuance of the stock dividend is:

Account	Debit	Credit
Stock Dividend Distributable—Common	40,000	
Common Stock		40,000
To record the issuance of the stock dividend.		

Recording Large Stock Dividends A stock dividend of more than 20 to 25% of the outstanding shares is a large stock dividend. Since one purpose of a large stock dividend is to reduce the market value of the stock so the shares can be traded more easily, firms do not use the current market value of the stock in the entry. They account for such dividends at their par or stated value rather than at their current market value. The laws of the state of incorporation or the board of directors establish the amounts for stocks without par or stated value.

To illustrate the treatment of a stock dividend of more than 20 to 25%, assume X Corporation has been authorized to issue 10,000 shares of $10 par value common stock, of which 5,000 shares are outstanding. X Corporation declared a 30% stock dividend (1,500 shares) on September 20, 1997, to be issued on October 15, 1997. The required entries are:

Month	Day	Account	Debit	Credit
Sept.	20	Retained Earnings (or Stock Dividends) (1,500 shares × $10)	15,000	
		Stock Dividend Distributable—Common		15,000
		To declare a 30% stock dividend.		
Oct.	15	Stock Dividend Distributable—Common	15,000	
		Common Stock		15,000
		To issue the 30% stock dividend.		

Note that although firms account for the small stock dividend at current market value, they account for the 30% stock dividend at par value (1,500 shares × $10 = $15,000). Because of the differences in accounting for large and small stock dividends, accountants must determine the relative size of the stock dividend before making any journal entries.

To see the effect of small and large stock dividends on stockholders equity, look at Illustration 13.3.

Stock Splits

A **stock split** is a distribution of 100% or more of additional shares of the issuing corporation's stock accompanied by a corresponding reduction in the par value per share. The corporation receives no assets in this transaction. A stock split causes a large reduction in the market price per share of the outstanding stock. A two-for-one split doubles the number of shares outstanding, a three-for-one split

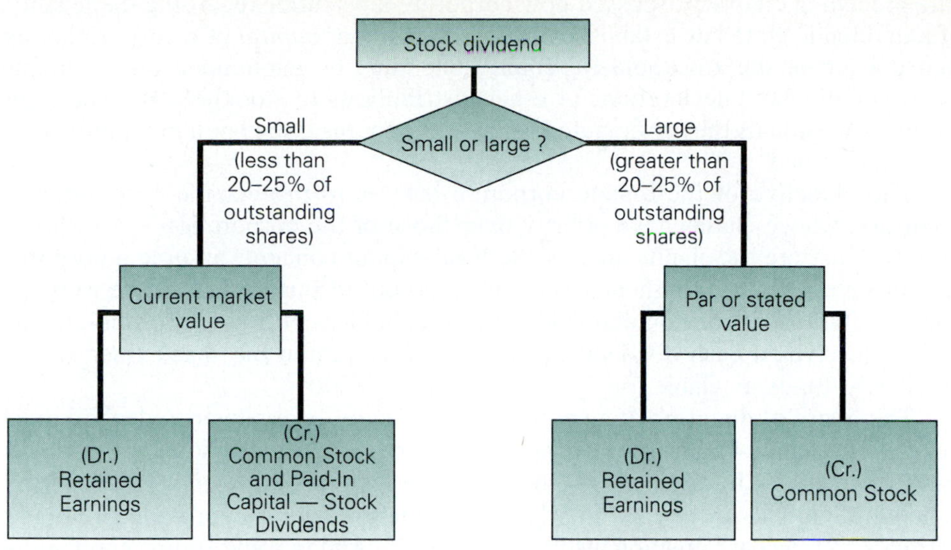

ILLUSTRATION 13.3
Stock Dividends

ILLUSTRATION 13.4 Summary of Effects of Stock Dividends and Stock Splits

	Total Stockholders' Equity	Common Stock	Paid-In Capital—Common	Retained Earnings	Number of Shares Outstanding	Par Value per Share
Stock dividends:						
Small	No effect	Increases	Increases*	Decreases	Increases	No effect
Large	No effect	Increases	No effect	Decreases	Increases	No effect
Stock splits	No effect	No effect	No effect	No effect	Increases	Decreases

* Assuming current market value is greater than par value.

triples the number of shares, and so on. The split reduces the par value per share at the same time so that the total dollar amount credited to Common Stock remains the same. For instance, a two-for-one split halves the par value per share.[2] If the corporation issues 100% more stock without a reduction in the par value per share, the transaction is a 100% stock dividend rather than a two-for-one stock split.

The entry to record a stock split depends on the particular circumstances. Usually, firms change only the number of shares outstanding and the par or stated value in the records. (The number of shares authorized may also change.) Thus, they would record a two-for-one stock split in which the par value of the shares decreases from $20 to $10 as follows:

Common Stock—$20 par value	100,000	
Common Stock—$10 par value		100,000
To record a two-for-one stock split; 5,000 shares of $20 par value common stock were replaced by 10,000 shares of $10 par value common stock.		

In Illustration 13.4, we summarize the effects of stock dividends and stock splits. Stock dividends and stock splits have no effect on the total amount of stockholders' equity. In addition, stock splits have no effect on the total amount of paid-in capital or retained earnings. They merely increase the number of shares outstanding and decrease the par value per share. Stock dividends increase paid-in capital and decrease retained earnings by equal amounts.

[2] If a corporation *reduces* the par value of its stock without issuing more shares, say, from $100 to $60 per share, then $40 per share must be removed from the appropriate capital stock account and credited to Paid-In Capital—Recapitalization. Further discussion of this process, called *recapitalization*, is beyond the scope of this text.

Legality of Dividends

The preceding chapter discussed how corporate laws differ regarding the legality of a dividend. State law establishes the *legal* or *stated capital* of a corporation as that portion of the stockholders' equity that must be maintained intact, unimpaired by dividend declarations or other distributions to stockholders. The legal capital often equals the par or stated value of the shares issued or a minimum price per share issued.

The objective of these state corporate laws is to protect the corporation's creditors, whose claims have priority over those of the corporation's stockholders. To illustrate the significance of the legal capital concept, assume a corporation in severe financial difficulty is about to go out of business. If there were no legal capital restrictions on dividends, the stockholders of that corporation might pay themselves a cash dividend or have the corporation buy back their stock, leaving no funds available for the corporation's creditors.

The board of directors of a corporation possesses sole power to declare dividends. The legality of a dividend generally depends on the amount of retained earnings available for dividends—not on the net income of any one period. Firms can pay dividends in periods in which they incurred losses, provided retained earnings and the cash position justify the dividend. And in some states, companies can declare dividends from current earnings despite an accumulated deficit. The financial advisability of declaring a dividend depends on the cash position of the corporation.

Liquidating Dividends

Normally, dividends are reductions of retained earnings since they are distributions of the corporation's net income. However, dividends may be distributions of contributed capital. These dividends are called **liquidating dividends.**

Accountants debit liquidating dividends to a paid-in capital account. Corporations should disclose to stockholders the source of any dividends that are not distributions of net income by indicating which paid-in capital account was debited as a result of the dividend. The legality of paying liquidating dividends depends on the source of the paid-in capital and the laws of the state of incorporation.

Retained Earnings Appropriations

The amount of retained earnings that a corporation may pay as cash dividends may be less than total retained earnings for several contractual or voluntary reasons. These contractual or voluntary restrictions or limitations on retained earnings are **retained earnings appropriations.** For example, a loan contract may state that part of a corporation's $100,000 of retained earnings is not available for cash dividends until the loan is paid. Or a board of directors may decide to use assets resulting from net income for plant expansion rather than for cash dividends. An example of a voluntary restriction was General Electric's annual report statement that cash dividends were limited "to support enhanced productive capability and to provide adequate financial resources for internal and external growth opportunities."

Companies formally record retained earnings appropriations by transferring amounts from Retained Earnings to accounts such as "Appropriation for Loan Agreement" or "Retained Earnings Appropriated for Plant Expansion." Even though some refer to retained earnings appropriations as *retained earnings reserves,* using the term *reserves* is discouraged.

Other reasons for appropriations of retained earnings include pending litigation, debt retirement, and contingencies in general. Such appropriations do not reduce total retained earnings. They merely disclose to balance sheet readers that a portion of retained earnings is not available for cash dividends. Thus, recording these appropriations guarantees that the corporation limits its outflow of cash dividends while repaying a loan, expanding a plant, or taking on some other costly endeavor. Recording retained earnings appropriations does not involve the setting aside of cash for the indicated purpose. The establishment of a separate fund would require a specific directive from the board of directors. The only entry required to record the appropriation of $25,000 of retained earnings to fulfill the provisions in a loan agreement is:

Retained Earnings	25,000	
Appropriation per Loan Agreement		25,000
To record restriction on retained earnings.		

When the retained earnings appropriation has served its purpose of restricting dividends and the loan has been repaid, the board of directors may decide to return the appropriation intact to Retained Earnings. The entry to do this is:

Appropriation per Loan Agreement	25,000	
Retained Earnings		25,000
To return balance in Appropriation per Loan Agreement account to Retained Earnings.		

Retained Earnings Appropriations on the Balance Sheet

On the balance sheet, retained earnings appropriations appear in the stockholders' equity section as follows:

Stockholders' equity:		
Paid-in capital:		
Preferred stock—8%, $50 par value; 500 shares authorized, issued, and outstanding	$25,000	
Common stock—$5 par value; 10,000 shares authorized, issued, and outstanding	50,000	
Total paid-in capital		$ 75,000
Retained earnings:		
Appropriated:		
Per loan agreement	$25,000	
Unappropriated	20,000	
Total retained earnings		45,000
Total stockholders' equity		$120,000

Note that a retained earnings appropriation does not reduce either stockholders' equity or total retained earnings but merely earmarks (restricts) a portion of retained earnings for a specific reason.

The formal practice of recording and reporting retained earnings appropriations is decreasing. Footnote explanations such as the following are replacing these appropriations:

> Note 7. Retained earnings restrictions. According to the provisions in the loan agreement, retained earnings available for dividends are limited to $20,000.

Such footnotes appear after the formal financial statements in "Notes to Financial Statements." The Retained Earnings account on the balance sheet would be referenced as follows: "Retained Earnings (see note 7) . . . $45,000."

Changes in the composition of retained earnings reveal important information about a corporation to financial statement users. A separate formal statement—the *statement of retained earnings*—discloses such changes.

Statement of Retained Earnings

A **statement of retained earnings** is a formal statement showing the items causing changes in unappropriated and appropriated retained earnings during a stated period of time. Changes in unappropriated retained earnings usually consist of the addition of net income (or deduction of net loss) and the deduction of dividends and appropriations. Changes in appropriated retained earnings consist of increases or decreases in appropriations.

ILLUSTRATION 13.5
Statement of Retained Earnings

WARD CORPORATION
Statement of Retained Earnings
For Year Ended December 31, 1997

Unappropriated retained earnings:		
January 1, 1997, balance		$180,000
Add: Net income		80,000
		$260,000
Less: Dividends	$15,000	
Appropriation for plant expansion	35,000	50,000
Unappropriated retained earnings, December 31, 1997		$210,000
Appropriated retained earnings:		
Appropriation for plant expansion, January 1, 1997, balance	$25,000	
Add: Increase in 1997	35,000	$ 60,000
Appropriation for contract obligation, January 1, 1997, balance		20,000
Appropriated retained earnings, December 31, 1997		$ 80,000
Total retained earnings, December 31, 1997		$290,000

Note Ward Corporation's statement of retained earnings in Illustration 13.5. The only new appropriation during 1997 was an additional $35,000 for plant expansion. Ward added this new $35,000 to the $25,000 beginning balance in that account and subtracted that amount from unappropriated retained earnings. An alternative to the statement of retained earnings is the statement of stockholders' equity.

STATEMENT OF STOCKHOLDERS' EQUITY

Most corporations include four financial statements in their annual reports: a balance sheet, an income statement, a statement of stockholders' equity (in place of a statement of retained earnings), and a statement of cash flows (discussed in Chapter 16). A **statement of stockholders' equity** is a summary of the transactions affecting the accounts in the stockholders' equity section of the balance sheet during a stated period. These transactions include activities affecting both paid-in capital and retained earnings accounts. Thus, the statement of stockholders' equity includes the information contained in a statement of retained earnings plus some additional information. The columns in the statement of stockholders' equity reflect the major account titles within the stockholders' equity section: the types of stock issued and outstanding, paid-in capital in excess of par (or stated) value, retained earnings, and treasury stock. Each row indicates the effects of major transactions affecting one or more stockholders' equity accounts.

Look at Illustration 13.6, a statement of stockholders' equity. The first row indicates the beginning balances of each account in the stockholders' equity section. This summary shows that Larkin Corporation issued 10,000 shares of common stock, declared a 5% stock dividend on common stock, repurchased 1,200 shares of treasury stock, earned net income of $185,000, and paid cash dividends on both its preferred and common stock. After the transactions' effects are indicated within each row, Larkin added or subtracted each column's components to determine the ending balance in each stockholders' equity account.

TREASURY STOCK

Objective 3
Account for the acquisition and reissuance of treasury stock.

Treasury stock is the corporation's own capital stock that it has issued and then reacquired; this stock has not been canceled and is legally available for reissuance. Because it has been issued, we cannot classify treasury stock as unissued stock.

ILLUSTRATION 13.6 Statement of Stockholders' Equity

LARKIN CORPORATION
Statement of Stockholders' Equity
For the Year Ended December 31, 1997

	$50 Par Value, 6% Preferred Stock	$20 Par Value Common Stock	Paid-In Capital in Excess of Par Value	Retained Earnings	Treasury Stock	Total
Balance, January 1, 1997	$250,000	$300,000	$200,000	$500,000	$(42,000)	$1,208,000
Issuance of 10,000 shares of common stock		200,000	100,000			300,000
5% stock dividend on common stock, 1,250 shares		25,000	27,500	(52,500)		-0-
Purchase of 1,200 shares of treasury stock					(48,000)	(48,000)
Net income				185,000		185,000
Cash dividends:						
Preferred stock				(15,000)		(15,000)
Common stock				(25,000)		(25,000)
Balance, December 31, 1997	$250,000	$525,000	$327,500	$592,500	$(90,000)	$1,605,000

Recall that when a corporation has additional authorized shares of stock that are to be issued after the date of original issue, in most states the preemptive right requires offering these additional shares first to existing stockholders on a pro rata basis. However, firms may reissue treasury stock without violating the preemptive right provisions of state laws; that is, treasury stock does not have to be offered to current stockholders on a pro rata basis.

A corporation may reacquire its own capital stock as treasury stock to: (1) cancel and retire the stock; (2) reissue the stock later at a higher price; (3) reduce the shares outstanding and thereby increase earnings per share; or (4) issue the stock to employees. If the intent of reacquisition is cancellation and retirement, the treasury shares exist only until they are retired and canceled by a formal reduction of corporate capital.

For dividend or voting purposes, most state laws consider treasury stock as issued but not outstanding, since the shares are no longer in the possession of stockholders. Also, accountants do not consider treasury shares outstanding in calculating earnings per share. However, they consider treasury shares outstanding for purposes of determining legal capital, which includes outstanding shares plus treasury shares.

In states that consider treasury stock as part of legal capital, the cost of treasury stock may not exceed the retained earnings at the date the shares are reacquired. This regulation protects creditors by preventing the corporation in financial difficulty from using funds to purchase its own stock instead of paying its debts. Thus, if a corporation is subject to such a law (as is assumed in this text), the retained earnings available for dividends must exceed the cost of the treasury shares on hand.

Acquisition and Reissuance of Treasury Stock

When firms reacquire treasury stock, they record the stock at cost as a debit in a stockholders' equity account called *Treasury Stock*.[3] They credit reissuances to the Treasury Stock account at the cost of acquisition. Any excess of the reissue price over cost represents additional paid-in capital and is credited to **Paid-In Capital—Common (Preferred) Treasury Stock Transactions.**

[3] Another acceptable method of accounting for treasury stock transactions is the par value method. We leave further discussion of the par value method to intermediate accounting texts.

To illustrate, assume that on February 18, 1997, the Hillside Corporation reacquired 100 shares of its outstanding common stock for $55 each. (The company's stockholders' equity consisted solely of common stock and retained earnings.) On April 18, 1997, the company reissued 30 shares for $58 each. The entries to record these events are:

1997				
Feb.	18	Treasury Stock—Common (100 shares × $55)	5,500	
		Cash		5,500
		Acquired 100 shares of treasury stock at $55.		
Apr.	18	Cash (30 shares × $58)	1,740	
		Treasury Stock—Common (30 shares × $55)		1,650
		Paid-In Capital—Common Treasury Stock Transactions		90
		Reissued 30 shares of treasury stock at $58; cost is $55 per share.		

When the reissue price of subsequent shares is less than the acquisition price, firms debit the difference between cost and reissue price to Paid-In Capital—Common Treasury Stock Transactions. This account, however, never develops a debit balance. By definition, no paid-in capital account can have a debit balance. If Hillside reissued an additional 20 shares at $52 per share on June 12, 1997, the entry would be:

June	12	Cash (20 shares × $52)	1,040	
		Paid-In Capital—Common Treasury Stock Transactions	60	
		Treasury Stock—Common (20 shares × $55)		1,100
		Reissued 20 shares of treasury stock at $52; cost is $55 per share.		

At this point, the credit balance in the Paid-In Capital—Common Treasury Stock Transactions account would be $30. If the remaining 50 shares are reissued on July 16, 1997, for $53 per share, the entry would be:

July	16	Cash (50 shares × $53)	2,650	
		Paid-In Capital—Common Treasury Stock Transactions	30	
		Retained Earnings	70	
		Treasury Stock—Common (50 shares × $55)		2,750
		Reissued 50 shares of treasury stock at $53; cost is $55 per share.		

Notice that Hillside has exhausted the Paid-In Capital—Common Treasury Stock Transactions account credit balance. If more than $30 is debited to that account, it would develop a debit balance. Thus, the remaining $70 of the excess of cost over reissue price is a special distribution to the stockholders involved and is debited to the Retained Earnings account.

Sometimes stockholders donate stock to a corporation. Since donated treasury shares have no cost to the corporation, accountants make only a memo entry when the shares are received.[4] The only formal entry required is to debit Cash and credit the Paid-In Capital—Donations account when the stock is reissued. For example, if donated treasury stock is sold for $5,000, the entry would be:

Cash	5,000	
Paid-In Capital—Donations		5,000
To record the sale of donated treasury stock.		

[4] The method illustrated here is called the *memo* method. Other acceptable methods of accounting for donated stock are the *cost* method and *par value* method. Intermediate accounting texts discuss these latter two methods.

ILLUSTRATION 13.7
Stockholders' Equity Section of the Balance Sheet

HYPOTHETICAL CORPORATION
Partial Balance Sheet
December 31, 1997

Stockholders' equity:		
Paid-in capital:		
Preferred stock—8%, $100 par value; 2,000 shares authorized, issued, and outstanding		$ 200,000
Common stock—$10 par value; authorized, 100,000 shares; issued, 80,000 shares of which 1,000 are held in the treasury	$800,000	
Stock dividend distributable on common stock on January 15, 1998, 7,900 shares	79,000	879,000
Paid-in capital—		
From common stock issuances	$ 40,000	
From stock dividends	60,000	
From treasury stock transactions	30,000	
From donations	50,000	180,000
Total paid-in capital		$1,259,000
Retained earnings:		
Appropriated:		
Per loan agreement	$250,000	
Unappropriated (restricted to the extent of $20,000, the cost of treasury shares held)	150,000	
Total retained earnings		400,000
Total paid-in capital and retained earnings		$1,659,000
Less: Treasury stock, common, 1,000 shares at cost		20,000
Total stockholders' equity		$1,639,000

Treasury Stock on the Balance Sheet

When treasury stock is held on a balance sheet date, it customarily appears at cost, as a deduction from the sum of total paid-in capital and retained earnings, as follows:

Stockholders' equity:		
Paid-in capital:		
Common stock—$10 par value; authorized and issued, 20,000 shares, of which 2,000 shares are in the treasury	$200,000	
Retained earnings (including $22,000 restricted by acquisition of treasury stock)	80,000	
Total paid-in capital and retained earnings		$280,000
Less: Treasury stock at cost, 2,000 shares		22,000
Total stockholders' equity		$258,000

AN ACCOUNTING PERSPECTIVE

BUSINESS INSIGHT Flowers Industries serves regional and national retail and food service markets with fresh and frozen baked goods and frozen specialty vegetables, fruits, and desserts. For 1992 and 1991, Flowers Industries reported common stock in treasury of 1,083,980 and 1,816,975 shares, respectively. Flowers deducted the cost of these shares from total paid-in capital and retained earnings.

Stockholders' Equity on the Balance Sheet

To summarize much of what we have discussed in Chapters 12 and 13, we present the stockholders' equity section of the balance sheet in Illustration 13.7. This partial balance sheet shows: (1) the amount of capital assigned to shares outstanding; (2) the capital contributed for outstanding shares in addition to that assigned to the shares; (3) other forms of paid-in capital; and (4) retained earnings, appropriated and unappropriated.

Net Income Inclusions and Exclusions

Objective 4
Describe the proper accounting treatment of discontinued operations, extraordinary items, and changes in accounting principle.

Accounting has long faced the problem of what to include in the net income reported for a period. Should net income include only the revenues and expenses related to normal operations? Or should it include the results of discontinued operations and unusual, nonrecurring gains and losses? And further, should the determination of net income for 1997, for example, include an item that can be clearly associated with a prior year, such as additional federal income taxes for 1996? Or should such items, including corrections of errors, be carried directly to retained earnings? How are the effects of making a change in accounting principle (like a change in depreciation methods) to be reported?

APB Opinion No. 9 (December 1966) sought to provide answers to some of these questions. The *Opinion* directed that unusual and nonrecurring items having an earnings or loss effect are extraordinary items (reported in the income statement) or prior period adjustments (reported in the statement of retained earnings). Extraordinary items are reported separately after net income from regular continuing activities.

In Illustrations 13.8 (p. 479) and 13.10 (p. 483), we show the reporting of discontinued operations, extraordinary items, changes in accounting principle, and prior period adjustments. For Illustrations 13.8 and 13.10, assume that the Anson Company has 1,000,000 shares of common stock outstanding and the company's earnings are taxed at 40%. Also, assume the following:

1. Anson sold its Cosmetics Division on August 1, 1997, at a loss of $500,000. The net operating loss of that division through July 31, 1997, was $2,000,000.
2. Anson had a taxable gain in 1997 of $40,000 from voluntary early retirement of debt (extraordinary item).
3. Anson changed depreciation methods in 1997 (change in accounting principle), and the cumulative effect of the changes was a $6,000 decrease in prior years' depreciation expense.
4. In 1997, Anson discovered that the $200,000 cost of land acquired in 1996 had been expensed for both financial accounting and tax purposes. A prior period adjustment was made in 1997.

Next, we explain the effects of these assumptions in greater detail.

Discontinued Operations

A **discontinued operation** occurs when a business sells a segment (usually an unprofitable department or division) to another company or abandons it. When a company discontinues a segment, it shows the relevant information in a special section of the income statement immediately after income from continuing operations and before extraordinary items. Two items of information appear:

1. The income or loss (net of tax effect) from the segment's operations for the portion of the current year before it was discontinued.
2. The gain or loss (net of tax effect) on disposal of the segment.

To illustrate, Anson's sale of its Cosmetics Division on July 31 led to a before-tax loss of $500,000. The after-tax loss was $500,000 × 60% = $300,000. The operating loss before taxes through July 31 was $2,000,000. The after-tax operating loss for that period was $2,000,000 × 60% = $1,200,000. Note this information on the income statement in Illustration 13.8.

Extraordinary Items

Prior to 1973, companies reported a gain or loss as an extraordinary item if it was *either* unusual in nature *or* occurred infrequently. As a result, companies were inconsistent in the financial reporting of certain gains and losses. This inconsistency led to the issuance of *APB Opinion No. 30* (September 1973). *Opinion No. 30* redefined **extraordinary items** as those unusual in nature *and* occurring infre-

ILLUSTRATION 13.8 Income Statement

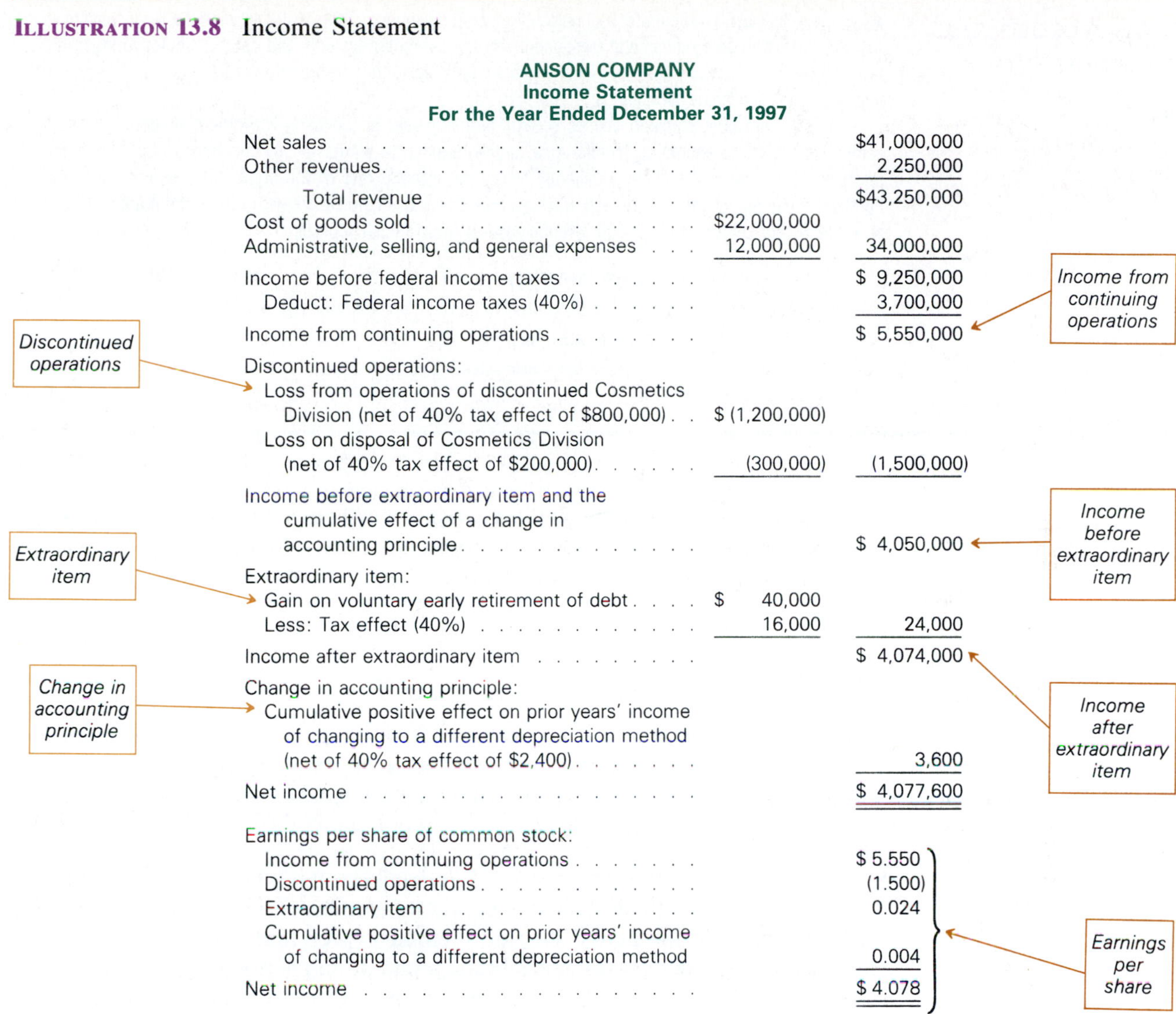

ANSON COMPANY
Income Statement
For the Year Ended December 31, 1997

Net sales		$41,000,000
Other revenues		2,250,000
Total revenue		$43,250,000
Cost of goods sold	$22,000,000	
Administrative, selling, and general expenses	12,000,000	34,000,000
Income before federal income taxes		$ 9,250,000
Deduct: Federal income taxes (40%)		3,700,000
Income from continuing operations		$ 5,550,000
Discontinued operations:		
Loss from operations of discontinued Cosmetics Division (net of 40% tax effect of $800,000)	$ (1,200,000)	
Loss on disposal of Cosmetics Division (net of 40% tax effect of $200,000)	(300,000)	(1,500,000)
Income before extraordinary item and the cumulative effect of a change in accounting principle		$ 4,050,000
Extraordinary item:		
Gain on voluntary early retirement of debt	$ 40,000	
Less: Tax effect (40%)	16,000	24,000
Income after extraordinary item		$ 4,074,000
Change in accounting principle:		
Cumulative positive effect on prior years' income of changing to a different depreciation method (net of 40% tax effect of $2,400)		3,600
Net income		$ 4,077,600
Earnings per share of common stock:		
Income from continuing operations		$ 5.550
Discontinued operations		(1.500)
Extraordinary item		0.024
Cumulative positive effect on prior years' income of changing to a different depreciation method		0.004
Net income		$ 4.078

quently. Note that both conditions must be met—unusual nature and infrequent occurrence. Accountants determine whether an item is unusual and infrequent in light of the environment in which the company operates. Examples of extraordinary items include gains or losses that are the direct result of a major catastrophy (a flood or hurricane where few have occurred before), a confiscation of property by a foreign government, or a prohibition under a newly enacted law. *FASB Statement No. 4* further directs that gains and losses from the voluntary early extinguishment (retirement) of debt are extraordinary items.

Extraordinary items are included in the determination of periodic net income, but are disclosed separately (net of their tax effects) in the income statement below "Income from continuing operations." As shown in Illustration 13.8, Anson reported the extraordinary items after reporting the loss from discontinued operations.

Gains or losses related to ordinary business activities are not extraordinary items regardless of their size. For example, material write-downs of uncollectible receivables, obsolete inventories, and intangible assets are not extraordinary items. However, such items may be separately disclosed as part of income from continuing operations.

AN ACCOUNTING PERSPECTIVE

BUSINESS INSIGHT Seagate Technology is a leading independent designer, manufacturer, and marketer of data storage products and components for the computer systems and data technology industries. Guilford Mills, Inc., produces, processes, and sells finished fabrics to manufacturers of apparel, automotive products, and home furnishings.

One of the most common causes of extraordinary gain is the early retirement of debt. Often, a company that sold debentures (bonds) at a high interest rate wants to buy the bonds back when the interest rate in the market falls sufficiently below the interest rate of the bond. After repurchasing the bonds, if the company still needs cash, it issues new bonds at the lower interest rate in the market. This is how these two companies reported a repurchase in their annual reports:

Seagate Technology	**1993**	**1992**	**1991**
Extraordinary gain on repurchase of debt (less applicable income taxes of $2,594) .	—	—	4,613
Guilford Mills, Inc.			
Extraordinary Item—Gain on purchase of convertible subordinated debentures, less applicable income taxes (Note 5)	—	—	2,360

In Illustration 13.9, note that in a sample of 600 companies for the years 1989–92, most companies do not report extraordinary items. Notice the huge increase in debt extinguishments in 1992, which probably resulted from the low interest rates in 1992.

Changes in Accounting Principle

Changes in accounting principle can materially alter a company's reported net income and financial position. **Changes in accounting principle** are changes in accounting methods pertaining to such items as inventory and depreciation. Such changes include a change in inventory valuation method from FIFO to LIFO or a change in depreciation method from accelerated to straight-line.

According to *APB Opinion No. 20,* a company should consistently apply the same accounting methods from one period to another. However, a company may make a change if the newly adopted method is preferable and if the change is adequately disclosed in the financial statements. In the period in which a company makes a change in accounting principle, it must disclose on the financial statements the nature of the change, its justification, and its effect on net income. Also, the company must show on the income statement for the year of the change (Illustration 13.8) the cumulative effect of the change on prior years' income (net of tax).

As an example of a change in accounting principle, assume that Anson purchased a machine on January 2, 1995, for $30,000. The machine has an estimated useful life of five years with no salvage value. Anson decided to depreciate the machine for financial reporting purposes using the sum-of-the-years'-digits method. At the beginning of 1997, the company decided to change to the straight-line method of depreciation. The cumulative effect of the change in accounting principle is as follows:

Under sum-of-the-years'-digits depreciation:		
Depreciation for 1995: $30,000 × 5/15	$10,000	
Depreciation for 1996: $30,000 × 4/15	8,000	
Balance in accumulated depreciation at beginning of 1997	$18,000	Difference $6,000
Under straight-line depreciation (if it had been used):		
Depreciation for 1995: $30,000/5	$ 6,000	
Depreciation for 1996: $30,000/5	6,000	
Balance that would have been in accumulated depreciation at beginning of 1997	$12,000	

ILLUSTRATION 13.9
Extraordinary Items

	1992	1991	1990	1989
Nature:				
Debt extinguishments	60	33	36	16
Operating loss carryforwards	17	20	24	26
Litigation settlements	2	1	2	3
Other	5	4	5	9
Total extraordinary items	84	58	67	54
Number of companies:				
Presenting extraordinary items	81	55	63	49
Not presenting extraordinary items	519	545	537	551
Total companies	600	600	600	600

Source: Based on American Institute of Certified Public Accountants, *Accounting Trends & Techniques* (New York: AICPA, 1993), p. 377.

The accumulated depreciation account balance would have been $6,000 less under the straight-line method. Also, depreciation expense over the two years would have been $6,000 less. Assume that federal income tax would have been $2.400 more ($6,000 × 0.4). The net effect of the change is $6,000 − $2,400 = $3,600. Therefore, Anson corrects the appropriate account balances by reducing (debiting) the accumulated depreciation account balance by $6,000, crediting an account entitled Cumulative Effect of Change in Accounting Principle for $3,600 (which is closed to Retained Earnings during the normal closing process), and crediting Federal Income Taxes Payable for $2,400. The journal entry would be:

	Debit	Credit
Accumulated Depreciation—Machinery	6,000	
Cumulative Effect of Change in Accounting Principle		3,600
Federal Income Taxes Payable		2,400
To record the effect of changing from sum-of-the-years'-digits depreciation to straight-line depreciation on machinery.		

Note the cumulative effect of changing to the straight-line depreciation method appears below "income from continuing operations" in Illustration 13.8 at the after-tax amount of $3,600. Discontinued operations, extraordinary items, and changes in accounting principle are reported in the above order below "income from continuing operations."

Prior Period Adjustments

Objective 5
Define prior period adjustments and show their proper presentation in the financial statements.

According to *FASB Statement No. 16*, **prior period adjustments** consist almost entirely of corrections of errors in previously published financial statements. Corrections of abnormal, nonrecurring errors that may have been caused by the improper use of an accounting principle or by mathematical mistakes are prior period adjustments. Normal, recurring corrections and adjustments, which follow inevitably from the use of estimates in accounting practice, are not treated as prior period adjustments. Also, mistakes corrected in the same year they occur are not prior period adjustments. To illustrate a prior period adjustment, suppose that Anson purchased land in 1996 at a total cost of $200,000 and recorded this amount in an expense account instead of in the Land account. Discovery of the error on May 1, 1997, after publication of the 1996 financial statements, would require a prior period adjustment. The adjustment would be recorded directly in the Retained Earnings account. Assuming the error had resulted in an $80,000 underpayment of taxes in 1996, the entry to correct the error would be:

			Debit	Credit
May	1	Land	200,000	
		Federal Income Taxes Payable		80,000
		Retained Earnings (or Prior Period Adjustment—Land)		120,000
		To correct an accounting error expensing land.		

AN ETHICAL PERSPECTIVE

Ace Chemical Company

Ace Chemical Company is a small, privately held manufacturer that has been operating at a profit for years. The current balance in the Cash account is $8 million, and the balance in Retained Earnings is $4 million. The company's plant assets consist of special purpose equipment that can produce only certain chemicals. The company has long-term debt with a principal balance of $10 million. Its officers (all of whom are stockholders) are concerned about the future prospects of the company. Many similar firms have been sued by customers and employees claiming that toxic chemicals produced by the company caused their health problems. No such suits have yet been filed against Ace, but the officers fully expect them to be filed within the next two years.

The company's stock is not listed on a stock exchange, nor has it recently been traded. The officers hold 70% of the stock and estimate that their total stockholdings have a current market value of about $8 million (although its value would be much lower if all the facts were known). They are worried that if suits are filed and the company loses, there will not even be enough remaining assets to satisfy creditors' claims, and the officers' stock would be worthless. Private legal counsel has informed the officers that the company is likely to lose any suits that are filed.

One of the officers suggested that they could at least receive something for their stock by having the company buy half of the shares held by the officers at a total price of $4 million. Another officer asked if such a treasury stock transaction would be legal. The response was that the transactions would be legal because it did not dip into the present legal capital of the company. Retained earnings would be reduced to a zero balance, but would not develop a debit balance as a result of the transaction.

Prior period adjustments do not appear on the income statements but in the current-year financial statements as adjustments to the opening balance of retained earnings on the statement of retained earnings (Illustration 13.10).

Accounting for Tax Effects

Most discontinued operations, extraordinary items, changes in accounting principle, and prior period adjustments affect the amount of income taxes a corporation must pay. To report the income tax effect, *FASB Statement No. 96* requires reporting all of these items *net of their tax effects,* as shown in Illustrations 13.8 and 13.10.[5] **Net-of-tax effect** means that items appear at the dollar amounts remaining after deducting the income tax effects. Thus, the total effect of a discontinued operation, an extraordinary item, a change in accounting principle, or a prior period adjustment appears in one place in the appropriate financial statement. The reference to "Income from continuing operations" on the income statement represents the results of transactions (including income taxes) that are normal for the business and may be expected to reoccur. Note that the tax effect of an item may appear separately, as it does for the gain on voluntary early retirement of debt in Illustration 13.8. Or the company may mention it parenthetically with only the net amount shown (see loss from discontinued operations and change in accounting principle in Illustration 13.8 and correction of error in Illustration 13.10).

Summary of Illustrative Financial Statements

1. Income from continuing operations of $5,550,000 (Illustration 13.8) is more representative of the continuing earning power of the company than is the net income figure of $4,077,600.
2. Following income, the special items from continuing operations appear at their actual impact on the company—that is, net of their tax effect.

[5] FASB, *Statement of Financial Accounting Standards No. 96*, "Accounting for Income Taxes" (Stamford. Conn., 1987). Copyright © by the Financial Accounting Standards Board, High Ridge Park, Stamford, Connecticut 06905, U.S.A.

ILLUSTRATION 13.10
Statement of Retained Earnings

ANSON COMPANY
Statement of Retained Earnings
For the Year Ended December 31, 1997

Retained earnings, January 1, 1997	$5,000,000
Prior period adjustment:	
Correction of error of expensing land (net of tax effect of $80,000)	120,000
Retained earnings, January 1, 1997, as adjusted	$5,120,000
Add: Net income	4,077,600
	$9,197,600
Less: Dividends	500,000
Retained earnings, December 31, 1997	$8,697,600

Prior period adjustment

AN ACCOUNTING PERSPECTIVE

BUSINESS INSIGHT Dover Corporation encompasses Dover Elevator International, Dover Resources, Dover Diversified, Dover Industries, and Dover Technologies. Dover provides a wide range of services. The following graph illustrates the growth of Dover Corporation's EPS:

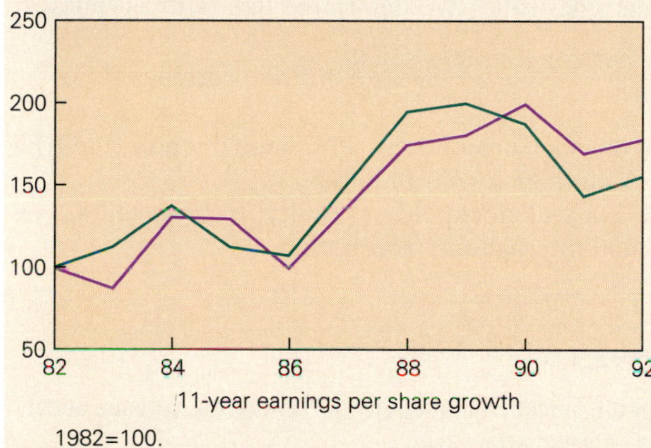

This graph compares Dover's EPS (shown in plum) with an industry average called S&P's 400 Industrial (shown in green). To understand financial ratios, one must compare the ratio to some form of industry average. As the graph indicates, Dover's EPS has steadily followed the industry in which it operates. Dover is in good shape in 1992 with an EPS well above the industry.

3. EPS is reported both before ($5.550) and after ($4.078) the discontinued operations, extraordinary item, and the cumulative effect of a change in accounting principle (Illustration 13.8).
4. The correction of the $200,000 error adds only $120,000 to retained earnings (Illustration 13.10). This result occurs because the mistake was included in the 1996 tax return and taxes were underpaid by $80,000. In the 1997 return, the $80,000 of taxes would have to be paid.

ANALYZING AND USING THE FINANCIAL RESULTS—EARNINGS PER SHARE AND PRICE-EARNINGS RATIO

Objective 6
Analyze and use the financial results—earnings per share and price-earnings ratio.

A major item of interest to investors and potential investors is how much a company earned during the current year, both in total and for each share of stock outstanding. Firms calculate the earnings per share amount only for the common shares of ownership. They compute **earnings per share (EPS)** as net income available to common stockholders divided by the average number of common shares outstanding during that period. **Income available to common stockholders** is net income less any dividends on preferred stock. They deduct the regular preferred dividend on cumulative preferred stock (but *not* a dividend in arrears) whether or not declared; however, they deduct only declared dividends on noncumulative preferred stock.

Bindley Western Industries
Bindley Western Industries is the fifth largest wholesale distributor of pharmaceuticals, health products, and beauty aids in the United States.

To illustrate, Bindley Western Industries had 10,139,662 weighted-average number of common shares outstanding with income available to common shareholders of $12,891,000 during 1993. Bindley Western Industries would compute EPS as follows:

$$\text{EPS} = \frac{\text{Income available to common stockholders}}{\text{Weighted-average number of common shares outstanding}}$$

$$= \frac{\$12{,}891{,}000}{10{,}139{,}662 \text{ shares}}$$

$$= \$1.27 \text{ per share}$$

Firms calculate EPS for each major category on the face of the income statement. In other words, they make an EPS calculation for income from continuing operations, discontinued operations, extraordinary items, changes in accounting principle, and net income. Note in Illustration 13.8 that Anson reports the EPS amounts at the bottom of its income statement.

VF Corporation
VF Corporation provides jeanswear, sportswear, intimate apparel, and occupational apparel.

The **price-earnings ratio** provides an index on whether a stock has future high income potential compared to other stocks. Stocks with future high income potential tend to have a high price-earnings ratio. We determine this ratio as follows:

$$\frac{\text{Current market price per share of common stock}}{\text{EPS}} = \text{Price-earnings ratio}$$

In the financial summary of the VF Corporation's 1992 annual report, the EPS is $2.75 and the price-earnings ratio high-low is 14.8–6.5.

This chapter completes the study of stockholders' equity. In Chapter 14, you learn about stock investments and international accounting.

Understanding The Learning Objectives

Objective 1
Identify the different sources of paid-in capital and describe how to present them on a balance sheet.

- Paid-in capital is presented in the stockholders' equity section of the balance sheet. Each source of paid-in capital is listed separately.
- Sources of paid-in capital are:
  1. Common stock.
  2. Preferred stock.
  3. In excess of par value or stated value (common and preferred).
  4. Stock dividends.
  5. Treasury stock transactions.
  6. Donations.

Objective 2
Account for a cash dividend, a stock dividend, a stock split, and a retained earnings appropriation.

- Cash dividend of 3% on $100,000 of outstanding common stock: declared on July 1 and paid on September 15.

July	1	Retained Earnings	3,000	
		Dividends Payable		3,000
Sept	15	Dividends Payable	3,000	
		Cash		3,000

Ten percent stock dividend on 10,000 shares of common stock outstanding; par value, $100; market value at declaration, $125 per share (declared on January 1 and paid on February 1).

Jan.	1	Retained Earnings (1,000 shares × $125)	125,000	
		Stock Dividend Distributable—Common (1,000 shares × $100)		100,000
		Paid-In Capital—Stock Dividends (1,000 shares × $25)		25,000
Feb.	1	Stock Dividend Distributable—Common	100,000	
		Common Stock		100,000

- Thirty percent stock dividend on 10,000 shares of common stock outstanding: declared on January 1 and payable on February 1; par value, $100.

Jan.	1	Retained Earnings (3,000 shares × $100)	300,000	
		Stock Dividend Distributable—Common		300,000
Feb.	1	Stock Dividend Distributable—Common	300,000	
		Common Stock		300,000

- Stock split: 1,000 shares of $50 par value common stock replaced by 2,000 shares of $25 par value common stock.

Common Stock—$50 par value	50,000	
Common Stock—$25 par value		50,000

- Retained earnings appropriation: $75,000 appropriated for plant expansion.

Retained Earnings	75,000	
Retained Earnings Appropriated for Plant Expansion		75,000

Objective 3
Account for the acquisition and reissuance of treasury stock.

- Treasury stock transactions: 100 shares of common stock were reacquired at $100 each and reissued for $105 each.

Treasury Stock—Common (100 shares × $100)	10,000	
Cash		10,000
Cash (100 shares × $105)	10,500	
Treasury Stock—Common (100 shares × $100)		10,000
Paid-In Capital—Common Treasury Stock Transactions (100 shares × $5)		500

Objective 4
Describe the proper accounting treatment of discontinued operations, extraordinary items, and changes in accounting principle.

- The income or loss (net of tax effect) from the segment's operations for the portion of the current year before it was discontinued is reported on the income statement below "Income from continuing operations."
- The gain or loss (net of tax effect) on disposal of the segment is also reported in that same section of the income statement.
- Extraordinary items are both unusual in nature and infrequent in occurrence. Extraordinary items appear on the income statement (net-of-tax effect) below "Income from continuing operations."
- In the period in which a change in principle is made, the nature of the change, its justification, and its effect on net income must be disclosed in the financial statements. Also, the cumulative effect of the change on prior years' income (net of tax effect) must be shown on the income statement for the year of the change below "Income from continuing operations."

Objective 5
Define prior period adjustments and show their proper presentation in the financial statements.

- Prior period adjustments consist of errors in previously published financial statements. Prior period adjustments appear (net-of-tax effect) as a correction to the beginning retained earnings balance on the statement of retained earnings.

Objective 6
Analyze and use the financial results—earnings per share and price-earnings ratio.

- EPS equals the income available to common stockholders divided by the weighted-average number of common shares outstanding. Income available to common stockholders is net income less any dividends on preferred stock. EPS provides information on the return of an investment in common stock.
- The price-earnings ratio equals the current market price per share of common stock divided by EPS. The price-earnings ratio indicates whether a stock has a future high income potential as compared to other stocks.

Demonstration Problem 13–A

Wylie Corporation has outstanding 10,000 shares of $150 par value common stock.

Required Prepare the entries to record:

a. The declaration of a cash dividend of $1.50 per share.

b. The declaration of a stock dividend of 10% at a time when the market value per share is $185.

c. The declaration of a stock dividend of 40% at a time when the market value per share is $195.

Solution to Demonstration Problem 13–A

		Debit	Credit
a.	Retained Earnings (or Dividends)	15,000	
	Dividends Payable		15,000
	To record declaration of a cash dividend.		
b.	Retained Earnings (or Stock Dividends) (1,000 shares × $185)	185,000	
	Stock Dividend Distributable—Common (1,000 shares × $150)		150,000
	Paid-In Capital—Stock Dividends		35,000
	To record declaration of a small stock dividend (10%).		
c.	Retained Earnings (or Stock Dividends) (4,000 shares × $150)	600,000	
	Stock Dividend Distributable—Common		600,000
	To record declaration of a large stock dividend (40%).		

Demonstration Problem 13–B

Following are selected transactions of Brackett Company:

1. The company reacquired 200 shares of its own $100 par value common stock, previously issued at $105 per share, for $20,600.
2. Fifty of the treasury shares were reissued at $110 per share, cash.
3. Seventy of the treasury shares were reissued at $95 per share, cash.
4. Stockholders of the corporation donated 100 shares of their common stock to the company.
5. The 100 shares of treasury stock received by donation were reissued for $9,000.

Required Prepare the necessary journal entries to record these transactions.

Solution to Demonstration Problem 13–B

		Debit	Credit
1.	Treasury Stock	20,600	
	Cash		20,600
	Acquired 200 shares at $20,600 ($103 per share).		
2.	Cash (50 shares × $110)	5,500	
	Treasury Stock—Common (50 shares × $103)		5,150
	Paid-In Capital—Common Treasury Stock Transactions		350
	Reissued 50 shares at $110 per share; cost is $5,150.		
3.	Cash (70 shares × $95)	6,650	
	Paid-In Capital—Common Treasury Stock Transactions (50 shares × $7)	350	
	Retained Earnings	210	
	Treasury Stock—Common (70 shares × $103)		7,210
	Reissued 70 shares at $95 per share; cost is $7,210.		
4.	Stockholders donated 100 shares of common stock to the company. (Only memo entry is made.)		
5.	Cash	9,000	
	Paid-In Capital—Donations (100 shares × $90)		9,000
	Reissued donated shares at $90 per share.		

Demonstration Problem 13–C

Selected account balances of Nexis Corporation at December 31, 1997, are:

Common Stock (no par value; 100,000 shares authorized, issued, and outstanding; stated value of $20 per share)	$2,000,000
Retained Earnings	570,000
Dividends Payable (in cash, declared December 15 on preferred stock)	16,000
Preferred Stock (8%, par value $200; 1,000 shares authorized, issued, and outstanding)	200,000
Paid-In Capital from Donation of Plant Site	100,000
Paid-In Capital in Excess of Par Value—Preferred	8,000

Required

Present in good form the stockholders' equity section of the balance sheet.

Solution to Demonstration Problem 13–C

NEXIS CORPORATION
Partial Balance Sheet
December 31, 1997

Stockholders' equity:		
Paid-in capital:		
Preferred stock—8%, par value $200; 1,000 shares authorized, issued, and outstanding	$ 200,000	
Common stock—no par value, stated value of $20 per share; 100,000 shares authorized, issued, and outstanding	2,000,000	
Paid-in capital from donation of plant site	100,000	
Paid-in capital in excess of par value—preferred	8,000	
Total paid-in capital		$2,308,000
Retained earnings		570,000
Total stockholders' equity		$2,878,000

New Terms

Cash dividends Cash distributions of accumulated earnings by a corporation to its stockholders. *467*

Changes in accounting principle Changes in accounting methods pertaining to such items as inventory and depreciation. *480*

Contributed capital See Paid-in capital.

Date of declaration (of dividends) The date the board of directors takes action in the form of a motion that dividends be paid. *466*

Date of payment (of dividends) The date of actual payment of a dividend, or issuance of additional shares for a stock dividend. *467*

Date of record (of dividends) The date of record established by the board that determines the stockholders who will receive dividends. *466*

Deficit A debit balance in the Retained Earnings account. *466*

Discontinued operation When a segment of a business is sold to another company or is abandoned. *478*

Dividends Distribution of earnings by a corporation to its stockholders. *466*

Dividends (cash) See Cash dividends.

Dividends (stock) See Stock dividends.

Donated capital Results from donation of assets to the corporation, which increases stockholders' equity. *465*

Earnings per share (EPS) Earnings to the common stockholders on a per share basis, computed as income available to common stockholders divided by the weighted-average number of common shares outstanding. *483*

Extraordinary items Items both unusual in nature and infrequent in occurrence; reported in the income statement net of their tax effects, if any. *478*

Income available to common stockholders Net income less any dividends on preferred stock. *483*

Liquidating dividends Dividends that are a return of contributed capital, not a distribution chargeable to retained earnings. *472*

Net-of-tax effect Used for discontinued operations, extraordinary items, changes in accounting principle, and prior period adjustments, whereby items are shown at the dollar amounts remaining after deducting the effects of such items on income taxes, if any, payable currently. *482*

Paid-in capital All of the contributed capital of a corporation, including that carried in capital stock accounts. When the words *paid-in capital* are included in the account title, the account contains capital contributed in addition to that assigned to the shares issued and recorded in the capital stock accounts. *464*

Paid-In Capital—Common (Preferred) Treasury Stock Transactions The account credited when treasury stock is reissued for more than its cost; this account is debited to the extent of its credit balance when such shares are reissued at less than cost. *475*

Price-earnings ratio The current market price per share of common stock divided by EPS. *484*

Prior period adjustments Consist almost entirely of corrections of errors in previously published financial statements. Prior period adjustments are reported in the statement of retained earnings net of their tax effects, if any. *481*

Retained earnings That part of stockholders' equity resulting from accumulated earnings; the account to which the results of corporate activity, including prior period adjustments, are carried and to which dividends and certain items resulting from capital transactions are charged. *465*

Retained earnings appropriations Contractual or voluntary restrictions or limitations on retained earnings that reduce the amount of dividends that may be declared. *472*

Statement of retained earnings A formal statement showing the items causing changes in unappropriated and appropriated retained earnings during a stated period of time. *473*

Statement of stockholders' equity A summary of the transactions affecting the accounts in the stockholders' equity section of the balance sheet during a stated period of time. *474*

Stock Dividend Distributable—Common account The stockholders' equity (paid-in capital) account that is credited for the par or stated value of the shares distributable when recording the declaration of a stock dividend. *469*

Stock dividends Dividends that are payable in additional shares of the declaring corporation's capital stock. *468*

Stock split A distribution of 100% or more of additional shares of the issuing corporation's stock, accompanied by a corresponding reduction in the par value per share. The purpose of a stock split is to cause a large reduction in the market price per share of the outstanding stock. *470*

Treasury stock Shares of capital stock issued and reacquired by the issuing corporation; they have not been formally canceled and are available for reissuance. *465*

SELF-TEST

TRUE-FALSE

Indicate whether each of the following statements is true or false.

1. The retained earnings balance of a corporation is part of its paid-in capital.
2. The purchase of treasury stock does not affect stockholders' equity.
3. Dividends are expenses since they decrease stockholders' equity.
4. A stock dividend reduces the retained earnings balance and permanently capitalizes the reduced portion of the retained earnings.
5. A retained earnings appropriation reduces the total stockholders' equity shown on the balance sheet.
6. Heavy frost damage suffered by a Florida citrus grower's orange trees would probably be reported as an extraordinary item.

MULTIPLE-CHOICE

Select the best answer for each of the following questions.

1. Which of the following is not included in paid-in capital?
   - **a.** Common Stock.
   - **b.** Paid-In Capital—Donations.
   - **c.** Stock Dividend Distributable.
   - **d.** Appropriation per Loan Agreement.
2. Atkins Company issued 10,000 shares of $20 par value common stock at $24 per share. Atkins reacquired 1,000 shares of its own stock at a cost of $30 per share. The entry to record the reacquisition is:

a.

Premium on Treasury Stock	10,000	
Treasury Stock	20,000	
Cash		30,000

b.

Premium on Treasury Stock	6,000	
Treasury Stock	24,000	
Cash		30,000

c.

Treasury Stock	30,000	
Cash		30,000

d.

Treasury Stock	20,000	
Paid-In Capital—Treasury Stock Transactions	10,000	
Cash		30,000

3. If the company reissues 500 shares of the treasury stock in (2) for $36 per share, the entry is:

a.

Cash	18,000	
Treasury Stock		15,000
Paid-In Capital—Treasury Stock Transactions		3,000

b.

Cash	18,000	
Treasury Stock		18,000

c.

Cash	18,000	
Treasury Stock		15,000
Retained Earnings		3,000

d. Cash 18,000
    Treasury Stock 10,000
    Retained Earnings 8,000

4. Treasury stock should be shown on the balance sheet as a:
   a. Reduction of the corporation's stockholders' equity.
   b. Current asset.
   c. Current liability.
   d. Investment asset.
5. An individual stockholder is entitled to receive any dividends declared on stock owned, provided the stock is held on the:
   a. Date of declaration.
   b. Date of record.
   c. Date of payment.
   d. Last day of a fiscal year.
6. ABC Corporation declared the regular quarterly dividend of $2 per share. ABC had issued 12,000 shares and subsequently reacquired 2,000 shares as treasury stock. What would be the total amount of the dividend?
   a. $24,000.
   b. $28,000.
   c. $20,000.
   d. $4,000.
7. Which item is not reported as a separate line item below income from continuing operations, net of tax effects, in the income statement?
   a. Extraordinary items.
   b. Prior period adjustments.
   c. Discontinued operations.
   d. Changes in accounting principle.

Now turn to page 499 to check your answers.

Questions

1. What are the two main elements of stockholders' equity in a corporation? Explain the difference between them.
2. Name several sources of paid-in capital. Would it suffice to maintain one account called *Paid-In Capital* for all sources of paid-in capital? Why or why not?
3. Does accounting for treasury stock resemble accounting for an asset? Is treasury stock an asset? If not, where is it properly shown on a balance sheet?
4. What are some possible reasons for a corporation to reacquire its own capital stock as treasury stock?
5. What is the purpose underlying the statutes that provide for restriction of retained earnings in the amount of the cost of treasury stock? Are such statutes for the benefit of stockholders, management, or creditors?
6. What is the effect of each of the following on the total stockholders' equity of a corporation: *(a)* declaration of a cash dividend, *(b)* payment of a cash dividend already declared, *(c)* declaration of a stock dividend, and *(d)* issuance of a stock dividend already declared?
7. The following dates are associated with a cash dividend of $80,000: July 15, July 31, and August 15. Identify each of the three dates, and give the journal entry required on each date, if any.
8. How should a declared but unpaid cash dividend be shown on the balance sheet? How should a declared but unissued stock dividend be shown?
9. On May 8, the board of directors of Tyler Corporation declared a dividend, payable on June 5, to stockholders of record on May 17. On May 10, James sold his capital stock in Tyler Corporation directly to Benton for $20,000, endorsing his stock certificate and giving it to Benton. Benton placed the stock certificate in her safe. On May 30, Benton sent the certificate to the transfer agent of Tyler Corporation for transfer. Who received the dividend? Why?
10. What are the possible reasons for a corporation to declare a stock dividend?
11. Why is a dividend consisting of the distribution of additional shares of the common stock of the declaring corporation not considered income to the recipient stockholders?
12. What is the difference between a small stock dividend and a large stock dividend?
13. What are liquidating dividends?
14. What is the purpose of a retained earnings appropriation?
15. What is a statement of stockholders' equity?
16. Describe a discontinued operation.
17. What are extraordinary items? Where and how are they reported?
18. Give an example of a change in accounting principle. How are the effects of changes in accounting principle reported?
19. What are prior period adjustments? Where and how are they reported?
20. Why are stockholders and potential investors interested in the amount of a corporation's EPS? What does the EPS amount reveal that total earnings do not?

The Coca-Cola Company

21. **Real World Question** From the consolidated statements of share-owners' equity of The Coca-Cola Company in the annual report booklet, identify the 1993 total amount for each of the following items:
   a. Sales to employees exercising stock options.
   b. Purchase of common stock for treasury.
   c. Total cash dividends.
   d. Balance—December 31, 1993.

MAYTAG

22. **Real World Question** Based on the financial statements of Maytag Corporation contained in the annual report booklet, what was the 1993 number of shares of common stock in treasury?

THE LIMITED, INC.

23. **Real World Question** Based on the balance sheet of The Limited, Inc., contained in the annual report booklet, what was the cost of treasury stock?

HARLAND

24. **Real World Question** Based on the financial statements of John H. Harland Company contained in the annual report booklet, what was the 1993 ending number of shares in treasury?

Exercises

Exercise 13–1
Prepare stockholders' equity section of balance sheet (L.O. 1)

The December 31, 1996, trial balance of Centinal Corporation had the following account balances:

Common Stock (no-par value; 200,000 shares authorized, issued, and outstanding; stated value of $40 per share)	$8,000,000
Notes Payable (12% due May 1, 1997)	1,000,000
Retained Earnings, Unappropriated	5,000,000
Dividends Payable in Cash (declared December 15, on preferred stock)	24,000
Appropriation per Loan Agreement	960,000
Preferred Stock (6%, par value $400; 2,000 shares authorized, issued, and outstanding)	800,000
Paid-In Capital in Excess of Stated Value—Common	600,000
Paid-In Capital in Excess of Par Value—Preferred	80,000

Present in proper form the stockholders' equity section of the balance sheet.

Exercise 13–2
Prepare journal entries for cash dividends (L.O. 2)

Hayman Company has issued all of its authorized 5,000 shares of $400 par value common stock. On February 1, 1996, the board of directors declared a dividend of $12 per share payable on March 15, 1996, to stockholders of record on March 1, 1996. Give the necessary journal entries.

Exercise 13–3
Prepare journal entries for cash dividend when treasury stock is held (L.O. 2)

The stockholders' equity section of Macon Company's balance sheet on December 31, 1996, shows 100,000 shares of authorized and issued $40 stated value common stock, of which 9,000 shares are held in the treasury. On this date, the board of directors declared a cash dividend of $4 per share payable on January 21, 1997, to stockholders of record on January 10. Give dated journal entries for these.

Exercise 13–4
Prepare journal entry for small stock dividend and discuss large stock dividend (L.O. 2)

Dator Company has outstanding 75,000 shares of common stock without par or stated value, which were issued at an average price of $80 per share, and retained earnings of $3,200,000. The current market price of the common stock is $120 per share. Total authorized stock consists of 500,000 shares.

a. Give the required entry to record the declaration of a 10% stock dividend.

b. If, alternatively, the company declared a 30% stock dividend, what additional information would you need before making a journal entry to record the dividend?

Exercise 13–5
Prepare journal entries for stock split and small stock dividend (L.O. 2)

Amtrox Corporation's stockholders' equity consisted of 60,000 authorized shares of $60 par value common stock, of which 30,000 shares had been issued at par, and retained earnings of $1,500,000. The company then split its stock, two for one, by changing the par value of the old shares and issuing new $30 par shares.

a. Give the required journal entry to record the stock split.

b. Suppose instead that the company declared and later issued a 10% stock dividend. Give the required journal entries, assuming that the market value on the date of declaration was $80 per share.

Exercise 13–6
Prepare journal entry for appropriation of retained earnings and explain (L.O. 2)

The balance sheet of Razor Company contains the following:

Appropriation per loan agreement	$900,000

a. Give the journal entry made to create this account.

b. Explain the reason for the appropriation's existence and its manner of presentation in the balance sheet.

Exercise 13–7
Prepare journal entries for reacquisition and reissuance of treasury stock (L.O. 3)

Beard Company had outstanding 50,000 shares of $40 stated value common stock, all issued at $48 per share, and had retained earnings of $1,600,000. The company reacquired 2,000 shares of its stock for cash at book value from the widow of a deceased stockholder.

a. Give the entry to record the reacquisition of the stock.

b. Give the entry to record the subsequent reissuance of this stock at $100 per share.

c. Give the entry required if the stock is instead reissued at $60 per share and there were no prior treasury stock transactions.

Exercise 13–8
Prepare journal entry(ies) for reissuance of donated stock (L.O. 3)

XYZ Company received 200 shares of its $200 stated value common stock on December 1, 1996, as a donation from a stockholder. On December 15, 1996, it reissued the stock for $62,400 cash. Give the journal entry or entries necessary for these transactions.

Exercise 13–9
Prepare income statement and statement of retained earnings (L.O. 2, 4)

Charcoal Company has revenues of $160 million, expenses of $128 million, a tax-deductible earthquake loss (its first such loss) of $8 million, and a tax-deductible loss of $12 million resulting from the voluntary early extinguishment (retirement) of debt. The assumed income tax rate is 40%. The company's beginning-of-the-year retained earnings were $60 million, and a dividend of $4 million was declared.

a. Prepare an income statement for the year.

b. Prepare a statement of retained earnings for the year.

Exercise 13–10
Prepare statement of retained earnings (L.O. 2, 5)

Waycross Company had retained earnings of $56,000 as of January 1, 1996. In 1996, Waycross Company had sales of $160,000, cost of goods sold of $96,000, and other operating expenses, excluding taxes, of $32,000. In 1996, Waycross Company discovered that it had, in error, depreciated land over the last three years resulting in a balance in the accumulated depreciation account of $40,000. The assumed tax rate for Waycross Company is 40%. Present in proper form a statement of retained earnings for the year ended December 31, 1996.

Exercise 13–11
Calculate EPS; present information in income statement format (L.O. 6)

The following information relates to Octagon Corporation for the year ended December 31, 1996:

Common stock outstanding.	75,000 shares
Income from continuing operations	$3,046,400
Loss on discontinued operations (net of tax)	480,000
Extraordinary gain (net of tax)	288,000

Calculate EPS for the year ended December 31, 1996. Present the information in the same format used in the corporation's income statement.

Exercise 13–12
Calculate EPS; comment on resulting amounts (L.O. 6)

Western Company had an average number of shares of common stock outstanding of 200,000 in 1996 and 215,000 in 1997. Net income for these two years was as follows:

1996	$2,208,000
1997	2,304,000

a. Calculate EPS for the years ended December 31, 1996, and 1997

b. What might the resulting figures tell a stockholder or a potential investor?

PROBLEMS

Problem 13–1
Prepare stockholders' equity section of balance sheet (L.O. 1)

The bookkeeper of Denzel Company has prepared the following incorrect statement of stockholders' equity for the year ended December 31, 1996:

Stockholders' equity:		
Paid-in capital:		
Preferred stock—6%, cumulative (8,000 shares)	$501,600	
Common stock—50,000 shares	1,428,000	
Total paid-in capital		$1,929,600
Retained earnings.		818,400
Total stockholders' equity		$2,748,000

The authorized stock consists of 12,000 shares of preferred stock with a $60 par value and 75,000 shares of common stock, $24 par value. The preferred stock was issued on two occasions: (1) 5,000 shares at par, and (2) 3,000 shares at $67.20 per share. The 50,000 shares of common stock were issued at $31.20 per share. Five thousand shares of treasury common stock were reacquired for $132,000. The bookkeeper deducted the cost of the treasury stock from the Common Stock account.

Required Prepare the correct stockholders' equity section of the balance sheet at December 31, 1996.

Problem 13–2
Prepare journal entries for cash dividend and small stock dividend (L.O. 2)

The only stockholders' equity items of Riley Company at June 30, 1996, are:

Stockholders' equity:		
Paid-in capital:		
Common stock—$400 par value, 10,000 shares authorized, 6,000 shares issued and outstanding	$2,400,000	
Paid-in capital in excess of par value	960,000	
Total paid-in capital		$3,360,000
Retained earnings		960,000
Total stockholders' equity		$4,320,000

On August 4, 1996, a 4% cash dividend was declared, payable on September 3. On November 16, a 10% stock dividend was declared. The shares were issued on December 1. The market value of the common stock was $720 per share on November 16 and $708 per share on December 1.

Required Prepare journal entries for these dividend transactions.

Problem 13–3
Prepare journal entries for retained earnings appropriation, asset acquisition, and stock dividend (L.O. 2)

Following are selected transactions of Piper Corporation:

1989

Dec. 31 The board of directors authorized the appropriation of $100,000 of retained earnings to provide for the future acquisition of a new plant site and the construction of a new building. (On the last day of the next six years, the same action was taken. You need not make entries for these six years.)

1994

Jan. 2 Purchased a new plant site for cash, $200,000.

Mar. 29 Entered into a contract for construction of a new building, payment to be made within 30 days following completion.

1996

Feb. 10 Following final inspection and approval of the new building, Dyer Construction Company was paid in full, $1,000,000.

Mar. 10 The board of directors authorized release of the retained earnings appropriated for the plant site and building.

Apr. 2 A 5% stock dividend on the 100,000 shares of $100 par value common stock outstanding was declared. The market price on this date was $110 per share.

Required Prepare journal entries for all of these transactions.

Problem 13–4
Present statement of retained earnings (L.O. 2)

Following are selected data of Cryer Corporation at December 31, 1996:

Net income for the year	$512,000
Dividends declared on preferred stock	72,000
Retained earnings appropriated during the year for future plant expansion	240,000
Dividends declared on common stock	64,000
Retained earnings, January 1, unappropriated	720,000
Directors ordered that the balance in the "Appropriation per loan agreement," related to a loan repaid on March 31, 1996, be returned to unappropriated retained earnings	480,000

Required Prepare a statement of retained earnings for the year ended December 31, 1996.

Problem 13–5
Prepare journal entries for stock dividend, treasury stock transactions, and retained earnings appropriation (L.O. 2, 3)

The stockholders' equity of Peter Company at January 1, 1996, is as follows:

Common stock—no-par value, stated value of $40; 100,000 shares authorized, 60,000 shares issued	$2,400,000
Paid-in capital in excess of stated value	400,000
Appropriation per loan agreement	150,400
Unappropriated retained earnings	848,000
Treasury stock (3,000 shares at cost)	(144,000)

During 1996, the following transactions occurred in the order listed:

1. Issued 10,000 shares of stock for $736,000.
2. Declared a 4% stock dividend when the market price was $96 per share.
3. Sold 1,000 shares of treasury stock for $86,400.
4. Issued stock certificates for the stock dividend declared in transaction 2.
5. Bought 2,000 shares of treasury stock for $134,400.
6. Increased the appropriation by $86,400 per loan agreement.

Required

Prepare journal entries as necessary for these transactions.

Problem 13–6
Prepare journal entries for treasury stock transactions and for cash dividend; present stockholders' equity section of balance sheet (L.O. 2, 3)

The stockholders' equity of Stackert Company on December 31, 1995, consisted of 1,000 authorized, issued, and outstanding shares of $72 cumulative preferred stock, stated value $240 per share, which were originally issued at $1,192 per share; 100,000 shares authorized, issued, and outstanding of no-par, $160 stated value common stock, which were originally issued at $160; and retained earnings of $1,120,000. Following are selected transactions and other data relating to 1996. No previous treasury stock transactions had occurred.

1. The company reacquired 2,000 shares of its common stock at $336.
2. One thousand of the treasury shares were reissued at $288.
3. Stockholders donated 1,000 shares of common stock to the company. These shares were immediately reissued at $256 to provide working capital.
4. The first quarter's dividend of $18 per share was declared and paid on the preferred stock. No other dividends were declared or paid during 1996.

The company suffered a net loss of $224,000 for the year 1996.

Required

a. Prepare journal entries for the preceding numbered transactions.
b. Prepare the stockholders' equity section of the December 31, 1996, balance sheet.

Problem 13–7
Prepare journal entries to close retained earnings appropriation and for treasury stock transactions and cash dividends; present statement of retained earnings and stockholders' equity section of balance sheet (L.O. 2, 3)

The following stockholders' equity section is from Jeblon Company's October 31, 1995, balance sheet:

Stockholders' equity:		
Paid-in capital:		
Preferred stock—$120 par value, 6%; 1,000 shares authorized; 350 shares issued and outstanding	$ 42,000	
Common stock—$12 par value; 100,000 shares authorized; 40,000 shares issued and outstanding	480,000	
Paid-in capital from donation of plant site	30,000	
Total paid-in capital		$552,000
Retained earnings:		
Appropriated:		
Appropriation for contingencies	$ 24,000	
Unappropriated	66,600	
Total retained earnings		90,600
Total stockholders' equity		$642,600

During the ensuing fiscal year, Jeblon Company entered into the following transactions:

1. The appropriation of $24,000 of retained earnings had been authorized in October 1995 because of the likelihood of an unfavorable court decision in a pending lawsuit. The suit was brought by a customer seeking damages for the company's alleged breach of a contract to supply the customer with certain products at stated prices in 1994. The suit was concluded on March 6, 1996, with a court order directing the company to pay $21,000 in damages. These damages were not deductible in determining the income tax liability. The board ordered the damages paid and the appropriation closed. The loss does not qualify as an extraordinary item.
2. The company acquired 1,000 shares of its own common stock at $18 in May 1996. On June 30, it reissued 500 of these shares at $14.40.
3. Dividends declared and paid during the year were 6% on preferred stock and 36 cents per share on common stock. Both dividends were declared on September 1 and paid on September 30, 1996.

For the fiscal year, the company had net income after income taxes of $22,800, excluding the loss of the lawsuit.

Required

a. Prepare journal entries for the preceding numbered transactions.

b. Prepare a statement of retained earnings for the year ended October 31, 1996.

c. Prepare the stockholders' equity section of the October 31, 1996, balance sheet.

Problem 13–8
Present income statement and statement of retained earnings (L.O. 2, 4, 5)

Selected data for Racker Company for 1996 are given below:

Common stock—$20 par value	$2,000,000
Sales, net	1,740,000
Selling and administrative expenses	320,000
Cash dividends declared and paid	120,000
Cost of goods sold	800,000
Depreciation expense	120,000
Interest revenue	20,000
Loss on write-down of obsolete inventory	40,000
Retained earnings (as of 12/31/95)	2,000,000
Operating loss on Candy Division up to point of sale in 1996	40,000
Loss on disposal of Candy Division	200,000
Earthquake loss	96,000
Cumulative negative effect on prior years' income of changing from straight-line to an accelerated method of computing depreciation	64,000

Assume the applicable federal income tax rate is 40%. All of the items of expense, revenue, and loss are included in the computation of taxable income. The earthquake loss resulted from the first earthquake experienced at the company's location. In addition, the company discovered that in 1995 it had erroneously charged to expense the $160,000 cost of a tract of land purchased that year and had made the same error on its tax return for 1995.

Required

a. Prepare an income statement for the year ended December 31, 1996.

b. Prepare a statement of retained earnings for the year ended December 31, 1996.

Alternate Problems

Problem 13–1A
Present stockholders' equity section of balance sheet (L.O. 1)

The trial balance of Lyle Corporation as of December 31, 1996, contains the following selected balances:

Notes Payable (17%, due May 1, 1998)	$2,000,000
Allowance for Uncollectible Accounts	30,000
Common Stock (without par value, $10 stated value; 300,000 shares authorized, issued, and outstanding)	3,000,000
Retained Earnings, Unappropriated	250,000
Dividends Payable (in cash, declared December 15 on preferred stock)	7,000
Appropriation for Pending Litigation	300,000
Preferred Stock (6%, $100 par value; 3,000 shares authorized, issued, and outstanding)	300,000
Paid-In Capital—Donations	200,000
Paid-In Capital in Excess of Par Value—Preferred	5,000

Required Present the stockholders' equity section of the balance sheet as of December 31, 1996.

Problem 13–2A
Prepare journal entries for cash dividend and small stock dividend (L.O. 2)

The stockholders' equity section of Giant Company's December 31, 1995, balance sheet follows:

Stockholders' equity:		
Paid-in-capital:		
Common stock—$120 par value; authorized, 2,000 shares; issued and outstanding, 1,000 shares	$120,000	
Paid-in capital in excess of par value	6,000	
Total paid-in capital		$126,000
Retained earnings		48,000
Total stockholders' equity		$174,000

On July 15, 1996, the board of directors declared a cash dividend of $12 per share, which was paid on August 1, 1996. On December 1, 1996, the board declared a stock dividend of 10%, and the shares were issued on December 15, 1996. Market value of the stock was $144 on December 1 and $168 on December 15.

Required

Prepare journal entries for these dividend transactions.

Problem 13–3A
Prepare journal entries for appropriations of retained earnings (L.O. 2)

The ledger of Eagle Company includes the following account balances on September 30, 1996:

Appropriation for Contingencies	$105,000
Appropriation for Plant Expansion	196,000
Retained Earnings, Unappropriated	350,000

During October 1996, the company took action to:

1. Increase the appropriation for contingencies by $30,000.
2. Decrease the appropriation for plant expansion by $80,000.
3. Establish an appropriation per loan agreement, with an annual increase of $24,000.
4. Declare a cash dividend of $70,000.

Required

Prepare the journal entries to record these transactions of Eagle Company.

Problem 13–4A
Prepare journal entries for retained earnings appropriation and small stock dividend (L.O. 2)

Following are selected transactions of Alice Corporation:

1991
Dec. 31 By action of the board of directors, $450,000 of retained earnings was appropriated to provide for future expansion of the company's main building. (On the last day of each of the next four years, the same action was taken. You need not make entries for these years.)

1996
Jan. 3 Obtained, at a cost of $4,500, a building permit to construct a new wing on the main plant building.
July 30 Paid $1,800,000 to Axel Construction Company for completion of the new wing.
Aug. 4 The board of directors authorized the release of the sum appropriated for expansion of the plant building.
4 The board of directors declared a 10% common stock dividend on the 25,000 shares of $500 par value common stock outstanding. The market price on this date was $660 per share.

Required

Prepare journal entries to record all of these transactions.

Problem 13–5A
Present statement of retained earnings (L.O. 2)

The following information relates to George Corporation for the year 1996:

Net income for the year	$ 840,000
Dividends declared on common stock	117,600
Dividends declared on preferred stock	67,200
Retained earnings, January 1, unappropriated	2,520,000
Appropriation for retirement of bonds	336,000
Balance in "Appropriation for possible loss of a lawsuit," no longer needed on December 31 because of a favorable court decision, is (by directors' order) returned to unappropriated retained earnings	420,000

Required

Prepare a statement of retained earnings for the year ended December 31, 1996.

Problem 13–6A
Prepare journal entries for treasury stock transactions and for cash dividends; present stockholders' equity section (L.O. 2, 3)

The stockholders' equity of Samuel Company as of December 31, 1995, consisted of 20,000 shares of authorized, issued, and outstanding $50 par value common stock, paid-in capital in excess of par of $240,000, and retained earnings of $400,000. Following are selected transactions for 1996:

May 1 Acquired 3,000 shares of its own common stock at $100 per share.
June 1 Reissued 500 shares at $120.
30 Reissued 700 shares at $90.
Oct. 1 Declared a cash dividend of $5 per share.
31 Paid the cash dividend declared on October 1.

Net income for the year was $80,000. No other transactions affecting retained earnings occurred during the year.

Required

a. Prepare general journal entries for these transactions.

b. Prepare the stockholders' equity section of the December 31, 1996, balance sheet.

Problem 13–7A
Prepare journal entries for stock transactions, cash dividend, small stock dividend, and retained earnings appropriation; prepare statement of retained earnings and stockholders' equity section of balance sheet (L.O. 2, 3)

The stockholders' equity section of Alonzo Company's December 31, 1995, balance sheet follows:

Stockholders' equity:		
Paid-in capital:		
Preferred stock—$120 par value, 5%; authorized, 5,000 shares; issued and outstanding, 2,500 shares		$ 300,000
Common stock—without par or stated value; authorized, 50,000 shares; issued, 25,000 shares of which 500 are held in treasury		450,000
Paid-in capital in excess of par—preferred		6,000
Total paid-in capital		$ 756,000
Retained earnings:		
Appropriated:		
For plant expansion	$ 30,000	
Unappropriated (restricted as to dividends to the extent of $12,000, the cost of the treasury stock held)	252,000	
Total retained earnings		282,000
Total paid-in capital and retained earnings		$1,038,000
Less: Treasury stock, common, at cost (500 shares)		12,000
Total stockholders' equity		$1,026,000

Following are selected transactions that occurred in 1996:

Jan. 13 Cash was received for 550 shares of previously unissued common stock at $26.40.
Feb. 4 A plot of land was accepted as payment in full for 500 shares of common stock, and the stock was issued. Closing market price of the common stock on this date was $24 per share.
Mar. 24 All of the treasury stock was reissued at $28.80 per share.
June 23 The regular semiannual dividend on the preferred stock was declared.
30 The preferred dividend was paid.
July 3 A 10% stock dividend was declared on the common stock. Market price on this date was $33.60.
18 The stock dividend shares were issued.
Oct. 4 The company reacquired 105 shares of its common stock at $28.80.
Dec. 18 The regular semiannual dividend on the preferred stock and a $0.48 per share dividend on the common stock were declared.
31 Both dividends were paid.
31 An additional appropriation of retained earnings of $6,000 for plant expansion was authorized.

Required

a. Prepare journal entries to record the 1996 transactions.

b. Prepare a statement of retained earnings for the year 1996, assuming net income for the year was $51,600.

c. Prepare the stockholders' equity section of the December 31, 1996, balance sheet.

Problem 13–8A
Present income statement and statement of retained earnings (L.O. 2, 4, 5)

Selected data of Dayton Company for the year ended December 31, 1996, are:

Sales, net	$1,000,000
Interest expense	90,000
Cash dividends on common stock	150,000
Selling and administrative expenses	245,000
Cash dividends on preferred stock	70,000
Rent revenue	400,000
Cost of goods sold	650,000
Flood loss (has never occurred before)	200,000
Interest revenue	90,000
Other revenue	150,000
Depreciation and maintenance on rental equipment	270,000
Stock dividend on common stock	300,000
Operating income on Plastics Division up to point of sale in 1996	50,000

Gain on disposal of Plastics Division	$ 25,000
Litigation loss (has never occurred before)	400,000
Cumulative positive effect on prior years' income of changing to a different depreciation method	80,000

Assume the applicable federal income tax rate is 40%. All of the preceding items of expense, revenue, and loss are included in the computation of taxable income. The litigation loss resulted from a court award of damages for patent infringement on a product that the company produced and sold in 1992 and 1993, but was discontinued in 1993. In addition, the company discovered that in 1995 it had erroneously charged to expense the $250,000 cost of a tract of land purchased that year and had made the same error on its tax return for 1995. Retained earnings as of January 1, 1996, were $5,600,000. Assume there were 10,000 shares of common stock and 5,000 shares of preferred stock outstanding for the entire year.

Required

Prepare an income statement and a statement of retained earnings for 1996.

BEYOND THE NUMBERS—CRITICAL THINKING

Business Decision Case 13–1
Determine amount of dividends received and effect on stock prices
(L.O. 2)

The stockholders' equity section of the Brown Corporation's balance sheet for June 30, 1996, follows:

Stockholders' equity:		
Paid-in capital:		
Common stock—$40 par value; authorized 200,000 shares; issued and outstanding 80,000 shares	$3,200,000	
Paid-in capital in excess of par value	1,920,000	
Total paid-in capital		$5,120,000
Retained earnings		3,040,000
Total stockholders' equity		$8,160,000

On July 1, 1996, the corporation's directors declared a 10% stock dividend distributable on August 2 to stockholders of record on July 16. On November 1, 1996, the directors voted a $4.80 per share annual cash dividend payable on December 2 to stockholders of record on November 16. For four years prior to 1996, the corporation had paid an annual cash dividend of $5.04.

As of July 1, 1996, Bob Jones owned 8,000 shares of Brown Corporation's common stock, which he had purchased four years earlier. The market value of his stock was $96 per share on July 1, 1996, and $87.27 per share on July 16, 1996.

Required

a. What amount of cash dividends will Jones receive in 1996? How does this amount differ from the amount of cash dividends Jones received in the previous four years?

b. Jones has asked you, his CPA, to explain why the price of the stock dropped from $96 to $87.27 on July 16, 1996. Write a memo to Jones explaining your answer.

c. Do you think Jones is better off as a result of the stock dividend and the $4.80 cash dividend than he would have been if he had just received the $5.04 cash dividend? Write a memo to Jones explaining your answer.

Business Decision Case 13–2
Analyze journal entries for impropriety and make subsequent corrections
(L.O. 2, 3)

The following journal entries are for Gypsy Corporation:

1.	Retained Earnings	12,000	
	Reserve for Uncollectible Accounts		12,000
	To record the adjusting entry for uncollectible accounts.		
2.	Retained Earnings	48,000	
	Reserve for Depreciation		48,000
	To record depreciation expense.		
3.	Retained Earnings	120,000	
	Appropriation for Plant Expansion		120,000
	To record retained earnings appropriation.		
4.	Retained Earnings	8,000	
	Stock Dividend Distributable—Common		8,000
	To record 10% stock dividend declaration (100 shares to be distributed—$80 par value, $120 market value).		

		Debit	Credit
5.	Stock Dividend Distributable—Common	8,000	
	Common Stock		8,000
	To record distribution of stock dividend.		
6.	Treasury Stock	32,000	
	Cash		32,000
	To record acquisition of 200 shares of $80 par value common stock at $160 per share.		
7.	Cash	17,600	
	Treasury Stock		17,600
	To record sale of 100 treasury shares at $176 per share.		
8.	Cash	6,800	
	Treasury Stock		6,800
	To record sale of 50 treasury shares at $136 per share.		
9.	Common Stock	16,000	
	Dividends Payable		16,000
	To record declaration of cash dividend.		
10.	Dividends Payable	16,000	
	Cash		16,000
	To record payment of cash dividend.		

Required The management of Gypsy Corporation has asked you, a CPA, to analyze these journal entries and decide whether each is correct. The explanations are all correct. Wherever a journal entry is incorrect, prepare the journal entry that should have been made.

Annual Report Analysis 13–3
Determine the number of shares of common stock issued and the cost of treasury stock. Compute EPS. (L.O. 3, 7)

Refer to the financial statements of The Coca-Cola Company in the annual report booklet. Note 11 discusses the treasury stock transactions during the 1993 fiscal period.

Required

a. Based on the information in the balance sheet and the note, determine the number of common shares issued and outstanding; and the average cost of treasury stock shares on hand at the end of 1993 and 1992, as shown on the balance sheets.

b. In writing, discuss what reasons Coca-Cola might have to acquire treasury stock.

c. Find Coca-Cola's EPS listed in its annual report. If the common stock's market price at December 31, 1993, was $44.63, what was the price-earnings ratio?

Ethics Case—Writing Experience 13–4
Answer questions based on the ethics case

Based on the ethics case on page 482, answer the following questions concerning Ace Chemical Company in writing:

a. Is this transaction fair to the creditors?

b. Why wouldn't the officers merely declare a $4 million cash dividend? Is the proposed treasury stock transaction fair to the other stockholders?

c. If you were one of the officers, would you feel comfortable in going ahead with this proposed treasury stock transaction?

Group Project 13–5
Library project—Compare features of accounting software packages

In teams of two to three students, go to the library to find articles evaluating accounting software packages. Use a periodicals index such as the *Accounting and Tax Index* or the *Business Periodicals Index* to locate these articles. Compare the cost and features of three accounting software packages. As a team, prepare a memorandum to the manager of a small retail business. Compare and contrast the three accounting software packages so the manager might decide which package to purchase. In the memorandum, cite the sources used in gathering the data and properly reference any direct quotes or paraphrasing. The heading of the memorandum should contain the date, to whom it is written, from whom, and the subject matter.

Answers To Self-Test

True-False

1. **False.** The paid-in capital of a corporation only includes capital contributed by stockholders or others. Thus, it does not include retained earnings.
2. **False.** The purchase of treasury stock reduces total stockholders' equity.
3. **False.** Dividends are distributions of earnings in the past and are not expenses.
4. **True.** A stock dividend permanently capitalizes a portion of retained earnings by decreasing retained earnings and increasing paid-in capital by an equal amount.
5. **False.** The purpose of a retained earnings appropriation is to disclose that a portion of retained earnings is not available for cash dividends. Thus, such an appropriation does not reduce total stockholders' equity.
6. **False.** Such damage occurs too frequently to be considered nonrecurring.

Multiple-Choice

1. **d.** Appropriation per Loan Agreement is part of retained earnings.
2. **c.** When treasury stock is reacquired, the stock is recorded at cost in a debit-balance stockholders' equity account, Treasury Stock.
3. **a.** The excess of the reissue price over the cost of treasury stock is recorded in the Paid-In Capital—Treasury Stock Transactions account.
4. **a.** Treasury stock is customarily shown as a deduction from total stockholders' equity.
5. **b.** The date of record determines who is to receive the dividends.
6. **c.** The total amount of dividends is computed as follows:

Total outstanding shares at declaration:	
(12,000 − 2,000) shares	10,000
Dividend per share	× $2
Total dividend amount	$20,000

7. **b.** Prior period adjustments are shown as adjustments to the opening balance of retained earnings on the statement of retained earnings.

14

Stock Investments

Cost, Equity, Consolidations; International Accounting

Learning Objectives

After studying this chapter, you should be able to:

1. Report stock investments and distinguish between the cost and equity methods of accounting for stock investments.
2. Prepare journal entries to account for short-term stock investments and for long-term stock investments of less than 20%.
3. Prepare journal entries to account for long-term stock investments of 20% to 50%.
4. Describe the nature of parent and subsidiary corporations.

(*continued*)

Often a large company attempts to take over a smaller company by acquiring a controlling interest (more than 50% of the outstanding shares) in that target company. Some of these takeover attempts are friendly (not resisted by the target company), and some are unfriendly (resisted by the target company). If the attempt is successful, the two companies become one business entity for accounting purposes, and consolidated financial statements are prepared. The company that takes over another company is the *parent company;* the company acquired is the *subsidiary company*. This chapter discusses accounting for parent and subsidiary companies.

When a corporation purchases the stock of another corporation, the method of accounting for the stock investment depends on the corporation's motivation for making the investment and the relative size of the investment. A corporation's motivation for purchasing the stock of another company may be as: (1) a short-term investment of excess cash; (2) a long-term investment in a substantial percentage of another company's stock to ensure a supply of a required raw material (for example, when large oil companies invest heavily in, or purchase outright, wildcat oil drilling companies); or (3) a long-term investment for expansion (when a company purchases another profitable company rather than starting a new business operation). On the balance sheet, the first type of investment is a current asset, and the last two types are long-term (noncurrent) investments. As explained in the chapter, the purchaser's level of ownership of the investee company determines whether the investment is accounted for by the cost method or the equity method.

The chapter appendix discusses international accounting. As businesses expand their operations across international borders, accountants must become aware of the accounting challenges this expansion presents.

Cost and Equity Methods

Investors in common stock can use two methods to account for their investments—the cost method or the equity method. Under both methods, they initially record the investment at cost (price paid at acquisition). Under the **cost method,** the investor company does not adjust the investment account balance subsequently for its share of the investee's reported income, losses, and dividends. Instead, the investor company receives dividends and credits them to a Dividends Revenue account. Under the **equity method,** the investor company adjusts the investment account for its share of the investee's reported income, losses, and dividends.

The Accounting Principles Board has identified the circumstances under which each method must be used. This chapter illustrates each of those circumstances. The general rules for determining the appropriate method of accounting follow:

Types of Common Stock Investment	Method of Accounting Required by Accounting Principles Board in Most Cases
All short-term investments	Cost
Long-term investments of:	
Less than 20%:	
If no significant influence	Cost
If significant influence	Equity
20%–50%	Equity
More than 50%	Cost or equity

(*concluded*)

5. Prepare consolidated financial statements through the use of a consolidated statement work sheet.
6. Identify the differences between purchase accounting and pooling of interests accounting.
7. Describe the uses and limitations of consolidated financial statements.
8. Analyze and use the financial results—dividend yield on common stock and payout ratio on common stock.
9. Discuss the differences in international accounting among nations (Appendix).

Accounting for Short-Term Stock Investments and for Long-Term Stock Investments of Less Than 20%

Objective 1
Report stock investments and distinguish between the cost and equity methods of accounting for stock investments.

Accountants use the cost method to account for all short-term stock investments. When a company owns less than 50% of the outstanding stock of another company as a long-term investment, the percentage of ownership determines whether to use the cost or equity method. A purchasing company that owns less than 20% of the outstanding stock of the investee company, and does not exercise significant influence over it, uses the cost method. A purchasing company that owns from 20% to 50% of the outstanding stock of the investee company or owns less than 20%, but still exercises significant influence over it, uses the equity method. Thus, firms use the cost method for all short-term stock investments and almost all long-term stock investments of less than 20%. For investments of more than 50%, they use either the cost or equity method because the application of consolidation procedures yields the same result.

Cost Method for Short-Term Investments and for Long-Term Investments of Less Than 20%

Objective 2
Prepare journal entries to account for short-term stock investments and for long-term stock investments of less than 20%.

When a company purchases stock (equity securities) as an investment, accountants must classify the stock according to management's intent. If management bought the security for the principal purpose of selling it in the near term, the security would be a **trading security.** If the stock will be held for a longer term, it is called an **available-for-sale security.** Trading securities are always current assets. Available-for-sale securities may be either current assets or noncurrent assets, depending on how long management intends to hold them. Each classification is accounted for differently. This topic will be discussed later in this chapter.

Securities can be transferred between classifications; however, there are specific rules that must be met for these transfers to be allowed. These rules will be addressed in intermediate accounting. Under the cost method, investors record stock investments at cost, which is usually the cash paid for the stock. They purchase most stocks from other investors (not the issuing company) through brokers who execute trades in an organized market, such as the New York Stock

Exchange. Thus, cost usually consists of the price paid for the shares, plus a broker's commission.

For example, assume that Brewer Corporation purchased as a near-term investment 1,000 shares of Cowen Company's $10 par value common stock at 14⅛, plus a $175 broker's commission. Brokers quote stock prices in dollars and fractions of one dollar; thus, 14⅛ means $14.125 per share. Brewer's entry to record its investment is:

Trading Securities [(1,000 shares × $14.125) + $175 commission]	14,300	
Cash		14,300
Purchased 1,000 shares of Cowen common stock as a near-term investment at 14⅛, plus commission.		

Accounting for Cash Dividends Received Investments in stock provide dividends revenue. As a general rule, investors debit cash dividends to Cash and credit Dividends Revenue. The only exception to this general rule is when a dividend declared in one accounting period is payable in the next. This exception allows a company to record the revenue in the proper accounting period. Assume that Cowen declared a $1 per share cash dividend on December 1, 1997, to stockholders of record as of December 20, payable on January 15, 1998. Brewer should make the following entry in 1997:

1997				
Dec.	1	Dividends Receivable	1,000	
		Dividends Revenue		1,000
		To record $1 per share cash dividend on Cowen common stock, payable January 15, 1998.		

When collecting the dividend on January 15, Brewer debits Cash and credits Dividends Receivable:

1998				
Jan.	15	Cash	1,000	
		Dividends Receivable		1,000
		To record the receipt of a cash dividend on Cowen common stock.		

Stock Dividends and Stock Splits As discussed in Chapter 13, a company might declare a stock dividend rather than a cash dividend. An investor does not recognize revenue on receipt of the additional shares from a stock dividend. The investor merely records the number of additional shares received and reduces the cost per share for each share held. For example, if Cowen distributed a 10% stock dividend in February 1998, Brewer, which held 1,000 shares at a cost of $14,300 (or $14.30 per share), would receive another 100 shares and would then hold 1,100 shares at a cost per share of $13 (computed as $14,300/1,100 shares). Similarly, when a corporation declares a stock split, the investor would note the shares received and the reduction in the cost per share.

Subsequent Valuation of Stock Investments under the Fair Market Value Method

FASB Statement No. 115 (1993) governs the subsequent valuation of **marketable equity securities** accounted for under the fair market value method.[1] Marketable refers to the fact that the stocks are readily saleable; equity securities are common and preferred stocks. The *Statement* also addresses the treatment of debt securities. The treatment of debt securities will be addressed in intermediate accounting classes.

[1] FASB, *Statement of Financial Accounting Standards No. 115*, "Accounting for Certain Marketable Securities" (Stamford, Conn., 1993). Copyright © by the Financial Accounting Standards Board, Stamford, Connecticut 06856, U.S.A. Quoted (or excerpted) with permission. Copies of the complete document are available from the FASB.

ILLUSTRATION 14.1
Stock Portfolio of Hanson Company

Company	No. of Shares	Cost per Share	Market Price per Share, 12/31/97	Total Cost	Total Market, 12/31/97	Increase/ (Decrease) in Market Value
A.	200	$35	$40	$ 7,000	$ 8,000	$ 1,000
B.	400	10	15	4,000	6,000	2,000
C.	100	90	50	9,000	5,000	(4,000)
				$20,000	$19,000	$(1,000)

Unrealized loss → expense

The FASB *Statement* requires that at year-end, companies adjust the carrying value of each of their two portfolios (trading securities and available-for-sale securities) to their fair market value. Fair market value is considered to be the market price of the securities or what a buyer or seller would pay to exchange the securities. An unrealized holding gain or loss will usually result in each portfolio.

TRADING SECURITIES To illustrate the application of the fair market value to trading securities, assume that Hanson Company has the securities shown in Illustration 14.1 in its trading securities portfolio. Applying the fair market value method reveals that the total fair market value of the trading securities portfolio is $1,000 less than its cost. The journal entry required at the end of 1997 is:

1997				
Dec.	31	Unrealized Loss on Trading Securities.	1,000	
		Trading Securities		1,000
		To record unrealized loss from market decline of trading securities.		

Note that the debit is to the Unrealized Loss on Trading Securities account. This loss is *unrealized* because the securities have not been sold. However, **the loss is reported in the income statement as a deduction in arriving at net income.** The credit in the preceding entry is to the Trading Securities account so as to adjust its balance to its fair market value. (An unrealized holding gain would be an addition to net income.)

If Hanson sold investment C on Janaury 1, 1998, the company would receive $5,000 (assuming no change in market values from the previous day). The loss on the sale results from market changes in 1997 rather than in 1998; the fair market value procedure placed that loss in the proper year. The entry for the sale is:

Cash	5,000	
Trading Security—Company C Stock		5,000

No adjustment needs be made to the unrealized loss account previously debited because the unrealized loss recorded in 1997 has flowed through the income statement and been closed to retained earnings through the closing process.

AVAILABLE-FOR-SALE SECURITIES Assume a marketable equity security that management does not intend to sell in the near term has a cost of $32,000 and a current market value on December 31, 1997, of $31,000. The treatment of the loss depends on whether it results from a temporary decline in market value of the stock or a permanent decline in the value. Assume first that the loss is related to a "temporary" decline in the market value of the stock. The required entry is:

1997				
Dec.	31	Unrealized Loss on Available-for-Sale Securities	1,000	
		Available-for-Sale Securities		1,000
		To record unrealized losses from market decline of available-for-sale securities.		

These accounts would appear on the balance sheet as follows:

HANSON COMPANY
Partial Balance Sheet
December 31, 1997

Investments (or Current Assets):*	
Available-for-sale securities	$31,000
Stockholders' equity:	
Capital stock	$xxx,xxx
Additional paid-in capital	x,xxx
Total paid-in capital	$xxx,xxx
Less: Unrealized loss on available-for-sale securities	1,000
	$xxx,xxx
Retained earnings	xx,xxx
Total stockholders' equity	$xxx,xxx

* Depending on the length of time management intends to hold the securities.

Note that the unrealized loss for available-for-sale securities appears in the balance sheet as a separate negative component of stockholders' equity rather than in the income statement (as it does for trading securities). An unrealized gain would be shown as a separate positive component of stockholders' equity. An unrealized loss or gain on available-for-sale securities is **not** included in the determination of net income because it is not expected to be realized in the near future. These securities are being held on a long-term basis and will probably not be sold soon.

The sale of an available-for-sale security results in a realized gain or loss and is reported on the income statement for the period. Any unrealized gain or loss on the balance sheet must be recognized at that time. Assume the stock discussed above is sold on January 1, 1998, for $31,000 (assuming no change in market value from the previous day) after the company had held the stock for three years. The entries to record this sale are:

Date		Account	Debit	Credit
1998 Jan.	1	Realized Loss on Available-for-Sale-Securities	1,000	
		Unrealized Loss on Available-for-Sale Securities		1,000
		Cash	31,000	
		Available-for-Sale Securities		31,000

The account debited in the first entry shows that the unrealized loss has been realized with the sale of the security; the amount is reported in the income statement. The second entry writes off the security and records the cash received and is similar to the entry for the sale of trading securities.

A loss on an individual security that is "permanent" is recorded as a realized loss and deducted in determining net income. The entry to record a permanent loss of $1,400 reads:

Account	Debit	Credit
Realized Loss on Available-for-Sale Securities	1,400	
Available-for-Sale Securities		1,400
To record loss in value of available-for-sale securities.		

No part of the $1,400 loss is subject to reversal if the market price of the stock recovers. The stock's reduced value is now its "cost." When this stock is later sold, the sale will be treated in the same manner as trading securities. The loss or gain has already been recognized on the income statement. Therefore, the entry would simply record the cash received and write off the security sold for its fair market value. If the market value of the security has fluctuated since the last time the account had been adjusted (end of the year), then an additional gain or loss may have to be recorded to account for this fluctuation.

AN ACCOUNTING PERSPECTIVE

BUSINESS INSIGHT The shift to FAS 115 is a recent development in accounting policies. SunTrust Banks, Inc., in its 1993 annual report included the following footnote explaining their adoption of FAS 115. Note the impact of this change on the reporting of SunTrust's investment in the common stock of The Coca-Cola Company. Reporting the investment at its fair market value yielded a gain of about $1 billion.

Investment Securities: The Company adopted Financial Accounting Standards Board Statement No. 115 (FAS 115) "Accounting for Certain Investments in Debt and Equity Securities" as of December 31, 1993. Under the standard, securities carried in the Trading Account continue to be so classified and are carried at market value with unrealized gains and losses charged to income. Investment securities are classified as either Available-For-Sale or Held-To-Maturity. Available-For-Sale securities are carried at market value with unrealized gains and losses, net of any tax effect, added or deducted directly from shareholders' equity. Held-To-Maturity [debt] securities are carried at amortized cost. The standard further requires that any investments in equity securities, including the Company's investment in common stock of The Coca-Cola Company, be classified as Available-For-Sale. The Company has also classified its investment in all other non-trading account securities as Available-For-Sale. Realized and unrealized gains and losses are determined using the specific identification method.

Investment securities were as follows at December 31:

	1993			
(In thousands)	**Amortized Cost**	**Carrying Value**	**Unrealized Gains**	**Unrealized Losses**
U.S. Treasury and other U.S. government agencies and corporations	$3,774,360	$ 3,813,946	$ 40,615	$ 1,029
States and political subdivisions	1,080,277	1,157,602	77,974	649
Mortgage-backed securities	4,319,345	4,343,360	36,780	12,765
Common stock of The Coca-Cola Company	110	1,076,946	1,076,836	–
Other securities	234,517	252,099	18,389	807
Total investment securities	$9,408,609	$10,643,953	$1,250,594	$15,250

THE EQUITY METHOD FOR LONG-TERM INVESTMENTS OF BETWEEN 20% AND 50%

Objective 3
Prepare journal entries to account for long-term stock investments of 20% to 50%.

When a company (the **investor**) purchases between 20% and 50% of the outstanding stock of another company (the **investee**) as a long-term investment, the purchasing company is said to have significant influence over the investee company. In certain cases, a company may have significant influence even when its investment is less than 20%. In either situation, the investor must account for the investment under the equity method.

When using the **equity method** in accounting for stock investments, the investor company must recognize its share of the investee company's income, regardless of whether or not it receives dividends. The logic behind this treatment is that the investor company may exercise influence over the declaration of dividends and thereby manipulate its own income by influencing the investee's decision to declare (or not declare) dividends.

Thus, when the investee reports income or losses, the investor company must recognize its share of the investee's income or losses. For example, assume that Tone Company (the investor) owns 30% of Dutch Company (the investee) and Dutch reports $50,000 net income in the current year. Under the equity method, Tone makes the following entry as of the end of 1997:

Investment in Dutch Company	15,000	
Income from Dutch Company ($50,000 × 0.30)		15,000
To recognize 30% of Dutch Company's net income.		

The $15,000 income from Dutch would be reported on Tone's 1997 income statement. The investment account is also increased by $15,000.

If the investee incurs a loss, the investor company debits a loss account and credits the investment account for the investor's share of the loss. For example, assume Dutch incurs a loss of $10,000 in 1998. Since it still owns 30% of Dutch, Tone records its share of the loss as follows:

Loss from Dutch Company ($10,000 × 0.30)	3,000	
Investment in Dutch Company		3,000
To record 30% of Dutch Company's loss.		

Tone would report the $3,000 loss on its 1988 income statement. The $3,000 credit reduces Tone's equity in the investee. Furthermore, because dividends are a distribution of income to the owners of the corporation, if Dutch declares and pays $20,000 in dividends, this entry would also be required for Tone:

Cash	6,000	
Investment in Dutch Company ($20,000 × 0.30)		6,000
To record receipt of 30% of dividends paid by Dutch Company.		

Under the equity method just illustrated, the Investment in Dutch Company account always reflects Tone's 30% interest in the net assets of Dutch.

Reporting for Stock Investments of More Than 50%

In recent years, many companies have expanded by purchasing a major portion, or all, of another company's outstanding voting stock. The purpose of such acquisitions ranges from ensuring a source of raw materials (such as oil), to desiring to enter into a new industry, or seeking income on the investment. Both corporations remain separate legal entities, regardless of the investment purpose. In this section, you learn how to account for business combinations.

Parent and Subsidiary Corporations

Objective 4
Describe the nature of parent and subsidiary corporations.

As stated in the introduction to this chapter, a corporation that owns more than 50% of the outstanding voting common stock of another corporation is the **parent company**. The corporation acquired and controlled by the parent company is the **subsidiary company**.

A parent company and its subsidiaries maintain their own accounting records and prepare their own financial statements. However, since a central management controls the parent and its subsidiaries and they are related to each other, the parent company usually must prepare one set of financial statements. These statements, called **consolidated statements,** consolidate the parent's financial statement amounts with its subsidiaries' and show the parent and its subsidiaries as a single enterprise.

According to *FASB Statement No. 94,* consolidated statements must be prepared (1) when one company owns more than 50% of the outstanding voting common stock of another company, and (2) unless control is likely to be temporary or if it does not rest with the majority owner (e.g., the company is in legal reorganization or bankruptcy).[3] Thus, almost all subsidiaries must be included in the consolidated financial statements under *FASB Statement No. 94*. Previously, the consolidated statements did not include subsidiaries in markedly dissimilar businesses than those of the parents.

Eliminations

Financial transactions involving a parent and one of its subsidiaries or between two of its subsidiaries are **intercompany transactions.** In preparing consolidated financial statements, parent companies eliminate the effects of intercompany transactions by making **elimination entries.** Elimination entries allow the presentation of all account balances as if the parent and its subsidiaries were a single economic enterprise. Elimination entries appear only on a consolidated statement

[3] FASB, *Statement of Financial Accounting Standards No. 94,* "Consolidation of All Majority-Owned Subsidiaries" (Stamford, Conn., 1987), p. 5. Copyright © by the Financial Accounting Standards Board, High Ridge Park, Stamford, Connecticut 06905, U.S.A.

AN ACCOUNTING PERSPECTIVE

BUSINESS INSIGHT The Clorox Company's retail products include laundry additives, home cleaning products, insecticides, charcoal, and salad dressing. The company's 1993 annual report includes the consolidated financial statements of the company and its majority-owned subsidiaries. Minority investments in foreign entities are accounted for under the equity method.

work sheet, not in the accounting records of the parent or subsidiaries. After elimination entries are prepared, the parent totals the amounts remaining for each account of the work sheet and prepares the consolidated financial statements.

To illustrate the need for elimination entries, assume Y Company organized the Z Company, receiving all of Z Company's $100,000 par value common stock for $100,000 cash. The parent records the following entry on its books:

Investment in Z Company	100,000	
Cash		100,000
To record an investment in Z Company. Purchased 100% of Z Company stock.		

Z Company, the subsidiary, records the following entry on its books:

Cash	100,000	
Common Stock		100,000
To record issuance of all of the common stock to Y Company.		

An elimination entry can offset the parent company's subsidiary investment account against the stockholders' equity accounts of the subsidiary. On the consolidated statements work sheet, the required elimination is:

Common Stock (Z Company)	100,000	
Investment in Z Company		100,000

This elimination is required because the parent company's investment in the stock of the subsidiary actually represents an equity interest in the net assets of the subsidiary. Unless the investment is eliminated, the same resources appear twice on the consolidated balance sheet—first as the investment account of the parent and second as the assets of the subsidiary. By eliminating Z Company's common stock, the parent avoids double counting stockholders' equity. Viewing the two companies as if they were one, the Z Company common stock is really not outstanding; it is held within the consolidated group.

Consolidated financial statements present financial data as though the companies were a single entity. Since no entity can owe an amount to itself or be due an amount from itself, Z Company must eliminate intercompany receivables and payables (amounts owed to and due from companies within the consolidated group) during the preparation of consolidated financial statements. For example, assume the parent company purchased $5,000 of bonds issued by its subsidiary company. Because no debt is owed to or due from any entity outside the consolidated enterprise, Y Company would eliminate those balances by an entry like the following that offsets the Investment in Bonds against the Bonds Payable:

Bonds Payable (subsidiary company)	5,000	
Investment in Bonds (parent company)		5,000
To eliminate intercompany bonds and bond investment.		

When preparing consolidated statements, the parent would similarly eliminate other intercompany balances.

CONSOLIDATED BALANCE SHEET AT TIME OF ACQUISITION

A parent company may acquire a subsidiary at its book value or at a cost above or below book value. Also, the parent may acquire 100% of the outstanding voting common stock of the subsidiary or some lesser percentage exceeding 50%.

ILLUSTRATION 14.2
Consolidated Balance Sheet Work Sheet (stock acquired at book value)

P COMPANY AND SUBSIDIARY S COMPANY
Work Sheet for Consolidated Balance Sheet
January 1, 1997 (date of acquisition)

	P Company	S Company	Eliminations Debit	Eliminations Credit	Consolidated Amounts
Assets					
Cash	26,000	12,000			38,000
Notes receivable	5,000			(2) 5,000	
Accounts receivable, net	24,000	15,000			39,000
Merchandise inventory	35,000	30,000			65,000
Investment in S Company	106,000			(1) 106,000	
Equipment, net	41,000	15,000			56,000
Buildings, net	65,000	35,000			100,000
Land	20,000	10,000			30,000
	322,000	117,000			328,000
Liabilities and Stockholders' Equity					
Accounts payable	18,000	6,000			24,000
Notes payable		5,000	(2) 5,000		
Common stock	250,000	100,000	(1) 100,000		250,000
Paid-in capital in excess of par value—common		4,000	(1) 4,000		-0-
Retained earnings	54,000	2,000	(1) 2,000		54,000
	322,000	117,000	111,000	111,000	328,000

Acquisition of Subsidiary at Book Value

Objective 5
Prepare consolidated financial statements through the use of a consolidated statement work sheet.

To consolidate its assets and liabilities with those of its subsidiaries, a parent company prepares a consolidated statement work sheet similar to the one in Illustration 14.2. A **consolidated statement work sheet** is an informal record on which elimination entries are made for the purpose of showing account balances as if the parent and its subsidiaries were a single economic enterprise. The first two columns of the work sheet show assets, liabilities, and stockholders' equity of the parent and subsidiary as they appear on each corporation's balance sheet. The pair of columns labeled Eliminations allows intercompany items to be offset and consequently eliminated from the consolidated statement. The final column shows the amounts that will appear on the consolidated balance sheet.

The work sheet in Illustration 14.2 consolidates the accounts of P Company and its subsidiary, S Company, on January 1, 1997. P Company acquired S Company on January 1, 1997, by purchasing all of its outstanding voting common stock for $106,000 cash, which was the book value of the stock. Book value is equal to stockholders' equity, or net assets (assets minus liabilities). Thus, common stock ($100,000), paid-in capital in excess of par value—common ($4,000), and retained earnings ($2,000) equal $106,000. When P Company acquired the S Company stock, P Company made the following entry:

Investment in S Company	106,000	
Cash		106,000
To record investment in S Company.		

The Investment in S Company account appears as an asset on P Company's balance sheet. By buying the subsidiary's stock, the parent acquired a 100% equity, or ownership, interest in the subsidiary's net assets. Thus, if both the investment account and the subsidiary's assets appear on the consolidated balance sheet, the same resources would be counted twice. The Common Stock and Retained Earnings accounts of the subsidiary also represent an equity interest in the subsidiary's assets. Therefore, P's investment in S Company must be offset against S Company's stockholders' equity accounts so that the subsidiary's assets and the ownership interest in these assets appear only once on the consolidated balance sheet. P Company accomplishes this elimination by entry *1* under Eliminations on the work sheet. The entry debits S Company's Common Stock for $100,000, Paid-In Capital in Excess of Par Value—Common for $4,000, and Retained Earnings for $2,000 and credits Investment in S Company for $106,000. In journal entry form, the elimination entry is:

Common Stock	100,000	
Paid-In Capital in Excess of Par Value—Common	4,000	
Retained Earnings	2,000	
Investment in S Company		106,000
To eliminate investment account and subsidiary stockholders' equity.		

Entry *2* eliminates the effect of an intercompany debt. On the date it acquired S Company, P Company loaned S Company $5,000. The loan is a $5,000 note receivable on P's books and a $5,000 note payable on S's books. If the elimination entry is not made on the work sheet, the consolidated balance sheet would show $5,000 owed to the consolidated enterprise by itself. From the viewpoint of the consolidated equity, neither an asset nor a liability exists. Therefore, entry *2* on the work sheet eliminates both the asset and liability. The entry debits Notes Payable and credits Notes Receivable for $5,000. In general journal form, entry *2* is:

Notes Payable	5,000	
Notes Receivable		5,000
To eliminate intercompany payable and receivable.		

Note that P Company makes elimination entries only on the consolidated statement work sheet; no elimination entries appear in the accounting records of either P Company or S Company. P Company uses the final work sheet column to prepare the consolidated balance sheet.

An Accounting Perspective

Uses of Technology Computer applications have greatly simplified the preparation of consolidated work sheets. Spreadsheet programs in particular expedite the process of constructing consolidated financial statements.

Acquisition of Subsidiary at a Cost above or below Book Value

In the previous example, P Company acquired 100% of S Company at a cost equal to book value. In some cases, firms acquire subsidiaries at a cost greater than or less than book value. For example, assume P Company purchased 100% of S Company's outstanding voting common stock for $125,000 (instead of $106,000). The book value of this stock is $106,000. Cost exceeds book value by $19,000. P Company's management may have paid more than book value because (1) the subsidiary's earnings prospects justify paying a price greater than book value or (2) the total fair market value of the subsidiary's assets exceeds their total book value.

According to the Accounting Principles Board *(APB Opinion No. 16)*, where cost exceeds book value because of expected above-average earnings, the investor labels the excess *goodwill* on the consolidated balance sheet. **Goodwill** is an intangible value attached to a business primarily due to above-average earnings prospects (as discussed in Chapter 11). On the other hand, if the excess is attributable to the belief that assets of the subsidiary are undervalued, then the investor increases the asset values on the consolidated balance sheet to the extent of the excess.[4] In Illustration 14.3, $4,000 is due to the undervaluation of land owned by

[4] *APB Accounting Principles* (Chicago: Commerce Clearing House, Inc., 1973), vol. II, p. 6655.

ILLUSTRATION 14.3
Consolidated Balance Sheet Work Sheet (stock acquired at more than book value)

P COMPANY AND SUBSIDIARY S COMPANY
Work Sheet for Consolidated Balance Sheet
January 1, 1997 (date of acquisition)

	P Company	S Company	Eliminations Debit	Eliminations Credit	Consolidated Amounts
Assets					
Cash	7,000	12,000			19,000
Notes receivable	5,000			(2) 5,000	
Accounts receivable, net	24,000	15,000			39,000
Merchandise inventory	35,000	30,000			65,000
Investment in S Company	125,000			(1) 125,000	
Equipment, net	41,000	15,000			56,000
Buildings, net	65,000	35,000			100,000
Land	20,000	10,000	(1) 4,000		34,000
Goodwill			(1) 15,000		15,000
	322,000	117,000			328,000
Liabilities and Stockholders' Equity					
Accounts payable	18,000	6,000			24,000
Notes payable		5,000	(2) 5,000		
Common stock	250,000	100,000	(1) 100,000		250,000
Paid-in capital in excess of par value—common		4,000	(1) 4,000		–0–
Retained earnings	54,000	2,000	(1) 2,000		54,000
	322,000	117,000	130,000	130,000	328,000

the company, and the remaining $15,000 of the excess of cost over book value is due to expected above-average earnings. As a result, P Company adds $4,000 of the $19,000 excess to Land, and identifies the other $15,000 as Goodwill on the work sheet (Illustration 14.3) and on the balance sheet (Illustration 14.4).

P Company establishes Goodwill as part of the first elimination entry. Elimination entry *1* in Illustration 14.3 involves debits to the subsidiary's Common Stock for $100,000, Paid-In Capital in Excess of Par Value—Common for $4,000, Retained Earnings for $2,000, Land for $4,000, and Goodwill for $15,000, and a credit to Investment in S Company for $125,000. In journal form, entry *1* is:

	Debit	Credit
Common Stock	100,000	
Paid-In Capital in Excess of Par Value—Common	4,000	
Retained Earnings	2,000	
Land	4,000	
Goodwill	15,000	
Investment in S Company		125,000
To eliminate investment and subsidiary stockholders' equity and to establish increased value of land and goodwill.		

Entry *2* is the same as elimination entry *2* in Illustration 14.2. Entry *2* eliminates the intercompany loan by debiting Notes Payable and crediting Notes Receivable for $5,000.

After these elimination entries are made, the company consolidates and extends the remaining amounts to the Consolidated Amounts column. It uses the amounts in this column to prepare the consolidated balance sheet in Illustration 14.4. Notice that the firm carries the $15,000 debit to Goodwill to the Consolidated Amounts column and lists it as an asset in the consolidated balance sheet.

As noted earlier, a company may purchase all or part of another company at more than book value and create goodwill on the consolidated balance sheet. The Accounting Principles Board, in *APB Opinion No. 17*, requires that all goodwill be

ILLUSTRATION 14.4
Consolidated Balance Sheet

P COMPANY AND SUBSIDIARY S COMPANY
Consolidated Balance Sheet
January 1, 1997

Assets		
Current assets:		
Cash	$ 19,000	
Accounts receivable, net	39,000	
Merchandise inventory	65,000	
Total current assets		$123,000
Property, plant, and equipment:		
Equipment, net	$ 56,000	
Buildings, net	100,000	
Land	34,000	
Total property, plant, and equipment		190,000
Goodwill		15,000
Total assets		$328,000
Liabilities and Stockholders' Equity		
Current liabilities:		
Accounts payable		$ 24,000
Stockholders' equity:		
Common stock	$250,000	
Retained earnings	54,000	
Total stockholders' equity		304,000
Total liabilities and stockholders' equity		$328,000

amortized over a period not to exceed 40 years. This amortization is necessary under the cost and equity methods. We leave a discussion of this topic to a more advanced text.

Under some circumstances, a parent company may pay less than book value of the subsidiary's net assets. In such cases, it is highly unlikely that a bargain purchase has been made. The most logical explanation is that some of the subsidiary's assets are overvalued. The Accounting Principles Board requires that firms use the excess of book value over cost to reduce proportionately the value of the noncurrent assets acquired (except long-term investments in marketable securities). If noncurrent assets are reduced to zero, the remaining dollar amount is a deferred credit.[5]

Acquisition of Less Than 100% of a Subsidiary

Sometimes a parent company acquires less than 100% of the outstanding voting common stock of a subsidiary. For example, assume P Company acquired 80% of S Company's outstanding voting common stock. P Company is the majority stockholder, but another group of stockholders owns the remaining 20% of the stock. Stockholders who own less than 50% of a subsidiary's outstanding voting common stock are *minority stockholders*, and their claim or interest in the subsidiary is the **minority interest.** Minority stockholders have an interest in the subsidiary's net assets and share the subsidiary's income or loss with the parent company.

Look at Illustration 14.5, the elimination entries required when P Company purchases 80% of S Company's stock for $90,000. The book value of the stock acquired by P Company is $84,800 (80% of $106,000). Assuming no assets are undervalued, P Company attributes the excess of cost ($90,000) over book value ($84,800) of $5,200 to S Company's above-average earnings prospects (goodwill).

[5] Ibid., p. 6655.

ILLUSTRATION 14.5
Consolidated Balance Sheet Work Sheet (80% of stock acquired at more than book value)

P COMPANY AND SUBSIDIARY S COMPANY
Work Sheet for Consolidated Balance Sheet
January 1, 1997 (date of acquisition)

	P Company	S Company	Eliminations Debit	Eliminations Credit	Consolidated Amounts
Assets					
Cash	42,000	12,000			54,000
Notes receivable	5,000			(2) 5,000	
Accounts receivable, net	24,000	15,000			39,000
Merchandise inventory	35,000	30,000			65,000
Investment in S Company	90,000			(1) 90,000	
Equipment, net	41,000	15,000			56,000
Buildings, net	65,000	35,000			100,000
Land	20,000	10,000			30,000
Goodwill			(1) 5,200		5,200
	322,000	117,000			349,200
Liabilities and Stockholders' Equity					
Accounts payable	18,000	6,000			24,000
Notes payable		5,000	(2) 5,000		
Common stock	250,000	100,000	(1) 100,000		250,000
Paid-in capital in excess of par value—common		4,000	(1) 4,000		-0-
Retained earnings	54,000	2,000	(1) 2,000		54,000
Minority interest				(1) 21,200	21,200
	322,000	117,000	116,200	116,200	349,200

Elimination entry *1* eliminates S Company's stockholders' equity by debiting Common Stock for $100,000, Paid-In Capital in Excess of Par Value—Common for $4,000, and Retained Earnings for $2,000. To establish minority interest, it credits a Minority Interest account for $21,200 (20% of $106,000). P Company eliminates the investment account by crediting Investment in S Company for $90,000. The $5,200 debited to Goodwill makes the debits equal the credits. In journal form, the elimination entry *1* is:

	Debit	Credit
Common Stock	100,000	
Paid-In Capital in Excess of Par Value—Common	4,000	
Retained Earnings	2,000	
Goodwill	5,200	
Investment in S Company		90,000
Minority Interest		21,200
To eliminate investment and subsidiary stockholders' equity and to establish minority interest and goodwill.		

Elimination entry *2* is the same as shown in Illustration 14.2. The entry eliminates intercompany debt by debiting Notes Payable and crediting Notes Receivable for $5,000.

On the consolidated balance sheet (Illustration 14.6), minority interest appears between the liabilities and stockholders' equity sections.

AN ACCOUNTING PERSPECTIVE

BUSINESS INSIGHT Borden, Inc., is a worldwide producer of food and nonfood products such as pasta, snacks, dairy products, and glue. In 1992, Borden held a 77.28% general partner interest in T.M.I. Associates, L.P., and an outside investor held a 22.72% limited partner interest. For financial reporting purposes, Bordon consolidated T.M.I. Associates' assets, liabilities, and earnings with its own and included the limited partner's interest in the financial statements as a minority interest.

ILLUSTRATION 14.6
Consolidated Balance Sheet

P COMPANY AND SUBSIDIARY S COMPANY
Consolidated Balance Sheet
January 1, 1997

Assets		
Current assets:		
Cash	$ 54,000	
Accounts receivable, net	39,000	
Merchandise inventory	65,000	
Total current assets		$158,000
Property, plant, and equipment:		
Equipment, net	$ 56,000	
Buildings, net	100,000	
Land	30,000	
Total property, plant, and equipment		186,000
Goodwill		5,200
Total assets		$349,200
Liabilities and Stockholders' Equity		
Liabilities:		
Accounts payable		$ 24,000
Minority interest		21,200
Stockholders' equity:		
Common stock	$250,000	
Retained earnings	54,000	
Total stockholders' equity		304,000
Total liabilities and stockholders' equity		$349,200

ACCOUNTING FOR INCOME, LOSSES, AND DIVIDENDS OF A SUBSIDIARY

When a subsidiary is operating profitably, its net assets and retained earnings increase. The subsidiary pays dividends to both the parent company and minority stockholders. The subsidiary records all transactions in its accounting records in a normal manner.

As noted earlier, two different methods used by an investor to account for investments in common stock are the cost and equity methods. A parent company may use either the cost or equity method of accounting for its investment in a consolidated subsidiary. This choice is allowed because the investment account is eliminated during the consolidation process; therefore, the results are identical after consolidation. To illustrate the consolidation process at a date after acquisition, we assume the parent company uses the equity method.

CONSOLIDATED FINANCIAL STATEMENTS AT A DATE AFTER ACQUISITION

Under the equity method, the investment account on the parent company's books increases and decreases as the parent records its share of the income, losses, and dividends reported by the subsidiary. Thus, the balance in the investment account differs after acquisition from its balance on the date of acquisition. Consequently, the amounts eliminated on the consolidated statements work sheet differ from year to year. As an illustration, assume the following facts:

1. P Company acquired 100% of the outstanding voting common stock of S Company on January 1, 1997. P Company paid $121,000 for stockholders' equity totaling $106,000. The excess of cost over book value is attributable to *(a)* an undervaluation of land amounting to $4,000 and *(b)* the remainder to S Company's above-average earnings prospects.

2. During 1997, S Company earned $20,000 from operations.
3. On December 31, 1997, S Company paid a cash dividend of $8,000.
4. S Company owes P Company $5,000 on a note at December 31.
5. Including its share (100%) of S Company's income, P Company earned $31,000 during 1997.
6. P Company paid a cash dividend of $10,000 during December 1997.
7. P Company uses the equity method of accounting for its investment in S Company.

The financial statements for the two companies as of December 31, 1997, are in the first two columns of Illustration 14.7.

The work sheet shown in Illustration 14.7 allows us to prepare a consolidated income statement, statement of retained earnings, and balance sheet. Notice that in Illustration 14.7, P Company has a balance of $20,000 in its Income of S Company account and a balance of $133,000 in its Investment in S Company account. These balances are the result of the following journal entries made by P Company in 1997:

1997				
Jan.	1	Investment in S Company	121,000	
		Cash		121,000
		To record 100% investment in subsidiary.		
Dec.	31	Investment in S Company	20,000	
		Income of S Company		20,000
		To record income of subsidiary.		
	31	Cash	8,000	
		Investment in S Company		8,000
		To record dividends received from subsidiary.		

The explanations for the elimination entries on the work sheet in Illustration 14.7 are as follows:

Entry *1*: During the year, S Company earned $20,000. P Company increased its investment account balance by $20,000. Entry *1* on the work sheet eliminates the subsidiary's income from the Investment in S Company account and the Income of S Company account ($20,000). This entry reverses the entry made on the books of P Company to recognize the parent's share of the subsidiary's income (the first December 31 journal entry).

Entry *2*: When S Company paid its cash dividend, P Company debited Cash and credited the investment account for $8,000 (the second December 31 journal entry). Entry *2* restores the investment account to its balance before the dividends from S Company were deducted. That is, P Company debits its investment account and credits S Company's dividends account for $8,000. On a consolidated basis, a company cannot pay a dividend to itself.

Entry *3*: Entry 3 eliminates the original investment account balance ($121,000) and the subsidiary's stockholders' equity accounts as of the date of acquisition (retained earnings of $6,000 and common stock of $100,000). The entry also establishes goodwill of $11,000 and increases land by $4,000 to account for the excess of acquisition cost over book value.

Entry *4*: Entry 4 eliminates the intercompany debt of $5,000.

After the first three entries have been made, the investment account contains a zero balance from the viewpoint of the consolidated entity.

After making the eliminations, P Company combines the corresponding amounts and places them in the Consolidated Amounts column. Notice that certain totals in the first two columns do not add across to the total in the Consolidated Amounts column. For instance, consolidated net income is $31,000, not

ILLUSTRATION 14.7
Consolidated Work Sheet One Year after Acquisition

P COMPANY AND SUBSIDIARY S COMPANY
Work Sheet for Consolidated Financial Statements
December 31, 1997

	P Company	S Company	Eliminations Debit	Eliminations Credit	Consolidated Amounts
Income Statement					
Revenue from sales	397,000	303,000			700,000
Income of S Company	20,000		(1) 20,000		
Cost of goods sold	(250,000)	(180,000)			(430,000)
Expenses (excluding depreciation and taxes)	(100,000)	(80,000)			(180,000)
Depreciation expense	(7,400)	(5,000)			(12,400)
Federal income tax expense	(28,600)	(18,000)			(46,600)
Net income—carried forward	31,000	20,000			31,000*
Statement of Retained Earnings					
Retained earnings—January 1:					
P Company	54,000				54,000
S Company		6,000	(3) 6,000		
Net income—brought forward	31,000	20,000			31,000*
	85,000	26,000			85,000*
Dividends:					
P Company	(10,000)				(10,000)
S Company		(8,000)		(2) 8,000	
Retained earnings—Dec. 31—carried forward	75,000	18,000			75,000*
Balance Sheet Assets					
Cash	38,000	16,000			54,000
Notes receivable	5,000			(4) 5,000	
Accounts receivable, net	25,000	18,000			43,000
Merchandise inventory	40,000	36,000			76,000
Investment in S Company	133,000		(2) 8,000	(3) 121,000	
				(1) 20,000	
Equipment, net	36,900	12,000			48,900
Buildings, net	61,700	33,000			94,700
Land	20,000	10,000	(3) 4,000		34,000
Goodwill			(3) 11,000		11,000
	359,600	125,000			361,600*
Liabilities and Stockholders' Equity					
Accounts payable	19,600	2,000			21,600
Notes payable	15,000	5,000	(4) 5,000		15,000
Common stock	250,000	100,000	(3) 100,000		250,000
Retained earnings—brought forward	75,000	18,000			75,000*
	359,600	125,000	154,000	154,000	361,600*

* Totals are determined vertically, not horizontally.

ILLUSTRATION 14.8
Consolidated Income Statement

P COMPANY AND SUBSIDIARY S COMPANY
Consolidated Income Statement
For the Year Ended December 31, 1997

Revenue from sales		$700,000
Cost of goods sold		430,000
Gross margin		$270,000
Expenses (excluding depreciation and taxes)	$180,000	
Depreciation expense	12,400	
Federal income tax expense	46,600	239,000
Net income		$ 31,000

ILLUSTRATION 14.9
Consolidated Statement of Retained Earnings

P COMPANY AND SUBSIDIARY S COMPANY
Consolidated Statement of Retained Earnings
For the Year Ended December 31, 1997

Retained earnings, January 1, 1997	$54,000
Net income	31,000
Subtotal	$85,000
Dividends	10,000
Retained earnings, December 31, 1997	$75,000

$31,000 plus $20,000. The firm carries the net income row in the Income Statement section forward to the net income row in the Statement of Retained Earnings section. Likewise, it carries the ending retained earnings row in the Statement of Retained Earnings section forward to the retained earnings row in the Balance Sheet section. P Company uses the final work sheet column to prepare the consolidated income statement (Illustration 14.8), the consolidated statement of retained earnings (Illustration 14.9), and the consolidated balance sheet (Illustration 14.10).[6] We ignore the amortization of goodwill in the illustration.

PURCHASE VERSUS POOLING OF INTERESTS

Objective 6
Identify the differences between purchase accounting and pooling of interests accounting.

In the illustrations in this chapter, we have assumed that the parent company acquired the subsidiary's common stock in exchange for cash. The acquiring company could also have used assets other than cash in the exchange. This transaction—the exchange of cash or other assets for the common stock of another company—is a **purchase.** When assets other than cash are used, the cost of the acquired company's stock is the fair market value of the assets given up or of the stock received, whichever can be more clearly and objectively determined.

A company can also acquire the common stock of another company by issuing its own common stock in exchange for the other company's common stock. When such an exchange occurs, the stockholders of both companies maintain a joint ownership interest in the combined company. Such a business combination involving the issuance of common stock in exchange for common stock is a **pooling of interests** if it meets all the criteria cited in *APB Opinion No. 16*. When a combination resulting from an exchange of stock does not qualify as a pooling of interests, we record it as a purchase.

The purchase and pooling of interests methods are not alternatives that can be applied to the same situation. Given the circumstances surrounding a particular business combination, only one of the two methods—purchase or pooling of interests—is appropriate. *APB Opinion No. 16* specifies that 12 conditions must be met before a business combination can be classified as a pooling of interests.

[6] The annual report booklet shows consolidated financial statements for actual corporations.

ILLUSTRATION 14.10
Consolidated Balance Sheet (one year after acquisition)

P COMPANY AND SUBSIDIARY S COMPANY
Consolidated Balance Sheet
December 31, 1997

Assets

Current assets:		
Cash	$ 54,000	
Accounts receivable, net	43,000	
Merchandise inventory	76,000	
Total current assets		$173,000
Property, plant, and equipment:		
Equipment, net	$ 48,900	
Buildings, net	94,700	
Land	34,000	
Total property, plant, and equipment		177,600
Goodwill		11,000
Total assets		$361,600

Liabilities and Stockholders' Equity

Current liabilities:		
Accounts payable	$ 21,600	
Notes payable	15,000	
Total liabilities		$ 36,600
Stockholders' equity:		
Common stock	$250,000	
Retained earnings	75,000	
Total stockholders' equity		325,000
Total liabilities and stockholders' equity		$361,600

For example, two of these conditions are (1) the combination must be completed in one transaction or be completed within one year in accordance with a specific plan, and (2) one corporation must issue only its common stock (no cash or other assets) in exchange for 90% or more of the voting common stock of another company. If all 12 conditions specified by the APB are met, companies can account for the resulting business combination as a pooling of interests. Otherwise, they must use the purchase method to account for the combination.

When using the pooling of interests method, the parent company records its investment at the book value of the subsidiary's net assets (assets minus liabilities). Since the investment is recorded at the book value, there can be no goodwill or changes in asset valuations from consolidation. The subsidiary's retained earnings at the date of acquisition become a part of the consolidated retained earnings, whereas under the purchase method they do not. Also, the pooling of interests method includes all subsidiary income for the year of acquisition in the consolidated net income. The purchase method includes in consolidated net income only that portion of the subsidiary's income that arises after the date of acquisition.

It is apparent that these two methods lead to significant differences in financial statement amounts. For instance, the purchase method uses any excess of investment cost over the book value of the ownership interest acquired to increase the value of any assets that are undervalued or that must be recognized as goodwill from consolidation. On the other hand, under the pooling of interests method, book value—rather than cost—is the amount of the investment. Thus, whenever cost exceeds book value, the purchase method records either more depreciation or more amortization than the pooling of interests method. Also, consolidated net income is smaller under the purchase method than under the pooling of interests method.

In Illustration 14.11, we show the number of business combinations involving the two methods that occurred in a sample of 600 companies for the years 1989–

Illustration 14.11
Business Combinations

	1992	1991	1990	1989
Pooling of interests				
Prior year financial statements restated	7	7	4	9
Prior year financial statements not restated	10	9	6	9
Total	17	16	10	18
Purchase method	182	160	190	219

Source: Based on American Institute of Certified Public Accountants, *Accounting Trends & Techniques* (New York: AICPA, 1993), p. 53.

92. The companies used the purchase method much more extensively than the pooling of interests method.

Uses and Limitations of Consolidated Statements

Objective 7
Describe the uses and limitations of consolidated financial statements.

Consolidated financial statements are of primary importance to stockholders, managers, and directors of the parent company. The parent company benefits from the income and other financial strengths of the subsidiary. Likewise, the parent company suffers from a subsidiary's losses and other financial weaknesses.

Consolidated financial statements are of limited use to the creditors and minority stockholders of the subsidiary. The subsidiary's creditors have a claim against the subsidiary alone; they cannot look to the parent company for payment. Minority stockholders in the subsidiary do not benefit or suffer from the parent company's operations. These minority stockholders benefit from the subsidiary's income and financial strengths; they suffer from the subsidiary's losses and financial weaknesses. Thus, the subsidiary's creditors and minority stockholders are more interested in the subsidiary's individual financial statements than in the consolidated statements. Because of these factors, annual reports always include the financial statements of the consolidated entity, and sometimes include the financial statements of certain subsidiary companies alone, but never include the parent company's financial statements alone.

Analyzing and Using the Financial Results—Dividend Yield on Common Stock and Payout Ratios

Objective 8
Analyze and use the financial results—dividend yield on common stock and payout ratio on common stock.

Investors often search for stock that fulfills their needs. To locate this stock, potential stockholders may use the dividend yield on common stock ratio or the payout ratio on common stock. To demonstrate these ratios, consider the 1992 annual report of ConAgra, Inc.

ConAgra
ConAgra, Inc., is a diversified, international food company that sells prepared foods and farming supplies.

	1992	1991
Dividend per share of common stock	$ .520	$ .445
Current market price per share	30.33	25.88
Earnings per share	1.50	1.42

Investors use the **dividend yield on common stock ratio** as a tool to compare stocks. Some investors favor stocks with a high dividend yield ratio and a high payout ratio. Other investors would rather have the corporation retain more of the funds and use them to attempt to increase future earnings and the market price of the stock. The formula for the dividend yield on common stock ratio is:

$$\text{Dividend yield on common stock ratio} = \frac{\text{Dividend per share of common stock}}{\text{Current market price per share}}$$

For ConAgra, the dividend yield on common stock ratios are:

1992: $.520/$30.33 = 1.71%
1991: $.445/$25.88 = 1.72%

To determine the relevance of this ratio, an investor compares these numbers to ratios calculated on other stocks.

Investors calculate the **payout ratio on common stock** as follows:

$$\text{Payout ratio on common stock} = \frac{\text{Dividend per share of common stock}}{\text{Earnings per share (EPS)}}$$

This ratio indicates whether a company pays out a large percentage of earnings as dividends or reinvests most of its earnings. When computing the payout ratio, remember that negative earnings per share result in an invalid calculation. ConAgra's payout ratios are:

1992: $.520/$1.50 = 34.67%
1991: $.445/$1.42 = 31.34%

Now that you have studied consolidated financial statements, you should realize the importance of presenting a complete picture of the business operations of a company. In Chapter 15 you learn about long-term financing, its advantages and disadvantages, and how bonds differ from stocks.

Understanding the Learning Objectives

Objective 1
Report stock investments and distinguish between the cost and equity methods of accounting for stock investments.

- Under the cost method, the investor company records its investment at the price paid at acquisition and does not adjust the investment account balance subsequently. The cost method is used for all short-term investments, long-term investments of less than 20% where the purchasing company does not exercise significant influence over the investee company, and may be used for long-term investments of more than 50%.
- Under the equity method, the investment is also initially recorded at acquisition price, but is then adjusted periodically for the investor company's share of the investee's reported income, losses, and dividends. The equity method is used for all long-term investments of between 20% and 50% and may be used for investments of more than 50%. This method is also used for investments of less than 20% if the purchasing company exercises significant influence over the investee company.

Objective 2
Prepare journal entries to account for short-term stock investments and for long-term stock investments of less than 20%.

- Under the cost method, the initial investment is debited to either Trading Securities or Available-for-Sale Securities, depending on whether the investment is a short-term or long-term investment.
- At the end of each accounting period, the company must adjust the carrying value of each investment. The fair market value method is applied independently to each of these portfolios.
- Under the cost method, dividends received are credited to Dividend Revenue.
- Under the equity method, the initial investment is debited to an Investment in (Company Name) account. Income, losses, and dividends result in increases or decreases to the investment account.

Objective 3
Prepare journal entries to account for long-term investments of 20% to 50%.

- The equity method must be used.
- The initial investment is debited to an Investment in (Company Name) account. The purchasing company's share of the investee's income is debited to the investment account, and the purchaser's share of the investee's losses and dividends is credited to the investment account as they are reported by the investee.

Objective 4
Describe the nature of parent and subsidiary corporations.

- A corporation that owns more than 50% of the outstanding voting common stock of another corporation is called the *parent company*.
- The corporation acquired and controlled by the parent company is known as the *subsidiary company*.
- A parent company and its subsidiaries maintain their own accounting records and prepare their own financial statements, but the parent company must also prepare consolidated financial statements. The consolidated financial statements consolidate the financial results of the parent and subsidiaries as a single enterprise.

- Consolidated financial statements must be prepared (1) when one company owns more than 50% of the outstanding voting stock of another company and (2) unless control is likely to be temporary or if it does not rest with the majority owner.
- In preparing consolidated financial statements, the effects of intercompany transactions must be eliminated by making elimination entries. Elimination entries are made only on a consolidated statement work sheet, not in the accounting records of the parent or subsidiaries.
- One elimination entry offsets the parent company's subsidiary investment account against the stockholders' equity accounts of the subsidiary. Intercompany receivables and payables also must be eliminated.

Objective 5
Prepare consolidated financial statements through the use of a consolidated statement work sheet.

- A consolidated financial statements work sheet is an informal record in which elimination entries are made for the purpose of showing account balances as if the parent and its subsidiaries were a single economic enterprise.
- A consolidated balance sheet work sheet is prepared at the time of acquisition. The first two columns of the work sheet show assets, liabilities, and stockholders' equity of the parent and subsidiary as they appear on each corporation's individual balance sheet. The next pair of columns shows the eliminations. The final column shows the amounts that appear on the consolidated balance sheet.
- A consolidated work sheet is prepared at various dates after acquisition. The first two columns show the income statements, statements of retained earnings, and balance sheets of the parent and subsidiary. The next pair of columns shows the eliminations. The final column shows the amounts that appear in the consolidated financial statements.

Objective 6
Identify the differences between purchase accounting and pooling of interests accounting.

- The exchange of cash or other assets for the common stock of another company is called a *purchase*. Any other combination that does not qualify as a pooling of interests must be accounted for as a purchase.
- When a company exchanges some of its own common stock for all or some of the other company's common stock, the business combination is classified as a pooling of interests (if certain other criteria are met). If a combination results from an exchange of stock but does not qualify as a pooling of interests, it must be recorded as a purchase.
- When the purchase method is used, the parent company's investment is recorded at cost, which may be greater than or less than book value. When the pooling of interests method is used, the parent company's investment is recorded at the book value of the subsidiary's net assets.

Objective 7
Describe the uses and limitations of consolidated financial statements.

- Consolidated financial statements are of primary importance to stockholders, managers, and directors of the parent company. On the other hand, consolidated financial statements are of limited use to the creditors and minority stockholders of the subsidiary.

Objective 8
Analyze and use the financial results—dividend yield on common stock and payout ratio on common stock.

- $\text{Dividend yield on common stock ratio} = \dfrac{\text{Dividend per share of common stock}}{\text{Current market price per share}}$
- This ratio helps investors to compare stocks.
- $\text{Payout ratio on common stock} = \dfrac{\text{Dividend per share of common stock}}{\text{Earnings per share (EPS)}}$
- This ratio indicates whether a company pays out a large percentage of earnings as dividends or reinvests most of its earnings.

Objective 9
Discuss the differences in international accounting among nations (Appendix).

- Accounting principles differ among nations because they were developed independently.
- There have been attempts at harmonizing accounting principles throughout the world.
- Differences in accounting principles exist between nations regarding foreign currency translation, inventory cost, and the effects of changing prices.

International Accounting

Appendix

In today's world, we do not find it surprising to discover a British bank in Atlanta, Coca-Cola in Paris, and French airplanes in Zaire. German automobile parts assembled in Spain are sold in the United States. Japan buys oil from Saudi Arabia and sells cameras in Italy. Soviet livestock eat American grain, and the British sip tea from Sri Lanka and China. Business has become truly international, but accounting, often described as the language of business, does not cross borders so easily.

Why Accounting Principles and Practices Differ among Nations

Objective 9
Discuss the differences in international accounting among nations.

Accounting principles and reporting practices differ from country to country, and international decision making is made more difficult by the lack of a common communication system. However, since business is practiced at an international level, accounting must find a way to provide its services at that level.

The problem is that accounting reflects the national economic and social environment in which it is practiced, and this environment is not the same in Bangkok as in Boston. Some economies, for example, are mainly agricultural. Others are based on manufacturing, trade, or service industries. Still others export natural resources, such as oil or gold, while a few derive most of their income from tourism. Accounting for inventories and natural resources, cost accounting techniques, and methods of foreign currency translation have a different orientation, emphasis, and degree of refinement in these different economies.

Other accounting differences stem from the various legal or political systems of nations. In centrally controlled economies, for instance, the state owns all or most of the property. It makes little sense to prescribe full disclosure of accounting procedures to protect investors when little or no private ownership of property exists. In these nations with centrally controlled economies, an accounting profession is virtually nonexistent. One of the great challenges for Western nations over the next few decades is to assist the nations of Eastern Europe to build an accounting profession within those nations to serve the companies that evolve under their new market-oriented economies. Some of these countries standardize their accounting methods and incorporate them into law.

In most market-oriented economies, the development of accounting principles and reporting practices is left mainly to the private sector. Where uniformity exists, it occurs more by general agreement or consensus of interested parties than by governmental decree. In countries where business firms are predominately family owned, disclosure practices usually are less complete than in countries where large, publicly held corporations dominate. The requirement in many countries that the financial statements must conform to tax returns contributes to diversity in accounting practices among countries.

The degree of development of the accounting profession and the general level of education of a country also influence accounting practices and procedures. Nations that lack a well-organized accounting profession may adopt, almost in total, the accounting methods of other countries. Commonwealth countries, for example, tend to follow British accounting standards; the former French colonies of Africa use French systems; Bermuda follows Canadian pronouncements; and the influence of the United States is widespread. At the same time, levels of expertise vary. In countries that have little knowledge or understanding of statistics, nothing is gained by advocating statistical accounting and auditing techniques. Accounting systems designed for electronic data processing are not helpful in countries where few or no businesses use computers.

Even in advanced countries, genuine differences of opinion exist regarding accounting theory and appropriate accounting methods. American standards, for example, require the periodic amortization of goodwill to expense, but British and Dutch standards do not. The lack of agreement on the objectives of financial statements and the lack of any effort in most countries to articulate objectives also contribute to diversity. Accounting methods also differ within nations. Most countries, including the United States, permit several depreciation methods and two or more inventory costing methods.

Attempted Harmonization of Accounting Practices

The question arises as to whether financial statements that reflect the economic and social environment of, say, France can also be useful to a potential American investor. Can some of the differences between French and American accounting be eliminated or at least explained so that French and American investors understand each other's financial reports and find them useful when they make decisions?

Several organizations are working to achieve greater understanding and harmonization of different accounting practices. These organizations include the Organization for Economic Cooperation and Development (OECD), the European Community (EC), the International Accounting Standards Committee (IASC), and the International Federation of Accountants (IFAC). These organizations study the information needs and accounting and reporting practices of different nations. Some of them issue pronouncements recommending specific practices and procedures for adoption by all members.

The IASC is making a significant contribution to the development of international accounting standards. It was founded in London in 1973 by the professional accountancy bodies of 10 countries: Australia, Canada, France, Germany, Ireland, Japan, Mexico, the Netherlands, the United Kingdom, and the United States. The IASC selects a topic for study from lists of problems submitted by the profession all over the world. After research and discussion by special committees, the IASC issues an exposure draft of a proposed standard for consideration by the profession and the business and financial communities. After about six months' further study of the topic in light of the comments received, the IASC issues the final international accounting standard. To date, it has issued approximately 30 standards on topics as varied as *Disclosure of Accounting Policies* (IAS 1), *Depreciation Accounting* (IAS 4), *Statement of Changes in Financial Position* (IAS 7), and *Revenue Recognition* (IAS 18). Setting international standards is not easy. If the standards are too detailed or rigid, the flexibility needed to reflect different national environments is lost. On the other hand, if pronouncements are vague and allow too many alternative methods, there is little point in setting international standards.

Since 1988, the IASC has striven to reduce the large number of existing alternatives allowed in its prior standards. In revising prior standards, there are sometimes conflicts between the IASC standards and US GAAP. Two examples of such conflicts are the IASC's proposed elimination of the completed contract method as an acceptable accounting procedure for long-term construction projects and the proposed amortization of goodwill over a maximum 5-year period unless a longer life is justifiable. If justification is shown, the maximum amortization period is 20 years. US GAAP currently requires amortization over a period not to exceed 40 years. However, the FASB is considering a change to a maximum 20-year amortization for goodwill to bring the IASC standards and US GAAP closer together. For tax purposes, the maximum amortization period is 15 years.

The IASC addressed the importance of the international harmonization of cash flow statements with the International Accounting Standard IAS 7, Cash Flow Statements. If accepted and complied with on a global basis, the harmonization of cash flow statements will have a significant effect on the use of cross border offerings for companies seeking global financing. A prospective finance-seeking company would be able to generate a cash flow statement that is accepted in all foreign markets. A cash flow statement that complies with IAS 7 would not require modification or the inclusion of additional data and would greatly simplify cross border offerings and any future reporting by foreign investors, thus encouraging global financing.[7]

One major problem is obtaining compliance with these standards. There is no organization, nor is there likely to be an organization, to ensure compliance with international standards. Adoption is left to national standard-setting bodies or legislatures, which may or may not adopt a recommended international standard. Generally, members commit themselves to support the objectives of the international body. The members promise to use their best endeavors to see that international standards are formally adopted by local professional accountancy bodies, by government departments or other authorities that control the securities markets, and by the industrial, business, and financial communities of their respective countries.

The American Institute of Certified Public Accountants (AICPA), for example, issued a revised statement in 1975 reaffirming its support for the implementation of international standards adopted by the IASC. The AICPA's position is that international accounting standards must be specifically adopted by the Financial Accounting Standards Board (FASB), which is not a member of the IASC, to achieve acceptance in the United States. However, if no significant difference exists between an international standard and U.S. practice, compliance with U.S. generally accepted accounting principles (GAAP) constitutes compliance with the international standard. Where a significant difference exists, the

[7] *IASC Insight*, December 1993, p. 4.

AICPA publishes the IASC standard together with comments on how it differs from GAAP in the United States and undertakes to urge the FASB to give early consideration to harmonizing the differences.[8] Significant support for IASC standards has also resulted from a resolution adopted by the World Federation of Stock Exchanges in 1975. The resolution binds members to require conformance with IASC standards in securities listing agreements.[9]

Although these developments are important for the international harmonization of accounting, the success of international pronouncements ultimately depends on the willingness of the members to support them. In some cases, national legislation is required and may be slow or difficult to pass. The EC, for example, issues Directives that must be accepted as compulsory objectives by the 12 member states (Belgium, Denmark, France, Germany, Greece, Ireland, Italy, Luxembourg, the Netherlands, Portugal, Spain, and the United Kingdom) but are translated into national legislation at the discretion of each member state. The EC's important *Fourth Directive* was adopted in 1978 to regulate the preparation, content, presentation, audit, and publication of the accounts and reports of companies. It applies to all limited-liability companies (corporations) registered in the EC, except banks and insurance companies. Under the directive, member states were to introduce legislation by July 1980 so that accounts in all EC countries would conform to the directive as of the fiscal year beginning January 1, 1982.

The general movement toward international harmonization of accounting standards is increasing in other areas of society. The accounting profession, national standard-setting bodies, universities, academic societies, and multinational corporations have all shown an increased interest in international accounting problems in recent years. The AICPA has an International Practice Division as a formal part of its organization. The American Accounting Association officially established an International Accounting section in 1976 and has approximately one dozen international accounting organizations as Associate Members. The University of Lancaster (England) and the University of Illinois have international accounting research centers that support research studies and conduct international conferences and seminars. Georgia State University received a Touche Ross & Co. grant to internationalize its accounting curriculum. Many universities currently offer courses in international business and accounting.

All this activity helps increase the flow of information and our understanding of the accounting and reporting practices in other parts of the world. Greater understanding improves the likelihood that unnecessary differences will be eliminated and enhances the general acceptance of international standards.

The difficulty of achieving harmonization was illustrated in a recent effort to gain international agreement on the treatment of goodwill.[10] The International Accounting Standards Committee issued an exposure draft, known as E32, that included a provision that goodwill be recorded as an asset and amortized against earnings over a period of five years. If a company wanted to use a longer period, it would have to justify and explain its position in the financial statements.

Currently, the United Kingdom and the Netherlands write off goodwill immediately against "reserves" (a part of stockholders' equity) and bypass the income statement. This method gives them an advantage when making acquisitions because future earnings are not reduced by the amortization of goodwill. Some countries record goodwill as an asset but have amortization periods that exceed five years. For instance, in the United States goodwill can be written off over a period not to exceed 40 years. Other countries, such as Holland, permit either approach.

Reuters
Reuters collects and distributes news and other information from major securities and commodities exchanges, as well as provides world news services and products.

Companies in the United Kingdom generally oppose the change because it would reduce reported earnings and would remove their advantage in making acquisitions. For example, the 1992 annual report of Reuters, based in the United Kingdom, indicates that accounting for goodwill under U.S. GAAP would result in a £21.9 million decrease in net income. However, British firms might be willing to support a change if the write-off period were longer, say, 20 years. The Dutch seem to be opposed to any change in their current accounting for goodwill. The French generally agree with the proposal but would like a longer write-off period. Arthur Wyatt, the U.S. delegate to the IASC, felt that executives of U.S. companies might oppose a five-year write-off period because it would reduce

[8] American Institute of Certified Public Accountants, *CPA Letter*, August 1975.

[9] *CA Magazine*, January 1975, p. 52.

[10] This discussion is based on an article by Anne O'Carroll, "IASC's Goodwill Proposal Draws Much Negative Criticism," *Corporate Accounting International*, no. 1 (November 1989), pp 8–9.

A Broader Perspective

Reuters: Summary of Differences between UK and US GAAP

Accounting principles

These consolidated financial statements have been prepared in accordance with UK GAAP, which differ in certain significant respects from US GAAP. A description of the relevant accounting principles which differ materially is given below.

Goodwill and other intangibles

Under UK GAAP, purchased goodwill arising after ascribing fair values to all assets acquired, other than separate intangible assets, may be written off against reserves. Under US GAAP, fair values are ascribed to all assets including separate intangibles. For the purpose of the US GAAP adjustments included in notes 35–37, the intangible assets and the resultant goodwill are being amortised to income over their estimated lives, not exceeding 20 years.

Software development costs

Under UK GAAP, costs of developing computer software products are expensed in the year in which they are incurred. Under US GAAP, the costs of developing computer software products subsequent to establishing technical feasibility are capitalised. The amortisation of the capitalised costs is based on the estimated useful economic lives of the products involved or on estimated future revenues if greater.

Employee costs

In 1992, Reuters changed its method of accounting under UK GAAP for its US post-retirement health care plan from a cash to an accruals basis. The new method is consistent with the US Statement of Financial Accounting Standard (FAS) Number 106. Under UK GAAP, Reuters has recorded the previously unrecognised obligation of £3.6 million (net of £1.8 million tax) as a prior year adjustment, whereas under US GAAP the amount has been written off in 1992 as a cumulative change in accounting principle.

Since 1990, options have been granted under Reuters save as you earn plans at a 20% discount which renders the grants "compensatory" as defined in Opinion 25 of the US Accounting Principles Board. Under UK GAAP, the related share issues are recorded at their discounted price when the options are exercised. Under US GAAP the discount is regarded as employee compensation and is accrued over the five-year vesting period of the grants.

Taxes on income

Under UK GAAP, deferred taxes are accounted for to the extent that it is considered probable that a liability or asset will crystallise in the foreseeable future. Under US GAAP, in accordance with FAS 109, deferred taxes are accounted for on all timing differences, including those arising from the US GAAP adjustments and a valuation allowance is established in respect of those deferred tax assets where it is more likely than not that some portion will not be realised. Effective 1 January 1992, Reuters has implemented FAS 109 in its US GAAP disclosures, having previously applied FAS 96 in 1991 and 1990. The different approaches for deferred tax enshrined in FAS 109, FAS 96 and the UK Statement of Standard Accounting Practice Number 15 have not led to any GAAP adjustments in 1992.

Dividends

Under UK GAAP, dividends are provided for in the year in respect of which they are declared or proposed. Under US GAAP, dividends and the related advance corporation tax are given effect only in the period in which dividends are formally declared.

Source: Reuters *1992 Annual Report.*

income and affect their compensation plans that are often tied to income. If harmonization is to be achieved regarding accounting for goodwill, compromise will be necessary.

The remainder of this appendix gives examples of the accounting methods used in different countries and of the concepts that underlie them to illustrate the difficulty of achieving international harmonization.

Foreign Currency Translation

Foreign currency translation is probably the most common problem in an international business environment. Foreign currency translation has two main components: accounting for transactions in a foreign currency and translating the financial statements of foreign enterprises into a different, common currency. This topic is presented here to give you an idea of the complexity of the harmonization effort.

Accounting for Transactions in a Foreign Currency

Suppose an American automobile dealership imports vehicles from Japan and promises to pay for them in yen 90 days after receiving them. If no change in the dollar-yen exchange rate occurs between the date the goods are received and the date the invoice is paid, no problem exists. The importer records both the purchase and the payment at the same dollar value. But if the yen appreciates against the dollar during the 90-day period, the importer must pay more dollars for the yen needed on the settlement date.[11] Which exchange rate should the importer use to record the purchase of the vehicles—the rate in effect on the purchase date or on the payment date?

One approach to the problem is to regard the purchase of the automobiles and settlement of the invoice as two separate transactions and record them at two different exchange rates. The difference between the amount recorded in Accounts Payable on the purchase date and the amount of cash paid on the settlement date is considered an exchange gain or loss. This approach, known as the time-of-transaction method, was the prescribed or predominant practice in 61 of 64 countries surveyed in 1979,[12] including the United States.[13] The time-of-transaction method is also the method recommended in the IASC's Statement No. 21, *Accounting for the Effects of Changes in Foreign Exchange Rates,* issued in July 1983.

Another approach, the time-of-settlement method, regards the transaction and its settlement as a single event. This method regards the amount recorded on the purchase date as an estimate of the settlement amount. It accounts for any fluctuations in the exchange rate between the purchase date and the settlement date as part of the transaction and not as a separate gain or loss. Consequently, it does not recognize the effect on earnings until the purchased items are sold.

Although the time-of-transaction method is widely used, the treatment of resulting exchange gains and losses is not uniform. If the gains or losses are realized (that is, if settlement is made within the same accounting period as the purchase), most countries recognize the gains and losses in the income statement for that period. If the **exchange gains or losses** are unrealized—that is, if they result from translating accounts payable (or accounts receivable for the vendor) at the balance sheet date—the treatment varies. Recording unrealized losses was the prescribed or predominant practice in 54 countries in 1979. Only 40 countries, however, similarly recognized exchange gains in income, the remaining nations preferring to defer them until settlement. In the United States, under the provisions of FASB *Statement No. 52,* we recognize both realized and unrealized transaction gains and losses in earnings of the period in which the exchange rate changes.

Translating Financial Statements

Companies translate the financial statements of foreign subsidiaries into a single common unit of measurement, such as the dollar, for purposes of consolidation. Considerable argument has arisen in recent years regarding the correct way to make this translation. That is, which exchange rate should a firm use to translate items in the balance sheet and income statement, and what treatment is appropriate for any resulting exchange gains and losses? Items translated at the historical rate cannot result in exchange gains or losses. However, items translated at the exchange rate in effect on the balance sheet date (the **current rate**) can result in exchange gains and losses if the current rate differs from the rate in effect when those items were recorded (the historical rate). If the current rate is used, a related question arises: Should the resulting exchange gains or losses be recognized immediately in income or deferred in some way?

The methods used to translate financial statements fall basically into two groups: translation of all items at the current rate and translation of some items at the current rate and others at the historical rates. The two groups are based on different concepts of both consolidation and international business.

The Current-Rate Approach The **current-rate or closing-rate approach** translates all assets and liabilities at the current rate, the exchange rate in effect on the balance sheet date. The main advantage of this method is its simplicity; it treats all items uniformly. The approach treats a foreign subsidiary is a separate unit from the domestic parent company. It considers the subsidiary's assets as being acquired largely out of local borrowing.

---

[11] This example ignores the possibility that the importer might obtain a forward exchange contract, a discussion of which is beyond the scope of this text.

[12] Price Waterhouse International, *International Survey*. Data on the different methods used and on the number of countries using each method described in these examples are derived substantially from this publication.

[13] FASB, *Statement of Financial Accounting Standards No. 8,* "Accounting for the Translation of Foreign Currency Transactions and Foreign Currency Financial Statements" (Stamford, Conn., 1975). The "time-of-transaction" method is also prescribed by FASB *Statement No. 52,* "Foreign Currency Translation" (Stamford, Conn., 1981), which supersedes FASB *Statement No. 8.*

Multinational groups, therefore, consist of entities that operate independently but contribute to a central fund of resources. Consequently, in consolidation, stockholders of the parent company are interested primarily in the parent company's net investment in the foreign subsidiary.

The Current/Historical-Rates Approach The **current/historical-rates approach** regards the parent company and its foreign subsidiaries as a single business undertaking. Assets owned by a foreign subsidiary are indistinguishable from assets owned by the parent company. Therefore, parent companies reflect foreign assets in consolidated statements in the same way that they report their similar assets, that is, at historical cost in the parent company's currency.

Firms commonly use three translation methods under this approach. The **current-noncurrent method** translates current assets and current liabilities at the current rate—the rate in effect on the balance sheet date—while noncurrent items are translated at their respective historical rates. The **historical rate** is the rate in effect when an asset or liability is originally recorded. The **monetary-nonmonetary method** uses the current rate for monetary assets and liabilities—that is, for those that have a fixed, nominal value in terms of the foreign currency—while historical rates are applied to nonmonetary items. The **temporal method** is a variation of the monetary-nonmonetary method. It translates cash, receivables and payables, and other assets and liabilities carried at current prices (for example, marketable securities carried at current fair market value) at the current rate of exchange. This method translates all other assets and liabilities at historical rates.

Disagreement over the appropriate translation method seems likely to continue because of the different concepts of parent-subsidiary relations on which they are founded. In 1979, only six countries prescribed a single method. The temporal method was required in Austria, Canada, Bermuda, Jamaica, and the United States (under FASB *Statement No. 8*), while Uruguay required the current-rate method. Since that time the United States and Canada have changed to the current-rate method (FASB *Statement No. 52*). Apart from these 6 nations, 24 countries, including most of Europe, Japan, and Australia, predominantly followed the current-rate approach, while in 25 countries, including Germany, South Africa, and most of Central and South America, some variation of the current/historical-rates approach was common practice.

The treatment of exchange gains and losses produced by translating items at the current rate varies and is not strictly related to the translation method used. In 1979, the predominant practice in 42 nations, including much of Europe, Latin America, Japan, and the United States, was to recognize all gains and losses immediately in income. Eighteen of these countries used the current-rate translation method, and 23 followed one of the current/historical-rates methods. Alternative treatments of translation gains and losses included recording them directly in stockholders' equity (Australia), recognizing some of them immediately in income and deferring others (United Kingdom), and recognizing some in income and deferring and amortizing others over the remaining life of the items concerned (Canada and Bermuda).

FASB *Statement No. 52* does not permit the immediate recognition of translation gains and losses in income in the United States. Instead, parent companies report them separately and accumulate them in a separate component of stockholders' equity until they sell or liquidate their investment in the foreign subsidiary. At this time the parent companies report translation gains or losses as part of the gain or loss on the sale or liquidation of the investment.

An Accounting Perspective

Business Insight Liz Claiborne, Inc., is a designer and marketer of an extensive range of women's apparel and related items and also designs sportswear and furnishings for men, in addition to marketing fragrance items. According to its 1992 annual report, the company translated assets and liabilities of non-U.S. subsidiaries at year-end exchange rates, and it translated related revenues and expenses at average rates of exchange in effect during the year. Foreign currency translation resulted in a $1.4 million negative adjustment of stockholders' equity.

Inventories

Variations in accounting for inventories relate principally to the basis for determining cost and whether cost, once determined, should be increased or decreased to reflect the fair market value of the inventories.

Determination of Cost

Although some countries occasionally use other methods, the three principal bases for determining inventory cost are first-in, first-out (FIFO); last-in, first-out (LIFO); and average cost.

The most frequently used methods in 1979 were FIFO and average cost. Each of these methods was predominant in 31 countries, although no country required the use of one method to the exclusion of the other. FIFO was more common in Europe, although Austria, France, Greece, and Portugal predominantly used an average method. FIFO also predominated in Australia, Canada, South Africa, and the United States. The average method was generally followed in Latin America, Japan, and much of Africa. LIFO was the principal method in only one country—Italy—although it was a common minority method in Japan, the United States, most of Latin America, and several European countries. LIFO was an unacceptable method in Australia, Brazil, France, Ireland, Malawi, Norway, Peru, and the United Kingdom. IASC's Statement No. 2, *Valuation and Presentation of Inventories in the Context of the Historical Cost System,* supports the preference of the majority of countries and recommends the use of FIFO or average cost.

Market Value of Inventories

Only seven countries in 1979 did not require or predominantly follow the principle that inventories should be carried at the lower-of-cost-or-market value. Five of these countries, including Japan, used cost, even when cost exceeded market value. In the other two countries—Portugal and Switzerland—most enterprises wrote down inventories to amounts below both cost and market value, a practice permitted by law.

The main difference in the countries that did use the lower-of-cost-or-market approach was in the interpretation of *market value*. Forty-eight countries equated market value with net realizable value, meaning estimated selling price in the ordinary course of business less costs of completion and necessary selling expenses. This view was essentially required in 22 countries, including Australia, France, Ireland, South Africa, and the United Kingdom. IASC Statement No. 2 also requires this interpretation. Austria, Greece, Italy, and Venezuela interpreted market value as replacement cost—the current cost of replacing the inventories in their present condition and location.

The United States defines market value as replacement cost, with the stipulation that it cannot exceed net realizable value or fall below net realizable value reduced by the normal profit margin. In 1979, Chile, the Dominican Republic, Mexico, Panama, and the Philippines also used this interpretation of market value.

Accounting for the Effects of Changing Prices

The final example of international differences illustrates an opportunity for international harmonization that is almost unique. Accounting for the effects of changing prices is a relatively recent development, so it may be possible to achieve a general international approach to the problem before national practices become too varied and too entrenched.

The FASB, in *Statement No. 33,* required two methods: general price-level (constant-dollar) accounting and current-cost accounting.[14] However, *Statement No. 82* eliminated the requirement to use the first of these methods.[15] The first approach attempts to reflect the effects of changes in general purchasing power on historical-cost financial statements, while the second is concerned with the impact of specific price changes. FASB *Statement No. 89* made reporting the effects of inflation completely optional.[16]

---

[14] FASB, *Statement of Financial Accounting Standards No. 33,* "Financial Reporting and Changing Prices" (Stamford, Conn., 1979).

[15] FASB, *Statement of Financial Accounting Standards No. 82,* "Financial Reporting and Changing Prices: Elimination of Certain Disclosures" (Stamford, Conn., 1984).

[16] FASB, *Statement of Financial Accounting Standards No. 89,* "Financial Reporting and Changing Prices" (Stamford, Conn., 1987).

A number of countries are concerned about the loss of relevance of historical-cost financial reporting in inflationary environments, and several have adopted one of the two standard approaches—constant dollar or current cost. Some countries, usually those with the longest history of severe inflation, have issued standards that are mandatory for all enterprises, or at least for large or publicly held entities. In other countries, the accounting profession recommends, but does not prescribe, a form of inflation-adjusted statements, usually as supplementary information. Few countries, however, are prepared to abandon the present system based on historical cost and nominal units of currency for their primary financial statements, at least until decision makers have had sufficient experience with inflation accounting to give an opinion on its utility. Exceptions to this view are Argentina, Brazil, and Chile, which now require incorporation of general price-level accounting in the primary financial statements of all enterprises.

The United Kingdom's standard, until it was withdrawn, prescribed the provision of current-cost information either in the primary financial statements or as supplementary statements or additional information. New Zealand requires a supplementary income statement and balance sheet on a current-cost basis. Australia and South Africa recommend, but do not yet require, similar supplementary current-cost statements. Germany recommends the incorporation of current-cost information in notes to the historical-cost financial statements; while in the Netherlands, some companies prepare the primary statements on a current-cost basis, and some provide only supplementary information.

The fact that the accountancy bodies of various nations are adopting neither a uniform approach nor a uniform application of any approach, even with something as relatively new as accounting for changing prices, highlights the difficulty of achieving international harmonization of accounting standards. Adoption of different approaches to accounting for changing prices by different countries will make the preparation of consolidated financial statements by multinational corporations especially difficult, while at the same time comparability of the financial reports of companies in different nations will be further reduced. However, even if all countries adopted a similar approach, a major barrier to comparability would still remain: the price indexes used in each country to compute adjustments for price changes are not comparable in composition, accuracy, frequency of publication, or timeliness.

Many accountants are reluctant to see current-cost-adjusted statements replace historical-cost financial statements because they believe historical cost is the most objective basis of valuation. However, business entities may be more likely to favor inflation accounting, once they become accustomed to it, because of its tax implications—assuming the tax law permits the method. Since inflation accounting generally leads to lower profit figures than those computed on the historical-cost basis, companies have a strong incentive to adopt inflation accounting in those countries where computation of the tax liability is based on reported net income. Governments, on the other hand, could then decide to prohibit the use of inflation accounting for tax purposes when a decline in tax revenues becomes apparent.

The current trend in the use of approaches to accounting for changing prices appears to be toward current-cost accounting and away from general price-level accounting. Some suggest that, of the two approaches, governments prefer current-cost accounting, and this preference may influence the decisions of the accounting profession in some countries. As one British writer has pointed out:

> No government wants to have the effects of its currency debasement measured by anyone—certainly not by every business enterprise in the country. Much better to point the finger at all those individual prices moving around because of the machinations of big business, big labour and big aliens.[17]

Whether current-cost accounting will become common practice or whether some combination of current-cost and general price-level accounting will gain favor should depend on the usefulness to decision makers of the information provided by each approach. One thing is clear: When inflation again becomes a problem, more countries will adopt some form of inflation accounting. The opportunity to achieve a higher level of international harmonization while national standards are still at the development stage should not be missed.

We have attempted in these few pages to provide a broad and general picture of the variety of accounting principles and reporting practices that exist across the world. Articu-

---

[17] P. H. Lyons, "Farewell to Historical Costs?" *CA Magazine*, February 1976, p. 23.

lation among countries is a challenging problem—and one that will receive increasing attention in the years to come.

Selected Bibliography

The following sources can provide additional information about international accounting:

Arthur Andersen & Co. (London). *European Review,* nos. 1–5 (January 1981–May 1982).

Choi, Frederick D. S., and Richard M. Levich. "Behavioral Effects of International Accounting Diversity." *Accounting Horizons,* vol. 5, no. 2 (June 1991), pp. 1–13.

Choi, Frederick D. S., and Gerhard G. Mueller. *An Introduction to Multinational Accounting.* Englewood Cliffs, N.J.: Prentice Hall, 1984.

Cohen, Jeffery R.; Lanie W. Pant; and David J. Sharp. "Culture-Based Ethical Conflicts Confronting Multinational Accounting Firms," *Accounting Horizons*, vol. 7, no. 3 (September 1993), pp. 1–13.

Gandy, Lisa A. "German and Japanese Annual Reports Lack Sufficient Information." *Corporate Accounting International,* no. 1 (November 1989), pp. 14–15.

Gray, Sidney J., and Clare B. Robert. "East-West Accounting Issues: A New Agenda." *Accounting Horizons,* vol. 5, no. 1 (March 1991), pp. 42–50.

Hauworth, William P., II. "A Comparison of Various International Proposals on Inflation Accounting: A Practitioner's View." Monograph, 1980.

Hobson, D. "International Harmonization." *Public Finance and Accountancy* (May 1983), pp. 34–36.

Horner, Lawrence D. "Efficient Markets and Universal Standards." *Chief Executive* (Winter 1985), p. 38.

International Financial Reporting Standards: Problems and Prospects. ICRA Occasional Paper No. 13. Lancaster, England: International Centre for Research in Accounting, University of Lancaster, 1977.

London, David Aron. "Soviets Begin to Westernize Accounting Standards with East-West Joint Ventures." *Corporate Accounting International,* no. 1 (November 1989), pp. 6–7.

O'Carroll, Anne. "IASC's Goodwill Proposal Draws Much Negative Criticism." *Corporate Accounting International,* no. 1 (November 1989), pp. 8–9.

Price Waterhouse International. *International Survey of Accounting Principles and Reporting Practices,* 1979.

Purvis, S. E. C., Helen Gernon, and Michael A. Diamond. "The IASC and Its Comparability Project: Prerequisite for Success." *Accounting Horizons,* vol. 5, no. 2 (June 1991), pp. 25–44.

Smith, Bradford E. "Red Revolution Jostles World Rule Makers." *Accounting Today* (January 22, 1990), p. 12.

Stamp, Edward. *The Future of Accounting and Auditing Standards. ICRA Occasional Paper No. 18*. Lancaster, England: International Centre for Research in Accounting, University of Lancaster, 1979.

Stamp, Edward, and Maurice Moonitz. "International Auditing Standards—Parts I and II." *The CPA Journal* LII, nos. 6 and 7 (June–July 1982).

Demonstration Problem 14–A

Following are selected transactions and other data for Kelly Company for 1997:

Mar. 21 Purchased 600 shares of Sly Company common stock at $48.75 per share, plus a $450 broker's commission. Also purchased 100 shares of Rob Company common stock at $225 per share, plus a $376 broker's commission. Both investments are expected to be temporary.

June 2 Received cash dividends of $1.50 per share on the Sly common shares and $3 per share on the Rob common shares.

Aug. 12 Received shares representing a 100% stock dividend on the Rob shares.

30 Sold 100 shares of Rob common stock at $120 per share, less a $360 broker's commission.

Sept. 15 Received shares representing a 10% stock dividend on the Sly common stock. Market price today was $52.50 per share.

Dec. 31 Per share market values for the two investments in common stock are Sly, $45.75, and Rob, $106.50. Both investments are considered temporary.

Required Prepare journal entries to record these transactions and the necessary adjustments for a December 31 closing.

Solution to Demonstration Problem 14–A

KELLY COMPANY
GENERAL JOURNAL

			Debit	Credit
1997				
Mar.	21	Trading Securities	52,576	
		Cash		52,576
		To record purchase of 600 shares of Sly common stock for $29,700 and 100 shares of Rob common stock for $22,876.		
June	2	Cash	1,200	
		Dividend Revenue		1,200
		To record cash dividends: $900 Sly, and $300 Rob.		
Aug.	12	Received 100 shares of Rob common stock as a 100% stock dividend. The new cost per share is $22,876 ÷ 200 shares = $114.38.		
	30	Cash	11,640	
		Trading Securities		11,438
		Gain on Sale of Trading Securities		202
		To record sale of trading securities: proceeds = $12,000 − $360; cost = $114.38 × 100 shares.		
Sept.	15	Received 60 shares of Sly common stock as a 10% stock dividend. New cost per share is $29,700 ÷ 660 shares = $45.		
Dec.	31	Unrealized Loss on Trading Securities	293	
		Trading Securities		293
		To write trading securities down to market value:		

	Cost	Market	Inc. (Dec.) in Market Value
Sly common stock	$29,700	$30,195*	$ 495
Rob common stock	11,438	10,650†	(788)
Total	$41,138	$40,845	$(293)

* $45.75 × 660 shares = $30,195.
† $106.50 × 100 shares = $10,650.

Demonstration Problem 14–B

Lanford Company acquired all of the outstanding voting common stock of Casey Company on January 2, 1997, for $300,000 cash. After the close of business on the date of acquisition, the balance sheets for the two companies were as follows:

	Lanford Company	Casey Company
Assets		
Cash	$ 75,000	$ 30,000
Accounts receivable, net	90,000	37,500
Notes receivable	15,000	7,500
Merchandise inventory	112,500	45,000
Investment in Casey Company	300,000	
Investment in bonds		30,000
Plant and equipment, net	303,000	195,000
Total assets	$895,500	$345,000

	Lanford Company	Casey Company
Liabilities and Stockholders' Equity		
Accounts payable	$ 75,000	$ 45,000
Notes payable	22,500	15,000
Bonds payable	225,000	
Common stock—$7.50 par value	300,000	150,000
Paid-in capital in excess of par value—common		60,000
Retained earnings	273,000	75,000
Total liabilities and stockholders' equity	$895,500	$345,000

On January 2, 1997, Casey Company borrowed $15,000 from Lanford Company by giving a note. On that same day, Casey Company purchased $30,000 of Lanford Company's bonds. The excess of cost over book value is attributable to Casey Company's above-average earnings prospects.

Prepare a work sheet for a consolidated balance sheet on the date of acquisition. *Required*

Solution to Demonstration Problem 14–B

LANFORD COMPANY AND SUBSIDIARY CASEY COMPANY
Work Sheet for Consolidated Balance Sheet
January 2, 1997 (date of acquisition)

	Lanford Company	Casey Company	Eliminations Debit	Eliminations Credit	Consolidated Amounts
Assets					
Cash	75,000	30,000			105,000
Accounts receivable, net	90,000	37,500			127,500
Notes receivable	15,000	7,500		(2) 15,000	7,500
Merchandise inventory	112,500	45,000			157,500
Investment in Casey Co.	300,000			(1) 300,000	
Investment in bonds		30,000		(3) 30,000	–0–
Plant and equipment, net	303,000	195,000			498,000
Goodwill			(1) 15,000		15,000
	895,500	345,000			910,500
Liabilities and Stockholders' Equity					
Accounts payable	75,000	45,000			120,000
Notes payable	22,500	15,000	(2) 15,000		22,500
Bonds payable	225,000		(3) 30,000		195,000
Common stock—$7.50 par	300,000	150,000	(1) 150,000		300,000
Paid-in capital in excess of par value—common		60,000	(1) 60,000		–0–
Retained earnings	273,000	75,000	(1) 75,000		273,000
	895,500	345,000	345,000	345,000	910,500

New Terms

Available-for-sale securities Securities purchased that will be held for longer than the near term. *501*

Consolidated statements The financial statements that result from consolidating the parent's financial statement amounts with those of its subsidiaries (after certain eliminations have been made). The consolidated statements reflect the financial position and results of operations of a single economic enterprise. *506*

Consolidated statement work sheet An informal record on which elimination entries are made to show account balances as if the parent and its subsidiaries were a single economic enterprise. *508*

Cost method A method of accounting for stock investments in which the investor company does not adjust the investment account balance for its share of the investee's reported income, losses, and dividends. Dividends received are credited to Dividends Revenue. *501*

Current/historical-rates approach Regards the parent company and its foreign subsidiaries as a single business undertaking. All assets are shown at historical cost in the parent company's currency. *526*

Current-noncurrent method Translates current assets and current liabilities at the current rate and noncurrent items at their historical rates. *526*

Current rate Exchange rate in effect on the balance sheet date. *525*

Current-rate or closing-rate approach The current-rate or closing rate method translates all assets and liabilities at the current rate, the exchange rate in effect on the balance sheet date. *526*

Dividend yield on common stock ratio Equal to dividend per share of common stock divided by the current market price per share. Investors use this ratio to compare stocks. *518*

Elimination entries Entries made on a consolidated statement work sheet to remove certain intercompany items and transactions. Elimination entries allow the presentation of all account balances as if the parent and its subsidiaries were a single economic enterprise. *507*

Equity method A method of accounting for stock investments where the investment account is adjusted periodically for the investor company's share of the investee's income, losses, and dividends as they are reported by the investee. *501, 505*

Exchange gains or losses (time-of-transaction method) The difference between the amount recorded in Accounts Payable on the purchase date and amount of cash paid on the settlement date. *525*

Goodwill An intangible value attached to a business primarily due to above-average earnings prospects. *509*

Historical rate The exchange rate in effect when an asset or liability is originally recorded. *526*

Intercompany transactions Financial transactions involving a parent and one of its subsidiaries or between two of the subsidiaries. *507*

Investee A company that has 20% to 50% of its stock purchased by another company (the investor) as a long-term investment. *505*

Investor A company that purchases 20% to 50% of another company (the investee) as a long-term investment. *505*

Marketable equity securities Readily saleable common and preferred stocks of other companies. *502*

Minority interest The claim or interest of the stockholders who own less than 50% of a subsidiary's outstanding voting common stock. The minority stockholders have an interest in the subsidiary's net assets and share the subsidiary's earnings with the parent company. *511*

Monetary-nonmonetary method Translates monetary assets and liabilities at the current rate and nonmonetary items at their historical rates. *526*

Parent company A corporation that owns more than 50% of the outstanding voting common stock of another corporation. *506*

Payout ratio on common stock Calculated by dividing dividend per share of common stock by earnings per share (EPS). The ratio indicates whether a company pays out a large percentage of earnings as dividends or reinvests most of its earnings. *519*

Pooling of interests A business combination that meets certain criteria specified in *APB Opinion No. 16,* including the issuance of common stock in exchange for common stock. *516*

Purchase A transaction in which one company issues cash or other assets to acquire common stock of another company. Also, any combination that does not qualify as a pooling of interests. *516*

Subsidiary company A corporation acquired and controlled by a parent corporation; control is established by ownership of more than 50% of the subsidiary's outstanding voting common stock. *506*

Temporal method Cash, receivables and payables, and other assets and liabilities carried at current prices are translated at the current rate of exchange. All other assets and liabilities are translated at historical rates. *526*

Trading securities Securities bought principally for sale in the near term. *501*

SELF-TEST

TRUE-FALSE

Indicate whether each of the following statements is true or false.

1. Under the cost method, the investment account is adjusted when dividends are received.
2. The cost method should be used when a corporation makes a long-term investment of less than 20%, and there is no significant control.
3. In a stock split, the investor does not recognize revenue, but reduces the cost per share of stock.
4. Trading securities and available-for-sale securities should be grouped separately in applying the fair market value rules.
5. When making elimination entries, the entries are made only on the consolidated statements work sheet and not on the accounting records of the parent and subsidiary.
6. (*Based on appendix*) Pronouncements issued by the International Accounting Standards Committee (IASC) must be followed by member nations.

Multiple-Choice

Select the best answer for each of the following questions.

1. In which of the following cases is the investor company limited to use of the equity method in accounting for its stock investments?
   - **a.** Short-term investments.
   - **b.** Long-term investments of less than 20%.
   - **c.** Long-term investments of 20%–50%.
   - **d.** Long-term investments of more than 50%.
2. Under the equity method, which of the following is true?
   - **a.** Dividends received reduce the investment account.
   - **b.** Dividends received increase the investment account.
   - **c.** The investor's share of net income decreases the investment account.
   - **d.** The investor's share of net loss increases the investment account.
3. When the fair market value rules are followed, which of the following is true when the market value of the stocks in the Trading Securities account falls below their cost?
   - **a.** The Unrealized Losses on Trading Securities account is credited.
   - **b.** The Recovery of Market Value of Trading Securities account is credited.
   - **c.** The Allowance for Market Decline of Current Marketable Equity Securities is debited.
   - **d.** The Unrealized Loss on Trading Securities is debited.
4. Under the equity method, the investment account always reflects only the:
   - **a.** Dividends paid by the investee corporation.
   - **b.** Investor's interest in the net assets of the investee.
   - **c.** Investor's share of net income.
   - **d.** Historical cost of the investment.
5. The excess of cost over the book value of an investment that is due to expected above-average earnings is labeled on the consolidated balance sheet as:
   - **a.** Goodwill.
   - **b.** Common stock.
   - **c.** Retained earnings.
   - **d.** Loss on investment.
6. (*Based on appendix*) Which of the following statements is true regarding the environment of international accounting?
   - **a.** More and more nations are switching to a market-oriented economy.
   - **b.** The accounting practices around the world are almost completely harmonized.
   - **c.** The other nations of the world are willing to accept accounting methods used in the United States as the best methods to use in their own countries.
   - **d.** The topic of international accounting is becoming less and less relevant over time.

Now turn to page 542 to check your answers.

Questions

1. For what reasons do corporations purchase the stock of other corporations?
2. Explain how marketable securities should be classified in the balance sheet.
3. Describe the valuation bases used for marketable equity securities.
4. Under what circumstances is the equity method used to account for stock investments?
5. Explain briefly the accounting for stock dividends and stock splits from the investor's point of view.
6. Of what significance is par value to the investing corporation?
7. What is the purpose of preparing consolidated financial statements?
8. Under what circumstances must consolidated financial statements be prepared?
9. Why is it necessary to make elimination entries on the consolidated statement work sheet? Are these elimination entries also posted to the accounts of the parent and subsidiary? Why or why not?
10. Why might a corporation pay an amount in excess of the book value for a subsidiary's stock? Why might it pay an amount less than the book value of the subsidiary's stock?
11. The item *Minority interest* often appears as one amount in the consolidated balance sheet. What does this item represent?
12. How do a subsidiary's earnings, losses, and dividends affect the investment account of the parent when the equity method of accounting is used?
13. When must each of the following methods be used to account for a business combination?
    - **a.** Purchase.
    - **b.** Pooling of interests.
14. List three differences between the purchase and pooling of interests methods of accounting for business combinations.
15. Why are consolidated financial statements of limited usefulness to the creditors and minority stockholders of a subsidiary?
16. Distinguish between a purchase and a pooling of interests.
17. (*Based on appendix*) Why do differences exist in accounting standards and practices from nation to nation?

18. (*Based on appendix*) How successful have efforts at harmonization been to date?

The Coca-Cola Company

19. **Real World Question.** Based on the financial statements of The Coca-Cola Company contained in the annual report booklet, what was the 1993 Investment in Coca-Cola Enterprises, Inc., balance? According to Note 3, what percentage of Coca-Cola Enterprises, Inc., does The Coca-Cola Company own? What method of accounting (cost or equity) does The Coca-Cola Company use for its investment? Why did its investment decrease from 1992 to 1993?

HARLAND

20. **Real World Question.** Based on the financial statements of John H. Harland Company contained in the annual report booklet, what was the 1993 ending investment balance? What was the net change from 1992?

Exercises

Exercise 14–1
Prepare entries for trading securities (L.O. 2)

On July 1, 1997, Mike Company purchased 200 shares of Sam Company capital stock as a temporary investment (trading securities) at $338.40 per share plus a commission of $360. On July 15, a 10% stock dividend was received. Mike received a cash dividend of $1.80 per share on August 12, 1997. On November 1, Mike sold all of the shares for $417.60 per share, less a commission of $360. Prepare entries to record all of these transactions in Mike Company's accounts if this investment is classified under current assets.

Exercise 14–2
Prepare entries for trading securities (L.O. 2)

Kron Company purchased 200 shares of Wiley Company stock at a total cost of $7,560 on July 1, 1997. At the end of the accounting year (December 31, 1997), the market value for these shares was $6,840. By December 31, 1998, the market value had risen to $7,920. This stock is the only marketable equity security that Kron Company owns. The company classifies the securities as trading securities. Give the entries necessary at the date of purchase and at December 31, 1997, and 1998.

Exercise 14–3
Apply fair market value method to marketable equity securities (L.O. 2)

Alley Company has marketable equity securities that have a fair market value at year-end that is $6,720 below their cost. Give the required entry if:

a. The securities are current assets classified as trading securities.

b. The securities are noncurrent assets classified as available-for-sale securities, and the loss is considered to be temporary.

c. The securities are noncurrent assets classified as available-for-sale securities, and the loss is considered to be permanent.

State where each of the accounts debited in **a, b,** and **c** would be reported in the financial statements.

Exercise 14–4
Prepare equity method entries for an investment (L.O. 1, 3)

Diez Company owns 75% of Crone Company's outstanding common stock and uses the equity method of accounting. Crone Company reported net income of $702,000 for 1997. On December 31, 1997, Crone Company paid a cash dividend of $189,000. In 1998, Crone Company incurred a net loss of $125,000. Prepare entries to reflect these events on Diez Company's books.

Exercise 14–5
Record investment at book value and elimination entry as of acquisition date (L.O. 5)

On February 1, 1997, Lowe Company acquired 100% of the outstanding voting common stock of TRD Company for $4,200,000 cash. The stockholders' equity of the TRD Company consisted of common stock, $3,360,000, and retained earnings, $840,000. Prepare *(a)* the entry to record the investment in TRD Company and *(b)* the elimination entry on the work sheet used to prepare a consolidated balance sheet as of the date of acquisition.

Exercise 14–6
Determine amount of goodwill (L.O. 5)

Given the facts in Exercise 14–5, how much would be recorded as goodwill in each of the following instances? The same amount was paid, but the parent company acquired a—

a. 90% interest.

b. 70% interest.

c. 55% interest.

Exercise 14–7
Record investment at more than book value and elimination entry as of acquisition date (L.O. 5)

Helen Corporation acquired, for cash, 80% of the outstanding voting common stock of Stone Company. After the close of business on the date of acquisition, Stone Company's stockholders' equity consisted of common stock, $2,940,000, and retained earnings, $1,092,000. The cost of the investment exceeded the book value by $151,200 and was attributable to above-average earnings prospects. Prepare *(a)* the entry to record the investment in Stone Company and *(b)* the elimination entry on the work sheet used to prepare consolidated financial statements as of the date of acquisition.

Exercise 14–8
Compute difference between cost and book value of common stock investments (L.O. 5)

On January 1, 1994, Company J acquired 85% of the outstanding voting common stock of Company K. On that date, Company K's stockholders' equity consisted of:

Stockholders' equity:	
Paid-in capital:	
Common stock, $90 par; 30,000 shares authorized, issued, and outstanding	$2,700,000
Retained earnings	675,000
Total stockholders' equity	$3,375,000

Compute the difference between cost and book value in each of the following cases:

a. Company J pays $2,868,750 cash for its interest in Company K.

b. Company J pays $3,375,000 cash for its interest in Company K.

c. Company J pays $2,610,000 cash for its interest in Company K.

Exercise 14–9
Compute book value, difference between cost and book value, and minority interest of an investment (L.O. 5)

The January 1, 1997, stockholders' equity section of Sawyer Company's balance sheet follows:

Stockholders' equity:	
Paid-in capital:	
Common stock—$72 par value: authorized, 200,000 shares; issued and outstanding, 150,000 shares	$10,800,000
Paid-in capital in excess of par value	1,800,000
Total paid-in capital	$12,600,000
Retained earnings	1,080,000
Total stockholders' equity	$13,680,000

Ninety percent of Sawyer Company's outstanding voting common stock was acquired by Tom Company on January 1, 1998, for $12,024,000. Compute *(a)* the book value of the investment, *(b)* the difference between cost and book value, and *(c)* the minority interest.

Exercise 14–10
Compute investment account balance at year-end and minority interest at beginning and end of year (L.O. 2, 5)

Company S purchased 90% of Company T's outstanding voting common stock on January 2, 1997. Company S paid $2,790,000 for its proportionate equity of $2,430,000, representing $1,620,000 common stock and $210,000 of retained earnings. The difference was due to undervalued land owned by Company T. Company T earned $324,000 during 1997 and paid cash dividends of $108,000.

a. Compute the balance in the investment account on December 31, 1997.

b. Compute the amount of the minority interest on (1) January 2, 1997, and (2) December 31, 1997.

PROBLEMS

Problem 14–1
Prepare entries for trading securities (L.O. 1, 2)

Koch Company acquired on July 15, 1997, 400 shares of Risner Company $360 par value capital stock at $349.20 per share plus a broker's commission of $864. On August 1, 1997, Koch Company received a cash dividend of $4.32 per share. On November 3, 1997, it sold 200 of these shares at $378 per share less a broker's commission of $576. On December 1, 1997, Risner Company issued shares comprising a 100% stock dividend declared on its capital stock on November 18.

On December 31, 1997, the end of Koch Company's calendar-year accounting period, the market quotation for Risner Company's common stock was $165.60 per share. The decline was considered to be temporary.

Required

a. Prepare journal entries to record all of these data assuming the securities are considered temporary investments classified as trading securities. Where should the accounts in the last entry appear in the financial statements?

b. Assume Risner Company has become a major customer so the shares are held for long-term affiliation purposes. Indicate how the investment should be shown in the balance sheet.

Problem 14–2
Prepare entries for trading securities; compare entries to those for available-for-sale securities (L.O. 1, 2)

On October 17, 1997, Abadie Company purchased the following common stocks (all trading securities) at the indicated per share prices that included commissions:

600 shares of X Company common stock @ $216	$129,600
1,000 shares of Y Company common stock @ $144	144,000
1,600 shares of Z Company common stock @ $72	115,200
	$388,800

On December 31, 1997, the market prices per share of the above common stocks were X, $223.20; Y, $136.80; and Z, $54.

Summarized, the cash dividends per share received in 1998 were X, $14.40; Y, $7.20; and Z, $5.40.

On December 31, 1998, the per share market prices were X, $252.80; Y, $115.20; and Z, $72.

All of these changes in market prices are considered temporary.

Required

a. Prepare journal entries for all of these transactions, including calendar year-end adjusting entries, assuming the shares of common stock acquired are considered trading securities.

b. If the securities acquired are considered available-for-sale securities, how would the entries made in **a** differ?

c. For both parts **a** and **b**, give the descriptions (titles) and the dollar amounts of the items that would appear in the income statements for 1997 and 1998.

Problem 14–3
Prepare equity method entries for an investment and eliminating entries for consolidated statements work sheet (L.O. 1, 3, 5)

On January 1, 1997, Creed Company acquired 80% of the outstanding voting common stock of Copeland Company for $2,016,000 cash. Creed Company uses the equity method. During 1997, Copeland reported $336,000 of net income and paid $144,000 in dividends. The stockholders' equity section of the December 31, 1996, balance sheet for Copeland follows:

Stockholders' equity:	
Paid-in capital:	
Common stock—$21 par	$2,100,000
Retained earnings	420,000
Total stockholders' equity	$2,520,000

Required

a. Prepare the general journal entries to record the investment and the effect of Copeland's income and dividends on Creed Company's accounts.

b. Prepare the elimination entry that would be made on the work sheet for a consolidated balance sheet as of the date of acquisition.

Problem 14–4
Prepare equity method entries for an investment (L.O. 1, 3, 5)

Marsh Company acquired 75% of the outstanding voting common stock of Rawlins Company for $2,889,600 cash on January 1, 1997. The investment is accounted for under the equity method. During 1997, 1998, and 1999, Rawlins Company reported the following:

	Net Income (loss)	Dividends Paid
1997	$715,680	$581,280
1998	(90,720)	–0–
1999	216,720	144,480

Required

a. Prepare general journal entries to record the investment and the effect of the subsidiary's income, losses, and dividends on Marsh Company's accounts.

b. Compute the balance in the investment account on December 31, 1999.

Problem 14–5
Prepare work sheet and consolidated balance sheet at acquisition (L.O. 5)

Penno Company acquired 100% of the outstanding voting common stock of Moran Company on January 2, 1997, for $2,700,000. At the end of business on the date of acquisition, the balance sheets for the two companies were as follows:

	Penno Company	Moran Company
Assets		
Cash	$ 315,000	$ 180,000
Accounts receivable, net	234,000	144,000
Notes receivable	360,000	90,000
Merchandise inventory	495,000	234,000
Investment in Moran Company	2,700,000	
Equipment, net	648,000	450,000
Buildings, net	1,890,000	990,000
Land	765,000	405,000
Total assets	$7,407,000	$2,493,000
Liabilities and Stockholders' Equity		
Accounts payable	$ 117,000	$ 135,000
Notes payable	90,000	108,000
Common stock—$45 par value	5,400,000	1,800,000
Retained earnings	1,800,000	450,000
Total liabilities and stockholders' equity	$7,407,000	$2,493,000

The excess of cost over book value is attributable to the above-average earnings prospects of Moran Company. On the date of acquisition, Moran Company borrowed $72,000 from Penno Company by giving a note.

Required

a. Prepare a work sheet for a consolidated balance sheet as of the date of acquisition.
b. Prepare a consolidated balance sheet for January 2, 1997.

Problem 14–6
Prepare work sheet for consolidated financial statements (L.O. 5)

Refer to Problem 14–5. Penno Company uses the equity method. Assume the following are from the adjusted trial balances of Penno Company and Moran Company on December 31, 1997:

	Penno Company	Moran Company
Debit Balance Accounts		
Cash	$ 351,000	$ 315,000
Accounts receivable, net	378,000	180,000
Notes receivable	315,000	45,000
Merchandise inventory, December 31	495,000	287,100
Investment in Moran Company	2,790,000	
Equipment, net	615,600	427,500
Buildings, net	1,814,400	950,400
Land	765,000	405,000
Cost of goods sold	1,800,000	630,000
Expenses (excluding depreciation and taxes)	720,000	270,900
Depreciation expense	108,000	62,100
Income tax expense	585,000	189,000
Dividends	540,000	108,000
Total of the accounts with debit balances	$11,277,000	$3,870,000
Credit Balance Accounts		
Accounts payable	$ 135,000	$ 180,000
Notes payable	144,000	90,000
Common stock—$45 par value	5,400,000	1,800,000
Retained earnings—January 1	1,800,000	450,000
Revenue from sales	3,600,000	1,350,000
Income of Moran Company	198,000	
Total of the accounts with credit balances	$11,277,000	$3,870,000

There is no intercompany debt at the end of the year.

Required

Prepare a work sheet for consolidated financial statements on December 31, 1997. Ignore the amortization of goodwill.

Problem 14–7
Prepare consolidated income statement, statement of retained earnings, and balance sheet (L.O. 5)

Using the work sheet from Problem 14–6, prepare the following items:

a. Consolidated income statement for the year ended December 31, 1997.
b. Consolidated statement of retained earnings for the year ended December 31, 1997.
c. Consolidated balance sheet for December 31, 1997.

Problem 14–8
Answer multiple-choice questions regarding international accounting (based on appendix) (L.O. 8)

Select the best answer to each of the following questions:

1. Methods used to account for transactions between companies in different nations when goods are received on one date and the invoice is paid on another date include:
   a. Time-of-transaction method.
   b. Time-of-settlement method.
   c. Current-rate method.
   d. **a** and **b** are correct.
2. Which of the following statements is false regarding translating the financial statements of foreign subsidiaries?
   a. Under the *current-rate approach*, all assets and liabilities are translated at the exchange rate in effect on the balance sheet date.
   b. Under the *current-noncurrent method,* current assets and current liabilities are translated at the current rate, and noncurrent items are translated at their historical rates.
   c. Under the *monetary-nonmonetary method,* nonmonetary assets and liabilities are translated at their historical rate.
   d. The nations of the world now have settled on the current-rate method.
3. Variations between nations in accounting for inventories include all *except* which of the following?
   a. The basis for determining cost.
   b. Whether cost should be increased or decreased to reflect changes in market value.
   c. Whether inventories should be written down to an amount below both cost and market.
   d. Whether standard costs should be used.
4. In accounting for the effects of inflation, the approach that seems to be favored by most nations that have adopted an approach is:
   a. Current cost.
   b. Constant dollar (general price-level) adjusted statements.
   c. A combination of **a** and **b** in one set of financial statements.
   d. Both **a** and **b** as two sets of financial statements.

Alternate Problems

Problem 14–1A
Prepare entries for available-for-sale securities (L.O. 1, 3)

On September 1, 1997, Gomez Company purchased the following long-term investments classified as available-for-sale securities:

1. Two thousand shares of Newberry Company capital stock at $219.60 plus broker's commission of $2,880.
2. One thousand shares of Reid Company capital stock at $352.80 plus broker's commission of $2,520.

Cash dividends of $9.00 per share on the Newberry capital stock and $7.20 per share on the Reid capital stock were received on December 7 and December 10, respectively.

On December 31, 1997, per share market values are Newberry, $230.40; and Reid, $327.60.

Required

a. Prepare journal entries to record these transactions.
b. Prepare the necessary adjusting entry(ies) at December 31, 1997, to adjust the carrying values assuming that market price changes are believed to be temporary. Where would the accounts appear in the financial statements?

Problem 14–2A
Prepare entries for trading securities (L.O. 1, 2)

Bogard, Inc., purchased on July 2, 1997, 240 shares of Lowery Company $180 par value common stock as a temporary investment at $288 per share, plus a broker's commission of $432.

On July 15, 1997, a cash dividend of $7.20 per share was received. On September 15, 1997, Lowery Company split its $180 par value common shares two for one.

On November 2, 1997, Bogard sold 200 shares of Lowery common stock at $180, less a broker's commission of $288.

Required

a. Prepare journal entries to record all of these above 1999 transactions.

b. How would you recommend that the remaining shares be classified in the December 31, 1997, balance sheet if still held at that date?

c. Assume the remaining shares were considered current assets classified as trading securities at the end of 1997, at which time their market value was $128 per share. Prepare any necessary adjusting entries for the end of 1997.

Problem 14–3A
Prepare equity method entries for an investment and eliminating entries for consolidated work sheet (L.O. 1, 3, 5)

Ward Company acquired 90% of the outstanding voting common stock of Sherman Company on January 1, 1997, for $3,780,000 cash. Ward Company uses the equity method. During 1997, Sherman reported $756,000 of net income and paid $252,000 in cash dividends. The stockholders' equity section of the December 31, 1996, balance sheet for Sherman follows:

Stockholders' equity:	
Paid-in capital:	
Common stock—$21.00 par	$3,360,000
Retained earnings	840,000
Total stockholders' equity	$4,200,000

Required

a. Prepare general journal entries to record the investment and the effect of Sherman's earnings and dividends on Ward Company's accounts.

b. Prepare the elimination entry that would be made on the work sheet for a consolidated balance sheet as of the date of acquisition.

Problem 14–4A
Prepare equity method entries for an investment (L.O. 1, 3, 5)

Conner Company acquired 70% of the outstanding voting common stock of Scott Company for $8,568,000 on January 1, 1997. The investment is accounted for under the equity method. During the years 1997–99, Scott Company reported the following:

	Net Income (loss)	Dividends Paid
1997	$1,454,880	$871,920
1998	372,960	223,440
1999	(23,520)	55,860

Required

a. Prepare general journal entries to record the investment and the effect of the subsidiary's income, losses, and dividends on Conner Company's accounts.

b. Compute the investment account balance on December 31, 1999.

Problem 14–5A
Prepare work sheet and consolidated balance sheet at acquisition (L.O. 5)

Jennings Company acquired all of the outstanding voting common stock of Dyer Company on January 2, 1997, for $2,160,000. On the date of acquisition, the balance sheets for the two companies were as follows:

	Jennings Company	Dyer Company
Assets		
Cash	$ 450,000	$ 135,000
Accounts receivable, net	216,000	180,000
Notes receivable	90,000	54,000
Merchandise inventory	684,000	432,000
Investment in Dyer Company	2,160,000	
Equipment, net	612,000	369,000
Buildings, net	1,665,000	828,000
Land	702,000	225,000
Total assets	$6,579,000	$2,223,000

Liabilities and Stockholders' Equity		
Accounts payable	$ 396,000	$ 180,000
Notes payable	108,000	126,000
Common stock—$60 par value	4,770,000	1,782,000
Retained earnings	1,305,000	135,000
Total liabilities and stockholders' equity	$6,579,000	$2,223,000

The management of Jennings Company thinks that the Dyer Company's land is undervalued by $81,000. The remainder of the excess of cost over book value is due to superior earnings potential.

On the date of acquisition, Dyer Company borrowed $90,000 from Jennings Company by giving a note.

Required

a. Prepare a work sheet for a consolidated balance sheet as of the date of acquisition.

b. Prepare a consolidated balance sheet for January 2, 1997.

Problem 14–6A
Prepare work sheet for consolidated financial statements (L.O. 5)

Refer back to Problem 14–5A. Jennings Company uses the equity method. Assume the following amounts are taken from the adjusted trial balances of Jennings Company and Dyer Company on December 31, 1997:

	Jennings Company	Dyer Company
Debit Balance Accounts		
Cash	$ 432,000	$ 182,148
Accounts receivable, net	276,768	207,000
Notes receivable	171,000	45,000
Merchandise inventory, December 31	765,000	504,000
Investment in Dyer Company	2,259,678	
Equipment, net	573,750	345,930
Buildings, net	1,581,750	786,600
Land	702,000	225,000
Cost of goods sold	4,032,000	1,080,000
Expenses (excluding depreciation and taxes)	1,080,000	405,000
Depreciation expense	121,500	64,470
Income tax expense	284,832	61,752
Dividends	238,500	89,100
Total of the accounts with debit balances	$12,518,778	$3,996,000
Credit Balance Accounts		
Accounts payable	$ 360,000	$ 189,000
Notes payable	135,000	90,000
Common stock—$90 par value	4,770,000	1,782,000
Retained earnings	1,305,000	135,000
Revenue from sales	5,760,000	1,800,000
Income of Dyer Company	188,778	
Total of the accounts with credit balances	$12,518,778	$3,996,000

There is no intercompany debt at the end of the year.

Required

Prepare a work sheet for consolidated financial statements on December 31, 1997. Ignore the amortization of goodwill.

Problem 14–7A
Prepare consolidated income statement, statement of retained earnings, and balance sheet (L.O. 5)

Using the work sheet from Problem 14–6A, prepare the following items:

a. Consolidated income statement for the year ended December 31, 1997.

b. Consolidated statement of retained earnings for the year ended December 31, 1997.

c. Consolidated balance sheet for December 31, 1997.

Problem 14–8A
Answer fill-in-the-blank questions regarding international accounting (based on appendix) (L.O. 8)

Supply the missing word(s) in the following statements:

a. Accounting must reflect the national ______________ and ______________ environment in which it is practiced.

b. Other accounting differences among nations stem from the legal or ______________ differences.

c. Commonwealth nations tend to adopt ______________ accounting standards.

d. Several organizations are working to achieve greater understanding and ______________ of accounting principles.

e. Ultimately, the success of international pronouncements depends on the willingness of the nations to ______________ them.

f. ______________ ______________ translation is probably the most common problem in an international business environment.

BEYOND THE NUMBERS—CRITICAL THINKING

Business Decision Case 14–1
Classify a portfolio of marketable equity securities as current or noncurrent investments (L.O. 1)

You are the CPA engaged to audit the records of Quigley Company. You find that your client has a portfolio of marketable equity securities that has a total market value of $300,000 less than the total cost of the portfolio. You ask the vice president for finance if the client expects to sell these securities in the coming year. He answers that he doesn't know. The securities will be sold if additional cash is needed to finance operations. When you ask for a cash forecast, you are told that a forecast has been prepared that covers the next year. It indicates no need to sell the marketable securities.

Required

Write a brief statement in which you explain how you would classify the client's portfolio of marketable securities in the balance sheet. Does it really make any difference whether the securities are classified as trading securities or available-for-sale securities? Explain.

Business Decision Case 14–2
Prepare a consolidated balance sheet at acquisition (L.O. 5)

On January 2, 1997, Tyler Company acquired 60% of the voting common stock of Yoshihara Company for $360,000 cash. The excess of cost over book value was due to above-average earnings prospects. Tyler has hired you to help it prepare consolidated financial statements and has already collected the following information for both companies as of January 2, 1997:

	Tyler Company	Yoshihara Company
Assets		
Cash	$ 36,000	$ 27,000
Accounts receivable, net	54,000	63,000
Merchandise inventory	144,000	108,000
Investment in Yoshihara Company	360,000	
Plant and equipment, net	468,000	369,000
Total assets	$1,062,000	$567,000
Liabilities and Stockholders' Equity		
Accounts payable	$ 72,000	$ 27,000
Common stock—$72 par	720,000	360,000
Retained earnings	270,000	180,000
Total liabilities and stockholders' equity	$1,062,000	$567,000

Required

a. Tyler believes that consolidated financial statements can be prepared simply by adding together the amounts in the two individual columns. Is he correct? If not, why not?

b. Prepare a consolidated balance sheet for the date of acquisition without preparing a consolidated statement work sheet.

Business Decision Case 14–3
Compute the dividend yield on common stock and the payout ratios. Analyze ratios (L.O. 8)

Lockheed Corporation researches, develops, and produces aerospace products and systems, such as military and civilian space systems, strategic fleet ballistic missiles, and tactical defense and communications systems.

Use the following excerpt from Lockheed Corporation's 1992 annual report to calculate the dividend yield on common stock and the payout ratios.

Consider the fact that Lockheed's Hercules plane flew thousands of missions in 1992 to Somalia and Sarajevo carrying tons of food, medicine, and relief supplies. In addition, 1992 saw a decrease in military spending. Explain how these two facts could be interrelated. Could these two facts affect the dividend yield on common stock ratio or the payout ratio on common stock? How?

	1992	1991	1990
Earnings per share			
Before cumulative effect of change in accounting principle	$ 5.65	$ 4.86	$ 5.30
Cumulative effect of change in accounting principle	(10.23)		
Net earnings (loss) per share	(4.58)	4.86	5.30
Dividends per share ($)	2.09	1.95	1.80
Stock price per common share ($)	56.88	44.00	33.63

Annual Report Analysis 14-4
Determine effect of differences between U.K. GAAP and U.S. GAAP on net income (Appendix)

Refer to the Reuters's annual report excerpt in "A Broader Perspective" on page 524. In writing, explain how the differences between the U.K. and the U.S. GAAP would affect Reuters's net income.

Group Project 14–5
Determine gain or loss on short-term investments

In teams of two or three students, select three companies you believe may be profitable short-term investments. Determine the current market prices for those companies' stocks from today's newspaper and the market prices six months ago. Calculate the gain or loss that your team would have recorded if it had purchased 500 shares of each company's stock six months ago and sold all of the shares today. Write a short memo to your instructor describing why you selected those companies and why you believe the market prices of their stocks increased or decreased. Also, be prepared to describe your analysis to the class.

Answers to Self-Test

True-False

1. **False.** Under the cost method of accounting for stock investments, the Dividend Revenue account, rather than the investment account, is adjusted.
2. **True.** For long-term investments of less than 20%, the cost method should be used.
3. **True.** Revenue is not recognized when there is a stock split. The new number of shares is recorded, and the cost per share is reduced.
4. **True.** Trading securities should be considered separately from available-for-sale securities in applying the fair market value method.
5. **True.** Eliminating entries are not made on the accounting records of the parent and subsidiary. Only the work sheet is affected by elimination entries made during consolidation.
6. **False.** The IASC can only recommend specific practices and procedures for adoption by member nations.

Multiple-Choice

1. **c.** The Accounting Principles Board has said that investors must use the equity method when accounting for long-term investments of 20% to 50%.
2. **a.** Under the equity method, dividends received reduce the investment account; the other choices are not true.
3. **d.** If the market value of securities falls below their cost, an unrealized loss account is debited.
4. **b.** Under the equity method, the investment account always reflects the investor's interest in the net assets of the investee.
5. **a.** If cost is greater than the book value of an investment because of expected above-average earnings, *APB Opinion No. 16* tells us that the excess cost should be labeled goodwill.
6. **a.** The move from communism toward democracy is causing East European nations and certain other nations to pursue market-oriented economies.

15

LONG-TERM FINANCING BONDS

In previous chapters, you learned that corporations obtain cash for recurring business operations from stock issuances, profitable operations, and short-term borrowing (current liabilities). However, when situations arise that require large amounts of cash, such as the purchase of a building, corporations also raise cash from long-term borrowing, that is, by issuing bonds. The issuing of bonds results in a Bonds Payable account.

LEARNING OBJECTIVES

After studying this chapter, you should be able to:

1. Describe the features of bonds and tell how bonds differ from shares of stock.
2. List the advantages and disadvantages of financing with long-term debt and prepare examples showing how to employ financial leverage.
3. Prepare journal entries for bonds issued at face value.
4. Explain how interest rates affect bond prices and what causes a bond to sell at a premium or a discount.

(continued)

BONDS PAYABLE

A **bond** is a long-term debt, or liability, owed by its issuer. Physical evidence of the debt lies in a negotiable *bond certificate*. In contrast to long-term notes, which usually mature in 10 years or less, bond maturities often run for 20 years or more.

Generally, a bond issue consists of a large number of $1,000 bonds rather than one large bond. For example, a company seeking to borrow $100,000 would issue one hundred $1,000 bonds rather than one $100,000 bond. This practice enables investors with less cash to invest to purchase some of the bonds.

Bonds derive their value primarily from two promises made by the borrower to the lender or bondholder. The borrower promises to pay (1) the **face value** or principal amount of the bond on a specific maturity date in the future and (2) periodic interest at a specified rate on face value at stated dates, usually semiannually, until the maturity date.

Large companies often have numerous long-term notes and bond issues outstanding at any one time. The various issues generally have different stated interest rates and mature at different points in the future. Companies present this information in the footnotes to their financial statements. Illustration 15.1 shows a portion of the long-term borrowings footnote from Du Pont's 1992 annual report. All of the items labeled debentures are bond issues outstanding. You can see that in 1992 Du Pont retired some of its bonds with relatively high interest rates (or possibly unfavorable provisions). In their place, the company issued new debenture bonds with an interest rate of 8.25%.

(*concluded*)

5. Apply the concept of present value to compute the price of a bond.
6. Prepare journal entries for bonds issued at a discount or a premium.
7. Prepare journal entries for bond redemptions and bond conversions.
8. Describe the ratings used for bonds.
9. Analyze and use the financial results—times interest earned ratio.
10. Explain future value and present value concepts and make required calculations (Appendix).

Comparison with Stock

A bond differs from a share of stock in several ways:

1. A bond is a debt or liability of the issuer, while a share of stock is a unit of ownership.
2. A bond has a maturity date when it must be paid. A share of stock does not mature; stock remains outstanding indefinitely unless the company decides to retire it.
3. Most bonds require stated periodic interest payments by the company. In contrast, dividends to stockholders are payable only when declared; even preferred dividends need not be paid in a particular period if the board of directors so decides.
4. Bond interest is deductible by the issuer in computing both net income and taxable income, while dividends are not deductible in either computation.

Selling (Issuing) Bonds

A company seeking to borrow millions of dollars generally is not able to borrow from a single lender. By selling (issuing) bonds to the public, the company secures the necessary funds.

Usually companies sell their bond issues through an investment company or a banker called an **underwriter.** The underwriter performs many tasks for the bond issuer, such as advertising, selling, and delivering the bonds to the purchasers. Often the underwriter guarantees the issuer a fixed price for the bonds, expecting to earn a profit by selling the bonds for more than the fixed price.

Objective 1
Describe the features of bonds and tell how bonds differ from shares of stock.

When a company sells bonds to the public, many purchasers buy the bonds. Rather than deal with each purchaser individually, the issuing company appoints a *trustee* to represent the bondholders. The **trustee** usually is a bank or trust company. The main duty of the trustee is to see that the borrower fulfills the provisions of the *bond indenture*. A **bond indenture** is the contract or loan agreement under which the bonds are issued. The indenture deals with matters such as the interest rate, maturity date and maturity amount, possible restrictions on dividends, repayment plans, and other provisions relating to the debt. An issuing company that does not adhere to the bond indenture provisions is in default. Then, the trustee takes action to force the issuer to comply with the indenture.

Characteristics of Bonds

Bonds may differ in some respects; they may be secured or unsecured bonds, registered or unregistered (bearer) bonds, and term or serial bonds. We discuss these differences next.

Certain bond features are matters of legal necessity, such as how a company pays interest and transfers ownership. Such features usually do not affect the issue price of the bonds. Other features, such as convertibility into common stock, are *sweeteners* designed to make the bonds more attractive to potential purchasers. These sweeteners may increase the issue price of a bond.

Secured Bonds A **secured bond** is a bond for which a company has pledged specific property to ensure its payment. Mortgage bonds are the most common secured bonds. A **mortgage** is a legal claim (lien) on specific property that gives the bondholder the right to possess the pledged property if the company fails to make required payments.

Unsecured Bonds An **unsecured bond** is a **debenture bond,** or simply a *debenture*. A debenture is an unsecured bond backed only by the general creditworthiness of the issuer, not by a lien on any specific property. A financially sound company can issue debentures more easily than a company experiencing financial difficulty.

December 31	1992	1991
9.13% debentures due 1999	$—	$ 78
7.50% debentures due 1999	—	45
8.88% debentures due 2001	—	140
6.00% debentures due 2001 ($660 face value, 13.95% yield to maturity)	395	381
Industrial development bonds due 2001–2022	304	265
8.45% debentures due 2004	—	171
8.50% debentures due 2006	158	182
9.38% debentures due 2009	—	170
8.50% debentures due 2016	284	285
8.25% debentures due 2022	399	—

Source: Du Pont's 1992 annual report.

Illustration 15.1
Du Pont's Long-Term Bonds (in millions)

Du Pont
Du Pont is a large chemical and diversified products company with 125,000 employees and recent annual sales of around $40 billion.

An Accounting Perspective

Business Insight Detroit Edison is an electric utility that serves 1.9 million customers in southeastern Michigan. It finances its properties with mortgage bonds. As of December 31, 1992, the company had $2.86 billion of long-term mortgage bonds outstanding. In the following note to its financial statements, the company described the additional mortgage bonds that could have been issued based on property additions and bond retirements:

> The Company's 1924 Mortgage and Deed of Trust ("Mortgage"), the lien of which covers substantially all of the Company's properties, provides for the issuance of additional bonds. At December 31, 1992, approximately $2.7 billion principal amount of Mortgage Bonds could have been issued on the basis of property additions, combined with an earnings test provision, assuming an interest rate of 8.35% on any such additional Mortgage Bonds. An additional $443 million principal amount of Mortgage Bonds could have been issued on the basis of bond retirements, after giving effect to the actual and planned 1993 issuances of $340 million of Mortgage Bonds.

Registered Bonds A **registered bond** is a bond with the owner's name on the bond certificate and in the register of bond owners kept by the bond issuer or its agent, the registrar. Bonds may be registered as to principal (or face value of the bond) or as to both principal and interest. Most bonds in our economy are registered as to principal only. For a bond registered as to both principal and interest, the issuer pays the bond interest by check. To transfer ownership of registered bonds, the owner endorses the bond and registers it in the new owner's name. Therefore, owners can easily replace lost or stolen registered bonds.

Unregistered (Bearer) Bonds An **unregistered (bearer) bond** is the property of its holder or bearer because the owner's name does not appear on the bond certificate or in a separate record. Physical delivery of the bond transfers ownership.

Coupon Bonds A **coupon bond** is a bond not registered as to interest. Coupon bonds carry detachable coupons for the interest they pay. At the end of each interest period, the owner clips the coupon for the period and presents it to a stated party, usually a bank, for collection.

Term Bonds and Serial Bonds A **term bond** matures on the same date as all other bonds in a given bond issue. **Serial bonds** in a given bond issue have maturities spread over several dates. For instance, one fourth of the bonds may mature on December 31, 1998, another one fourth on December 31, 1999, and so on.

Callable Bonds A **callable bond** contains a provision that gives the issuer the right to call (buy back) the bond before its maturity date. The provision is similar to the call provision of some preferred stocks. A company is likely to exercise this call right when its outstanding bonds bear interest at a much higher rate than the company would have to pay if it issued new but similar bonds. The exercise of the call provision normally requires the company to pay the bondholder a call premium of about $30 to $70 per $1,000 bond. A **call premium** is the price paid in excess of face value that the issuer of bonds must pay to redeem (call) bonds before their maturity date.

Convertible Bonds A **convertible bond** is a bond that may be exchanged for shares of stock of the issuing corporation at the bondholder's option. A convertible bond has a stipulated conversion rate of some number of shares for each $1,000 bond. Although any type of bond may be convertible, issuers add this feature to make risky debenture bonds more attractive to investors.

Bonds with Stock Warrants A **stock warrant** allows the bondholder to purchase shares of common stock at a fixed price for a stated period. Warrants issued with long-term debt may be nondetachable or detachable. A bond with *nondetachable warrants* is virtually the same as a convertible bond; the holder must surrender the bond to acquire the common stock. *Detachable warrants* allow bondholders to keep their bonds and still purchase shares of stock through exercise of the warrants.

Junk Bonds **Junk bonds** are high-interest rate, high-risk bonds. Many junk bonds issued in the 1980s financed corporate restructurings. These restructurings took the form of management buyouts (called leveraged buyouts or LBOs), hostile takeovers of companies by outside parties, or friendly takeovers of companies by outside parties. In the early 1990s, junk bonds lost favor because many issuers defaulted on their interest payments. Some issuers declared bankruptcy or sought relief from the bondholders by negotiating new debt terms.

Advantages of Issuing Debt

Objective 2
List the advantages and disadvantages of financing with long-term debt and prepare examples showing how to employ financial leverage.

Several advantages come from raising cash by issuing bonds rather than stock. First, the current stockholders do not have to dilute or surrender their control of the company when funds are obtained by borrowing rather than issuing more shares of stock. Second, it may be less expensive to issue debt rather than additional stock because the interest payments made to bondholders are tax deductible while dividends are not. Finally, probably the most important reason to issue bonds is that the use of debt may increase the earnings of stockholders through favorable financial leverage.

Favorable Financial Leverage A company has **favorable financial leverage** when it uses borrowed funds to increase earnings per share (EPS) of common stock. An increase in EPS usually results from earning a higher rate of return than the rate of interest paid for the borrowed money. For example, suppose a company borrowed money at 10% and earned a 15% rate of return. The 5% difference increases earnings.

Illustration 15.2 provides a more comprehensive example of favorable financial leverage. The two companies in the illustration are identical in every respect except in the way they are financed. Company A issued only capital stock, while Company B issued equal amounts of 10% bonds and capital stock. Both companies have $20,000,000 of assets, and both earned $4,000,000 of income from operations. If we divide income from operations by assets ($4,000,000 ÷ $20,000,000), we see that both companies earned 20% on assets employed. Yet B's stockholders fared far better than A's. The ratio of net income to stockholders' equity is 18% for B, while it is only 12% for A.

Assume that both companies issued their stock at the beginning of 1997 at $10 per share. B's $1.80 EPS are 50% greater than A's $1.20 EPS. This EPS difference

ILLUSTRATION 15.2
Favorable Financial Leverage

COMPANIES A AND B CONDENSED STATEMENTS
Balance Sheets
December 31, 1997

	Company A	Company B
Total assets	$20,000,000	$20,000,000
Bonds payable, 10%		$10,000,000
Stockholders' equity (capital stock)	$20,000,000	10,000,000
Total equities	$20,000,000	$20,000,000

Income Statements
For the Year Ended December 31, 1997

	Company A	Company B
Income from operations	$ 4,000,000	$ 4,000,000
Interest expense		1,000,000
Income before federal income taxes	$ 4,000,000	$ 3,000,000
Deduct: Federal income taxes (40%)	1,600,000	1,200,000
Net income	$ 2,400,000	$ 1,800,000
Number of common shares outstanding	2,000,000	1,000,000
Earnings per share (EPS) (Net income ÷ Number of common shares outstanding)	$1.20	$1.80
Rate of return on assets employed (Income from operations ÷ Total assets; both companies $4,000,000/$20,000,000)	20%	20%
Rate of return on stockholders' equity (Net income ÷ Stockholders' equity):		
Company A ($2,400,000/$20,000,000)	12%	
Company B ($1,800,000/$10,000,000)		18%

probably would cause B's shares to sell at a substantially higher market price than A's shares. B's larger EPS would also allow a larger dividend on B's shares.

Company B in Illustration 15.2 is employing financial leverage, or **trading on the equity.** The company is using its stockholders' equity as a basis for securing funds on which it pays a fixed return. Company B expects to earn more from the use of such funds than their fixed after-tax cost. As a result, Company B increases its rate of return on stockholders' equity and EPS.[1]

Disadvantages of Issuing Debt

Several disadvantages accompany the use of debt financing. First, the borrower has a fixed interest payment that must be met each period to avoid default. Second, use of debt also reduces a company's ability to withstand a major loss. For example, assume that instead of having net income, both Company A and Company B in Illustration 15.2 sustain a net loss in 1997 of $11,000,000. At the end of 1997, Company A will still have $9,000,000 of stockholders' equity and can continue operations with a chance of recovery. Company B, on the other hand, would have negative stockholders' equity of $1,000,000 and the bondholders could force the company to liquidate if B could not make interest payments as they came due. The result of sustaining the loss by the two companies is as follows:

COMPANIES A AND B
Partial Balance Sheets
December 31, 1997

	Company A	Company B
Stockholders' equity:		
Paid-in capital:		
Common stock	$ 20,000,000	$ 10,000,000
Retained earnings	(11,000,000)	(11,000,000)
Total stockholders' equity	$ 9,000,000	$ (1,000,000)

[1] Issuing bonds is only one method of using leverage. Other methods of using financial leverage include issuing preferred stock or long-term notes.

A third disadvantage of debt financing is that it also causes a company to experience unfavorable financial leverage when income from operations falls below a certain level. **Unfavorable financial leverage** results when the cost of borrowed funds exceeds the revenue they generate; it is the reverse of *favorable financial leverage*. In the previous example, if income from operations fell to $1,000,000, the rates of return on stockholders' equity would be 3% for A and zero for B, as shown in this schedule:

COMPANIES A AND B
Income Statements
For the Year Ended December 31, 1997

	Company A	Company B
Income from operations	$1,000,000	$1,000,000
Interest expense		1,000,000
Income before federal income taxes	$1,000,000	$ –0–
Deduct: Federal income taxes (40%)	400,000	–0–
Net income	$ 600,000	$ –0–
Rate of return on stockholders' equity:		
Company A ($600,000/$20,000,000)	3%	
Company B ($0/$10,000,000)		0%

The fourth disadvantage of issuing debt is that loan agreements often require maintaining a certain amount of working capital (Current assets − Current liabilities) and place limitations on dividends and additional borrowings.

Accounting for Bonds Issued at Face Value

When a company issues bonds, it incurs a long-term liability on which periodic interest payments must be made, usually twice a year. If interest dates fall on other than balance sheet dates, the company must accrue interest in the proper periods. The following examples illustrate the accounting for bonds issued at face value on an interest date and issued at face value between interest dates.

Objective 3
Prepare journal entries for bonds issued at face value.

BONDS ISSUED AT FACE VALUE ON AN INTEREST DATE Valley Company's accounting year ends on December 31. On December 31, 1997, Valley issued 10-year, 12% bonds with a $100,000 face value, for $100,000. The bonds are dated December 31, 1997, call for semiannual interest payments on June 30 and December 31, and mature on December 31, 2007. Valley made the required interest and principal payments when due. The entries for the 10 years are as follows:

On December 31, 1997, the date of issuance, the entry is:

Date		Account	Debit	Credit
1997 Dec.	31	Cash	100,000	
		Bonds Payable		100,000
		To record bonds issued at face value.		

On each June 30 and December 31 for 10 years, beginning June 30, 1998 (ending June 30, 2007), the entry would be:

Date		Account	Debit	Credit
Each year June	30			
and Dec.	31	Bond Interest Expense ($100,000 × 0.12 × ½)	6,000	
		Cash		6,000
		To record periodic interest payment.		

On December 31, 2007, the maturity date, the entry would be:

Date		Account	Debit	Credit
2007 Dec.	31	Bond Interest Expense	6,000	
		Bonds Payable	100,000	
		Cash		106,000
		To record final interest and bond redemption payment.		

Note that Valley does not need adjusting entries because the interest payment date falls on the last day of the accounting period. The income statement for each of the 10 years 1998–2007 would show Bond Interest Expense of $12,000 ($6,000 × 2); the balance sheet at the end of each of the years 1997–2005 would report bonds payable of $100,000 in long-term liabilities. At the end of 2006, Valley would reclassify the bonds as a current liability because they will be paid within the next year.

The real world is more complicated. For example, assume the Valley bonds were dated October 31, 1997, issued on that same date, and pay interest each April 30 and October 31. Valley must make an adjusting entry on December 31 to accrue interest for November and December. That entry would be:

1997				
Dec.	31	Bond Interest Expense ($100,000 × 0.12 × 2/12)	2,000	
		Bond Interest Payable		2,000
		To accrue two months' interest expense.		

The April 30, 1998, entry would be:

1998				
Apr.	30	Bond Interest Expense ($100,000 × 0.12 × 4/12)	4,000	
		Bond Interest Payable	2,000	
		Cash		6,000
		To record semiannual interest payment.		

The October 31, 1998, entry would be:

1998				
Oct.	31	Bond Interest Expense	6,000	
		Cash		6,000
		To record semiannual interest payment.		

Each year Valley would make similar entries for the semiannual payments and the year-end accrued interest. The firm would report the $2,000 Bond Interest Payable as a current liability on the December 31 balance sheet for each year.

Bonds Issued at Face Value between Interest Dates Companies do not always issue bonds on the date they start to bear interest. Regardless of when the bonds are physically issued, interest starts to accrue from the most recent interest date. Firms report bonds to be selling at a stated price "plus accrued interest." The issuer must pay holders of the bonds a full six months' interest at each interest date. Thus, investors purchasing bonds after the bonds begin to accrue interest must pay the seller for the unearned interest accrued since the preceding interest date. The bondholders are reimbursed for this accrued interest when they receive their first six months' interest check.

Using the facts for the Valley bonds dated December 31, 1997, suppose Valley issued its bonds on May 31, 1998, instead of on December 31, 1997. The entry required is:

1998				
May	31	Cash	105,000	
		Bonds Payable		100,000
		Bond Interest Payable ($100,000 × 0.12 × 5/12)		5,000
		To record bonds issued at face value plus accrued interest.		

This entry records the $5,000 received for the accrued interest as a debit to Cash and a credit to Bond Interest Payable.

The entry required on June 30, 1998, when the full six months' interest is paid, is:

1998				
June	30	Bond Interest Expense ($100,000 × 0.12 × 1/12)	1,000	
		Bond Interest Payable	5,000	
		Cash		6,000
		To record bond interest payment.		

This entry records $1,000 interest expense on the $100,000 of bonds that were outstanding for one month. Valley collected $5,000 from the bondholders on May 31 as accrued interest and is now returning it to them.

Bond Prices and Interest Rates

Objective 4
Explain how interest rates affect bond prices and what causes a bond to sell at a premium or a discount.

The price of a bond issue often differs from its face value. The amount a bond sells for above face value is a **premium.** The amount a bond sells for below face value is a **discount.** A difference between face value and issue price exists whenever the market rate of interest for similar bonds differs from the contract rate of interest on the bonds. The **market interest rate** (also called the effective rate or yield) is the minimum rate of interest that investors accept on bonds of a particular risk category. The higher the risk category, the higher the minimum rate of interest that investors accept. The **contract rate of interest** is also called the *stated, coupon,* or *nominal rate*. Firms state this rate in the bond indenture, print it on the face of each bond, and use it to determine the amount of cash paid each interest period. The market rate fluctuates from day to day, responding to factors such as the interest rate the Federal Reserve Board charges banks to borrow from it; government actions to finance the national debt; and the supply of, and demand for, money.

Market and contract rates of interest are likely to differ. Issuers must set the contract rate before the bonds are actually sold to allow time for such activities as printing the bonds. Assume, for instance, that the contract rate for a bond issue is set at 12%. If the market rate is equal to the contract rate, the bonds will sell at their face value. However, by the time the bonds are sold, the market rate could be higher or lower than the contract rate. As shown in Illustration 15.3, if the market rate is lower than the contract rate, the bonds will sell for more than their face value. Thus, if the market rate is 10% and the contract rate is 12%, the bonds will sell at a premium as the result of investors bidding up their price. However, if the market rate is higher than the contract rate, the bonds will sell for less than their face value. Thus, if the market rate is 14% and the contract rate is 12%, the bonds will sell at a discount. Investors are not interested in bonds bearing a contract rate less than the market rate unless the price is reduced. Selling bonds at a premium or a discount allows the purchasers of the bonds to earn the market rate of interest on their investment.

Computing Bond Prices

Objective 5
Apply the concept of present value to compute the price of a bond.

Computing long-term bond prices involves finding **present values** using compound interest. The appendix to this chapter explains the concepts of future value and present value. If you do not understand the present value concept, read the appendix before continuing with this section.

Buyers and sellers negotiate a price that yields the going rate of interest for bonds of a particular risk class. The price investors pay for a given bond issue is equal to the present value of the bonds. To compute present value, we discount the promised cash flows from the bonds—principal and interest—using the market, or effective, rate. We use the market rate because the bonds must yield at least this rate or investors are attracted to alternative investments. The life of the bonds is stated in interest (compounding) periods. The interest rate is the effective rate per interest period, which is found by dividing the annual rate by the number of times interest is paid per year. For example, if the annual rate is 12%, the semiannual rate would be 6%.

Issuers usually quote bond prices as percentages of face value—100 means 100% of face value, 97 means 97% of face value, and 103 means 103% of face value. For example, one hundred $1,000 face value bonds issued at 103 have a price of $103,000. Regardless of the issue price, at maturity the issuer of the bonds must pay the investor(s) the face value of the bonds.

ILLUSTRATION 15.3
Bond Premiums and Discounts

	Market Rate	Contract Rate
Bonds sell at a *premium* if Market rate < Contract rate	10%	12%
Bonds sell at *face value* if Market rate = Contract rate	12%	12%
Bonds sell at a *discount* if Market rate > Contract rate	14%	12%

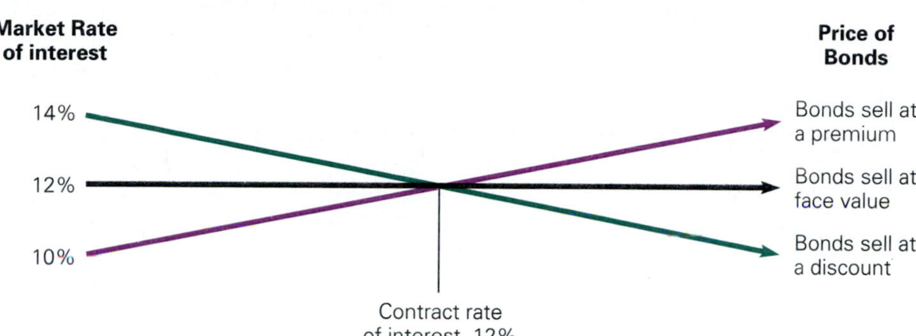

BONDS ISSUED AT FACE VALUE The following example illustrates the specific steps in computing the price of bonds. Assume Carr Company issues 12% bonds with a $100,000 face value to yield 12%. Dated and issued on June 30, 1997, the bonds call for semiannual interest payments on June 30 and December 31, and mature on June 30, 2000.[2] The bonds would sell at face value because they offer 12% and investors seek 12%. Potential purchasers have no reason to offer a premium or demand a discount. One way to prove the bonds would be sold at face value is by showing that their present value is $100,000:

	Cash Flow	×	Present Value Factor	=	Present Value
Principal of $100,000 due in six interest periods multiplied by present value factor for 6% from Table A.3 of the Appendix (end of text)	$100,000	×	0.70496	=	$ 70,496
Interest of $6,000 due at end of each of six interest periods multiplied by present value factor for 6% from Table A.4 of the Appendix (end of text)	6,000	×	4.91732	=	29,504
Total price (present value)					$100,000

According to this schedule, investors who seek an effective rate of 6% per six-month period should pay $100,000 for these bonds. Notice that the same number of interest periods and semiannual interest rates occur in discounting both the principal and interest payments to their present values. The entry to record the sale of these bonds on June 30, 1997, debits Cash and credits Bonds Payable for $100,000.

BONDS ISSUED AT A DISCOUNT Assume the $100,000, 12% Carr bonds are sold to yield a current market rate of 14% annual interest, or 7% per semiannual period. Carr computes the present value (selling price) of the bonds as follows:

[2] Bonds do not normally mature in such a short time; we use a three-year life for illustrative purposes only.

	Cash Flow	×	Present Value Factor	=	Present Value
Principal of $100,000 due in six interest periods multiplied by present value factor for 7% from Table A.3, Appendix (end of text)	$100,000	×	0.66634	=	$66,634
Interest of $6,000 due at end of each of six interest periods multiplied by present value factor for 7% from Table A.4, Appendix (end of text)	6,000	×	4.76654	=	28,599
Total price (present value)					$95,233

Note that in computing the present value of the bonds, Carr uses the actual $6,000 cash interest payment that will be made each period. The amount of cash the company pays as interest does not depend on the market interest rate. However, the market rate per semiannual period—7%—does change, and Carr uses this new rate to find interest factors in the tables.

Objective 6
Prepare journal entries for bonds issued at a discount or a premium.

The journal entry to record issuance of the bonds is:

1997				
June	30	Cash	95,233	
		Discount on Bonds Payable	4,767	
		Bonds Payable		100,000
		To record bonds issued at a discount.		

In recording the bond issue, Carr credits Bonds Payable for the face value of the debt. The company debits the difference between face value and price received to Discount on Bonds Payable, a contra account to Bonds Payable. Carr reports the bonds payable and discount on bonds payable in the balance sheet as follows:

Long-term liabilities:		
Bonds payable, 12%, due June 30, 2000	$100,000	
Less: Discount on bonds payable	4,767	$95,233

The $95,233 is the carrying value, or *net liability,* of the bonds. **Carrying value** is the face value of the bonds minus any unamortized discount or plus any unamortized premium. The next section discusses unamortized premium on bonds payable.

Bonds Issued at a Premium Assume that Carr issued the $100,000 face value of 12% bonds to yield a current market rate of 10%. The bonds would sell at a premium calculated as follows:

	Cash Flow	×	Present Value Factor	=	Present Value
Principal of $100,000 due in six interest periods multiplied by present value factor for 5% from Table A.3, Appendix (end of text)	$100,000	×	0.74622	=	$ 74,622
Interest of $6,000 due at end of each of six interest periods multiplied by present value factor for 5% from Table A.4, Appendix (end of text)	6,000	×	5.07569	=	30,454
Total price (present value)					$105,076

The journal entry to record the issuance of the bonds is:

1997				
June	30	Cash	105,076	
		Bonds Payable		100,000
		Premium on Bonds Payable		5,076
		To record bonds issued at a premium.		

The carrying value of these bonds at issuance is $105,076, consisting of the face value of $100,000 and the premium of $5,076. The premium is an adjunct account shown on the balance sheet as an addition to bonds payable as follows:

Long-term liabilities:		
Bonds payable, 12%, due June 30, 2000	$100,000	
Add: Premium on bonds payable	5,076	$105,076

Discount/Premium Amortization

When a company issues bonds at a premium or discount, the amount of bond interest expense recorded each period differs from bond interest payments. A discount increases and a premium decreases the amount of interest expense. For example, if Carr issues bonds with a face value of $100,000 for $95,233, the total interest cost of borrowing would be $40,767: $36,000 (which is six payments of $6,000) plus the discount of $4,767. If the bonds had been issued at $105,076, the total interest cost of borrowing would be $30,924: $36,000 less the premium of $5,076. The $4,767 discount or $5,076 premium must be allocated or charged to the six periods that benefit from the use of borrowed money. Two methods are available for amortizing a discount or premium on bonds—the straight-line method and the effective interest rate method.

The straight-line method records interest expense at a *constant amount;* the effective interest rate method records interest expense at a *constant rate*. *APB Opinion No. 21* states that the straight-line method may be used only when it does not differ materially from the effective interest rate method. In many cases, the differences are not material.

The Straight-Line Method The **straight-line method of amortization** allocates an equal amount of discount or premium to each month the bonds are outstanding. The issuer calculates the amount by dividing the discount or premium by the total number of months from the date of issuance to the maturity date. For example, if it sells $100,000 face value bonds for $95,233, Carr would charge the $4,767 discount to interest expense at a rate of $132.42 per month (equal to $4,767/36). Total discount amortization for six months would be $794.52, computed as follows: $132.42 × 6. Interest expense for each six-month period then would be $6,794.52, calculated as follows: $6,000 + ($132.42 × 6). The entry to record the expense on December 31, 1997, would be:

1997				
Dec.	31	Bond Interest Expense	6,794.52	
		Cash		6,000.00
		Discount on Bonds Payable ($132.42 × 6)		794.52
		To record interest payment and discount amortization.		

By the maturity date, all of the discount would have been amortized.

To illustrate the straight-line method applied to a premium, recall that earlier Carr sold its $100,000 face value bonds for $105,076. Carr would amortize the $5,076 premium on these bonds at a rate of $141 per month, equal to $5,076/36. The entry for the first period's semiannual interest expense on bonds sold at a premium is:

1997				
Dec.	31	Bond Interest Expense	5,154	
		Premium on Bonds Payable ($141 × 6)	846	
		Cash		6,000
		To record interest payment and premium amortization.		

By the maturity date, all of the premium would have been amortized.

The Effective Interest Rate Method *APB Opinion No. 21* recommends an amortization procedure called the **effective interest rate method,** or simply the **interest method.** Under the interest method, interest expense for any interest period is equal to the effective (market) rate of interest on the date of issuance times the carrying value of the bonds at the beginning of that interest period.

Using the Carr example of 12% bonds with a face value of $100,000 sold to yield 14%, the carrying value at the beginning of the first interest period is the selling price of $95,233. Carr would record the interest expense for the first semiannual period as follows:

1997				
Dec.	31	Bond Interest Expense ($95,233 × 0.14 × ½)	6,666	
		Cash ($100,000 × 0.12 × ½)		6,000
		Discount on Bonds Payable		666
		To record discount amortization and interest payment.		

Note that interest expense is the carrying value times the effective interest rate. The cash payment is the face value times the contract rate. The discount amortized for the period is the difference between the two amounts.

After the preceding entry, the carrying value of the bonds is $95,899, or $95,233 + $666. Carr reduced the balance in the Discount on Bonds Payable account by $666 to $4,101, or $4,767 − $666. Assuming the accounting year ends on December 31, the entry to record the payment of interest for the second semiannual period on June 30, 1998, is:

1998				
June	30	Bond Interest Expense ($95,899 × 0.14 × ½)	6,713	
		Cash ($100,000 × 0.12 × ½)		6,000
		Discount on Bonds Payable		713
		To record discount amortization and interest payment.		

Carr can also apply the effective interest rate method to premium amortization. If the Carr bonds had been issued at $105,076 to yield 10%, the premium would be $5,076. The firm calculates interest expense in the same manner as for bonds sold at a discount. However, the entry would differ somewhat, showing a debit to the premium account. The entry for the first interest period is:

1997				
Dec.	31	Bond Interest Expense ($105,076 × 0.10 × ½)	5,254	
		Premium on Bonds Payable	746	
		Cash ($100,000 × 0.12 × ½)		6,000
		To record interest payment and premium amortization.		

After the first entry, the carrying value of the bonds is $104,330, or $105,076 − $746. The premium account now carries a balance of $4,330, or $5,076 − $746. The entry for the second interest period is:

1998				
June	30	Bond Interest Expense ($104,330 × 0.10 × ½)	5,216*	
		Premium on Bonds Payable	784	
		Cash ($100,000 × 0.12 × ½)		6,000
		To record interest payment and premium amortization.		
		* Rounded down.		

Discount and Premium Amortization Schedules A discount amortization schedule (Illustration 15.4) and a premium amortization schedule (Illustration 15.5) aid in preparing entries for interest expense. Usually, companies prepare such schedules when they first issue bonds, often using computer programs designed for this purpose. The companies then refer to the schedules whenever they make journal entries to record interest. Note that in each period the amount of interest expense changes; interest expense gets larger when a discount is involved and smaller when a premium is involved. This fluctuation occurs because the carrying value to which a constant interest rate is applied changes each interest payment date. With a discount, carrying value increases; with a premium, it decreases. However, the actual cash paid as interest is always a constant amount determined by multiplying the bond's face value by the contract rate.

ILLUSTRATION 15.4
Discount Amortization Schedule for Bonds Payable

(A) Interest Payment Date	Bond (B) Interest Expense Debit (E × 0.14 × ½)	(C) Cash Credit ($100,000 × 0.12 × ½)	(D) Discount on Bonds Payable Credit (B − C)	(E) Carrying Value of Bonds Payable (previous balance in E + D)
Issue price				$ 95,233
12/31/97	$ 6,666	$ 6,000	$ 666	95,899
6/30/98	6,713	6,000	713	96,612
12/31/98	6,763	6,000	763	97,375
6/30/99	6,816	6,000	816	98,191
12/31/99	6,873	6,000	873	99,064
6/30/2000	6,936*	6,000	936	100,000
	$40,767	$36,000	$4,767	

* Includes rounding difference.

ILLUSTRATION 15.5
Premium Amortization Schedule for Bonds Payable

(A) Interest Payment Date	(B) Bond Interest Expense Debit (E × 0.10 × ½)	(C) Cash Credit ($100,000 × 0.12 × ½)	(D) Premium on Bonds Payable Debit (C − B)	(E) Carrying Value of Bonds Payable (previous balance in E − D)
Issue price				$105,076
12/31/97	$ 5,254	$ 6,000	$ 746	104,330
6/30/98	5,216*	6,000	784	103,546
12/31/98	5,177	6,000	823	102,723
6/30/99	5,136	6,000	864	101,859
12/31/99	5,093	6,000	907	100,952
6/30/2000	5,048	6,000	952	100,000
	$30,924	$36,000	$5,076	

* Rounded down.

Recall that the issue price was $95,233 for the discount situation and $105,076 for the premium situation. The total interest expense of $40,767 for the discount situation in Illustration 15.4 is equal to $36,000 (which is six $6,000 payments) plus the $4,767 discount. This amount agrees with the earlier computation of total interest expense. In Illustration 15.5, total interest expense in the premium situation is $30,924, or $36,000 (which is six $6,000 payments) less the $5,076 premium. In both illustrations, at the maturity date the carrying value of the bonds is equal to the face value because the discount or premium has been fully amortized.

ADJUSTING ENTRY FOR PARTIAL PERIOD Illustrations 15.4 and 15.5 also would be helpful if Carr must accrue interest for a partial period. Instead of a calendar-year accounting period, assume the fiscal year of the bond issuer ends on August 31. Using the information provided in the premium amortization schedule (Illustration 15.5), the adjusting entry needed on August 31, 1997, is:

Date		Account	Debit	Credit
1997				
Aug.	31	Bond Interest Expense ($5,254 × 2/6)	1,751	
		Premium on Bonds Payable ($746 × 2/6)	249	
		Bond Interest Payable ($6,000 × 2/6)		2,000
		To record two months' accrued interest.		

This entry records interest for two months, July and August, of the six-month interest period ending on December 31, 1997. The first line of Illustration 15.5 shows the interest expense and premium amortization for the six months. Thus, the previous entry records two sixths (or one third) of the amounts for this six-month period. Carr would record the remaining four months' interest when making the first payment on December 31, 1997. That entry reads:

1997				
Dec.	31	Bond Interest Payable	2,000	
		Bond Interest Expense ($5,254 × 4/6)	3,503	
		Premium on Bonds Payable ($746 × 4/6)	497	
		Cash		6,000
		To record four months' interest expense and semiannual interest payment.		

During the remaining life of the bonds, Carr would make similar entries for August 31 and December 31. The amounts would differ, however, because Carr uses the interest method of accounting for bond interest. The entry for each June 30 would be as indicated in Illustration 15.5.

Redeeming Bonds Payable

Objective 7
Prepare journal entries for bond redemptions and bond conversions.

Bonds may be (1) paid at maturity, (2) called, or (3) purchased in the market and retired. Bonds may also be retired by being converted into stock. Each action is either a redemption of bonds or the extinguishment of debt. A company that pays its bonds at maturity would have already amortized any related discount or premium and paid the last interest payment. The only entry required at maturity would debit Bonds Payable and credit Cash for the face amount of the bonds as follows:

2000				
June	30	Bonds Payable	100,000	
		Cash		100,000
		To pay bonds on maturity date.		

An issuer may redeem some or all of its outstanding bonds before maturity by calling them. The issuer may also purchase bonds in the market and retire them. In either case, the accounting is the same. Assume that on January 1, 1999, Carr calls bonds totaling $10,000 of the $100,000 face value bonds in Illustration 15.5 at 103, or $10,300. Even though accrued interest would be added to the price, assume that the interest due on this date has been paid. A look at the last column on the line dated 12/31/98 in Illustration 15.5 reveals that the carrying value of the bonds is $102,723, which consists of Bonds Payable of $100,000 and Premium on Bonds Payable of $2,723. Since 10% of the bond issue is being redeemed, Carr must remove 10% from each of these two accounts. The firm incurs a loss for the excess of the price paid for the bonds, $10,300, over their carrying value, $10,272. The required entry is:

1999				
Jan.	1	Bonds Payable	10,000	
		Premium on Bonds Payable ($2,723 ÷ 10)	272	
		Loss on Bond Redemption ($10,272 − $10,300)	28	
		Cash		10,300
		To record bonds redeemed.		

According to *FASB Statement No. 4,* gains and losses from *voluntary early* retirement of bonds are extraordinary items, if material. We report such gains and losses in the income statement, net of their tax effects, as described in Chapter 13.

Serial Bonds

To avoid the burden of redeeming an entire bond issue at one time, companies sometimes issue **serial bonds** that mature over several dates. Assume that on June 30, 1992, Jasper Company issued $100,000 face value, 12% serial bonds at 100. Interest is payable each year on June 30 and December 31. A total of $20,000 of the bonds mature each year starting on June 30, 1997. Jasper has a calendar-year accounting period. Entries required for 1997 for interest expense and maturing debt are:

			Debit	Credit
1997				
June	30	Bond Interest Expense ($100,000 × 0.12 × ½)	6,000	
		Cash		6,000
		To record interest payment.		
	30	Serial Bonds Payable	20,000	
		Cash		20,000
		To record retirement of serial debt.		
Dec.	31	Bond Interest Expense ($80,000 × 0.12 × ½)	4,800	
		Cash		4,800
		To record payment of semiannual interest expense.		

Note that Jasper calculates the interest expense for the last six months of 1997 only on the remaining outstanding debt ($100,000 original issue less the $20,000 that matured on June 30, 1997). Each year after the bonds maturing that year are retired, interest expense decreases proportionately. Jasper reports the $20,000 amount maturing the next year as a current liability on each year-end balance sheet. The remaining debt is a long-term liability.

Bond Redemption or Sinking Funds

Naturally, bond investors are concerned about the safety of their investments. They fear the company may default on paying the entire principal at the maturity date. This concern has led to provisions in some bond indentures that require companies to make periodic payments to a **bond redemption fund,** often called a **sinking fund.** The fund trustee uses these payments to redeem a stated amount of bonds annually and pay the accrued bond interest. The trustee determines which bonds to call and uses the cash deposited in the fund only to redeem these bonds and pay their accrued interest.

To illustrate, assume Hand Company has 12% coupon bonds outstanding that pay interest on March 31 and September 30 and were issued at face value. The bond indenture requires that Hand pay a trustee $53,000 each September 30. The entry for the payment to the trustee is:

			Debit	Credit
Sept.	30	Sinking Fund	53,000	
		Cash		53,000
		To record payment to trustee of required deposit.		

The trustee calls $50,000 of bonds, pays for the bonds and accrued interest, and notifies Hand. The trustee also bills Hand for its fee and expenses incurred of $325. Assuming no interest has been recorded on these bonds for the period ended September 30, the entries are:

			Debit	Credit
Sept.	30	Bonds Payable	50,000	
		Bond Interest Expense	3,000	
		Sinking Fund		53,000
		To record bond redemption and interest paid by trustee.		
	30	Sinking Fund Expense	325	
		Cash		325
		To record trustee fee and expenses.		

If a balance exists in the Sinking Fund account at year-end, Hand includes it in a category labeled Investments or Other Assets on the balance sheet. Hand would describe the $50,000 of bonds that must be retired during the coming year as "Current maturity of long-term debt" and report it as a current liability on the balance sheet.

The existence of a sinking fund does not necessarily mean that the company has created a retained earnings appropriation entitled "Appropriation for Bonded Indebtedness." A sinking fund usually is contractual (required by the bond inden-

Occidental Petroleum
Occidental Petroleum Corporation is an international oil, gas, and chemical company, with recent annual sales of about $9 billion.

ture), and an appropriation of retained earnings is simply an announcement by the board of directors that dividend payments will be limited over the term of the bonds. The former requires cash to be paid in to a trustee, and the latter restricts retained earnings available for dividends to stockholders. Also, even if the indenture does not require a sinking fund, the corporation may decide to (1) pay into a sinking fund and not appropriate retained earnings, (2) appropriate retained earnings and not pay into a sinking fund, (3) do neither, or (4) do both.

AN ACCOUNTING PERSPECTIVE

BUSINESS INSIGHT Regarding sinking fund payments and the amortization of Discount on Bonds Payable, Occidental Petroleum Corporation had the following note in its 1992 annual report:

> At December 31, 1992, minimum principal payments on senior funded debt, including sinking fund requirements subsequent to December 31, 1993, aggregated $5.638 billion, of which $292 million was due in 1994, $221 million in 1995, $622 million in 1996, $730 million in 1997, $289 million in 1998, and $3.484 billion thereafter. Unamortized discount is generally being amortized to interest expense on the effective interest method over the lives of the related issues.

Convertible Bonds

A company may add to the attractiveness of its bonds by giving the bondholders the option to convert the bonds to shares of the issuer's common stock. In accounting for the conversions of **convertible bonds,** a company treats the carrying value of bonds surrendered as the capital contributed for shares issued.

Suppose a company has $10,000 face value of bonds outstanding. Each $1,000 bond is convertible into 50 shares of the issuer's $10 par value common stock. On May 1, when the carrying value of the bonds was $9,800, investors presented all of the bonds for conversion. The entry required is:

Date		Account	Debit	Credit
May	1	Bonds Payable	10,000	
		Discount on Bonds Payable		200
		Common Stock ($10,000 ÷ $1,000 = 10 bonds; 10 bonds × 50 shares × $10 par)		5,000
		Paid-In Capital in Excess of Par Value—Common		4,800
		To record bonds converted to common stock.		

The entry eliminates the $9,800 book value of the bonds from the accounts by debiting Bonds Payable for $10,000 and crediting Discount on Bonds Payable for $200. It credits Common Stock for the par value of the 500 shares issued (500 shares × $10 par). The excess amount ($4,800) is credited to Paid-In Capital in Excess of Par Value—Common.

AN ACCOUNTING PERSPECTIVE

BUSINESS INSIGHT **CBS, Inc.,** one of the three major television networks, has the largest total-day share of audience. Its 1992 annual report described the principal terms of its convertible, callable, debenture bonds:

> The 5% convertible debentures are due April 7, 2002. At the holder's option, each five thousand dollar debenture is convertible into 25 shares of the Company's common stock at any time prior to redemption or maturity. At December 31, 1992, there were 1,952,000 shares of common stock reserved for issuance upon conversion of these debentures. The debentures are redeemable [callable], in whole or in part, at the option of the Company, subject to certain restrictions, at a redemption price that declines from 102.5 percent of the principal amount during the 12-month period ending April 6, 1993, to 100 percent on April 7, 1997, and thereafter, together in each case with accrued interest to the date fixed for redemption. However, if certain events occur involving U.S. taxes or U.S. information reporting requirements, the Company may redeem all the outstanding debentures at par value plus accrued interest.

BOND RATING SERVICES

Objective 8
Describe the ratings used for bonds.

The two leading bond rating services are Moody's Investors Service and Standard & Poor's Corporation. The bonds are rated as to their riskiness. The ratings used by these services are:

	Moody's	Standard & Poor's
Highest quality to upper medium	Aaa	AAA
	Aa	AA
	A	A
Medium to speculative	Baa	BBB
	Ba	BB
	B	B
Poor to lowest quality	Caa	CCC
	Ca	CC
	C	C
In default, value is questionable		DDD
		DD
		D

Normally, Moody's rates junk bonds at Ba or below and Standard & Poor's at BB or below. As a company's prospects change over time, the ratings of its outstanding bonds change because of the higher or lower probability that the company can pay the interest and principal on the bonds when due. A severe recession may cause many companies' bond ratings to decline.

Bond prices appear regularly in certain newspapers. For instance, *The Wall Street Journal* recently quoted Citicorp's bonds as follows:

Issue (Rating: Moody's/S&P)	Coupon	Maturity	Price	Change	Yield	Change
Citicorp (Baa/BBB)	8.000	02/01/03	107.728	−0.291	6.880	0.040

The information indicates that the bonds are rated Baa by Moody's and BBB by Standard & Poor's. Thus, the two rating services agree as to the riskiness of the bonds. The bonds carry a coupon rate of 8%. The bonds mature on February 1, 2003. The current price is $107.728 per hundred, or $1,077.28 for a $1,000 bond. The price the preceding day was $108.109, since the change was −0.291. The current price yields a return to investors of 6.88%, which is a change of .04% from the preceding day. As the market rate of interest changes from day to day, the market price of the bonds varies inversely. Thus, if the market rate of interest increases, the market price of bonds decreases, and vice versa.

An Accounting Perspective

Business Insight Companies sometimes invest in the bonds of other companies. According to FASB Statement No. 115 (covered in Chapter 14), investments in these bonds fall into three categories—trading securities, available-for-sale securities, or held-to-maturity securities. The bonds would be classified as trading securities if they were acquired principally for the purpose of selling them in the near future. If the bonds were to be held for a longer period of time, but not until maturity, they would be classified as available-for-sale securities. Bonds that will be held to maturity are classified as held-to-maturity securities. All trading securities are current assets. Available-for-sale securities are either current assets or long-term assets, depending on how long management intends to hold them. Discounts and premiums on bonds classified as trading and available-for-sale securities are not amortized because management does not know how long they will be held. Held-to-maturity securities are long-term assets. Discounts and premiums on bonds classified as held-to-maturity securities are amortized by the holder of the bonds in the same manner as for the issuer of the bonds. Further discussion of investments in bonds is reserved for an intermediate accounting course.

Analyzing and Using the Financial Results—Times Interest Earned Ratio

Objective 9
Analyze and use the financial results—times interest earned ratio.

The **times interest earned ratio** (or *interest coverage ratio*) indicates the ability of a company to meet required interest payments when due. We calculate the ratio as follows:

$$\text{Times interest earned ratio} = \frac{\text{Income before interest and taxes (IBIT)}}{\text{Interest expense}}$$

An Ethical Perspective

Rawlings Furniture Company

The Rawlings brothers inherited 300,000 shares (30%) of the common stock of the Rawlings Furniture Company from their father, who had founded the company 55 years earlier. One brother served as president of the company, and the other two brothers served as vice presidents. The company, which produced a line of fine furniture sold nationwide, earned an average of $4 million per year. Located in Jamesville, New York, the company had provided steady employment for approximately 10% of the city's population. The city had benefited from the revenues the company attracted to the area and from the generous gifts provided by the father.

The remainder of the common stock was widely held and was traded in the over-the-counter market. No other stockholder held more than 4% of the stock. The stock had recently traded at $30 per share. The company has $10 million of 10% bonds outstanding, which mature in 15 years.

The brothers enjoyed the money they received from the company, but did not enjoy the work. They also were frustrated by the fact that they did not own a controlling interest (more than 50%) of the company. If they had a controlling interest, they could make important decisions without obtaining the agreement of the other stockholders.

With the assistance of a New York City brokerage house, the brothers decided to pursue a plan that could increase their wealth. The company would offer to buy back shares of common stock at $40 per share. These shares would then be canceled, and the Rawlings brothers would have a controlling interest. The stock buy-back would be financed by issuing 10-year, 18%, high-interest junk bonds. The brokerage house had located some financial institutions willing to buy the bonds. The interest payments on the junk bonds would be $3 million per year. The brothers thought the company could make these payments unless the country entered a recession. If need be, wage increases could be severely restricted or eliminated and the company's pension plan could be terminated. If the junk bonds could be paid at maturity, the brothers would own a controlling interest in what could be an extremely valuable company. If the interest payments could not be met or if the junk bonds were defaulted at maturity, the company could eventually be forced to liquidate. The risks are high, but so are the potential rewards.

If another buyer entered the picture at this point and bid an even higher amount for the stock, the brothers could sell their shares and exit the company. Two of the brothers hoped that another buyer might bid as much as $50 per share so they could sell their shares and pursue other interests. The changes a new buyer might make are unpredictable at this point.

Income before interest and taxes (IBIT), also called "earnings before interest and taxes (EBIT)," is the numerator because there would be no income taxes if interest expense is equal to or greater than IBIT. To find IBIT when the income statement is not complex, take net income and add back interest expense and taxes. However, in complex situations, when there are discontinued operations, changes in accounting principle, extraordinary items, interest revenue, and/or other similar items, analysts often use "operating income" to represent IBIT. The higher the ratio, the more comfortable creditors feel about receiving interest payments in the future.

The times interest earned ratios for 1992 for several companies (described in footnotes on the next page) were as follows:

Company	Earnings Before Interest and Taxes	Interest Expense	Times Interest Earned Ratio
Exxon Corporation[a]	$8,031,000,000	$ 784,000,000	10.24
Ralston Purina Company[b]	777,500,000	242,900,000	3.20
J. P. Morgan & Co., Inc.[c]	7,322,000,000	5,573,000,000	1.31
Pitney Bowes, Inc.[d]	510,678,000	227,257,000	2.25
Barnett Banks, Inc.[e]	1,446,646,000	1,143,680,000	1.26

You can see from these data that a great deal of variability exists in the times interest earned ratios for real companies. Recall, however, that 1992 was a recession year causing many companies to report lower earnings. Some companies that issued high-interest junk bonds in the 1980s defaulted on their interest payments and had to declare Chapter 11 bankruptcy or renegotiate payment terms with bondholders. Other companies with high-interest bonds issued new low-interest bonds and used the proceeds to retire the high-interest bonds.

Chapter 16 discusses the fourth major financial statement—the statement of cash flows, which we mentioned in Chapter 1. This statement shows the cash inflows and outflows from operating, investing, and financing activities.

Understanding the Learning Objectives

Objective 1
Describe the features of bonds and tell how bonds differ from shares of stock.

- A bond is a liability (with a maturity date) that bears interest that is deductible in computing both net income and taxable income.
- A stock is a unit of ownership on which a dividend is paid only if declared, and dividends are not deductible in determining net income or taxable income.
- Bonds may be secured or unsecured, registered or unregistered, callable, and/or convertible.

Objective 2
List the advantages and disadvantages of financing with long-term debt and prepare examples showing how to employ financial leverage.

- Advantages include stockholders retaining control of the company, tax deductibility of interest, and possible creation of favorable financial leverage.
- Disadvantages include having to make a fixed interest payment each period, reduction in a company's ability to withstand a major loss, possible limitations on dividends and future borrowings, and possible reduction in earnings per share caused by unfavorable financial leverage.

Objective 3
Prepare journal entries for bonds issued at face value.

- If bonds are issued at face value on an interest date, no accrued interest is recorded.
- If bonds are issued between interest dates, accrued interest must be recorded.

Objective 4
Explain how interest rates affect bond prices and what causes a bond to sell at a premium or a discount.

- If the market rate is lower than the contract rate, bonds sell for more than their face value, and a premium is recorded.
- If the market rate is higher than the contract rate, bonds sell for less than their face value, and a discount is recorded.

Objective 5
Apply the concept of present value to compute the price of a bond.

- The present value of the principal plus the present value of the interest payments is equal to the price of the bond.
- The contract rate of interest is used to determine the amount of future cash interest payments.
- The effective rate of interest is used to discount the future payment of principal and of interest back to the present value.

---

[a] Exxon Corporation is one of the largest oil companies in the world, with recent annual sales of approximately $120 billion.

[b] Ralston Purina Company is one of the world's largest producers of pet foods, fresh bakery products, dry cell battery products, breakfast cereals, and polymers.

[c] J. P. Morgan & Co., Inc., is a global banking firm that serves clients with complex financial needs.

[d] Pitney Bowes Inc., is a multinational company providing mailing, shipping, copying, dictating, communications recording, and facsimile systems; item identification and tracking systems and supplies; mailroom, reprographics, and related management services; and product financing.

[e] Barnett Banks, Inc., is the leading financial institution in Florida and the 18th largest in the United States.

Objective 6
Prepare journal entries for bonds issued at a discount or a premium.

- When bonds are issued, Cash is debited, and Bonds Payable is credited. For bonds issued at a discount, Discount on Bonds Payable is also debited. For bonds issued at a premium, Premium on Bonds Payable is also credited. For bonds issued between interest dates, Bond Interest Payable is also credited.
- Any premium or discount must be amortized over the period the bonds are outstanding.
- Under the effective interest rate method, interest expense for any period is equal to the effective (market) rate of interest at date of issuance times the carrying value of the bond at the beginning of that interest period.
- Under the straight-line method of amortization, an equal amount of discount or premium is allocated to each month the bonds are outstanding.

Objective 7
Prepare journal entries for bond redemptions and bond conversions.

- When bonds are redeemed before they mature, a loss or gain (an extraordinary item, if material) on bond redemption may occur.
- A bond sinking fund might be required in the bond indenture.
- Bonds may be convertible into shares of stock. The carrying value of the bonds is the capital contributed for shares of stock issued.

Objective 8
Describe the ratings used for bonds.

- Bonds are rated as to their riskiness.
- The two leading bond rating services are Moody's Investors Services and Standard & Poor's Corporation.
- Each of these services has its own rating scale. For instance, the highest rating is Aaa (Moody's) and AAA (Standard & Poor's).

Objective 9
Analyze and use the financial results—times interest earned ratio.

- The times interest earned ratio indicates a company's ability to meet interest payments when due.
- The ratio is equal to income before interest and taxes (IBIT) divided by interest expense.

Objective 10
Explain future value and present value concepts and make required calculations (Appendix).

- The future value of an investment is the amount to which a sum of money invested today will grow in a stated time period at a specified interest rate.
- Present value is the current worth of a future cash receipt and is the reciprocal of future value. To discount future receipts is to bring them back to their present values.

Appendix: Future Value and Present Value

Managers apply the concepts of interest, future value, and present value in making business decisions. Therefore, accountants need to understand these concepts to properly record certain business transactions.

The Time Value of Money

Objective 10
Explain future value and present value concepts and make required calculations.

The concept of the *time value of money* stems from the logical preference for a dollar today rather than a dollar at any future date. Most individuals prefer having a dollar today rather than at some future date because (1) the risk exists that the future dollar will never be received; and (2) if the dollar is on hand now, it can be invested, resulting in an increase in total dollars possessed at that future date.

Most business decisons involve a comparison of cash flows in and out of the company. To be useful in decision making, such comparisons must be in dollars of the same point in time. That is, the dollars held now must be accumulated or rolled forward, or future dollars must be discounted or brought back to the present dollar value, before comparisons are valid. Such comparisons involve future value and present value concepts.

Future Value

The **future value or worth** of any investment is the amount to which a sum of money invested today grows during a stated period of time at a specified interest rate. The interest involved may be simple interest or compound interest. **Simple interest** is interest on princi-

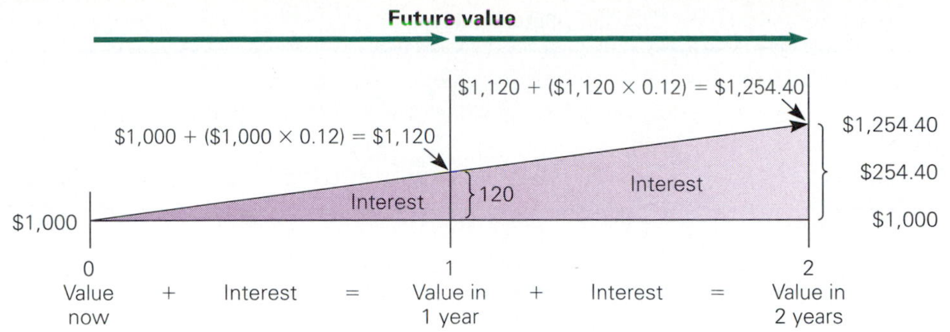

ILLUSTRATION 15.6
Compound Interest and Future Value

pal only. For example, $1,000 invested today for two years at 12% simple interest grows to $1,240 since interest is $120 per year. The principal of $1,000, plus 2 × $120, is equal to $1,240. **Compound interest** is interest on principal and on interest of prior periods. For example, $1,000 invested for two years at 12% compounded annually grows to $1,254.40 as follows:

Principal or present value	$1,000.00
Interest, year 1 = $1,000 × 0.12 =	120.00
Value at end of year 1	$1,120.00
Interest, year 2 = $1,120 × 0.12 =	134.40
Value at end of year 2 (future value)	$1,254.40

In Illustration 15.6, we graphically portray these computations of future worth and show how $1,000 grows to $1,254.40 with a 12% interest rate compounded annually. The effect of compounding is $14.40—the interest in the second year that was based on the interest computed for the first year, or $120 × 0.12 = $14.40.

Interest tables ease the task of computing the future worth to which any invested amount will grow at a given rate for a stated period. An example is Table A.1 in the Appendix at the end of this text. To use the Appendix tables, first determine the number of compounding periods involved. A compounding period may be any length of time, such as a day, a month, a quarter, a half-year, or a year, but normally not more than a year. The number of compounding periods is equal to the number of years in the life of the investment times the number of compoundings per year. Five years compounded annually is five periods, five years compounded quarterly is 20 periods, and so on.

Second, determine the interest rate per compounding period. Interest rates are usually quoted in annual terms; in fact, federal law requires statement of the interest rate in annual terms in some situations. Divide the annual rate by the number of compounding periods per year to get the proper rate per period. Only with an annual compounding period will the annual rate be the rate per period. All other cases involve a lower rate. For example, if the annual rate is 12% and interest is compounded monthly, the rate per period (one month) will be 1%.

To use the tables, find the number of periods involved in the Period column. Move across the table to the right, stopping in the column headed by the Interest Rate per Period, which yields a number called a *factor*. The factor shows the amount to which an investment of $1 will grow for the periods and the rate involved. To compute the future worth of the investment, multiply the number of dollars in the given situation by this factor. For example, suppose your parents tell you that they will invest $8,000 at 12% for four years and give you the amount to which this investment grows if you graduate from college in four years. How much will you receive at the end of four years if the interest rate is 12% compounded annually? How much will you receive if the interest rate is 12% compounded quarterly?

To calculate these amounts, look at the end-of-text Appendix, Table A.1. In the intersection of the 4 period row and the 12% column, you find the factor 1.57352. Multiplying this factor by $8,000 yields $12,588.16, the answer to the first question. To answer the second question, look at the intersection of the 16 period row and the 3% column. The factor is 1.60471, and the value of your investment is $12,837.68. The more frequent compounding would add $12,837.68 − $12,588.16 = $249.52 to the value of your investment. The reason for this difference in amounts is that 12% compounded quarterly is a higher rate than 12% compounded annually.

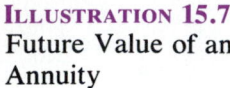

Illustration 15.7
Future Value of an Annuity

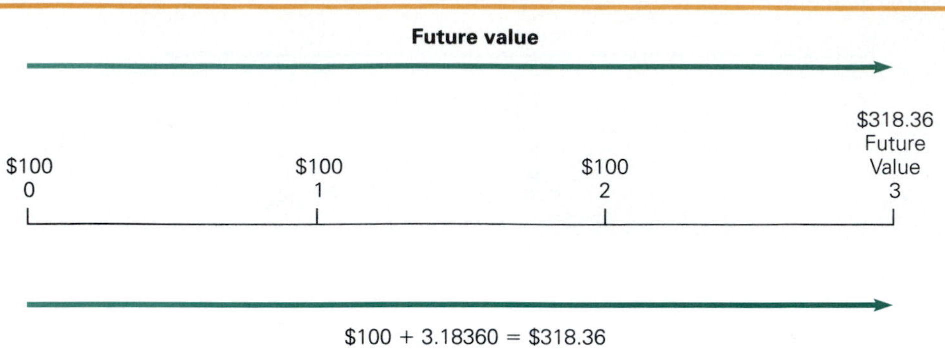

Future Value of an Annuity

An **annuity** is a series of equal cash flows (often called *rents*) spaced equally in time. The semiannual interest payments received on a bond investment are a common example of an annuity. Assume that $100 will be received at the end of each of the next three semiannual periods. The interest rate is 6% per semiannual period. Using Table A.1 in the Appendix, we find the future value of each of the $100 receipts as follows:

Future value (after three periods) of $100 received at the end of the—		
First period:	1.12360 × $100 =	$112.36
Second period:	1.06000 × 100 =	106.00
Third period:	1.00000 × 100 =	100.00
Total future value		$318.36

Such a procedure would become quite tedious if the annuity consisted of many receipts. Fortunately, tables are available to calculate the total future value directly. See the Appendix, Table A.2. For the annuity just described, you can identify one single factor by looking at the 3 period row and 6% column. The factor is 3.18360 (the sum of the three factors shown above), and when multiplied by $100, yields $318.36, which is the same answer. In Illustration 15.7, we graphically present the future value of an annuity.

Present Value

Present value is the current worth of a future cash receipt and is the reciprocal of future value. In future value, we calculate the future value of a sum of money possessed now. In present value, we calculate the current worth of rights to future cash receipts possessed now. We discount future receipts by bringing them back to their present values.

Assume that you have the right to receive $1,000 in one year. If the appropriate interest rate is 12% compounded annually, what is the present value of this $1,000 future cash receipt? You know that the present value is less than $1,000 because $1,000 due in one year is not worth $1,000 today. You also know that the $1,000 due in one year is equal to some amount, P, plus interest on P at 12% for one year. Thus, $P + 0.12P = \$1,000$, or $1.12P = \$1,000$. Dividing $1,000 by 1.12, you get $892.86; this amount is the present value of your future $1,000. If the $1,000 was due in two years, you would find its present value by dividing $892.86 by 1.12, which equals $797.20. Portrayed graphically, present value looks similar to future value, except for the direction of the arrows (Illustration 15.8).

Table A.3 (end-of-text Appendix) contains present value factors for combinations of a number of periods and interest rates. We use Table A.3 in the same manner as Table A.1. For example, the present value of $1,000 due in four years at 16% compounded annually is $552.29, computed as $1,000 × 0.55229. The 0.55229 is the present value factor found in the intersection of the 4 period row and the 16% column.

As another example, suppose that you wish to have $4,000 in three years to pay for a vacation in Europe. If your investment increases at a 20% rate compounded quarterly, how much should you invest now? To find the amount, you would use the present value factor found in Table A.3, 12 period row, 5% column. This factor is 0.55684, which means that an investment of about 55½ cents today would grow to $1 in 12 periods at 5% per period. To have $4,000 at the end of three years, you must invest 4,000 times this factor (0.55684), or $2,227.36.

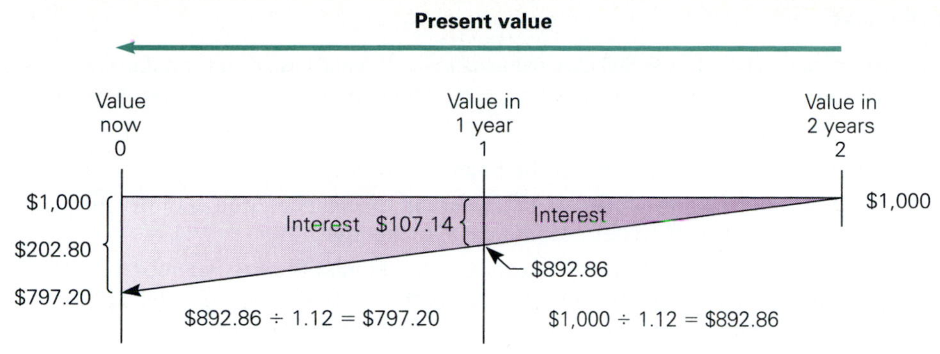

ILLUSTRATION 15.8
Compound Interest and Present Value

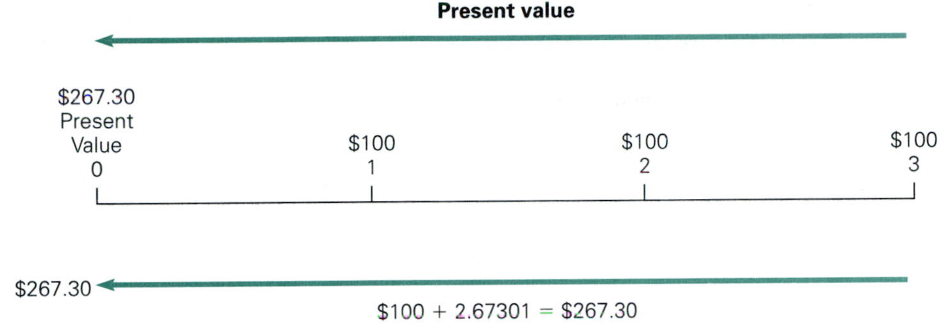

ILLUSTRATION 15.9
Present Value of an Annuity

Present Value of an Annuity

The semiannual interest payments on a bond are a common example of an annuity. As an example of calculating the present value of an annuity, assume that $100 is received at the end of each of the next three semiannual periods. The interest rate is 6% per semiannual period. By using Table A.3 (Appendix), you can find the present value of each of the three $100 payments as follows:

Present value of $100 due in:	
1 period: 0.94340 × $100 =	$ 94.34
2 periods: 0.89000 × 100 =	89.00
3 periods: 0.83962 × 100 =	83.96
Total present value	$267.30

Such a procedure could become quite tedious if the annuity consisted of a large number of payments. Fortunately, tables are also available showing the present values of an annuity of $1 per period for varying interest rates and periods. See the end-of-text Appendix, Table A.4. For the annuity just described, you can obtain a single factor from the table to represent the present value of an annuity of $1 per period for three (semiannual) periods at 6% per (semiannual) period. This factor is 2.67301; it is equal to the sum of the present value factors for $1 due in one period, $1 in two periods, and $1 in three periods found in the Appendix, Table A.3. When this factor is multiplied by $100, the number of dollars in each payment, it yields the present value of the annuity, $267.30. In Illustration 15.9, we graphically present the present value of this annuity and show how to find the present value of the three $100 cash flows by multiplying the $100 by a present value of an annuity factor, 2.67301.

Suppose you won a lottery that awarded you a choice of receiving $10,000 at the end of each of the next five years or $35,000 cash today. You believe you can earn interest on invested cash at 15% per year. Which option should you choose? To answer the question, compute the present value of an annuity of $10,000 per period for five years at 15%. The present value is $33,521.60, or $10,000 × 3.35216. You should accept the immediate payment of $35,000 since it has the larger present value.

Demonstration Problem

Jackson Company issued $100,000 face value of 15%, 20-year junk bonds on April 30, 1997. The bonds are dated April 30, 1997, call for semiannual interest payments on April 30 and October 31, and are issued to yield 16% (8% per period).

Required

a. Compute the amount received for the bonds.

b. Prepare an amortization schedule. Enter data in the schedule for only the first two interest periods. Use the effective interest rate method.

c. Prepare journal entries to record issuance of the bonds, the first six months' interest expense on the bonds, the adjustment needed on December 31, 1997 (assuming Jackson's accounting year ends on that date), and the second six months' interest expense on April 30, 1998.

Solution to Demonstration Problem

a. Price received:

Present value of principal: $100,000 × 0.04603	
(see Appendix, Table A.3, 40 period row, 8% column)	$ 4,603
Present value of interest: $7,500 × 11.92461	
(see Appendix, Table A.4, 40 period row, 8% column)	89,435
Total	$94,038

b.

(A) Interest Payment Date	(B) Bond Interest Expense Debit (E × 0.16 × ½)	(C) Cash Credit ($100,000 × 0.15 × ½)	(D) Discount on Bonds Payable Credit (B − C)	(E) Carrying Value of Bonds Payable (previous balance in E + D)
Issue price				$94,038
10/31/97	$7,523	$7,500	$23	94,061
4/30/98	7,525	7,500	25	94,086

c.

JACKSON COMPANY
GENERAL JOURNAL

Date		Account	Debit	Credit
1997				
Apr.	30	Cash	94,038	
		Discount on Bonds Payable	5,962	
		Bonds Payable		100,000
		Issued $100,000 face value of 20-year, 15% bonds to yield 16%.		
Oct.	31	Bond Interest Expense	7,523	
		Discount on Bonds Payable		23
		Cash		7,500
		Paid semiannual bond interest expense.		
Dec.	31	Bond Interest Expense ($7,525 × ⅓)	2,508	
		Discount on Bonds Payable		8
		Bond Interest Payable ($7,500 × ⅓)		2,500
		To record accrual of two months' interest expense.		
1998				
Apr.	30	Bond Interest Payable	2,500	
		Bond Interest Expense ($7,525 × ⅔)	5,017	
		Discount on Bonds Payable		17
		Cash		7,500
		Paid semiannual bond interest expense.		

New Terms

Annuity A series of equal cash flows spaced in time. *564*

Bearer bond See Unregistered bond.

Bond A long-term debt, or liability, owed by its issuer. A *bond certificate*, a negotiable instrument, is the formal, physical evidence of the debt owed. *543*

Bond indenture The contract or loan agreement under which bonds are issued. *544*

Bond redemption (or sinking) fund A fund used to bring about the gradual redemption of a bond issue. *557*

Callable bond A bond that gives the issuer the right to call (buy back) the bond before its maturity date. *545*

Call premium The price paid in excess of face value that the issuer of bonds must pay to redeem (call) bonds before their maturity date. *546*

Carrying value (of bonds) The face value of bonds minus any unamortized discount or plus any unamortized premium. Sometimes referred to as **net liability** on the bonds. *552*

Compound interest Interest calculated on the principal and on interest of prior periods. *563*

Contract rate of interest The interest rate printed on the bond certificates and specified on the bond indenture; also called the **stated, coupon,** or **nominal rate.** *550*

Convertible bond A bond that may be exchanged for shares of stock of the issuing corporation at the bondholders' option. *564, 558*

Coupon bond A bond not registered as to interest; it carries detachable coupons that are to be clipped and presented for payment of interest due. *545*

Debenture bond An unsecured bond backed only by the general creditworthiness of its issuer. *544*

Discount (on bonds) Amount a bond sells for below its face value. *550*

Effective interest rate method (interest method) A procedure for calculating periodic interest expense (or revenue) in which the first period's interest is computed by multiplying the carrying value of bonds payable (bond investments) by the market rate of interest at the issue date. The difference between computed interest expense (revenue) and the interest paid (received), based on the contract rate times face value, is the discount or premium amortized for the period. Computations for subsequent periods are based on the carrying value at the beginning of the period. *553*

Face value Principal amount of a bond. *543*

Favorable financial leverage An increase in EPS and the rate of return on stockholders' equity resulting from earning a higher rate of return on borrowed funds than the fixed cost of such funds. **Unfavorable financial leverage** results when the cost of borrowed funds exceeds the income they generate, resulting in decreased income to stockholders. *546*

Future value or worth The amount to which a sum of money invested today will grow during a stated period of time at a specified interest rate. *562*

Interest method See Effective interest rate method.

Junk bonds High-interest rate, high-risk bonds; many were issued in the 1980s to finance corporate restructurings. *546*

Market interest rate The minimum rate of interest investors will accept on bonds of a particular risk category. Also called **effective rate** or **yield.** *550*

Mortgage A legal claim (lien) on specific property that gives the bondholder the right to possess the pledged property if the company fails to make required payments. A bond secured by a mortgage is called a **mortgage bond.** *544*

Premium (on bonds) Amount a bond sells for above its face value. *550*

Present value The current worth of a future cash receipt(s); computed by discounting future receipts at a stipulated interest rate. *550, 564*

Registered bond A bond with the owner's name on the bond certificate and in the register of bond owners kept by the bond issuer or its agent, the registrar. *545*

Secured bond A bond for which a company has pledged specific property to ensure its payment. *544*

Serial bonds Bonds in a given bond issue with maturities spread over several dates. *545, 556*

Simple interest Interest on principal only. *562*

Sinking fund See Bond redemption fund.

Stock warrant A right that allows the bondholder to purchase shares of common stock at a fixed price for a stated period of time. Warrants issued with long-term debt may be **detachable** or **nondetachable.** *546*

Straight-line method of amortization A procedure that, when applied to bond discount or premium, allocates an equal amount of discount or premium to each period in the life of a bond. *553*

Term bond A bond that matures on the same date as all other bonds in a given bond issue. *545*

Times interest earned ratio Income before interest and taxes (IBIT) divided by interest expense. In complex situations, "operating income" is often used to represent IBIT. *559*

Trading on the equity A company using its stockholders' equity as a basis for securing funds on which it pays a fixed return. *547*

Trustee Usually a bank or trust company appointed to represent the bondholders and to enforce the provisions of the bond indenture against the issuer. *544*

Underwriter An investment company or a banker that performs many tasks for the bond issuer in issuing bonds; may also guarantee the issuer a fixed price for the bonds. *544*

Unfavorable financial leverage Results when the cost of borrowed funds exceeds the revenue they generate; it is the reverse of **favorable financial leverage.** *548*

Unregistered (bearer) bond Ownership transfers by physical delivery. *545*

Unsecured bond A **debenture bond,** or simply a **debenture.** *544*

SELF-TEST

TRUE-FALSE

Indicate whether each of the following statements is true or false.

1. An unsecured bond is called a debenture bond.
2. Callable bonds may be called at the option of the holder of the bonds.
3. Favorable financial leverage results when borrowed funds are used to increase earnings per share of common stock.
4. If the market rate of interest exceeds the contract rate, the bonds are issued at a discount.
5. The straight-line method of amortization is the recommended method.

MULTIPLE-CHOICE

Select the best answer for each of the following questions.

1. Harner Company issued $100,000 of 12% bonds on March 1, 1997. The bonds are dated January 1, 1997, and were issued at 96 plus accrued interest. The entry to record the issuance would be:

a.

Cash	98,000	
Discount on Bonds Payable	4,000	
Bonds Payable		100,000
Bond Interest Payable		2,000

b.

Cash	102,000	
Bonds Payable		100,000
Bond Interest Payable		2,000

c.

Cash	96,000	
Discount on Bonds Payable	4,000	
Bonds Payable		100,000

d. None of the above.

2. If the bonds in (1) had been issued at 104, the entry to record the issuance would have been:

a.

Cash	104,000	
Bonds Payable		100,000
Premium on Bonds Payable		4,000

b.

Cash	102,000	
Bonds Payable		100,000
Bond Interest Payable		2,000

c.

Cash	106,000	
Bonds Payable		100,000
Premium on Bonds Payable		4,000
Bond Interest Expense		2,000

d. None of the above.

3. On January 1, 1997, the Alvarez Company issued $400,000 face value of 8%, 10-year bonds for cash of $328,298, a price to yield 11%. The bonds pay interest semiannually and mature on January 1, 2004. Using the effective interest rate method, the bond interest expense for the first six months of 1998 would be:

a. $36,113.
b. $18,056.
c. $32,000.
d. $16,000.

4. If the straight-line amortization method had been used in (**3**), the interest expense for the first six months would have been:

a. $39,170.
b. $32,000.
c. $18,000.
d. $19,585.

5. Assume a company has net income of $100,000, income tax expense of $40,000, and interest expense of $20,000. The times interest earned ratio is:

a. 5 times
b. 7 times
c. 8 times
d. 9 times

Now turn to page 574 to check your answers.

QUESTIONS

1. What are the advantages of obtaining long-term funds by the issuance of bonds rather than additional shares of capital stock? What are the disadvantages?
2. What is a bond indenture? What parties are usually associated with it? Explain why.
3. Explain what is meant by the terms *coupon, callable, convertible,* and *debenture.*
4. What is meant by the term *trading on the equity?*
5. When bonds are issued between interest dates, why should the issuing corporation receive cash equal to the amount of accrued interest (accrued since the preceding interest date) in addition to the issue price of the bonds?
6. Why might it be more accurate to describe a sinking fund as a bond redemption fund?
7. Indicate how each of the following items should be classified in a balance sheet on December 31, 1996.
   a. Cash balance in a sinking fund.
   b. Accrued interest on bonds payable.
   c. Debenture bonds payable due in 2006.

d. Premium on bonds payable.
e. First-mortgage bonds payable, due July 1, 1997.
f. Discount on bonds payable.
g. First National Bank—Interest account.
h. Convertible bonds payable due in 1999.

8. Why is the effective interest rate method of computing periodic interest expense considered theoretically preferable to the straight-line method?
9. Why would an investor whose intent is to hold bonds to maturity pay more for the bonds than their face value?
10. Of what use is the times interest earned ratio?

EXERCISES

Exercise 15–1
Record issuance of bonds at face value, adjusting entry, and payment of interest (L.O. 3)

On September 30, 1997, Santiago's Construction Company issued $240,000 face value of 12%, 10-year bonds dated August 31, 1997, at 100, plus accrued interest. Interest is paid semiannually on February 28 and August 31. Santiago's accounting year ends on December 31. Prepare journal entries to record the issuance of these bonds, the accrual of interest at year-end, and the payment of the first interest coupon.

Exercise 15–2
Compute bond interest expense; show how bond price was determined (L.O. 4–6)

On December 31, 1996, Dexter Office Equipment Company issued $800,000 face value of 8%, 10-year bonds for cash of $700,303, a price to yield 10%. The bonds pay interest semiannually and mature on December 31, 2006.

a. State which is higher, the market rate of interest or the contract rate.
b. Compute the bond interest expense for the first six months of 1996, using the interest method.
c. Show how the $700,303 price must have been determined.

Exercise 15–3
Calculate interest expense using straight-line amortization (L.O. 6)

Compute the annual interest expense on the bonds in Exercise 15–2, assuming the bond discount is amortized using the straight-line method.

Exercise 15–4
Prepare entry to record interest payment (L.O. 6)

After recording the payment of the interest coupon due on June 30, 1997, the accounts of Thuss Sailboat, Inc., showed Bonds Payable of $600,000 and Premium on Bonds Payable of $21,144. Interest is payable semiannually on June 30 and December 31. The five-year, 12% bonds have a face value of $600,000 and were originally issued to yield 10%. Prepare the journal entry to record the payment of interest on December 31, 1997. Use the interest method. (Round all amounts to the nearest dollar.)

Exercise 15–5
Record call of bonds and payment of interest (L.O. 7)

On June 30, 1997 (a semiannual interest payment date), Holiday Rollerblade Company redeemed all of its $200,000 face value of 10% bonds outstanding by calling them at 106. The bonds were originally issued on June 30, 1993, at 100. Prepare the journal entry to record the payment of the interest and the redemption of the bonds on June 30, 1997.

Exercise 15–6
Record accrued interest and purchase and retirement of bonds (L.O. 7)

On August 31, 1996, as part of the provisions of its bond indenture, South Pacific Cruise Line, Inc., acquired $240,000 of its outstanding bonds on the open market at 96 plus accrued interest. These bonds were originally issued at face value and carry a 12% interest rate, payable semiannually. The bonds are dated November 30, 1985, and pay semiannual interest on May 31 and November 30. Prepare the journal entries required to record the accrual of the interest to the acquisition date on the bonds acquired and the acquisition of the bonds.

Exercise 15–7
Record sinking fund transactions (L.O. 7)

Chicago Heating Systems, Inc., is required to make a deposit of $36,000 plus semiannual interest expense of $1,080 on October 31, 1996, to the trustee of its sinking fund so that the trustee can redeem $36,000 of the company's bonds on that date. The bonds were issued at 100. Prepare the journal entries required on October 31 to record the sinking fund deposit, the bond retirement, payment of interest (due on that date), and payment of trustee expenses, assuming the latter is $200.

Exercise 15–8
Record conversion of bonds into capital stock(L.O. 7)

After interest was paid on September 30, 1997, $30,000 face value of Jake's Video Rentals, Inc., outstanding bonds were converted into 4,000 shares of the company's $5 par value common stock. Prepare the journal entry to record the conversion, assuming the bonds were issued at 100.

Exercise 15–9
Calculate times interest earned ratios for a company and comment (L.O. 9)

A recent annual report of Rite Aid Corporation showed the following amounts as of the dates indicated:

	Years Ended		
	February 27, 1993	February 29, 1992	March 2, 1991
Earnings before interest (and taxes)	$247,469,000	$242,802,000	$227,085,000
Interest expense	32,888,000	40,821,000	52,400,000

Calculate the times interest earned ratio for each year and comment on the results.

Exercise 15–10
Determine present value of a lump-sum payment (based on appendix) (L.O. 10)

What is the present value of a lump-sum payment of $40,000 due in five years if the market rate of interest is 10% per year (compounded annually) and the present value of $1 due in five periods at 10% is 0.62092?

Exercise 15–11
Determine present value of an annuity (based on appendix) (L.O. 10)

What is the present value of a series of semiannual payments of $1,000 due at the end of each six months for the next five years if the market rate of interest is 10% per year and the present value of an annuity of $1 for 10 periods at 5% is 7.72173?

Exercise 15–12
Determine present value for lottery winnings (based on appendix) (L.O. 10)

Sam Williams bought a ticket in the New York State lottery for $1, hoping to strike it rich. To his amazement, he won $2,000,000. Payment was to be received in equal amounts at the end of each of the next 20 years. Williams heard from relatives and friends he had not heard from in years. They all wanted to renew their relationship with this new millionaire. Federal and state income taxes were going to be about 40% (36% for federal and 4% for state) on each year's income from the lottery check. The discount rate to use in all present value calculations is 12%.

a. How much will Williams actually receive after taxes each year?

b. Is Williams a multimillionaire according to the present value of his cash inflow after taxes?

c. What is the present value of the net amount the state has to pay out? Remember that the state gets part of the money back in the form of taxes.

Exercise 15–13
Determine future value of an annuity (based on appendix) (L.O. 10)

After Sam Williams won $2,000,000 in the New York State lottery, he decided to purchase $10,000 of lottery tickets at the end of each year for the next 20 years. He was hoping to hit the lottery again, but he never did. If the state can earn 12% on ticket revenue received, how much will the annuity of $10,000 from Williams grow to by the end of 20 years?

PROBLEMS

Problem 15–1
Record issuance of bonds and payment of interest (L.O. 3)

On June 1, 1996, True Auto Parts, Inc., issued $90,000 of 10-year, 16% bonds dated April 1, 1996, at 100. Interest on bonds is payable semiannually on presentation of the appropriate coupon. All of the bonds are of $1,000 denomination. The company's accounting period ends on June 30, with semiannual statements prepared on December 31 and June 30. The interest payment dates are April 1 and October 1.

All of the first coupons on the bonds are presented to the company's bank and paid on October 2, 1996. All but one of the second coupons are similarly received and paid on April 1, 1997.

Required Prepare all necessary journal entries for these transactions through April 1, 1997, including the adjusting entry needed at June 30, 1996.

Problem 15–2
Compute two prices for bond issue and first period's interest (L.O. 5, 6)

Water Filtration, Inc., is going to issue $800,000 face value of 10%, 15-year bonds. The bonds are dated June 30, 1996, call for semiannual interest payments, and mature on June 30, 2011.

Required

a. Compute the price investors should offer if they seek a yield of 8% on these bonds. Also, compute the first six months' interest, assuming the bonds are issued at this price. Use the interest method and calculate all amounts to the nearest dollar.

b. Repeat part **a**, assuming investors seek a yield of 12%.

Problem 15–3
Record bond interest expense payment and accrual for partial period (L.O. 6)

On July 1, 1996, North Carolina Table Company issued $900,000 face value of 10%, 10-year bonds. The bonds call for semiannual interest payments and mature on July 1, 2006. The company received cash of $796,770, a price that yields 12%.

Required

Assume that the company's fiscal year ends on March 31. Prepare journal entries (to the nearest dollar) to record the bond interest expense on January 1, 1997, and the adjustment needed on March 31, 1997, using the interest method. Calculate alll amounts to the nearest dollar.

Problem 15–4
Compute price of bonds; prepare amortization schedule; journalize bond issuance and interest payment (L.O. 5, 6)

Massey Company issued $200,000 face value of 16%, 20-year junk bonds on July 1, 1997. The bonds are dated July 1, 1997, call for semiannual interest payments on July 1 and January 1, and were issued to yield 12% (6% per period).

Required

a. Compute the amount received for the bonds.
b. Prepare an amortization schedule similar to that in Illustration 15.5. Enter data in the schedule for only the first two interest periods. Use the interest method.
c. Prepare journal entries to record issuance of the bonds, the first six months' interest expense on the bonds, and the adjustment needed on May 31, 1998, assuming Massey's fiscal year ends on that date.

Problem 15–5
Compute price of bonds; prepare amortization schedule; journalize bond issuance, payment of first period's interest, and accrual of partial period's interest (L.O. 5, 6)

Jamestown Furniture Company issued $200,000 face value of 18%, 20-year junk bonds on October 1, 1996. The bonds are dated October 1, 1996, call for semiannual interest payments on April 1 and October 1, and are issued to yield 16% (8% per period).

Required

a. Compute the amount received for the bonds.
b. Prepare an amortization schedule similar to that in Illustration 15.5. Enter data in the schedule for only the first two interest periods. Use the interest method and make all calculations to the nearest dollar.
c. Prepare entries to record the issuance of the bonds, the first six months' interest on the bonds, and the adjustment needed on June 30, 1997, assuming the company's fiscal year ends on that date.

Problem 15–6
Record serial bond transactions, and show financial reporting (L.O. 7)

Dallas Clothing Company issued $300,000 of 12% serial bonds on July 1, 1996, at face value. The bonds are dated July 1, 1996; call for semiannual interest payments on July 1 and January 1; and mature at the rate of $60,000 per year, with the first maturity date falling on July 1, 2001. The company's accounting period ends on September 30.

Required

Prepare journal entries to record the interest payment of July 1, 2001; the maturing of $60,000 of bonds on July 1, 2001; and the adjusting entry needed on September 30, 2001. Also, show how the bonds would be presented in the company's balance sheet for September 30, 2001.

ALTERNATE PROBLEMS

Problem 15–1A
Record issuance of bonds, payment of bonds, payment of interest, and partial period accrual (L.O. 3)

On December 1, 1996, California Waste Management Company issued $150,000 of 10-year, 9% bonds dated July 1, 1996, at 100. Interest on the bonds is payable semiannually on July 1 and January 1. All of the bonds are registered. The company's accounting period ends on March 31. Quarterly financial statements are prepared.

The company deposits a sum of money sufficient to pay the semiannual interest on the bonds in a special checking account in First National Bank and draws interest payment checks on this account. The deposit is made the day before the checks are drawn.

Required Prepare journal entries to record the issuance of the bonds; the December 31 adjusting entry; the January 1, 1997, interest payment; and the adjusting entry needed on March 31, 1997, to prepare quarterly financial statements.

Problem 15–2A
Compute two prices on bond issue and first period's interest (L.O. 5, 6)

Nifty Toy Company is seeking to issue $800,000 face value of 10%, 20-year bonds. The bonds are dated June 30, 1996, call for semiannual interest payments, and mature on June 30, 2016.

Required

a. Compute the price investors should offer if they seek a yield of 8% on these bonds. Also, compute the first six months' interest assuming the bonds are issued at that price. Use the interest method and calculate all amounts to the nearest dollar.

b. Repeat part **a** assuming investors seek a yield of 12%.

Problem 15–3A
Record bond interest expense and accrual for partial period (L.O. 6)

On July 1, 1996, Big Ben Clock Company issued $200,000 face value of 8%, 10-year bonds. These bonds call for semiannual interest payments and mature on July 1, 2006. The company received cash of $175,076, a price that yields 10%.

Required

Assume that the company's fiscal year ends on March 31. Prepare journal entries to record the bond interest expense on January 1, 1997, and the adjustment needed on March 31, 1997, using the interest method. Calculate all amounts to the nearest dollar.

Problem 15–4A
Compute price of bonds; prepare amortization schedule; journalize bond issuance; and accrue interest (L.O. 5, 6)

Bendix Company issued $300,000 face value of 15%, 20-year bonds on October 1, 1997. The bonds are dated October 1, 1997, call for semiannual interest payments on April 1 and October 1, and are issued to yield 16% (8% per period).

Required

a. Compute the amount received for the bonds.

b. Prepare an amortization schedule similar to that in Illustration 15.4. Enter data in the schedule for only the first two interest periods. Use the interest method.

c. Prepare journal entries to record issuance of the bonds, the first six months' interest expense on the bonds, and the adjustment needed on May 31, 1998, assuming Bendix's fiscal year ends on that date.

Problem 15–5A
Compute price of bonds; prepare amortization schedule; journalize bond issuance; and record two interest payments (L.O. 5, 6)

Software Systems, Inc., issued $200,000 face value of 10%, 20-year bonds on July 1, 1996. The bonds are dated July 1, 1996, call for semiannual interest payments on July 1 and January 1, and are issued to yield 12% (6% per period).

Required

a. Compute the amount received for the bonds.

b. Prepare an amortization schedule similar to that in Illustration 15.4. Enter data in the schedule for only the first two interest periods. Use the interest method and calculate all amounts to the nearest dollar.

c. Prepare entries to record the issuance of the bonds, the first six months' interest on the bonds, and the adjustment needed on June 30, 1997, assuming Software System's fiscal year ends on that date.

Problem 15–6A
Record serial bond transactions, and show financial reporting (L.O. 7)

Solar Energy Company issued $200,000 of 12% bonds on July 1, 1996, at face value. The bonds are dated July 1, 1996, call for semiannual payments on July 1 and January 1, and mature at the rate of $20,000 per year on July 1, beginning in 2001. The company's accounting period ends on September 30.

Required

a. Prepare journal entries to record the interest expense and payment for the six months ending July 1, 2001; the maturing of the bonds on July 1, 2001; and the adjusting entries needed on September 30, 2001.

b. Show how the bonds would be presented in the company's balance sheet for September 30, 2001.

BEYOND THE NUMBERS—CRITICAL THINKING

Business Decision Case 15–1
Analyze two financing proposals; decide whether investment should be made (L.O. 2)

A company is trying to decide whether to invest $2 million on plant expansion and $1 million to finance a related increase in inventories and accounts receivable. The $3 million expansion is expected to increase business volume substantially. Profit forecasts indicate that income from operations will rise from $1.6 million to $2.2 million. The income tax rate will be about 40%. Net income last year was $918,000. Interest expense on debt now outstanding is $70,000 per year. There are 200,000 shares of common stock currently outstanding.

The $3 million needed can be obtained in two alternative ways:

1. Finance entirely by issuing additional shares of common stock at an expected issue price of $75 per share.
2. Finance two thirds with bonds, one third with additional stock. The bonds would have a 20-year life, bear interest at 10%, and sell at face value. The issue price of the stock would be $80 per share.

Required

Should the investment be made? If so, explain which financing plan you would recommend. (Hint: Calculate earnings per share for last year and for future years under each of the alternatives.)

Business Decision Case 15–2
Answer questions regarding annual report (L.O. 7)

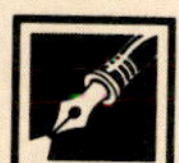

A recent annual report of Fuqua Industries (now Actava Group, Inc.) contained the following paragraph in the notes to the financial statements:

The 9⅞% Senior Subordinated Debentures are redeemable at the option of Fuqua at 103.635% of the principal amount plus accrued interest if redeemed prior to March 15, 1990, and at decreasing prices thereafter. Mandatory sinking fund payments of $3,000,000 (which Fuqua may increase to $6,000,000 annually) began in 1982 and are intended to retire, at par plus accrued interest, 75% of the issue prior to maturity.

Required

Answer the following questions:

a. What does the term *debentures* mean?
b. How much is the call premium initially? Does this premium decrease over time?
c. Under what circumstances might the company want to increase the sinking fund payments?

Business Decision Case 15–3
Answer questions regarding bond yields (L.O. 8)

The April 29, 1994, issue of *The Wall Street Journal* contained a table showing yield comparisons for groups of corporate bonds. The following data have been adapted from the table:

	Yield Percentage			
	As of		52-week	
Risk category	4/28	4/27	High	Low
1–10 year maturities:				
High quality	7.08%	6.94%	7.16%	5.32%
Medium quality	7.41	7.26	7.49	5.76
Over 10 year maturities:				
High quality	7.91	7.81	8.06	6.93
Medium quality	8.36	8.25	8.49	7.29
High-yield bonds	10.45	10.48	10.53	9.25

Standard & Poor's ratings were:

High quality	AAA to AA
Medium quality	A to BBB
High-yield	BB to C

Required

Prepare written answers to the following questions.

a. In each column of numbers, why do the yield rates increase from top to bottom?
b. For the high quality and medium quality bonds, what could account for the increase in the yield rates from 4/27/94 to 4/28/94? Take into consideration the economic events occurring at about that time.

c. Which risk class of bonds was closest to its 52-week high on 4/28/94? What could have been the cause?

Annual Report Analysis 15–4
Calculate times interest earned ratio for three companies and prepare written comments on results (L.O. 9)

Refer to the annual report booklet and determine the times interest earned ratios for 1993 for The Coca-Cola Company, Maytag Corporation, and The Limited, Inc. Use "operating income" to represent IBIT. Prepare written comments on the results of your analysis.

Annual Report Analysis 15–5
Decide whether to convert or surrender bonds (real world problem) (L.O. 7)

A recent annual report of Emhart Corporation contained the following paragraph in its notes to the financial statements:

> The 6¾% convertible subordinated debentures may be converted into shares of common stock at a price of $26.50 per share at any time prior to maturity. They are redeemable at prices decreasing from 105 percent of face amount currently to 100 percent in July 1993. At December 31, 1988, a total of 1,886,794 common shares were reserved for the conversion of the debentures.

Required Answer the following questions:

a. If you held one $1,000 bond, how many shares of stock would you receive if you converted the bond into shares of stock? (Hint: You can use the principal amount of the bond to buy shares of stock at the stated price.)

b. Assume you held one $1,000 bond and the bond was called by the company at a price of 105% of the face amount. If the current market price per share of the stock was $29, would you convert the bond into shares of stock or would you surrender the bond? Explain.

Ethics Case—Writing Experience 15–6
Answer questions regarding ethics case

Refer to "An Ethical Perspective" on page 560. Write out the answers to the following questions:

a. What motivates the brothers to pursue this new strategy?

b. Are the brothers the only ones assuming the risks?

c. How will workers, the city, the holders of the original bond issue, and the other present stockholders be affected if the junk bonds are issued and are then defaulted?

d. How might these parties (stakeholders) be affected if a new buyer outbids the management?

e. What ethical considerations are involved?

Group Project 15–7
Write a paper on a specific topic

In groups of two or three students, write a two-page, double-spaced paper on one of the following topics:

The Use of Junk Bonds in the 1980s
Why Market Rates of Interest and Prices of Bonds Are Inversely Related
How a Company Can Force Conversion of Callable, Convertible Bonds
How Bond Sinking Funds Work

Do some library research on your topic and properly cite your sources. Make your analysis convincing. Your paper should be neat, contain no spelling or grammatical errors, and be the result of several drafts. Use a word processing program to prepare your paper if possible. Your paper should have a cover page with the title and the authors' names.

ANSWERS TO SELF-TEST

TRUE-FALSE

1. **True.** These unsecured bonds are called debenture bonds and are backed only by the general credit-worthiness of the issuer.
2. **False.** Callable bonds may be called at the option of the issuer.
3. **True.** This statement is the definition of favorable financial leverage. However, unfavorable financial leverage can result when favorable financial leverage was planned. Unfavorable financial leverage will result if income before interest and taxes is much lower than anticipated. Then earnings per share for the common stockholders would be lower than they would have been without the borrowing.
4. **True.** Purchasers will not be willing to pay the face amount if the market rate of interest exceeds the contract rate. By paying less than the face value, purchasers can earn the market rate of interest on the bonds.
5. **False.** The effective interest rate method is the recommended method. The straight-line method may be used only when the results are not materially different from the interest method.

MULTIPLE-CHOICE

1. **a.** The discount of $4,000 must be recorded. Also, the accrued interest must be recognized ($100,000 × 12% × 2/12 = $2,000).
2. **c.** The premium is $4,000, and the accrued interest is $2,000. Both must be recognized.
3. **b.** The interest is ($328,298 × 0.11 × 1/2) = $18,056.
4. **d.** The interest would have been ($400,000 × 0.04) + ($71,702/20) = $19,585.
5. **c.** Income before interest and taxes is ($100,000 + $40,000 + $20,000) = $160,000. This total of $160,000 divided by interest of $20,000 = 8 times.

V

Analysis of Financial Statements Using the Statement of Cash Flows

Part Outline

A Manager's Perspective

Don Lehman

Principal Accountant

The Coca-Cola Company

After working for three and half years as a "Big Six" auditor, I moved to The Coca-Cola Company in the corporate finance division, working primarily on the company's external financial reporting. I was project manager for the financial section of the company's Annual Report to Share Owners for two years, and I also coordinated with the

field divisions and the external auditors to implement two of the recently issued accounting standards.

As part of my responsibilities, I work with people from every part of the Company—Marketing, Operations, Legal, Human Resources, etc. I am often a financial division "representative" on committees or task forces. I have found that many of the non-financial people I work with in these situations have a relatively broad knowledge of finance and some knowledge of basic accounting. Many of these people came from accounting backgrounds, and others have sought additional training or education. This working knowledge of accounting is extremely important in getting team assignments completed quickly, because the team members can focus immediately on a solution with the best possible financial impact.

Almost every decision made here, as at most companies, is based on its eventual impact on the company's financial results, so a solid background in accounting and finance is an advantage for persons in non-financial roles who are trying to understand how their actions will be evaluated. The fundamental concepts that define assets, equity, and expenses are crucial to making informed management decisions at every level of every business. While learning all the accounting rules for employee benefits and equity-method investees is not necessary for every student, a good understanding of accounting principles is an essential building-block for your career.

16

Analysis Using the Statement of Cash Flows

The income statement, statement of stockholders' equity (or statement of retained earnings), and the balance sheet do not answer all the questions raised by users of financial statements. Such questions include: How much cash was generated by the company's operations? How can the Cash account be overdrawn when my accountant said the business was profitable? Why is such a profitable company able to pay only small dividends? How much was spent for new plant and equipment, and where did the company get the cash for the expenditures? How was the company able to pay a dividend when it incurred a net loss for the year?

In this chapter, you will learn about the statement of cash flows, which answers these questions. The statement of cash flows is another major required financial statement; it shows important information not shown directly in the other financial statements.

Learning Objectives

After studying this chapter, you should be able to:

1. Explain the purposes and uses of the statement of cash flows.
2. Describe the content of the statement of cash flows and where certain items would appear on the statement.
3. Describe how to calculate cash flows from operating activities under both the direct and indirect methods.

(*continued*)

Purposes of the Statement of Cash Flows

In November 1987, the Financial Accounting Standards Board issued *Statement of Financial Accounting Standards No. 95,* "Statement of Cash Flows."[1] The *Statement* became effective for annual financial statements for fiscal years ending after July 15, 1988. Thus, the statement of cash flows is now one of the major financial statements issued by a company. The statement of cash flows replaced the statement of changes in financial position, on which *funds* were generally defined as working capital. **Working capital** is equal to current assets minus current liabilities.

The main purpose of the statement of cash flows is to report on the cash receipts and cash disbursements of an entity during an accounting period. Broadly defined, *cash* includes both cash and cash equivalents, such as short-term invest-

[1] FASB, *Statement of Financial Accounting Standards No. 95,* "Statement of Cash Flows" (Stamford, Conn., 1987). Copyright by the Financial Accounting Standards Board, High Ridge Park, Stamford, Connecticut 06905. U.S.A. Quoted (or excerpted) with permission. Copies of the complete document are available from the FASB.

(*concluded*)

4. Prepare a statement of cash flows, under both the direct and indirect methods, showing cash flows from operating activities, investing activities, and financing activities.
5. Analyze a statement of cash flows of a real company.
6. Analyze and use the financial results—cash flow per share of common stock, cash flow margin, and cash flow liquidity ratios.
7. Use a working paper to prepare a statement of cash flows (Appendix).

ments in Treasury bills, commercial paper, and money market funds. Another purpose of this statement is to report on the entity's investing and financing activities for the period. As shown in Illustration 16.1, the statement of cash flows reports the effects on cash during a period of a company's operating, investing, and financing activities. Firms show the effects of significant investing and financing activities that do not affect cash in a schedule separate from the statement of cash flows.

Uses of the Statement of Cash Flows

Objective 1
Explain the purposes and uses of the statement of cash flows.

The **statement of cash flows** summarizes the effects on cash of the operating, investing, and financing activities of a company during an accounting period; it reports on past management decisions on such matters as issuance of capital stock or the sale of long-term bonds. This information is available only in bits and pieces from the other financial statements. Since cash flows are vital to a company's financial health, the statement of cash flows provides useful information to management, investors, creditors, and other interested parties.

Management Uses

The statement of cash flows presents the effects on cash of all significant operating, investing, and financing activities. By reviewing the statement, management can see the effects of its past major policy decisions in quantitative form. The statement may show a flow of cash from operating activities large enough to finance all projected capital needs internally rather than having to incur long-term debt or issue additional stock. Alternatively, if the company has been experiencing cash shortages, management can use the statement to determine why such shortages are occurring. Using the statement of cash flows, management may also recommend to the board of directors a reduction in dividends to conserve cash.

Investor and Creditor Uses

The information in a statement of cash flows assists investors, creditors, and others in assessing the following:

1. Enterprise's ability to generate positive future net cash flows.
2. Enterprise's ability to meet its obligations.
3. Enterprise's ability to pay dividends.
4. Enterprise's need for external financing.
5. Reasons for differences between net income and associated cash receipts and payments.
6. Effects on an enterprise's financial position of both its cash and noncash investing and financing transactions during the period (disclosed in a separate schedule).

Information in the Statement of Cash Flows

Objective 2
Describe the content of the statement of cash flows and where certain items would appear on the statement.

The statement of cash flows classifies cash receipts and disbursements as operating, investing, and financing cash flows. Both inflows and outflows are included within each category. Look at Illustration 16.2 to see how activities can be classified to prepare a statement of cash flows.

Operating activities generally include the cash effects (inflows and outflows) of transactions and other events that enter into the determination of net income. *Cash inflows* from operating activities affect items that appear on the income statement and include: (1) cash receipts from sales of goods or services; (2) interest received from making loans; (3) dividends received from investments in equity securities; (4) cash received from the sale of trading securities; and (5) other cash

Investing and financing activities that do not affect cash are shown in a separate schedule.

ILLUSTRATION 16.1
Statement of Cash Flows—Basic Content

ILLUSTRATION 16.2
Rules for Classifying Activities in the Statement of Cash Flows

Operating activities Cash effects of transactions and other events that enter into the determination of net income

- Cash inflows from:
  - Sales of goods or services
  - Interest
  - Dividends
  - Sale of trading securities
  - Other sources not related to investing or financing activities (e.g., insurance settlements)
- Cash outflows for:
  - Merchandise inventory
  - Salaries and wages
  - Interest
  - Purchase of trading securities
  - Other expenses
  - Other items not related to investing or financing activities (e.g., contributions to charities)

Investing activities Transactions involving the acquisition or disposal of noncurrent assets

- Cash inflows from:
  - Sale of property, plant, and equipment
  - Sale of available-for-sale and held-to-maturity securities
  - Collection of loans
- Cash outflows for:
  - Purchase of property, plant, and equipment
  - Purchase of available-for-sale and held-to-maturity securities
  - Making of loans

Financing activities Transactions with creditors and owners

- Cash inflows from:
  - Issuing capital stock
  - Issuing debt (bonds, mortgages, notes, and other short- or long-term borrowing of cash)
- Cash outflows for:
  - Purchase of treasury stock
  - Payment of debt (principal only)
  - Cash dividends

receipts that do not arise from transactions defined as investing or financing activities, such as amounts received to settle lawsuits, proceeds of certain insurance settlements, and refunds from suppliers.

Cash outflows for operating activities affect items that appear on the income statement and include payments: (1) to acquire inventory; (2) to other suppliers and employees for other goods or services; (3) to lenders and other creditors for interest; (4) for purchases of trading securities; and (5) all other cash payments that do not arise from transactions defined as investing or financing activities, such as taxes and payments to settle lawsuits, cash contributions to charities, and cash refunds to customers.

Investing activities generally include transactions involving the acquisition or disposal of noncurrent assets. Thus, *cash inflows* from investing activities include cash received from: (1) the sale of property, plant, and equipment; (2) the sale of available-for-sale and held-to-maturity securities; and (3) the collection of long-term loans made to others. *Cash outflows* for investing activities include cash paid: (1) to purchase property, plant, and equipment; (2) to purchase available-for-sale and held-to-maturity securities; and (3) to make long-term loans to others.

Financing activities generally include the cash effects (inflows and outflows) of transactions and other events involving creditors and owners. *Cash inflows* from financing activities include cash received from issuing capital stock and bonds, mortgages, and notes, and from other short- or long-term borrowing. *Cash outflows* for financing activities include payments of cash dividends or other distributions to owners (including cash paid to purchase treasury stock) and repayments of amounts borrowed. Payment of interest is not included because interest expense appears on the income statement and is, therefore, included in operating activities. Cash payments to settle accounts payable, wages payable, and income taxes payable are not financing activities. These payments are operating activities.

A Separate Schedule for Significant Noncash Investing and Financing Activities

Information about all material investing and financing activities of an enterprise that do not result in cash receipts or disbursements during the period appear in a separate schedule, rather than in the statement of cash flows. The disclosure may be in narrative form. For instance, assume a company issued a mortgage note to acquire land and buildings. A separate schedule might appear as follows:

Schedule of noncash financing and investing activities:	
Mortgage note issued to acquire land and buildings	$35,000

An Accounting Perspective

Business Insight In a supplemental schedule of noncash investing and financing activities, Johnson & Johnson reported one item as follows:

Treasury stock issued for employee compensation and stock option plans, net of cash proceeds	$163 million

The company included the cash proceeds amount from the exercise of stock options ($74 million) in the cash flows from financing activities section of the statement of cash flows.

Cash Flows from Operating Activities

Objective 3
Describe how to calculate cash flows from operating activities under both the direct and indirect methods.

Cash flows from operating activities show the net amount of cash received or disbursed during a given period for items that normally appear on the income statement. You can calculate these cash flows using either the direct or indirect method. The **direct method** deducts from cash sales only those operating expenses that *consumed cash*. This method converts each item on the income statement *directly* to a cash basis. Alternatively, the **indirect (addback) method** starts with accrual basis net income and *indirectly* adjusts net income for items that affected reported net income but did not involve cash.

The *Statement of Financial Accounting Standards No. 95* encourages use of the direct method but permits use of the indirect method. Companies use the indirect method much more frequently, as shown in the following table. Whenever given a choice between the indirect and direct methods in similar situations, accountants choose the indirect method almost exclusively.

Method of Reporting Cash Flows from Operating Activities

	Number of Companies			
	1992	**1991**	**1990**	**1989**
Indirect method	585	585	585	583
Direct method	15	15	15	17
Total companies presenting statement of cash flows	600	600	600	600

Source: American Institute of Certified Public Accountants, *Accounting Trends & Techniques* (New York: AICPA, 1993), p. 452.

The direct method converts each item on the income statement to a cash basis. For instance, assume that sales are stated at $100,000 on an accrual basis. If accounts receivable increased by $5,000, cash collections from customers would be $95,000, calculated as $100,000 – $5,000. The direct method also converts all remaining items on the income statement to a cash basis, as we will illustrate later.

The indirect method adjusts net income (rather than adjusting individual items in the income statement) for (1) changes in current assets (other than cash) and current liabilities, and (2) items that were included in net income but did not affect cash.

The most common example of an operating expense that does not affect cash is depreciation expense. The journal entry to record depreciation debits an expense account and credits an accumulated depreciation account. This transaction has no effect on cash and, therefore, should not be included when measuring cash from operations. Because accountants deduct depreciation in computing net income, net income understates cash from operations. Under the indirect method, since net income is a starting point in measuring cash flows from operating activities, depreciation expense must be added back to net income.

Consider the following example. Company A had net income for the year of $20,000 after deducting depreciation of $10,000, yielding $30,000 of positive cash flows. Thus, Company A had $30,000 of positive cash flows from operating activities. Company B had a net loss for the year of $4,000 after deducting $10,000 of depreciation. Although Company B experienced a loss, it had $6,000 of positive cash flows from operating activities, as shown here:

	Company A	Company B
Net income (loss)	$20,000	$(4,000)
Add depreciation expense (which did not require use of cash)	10,000	10,000
Positive cash flows from operating activities	$30,000	$ 6,000

Company B's loss would have had to exceed $10,000 to generate negative cash flows from operating activities.

Companies add other expenses and losses back to net income because they do not actually use company cash; they call these addbacks **noncash charges or expenses.** Besides depreciation, the items added back include amounts of depletion that were expensed, amortization of intangible assets such as patents and goodwill, amortization of discount on bonds payable, and losses from disposals of noncurrent assets.

AN ACCOUNTING PERSPECTIVE

BUSINESS INSIGHT Like many other companies, Procter & Gamble Company (P & G) included a provision for corporate restructuring in the cash flows from operating activities section of its 1993 statement of cash flows. P & G added $2.705 million back to net income because this expense did not represent a cash outflow in 1993. In the notes accompanying the financial statements, P & G described its restructuring as follows:

> The worldwide program covers (*a*) manufacturing consolidations involving the closing of an estimated 30 plants, and (*b*) other organizational restructuring with the focus on reducing overhead costs. Together this will result in a workforce reduction of about 13,000 employees over the next four years. Costs associated with disposal of property, plant, and equipment; voluntary personnel separations; and early retirement incentives are included in the provision.

Many companies decided to follow this strategy in the early 1990s. Some of the people who were terminated formed their own small businesses, which then created new jobs.

To illustrate the addback of losses from disposals of noncurrent assets, assume that Quick Company sold a piece of equipment for $6,000. The equipment had cost $10,000 and had accumulated depreciation of $3,000. The journal entry to record the sale is:

	Debit	Credit
Cash	6,000	
Accumulated Depreciation	3,000	
Loss on Sale of Equipment	1,000	
Equipment		10,000
To record disposal of equipment at a loss.		

Quick would show the $6,000 inflow from the sale of the equipment as a cash inflow from investing activities on its statement of cash flows. Although Quick deducted the loss of $1,000 in calculating net income, it recognized the total $6,000 effect on cash (which reflects the $1,000 loss) as resulting from an investing activity. Thus, Quick must add the loss back to net income in converting net income to cash flows from operating activities to avoid double-counting the loss.

Certain revenues and gains included in arriving at net income do not provide cash; these items are **noncash credits or revenues.** Quick should deduct these revenues and gains from net income to compute cash flows from operating activities. Such items include gains from disposals of noncurrent assets, income from investments carried under the equity method, and amortization of premiums on bonds payable.

To illustrate why we deduct the gain on the disposal of a noncurrent asset from net income, assume that Quick sold the equipment just mentioned for $9,000. The journal entry to record the sale is:

Cash	9,000	
Accumulated Depreciation	3,000	
Equipment		10,000
Gain on Sale of Equipment		2,000
To record disposal of equipment at a gain.		

Quick shows the $9,000 inflow from the sale of the equipment on its statement of cash flows as a cash inflow from investing activities. Thus, it has already recognized the total $9,000 effect on cash (including the $2,000 gain) as resulting from an investing activity. Since the $2,000 gain is also included in calculating net income, Quick must deduct the gain in converting net income to cash flows from operating activities to avoid double-counting the gain.

Steps in Preparing Statement of Cash Flows

Objective 4
Prepare a statement of cash flows, under both the direct and indirect methods, showing cash flows from operating activities, investing activities, and financing activities.

Accountants follow specific procedures when preparing a statement of cash flows. We show these procedures using the financial statements and additional data for Welby Company in Illustration 16.3.

After determining the change in cash, the first step in preparing the statement of cash flows is to calculate the cash flows from operating activities, using either the direct or indirect method. The second step is to analyze all of the noncurrent accounts and additional data for changes resulting from investing and financing activities. The third step is to arrange the information gathered in steps 1 and 2 into the proper format for the statement of cash flows.

Step 1: Determining Cash Flows from Operating Activities—Direct Method

The direct method converts the income statement from the accrual basis to the cash basis. Accountants must consider changes in balance sheet accounts that are related to items on the income statement. The accounts involved are all current assets or current liabilities. The following schedule shows which balance sheet accounts are related to the items on Welby's income statement:

Income Statement Items	Related Balance Sheet Accounts	Cash Flows from Operating Activities
Sales	Accounts Receivable	Cash received from customers
Cost of goods sold	Accounts Payable and Merchandise Inventory	Cash paid for merchandise
Operating expenses and taxes	Accrued Liabilities and Prepaid Expenses	Cash paid for operating expenses

For other income statement items, the relationship is often obvious. For instance, salaries payable relates to salaries expense, federal income tax payable relates to federal income tax expense, prepaid rent relates to rent expense, and so on.

The table on the next page shows how income statement items are affected by the balance sheet accounts.

ILLUSTRATION 16.3
Financial Statements and Other Data

WELBY COMPANY
Comparative Balance Sheets
December 31, 1997, and 1996

	1997	1996	Increase/ (Decrease)
Assets			
Cash	$ 21,000	$ 10,000	$11,000
Accounts receivable, net	30,000	20,000	10,000
Merchandise inventory	26,000	30,000	(4,000)
Equipment	70,000	50,000	20,000
Accumulated depreciation—Equipment	(10,000)	(5,000)	(5,000)
Total assets	$137,000	$105,000	$32,000
Liabilities and Stockholders' Equity			
Accounts payable	$ 9,000	$ 15,000	$ (6,000)
Accrued liabilities payable	2,000	-0-	2,000
Common stock ($10 par value)	90,000	60,000	30,000
Retained earnings	36,000	30,000	6,000
Total liabilities and stockholders' equity	$137,000	$105,000	$32,000

WELBY COMPANY
Income Statement
For the Year Ended December 31, 1997

Sales		$140,000
Cost of goods sold		100,000
Gross margin		$ 40,000
Operating expenses		
(other than depreciation)	$25,000	
Depreciation expense	5,000	30,000
Net income		$ 10,000

Additional data

1. Equipment purchased for cash during 1997 amounted to $20,000.
2. Common stock with a par value of $30,000 was issued at par for cash.
3. Cash dividends declared and paid in 1997 totaled $4,000.

Accrual Basis			Cash Basis (Cash Flows from Operating Activities)
Sales	+ Decrease or − Increase in Accounts Receivable	=	Cash received from customers
Cost of goods sold	+ Increase or − Decrease in Merchandise Inventory *and* + Decrease or − Increase in Accounts Payable	=	Cash paid for merchandise
Operating expenses	+ Decrease or − Increase in related accrued liability *and/or* + Increase or − Decrease in related prepaid expense	=	Cash paid for operating expenses

Noncash operating expenses (such as depreciation expense and amortization expense), revenues, gains, and losses are reduced to zero in the cash basis income statement.

As a general rule, an increase in a current asset (other than cash) decreases cash inflow or increases cash outflow. Thus, when accounts receivable increases, sales revenue on a cash basis decreases (some customers who bought merchandise have not yet paid for it). When inventory increases, cost of goods sold on a cash basis increases (increasing cash outflow). When a prepaid expense increases, the related operating expense on a cash basis increases. (For example, a company not only paid for insurance expense but also paid cash to increase prepaid insurance.) The effect on cash flows is just the opposite for decreases in these other current assets.

An increase in a current liability increases cash inflow or decreases cash outflow. Thus, when accounts payable increases, cost of goods sold on a cash basis decreases (instead of paying cash, the purchase was made on credit). When an accrued liability (such as salaries payable) increases, the related operating expense (salaries expense) on a cash basis decreases. (For example, the company incurred more salaries than it paid.) Decreases in current liabilities have just the opposite effect on cash flows.

Welby Company had no prepaid expenses. The current assets and current liabilities affecting the income statement items changed as follows:

	Increase	Decrease
Accounts receivable	$10,000	
Merchandise inventory		$4,000
Accounts payable		6,000
Accrued liabilities payable	2,000	

Thus, Welby converted its income statement to a cash basis as shown in Illustration 16.4.

Alternate Step 1: Determining Cash Flows from Operating Activities—Indirect Method

The indirect method makes certain adjustments to convert net income to cash flows from operating activities. Welby must analyze the effects of changes in current accounts (other than cash) on cash. The firm should also take into account noncash items such as depreciation that affected net income but not cash. Welby had only one such item—depreciation expense of $5,000. Applying these adjustments to Welby's financial statements and other data in Illustration 16.3 yields the following schedule:

Cash flows from operating activities:		
Net income	$ 10,000	
Adjustments to reconcile net income to net cash provided by operating activities:		
Increase in accounts receivable	(10,000)	
Decrease in merchandise inventory	4,000	
Decrease in accounts payable	(6,000)	
Increase in accrued liabilities payable	2,000	
Depreciation expense	5,000	
Net cash provided by operating activities		$5,000

Notice that both the direct and indirect methods result in $5,000 net cash provided by operating activities.

You can use the following table to make the adjustments to net income for the changes in current assets and current liabilities:

For changes in these current assets and current liabilities:	Make these adjustments to convert accrual basis net income to cash basis net income:	
	Add	**Deduct**
Accounts receivable	Decrease	Increase
Merchandise inventory	Decrease	Increase
Prepaid expenses	Decrease	Increase
Accounts payable	Increase	Decrease
Accrued liabilities payable	Increase	Decrease

ILLUSTRATION 16.4
Working Paper to Convert Income Statement from Accrual Basis to Cash Basis

WELBY COMPANY
Working Paper to Convert Income Statement from Accrual Basis to Cash Basis
For the Year Ended December 31, 1997

	Accrual Basis		Add	Deduct	Cash Basis (Cash Flows from Operating Activities)	
Sales		$140,000		$10,000*		$130,000
Cost of goods sold	$100,000		$6,000†	4,000‡	$102,000	
Operating expenses	25,000			2,000§	23,000	
Depreciation expense	5,000			5,000	-0-	
		130,000				125,000
Net income		$ 10,000				$ 5,000

* Increase in Accounts Receivable.
† Decrease in Accounts Payable.
‡ Decrease in Merchandise Inventory.
§ Increase in Accrued Liabilities Payable.

Note that you would handle all changes in current asset accounts in a similar manner. All changes in current liability accounts require the opposite treatment of the current asset changes. Use this table in making these adjustments:

For Changes in—	Add the Changes to Net Income	Deduct the Changes from Net Income
Current assets	Decreases	Increases
Current liabilities	Increases	Decreases

In applying the rules in this table, add a decrease in a current asset to net income, and deduct an increase in a current asset from net income. For current liabilities, add increases to net income, and deduct decreases from net income.

Under the indirect method, the amount of cash flows from operating activities is calculated as follows:

Accrual basis net income
+ or − Changes in noncash current asset and current liability accounts
+ Expenses and losses not affecting cash
− Revenues and gains not affecting cash
= Cash flows from operating activities

Step 2: Analyzing the Noncurrent Accounts and Additional Data

After analyzing the changes in current accounts for their effect on cash, we examine the noncurrent accounts and additional data. Remember that a change in a noncurrent account usually comes about because cash is received or disbursed.

In the Welby example, we must analyze four noncurrent accounts: Retained Earnings, Equipment, Accumulated Depreciation—Equipment, and Common Stock.

1. The analysis of the noncurrent accounts can begin with any of the noncurrent accounts; we begin by reviewing the Retained Earnings account. Retained Earnings is the account to which net income or loss for the period was closed. The $6,000 increase in this account consists of $10,000 of net income less $4,000 of dividends paid.

Retained Earnings

		Beg. bal.	30,000
Dividends	4,000	Net income	10,000
		End. bal.	36,000

The net income amount is in the income statement. We enter both net income and dividends on the statement of cash flows in Illustration 16.5, Part B. The $10,000 net income is the starting figure in determining cash flows from operating activities. Thus, we enter the net income of $10,000 on the statement in the cash flows from operating activities section.

2. The Equipment account increased by $20,000 during the year. The additional data indicate that $20,000 of equipment was purchased during the period. A purchase of equipment is a deduction in the cash flows from investing activities section.
3. The $5,000 increase in the Accumulated Depreciation—Equipment account equals the amount of depreciation expense in the income statement for the period. As shown earlier, because depreciation does not affect cash, under the indirect (addback) method we add it back to net income on the statement of cash flows to convert accrual net income to a cash basis.
4. The $30,000 increase in common stock resulted from the issuance of stock at par value, as disclosed in the additional data (item 2) in Illustration 16.3. An issuance of stock in the statement of cash flows is a positive amount in the cash flows from financing activities section.

Step 3: Arranging Information in the Statement of Cash Flows

After we have analyzed the noncurrent accounts, we can prepare the statement of cash flows from the information generated. Part A of Illustration 16.5 presents the statement of cash flows for Welby using the direct method. Part B shows the statement of cash flows for Welby using the indirect method. The Appendix to this chapter shows how a working paper can be used to assist in preparing a statement of cash flows for the Welby Company under the indirect method. However, we believe you will gain a greater conceptual understanding by not using a working paper.

The statement of cash flows has three major sections: cash flows from operating activities, cash flows from investing activities, and cash flows from financing activities. The format in the operating activities section differs for the direct and indirect methods. The direct method adjusts each item in the income statement to a cash basis. The indirect method makes these same adjustments but to net income rather than to each item in the income statement. Both methods eliminate not only the effects of noncash items, such as depreciation, but also gains and losses on sales of plant assets.

The only item in the cash flows from investing activities section is the cash outflow of $20,000 for the purchase of equipment. In a more complex situation, other items could be included in this category.

Two items are under the cash flows from financing activities section. The issuance of common stock resulted in a cash inflow of $30,000. The payment of dividends resulted in a cash outflow of $4,000.

The last line of the statement is the $11,000 increase in cash for the year. Other examples could result in a decrease in cash for the year.

An Accounting Perspective

Business Insight In its 1992 consolidated statement of cash flows, Bristol-Meyers Squibb Company reported proceeds from the sale of a business of $1.15 billion among its cash flows from investing activities. In a letter to stockholders, the company stated:

> In 1992, we also took a new look at our business categories. This led to a decision to divest The Drackett Company, a subsidiary that has made many important contributions to our growth and success since it was acquired in 1965, as we determined that the household products business no longer fits the strategic direction of our company, which increasingly is focused on health care and personal care products. We sold The Drackett Company to S. C. Johnson & Son, Inc., for $1.15 billion in cash in December.

Many companies are deciding to focus on the activities they do best to reduce their business risk. In the 1980s, business gurus taught that management skills successfully applied in one area of activity could be equally effective in almost any other area. Now the managements of some companies seem to be discarding this philosophy.

ILLUSTRATION 16.5 Statement of Cash Flows—Welby Company

A. Direct Method

WELBY COMPANY
Statement of Cash Flows
For the Year Ended December 31, 1997

Cash flows from operating activities:		
Cash received from customers	$ 130,000	
Cash paid for merchandise	(102,000)	
Cash paid for operating expenses	(23,000)	
Net cash provided by operating activities		$ 5,000
Cash flows from investing activities:		
Purchase of equipment		(20,000)
Cash flows from financing activities:		
Proceeds from issuing common stock	$ 30,000	
Paid cash dividends	(4,000)	
Net cash provided by financing activities		26,000
Net increase (decrease) in cash		$ 11,000

This portion differs between the two versions

This portion is the same in both versions

B. Indirect Method

WELBY COMPANY
Statement of Cash Flows
For the Year Ended December 31, 1997

Cash flows from operating activities:		
Net income	$ 10,000	
Adjustments to reconcile net income to net cash provided by operating activities:		
Increase in accounts receivable	(10,000)	
Decrease in merchandise inventory	4,000	
Decrease in accounts payable	(6,000)	
Increase in accrued liabilities payable	2,000	
Depreciation expense	5,000	
Net cash provided by operating activities		$ 5,000
Cash flows from investing activities:		
Purchase of equipment		(20,000)
Cash flows from financing activities:		
Proceeds from issuing common stock	$ 30,000	
Paid cash dividends	(4,000)	
Net cash provided by financing activities		26,000
Net increase (decrease) in cash		$ 11,000

ANALYSIS OF THE STATEMENT OF CASH FLOWS

Objective 5
Analyze a statement of cash flows of a real company.

Business students will benefit throughout their careers from knowing how to analyze a statement of cash flows. We will use the consolidated statement of cash flows from the 1993 Annual Report of the Colgate-Palmolive Company to illustrate the analysis. The company manufactures and markets a wide variety of products in the U.S. and around the world in two distinct business segments—(1) oral, personal, and household care, and (2) specialty marketing. Principal global trademarks include Colgate, Palmolive, Mennen, Ajax, Fab, and Science Diet. This same company will be used in the next chapter to illustrate the complete analysis and interpretation of all of the financial statements.

ILLUSTRATION 16.6
Consolidated Statements of Cash Flows for the Colgate-Palmolive Company—Indirect Method

($ Millions)	1993	1992	1991
Operating Activities			
Net income	$ 189.9	$ 477.0	$ 124.9
Adjustments to reconcile net income to net cash provided by operations:			
Cumulative effect on prior years of accounting changes	358.2	—	—
Restructured operations, net	(77.0)	(92.0)	319.0
Depreciation and amortization	209.6	192.5	146.2
Deferred income taxes and other liabilities	53.6	(25.8)	(38.4)
Cash effects of changes in:*			
Receivables	(103.6)	(38.0)	(58.2)
Inventories	31.7	28.4	45.8
Other current assets	(4.6)	10.6	(11.9)
Payables and accruals	52.6	(10.0)	(41.7)
Net cash provided by operations	$ 710.4	$ 542.7	$ 485.7
Investing Activities			
Capital expenditures	$(364.3)	$(318.5)	$(260.7)
Payment for acquisitions, net of cash acquired	(171.2)	(170.1)	(269.6)
Sale of marketable securities and other investments†	33.8	79.9	36.8
Investments in less-than-majority-owned companies and other	(12.5)	(6.6)	(12.7)
Other, net	61.7	17.4	(30.1)
Net cash used for investing activities	$(452.5)	$(397.9)	$(536.3)
Financing Activities			
Principal payments on debt	$(200.8)	$(250.1)	$(311.4)
Proceeds from issuance of debt, net	782.1	262.6	51.0
Proceeds from outside investors	60.0	—	—
Dividends paid	(231.4)	(200.7)	(157.1)
Purchase of common stock	(657.2)	(20.5)	(.2)
Proceeds from issuance of common stock	—	—	445.5
Proceeds from exercise of stock options	21.8	22.6	30.4
Net cash (used for) provided by financing activities	$(225.5)	$(186.1)	$ 58.2
Effect of exchange rate changes on cash and cash equivalents	(6.2)	(9.3)	(5.5)
Net increase (decrease) in cash and cash equivalents	$ 26.2	$ (50.6)	$ 2.1
Cash and cash equivalents at beginning of year	117.9	168.5	166.4
Cash and cash equivalents at end of year	$ 144.1	$ 117.9	$ 168.5

* These changes are shown net of the effects of acquisitions and dispositions, since the total effect of acquisitions and dispositions would be shown under the investing activities section or included in other items in the operating activities section.

† For all fiscal years beginning after December 15, 1993, sales and purchases of trading securities must be shown under the operating activities section. Available-for-sale and held-to-maturity securities (e.g., investments in bonds held to maturity) are still shown under the investing activities section.

Colgate-Palmolive Company's Consolidated Statements of Cash Flows

Illustration 16.6 shows the consolidated statements of cash flows for the years 1993, 1992, and 1991 for the Colgate-Palmolive Company. We also include portions of Management's Discussion and Analysis of the 1993 statement of cash flows. We will then discuss the statement further, explaining various items and illustrating how the information might be used for decision making.

Management's Discussion and Analysis

The following paragraphs were taken from Colgate-Palmolive's *1993 Annual Report*.

Liquidity and Capital Resources*

Net cash provided by operations increased to $710.4 [$ millions] in 1993 compared with $542.7 in 1992 and $485.7 in 1991. The improvement in cash generated by operating activities from 7.7% of sales in 1992 to 9.9% of sales in 1993 reflects the Company's improving

* Source: The Colgate-Palmolive Company *1993 Annual Report*, pp. 20–21.

Cash Provided by Operations (in $ millions)

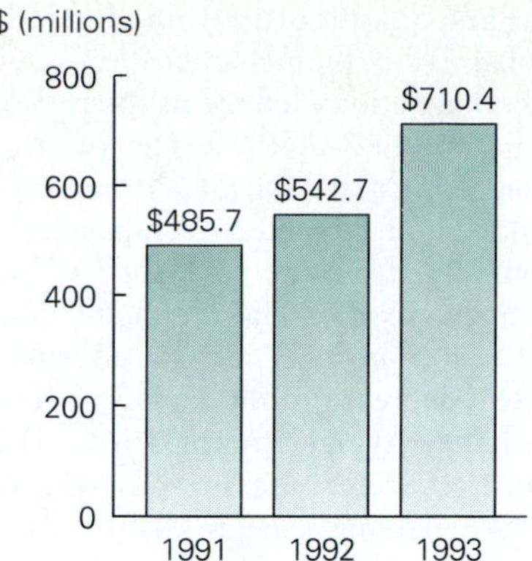

profitability and continued management emphasis on working capital. Cash generated from operations was used to finance acquisitions, repurchase shares and fund an increased dividend level.

The Company has additional sources of liquidity available in the form of lines of credit maintained with various banks. Such lines of credit amounted to $1,303.2 at December 31, 1993. The Company also has the ability to issue commercial paper at favorable interest rates to meet short-term liquidity needs. These borrowings carry a Standard & Poor's rating of A1 and a Moody's rating of P1.

During the 1993 first quarter, the Company repaid outstanding debt totaling $85.7, which included $50.0 of 8.9% Swiss franc notes due in 1993. During the third quarter, the Company redeemed $79.0 of its 9.625% debentures issue due 2017.

. . . In the fourth quarter of 1993, $230.0 of medium-term notes were issued . . . in addition to $169.2 issued in the fourth quarter of 1992. These notes are rated A1/A+ by Moody's and Standard & Poor's, respectively.

During the third quarter of 1993, the Company participated in the formation of a business which purchases receivables, including Company receivables. Outside institutions invested $60.0 in this entity. The Company consolidates this entity, and the amounts invested by the outside institutions are classified as a minority interest.

Colgate's reputation, global presence and strong capital position afford it access to debt and equity markets around the world, enabling the Company to raise funds with a low effective cost. . .

Capital expenditures in 1993 were $364.3 or 5.1% of sales as compared with $318.5 in 1992 and $260.7 in 1991. The increase in 1993 spending was focused primarily on projects that yield high aftertax returns, thereby reducing the Company's cost structure. Capital expenditures for 1994 are expected to continue at or slightly above the current rate of approximately 5% of sales.

Other investing activities in 1993, 1992 and 1991 included strategic acquisitions and equity investments worldwide. In October 1993, the Company acquired the liquid hand and body soap brands of S.C. Johnson Wax in Europe, the South Pacific and other international locations. During the year, the Company also acquired the Cristasol glass cleaner business in Spain, increased ownership of its Indian operation to majority control and made other investments. The aggregate purchase price of all 1993 acquisitions was $222.5.

Acquisitions totaled $718.4 in 1992 and $339.4 in 1991 and included businesses in the household care, fabric care, personal care and oral care categories. In March 1992, the Company acquired The Mennen Company for an aggregate purchase price of approximately $670.0. The purchase price was paid with 11.6 million unregistered shares of the Company's common stock and $127.0 in cash. Other acquisitions included significant ownership positions in joint ventures in China and Eastern Europe, The Murphy-Phoenix Company and the Plax worldwide business excluding the United States, Canada and Puerto Rico. Goodwill and other intangible assets increased as a result of these acquisitions.

During 1993, the Company repurchased common shares in the open market and private transactions to provide for employee benefit plans and to maintain its target capital structure. Aggregate repurchases for the year approximated 12 million shares with a total purchase price of $673.0. In the first quarter of 1994, the Board of Directors authorized the repurchase of up to an additional five million shares.

The ratio of debt to total capitalization (defined as the ratio of debt to debt plus equity) increased to 48% during 1993 from 30% in 1992. The return on average shareholders' equity, before accounting changes, increased to 24% from 21% during the same period as this shift towards targeted capitalization benefited overall shareholder return. The decrease in debt to total capitalization in 1992 from the 1991 level of 36% reflects the issuance of shares in connection with the acquisition of The Mennen Company.

Dividend payments were $240.8 in 1993 ($231.4 aftertax), up from $211.1 ($200.7 aftertax) in 1992, reflecting a 16% increase in the common dividend effective in the third quarter of 1993. Common dividend payments increased to $1.34 per share in 1993 from $1.15 per share in 1992. The Series B Preference Stock dividends were declared and paid at the stated rate of $4.88 per share. The increase in dividend payments in 1992 over 1991 reflects a 17% increase in the common dividend effective in the third quarter of 1992.

Internally generated cash flows appear to be adequate to support currently planned business operations and capital expenditures. However, certain events, such as significant acquisitions, could require external financing.

The Company is a party to various superfund and other environmental matters and is contingently liable with respect to lawsuits, taxes and other matters arising out of the normal course of business. While it is possible that the Company's cash flows and results of operations in particular quarterly or annual periods could be affected by the one-time impacts of the resolution of such contingencies, it is the opinion of management that the ultimate disposition of these matters, to the extent not previously provided for, will not have a material impact on the Company's financial condition or ongoing cash flows and results of operations.

Explanation of Items in Colgate-Palmolive Company's Consolidated Statements of Cash Flows

Refer to Illustration 16.6. First we will discuss the items in the operating activities section of the statement of cash flows, then we will discuss investing activities and financing activities.

Operating Activities The company used the indirect method of calculating net cash provided by operations. Various adjustments were made to convert accrual based net income to cash basis net income.

The "cumulative effect on prior years of accounting changes" is an item you studied in Chapter 13. Because of its large size, this particular item probably resulted from implementation of *FASB Statement 106*, relating to the recognition of postretirement benefits. Net income was reduced substantially in 1993 because of this item, but no cash outflow resulted. Therefore, the item was added back to net income.

The "restructured operations, net" item resulted from the fact that many companies restructured their operations during the early 1990s by closing plants and significantly reducing their work forces. Some companies recognized a net loss from restructuring and others recognized a net gain. Apparently, the Colgate-Palmolive Company recognized a net gain in 1993 because it deducted the item from net income on the statement of cash flows. The actual cash flows from restructuring will occur in a later period.

"Depreciation and amortization" includes depreciation on plant assets and amortization of intangible assets, such as goodwill. Goodwill had increased because of using the purchase method (discussed in Chapter 14) to account for the acquisition of other companies and segments of other companies. Depreciation and amortization are noncash charges against revenues and must be added back to net income.

The "deferred income taxes and other liabilities" item results primarily from the fact that income tax expense on the income statement was higher than the actual income taxes paid. This phenomenon occurs because of using a different method for tax and accounting purposes for such items as depreciation.

Receivables and other current assets increased (causing cash to decrease), while inventories decreased (causing cash to increase). Payables and accruals increased (causing cash to increase). (These increases and decreases are net of any amounts related to acquisitions, dispositions, or amounts that are included elsewhere, such as in "restructured operations, net.")

Investing Activities "Capital expenditures" include the purchase of plant assets, such as new machinery and equipment, to modernize production facilities. Companies, including the Colgate-Palmolive Company, normally select those capital expenditures with the highest rate of return. For instance, if funds are limited (and they normally are) and two capital investments (a machine and a mainframe computer) are being considered, one yielding a 20% return and the other yielding a 25% return, the company will normally select the one with the 25% return.

"Payment for acquisitions, net of cash acquired" shows the amount spent in acquiring other companies and segments of other companies, net of the amount of cash held by those companies and obtained as a part of the acquisition. "Management's Discussion and Analysis" (quoted above) identified some of these acquisitions.

The company sold "marketable securities and other investments." These securities normally consist of stocks, bonds, and other instruments of other companies. For fiscal years beginning after December 15, 1993, marketable securities must be identified as trading securities, available-for-sale securities, or held-to-maturity securities. Trading securities and available-for-sale securities were discussed in some detail in Chapter 14. Held-to-maturity securities were mentioned briefly in Chapter 15. These held-to-maturity securities are debt securities (such as bonds of other companies) that the company has purchased and has both the intent and ability to hold to maturity. As mentioned earlier, the proceeds from sales and purchases of trading securities must be shown as cash flows from operating activities, and the proceeds from sales and purchases of available-for-sale and held-to-maturity securities must be shown as cash flows from investing activities.

"Investments in less-than-majority-owned companies and other" represent investments in other companies where the Colgate-Palmolive Company holds less than a 50% interest.

Financing Activities The company paid off some old debt and incurred new debt. During the early 1990s, many companies substituted new debt with a low interest rate for old debt with a high interest rate, just as homeowners refinanced their homes to lower their interest rate. This successful use of leverage increased the return on average stockholders' equity (ignoring the one-time charge resulting from the cumulative effect on prior years of accounting changes).

As stated in "Management's Discussion and Analysis," the "proceeds from outside investors" resulted from the other participants in the formation of a business that purchases receivables. The Colgate-Palmolive Company holds more than a 50% share in this business, but some minority interest is present.

The company bought back some of its own stock (treasury stock). Companies often buy back their own shares because they (1) need the shares to issue to employees or officers under stock option plans, (2) want to bolster the market price of the stock, or (3) hope to later sell the stock at a substantially higher price.

"Dividends paid" and "proceeds from issuance of common stock" are items that should be familiar to you. The company has not issued common stock since 1991, when common stock shares were issued to acquire the Mennen Company. Dividends paid increased each year over this three-year period.

"Proceeds from exercise of stock options" represents the proceeds received from employees and officers who exercised their stock options. Stock options are usually granted to employees to encourage them to work efficiently to increase profitability, which should increase the market price of the stock. Stock options made available to officers are for the same purpose or to attract or retain a talented executive. Normally, an option gives the recipient the right to buy a certain number of shares at a stated price within a given timeframe. For instance, the president of a company may be granted an option to buy 10,000 shares at $40 per share any time after two years from that date and before six years from that date. Assume that the current market price is $38. If the market price of the stock rises to $80 at some time during the option period, the president could buy the shares at $40 and then hold them or sell them at the higher market price. Executives of companies have become multimillionaires by exercising their stock options. The employees and executives of the Colgate-Palmolive Company paid the company between $21.8 million and $30.4 million per year to exercise their stock options during the three-year period.

Use of the Cash Flow Information for Decision Making

We will discuss some examples of the ways that the information in the statement of cash flows can be used by management, stockholders, and creditors to make decisions. Each of these parties would use more than the statement of cash flows to perform an analysis of the company's performance, but we will restrict ourselves to the statement of cash flows. The next chapter shows a more complete analysis of the Colgate-Palmolive Company's performance.

Management Management is the first to see the information contained in the statement of cash flows. You have already read portions of "Management's Discussion and Analysis" concerning the information contained in that statement. Management concluded that the amount of internally generated cash flows (net cash provided by operations) appears adequate to support currently planned business operations and capital expenditures. Thus, unless the company engages in a significant acquisition it will not have to sell more stock or borrow more funds in the foreseeable future. Also, the company apparently replaced some of its high interest rate debt ($200.8 million) with lower interest rate debt ($782.1 million). Many companies did this same thing in the early 1990s to take advantage of the low interest rates available.

Stockholders Stockholders can see that dividend payments ($231.4 million) are comfortably covered by net cash provided by operations ($710.4 million). They can also see that if the amount identified as the cumulative effect on prior years of accounting changes (postretirement benefits) had not been charged against income, net income in 1993 would have been $548.1 million, ignoring tax effects. Thus, profitability from "normal" operations continues to increase. The company continues to invest in its future by making capital expenditures ($364.3 million) to modernize its productive facilities. The repurchase of its own stock ($657.2 million) decreases the number of shares outstanding, although some of the stock will undoubtedly be reissued in the future as employees and executives exercise their stock options. Any net reduction in the number of shares outstanding will tend to increase earnings per share and help to increase the market price per share in the future. Also, the company may decide to increase dividends per share in the future. These favorable factors might induce present stockholders to retain their stock or even increase their holdings. Potential stockholders might also be attracted to the stock.

Creditors One item of interest might be the large increase of $103.6 million in the amount of receivables. However, many companies experienced an increase in receivables and uncollectible accounts expense because of the recession in the early 1990s. An encouraging factor is the increasing amount of net cash provided by operations. Also comforting to creditors is the information in Management's Discussion and Analysis that the company has access to $1,303.2 million in lines of credit and that it can issue commercial paper at favorable rates. Another comforting statement in "Management's Discussion and Analysis" is that the company has "access to debt and equity markets around the world, enabling the company to raise funds with a low effective cost." This information would support a decision to loan the company more funds, should such a request be forthcoming.

The preceding discussions are merely examples of how the information contained in the statement of cash flows might be analyzed to make decisions. The next section describes three ratios that can provide further analyses of cash flows.

Analyzing and Using the Financial Results—Cash Flow per Share of Common Stock, Cash Flow Margin, and Cash Flow Liquidity Ratios

Objective 6
Analyze and use the financial results—cash flow per share of common stock, cash flow margin, and cash flow liquidity ratios.

The information in the statement of cash flows provides a basis for analyzing financial results. However, further analysis is possible through the use of three ratios relating to cash flow: the cash flow per share of common stock, cash flow margin, and cash flow liquidity ratios. The ratios shown below are based on 1993 results for the Colgate-Palmolive Company and 1992 results for the other companies.

The **cash flow per share of common stock ratio** is equal to the net cash provided by operations divided by the average number of shares of common stock outstanding. This ratio indicates the company's ability to pay dividends and liabilities. The higher the ratio, the greater the ability to pay. The cash flow per share of common stock ratios for the companies were:

Company	Net Cash Provided by Operating Activities	Average Shares of Common Stock Outstanding*	Cash Flow per Share
Colgate-Palmolive Company	$710,400,000	154,748,503	$4.59
Ralston Purina Company.	577,900,000	107,119,104	5.39
Occidental Petroleum Corporation . . .	550,000,000	301,895,500	1.82
Kimberly-Clark Corporation.	814,500,000	160,450,000	5.08

* To determine the average number of shares, add the beginning and ending numbers outstanding and divide by two. No information was available about when new shares were issued.

The **cash flow margin ratio** is equal to net cash provided by operating activities divided by net sales. This ratio is a measure of a company's ability to turn sales revenue into cash. The higher the ratio, the better. The cash flow margin ratios for the companies were:

Company	Net Cash Provided by Operating Activities	Net Sales	Cash Flow Margin
Colgate-Palmolive Company	$710,400,000	$7,141,300,000	9.95%
Ralston Purina Company	577,900,000	7,752,400,000	7.45
Occidental Petroleum Corporation	550,000,000	8,494,000,000	6.48
Kimberly-Clark Corporation	814,500,000	7,091,100,000	11.49

The **cash flow liquidity ratio** is equal to the total of cash, marketable securities, and net cash provided by operating activities divided by current liabilities. This ratio is a test of a company's short-term, debt-paying ability. The higher the ratio, the better. The cash flow liquidity ratios for the companies were:

Company	Cash, Marketable Securities, and Net Cash Provided by Operating Activities	Current Liabilities	Cash Flow Liquidity Ratio
Colgate-Palmolive Company	$921,600,000	$1,394,000,000	.66 times
Ralston Purina Company	637,400,000	1,745,300,000	.37 times
Occidental Petroleum Corporation	640,000,000	2,290,000,000	.28 times
Kimberly-Clark Corporation	855,600,000	1,822,800,000	.47 times

On the first of these measures, Ralston Purina Company and Kimberly-Clark Corporation seem to be in the strongest position, although all of the companies are

A Broader Perspective

Archer Daniels Midland—Indirect Method

Archer Daniels Midland
Archer Daniels Midland Company processes and merchandises virtually every commodity grown by farmers.

ARCHER DANIELS MIDLAND COMPANY
Consolidated Statements of Cash Flows
For the Years Ended June 30, 1992, 1991, and 1990
($ thousands)

	1992	1991	1990
Operating activities			
Net earnings	$ 503,757	$ 466,678	$ 483,522
Adjustments to reconcile to net cash provided by operations			
Depreciation and amortization	293,729	261,367	248,113
Deferred income taxes	30,415	23,899	21,005
Amortization of long-term debt discount	26,044	24,954	22,047
Other	(13,662)	(75,627)	(35,923)
Changes in operating assets and liabilities			
Receivables	(54,066)	15,078	(2,157)
Inventories	(92,355)	(75,269)	63,192
Prepaid expenses	(1,843)	(14,159)	(10,845)
Accounts payable, accrued expenses and taxes	176,875	51,436	(78,105)
Total operating activities	$ 868,894	$ 678,357	$ 710,849
Investing activities			
Purchases of property, plant, and equipment	$(479,528)	$(467,712)	$(327,397)
Business acquisitions	(21,197)	(344,775)	(185,142)
Investments in and advances to affiliates	(88,237)	(10,852)	3,758
Purchases of marketable securities	(1,004,824)	(765,954)	(1,217,646)
Proceeds from sales of marketable securities	773,816	1,007,406	1,039,007
Purchases of treasury stock	(85,889)	(97,253)	(10,928)
Total investing activities	$(905,859)	$(679,140)	$(698,348)
Financing activities			
Long-term debt borrowings	$ 594,355	$ 302,352	$ 9,154
Long-term debt payments	(210,616)	(32,813)	(21,288)
Cash dividends and other	(30,009)	(29,539)	(25,556)
Total financing activities	$ 353,730	$ 240,000	$ (37,690)
Increase (decrease) in cash and cash equivalents	$ 316,765	$ 239,217	$ (25,189)
Cash and cash equivalents beginning of period	647,595	408,378	433,567
Cash and cash equivalents end of period	$ 964,360	$ 647,595	$ 408,378

Source: Archer Daniels Midland Company 1992 Annual Report.

financially sound. On the second measure, Kimberly-Clark and Colgate-Palmolive have the highest cash flow margin ratios. On the third measure, Colgate-Palmolive seems to be in the strongest position. However, a more valid comparison on each of these measures would be made if each of these companies was compared with other companies in their industry. Dun & Bradstreet's Industry Norms and Key Business Ratios can be used for this purpose. (This source could also be used for comparisons of ratios in the next chapter.) A complete analysis using the techniques described in the next chapter would provide additional information about the strengths and weaknesses of each of these companies.

Understanding the Learning Objectives

Objective 1
Explain the purposes and uses of the statement of cash flows.

- The statement of cash flows summarizes the effects on cash of the operating, financing, and investing activities of a company during an accounting period.
- Management can see the effects of its past major policy decisions in quantitative form.
- Investors and creditors can assess the entity's ability to generate positive future net cash flows, to meet its obligations, and to pay dividends, and can assess the need for external financing.

Objective 2
Describe the content of the statement of cash flows and where certain items would appear on the statement.

- Operating activities generally include the cash effects (inflows and outflows) of transactions and other events that enter into the determination of net income. The cash flows from operating activities can be measured in two ways. The direct method deducts from cash sales only those operating expenses that consumed cash. The indirect method starts with net income and adjusts net income for items that affected reported net income but did not involve cash.
- Investing activities generally include transactions involving the acquisition or disposal of noncurrent assets.
- Financing activities generally include the cash effects (inflows and outflows) of transactions and other events involving creditors and owners.

Objective 3
Describe how to calculate cash flows from operating activities under both the direct and indirect methods.

- The direct method deducts from cash sales only those operating expenses that consumed cash. The FASB recommends use of the direct method.
- The indirect method starts with accrual basis net income and indirectly adjusts net income for items that affected reported net income but did not involve cash. A large majority of companies use the indirect method.

Objective 4
Prepare a statement of cash flows, under both the direct and indirect methods, showing cash flows from operating activities, investing activities, and financing activities.

- The first step is to determine the cash flows from operating activities. Either the direct or indirect method may be used.
- The second step is to analyze all the noncurrent accounts for changes in cash resulting from investing and financing activities.
- The third step is to arrange the information gathered in steps 1 and 2 into the format required for the statement of cash flows.

Objective 5
Analyze a statement of cash flows of a real company.

- Business students will benefit throughout their careers from knowing how to analyze a statement of cash flows.
- "Management's Discussion and Analysis" in the annual report provides part of the analysis.
- Inspection of the statement of cash flows together with "Management's Discussion and Analysis" will provide the most insight as to the cash flow situation.

Objective 6
Analyze and use the financial results—cash flow per share of common stock, cash flow margin, and cash flow liquidity ratios.

- The cash flow per share of common stock ratio tests a company's ability to pay dividends and liabilities and is equal to net cash provided by operating activities divided by the average number of shares of common stock outstanding.
- The cash flow margin ratio measures a company's ability to turn sales revenue into cash and is equal to net cash provided by operating activities divided by net sales.
- The cash flow liquidity ratio tests a company's short-term, debt-paying ability and is equal to the total of cash, marketable securities, and net cash provided by operating activities divided by current liabilities.

Objective 7
Use a working paper to prepare a statement of cash flows (Appendix).

- A work sheet can be used to assist in preparing a statement of cash flows.
- A company's comparative balance sheets, income statement, and additional data are used to prepare the work sheet.
- The work sheet technique makes the recording of the effects of transactions on cash flows almost a mechanical process.

Use of a Working Paper to Prepare a Statement of Cash Flows

Appendix

Objective 7
Use a working paper to prepare a statement of cash flows.

This appendix shows how a work sheet could be used to assist in preparing a statement of cash flows. We use the comparative balance sheets, income statement, and additional data for the Welby Company, shown on page 585, as the basis for this example.

Look at the working paper in Illustration 16.7 for Welby Company, which we use to analyze the transactions and prepare the statement of cash flows. While discussing the steps in preparing the working paper, we describe the items and trace their effects in the entries.

1. Enter the beginning account balances of all balance sheet accounts in the first column and the ending account balances in the fourth column. Notice that the debit items precede the credit items.
2. Total the debits and credits in the first and fourth columns to make sure that debits equal credits in each column.
3. Write "Cash Flows from Operating Activities" immediately below the total of the credit items. Skip sufficient lines for recording adjustments to convert accrual net income to cash flows from operating activities. Then write "Cash Flows from Investing Activities" and allow enough space for those items. Finally, write "Cash Flows from Financing Activities" and allow enough space for those items.
4. Enter entries for analyzing transactions in the second and third columns. The entries serve two functions: (*a*) they explain the change in each account; and (*b*) they classify the changes into operating, investing, and financing activities. We discuss these entries individually in the next section.
5. Total the debits and credits in the second and third columns; they should be equal. You will have one pair of totals for the balance sheet items and another pair for the bottom portion of the working paper. We use the bottom portion of the working paper to prepare the statement of cash flows.

Completing the Working Paper

To complete the working paper in Illustration 16.7, we must analyze the change in each noncash balance sheet account. The focus of this working paper is on cash and every change in cash means a change in a noncash balance sheet account. After we have made the proper entries to analyze all changes in noncash balance sheet accounts, the working paper shows all activities affecting cash flows. The following explanations are keyed to the entry numbers on the working paper:

Entry *0*. In comparing the beginning and ending cash balances, we determine the change in the Cash account during the year is an $11,000 increase. An entry on the working paper debits Cash for $11,000 and credits Increase in Cash for Year near the bottom of the schedule. This *0* entry does not explain the change in cash but is the "target" of the analysis. The entry sets out the change in cash that the statement seeks to explain. No further attention need be paid to cash in completing the working paper.

We now direct our attention toward changes in other balance sheet accounts. These accounts can be dealt with in any order; first, we record the net income for the period and analyze the current assets (other than cash) and the current liabilities. Second, we analyze the changes in the noncurrent accounts.

Entry *1*. The income statement shows a net income for 1997 of $10,000. Entry *1* records the $10,000 as the starting point in measuring cash flows from operating activities and credits Retained Earnings as a partial explanation of the change in that account.

The next task is to analyze changes in current accounts other than Cash. The current accounts of Welby Company are closely related to operations, and their changes are included in converting net income to cash flows from operating activities.

Entry *2*. We deduct the $10,000 increase in accounts receivable from net income when converting it to cash flows from operating activities. If accounts receivable increased, sales to customers exceeded cash received from customers. To convert net income to a cash basis, we must deduct the $10,000.

The working paper technique makes the recording of these effects almost mechanical. By debiting Accounts Receivable for $10,000, we increase it from $20,000 to $30,000. If Accounts Receivable is debited, we must credit an item that can be entitled "Increase in Accounts Receivable." We deduct the increase from net income in converting it to cash flows from operating activities.

Entry *3* is virtually a duplicate of entry *2*, except it involves merchandise inventory rather than receivables and is a decrease rather than an increase.

Entry *4* records the effect of a decrease in accounts payable on net income in converting it to cash flows from operating activities.

Entry *5* records the effect of an increase in accrued liabilities payable in converting net income to cash flows from operating activities.

ILLUSTRATION 16.7 Working Paper for Statement of Cash Flows

WELBY COMPANY
Working Paper for Statement of Cash Flows
For the Year Ended December 31, 1997

	Account Balances 12/31/96	Analysis of Transactions for 1997 Debit	Analysis of Transactions for 1997 Credit	Account Balances 12/31/97
Debits				
Cash	10,000	*(0)* 11,000		21,000
Accounts Receivable, Net	20,000	*(2)* 10,000		30,000
Merchandise Inventory	30,000		*(3)* 4,000	26,000
Equipment	50,000	*(7)* 20,000		70,000
Totals	110,000			147,000
Credits				
Accumulated Depreciation—Equipment	5,000		*(6)* 5,000	10,000
Accounts Payable	15,000	*(4)* 6,000		9,000
Accrued Liabilities Payable	–0–		*(5)* 2,000	2,000
Common Stock ($10 par value)	60,000		*(8)* 30,000	90,000
Retained Earnings	30,000	*(9)* 4,000	*(1)* 10,000	36,000
Totals	110,000	51,000	51,000	147,000
Cash Flows from Operating Activities:				
Net Income		*(1)* 10,000		
Increase in Accounts Receivable			*(2)* 10,000	
Decrease in Merchandise Inventory		*(3)* 4,000		
Decrease in Accounts Payable			*(4)* 6,000	
Increase in Accrued Liabilities Payable		*(5)* 2,000		
Depreciation Expense		*(6)* 5,000		
Cash Flows from Investing Activities:				
Purchase of Equipment			*(7)* 20,000	
Cash Flows from Financing Activities:				
Proceeds from Issuing Common Stock		*(8)* 30,000		
Payment of Cash Dividends			*(9)* 4,000	
Increase in Cash for Year			*(0)* 11,000	
		51,000	51,000	

Next, we analyze the changes in the noncurrent balance sheet accounts.

Entry *6*. We add the $5,000 depreciation back to net income and credit the respective accumulated depreciation account. You can find the depreciation expense (1) on the income statement, or (2) by solving for the credit needed to balance the accumulated depreciation account on the balance sheet.

Accumulated Depreciation—Equipment

	Beg. bal. 5,000
	(6) 5,000
	End. bal. 10,000

Entry *7*. We debit the Equipment account and credit "Purchase of Equipment" in the investing activities section for the $20,000 cash spent to acquire new plant assets (equipment).

Entry *8*. We show the $30,000 cash received from sale of common stock as a financing activity. The entry also explains the change in the Common Stock account. If stock had been sold for more than its stated value of $50 per share, we would record the excess in a separate Paid-In Capital in Excess of Stated Value account. However, we would report the total amount of cash received from the issuance of common stock as a single figure on the statement of cash flows. Only this total amount received is significant to creditors and other users of the financial statements trying to judge the solvency of the company.

Entry 9. We debit Retained Earnings and credit Payment of Cash Dividends for the $4,000 dividends declared and paid. The entry also completes the following explanation of the change in Retained Earnings. Notice that on the statement of cash flows, the dividends must be paid to be included as a cash outflow from financing activities.

Retained Earnings

		Beg. bal.	30,000
(9)	4,000	*(1)*	10,000
		End. bal.	36,000

Preparing the Statement of Cash Flows

Using the data in the lower section of the working paper, we would prepare the statement of cash flows under the indirect method shown in Illustration 16.5 (Part B) on page 589.

Demonstration Problem

The following comparative balance sheets are for Dells Corporation as of June 30, 1997, and June 30, 1996. Also provided is the statement of income and retained earnings for the year ended June 30, 1997, with additional data.

DELLS CORPORATION
Comparative Balance Sheets
June 30, 1997, and 1996

	1997	1996	Increase (Decrease)
Assets			
Current assets:			
Cash	$ 30,000	$ 80,000	$ (50,000)
Accounts receivable, net	160,000	100,000	60,000
Merchandise inventory	100,000	70,000	30,000
Prepaid rent	20,000	10,000	10,000
Total current assets	$310,000	$260,000	$ 50,000
Property, plant, and equipment:			
Equipment	$400,000	$200,000	$200,000
Accumulated depreciation—equipment	(60,000)	(50,000)	(10,000)
Total property, plant, and equipment	$340,000	$150,000	$190,000
Total assets	$650,000	$410,000	$240,000
Liabilities and Stockholders' Equity			
Current liabilities:			
Accounts payable	$ 50,000	$ 40,000	$ 10,000
Notes payable—bank	–0–	50,000	(50,000)
Salaries payable	10,000	20,000	(10,000)
Federal income taxes payable	30,000	20,000	10,000
Total current liabilities	$ 90,000	$130,000	$ (40,000)
Stockholders' equity:			
Common stock, $10 par	$300,000	$100,000	$200,000
Paid-in capital in excess of par	50,000	–0–	50,000
Retained earnings	210,000	180,000	30,000
Total stockholders' equity	$560,000	$280,000	$280,000
Total liabilities and stockholders' equity	$650,000	$410,000	$240,000

DELLS CORPORATION
Statement of Income and Retained Earnings
For the Year Ended June 30, 1997

Sales		$1,000,000
Cost of goods sold	$600,000	
Salaries and wages expense	200,000	
Rent expense	40,000	
Depreciation expense	20,000	
Interest expense	3,000	
Loss on sale of equipment	7,000	870,000
Income before federal income taxes		$ 130,000
Deduct: Federal income taxes		60,000
Net income		$ 70,000
Retained earnings, July 1, 1996		180,000
		$ 250,000
Deduct: Dividends		40,000
Retained earnings, June 30, 1997		$ 210,000

Additional data

1. Equipment with a cost of $20,000, on which $10,000 of depreciation had been recorded, was sold for $3,000 cash. Additional equipment was purchased for $220,000.
2. Stock was issued for $250,000 cash.
3. The $50,000 bank note was paid.

Required

Using the data given for Dells Corporation:

a. Prepare a statement of cash flows—indirect method.

b. Prepare a working paper to convert net income from an accrual basis to a cash basis. Then prepare a partial statement of cash flows—direct method, showing only the cash flows from operating activities section.

Solution to Demonstration Problem

a.

DELLS CORPORATION
Statement of Cash Flows—Indirect Method
For the Year Ended June 30, 1997

Cash flows from operating activities:		
Net income	$ 70,000	
Adjustments to reconcile net income to net cash provided by operating activities:		
Increase in accounts receivable	(60,000)	
Increase in merchandise inventory	(30,000)	
Increase in prepaid rent	(10,000)	
Increase in accounts payable	10,000	
Decrease in salaries payable	(10,000)	
Increase in federal income taxes payable	10,000	
Loss on sale of equipment	7,000	
Depreciation expense	20,000	
Net cash provided by operating activities		$ 7,000
Cash flows from investing activities:		
Proceeds from sale of equipment	$ 3,000	
Purchase of equipment	(220,000)	
Net cash used by investing activities		(217,000)
Cash flows from financing activities:		
Proceeds from issuing common stock	$ 250,000	
Repayment of bank note	(50,000)	
Dividends paid	(40,000)	
Net cash provided by financing activities		160,000
Net increase (decrease) in cash		$ (50,000)

b.

DELLS CORPORATION
Working Paper to Convert Income Statement from Accrual Basis to Cash Basis
For the Year Ended June 30, 1997

	Accrual Basis		Add	Deduct	Cash Basis (Cash Flows from Operating Activities)	
Sales		$1,000,000		$60,000[a]		$940,000
Cost of goods sold	$600,000		$30,000[b]	10,000[c]	$620,000	
Salaries and wages expense	200,000		10,000[d]		210,000	
Rent expense	40,000		10,000[e]		50,000	
Depreciation expense	20,000			20,000	–0–	
Interest expense	3,000				3,000	
Loss on sale of equipment	7,000			7,000	–0–	
Federal income taxes	60,000			10,000[f]	50,000	
		930,000				933,000
Net income		$ 70,000				$ 7,000

[a] Increase in Accounts Receivable.
[b] Increase in Merchandise Inventory.
[c] Increase in Accounts Payable.
[d] Decrease in Salaries Payable.
[e] Increase in Prepaid Rent.
[f] Increase in Federal Income Taxes Payable.

DELLS CORPORATION
Partial Statement of Cash Flows—Direct Method
For the Year Ended June 30, 1997

Cash flows from operating activities:		
Cash received from customers	$ 940,000	
Cash paid for merchandise	(620,000)	
Salaries and wages paid	(210,000)	
Rent paid	(50,000)	
Interest paid	(3,000)	
Federal income taxes paid	(50,000)	
Net cash provided by operating activities		$7,000

NEW TERMS

Cash flow liquidity ratio Cash and marketable securities plus net cash provided by operating activities divided by current liabilities. *595*

Cash flow margin ratio Net cash provided by operating activities divided by net sales. *595*

Cash flow per share of net common stock ratio Net cash provided by operating activities divided by the average number of shares of common stock outstanding. *595*

Cash flows from operating activities The net amount of cash received or disbursed during a given period on items that normally appear on the income statement. *582*

Direct method Deducts from cash sales only those operating expenses that consumed cash. *582*

Financing activities Generally include the cash effects of transactions and other events involving creditors and owners. Cash payments made to settle current liabilities such as accounts payable, wages payable, and income taxes payable are not financing activities. These payments are operating activities. *581*

Indirect method A method of determining cash flows from operating activities that starts with net income and indirectly adjusts net income for items that do not involve cash. Also called the **addback** method. *582*

Investing activities Generally include transactions involving the acquisition or disposal of noncurrent assets. Examples include cash received or paid from the sale or purchase of property, plant, and equipment; available-for-sale and held-to-maturity securities; and loans made to others. *581*

Noncash charges or expenses Expenses and losses that are added back to net income because they do not actually use cash of the company. The items added back include amounts of depreciation on plant assets, depletion that was expensed, amortization of intangible assets such as patents and goodwill, amortization of discount on bonds payable, and losses from disposals of noncurrent assets. *583*

Noncash credits or revenues Revenues and gains included in arriving at net income that do not provide cash; examples include gains from disposals of noncurrent assets, income from investments carried under the equity method, and amortization of premium on bonds payable. *584*

Operating activities Generally include the cash effects of transactions and other events that enter into the determination of net income. *580*

Statement of cash flows A statement that summarizes the effects on cash of the operating, investing, and financing activities of a company during an accounting period. Both inflows and outflows are included in each category. The statement of cash flows must be prepared each time an income statement is prepared. *580*

Working capital Equal to current assets minus current liabilities. *579*

Self-Test

True-False

Indicate whether each of the following statements is true or false.

1. The requirement for a statement of cash flows was preceded by the requirement for the statement of changes in financial position.
2. The statement of cash flows is one of the major financial statements.
3. Investing activities are transactions with creditors and owners.
4. The direct method of calculating cash flows from operations is encouraged by the FASB and is the predominant method used.
5. Issuance of capital stock and the subsequent reacquisition of some of those shares would both be financing activities.

Multiple-Choice

Select the best answer for each of the following questions.

1. Which of the following statements is true?
   a. The direct method of calculating cash flows from operations starts with net income and adjusts for noncash revenues and expenses and changes in current assets and current liabilities.
   b. The indirect method of calculating cash flows from operations adjusts each item in the income statement to a cash basis.
   c. The description in *(a)* and *(b)* should be reversed.
   d. The direct method is easier to use than the indirect method.
2. Investing activities include all of the following except:
   a. Payment of debt.
   b. Collection of loans.
   c. Making of loans.
   d. Sale of available-for-sale and held-to-maturity securities.
3. If sales on an accrual basis are $500,000 and accounts receivable increased by $30,000, the cash received from customers would be:
   a. $500,000.
   b. $470,000.
   c. $530,000.
   d. Cannot be determined.
4. Assume cost of goods sold on an accrual basis is $300,000, accounts payable increased by $20,000, and inventory increased by $50,000. Cash paid for merchandise is:
   a. $370,000.
   b. $230,000.
   c. $270,000.
   d. $330,000.
5. Assume net income was $200,000, depreciation expense was $10,000, accounts receivable increased by $15,000, and accounts payable increased by $5,000. The amount of cash flows from operating activities is:
   a. $200,000.
   b. $180,000.
   c. $210,000.
   d. $190,000.

Now turn to page 619 to check your answers.

Questions

1. What are the purposes of the statement of cash flows?
2. What are some of the uses of the statement of cash flows?
3. What information is contained in the statement of cash flows?
4. Which activities are generally included in operating activities?
5. Which activities are included in investing activities?
6. Which activities are included in financing activities?
7. Where should investing and financing activities that do not involve cash flows be reported?
8. Explain the difference between the direct and indirect methods for computing cash flows from operating activities.

9. What are noncash expenses? How are they treated in computing cash flows from operating activities?
10. Describe the treatment of a gain on the sale of equipment in preparing a statement of cash flows under the indirect method.
11. Depreciation is sometimes referred to as a source of cash. Is it a source of cash? Explain.
12. Why is it unlikely that cash flows from operating activities will be equal to net income for the same period?
13. If the net income for a given period is $25,000, does this mean there is an increase in cash of the same amount? Why or why not?
14. Why might a company have positive cash flows from operating activities even though operating at a net loss?
15. Indicate the type of activity each of the following transactions represents (operating, investing, or financing) and whether it is an inflow or an outflow.
    - **a.** Sold goods.
    - **b.** Purchased building.
    - **c.** Issued capital stock.
    - **d.** Received cash dividends.
    - **e.** Paid cash dividends.
    - **f.** Purchased treasury stock.
    - **g.** Sold available-for-sale securities.
    - **h.** Made a loan.
    - **i.** Paid interest on loan.
    - **j.** Paid bond principal.
    - **k.** Received proceeds of insurance settlement.
    - **l.** Made contribution to charity.
16. Refer to "A Broader Perspective" on page 596. Answer the following questions:
    - **a.** What was the major investing activity in all three years?
    - **b.** Was there a net negative or positive cash flow from investing activities?
    - **c.** Was the positive cash flow from investing activities large enough to pay the cash dividends?
17. **Real World Question** Refer to the annual report booklet. Of the four companies represented, which ones use the direct method of reporting cash flows from operating activities and which ones use the indirect method?

Exercises

Exercise 16–1
Report specific items on statement of cash flows
(L.O. 2, 4)

Indicate how the following data should be reported in a statement of cash flows. A company paid $300,000 cash for land. A building was acquired for $2,500,000 by assuming a mortgage on the building.

Exercise 16–2
Calculate the amount of cash paid for merchandise
(L.O. 3)

Cost of goods sold in the income statement for the year ended 1997 was $210,000. The balances in Merchandise Inventory and Accounts Payable were:

	January 1, 1997	December 31, 1997
Merchandise Inventory	$160,000	$180,000
Accounts Payable.	44,000	36,000

Calculate the amount of cash paid for merchandise for 1997.

Exercise 16–3
Show effects of conversion from accrual to cash basis income
(L.O. 3)

Fill in the following chart, showing how increases and decreases in these accounts affect the conversion of accrual basis income to cash basis income:

	Add	Deduct
Accounts Receivable		
Merchandise Inventory		
Prepaid Expenses		
Accounts Payable		
Accrued Liabilities Payable		

Exercise 16–4
Compute cash flows from operating activities
(L.O. 3)

The income statement of a company shows net income of $100,000; merchandise inventory on January 1 was $76,500 and on December 31 was $94,500; accounts payable for merchandise purchases were $57,000 on January 1 and $68,000 on December 31. Compute the cash flows from operating activities under the indirect method.

Exercise 16–5
Compute cash flows from operating activities
(L.O. 3)

The operating expenses and taxes (including $80,000 of depreciation) of a company for a given year were $600,000. Net income was $450,000. Prepaid insurance decreased from $18,000 to $14,000 during the year, while wages payable increased from $22,000 to $36,000 during the year. Compute the cash flows from operating activities under the indirect method.

Exercise 16–6
Indicate treatment of dividend (L.O. 2, 4)

Dividends payable increased by $10,000 during a year in which total dividends declared were $120,000. What amount appears for dividends paid in the statement of cash flows?

Exercise 16–7
Compute cash used to purchase plant assets (L.O. 2, 4)

Following are balance sheet data for Discount Quality Merchandise, Inc.:

	December 31	
	1998	1997
Cash	$ 47,000	$ 26,000
Accounts receivable, net	141,000	134,000
Merchandise inventory	83,000	102,000
Prepaid expenses	9,000	11,000
Plant assets (net of accumulated depreciation)	235,000	230,000
Accounts payable	122,000	127,000
Accrued liabilities payable	40,000	41,000
Capital stock	300,000	300,000
Retained earnings	53,000	35,000

Assume that the depreciation recorded in 1998 was $15,000. Compute the cash spent to purchase plant assets, assuming no assets were sold or scrapped in 1998.

Exercise 16–8
Prepare statement of cash flows (L.O. 4)

Use the data in Exercise 16–7. Assume the net income for 1998 was $24,000, depreciation was $15,000, and dividends declared and paid were $6,000. Prepare a statement of cash flows—indirect method.

Exercise 16–9
Report specific items on statement of cash flows (L.O. 2, 4)

The following data are from a company's Automobile and the Accumulated Depreciation—Automobile accounts:

Automobile

Date		Debit	Credit	Balance
Jan. 1	Balance brought forward			16,000
July 1	Traded for new auto		16,000	-0-
	New auto	31,000		31,000

Accumulated Depreciation—Automobile

Date		Debit	Credit	Balance
Jan. 1	Balance brought forward			12,000
July 1	One-half year's depreciation		2,000	14,000
	Auto traded	14,000		-0-
Dec. 31	One-half year's depreciation		4,000	4,000

The old auto was traded for a new one, with the difference in values paid in cash. The income statement for the year shows a loss on the exchange of autos of $1,200.

Indicate the dollar amounts, the descriptions of these amounts, and their exact locations in a statement of cash flows—indirect method.

PROBLEMS

Problem 16–1
Prepare working paper to convert income statement to cash basis; prepare cash flows from operating activities under both methods (L.O. 2, 3)

The income statement and other data of Dalton Carpet Outlet, Inc., follow:

DALTON CARPET OUTLET, INC.
Income Statement
For the Year Ended December 3, 1997

Sales		$460,000
Cost of goods sold		190,000
Gross margin		$270,000
Operating expenses (other than depreciation)	$70,000	
Depreciation expense	20,000	90,000
Net income		$180,000

Changes in current assets (other than cash) and current liabilities during the year were:

	Increase	Decrease
Accounts receivable		$10,000
Merchandise inventory	$ 8,000	
Prepaid insurance	4,000	
Accounts payable	14,000	
Accrued liabilities payable	2,000	

Depreciation was the only noncash item affecting net income.

Required

a. Prepare a working paper to calculate cash flows from operating activities under the *direct method.*

b. Prepare the cash flows from operating activities section of the statement of cash flows under the *direct method.*

c. Prove that the same cash flows amount will be obtained under the indirect method by preparing the cash flows from operating activities section of the statement of cash flows under the *indirect method.* You need not prepare a working paper.

Problem 16–2
Prepare statement of cash flows under the indirect method (L.O. 4)

The following comparative balance sheets and other data are for Mobile Telephone Sales, Inc.:

MOBILE TELEPHONE SALES, INC.
Comparative Balance Sheets
December 31, 1998 and 1997

	1998	1997
Assets		
Cash	$ 76,105	$ 51,000
Accounts receivable, net	26,075	24,250
Merchandise inventory	30,000	35,000
Supplies on hand	1,750	2,550
Prepaid insurance	1,400	1,200
Land	180,000	142,500
Equipment	270,000	300,000
Accumulated depreciation—equipment	(75,000)	(67,500)
Total assets	$510,330	$489,000
Liabilities and Stockholders' Equity		
Accounts payable	$ 45,330	$ 76,300
Salaries payable	4,000	2,000
Accrued liabilities payable	2,000	8,250
Long-term note payable	150,000	150,000
Common stock ($5 par)	185,000	165,000
Paid-in capital in excess of par	32,500	–0–
Retained earnings	91,500	87,450
Total liabilities and stockholders' equity	$510,330	$489,000

Additional data

1. Land was bought for $37,500 cash. The company intends to build a building on the land. Currently the company leases a building for its operations.
2. Equipment costing $50,000 with accumulated depreciation of $30,000 was sold for $23,500 (a gain of $3,500), and equipment costing $20,000 was purchased for cash.
3. Depreciation expense for the year was $37,500.
4. Common stock was issued for $52,500 cash.
5. Dividends declared and paid in 1998 totaled $32,950.
6. Net income was $37,000.

Required Prepare a statement of cash flows under the indirect method.

Problem 16–3
Analyze GTE Corporation's statement of cash flows (L.O. 5, 6)

GTE Corporation is the fourth-largest publicly owned telecommunications company in the world. This company is the largest U.S.-based local telephone company and is the second-largest cellular service provider in the United States. GTE Corporation's 1993 statement of cash flows is shown below, followed by Management's Financial Review regarding information contained in the statement of cash flows.

GTE CORPORATION AND SUBSIDIARIES
Consolidated Statements of Cash Flows
For the Years Ended December 31
($ millions)

	1993	1992	1991
Cash Flows from Operations:			
Income from continuing operations	$ 990	$ 1,787	$ 1,529
Adjustments to reconcile income to net cash from continuing operations:			
Depreciation and amortization	3,419	3,289	3,254
Restructuring and merger costs	1,840	—	342
Deferred taxes and investment tax credits	(864)	37	37
Change in current assets and current liabilities, excluding the effects of acquisitions and dispositions	(13)	(268)	(732)
Other—net	(95)	(13)	213
Net cash from continuing operations	$ 5,277	$ 4,832	$ 4,643
Net cash from discontinued operations	—	—	141
Net cash from operations	$ 5,277	$ 4,832	$ 4,784
Cash Flows from Investing:			
Capital expenditures	$(3,893)	$(3,909)	$(3,965)
Acquisitions and investments	(46)	(84)	(1,132)
Proceeds from sales of assets	2,267	662	177
Other—net	(66)	55	(104)
Net cash used in investing	$(1,738)	$(3,276)	$(5,024)
Cash Flows from Financing:			
GTE common stock issued	$ 383	$ 1,513	$ 412
Long-term debt issued	2,325	590	3,958
Long-term debt and preferred stock retired	(4,836)	(2,002)	(1,539)
Dividends to shareholders of parent	(1,744)	(1,572)	(1,447)
Increase (decrease) in short-term obligations, excluding current maturities	304	(254)	(1,094)
Other—net	(3)	6	5
Net cash provided from/(used in) financing	$(3,571)	$(1,719)	$ 295
Increase (decrease) in cash and temporary cash investments	$ (32)	$ (163)	$ 55
Cash and temporary cash investments:			
Beginning of year	354	517	462
End of year	$ 322	$ 354	$ 517

Management's Discussion and Analysis*

Capital Investment, Resources and Liquidity

GTE's cash flow from operations increased from $4.8 billion in 1992 to $5.3 billion in 1993 and, together with nearly $400 million raised through employee stock purchase and dividend reinvestment plans, provided the funds required for dividends of $1.7 billion and capital expenditures of $3.9 billion.

In 1993, GTE redeemed in advance of scheduled maturity $2.1 billion of high-coupon debt issues and recognized an extraordinary charge of $90 million for the expenses associated with these redemptions. GTE also issued $2.3 billion of long-term debt during 1993, which was used to refinance maturing issues and to begin refinancing the high-coupon redemptions. The remaining refinancing related to high-coupon redemptions is expected to be completed during the first half of 1994.

During 1993, GTE made substantial progress in its program to sell or trade a small percentage of local-exchange telephone properties (representing less than 5% of its U.S. access lines) that had been identified as non-strategic. GTE completed about half of the expected transactions through the sale or exchange of 440,000 net access lines for $1 billion in cash. GTE also entered into definitive agreements for the sale of over 400,000 additional access lines for $.9 billion in cash. These transactions are subject to various government and regulatory approvals and the transfers of ownership, and are expected to occur on a state-by-state basis throughout 1994. GTE plans to continue to reduce debt with the net proceeds from these transactions.

Capital expenditures in 1994 are expected to increase slightly from the 1993 level, as accelerating investment in fiber optics and other enabling technologies for broadband services together with continued expansion of the cellular business more than offset the declining requirements for conversion to

* Source: GTE Corporation's 1993 Annual Report, pp. 18–19.

digital switching. Cash requirements to implement the re-engineering plan at Telephone Operations are expected to be largely offset by cost savings. Dividends and the capital requirements for GTE's businesses should continue to be funded largely with cash from operations and the funds generated from the employee stock purchase and dividend reinvestment plans. However, GTE's strong financial position allows ready access to worldwide capital markets for any additional requirements.

The issuance of long-term debt during 1994 is expected to be related largely to refinancing activity and is likely to increase compared with 1993 when refinancing also accounted for most of the new issuances.

Required Based on the information provided, prepare written responses to the following questions.

a. Does it appear that the company can continue to pay dividends at the current level? Explain.

b. What is unique about the first and fifth items on the statement of cash flows?

c. Does it appear that the company is modernizing its productive capacity? Explain.

d. Does it appear that the company is taking advantage of the lower interest rates existing in the early 1990's? Explain.

e. Given the following data, calculate the cash flow per share of common stock ratio, the cash flow margin ratio, and the cash flow liquidity ratio.

Average shares of common stock outstanding	945.6 million
Net sales	$19,748 million
Cash and marketable securities	322 million
Current liabilities	7,933 million

How do these ratios compare with the ratios shown for other companies on page 595?

Problem 16–4
Analyze Eli Lilly and Company's statement of cash flows (L.O. 5, 6)

Eli Lilly and Company is one of the world's largest pharmaceutical companies. The company has decided to focus its attention on certain diseases. The targeted disease categories include central-nervous-system diseases, endocrine diseases, infectious diseases, cancer, and cardiovascular diseases. The company's 1993 statement of cash flows is shown below, followed by Management's Discussion and Analysis regarding information contained in the statement of cash flows.

ELI LILLY AND COMPANY AND SUBSIDIARIES
Consolidated Statements of Cash Flows
For the Years Ended December 31
($ millions)

	1993	1992	1991
Cash Flows from Operating Activities			
Net income	$ 480.2	$ 708.7	$ 1,314.7
Adjustments to Reconcile Net Income to Cash Flows from Operating Activities			
Depreciation and amortization	398.3	368.1	299.5
Change in deferred taxes	(231.6)	(184.3)	(13.7)
Restructuring and special charges—net of payments	1,041.3	565.7	—
Cumulative effect of changes in accounting principles	10.9	118.9	—
Other noncash (income)—net	(53.1)	(16.2)	(8.7)
Changes in operating assets and liabilities:			
Receivables—(increase) decrease	(32.1)	28.1	(122.2)
Inventories—increase	(192.3)	(198.4)	(116.1)
Other assets—increase	(104.5)	(48.8)	(140.3)
Accounts payable and other liabilities—increase	199.8	141.7	41.4
Net Cash Flows from Operating Activities	$1,516.9	$1,483.5	$ 1,254.6
Cash Flows from Investing Activities			
Additions to property and equipment	$ (633.5)	$ (912.9)	$(1,142.4)
Disposals of property and equipment	5.4	10.6	28.5
Additions to intangibles and other assets	(70.1)	(59.6)	(100.9)
Net proceeds from divestiture	—	98.9	—
Reductions of investments	889.3	764.2	1,301.7
Additions to investments	(1,001.7)	(740.2)	(942.6)
Acquisitions	(56.1)	(89.2)	—
Net Cash Used for Investing Activities	$ (866.7)	$ (928.2)	$ (855.7)

Cash Flows from Financing Activities			
Dividends paid	$ (708.4)	$ (643.7)	$ (582.7)
Warrant exercises	—	—	955.7
Purchase of common stock and other capital transactions	(25.8)	(68.5)	(69.2)
Issuance under stock plans	19.8	26.0	39.3
Decrease in short-term borrowings	(152.7)	(104.9)	(713.9)
Additions to long-term debt	383.8	205.5	152.6
Reductions of long-term debt	(39.8)	(3.0)	(60.0)
Net Cash Used for Financing Activities	$ (523.1)	$ (588.6)	$ (278.2)
Effect of exchange rate changes on cash	(19.9)	(13.5)	8.3
Net increase (decrease) in cash and cash equivalents	$ 107.2	$ (46.8)	$ 129.0
Cash and cash equivalents at the beginning of year	432.4	479.2	350.2
Cash and Cash Equivalents at End of Year	$ 539.6	$ 432.4	$ 479.2

See notes to consolidated financial statements [not included].

Management's Discussion and Analysis*

Financial Condition

The company maintained its sound financial position in 1993 despite the impacts of the restructuring and special charges taken in both 1993 and 1992. The cash generated from operations provided the resources to fund capital expenditures, dividends, and acquisitions. In 1993, the company issued additional long-term debt of $350 million to take advantage of favorable long-term interest rates.

Capital expenditures during 1993 were approximately $279 million less than in 1992, as work progressed toward completion of new manufacturing facilities, including environmental control systems, and development, research, and administrative facilities. The company expects a continued decline in near-term capital-expenditure requirements. Sufficient liquidity exists to meet these near-term capital-expenditure requirements.

The company is a 40 percent partner with The Dow Chemical Company in DowElanco, a global agricultural products joint venture. The company holds [an] option, which can be exercised after October 31, 1994, requiring Dow to purchase the company's interest in DowElanco at a fair market value.

The company's strong financial position contributes to its ability to finance growth. Liquidity is substantial as evidenced by the company's ability to generate cash from operations, debt-to-equity ratio, and substantial debt capacity. These factors give the company the ability and flexibility to meet its obligations, to pay dividends, and to continue to invest in growth opportunities. The highest long-term debt rating of AAA for the company was reaffirmed by Standard & Poor's in December 1993; however, the company's long-term debt rating was lowered to Aa1 from AAA by Moody's in January 1994.

Dividends of $2.42 per share were paid in 1993, a 10 percent increase from the $2.20 per share paid in 1992. Dividends of $2.20 per share were paid in 1992, a 10 percent increase from the $2.00 per share paid in 1991. The year 1993 was the 109th consecutive year that the company made dividend payments and the 26th consecutive year in which dividends have been increased.

Required

Based on the information provided, prepare written responses to the following questions.

a. Does it appear that the company can continue to pay dividends at the current level? Explain.

b. What was one of the major reasons for the lower net income during 1992 and 1993?

c. Does it appear that the company is modernizing its productive capacity? Explain.

d. Does it appear that the company is taking advantage of the lower interest rates existing in the early 1990s? Explain. If you were a long-term creditor, is there any information in Management's Discussion and Analysis that would be of some concern?

e. What is the likely cause of the reductions and additions in investments?

f. Given the following data, calculate the cash flow per share of common stock ratio, the cash flow margin ratio, and the cash flow liquidity ratio.

Average shares of common stock outstanding	293 million
Net sales	$6,452.4 million
Cash and marketable securities	987.1 million
Current liabilities	2,928 million

How do these ratios compare with the ratios shown for other companies on page 595?

* Source: Eli Lilly and Company's 1993 Annual Report, pp. 13, 16.

Problem 16–5
Prepare working paper and statement of cash flows under the indirect method (Appendix) (L.O. 7)

The following comparative balance sheets and other data are for Tent & Awning Sales, Inc.:

TENT & AWNING SALES, INC.
Comparative Balance Sheets
June 30, 1998 and 1997

	1998	1997
Assets		
Cash	$ 441,800	$ 332,600
Accounts receivable, net	750,750	432,900
Merchandise inventory	819,000	850,200
Prepaid insurance	3,900	5,850
Land	312,000	351,000
Buildings	2,184,000	1,209,000
Machinery and tools	858,000	468,000
Accumulated depreciation—machinery and tools	(809,250)	(510,900)
Total assets	$4,560,200	$3,138,650
Liabilities and Stockholders' Equity		
Accounts payable	$ 226,750	$ 275,500
Accrued liabilities payable	185,800	111,700
Bank loans (due in 2000)	56,550	66,300
Mortgage bonds payable	382,200	185,250
Common stock—$100 par	1,755,000	585,000
Paid-in capital in excess of par	58,500	–0–
Retained earnings	1,895,400	1,914,900
Total liabilities and stockholders' equity	$4,560,200	$3,138,650

Additional data

1. Net income for the year was $128,000.
2. Depreciation for the year was $356,850.
3. There was a gain of $7,800 on the sale of land. The land was sold for $46,800.
4. The additional mortgage bonds were issued at face value as partial payment for a building valued at $975,000. The amount of cash paid was $778,050.
5. Machinery and tools were purchased for $448,500 cash.
6. Fully depreciated machinery with a cost of $58,500 was scrapped and written off.
7. Additional common stock was issued at $105 per share. The total proceeds were $1,228,500.
8. Dividends declared and paid were $147,500.
9. A payment was made on the bank loan, $9,750.

Required

a. Prepare a working paper for a statement of cash flows.
b. Prepare a statement of cash flows under the indirect method. Prepare a separate schedule of noncash investing and financing activities.

ALTERNATE PROBLEMS

Problem 16–1A
Prepare working paper to convert income statement to cash basis; prepare cash flows from operating activities under both methods (L.O. 2, 3)

The following income statement and other data are for Auto Glass Specialists, Inc.:

AUTO GLASS SPECIALISTS, INC.
Income Statement
For the Year Ended December 31, 1997

Sales		$900,000
Cost of goods sold		250,000
Gross margin		$650,000
Operating expenses (other than depreciation)	$120,000	
Depreciation expense	40,000	160,000
Net income		$490,000

Changes in current assets (other than cash) and current liabilities during the year were:

	Increase	Decrease
Accounts receivable	$30,000	
Merchandise inventory		$50,000
Prepaid insurance	16,000	
Accounts payable		30,000
Accrued liabilities payable	8,000	

Depreciation was the only noncash item affecting net income.

Required

a. Prepare a working paper to calculate cash flows from operating activities under the *direct method.*

b. Prepare the cash flows from operating activities section of the statement of cash flows under the *direct method.*

c. Prove that the same cash flows amount is obtained under the indirect method by preparing the cash flows from operating activities section of the statement of cash flows under the *indirect method.* You need not prepare a working paper.

Problem 16–2A
Prepare statement of cash flows under the indirect method (L.O. 4)

The following information relates to Nursery & Garden Center, Inc. The company leases a building adjacent to its land.

NURSERY & GARDEN CENTER, INC.
Comparative Balance Sheets
December 31, 1998 and 1997

	1998	1997
Assets		
Cash	$ 44,500	$ 52,000
Accounts receivable, net	59,000	60,000
Merchandise inventory	175,000	120,000
Equipment	412,500	315,000
Accumulated depreciation—equipment	(120,000)	(105,000)
Land	75,000	15,000
Total assets	$646,000	$457,000
Liabilities and Stockholders' Equity		
Accounts payable	$ 43,750	$ 40,750
Accrued liabilities payable	2,250	3,750
Capital stock—common—$10 par	375,000	300,000
Paid-in capital in excess of par	150,000	75,000
Retained earnings	75,000	37,500
Total liabilities and stockholders' equity	$646,000	$457,000

Additional data

1. Net income was $97,500 for the year.
2. Fully depreciated equipment costing $15,000 was sold for $3,750 (a gain of $3,750), and equipment costing $112,500 was purchased for cash.
3. Depreciation expense for the year was $30,000.
4. Land was purchased, $60,000.
5. An additional 7,500 shares of common stock were issued for cash at $20 per share (total proceeds, $150,000).
6. Cash dividends of $60,000 were declared and paid.

Required

Prepare a statement of cash flows under the indirect method.

Problem 16–3A
Analyze Raytheon Company's statement of cash flows (L.O. 5, 6)

Raytheon Company is a diversified, international, multi-industry, technology-based company ranked among the 100 largest U.S. industrial corporations. In 1993, the U.S. government accounted for about 49% of sales, including the Patriot Air Defense System. The company has four major segments: Electronics, Major Appliances, Aircraft Products, and Energy and Environmental. The company is finding new opportunities to diversify defense technology into commercial markets. Raytheon Company's 1993 statement of cash flows is shown below, followed by Management's Discussion and Analysis regarding information contained in the statement of cash flows.

RAYTHEON COMPANY AND SUBSIDIARIES
Consolidated Statements of Cash Flows
Years Ended December 31
($ thousands)

	1993	1992	1991
Cash flows from operating activities			
Net income	$ 692,991	$ 635,073	$ 591,762
Adjustments to reconcile net income to net cash provided by operating activities, net of the effect of acquired companies			
Depreciation	277,946	302,133	306,117
(Increase) decrease in accounts receivable	(38,478)	79,749	42,297
(Increase) decrease in contracts in process	3,658	(106,657)	(177,259)
(Increase) decrease in inventories	(98,270)	(36,560)	1,433
(Increase) decrease in long-term receivables	48,356	(13,220)	98,704
Increase (decrease) in advance payments	106,107	(96,794)	(75,973)
(Decrease) in accounts payable	(3,167)	(22,743)	(543)
Increase (decrease) in federal and foreign income taxes	95,073	(27,853)	10,663
Other adjustments, net	(134,159)	(21,603)	(48,627)
Net cash provided by operating activities	$ 950,057	$ 691,525	$ 748,574
Cash flows from investing activities			
Additions to property, plant, and equipment	$(256,131)	$(307,726)	$(348,536)
Disposals of property, plant, and equipment	36,516	58,282	45,370
(Increase) decrease in other assets	14,825	(4,140)	(20,407)
Payment for purchase of acquired companies	(566,400)	—	—
All other, net	(904)	36,603	9,530
Net cash used in investing activities	$(772,094)	$(216,981)	$(314,043)
Cash flows from financing activities			
Dividends	$(189,827)	$(178,721)	$(162,589)
Increase (decrease) in short-term debt	166,407	(397,705)	(320,719)
(Decrease) in long-term debt	(894)	(13,980)	(7,116)
Purchase of treasury shares	(114,398)	—	—
Proceeds under common stock plans	68,966	70,384	74,377
All other, net	(7,169)	(2,251)	(6,735)
Net cash (used in) financing activities	$ (76,915)	$(522,273)	$(422,782)
Effect of foreign exchange rates on cash	$ 343	$ 329	$(1,023)
Net increase (decrease) in cash and cash equivalents	$ 101,391	$ (47,400)	$ 10,726
Cash and cash equivalents at beginning of year	88,730	136,130	125,404
Cash and cash equivalents at end of year	$ 190,121	$ 88,730	$ 136,130

Management's Discussion and Analysis*

For the year ended December 31, 1993, cash flows from operating activities provided $950.1 million and short-term debt was increased to provide additional funds of $166.4 million. These total funds of $1,116.5 million were used to fund additions to property, plant, and equipment of $256.1 million, to pay dividends of $189.8 million, to purchase treasury shares for $114.4 million and for the acquisition of Corporate Jets and Ebasco for a net expenditure of $566.4 million. Cash and cash equivalents increased by $101.4 million during the year.

Contracts in process were $2.024 billion at December 31, 1993, as compared with $1.863 billion at December 31, 1992. The increase was principally due to the acquisition of Ebasco.

Inventories increased to $1.500 billion at year-end 1993 from $1.051 billion in 1992 principally as a result of the acquisitions of Corporate Jets and Ebasco and an increase in commercial aircraft inventories.

Other assets increased to $1.226 billion at year-end 1993 from $819 million at the end of 1992 principally due to the goodwill associated with the acquisitions made during 1993.

Advance payments, less related contracts in process balances, increased to $376.1 million at year-end 1993 from $210.9 million at the end of 1992 due mainly to advance payments received on foreign engineering and construction programs.

The company is working with the U.S. Government and the Kingdom of Saudi Arabia on the financing of certain defense contracts and expects to conclude a satisfactory arrangement.

---

* Source: Raytheon Company's 1993 Annual Report, pp. 36–37.

Total debt at the end of 1993 was $898 million as compared with $732 million at the end of 1992. The company expects that the cash flow from operations will be sufficient to meet the funding requirements of the company in 1994.

During 1993, the company sold $288.5 million of general aviation and $101.5 million of commuter long-term receivables to a bank syndicate.

Lines of credit with certain commercial banks exist as a stand-by facility to support the issuance of commercial paper by the company. These lines of credit were $1.11 billion and $1.12 billion as of December 31, 1993, and December 31, 1992, respectively. Through the end of 1993, there have been no borrowings under these lines of credit.

Capital expenditures decreased to $256.1 million in 1993 from $307.7 million in 1992. Capital expenditures for the year 1994 are expected to approximate the 1993 amount.

Dividends declared to stockholders in 1993 increased to $189.8 million from $178.7 million in 1992. The dividend declared per common share was increased by 5.7 percent to $1.40 in 1993 versus $1.325 in 1992.

In November 1992, to counter the dilution due to exercise of stock options, the Board of Directors authorized the purchase of up to two million shares of the company's common stock per year over the next five years. During 1993, 1,978,000 shares were purchased under this authorization at a cost of $114.4 million . . .

In August 1993, the company acquired the Corporate Jets business of British Aerospace Public Limited Company for $372 million. Corporate Jets manufactures medium-sized business jets. In December 1993, the company purchased the principal operating assets of Ebasco Services, Inc., for $210 million. Earlier in 1993, the company acquired the assets of Harbert Construction Company, the assets of Menumaster, Inc., three engineering businesses from Gibbs & Hill, Inc. and Applied Remote Technology. The results of operations of the above companies have been included in the consolidated results of the company.

Required

Based on the information provided, prepare written responses to the following questions.

a. Does it appear that the company can continue to pay dividends at the current level? Explain.

b. Does it appear that the company is modernizing its productive capacity? Explain.

c. Does it appear that the company is taking advantage of the lower interest rates existing in the early 1990s? Explain.

d. Raytheon is a large defense contractor. Does it appear that the company is reducing its productive facilities as a result of the end of the Cold War?

e. Why did the company reacquire so much of its own stock (treasury stock)?

f. Given the following data, calculate the cash flow per share of common stock ratio, the cash flow margin ratio, and the cash flow liquidity ratio.

Average shares of common stock outstanding	135.4 million
Net sales	$9,201 million
Cash and marketable securities	190 million
Current liabilities	2,910 million

How do these ratios compare with the ratios shown for other companies on page 595?

Problem 16–4A
Analyze International Flavors & Fragrances Inc.'s statement of cash flows (L.O. 5, 6)

International Flavors & Fragrances Inc. is a leading creator and manufacturer of flavors and fragrances used by others to impart or improve flavor or fragrance in a wide variety of consumer products. Fragrance products are sold principally to makers of perfumes and cosmetics, hair and other personal care products, soaps and detergents, household and other cleaning products, and area fresheners. The company's 1993 statement of cash flows is shown below, followed by Management's Discussion and Analysis regarding information contained in the statement of cash flows.

INTERNATIONAL FLAVORS & FRAGRANCES INC.
Consolidated Statement of Cash Flows
Years Ended December 31
($ thousands)

	1993	1992	1991
Cash flows from operating activities:			
Net income	$ 202,471	$ 170,594	$ 168,674
Adjustments to reconcile to net cash provided by operations:			
Depreciation	35,067	34,023	29,393
Accounting changes, net of tax	—	6,089	—
Nonrecurring charge	—	20,033	—
Deferred income taxes	615	4,933	(2,921)
Changes in assets and liabilities:			
Current receivables	(36,614)	(19,248)	(12,369)
Inventories	(17,144)	(18,711)	(13,088)
Current payables	24,933	16,253	20,808
Other, net	(3,042)	(10,385)	(6,199)
Net cash provided by operations	$ 206,286	$ 203,581	$ 184,298
Cash flows from investing activities:			
Short-term investments, net	$ 89,785	$ 49,936	$ (30,971)
Additions to property, plant and equipment, net of minor disposals	(81,134)	(49,446)	(53,314)
Net cash provided by (used in) investing activities	$ 8,651	$ 490	$ (84,285)
Cash flows from financing activities:			
Cash dividends paid to shareholders	$(114,555)	$(104,495)	$ (91,714)
Increase (decrease) in bank loans	18,029	(1,135)	2,609
Proceeds from issuance of stock under stock option plans	3,722	5,229	3,928
Purchase of treasury stock	(125,734)	(17,939)	(9,048)
Net cash used in financing activities	$(218,538)	$(118,340)	$ (94,225)
Effect of exchange rate changes on cash and cash equivalents	$ (19,992)	$ (8,908)	$ (281)
Net change in cash and cash equivalents	$ (23,593)	$ 76,823	$ 5,507
Cash and cash equivalents at beginning of year	210,798	133,975	128,468
Cash and cash equivalents at end of year	$ 187,205	$ 210,798	$ 133,975

See Notes to Consolidated Financial Statements [not included].

Management's Discussion and Analysis*

Financial Condition

The favorable cash flow from operations for the Company, as shown in the Consolidated Statement of Cash Flows, reflects the continuing growth of sales and earnings.

The financial condition of the Company continued to be strong during 1993. Cash, cash equivalents and short-term investments totalled $311,278,000 at December 31, 1993 compared to $429,972,000 and $410,001,000 at December 31, 1992 and 1991, respectively. Short-term investments held by the Company are high quality, readily marketable instruments. Working capital totalled $652,436,000 at year-end 1993, compared to $770,412,000 and $736,933,000, at December 31, 1992 and 1991, respectively. The reduction in cash, cash equivalents and short-term investments, and working capital is primarily attributable to the purchase of treasury shares in connection with the Company's authorized share repurchase program. Gross additions to property, plant and equipment were $82,286,000, $51,095,000 and $54,121,000 in the years 1993, 1992 and 1991, respectively, and are expected to approximate $100,000,000 in 1994.

In December 1993, the Board of Directors declared a three-for-one stock split. The additional shares were distributed on January 19, 1994 to shareholders of record on December 28, 1993. All share and per share amounts in this report reflect this stock split.

In September 1992, the Board of Directors authorized the repurchase of up to 7.5 million shares of the Company's common stock on the open market or through private transactions, as market and business conditions warrant. The reacquired shares are available for use under the Company's employee benefit plans and for general corporate purposes. At December 31, 1993, approximately 4.0 million shares had been repurchased under this program.

* Source: International Flavors & Fragrances Inc.'s 1993 Annual Report, p. 32.

The Company anticipates that its growth and capital expenditure programs, and the above share repurchase plan will continue to be funded mainly from internal sources.

During 1993, the Company paid dividends to shareholders totalling $114,555,000, while $104,495,000 was paid in 1992 and $91,714,000 in 1991. In January 1994, the cash dividend was increased 8% to an annual rate of $1.08 per share. This increase follows an increase of 10% in January 1993 and 13% in January 1992. The Company believes these increases in dividends to the shareholders can be made without limiting future growth and expansion.

Required

Based on the information provided, prepare written responses to the following questions.

a. Does it appear that the company can continue to pay dividends at the current level? Explain.

b. What major events occurred regarding the company's capital stock?

c. Does it appear that the company is expanding its productive capacity? Explain.

d. Does it appear that the company is taking advantage of the lower interest rates existing in the early 1990s? Explain.

e. Besides operations, what was one of the major sources of cash in 1993?

f. Given the following data, calculate the cash flow per share of common stock ratio, the cash flow margin ratio, and the cash flow liquidity ratio.

Average shares of common stock outstanding	114 million
Net sales	$1,188.6 million
Cash and marketable securities	311.3 million
Current liabilities	226.6 million

How do these ratios compare with the ratios shown for other companies on page 595?

Problem 16–5A
Prepare working paper and statement of cash flows under the indirect method (Appendix)
(L.O. 7)

The following information is from the accounting records of Discount Office Supplies, Inc., for the fiscal years 1998 and 1997:

DISCOUNT OFFICE SUPPLIES, INC.
Comparative Balance Sheets
June 30, 1998 and 1997

	1998	1997
Assets		
Cash	$ 66,250	$ 61,000
Accounts receivable, net	84,000	42,000
Merchandise inventory	42,000	48,250
Prepaid expenses	7,875	12,125
Land	94,500	78,750
Buildings	199,500	147,000
Accumulated depreciation—buildings	(31,500)	(26,250)
Equipment	257,250	210,000
Accumulated depreciation—equipment	(78,750)	(63,000)
Total assets	$641,125	$509,875
Liabilities and Stockholders' Equity		
Accounts payable	$ 73,500	$ 47,250
Accrued liabilities payable	50,500	55,750
Five-year note payable	52,500	–0–
Capital stock—$50 par	420,000	367,500
Retained earnings	44,625	39,375
Total liabilities and stockholders' equity	$641,125	$509,875

Additional data

1. Net income for year ended June 30, 1998, was $56,250.
2. Additional land was acquired for cash, $15,750.
3. No equipment or building retirements occurred during the year.
4. Equipment was purchased for cash, $47,250.
5. The five-year note for $52,500 was issued to pay for a building erected on land leased by the company.
6. Stock was issued at par for cash, $52,500.
7. Dividends declared and paid were $51,000.

Required

a. Prepare a working paper for a statement of cash flows.

b. Prepare a statement of cash flows under the indirect method. Prepare a separate schedule of noncash investing and financing activities.

BEYOND THE NUMBERS—CRITICAL THINKING

Business Decision Case 16–1
Prepare a statement of cash flows using the indirect method and answer owner's questions (L.O. 1, 2, 4)

U.S.A. Sports, Inc., is a sports equipment sales company. During 1998, the company replaced $18,000 of its fully depreciated equipment with new equipment costing $23,000. Although a midyear dividend of $5,000 was paid, the company found it necessary to borrow $5,000 from its bank on a two-year note. Further borrowing may be needed since the Cash account is dangerously low at year-end.

Following are the income statement and "cash flow statement," as the company's accountant calls it, for 1998.

U.S.A. SPORTS, INC.
Income Statement
For the Year Ended December 31, 1998

Sales		$195,000
Cost of goods sold	$140,000	
Operating expenses and taxes	49,700	189,700
Net income		$ 5,300

U.S.A. SPORTS, INC.
Cash Flow Statement
For the Year Ended December 31, 1998

Cash received:		
From operations:		
Net income		$ 5,300
Depreciation		5,000
Total cash from operations		$10,300
Note issued to bank		5,000
Mortgage note issued		16,000
Total funds provided		$31,300
Cash paid:		
New equipment	$23,000	
Dividends	5,000	28,000
Increase in cash		$ 3,300

The company's president is very concerned about what he sees in these statements and how it relates to what he knows has actually happened. He turns to you for help. Specifically, he wants to know why the cash flow statement shows an increase in cash of $3,300 when he knows the cash balance decreased from $15,000 to $500 during the year. Also, why is depreciation shown as providing cash?

You believe you can answer the president's questions after receiving the following condensed balance sheet data:

U.S.A. SPORTS, INC.
Comparative Balance Sheets
December 31, 1998 and 1997

	December 31	
	1998	1997
Assets		
Current assets:		
Cash	$ 500	$ 15,000
Accounts receivable, net	17,800	13,200
Merchandise inventory	28,500	17,500
Prepaid expenses	700	300
Total current assets	$ 47,500	$ 46,000
Property, plant, and equipment:		
Equipment	$ 40,000	$ 35,000
Accumulated depreciation—equipment	(11,000)	(24,000)
Total property, plant, and equipment	$ 29,000	$ 11,000
Total assets	$ 76,500	$ 57,000

Liabilities and Stockholders' Equity

Current liabilities:		
Accounts payable	$ 8,700	$ 10,000
Accrued liabilities payable	600	1,100
Total current liabilities	$ 9,300	$ 11,100
Long-term liabilities:		
Notes payable	5,000	–0–
Mortgage note payable	16,000	–0–
Total liabilities	$ 30,300	$ 11,100
Stockholders' equity:		
Common stock	$ 40,000	$ 40,000
Retained earnings	6,200	5,900
Total stockholders' equity	46,200	45,900
Total liabilities and stockholders' equity	$ 76,500	$ 57,000

Required Prepare a correct statement of cash flows using the indirect method that shows why U.S.A. Sports, Inc., is having such a difficult time keeping sufficient cash on hand. Also, answer the president's questions.

Business Decision Case 16–2
Prepare a schedule showing cash flows from operating activities under the indirect method and decide whether certain goals can be met (L.O. 4)

Following are comparative balance sheets for Vinyl Siding, Inc.:

VINYL SIDING, INC.
Comparative Balance Sheets
December 31, 1998 and 1997

	1998	1997
Assets		
Cash	$ 80,000	$ 57,500
Accounts receivable, net	60,000	45,000
Merchandise inventory	90,000	52,500
Land	67,500	60,000
Buildings	90,000	90,000
Accumulated depreciation—buildings	(30,000)	(27,000)
Equipment	285,000	225,000
Accumulated depreciation—equipment	(52,500)	(48,000)
Goodwill	120,000	150,000
Total assets	$710,000	$605,000
Liabilities and Stockholders' Equity		
Accounts payable	$ 95,000	$ 65,000
Accrued liabilities payable	30,000	22,500
Capital stock	315,000	300,000
Paid-in capital—stock dividends	75,000	67,500
Paid-in capital—land donations	15,000	–0–
Retained earnings	180,000	150,000
Total liabilities and stockholders' equity	$710,000	$605,000

An analysis of the Retained Earnings account for the year reveals the following:

Balance, January 1, 1998		$150,000
Add: Net income for the year		107,500
		$257,500
Less: Cash dividends	$55,000	
Stock dividends	22,500	77,500
Balance, December 31, 1998		$180,000

Additional data

a. Equipment with a cost of $30,000 on which $27,000 of depreciation had been accumulated was sold during the year at a loss of $1,500. Included in net income is a gain on the sale of land of $9,000.

b. The president of the company has set two goals for 1999: (1) increase cash by $40,000 and (2) increase cash dividends by $35,000. The company's activities in 1999 are expected to be quite similar to those of 1998, and no new fixed assets will be acquired.

Required Prepare a schedule showing cash flows from operating activities under the indirect method for 1998. Can the company meet its president's goals for 1999? Explain.

Annual Report Analysis 16–3
Decide whether four companies can maintain their current dividends (real world problem)
(L.O. 1)

Refer to the annual report booklet. Evaluate the ease with which each of the four companies represented will be able to maintain their dividend payments in the future at 1993 amounts. (Hint: Compare current dividend amounts with net cash provided by operating activities.) Rank the companies in their ability to maintain their dividend payments by dividing their net cash provided by operating activities by their dividends paid.

Annual Report Analysis 16–4
Analyze a company's statement of cash flows and answer questions
(L.O. 5)

Refer to "A Broader Perspective" on page 596 and answer the following questions:

a. Over the last three years from which major activities (operations, investing, financing) has Archer Daniels Midland Company received net cash inflows and on which major activities have they spent the funds?
b. What relationship do you see between "Depreciation and amortization" and "Purchases of property, plant, and equipment"?
c. What were the two major sources of cash outflows to stockholders and which was larger?
d. By how much did the investments in marketable securities grow or shrink over the three-year period?
e. By how much did long-term debt grow or shrink over the three-year period?
f. If you were a stockholder, would you feel uncertain or confident that this company will be able to pay future dividends at the same rate as in the past?
g. For what reason or reasons might the company be buying back its own stock?
h. For the latest year, did the current assets (other than cash) and current liabilities go up or down?
i. From the information that is available, does it appear that the company is performing well or poorly?

Annual Report Analysis 16–5
For four real companies, calculate cash flow per share of common stock, cash flow margin, and cash flow liquidity ratios and then comment
(L.O. 6)

Refer to the annual report booklet. For each of the four companies—The Coca-Cola Company; Maytag Corporation; The Limited, Inc.; and John H. Harland—calculate the following ratios for 1993:

a. Cash flow per share of common stock ratio
b. Cash flow margin ratio
c. Cash flow liquidity ratio

Then comment on the results.

Group Project 16–6
Write a paper on a specific topic

In groups of two or three students write a two-page, double-spaced paper on one of the following topics:

Which Is Better, the Direct or Indirect Method (of calculating net cash provided by operating activities)?

Analysis of the Archer Daniels Midland Cash Flow Statement (shown in "A Broader Perspective" in this chapter)

Analysis of The Coca-Cola Company's Cash Flow Statement (shown in the annual report booklet)

Your analysis should be convincing and have no spelling or grammatical errors. Your paper should be neat and the result of several drafts. The paper should have a cover page with the title and the authors' names. Use a word processing program if possible.

Answers to Self-Test

True-False

1. **True.** Before July 1988, the statement of changes in financial position was required. This statement usually emphasized changes in working capital rather than changes in cash.
2. **True.** The statement of cash flows must be published every time an income statement is published.
3. **False.** Investing activities are transactions involving the acquisition or disposal of noncurrent assets. Transactions with creditors and owners are financing activities.
4. **False.** While the direct method is the method encouraged by the FASB, it is not the predominant method in use. In a recent study, only about 3% of the companies surveyed used the direct method.
5. **True.** Both of these transactions are with owners and, therefore, would be financing activities.

Multiple-Choice

1. **c.** The descriptions in *(a)* and *(b)* would be correct if they were reversed. The indirect method is easier to use, and this characteristic is probably the main reason why it is used by most companies.
2. **a.** Payment of debt is a financing activity because it is a transaction with creditors. All of the others are investing activities because they are transactions involving the acquisition or disposal of noncurrent assets.
3. **b.** Sales of $500,000 minus the increase in accounts receivable of $30,000 = $470,000.
4. **d.** Cost of goods sold of $300,000, less the increase in accounts payable of $20,000, plus the increase in inventory of $50,000 = $330,000.
5. **a.** Net income of $200,000, plus depreciation of $10,000, less the increase in accounts receivable of $15,000, plus the increase in accounts payable of $5,000 = $200,000.

17

Analysis and Interpretation of Financial Statements

Learning Objectives

After studying this chapter, you should be able to:

1. Describe and explain the objectives of financial statement analysis.
2. Describe the sources of information for financial statement analysis.
3. Calculate and explain changes in financial statements using horizontal analysis, vertical analysis, and trend analysis.
4. Perform ratio analysis on financial statements using liquidity ratios, long-term solvency ratios, profitability tests, and market tests.
5. Describe the considerations used in financial statement analysis.

The two primary objectives of every business are solvency and profitability. Solvency is the ability of a company to pay debts as they come due; it is reflected on the company's balance sheet. Profitability is the ability of a company to generate income; it is reflected on the company's income statement. Generally, all those interested in the affairs of a company are especially interested in solvency and profitability.

This chapter discusses several common methods of analyzing and relating the data in financial statements and, as a result, gaining a clear picture of the solvency and profitability of a company. Internally, management analyzes a company's financial statements as do external investors, creditors, and regulatory agencies. Although these users have different immediate goals, their overall objective in financial statement analysis is the same—to make predictions about an organization as an aid in decision making.

Objectives of Financial Statement Analysis

Management's analysis of financial statements primarily relates to parts of the company. Using this approach, management can plan, evaluate, and control operations within the company. Management obtains any information it wants about the company's operations by requesting special-purpose reports. It uses this information to make difficult decisions, such as which employees to lay off and when to expand operations. Our primary focus in this chapter, however, is not on the special reports accountants prepare for management. Rather, it is on the information needs of persons outside the firm.

Investors, creditors, and regulatory agencies generally focus their analysis of financial statements on the company as a whole. Since they cannot request special-purpose reports, external users must rely on the general-purpose financial

---

This chapter uses the following source: Colgate-Palmolive Company, *1993 Annual Report, Succeeding in a Changing World* . . . Colgate-Palmolive Company, New York, New York, 1993.

statements that companies publish. These statements include a balance sheet, an income statement, a statement of stockholders' equity, a statement of cash flows, and the explanatory notes that accompany the financial statements.

Objective 1
Describe and explain the objectives of financial statement analysis.

Users of financial statements need to pay particular attention to the explanatory notes, or the financial review, provided by management in annual reports. This integral part of the annual report provides insight into the scope of the business, the results of operations, liquidity and capital resources, new accounting standards, and geographic area data. Moreover, this section provides an economic outlook that an analyst may find very helpful when considering the possible future profitability of the company.

Financial Statement Analysis

Financial statement analysis consists of applying analytical tools and techniques to financial statements and other relevant data to obtain useful information. This information reveals significant relationships between data and trends in those data that assess the company's past performance and current financial position. The information shows the results or consequences of prior management decisions. In addition, analysts use the information to make predictions that may have a direct effect on decisions made by users of financial statements.

Present and potential investors are interested in the future ability of a company to earn profits—its profitability. These investors wish to predict future dividends and changes in the market price of the company's common stock. Since both dividends and price changes are likely to be influenced by earnings, investors may predict earnings. The company's past earnings record is the logical starting point in predicting future earnings.

Some outside parties, such as creditors, are more interested in predicting a company's solvency than its profitability. The **liquidity** of the company affects its short-term solvency. The company's liquidity is its state of possessing liquid assets, such as cash and other assets easily converted to cash. Because companies must pay short-term debts soon, liquid assets must be available for their payment. For example, a bank asked to extend a 90-day loan to a company would want to know the company's projected short-term liquidity. Of course, the company's predicted ability to repay the 90-day loan is likely to be based at least partially on its past ability to pay off debts.

Long-term creditors are interested in a company's long-term solvency, which is usually determined by the relationship of a company's assets to its liabilities. Generally, we consider a company to be solvent when its assets exceed its liabilities so that the company has a positive stockholders' equity. The larger the assets are in relation to the liabilities, the greater the long-term solvency of the company. Thus, the company's assets could shrink significantly before its liabilities would exceed its assets and destroy the company's solvency.

Investors perform several types of analyses on a company's financial statements. All of these analyses rely on comparisons or relationships of data that enhance the utility or practical value of accounting information. For example, knowing that a company's net income last year was $100,000 may or may not, by itself, be useful information. Some usefulness is added when we know that the prior year's net income was $25,000. And even more useful information is gained if we know the amounts of sales and assets of the company. Such comparisons or relationships may be expressed as:

1. Absolute increases and decreases for an item from one period to the next.
2. Percentage increases and decreases for an item from one period to the next.
3. Percentages of single items to an aggregate total.
4. Trend percentages.
5. Ratios.

Earlier chapters have discussed and illustrated many of these analysis techniques. However, in this chapter we apply all of these techniques in analyzing Colgate-Palmolive Company's performance for 1993.

Items 1 and 2 make use of comparative financial statements. **Comparative financial statements** present the same company's financial statements for one or two successive periods in side-by-side columns. The calculation of dollar changes or percentage changes in the statement items or totals is **horizontal analysis.** This analysis detects changes in a company's performance and highlights trends.

Analysts also use vertical analysis of a single financial statement, such as an income statement. **Vertical analysis** (item 3) consists of the study of a single financial statement in which each item is expressed as a *percentage of a significant total.* Vertical analysis is especially helpful in analyzing income statement data such as the percentage of cost of goods sold to sales.

Financial statements that show only percentages and no absolute dollar amounts are **common-size statements.** All percentage figures in a common-size balance sheet are percentages of total assets while all the items in a common-size income statement are percentages of net sales. The use of common-size statements facilitates vertical analysis of a company's financial statements.

Trend percentages (item 4) are similar to horizontal analysis except that comparisons are made to a selected base year or period. Trend percentages are useful for comparing financial statements over several years because they disclose changes and trends occurring through time.

Ratios (item 5) are expressions of logical relationships between items in the financial statements of a single period. Analysts can compute many ratios from the same set of financial statements. A ratio can show a relationship between two items on the same financial statement or between two items on different financial statements (e.g., balance sheet and income statement). The only limiting factor in choosing ratios is the requirement that the items used to construct a ratio have a logical relationship to one another.

Sources of Information

Financial information about publicly owned corporations can come from different sources such as published reports, government reports, financial service information, business publications, newspapers, and periodicals.

Published Reports

Objective 2
Describe the sources of information for financial statement analysis.

Public corporations must publish annual financial reports. The annual report booklet gives such 1993 data for The Coca-Cola Company; John H. Harland Company; The Limited, Inc.; and Maytag Corporation. The major sections of an annual report are:

1. Consolidated financial statements Consolidated financial statements include a balance sheet containing two years of comparative data; an income statement containing three years of comparative data; a statement of cash flows containing three years of comparative data; and a statement of shareholders' equity containing three years of comparative data. For examples of each statement, refer to the annual report booklet.

2. Notes to consolidated financial statements Notes to consolidated financial statements provide an in-depth look into the numbers contained in the financial statements. The notes usually contain sections on significant accounting policies, long-term debt, leases, stock option plans, etc. These explanations allow stockholders to look beyond the numbers to the events that triggered the dollar amount recorded in the financial statements.

Chesapeake Corporation is a paper and packaging company.

3. Letters to stockholders Most annual reports are introduced with a letter to the stockholders. The letter often includes information about the company's past history, its mission, current year operating results, and the company's future goals. For example, in the Chesapeake Corporation's 1992 annual report, the chairman of the board and the president and chief executive officer included in their letter to the stockholders a description of their mission and future company goals, entitled Vision 2000 strategy, as follows:

Mission

Chesapeake's mission is to increase the wealth of our stockholders while fulfilling, with integrity, our responsibilities to our employees, customers, suppliers, the public and the environment.

Vision 2000 Strategy

We will conduct our business in accordance with these goals and principles:

- Maintain high ethical standards
- Be innovative and look beyond the obvious
- Be proactive and strive to be different
- Have respect for people as individuals
  Maintain a clean, safe, injury-free workplace
  Provide the appropriate authority and responsibility to make decisions in a decentralized environment
  Utilize the individual talents of our people
  Reward employee innovation, participation and performance
  Achieve a high degree of ownership and commitment
- Continually improve our cost positions and our asset utilization
- Be at least 15 minutes ahead of our competition
- Provide value to our customers through continuous improvement
- Be good stewards of the environment
- Serve our country and communities to the best of our abilities

As the strategy statement indicates, we will manage the company for cash flow and value creation. We are committed to growth, reducing our capital intensity and managing our cyclicality. We have also established financial goals for the year 2000. Our growth target is to have $2 billion in sales by the year 2000. Our profitability target is to achieve an average annual return on equity of 15%. We also will work to control our cyclicality so that our return on equity will not be lower than 10% in any year. The industry in which we participate is the most capital intensive in the United States, and our strategy is intended to achieve a sales to asset ratio of 1.25 : 1 by the year 2000 while keeping our debt at reasonable levels.

4. **Reports of independent accountants** The Securities and Exchange Commission (SEC) requires the financial statements of certain companies to be audited. The report of independent accountants, found at the end of the financial statements, provides assurance that the financial statements prepared by the company have been audited and are free of material misstatements. The report also may include a paragraph highlighting the significant accounting policies that the company has changed recently.

5. **Management discussion and analysis** The management discussion and analysis section of the annual report provides management's view of the performance of the company. The analysis is based on the financial statements, the conditions of the industry, and ratios.

Government Reports

Publicly held companies must file detailed annual reports (Form 10–K), quarterly reports (Form 10–Q), and special events reports (Form 8–K) with the Securities and Exchange Commission. These reports are available to the public for a small charge and sometimes contain more detailed information than the published reports.

Financial Service Information, Business Publications, Newspapers, and Periodicals

Financial statement information is often more meaningful when users compare it with industry norms. Two firms that provide information on individual companies and industries are Moody's Investors Service and Standard & Poor's. Dun & Bradstreet Companies, Inc., publishes *Key Business Ratios* and Robert Morris Associates publishes *Annual Statement Studies;* both provide information for specific industries. Standard & Poor's *Industry Surveys* contains background descriptions and the economic outlook for different industries.

Business publications such as *The Wall Street Journal, Barron's, Forbes,* and *Fortune* also report industry financial news. Because financial statement users must be knowledgeable about current developments in business, the information in financial newspapers and periodicals is very valuable to them.

Horizontal Analysis and Vertical Analysis: An Illustration

Objective 3
Calculate and explain changes in financial statements using horizontal analysis, vertical analysis, and trend analysis.

The comparative financial statements of the Colgate-Palmolive Company will serve as a basis for an example of horizontal analysis and vertical analysis of a balance sheet and a statement of income and retained earnings. Recall that horizontal analysis calculates changes in comparative statement items or totals, whereas vertical analysis consists of a comparison of items on a single financial statement.

Analysis of a Balance Sheet

The Colgate-Palmolive Company manufactures and markets toothpastes, oral rinses and toothbrushes, bar and liquid soaps, shampoos, conditioners, deodorants, detergents, and cleansers.

Imagine that you are a prospective investor interested in Colgate-Palmolive Company. You have acquired the 1993 Annual Report of the company and want to perform some horizontal and vertical analyses of the financial statements.

First, we begin with the balance sheets. Illustration 17.1 shows the comparative balance sheets for 1993 and 1992 in Columns (1) and (2). Take a few minutes to study the balance sheets. Then place Illustration 17.2, containing Columns (3) and (4), over Illustration 17.1. Columns (3) and (4) show the horizontal analysis that would be performed on the comparative balance sheets.

Column (3) shows the change that occurred in each item between December 31, 1992, and December 31, 1993. If the change between the two dates is an increase from 1992 to 1993, the change is a positive figure. If the change is a decrease, the change is a negative figure and is shown in parentheses. Column (4) shows the percentage change in each item. You can calculate the percentage change by dividing the dollar change by the dollar balance of the earlier year (1992). While examining the horizontal analysis in Illustration 17.2 note that:

1. Total current assets have increased $75.3 million, consisting largely of a $111.8 million increase in net receivables, while total current liabilities have increased only $34.5 million.
2. Total liabilities have increased $1,071.9 million, while total assets only increased by $327.1 million.

Next, study Column (4) in Illustration 17.2, which expresses as a percentage the dollar change in Column (3). Frequently, these percentage increases are more informative than absolute amounts, as illustrated by the current asset and current liability changes. Although the absolute amount of current assets has increased more than twice the amount of current liabilities, the percentages reveal the current assets increased 3.8%, while current liabilities increased 2.5%. Thus, current assets are increasing at a slightly faster rate than current liabilities. This fact indicates that the company will be able to pay its debts as they come due.

Studying the percentages in Column (4) could lead to several other observations. For instance, the 61.9% increase in long-term debt indicates that interest charges will be higher in the future, having a negative effect on future net income. The 1.9% decrease in retained earnings could be a sign of decreased dividends in the future; however, the increase in cash of 22.2% could offset this conclusion.

Now place Illustration 17.3, containing Columns (5) and (6), over Illustration 17.2 to see the vertical analysis that would be performed. A vertical analysis of Colgate-Palmolive's balance sheet discloses each account's significance to total assets or total equities. This comparison aids in assessing the importance of the changes in each account. Columns (5) and (6) in Illustration 17.3 express the dollar amount of each item in Columns (1) and (2) as a percentage of total assets or equities. For example, although other assets declined $76.2 million in 1993, the decrease of 18.5% in the account represents only approximately 5.8% of total assets and, therefore, probably does not have great significance. Vertical analysis also shows that total debt financing increased from 51.8% of total equities (liabilities and stockholders' equity) in 1992, to 67.5% in 1993. At the same time, the percentage of stockholder financing to total assets of the company decreased from 48.2% to 32.5%.

Analysis of Statement of Income and Retained Earnings

Illustration 17.4 provides the information needed to analyze Colgate-Palmolives' comparative statements of income and retained earnings. Such a statement merely combines the income statement and the statement of retained earnings. Columns (7) and (8) in Illustration 17.4 show the dollar amounts for the years 1993 and 1992, respectively. Study these statements for a few minutes. Then place Illustration 17.5, containing Columns (9) and (10), over Illustration 17.4 to show the horizontal analysis that would be performed on Colgate-Palmolive's comparative statements of income and retained earnings. Columns (9) and (10) show the absolute and percentage increase and decrease in each item from 1992 to 1993. The absolute change is determined by deducting the 1992 amount from the 1993 amount. If the change between two dates is an increase from 1992 to 1993, the change is a positive figure. If the change is a decrease, the change is a negative figure and is shown in parentheses. You calculate the percentage change by dividing the dollar change by the dollar amount for 1992.

The horizontal analysis shows that sales increased a total of $134.1 million, an increase of 1.9%. Since cost of goods sold increased by a much smaller amount ($21.5 million), gross profit increased by $112.6, or 3.4%. Total expenses increased by only $4.3 million in spite of the $50.6 million increase in "other expense." Regarding the $358.2 million cumulative effect on prior years of accounting changes, management stated, "Included in 1993 net income and per share amounts is the cumulative one-time impact on prior years of adopting new mandatory accounting standards effective January 1, 1993 for income taxes, other postretirement benefits, and postemployment benefits." Since these one-time charges will not be incurred in the future, analysts forecasting future earnings might focus on the "income before changes in accounting" (called "income from continuing operations" in Chapter 13), which increased by $71.1 million, or 14.9%.

Now place Illustration 17.6, containing Columns (11) and (12), over Illustration 17.5 to see the vertical analysis that would be performed. Columns (11) and (12) express the dollar amount of each item in Columns (7) and (8) as a percentage of net sales. Even though cost of goods sold increased in 1993, it remained a fairly constant percentage of net sales. Therefore, gross profit as a percentage of net sales increased only slightly. The percentage of expenses to net sales remained fairly constant, thus yielding only a slight increase in income before changes in accounting as a percentage of net sales. The cumulative effect on prior years of accounting changes had a negative impact on net income that was equal to 5% of net sales. Thus, instead of net income being 7.7% of net sales, it was only 2.7% of net sales.

Many times, "a picture is worth a thousand words." Colgate-Palmolive Company included some bar graphs in its 1993 Annual Report that show some of the information in the comparative financial statements. Several of the graphs include data from earlier years as well. Illustration 17.7 shows the relationship between net sales and gross profit for the years 1991 through 1993.

Illustration 17.8 shows the percentage of gross profit to sales for the years 1984 through 1993. The percentage has increased steadily over that period from 39.2% to 47.8% of net sales.

Illustration 17.9 shows income from continuing operations for the years 1991 through 1993. This graph shows that 1993 income from continuing operations

ILLUSTRATION 17.1 Comparative Balance Sheets

COLGATE-PALMOLIVE COMPANY
Comparative Balance Sheets
December 31, 1993 and 1992
(in millions)

	December 31	
	(1) 1993	**(2) 1992**
Assets		
Current Assets		
Cash and cash equivalents	$144.1	$117.9
Marketable securities	67.1	102.6
Receivables, net	988.3	876.5
Inventories	678.0	695.6
Other current assets	192.9	202.5
Total current assets	$2,070.4	$1,995.1
Property, plant and equipment, net	1,766.3	1,596.8
Goodwill and other intangible assets, net	1,589.0	1,430.5
Other assets	335.5	411.7
	$5,761.2	$5,434.1
Liabilities and Shareholders' Equity		
Current liabilities		
Notes and loans payable	$169.4	$132.0
Current portion of long-term debt	15.5	59.4
Accounts payable	599.3	563.0
Accrued income taxes	59.4	33.9
Other accruals	550.4	571.2
Total current liabilities	$1,394.0	$1,359.5
Long-term debt	1,532.4	946.5
Deferred income taxes	266.2	171.3
Other liabilities	693.6	337.0
	$3,886.2	$2,814.3
Shareholders' Equity		
Preferred stock	$414.3	$418.3
Common stock, $1 par value (500,000,000 shares authorized, 183,213,295 shares issued)	183.2	183.2
Additional paid-in capital	1,000.9	985.3
Retained earnings	2,163.4	2,204.9
Cumulative translation adjustment	(372.9)	(308.5)
	$3,388.9	$3,483.2
Unearned compensation	(389.9)	(396.1)
Treasury stock, at cost	(1,124.0)	(467.3)
Total shareholders' equity	$1,875.0	$2,619.8
	$5,761.2	$5,434.1

* Dollars = (1) − (2); Percent = (3)/(2).
† Difference due to rounding.
Source: Colgate-Palmolive Company, *1993 Annual Report, Succeeding in a Changing World . . .* (New York: Colgate-Palmolive Company, 1993). Used with permission.

ILLUSTRATION 17.4 Comparative Statements of Income and Retained Earnings

COLGATE-PALMOLIVE COMPANY
Comparative Statements of Income and Retained Earnings
For the years ended December 31, 1993 and 1992
($ millions)

	Year Ended December 31	
	(7) 1993	(8) 1992
Net sales	$7,141.3	$7,007.2
Cost of sales	3,729.9	3,708.4
Gross profit	$3,411.4	$3,298.8
Selling, general and administrative expenses	2,457.1	2,500.2
Other expense (income)	71.3	20.7
Interest expense, net of interest income of $22.7, $28.1 and $33.4, respectively	46.8	50.0
Income before income taxes	$836.2	$727.9
Provision for income taxes	288.1	250.9
Income before changes in accounting	$548.1	$477.0
Cumulative effect on prior years of accounting changes	(358.2)	0
Net income	$189.9	$477.0
Retained earnings, January 1	2,204.9	1,928.6
	$2,394.8	$2,405.6
Dividends declared		
Series B Convertible preferred stock, net of tax	21.1	20.2
Preferred stock	0.5	0.5
Common stock	209.8	180.0
Retained earnings, December 31	$2,163.4	$2,204.9

* Dollars = (7) − (8); Percent = (9)/(8).

Source: Colgate-Palmolive Company, *1993 Annual Report, Succeeding in a Changing World* . . . (New York: Colgate-Palmolive Company, 1993). Used with permission.

would have increased by 15% over 1992 if it had not been for the cumulative effect on prior years of changes in accounting principle.

Having completed the horizontal analysis and vertical analysis of Colgate-Palmolive's balance sheet and statement of income and retained earnings, you are ready to study trend percentages and ratio analysis. The last section in this chapter discusses some final considerations in financial statement analysis. Professional financial statement analysts use several tools and techniques to determine the solvency and profitability of companies.

Trend Percentages

Trend percentages, also referred to as *index numbers*, help you to compare financial information over time to a base year or period. You can calculate trend percentages by:

1. Selecting a base year or period.
2. Assigning a weight of 100% to the amounts appearing on the base-year financial statements.
3. Expressing the corresponding amounts on the other years' financial statements as a percentage of base-year or period amounts. Compute the percentages by dividing nonbase-year amounts by the corresponding base-year amounts and then multiplying the result by 100.

The following information for Colgate-Palmolive illustrates the calculation of trend percentages:

($ millions)	1991	1992	1993
Net sales	$6,060.3	$7,007.2	$7,141.3
Cost of goods sold	3,296.3	3,708.4	3,729.9
Gross profit	$2,764.0	$3,298.8	$3,411.4
Operating expenses	2,546.1	2,570.9	2,575.2
Income before income taxes	$ 217.9	$ 727.9	$ 836.2

If 1991 is the base year, to calculate trend percentages for each year divide net sales by $6,060.3 million; cost of goods sold by $3,296.3 million; gross profit by $2,764.0 million; operating profit by $2,546.1 million; and income before income taxes by $217.9 million. After all divisions have been made, multiply each result by 100. The resulting percentages reflect trends as follows:

	1991	1992	1993
Net sales	100.0%	115.6%	117.8%
Cost of goods sold	100.0	112.5	113.2
Gross profit	100.0	119.3	123.4
Operating expenses	100.0	101.0	101.1
Income before income taxes	100.0	334.1	383.8

These trend percentages indicate the changes taking place in the organization and highlight the direction of these changes. For instance, the percentage of sales is increasing each year compared to the base year. Cost of goods sold increased at a lower rate than net sales, causing gross profit to increase at a higher rate than net sales. Operating expenses hardly increased at all, leading to significant increases in income before income taxes. Percentages provide clues to an analyst about which items need further investigation or analysis. In reviewing trend percentages, a financial statement user should pay close attention to the trends in related items, such as the cost of goods sold in relation to sales. Trend analysis that shows a constantly declining gross margin (profit) rate may be a signal that future net income will decrease.

As useful as trend percentages are, they have one drawback. Expressing changes as percentages is usually straightforward as long as the amount in the

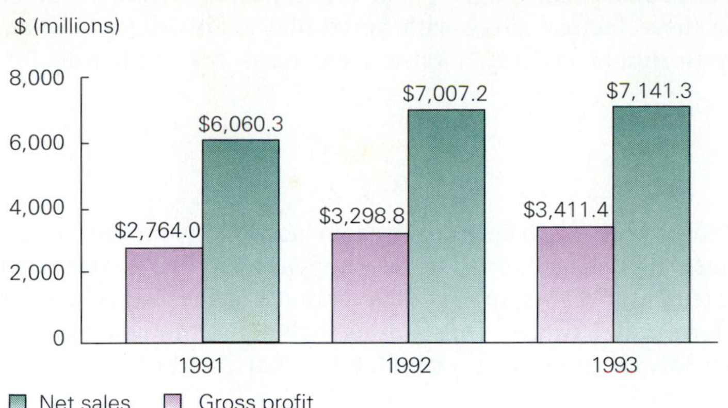

ILLUSTRATION 17.7
Net Sales and Gross Profit ($ millions)

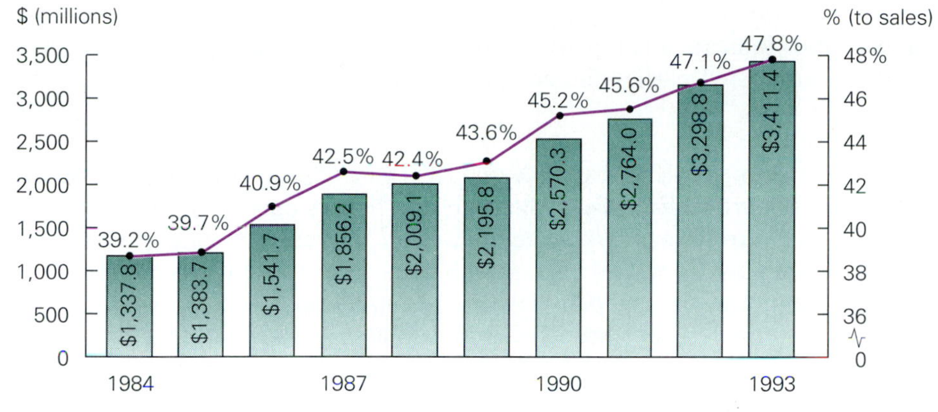

ILLUSTRATION 17.8
Gross Profit ($ millions; percent to sales)

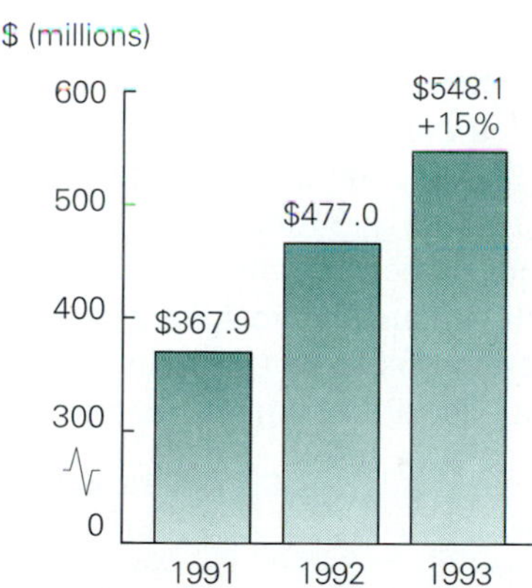

Excluding the impact of an accounting change in 1993 and a restructuring charge in 1991.

ILLUSTRATION 17.9
Income ($ millions)

base year or period is positive—that is, not zero or negative. Analysts cannot express a $30,000 increase in notes receivable as a percentage if the increase is from zero last year to $30,000 this year. Nor can they express an increase from a loss last year of $10,000 to income this year of $20,000 in percentage terms.

Proper analysis does not stop with the calculation of increases and decreases in amounts or percentages over several years. Such changes generally indicate areas worthy of further investigation and are merely clues that may lead to significant findings. Accurate predictions depend on many factors, including economic and political conditions; management's plans regarding new products, plant expansion, and promotional outlays; and the expected activities of competitors. Considering these factors along with horizontal analysis, vertical analysis, and trend analysis should provide a reasonable basis for predicting future performance.

Ratio Analysis

Objective 4
Perform ratio analysis on financial statements using liquidity ratios, long-term solvency ratios, profitability tests, and market tests.

Logical relationships exist between certain accounts or items in a company's financial statements. These accounts may appear on the same statement or on two different statements. We set up the dollar amounts of the related accounts or items in fraction form called *ratios*. These ratios include: (1) liquidity ratios; (2) equity, or long-term solvency, ratios; (3) profitability tests; and (4) market tests.

Liquidity Ratios

Liquidity ratios indicate a company's short-term debt-paying ability. Thus, these ratios show interested parties the company's capacity to meet maturing current liabilities.

Current, or Working Capital, Ratio Working capital is the excess of current assets over current liabilities. The ratio that relates current assets to current liabilities is the **current,** or **working capital, ratio.** The current ratio indicates the ability of a company to pay its current liabilities from current assets and, thus, shows the strength of the company's working capital position.

You can compute the current ratio by dividing current assets by current liabilities:

$$\text{Current ratio} = \frac{\text{Current assets}}{\text{Current liabilities}}$$

The ratio is usually stated as a number of dollars of current assets to one dollar of current liabilities (although the dollar signs usually are omitted). Thus, for Colgate-Palmolive in 1993, when current assets totaled \$2,070.4 million and current liabilities totaled \$1,394.0 million, the ratio is 1.49 : 1, meaning that the company has \$1.49 of current assets for each \$1.00 of current liabilities.

The current ratio provides a better index of a company's ability to pay current debts than does the absolute amount of working capital. To illustrate, assume that we are comparing Colgate-Palmolive to Company B. For this example, use the following totals for current assets and current liabilities:

	Colgate-Palmolive	Company B
Current assets (a)	\$2,070.4	\$130.0
Current liabilities (b)	1,394.0	62.4
Working capital (a − b)	\$ 676.4	\$ 67.6
Current ratio (a/b)	1.49 : 1	2.08 : 1

Colgate-Palmolive has 10 times as much working capital as Company B. However, Company B has a superior debt-paying ability since it has \$2.08 of current assets for each \$1.00 of current liabilities. Colgate-Palmolive is not far behind with \$1.49 of current assets for each \$1.00 of current liabilities.

Short-term creditors are particularly interested in the current ratio since the conversion of inventories and accounts receivable into cash is the primary source from which the company obtains the cash to pay short-term creditors. Long-term creditors are also interested in the current ratio because a company that is unable to pay short-term debts may be forced into bankruptcy. For this reason, many bond indentures, or contracts, contain a provision requiring that the borrower maintain at least a certain minimum current ratio. A company can increase its current ratio by issuing long-term debt or capital stock or by selling noncurrent assets.

A company must guard against a current ratio that is too high, especially if caused by idle cash, slow-paying customers, and/or slow-moving inventory. Decreased net income can result when too much capital that could be used profitably elsewhere is tied up in current assets.

Refer to Illustration 17.2. The Colgate-Palmolive Company data in Column (4) indicate that current assets are increasing more rapidly than current liabilities. We could also make such an observation directly by looking at the change in the current ratio. Colgate-Palmolive's current ratios for 1993 and 1992 follow:

	December 31		Amount of
($ millions)	1993	1992	Increase
Current assets (a)	$2,070.4	$1,995.1	$75.3
Current liabilities (b)	1,394.0	1,359.5	34.5
Working capital (a − b)	$ 676.4	$ 635.6	$40.8
Current ratio (a/b)	1.49 : 1	1.47 : 1	

Colgate-Palmolive's working capital increased by $40.8 million, or 6.4% ($40.8/$635.6), and its current ratio increased from 1.47 : 1 to 1.49 : 1. Together, these figures reflect that its current assets increased faster than its current liabilities.

Acid-Test (Quick) Ratio The current ratio is not the only measure of a company's short-term debt-paying ability. Another measure, called the **acid-test (quick) ratio,** is the ratio of quick assets (cash, marketable securities, and net receivables) to current liabilities. Analysts exclude inventories and prepaid expenses from current assets to compute quick assets because they might not be readily convertible into cash. The formula for the acid-test ratio is:

$$\text{Acid-test ratio} = \frac{\text{Quick assets}}{\text{Current liabilities}}$$

Short-term creditors are particularly interested in this ratio, which relates the pool of cash and immediate cash inflows to immediate cash outflows.

The acid-test ratios for 1993 and 1992 for Colgate-Palmolive are:

	December 31		Amount of
($ millions)	1993	1992	Increase
Quick Assets (a)	$1,199.5	$1,097.0	$102.5
Current Liabilities (b)	1,394.0	1,359.5	34.5
Net quick assets (a − b)	$ (194.5)	$ (262.5)	$ 68.0
Acid-Test Ratio (a/b)	.86 : 1	.81 : 1	

In deciding whether the acid-test ratio is satisfactory, investors consider the quality of the marketable securities and receivables. An accumulation of poor-quality marketable securities or receivables, or both, could cause an acid-test ratio to appear deceptively favorable. When referring to marketable securities, poor quality means securities likely to generate losses when sold. Poor-quality receivables may be uncollectible or not collectible until long past due. The quality of receivables depends primarily on their age, which can be assessed by preparing an aging schedule or by calculating the accounts receivable turnover. (Refer to Chapter 9 for a discussion of an accounts receivable aging schedule.)

Cash Flow Liquidity Ratio Another approach to measuring short-term liquidity is the **cash flow liquidity ratio.** The numerator, as an approximation of cash resources, consists of (1) cash and marketable securities, or liquid current assets, and (2) net cash provided by operating activities, or the cash generated from the company's operations. This reflects the company's ability to sell inventory and collect accounts receivable. The formula for the cash flow liquidity ratio is:

$$\frac{\text{Cash and marketable securities} + \text{Net cash provided by operating activities}}{\text{Current liabilities}}$$

For 1993, Colgate-Palmolive has $144.1 million in cash and cash equivalents, $67.1 million in marketable securities, $1,394.0 million in current liabilities, and $710.4 million in cash provided by operating activities. Its cash flow liquidity ratio is:

$$\frac{\$144.1 + \$67.1 + \$710.4}{\$1,394.0} = .66 \text{ times}$$

This indicates that the company is going to have to rely on some other sources of funding to pay its current liabilities. The company's liquid current assets will only cover about two-thirds of the current liabilities. Possibly net cash provided by operations will be substantially higher in 1994.

ACCOUNTS RECEIVABLE TURNOVER **Turnover** is the relationship between the amount of an asset and some measure of its use. **Accounts receivable turnover** is the number of times per year that the average amount of receivables is collected. To calculate this ratio, divide net credit sales (or net sales) by average net accounts receivable; that is, accounts receivable after deducting the allowance for uncollectible accounts:

$$\text{Accounts receivable turnover} = \frac{\text{Net credit sales (or net sales)}}{\text{Average net accounts receivable}}$$

When a ratio compares an income statement item (like net credit sales) with a balance sheet item (like net accounts receivable), the balance sheet item should be an average. Ideally, analysts calculate average net accounts receivable by averaging the end-of-month balances or end-of-week balances of net accounts receivable outstanding during the period. The greater the number of observations used, the more accurate the resulting average. Often, analysts average only the beginning-of-year and end-of-year balances because this information is easily obtainable from comparative financial statements. Sometimes a formula calls for the use of an average balance, but only the year-end amount is available. Then the analyst must use the year-end amount.[1]

In theory, the numerator of the accounts receivable turnover ratio consists of only net credit sales because those are the only sales that generate accounts receivable. However, if cash sales are relatively small or their proportion to total sales remains fairly constant, analysts can obtain reliable results by using total net sales. In most cases, the analyst may have to use total net sales because the separate amounts of cash sales and credit sales are not reported on the income statement.

Colgate-Palmolive's accounts receivable turnover ratios for 1993 and 1992 follow. Net accounts receivable on January 1, 1992, totaled $744.2 million.

	December 31		Amount of
($ millions)	1993	1992	Increase
Net sales (a)	$7,141.3	$7,007.2	$134.1
Net accounts receivable:			
January 1	$ 876.5	$ 744.2	$132.3
December 31	988.3	876.5	111.8
Total (b)	$1,864.8	$1,620.7	$244.1
Average net receivables (c) (b/2 = c)	$ 932.4	$ 810.4	
Turnover of accounts receivable (a/c)	7.66	8.65	

[1] These general comments about the use of averages in a ratio apply to the other ratios involving averages discussed in this chapter.

The accounts receivable turnover ratio provides an indication of how quickly the company collects receivables. The accounts receivable turnover ratio for 1993 indicates that Colgate-Palmolive collected, or turned over, its accounts receivable slightly more than seven times. The ratio is better understood and more easily compared with a company's credit terms if we convert it into a number of days, as is illustrated in the next ratio.

Number of Days' Sales in Accounts Receivable The **number of days' sales in accounts receivable** ratio is also called the *average collection period for accounts receivable*. Calculate it as follows:

$$\text{Number of days' sales in accounts receivable (average collection period for accounts receivable)} = \frac{\text{Number of days in year (365)}}{\text{Accounts receivable turnover}}$$

The turnover ratios for Colgate-Palmolive show that the number of days' sales in accounts receivable increased from about 42 days (365/8.65) in 1992 to 48 days (365/7.66) in 1993. The change means that the average collection period for the company's accounts receivable increased from 42 to 48 days. Possibly the worsening of the recession in 1993 was the cause.

An Accounting Perspective

Business Insight The number of days' sales in accounts receivable ratio measures the average liquidity of accounts receivable and indicates their quality. Generally, the shorter the collection period, the higher the quality of receivables. However, the average collection period varies by industry; for example, collection periods are short in utility companies and much longer in some retailing companies. A comparison of the average collection period with the credit terms extended customers by the company provides further insight into the quality of the accounts receivable. For example, receivables with terms of 2/10, n/30 and an average collection period of 75 days need to be investigated further. It is important to determine why customers are paying their accounts much later than expected.

Inventory Turnover A company's inventory turnover ratio shows the number of times its average inventory is sold during a period. You can calculate **inventory turnover** as follows:

$$\text{Inventory turnover} = \frac{\text{Cost of goods sold}}{\text{Average inventory}}$$

When comparing an income statement item and a balance sheet item, measure both in comparable dollars. Notice that we measure the numerator and denominator in cost rather than sales dollars. (Earlier, when calculating accounts receivable turnover, we measured both numerator and denominator in sales dollars.) Inventory turnover relates a measure of sales volume to the average amount of goods on hand to produce this sales volume.

Colgate-Palmolive's inventory on January 1, 1992, was $675.9 million. The following schedule shows that the inventory turnover increased slightly from 5.41 times per year in 1992 to 5.43 times per year in 1993. To convert these turnover ratios to the number of days it takes the company to sell its entire stock of inventory, divide 365 by the inventory turnover. Colgate-Palmolive's average inventory sold in about 67 days (365/5.43 and 365/5.41) in both 1993 and 1992.

($ millions)	1993	1992	Amount of Increase or (Decrease)
Cost of goods sold (a)	$3,729.9	$3,708.4	$21.5
Merchandise inventory:			
January 1	$ 695.6	$ 675.9	$19.7
December 31	678.0	695.6	(17.6)
Total (b)	$1,373.6	$1,371.5	$ 2.1
Average inventory (c) (b/2 = c)	$ 686.8	$ 685.8	
Turnover of inventory (a/c)	5.43	5.41	

Other things being equal, a manager who maintains the highest inventory turnover ratio is the most efficient. Yet, other things are not always equal. For example, a company that achieves a high inventory turnover ratio by keeping extremely small inventories on hand may incur larger ordering costs, lose quantity discounts, and lose sales due to lack of adequate inventory. In attempting to earn satisfactory income, management must balance the costs of inventory storage and obsolescence and the cost of tying up funds in inventory against possible losses of sales and other costs associated with keeping too little inventory on hand.

Total Assets Turnover **Total assets turnover** shows the relationship between the dollar volume of sales and the average total assets used in the business. We calculate it as follows:

$$\text{Total assets turnover} = \frac{\text{Net sales}}{\text{Average total assets}}$$

This ratio measures the efficiency with which a company uses its assets to generate sales. The larger the total assets turnover, the larger the income on each dollar invested in the assets of the business. For Colgate-Palmolive, the total asset turnover ratios for 1993 and 1992 follow. Total assets as of January 1, 1992, were $4,510.6 million.

($ millions)	1993	1992	Amount of Increase
Net sales (a)	$ 7,141.3	$7,007.2	$ 134.1
Total assets:			
January 1	$ 5,434.1	$4,510.6	$ 923.5
December 31	5,761.2	5,434.1	327.1
Total (b)	$11,195.3	$9,944.7	$1,250.6
Average total assets (c) (b/2 = c)	$ 5,597.7	$4,972.4	
Turnover of total assets (a/c)	1.28 : 1	1.41 : 1	

Each dollar of total assets produced $1.41 of sales in 1992 and $1.28 of sales in 1993. In other words, between 1992 and 1993, Colgate-Palmolive had a decrease of $.13 of sales per dollar of investment in assets.

Equity, or Long-Term Solvency, Ratios

Equity, or long-term solvency, ratios show the relationship between debt and equity financing in a company.

Equity (Stockholders' Equity) Ratio The two basic sources of assets in a business are owners (stockholders) and creditors; the combined interests of the two groups are *total equities*. In ratio analysis, however, the term *equity* generally refers only to stockholders' equity. Thus, the **equity (stockholders' equity) ratio** indicates the proportion of total assets (or total equities) provided by stockholders (owners) on any given date. The formula for the equity ratio is:

$$\text{Equity ratio} = \frac{\text{Stockholders' equity}}{\text{Total assets (or total equities)}}$$

Colgate-Palmolive's liabilities and stockholders' equity from Illustration 17.1 follow. Colgate-Palmolive's equity ratio decreased from 48.2% in 1992 to 32.5% in 1993. Illustration 17.1 shows that stockholders decreased their proportionate equity in the company's assets due largely to the reacquisition of preferred stock and the increase in dividends (which reduces retained earnings).

	December 31, 1993		December 31, 1992	
($ millions)	Amount	Percent	Amount	Percent
Current liabilities	$1,394.0	24.2%	$1,359.5	25.0%
Long-term liabilities	2,492.2	43.3	1,454.8	26.8
Total liabilities	$3,886.2	67.5	$2,814.3	51.8
Total stockholders' equity	1,875.0	32.5	$2,619.8	48.2
Total equity (equity to total assets)	$5,761.2	100.0%	$5,434.1	100.0%

The equity ratio must be interpreted carefully. From a creditor's point of view, a high proportion of stockholders' equity is desirable. A high equity ratio indicates the existence of a large protective buffer for creditors in the event a company suffers a loss. However, from an owner's point of view, a high proportion of stockholders' equity may or may not be desirable. If the business can use borrowed funds to generate income in excess of the net after-tax cost of the interest on such funds, a lower percentage of stockholders' equity may be desirable.

To illustrate the effect of higher leveraging (i.e., a larger proportion of debt), assume that Colgate-Palmolive could have financed an increase in its productive capacity with $40 million of 6% bonds instead of issuing 5 million additional shares of common stock. The effect on income for 1993 would be as follows, assuming a federal income tax rate of 40%:

Net income as presently stated (Illustration 17.4)	$189,900,000
Deduct additional interest on debt (0.06 × $40 million)	2,400,000
	$187,500,000
Add reduced taxes due to interest deduction (.4 × 2,400,000)	960,000
Adjusted net income	$188,460,000

As shown, increasing leverage by issuing bonds instead of common stock reduces net income. However, there are also fewer shares of common stock outstanding. Assume the company has 183 million shares of common stock outstanding. Earnings per share (EPS) with the additional debt would be $1.03 (or $188,460,000/183 million shares), and EPS with the additional stock would be $1.01 (or $189,900,000/188 million shares).

Since investors place heavy emphasis on EPS amounts, many companies in recent years have introduced large portions of debt into their capital structures to increase EPS, especially since interest rates were relatively low in the early 1990s.

We should point out, however, that too low a percentage of stockholders' equity (too much debt) has its dangers. Financial leverage magnifies losses per share as well as EPS since there are fewer shares of stock over which to spread the losses. A period of business recession may result in operating losses and shrinkage in the value of assets, such as receivables and inventory, which in turn may lead to an inability to meet fixed payments for interest and principal on the debt. As a result, the company may be forced into liquidation, and the stockholders could lose their entire investments.

Stockholders' Equity to Debt (Debt to Equity) Ratio Analysts express the relative equities of owners and creditors in several ways. To say that creditors held a 67.5% interest in the assets of Colgate-Palmolive on December 31, 1992, is equivalent to saying stockholders held a 32.5% interest. Another way of expressing this relationship is the **stockholders' equity to debt ratio:**

$$\text{Stockholders' equity to debt ratio} = \frac{\text{Stockholders' equity}}{\text{Total debt}}$$

Such a ratio for Colgate-Palmolive would be .93 : 1 (or $2,619.8 million/$2,814.3 million) on December 31, 1992, and .48 : 1 (or $1,875.0 million/$3,886.2 million) on December 31, 1993. This ratio is often inverted and called the **debt to equity ratio.** Some analysts use only long-term debt rather than total debt in calculating these ratios. These analysts do not consider short-term debt to be part of the capital structure since it is paid within one year.

Profitability Tests

Profitability is an important measure of a company's operating success. Generally, we are concerned with two areas when judging profitability: (1) relationships on the income statement that indicate a company's ability to recover costs and expenses, and (2) relationships of income to various balance sheet measures that indicate the company's relative ability to earn income on assets employed. Each of the following ratios utilizes one of these relationships.

Rate of Return on Operating Assets The best measure of earnings performance without regard to the sources of assets is the relationship of net operating income to operating assets, the **rate of return on operating assets.** This ratio shows the earning power of the company as a bundle of assets. By disregarding both nonoperating assets and nonoperating income elements, the rate of return on operating assets measures the profitability of the company in carrying out its primary business functions. We can break the ratio down into two elements—the operating margin and the turnover of operating assets.

Operating margin reflects the percentage of each dollar of net sales that becomes net operating income. Net operating income excludes **nonoperating income elements** such as extraordinary items, cumulative effect on prior years of changes in accounting principle, losses or gains from discontinued operations, interest revenue, and interest expense. Another name for net operating income is "income before interest and taxes" (IBIT). The formula for operating margin is:

$$\text{Operating margin} = \frac{\text{Net operating income}}{\text{Net sales}}$$

Turnover of operating assets shows the amount of sales dollars generated for each dollar invested in operating assets. **Operating assets** are all assets actively used in producing operating revenues. Typically, we use year-end operating assets, even though in theory an average would be better. **Nonoperating assets** are owned by a company but not used in producing operating revenues, such as land held for future use, a factory building rented to another company, and long-term bond investments.

Analysts do not use these nonoperating assets in evaluating earnings performance. Nor do they use total assets that include nonoperating assets not contributing to the generation of sales. The formula for the turnover of operating assets is:

$$\text{Turnover of operating assets} = \frac{\text{Net sales}}{\text{Operating assets}}$$

The rate of return on operating assets of a company is equal to its operating margin multiplied by turnover of operating assets. The more a company earns per dollar of sales and the more sales it makes per dollar invested in operating assets, the higher is the return per dollar invested. To find the rate of return on operating assets, use the following formulas:

$$\text{Rate of return on operating assets} = \text{Operating margin} \times \text{Turnover of operating assets}$$

or

$$\text{Rate of return on operating assets} = \frac{\text{Net operating income}}{\text{Net sales}} \times \frac{\text{Net sales}}{\text{Operating assets}}$$

Because net sales appears in both ratios (once as a numerator and once as a denominator), we can cancel it out, and the formula for rate of return on operating assets becomes:

$$\text{Rate of return on operating assets} = \frac{\text{Net operating income}}{\text{Operating assets}}$$

For analytical purposes, the formula should remain in the form that shows margin and turnover separately, since it provides more information.

The rates of return on operating assets for Colgate-Palmolive for 1993 and 1992 are:

($ millions)	1993	1992	Amount of Increase or (Decrease)
Net operating income (a)*	$ 883.0	$ 777.9	$105.1
Net sales (b)	$7,141.3	$7,007.2	$134.1
Operating assets (c)†	$5,761.2	$5,434.1	$327.1
Operating margin (a/b)	12.36%	11.10%	
Turnover of operating assets (b/c)	1.24 times	1.29 times	
Rate of return on operating assets (a/c)	15.33%	14.32%	

* Calculated as income before income taxes plus net interest expense. This method excludes nonoperating items.

† Colgate-Palmolive Company had no nonoperating assets, so we used total assets in the calculation.

An Accounting Perspective

Business Insight Companies that are to survive in the economy must attain some minimum rate of return on operating assets. However, they can attain this minimum rate of return in many different ways. To illustrate, consider a grocery store and a jewelry store, each with a rate of return of 8% on operating assets. The grocery store normally would attain this rate of return with a low margin and a high turnover, while the jewelry store would have a high margin and a low turnover, as shown here:

	Margin ×	Turnover =	Rate of Return on Operating Assets
Grocery store	1%	× 8.0 times =	8%
Jewelry store	20	× 0.4 =	8

Net Income to Net Sales (Return on Sales) Ratio Another measure of a company's profitability is the **net income to net sales** ratio, calculated as follows:

$$\text{Net income to net sales} = \frac{\text{Net income}}{\text{Net sales}}$$

This ratio measures the proportion of the sales dollar that remains after deducting all expenses. The computations for Colgate-Palmolive for 1993 and 1992 are:

($ millions)	1993	1992	Amount of Increase or (Decrease)
Net income (a)	$ 189.9	$ 477.0	$(287.1)
Net sales (b)	$7,141.3	$7,007.2	$ 134.1
Ratio of net income to net sales (a/b)	2.66%	6.81%	

Although the ratio of net income to net sales indicates the net amount of profit decreased on each sales dollar, exercise care in using and interpreting this ratio. The net income includes all nonoperating items that may occur only in a particular period; therefore, net income includes the effects of such things as extraordinary items, changes in accounting principle, effects of discontinued operations, and interest charges. Thus, a period that contains the effects of an extraordinary item is not comparable to a period that contains no extraordinary items. Also, since interest expense is deductible in the determination of net income while dividends are not, the methods used to finance a company's assets affect net income.

Illustration 17.10 shows graphically what net income to net sales for 1993 would have been without the decrease caused by the one-time cumulative effect on prior years of changes in accounting principle. By including this graph in its annual report, the company is showing that the "normal" return on sales increased steadily over the three years shown.

RETURN ON AVERAGE COMMON STOCKHOLDERS' EQUITY From the stockholders' point of view, an important measure of the income-producing ability of a company is the relationship of **return on average common stockholders' equity,** also called *rate of return on average common stockholders' equity,* or simply the **return on equity (ROE).** Although stockholders are interested in the ratio of operating income to operating assets as a measure of management's efficient use of assets, they are even more interested in the return the company earns on each dollar of stockholders' equity. The formula for return on average common stockholders' equity if no preferred stock is outstanding is:

$$\text{Return on average common stockholders' equity} = \frac{\text{Net income}}{\text{Average common stockholders' equity}}$$

When a company has preferred stock outstanding, the numerator of this ratio becomes net income minus the annual preferred dividends, and the denominator becomes the average book value of common stock. As described in Chapter 12, the book value of common stock is equal to total stockholders' equity minus

ILLUSTRATION 17.10
Return on Sales
(% to sales)

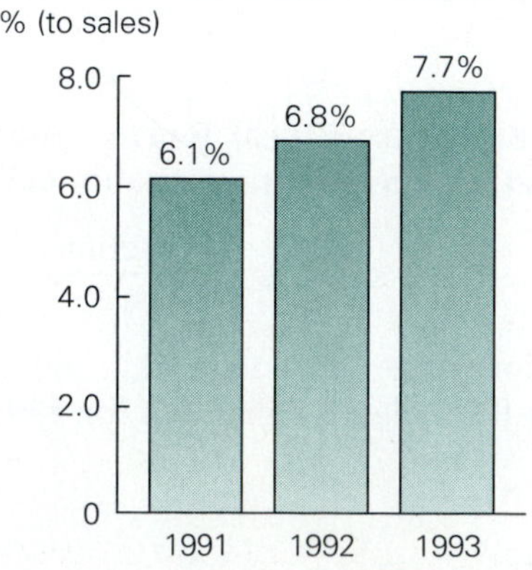

Excluding the impact of an accounting change in 1993 and a restructuring charge in 1991.

(1) the liquidation value (usually equal to par value) of preferred stock and (2) any dividends in arrears on cumulative preferred stock. Thus, the formula becomes:

$$\text{Return on average common stockholders' equity} = \frac{\text{Net income} - \text{Preferred stock dividends}}{\text{Average book value of common stock}}$$

The Colgate-Palmolive Company has preferred stock outstanding. The ratios for Colgate-Palmolive follow. Total common stockholders' equity on January 1, 1992, was $1,445.0 million.

($ millions)	1993	1992	Amount of Increase or (Decrease)
Net income − Preferred stock dividends (a)	$ 168.3	$ 456.3	$(288.0)
Total common stockholders' equity (book value of common stock):*			
January 1	$2,201.5	$1,445.0	$ 756.5
December 31	1,460.7	2,201.5	(740.8)
Total (b)	$3,662.2	$3,646.5	$ 15.7
Average common stockholder's equity: (c) (b/2 = c)	$1,831.1	$1,823.3	
Return on common stockholders' equity (a/c)	9.19%	25.03%	

* Total stockholders' equity − Par value of preferred stock

The stockholders would regard the decrease in the ratio from 25.03% to 9.19% unfavorably. This ratio indicates that for each dollar of capital invested by a common stockholder, the company earned slightly less than 10 cents in 1993.

AN ACCOUNTING PERSPECTIVE

BUSINESS INSIGHT Sometimes, two companies have the same return on assets but have different returns on stockholders' equity, as shown here:

	Company 1	Company 2
Return on assets	12.0%	12.0%
Return on stockholders' equity	6.4	8.0

The difference of 1.6% in Company 2's favor is the result of Company 2's use of borrowed funds, particularly long-term debt, in its capital structure. Use of these funds (or preferred stock with a fixed return) is called trading on the equity. When a company is trading profitably on the equity, it is generating a higher rate of return on its borrowed funds than it is paying for the use of the funds. The excess, in this case 1.6%, is accruing to the benefit of the common stockholders, because their earnings are being increased.

Companies that magnify the gains from this activity for the stockholders are using *leverage*. Using leverage is a risky process because losses also can be magnified, to the disadvantage of the common stockholders. We discussed trading on the equity and leverage in Chapter 15.

Reinforcing Problem
E17-4 Compute cash flow margin

CASH FLOW MARGIN The cash flow margin measures a company's overall efficiency and performance. The **cash flow margin** indicates the ability of a company to translate sales into cash. Measuring the amount of cash a company generates from every dollar of sales is important because a company needs cash to service debt, pay dividends, and invest in new capital assets. The formula for the cash flow margin is:

$$\text{Cash flow margin} = \frac{\text{Net cash provided by operating activities}}{\text{Net sales}}$$

Thus, we calculate Colgate-Palmolive's 1993 cash flow margin as follows:

$$\frac{\$710.4 \text{ million net cash provided by operating activities}}{\$7{,}141.3 \text{ million net sales}} = 9.95\%$$

Earnings per Share of Common Stock Probably the measure used most widely to appraise a company's operations is **earnings per share (EPS)** of common stock. EPS is equal to earnings available to common stockholders divided by the weighted-average number of shares of common stock outstanding. The financial press regularly publishes actual and forecasted EPS amounts for publicly traded corporations, together with period-to-period comparisons. The Accounting Principles Board noted the significance attached to EPS by requiring that such amounts be reported on the face of the income statement.[2] (Chapter 13 illustrates how earnings per share should be presented on the income statement.)

The calculation of EPS may be fairly simple or highly complex depending on a corporation's capital structure. A company has a simple capital structure if it has no outstanding securities (e.g., convertible bonds, convertible preferred stocks, warrants, or options) that can be exchanged for common stock. If a company has such securities outstanding, it has a complex capital structure.

A company with a simple capital structure reports a single EPS amount, which is calculated as follows:

$$\text{EPS of common stock} = \frac{\text{Earnings available to common stockholders}}{\text{Weighted-average number of common shares outstanding}}$$

The amount of earnings available to common stockholders is equal to net income minus the current year's preferred dividends, whether such dividends have been declared or not.

Determining the Weighted-Average Number of Common Shares The denominator in the EPS fraction is the weighted-average number of common shares outstanding for the period. If the number of common shares outstanding did not change during the period, the weighted-average number of common shares outstanding would, of course, be the number of common shares outstanding at the end of the period. The balance in the Common Stock account of Colgate-Palmolive (Illustration 17.1) was $183.2 million on December 31, 1993. The common stock had a $1 par value. Assuming no common shares were issued or redeemed during 1993, the weighted-average number of common shares outstanding would be 183.2 million (or $183.2 million/$1 per share). (Normally, common treasury stock reacquired and reissued are also included in the calculation of the weighted-average number of common shares outstanding. We ignore treasury stock transactions to simplify the illustrations.)

If the number of common shares changed during the period, such a change increases or decreases the capital invested in the company and should affect earnings available to stockholders. To compute the weighted-average number of common shares outstanding, we weight the change in the number of common shares by the portion of the year that those shares were outstanding. Shares are outstanding only during those periods that the related capital investment is available to produce income.

To illustrate, assume that during 1992 Colgate-Palmolive's common stock balance increased by $11.7 million (11.7 million shares). Assume that the company issued 9.5 million of these shares on April 1, 1992, and the other 2.2 million shares on October 1, 1992. The computation of the weighted-average number of common shares outstanding would be:

171.5 million shares × 1 year	171.5 million
9.5 million shares × ¾ year (April–December)	7.125 million
2.2 million shares × ¼ year (October–December)	.55 million
Weighted-average number of common shares outstanding	179.175 million

[2] Accounting Principles Board, *Opinion No. 15,* "Reporting Earnings per Share" (New York: AICPA, 1969), par. 12.

An alternate method looks at the total number of common shares outstanding, weighted by the portion of the year that the number of shares was outstanding, as follows:

171.5 million shares × ¼ year (January–March)	42.875 million
181.0 million shares × ½ year (April–September).	90.5 million
183.2 million shares × ¼ year (October–December)	45.8 million
Weighted-average number of shares outstanding	179.175 million

Another alternate method is:

171.5 million shares ×	3 months	=	514.5 million share-months
181.0 million shares ×	6 months	=	1,086.0 million share-months
183.2 million shares ×	3 months	=	549.6 million share-months
	12 months		2,150.1 million share-months

2,150.1 million share-months/12 months = 179.175 million shares

Note that all three methods yield the same result. In 1993, the balance in the common stock account did not change as it had during 1992. Therefore, the weighted-average number of common shares outstanding during 1993 is equal to the number of common shares issued, 183.2 million. The EPS of common stock for the Colgate-Palmolive Company are:

($ millions)	1993	1992	Amount of Increase or (Decrease)
Net income—preferred dividends (a)	$168.3	$456.3	$(288.0)
Average number of shares of common stock outstanding (b).	183.2	179.175	4.025
EPS of common stock (a/b)	$ 0.92	$ 2.55	

Colgate-Palmolive's stockholders would probably view the decrease of approximately 63.9% ([$0.92 − $2.55]/$2.55) in EPS from $2.55 to $0.92 unfavorably.

EPS and Stock Dividends or Splits Increases in shares outstanding as a result of a stock dividend or stock split do not require weighting for fractional periods. Such shares do not increase the capital invested in the business and, therefore, do not affect income. All that is required is to restate all prior calculations of EPS using the increased number of shares. For example, assume a company reported EPS for 1996 as $1 (or $100,000/100,000 shares) and earned $150,000 in 1997. The only change in common stock over the two years was a two-for-one stock split on December 1, 1997, which doubled the shares outstanding to 200,000. The firm would restate EPS for 1996 as $0.50 (or $100,000/200,000 shares) and as $0.75 ($150,000/200,000 shares) for 1997.

Primary EPS and Fully Diluted EPS In the merger wave of the 1960s, corporations often issued securities to finance their acquisitions of other companies. Many of the securities issued were *calls on common* or possessed *equity kickers*. These terms mean that the securities were convertible to, or exchangeable for, shares of their issuers' common stock. As a result, many complex problems arose in computing EPS. *APB Opinion No. 15* provides guidelines for solving these problems. A company with a complex capital structure must present at least two EPS calculations, primary EPS and fully diluted EPS. Because of the complexities involved in the calculations, we reserve further discussion of these two EPS calculations for an intermediate accounting text.

TIMES INTEREST EARNED RATIO Creditors, especially long-term creditors, want to know whether a borrower can meet its required interest payments when these payments come due. The **times interest earned ratio,** or *interest coverage ratio,* is an indication of such an ability. It is computed as follows:

$$\text{Times interest earned ratio} = \frac{\text{Income before interest and taxes (IBIT)}}{\text{Interest expense}}$$

The ratio is a rough comparison of cash inflows from operations with cash outflows for interest expense. Income before interest and taxes (IBIT) is the numerator because there would be no income taxes if interest expense is equal to or greater than IBIT. (To find income before interest and taxes, take net income from continuing operations and add back the net interest expense and taxes.) Analysts disagree on whether the denominator should be (1) only interest expense on long-term debt, (2) total interest expense, or (3) net interest expense. We will use net interest expense in the Colgate-Palmolive Company illustration.

For Colgate-Palmolive, the net interest expense is $46.8 million (interest expense of $69.5 less interest revenue of $22.7). With an IBIT of $883 million, the times interest earned ratio is 18.87, calculated as:

$$\frac{\$883}{\$46.8} = 18.87 \text{ times}$$

The company earned enough during the period to pay its interest expense almost 19 times over.

Illustration 17.11 shows earnings before interest and taxes for the Colgate-Palmolive Company for the years 1991–1993.

Low or negative interest coverage ratios suggest that the borrower could default on required interest payments. A company is not likely to continue interest payments over many periods if it fails to earn enough income to cover them. On the other hand, interest coverage of 10 to 20 times suggests that the company is not likely to default on interest payments. Colgate-Palmolive's interest coverage of 18.87 falls in this range.

Times Preferred Dividends Earned Ratio Preferred stockholders, like bondholders, must usually be satisfied with a fixed-dollar return on their investments. They are interested in the company's ability to make preferred dividend payments each year. We can measure this ability by computing the **times preferred dividends earned ratio** as follows:

$$\text{Times preferred dividends earned ratio} = \frac{\text{Net income}}{\text{Annual preferred dividends}}$$

Colgate-Palmolive has a net income of $189.9 million and preferred dividends of $21.6 million. The number of times the annual preferred dividends are earned for 1993 is:

$$\frac{\$189.9}{\$21.6} = 8.79:1, \text{ or } 8.79 \text{ times}$$

Illustration 17.11
Earnings before Interest and Taxes ($ millions)

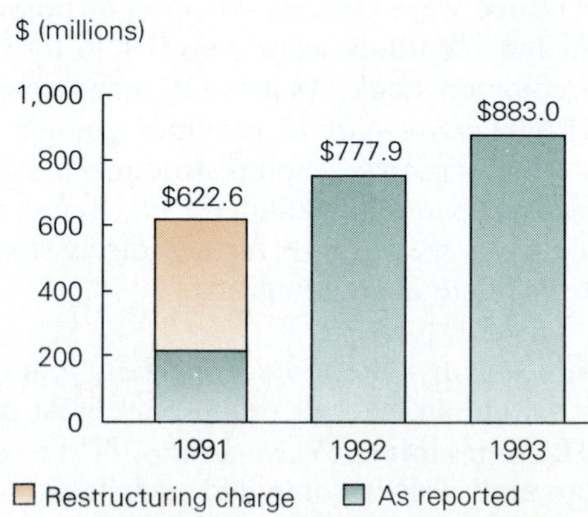

The higher this rate, the higher is the probability that the preferred stockholders will receive their dividends each year.

Market Tests

Analysts compute certain ratios using information from the financial statements and information about the market price of the company's stock. These tests help investors and potential investors assess the relative merits of the various stocks in the marketplace.

The **yield** on a stock investment refers to either an earnings yield or a dividends yield.

Earnings Yield on Common Stock You can calculate a company's earnings yield per share of common stock as follows:

$$\text{Earnings yield on common stock} = \frac{\text{EPS}}{\text{Current market price per share of common stock}}$$

Assume Colgate-Palmolive has common stock with an EPS of \$3.38 and that the quoted market price of the stock on the New York Stock Exchange is \$62.38. (We have excluded a mandated 1993 adjustment for accounting changes in using the \$3.38 EPS amount. See Illustration 17.12.) The **earnings yield on common stock** would be:

$$\frac{\$3.38}{\$62.38} = 5.42\%$$

Price-Earnings Ratio When inverted, the earnings yield on common stock is the **price-earnings ratio.** To compute the price-earnings ratio:

$$\text{Price-earnings ratio} = \frac{\text{Current market price per share of common stock}}{\text{EPS}} = \frac{\$62.38}{\$3.38} = 18.46:1$$

Investors would say that this stock is selling at 18 times earnings, or at a multiple of 18. These investors might have a specific multiple in mind that indicates whether the stock is underpriced or overpriced. Different investors have different estimates of the proper price-earnings ratio for a given stock and also different estimates of the future earnings prospects of the company. These different estimates may cause one investor to sell stock at a particular price and another investor to buy at that price.

Payout Ratio on Common Stock Using dividend yield, investors can compute the payout ratio on common stock. To calculate **payout ratio on common stock,**

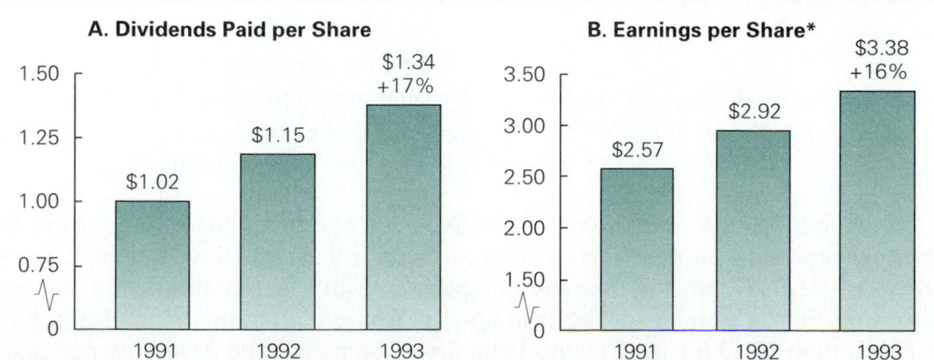

* Excluding the impact of an accounting change in 1993 and a restructuring charge in 1991.

Illustration 17.12
Dividends and Earnings per Share

divide the dividend per share of common stock ($1.34, per Illustration 17.12) by EPS. The payout ratio for Colgate-Palmolive's stock in 1993 is:

$$\text{Payout ratio on common stock} = \frac{\text{Dividend per share of common stock}}{\text{EPS}} = \frac{\$1.34}{\$3.38} = 39.6\%$$

A payout ratio of 39.6% means that the company paid out 39.6% of its earnings in the form of dividends. (If preferred dividends had been deducted in calculating EPS, EPS would have been about $3.25, and the payout ratio would have been 41.2%.) Some investors are attracted by the stock of companies that pay out a large percentage of their earnings. Other investors are attracted by the stock of companies that retain and reinvest a large percentage of their earnings. The tax status of the investor has a great deal to do with this preference. Investors in high tax brackets often prefer to have the company reinvest the earnings with the expectation that this reinvestment results in share price appreciation.

Dividend Yield on Common Stock The dividend paid per share of common stock is also of much interest to common stockholders. When the current annual dividend per share of common stock is divided by the current market price per share of common stock, the result is called the **dividend yield on common stock.** Colgate-Palmolive Company's December 31, 1993, common stock price was $62.38 per share. Its dividends per share were $1.34. The company's dividend yield on common stock was:

$$\text{Dividend yield on common stock} = \frac{\text{Dividend per share of common stock}}{\text{Current market price per share of common stock}} = \frac{\$1.34}{\$62.38} = 2.15\%$$

Dividend Yield on Preferred Stock Preferred stockholders, as well as common stockholders, are interested in dividend yields. The computation of the **dividend yield on preferred stock** is similar to the common stock dividend yield computation. Considering Colgate-Palmolive's $4.25 dividend per share of preferred stock with a current market price of $73.50 per share, we compute the dividend yield on preferred stock as follows:

$$\text{Dividend yield on preferred stock} = \frac{\text{Dividend per share of preferred stock}}{\text{Current market price per share of preferred stock}} = \frac{\$4.25}{\$73.50} = 5.78\%$$

Through the use of dividend yield rates, we can compare different preferred stocks having different annual dividends and different market prices.

Cash Flow per Share of Common Stock Investors calculate the **cash flow per share of common stock** ratio as follows:

$$\text{Cash flow per share of common stock} = \frac{\text{Net cash provided by operating activities}}{\text{Average number of shares of common stock outstanding}}$$

Currently, *FASB Statement No. 95* does not permit the use of this ratio for external reporting purposes. However, some mortgage and investment banking firms do use this ratio to judge the company's ability to pay dividends and pay liabilities. For an example of the cash flow per share of common stock ratio, look at Illustration 17.13 for the Colgate-Palmolive Company. The cash flow per share of common stock has increased steadily over the period 1991–1993.

ILLUSTRATION 17.13
Colgate-Palmolive Company's Cash Flow per Share of Common Stock

($ million, except per share data)	Fiscal Year 1993	1992	1991
Operating cash flow data:			
Net income	$189.9	$477.0	$124.9
Cumulative effect on prior years of accounting changes	358.2		
Restructured operations, net	(77.0)	(92.0)	319.0
Depreciation and amortization	209.6	192.5	146.2
Deferred income taxes and other liabilities	53.6	(25.8)	(38.4)
Cash effect of changes in:			
Receivables	(103.6)	(38.0)	(58.2)
Inventories	31.7	28.4	45.8
Other current assets	(4.6)	10.6	(11.9)
Payables and accruals	52.6	(10.0)	(41.7)
Cash provided by operating activities (a)	$710.4	$542.7	$485.7
Average shares outstanding (b)	149.3	160.2	147.3
Cash flow per share of common stock (a) ÷ (b)	$4.76	$3.39	$3.30

A Broader Perspective

BellSouth Corporation

The following data are typical of those provided by companies in their annual reports to stockholders:

($ millions, except per share amounts)	1991	1990	1989	1988	1987
Operating revenues	$14,445.5	$14,345.4	$13,996.3	$13,596.9	$12,229.9
Operating expenses	11,641.3	11,314.7	10,999.3	10,557.2	9,027.8
Net income	1,471.5	1,631.5	1,741.1	1,665.5	1,664.8
Earnings per share	3.04	3.38	3.64	3.51	3.46
Dividends per share	2.76	2.68	2.52	2.36	2.20
Book value per share	26.93	26.28	27.21	25.52	24.89
Weighted-average common shares outstanding (millions)	484.3	482.4	477.7	474.9	481.2
Total assets	$30,941.7	$30,206.8	$30,049.8	$28,472.4	$27,416.5
Capital expenditures	3,102.4	3,190.7	3,222.6	3,207.3	3,058.6
Return to average common equity	11.3%	12.8%	13.7%	13.8%	14.2%
Debt ratio	41.3%	40.7%	38.0%	39.8%	37.3%
Employees (end of year)	96,084	101,945	101,230	100,280	98,700
Telephone employees (end of year)	82,245	85,967	86,728	88,801	87,560

Earnings per Share
$ (per share)

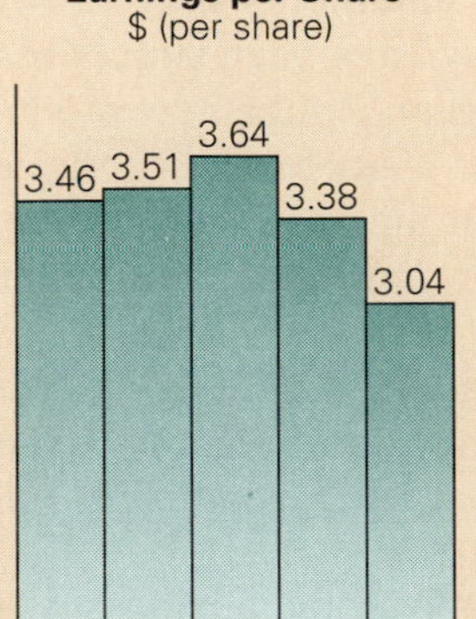

Earnings per share of $3.04 in 1991 included one-time charges of $0.21.

Net Income
$ (in billions)

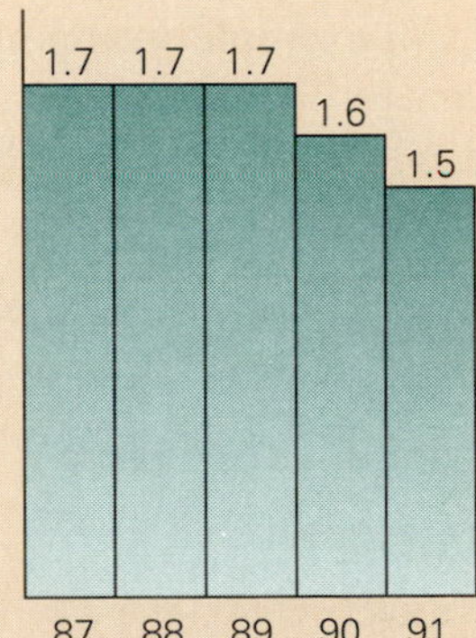

Rate reductions totaling $327 million had a significant impact on 1991 earnings.

Dividends per Share
$ (per share)

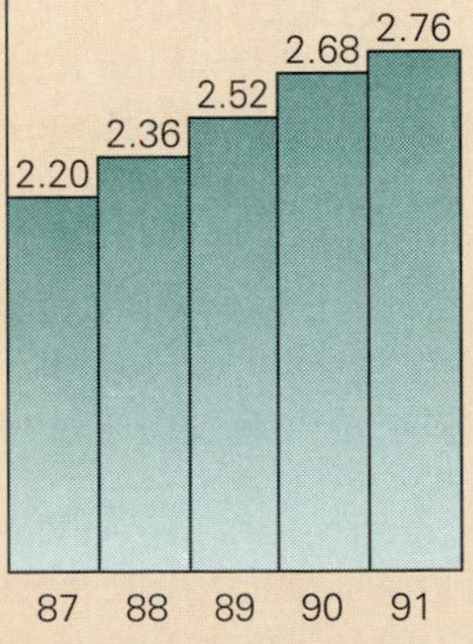

BellSouth increased the dividend in 1991 for the seventh consecutive year.

Access Lines in Service
(in millions)

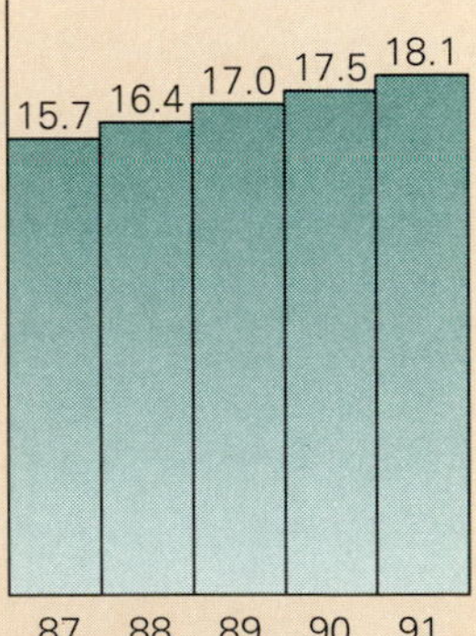

Telephone access lines increased 3.2 percent during 1991, highest growth rate in the nation.

Final Considerations in Financial Statement Analysis

Objective 5
Describe the considerations used in financial statement analysis.

Standing alone, a single financial ratio may not be informative. Investors gain greater insight by computing and analyzing several related ratios for a company. Illustration 17.14 summarizes the ratios presented in this chapter, and Illustration 17.15 presents them graphically.

Financial analysis relies heavily on informed judgment. As guides to aid comparison, percentages and ratios are useful in uncovering potential strengths and weaknesses. However, the financial analyst should seek the basic causes behind changes and established trends.

An Accounting Perspective

Uses of Technology Most companies calculate some of the ratios we have discussed, if not all of them. To efficiently and effectively perform these calculations, accountants use computers. Some programs that gather information in the preparation of financial statements calculate the ratios at the end of a period. Accountants also create spreadsheets to perform this task. Remember, to interpret the numbers correctly, investors and management must compare these ratios with the industry in which the company operates.

Need for Comparable Data

Analysts must be sure that their comparisons are valid—especially when the comparisons are of items for different periods or different companies. They must follow consistent accounting practices if valid interperiod comparisons are to be made. Comparable intercompany comparisons are more difficult to secure. Accountants cannot do much more than disclose the fact that one company is using FIFO and another is using LIFO for inventory and cost of goods sold computations. Such a disclosure alerts analysts that intercompany comparisons of inventory turnover ratios, for example, may not be comparable.

Also, when comparing a company's ratios to industry averages provided by an external source such as Dun & Bradstreet, the analyst should calculate the company's ratios in the same manner as the reporting service. Thus, if Dun & Bradstreet uses net sales (rather than cost of goods sold) to compute inventory turnover, so should the analyst. Net sales is sometimes preferable because all companies do not compute and report cost of goods sold amounts in the same manner.

Influence of External Factors

Facts and conditions not disclosed by the financial statements may, however, affect their interpretation. A single important event may have been largely responsible for a given relationship. For example, competitors may put a new product on the market, making it necessary for the company under study to reduce the selling price of a product suddenly rendered obsolete. Such an event would severely affect the percentage of gross margin to net sales. Yet there may be little chance that such an event will happen again.

Analysts must consider general business conditions within the industry of the company under study. A corporation's downward trend in earnings, for example, is less alarming if the industry trend or the general economic trend is also downward.

Investors also need to consider the seasonal nature of some businesses. If the balance sheet date represents the seasonal peak in the volume of business, for example, the ratio of current assets to current liabilities may be much lower than if the balance sheet date is in a season of low activity.

Potential investors should consider the market risk associated with the prospective investment. They can determine market risk by comparing the changes in

ILLUSTRATION 17.14 Summary of Ratios

Liquidity Ratios	**Formula**	**Significance**
Current, or working capital, ratio	Current assets ÷ Current liabilities	Test of debt-paying ability
Acid-test (quick) ratio	Quick assets (Cash + Marketable securities + Net receivables) ÷ Current liabilities	Test of immediate debt-paying ability
Cash flow liquidity ratio	(Cash and marketable securities + Net cash provided by operating activities) ÷ Current liabilities	Test of short-term, debt-paying ability
Accounts receivable turnover	Net credit sales (or net sales) ÷ Average net accounts receivable	Test of quality of accounts receivable
Number of days' sales in accounts receivable (average collection period of accounts receivable)	Number of days in year (365) ÷ Accounts receivable turnover	Test of quality of accounts receivable
Inventory turnover	Cost of goods sold ÷ Average inventory	Test of whether or not a sufficient volume of business is being generated relative to inventory
Total assets turnover	Net sales ÷ Average total assets	Test of whether or not the volume of business generated is adequate relative to amount of capital invested in the business
Equity, or Long-Term Solvency, Ratios		
Equity (stockholders' equity) ratio	Stockholders' equity ÷ Total assets (or total equities)	Index of long-run solvency and safety
Stockholders' equity to debt (debt to equity) ratio	Stockholders' equity ÷ Total debt	Measure of the relative proportion of stockholders' and of creditors' equities
Profitability Tests		
Rate of return on operating assets	Net operating income ÷ Operating assets or Operating margin × Turnover of operating assets	Measure of managerial effectiveness
Net income to net sales (return on sales)	Net income ÷ Net sales	Indicator of the amount of net profit on each dollar of sales
Return on average common stockholders' equity	Net income ÷ Average common stockholders' equity	Measure of what a given company earned for its stockholders from all sources as a percentage of the common stockholders' investment
Cash flow margin	Net cash provided by operating activities ÷ Net sales	Measure of the ability of a firm to translate sales into cash
EPS of common stock	Earnings available to common stockholders ÷ Weighted-average number of common shares outstanding	Measure of the return to investors
Times interest earned ratio	Income before interest and taxes ÷ Interest expense	Test of the likelihood that creditors will continue to receive their interest payments
Times preferred dividends earned ratio	Net income ÷ Annual preferred dividends	Test of the likelihood that preferred stockholders will receive their dividend each year
Market Tests		
Earnings yield on common stock	EPS ÷ Current market price per share of common stock	Comparison with other common stocks
Price-earnings ratio	Current market price per share of common stock ÷ EPS	Index of whether a stock is relatively cheap or expensive based on the ratio
Payout ratio on common stock	Dividend per share of common stock ÷ EPS	Index of whether company pays out a large percentage of earnings as dividends or reinvests most of its earnings
Dividend yield on common stock	Dividend per share of common stock ÷ Current market price per share of common stock	Comparisons with other common stocks
Dividend yield on preferred stock	Dividend per share of preferred stock ÷ Current market price per share of preferred stock	Comparison with other preferred stocks
Cash flow per share of common stock	Net cash provided by operating activities ÷ Average number of shares of common stock outstanding	Test of ability to pay dividends and liabilities

ILLUSTRATION 17.15 Graphic Depiction of Financial Statement Analysis Utilizing Financial Ratios

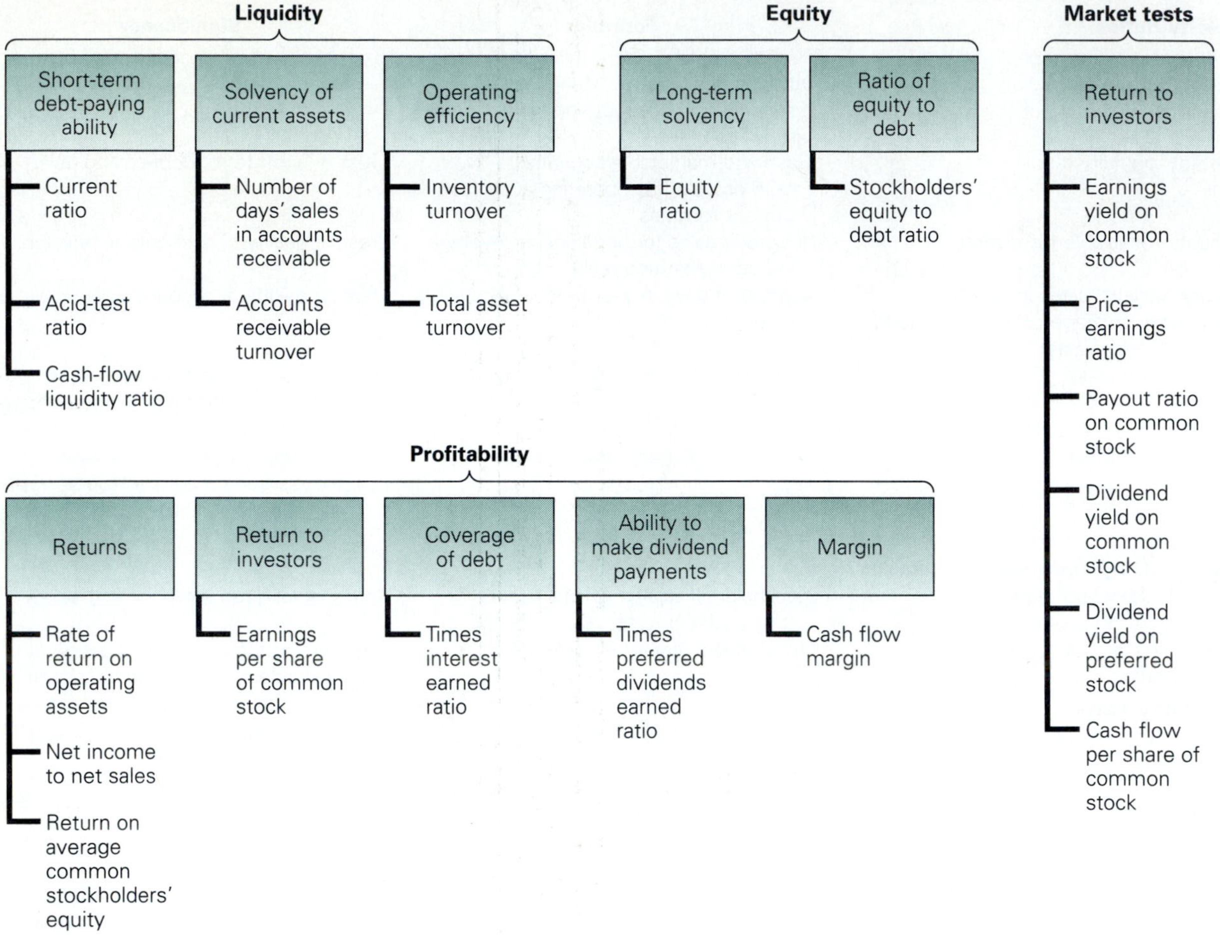

Liquidity
Short-term debt-paying ability
Current ratio
Acid-test ratio
Cash-flow liquidity ratio
Solvency of current assets
Number of days' sales in accounts receivable
Accounts receivable turnover
Operating efficiency
Inventory turnover
Total asset turnover
Equity
Long-term solvency
Equity ratio
Ratio of equity to debt
Stockholders' equity to debt ratio
Market tests
Return to investors
Earnings yield on common stock
Price-earnings ratio
Payout ratio on common stock
Dividend yield on common stock
Dividend yield on preferred stock
Cash flow per share of common stock
Profitability
Returns
Rate of return on operating assets
Net income to net sales
Return on average common stockholders' equity
Return to investors
Earnings per share of common stock
Coverage of debt
Times interest earned ratio
Ability to make dividend payments
Times preferred dividends earned ratio
Margin
Cash flow margin

ILLUSTRATION 17.16
Five-Year Cumulative Total Return*

$
300
250
200
150
100
1988
1989
1990
1991
1992
1993
$302 Colgate–Palmolive
$237 Peer Group†
$197 S & P 500

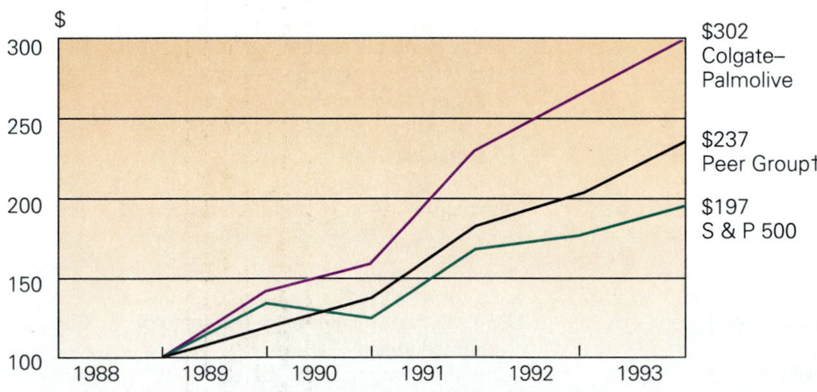

* $100 invested on 12/31/88 including reinvestment of dividends.
† The Peer Group index consists of Avon Products, Clorox Company, The Dial Corp., Dow Chemical, Eastman Kodak, Gillette Company, Ralston Purina, Procter & Gamble, Quaker Oats, and Unilever N.V.

the price of a stock in relation to the changes in the average price of all stocks. Illustration 17.16 shows the performance of Colgate-Palmolive Company's stock compared to its peer group of companies and Standard & Poor's 500 group of companies.

Potential investors should realize that acquiring the ability to make informed judgments is a long process and does not occur overnight. Using ratios and percentages without considering the underlying causes may lead to incorrect conclusions.

Need for Standards of Comparison

Relationships between financial statement items also become more meaningful when standards are available for comparison. Comparisons with standards provide a starting point for the analyst's thinking and lead to further investigation and, ultimately, to conclusions and business decisions. Such standards consist of (1) those in the analyst's own mind as a result of experience and observations, (2) those provided by the records of past performance and financial position of the business under study, and (3) those provided about other enterprises. Examples of the third standard are data available through trade associations, universities, research organizations (such as Dun & Bradstreet and Robert Morris Associates), and governmental units (such as the Federal Trade Commission).

In financial statement analysis, remember that standards for comparison vary by industry, and financial analysis must be carried out with knowledge of specific industry characteristics. For example, a wholesale grocery company would have large inventories available to be shipped to retailers and a relatively small investment in property, plant, and equipment, while an electric utility company would have no merchandise inventory (except for repair parts) and a large investment in property, plant, and equipment.

Even within an industry, variations may exist. Acceptable current ratios, gross margin percentages, debt to equity ratios, and other relationships vary widely depending on unique conditions within an industry. Therefore, it is important to know the industry to make comparisons that have real meaning.

This chapter concludes our coverage of financial accounting. Chapter 18 is the first of our chapters on *managerial* accounting. However, you should realize that it is impossible to completely separate financial and managerial accounting information into neat packages. Managers use both the published financial statements and managerial accounting information in making decisions. Also, some of the concepts covered in managerial accounting (e.g., job costing and process costing) have a direct impact on the formal financial statements. Many accountants are attracted to managerial accounting because it is not constrained by having to conform to generally accepted accounting principles. Instead, management accountants can provide to management whatever information in whatever form management requests.

UNDERSTANDING THE LEARNING OBJECTIVES

Objective 1
Describe and explain the objectives of financial statement analysis.

- A company's financial statements are analyzed internally by management and externally by investors, creditors, and regulatory agencies.
- Management's analysis of financial statements primarily relates to parts of the company. Management is able to obtain specific, special-purpose reports to aid in decision making.
- External users focus their analysis of financial statements on the company as a whole. They must rely on the general-purpose financial statements that companies publish.
- Financial statement analysis consists of applying analytical tools and techniques to financial statements and other relevant data to obtain useful information.
- This information is the significant relationships between data and trends in those data assessing the company's past performance and current financial position.
- The information is useful for making predictions that may have a direct effect on decisions made by many users of financial statements.
- Present and potential company investors use this information to assess the profitability of the firm.

- Outside parties and long-term creditors sometimes are interested in a company's solvency, and thus use the information in predicting the company's solvency.

Objective 2
Describe the sources of information for financial statement analysis.

- Published reports are one source of financial information. Published reports include financial statements, explanatory notes, letters to stockholders, reports of independent accountants, and management's discussion and analysis (MDA).
- Government reports are another source of financial information and include Form 10-K, Form 10-Q, and Form 8-K. These reports are available to the public for a small charge.
- Financial service information, business publications, newspapers, and periodicals offer meaningful financial information to external users. Moody's Investors Services; Standard & Poor's; Dun & Bradstreet, Inc.; and Robert Morris Associates all provide useful industry information. Business publications, such as *The Wall Street Journal* and *Forbes,* also report industry financial news.

Objective 3
Calculate and explain changes in financial statements using horizontal analysis, vertical analysis, and trend analysis.

- Horizontal analysis is the calculation of dollar changes or percentage changes in comparative statement items or totals. Use of this analysis helps detect changes in a company's performance and highlights trends.
- Vertical analysis consists of a study of a single financial statement in which each item is expressed as a percentage of a significant total. Use of this analysis is especially helpful in analyzing income statement data such as the percentage of cost of goods sold to sales or the percentage of gross margin to sales.
- Trend analysis compares financial information over time to a base year. The analysis is calculated by:
  1. Selecting a base year or period.
  2. Assigning a weight of 100% to the amounts appearing on the base-year financial statements.
  3. Expressing the corresponding amounts shown on the other years' financial statements as a percentage of base-year or period amounts. The percentages are computed by dividing nonbase-year amounts by the corresponding base-year amounts and then multiplying the results by 100.

  Trend analysis indicates changes that are taking place in an organization and highlights the direction of these changes.

Objective 4
Perform ratio analysis on financial statements using liquidity ratios, long-term solvency ratios, profitability tests, and market tests.

- **Liquidity ratios** indicate a company's short-term debt-paying ability. These ratios include (1) current, or working capital, ratio; (2) acid-test (quick) ratio; (3) cash flow liquidity ratio; (4) accounts receivable turnover; (5) number of days' sales in accounts receivable; (6) inventory turnover; and (7) total assets turnover.
- **Equity, or long-term solvency, ratios** show the relationship between debt and equity financing in a company. These ratios include (1) equity (stockholders' equity) ratio and (2) stockholders' equity to debt ratio.
- **Profitability tests** are an important measure of a company's operating success. These tests include (1) rate of return on operating assets, (2) net income to net sales, (3) net income to average common stockholders' equity, (4) cash flow margin, (5) earnings per share of common stock, (6) times interest earned ratio, and (7) times preferred dividends earned ratio.
- **Market tests** help investors and potential investors assess the relative merits of the various stocks in the marketplace. These tests include (1) earnings yield on common stock, (2) price-earnings ratio, (3) dividend yield on common stock, (4) payout ratio on common stock, (5) dividend yield on preferred stock, and (6) cash flow per share of common stock.
- For a complete summary and a graphic depiction of all liquidity, long-term solvency, profitability, and market test ratios, see Illustrations 17.14 and 17.15.

Objective 5
Describe the considerations used in financial statement analysis.

- **Need for comparative data:** Analysts must be sure that their comparisons are valid—especially when the comparisons are of items for different periods or different companies.
- **Influence of external factors:** A single important event, such as the unexpected placing of a product on the market by a competitor, may affect the interpretation of the financial statements. Also, the general business conditions and the possible seasonal nature of the business must be taken into consideration, since these factors could have an impact on the financial statements.

- **Impact of inflation:** Since financial statements fail to reveal the impact of inflation on the reporting entity, one must make sure that the items being compared are all comparable; that is, the impact of inflation has been taken into consideration.
- **Need for comparative standards:** In financial statement analysis, remember that standards for comparison vary by industry, and financial analysis must be carried out with knowledge of specific industry characteristics.

DEMONSTRATION PROBLEM 17–A

Comparative financial statements of Kellogg Company for 1991 and 1992 follow:

Kellogg Company
Kellogg Company is one of the world's largest breakfast cereal companies.

KELLOGG COMPANY
Comparative Income Statements
For the Years Ended December 31, 1991, and 1992
($ millions)

	1992	1991
Net revenues	$6,227.4	$5,801.2
Cost of goods sold	2,987.7	2,828.7
Gross margin	$3,239.7	$2,972.5
Operating expenses	2,140.1	1,930.0
Nonoperating expense (interest)	29.2	58.3
Income before income taxes	$1,070.4	$ 984.2
Income taxes	387.6	378.2
Net income before effect of accounting change	$ 682.8	$ 606.0
Cumulative effect of accounting change	(251.6)	0
Net earnings	$ 431.2	$ 606.0

KELLOGG COMPANY
Comparative Balance Sheets
December 31, 1992,and 1991
($ millions)

	1992	1991
Assets		
Cash and temporary investments	$ 126.3	$ 178.0
Accounts receivable, net	519.1	420.0
Inventories	416.4	401.1
Deferred income taxes	66.2	63.5
Prepaid expenses	108.6	110.4
Property, net	2,662.7	2,646.5
Intangible assets	53.3	49.8
Other assets	62.4	56.5
Total assets	$4,015.0	$3,925.8
Liabilities and Stockholders' Equity		
Current liabilities	$1,071.0	$1,324.4
Long-term liabilities	998.8	441.6
Common stock	77.5	77.4
Capital in excess of par value	69.2	60.2
Retained earnings	3,033.9	2,889.1
Treasury stock	(1,105.0)	(880.9)
Currency translation adjustment	(130.4)	14.0
Total liabilities and stockholders' equity	$4,015.0	$3,925.8

Required

a. Prepare comparative common-size income statements for 1992 and 1991.

b. Perform a horizontal analysis of the comparative balance sheets.

c. Comment on the results of **a** and **b**.

Solution to Demonstration Problem 17–A

a.

KELLOGG COMPANY
Common-Size Comparative Income Statements
For the Years Ended December 31, 1991, and 1992

	Percent	
	1992	**1991**
Net revenues	100.00%	100.00%
Cost of goods sold	47.98	48.76
Gross margin	52.02%	51.24%
Operating expenses	34.37	33.27
Nonoperating expense (interest)	0.47	1.00
Income before income taxes	17.19%*	16.97%
Income taxes	6.22	6.52
Net income before effect of accounting change	10.96%*	10.45%
Cumulative effect of accounting change	−4.04	0.00
Net earnings	6.92%	10.45%

* Difference due to rounding.

b.

KELLOGG COMPANY
Comparative Balance Sheets
December 31, 1992, and 1991
($ millions)

			Increase or Decrease	
	1992	**1991**	**1992 Amount**	**1991 Percent**
Assets				
Cash and temporary investments	$ 126.3	$ 178.0	$(51.7)	(29.04)%
Accounts receivable, net	519.1	420.0	99.1	23.60
Inventories	416.4	401.1	15.3	3.81
Deferred income taxes	66.2	63.5	2.7	4.25
Prepaid expenses	108.6	110.4	(1.8)	(1.63)
Property, net	2,662.7	2,646.5	16.2	0.61
Intangible assets	53.3	49.8	3.5	7.03
Other assets	62.4	56.5	5.9	10.44
Total assets	$4,015.0	$3,925.8	$89.2	2.27%
Liabilities and Stockholders' Equity				
Current liabilities	$1,071.0	$1,324.4	$(253.4)	(19.13)%
Long-term liabilities	998.8	441.6	557.2	126.18
Common stock	77.5	77.4	0.1	0.13
Capital in excess of par value	69.2	60.2	9.0	14.95
Retained earnings	3,033.9	2,889.1	144.8	5.01
Treasury stock	(1,105.0)	(880.9)	(224.1)	25.44
Currency translation adjustment	(130.4)	14.0	(144.4)	(1,031.43)
Total liabilities and stockholders' equity	$4,015.0	$3,925.8	$ 89.2	2.27%

c. The $426.2 million increase in net revenues yielded a $267.2 million increase in gross margin because the gross margin rate rose from 51.24% to 52.02%. Operating expenses increased as a percentage of sales from 33.27% to 34.37%; however, the increase in gross margin coupled with the smaller increase in expenses yielded an overall increase in net income before the effect of the accounting changes. (The cumulative effect of accounting changes will probably not exist in the forthcoming year. When analyzing Kellogg's performance in 1992, an investor should note this fact.)

The balance sheet of Kellogg Company changed significantly. The company probably financed increases in accounts receivable, inventories, and property through decreased cash and increased long-term liabilities and retained earnings. The recession may have been responsible for the huge increase in 1992 in accounts receivable (slower collections).

DEMONSTRATION PROBLEM 17–B

Xerox
Xerox Corporation is a global enterprise serving the document processing market.

The balance sheet and supplementary data for Xerox Corporation follow:

XEROX CORPORATION
Balance Sheet with IOFS on an Equity Basis
December 31, 1992
($ millions)

	1992
Assets	
Cash	$ 2
Accounts receivable, net	1,751
Finance receivables, net	3,162
Inventories	2,257
Deferred taxes and other current assets	864
Total current assets	$ 8,036
Finance receivables due after one year, net	$ 5,337
Land, buildings, and equipment, net	2,150
Investments in affiliates, at equity	957
Investment in insurance and other financial services, net	2,955
Investment in discontinued operations, net	1,171
Other assets	660
Total assets	$21,266
Liabilities and Shareholders' Equity	
Short-term debt and current portion of long-term debt	$ 2,533
Accounts payable	544
Accrued compensation and benefit costs	722
Unearned income	363
Other current liabilities	1,296
Total current liabilities	$ 5,458
Long-term debt	$ 8,105
Liabilities for postretirement medical benefits	927
Deferred taxes and other liabilities	1,625
Deferred ESOP benefits	(681)
Minorities' interests in equity of subsidiaries	885
Preferred stock	1,072
Common shareholders' equity (108.1 million)	3,875
Total liabilities and shareholders' equity	$21,266

Supplementary data for 1992 (in millions)

1. Net loss, $1,020.
2. Cost of goods sold, $4,033.
3. Net sales, $14,681.
4. Inventory, January 1, $2,091.
5. Net interest expense, $570.
6. Net income before interest and taxes, $43.
7. Net accounts receivable on January 1, $1,781.
8. Total assets on January 1, $20,624.

Required

Compute the following ratios:

a. Current ratio.
b. Acid-test ratio.
c. Accounts receivable turnover.
d. Inventory turnover.
e. Total assets turnover.
f. Equity ratio.
g. EPS of common stock.
h. Times interest earned ratio.

Solution to Demonstration Problem 17–B

a. Current ratio:

$$\frac{\text{Current assets}}{\text{Current liabilities}} = \frac{\$8{,}036{,}000{,}000}{\$5{,}458{,}000{,}000} = 1.47:1$$

b. Acid-test ratio:

$$\frac{\text{Quick assets}}{\text{Current liabilities}} = \frac{\$4{,}915{,}000{,}000}{\$5{,}458{,}000{,}000} = .9:1$$

c. Accounts receivable turnover:

$$\frac{\text{Net sales}}{\text{Average net accounts receivable}} = \frac{\$14{,}681{,}000{,}000}{\$1{,}766{,}000{,}000} = 8.3 \text{ times}$$

d. Inventory turnover:

$$\frac{\text{Cost of goods sold}}{\text{Average inventory}} = \frac{\$4{,}033{,}000{,}000}{\$2{,}174{,}000{,}000} = 1.86 \text{ times}$$

e. Total assets turnover:

$$\frac{\text{Net sales}}{\text{Average total assets}} = \frac{\$14{,}681{,}000{,}000}{\$20{,}945{,}000{,}000} = .7 \text{ times}$$

f. Equity ratio:

$$\frac{\text{Stockholders' equity}}{\text{Total assets}} = \frac{\$4{,}947{,}000{,}000}{\$21{,}266{,}000{,}000} = 23.26\%$$

g. EPS of common stock:

$$\frac{\text{Earnings available to common stockholders}}{\text{Weighted-average number of common shares outstanding}} = \$0 \text{ because of net loss of } \$1{,}020{,}000{,}000$$

h. Times interest earned ratio:

$$\frac{\text{Income before interest and taxes}}{\text{Interest expense}} = \frac{\$43{,}000{,}000}{\$570{,}000{,}000} = .075:1, \text{ or } .075 \text{ times}$$

New Terms

Accounts receivable turnover Net credit sales (or net sales) divided by average net accounts receivable. *630*

Acid-test (quick) ratio Ratio of quick assets (cash, marketable securities, and net receivables) to current liabilities. *629*

Cash flow liquidity ratio Cash and marketable securities plus net cash provided by operating activities divided by current liabilities. *629*

Cash flow margin Net cash provided by operating activities divided by net sales. *637*

Cash flow per share of common stock Net cash provided by operating activities divided by the average number of shares of common stock outstanding. *642*

Common-size statements Show only percentages and no absolute dollar amounts. *622*

Comparative financial statements Present the same company's financial statements for two or more successive periods in side-by-side columns. *622*

Current ratio Also called *working capital ratio*. Current assets divided by current liabilities. *628*

Debt to equity ratio Total debt divided by stockholders' equity. *634*

Dividend yield on common stock Dividend per share of common stock divided by current market price per share of common stock. *642*

Dividend yield on preferred stock Dividend per share of preferred stock divided by current market price per share of preferred stock. *642*

Earnings per share (EPS) The amount of earnings available to common stockholders (which equals net income less preferred dividends) divided by weighted-average number of shares of common stock outstanding. *638*

Earnings yield on common stock Ratio of current EPS to current market price per share of common stock. *641*

Equity (stockholders' equity) ratio The ratio of stockholders' equity to total assets (or total equities). *632*

Horizontal analysis Analysis of a company's financial statements for two or more successive periods showing percentage and/or absolute changes from prior year. This type of analysis helps detect changes in a company's performance and highlights trends. *622*

Inventory turnover Cost of goods sold divided by average inventory. *631*

Liquidity Company's state of possessing liquid assets, such as (1) cash and (2) other assets that will soon be converted to cash. *621*

Net income to net sales Net income divided by net sales. *635*

Nonoperating assets Assets owned by a company but not used in producing operating revenues. *634*

Nonoperating income elements Elements excluded from net operating income because they are not directly related to operations; includes such elements as extraordinary items, cumulative effect on prior year of changes in accounting principle, losses or gains from discontinued operations, interest revenue, and interest expense. *634*

Number of days' sales in accounts receivable The number of days in a year (365) divided by the accounts receivable turnover. Also called the **average collection period for accounts receivable.** *631*

Operating assets All assets actively used in producing operating revenues. *634*

Operating margin Net operating income divided by net sales. *634*

Payout ratio on common stock The ratio of dividends per share of common stock divided by EPS. *641*

Price-earnings ratio The ratio of current market price per share of common stock divided by the EPS of the stock. *641*

Rate of return on operating assets (Net operating income ÷ Net sales) × (Net sales ÷ Operating assets). Result is equal to net operating income divided by operating assets. *634*

Return on average common stockholders' equity Net income divided by average common stockholders' equity; often called **rate of return on average common stockholders' equity,** or simply **return on equity (ROE).** *636*

Return on equity (ROE) Net income divided by average common stockholders' equity. *636*

Stockholders' equity to debt ratio Stockholders' equity divided by total debt; often used in inverted form and called the **debt to equity ratio.** *634*

Times interest earned ratio A ratio computed by dividing income before interest and taxes by interest expense (also called **interest coverage ratio**). *639*

Times preferred dividends earned ratio Net income divided by annual preferred dividends. *640*

Total assets turnover Net sales divided by average total assets. *632*

Trend percentages Similar to horizontal analysis except that a base year or period is selected, and comparisons are made to the base year or period. *622*

Turnover The relationship between the amount of an asset and some measure of its use. See Accounts receivable turnover, Inventory turnover, and Total assets turnover. *630*

Turnover of operating assets Net sales divided by operating assets. *634*

Vertical analysis The study of a single financial statement in which each item is expressed as a percentage of a significant total; for example, percentages of sales calculations. *622*

Yield (on stock) The yield on a stock investment refers to either an earnings yield or a dividend yield. Also see Earnings yield on common stock and Dividend yield on common stock and preferred stock. *641*

Self-Test

True-False

Indicate whether each of the following statements is true or false.

1. An objective of financial statement analysis is to provide information about the company's past performance and current financial position.
2. Vertical analysis helps detect changes in a company's performance over several periods and highlights trends.
3. Common-size statements provide information about changes in dollar amounts relative to the previous periods.
4. Liquidity ratios show a company's capacity to pay maturing current liabilities.
5. A company that is quite profitable may find it difficult to pay its accounts payable.
6. Financial statement analysts must be sure that comparable data are used among companies to make the comparisons valid.

Multiple-Choice

Select the best answer for each of the following questions.

The following data were abstracted from the December 31, 1997, balance sheet of Andrews Company (use for questions 1 and 2):

Cash	$136,000
Marketable securities	64,000
Accounts and notes receivable, net	184,000
Merchandise inventory	244,000
Prepaid expenses	12,000
Accounts and notes payable, short term	256,000
Accrued liabilities	64,000
Bonds payable, long term	400,000

1. The current ratio is:
   a. 1 : 2.
   b. 2 : 1.
   c. 1.2 : 1.
   d. 3 : 1.
2. The acid-test ratio is:
   a. 1 : 2.
   b. 2 : 1.
   c. 1.2 : 1.
   d. 3 : 1.

Benson Company shows the following data on its 1997 financial statements (use for questions 3–5):

Accounts receivable, January 1	$ 720,000
Accounts receivable, December 31	960,000
Merchandise inventory, January 1	900,000
Merchandise inventory, December 31	1,020,000
Gross sales	4,800,000
Sales returns and allowances	180,000
Net sales	4,620,000
Cost of goods sold	3,360,000
Income before interest and taxes	720,000
Interest on bonds	192,000
Net income	384,00

3. The accounts receivable turnover is:
   a. 5.5 times per year.
   b. 5.714 times per year.
   c. 5 times per year.
   d. 6.667 times per year.
4. The inventory turnover is:
   a. 5 times per year.
   b. 4.8125 times per year.
   c. 3.5 times per year.
   d. 4 times per year.
5. The times interest earned ratio is:
   a. 4.75 times per year.
   b. 3.75 times per year.
   c. 2 times per year.
   d. 3 times per year.

Now turn to page 670 to check your answers.

QUESTIONS

1. What are the major sources of financial information for publicly owned corporations?
2. The higher the accounts receivable turnover rate, the better off the company is. Do you agree? Why?
3. Can you think of a situation where the current ratio is very misleading as an indicator of short-term, debt-paying ability? Does the acid-test ratio offer a remedy to the situation you have described? Describe a situation where the acid-test ratio does not suffice either.
4. Before the Marvin Company issued $20,000 of long-term notes (due more than a year from the date of issue) in exchange for a like amount of accounts payable, its current ratio was 2 : 1 and its acid-test ratio was 1 : 1. Will this transaction increase, decrease, or have no effect on the current ratio and acid-test ratio? What would be the effect on the equity ratio?
5. Through the use of turnover rates, explain why a firm might seek to increase the volume of its sales even though such an increase can be secured only at reduced prices.
6. Indicate which of the relationships illustrated in the chapter would be best to judge:
   a. The short-term debt-paying ability of the firm.
   b. The overall efficiency of the firm without regard to the sources of assets.
   c. The return to owners (stockholders) of a corporation.
   d. The safety of long-term creditors' interest.
   e. The safety of preferred stockholders' dividends.
7. Indicate how each of the following ratios or measures is calculated:
   a. Payout ratio.
   b. Earnings per share of common stock.
   c. Price-earnings ratio.
   d. Earnings yield on common stock.
   e. Dividend yield on preferred stock.
   f. Times interest earned.
   g. Times preferred dividends earned.
   h. Return on average common stockholders' equity.
   i. Cash flow margin.
8. How is the rate of return on operating assets determined? Is it possible for two companies with operating margins of 5% and 1%, respectively, to both have a rate of return of 20% on operating assets? How?
9. Cite some of the possible deficiencies in accounting information, especially regarding its use in analyzing a particular company over a 10-year period.

The Coca-Cola Company

10. **Real World Question** From the financial highlights of The Coca-Cola Company in the annual report booklet, determine the percentage change in operating income from 1992 to 1993.

The Coca-Cola Company

11. **Real World Question** From the financial highlights of The Coca-Cola Company in the annual report

booklet, determine the 1993 net income per common share.

The Coca-Cola Company

12. **Real World Question** From the financial highlights of The Coca-Cola Company in the annual report booklet, determine the 1993 cash dividends per common share.

The Coca-Cola Company

13. **Real World Question** From the financial statements of The Coca-Cola Company in the annual report booklet, determine the 1993 cash flow margin.

EXERCISES*

Exercise 17–1
Perform horizontal and vertical analysis (L.O. 2)

Income statement data for Sargent Company for 1997 and 1996 follow:

	1997	1996
Net sales.	$1,305,000	$968,000
Cost of goods sold	914,800	628,200
Selling expenses	198,400	175,000
Administrative expenses	117,400	99,200
Federal income taxes	28,800	27,000

Prepare a horizontal and vertical analysis of the income data in a form similar to Illustration 17.2. Comment on the results of this analysis.

Exercise 17–2
Determine effects of various transactions on the current ratio (L.O. 3)

A company engaged in the following three independent transactions:

1. Merchandise purchased on account, $1,200,000.
2. Machinery purchased for cash, $1,200,000.
3. Capital stock issued for cash, $1,200,000.
   a. Compute the current ratio after each of these transactions assuming current assets were $1,600,000 and the current ratio was 1 : 1 before the transactions occurred.
   b. Repeat Part **a** assuming the current ratio was 2 : 1.
   c. Repeat Part **a** assuming the current ratio was 1 : 2.

Exercise 17–3
Compute average number of days receivables are outstanding; determine effect of increase in turnover (L.O. 3)

A company has sales of $1,840,000 per year. Its average net accounts receivable balance is $460,000.

a. What is the average number of days accounts receivable are outstanding?
b. By how much would the capital invested in accounts receivable be reduced if the turnover could be increased to 6 without a loss of sales?

Exercise 17–4
Compute cash flow margin

Settle Corporation had the following selected financial data for December 31, 1995:

Net sales	$900,000
Cost of goods sold.	540,000
Operating expenses	157,500
Net income	97,500
Total assets.	500,000
Net cash provided by operating activities	12,500

Compute the cash flow margin.

* By using the ratio module in the General Ledger Applications Software (GLAS) package, you can work any of the exercises or problems that deal with ratios.

Exercise 17–5
Compute inventory turnover (L.O. 2)

From the following partial income statement, calculate the inventory turnover for the period.

Net sales		$1,014,000
Cost of goods sold:		
Beginning inventory	$117,000	
Purchases	663,000	
Cost of goods available for sale	$780,000	
Less: Ending inventory	132,600	
Cost of goods sold		647,400
Gross margin		$ 366,600
Operating expenses		163,800
Net operating income		$ 202,800

Exercise 17–6
Compute rate of return on operating assets (L.O. 3)

Western, Inc., had net sales of $1,760,000, gross margin of $748,000, and operating expenses of $452,000. Total assets (all operating) were $1,540,000. Compute Western's rate of return on operating assets.

Exercise 17–7
Compute return on common stockholders' equity (L.O. 3)

Turtle Company began the year 1996 with total stockholders' equity of $1,200,000. Its net income for 1996 was $320,000, and $53,400 of dividends were declared. Compute the rate of return on average stockholders' equity for 1996. No preferred stock was outstanding.

Exercise 17–8
Compute EPS (L.O. 3)

Lindsay Company had 30,000 shares of common stock outstanding on January 1, 1996. On April 1, 1996, it issued 10,000 additional shares for cash. The amount of earnings available for common stockholders for 1996 was $300,000. What amount of EPS of common stock should the company report?

Exercise 17–9
Compute weighted-average number of shares outstanding (L.O. 3)

Welch Company started 1997 with 400,000 shares of common stock outstanding. On March 31, it issued 48,000 shares for cash, and on September 30, it purchased 40,000 shares of its own stock for cash. Compute the weighted-average number of common shares outstanding for the year.

Exercise 17–10
Compute EPS for current and prior year (L.O. 3)

A company reported EPS of $2 (or $1,200,000/600,000 shares) for 1995, ending the year with 600,000 shares outstanding. In 1996, the company earned net income of $3,840,000, issued 160,000 shares of common stock for cash on September 30, and distributed a 100% stock dividend on December 31, 1996. Compute EPS for 1996, and compute the adjusted earnings per share for 1995 that would be shown in the 1996 annual report.

Exercise 17–11
Compute times interest earned (L.O. 3)

A company paid interest of $16,000, incurred federal income taxes of $44,000, and had net income (after taxes) of $56,000. How many times was interest earned?

Exercise 17–12
Compute times dividends earned and dividend yield (L.O. 3)

Brad Company had 20,000 shares of $300 par value, 8% preferred stock outstanding. Net income after taxes was $2,880,000. The market price per share was $360.

a. How many times were the preferred dividends earned?

b. What was the dividend yield on the preferred stock assuming the regular preferred dividends were declared and paid?

Exercise 17–13
Compute EPS and price-earnings ratio (L.O. 3)

A company had 40,000 weighted-average number of shares of $160 par value common stock outstanding. The amount of earnings available to common stockholders was $400,000. Current market price per share is $360. Compute the EPS and the price-earnings ratio.

PROBLEMS

Problem 17–1
Perform horizontal and vertical analysis and comment on the results
(L.O. 2)

Fruit of the Loom is one of the largest manufacturers of knit apparel in the world and has maintained a position of leadership as a vertically integrated low-cost producer in the industry. Fruit of the Loom's comparative statements of income and retained earnings for 1993 and 1992 are given below.

FRUIT OF THE LOOM
Consolidated Statement of Earnings
For the Years Ended December 31, 1993, and 1992
($ thousands, except per share data)

	1993	1992
Net sales	$1,884,400	$1,855,100
Cost of sales	(1,237,000)	(1,194,800)
Gross earnings	$ 647,400	$ 660,300
Selling, general and administrative expenses	(240,100)	(225,000)
Goodwill amortization	(25,800)	(25,400)
Operating earnings	$ 381,500	$ 409,900
Interest expense	(72,700)	(82,100)
Gain on Acme Boot investment	67,300	—
Other expense–net	(9,000)	(7,900)
Earnings before income tax expense, extraordinary items and cumulative effect of change in accounting principle	$ 367,100	$ 319,900
Income tax expense	(154,300)	(131,400)
Earnings before extraordinary items and cumulative effect of change in accounting principle	$ 212,800	$ 188,500
Extraordinary items–loss on early retirement of debt and debt redemption	(8,700)	(9,900)
Earnings before cumulative effect of change in accounting principle	$ 204,100	$ 178,600
Cumulative effect of change in accounting for income taxes	3,400	—
Net earnings	$ 207,500	$ 178,600
Retained Earnings, January 1	412,800	234,200
Retained Earnings, December 31	$ 620,300	$ 412,800

FRUIT OF THE LOOM
Consolidated Balance Sheet
As of December 31, 1993, and 1992

	December 31,	
Assets	**1993**	**1992**
	(in thousands of dollars)	
Current assets:		
Cash and cash equivalents (including restricted cash)	$ 74,200	$ 57,400
Notes and accounts receivable (less allowance for possible losses of $16,100,000 and $14,300,000, respectively)	239,700	233,400
Inventories		
Finished goods	454,500	308,300
Work in process	94,000	85,300
Materials and supplies	25,600	21,400
Other	54,700	37,800
Total current assets	$ 942,700	$ 743,600
Property, plant and equipment:		
Land	$ 9,100	$ 8,200
Buildings, structures, and improvements	325,200	248,200
Machinery and equipment	867,900	673,600
Construction in progress	31,700	47,600
Total property, plant, and equipment	$1,233,900	$ 977,600
Less accumulated depreciation	367,900	290,500
Net property, plant, and equipment	$ 866,000	$ 687,100
Other assets:		
Goodwill (less accumulated amortization of $207,200,000 and $181,400,000, respectively)	$ 895,300	$ 810,800
Other	30,000	40,400
Total other assets	$ 925,300	$ 851,200
Total assets	$2,734,000	$2,281,900

Liabilities and Stockholders' Equity	December 31, 1993	1992
Current Liabilities:		
Short-term notes payable	$ —	$ 65,100
Current maturities of long-term debt	34,000	123,100
Trade accounts payable	78,100	80,500
Accrued payroll and vacation pay	25,700	26,500
Accrued pension	18,700	18,600
Accrued insurance obligations	15,500	12,500
Accrued advertising and promotion	15,400	24,300
Interest payable	14,300	11,600
Other accounts payable and accrued expenses	48,800	71,400
Total current liabilities	$ 250,500	$ 433,600
Noncurrent liabilities:		
Long-term debt	$1,194,000	$ 756,300
Net deferred income taxes	51,000	49,100
Other	191,500	187,900
Total noncurrent liabilities	$1,436,500	$ 993,300
Common stockholders' equity:		
Common stock and capital in excess of par value, $.01 par value; authorized, Class A, 200,000,000 shares, Class B, 30,000,000 shares; issued and outstanding:		
Class A Common Stock, 69,032,919 and 68,843,592 shares, respectively	$ 459,600	$ 454,000
Class B Common Stock, 6,690,976 and 6,710,128 shares, respectively	4,400	4,400
Retained earnings	620,300	412,800
Currency translation adjustments	(37,300)	(16,200)
Total common stockholders' equity	$1,047,000	$ 855,000
Total liabilities and stockholders' equity	$2,734,000	$2,281,900

Required

a. Perform a horizontal and vertical analysis of Fruit of the Loom's financial statements in a manner similar to those illustrated in this chapter.

b. Comment on the results of the analysis in Part **a**.

Problem 17–2
Perform trend analysis and comment on the results (L.O. 2)

Deere & Company manufactures, distributes, and finances a full range of agricultural equipment; a broad range of industrial equipment for construction, forestry, and public works; and a variety of lawn and grounds care equipment. The company also provides credit, health care, and insurance products for businesses and the general public. Consider the following information from the Deere & Company 1993 Annual Report:

($ millions)	1990	1991	1992	1993
Sales	$7,875	$7,055	$6,961	$7,754
Cost of goods sold	5,424	4,894	4,892	5,375
Gross margin	$2,451	$2,161	$2,069	$2,379
Operating expenses	1,864	2,187	2,025	2,107
Net operating income	$ 587	($26)	$ 44	$ 272

Required

a. Prepare a statement showing the trend percentages for each item using 1990 as the base year.

b. Comment on the trends noted.

Problem 17–3
Compute working capital, current ratio, and acid-test ratio (L.O. 3)

The following data are for Breed Company:

	December 31	
	1997	1996
Allowance for uncollectible accounts	$ 36,000	$ 28,500
Prepaid expenses	17,250	22,500
Accrued liabilities	105,000	93,000
Cash in Bank A	547,500	487,500
Wages payable	-0-	18,750
Accounts payable	357,000	292,500
Merchandise inventory	671,250	718,500
Bonds payable, due in 2001	307,500	297,000
Marketable securities	108,750	73,500
Notes payable (due in six months)	150,000	97,500
Accounts receivable	453,750	435,000
Cash flow from operating activities	96,000	90,000

Required

a. Compute the amount of working capital at both year-end dates.

b. Compute the current ratio at both year-end dates.

c. Compute the acid-test ratio at both year-end dates.

d. Compute the cash flow liquidity ratio at both year-end dates.

e. Comment briefly on the company's short-term financial position.

Problem 17–4
Determine effects of various transactions on working capital and current ratio (L.O. 3)

On December 31, 1997, Duggan Company's current ratio was 3 : 1 before the following transactions were completed:

1. Purchased merchandise on account.
2. Paid a cash dividend declared on November 15, 1997.
3. Sold equipment for cash.
4. Temporarily invested cash in marketable securities.
5. Sold obsolete merchandise for cash (at a loss).
6. Issued 10-year bonds for cash.
7. Wrote off goodwill to retained earnings.
8. Paid cash for inventory.
9. Purchased land for cash.
10. Returned merchandise that had not been paid for.
11. Wrote off an account receivable as uncollectible. Uncollectible amount is less than the balance in the Allowance for Uncollectible Accounts.
12. Accepted a 90-day note from a customer in settlement of customer's account receivable.
13. Declared a stock dividend on common stock.

Consider each transaction independently of all the others.

Required

a. Indicate whether the amount of working capital will increase, decrease, or be unaffected by each of the transactions.

b. Indicate whether the current ratio will increase, decrease, or be unaffected by each of the transactions.

Problem 17–5
Compute rate of return on operating assets and demonstrate effects of various transactions on this rate of return (L.O. 3)

Cotton Company has net operating income of $250,000 and operating assets of $1,000,000. Its net sales are $2,000,000.

The accountant for the company computes the rate of return on operating assets after computing the operating margin and the turnover of operating assets.

Required

a. Show the computations the accountant made.

b. Indicate whether the operating margin and turnover increase or decrease after each of the following changes. Then determine what the actual rate of return on operating assets would be. The events are not interrelated; consider each separately, starting from the original earning power position. No other changes occurred.

1. Sales increased by $80,000. There was no change in the amount of operating income and no change in operating assets.
2. Management found some cost savings in the manufacturing process. The amount of reduction in operating expenses was $20,000. The savings resulted from the use of less materials to manufacture the same quantity of goods. As a result, average inventory was $8,000 lower than it otherwise would have been. Operating income was not affected by the reduction in inventory.
3. The company invested $40,000 of cash (received on accounts receivable) in a plot of land it plans to use in the future (a nonoperating asset); income was not affected.
4. The federal income tax rate increased and caused income tax expense to increase by $10,000. The taxes have not yet been paid.
5. The company issued bonds and used the proceeds to buy $200,000 of machinery to be used in the business. Interest payments are $10,000 per year. Net operating income increased by $50,000 (net sales did not change).

Problem 17–6
Compute EPS, rate of return on sales and stockholders' equity, and number of times interest earned for two years (L.O. 3)

Polaroid Corporation designs, manufactures, and markets worldwide instant photographic cameras and films, electronic imaging recording devices, conventional films, and light polarizing filters and lenses. The following information is for Polaroid:

($ millions)	1992	1991
Net sales	$2,152.3	$2,070.6
Income before interest and taxes	221.6	1,141.6
Net income	99.0	683.7
Interest expense	58.5	58.4
Stockholders' equity (on December 31, 1990, $207.7)	808.9	772.9
Common stock, par value $1, December 31	75.4	75.4

Required Compute the following for both 1992 and 1991. Then compare and comment.

a. EPS of common stock.

b. Net income to net sales.

c. Net income to average common stockholders' equity.

d. Times interest earned ratio.

Problem 17–7
Compute numerous standard ratios (L.O. 3)

With operations in 21 countries, Scott Paper Company sells a broad range of products for personal care, environmental cleaning and wiping, and health care. The following balance sheet and supplementary data are for Scott Paper for 1992.

SCOTT PAPER COMPANY
Consolidated Balance Sheet
For December 26, 1992
($ millions)

		1992
Assets		
Current assets		
Cash and cash equivalents		$ 141.7
Receivables		647.1
Inventories		537.2
Prepaid items and other		65.5
Total current assets		$1,391.5
Plant assets, at cost	$7,059.1	
Accumulated depreciation	(3,090.6)	3,968.5
Timber resources, at cost less timber harvested		111.7
Investments in international equity affiliates		246.2
Investments in and advances to other equity affiliates		88.1
Notes receivable, goodwill and other assets		493.6
Total assets		$6,299.6
Liabilities and Shareholders' Equity		
Current liabilities		
Payable to suppliers and others		$1,205.9
Current maturities of long-term debt		255.3
Accrued taxes on income		54.3
Total current liabilities		$1,515.5
Long-term debt		2,030.6
Deferred income taxes and other liabilities		728.6
Total liabilities		$4,274.7
Preferred shares		7.1
Common shareholders' equity		
Common shares ($1 par value)	$ 445.1	
Reinvested earnings	1,708.3	
Cumulative translation adjustment	(121.6)	
Treasury shares	(14.0)	2,017.8
Total liabilities and shareholders' equity		$6,299.6

Supplementary data for 1992 (in millions)

1. Net income, $167.2.
2. Income before interest and taxes, $414.5.
3. Cost of goods sold, $3,626.2.
4. Net sales, $4,886.2.
5. Inventory on December 28, 1991, $570.7.
6. Total interest expense for the year, $188.8.

Required

Calculate the following ratios and show your computations.

a. Current ratio.
b. Net income to average common stockholders' equity.
c. Inventory turnover.
d. Number of days' sales in accounts receivable (assume 365 days in 1992).
e. EPS of common stock (ignore treasury stock).
f. Times interest earned ratio.
g. Equity ratio.
h. Net income to net sales.
i. Total assets turnover.
j. Acid-test ratio.

Problem 17–8
Determine effects on ratios of change in accounting method (FIFO to LIFO) (L.O. 3)

Rusty Company currently uses the FIFO method to account for its inventory but is considering a switch to LIFO before the books are closed for the year. Selected data for the year are:

Merchandise inventory, January 1	$ 715,000
Current assets	1,801,800
Total assets (operating)	2,860,000
Cost of goods sold (FIFO)	1,115,400
Merchandise inventory, December 31 (LIFO)	772,200
Merchandise inventory, December 31 (FIFO)	943,800
Current liabilities	572,000
Net sales	1,916,200
Operating expenses	457,600

Required

a. Compute the current ratio, inventory turnover ratio, and rate of return on operating assets assuming the company continues using FIFO.

b. Repeat Part **a** assuming the company adjusts its accounts to the LIFO inventory method.

Alternate Problems

Problem 17–1A
Perform horizontal and vertical analysis and comment on the results (L.O. 2)

Bethlehem Steel Corporation is one of the leading U.S. producers of steel plate and corrosion-resistent coated sheet steel used in the automotive markets. Bethlehem Steel's comparative statements of income and retained earnings and consolidated balance sheet for 1993 and 1992 follow.

BETHLEHEM STEEL
Consolidated Statements of Income
For Years Ended 1993 and 1992
($ millions, except per share data)

	1993	1992
Net Sales	$4,323.4	$4,007.9
Costs and Expenses:		
Cost of sales	$3,834.2	$3,789.9
Depreciation (Note A)	277.5	261.7
Selling, administration and general expense	156.9	159.3
Estimated restructuring losses (Note D)	350.0	—
Total Costs and Expenses	$4,618.6	$4,210.9
Loss from Operations	$ (295.2)	$ (203.0)
Financing Income (Expense):		
Interest and other income	7.1	4.9
Interest and other financing costs	(63.2)	(57.2)
Loss before Income Taxes and Cumulative Effect of Changes in Accounting	$ (351.3)	$ (255.3)
Benefit (Provision) for Income Taxes (Note E)	85.0	45.0
Loss before Cumulative Effect of Changes in Accounting [($3.37), ($2.86) and ($11.01) per share]	$ (266.3)	$ (210.3)
Cumulative Effect of Changes in Accounting [($4.15) per share] (Note B)	—	(340.0)
Net Loss	$ (266.3)	$ (550.3)
Retained Earnings, January 1	(673.6)	(123.3)
	$ (939.9)	$ (673.6)
Dividends	0	0
Retained Earnings, December 31	$ (939.9)	$ (673.6)

BETHLEHEM STEEL CORPORATION
Consolidated Balance Sheets
December 31, 1992, and 1993
($ millions, except per share data)

	1993		1992	
Assets				
Current Assets:				
Cash and cash equivalents (Note A)		$ 228.9		$ 208.2
Receivables, less allowances of $16.3 and $15.7 (Note F)		503.2		403.3
Inventories (Notes A, B and F):				
Raw materials and supplies	$ 341.9		$ 373.7	
Finished and semifinished products	494.8		455.0	
Contract work in progress less billings of $10.3 and $5.3	15.8		23.8	
Total inventories		852.5		852.5
Other current assets		6.5		5.5
Total Current Assets		$1,591.1		$1,469.5
Property, Plant and Equipment, less accumulated depreciation of $4,107.0 and $4,255.1 (Note A)		2,634.3		2,804.5
Investments and Miscellaneous Assets (Note A)		124.0		150.2
Deferred Income Tax Asset—net (Note E)		926.7		829.2
Intangible Asset—Pensions (Note I)		600.6		239.6
Total Assets		$5,876.7		$5,493.0
Liabilities and Stockholders' Equity				
Current Liabilities:				
Accounts payable		$ 360.9		$ 375.7
Accrued employment costs		130.1		132.8
Postretirement benefits other than pensions (Note J)		132.3		122.0
Accrued taxes (Note E)		65.4		67.5
Debt and capital lease obligations (Notes F and G)		95.5		69.2
Other current liabilities		130.0		126.0
Total Current Liabilities		$ 914.2		$ 893.2
Pension Liability (Notes D and I)		1,613.6		1,188.7
Postretirement Benefits Other Than Pensions (Notes D and J)		1,448.3		1,417.9
Long-term Debt and Capital Lease Obligations (Notes F and G)		718.3		726.8
Other Long-term Liabilities		485.7		477.0
Total Liabilities		$5,180.1		$4,703.6
Stockholders' Equity (Notes K, L and M):				
Preterred Stock–at $1 per share par value (aggregate liquidation preference of $481.2); Authorized 20,000,000 shares	11.6		6.5	
Preference Stock–at $1 per share par value (aggregate liquidation preference of $95.1); Authorized 20,000,000 shares	2.8		2.9	
Common Stock–at $1 per share par value; Authorized 150,000,000 shares; Issued 93,412,852 and 92,511,105 shares	93.4		92.5	
Held in Treasury, 2,003,760 and 2,001,677 shares at cost	(59.7)		(59.7)	
Additional Paid-in Capital	1,588.4		1,420.8	
Retained Deficit (Note B)	(939.9)		(673.6)	
Total Stockholders' Equity			696.6	789.4
Total Liabilities and Stockholders' Equity			$5,876.7	$5,493.0

Required

a. Perform a horizontal and vertical analysis of Bethlehem Steel's financial statements in a manner similar to Illustrations 17.1 and 17.2.

b. Comment on the results obtained.

Problem 17–2A
Perform trend analysis and comment on the results (L.O. 2)

Ford Motor Company is the world's second-largest producer of cars and trucks and ranks among the largest providers of financial services in the United States. The following information pertains to Ford:

($ millions)	1990	1991	1992
Sales	$81,844.0	$72,050.9	$84,407.2
Cost of sales	77,528.4	71,826.6	81,747.7
Gross margin	$ 4,315.6	$ 224.3	$ 2,659.5
Operating Expenses	4,000.0	3,993.4	4,434.5
Net operating income	$ 315.6	$ (3,769.1)	$ (1,775.0)

Required

a. Prepare a statement showing the trend percentages for each item, using 1990 as the base year.

b. Comment on the trends noted.

Problem 17–3A
Compute working capital, current ratio, and acid-test ratio (L.O. 3)

The following data are for Mills Company:

	December 31	
	1997	1996
Notes payable (due in 90 days)	$ 37,600	$ 30,000
Merchandise inventory	120,000	104,000
Cash	50,000	64,000
Marketable securities	24,800	15,000
Accrued liabilities	9,600	11,000
Accounts receivable	94,000	92,000
Accounts payable	56,000	36,000
Allowance for uncollectible accounts	12,000	7,600
Bonds payable, due 2001	78,000	80,000
Prepaid expenses	3,200	3,680
Cash flow from operating activities	30,000	20,000

Required

a. Compute the amount of working capital at both year-end dates.

b. Compute the current ratio at both year-end dates.

c. Compute the acid-test ratio at both year-end dates.

d. Compute the cash flow liquidity ratio at both year-end dates.

e. Comment briefly on the company's short-term financial position.

Problem 17–4A
Determine effects of various transactions on working capital and current ratio (L.O. 3)

Rose Products, Inc., has a current ratio on December 31, 1996, of 2 : 1 before the following transactions were completed:

1. Sold a building for cash.
2. Exchanged old equipment for new equipment. (No cash was involved.)
3. Declared a cash dividend on preferred stock.
4. Sold merchandise on account (at a profit).
5. Retired mortgage notes that would have matured in 2004.
6. Issued a stock dividend to common stockholders.
7. Paid cash for a patent.
8. Temporarily invested cash in government bonds.
9. Purchased inventory for cash.
10. Wrote off an account receivable as uncollectible. Uncollectible amount is less than the balance of the Allowance for Uncollectible Accounts.
11. Paid the cash dividend on preferred stock that was declared earlier.
12. Purchased a computer and gave a two-year promissory note.
13. Collected accounts receivable.
14. Borrowed from the bank on a 120-day promissory note.
15. Discounted a customer's note. Interest expense was involved.

Required

Consider each transaction independently of all the others.

a. Indicate whether the amount of working capital will increase, decrease, or be unaffected by each of the transactions.

b. Indicate whether the current ratio will increase, decrease, or be unaffected by each of the transactions.

Problem 17–5A
Compute rate of return on operating assets and demonstrate effects of various transactions on this rate of return (L.O. 3)

The following selected data are for three companies:

	Operating Assets	Net Operating Income	Net Sales
Company 1	$ 702,000	$ 93,600	$ 1,029,600
Company 2	4,212,000	304,200	9,360,000
Company 3	18,720,000	2,457,000	17,550,000

Required

a. Determine the operating margin, turnover of operating assets, and rate of return on operating assets for each company.

b. In the subsequent year, the following changes took place (no other changes occurred):

Company 1 bought some new machinery at a cost of $78,000. Net operating income increased by $6,240 as a result of an increase in sales of $124,800.

Company 2 sold some equipment it was using that was relatively unproductive. The book value of the equipment sold was $312,000. As a result of the sale of the equipment, sales declined by $156,000, and operating income declined by $3,120.

Company 3 purchased some new retail outlets at a cost of $3,120,000. As a result, sales increased by $4,680,000, and operating income increased by $249,600.

1. Which company has the largest absolute change in—
   - **a.** Operating margin ratio?
   - **b.** Turnover of operating assets?
   - **c.** Rate of return on operating assets?
2. Which one realized the largest dollar change in operating income? Explain this change in relation to the changes in the rate of return on operating assets.

Problem 17–6A
Compute EPS, rate of return on sales and stockholders' equity, and number of times interest earned for two years (L.O. 3)

The largest spice company in the world, McCormick & Company, Inc., produces a diverse array of specialty foods. The following information is for McCormick & Company, Inc.:

($ millions)	1992	1991
Net sales	$1,471,369	$1,427,902
Income before interest and taxes	169,208	142,412
Net income	95,217	80,924
Interest expense	30,895	27,464
Stockholders' equity	437,938	389,203
Common stock, no par value, November 30	122,743	100,257

Assume average common shares outstanding for 1992 and 1991 are 81,918 and 82,396 (in millions), respectively.

Required

Compute the following for both 1992 and 1991. Then compare and comment. Assume stockholders' equity for 1990 is $364,400.

a. EPS of common stock.

b. Net income to net sales.

c. Return on average common stockholders' equity.

d. Times interest earned ratio.

Problem 17–7A
Compute numerous standard ratios (L.O. 3)

AT&T is a global company that provides communications services and products, as well as network equipment and computer systems, to businesses, consumers, telecommunications service providers, and government agencies. The following consolidated balance sheet and supplementary data are for AT&T for 1992:

AT&T AND SUBSIDIARIES
Consolidated Balance Sheet
December 31, 1992
($ millions except per share amounts)

	1992
Assets	
Cash and temporary cash investments	$ 1,310
Receivables less allowances of $829 and $936	
Accounts receivable	11,040
Finance receivables	8,569
Inventories	2,659
Deferred income taxes	2,118
Other current assets	818
Total current assets	$26,514
Property, plant and equipment—net	19,358
Investments	864
Finance receivables	3,643
Prepaid pension costs	3,480
Other assets	3,329
Total assets	$57,188
Liabilities and Deferred Credits	
Accounts payable	$ 5,045
Payroll and benefit-related liabilities	3,336
Debt maturing within one year	7,600
Dividends payable	443
Other current liabilities	4,962
Total current liabilities	$21,386
Long-term debt including capital leases	8,604
Other liabilities	2,634
Deferred income taxes	4,660
Unamortized investment tax credits	350
Other deferred credits	181
Total liabilities and deferred credits	$37,815
Minority interests	$ 452
Shareowners' Equity	
Common shares—par value $1 per share	$ 1,340
Authorized shares: 2,000,000,000 at December 31, 1992	
1,500,000,000 at December 31, 1991	
Outstanding shares: 1,339,831,000 at December 31, 1992	
1,309,352,000 at December 31, 1991	
Additional paid-in capital	11,425
Guaranteed ESOP obligation	(407)
Foreign currency translation adjustments	65
Retained earnings	6,498
Total shareowners' equity	$18,921
Total liabilities and shareowners' equity	$57,188

Supplementary data for 1992 (in millions)

1. Interest expense, $663.
2. Net sales, $64,904.
3. Cost of goods sold, $39,710.
4. Net income, $3,807.
5. Income before interest and taxes, $6,621.
6. Inventories, December 31, 1991, $3,125.

Required

Calculate the following ratios and show your computations.

a. Current ratio.
b. Net income to average common stockholders' equity.
c. Inventory turnover.
d. Number of days' sales in accounts receivable (assume 365 days in 1992).
e. EPS of common stock.
f. Times interest earned ratio.
g. Equity ratio.
h. Net income to net sales.
i. Total assets turnover.
j. Acid-test ratio.

Problem 17–8A
Determine effects on ratios of change in accounting method (FIFO to LIFO) (L.O. 3)

Drew Company is considering switching from the FIFO method to the LIFO method of accounting for its inventory before it closes its books for the year. The January 1 merchandise inventory was $432,000. Following are data compiled from the adjusted trial balance at the end of the year:

Merchandise inventory, December 31 (FIFO)	$ 504,000
Current liabilities	360,000
Net sales	1,260,000
Operating expenses	387,000
Current assets	945,000
Total assets (operating)	1,440,000
Cost of goods sold	729,000

If the switch to LIFO takes place, the December 31 merchandise inventory would be $450,000.

Required

a. Compute the current ratio, inventory turnover ratio, and rate of return on operating assets assuming the company continues using FIFO.
b. Repeat Part **a** assuming the company adjusts its accounts to the LIFO inventory method.

BEYOND THE NUMBERS—CRITICAL THINKING

Business Decision Case 17–1
Compute net income, identify reason for cash increase, state main sources of financing, and indicate further analyses needed (L.O. 2, 3)

The comparative balance sheets of the Champ Corporation for December 31, 1997, and 1996 follow:

CHAMP CORPORATION
Comparative Balance Sheets
December 31, 1997, and 1996

	1997	1996
Assets		
Cash	$240,000	$ 48,000
Accounts receivable, net	43,200	57,600
Merchandise inventory	192,000	201,600
Plant and equipment, net	134,400	144,000
Total assets	$609,600	$451,200
Liabilities and Stockholders' Equity		
Accounts payable	$ 48,000	$ 48,000
Common stock	336,000	336,000
Retained earnings	225,600	67,200
Total liabilities and stockholders' equity	$609,600	$451,200

Based on your review of the comparative balance sheets, determine the following:

a. What was the net income for 1997 assuming there were no dividend payments?

b. What was the primary source of the large increase in the cash balance from 1996 to 1997?

c. What are the two main sources of assets for Champ Corporation?

d. What other comparisons and procedures would you use to complete the analysis of the balance sheet?

Business Decision Case 17–2
Compute turnover ratios for four years and number of days' sales in accounts receivable; evaluate effectiveness of company's credit policy (L.O. 3)

As Joiner Manufacturing Company's internal auditor, you are reviewing the company's credit policy. The following information is from Joiner's annual reports for 1994, 1995, 1996, and 1997:

	1994	1995	1996	1997
Net accounts receivable	$ 540,000	$1,080,000	$1,350,000	$1,800,000
Net sales	5,400,000	6,975,000	8,550,000	9,900,000

Management has asked you to calculate and analyze the following in your report:

a. If cash sales account for 30% of all sales and credit terms are always 1/10, n/60, determine all turnover ratios possible and the number of days' sales in accounts receivable at all possible dates. (The number of days' sales in accounts receivable should be based on year-end accounts receivable and net credit sales.)

b. How effective is the company's credit policy?

Business Decision Case 17–3
Analyze investment alternatives (L.O. 2, 3)

Lisa French has consulted you about the possibility of investing in one of three companies (Avery Inc., Brigade Company, or Calico Corp.) by buying its common stock. The companies' shares are selling at about the same price. The long-term capital structures of the companies are as follows:

	Avery Inc.	Brigade Company	Calico Corp.
Bonds with a 10% interest rate			$1,200,000
Preferred stock with an 8% dividend rate		$1,200,000	
Common stock, $10 par value	$2,400,000	1,200,000	1,200,000
Retained earnings	192,000	192,000	192,000
Total long-term equity	$2,592,000	$2,592,000	$2,592,000
Number of common shares outstanding	240,000	120,000	120,000

French has already consulted two investment advisers. One adviser believes that each of the companies will earn $150,000 per year before interest and taxes. The other adviser believes that each company will earn about $480,000 per year before interest and taxes. French has asked you to write a report covering these points:

a. Compute each of the following, using the estimates made by the first and second advisers.

1. Earnings available for common stockholders assuming a 40% tax rate.
2. EPS of common stock.
3. Rate of return on total stockholders' equity.

b. Which stock should French select if she believes the first adviser?

c. Are the stockholders as a group (common and preferred) better off with or without the use of long-term debt in the companies?

Annual Report Analysis 17–4
Analyze management's objectives and performance from the viewpoints of a creditor and an investor (real world problem)
(L.O. 2, 3)

The following selected financial data excerpted from the 1993 annual report of Maytag Corporation represents the summary information which management presented for interested parties to review:

MAYTAG CORPORATION
Selected Financial Data
($ thousands except per share data)

	1993*	1992†	1991	1990	1989‡
Net sales	$2,987,054	$3,041,223	$2,970,626	$3,056,833	$3,088,753
Cost of sales	2,262,942	2,339,406	2,254,221	2,309,138	2,312,645
Income taxes	38,600	15,900	44,400	60,500	75,500
Income (loss) from continuing operations	51,270	(8,354)	79,017	98,905	131,472
Percent of income (loss) from continuing operations to net sales	1.7%	(.3%)	2.7%	3.2%	4.3%
Income (loss) from continuing operations per share	$ .48	$ (.08)	$ .75	$ .94	$ 1.27
Dividends paid per share	.50	.50	.50	.95	.95
Average shares outstanding (in thousands)	106,252	106,077	105,761	105,617	103,694
Working capital	$ 406,181	$ 452,626	$ 509,025	$ 612,802	$ 650,905
Depreciation of property, plant and equipment	102,459	94,032	83,352	76,836	68,077
Additions to property, plant and equipment	99,300	129,891	143,372	141,410	127,838
Total assets	2,469,498	2,501,490	2,535,068	2,586,541	2,436,319
Long-term debt	724,695	789,232	809,480	857,941	876,836
Total debt to capitalization	60.6%	58.7%	45.9%	47.7%	50.6%
Shareowners' equity per share of Common stock	$ 5.50	$ 5.62	$ 9.50	$ 9.60	$ 8.89

* Includes $60.4 million in pretax charges ($50 million in a special charge and $10.4 million in selling, general and administrative expenses) for additional costs associated with two Hoover Europe "free flights" promotion programs.

† Includes a $95 million pretax charge relating to the reorganization of the North American and European business units and before cumulative effect of accounting changes.

‡ These amounts reflect the acquisition of Hoover on January 26, 1989.

Required

a. As a creditor, what do you believe management's objectives should be? Which of the preceding items of information would assist a creditor in judging management's performance?

b. As an investor, what do you believe management's objectives should be? Which of the preceding items of information would assist an investor in judging management's performance?

c. What other information might be considered useful?

Annual Report Analysis 17–5
Discuss payout ratio

Refer to the excerpt from BellSouth Corporation's annual report, in "A Broader Perspective" (page 643). Explain why the dividends per share continued to increase despite a steady decline in net income and earnings per share since 1989.

Group Project 17–6
Analyze an annual report

Choose a company the class wants to know more about and obtain its annual report. In groups of two or three students, calculate either the liquidity, equity, profitability, or market test ratios. Each group should select a spokesperson to tell the rest of the class the results of the group's calculations. Finally, the class should decide whether or not to invest in the corporation based on the ratios they calculated.

Answers to Self-Test

True-False

1. **True.** Financial statement analysis consists of applying analytical tools and techniques to financial statements and other relevant data to obtain useful information.
2. **False.** Horizontal analysis provides useful information about the changes in a company's performance over several periods by analyzing comparative financial statements of the same company for two or more successive periods.
3. **False.** Common-size statements show only percentage figures, such as percentages of total assets and percentages of net sales.
4. **True.** Liquidity ratios such as the current ratio and acid-test ratio indicate a company's short-term debt-paying ability.
5. **True.** The accrual net income shown on the income statement is not cash basis income and does not indicate cash flows.
6. **True.** Analysts must use comparable data when making comparisons of items for different periods or different companies.

Multiple-Choice

1. **b.** Current assets:

   $136,000 + $64,000 + $184,000
   + $244,000 + $12,000 = $640,000

   Current liabilities:

   $256,000 + $64,000 = $320,000

   Current ratio:

   $640,000/$320,000 = 2 : 1

2. **c.** Quick assets:

   $136,000 + $64,000 + $184,000 = $384,000

   Current liabilities:

   256,000 + $64,000 = $320,000

   Acid-test ratio:

   $384,000/$320,000 = 1.2 : 1

3. **a.** Net sales:

   $4,620,000

   Average accounts receivable:

   ($720,000 + $960,000)/2 = $840,000

   Accounts receivable turnover:

   $4,620,000/$840,000 = 5.5

4. **c.** Cost of goods sold:

   $3,360,000

   Average inventory:

   ($900,000 + $1,020,000)/2 = $960,000

   Inventory turnover:

   $3,360,000/$960,000 = 3.5

5. **b.**

Income before interest and taxes	$720,000
Interest on bonds	192,000

   Times interest earned ratio:

   $720,000/$192,000 = 3.75 times

VI

Product Costing

Part Outline

A Manager's Perspective

Ann Francis

Manager, Consumer Affairs Administration
The Coca-Cola Company

Regardless of the area of business in which they choose to make their careers, students, especially when they reach the management level, will inevitably have financial responsibilities. As a manager, I need to understand some basic accounting information in order to make decisions and to process the information flow in and out of my office.

For example, I manage a department budget, and it is my responsibility to track cash inflow and outflow on a regular basis to ensure that the budget is administered appropriately. I track all our invoices, then reconcile them with a "Deck" report, which we receive from accounting. I also order supplies for our department, and that needs to be managed within a budget as well.

Every year we review our department's past expenditures and our anticipated expenditures, then establish a budget for the next year. At this point, we also make decisions about capital expenditures such as purchasing new computer equipment, and those plans are worked into the capital budget.

Aside from general administration, I am also responsible for a program called "Coca-Cola Cares," an employee hotline set up in 1992 to provide a vehicle for employees to report any problems they notice in the marketplace such as broken vending machines or inappropriate use of our trademark. I receive weekly and monthly reports to assess improvements based on increases and decreases in the number of calls we receive.

Another group under my management is telemarketing services, an internal service set up to help Coca-Cola associates with market research and customer service projects. Since independent telemarketing services can be very expensive, this system allows us to maintain high quality service to Coca-Cola customers in the most economically feasible way.

18

Managerial Accounting Concepts/Job Costing

Have you ever considered starting or running a business, or know someone who has? Have you considered providing management skills to a nonprofit organization? If so, then you realize that good decisions are based on good information.

Managerial accounting helps managers make good decisions. Managerial accounting provides information about the cost of goods and services, whether a product is profitable, whether to invest in a new business venture, and how to budget. It compares actual performance to planned performance and facilitates many other important decisions critical to the success of organizations.

The remaining chapters in this book focus on managerial accounting. This chapter provides an overview of managerial accounting, defines cost terms, and shows how to determine the cost of a particular type of product known as a *job*.

Learning Objectives

After studying this chapter, you should be able to:

1. Compare and contrast managerial accounting and financial accounting.
2. Describe the basic components of a product's cost.
3. Explain the difference between product costs and period costs.
4. Compare financial reporting by a merchandiser to that of a manufacturer, and prepare a statement of cost of goods manufactured, an income statement, and a balance sheet for a manufacturer.

(*continued*)

Compare Managerial Accounting with Financial Accounting

Whereas financial accounting provides financial information primarily for external use, **managerial accounting** information is for internal use. By reporting on the financial activities of the organization, financial accounting provides information needed by investors and creditors.

Most managerial decisions require data more detailed than that provided by external financial reports. For instance, in their external financial statements, large corporations such as General Electric Company show single amounts on their balance sheets for inventory and on their income statements for the cost of goods sold. However, managers need more detailed data about the cost of each of several hundred products.

We show the fundamental differences between managerial and financial accounting in the chart on page 677.

Accountants currently face a big challenge: designing information systems with sufficient flexibility to provide data for multiple purposes. Some people at

(concluded)

5. Explain the pattern of cost flows for a company.
6. Compare and contrast different production methods and accounting systems.
7. Describe job cost flows and determine the cost of jobs.
8. Explain how and why predetermined overhead rates are computed.
9. Describe the differences in net income under absorption costing and variable costing. (Appendix)

lower levels in the organization need detailed information, but not the big picture provided by a company's income statement. However, managers at top levels need to see the big picture.

Most of you will use accounting information. Therefore, you need to know enough about accounting to communicate with accountants to get the information you need for decision making.

Ethical Issues

Managerial accountants face many choices involving ethics. For example, managers are responsible for achieving financial targets such as net income for a company's division. Managers who fail to achieve these targets may lose their jobs. If a division or company is having trouble achieving financial performance targets, managers may be tempted to manipulate the accounting numbers. Whether your career is in the public or private sector, you are likely to encounter cases where you or people you know are tempted to commit financial fraud, which is the intentional misrepresentation of financial results.

In its Standards of Ethical Conduct for Management Accountants, the Institute of Management Accountants (IMA) states that management accountants have an obligation to maintain the highest levels of ethical conduct by maintaining professional competency, refraining from disclosing confidential information, and maintaining integrity and objectivity in their work.[1]

The standards recommend that people faced with ethical conflicts follow the company's established policies that deal with such conflicts. If the policies do not resolve the conflict, accountants should consider discussing the matter with their superiors, potentially going as high as the audit committee of the board of directors. In extreme cases, the accountants may have no alternative but to resign.

Objective 1
Compare and contrast managerial accounting and financial accounting.

Merchandiser and Manufacturer Accounting: Differences in Cost Concepts

Cost is a financial measure of the resources used or given up to achieve a stated purpose. **Product costs** are the costs a company assigns to units produced. Product costs are the costs of making a product, such as an automobile; the cost of making and serving a meal in a restaurant; or the cost of teaching a class in a university.

Objective 2
Describe the basic components of a product's cost.

Basic Product Cost Components

Manufacturing companies use the most complex product costing methods. To ensure that you understand how and why product costing is done in manufacturing companies, we use many manufacturing company examples. However, since many of you could have careers in service or merchandising companies, we also use nonmanufacturing examples.

In manufacturing companies, a product's cost is made up of three cost elements: direct material costs, direct labor costs, and manufacturing overhead costs.

Direct Materials **Materials** are unprocessed items used in the manufacturing process. **Direct materials** are those materials used only in making the product and are clearly and easily traceable to a particular product. For example, iron ore is a direct material to a steel company because the iron ore is clearly traceable to the

[1] See *Standards of Ethical Conduct for Management Accountants* (Montvale, N.J.: Institute of Management Accountants, June 1, 1983.) The institute's former name was the National Association of Accountants.

Financial Accounting	Managerial Accounting
Users	
External users of information—usually shareholders, financial analysts, and creditors.	Internal users of information—usually managers.
Compliance with Generally Accepted Accounting Principles	
Must comply with generally accepted accounting principles.	Need not comply with generally accepted accounting principles. Internal cost/benefit evaluation determines how much information is enough.
Future versus Past	
Uses historical data.	May use estimates of the future for budgeting and decision making.
Detail Presented	
Presents summary data.	More detailed data are presented about product costs, revenues, and profits.

finished product, steel. In turn, steel becomes a direct material to an automobile manufacturer.

Some materials (such as glue and thread used in manufacturing furniture) may become part of the finished product, but tracing those materials to a particular product would require more effort than is sensible. Such materials, called *indirect materials* or *supplies,* are included in manufacturing overhead. **Indirect materials** are materials used in the manufacture of a product that cannot, or will not for practical reasons, be traced directly to the product being manufactured. Indirect materials are part of overhead, which we will discuss later.

Direct Labor **Direct labor** costs include the labor costs of all employees actually working on materials to convert them into finished goods. As with direct material costs, direct labor costs of a product include only those labor costs clearly traceable to, or readily identifiable with, the finished product. The wages

An Ethical Perspective

High Pressure Sales Tactics and Creative Accounting

Perhaps the most common financial fraud is premature recording of revenues. For instance, a manager or accountant recorded a sale before the end of Year 1 when, in fact, the sale occurred in Year 2. That sale and its profits appear on the Year 1 financial statements, instead of the Year 2 financial statements. A company known as Comserv provides an example of this type of fraud.

Comserv was a software development company that installed specialized software for companies. Comserv recorded revenue for a software installation as follows: First, it recorded a portion of the revenue when the customer signed a contract. Second, it recorded the rest of the revenue when the installation was complete. This approach complied with generally accepted accounting principles for external reporting and with company policy for internal reporting.

Using this method, salespeople had incentives to pressure customers to sign contracts before the end of the fiscal year. Subsequent investigations by Comserv's external auditors and the Securities and Exchange Commission uncovered several fraudulent activities. For instance, employees backdated sales contracts by recording a contract signed on January 28 of Year 2 as being signed on December 28 of Year 1. (The end of the fiscal year was December 31.)

Comserv salespeople also persuaded customers to sign contracts for software installations before the end of the fiscal year while providing a separate side agreement that allowed customers to withdraw from the deal at a later date. Because of this side agreement, the company should not have recorded revenue at the time the contract was signed. Comserv should have waited until customers could no longer withdraw from the contract. The accounting department, not knowing of the separate side agreement, recorded revenue at the time of the contract.

The Securities and Exchange Commission alleged many people at Comserv were involved in fraudulent activities, including salespeople and accountants who unwittingly supported these activities. In the end, several people were charged with committing fraud by the Securities and Exchange Commission, and the company was taken over by another company in the computer software industry.

Based on the authors' research of Securities and Exchange Commission files and court testimony.

ILLUSTRATION 18.1
Manufacturing Overhead Costs

Indirect labor:
- Janitors
- Supervisors
- Materials storeroom personnel
- Cost accountant

Indirect materials:
- Oil
- Nails

Repairs and maintenance on factory buildings and equipment
Payroll taxes and fringe benefits for manufacturing employees
Depreciation on factory buildings and equipment
Insurance and taxes on factory property and inventories
Utilities for factory buildings

paid to a construction worker, a pizza delivery driver, and an assembler in an electronics company are examples of direct labor.

To determine direct labor cost, companies usually multiply the number of hours of direct labor by the hourly wage rate. Many employees receive fringe benefits—employers pay for payroll taxes, pension costs, and paid vacations. These fringe benefit costs can significantly increase the direct labor hourly wage rate. Some companies treat fringe benefit costs as direct labor. Other companies include fringe benefit costs in overhead if they can be traced to the product only with great difficulty and effort.

Firms do not account for some labor costs (for example, wages of materials handlers, custodial workers, and supervisors) as direct labor because the expense of tracing these costs to product units would be too great. These labor costs, called *indirect labor,* are part of overhead. **Indirect labor** consists of the cost of labor that cannot, or will not for practical reasons, be traced to the products being manufactured.

OVERHEAD In a manufacturing company, overhead is generally called *manufacturing overhead.* (You may also see other names for manufacturing overhead, such as *factory overhead, factory indirect costs,* or *factory burden.*) Service companies use *service overhead,* and construction companies use *construction overhead.* Any of these companies may just use *overhead* rather than specifying it as manufacturing overhead, service overhead, or construction overhead. Some people confuse overhead with selling and administrative costs. Overhead is part of making the good or providing the service, whereas selling costs result from sales activity and administrative costs result from running the business.

In general, **overhead** refers to all costs of making the product or providing the service except those classified as direct materials or direct labor. (Some service organizations have direct labor but not direct materials.) In manufacturing companies, **manufacturing overhead** includes all manufacturing costs except those accounted for as direct materials and direct labor. Manufacturing overhead costs are manufacturing costs that must be incurred but that cannot or will not be traced directly to specific units produced. In addition to direct materials and direct labor, manufacturing overhead includes depreciation and maintenance on machines, supervisors' salaries, and factory utility costs. Look at Illustration 18.1 for more manufacturing overhead costs.

Selling Costs **Selling costs** are costs incurred to obtain customer orders and get the finished product in the customers' possession. Advertising, market research, sales salaries and commissions, and delivery and storage of finished goods are selling costs. The costs of delivery and storage of finished goods are selling costs because they are incurred after production has been completed. Therefore, the costs of storing materials are part of manufacturing overhead, whereas the costs of storing finished goods are a part of selling costs. Remember that retailers, wholesalers, manufacturers, and service organizations all have selling costs.

Administrative Costs **Administrative costs** are nonmanufacturing costs that include the costs of top administrative functions and various staff departments such as accounting, data processing, and personnel. Executive salaries, clerical salaries, office expenses, office rent, donations, research and development costs, and legal costs are administrative costs. As with selling costs, all organizations have administrative costs.

Product and Period Costs

Objective 3
Explain the difference between product costs and period costs.

Companies also classify costs as product costs and period costs. **Product costs** are the costs incurred in making products. These costs include the costs of direct materials, direct labor, and manufacturing overhead. Manufacturing companies and some service companies that have inventories call product costs inventoriable costs.

Period costs are closely related to periods of time rather than units of products. For this reason, firms expense (deduct from revenues) period costs in the period in which they are incurred. Accountants treat all selling and administrative costs as period costs for external financial reporting.

To illustrate, assume a company pays its sales manager a fixed salary. Even though the manager may be working on projects to benefit the company in future accounting periods, it expenses the sales manager's salary in the period incurred because the expense cannot be traced to the production of a specific product.

An Accounting Perspective

Business Insight Many service organizations have inventories. For example, consulting firms, public accounting firms, and law firms have inventories of work not yet billed to clients. The inventories in service companies are less tangible than the inventories in manufacturing companies. Inventories represent the time and talent that has gone into the job. In service companies, this includes working papers and documents or simply the ideas of the people doing the work.

Financial Reporting by Manufacturing Companies

Objective 4
Compare financial reporting by a merchandiser to that of a manufacturer, and prepare a statement of cost of goods manufactured, an income statement, and a balance sheet for a manufacturer.

Many of you will work in manufacturing companies or provide services for them. Others will work in retail or service organizations that do business with manufacturers. This section will help you understand how manufacturing companies work and how to read both their internal and external financial statements.

Assume you own a bicycle store and purchase bicycles and accessories to sell to customers. To determine your profitability, you would subtract the cost of bicycles and accessories from your gross sales as cost of goods sold. However, if you owned the manufacturing company that made the bicycles, you would base your cost of goods sold on the cost of manufacturing those bicycles. Accounting for manufacturing costs is more complex than accounting for costs of merchandise purchased that is ready for sale.

Perhaps the most important accounting difference between merchandisers and manufacturers relates to the differences in the nature of their activities. A merchandiser purchases finished goods ready to be sold. On the other hand, a manufacturer must purchase raw materials and use production equipment and employee labor to transform the raw materials into finished products.

Thus, while a merchandiser has only one type of inventory—merchandise available for sale—a manufacturer has three types—unprocessed *materials*, partially complete *work in process*, and ready-for-sale *finished goods*. Instead of one, three different inventory accounts are necessary to show the cost of inventory in various stages of production. Looking at Illustration 18.2, you can see how the inventory cost flows differ between manufacturing and merchandising companies.

Illustration 18.2
Comparison of Inventory Cost Flows

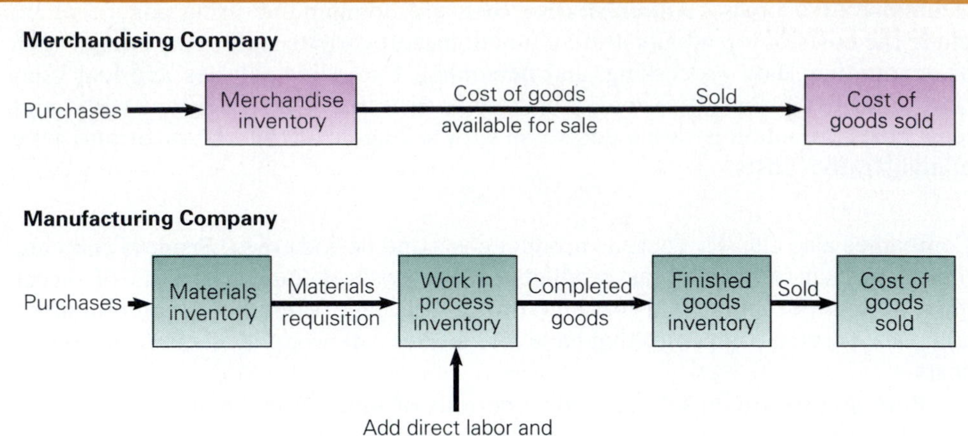

Illustration 18.3
Cost of Goods Sold Comparison

Merchandiser

Cost of goods sold:	
Merchandise inventory, January 1	$ 25,000
Net cost of purchases	165,000
Cost of goods available for sale	$190,000
Merchandise inventory, December 31	30,000
Cost of goods sold.	$160,000

Manufacturer

Cost of goods sold:	
Finished goods inventory, January 1	$ 50,000
Cost of goods manufactured (from statement of cost of goods manufactured)	1,100,000
Cost of goods available for sale	$1,150,000
Finished goods inventory, December 31	60,000
Cost of goods sold	$1,090,000

We compare a manufacturer's cost of goods sold section of the income statement to that same section of the merchandiser's income statement in Illustration 18.3. There are two major differences in these cost of goods sold sections: (1) goods ready to be sold are referred to as *merchandise inventory* by a merchandiser and *finished goods inventory* by a manufacturer, and (2) the *net cost of purchases* for a merchandiser is equivalent to the cost of goods manufactured by a manufacturer.

The Statement of Cost of Goods Manufactured

The **statement of cost of goods manufactured** supports the cost of goods sold figure on the income statement. (See the $1,100,000 cost of goods manufactured in Illustration 18.3.) The two most important numbers on this statement are the cost to manufacture and the cost of goods manufactured. Be careful not to confuse the terms *cost to manufacture* and *cost of goods manufactured* with each other or with the cost of goods sold. We depict the relationship among these terms in Illustration 18.4.

Cost to manufacture includes the costs of all resources put into production during the period. **Cost of goods manufactured** consists of the cost of all goods completed during the period. It includes cost to manufacture plus the beginning work in process inventory minus the ending work in process inventory. **Cost of goods sold** includes the cost of goods manufactured plus the beginning finished goods inventory minus the ending finished goods inventory.

Look at Illustration 18.5, the statement of cost of goods manufactured for Farside Manufacturing Company for 1997. Farside Manufacturing makes calendars and books that some people find comical.

Note how the statement shows the costs incurred for direct materials, direct labor, and manufacturing overhead. The statement totals these three costs as cost

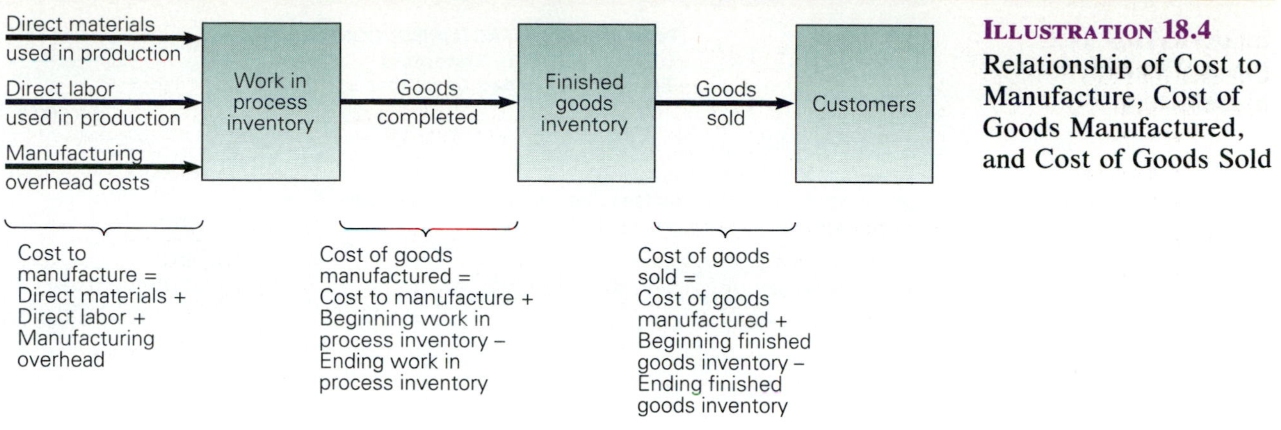

ILLUSTRATION 18.4
Relationship of Cost to Manufacture, Cost of Goods Manufactured, and Cost of Goods Sold

ILLUSTRATION 18.5
Statement of Cost of Goods Manufactured

FARSIDE MANUFACTURING COMPANY
Statement of Cost of Goods Manufactured
For the Year Ended December 31, 1997

Direct materials		
Materials inventory, January 1	$ 40,000	
Materials purchases	480,000	
Materials available for use	$520,000	
Less: Materials inventory, December 31	30,000	
Materials used		$ 490,000
Direct labor		380,000
Manufacturing overhead		
Indirect labor	$120,000	
Maintenance and repairs expense	60,000	
Factory utilities expense	10,000	
Depreciation expense—factory building	20,000	
Depreciation expense—factory equipment	30,000	
Other expense—factory	20,000	
Total manufacturing overhead		260,000
Cost to manufacture		$1,130,000
Add: Work in process inventory, January 1		30,000
		$1,160,000
Less: Work in process inventory, December 31		60,000
Cost of goods manufactured		$1,100,000

to manufacture during the period. When adding beginning work in process inventory and deducting ending work in process inventory from the cost to manufacture, we obtain cost of goods manufactured or completed. Cost of goods sold does not appear on the cost of goods manufactured statement but on the income statement.

The Income Statement

To make the manufacturer's income statement more understandable to readers of the financial statements, accountants do not show all of the details that appear in the cost of goods manufactured statement. In Illustration 18.6, we show the income statement for Farside Manufacturing Company. Notice in Illustration 18.6 the relationship of the statement of cost of goods manufactured to the income statement.

The cost of goods manufactured appears in the cost of goods sold section of the income statement. The cost of goods manufactured is in the same place that purchases would be presented on a merchandiser's income statement. We add cost of goods manufactured to beginning finished goods inventory to derive cost of

ILLUSTRATION 18.6
Income Statement of a Manufacturer

FARSIDE MANUFACTURING COMPANY
Income Statement
For the Year Ended December 31, 1997

Sales		$1,800,000
Cost of goods sold:		
Finished goods inventory, January 1	$ 50,000	
Cost of goods manufactured (see statement of cost of goods manufactured in Illustration 18.5)	1,100,000	
Cost of goods available for sale	$1,150,000	
Less: Finished goods inventory, December 31	60,000	
Cost of goods sold		1,090,000
Gross margin		$ 710,000
Operating expenses:		
Selling expenses	$ 300,000	
Administrative expenses	200,000	
Total operating expenses		500,000
Income from operations		$ 210,000

Note: Income statements presented in external financial statements also include nonoperating revenues and expenses and income taxes.

goods available for sale. This is similar to the merchandiser who presents purchases added to beginning merchandise to derive goods available for sale.

When financial statements are released to the public, it is common to further simplify the income statement. These simplified statements show only the items and amounts in the right column of Illustration 18.6, not the details in the left column.

The Balance Sheet

Unlike a merchandiser's balance sheet that reports a single inventory amount, the balance sheet for a manufacturer typically shows materials, work in process, and finished goods inventories separately. A manufacturer's balance sheet may also show greater detail in the property, plant, and equipment section because of the significant investment in plant assets.

THE GENERAL COST ACCUMULATION MODEL

Product and Cost Flows

Objective 5
Explain the pattern of cost flows for a company.

In general, companies match the flow of costs to the physical flow of products through the production process, as shown in Illustration 18.7. They place materials received from suppliers in the materials storeroom. They also record the cost of those materials when purchasing them. As they are needed for production, the materials move from the materials storeroom to the production departments, and their cost is assigned to those production departments, as shown in Illustration 18.7.

During production, the materials processed by workers and machines become partially manufactured products. At any time during production, these partially manufactured products are collectively known as **work in process.** For example, if accountants compute the inventory when the company has partially finished products at the end of the year, this inventory is work in process inventory.

Completed products are **finished goods.** When the products are completed and transferred to the finished goods storeroom, the company removes their costs from Work in Process Inventory and assigns them to Finished Goods Inventory. As the goods are sold, the company transfers related costs from Finished Goods Inventory to Cost of Goods Sold.

The accounting flow of costs follows the physical flow of the manufacturing process in most companies. Some companies use an alternative approach that we discuss in Chapter 20. In this chapter and the next, we assume costs follow the physical flow of products.

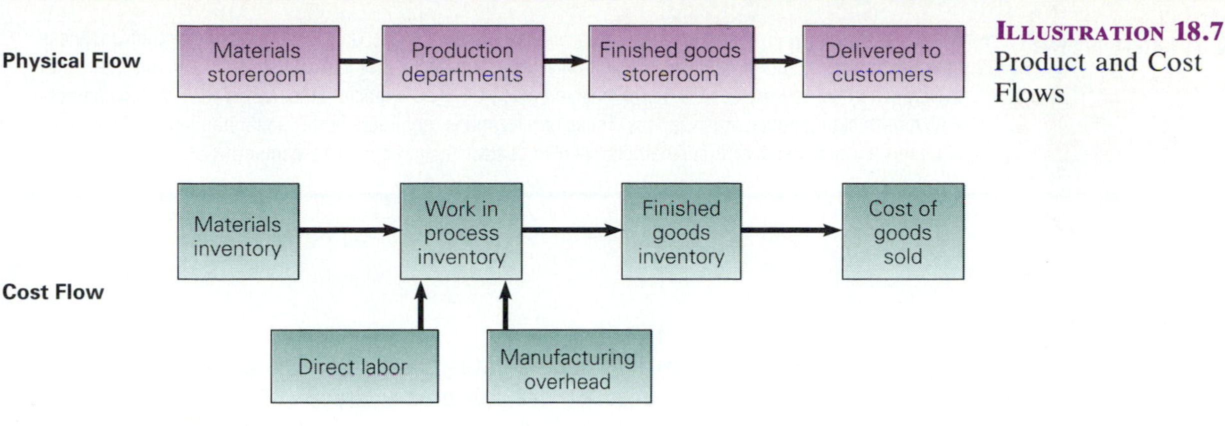

ILLUSTRATION 18.7
Product and Cost Flows

ILLUSTRATION 18.8
Production Activities and Types of Accounting Systems

Type of Production	Accounting System	Type of Product
Job shop Hospital, custom home builder, consulting firm	Job costing	Customized
Batch production Furniture manufacturer, winery	Mostly job costing	Several different products
Repetitive manufacturing Computer terminals, bicycles, clothing	Mostly process costing (operations)	Few new products
Continuous flow processing Oil refinery, paint, chemicals	Process costing	Standardized

Cost Accounting Systems for Different Types of Production

Objective 6
Compare and contrast different production methods and accounting systems.

In discussing product costing, we described how accountants and managers assign costs to products. Recall that products can be either goods or services, so this discussion applies to service and merchandising companies as well as to manufacturing companies.

In Illustration 18.8, we show how various companies choose different accounting systems, depending on their products. First, companies producing individual, unique products known as *jobs* use job costing (also called *job order costing*). Companies such as Morrison-Knudsen, a construction company, and Andersen Consulting, a consulting firm, produce jobs and use job costing.

Morrison-Knudsen
Morrison-Knudsen is a multinational construction company whose products include highways and dams.

Andersen Consulting
Andersen Consulting is a multinational consulting company that specializes in information systems consulting.

Second, some companies, like furniture manufacturers, produce batches of products. They produce all of the components of a single product (e.g., coffee tables) in one batch. They would then produce the components of another product (e.g., dining room sets) in a new batch. (Some university food service companies prepare meals this way.) Companies such as these use job costing methods to accumulate the cost of each batch.

The last two types of production in Illustration 18.8 use process costing methods described in Chapter 19, so we give just a brief overview here. Repetitive manufacturing lends itself to the use of automated equipment that minimizes the amount of manual material handling. Automobile assembly plants, food processing plants, and computer terminal assembly plants use repetitive manufacturing.

Continuous flow processing is the opposite of job shops. Companies using this process continuously mass-produce a single, homogeneous product. Companies use process cost systems in manufacturing paint, grinding flour, and refining oil.

An Accounting Perspective

Business Insight Engineers for automobile companies in the United States believe that Japanese manufacturers can build cars for considerably less than their U.S. counterparts. Many hospitals that thrived when health care costs were reimbursed faced troubled financial times when they had to compete with health maintenance organizations. These organizations required a better understanding of their costs. It's simple. Companies with competitors have to control their costs to be competitive.

Job Costing

Objective 7
Describe job cost flows and determine the cost of jobs.

A **job cost system (job costing)** accumulates costs incurred according to the individual jobs. Companies generally use job cost systems when they can identify separate products or when they produce goods to meet a customer's particular needs.

Who uses job costing? Examples include homebuilders who design specific houses for each customer and accumulate the costs separately for each job, and caterers who accumulate the costs of each banquet separately. Consulting, law, and public accounting firms use job costing to measure the costs of serving each client. Motion pictures, printing, and other industries where unique jobs are produced use job costing. Hospitals also use job costing to determine the cost of each patient's care.

Assume Creative Printers is a company run by a group of students who use desktop publishing to produce specialty books and instruction manuals. Creative Printers uses job costing. Creative Printers keeps track of the time and materials (mostly paper) used on each job.

The company compares the cost of each job with the revenue received to be sure the jobs are profitable. Sometimes the company learns that certain jobs are too costly considering the prices they can charge. For example, Creative Printers recently learned that cookbooks were not profitable. On the other hand, printing instruction manuals was quite profitable, so the company has focused more on the instruction manual market. To illustrate a job costing system, this section describes the transactions for the month of July for Creative Printers.

On July 1, Creative Printers had these beginning inventories:

Materials inventory	$20,000
Work in process inventory (Job No. 106: direct materials, $4,200; direct labor, $5,000; and overhead, $4,000)	13,200
Finished goods inventory (Job No. 105)	5,500

Creative Printing had completed Job No. 105, a set of gardening books, but had not shipped them to the customer as of June 30. They had Job No. 106, a set of instruction manuals for computer software, in process at the beginning of July and completed it in July. They started Job No. 107, a travel guide for visitors to Southeast Asia, in July but had not completed it.

The transactions and the journal entries to record these transactions follow. In Illustration 18.9, we show the flow of costs through accounts and the beginning balances just presented.

1. During July, Creative Printers purchased $25,000 of materials on account. This purchase included both direct materials, such as paper, and indirect materials, such as printing supplies and computer supplies.

Materials Inventory	25,000	
Accounts Payable		25,000
To record purchase of materials.		

2. During July, Creative Printers sent direct materials from the materials storeroom to jobs as follows: $9,000 to Job No. 106, and $14,000 to Job No. 107. The company also sent indirect materials of $1,000 to jobs. It charged indirect

ILLUSTRATION 18.9 Job Cost Flows—Creative Printers

Materials Inventory	
July 1 balance 20,000	
(1)25,000	(2)24,000
July 31 balance 21,000	

Payroll Summary	
Incurred 25,000	Distributed (3)25,000

Overhead	
Indirect materials (2)1,000	Applied to production (4)16,000
Indirect labor (3)5,000	
Other overhead (7)9,800	
	Overapplied balance 200

Work in Process Inventory—Job No. 106	
Beginning inventory:	
Materials 4,200	
Labor 5,000	
Overhead 4,000	
Total 13,200	
Current period:	Completed (5)29,400
Mats. (2) 9,000	
Labor (3) 4,000	
Ovrhd. (4) 3,200	
Total 16,200	
Ending inventory –0–	

Work in Process Inventory—Job No. 107	
Beginning inventory –0–	
Current period:	
Mats. (2)14,000	
Labor (3)16,000	
Ovrhd. (4)12,800	
Total 42,800	
Ending inventory:	
Materials 14,000	
Labor 16,000	
Overhead 12,800	
Total 42,800	

Finished Goods Inventory	
July 1 balance 5,500	Sold (6)5,500
Completed (5)29,400	
July 31 balance 29,400	

Cost of Goods Sold	
Sold (6) 5,500	

Note: Numbers in parentheses refer to journal entries in the text. We show only the entries or parts of entries that deal with cost flows.

materials to overhead, not to each job, because the company does not keep track of how much indirect materials it uses on each job. (Manufacturing companies often use Manufacturing Overhead for the Overhead account. We generally use the Overhead account for both manufacturing and nonmanufacturing companies in this chapter.) Each job has a separate Work in Process Inventory account to keep track of the particular job's costs.

Work in Process Inventory—Job No. 106	9,000	
Work in Process Inventory—Job No. 107	14,000	
Overhead (or Manufacturing Overhead)	1,000	
Materials Inventory		24,000
To record direct and indirect materials sent from the storeroom to jobs.		

See Illustration 18.9 for the flow of materials from Materials Inventory to the Work in Process and Overhead accounts.

3. Production workers keep track of the time spent on each job at Creative Printers. Based on that information, the company assigned production-related labor costs to jobs and to Overhead as follows: $4,000 to Job No. 106, $16,000 to Job No. 107, and indirect labor of $5,000 to Overhead.

Work in Process Inventory—Job No. 106	4,000	
Work in Process Inventory—Job No. 107	16,000	
Overhead	5,000	
Payroll Summary		25,000
To distribute labor costs to jobs and overhead.		

The entry to record payroll incurred during the accounting period (not shown) includes a debit to Payroll Summary and a credit to liability accounts to show payables for fringe benefits, such as health insurance, payroll taxes, and employee wages. In entry (3) the payroll summary is distributed to the jobs and overhead. Look at Illustration 18.9 to see the assignment of labor costs to the Work in Process and Overhead accounts.

4. The company assigns overhead to each job in the following manner: Creative Printers charges indirect materials to jobs based on each job's usage of materials; it charges indirect labor to jobs based on each job's usage of labor; and it charges all other overhead to jobs on the basis of the machine-hours each job uses.

By definition, overhead cannot be traced directly to jobs. Instead, we use *cost drivers* to assign overhead to jobs. A **cost driver** is a measure of activities, such as machine-hours, that is the cause of costs. To assign overhead to jobs, the cost driver should be the cause of the overhead costs, or at least be reasonably associated with the overhead costs. Just as automobile mileage is a good cost driver for measuring the cause of gasoline consumption, machine-hours is a measure of what causes energy costs. By assigning energy costs to jobs based on the number of machine-minutes or hours the job uses, we have a pretty good idea of the energy costs required to produce the job.

Creative Printers assigns overhead (such as machine maintenance) to jobs on a machine-hour basis. This makes good sense if machine maintenance is based on hours of usage, similar to having car maintenance done every 6,000 miles.

Creative Printers also assigns overhead (such as building depreciation) to jobs on a machine-hour basis, which is less logical. However, Creative Printers' management does not believe the time and trouble of developing a more sophisticated method of assigning building depreciation to jobs is justified. For example, management did not believe better overhead allocation would sufficiently improve company profits to justify hiring another accountant to improve its overhead allocation method.

Creative Printers allocates overhead to each job as follows:

Materials basis: Overhead is assigned to a job at the rate of 5% of the cost of materials used on the job.

Labor basis: Overhead is assigned at the rate of 25% of the cost of labor used on the job.

Machine-hours basis: Overhead is assigned to a job at the rate of $2 per machine-hour used on the job.

For now, assume these overhead rates are correct. Later in the chapter we discuss how companies derive these overhead rates. Creative Printers assigned overhead to Jobs 106 and 107 as follows:

Job 106		**Overhead assigned to Job 106:**	
Materials	$9,000	5% × $9,000	$ 450
Labor cost	$4,000	25% × $4,000	1,000
Machine-hours	875 hours	$2 × 875 hours	1,750
		Total overhead assigned to Job 106	$3,200

Job 107		**Overhead assigned to Job 107:**	
Materials	$14,000	5% × $14,000	$ 700
Labor cost	$16,000	25% × $16,000	4,000
Machine-hours	4,050 hours	$2 × 4,050 hours	8,100
		Total overhead assigned to Job 107	$12,800

Here is the journal entry to assign overhead to jobs:

Work in Process Inventory—Job No. 106	3,200	
Work in Process Inventory—Job No. 107	12,800	
Overhead		16,000
To record application of overhead to jobs.		

See Illustration 18.9 for the application of overhead to jobs.

5. Job No. 106 was completed. Job 106 cost $29,400 for the total work done on the job, including costs in beginning Work in Process Inventory on July 1 and costs added during July. This entry records the completion of Job 106:

Finished Goods Inventory	29,400	
Work in Process Inventory—Job No. 106		29,400
To record completed production for July.		

See Illustration 18.9 for the flow of costs from Work in Process Inventory to Finished Goods Inventory.

6. Job No. 105 was sold on account in July for $9,000. These entries record the sale and the related cost of goods sold:

Accounts Receivable	9,000	
Sales		9,000
To record sales on account for July.		
Cost of Goods Sold	5,500	
Finished Goods Inventory		5,500
To record cost of goods sold in July (Job 105).		

7. The company applied overhead to the jobs in entry (4) based on a predetermined overhead rate. Many of the actual overhead costs are not known until the end of the month or later. For example, the company would not receive its utility bill for July until sometime in August. In addition to the indirect materials and indirect labor recorded in entries (2) and (3), Creative Printers incurred these other overhead costs for July:

Machinery repairs and maintenance	$4,500
Utilities, including energy costs to run machines	1,000
Depreciation of building and machines	2,500
Other overhead	1,800
Total overhead incurred in July other than indirect materials and indirect labor	$9,800

To prepare the journal entry, we debit the Overhead account for the actual costs. Then we credit Accounts Payable for the machinery repairs and maintenance, utilities, and other overhead. (We assume an outside contractor does the maintenance and repairs.) The amount is $7,300 ($4,500 + $1,000 + $1,800). And, finally we credit Accumulated Depreciation for $2,500. Here is the journal entry:

Overhead	9,800	
Accounts Payable		7,300
Accumulated Depreciation		2,500
To record actual overhead costs for July.		

At this point, you may want to review the flow of costs through the inventory accounts in Illustration 18.9. Note that Illustration 18.9 shows only the inventory accounts, Payroll Summary, Overhead, and Cost of Goods Sold, not all of the accounts in the preceding entries.

ILLUSTRATION 18.10
Transfer Overapplied Overhead to Cost of Goods Sold

Overhead		Cost of Goods Sold	
1,000*	16,000*	5,500*	Transfer from Overhead (8)200
5,000*			
9,800*			
	Overapplied balance 200	Cost of Goods Sold for July 5,300	
Transfer to Cost of Goods Sold (8)200			
–0–			

* These amounts are from Illustration 18.9.

8. At the end of the month, the Overhead account contains **overapplied overhead** of $200 as shown in Illustration 18.9. Companies generally transfer the balance of the Overhead account to Cost of Goods Sold at the end of the accounting period. Some companies do this monthly; others do it quarterly or annually. The journal entry to transfer Creative Printers' overhead balance to Cost of Goods Sold for the month of July is as follows:

Overhead	200	
Cost of Goods Sold		200
To transfer the overhead balance to Cost of Goods Sold.		

See the adjusted Cost of Goods Sold and the Overhead accounts in Illustration 18.10.

Why does entry (8) reduce the Cost of Goods Sold by $200? The overhead applied to the jobs was too high—it was overapplied. Thus, the cost of jobs was overstated. Although those jobs are still in Work in Process or Finished Goods Inventory, companies usually adjust the Cost of Goods Sold account instead of each inventory account. Adjusting each inventory account for a small overhead adjustment is usually not a good use of managerial and accounting time and effort. All jobs appear in Cost of Goods Sold sooner or later, so companies simply adjust Cost of Goods Sold instead of the inventory accounts.

In this book, we assume companies transfer overhead balances to Cost of Goods Sold. We leave the more complicated procedure of allocating overhead balances to inventory accounts to textbooks on cost accounting.

Although Creative Printers had overapplied overhead, it could just as easily have had **underapplied overhead.** If overhead had been underapplied, the company would have debited Cost of Goods Sold and credited Overhead to transfer the overhead balance.

Sometime in July or August, Creative Printers would collect its receivables in cash and pay its payables. The accounts payable for July amount to $32,300 ($25,000 for the materials purchase + $7,300 payables for overhead costs). The payroll liabilities amount to $25,000. Here are the entries recording Creative Printers' payment of payables and payroll liabilities, and the collection of its receivables of $9,000:

Accounts Payable	32,300	
Cash		32,300
Payroll Liabilities	25,000	
Cash		25,000
Cash	9,000	
Accounts Receivable		9,000

Note that in Illustration 18.11 we present the income statement for Creative Printers. Assume the selling and administrative expenses for July are $3,000.

ILLUSTRATION 18.11
Creative Printers—Income Statement

CREATIVE PRINTERS Income Statement For the Month Ended July 31, 1997		
Sales		$9,000
Cost of goods sold:		
Finished goods inventory, July 1	$ 5,500	
Cost of goods manufactured	29,400	
Cost of goods available for sale	$34,900	
Less: Finished goods inventory, July 31	29,400	
Cost of goods sold		5,500
Gross margin		$3,500
Selling and administrative expenses		3,000
Net income		$ 500

Managerial Uses of Cost Information

Managers would use the preceding cost information for several purposes: First, they would compare the actual costs of the job with expected costs, both as the work is being done and after the job has been completed. Later chapters discuss the role of managerial accounting in performance evaluation. Second, managers would assess the profitability of jobs. For example, Job 105 had revenue of $9,000 and costs of $5,500, leaving a gross margin of $3,500.

Third, managers would compare actual overhead on the left side of the Overhead account, with the overhead applied to jobs on the right side. If the actual overhead exceeds the applied overhead, they may wish to learn why the actual overhead is so high. Also, they may ask the accountants to increase the overhead applied to jobs to give them a better idea of the cost of jobs. If the actual is less than the applied overhead, they may ask the accountants to reduce the overhead applied to jobs.

PREDETERMINED OVERHEAD RATES

Objective 8
Explain how and why predetermined overhead rates are computed.

Creative Printers used predetermined rates to apply overhead to jobs. For example, they determined the 5% rate used to apply materials-related overhead to jobs before the month of July. Most manufacturing and service organizations use predetermined rates.

To calculate a **predetermined overhead rate,** a company divides the estimated total overhead costs for a period by an expected level of activity. This activity could be total expected machine-hours, total expected direct labor-hours, or total expected direct labor cost for the period. Companies set predetermined overhead rates at the beginning of the year in which they will use them. Thus, the rates for July may have been computed in November or December of the previous year. This formula computes a predetermined rate:

$$\text{Predetermined overhead rate} = \frac{\text{Estimated overhead costs}}{\text{Expected level of activity (such as machine-hours)}}$$

To demonstrate, assume the accountants at Creative Printers estimated overhead related to machine usage to be $120,000 for the year and estimated the machine usage for the year to be 60,000 machine-hours. Thus, the predetermined overhead rate would be $2 per hour, calculated as follows:

$$\text{Predetermined overhead rate} = \frac{\text{Estimated overhead costs}}{\text{Expected machine-hours}}$$

$$\text{Predetermined overhead rate} = \frac{\$120{,}000}{60{,}000 \text{ machine-hours}}$$

$$= \$2 \text{ per machine-hour}$$

Some companies compute the overhead rate after the fact; that is, after the jobs are done and the overhead costs are known. The formula to calculate an **actual overhead rate** is:

$$\text{Actual overhead rate} = \frac{\text{Total actual overhead costs}}{\text{Total actual manufacturing activity}}$$

Recall that we measured manufacturing activity using machine-hours, labor-hours, labor costs, materials costs, or some other cost driver.

Reasons for Using Predetermined Rates Most companies use predetermined overhead rates instead of actual overhead rates for the following reasons:

1. A company usually does not incur overhead costs uniformly throughout the year. For example, heating costs are greater during winter months. However, allocating more overhead costs to a job produced in the winter compared to one produced in the summer may serve no useful purpose.

2. Some overhead costs, like factory building depreciation, are fixed costs. If the volume of goods produced varies from month to month, the actual rate varies from month to month, even though the total cost is constant from month to month. The predetermined rate, on the other hand, is constant from month to month.

3. Predetermined rates make it possible for companies to estimate job costs sooner. Using a predetermined rate, companies can assign overhead costs to production when they assign direct materials and direct labor costs. Without a predetermined rate, companies do not know the costs of production until the end of the month or even later when bills arrive. For example, the electric bill for July will probably not arrive until August. If Creative Printers had used actual overhead, the company would not have determined the costs of its July work until August. It is better to have a good estimate of costs when doing the work instead of waiting a long time for only a slightly more accurate number.

An Accounting Perspective

Uses of Technology Recently, many high-tech companies have installed computer-assisted methods of manufacturing, merchandising, or providing services. These new technologies have had a major impact on managerial accounting. For example, where robots and computer-assisted manufacturing methods have replaced people, labor costs have shrunk from 20% to 40% of product costs to less than 5%. Accounting in traditional settings required much more work to keep track of labor costs than is necessary in current systems. On the other hand, in highly automated environments, accountants have had to become more sophisticated in finding the causes of overhead costs, which have become a larger part of total product cost.

Understanding the Learning Objectives

Objective 1
Compare and contrast managerial accounting and financial accounting.

- Financial accounting refers to providing financial information primarily for external use. Managerial accounting information is intended for internal use to provide more detailed information to managers.

Objective 2
Describe the basic components of a product's cost.

- In manufacturing companies, a product's cost is made up of three cost elements: direct materials costs, direct labor costs, and manufacturing overhead costs.
- Direct materials costs are clearly and easily traceable to the product.
- Direct labor costs include only those labor costs clearly traceable to, or readily identifiable with, the finished product.
- Overhead costs (1) include all costs of making the product except direct materials and direct labor costs; (2) are costs that must be incurred in making the product but cannot or will not be traced directly to specific units produced; and (3) include a

number of costs related to the production process, such as depreciation and maintenance on machines, supervisors' salaries, and utility costs for production facilities.

Objective 3
Explain the difference between product costs and period costs.

- Product costs are costs incurred in making products. These costs include costs of direct materials, direct labor, and overhead.
- Period costs are not assigned to units of a product but are related more closely to periods of time. For this reason, period costs are expensed (deducted from revenues) in the period in which they are incurred.

Objective 4
Compare financial reporting by a merchandiser to that of a manufacturer, and prepare a statement of cost of goods manufactured, an income statement, and a balance sheet for a manufacturer.

- The major difference between a merchandiser and a manufacturer is in the types of inventories carried.
- The statement of cost of goods manufactured supports the cost of goods sold figure on the income statement and has two important calculations: (1) Cost to manufacture, which includes the costs of all resources put into production during the period and (2) Cost of goods manufactured, which consists of the cost of all goods completed during the period.
- The manufacturer's balance sheet shows materials, work in process, and finished goods inventories separately.

Objective 5
Explain the pattern of cost flows for a company.

- The accounting flow of costs using perpetual procedure follows the physical flow of the manufacturing process.
- Accountants record the flow of direct materials costs from Materials Inventory into Work in Process Inventory. They add the costs of direct labor and overhead to Work in Process Inventory. When the products are completed and transferred to the finished goods storeroom, accountants transfer their costs from Work in Process Inventory to Finished Goods Inventory. As the goods are sold, the related costs are transferred from Finished Goods Inventory to Cost of Goods Sold.

Objective 6
Compare and contrast different production methods and accounting systems.

- Companies producing individual, unique products known as jobs use job costing (also called *job order costing*).
- Companies such as furniture manufacturers produce batches of products and use job costing methods to accumulate the cost of each batch.
- Repetitive manufacturing companies (automobile assembly plants) and companies producing in a continuous flow (oil refineries) use process costing, discussed in the next chapter.

Objective 7
Describe job cost flows and determine the cost of jobs.

- A job cost system (job costing) is a cost system that accumulates costs incurred according to the individual jobs. Each job has its own Work in Process Inventory account.

Objective 8
Explain how and why predetermined overhead rates are computed.

- The formula for the predetermined overhead rate is:

$$\text{Predetermined overhead rate} = \frac{\text{Estimated overhead costs}}{\text{Expected level of activity (such as machine-hours)}}$$

Objective 9
Describe the differences in net income under absorption costing and variable costing. (Appendix)

- Under variable costing, all the fixed manufacturing overhead costs are charged off (as period costs) during the period rather than being deferred and carried forward (as product costs) to the next period as part of inventory cost.
- Under absorption costing, all manufacturing costs are treated as product costs, including fixed manufacturing overhead.

APPENDIX

Objective 9
Describe the differences in net income under absorption costing and variable costing.

VARIABLE VERSUS ABSORPTION COSTING

Under **absorption costing,** companies treat all manufacturing costs, including both fixed and variable manufacturing costs, as product costs. Under **variable costing,** companies treat only variable manufacturing costs as product costs. Total variable costs change proportionately with changes in total activity, while fixed costs do not change as activity levels change. These variable manufacturing costs are usually made up of direct materials, variable manufacturing overhead, and direct labor. (Direct labor can be a fixed cost if the company chooses not to decrease or increase its direct labor force as volume changes. Unless otherwise stated, we treat direct labor as a variable cost.)

Variable costing (also known as *direct costing*) treats all fixed manufacturing costs as period costs to be charged to expense in the period received. The logic behind this expensing of fixed manufacturing costs is that the company would incur such costs whether a plant was in production or idle. Therefore, these fixed costs do not specifically relate to the manufacture of products.

Look at Illustration 18.12, Bradley Company's income statements for May 1997 using absorption costing on top and variable costing on the bottom. Notice that Bradley's variable costing income statement carries the goods in inventory at $3.30 per unit rather than at the $3.90 full cost. The statement shows all variable costs as deductions from sales to disclose the contribution margin for the month. It classifies all fixed costs as period costs no matter what the source of the cost (manufacturing, selling, or administrative).

ILLUSTRATION 18.12
Comparative Income Statements

Income Statement under Absorption Costing

BRADLEY COMPANY
Income Statement
For the Period Ending May 31, 1997

Sales (9,000 units at $8)		$72,000
Cost of goods sold:		
Variable costs of production (10,000 units at $3.30)	$33,000	
Fixed overhead costs	6,000	
Total costs of producing 10,000 units	$39,000	
Less: Ending inventory (1,000 units at $3.90)	3,900	35,100
Gross margin on sales		$36,900
Operating expenses:		
Selling expenses ($15,000 fixed plus 9,000 at $0.20 each)	$16,800	
Administrative expenses	12,000	28,800
Income before income taxes		$ 8,100

Contribution Margin Income Statement under Variable Costing

BRADLEY COMPANY
Income Statement
For the Period Ending May 31, 1997

Sales (9,000 units at $8)		$72,000
Variable costs		
Variable production costs incurred (10,000 units at $3.30)	$33,000	
Less: Ending inventory (1,000 units at $3.30)	3,300	29,700
Manufacturing margin		$42,300
Variable selling expenses (9,000 units at $0.20)		1,800
Contribution margin		$40,500
Fixed costs:		
Manufacturing overhead	$ 6,000	
Selling expenses	15,000	
Administrative expenses	12,000	33,000
Income before income taxes		$ 7,500

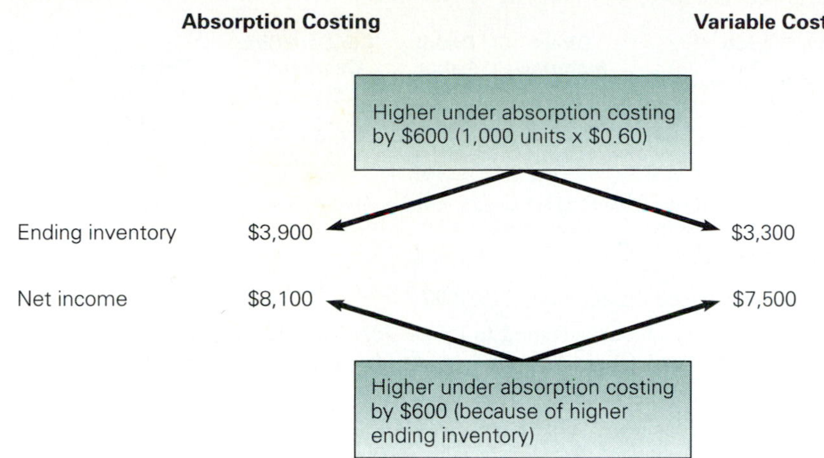

ILLUSTRATION 18.13
Comparison of Results under Absorption and Variable Costing

Comparing the Two Methods

In comparing the two income statements in Illustration 18.12, notice the $600 difference in net income for the month and a $600 difference in ending inventory valuation, as shown in Illustration 18.13. These differences are due to the treatment of fixed manufacturing costs. Under absorption costing, each unit in ending inventory carries $0.60 of fixed overhead cost as part of product cost. At the end of the month, Bradley has 1,000 units in inventory. Therefore, ending inventory under absorption costing includes $600 of fixed manufacturing overhead costs ($0.60 × 1,000 units) and is valued at $600 more than under variable costing.

Under variable costing, companies charge off, or expense, all the fixed manufacturing costs during the period rather than deferring their expense and carrying them forward to the next period as part of inventory cost. Therefore, $6,000 of fixed manufacturing costs appear on the variable costing income statement as an expense, rather than $5,400 ($6,000 fixed overhead costs − $600 fixed manufacturing included in inventory) under absorption costing. Consequently, income before income taxes under variable costing is $600 less than under absorption costing because more expense is charged off during the period.

Finally, remember that the difference between the absorption costing and variable costing methods is solely in the treatment of fixed manufacturing overhead costs and income statement presentation. Both methods treat selling and administrative expenses as period costs. Regarding selling and administrative expenses, the only difference is their placement on the income statement and the segregation of variable and fixed selling and administrative expenses. Variable selling and administrative expenses are not part of product cost under either method.

As a general rule, relate the difference in net income under absorption costing and variable costing to the change in inventories. Assuming a relatively constant level of production, if inventories increase during the year, production exceeded sales and reported income before federal income taxes is less under variable costing than under absorption costing. Conversely, if inventories decreased, then sales exceeded production, and income before income taxes is larger under variable costing than under absorption costing.

Variable costing is not currently acceptable for income measurement or inventory valuation in external financial statements that must comply with generally accepted accounting principles (GAAP) in the United States. However, managers often use variable costing for internal company reports.

DEMONSTRATION PROBLEM 18–A

Good Earth Construction Company uses a job cost system to account for the houses it builds. Each house is a separate job. As of January 1, 1997, its records showed:

Inventories:	
Materials and supplies	$ 48,000
Work in process (Job Nos. 212 and 213)	103,200
Finished goods (Job No. 211)	120,000

The work in process inventory consists of two jobs:

Job No.	Direct Materials	Direct Labor	Construction Overhead*	Total
212	$18,000	$24,000	$12,000	$ 54,000
213	20,400	19,200	9,600	49,200
	$38,400	$43,200	$21,600	$103,200

* Construction overhead is treated just like overhead in the text examples.

Cost and sales data for 1997:

1. Materials purchased on account, $198,000.
2. Labor costs: Direct labor assigned to jobs—Job No. 212, $48,000; Job No. 213, $96,000; Job No. 214 (started in 1997), $144,000; supervision and other indirect labor, $120,000.
3. Materials used: Job No. 212, $31,200; Job No. 213, $57,600; Job No. 214, $96,000; and indirect materials, $4,800.
4. Overhead is assigned to jobs at the rate of 50% of the actual direct labor costs incurred on each job.
5. Job Nos. 212 and 213 were completed.
6. Jobs 211 and 212 were sold for $540,000.
7. Construction overhead costs incurred, other than indirect materials and indirect labor: depreciation, $12,000; heat, light, power, and miscellaneous, $12,000.

Required Prepare journal entries to record the preceding data and close any underapplied or overapplied overhead to Cost of Goods Sold.

Solution to Demonstation Problem 18–A

GOOD EARTH CONSTRUCTION COMPANY
General Journal

	Account	Debit	Credit
(1)	Materials Inventory	198,000	
	Accounts Payable		198,000
	To record materials purchased on account.		
(2)	Work in Process Inventory—Job No. 212	48,000	
	Work in Process Inventory—Job No. 213	96,000	
	Work in Process Inventory—Job No. 214	144,000	
	Construction Overhead	120,000	
	Payroll Summary		408,000
	To distribute labor costs to jobs and overhead.		
(3)	Work in Process Inventory—Job No. 212	31,200	
	Work in Process Inventory—Job No. 213	57,600	
	Work in Process Inventory—Job No. 214	96,000	
	Construction Overhead	4,800	
	Materials Inventory		189,600
	To record direct and indirect materials sent from storeroom to jobs.		
(4)	Work in Process Inventory—Job No. 212	24,000	
	Work in Process Inventory—Job No. 213	48,000	
	Work in Process Inventory—Job No. 214	72,000	
	Construction Overhead		144,000
	To record overhead allocated to jobs using the predetermined rate of 50% of direct labor cost: Job No. 212, $24,000 (50% × $48,000); Job No. 213, $48,000 (50% × 96,000); and Job No. 214, $72,000 (50% × $144,000).		
(5)	Finished Goods Inventory	408,000	
	Work in Process Inventory—Job No. 212		157,200
	Work in Process Inventory—Job No. 213		250,800
	To record completion of Jobs 212 and 213.		

The following amounts were computed by adding beginning Work in Process balances to the current month's debits to Work in Process for direct materials, direct labor, and construction overhead:

Job No. 212: $157,200 ($54,000 + $31,200 + $48,000 + $24,000)
Job No. 213: 250,800 ($49,200 + $57,600 + $96,000 + $48,000)
$408,000

		Debit	Credit
(6)	Accounts Receivable	540,000	
	Sales		540,000
	To record sales on account.		
	Cost of Goods Sold	277,200	
	Finished Goods Inventory		277,200
	To record cost of goods sold ($120,000 + $157,200 = $277,200).		
(7)	Construction Overhead	24,000	
	Accumulated Depreciation		12,000
	Various accounts (Accounts Payable, Accrued Liabilities Payable, Cash, etc.)		12,000
	To record various construction overhead costs incurred.		
(8)	Cost of Goods Sold	4,800	
	Construction Overhead		4,800
	To close underapplied construction overhead (actual = $148,800, applied = $144,000).		

Demonstration Problem 18–B

Companies use different bases in computing their predetermined overhead rates. From the following estimated data, compute the predetermined rate used by each company.

	Company A	Company B	Company C
Machine-hours	103,000	212,000	125,000
Direct labor-hours	52,000	48,000	39,000
Direct labor cost	$650,000	$735,000	$420,000
Overhead costs	$845,000	$864,000	$750,000

Basis for determining predetermined overhead rate:

Company	Basis
A	Direct labor cost
B	Direct labor-hours
C	Machine-hours

Solution to Demonstration Problem 18–B

Company A:

$$\text{Predetermined overhead rate} = \frac{\$845,000}{\$650,000} = 130\% \text{ of direct labor cost}$$

Company B:

$$\text{Predetermined overhead rate} = \frac{\$864,000}{48,000 \text{ hours}} = \$18 \text{ per direct labor-hour}$$

Company C:

$$\text{Predetermined overhead rate} = \frac{\$750,000}{125,000 \text{ hours}} = \$6 \text{ per machine-hour}$$

New Terms

Absorption costing (Appendix) A concept of costing under which all manufacturing costs, including both fixed and variable manufacturing costs, are accounted for as product costs. *692*

Actual overhead rate Total actual manufacturing overhead divided by total actual manufacturing activity. *690*

Administrative costs Costs of managing the organization, including the costs of top administrative functions and various staff departments such as accounting, data processing, and personnel. *679*

Cost A financial measure of the resources used or given up to achieve a stated purpose. *676*

Cost driver Activity or transaction that causes costs to be incurred. Machine-hours can be a cost driver for costs of energy to run machines, for example. *686*

Cost of goods manufactured Consists of the total costs of all goods completed during the period; includes cost to manufacture plus beginning work in process inventory minus ending work in process inventory. *680*

Cost of goods sold Cost of goods manufactured plus the beginning finished goods inventory minus the ending finished goods inventory. *680*

Cost to manufacture Includes the direct materials, direct labor, and manufacturing overhead incurred during the period. *680*

Direct labor Labor costs of all employees actually working on materials to convert them to finished goods. Direct labor costs are directly traced to particular products in contrast to indirect labor costs. *677*

Direct materials Materials that are used only in making the product and are clearly and easily traceable to a particular product. *676*

Finished goods Completed manufactured products ready to be sold. Finished Goods Inventory is the title of an inventory account maintained for such products. *682*

Indirect labor The cost of labor that cannot, or will not for practical reasons, be traced to the goods being produced or the services being provided. *678*

Indirect materials Materials used in making a product that cannot, or will not for practical reasons, be traced directly to particular products. *677*

Job cost system (job costing) A manufacturing cost system that accumulates costs incurred to produce a product according to individual jobs, such as a building, a consulting job, or a batch of 100 computer desks. *684*

Managerial accounting Managerial accounting information is intended for internal use. The purpose is to generate information managers can use to make good decisions. *675*

Manufacturing overhead All manufacturing costs except for those costs accounted for as direct materials and direct labor. *678*

Materials Unprocessed items used in the manufacturing process. *676*

Overapplied (overabsorbed) overhead The amount by which the overhead applied to production exceeds the actual overhead costs incurred in that same period. *688*

Overhead All costs of making goods or providing services except for those costs classified as direct materials and direct labor. See manufacturing overhead for overhead in manufacturing companies. *678*

Period costs Costs related more closely to periods of time than to products produced. Period costs cannot be traced directly to the manufacture of a specific product; they are expensed in the period in which they are incurred. *679*

Predetermined overhead rate Calculated by dividing estimated total overhead costs for a period by the expected level of activity, such as total expected machine-hours or total expected direct labor-hours for the period. *689*

Product costs Costs a company assigns to units produced. In manufacturing companies, these costs are direct materials, direct labor, and manufacturing overhead. In service companies that have no materials, these costs are direct labor and overhead. *676, 679*

Selling costs Costs incurred to obtain customer orders and distribute the finished product to the customer. *678*

Statement of cost of goods manufactured An accounting report showing the cost to manufacture and the cost of goods manufactured. *680*

Underapplied (underabsorbed) overhead The amount by which actual overhead costs incurred in a period exceed the overhead applied to production in that period. *688*

Variable costing (also called *direct costing*) (Appendix) A concept of costing under which only variable manufacturing costs are accounted for as product costs and charged to the units produced during a period. All fixed manufacturing costs are charged to expense in the period in which they are incurred. *692*

Work in process Partially manufactured products; a Work in Process Inventory account is maintained for such products. *682*

Self-Test

True-False

Indicate whether each of the following statements is true or false.

1. Managerial accounting is for external use and gives less detailed information than financial accounting.
2. A manufacturer produces speedboats, and each one requires a motor. The motors are considered direct materials and are product costs.
3. A Pepsi-Cola bottling plant is an example of a company that would use a job cost system.
4. A predetermined overhead rate is calculated by dividing the expected level of activity by the estimated total overhead cost.

5. Overhead cannot be entered in Work in Process Inventory when using a predetermined overhead rate. Only when the actual overhead costs are determined is the overhead entered.

6. Selling and administrative expenses are part of period costs under both absorption and variable costing methods.

Multiple-Choice

Select the best answer for each of the following questions.

1. Under which cost category are indirect material costs included?
   - **a.** Direct materials.
   - **b.** Overhead.
   - **c.** Direct labor.
   - **d.** None of the above.
2. For financial accounting and external reporting purposes, all selling and administrative expenses are treated as:
   - **a.** Period costs.
   - **b.** Selling costs.
   - **c.** Manufacturing overhead costs.
   - **d.** Product costs.
3. What are the differences between the cost of goods sold sections in a manufacturer's and a merchandiser's income statements?
   - **a.** A merchandiser uses Merchandise Inventory and Direct Labor, whereas a manufacturer uses Finished Goods Inventory and Cost of Goods Manufactured.
   - **b.** A merchandiser uses Merchandise Inventory and Cost of Goods Available for Sale, whereas a manufacturer uses Finished Goods Inventory and Cost of Goods Available for Sale.
   - **c.** A merchandiser uses Work in Process Inventory and Cost of Goods Sold, whereas a manufacturer uses Finished Goods Inventory and Cost of Goods Sold.
   - **d.** None of the above.
4. A job cost system is used:
   - **a.** When there are dissimilar products.
   - **b.** By manufacturers and service companies.
   - **c.** When goods are produced to meet a customer's particular needs.
   - **d.** All of the above.
5. Which of the following best describes the advantages of using a predetermined overhead rate?
   - **a.** Overhead costs are applied evenly throughout the year rather than fluctuating from month to month.
   - **b.** Predetermined rates require managers to wait until long after the accounting period to get an estimate of product costs.
   - **c.** Total unit costs of production are known sooner than using actual overhead rates, and overhead costs are evenly distributed throughout the year.
   - **d.** Both (a) and (c) above.
6. The expected level of activity in a production center is 30,000 machine-hours. Estimated overhead costs are indirect materials and indirect labor, $360,000; other overhead, $90,000. Which of the following is the predetermined overhead rate per machine-hour?
   - **a.** $3.
   - **b.** $12.
   - **c.** $15.
   - **d.** $20.
7. You are given the following data relating to a company:

Estimated manufacturing overhead per year	$24,000
Expected level of activity per year	40,000 machine-hours
Predetermined overhead rate	$0.60 per machine-hour
Actual overhead costs incurred during year	$22,500
Actual machine-hours	35,000

Which of the following are the correct journal entries for the preceding data?

		Debit	Credit
a.	Manufacturing Overhead	22,500	
	Various accounts		22,500
	Work in Process Inventory	21,000	
	Manufacturing Overhead		21,000
b.	Manufacturing Overhead	22,500	
	Various accounts		22,500
	Work in Process Inventory	15,428	
	Manufacturing Overhead		15,428
c.	Manufacturing Overhead	24,000	
	Various accounts		24,000
	Work in Process Inventory	15,428	
	Manufacturing Overhead		15,428
d.	Various accounts	22,500	
	Manufacturing Overhead		22,500
	Manufacturing Overhead	15,428	
	Work in Process Inventory		15,428

Now turn to page 706 to check your answers.

Questions

1. What are the major differences between managerial and financial accounting?
2. Identify the three elements of cost incurred in manufacturing a product and indicate the distinguishing characteristics of each.
3. Why might a company claim that the total cost of employing a person is $10.30 per hour when the employee's wage rate is $6.50 per hour? How should this difference be classified and why?
4. Why are certain costs referred to as period costs? What are the major types of period costs incurred by a manufacturer?

5. Explain why the income statement of a manufacturing company differs from the income statement of a merchandising company.
6. What is the general content of a statement of cost of goods manufactured? What is its relationship to the income statement?
7. What is the relationship between cost flows in the accounts and the flow of physical products through a factory?
8. Define a job cost system and give an example of a situation in which it can be used.
9. What are the major reasons for using predetermined manufacturing overhead rates?
10. What is the formula for computing a predetermined overhead rate? If the expected level of activity in a production center is 50,000 machine-hours and the estimated overhead costs are $750,000, what is the predetermined overhead rate? Show the calculation.
11. What is underapplied and overapplied overhead? What type of balance does each have in the Overhead account?
12. Direct materials were issued to the following jobs: Material A was issued to Job No. 101, $2,000; Job No. 102, $1,000; and Job No. 103, $5,000. Material B was issued to Job No. 101, $5,000; Job No. 102, $2,000; and Job No. 103, $3,000. Indirect materials were issued to all jobs, $3,000.
Record the direct and indirect materials in journal entry form.
13. **Real World Question** Assume Domino's Pizza is considering offering a new product—a 6-inch pizza. Why would it matter if Domino's Pizza knows how much it costs to produce and deliver this 6-inch pizza?
14. **Real World Question** Why is it becoming more important that the managers of hospitals understand their product costs?
15. **Real World Question** Besides law firms and public accounting firms, name three service organizations that produce jobs.
16. (Appendix) Under what specific circumstances would you expect net income to be larger under variable costing than under absorption costing? What is the reason for this difference?

EXERCISES

Exercise 18–1
Classify costs (L.O. 2)

The following costs are incurred by an electrical appliance manufacturer. Classify these costs as direct materials, direct labor, manufacturing overhead, selling, or administrative.

a. President's salary.
b. Cost of electrical wire used in making appliances.
c. Cost of janitorial supplies (the janitors work in the factory).
d. Wages of assembly-line workers.
e. Cost of promotional displays.
f. Assembly-line supervisor's salary.
g. Cost accountant's salary (the accountant works in the factory).
h. Cost of cleaner used to clean appliances when they are completed.
i. Cost of aluminum used for toasters.
j. Cost of market research survey.

Exercise 18–2
Classify items as product or period costs (L.O. 3)

Classify the costs listed in Exercise 18–1 as either product costs or period costs.

Exercise 18–3
Compute cost of goods sold (L.O. 4)

Friendship Company makes products for the Olympic Games. The following data are for the year ended December 31, 1996:

Materials inventory, January 1, 1996	$ 90,000
Materials inventory, December 31, 1996	130,000
Materials purchases	350,000
Direct labor	450,000
Work in process inventory, January 1, 1996	60,000
Work in process inventory, December 31, 1996	80,000
Manufacturing overhead	260,000
Finished goods inventory, January 1, 1996	160,000
Finished goods inventory, December 31, 1996	280,000

Prepare a Cost of Goods Manufactured Statement and compute the cost of goods sold.

Exercise 18–4
Compute job costs; prepare journal entries to record production activities (L.O. 7)

In June, Socks Company worked only on Job No. 714 and completed it on June 30. There were no prior costs accumulated on Job No. 714 before June 1. During the month, the company purchased and used $5,400 of direct materials, used 2,000 machine-hours, and incurred $9,600 of direct labor costs. Assuming manufacturing overhead is applied at the rate of $6 per machine-hour, what is the total cost of Job No. 714? Prepare journal entries to assign the materials, labor, and manufacturing overhead costs to production and to record the transfer of Job No. 714 to Finished Goods Inventory.

Exercise 18–5
Compute job costs; prepare journal entries to record production activities (L.O. 7)

At the end of the second week in March, Job No. 301 has an accumulated total cost of $18,900. In the third week, $4,500 of direct materials were used on Job 301, 300 hours of direct labor were charged to the job at $20 per hour, and manufacturing overhead was applied on the basis of $20 per machine-hour for overhead. Job No. 301 was the only job worked on in the third week. It was also completed in the third week. Job No. 301 used 160 machine-hours during the third week in March. Compute the cost of Job No. 301, and give the journal entry required to record its completion and transfer to Finished Goods Inventory.

Exercise 18–6
Compute overhead rates (L.O. 8)

Different companies use different bases in computing their predetermined overhead rates. From the following estimated data, compute the predetermined rate to be used by each company:

	Company		
	Alpha	**Charlie**	**Zorba**
Machine-hours	200,000	420,000	250,000
Direct labor-hours	100,000	96,000	78,000
Direct labor cost	$1,600,000	$1,470,000	$820,000
Manufacturing overhead cost	$800,000	$864,000	$750,000

Basis for determining predetermined overhead rate:

Company	**Basis**
Alpha	Direct labor cost
Charlie	Direct labor-hours
Zorba	Machine-hours

Exercise 18–7
Prepare journal entry to transfer underapplied or overapplied overhead to Cost of Goods Sold (L.O. 7, 8)

Refer to Exercise 18–6. Assume the actual hours and cost data were:

Actual	**Alpha**	**Charlie**	**Zorba**
Manufacturing overhead	$900,000	$800,000	$750,000
Direct labor cost	$1,700,000	$1,400,000	$800,000
Direct labor-hours	90,000	92,000	76,000
Machine-hours	210,000	400,000	260,000

a. Compute overapplied or underapplied overhead for each company.

b. Prepare journal entries to transfer overapplied or underapplied overhead to Cost of Goods Sold for each company.

Exercise 18–8
Demonstrate job cost flows in a service organization (L.O. 7)

Anderhouse and Touche Consultants uses a job cost system and had the following activity during December:

1. There were no jobs in beginning Work in Process or Finished Goods Inventory.
2. Three jobs were started: Nos. 222, 223, and 224. Job No. 222 was completed and the customer was billed for $5,000 on account. Job No. 223 was completed and in Finished Goods Inventory awaiting billing to the client at the end of the month. Job No. 224 was still in process at month end.
3. Direct labor costs incurred for:

Job No. 222	100 hours @ $21/hour
Job No. 223	150 hours @ $18/hour
Job No. 224	60 hours @ $17/hour

4. Assume overhead is applied at the rate of $10 per labor-hour.
5. Actual overhead was $3,200.

Required

Prepare journal entries to record the preceding data, as well as the transfer of underapplied or overapplied overhead to Cost of Goods Sold.

Exercise 18–9
Prepare income statements using absorption and variable costing (based on Appendix) (L.O. 9)

The following data relate to Gore Company for the year ended December 31, 1996:

Cost of production:	
Direct materials (variable)	$180,000
Direct labor (variable)	252,000
Manufacturing overhead:	
Variable	90,000
Fixed	180,000
Sales commissions (variable)	54,000
Sales salaries (fixed)	36,000
Administrative expenses (fixed)	72,000
Units produced	75,000
Units sold (at $18 each)	60,000

There were no beginning inventories. Assume direct materials and direct labor are variable costs. Prepare two income statements—a variable costing income statement and an absorption costing income statement.

PROBLEMS

Problem 18–1
Classify costs (L.O. 2)

Sunspot, Inc., is considering a new sunscreen packet that contains a skin wipe with sunscreen on it. These would be particularly useful for people who do not want to carry a bottle of sunscreen, according to Sunspot's marketing manager. Classify the following costs of this new product as direct materials, direct labor, manufacturing overhead, selling, or administrative.

a. President's salary.
b. Packages used to hold the skin wipes.
c. Cleaning materials used to clean the skin wipe packages.
d. Wages of workers who package the product.
e. Cost of advertising the product.
f. The salary of the supervisor of the workers who package the product.
g. Cost accountant's salary (the accountant works in the factory).
h. Cost of a market research survey.
i. Sales commissions paid as a percent of sales.
j. Depreciation of administrative office building.

Problem 18–2
Classify items as product or period costs (L.O. 3)

Classify the costs listed in Problem 18–1 as either product costs or period costs.

Problem 18–3
Prepare statement of cost of goods manufactured and an income statement (L.O. 4)

Presley Manufacturing Company produces videotapes of musical performances. A newly hired executive of the company has asked you to sort through the records and prepare a statement of the company's cost of goods manufactured. You find the following data from records prepared by Presley Manufacturing Company for the year ended December 31, 1996:

Inventories:	
Beginning Direct Materials Inventory, January 1, 1996	$ 12,000
Ending Direct Materials Inventory, December 31, 1996	21,000
Beginning Work in Process Inventory, January 1, 1996	20,000
Ending Work in Process Inventory, December 31, 1996	19,000
Materials Purchases	100,000
Direct Labor	80,000
Indirect Labor	30,000
Factory Utilities Expense	14,000
Factory Supplies Expense	10,000
Depreciation Expense—Factory Building	28,000
Depreciation Expense—Equipment	21,000
Other Manufacturing Overhead	50,000

You also learn that beginning Finished Goods Inventory on January 1, 1996, was $40,000 and ending Finished Goods Inventory on December 31, 1996, was $10,000. Sales for the year were $800,000. Selling expenses were $100,000 and administrative expenses were $150,000.

Required

a. Prepare a statement of cost of goods manufactured for Presley Manufacturing Company for the year ended December 31, 1996.

b. Prepare an income statement for Presley Manufacturing Company for the year ended December 31, 1996.

Problem 18–4
Demonstrate job costing (L.O. 7)

High-Tech House Company uses a job cost system to account for its jobs, which are prefabricated houses. As of January 1, 1997, its records showed inventories as follows:

Materials and supplies	$50,000
Work in process (Job Nos. 22 and 23)	90,000
Finished goods (Job No. 21)	70,000

The work in process inventory consisted of two jobs:

Job No.	Direct Materials	Direct Labor	Manufacturing Overhead	Total
22	$18,000	$20,000	$10,000	$48,000
23	20,000	14,000	8,000	42,000
	$38,000	$34,000	$18,000	$90,000

Cost and sales data for 1997:

1. Materials purchased on account, $200,000.
2. Direct materials used: Job No. 22, $30,000; Job No. 23, $60,000; Job No. 24, $90,000. Indirect materials used, $5,000.
3. Direct labor costs: Job No. 22, $50,000; Job No. 23, $100,000; and Job No. 24, $40,000. Indirect labor costs, $40,000.
4. Overhead is assigned to jobs at $50 per machine-hour. Job No. 22 used 500 machine-hours, Job No. 23 used 1,000 machine-hours, and Job No. 24 used 300 machine-hours in January.
5. Job Nos. 22 and 23 were completed and transferred to Finished Goods Inventory.
6. Job Nos. 21 and 22 were sold for $600,000, total.
7. Manufacturing overhead costs incurred, other than indirect materials and indirect labor, were depreciation, $40,000, and heat, light, power, miscellaneous, $20,000.

Required

a. Prepare journal entries to assign the preceding costs to jobs. Show the appropriate entries debiting Finished Goods Inventory and Cost of Goods Sold. Transfer overapplied or underapplied overhead to Cost of Goods Sold.

b. Assuming selling and administrative expenses were $50,000, prepare an income statement for 1997.

Problem 18–5
Job costing in a service organization (L.O. 7)

Earthworm Landscaping Company uses a job cost system. As of January 1, 1997, its records showed the following inventory balances:

Materials (shrubs, trees, etc.)	$27,000
Work in Process	51,600
Finished Goods (Job No. 211)	60,000

The Work in Process Inventory consisted of two jobs:

Job No.	Direct Materials	Direct Labor	Manufacturing Overhead	Total
212 10 Downing St.	$ 9,000	$12,000	$ 4,800	$25,800
213 1010 Wilshire Blvd.	10,200	9,600	6,000	25,800
	$19,200	$21,600	$10,800	$51,600

Here are data for the company for January:

1. Materials purchased, $96,000.
2. Landscaping direct labor costs: direct labor to Job No. 212, $24,000; to Job No. 213, $48,000; and to Job No. 214, $72,000. Indirect labor, $60,000.
3. Direct materials used: direct materials for Job No. 212, $15,600; for Job No. 213, $28,800; and for Job No. 214, $48,000. Supplies (indirect materials) used amounted to $2,400.

4. Overhead is assigned to jobs at $6 per labor-hour, with 8,000 labor-hours to Job 212 and 2,000 labor-hours each to Jobs 213 and 214.
5. Jobs 212 and 213 were completed and in Finished Goods Inventory at the end of January.
6. Sales revenues for January were $90,000; cost of goods sold, $60,000 for Job No. 211 that was in Finished Goods Inventory on January 1, 1997.
7. Overhead costs incurred other than indirect labor and indirect materials were depreciation, $6,000, and utilities, fuel, and miscellaneous, $6,000.

Required

a. Prepare journal entries to record the preceding transactions, including the transfer of underapplied or overapplied overhead to Cost of Goods Sold.
b. Assuming selling and administrative expenses were $20,000, prepare an income statement for January.

Problem 18–6
Compute predetermined overhead rate and transfer underapplied or overapplied overhead to Cost of Goods Sold (L.O. 8)

Long-Haul Truck Lines transports computer equipment for various computer manufacturers. Long-Haul applied overhead to jobs using a predetermined overhead rate based on truck miles. Estimated data for 1997 are:

Estimated truck miles	10 million
Estimated overhead for hauling operations (equivalent to manufacturing overhead)	$12 million

Required

a. Compute the predetermined overhead rate per mile.
b. Assume that in 1997, actual manufacturing overhead for hauling operations amounted to $15 million, and 12 million truck miles were driven. Compute the amount of underapplied or overapplied manufacturing overhead for 1997.
c. Prepare the journal entry to transfer underapplied or overapplied overhead to Cost of Goods Sold.

Problem 18–7
Prepare income statements under absorption and variable costing; discuss reasons for differences (based on Appendix) (L.O. 9)

Sullivan Company uses an absorption costing system in accounting for the single product it manufactures. The following selected data are for the year 1996:

Sales (10,000 units)	$180,000
Direct materials used (variable cost)	64,800
Direct labor costs (variable cost)	21,600
Variable manufacturing overhead	6,480
Fixed manufacturing overhead	8,640
Variable selling and administrative expenses	10,800
Fixed selling and administrative expenses	36,000

The company produced 12,000 units and sold 10,000 units. Direct materials and direct labor are variable costs. One unit of direct material goes into each unit of finished goods. Overhead rates are based on a volume of 12,000 units and are $0.54 and $0.72 per unit for variable and fixed overhead, respectively. The only beginning or ending inventory is the 2,000 units of finished goods on hand at the end of 1996.

Required

a. Prepare an income statement for 1996 under variable costing.
b. Prepare an income statement for 1996 under absorption costing.
c. Explain the reason for the difference in net income between (**a**) and (**b**).

Alternate Problems

Problem 18–1A
Classify costs (L.O. 2)

Rainstop, Inc., is considering producing a new type of umbrella. This new pocket-sized umbrella would fit into a coat pocket or purse. Classify the following costs of this new product as direct materials, direct labor, manufacturing overhead, selling, or administrative.

a. Cost of advertising the product.
b. Fabric used to make the umbrellas.
c. Maintenance of cutting machines used to cut the umbrella fabric so it will fit the umbrella frame.

d. Wages of workers who assemble the product.
e. President's salary.
f. The salary of the supervisor of the people who assemble the product.
g. Wages of the product tester who stands in a shower to make sure the umbrellas don't leak.
h. Cost of market research survey.
i. Salary of the company's sales managers.
j. Depreciation of administrative office building.

Problem 18–2A
Classify items as product or period costs (L.O. 3)

Classify the costs listed in Problem 18–1A as either product costs or period costs.

Problem 18–3A
Prepare statement of cost of goods manufactured and an income statement (L.O. 4)

Good Vibrations, Inc., is a producer of music compact discs (CDs) and tapes. The following account balances are for the year ended December 31, 1996:

Administrative Expenses	$ 30,000
Depreciation Expense—Manufacturing Equipment	25,000
Direct Labor	234,000
Manufacturing Supplies Expense	20,000
Indirect Labor	18,000
Beginning Inventories, January 1, 1996:	
Direct Materials	7,000
Work in Process	10,000
Finished Goods	64,000
Ending Inventories, December 31, 1996:	
Direct Materials	22,000
Work in Process	28,000
Finished Goods	46,000
Direct Materials Purchases	108,000
Rent Expense—Factory	14,000
Sales	700,000
Selling Expense	36,000
Other Manufacturing Overhead	63,000

Required

a. Prepare a statement of cost of goods manufactured for Good Vibrations, Inc., for 1996.
b. Prepare an income statement for the year ended December 31, 1996.

Problem 18–4A
Job costing in a service organization (L.O. 7)

Exotic Eats Food Preparation uses a job cost system. Its activities in November 1997, its first month of operations, were as follows:

	Job		
	First-Rate University	**Active Life Home**	**Precocious School**
Direct materials cost (food)	$54,000	$36,000	$81,000
Direct labor cost	$45,000	$40,500	$54,000
Labor-hours	2,900	3,500	3,800

The company applies overhead at a rate of $16 per labor-hour. It completed all jobs in November. The total revenue for the three jobs was $400,000. The actual overhead for the month was $160,000, of which $120,000 should be credited to Accounts Payable and $40,000 should be credited to Accumulated Depreciation.

Required

Prepare journal entries to record the costs of jobs and to record the transfer of completed jobs to Finished Goods Inventory and to Cost of Goods Sold. Transfer any underapplied or overapplied overhead to Cost of Goods Sold. The company had no beginning or ending inventories.

Problem 18–5A
Compute predetermined overhead rate and underapplied or overapplied overhead (L.O. 8)

Costner Company applied overhead to production using a predetermined overhead rate based on machine-hours. Budgeted data for 1997 are:

Budgeted machine-hours	75,000
Budgeted manufacturing overhead	$435,000

Required

a. Compute the predetermined overhead rate.

b. Assume that in 1997, actual manufacturing overhead amounted to $498,750, and 86,000 machine-hours were used. Compute the amount of underapplied or overapplied manufacturing overhead for 1997.

c. Prepare the journal entry to transfer underapplied or overapplied overhead to Cost of Goods Sold.

Beyond the Numbers—Critical Thinking

Business Decision Case 18–1
Classify costs (L.O. 3)

Companies often do work on a cost-reimbursement basis. That is, Company B reimburses Company A for the cost of doing work for Company B. Suppose your company has a contract that calls for reimbursement of direct materials and direct labor, but not overhead. Following are costs that various organizations incur; they fall into three categories: direct materials (DM), direct labor (DL), or overhead (OH).

1. Glue used to attach labels to bottles containing a patented medicine.
2. Compressed air used in operating paint sprayers for Student Painters, a company that paints houses and apartments.
3. Insurance on a factory building and equipment.
4. A production department supervisor's salary.
5. Rent on factory machinery.
6. Iron ore in a steel mill.
7. Oil, gasoline, and grease for forklift trucks in a manufacturing company's warehouse.
8. Services of painters in building construction.
9. Cutting oils used in machining operations.
10. Cost of paper towels in a factory employees' washroom.
11. Payroll taxes and fringe benefits related to direct labor.
12. The plant electricians' salaries.
13. Crude oil to an oil refinery.
14. Copy editor's salary in a book publishing company.

Required

a. Classify each of these items as direct materials, direct labor, or overhead.

b. Assume your classifications could be challenged in a court case. Indicate to your attorneys which of your answers for Part (**a**) might be successfully disputed by the opposing attorneys. In which answers are you completely confident?

Business Decision Case 18–2
Evaluating job profitability (L.O. 7)

Creative Painters Company uses a job cost system. As of January 1, 1997, its records showed the following inventory balances:

Materials	$ 7,000
Work in Process	50,000
Finished Goods	0

The Work in Process Inventory consisted of two jobs:

Job No.	Direct Materials	Direct Labor	Overhead	Total
100 Community housing	$ 9,000	$12,000	$ 4,000	$25,000
101 Regal Apartments	10,000	9,000	6,000	25,000
	$19,000	$21,000	$10,000	$50,000

Here are data for the company for January:

1. Materials purchased, $90,000.
2. Direct labor costs: direct labor to Job No. 100, $20,000; to Job No. 101, $48,000; and to Job No. 102 (a new job), $50,000. Indirect labor, $10,000.
3. Direct materials used: direct materials for Job No. 100, $15,600; for Job No. 101, $28,800; and for Job No. 102, $48,000. Supplies (indirect materials) used amounted to $4,000.

4. Overhead is assigned to jobs at $5 per labor-hour, with 1,000 labor-hours to Job 100 and 2,000 labor-hours each to Jobs 101 and 102.
5. All three jobs were completed in January.
6. Sales revenues for January were $350,000 for the three jobs.
7. Overhead costs incurred other than indirect labor and indirect materials were depreciation, $6,000, and utilities, fuel, and miscellaneous, $6,000.

Management is concerned about the relationship between costs incurred on jobs and the costs expected to be incurred, and has asked for your help. Here are the expected total costs (direct materials, direct labor, and overhead) for the three jobs:

Job 100	$ 60,000
Job 101	120,000
Job 102	130,000

These cost estimates cover the entire job, including both costs in beginning Work in Process Inventory and costs incurred during January.

Required

a. Compare the costs incurred on each job, including the costs in beginning Work in Process Inventory and costs incurred during January with the expected costs. Is the company keeping its costs below the expected costs for each job?
b. Prepare an income statement for January 1997 assuming selling and administrative expenses for January were $50,000. Don't forget to transfer any underapplied or overapplied overhead balance to Cost of Goods Sold.
c. Is the company profitable (that is, showing net income greater than zero)? What suggestions can you make for management to help increase the company's net income?

Writing Assignment 18–3
Write short explanation of financial results

Refer to Problem 18–3 on page 700. Assume the newly hired executive is a whiz at marketing, but a person whose eyes glaze over at the sight of a number. The executive wants you to explain the financial results for the year in words. Essentially, assume the executive has not seen the financial statements prepared in Problem 18–3. What would you say to convey the message in the financial statements? Keep it short—less than 100 words.

Ethics Case—Writing Experience 18–4
Answer questions regarding ethics case

Refer to the Ethical Perspective discussion of Comserv's activities on page 677. As a salesperson, how would you respond if your boss asked you to backdate contracts from January 3, 1997, to December 28, 1996? What if you were asked to backdate the contracts from February 1, 1997, to December 28, 1996? Assume December 31 is the company's fiscal year-end.

Group Project—Ethical Perspective 18–5
Develop group response to ethics case

Refer to the discussion of Comserv's activities on page 677. As a salesperson, suppose your boss asked you to write a side agreement that allowed a customer to back out of a contract, and insisted that you not reveal the side contract to anyone else in your organization. You like your job a lot, and you will probably lose it if you don't comply with your boss's wish. In groups of three, discuss how you would respond to your boss. Try to develop a creative way to handle this situation. Choose a group spokesperson to report to the class.

Answers to Self-Test

True-False

1. **False.** Managerial accounting is for internal use by managers, not external use, and gives more detailed information than financial accounting.
2. **True.** The motors are direct materials, and they are product costs.
3. **False.** Because bottling soft drinks is a process, the plant would not use job costing.
4. **False.** The answer is the opposite. The estimated total overhead is the numerator, and the expected level of activity is the denominator.
5. **False.** Overhead can be applied to jobs during the period.
6. **True.** Selling and administrative expenses are part of period costs under both absorption and variable costing methods.

Multiple-Choice

1. **b.** Indirect materials are included under overhead.
2. **a.** Selling and administrative expenses are period costs for financial accounting purposes.
3. **b.** A merchandiser uses Merchandise Inventory and Cost of Goods Available for Sale, whereas a manufacturer uses Finished Goods Inventory and Cost of Goods Available for Sale.
4. **d.** All of the answers are true.
5. **d.** Both (**a**) and (**c**) are advantages of using a predetermined overhead rate.
6. **c.** $15 = ($360,000 + $90,000)/30,000 machine-hours.
7. **a.**

Manufacturing Overhead	22,500	
Various accounts		22,500
Work in Process Inventory	21,000	
Manufacturing Overhead		21,000

Note the predetermined overhead rate times the actual activity is $0.60 × 35,000 machine-hours = $21,000.

19

PROCESS COST SYSTEMS

This chapter continues the discussion of the two major types of cost accumulation systems. In Chapter 18, we explained and illustrated job costing. The **job cost system (job costing)** accumulates costs incurred to produce a product according to individual jobs. Construction companies, public accounting firms, book publishers, and architectural firms are examples of companies that use job costing.

We will also discuss another cost accumulation system, process costing. The chapter begins with a discussion of the nature of a process cost system. We review the similarities and differences between job costing and process costing. We also present an extended illustration of process costing that includes a discussion of equivalent units of production and the production cost report. In the chapter appendixes, we discuss and illustrate FIFO process costing and the allocation of joint product costs.

NATURE OF A PROCESS COST SYSTEM

Many businesses produce large quantities of a single product or similar products. Pepsi-Cola makes soft drinks, Georgia-Pacific Corporation produces lumber, and Kellogg Company produces breakfast cereals on a continuous basis over long periods. For these kinds of products, companies do not have separate jobs. Instead, production is an ongoing process.

A **process cost system (process costing)** accumulates costs incurred to produce a product according to the processes or departments a product goes through on its way to completion. Companies making paint, gasoline, steel, rubber, plastic, and similar products use process costing. In these types of operations, accountants must accumulate costs for each process or department involved in making the product. Accountants compute the cost per unit by first accumulating costs for the entire period (usually a month) for each process or department. Second, they divide the accumulated costs by the number of units produced (tons, pounds, gallons, or feet) in that process or department.

In "A Broader Perspective," we describe production in bottling and canning plants that use a process cost system.

LEARNING OBJECTIVES

After studying this chapter, you should be able to:

1. Describe the types of operations that require a process cost system.
2. Distinguish between process and job costing systems.
3. Discuss the concept of equivalent units in a process cost system.
4. Compute equivalent units of production and unit costs under the average cost procedure.
5. Prepare a production cost report for a process cost system and discuss its relationship to the Work in Process Inventory account.

(continued)

(*concluded*)

6. Distinguish between normal and abnormal spoilage.
7. Compute equivalent units of production and unit costs under the first-in first-out (FIFO) system (Appendix 19–A).
8. Discuss how joint costs are allocated to joint products (Appendix 19–B).

Job costing and process costing have important similarities:

1. Both job and process cost systems have the same *goal:* to determine the cost of products.
2. Both job and process cost systems have the same *cost flows*. Accountants record production in separate accounts for materials inventory, labor, and overhead. Then, they transfer the costs to a Work in Process Inventory account.
3. Both job and process cost systems use *predetermined overhead rates* (defined in Chapter 18) to apply overhead.

Job costing and process costing systems also have their significant differences:

1. *Types of products produced*. Companies that use job costing work on many different jobs with different production requirements during each period. Companies that use process costing produce a single product, either on a continuous basis or for long periods. All the products that the company produces under process costing are the same.
2. *Cost accumulation procedures employed*. Job costing accumulates costs by individual jobs. Process costing accumulates costs by process or department.
3. *Work in Process Inventory accounts*. Job cost systems have one Work in Process Inventory account for each job. Process cost systems have a Work in Process Inventory account for each department or process.

Objective 1
Describe the types of operations that require a process cost system.

Objective 2
Distinguish between process and job costing systems.

Illustration 19.1 shows the cost flows in a process cost system that processes the products in a specified sequential order. That is, the production and processing of products begin in Department A. From Department A, products go to Department B. Department B inputs direct materials and further processes the products. Then Department B transfers the products to Finished Goods Inventory. For illustration purposes, we assume that all the process cost systems in this chapter are sequential. There are many production flow combinations; Illustration 19.2 presents three possible production flow combinations.

Process Costing Illustration

Assume that Jax Company manufactures and sells a chemical product used to clean kitchen counters and sinks. The company processes the product in two departments. Department A crushes powders and blends the basic materials. Department B packages the product and transfers it to finished goods. Illustration 19.3 shows this manufacturing process.

The June production and cost data for Jax Company are:

	Department A	Department B
Beginning inventory	-0-	-0-
Units started, completed, and transferred	11,000	9,000
Units on hand June 30, partially completed	-0-	2,000
Direct materials	$16,500	$1,100
Direct labor	2,500	2,880
Actual overhead	7,500	8,600
Applied overhead	7,400	8,880

(Jax's accountant applies manufacturing overhead in Departments A and B based on the machine-hours used in production.) From these data, we can construct and summarize the Work in Process Inventory—Department A account as shown on page 710.

A Broader Perspective

Producing Cans of Coca-Cola®

How was the Diet Coke® I just finished drinking produced? A Coca-Cola bottling plant purchased cola syrup or a concentrate from The Coca-Cola Company, combined it with carbonated water, put it in cans, and sealed the cans. (Although these plants are usually called bottling plants, they also produce cans of Coke®.)

In a bottling plant, the first process combines the syrup or concentrate with carbonated water to make cola. In a second process, empty cans are rinsed and inspected. A third process combines these two materials by pouring the cola into the cans. Next, tops are placed on the cans. Finally, the cans are combined into packages. This completes the work in process stage.

The product enters finished goods inventory when it is sent to the warehouse. The product becomes cost of goods sold to the bottling plants when it is shipped to distributors or retail outlets.

Source: Based on the authors' research and documents provided by The Coca-Cola Company. Coca-Cola, Diet Coke, and Coke are registered trademarks of The Coca-Cola Company.

Illustration 19.1
Cost Flows in a Process Cost System

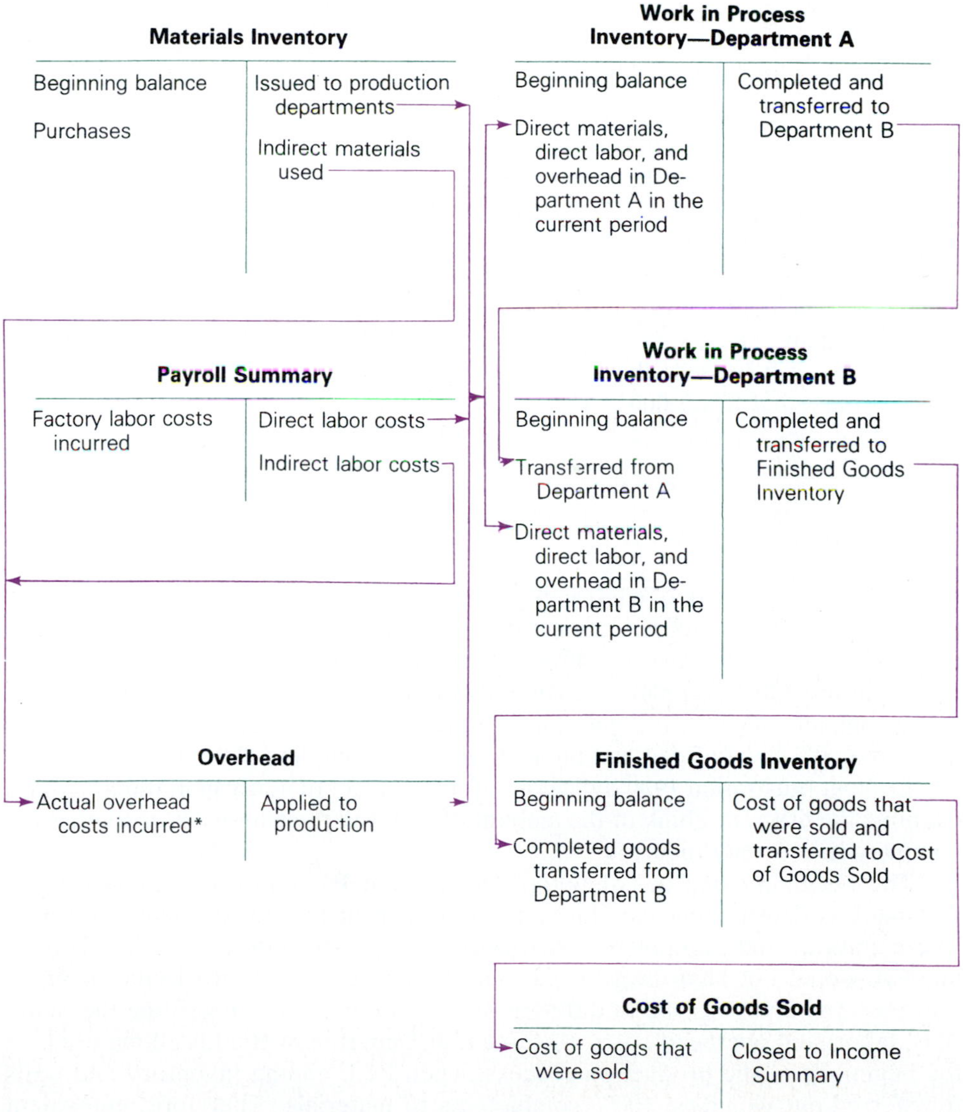

Materials Inventory

Beginning balance	Issued to production departments →
Purchases	Indirect materials used →

Payroll Summary

Factory labor costs incurred	Direct labor costs →
	Indirect labor costs →

Overhead

→ Actual overhead costs incurred*	Applied to production →

Work in Process Inventory—Department A

Beginning balance	Completed and transferred to Department B →
→ Direct materials, direct labor, and overhead in Department A in the current period	

Work in Process Inventory—Department B

Beginning balance	Completed and transferred to Finished Goods Inventory →
→ Transferred from Department A	
→ Direct materials, direct labor, and overhead in Department B in the current period	

Finished Goods Inventory

Beginning balance	Cost of goods that were sold and transferred to Cost of Goods Sold →
→ Completed goods transferred from Department B	

Cost of Goods Sold

→ Cost of goods that were sold	Closed to Income Summary

* Includes indirect materials, indirect labor, and other overhead.

Work in Process Inventory—Department A

Direct materials	16,500	Transferred to Department B:	
Direct labor	2,500	11,000 units @ $2.40	26,400
Applied overhead	7,400		
Balance	-0-		

Department A completed all the units it started in June and transferred them to Department B. So all the costs assigned to these units were transferred to Department B. Jax's accountant computed the unit costs in Department A by dividing the $26,400 total costs by the 11,000 units completed and transferred. The result is $2.40, the average unit cost of 11,000 units.

Computations are seldom this simple; one complication is partially completed inventories. Consider Department B, for example. Before Department B transfers the cost of completed units, its Work in Process Inventory account for June is as follows:

Work in Process Inventory—Department B

Transferred in from Department A	26,400	
Direct materials	1,100	
Direct labor	2,880	
Applied overhead	8,880	
Balance	39,260	

Recall that direct materials, direct labor, and applied overhead are product costs; that is, the costs attach to the product. Thus, Transferred in from Department A in the T-account represents the direct materials, direct labor, and applied overhead costs assigned to products in Department A. These costs have followed the physical units to Department B.

Now, Jax's accountant must divide the $39,260 total costs charged to Department B in June between the units transferred out and those remaining on hand in the department. The accountant cannot divide $39,260 by 11,000 units to get an average unit cost because the 11,000 units are not alike. Department B has 9,000 finished units and has 2,000 partially finished units. To solve this problem, the accountant uses the concept of equivalent units of production, which we discuss next.

Equivalent Units of Production

Objective 3
Discuss the concept of equivalent units in a process cost system.

Essentially, the concept of **equivalent units** involves expressing a given number of partially completed units as a smaller number of fully completed units. For example, if we bring 1,000 units to a 40% state of completion, this is equivalent to 400 units that are 100% complete. Accountants base this concept on the supposition that a company must incur approximately the same amount of costs to bring 1,000 units to a 40% level of completion as it would to complete 400 units.

Look at Illustration 19.4, a diagram of the concept of equivalent units. As you examine the diagram, think of the amount of water in the glasses as costs that the company has already incurred.

Objective 4
Compute equivalent units of production and unit costs under the average cost procedure.

The beginning step in computing Department B's equivalent units for Jax Company is determining the stage of completion of the 2,000 unfinished units. These units are 100% complete as to **transferred-in costs;** if they were not, Department A would not have transferred them to Department B. In Department B, however, the units may be in different stages of completion regarding the materials, labor, and overhead costs. Assume that Department B adds all materials at the beginning of the production process. Then both ending inventory and units transferred out would be 100% complete as to materials. Therefore, equivalent production for materials would be 11,000 units.

ILLUSTRATION 19.2
Possible Production Flow Combinations

A. One product is processed sequentially, yielding one final product.

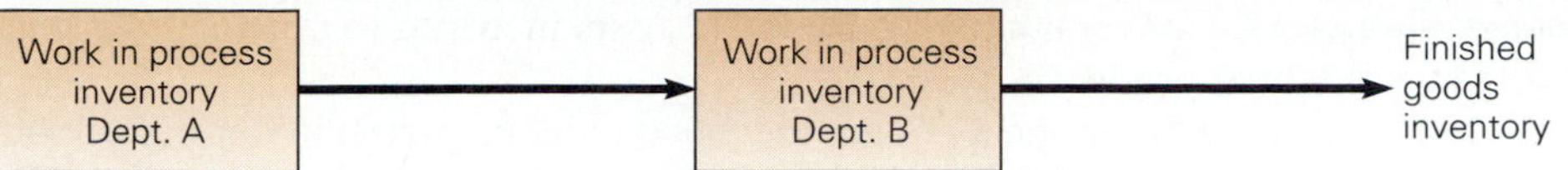

B. Two products are combined and then processed further to yield one final product.

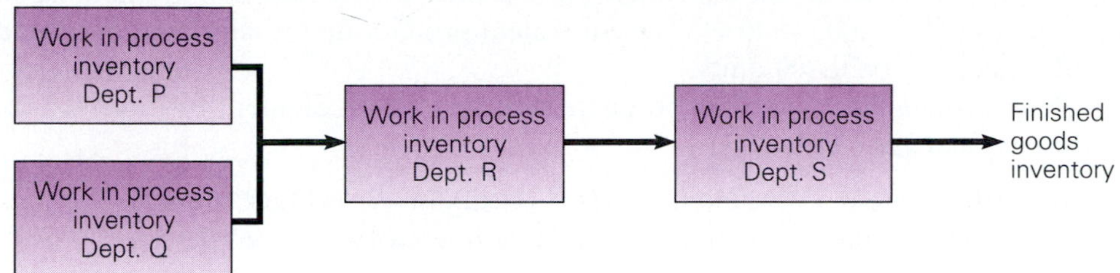

C. One product is further processed in two different ways, yielding two different final products.

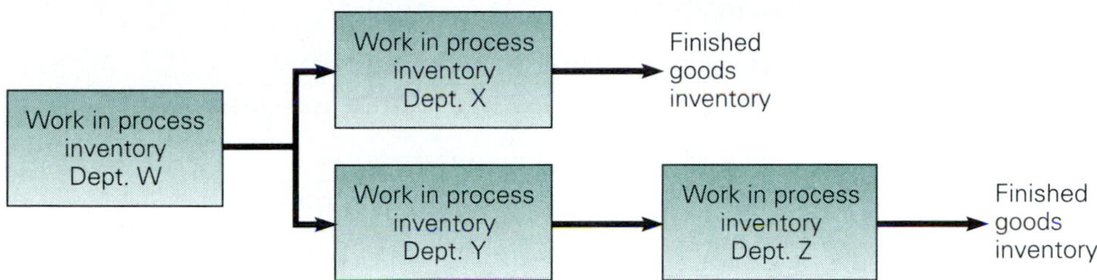

ILLUSTRATION 19.3
Product Flows in a Process Cost System (Jax Company example)

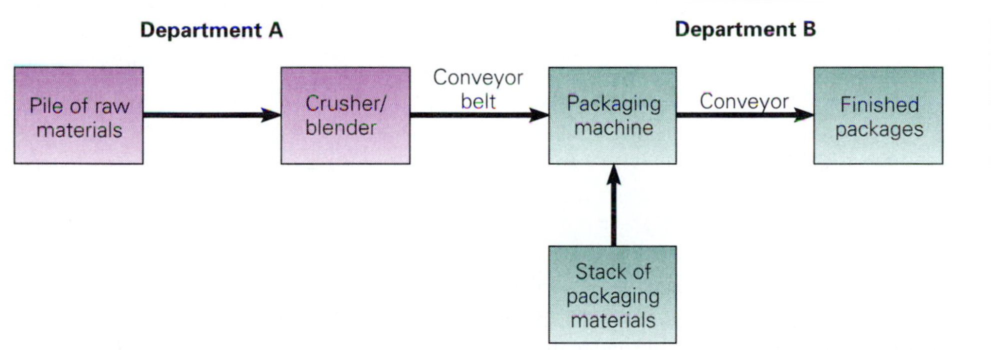

ILLUSTRATION 19.4
The Concept of Equivalent Units

8 glasses of water 50% full
are equivalent to
4 glasses of water 100% full

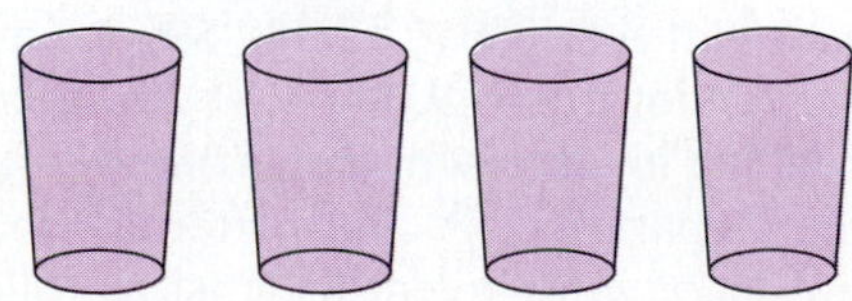

Accountants often assume that units are at the same stage of completion for both labor and overhead. Accountants call the combined labor and overhead costs **conversion costs.** Conversion costs are those costs incurred to convert raw materials into the final product.

Let's assume that on the average, the 2,000 units in ending inventory are 40% complete as to conversion costs. This means that Department B transferred out 9,000 units fully completed and brought 2,000 units to a 40% completion state. Department B now has an equivalent of 800 fully completed units remaining in inventory (800 = 2,000 × 40%). The equivalent production for labor and overhead would therefore be 9,800 units.

The formula for equivalent production for each cost element (transferred-in, materials, and conversion) is:

$$\text{Equivalent production} = \text{Units completed} + \left(\text{Units in ending inventory} \times \text{Percentage complete}\right)$$

When we know the equivalent units of production, we can compute unit costs for transferred-in, materials, and conversion elements. The average unit cost formulas for each cost element are:

$$\text{Unit cost for transferred-in} = \frac{\text{Total transferred-in costs}}{\text{Equivalent units, transferred-in}}$$

$$\text{Unit cost for materials} = \frac{\text{Total materials costs}}{\text{Equivalent units, materials}}$$

$$\text{Unit cost for conversion} = \frac{\text{Total conversion costs}}{\text{Equivalent units, conversion}}$$

Now we can compute unit costs for each cost element in Department B as follows:

	Transferred-In	Materials	Conversion	Total
Costs to be accounted for:				
Charged to Department B	$26,400	$ 1,100	$11,760*	$39,260
Equivalent units	11,000	11,000	9,800†	
Unit costs	$2.40	$0.10	$1.20	$3.70

* Conversion costs consist of direct labor + overhead ($2,880 + $8,880).

† Units transferred out (9,000) + equivalent units in ending inventory (800).

We can use the $3.70 computed unit costs to divide Department B's $39,260 June costs between the units completed and transferred out and the units remaining in the department's ending inventory. We do this in the following table:

	Transferred-In (@ $2.40)	Materials (@ $0.10)	Conversion (@ $1.20)	Total
Costs accounted for:				
Units completed and transferred out (9,000 units)	$21,600	$ 900	$10,800	$33,300
Units remaining in ending inventory (2,000 units)	4,800	200	960*	5,960
Costs accounted for	$26,400	$1,100	$11,760	$39,260

* Equivalent units = 800 units.

The $33,300 total costs transferred out of Department B consist of $21,600 transferred in from Department A (9,000 × $2.40), $900 of materials costs (9,000 × $0.10), and $10,800 of conversion costs (9,000 × $1.20), or a total cost of $3.70 per unit. The 2,000 units of ending inventory in Department B are fully complete as to costs transferred in from Department A and materials and 40% complete as to conversion. We calculate the ending inventory cost as follows:

Costs from Department A (2,000 × $2.40)		$4,800
Costs added by Department B:		
Materials (2,000 × $0.10)	$200	
Conversion (800 equivalent units × $1.20)	960	1,160
Total cost of ending inventory		$5,960

Jax carries units transferred out of Department B in finished goods inventory at a cost of $3.70 each until they are sold. Then, Jax charges the cost of units sold to Cost of Goods Sold.

An Accounting Perspective

Business Insight Companies using processes are often highly automated. Conversion costs are made up mostly of overhead with little direct labor. If possible, tour a canning or bottling plant, a lumber mill, an oil refinery, or a cereal processing plant. You will see lots of machinery and some people operating machines and inspecting the product. You probably won't see many people producing the product by hand, however.

Journal Entry Analysis

We have discussed how to determine the costs of each cost element placed in production, transferred to finished goods inventory, and charged to cost of goods sold. Now let's look at the summary of the journal entries for these activities for the month of June.

		Debit	Credit
1.	Work in Process Inventory—Department A	16,500	
	Work in Process Inventory—Department B	1,100	
	Materials Inventory		17,600
	To record materials placed in production in June.		
2.	Work in Process Inventory—Department A	2,500	
	Work in Process Inventory—Department B	2,880	
	Payroll Summary		5,380
	To assign labor costs to departments (assuming that all such costs are chargeable directly to production departments).		
3.	Work in Process Inventory—Department A	7,400	
	Work in Process Inventory—Department B	8,880	
	Overhead (or Manufacturing Overhead)		16,280
	To apply overhead to production.		
4.	Work in Process Inventory—Department B	26,400	
	Work in Process Inventory—Department A		26,400
	To record transfer of goods from Department A to Department B.		
5.	Overhead (or Manufacturing Overhead)	16,100	
	Various accounts—Cash, Accounts Payable, Accruals, and Accumulated Depreciation		16,100
	To record actual overhead costs incurred in June.		
6.	Finished Goods Inventory	33,300	
	Work in Process Inventory—Department B		33,300
	To record transfer of completed goods from Department B to finished goods.		

If Jax Company sold 6,000 of these completed units in June at $10 per unit on account, it would make the following entries:

		Debit	Credit
7.	Accounts Receivable	60,000	
	Sales		60,000
	To record sales on account.		
8.	Cost of Goods Sold	22,200	
	Finished Goods Inventory		22,200
	To record cost of goods sold in June, 6,000 units @ $3.70.		

Production Cost Report

The key document in a process costing system is the production cost report. A **production cost report** shows both the flow of units and the flow of costs through a processing center. It also shows how accountants divide these costs between the cost of units completed and transferred out and the cost of units still in the processing center's ending inventory. This report makes the equivalent unit and unit cost computations easier.

Objective 5
Prepare a production cost report for a process cost system and discuss its relationship to the Work in Process Inventory account.

To illustrate the preparation of a production cost report with partially completed beginning and ending inventories, assume the following June 1997 data for Department 3 of Storey Company:

Units		
Units in beginning inventory, complete as to materials, 60% complete as to conversion costs		6,000
Units transferred in from Department 2		18,000
Units completed and transferred out		16,000
Units in ending inventory, completed as to materials, 50% complete as to conversion costs		8,000
Costs		
Cost of beginning inventory:		
Costs transferred in from Department 2 in May	$12,000	
Materials added in May in Department 3	6,000	
Conversion costs (labor and overhead)	3,000	$21,000
Costs transferred in from Department 2 in June		37,200
Costs added in Department 3 in June:		
Materials	$18,480	
Conversion (equal amounts of labor and overhead)	18,000	36,480
Total costs in beginning inventory and placed in production in Department 3 in June		$94,680

The preparation of the production cost report includes the following four steps:

1. Trace the physical flow of the units through the production department.
2. Convert actual units to equivalent units.
3. Compute unit costs for each cost element.
4. Distribute the total cost between the units completed and transferred out and the units remaining in the ending inventory.

Using the June data, Storey developed the production cost report for Department 3 shown in Illustration 19.5.

The first step in the preparation of a production cost report is to trace the physical flow of actual units in and out of Department 3. The units section in Illustration 19.5 shows that Department 3 had 6,000 units in the June beginning inventory. Department 3 also had 18,000 units transferred in from Department 2. This makes a total of 24,000 units for which Department 3 must account.

Of these 24,000 units, Department 3 completed and transferred out 16,000 units (either to the next processing department or to finished goods). At the end of the month, Department 3 had 8,000 partially completed units. These 8,000 units are the June ending inventory. Now we are ready for the second step in the preparation of the production cost report—to convert actual units to equivalent units.

Storey Company's cost of production report uses the *average cost procedure*. Under the **average cost procedure,** the number of equivalent units for each cost element equals the number of units transferred out plus the number of equivalent units of that cost element in the ending inventory. The average cost procedure does not consider the number of units in the beginning inventory and the degree of completion of the beginning inventory. Alternatively, Storey could use First-in, First-out (FIFO) or Last-in, First-out (LIFO). We use the average cost procedure in this chapter because it is simpler and commonly used in practice.

ILLUSTRATION 19.5 Production Cost Report

STOREY COMPANY
Production Cost Report—Department 3
For the Month of June 1997

Units	Actual Units	Equivalent Units Transferred-In	Materials	Conversion
Units in beginning inventory	6,000			
Units transferred in from Department 2	18,000			
Units to be accounted for	24,000			
Units completed and transferred out	16,000	16,000	16,000	16,000
Units in ending inventory*	8,000	8,000	8,000	4,000
Units accounted for	24,000	24,000	24,000	20,000

Costs	Transferred-In	Materials	Conversion	Total
Costs to be accounted for:				
Costs in beginning inventory	$12,000	$ 6,000	$ 3,000	$21,000
Costs transferred in from Department 2 in June	37,200			37,200
Costs added in Department 3		18,480	18,000	36,480
Costs to be accounted for	$49,200	$24,480	$21,000	$94,680
Equivalent units (as above)	24,000	24,000	20,000	
Unit cost (per equivalent unit)†	$2.05	$1.02	$1.05	$4.12
Costs accounted for:				
Units completed and transferred out (16,000 units)	$32,800	$16,320	$16,800	$65,920
Units remaining in ending inventory (8,000 units)*	16,400	8,160	4,200	28,760
Costs accounted for	$49,200	$24,480	$21,000	$94,680

* Inventory is complete as to materials added, 50% complete as to conversion.
† Unit cost equals costs to be accounted for divided by equivalent units.

Storey's units in the ending inventory are fully complete as to costs transferred in and materials cost. Therefore, the number of equivalent units for each of these cost elements is 24,000 (16,000 units completed and transferred out + [8,000 units in the ending inventory × 100% complete for transferred-in costs and materials costs]). The 8,000 units remaining in ending inventory are 50% complete as to conversion. Therefore, there are 20,000 equivalent units with regards to conversion—16,000 units transferred out plus 8,000 units that were 50% complete.

Once a company has computed its equivalent units, it must calculate the unit costs. This is the third step in preparing the production cost report. Each cost element of production—costs transferred in, materials, and conversion—has accumulated costs. Notice in Illustration 19.5 that for each cost element, we total the costs of beginning inventory and costs of the current month. We refer to the total costs charged to a department as costs to be accounted for. These costs either have been transferred out or appear in the ending inventory of Department 3.

To determine the cost per equivalent unit for each cost element, divide the total cost for each cost element by the equivalent units of production related to that cost element. (Since we totaled all costs for each cost element before the division, we can average the computed unit costs across the current and prior period.) Illustration 19.5 shows the average per unit costs for June as transferred-in costs, $2.05; materials costs, $1.02; and conversion costs, $1.05. In monitoring these costs closely for cost control purposes, management watches for extreme fluctuations from one month to the next.

The last step in preparing the production cost report is to allocate costs between the units completed and transferred out and the units remaining in ending inventory. The units transferred out were fully complete as to all elements of production. Therefore, we can multiply the 16,000 units by $4.12, the total cost per unit. The result, $65,920, is the amount Storey assigns to the next department as cost transferred in or to finished goods as the cost of completed current period production. We now compute the cost of ending inventory as follows:

8,000 equivalent units transferred in @ $2.05	$16,400
8,000 equivalent units of materials costs @ $1.02	8,160
4,000 equivalent units of conversion costs @ $1.05	4,200
Total cost of ending inventory	$28,760

The sum of the ending inventory cost and the cost of the units transferred out must equal the total costs to be accounted for. This built-in check determines whether the company has properly followed the procedures of cost allocation. As shown in the production cost report, Department 3 adds the $65,920 costs transferred out to the $28,760 ending inventory cost. The total equals the $94,680 for which Department 3 must account.

Some companies replace the production cost report with three schedules. The first schedule is the schedule of equivalent production. This schedule computes the equivalent units of production for the period for transferred-in, materials, and conversion costs. The second schedule is the unit cost analysis schedule. This schedule sums all the costs charged to the Work in Process Inventory account of each production process department. Then it calculates the cost per equivalent unit for transferred-in, materials, and conversion costs. The third schedule is the cost summary schedule. This schedule uses the results of the preceding two schedules to distribute the total costs accumulated during the period among all the units of output. Companies generally show these three schedules in a process cost analysis report.

FIFO Method

Companies that use a process cost system may use the **first-in, first-out (FIFO) method** instead of the average cost procedure. Generally, under FIFO, the equivalent number of units for each cost element consists of:

1. Work needed to complete the units in beginning inventory.
2. Work done on units started and completed during the period.
3. Work done on partially completed units in ending inventory.

Appendix 19–A, at the end of this chapter, illustrates this method.

Now that you have studied both job costing in Chapter 18 and process costing in this chapter, you can appreciate why manufacturing companies must accurately account for product unit costs. Without accurate cost accounting information, a manufacturing company cannot determine the cost of its products for managerial decision making or prepare accurate financial statements.

Process Costing in Service Organizations

Service organizations that provide similar services to a variety of customers are potential users of process costing. For example, a clinic dispensing flu shots, a delicatessen selling only pastrami sandwiches, and a photo shop that processes pictures could use process costing. In manufacturing, the difficult task is to match period costs with the units produced that period, which is why companies compute equivalent units of production. (And that is what most people find difficult about process costing.)

Generally, service companies complete the service by the end of the period and have no work in process at the end of the period. Nurses do not leave for home halfway through giving a flu shot, and the delicatessen does not partially serve a sandwich one month and complete it the next. Consequently, there is no need to compute equivalent units, which simplifies process costing.

Note that some service companies do have partially completed work at the end of the period. Certain types of dry cleaning and photo processing may still be in process at the end of a period. You could apply the methods described in this chapter for manufacturing to those service companies. For materials, you could substitute any significant supplies, and for conversion costs, service labor and overhead.

SPOILAGE

Objective 6
Distinguish between normal and abnormal spoilage.

If you have ever tried to make something that did not work out, you know the concept of *spoilage*. **Spoilage** refers to the loss of goods during production. For example, suppose some of the cans are dented during the canning of tuna fish. Accountants would treat the cost of the dented cans of tuna fish as spoilage.

Accountants treat spoilage either as normal spoilage or abnormal spoilage. **Normal spoilage** occurs in the normal production process. Accountants generally assign normal spoilage costs to the good units produced. According to one method found in practice, accountants divide the total cost of production by the good units produced.

For example, suppose the total cost of producing tuna fish for one day is \$100,000. The company produced 220,000 cans of tuna fish, but 20,000 cans of tuna fish did not meet quality inspection requirements. Consequently, these 20,000 units were considered to be spoiled in the normal production process. One way accountants deal with the cost of such normal spoilage is to compute the cost of one good unit by dividing total production costs by the number of good cans of tuna fish produced. That is:

$$\text{Cost per good unit} = \frac{\$100{,}000}{200{,}000 \text{ good units produced}}$$

$$= \$0.50 \text{ per good unit produced}$$

Abnormal spoilage exceeds the amount expected under normal operating conditions. For example, if denting the tuna fish cans is unusual, accountants would treat the cost of those dented cans of tuna fish as abnormal spoilage. Whereas normal spoilage costs are assigned to good products, abnormal spoilage costs are typically expensed. Thus, accountants treat normal spoilage as a product cost and abnormal spoilage as a period cost.

Spoilage and Total Quality Management

Advocates of total quality management may prefer to classify all spoilage as abnormal. Normal spoilage costs are buried in the costs of the good products. Unless management personnel ask for a special analysis of spoilage costs, they will not know whether the spoilage costs are a small percent or a large percent of product costs. For example, management could see a report on tuna fish production costs stating the cost is \$0.50 per can, but they do not know how much of the \$0.50 was the cost of spoilage.

We recommend that accountants report spoilage costs to management, whether normal spoilage or abnormal spoilage, so management can make informed decisions to reduce spoilage.

UNDERSTANDING THE LEARNING OBJECTIVES

Objective 1
Describe the types of operations that require a process cost system.

- Process cost systems are used for businesses that produce products on a continuous basis over long periods.
- Paint, paper, chemicals, gasoline, beverages, and food products should be accounted for under a process cost system.

Objective 2
Distinguish between process and job costing systems.

- Types of products produced under each system: Companies that use job costing work on many different jobs with different production requirements during each period. Companies that use process costing produce a single product, either on a continuous basis or for long periods.
- Cost accumulation procedures used under each system: Job costing accumulates costs by individual jobs. Process costing accumulates costs by process or department.
- Work in Process accounts: Job cost systems have a Work in Process Inventory account for each job. Process cost systems have a Work in Process Inventory account for each department or process.

Objective 3
Discuss the concept of equivalent units in a process cost system.

- Whenever partially completed inventories are present, the number of equivalent units of production must be computed. Basically, the concept of equivalent units involves expressing a given number of partially completed units as a smaller number of fully completed units.
- As a simple example of equivalent units, two apples that are half eaten are equivalent to one whole apple eaten. In manufacturing, we estimate the degree of completion for a group of products with respect to transferred-in, materials, and conversion (direct labor and overhead). Accountants base the concept of equivalent units on the supposition that a company must incur approximately the same costs to partially complete a large number of units as to totally complete a smaller number of units.

Objective 4
Compute equivalent units of production and unit costs under the average cost procedure.

- Accountants compute equivalent units of production for transferred-in units, materials, and conversion. For each of these categories, the number of units transferred out is added to the equivalent units remaining in ending work in process in the department.
- Unit costs for the three categories—transferred-in units, materials, and conversion—are determined by dividing the equivalent units into the cost in beginning inventory plus the costs transferred in or added in the department during this period.

Objective 5
Prepare a production cost report for a process cost system and discuss its relationship to the Work in Process Inventory account.

- A production cost report shows both the flow of units and the flow of costs through a processing center. The report is divided into two parts. The first part traces the physical flow of the units through the production department and converts actual units to equivalent units. The second part shows the costs to be accounted for, computes unit costs based on equivalent units as determined in the first part, and shows how the costs were accounted for by adding the costs completed and transferred out with the costs remaining in ending inventory. The costs to be accounted for and the costs accounted for must balance.
- The production cost report provides a check on the Work in Process Inventory account. Each processing department normally has its own Work in Process Inventory account and related production cost report. The separate items that make up work in process inventory—direct labor, direct materials, applied overhead, and cost of units transferred in and out—can be traced from the production cost report to the Work in Process Inventory account (and vice versa) during a given period.

Objective 6
Distinguish between normal and abnormal spoilage.

- Normal spoilage occurs in the normal course of production and is treated as a product cost. Abnormal spoilage exceeds the spoilage that occurs in the normal course of production and is treated as a period cost.

Objective 7
Compute equivalent units of production and unit costs under the first-in, first-out (FIFO) system (Appendix 19–A).

- Equivalent units of production are computed by taking the equivalent units of work done to complete the beginning inventory, plus units started and completed during the current period, plus equivalent units of work done on the ending inventory. As is true under the average cost method, the equivalent units usually differ between materials and conversion.
- Unit costs for the three categories—transferred-in units, materials, and conversion—are determined by dividing cost to be accounted for during the period by units produced during the period.

- The physical measures method allocates joint product costs based on physical measures, such as units, pounds, or liters.
- The relative sales value method is the most commonly used method to allocate joint product costs. It is based on the relative sales values of the products at the split-off point.

Objective 8
Discuss how joint costs are allocated to joint products (Appendix 19–B).

The FIFO Process Cost Method

Appendix 19–A

Objective 7
Compute equivalent units of production and unit costs under the first-in, first-out (FIFO) system.

In this chapter, the discussion assumed the use of the average cost method for determining unit costs under process costing. Another acceptable method for determining unit cost under process costing is the first-in, first-out (FIFO) cost method. This appendix presents a detailed illustration of the FIFO process costing system.

The following table shows how the computation of equivalent units differs between the average cost method and the FIFO cost method:

Average Cost Method	FIFO Cost Method
Equivalent units of production = Units completed this period + Equivalent units of work done on the ending inventory	Equivalent units of production = Equivalent units of work done to complete the beginning inventory + Units started and completed this period + Equivalent units of work done on the ending inventory

To illustrate the computation of equivalent units under the FIFO method, assume the following facts:

Beginning inventory, 3,000 units, 40% complete
Units started this period, 10,000 units
Ending inventory, 5,000 units, 20% complete

The equivalent production for the period would be:

Equivalent units of work done to complete the beginning inventory (3,000 × 0.60)	1,800
Units started and completed this period (10,000 − 5,000 in ending inventory)	5,000
Equivalent units of work done to partially complete the ending inventory (5,000 × 0.20) . .	1,000
Equivalent units of production	7,800

As is true under the average cost method, the equivalent units usually differ between materials and conversion.

FIFO Process Costing—An Illustration

To illustrate more completely the operation of the FIFO process cost method, we use an example of the month of June production costs for a company having Departments A and B. Both departments add materials only at the beginning of processing. Department A has no May 31 inventory. The May 31 inventory in Department B consists of 2,000 units that are fully complete as to materials and 50% complete as to conversion. This inventory has accumulated costs of $6,180.

The following transactions and additional data summarize manufacturing operations in both departments for June:

1. Raw materials purchased on account, $25,000.
2. Direct materials issued: Department A (14,000 units at $1.50), $21,000; and Department B (10,000 units at $0.13), $1,300. Indirect materials issued: Department A, $400; and Department B, $200.
3. Labor costs: direct labor, Department A, $6,600, Department B, $5,400; and indirect labor, building occupancy department, $3,000.
4. Manufacturing overhead is applied as follows: $5,280 in Department A and $5,400 in Department B.

5. Other manufacturing overhead incurred:

Repairs (on account)	$2,100
Depreciation	3,000
Utilities (on account)	3,000
	$8,100

6. Production reports show the following for June:

	Department A	Department B
Beginning inventory	–0–	2,000
Units started	14,000	10,000
Units completed and transferred	10,000	9,000
Units in inventory, June 30	4,000	3,000
Estimated percentage of completion	50	33⅓

7. Sales for the month on account, 15,000 units at $6 per unit.
8. The company computed cost of goods sold at $55,866 on a FIFO basis.

The general journal entries and their explanations follow:

		Debit	Credit
1.	Materials Inventory	25,000	
	Accounts Payable		25,000
	To record materials purchased on account.		
2.	Work in Process—Department A	21,000	
	Work in Process—Department B	1,300	
	Manufacturing Overhead	600	
	Materials Inventory		22,900
	To record direct and indirect materials used.		
3.	Work in Process—Department A	6,600	
	Work in Process—Department B	5,400	
	Manufacturing Overhead	3,000	
	Payroll Summary		15,000
	To distribute labor costs to departments.		
4.	Work in Process—Department A	5,280	
	Work in Process—Department B	5,400	
	Manufacturing Overhead		10,680
	To record assignment of overhead to production.		
5.	Manufacturing Overhead	8,100	
	Accounts Payable		5,100
	Accumulated Depreciation—Plant and Equipment		3,000
	To record various overhead costs incurred.		
6.	Work in Process—Department B	24,900	
	Work in Process—Department A		24,900
	To record transfer of completed production from Department A to Department B. (For details of computation, see production cost report of Department A in Illustration 19.6.)		
	Finished Goods	34,120	
	Work in Process—Department B		34,120
	To record transfer of completed production from Department B to storeroom. (For details of computation, see production cost report for Department B in Illustration 19.7.)		
7.	Accounts Receivable	90,000	
	Sales		90,000
	To record sales for the month.		
8.	Cost of Goods Sold	55,866	
	Finished Goods		55,866
	To record cost of goods sold.		

The Production Cost Report

As noted in the journal entries for June's manufacturing operations, the production cost report provided the dollar amounts of certain entries. For product costing purposes, the production cost report is the primary report in a process cost system. The chapter illustra-

ILLUSTRATION 19.6
Production Cost Report—Department A

DEPARTMENT A
Production Cost Report
For the Month Ended June 30, 1997

Units			
Units in beginning inventory		–0–	
Units started during period		14,000	
Units to be accounted for		14,000	
Units completed and transferred out		10,000	
Units in ending inventory		4,000	
Units accounted for		14,000	
Costs	**Equivalent Units**	**Total Cost**	**Current Unit Cost**
Costs to be accounted for:			
Costs added during the month:			
Direct materials	14,000*	$21,000	$1.50
Conversion	12,000*	11,880	0.99
Costs added in month and costs to be accounted for		$32,880	$2.49
Costs accounted for:			
Cost of ending inventory:			
Direct materials (4,000 × 100% × $1.50)		$ 6,000	
Conversion (4,000 × 50% × $0.99)		1,980	
Total cost of ending inventory		$ 7,980	
Cost of 10,000 units transferred out		24,900	$2.49
Costs accounted for		$32,880	

* Supporting computations and data:

	Materials	**Conversion**
Computations of equivalent units:		
Equivalent units to complete beginning inventory	–0–	–0–
Units started and completed	10,000	10,000
Equivalent units in partially completed ending inventory	4,000	2,000
Equivalent units of production for month	14,000	12,000

Ending inventory is 100% complete for materials and 50% complete as to processing or conversion costs.

tion of the production cost report shows the units and costs charged to a department, the disposition of these units and costs, and, typically, some of the supporting details and computations.

PRODUCTION COST REPORT—DEPARTMENT A To illustrate flexibility in format, Illustration 19.6 shows the production cost report for Department A in a different format than the one in the chapter. Note that Department A placed 14,000 units into production. Then, Department A completed and transferred out 10,000 units. Department A retained the remaining 4,000 partially completed units in the department. The footnote in the illustration shows the computation of equivalent units.

The costs section of the report shows that the only costs to be accounted for were those added in the department in June. These costs include $21,000 for materials and $11,880 for conversion, totaling $32,880. Department A had no beginning inventory and no transfers in. Note how Department A determines its unit costs for each of the two elements of manufacturing costs ($1.50 for materials and $0.99 for conversion). The total current unit cost is $2.49. The report shows the disposition of the costs—the cost of the units transferred to Department B ($24,900) and the amount of ending inventory remaining in Department A ($7,980 based on current unit costs). The units transferred to Department B have the same unit cost as the unit cost in Department A for the month. The current unit cost and the cost of the transferred units is not always the same, as we will show for Department B in Illustration 19.7.

PRODUCTION COST REPORT—DEPARTMENT B The production cost report for Department B (Illustration 19.7) is similar to that of Department A. Note how the report

ILLUSTRATION 19.7
Production Cost Report—Department B

DEPARTMENT B
Production Cost Report
For the Month Ended June 30, 1997

Units			
Units in beginning inventory		2,000	
Units started during period		10,000	
Units to be accounted for		12,000	
Units completed and transferred out		9,000	
Units in ending inventory		3,000	
Units accounted for		12,000	

Costs	**Equivalent Units**	**Total Cost**	**Current Unit Cost**
Costs to be accounted for:			
Costs added during the month:			
Direct materials	10,000*	$ 1,300	$0.13
Conversion	9,000*	10,800	1.20
Costs added during the month		$12,100	$1.33
Costs in beginning inventory		6,180	
Costs transferred in from Department A		24,900	
Total costs to be accounted for		$43,180	
Costs accounted for:			
Cost of ending inventory:			
Transferred in from Department A (3,000 units at $2.49)		$ 7,470	
Direct materials (3,000 × 100% × $0.13)		390	
Conversion (3,000 × ⅓ × $1.20)		1,200	
Total cost of ending inventory		$ 9,060	
Cost of 9,000 units transferred out		34,120	$3.791
Costs accounted for		$43,180	

* Supporting computations and data:

	Materials	**Conversion**
Computations of equivalent units:		
Equivalent units to complete beginning inventory	-0-	1,000
Units started and completed	7,000	7,000
Equivalent units in partially completed ending inventory	3,000	1,000
Equivalent units of production for the month	10,000	9,000

Beginning and ending inventories are complete as to materials. Beginning inventory is 50% complete and ending inventory 33⅓% complete as to processing.

highlights the current unit cost of the operations performed in the department. Note also that Department B must account for the costs in the beginning inventory and the cost of the units transferred in from Department A. Department B determines the cost of the ending inventory through the use of the current month's unit cost ($1.33). All of Department B's other costs are included in the costs of the 9,000 units transferred to Finished Goods.

In the production cost report in Illustration 19.7, we determine the cost of units transferred out by subtracting the cost of the ending inventory from the total costs to be accounted for ($43,180 − $9,060 = $34,120). We can compute average unit cost of $3.791 by dividing $34,120 by the 9,000 units transferred out.

APPENDIX 19–B ALLOCATION OF JOINT PRODUCT COSTS

Objective 8
Discuss how joint costs are allocated to joint products.

A company incurs **joint product costs** (or common costs) when it produces two or more products through the same production process or from a common raw material. The company produces these products simultaneously. The products are not identifiable as different individual products until a particular point in the manufacturing process known as the *split-off point*.

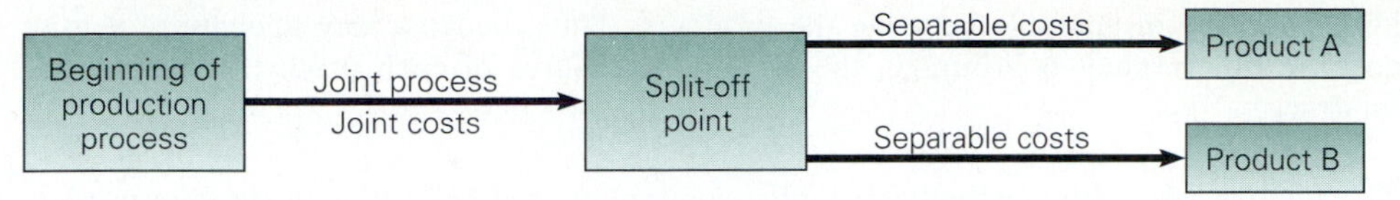

ILLUSTRATION 19.8
Joint Production Process

The **split-off point** is a certain stage of production at which the separate products become identifiable from a common processing unit. We refer to any costs beyond the split-off point as separable costs because they can be directly traced to individual products. Examples of joint products are petroleum products, lumber, flour milling, dairy products, and chemicals. In Illustration 19.8, we show the joint production process.

By definition, joint product costs are not identified with individual products. Any allocation of joint costs to one of the products is inherently arbitrary. Many companies do not allocate joint costs to particular products for managerial decision making because the allocated numbers could be misleading to decision makers.[1] The accounting problem we face is how to allocate the joint costs that a company incurred before the products become separately identified. Commonly used methods to allocate joint costs are the *physical measures method* and the *relative sales value method*.

Physical Measures Method

The **physical measures method** allocates joint product costs on the basis of physical measures such as units, pounds, or liters.

To illustrate, assume that Roy Company produces two grades of oil, product A and product B, through a joint process. The cost and production data of Roy Company for July are:

	Product A	Product B	Total
Units (barrels) produced	15,000	25,000	40,000
Unit selling price at split-off	$15	$6	
Revenue at split-off	$225,000	$150,000	
Joint product costs:			
Direct materials			$125,000
Direct labor			105,000
Manufacturing overhead			70,000
			$300,000

The physical measures method uses a ratio of the physical volume of each product to total volume as a basis for allocation of joint costs. We compute the allocation cost to each product as follows:

	Total Barrels	Ratio	Joint Costs	Allocated Joint Costs
Product A	15,000	$\frac{15,000}{40,000}$ ×	$300,000	$112,500
Product B	25,000	$\frac{25,000}{40,000}$ ×	$300,000	187,500
	40,000			$300,000

If Roy Company sells both products without further processing, the gross margin for product A is $112,500, or $225,000 less $112,500. Product B incurs a loss of $37,500, or $150,000 less $187,500. Even though the physical measures method is easy to use, it often has no relationship to the revenue-generating power of each product. In this instance, product B suffers a loss of $37,500 because the company allocated a high portion of joint costs based on product B's high volume even though its selling price is less than that of product A.

[1] For example, a survey of oil refineries indicated that seven of the nine companies did not allocate joint costs. See K. Slater and C. Wooton, *A Study of Joint and By-Product Costing in the U.K.* (Reprint, London: Chartered Institute of Management Accountants, 1988), p. 110.

Keep in mind that the joint costs cannot really be assigned to one product because joint costs are inseparable between the products. Thus, because any allocation of joint costs to one product is arbitrary, the resulting measures of each product's income are arbitrary.

Relative Sales Value Method

The **relative sales value method** is the most commonly used basis to allocate joint product costs at the split-off point. Accountants base the relative sales value method on the assumption that the market value of each product is the most reasonable basis for allocating joint costs.

Using the relative sales value method, Roy Company would allocate the joint costs as follows:

	Sales Value at Split-off	Ratio	Joint Costs	Allocated Joint Costs
Product A:				
($15 × 15,000)	$225,000	$\frac{\$225,000}{\$375,000}$	× $300,000	$180,000
Product B:				
($6 × 25,000)	150,000	$\frac{\$150,000}{\$375,000}$	× $300,000	120,000
	$375,000			$300,000

The allocation ratios of 60% and 40%, respectively, for product A and product B result in allocated joint costs of $180,000 to product A, and $120,000 to product B.

To compare the physical measures method and the relative sales value method, assume Roy Company has no inventory at the end of July. A partial July income statement would appear as shown:

	Product A		Product B	
	Physical Measures Method	Relative Sales Value Method	Physical Measures Method	Relative Sales Value Method
Sales	$225,000	$225,000	$150,000	$150,000
Cost of goods sold	112,500	180,000	187,500	120,000
Gross margin	$112,500	$ 45,000	$ (37,500)	$ 30,000
Gross margin percentage	50%	20%	(25%)	20%

As you can see, under the relative sales value method both products have the same gross margin percentage of 20%.

Demonstration Problem

Zarro, Inc., uses a process cost system to accumulate the costs it incurs to produce aluminum awning stabilizers from recycled aluminum cans. The May 1 inventory consisted of 36,000 units, fully complete as to materials and 80% complete as to conversion. The beginning inventory cost of $288,000 consisted of $216,000 of costs transferred in from the molding department, $30,000 of finishing department materials costs, and $42,000 of finishing department conversion costs (conversion costs are direct labor and overhead). The costs incurred in the finishing department for May appear as follows:

Costs from molding department (excluding costs in beginning inventory) . .		$720,000
Costs added in finishing department in May (excluding costs in beginning inventory):		
Materials	$ 63,600	
Conversion costs	131,376	194,976
		$914,976

The finishing department received 120,000 units from the molding department in May. During May, 127,200 units were completed by the finishing department and transferred out. As of May 31, 28,800 units, complete as to materials and 60% complete as to conversion, were left in inventory of the finishing department.

Required

a. Prepare a production cost report for the finishing department for May.

b. Compute the average unit cost for conversion in the finishing department in April.

Solution to Demonstration Problem

a.

ZARRO, INC.
Finishing Department
Production Cost Report
For the Month Ending May 31

Units	Actual Units	Equivalent Units: Transferred-In	Materials	Conversion
Units in May 1 inventory	36,000			
Units transferred in	120,000			
Units to be accounted for	156,000			
Units completed and transferred out	127,200	127,200	127,200	127,200
Units in May 31 inventory*	28,800	28,800	28,800	17,280†
Units accounted for	156,000	156,000	156,000	144,480

* Inventory is complete as to materials, 60% complete as to conversion.
† (28,800 × 60% = 17,280).

Costs	Transferred-In	Materials	Conversion	Total
Costs to be accounted for:				
Costs in May 1 inventory	$216,000	$ 30,000	$ 42,000	$ 288,000
Costs transferred in	720,000			720,000
Costs added in department		63,600	131,376	194,976
Costs to be accounted for	$936,000	$ 93,600	$173,376	$1,202,976
Equivalent units (as above)	156,000	156,000	144,480	
Unit costs	$6.00	$0.60	$1.20	$7.80
Costs accounted for:				
Units completed and transferred out (127,200 units)	$763,200	$ 76,320	$152,640	$ 992,160
Units remaining in May 31 inventory (28,800 units)	172,800	17,280	20,736*	210,816
Costs accounted for	$936,000	$ 93,600	$173,376	$1,202,976

* 17,280 equivalent units × $1.20 = $20,736.

b. The average unit cost for conversion in the finishing department in April was $1.46, calculated as ($42,000/[0.8 × 36,000]).

New Terms

Abnormal spoilage Spoilage that exceeds the amount expected under normal operating conditions. *717*

Average cost procedure A method of computing equivalent units where the number of equivalent units for each cost element equals the number of units transferred out plus the number of equivalent units of that cost element in the ending inventory. *714*

Conversion costs Costs of converting raw materials into the final product. Direct labor plus overhead. *712*

Equivalent units A method of expressing a given number of partially completed units as a smaller number of fully completed units; for example, bringing 1,000 units to a 75% level of completion is the equivalent of bringing 750 units to a 100% level of completion. *710*

First-in, first-out (FIFO) method A method of determining unit cost. This method computes equivalent units by adding equivalent units of work needed to complete the units in beginning inventory, work done on units started and completed during the period, and work done on partially completed units in ending inventory. *716*

Job cost system (job costing) A manufacturing cost system that accumulates costs incurred to produce a product according to individual jobs. *707*

Joint product costs Costs incurred when a company produces two or more products through the same production process or from a common raw material. *722*

Normal spoilage Spoilage that occurs in the normal production process. *717*

Physical measures method A method of allocating joint product costs on the basis of physical measures such as units, pounds, or liters. *723*

Process cost system (process costing) A manufacturing cost system that accumulates costs incurred to produce a product according to the processes or departments a product goes through on its way to completion. *707*

Production cost report A report that shows both the flow of units and the flow of costs through a processing center. It also shows how accountants divide these costs between the cost of units completed and transferred out and the cost of units still in the processing center's ending inventory. *714*

Relative sales value method A method of allocating joint product costs on the basis of the relative market value at the split-off point. *724*

Split-off point A certain stage of production at which the separate products become identifiable from a common processing unit. *723*

Spoilage The loss of goods during production. *717*

Transferred-in costs Costs associated with physical units that were accumulated in previous processing centers. *710*

Self Test

True-False

Indicate whether each of the following statements is true or false.

1. In process costing, costs are accumulated by process or department.
2. Both job and process cost systems have one Work in Process Inventory account.
3. The first step in computing equivalent units is to determine the amount of materials being used.
4. Abnormal spoilage is treated as a product cost.
5. (Based on Appendix 19–B.) A commonly used basis to allocate joint product costs is the relative sales value of the products at the split-off point.

Multiple Choice

Select the best answer for each of the following questions.

1. Which of the following does not apply to process costing?
   a. Uses the equivalent unit concept.
   b. Includes overhead in product costs.
   c. Costs of production are first recorded in Work in Process Inventory accounts then transferred to Finished Goods Inventory and Cost of Goods Sold.
   d. Keeps track of the actual cost of each individual unit produced.
2. Which of the following formulas is the correct formula for equivalent units of production under the average cost procedure?
   a. $\text{Units completed} - \left[\text{Units in ending inventory} \times \text{Percentage complete}\right] = \text{Equivalent production}$
   b. $\text{Units completed} - \left[\text{Units in beginning inventory} \times \text{Percentage complete}\right] = \text{Equivalent production}$
   c. $\text{Units completed} + \left[\text{Units in ending inventory} \times \text{Percentage complete}\right] = \text{Equivalent production}$
   d. None of the above.
3. Using the following data, compute the ending inventory cost:

   1,000 units are in ending inventory in Department B. The unit cost of goods transferred in from Department A is $1.20. The 1,000 units are fully complete as to materials and 20% complete as to conversion. The unit cost for materials is $0.05, and conversion unit cost equals $0.60.

   a. $1,370. c. $1,320.
   b. $1,170. d. $1,250.
4. A production cost report reports which of the following:
   a. Units in a production department.
   b. Costs related to production.
   c. Unit costs.
   d. Equivalent units.
   e. All of the above are included in the production cost report.
5. (Based on Appendix 19–A) Compute the equivalent units of production under the FIFO method using this data:

   Beginning inventory, 1,500 units—40% complete
   Units started this period, 5,000 units
   Ending inventory, 2,500 units—20% complete

   a. 3,000. c. 3,400.
   b. 3,900. d. 3,600.

Now refer to page 732 to check your answers.

QUESTIONS

1. Define process costing and describe the types of companies that use process costing.
2. How does a process cost system differ from a job costing system?
3. Would a lumber mill use process or job costing?
4. What is meant by the term *equivalent units*? Of what use is the computation of the numbers of equivalent units of production?
5. Distinguish between the number of units completed and transferred during a period and the equivalent units for the same period.
6. Under what circumstances would the number of equivalent units of materials differ from the number of equivalent units of labor and overhead in the same department in the same period? Under what circumstances would they be the same?
7. When transferring goods from one department to another, which accounts require journal entries?
8. Units are usually assumed to be at the same stage of completion for both labor and overhead. What is the reason for this assumption?
9. What is the basic information conveyed by a production cost report?
10. What are the four steps in preparing a production cost report?
11. What is meant by average cost procedure? What other two cost flow assumptions could be used?
12. Would an automobile plant that makes specialty race cars use job costing or process costing? Would an automobile plant that makes all terrain vehicles use job costing or process costing? Explain your answer.
13. What is the difference between normal and abnormal spoilage?
14. Why might an advocate of total quality management prefer to see all spoilage labeled as abnormal?
15. Show the differences between computing equivalent units of production using the average cost method and FIFO cost method (Appendix 19–A).
16. Describe the relative sales value method and show how it is used (Appendix 19–B).
17. **Real World Question** Refer to "A Broader Perspective" on page 709. Describe the different processes used in a cola bottling plant.

The Coca-Cola Company

18. **Real World Question** Refer to The Coca-Cola Company's annual report in the annual report booklet. Does The Coca-Cola Company use a process cost system or a job costing system? Why?
19. **Real World Question** Name five companies that probably use process costing.

EXERCISES

Exercise 19–1
Compute equivalent units (L.O. 3)

Using the average cost method, compute the equivalent units of production in each of the following cases:

a. Units started in production during the month, 36,000; units completed and transferred, 26,400; and units in process at the end of the month (100% complete as to materials; 60% complete as to conversion), 9,600.

b. Units in process at the beginning of the month (100% complete as to materials; 30% complete as to processing), 6,000; units started during the month, 24,000; and units in process at the end of the month (100% complete as to materials; 40% complete as to conversion), 12,000.

Exercise 19–2
Compute equivalent units (L.O. 3)

In Department C, materials are added at the beginning of the process. There were 1,000 units in beginning inventory, 10,000 units were started during the month, and 7,000 units were completed and transferred to finished goods inventory. The ending inventory in Department C in June was 20% complete as to conversion costs. Under the average cost method, what are the equivalent units of production for materials and conversion?

Exercise 19–3
Compute equivalent units (L.O. 3)

In Department D, materials are added uniformly throughout processing. The beginning inventory was considered 80% complete, as was the ending inventory. Assume that there were 3,000 units in the beginning inventory and 10,000 in the ending inventory, and that 40,000 units were completed and transferred out of Department D. What are the equivalent units for the period using the average cost method?

Exercise 19–4
Compute costs of the units completed and transferred (L.O. 4)

If in Exercise 19–3 the total costs charged to the department amounted to $480,000, including the $24,000 cost of the beginning inventory, what is the cost of the units completed and transferred?

Exercise 19–5
Calculate cost per equivalent unit; determine costs of units transferred out (L.O. 4)

The following data relate to Work in Process—Department C, in which all materials are added at the start of processing:

Work in Process—Department C: Inventory, March 1:	
Materials cost (1,200 pounds; 100% complete)	$ 7,020
Conversion cost (20% complete)	990
Costs incurred this period:	
Direct materials used (9,000 pounds at $4.02)	$36,180
Direct labor	10,880
Overhead	17,820
Inventory, March 31:	
Materials cost (1,800 pounds, 100% complete)	?
Conversion cost (1,800 pounds, 80% complete)	?
Pounds of product transferred out: 8,400	

Using these data, compute:

a. The unit cost per equivalent unit for materials and conversion (use the average cost method).

b. The cost of the product transferred out.

Problems

Problem 19–1
Calculate equivalent units, costs per equivalent units, cost of goods completed, and cost of ending inventory (L.O. 4)

The following data refer to a production center of Pure Aqua Company, a producer of flavored mineral water:

Work in process inventory, August 1, 4,000 units (units equal 12-bottle cases):	
Direct materials	$ 6,000
Direct labor	3,000
Manufacturing overhead applied	4,000
	$13,000
Units started in August	12,000
Costs incurred in August:	
Direct materials	$18,000
Direct labor	24,000
Manufacturing overhead applied	30,000

The beginning inventory was 100% complete for materials and 50% complete for conversion costs.

The ending inventory on August 31 consisted of 6,000 units (100% complete for materials, 70% complete for conversion costs).

Required Compute the following:

a. Number of units completed and transferred to finished goods inventory.

b. The equivalent units of production for materials and conversion costs using the average cost method.

c. Cost per equivalent unit for materials and conversion costs.

d. Cost of units completed and transferred.

e. Cost of ending inventory.

Problem 19–2
Prepare a production cost report (L.O. 5)

The following information relates to Sunbelt Company for its line of sunscreen products for the month ended March 31:

Units in beginning inventory (units equal cases of product)	5,400
Cost of units in beginning inventory:	
Materials	$ 40,500
Conversion	$ 18,900
Units placed in production	108,000
Cost incurred during current period:	
Materials	$239,598
Conversion	$215,310
Units remaining in ending inventory (100% complete as to materials, 60% complete as to conversion)	6,000

Required Prepare a production cost report for the month ended March 31, using the average cost method.

Problem 19–3
Prepare a production cost report (L.O. 5)

Healthbar Company uses a process cost system to account for the costs incurred in making its single product, a health food. This product is processed in Department A and then in Department B. Materials are added in both departments. Production for May was as follows:

	Department A	Department B
Units started or transferred in	200,000	160,000
Units completed and transferred out	160,000	120,000
Stage of completion of May 31 inventory:		
Materials	100%	80%
Conversion.	50%	40%
Costs incurred this month:		
Direct materials costs	$200,000	$304,000
Conversion costs	$540,000	$272,000

There was no May 1 inventory in either department.

Required

a. Prepare a production cost report for Department A in May.

b. Prepare a production cost report for Department B in May.

Problem 19–4
Prepare a production cost report (L.O. 5)

A bottling company bottles soft drinks using a process cost system. Following are cost and production data for the mixing department for June:

	Units	Materials Costs	Conversion Costs
Inventory, June 1	56,000	$11,620	$16,240
Placed in production in June	133,000	29,680	41,720
Inventory, June 30	63,000	?	?

The June 30 inventory was 100% complete as to materials and 30% complete as to conversion.

Required

Prepare a production cost report for the month ended June 30 using the average cost method.

Problem 19–5
Prepare a production cost report using FIFO (based on Appendix 19–A) (L.O. 7)

Refer to the facts given in Problem 19–4. Assume the beginning inventory on June 1 was 100% complete as to materials and 25% complete as to conversion.

Required

a. Prepare a production cost report for the month ended June 30, using FIFO. Round unit costs to the nearest cent.

b. Why are ending inventory amounts different than those for Problem 19–4?

Problem 19–6
Allocate joint costs to joint products (based on Appendix 19–B) (L.O. 8)

Georgia Timber Company produces two products from logs, Grade A lumber and Grade B lumber. The following events took place in June:

	Grade A	Grade B	Total
Units produced	40,000	60,000	100,000
Unit selling price at split-off	$2.00	$1.00	
Joint costs	?	?	$120,000

Required

a. Allocate the joint costs to the two products using the physical measures method.

b. Allocate the joint costs to the two products using the relative sales value method.

c. Explain the difference in unit costs using the two methods.

d. What are advantages of the relative sales value method if all of Grade A lumber has been sold and none of Grade B lumber has been sold at the end of a month?

Alternate Problems

Problem 19–1A
Calculate equivalent units, costs per equivalent units, cost of goods completed, and cost of ending inventory (L.O. 4)

Sipp-Fizz is a soft drink bottler. These data are for its March production:

Work in process inventory, March 1, 3,000 units (units equal cases):	
Direct materials	$ 6,300
Direct labor	3,000
Manufacturing overhead (1,500 machine-hours at $3 per machine-hour)	4,500
	$13,800
Units started in March	9,000
Costs incurred in March:	
Direct materials	$18,180
Direct labor	27,600
Manufacturing overhead applied (13.800 machine-hours)	?

The ending inventory consisted of 4,500 units (100% complete as to materials, 60% complete as to conversion).

Required Compute the following:

a. Number of units completed and transferred to finished goods inventory.

b. The equivalent units of production for materials and conversion costs using the average cost method.

c. Cost per equivalent unit for materials and conversion costs.

d. Cost of units completed and transferred.

e. Cost of ending inventory.

Problem 19–2A
Prepare a production cost report (L.O. 5)

The following data pertain to a production center of Aromatic Company, a perfume maker:

	Units	Materials Costs	Conversion Costs
Inventory, October 1	140,000	$12,000	$16,000
Placed in production in October	400,000	20,000	20,000
Inventory, October 31	200,000	?	?

The October 31 inventory was 100% complete as to materials and 20% complete as to conversion costs.

Required Prepare a production cost report for the month ended October 31, using the average cost method.

Problem 19–3A
Prepare a production cost report (L.O. 5)

Shine Company produces a hair conditioner and determines product costs using a process cost system. The product is moved through two departments, mixing and bottling. Production and cost data for the bottling department in August follow.

Work in process, August 1 (60,000 pints):	
Costs transferred in	$30,000
Materials costs	15,000
Conversion costs	9,000
Costs incurred in August:	
Transferred in (200,000 pints)	$100,000
Materials costs	50,000
Conversion costs	40,000

All materials are added at the beginning of the bottling process. Ending inventory consists of 50,000 pints, 100% complete as to materials and 40% complete as to conversion.

Required Prepare a production cost report for August using the average cost method.

Beyond the Numbers—Critical Thinking

Business Decision Case 19–1
Determine how production costs should be allocated (L.O. 3, 4, and 5)

Mountain High Company produces bicycles. While the company has developed a per unit cost, it has not been able to break down its costs in each of its three departments: frames, assembling, and finishing. Karol Ring, the production manager, has been concerned with cost overruns during July in the frames department, which produces the bicycle frames.

On July 1, the frames department had 6,000 units in its work in process inventory. These units were 100% complete as to materials and 40% complete as to conversion. The department had incurred $12,000 in materials costs and $90,000 in conversion costs in processing these 6,000 units.

The department handled 30,000 units during the month, including the 6,000 units in beginning inventory on July 1. At the end of the month, the department's work in process included 3,600 units that were 100% complete as to materials and 30% complete as to conversion. The month's costs were allocated on the number of units processed during the month as follows:

	Materials	Conversion
Costs	$60,000	$300,000
Units handled during month	30,000	30,000
Cost per unit	$2	$10

The $12 per unit cost was assigned in a way that resulted in the following costs:

	Beginning Work in Process	Work Started and Completed	Ending Work in Process
Cost per unit incurred during the month:			
Units	6,000	20,400	3,600
Cost per unit	$12	$12	$12

Ring realized that this per unit cost is incorrect and asks you to develop a better method of computing these costs for the month ended July 31.

Required

a. How would you recommend that July's costs be assigned to the units produced? How would this differ from the present method?

b. To justify your recommendation, recalculate July's costs using your recommendation. Present your analysis in a production cost report.

Ethics Case—Writing Experience 19–2
Respond to questions regarding the ethics case

Bill Merino works in the inventory control group at a company that produces stone-washed jeans. A good friend manages the Stitching Department at the same company. At the end of a recent month, Merino reviewed the Stitching Department's production cost report and found the department had no beginning Work in Process Inventory, had started 27,000 pairs of jeans, and had produced only 24,000 pairs. That leaves 3,000 pairs in ending inventory, Merino thought, that's a lot of jeans they didn't finish.

Later, Merino visited his friend who managed the Stitching Department. "Why all the ending inventory?" he asked.

"One of the new workers set several machines wrong, and the stitching was bad on 2,400 pairs," the manager replied. "We set those aside, and we'll fix them when we have some free time. The other 600 pairs are complete now, and have been transferred out. Our entire operation was slower because of the machine problem."

"Company policy is to send all defective products to the Rework Department. They can fix the jeans. That's their job," Merino said.

"No way!" exclaimed the Stitching Department manager. "We'd all be in trouble if plant management finds out. The worker who messed up would probably be fired. I don't want that. This is our little problem, and we'll take care of it."

Required

a. What should Merino do?

b. Would your answer to (**a**) change if Merino learned that the Stitching Department had fixed the jeans and sent them on to the next department?

Annual Report Analysis 19–3
Determine the effect of an assumed error on Coca-Cola's 1993 financial statements.

Refer to The Coca-Cola Company's annual report in the annual report booklet. Suppose Coca-Cola made an error in estimating the stage of completion of their work in process inventory in 1993. Suppose the costs in beginning inventory and the costs transferred in were correct, but the company overstated the stage of completion for both materials and conversion costs in ending Work in Process Inventory causing ending Work in Process Inventory to be 10% too high. The beginning and ending Finished Goods Inventory amounts are correct. What effect would this error have on Coca-Cola's 1993 financial statements?

Group Project 19–4
Allocation of joint costs (based on Appendix 19–B) (L.O. 8)

In groups of 3 or 4 students, write a paper on the topic, "How scientific is the allocation of joint costs to products?" Prepare the paper on a computer and prepare and edit several drafts before turning in the final paper. Use examples to demonstrate your points.

Answers to Self-Test

True-False

1. **True.** In process costing, costs are accumulated by process or department.
2. **False.** Job cost systems have one Work in Process Inventory account for each job, and process cost systems have a Work in Process Inventory account for each process or department.
3. **False.** The initial step in computing equivalent units is to determine either the stage of completion or the number of partially complete units.
4. **False.** Abnormal spoilage is treated as a period cost.
5. **True.** The relative sales value of the products at the split-off point is a commonly used basis to allocate joint product costs.

Multiple-Choice

1. **d.** Process costing does not keep track of the actual cost of each individual unit produced.
2. **c.** $$\text{Units completed} + \left[\text{Units in ending inventory} \times \text{Percentage complete}\right] = \text{Equivalent production}$$
3. **a.** $1,370 [$1,200 + (1,000 × $.05) + (200 × $.60)]
4. **e.** Items **a** through **d** are included in the production cost report.
5. **b.** The equivalent production for the period would be:

Equivalent units of work done to complete the beginning inventory (1,500 × 0.60)	900
Units started and completed this period (5,000 − 2,500) in ending inventory	2,500
Equivalent units of work done to partially complete the ending inventory (2,500 × 0.20)	500
Equivalent units of production	3,900

Comprehensive Review Problem

This problem covers material discussed in Chapters 18 and 19. Topics include product costing, cost flows, job costing, and underapplied/overapplied overhead.

The NoTech Company assembles personal computers. Personal computers go through several departments where subassemblies are unpacked and checked, the circuit board is attached, the product is tested and repaired if defective, and the computers are packed carefully for shipping. Each order is treated as a job, and the entire job is shipped at once. The company keeps track of costs by job and calculates the equivalent stage of completion for each job based on machine-hours.

Although the company has grown rapidly, it has yet to show a profit. You have been called in as a consultant. Management believes some jobs are profitable and others are not, but it's not clear which are profitable. The accounting system is almost nonexistent; however, you piece together the following information for April:

1. Production:
   a. Completed Job No. 101.
   b. Started and completed Job No. 102.
   c. Started Job No. 103.
2. Inventory values:
   a. Work in process inventory:

March 31: Job No. 101	
Direct materials	$60,000
Direct labor	9,600
Overhead	14,400
April 30: Job No. 103	
Direct materials	$45,000
Direct labor	10,400
Overhead	15,600

   b. Job No. 101 was exactly one-half finished in direct labor-hours and machine-hours at the beginning of April, and Job No. 103 was exactly one-half complete in direct labor-hours and machine-hours at the end of April. However, all of the direct materials necessary to do the entire job were charged to each job as soon as the job was started.
   c. There were no direct materials inventories or finished goods inventories at either March 31 or April 30.
3. Manufacturing overhead is applied at $30 per machine-hour. The company used 1,600 machine-hours during April, 480 machine-hours on Job 101 and 600 machine-hours on Job 102. The actual overhead for the month of April was $50,000.
4. Cost of goods sold (before adjustment for overapplied or underapplied overhead):

Job No. 101:		Job No. 102	
Materials	$60,000	Materials	?
Labor.	?	Labor.	?
Overhead	?	Overhead	?
Total	?	Total	?

5. Overhead was applied to jobs using the predetermined rate of $30 per machine-hour. The same rate had been used since the company began operations. Over- or underapplied overhead is debited or credited to Cost of Goods Sold.
6. All direct materials were purchased on account. Direct materials purchased in April amounted to $150,000.
7. Direct labor costs charged to jobs in April were $32,000. All labor costs were the same rate per hour for April for all laborers.

Required

a. Compute the cost of each job, whether in inventory or sold.
b. Show the transactions in journal entry form. Use a separate Work in Process Inventory account for each job.
c. Prepare an income statement for April assuming revenue was $250,000 and selling and administrative expenses were $60,000.

20

Using Accounting for Quality and Cost Management

Learning Objectives

After studying this chapter, you should be able to:

1. Describe why managers need good accounting information to be competitive in the new production environment.
2. Identify ways to improve quality.
3. Develop measures of performance that help achieve high quality.
4. Explain how just-in-time purchasing and production can reduce costs and improve quality.
5. Compare and contrast accounting in just-in-time settings with accounting in traditional settings.

(continued)

Importance of Good Accounting Information

Have you ever purchased a product and found it to be defective? If so, you may have sworn to yourself that you would never buy one of those again. By doing so, you have demonstrated why high-quality products are essential for business success. Successful companies remain in business by seeking continual improvement in the quality of their products. For example, J. Peterman and Company, a merchandising company that sells through catalogs, tells its customers to please hassle them if not completely satisfied. Nordstrom's department stores, Southwest Airlines Company, and Toyota Motor Corp. are companies that have built reputations based on the notion of hassle us if you are not completely satisfied.

In its plant near Nashville, Tennessee, Nissan Motor Corporation places some of the previous day's production of cars and trucks in the lobby with charts showing the number of production defects for that day. Displaying products and reporting on performance gives workers a sense of pride in their work and an incentive to reduce defects.

Quality and the New Production Environment

Attention to quality is an important feature of the new production environment. The phrase, *new production environment,* refers to an environment in which company managers are concerned with (1) improving customer service and product quality and (2) reducing costs. Both actions are necessary to stay competitive.

In the new production environment, new technology is helping managers improve quality and reduce costs. Computer-assisted manufacturing enables managers to reduce inventories, yet respond quickly to customers' needs. For example, robots perform certain repetitive functions more reliably than humans. Computerized airline reservations systems also provide better customer service at a lower cost to airlines.

The new production environment is rooted in the new management philosophies that we discuss in this chapter. For example, managers now use nonfinancial as well as financial measures of quality performance. Many companies have adopted a just-in-time philosophy for managing purchasing and production. Managerial accountants are restructuring costing systems to provide activity-based costs resulting in better managerial decision making. Many observers believe that the United States industry has fallen behind foreign competitors because managers and accountants have not worked together to produce the information management needs to make good decisions.

(*concluded*)

6. Define activity-based costing and explain its benefit to companies.
7. List the four steps in activity-based costing.
8. Compare product costs using activity-based costing with product costs using traditional costing methods.
9. Describe the strategic and behavioral advantages of activity-based management.

Improving Quality

Objective 1
Describe why managers need good accounting information to be competitive in the new production environment.

To make decisions about the costs and benefits of quality, we need to know what those costs and benefits of quality are. Managers at Texas Instruments have placed the costs of quality in these four categories:[1]

1. *Prevention costs.* Prevention costs cover the cost of preventing poor-quality products from being produced. Prevention costs include training employees to do quality work.
2. *Appraisal costs.* Appraisal costs are the costs of detecting poor-quality products. Appraisal costs include the costs of inspecting materials when purchased and product testing during production.
3. *Internal failure costs.* Internal failure costs are the costs of producing poor-quality products detected before products are shipped to customers. Internal failure costs include the costs of reworking poor-quality products to bring their quality up to specifications.
4. *External failure costs.* External failure costs are the costs incurred because customers purchased poor-quality products. External failure costs include the costs of dealing with returned products and future lost profits because customers are dissatisfied.

The manager's task is to minimize the sum of these costs. By incurring substantial costs of prevention, for example, a company might reduce costs of appraisal, internal failure, and external failure costs. This idea is a modern adaptation of the old saying, "An ounce of prevention is worth a pound of cure." Small prevention costs may even result in large cost savings in the other three categories.

Objective 2
Identify ways to improve quality.

Assume Diana's Secret is a company that sells clothing through catalogs. A marketing manager concerned about customer satisfaction noticed a substantial amount of returned merchandise. Upon investigating, the manager discovered that most returns were due to an incorrect color or size; most of these errors could be traced to mistakes made by order takers who had not been adequately trained.

The company decided to invest $5,000 per month in a training program for order takers. After the training program started, the amount of returned merchandise dropped dramatically. Working with people in the marketing department, accountants estimated the company saved $4,000 per month by having less returned merchandise and fewer refilled orders. In addition, marketing managers believed Diana's Secret's profits increased by $2,000 to $10,000 per month because of increased customer satisfaction. Management considered the $5,000 cost of prevention to be justified by the benefits of reduced returned merchandise and increased customer satisfaction.

The key quality concept in the new production environment is total quality management. **Total quality management (TQM)** is defined as managing the entire organization so it excels in its goods and services that are important to the cus-

[1] "Texas Instruments: Cost of Quality (A)" (Boston: Harvard Business School, Case 9-189-029).

ILLUSTRATION 20.1
Control Chart for Defective Products

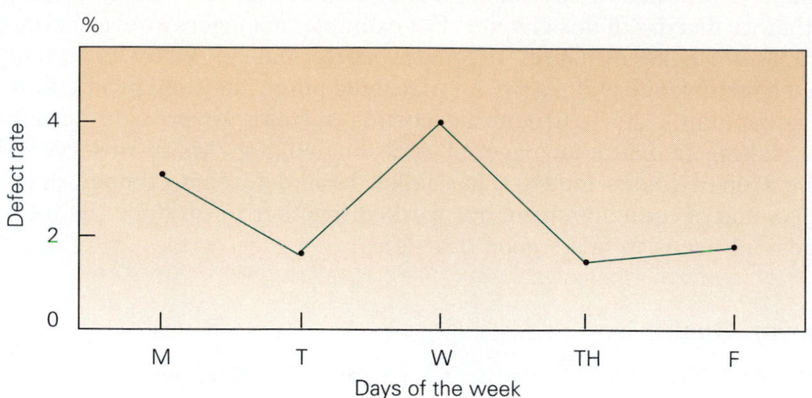

tomer. The key ideas are that the organization strives for excellence and that quality is ultimately defined by the customer.

CUSTOMER-DRIVEN QUALITY STANDARDS Total quality management means that your goods and services are not excellent until the customer says they are excellent. It is not enough for production managers or engineers to say an automobile is well-designed and produced; customers must say they like it—a lot. TQM means translating customer needs and wants into specifications for product design. Southwest Airlines learned that customers want flights to leave and arrive on time. No amount of free alcoholic beverages served to placate customers made up for late arrivals, missed connections, missed meetings, and missed birthday parties. So Southwest Airlines went to work to improve those things its customers wanted most; namely, on-time departures and arrivals. (Actually, the customers wanted on-time arrivals more than on-time departures, but you don't get on-time arrivals without on-time departures.)

Methods to Identify Quality Problems

How do companies identify quality problems? Three methods managers use to identify quality problems are the following:

1. Control charts.
2. Pareto diagrams.
3. Cause and effect analyses.

CONTROL CHARTS **Control charts** help managers distinguish between random or routine variations in quality and variations that should be investigated. For example, the managers of CD, Inc., expect some returned merchandise and do not panic because a customer returns merchandise. They use a control chart to plot data that shows trends or unusually high rates of returned merchandise.

Look at Illustration 20.1, a control chart for product defects in producing compact disc players at CD, Inc. Every compact disc player is tested to assure it works. Those products failing the test are reworked or scrapped, an example of *internal failure cost*. Management expects an average failure rate of 2% of the daily production. Management has set an upper limit for failure at 4% of daily production. If the failure rate exceeds 4%, management investigates to find out what is causing such a high rate.

Quality testers continuously record failure rates at CD, Inc. Managers can call up the results on their computers at any time. Note in Illustration 20.1 that Wednesday's results exceeded the 4% limit. Management investigated the problem Wednesday afternoon and found a machine improperly installing a switch. The machine was fixed Wednesday night and production returned to normal on Thursday.

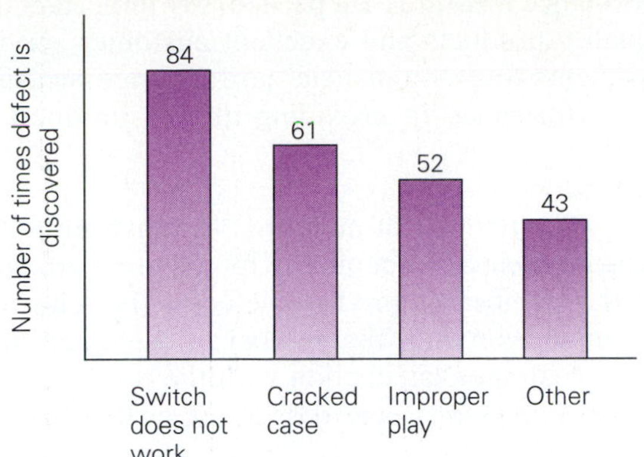

ILLUSTRATION 20.2
Pareto Diagram for Production at CD, Inc.

PARETO DIAGRAMS **Pareto diagrams** indicate how frequently each type of failure occurs. Note the Pareto diagram for compact disc player production at CD, Inc., in Illustration 20.2. Pareto diagrams have more information than simple control charts, but they require quality testers to classify and report defects. Managers learn more about the causes of problems from Pareto diagrams than they do from control charts.

CAUSE-AND-EFFECT ANALYSIS **Cause-and-effect analysis** identifies potential causes of defects. Consider the problem of cracked compact disc player cases, for example. Cracked cases could be due to breakage during production, faulty materials, or other handling problems. Managers must know the cause of problems to solve them. It makes no sense to focus on product handling, for example, if the problem is purchasing poor-quality materials.

QUALITY AND CUSTOMER SATISFACTION MEASURES

Objective 3
Develop measures of performance that help achieve high quality.

Quality-oriented organizations continually monitor the quality of their products and solicit feedback from customers to assess their satisfaction with goods and services. For instance, in Illustration 20.3 the second nonfinancial measure deals with delivery performance. Delivery performance is critical to success for companies such as American Airlines, Amtrak, Illinois Central and other metropolitan transit systems, Federal Express, United Parcel Service, and other delivery services.

The success of Lands' End, L. L. Bean, Territory Beyond, and other companies that sell through catalogs depends on quick delivery of their merchandise. Bottlers of soft drinks such as PepsiCola and canneries like Campbell Soup require precisely timed deliveries of cans and bottles. Ideally, the truck or railroad car unloads containers right onto the production line.

ILLUSTRATION 20.3
Nonfinancial Performance Measures

Performance Measure	Objective
1. Quality control	
Number of customer complaints	Create customer satisfaction (or even customer delight)
Number of defects	Make a high-quality product
2. Delivery performance	
Percentage of on-time deliveries	Increase on-time deliveries
3. Materials waste	
Scrap and waste as a percentage of total materials used	Decrease scrap and waste; improve the quality of products
4. Machine downtime	
Percentage of time machines are not working	Decrease machine downtime; increase on-time delivery to customers

Nonfinancial Performance Measures

Nonfinancial performance measures are particularly important to motivate people to provide high-quality products and excellent customer service. For example, Illustration 20.3 presents four nonfinancial performance measures used by managers to evaluate performance in providing quality products and service at a reasonable cost.

Quality Control The first set of measures in Illustration 20.3 reflect quality control. Firms measure their product quality by the number and type of customer complaints or by the number of product defects. By reducing the number of product defects, companies reduce the number of customer complaints. The objective is to increase customer satisfaction with the product, reduce the costs of dealing with customer complaints, and reduce the costs of repairing products or providing a new service.

Delivery Performance The second type of nonfinancial measure in Illustration 20.3 deals with delivery performance. As we noted earlier, delivery performance is critical for many companies. Domino's Pizza once based its success on 30 minute delivery service. The objective is to deliver goods and services when promised. To achieve this objective, companies keep track of the percentage of total deliveries that are on time.

Materials Waste Companies can take several steps to reduce materials waste, the third type of nonfinancial measure. They can purchase a higher quality of raw materials so there is less waste from defective materials, increase employee training so workers make fewer mistakes, and improve the production process. Reducing waste can improve quality. The causes of waste are often the causes of poor quality. For example, waste may reflect the poor training of employees. Improving training could improve the quality of their work on all products, not just those that result in waste. Generally, workers are motivated to find ways to reduce waste when companies keep track of the quantity of materials wasted every day. Companies sometimes provide immediate feedback to workers the next day, often in the form of large charts showing the previous day's waste.

Machine Downtime The fourth type of nonfinancial measure, machine downtime, is very important in all companies. At the New United Motor Mfg. Inc. (NUMMI) plant, a joint venture of General Motors and Toyota, line workers have the authority to stop the assembly line when they see something wrong. It should come as no surprise that such an action brings a lot of attention to the problem from many people in the plant. Stopping production causes a loss of output while people wait for the machinery to start up. Machine downtime also can cause customer dissatisfaction and loss of sales. You may have experienced this dissatisfaction at a bank when you could not be served because the computer was down, or when your airline flight was canceled because of an airplane's maintenance problems.

Motivation Effects

People like to take pride in their work. Surveys indicate that workers prefer to do high-quality work rather than low-quality work. Companies generally find that workers respond favorably to performance measures and incentives measuring and rewarding high-quality work.

Strategic Advantages of High Quality

Many companies use high quality as their strategic advantage. For example, Federal Express entered the air courier business with a promise that it would guarantee delivery the next day by mid-morning. By continually delivering on this promise, the company built up trust in its customers. Toyota and Motorola are other well-known companies that have used product quality to compete effectively.

Benchmarking

Benchmarking is the continuous process of measuring how well one is doing against performance levels either inside or outside of the organization. For instance, students often benchmark by comparing their performance against the professor's standards or other students' performance. Students often are interested in how well graduates of their school compare to graduates of other schools on CPA exams, bar exams, or other standardized exams.

Companies are benchmarking in a similar way. American Airlines looks at its own on-time arrival performance by computing the percentage of its flights that land within 15 minutes of their scheduled arrival time. The company compares the results with its own past experience and with its competitors' performance. American Airlines also compares its own percent of lost luggage to its own past experience and the performance of major competitors such as United Airlines and Delta Air Lines.

Benchmarking transforms the theory of quality products or service into practice. Benchmarking focuses attention on the objective. When American Airlines benchmarks on-time arrivals, it focuses the attention of its pilots, ground crews, mechanics, and everyone else on ways to improve on-time arrival performance.

Accounting Perspective

Managers Executed for Poor Quality

Business Insight Eighteen managers were executed for poor product quality in a refrigerator plant on the outskirts of Beijing. The managers—12 men and 6 women—were taken to a rice paddy outside of the factory and shot while plant workers watched.

A government official stated the action was required for committing unpardonable sins against the people of China. Apparently, workers complained the managers were forcing the production of poor quality products. When workers complained that components did not meet specifications and the refrigerators did not function as required, the managers told them to ship the products. Customers also had complained. This factory had a reputation for turning out poor quality products.

Source: *Wall Street Journal*, October 17, 1989.

Just-in-Time Method

Objective 4
Explain how just-in-time purchasing and production can reduce costs and improve quality.

Recent innovations in purchasing, production, and inventory management have the potential to revolutionize companies. One of these innovations is the **just-in-time (JIT) method.** Companies that use just-in-time methods purchase materials just in time for production, produce parts just when needed in the production process, and complete finished goods just in time for sale.

The principal feature of the just-in-time system is that production does not begin on an item until an order is received. When a company receives an order it buys the raw materials and the production cycle begins. As soon as the order is filled, production ends. Consequently, just-in-time requires immediate correction of processes or people making defective products because there is no inventory where defective products can await reworking or scrapping.

In theory, a JIT system eliminates the need for inventories because no production takes place until the company knows its products will be sold. As a practical matter, companies using this system normally have a backlog of orders so they can keep their production operations going. The benefits of the JIT system would be lost if a company had to shut down its operations for lengthy periods while waiting for new orders.

Just-in-Time and Quality

Just-in-time helps assure quality. If a unit is defective, employees cannot simply put it aside in inventory. Production workers and machines must do it right the first time.

Flexible Manufacturing

To achieve just-in-time production, many companies install a system of flexible manufacturing. A flexible manufacturing system is computer-based; it enables companies to make a variety of products with a minimum of setup time. The system does what its name implies: it enables companies to be flexible in making products just-in-time to fill customers' orders.

For example, consider a company that makes after-market running boards for trucks. Customers install these running boards on trucks after they purchase them. By using flexible manufacturing, the company that makes these running boards produces one set of running boards for a particular model of Jeep, then one set for a particular Toyota model, and so forth to fill customer orders. A traditional production system, by contrast, would produce numerous sets of running boards for the Jeep, which would remain in inventory until needed to fill customer orders. The traditional company would then produce numerous sets of running boards for the Toyota and place them in inventory until needed to fill customer orders.

Lean Production

Just-in-time is part of a lean production philosophy that has helped many companies successfully reduce costs and increase quality. One feature of lean production is the absence of shelves, floor space, and other places used to store partially finished products. For an example of lean production, imagine you are building a house and you have just enough materials arriving just when you need them. You don't have extra lumber lying about in case you make a mistake cutting the boards the first time. If your supplier of plumbing products doesn't deliver in time for your needs, you have to shut down production until the plumbing products arrive. As you can see, lean production requires high levels of efficiency and quality.

AN ACCOUNTING PERSPECTIVE

BUSINESS INSIGHT Holiday Inn learned some lessons when they hired D&B Software to develop a computerized reservation system. David Peach, a Holiday Inn vice president, said, "I think you need to take what the vendors say and really go back to them with your proposals and make sure the system specifications meet the software requirements." (From "Holiday Inn Hits Snags in Its Plans for Client/Server Setup," *Computerworld*, April 18, 1994.)

Effect of Just-in-Time on Accounting

Objective 5
Compare and contrast accounting in just-in-time settings with accounting in traditional settings.

Accountants using traditional costing methods assign costs to products as they go through the production steps. Assigning costs to products is time-consuming and expensive, not only for accountants, but also for workers and managers. One of the reasons for assigning costs as products proceed through production steps is to know the value of work-in-process inventory at the end of an accounting period. Suppose a product has completed the first three steps in a six-step production process at the end of the month. By assigning costs at each step along the way, accountants know the cost of the product at the end of the third step.

Accountants in JIT production facilities do not have to compute the cost of work-in-process inventories. There are no such inventories. Instead, accountants assign costs directly to Finished Goods Inventory or Cost of Goods Sold accounts. Companies have been known to save the time of two or three full-time accountants by assigning costs directly to Finished Goods Inventory or Cost of Goods Sold. Since JIT production responds to the receipt of an order for goods, a JIT accounting system normally debits all costs directly to cost of goods sold and bypasses the usual inventory accounts. When it is necessary to report inventory amounts in the financial statements, accountants back the inventory amounts out of the Cost of Goods Sold account using a method called *backflush costing*. **Backflush costing** is a method of assigning costs to inventories backwards from

Finished Goods Inventory or Cost of Goods Sold to Work in Process Inventory accounts.

For example, say Arizona Sunscreen Company uses the JIT method. Direct materials costs are $3.00 per bottle and other manufacturing costs are $1.50 per bottle. The company received an order for 10,000 bottles of sunscreen. Materials costs were $30,000 and other manufacturing costs were $15,000. Assume that $6,000 of these other costs are wages and the remaining $9,000 were applied to production from overhead. Assume also the company had an inventory of $4,500 left in work in process as of the date financial statements were prepared.

Traditional Methods Using traditional methods of recording costs, the costs would flow through the inventory accounts to Cost of Goods Sold as shown by the following journal entries:

	Debit	Credit
(1) Materials Inventory	30,000	
Accounts Payable		30,000
To record the purchase of materials.		
(2) Work in Process Inventory	45,000	
Materials Inventory		30,000
Payroll Summary		6,000
Overhead (applied)		9,000
To record production costs in the work in process account.		
(3) Finished Goods Inventory	40,500	
Work in Process Inventory		40,500
To transfer product from work in process to finished goods.		
(4) Cost of Goods Sold	40,500	
Finished Goods Inventory		40,500
To record the cost of the goods sold.		

Just-in-Time and Backflush Costing Using a just-in-time accounting system, the accountants would initially assume the company has no inventories. Therefore, they would debit all costs directly to Cost of Goods Sold, as follows:

	Debit	Credit
(1) Cost of Goods Sold	30,000	
Accounts Payable		30,000
To record the use of materials.		
(2) Cost of Goods Sold	15,000	
Payroll Summary		6,000
Overhead (applied)		9,000
To record other manufacturing costs.		

Upon learning the company has $4,500 of inventory in work in process, the accountants would back out $4,500 from Cost of Goods Sold, as follows:

	Debit	Credit
(3) Work in Process Inventory	4,500	
Cost of Goods Sold		4,500
To record inventory.		

This last entry is the backflush costing step. These entries appear in T-accounts in Illustration 20.4.

Just-in-time production simplifies accounting procedures. If the costs of these sunscreen bottles were charged into production using traditional costing methods, it would be necessary to debit the materials costs to a Materials Inventory account. As the materials were used, their costs would be transferred to Work in Process Inventory and other manufacturing costs would be charged to Work in Process Inventory. As goods were completed, costs would be transferred out of Work in Process Inventory, into Finished Goods Inventory, and, finally, into Cost of Goods Sold. Illustration 20.4 contrasts traditional versus just-in-time cost flows.

ILLUSTRATION 20.4 Traditional versus Just-in-Time Cost Flows

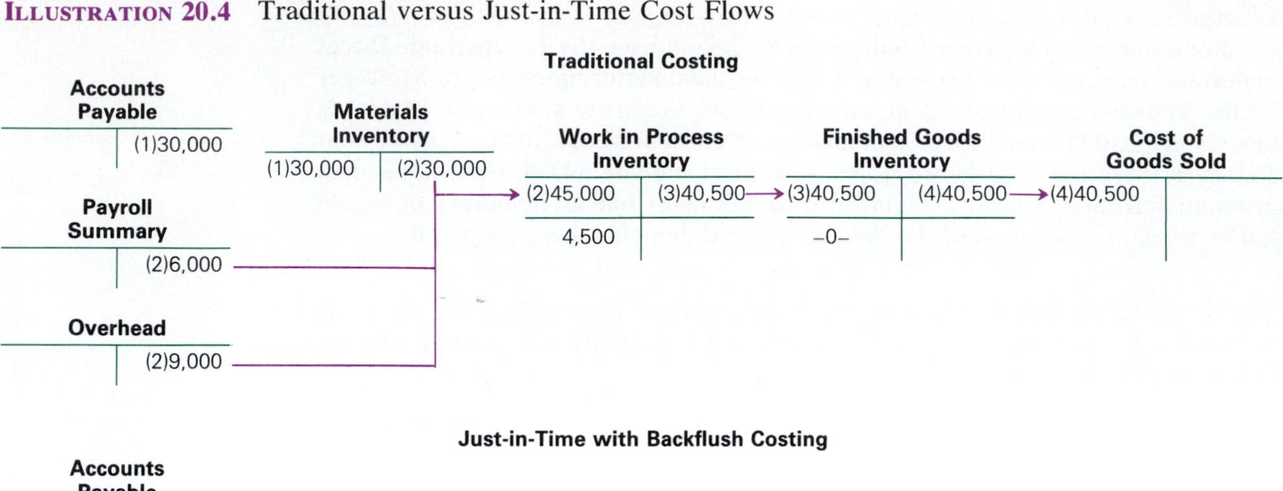

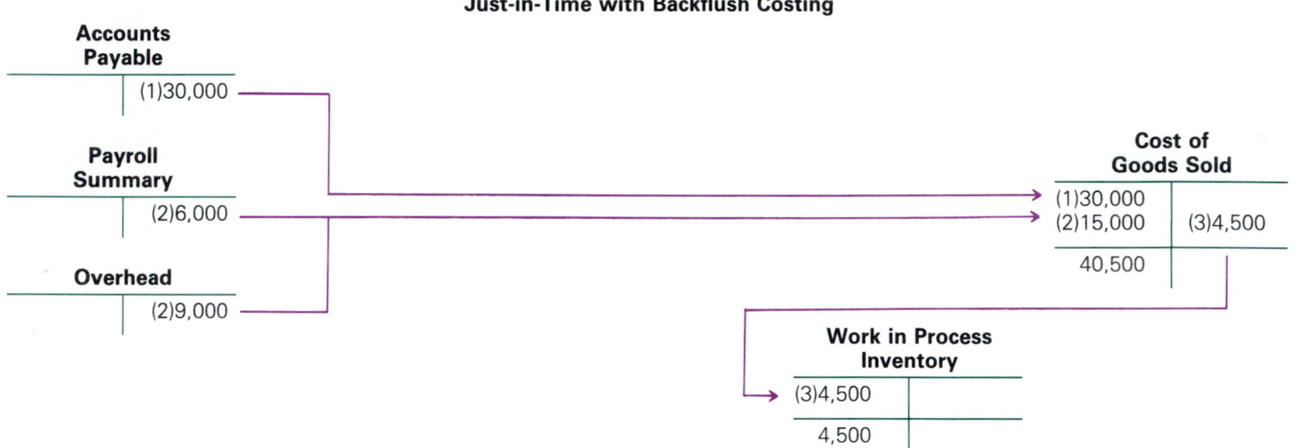

Advantages of Just-in-Time Systems

By reducing inventories, a just-in-time system offers potentially great cost savings. As noted earlier, it simplifies the accounting system. By reducing inventories, it releases investment dollars for use elsewhere, and frees space that the inventory previously occupied. Companies also have found that reducing inventories where defective products could be hidden helps management detect production problems more quickly. By tying JIT to quality improvement programs, companies move toward zero defect production.

ACTIVITY-BASED COSTING

Objective 6
Define activity-based costing and explain its benefit to companies.

Suppose you go to a movie theater that has five screens showing five different movies. Jerome Justin works for the movie theater selling tickets for all five movies. Suppose management wants to know the cost of selling tickets per movie and asks you to assign Justin's wages to each of the five movies. How would you assign his wages?

You could simply divide Justin's wages by the number of movies and allocate 20% of his salary to each movie. Or you could figure out how many tickets he sold to each movie, and allocate his wages on the basis of ticket sales. For example, if 50% of the ticket sales were for *Terminator 10,* you might allocate 50% of Justin's wages to *Terminator 10*. You probably also could think of additional ways to allocate Justin's wages. No matter how we allocate Justin's wages, his wages would not be directly traceable to one of the movies if he sold tickets for all five movies. In short, the allocation of Justin's wages to a particular movie is at least somewhat arbitrary because alternative methods could allocate different amounts of Justin's wages to each movie. Justin's wages would be indirect costs to the different movies because his wages could not be directly assigned to any one of the movies. By definition, the allocation of indirect costs is at least somewhat arbitrary. Nevertheless, accountants have discovered that they can improve the ways costs are assigned, such as to movies in this case, by using activity-based costing. **Activity-based costing** is a costing method that assigns costs to activities and to the products based on each product's use of activities. Activity-based costing is based on the premise: Products consume activities; activities consume resources.

Numerous companies, such as Hewlett-Packard, Procter & Gamble, Caterpillar, and IBM, have implemented activity-based costing. Activity-based costing (ABC) has revealed startling information in these companies. For example, after installing new costing methods, Tektronix Inc. found that one of its products, a printed circuitboard, was generating negative margins of 46%.[2]

Activity-based costing identifies the activities generating costs and assigns costs to those activities. Take the earlier Justin example. By focusing on Justin's activities, management could learn what caused costs and find ways to improve Justin's efficiency. Suppose that by studying Justin's activities, management learns he spends 40% of his time answering questions about movies, 40% of his time selling tickets, and 20% doing nothing. Based on this information, management could think about better ways to use Justin's time. By improving their signs and posting information about the movies, management could reassign Justin to other tasks.

Activity-Based Management

Closely related to activity-based costing is the notion of activity-based management. Using activity-based management, managers identify which activities consume resources but do not assign costs to them. Consider Justin and the movie theater again. Using activity-based management, managers would identify what Justin did with his time and perhaps find ways to help him become more efficient. Using activity-based costing, they would assign costs to those activities. Activity-based management often provides much of the insight of activity-based costing without the time and effort of assigning costs to activities.

The following discussion at a textile company that make jeans demonstrates important issues about the difficulty with traditional cost allocation methods and the advantages of activity-based costing. The participants are concerned about their company's ability to compete with foreign manufacturers that have lower labor costs. Many people in the company believe the company's managerial accounting system provides inadequate information. In this discussion, George, a managerial accountant, reports on his recent study of activity-based costing.

George (managerial accountant): I have been reading a lot of articles about companies like Ford and Hewlett-Packard that have discovered major problems with their cost systems. Their symptoms are similar to ours. Namely, they can't lower prices to be competitive on high-volume products, and their profits are shrinking.

Pam (company president): That sounds like us! What are they doing about it?

George: Well, they're putting in a new type of cost system called activity-based costing, or ABC for short. This system gives more detailed and better estimates of product costs, which helps their friends in marketing set prices. Applying this to ourselves, we may find, for example, that activity-

[2] "A Bean-Counter's Best Friend," *Business Week/Quality*, 1991, pp. 42–43.

A Broader Perspective

Hewlett-Packard Company

When a division of Hewlett-Packard Company introduced the just-in-time production method, the accountants found their traditional methods of cost accounting were no longer applicable. Reducing the work in process and finished goods inventories meant the accountants no longer needed to keep detailed records for inventory valuation.

Lowering inventories to immaterial levels for financial reporting purposes reduces the amount of accounting time required to make journal entries to transfer costs between inventory accounts. This Hewlett-Packard plant saved an estimated 100,000 journal entries per month by simplifying the accounting for work in process inventories.

JIT did not eliminate the need for product costing. Managers needed to know how much products cost so they could make decisions, plan, and evaluate performance. After simplifying inventory accounting at the Hewlett-Packard plant, the accountants turned their attention to providing better information in a form managers could understand and use. The accountants found their new role in helping managers plan and control production exciting and challenging.

Source: Based on an article by R. Hunt, L. Garrett, and C. M. Merz, "Direct Labor Cost Not Always Relevant at H-P," *Management Accounting,* February 1985, pp. 58–62.

based costing could reveal that the cost of skirts is lower than we thought, meaning we could lower our prices.

Lynn (vice president of marketing): That would be good news, but I thought costs were pretty cut-and-dried. How can a product cost less under one cost system than under another?

George: Actually, Lynn, the product doesn't cost less under one system or another. Our problem is that no cost system measures costs perfectly. We are able to trace some costs directly to the product. For example, we are pretty accurate in measuring the cost of denim, which is a direct material, in each of our shirts, pants, jackets, and so forth.

Overhead costs are another matter. Overhead includes costs like electricity to run machines and salaries of product designers and inspectors. All these costs are allocated to products. We know quality control inspectors cost money, but we don't know how much of that cost is caused by a particular jacket or pair of pants. So we make some assumptions about the relation between products and overhead costs. For example, we typically allocate overhead based on machine-hours required to stitch and fasten snaps. While that is probably a reasonable way to allocate the costs of electricity to run machines, its not a desirable way to allocate the cost of quality control inspectors.

Pam: As I understand it, overhead allocation is somewhat arbitrary. How will activity-based costing help?

George: Activity-based costing provides more accurate information because we can identify which activities cause costs, and we can determine the cost of the activity. Activity-based costing identifies and measures the costs of performing the activities that go into a product much better than traditional cost methods. For example, if a particular jacket requires 10 inspections for a production run of 1,000 jackets, we figure out the cost of those inspections and assign that cost to the production run for this particular jacket.

Martha (vice president of production): That makes sense to me. But exactly how would activity-based costing help us cut production costs?

George: Once we identify activities that cause costs, we can eliminate or modify costly activities. For example, if we find that a jacket requires too many costly inspections, we could redesign the jacket to reduce the need for inspections. Our current cost system allocates all overhead costs, including inspection costs, to products based on machine-hours. We really don't know how much it costs to make an inspection and how much inspection cost is required by each product.

Pam: George, why haven't you used activity-based costing before?

George (feeling somewhat defensive): Because activity-based costing provides more information, it takes more time than traditional cost systems. New accounting methods sound great in theory, but there must be enough benefit from improved management decisions to justify the additional work required to provide numbers. Until now, I did not think activity-based costing would pass a cost-benefit test.

Pam: I see many benefits in better pricing, reducing the costs of high-cost activities, and possibly dropping some products if we learn that their costs are too high. Our long-term strategy calls for new product lines in new markets where we are low-cost, low-price producers. We need the best cost information we can get to succeed in those markets. George, what do you need to get started developing an activity-based costing system for us?

George: I need a lot of support. Installing a new cost system requires teamwork between management, accounting, marketing, engineering, production, purchasing, and everybody else. This is not something to be done in an ivory tower.

Remember these important points about activity-based costing:

1. The allocation of indirect costs is at least somewhat arbitrary, even using sophisticated accounting methods.
2. Activity-based costing provides more detailed measures of costs than traditional allocation methods.
3. Activity-based costing can help marketing people by providing more accurate product cost numbers for decisions about pricing and which unprofitable products the company should eliminate.
4. Production also benefits because activity-based costing provides better information about the cost of each activity. In practice, ABC helps managers identify cost causing activities. To manage costs, production managers learn to manage the activities that cause costs.
5. Activity-based costing provides more information about product costs than traditional methods but requires more record-keeping. Managers must decide whether the benefits or improved decisions justify the additional record-keeping cost.
6. Installing activity-based costing requires teamwork among accountants, production managers, marketing managers, and other nonaccounting people.

Next, we discuss the methods used for activity-based costing and illustrate them with an example.

Methods Used for Activity-Based Costing

Objective 7
List the four steps in activity-based costing.

Activity-based costing requires accountants to use the following four steps:

1. *Identify the activities that consume resources and assign costs to those activities*. Purchasing materials would be an activity, for example.
2. *Identify the cost drivers associated with each activity*. A **cost driver** is an activity or transaction that causes costs to be incurred. For the purchasing materials activity, the cost drivers could be the number of orders placed or the number of items ordered. Each activity could have multiple cost drivers.
3. *Compute a cost rate per cost driver unit*. The cost driver rate could be the cost per purchase order, for example.
4. *Assign costs to products by multiplying the cost driver rate times the volume of cost driver units consumed by the product*. For example, the cost

per purchase order times the number of orders required for Product A for the month of December would measure the cost of the purchasing activity for Product A for December.

The next section describes these four steps.

Step 1: Identifying the Activities That Consume Resources

Step one is often the most interesting and challenging part of the exercise. This step requires people to understand all of the activities required to make the product. Imagine the activities involved in making a simple product like a pizza—ordering, receiving and inspecting materials, making the dough, putting on the ingredients, baking, and so forth. Or imagine the activities involved in making a complex product such as an automobile or computer.

Complexity as an Activity That Consumes Resources One of the lessons of activity-based costing has been that the more complex the business, the higher the indirect costs. Imagine that each month you produce 100,000 gallons of vanilla ice cream and your friend produces 100,000 gallons of 39 different flavors of ice cream. Further, assume your ice cream is sold only in one liter containers, while your friend sells ice cream in various containers. Your friend has more complicated ordering, storage, product testing (one of the more desirable jobs, nevertheless), and packing in containers. Your friend has more machine setups, too. Presumably, you can set the machinery to one setting to obtain the desired product quality and taste. Your friend has to set the machines each time a new flavor is produced. Although both of you produce the same total volume of ice cream, it is not hard to imagine that your friend's overhead costs would be considerably higher.

Step 2: Choosing Cost Drivers

In Illustration 20.5, we present several examples of the cost drivers companies use. Most cost drivers are related to either the volume of production or to the complexity of the production or marketing process. In deciding which cost drivers to use, managers consider these three factors:

1. *Causal relation.* Choosing a cost driver that causes the cost is ideal. For example, suppose students in biology classes are messier than students in history classes. As a result, the university does more maintenance per square foot in biology classrooms and labs than in history classrooms. Further, it is possible to keep track of the time maintenance people spend cleaning classrooms and labs. The university could assign maintenance costs based on the time spent in history classrooms and in biology classrooms and labs, respectively, to the history and biology departments.
2. *Benefits received.* Choose a cost driver so costs are assigned in proportion to benefits received. For example, if the physics department in a university benefits more from the university's supercomputer than the German department does, the university should select a cost driver that recognizes such differences in benefits. The cost driver could be the number of faculty and/or students in each department who use the computer.
3. *Reasonableness.* Some costs that cannot be linked to products based on causality or benefits received are assigned on the basis of reasonableness.

Step 3: Computing a Cost Rate per Cost Driver

In general, predetermined rates for allocating indirect costs to products are computed as follows:

$$\text{Predetermined indirect cost rate} = \frac{\text{Estimated indirect cost}}{\text{Estimated volume of the allocation base}}$$

This formula applies to all indirect costs, whether manufacturing overhead, administrative costs, distribution costs, selling costs, or any other indirect cost.

ILLUSTRATION 20.5
Cost Drivers

Cost Driver	Cost Assigned by Cost Driver
Miles driven	Automobile costs
Machine-hours	Electricity to run machines
Customers served	Overhead in a bank
Flight hours	Airplane maintenance costs
Number of customers	Selling costs

Using activity-based costing, we first define the notion of an activity center. An **activity center** is a unit of the organization that performs some activity. For example, the costs of setting up machines would be assigned to the activity center that sets up machines. This means that each activity has associated costs. When the cost driver is the number of inspections, for example, the company must keep track of the cost of inspections.

Step 4: Assigning Costs to Products

Workers and machines perform activities on each product as it is produced. Accountants allocate costs to products by multiplying each activity's indirect cost rate by the volume of activity used in making the product.

Activity-Based Costing Illustrated

Objective 8
Compare product costs using activity-based costing with product costs using traditional costing methods.

The following example illustrates how unit costs are computed when companies use activity-based costing. We contrast the results using activity-based costing to those using a departmental rate.

Assume High Challenge Company makes two products, touring bicycles and mountain bicycles. The touring bicycles product line is a high-volume line, while the mountain bicycle is a low-volume, specialized product.

TRADITIONAL COSTING METHOD Using a traditional costing method, assume that High Challenge Company followed this procedure to allocate manufacturing overhead costs to the two products for the month of January 1997.

1. Managers and accountants developed an overhead rate based on the following data for 1997:

Overhead for Department A for 1997	$2,000,000
Machine-hours worked during 1997 in Department A	20,000 hours
Department A overhead rate ($2,000,000/20,000 hours)	$100 per machine-hour

2. To compare activity-based costing with the company's traditional method, the accountants selected the month of January to study. At the end of January 1997 the following information was available for the month:

Actual machine-hours used in January 1997	
Touring bicycle products	1,500
Mountain bicycle products	500
Total	2,000

3. Using a traditional costing method, accountants then allocated overhead to the products worked on in January using the overhead rate of $100 per hour times the machine-hours worked on each product in Department A during January:

Overhead allocated to products worked on in January:	
Touring bicycles ($100 × 1,500 hours)	$150,000
Mountain bicycles ($100 × 500 hours)	50,000
Total overhead	$200,000

Assigning Costs Using Activity-Based Costing

In using activity-based costing, the company identified four activities that were important cost drivers and a cost driver used to allocate overhead. These activities were (1) purchasing materials, (2) setting up machines when a new product was started, (3) inspecting products, and (4) operating machines.

ILLUSTRATION 20.6
Overhead Rates for Activity-Based Costing

(1) Activity	(2) Cost Driver Used to Allocate Overhead Cost Driver	(3) Overhead Cost for the Activity	(4) Cost Driver Units for 1997	(5) Rate: Column (3) ÷ Column (4)
1. Purchasing materials	Pieces of materials in each unit	$200,000	100,000 pieces	$2/piece
2. Machine setups	Machine setups	800,000	400 setups	$2,000/setup
3. Inspections	Inspection hours	400,000	4,000 hours	$100/hour
4. Running machines	Machine-hours	600,000	20,000 hours	$30/hour
Total overhead		$2,000,000		

Accountants estimated the overhead and the volume of events for each activity. For example, management estimated the company would purchase 100,000 pieces of materials that would require overhead costs of $200,000 for the year. These overhead costs included salaries of people to purchase, inspect, and store materials. Consequently, each piece of material used to make a product would be assigned an overhead cost of $2.00 ($200,000/100,000 pieces).

These estimates made in 1996 were used during all of 1997. In practice, companies most frequently set rates for the entire year, although some set rates for shorter periods, such as a quarter. Look at the overhead rates computed for the four activities in Illustration 20.6. Note that the total overhead for 1997 is $2,000,000 using activity-based costing, just as it was using a traditional costing method. The total amount of overhead should be the same whether using activity-based costing or traditional methods of cost allocation to products. The primary difference between activity-based costing and the traditional allocation methods is the amount of detail; particularly, the number of activities used to assign overhead costs to products. Traditional allocation uses just one activity—such as machine-hours. Activity-based costing used four activities in this case. In practice, companies using activity-based costing generally use more than four activities because more than four activities are important. We used four to keep the illustration as simple as possible. (Many companies that use traditional allocation methods use just one activity, as we have in this example.)

For January 1997, the High Challenge Company has the following information about the actual number of cost driver units for each of the two products:

	Touring Bicycles	Mountain Bicycles
1. Purchasing materials	6,000 pieces	4,000 pieces
2. Machine setups	10 setups	30 setups
3. Inspections	200 hours	200 hours
4. Running machines	1,500 hours	500 hours

Multiplying the actual activity events for each product times the predetermined rates computed earlier resulted in the overhead allocated to the two products shown in Illustration 20.7. Now we can compare the overhead allocated to the two product lines using the traditional method and activity-based costing, as follows:

	Touring Bicycles	Mountain Bicycles
Traditional method	$150,000	$ 50,000
Activity-based costing	97,000	103,000

UNIT COSTS Assume High Challenge Company produced 1,000 units of touring bicycles and 200 units of mountain bicycles in January. The direct materials cost is $100 per unit for touring bicycles and $200 per unit for mountain bicycles. Direct labor cost is $20 per unit for touring bicycles and $30 per unit for mountain bicycles. Comparing the overhead allocations using the department allocation and

ILLUSTRATION 20.7
Overhead Costs Assigned to Products Using Activity-Based Costing

Activity	Rate	Touring Bicycles: Actual Cost Driver Units	Touring Bicycles: Cost Allocated to Product	Mountain Bicycles: Actual Cost Driver Units	Mountain Bicycles: Cost Allocated to Product
1. Purchasing materials	$2/piece	6,000 pieces	$12,000	4,000 pieces	$ 8,000
2. Machine setups	$2,000/setup	10 setups	20,000	30 setups	60,000
3. Inspections	$100/hour	200 hours	20,000	200 hours	20,000
4. Running machines	$30/hour	1,500 hours	45,000	500 hours	15,000
Total cost allocated to each product			$97,000		$103,000

ILLUSTRATION 20.8
Comparison of Product Costs Using Traditional Costing and Activity-Based Costing

	Traditional Costing: Touring Bicycles	Traditional Costing: Mountain Bicycles	Activity-Based Costing: Touring Bicycles	Activity-Based Costing: Mountain Bicycles
Direct materials	$100	$200	$100	$200
Direct labor	20	30	20	30
Overhead	150[a]	250[b]	97[c]	515[d]
Total	$270	$480	$217	$745

[a] $150 = overhead cost allocation to products using departmental rate divided by number of units produced = $150,000/1,000 units.

[b] $250 = overhead cost allocation to products using departmental rate divided by number of units produced = $50,000/200 units.

[c] $97 = overhead cost allocation to products using activity-based costing divided by number of units produced = $97,000/1,000 units.

[d] $515 = overhead cost allocation to products using activity-based costing divided by number of units produced = $103,000/200 units.

the activity-based costing allocation reveals the differences in unit costs, as we show in Illustration 20.8.

ANALYSIS More overhead is allocated to the lower volume mountain bicycles using activity-based costing. The mountain bicycles are allocated more overhead per unit primarily because activity-based costing recognizes the need for more setups for mountain bicycles and for as many inspection hours for the more specialized mountain bicycles as for the higher volume touring bicycles. By failing to assign costs to all of the activities, touring bicycles were subsidizing mountain bicycles. Many companies have found themselves in similar situations. Activity-based costing has revealed that low-volume, specialized products have been the cause of greater costs than managers had realized.

IMPACT OF NEW PRODUCTION ENVIRONMENT ON COST DRIVERS

When cost systems were first developed in industry, companies were far more labor intensive than they are today. The majority of the overhead cost was related to the support of labor, so it made sense to allocate overhead to products based on the amount of labor in the products. Labor is still a major product cost in many companies, especially service organizations such as public accounting firms. Often they allocate overhead to products (which are called *jobs*) on the basis of the amount of labor in the product.

As manufacturers and service companies have become more automated, direct labor has become less appropriate as a basis for allocating overhead. Direct labor has shrunk to less than 5% of product costs in many companies and overhead has increased. Thus, companies that continue to allocate overhead to products based on direct labor are seeing rates increase as high as 500% or more. (Some overhead rates are more than 1,000% of direct labor costs.)

When labor is such a small part of product costs, there is little—if any—relationship between labor and overhead. Further, small errors in assigning labor to products are magnified many times when overhead rates are several hundred percent of labor costs, or more.

Finally, allocating overhead on the basis of direct labor sends signals that direct labor is more expensive than it really is. This also creates tremendous incentives to reduce the labor content of products. While this may be desirable in particular circumstances, such decisions should be based on accurate cost numbers, not numbers heavily biased because of an arbitrary cost allocation method.

Activity-Based Costing in Marketing

Activity-based costing is not limited to the cost of producing goods and services; companies also apply it to marketing or administrative activities. The principles and methods are the same as discussed earlier: (1) identify activities or cost drivers, (2) compute an indirect cost rate for each activity, and (3) allocate indirect costs by multiplying the indirect cost rate for each activity by the volume of activities.

Instead of computing a cost of production, however, accountants compute a cost of performing an administrative or marketing service. Tissue products, for example, can be sold to grocery stores, convenience stores, the industrial market, and other channels of distribution. Each channel has different activities:

- Convenience stores would require many shipments in small orders and considerable marketing support.
- Grocery stores would require relatively large shipments, a variety of products, and considerable marketing support.
- Industrial users would involve brokers, minimum marketing support, and large orders.[3]

The cost of alternative channels of distribution is useful to marketing managers who make decisions about which channel to use. In this case, obvious cost drivers would include the number of shipments per period, size of shipment, number of products in a shipment, and measures of merchandising support.

Strategic Use of Activity-Based Management

Objective 9
Describe the strategic and behavioral advantages of activity-based management.

Many believe activity-based costing offers strategic opportunities for companies.[4] One of the key ways companies develop a competitive advantage is by becoming low-cost producers or sellers. Companies such as Wal-Mart Stores in retailing, United Parcel Service in delivery services, and Southwest Airlines in the airline industry have created competitive advantages by reducing costs. Michael Porter, among others, has pointed out that certain companies have learned to use the information they have gained from their cost systems to make substantial price cuts to increase market share.[5]

Activity-based costing plays an important role in companies' strategies and long-range plans to develop a competitive cost advantage. Activity-based costing focuses attention on activities. Cost reduction generally requires a change in activities. Although top management can send notices asking company employees to reduce costs, the implementation requires a change in activities. If you have been in school during a period when education costs were cut, you know that

---

[3] See J. M. Reeve, "Cost Management in Continuous-Process Environments," in *Emerging Practices in Cost Management*, ed. Barry J. Brinker (New York: Warren, Gorham & Lamont, 1992), pp. F3-1–13.

[4] See J. Shank and V. Govindarajan, *Strategic Cost Analysis* (Homewood, IL: Richard D. Irwin, 1989), for an extensive discussion of the strategic use of cost analysis.

[5] M. E. Porter, *Competitive Advantage* (New York: Free Press, 1985).

achieving the cut required a change in activities such as canceled classes, larger class sizes, and reduced services. It is impossible to know the effect of a change in activities on costs without the cost information provided by activity-based costing.

Behavioral and Implementation Issues

Accountants cannot implement activity-based costing without becoming familiar with the operations of the company. In identifying activities, accountants team up with management and people from production, engineering, marketing, and other departments in identifying the activities that drive the company's costs. This often creates discomfort at first as accountants are forced to deal with unfamiliar areas; in the long-run their familiarity with the company's operating activities can improve their contribution to the company. Nonaccounting personnel also feel a greater sense of ownership of the numbers reported by the accounting system so accounting improves its credibility among nonaccountants.

One of the problems encountered when implementing activity-based costing is the failure to get influential people in the organization to buy into the process. Accounting methods in companies are like rules in sports; people become accustomed to playing by the rules and oppose change to something unknown.

For example, two analysts at one company spent several months of their time and hundreds of hours of computer time to develop an activity-based costing system. Their analysis revealed several hundred products that were clearly unprofitable and should be eliminated. However, the key managers who made product elimination decisions agreed to drop only about 20 products. Why? The analysts had failed to talk to these key managers early in the process. When presented with the final results, these managers raised numerous objections that the analysts had not anticipated. *Moral*: If you are involved in trying to make a change, get all of the people who are important to that change to buy into the process early.

Opportunities to Improve Activity-Based Costing in Practice

The use of activity-based costing in industry is relatively new. Companies are continually encountering limitations and finding ways to improve activity-based costing. A philosopher once said that our knowledge is like a circle; the more we know, the larger the circle. But the larger the circle, the greater its boundary and the more we realize the limits of our knowledge. Activity-based costing has shown managers they have much to learn about the cost of the activities required to make their products.

Understanding The Learning Objectives

- The new production environment refers to an environment in which company managers are concerned with (1) improving quality and (2) reducing costs. Accounting information can help managers assess the costs of quality and reduce the costs of making products.

Objective 1
Describe why managers need good accounting information to be competitive in the new production environment.

- Three methods managers use to identify quality problems are control charts, Pareto diagrams, and cause and effect analyses.
- Knowing the four costs of quality—prevention, appraisal, internal failure, and external failure—can help managers minimize the cost of quality while providing high-quality products to customers.

Objective 2
Identify ways to improve quality.

Objective 3
Develop measures of performance that help achieve high quality.

- Four such measures are quality control, delivery performance, materials waste, and machine downtime.
- Managers can use benchmarking to focus attention on measuring how well one is doing against levels of performance either inside or outside of the organization.

Objective 4
Explain how just-in-time purchasing and production can reduce costs and improve quality.

- JIT substantially reduces or eliminates the need for inventories and improves quality by eliminating the flexibility provided by inventories. Products must be produced properly the first time.

Objective 5
Compare and contrast accounting in just-in-time settings with accounting in traditional settings.

- Just-in-time accounting procedures normally debit all costs directly to cost of goods sold and bypass the usual inventory accounts. When it is necessary to report inventories in financial statements, the inventory amounts are backed out of the Cost of Goods Sold account.

Objective 6
Define activity-based costing and explain its benefit to companies.

- Activity-based costing is a costing method that assigns costs to activities and then to the products based on each product's use of activities. Activity-based costing is based on the premise that products consume activities; activities consume resources.
- Companies benefit from activity-based costing because managers have more detailed information about the cost of activities and better product cost information.

Objective 7
List the four steps in activity-based costing.

- First, identify the activities that consume resources and assign costs to those activities. Second, identify the cost drivers associated with each activity. Third, compute a cost rate per cost driver unit. Fourth, assign costs to products by multiplying the cost driver rate times the volume of cost driver units consumed by the product.

Objective 8
Compare product costs using activity-based costing with product costs using traditional costing methods.

- In many companies, activity-based costing has revealed that low-volume, specialized products have been more costly than managers had realized.

Objective 9
Describe the strategic and behavioral advantages of activity-based management.

- By focusing attention on activities that cause costs, activity-based management helps managers eliminate activities that consume resources, thereby becoming more efficient and competitive.

Demonstration Problem

To continue the text example, consider December 1997 for High Challenge Company. Recall that the departmental overhead rate for 1997 was $100 per machine-hour. The following information for December is available:

	Touring Bicycles	Mountain Bicycles
Machine-hours	2,000	1,000
Units	1,300	400
Activities		
1. Purchasing materials	10,000 pieces	10,000 pieces
2. Machine setups	15 setups	40 setups
3. Inspections	200 hours	400 hours
4. Running machines	2,000 hours	1,000 hours

Compute the costs in total and per unit for touring bicycle and mountain bicycle products using both the traditional method based on machine-hours to allocate overhead and the activity-based costing rates. The actual activity levels for December are given in this problem; however, you should use the rates presented earlier in the text. Do not assume that the total overhead assigned to products for December using activity-based costing necessarily equals the total overhead allocated using the departmental allocation rate. Assume the direct materials costs are $100 and $200 per unit for touring bicycles and mountain bicycles, respectively; and direct labor costs are $20 and $30 per unit, respectively. Production was 1,300 touring bicycles and 400 mountain bicycles. Round unit costs to the nearest dollar.

Solution to Demonstration Problem

Overhead costs allocated to products using the traditional method:

Touring bicycles ($100 × 2,000 machine-hours)	$200,000
Mountain bicycles ($100 × 1,000 machine-hours)	100,000
Total	$300,000

Overhead costs assigned to products using activity-based costing:

		Touring Bicycles		Mountain Bicycles	
Activity	**Rate**	**Actual Cost Driver Units**	**Cost Allocated to Product**	**Actual Cost Driver Units**	**Cost Allocated to Product**
1. Purchasing materials	$2/piece	10,000 pieces	$ 20,000	10,000 pieces	$ 20,000
2. Machine setups	$2,000/setup	15 setups	30,000	40 setups	80,000
3. Inspections	$100/hour	200 hours	20,000	400 hours	40,000
4. Running machines	$30/hour	2,000 hours	60,000	1,000 hours	30,000
Total cost allocated to each product			$130,000		$170,000

Comparison of product costs using traditional costing and activity-based costing:

	Traditional Costing		Activity-Based Costing	
	Touring Bicycles	**Mountain Bicycles**	**Touring Bicycles**	**Mountain Bicycles**
Direct materials	$100	$200	$100	$200
Direct labor	20	30	20	30
Overhead	154[a]	250[b]	100[c]	425[d]
Total	$274	$480	$220	$655

[a] $154 = overhead cost allocation to products using departmental rate divided by number of units produced = $200,000/1,300 units.

[b] $250 = overhead cost allocation to products using department rate divided by number of units produced = $100,000/400 units.

[c] $100 = overhead cost allocation to products using activity-based costing divided by number of units produced = $130,000/1,300 units.

[d] $425 = overhead cost allocation to products using activity-based costing divided by number of units produced = $170,000/400 units.

New Terms

Activity-based costing A costing method that first assigns costs to activities, then assigns costs to products based on their consumption of activities. *743*

Activity center An activity center is a unit of the organization that performs some activity. *747*

Backflush costing Backflush costing is a method of assigning costs to inventories backwards from Finished Goods Inventory or Cost of Goods Sold to Work in Process Inventory accounts. *740*

Benchmarking Benchmarking is the continuous process of measuring how well one is doing against performance levels either inside or outside of the organization. *739*

Cause-and-effect analysis Cause-and-effect analysis identifies potential causes of defects. *737*

Control charts Control charts help managers distinguish between random or routine variations in quality and variations that they should investigate. *736*

Cost driver A cost driver is an activity or transaction that causes costs to be incurred. *745*

Just-in-time (JIT) method The just-in-time method manages purchasing and production so that materials are purchased just in time for production, parts are produced just when needed for the next step in the production process, and finished goods are completed just in time for sale. *739*

Pareto diagrams Pareto diagrams indicate how frequently each type of failure occurs. *737*

Total quality management (TQM) Defined as managing the entire organization so it excels in its goods and services that are important to the customer. *735*

SELF-TEST

TRUE-FALSE

Indicate whether each of the following statements is true or false.

1. In Texas Instruments' cost of quality program, the managers' task was to maximize the sum of prevention, appraisal, internal failure, and external failure costs.
2. Control charts are a means of distinguishing between random or routine variation in product quality and variations that managers should investigate.
3. The allocation of indirect costs is never arbitrary.
4. A cost driver is an activity or transaction that causes costs to be incurred.
5. The formula for computing an indirect cost rate has the cost in the numerator and the volume of the cost driver or allocation base in the denominator.

MULTIPLE-CHOICE

Select the best answer for each of the following questions.

1. The new production environment refers to an environment in which company managers are concerned with:
   - **a.** Improving customer service and product quality.
   - **b.** Reducing costs.
   - **c.** Increasing government regulation.
   - **d.** **a** and **b** above.
   - **e.** All of the above.
2. Just-in-time production and purchasing methods:
   - **a.** Must be used in conjunction with activity-based costing.
   - **b.** Require government regulation.
   - **c.** Eliminate the need for inventories in theory because production does not take place until it is known the item will be sold.
   - **d.** Require the use of Pareto charts.
   - **e.** All of the above.
3. UR Company has two products, U and R. Overhead costs are presently allocated to the two products based on the labor-hours used to produce each product. It takes one labor-hour to make one unit of each product. The chief financial officer has suggested converting to activity-based costing. She collected the data shown below for three cost drivers and activities to be used under activity-based costing:

Activity	Cost Driver	Amount	Cost Driver Volume U	R
Production setups	Number of setups	$ 82,000	8	12
Quality control	Number of inspections	48,000	56	24
Packaging costs	Number of units produced	130,000	80,000	50,000
Total overhead		$260,000		

   What is the total overhead allocated to Product U using the current method of allocating overhead based on labor-hours (80,000 labor-hours for U and 50,000 labor-hours for R)?
   - **a.** $113,600.
   - **b.** $130,000.
   - **c.** $146,400.
   - **d.** $160,000.
   - **e.** None of the above.
4. Refer to the facts for question **(3)**. What is the overhead per unit assigned to Product R using activity-based costing? (Round to the nearest cent.)
   - **a.** $2.60.
   - **b.** $2.27.
   - **c.** $2.00.
   - **d.** $1.83.
   - **e.** None of the above.

Now turn to page 762 to check your answers.

QUESTIONS

1. To what does the phrase *new production environment* refer?
2. Explain the purpose of using control charts, Pareto diagrams, and cause and effect analyses. You may find it useful to use examples.
3. Audio Company makes compact disc players. After producing a compact disc player, the company tests it, then scraps it because it doesn't work. Is this an example of an internal failure cost, an appraisal cost, or a prevention cost in the Texas Instruments' cost of quality program?
4. A company's performance measure is the number of customer complaints. Why would the company measure the number of customer complaints?
5. A company's performance measure is the percentage of time that machines are not working. Why would the company measure the percentage of time that the machines are not working?
6. How could reducing materials waste during production improve the quality of products?
7. What is benchmarking? Give an example of benchmarking that you might use.
8. What is the benefit to American Airlines of benchmarking on-time airplane arrivals?
9. How does just-in-time help assure quality of production?
10. Elimination of inventories through a just-in-time (JIT) method is believed to result in different types of cost savings. Give an example of a type of savings from JIT.
11. What is the difference between accounting for costs using a JIT method and using traditional cost flows through inventory accounts?
12. What operating conditions are necessary for a company to make use of a JIT method?
13. What is the difference between activity-based costing and activity-based management?
14. Activity-based costing methods use four steps in computing a product's cost. What are these steps?
15. "Activity-based costing is great for manufacturing plants, but doesn't really address the needs of the service sector." Do you agree with this statement? Explain.
16. What is a cost driver? Give three examples.
17. The vice president of marketing wonders how products can cost less under one cost system than under another. How would you respond to her question "Aren't costs cut-and-dried?"
18. A drawback to activity-based costing is that it requires more record-keeping and extensive teamwork between all departments. What are the potential benefits of a more detailed product cost system?
19. Give three criteria for choosing cost drivers for allocating costs to products.
20. "Activity-based costing is for accountants and production managers. I plan to be a marketing specialist so ABC won't help me." Do you agree with this statement? Explain.
21. Observe the workings of a food service or coffee house. What activities are being performed? Give examples of some cost drivers that cause the cost of those activities. (For example, cooking food is an activity; the number of meals could be a cost driver for the cooking activity.)
22. Observe the workings of a bank, credit union, or savings and loan institution. What activities are being performed? Give examples of some cost drivers that cause the cost of those activities. (For example, opening checking accounts is an activity; the number of accounts opened could be a cost driver for the opening accounts activity.)
23. Activity-based costing assigns costs to activities that consume resources and to the products based on each product's use of activities. What is a benefit of this approach compared to a traditional approach that allocates costs to products based on the machine-hours used to produce the product?
24. **Real World Question** Refer to the discussion on page 744 of the impact of just-in-time on accounting methods at Hewlett-Packard. What effect did the implementation have on the Hewlett-Packard plant's accounting methods?
25. **Real World Question** Why did Domino's Pizza once make such a big deal out of delivering pizzas within 30 minutes?

EXERCISES

Exercise 20–1
Costs of quality (L.O. 2)

Classify Moe Company's costs for a typical month into prevention costs, appraisal costs, internal failure costs, and external failure costs:

Inspection at the end of the production process	$20,000
Scrap	18,000
Design work to improve the way products are made	24,000
Cost of customer complaints	40,000
Employee training	12,000
Incoming materials inspection	10,000

Suppose Moe Company could increase employee training at a cost of $15,000 per month, and thereby reduce internal failure and external failure costs by 20% each per month.

(Appraisal costs would not be affected.) Would this be a wise thing for Moe Company to do?

Exercise 20–2
Measuring performance to achieve quality (L.O. 3)

You have been hired by a food service organization on campus to help assess the quality of food services in the student union building. The following food service information is for the month of February:

Customer complaints	120
Waste as a percentage of total food prepared	15%
Cases of food poisoning	2

What additional information would you like to have to assess the quality of the food service organization's performance?

Exercise 20–3
Compare cost flows using just-in-time and backflush costing with traditional cost flows (L.O. 5)

Mountain Peripherals, Inc., manufactures networking devices for personal computer systems, using just-in-time methods. After receiving an order for 600 devices, the company bought materials costing $7,000 to fill this order. It incurred labor and overhead costs of $24,000, of which $5,000 was for wages and the rest overhead.

After the production was finished, but before all goods were sold, the company needed to compute an inventory cost for financial statement purposes. The cost of finished goods inventory was $1,240.

Required

a. Use T-accounts to show the flow of costs under a traditional costing system.

b. Prepare journal entries for these transactions using backflush costing.

c. Use T-accounts to show the flow of costs using a JIT system with backflush costing.

Exercise 20–4
Activity-based costing versus traditional costing (L.O. 7, 8)

Soundoff Corporation produces two types of compact discs (CDs), one is to install on touring bicycles and the other is a high-grade product for home and car use. The touring bicycles' CDs are designed for durability rather than accurate sound reproduction. The company only recently began producing the higher-quality disc. Management believes the accounting system may not be accurately allocating costs to products.

Management asked you to investigate the cost allocation problem. You found that manufacturing overhead is currently assigned based on the direct labor costs in the products. For your investigation, you are using data from last year. Last year's manufacturing overhead was $880,000 based on production of 320,000 touring bicycle CDs and 100,000 high-grade CDs. Direct labor and direct materials costs were as follows:

	Touring Bicycle	High Grade	Total
Direct labor	$180,000	$ 60,000	$240,000
Materials	120,000	112,000	232,000

Management believes three activities cause overhead costs. The cost drivers and related costs for your analysis are as follows:

		Activity Level		
Cost Drivers	Costs Assigned	Touring Bicycle	High Grade	Total
Number of production runs	$400,000	40	10	50
Quality tests performed	360,000	12	18	30
Shipping orders processed	120,000	100	50	150
Total overhead	$880,000			

Required

a. How much of the overhead would be assigned to each product if the three cost drivers are used to allocate overhead? What would be the cost per unit (including materials, labor, and overhead) for each product if overhead is assigned to products using the three cost drivers?

b. How much of the overhead would be assigned to each product if direct labor costs had been used as the basis for allocating overhead to each product? What would be the cost per unit (including materials, labor, and overhead) for each product if overhead is allocated to products using direct labor cost as the allocation base?

Exercise 20–5
Activity-based costing versus traditional costing (L.O. 7, 8)

Greenthumb, Inc., is a lawn and garden service. The company originally specialized in serving small residential clients; recently it has started contracting for work on larger office building grounds.

Employees worked a total of 10,000 hours last year, 6,500 on residential jobs and 3,500 on commercial jobs. Wages amounted to $10 per hour for all work done. Materials used are included in overhead and called *supplies*. All overhead is allocated on the basis of labor-hours worked, which is also the basis for customer charges. Greenthumb can charge $30 per hour for residential work but, because of greater competition for commercial accounts, only $20 per hour for commercial work.

Required

a. Using labor-hours as the basis for allocating overhead, what was the gross margin (revenues minus labor and overhead expense) for (1) commercial and (2) residential service? Assume overhead was $50,000.

b. Overhead consists of transportation, lawn mowing and landscaping equipment costs, depreciation on equipment, supplies, fuels, and maintenance. These costs can be traced to the following activities:

Activity	Cost Driver	Cost	Activity Level	
			Commercial	Residential
Transportation	Clients serviced	$10,000	15	45
Equipment costs: fuel maintenance, depreciation	Equipment hours	25,000	3,000	2,000
Supplies	Square yards serviced per year	15,000	100,000	50,000
Total overhead		$50,000		

Recalculate gross margin for commercial and residential services based on these cost driver bases.

c. Would you advise Greenthumb to drop either the residential or commercial service based on your analysis? Explain.

PROBLEMS

Problem 20–1
Costs of quality
(L.O. 2, 3)

Here are cost items from Rockets Company's accounts for a typical month:

Inspection at the end of the production process	$40,000
Cost of returned goods	18,000
Design work to improve the way products are made	24,000
Repairs to satisfy customer complaints	10,000
Employee training	12,000
Incoming materials inspection	10,000
Scrap	18,000

Required

a. Classify these items into prevention costs, appraisal costs, internal failure costs, and external failure costs.

b. Suppose Rockets Company could spend an additional $20,000 per month on design work to improve the way products are made, and thereby reduce internal failure and external failure costs by 30 percent each per month. (Appraisal costs would not be affected.) Would this be a wise thing for Rockets Company to do?

c. Give two examples of additional nonfinancial quality measures that Rockets Company could use to help improve quality. (Hint: See Illustration 20.3.)

Problem 20–2
Measuring performance to achieve quality (L.O. 3)

You have been hired by Student Health Services to help assess the quality of health care services on campus. This health care information is for the month of March:

Patient complaints	60
Average patient waiting time	22 minutes
Cases of missed diagnosis	2
Lawsuits filed against the Student Health Services	1

Required

What additional information would you like to have to assess the quality of the health care organization's performance?

Problem 20–3
Compare JIT accounting to a traditional system
(L.O. 5)

Minnesota Precision Instruments produces sensitive heat measurement meters. The company has a large backlog of orders and no beginning inventories because all units in production last year were sold by the end of the year. At the start of this year, an order was received for 4,000 meters.

The company purchased and used $210,000 of materials in production for this order. Direct labor costs of $640,000 were incurred, and overhead costs of $1,040,000 were applied. Goods representing 10% of these costs were still in finished goods inventory at the end of the period.

Required

a. Use T-accounts to show the flow of costs under a traditional costing system.
b. Prepare journal entries for these transactions using backflush costing.
c. Use T-accounts to show the flow of costs using a JIT system with backflush costing.

Problem 20–4
Activity-based costing versus traditional costing
(L.O. 7, 8)

Timepiece Corporation manufactures travel clocks and watches. Overhead costs are currently allocated using direct labor-hours, but the controller has recommended using an activity-based costing system based on the following data:

			Activity Level	
Activity	**Cost Driver**	**Cost**	**Travel Clocks**	**Watches**
Production setup	Setups	$100,000	10	15
Material handling and requisition	Parts	30,000	12	18
Packaging and shipping	Units shipped	60,000	40,000	60,000
Total overhead		$190,000		

Required

a. Compute the amount of total overhead allocated to each of the products under activity-based costing.
b. Compute the amount of total overhead allocated to each product using labor-hours as the allocation base. Assume labor-hours required to assemble each unit are .5 per travel clock and 1.0 per watch, and that 40,000 travel clocks and 60,000 watches were produced.
c. Should the company follow the controller's recommendations?

Problem 20–5
Activity-based costing versus traditional costing
(L.O. 7, 8)

Sparkle Company makes three types of sunglasses: Nerds, Stars, and Fashions. Sparkle presently allocates overhead to products using a rate based on direct labor-hours. A consultant recommended that Sparkle switch to activity-based costing. Management decided to give ABC a try and identified the following activities, cost drivers, and costs for a typical year for each activity center. Use this information to compute the overhead rates for each cost driver.

Activity	Recommended Cost Driver	Costs	Cost Driver Units
Production setup	Production runs	$ 30,000	100
Order processing	Orders	50,000	200
Materials handling	Pounds of materials used	20,000	8,000
Equipment depreciation and maintenance	Machine-hours	60,000	10,000
Quality management	Inspections	50,000	40
Packing and shipping	Units shipped	40,000	20,000
Total overhead		$250,000	

In addition, there are 2,500 direct labor-hours in a typical year.

Assume the following activities occurred in February of 1997:

	Nerds	Stars	Fashions
Units produced	1,000	500	400
Direct materials costs	$4,000	$2,500	$2,000
Direct labor-hours	100	100	89
Orders	8	8	4
Production runs	2	4	8
Pounds of material	400	200	200
Machine-hours	500	300	300
Inspections	2	2	2
Units shipped	1,000	500	300

Direct labor costs are $15 per hour.

Required

a. Compute an overhead allocation rate (1) for each of the cost drivers recommended by the consultant and (2) for direct labor.

b. Management wants to compare the product costs using ABC and the traditional method for the month of February. Compute the production costs for each product for February using direct labor-hours as the allocation base. (Note: Production costs are direct materials, direct labor, and overhead.)

c. To derive product costs under ABC, compute the production costs for each product for February using the cost drivers recommended by the consultant.

d. Management has seen your numbers and wants to know how you account for the discrepancy between the product costs using direct labor-hours as the allocation base and using activity-based costing. Write a brief response to management.

Problem 20–6
Activity-based costing; prepare income statements (L.O. 7, 8)

Magic Photography offers two types of services, deluxe portraits and family portraits. Last year, Magic had the following costs and revenues:

MAGIC PHOTOGRAPHY
Income Statement

	Deluxe	Family	Total
Revenue	$360,000	$400,000	$760,000
Direct materials	50,000	50,000	100,000
Direct labor	180,000	120,000	300,000
Indirect costs:			
Administration	______	______	50,000
Production setup	______	______	100,000
Quality control	______	______	50,000
Distribution	______	______	40,000
Operating profit	______	______	$120,000

Magic Photography currently uses labor costs to allocate all overhead, but management is considering implementing an activity-based costing system. After interviewing the sales and production staff, management decides to allocate administrative costs on the basis of direct labor costs and to use the following bases to allocate the remaining overhead:

		Cost Driver Units	
Activity	**Cost Driver**	**Deluxe**	**Family**
Production setup	Photo sessions	150	250
Quality control	Customer inspections	300	200
Sales and marketing	Advertisements	60	40

Required

a. Complete the income statement using these activity bases.

b. Write a report describing how management might use activity-based costing to reduce costs.

c. Restate the income statement for Magic Photography using direct labor costs as the only overhead allocation base.

d. Write a report to management stating why product line profits differ using activity-based costing compared to the traditional approach. Indicate whether the activity-based costing method provides more accurate information and why (if you believe it does provide more accurate information). Indicate in your report how the use of labor-based overhead allocation could result in Magic Photography management making suboptimal decisions.

ALTERNATE PROBLEMS

Problem 20–1A
Costs of quality (L.O. 2, 3)

These cost items are from Huskies Company's accounts for a typical month:

Design work to improve the way products are made	$24,000
Warranty work to satisfy customer complaints	12,000
Employee training	18,000
Incoming materials inspection	20,000
Scrap	18,000
Cost of returned goods	24,000
Inspection at the end of the production process	30,000

Required

a. Classify these items into prevention costs, appraisal costs, internal failure costs, and external failure costs.

b. Suppose Huskies Company could spend an additional $20,000 per month on incoming materials inspection, and thereby reduce internal failure and external failure costs by 20% each per month. Would this be a wise thing for Huskies Company to do?

c. Give two examples of additional nonfinancial quality measures that Huskies Company could use to help improve quality. (Hint: See Illustration 20.3.)

Problem 20–2A
Measuring performance to achieve quality (L.O. 3)

You have been hired by Bucks 'R' Us Bank to help assess the quality of their services. You have been looking over the following information for the month of May:

Number of customer complaints	120
Minutes the average customer waits	3.8
Number of banking errors (for example, funds deposited in the wrong account)	23

Required

What additional information would you like to have to assess the quality of the bank's performance?

Problem 20–3A
Compare JIT accounting to a traditional system (L.O. 7)

Ohio Instruments produces high-tech devices. The company has a large backlog of orders and had no beginning inventories because all units in production last year were sold by the end of the year. At the start of this year, the firm received an order for 2,000 items.

The company purchased and used $400,000 of materials in production for this order. Direct labor costs of $300,000 and overhead costs of $800,000 were incurred. Goods representing 10% of these costs were still in finished goods inventory at the end of the period.

Required

a. Use T-accounts to show the flow of costs under a traditional costing system.

b. Prepare journal entries for these transactions using backflush costing.

c. Use T-accounts to show the flow of costs using a JIT system with backflush costing.

Problem 20–4A
Activity-based costing; nonmanufacturing (L.O. 7)

The manager of Outdoor Adventures uses activity-based costing to compute the costs of her raft trips. Each raft holds six paying customers and a guide. She offers two types of raft trips, a three-day float trip for beginners, and a three-day white-water trip for seasoned rafters. The breakdown of costs is as follows:

Activities (with Cost Drivers)	Costs per Float Trip	Costs per White-Water Trip
Advertising (trips)	$215	$215
Permit to use the river (trips)	30	50
Equipment use (trips, people)	20 + $5 per person	40 + $8 per person
Insurance (trips)	75	150
Paying guide (trips, guides)	300 per guide	400 per guide
Food (people)	60 per person	60 per person

Required

a. Compute the cost of a 28-person (including guides) float trip with four rafts and four guides.

b. Compute the cost of a 28-person (including guides) white-water trip with four rafts and four guides.

c. How much should the manager charge each customer if she wants to cover her costs?

Problem 20–5A
Activity-based costing; prepare income statements (L.O. 7, 8)

Fleetfoot, Inc., manufactures two types of shoes, B-Ball and Marathon. The B-Ball shoe has a complex design that uses gel-filled compartments to provide support. The Marathon shoe is simpler to manufacture and uses conventional foam padding. Last year, Fleetfoot had the following revenues and costs:

FLEETFOOT, INC.
Income Statement

	B-Ball	Marathon	Total
Revenue	$390,000	$368,000	$758,000
Direct materials	110,000	100,000	210,000
Direct labor	80,000	40,000	120,000
Indirect costs:			
Administration	______	______	40,000
Production setup	______	______	90,000
Quality control	______	______	60,000
Advertising	______	______	120,000
Net income before taxes	______	______	$118,000

Fleetfoot currently uses labor costs to allocate all overhead, but management is considering implementing an activity-based costing system. After interviewing the sales and production staff, management decides to allocate administrative costs on the basis of direct labor costs, but to use the following bases to allocate the remaining overhead:

		Activity Level	
Activity	Cost Drivers	B-Ball	Marathon
Production setup	Production runs	20	20
Quality control	Inspections	40	20
Advertising	Advertisements	12	48

Required

a. Complete the income statement using these activity bases.

b. Write a brief report indicating how management could use activity-based costing to reduce costs.

c. Restate the income statement for Fleetfoot, Inc., using direct labor costs as the only overhead allocation base.

d. Write a report to management stating why product line profits differ using activity-based costing compared to the traditional approach. Indicate whether the activity-based costing method provides more accurate information and why (if you believe it does provide more accurate information). Indicate in your report how the use of labor-based overhead allocation could result in Fleetfoot management making sub-optimal decisions.

Beyond the Numbers—Critical Thinking

Business Decision Case 20–1
Benefits of activity-based costing

Many companies recognize that their cost systems are inadequate for today's global market. Managers in companies selling multiple products are making important product decisions based on distorted cost information.

Write a short paper describing the benefits management should expect from implementing activity-based costing.

Business Decision Case 20–2
Writing Assignment

A company that makes Halloween costumes is considering using just-in-time purchasing and production methods. Write a short paper describing the problems this company might face in using just-in-time.

Business Decision Case 20–3
Writing Assignment

Managers at Texas Instruments developed these four cost-of-quality categories: prevention costs, appraisal costs, internal failure costs, and external failure costs. Give an example of a cost for each of these four categories. Would minimizing the sum of these four costs assure high-quality products? Why or why not? Write a short paper summarizing your analysis.

Group Project 20–4
React to cynic's comments regarding activity-based costing

The chapter listed the following six important points to remember about activity-based costing. Following each point are the comments of a cynic in italics. After forming six groups, discuss one of these points in each group. How would you respond to the cynic's comments? (It's okay to agree; even cynics have good points to make.) Choose one group member to report your group's response to the class.

1. The allocation of indirect costs is at least somewhat arbitrary, even using sophisticated accounting methods. (“*This means no method gives you a true cost; all are arbitrary. So why go to the trouble of implementing ABC?*”)
2. Activity-based costing provides more detailed measures of costs than traditional allocation methods. (“*Who needs more detail? Life is already too complicated.*”)
3. Activity-based costing can help marketing people by providing more accurate product cost numbers for decisions about pricing and which unprofitable products the company should eliminate. (“*Why should accountants want to help marketing people?*”)
4. Production also benefits because activity-based costing provides better information about the cost of each activity. In practice, ABC helps managers identify cost causing activities. To manage costs, production managers learn to manage the activities that cause costs. (“*If production people know their jobs, they don't need help from accountants.*”)
5. Activity-based costing provides more information about product costs than traditional methods but requires more record-keeping. Managers must decide whether the benefits of improved decisions justify the additional record-keeping cost. (“*ABC sounds like a lot of work. Why bother?*”)
6. Installing activity-based costing requires teamwork among accountants, production managers, marketing managers, and other nonaccounting people. (“*You'll never get these people to work together. Accountants and marketing people? You've got to be kidding!*”)

Answers to Self-Test

True-False

1. **False.** The managers' task is to minimize these costs, not maximize them.
2. **True.** Control charts are a means of distinguishing between random or routine variation in product quality and variations that managers should investigate.
3. **False.** To the contrary, the allocation of indirect costs is, by definition, at least somewhat arbitrary.
4. **True.** A cost driver is an activity or transaction that causes costs to be incurred.
5. **True.** The formula for computing an indirect cost rate has the cost in the numerator and the volume of the cost driver or allocation base in the denominator.

Multiple-Choice

1. **d.** The new production environment refers to an environment in which company managers are concerned with improving customer service and product quality, and reducing costs.
2. **c.** Production does not begin on an item until an order is received.
3. **d.** $160,000
   $260,000/(80,000 hours + 50,000 hours) = $2.
   $2 × 80,000 hours = $160,000.
4. **b.** $2.27
   First find the rates:
   $82,000/(8 + 12) = $4,100. $48,000/(56 + 24) = $600.
   $130,000/(80,000 + 50,000) = $1.
   Next assign overhead to Product R:
   ($4,100 × 12) + ($600 × 24) + (50,000 × $1)
   = $49,200 + $14,400 + $50,000 = $113,600.
   Now find the unit cost:
   $113,600/50,000 units = $2.27.

VII

USING COST INFORMATION FOR DECISION-MAKING

PART OUTLINE

A MANAGER'S PERSPECTIVE

Renee Vaughn
Manager, Administration and Special Projects
Public and Media Relations
The Coca-Cola Company

I am responsible for providing scheduling and assisting with staffing with the Public and Media Relations group. This requires anticipating needs for the group and planning accordingly. I also administer budgets for three departments (about 35 employees).

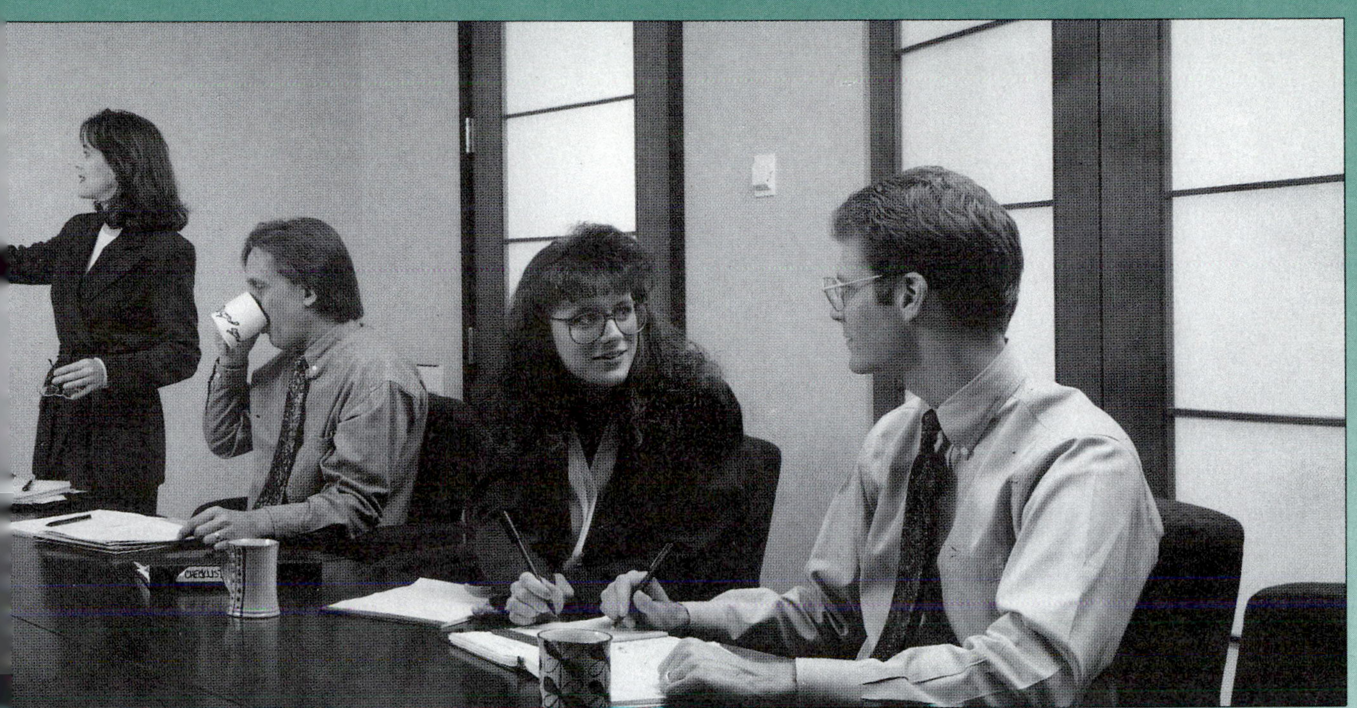

I began my professional career in an elementary school district administration office, serving as an administrative assistant for the superintendent of schools. I learned to plan and manage budgets in that capacity. At The Coca-Cola Company, once a budget is created at the departmental level, it is tracked on a monthly basis by reviewing all spending by account and total. We also review a rolling estimate of annual expenses and adjust the budget accordingly.

We plan for non-project capital budgeting a year in advance, which enables us to order computer, fax, and other office equipment as well as make other necessary major purchases. If an unforeseen need develops, we will review our plan and make revisions as necessary on a case-by-case basis.

21

COST-VOLUME-PROFIT ANALYSIS

Assume that a student organization wants to show movies on campus. The organization can rent a particular movie for one weekend for $1,000. Rent for an auditorium, salaries for ticket takers and other personnel, and other fixed costs would amount to $800 for the weekend. The organization would sell tickets for $4 per person. In addition, profits from the sale of soft drinks, popcorn, and candy are estimated to be $1 per ticket holder. How many people would have to buy tickets to justify renting the movie? (The answer is in the solution to Demonstration Problem 21–B at the end of this chapter.)

Solving problems like this requires an understanding of the relationship between costs, revenue, and volume. This chapter discusses the use of cost-volume-profit analysis for decision making and planning. (Although accountants call this topic *cost-volume-profit* analysis, it could just as easily have been called *cost-volume-revenue* analysis.) All of the analysis in this chapter is on a before-tax basis.

In this chapter we will focus on short-run decisions. The term **short run** describes a time frame during which a company's management cannot change the effects of certain past decisions. The short run is one year or less for practical purposes. For example, General Motors Corporation's decision to offer a special rebate starting January 5 and expiring on January 31 would be a short-run decision. In contrast, GM's decision to start the Saturn Corporation was a long-run decision.

In the short run, we assume many costs, such as building rental expense, are fixed and unchangeable. However, all costs are subject to change in the long run. Although we identify particular costs as fixed in this chapter, you should realize that costs fixed in the short run may change in the long run. Someday the building rental agreement will change, so the building rental expense will change.

LEARNING OBJECTIVES

After studying this chapter, you should be able to:

1. Explain and describe cost behavior patterns.
2. Separate mixed costs into fixed and variable components using the scatter diagram and high-low method.
3. Explain the relationship among costs, volume, revenue, and profits.
4. Find the break-even point.
5. Compute the margin of safety.
6. Demonstrate applications of cost-volume-profit analysis.

(continued)

COST BEHAVIOR PATTERNS

Illustration 21.1 shows four basic cost behavior patterns: fixed, variable, mixed (semivariable), and step. As discussed in earlier chapters, **fixed costs** remain constant (in total) over some relevant range of output. Often, we describe them as

(concluded)

7. List the assumptions underlying cost-volume-profit analysis.
8. Describe how computer spreadsheets expand your capability to use cost-volume-profit analysis.
9. Describe the impact of automation on fixed-variable cost relationships.

time-related costs. Depreciation, insurance, property taxes, and administrative salaries are examples of fixed costs. Recall that so-called fixed costs are fixed in the short run but not necessarily in the long run.

For example, a local high-tech company did not lay off employees during a recent decrease in business volume because the management did not want to hire and train new people when business picked up again. Management treated direct labor as a fixed cost in this situation. Although volume decreased, direct labor costs remained fixed.

In contrast to fixed costs, **variable costs** vary (in total) directly with changes in volume of production or sales. In particular, total variable costs change as total volume changes. If pizza production increases from 100 10-inch pizzas to 200 10-inch pizzas per day, the amount of dough required per day to make 10-inch pizzas would double. The dough is a variable cost of pizza production. Direct materials and sales commissions are variable costs.

Direct labor is a variable cost in many cases. If the total direct labor cost increases as the volume of output increases and decreases as volume decreases, direct labor is a variable cost. Piecework pay is an excellent example of direct labor as a variable cost. In addition, direct labor is frequently a variable cost for workers paid on an hourly basis, as the volume of output increases, more workers are hired. However, sometimes the nature of the work or management policy does not allow direct labor to change as volume changes and direct labor can be a fixed cost.

Objective 1
Explain and describe cost behavior patterns.

Mixed costs have both fixed and variable characteristics. A **mixed cost** contains a fixed portion of cost incurred even when the facility is idle, and a variable portion that increases directly with volume. Electricity is an example of a mixed cost. A company must incur a certain cost for basic electrical service. As the company increases its volume of activity, it runs more machines and runs them longer. The firm also may extend its hours of operation. As activity increases, so does the cost of electricity.

Managers usually separate mixed costs into their fixed and variable components for decision-making purposes. They include the fixed portion of mixed costs with other fixed costs, while assuming the variable part changes with volume. Look at Illustration 21.2 to see how to separate the fixed and variable portions of a mixed cost such as electricity.

A **step cost** remains constant at a certain fixed amount over a range of output (or sales). Then, at certain points, the step costs increase to higher amounts. Visually, step costs appear like stair steps, as shown in Illustration 21.1.

Supervisors' salaries are an example of a step cost when companies hire additional supervisors as production increases. For instance, the local McDonald's restaurant has one supervisor until sales exceed 100 meals during the lunch hour. If sales regularly exceed 100 meals during that hour, the company adds a second supervisor. In Illustration 21.3, we show a step cost for supervisors' salaries, assuming each supervisor is paid $2,000 per month. Step costs are sometimes labeled as step variable costs (many small steps) or step fixed costs (only a few large steps).

McDonald's
McDonald's Corporation is an international fast-food restaurant chain.

Although we have described four different cost patterns (fixed, variable, mixed, and step), we simplify our discussions in this chapter by assuming managers can separate mixed and step costs into fixed and variable components.

Curvilinear Cost Patterns

Many costs do not vary in a strictly linear relationship with volume. Rather, costs may vary in a curvilinear pattern—a 10% increase in volume may yield an 8% change in costs at lower output levels and an 11% change in costs at higher output levels. We show a curvilinear cost pattern in Illustration 21.4.

One way to deal with a curvilinear cost pattern is to assume a linear relationship between costs and volume within some relevant range. The **relevant range** is the range of production or sales volume over which the assumptions about cost behavior are valid. Look at Illustration 21.5 to see how to apply the relevant range

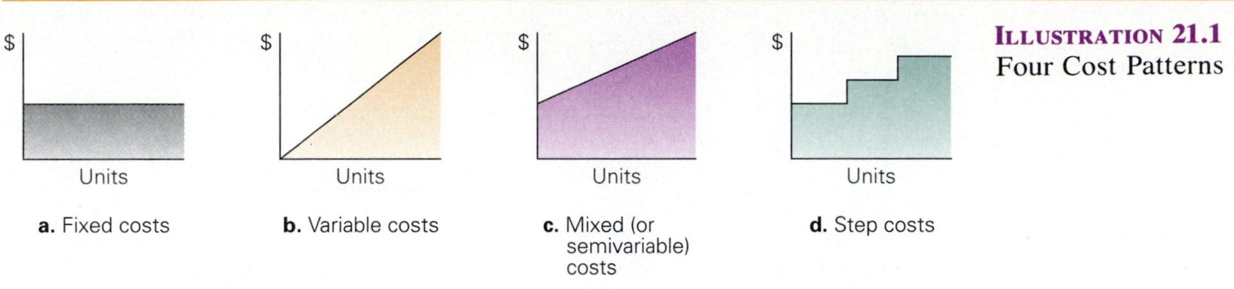

ILLUSTRATION 21.1
Four Cost Patterns

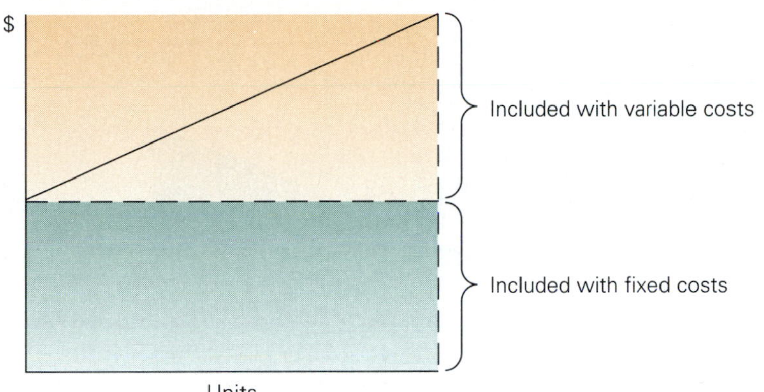

ILLUSTRATION 21.2
Separation of Mixed Costs into Fixed and Variable Parts

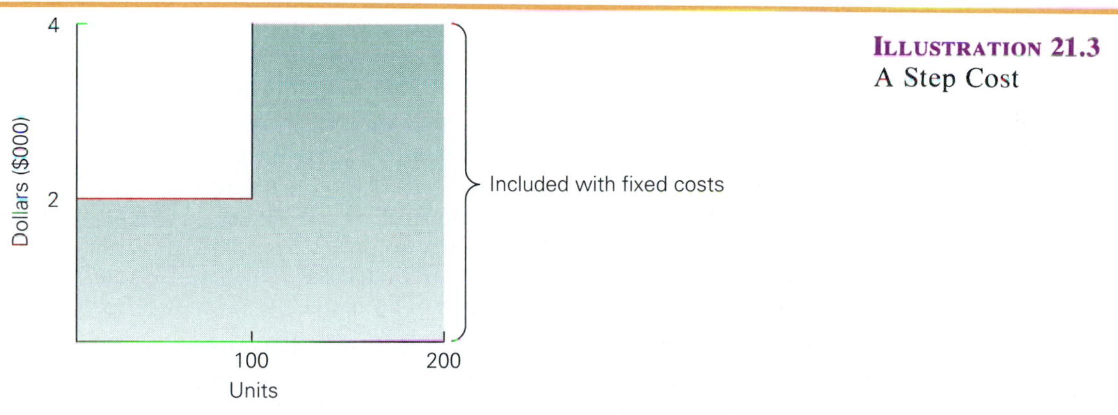

ILLUSTRATION 21.3
A Step Cost

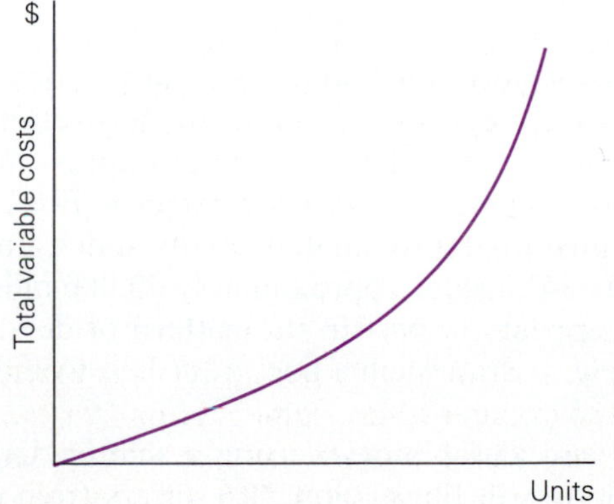

ILLUSTRATION 21.4
Curvilinear Cost Pattern

ILLUSTRATION 21.5
Relevant Range

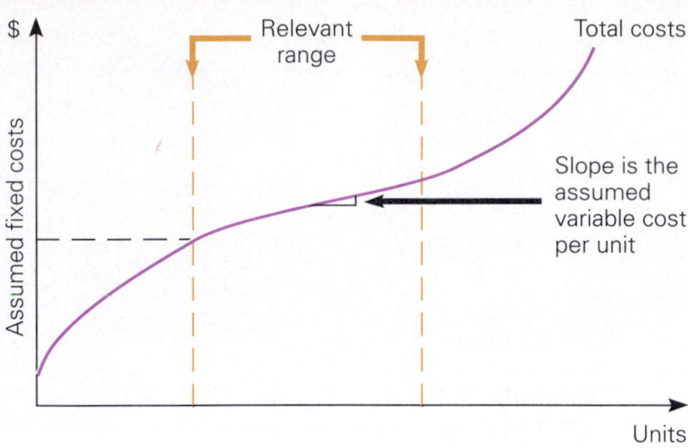

ILLUSTRATION 21.6
Scatter Diagram

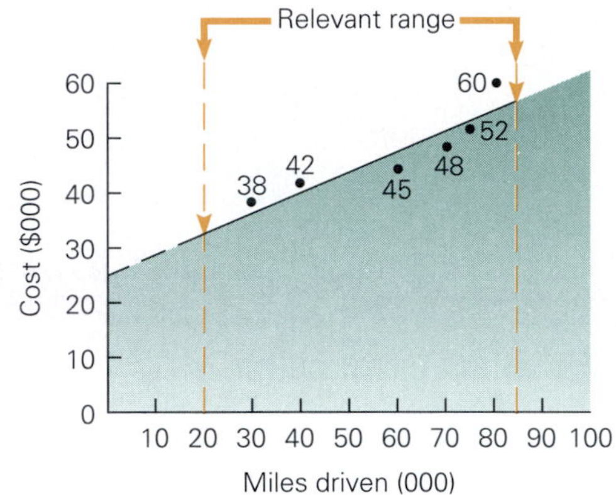

to a portion of the curvilinear cost curve. Within that relevant range, the total cost varies linearly with volume, at least approximately. Outside of the relevant range, we presume the assumptions about cost behavior may be invalid.

Costs rarely behave in the simple way that would make life easy for decision makers. Even within the relevant range, the assumed cost behavior is usually only *approximately* linear. As decision makers, we have to live with the fact that cost estimates are not as precise as physical or engineering measurements.

METHODS FOR ANALYZING COSTS

Objective 2
Separate mixed costs into fixed and varible components using the scatter diagram and high-low method.

You can use several methods to break down a mixed cost into its fixed and variable cost components. We present two of these methods—the scatter diagram and the high-low method.

Scatter Diagram

FedEx
Federal Express is an international delivery service known for its reliability in delivering packages on time.

A **scatter diagram** shows plots of actual costs incurred for various levels of activity. Assume the dots on the scatter diagram in Illustration 21.6 represent total actual maintenance costs per month for a Federal Express fleet of delivery trucks. Each dot represents one month's activity for one city. For example, the left point represents a $38,000 cost for approximately 30,000 miles a month. The next point to the right represents $42,000 for approximately 40,000 miles for another month. We drew a line that appears to best fit the pattern of dots. The line we drew is subjective. If you were to draw such a line, your line would probably differ from ours.

Estimating fixed and variable costs using a scatter diagram is subjective. If your line through the dots in Illustration 21.6 differs from ours, you would estimate different fixed and variable costs. Your line and cost estimates would not necessarily be right or wrong compared to ours, just different.

In Illustration 21.6, our line intersects the vertical axis at $25,000, which we estimate to be the fixed portion of the mixed cost. We estimate the line would pass through a point representing a cost of $57,000 at a volume of 80,000 miles. Thus, our line rises from $25,000, representing 0 (zero) miles, to $57,000 over a volume of 80,000 miles on the horizontal axis. Based on that information, we can now compute the variable cost portion of the mixed cost as follows:

$$\frac{\$57{,}000 - \$25{,}000}{80{,}000 \text{ miles} - 0 \text{ miles}} = \$0.40 \text{ per mile}$$

Using this result, we estimate the company's truck maintenance costs are $25,000 per month plus 40 cents for every mile driven.

High-Low Method

You can also use the **high-low method** to identify the elements of mixed costs. This method uses only the highest and lowest points (levels of operation) on a scatter diagram to fit a line to the data.

To illustrate, the lowest point in Illustration 21.6 is $38,000 of expense at 30,000 miles driven, and the highest point is $60,000 at 80,000 miles. Calculate the amount of variable cost per mile as follows:

$$\frac{\text{Change in cost}}{\text{Change in units}} = \frac{\$60{,}000 - \$38{,}000}{80{,}000 \text{ miles} - 30{,}000 \text{ miles}} = \frac{\$22{,}000}{50{,}000 \text{ miles}} = \frac{\$0.44}{\text{per mile}}$$

To compute the fixed portion:

Total cost at 80,000 miles	$60,000
Less: Variable cost at that level of output (80,000 × $0.44)	35,200
Fixed cost at all levels of mileage within the relevant range	$24,800

The high-low method is less precise than the scatter diagram because it uses only two data points in the computation. Either or both points may not be representative of the data as a whole.

Many people use more sophisticated statistical techniques to divide mixed costs into fixed and variable portions. Statistics and cost accounting texts discuss these techniques.

Now that you understand cost patterns and how to analyze costs, we will apply these concepts to the specific tools that managers use in short-term decision making. The first of these tools is cost-volume-profit (CVP) analysis.

Cost-Volume-Profit (CVP) Analysis

Objective 3
Explain the relationship among costs, volume, revenue, and profits.

Companies use **cost-volume-profit (CVP) analysis** (also called break-even analysis) to determine what effects changes in their selling prices, costs, and/or volume will have on profits in the short run. A careful and accurate cost-volume-profit (CVP) analysis requires knowledge of costs and their fixed or variable behavior as volume changes.

Cost-Volume-Profit Chart

A **cost-volume-profit chart** is a graph that shows the relationships among sales, costs, volume, and profit. Look at Illustration 21.7, a cost-volume-profit chart for Video Productions, a company that produces videotapes. Each tape sells for $20. The variable cost per tape is $12, and the fixed costs per month are $40,000.

The total cost line in Illustration 21.7 represents the fixed costs of $40,000 plus $12 per unit. Thus, if Video Productions produces and sells 6,000 tapes, the company's total costs are $112,000, made up of $40,000 fixed costs and $72,000 total variable costs ($72,000 = $12 per unit × 6,000 units produced and sold).

The total revenue line in Illustration 21.7 shows how revenue increases as volume increases. Total revenue is $120,000 for sales of 6,000 tapes ($120,000 = $20 per unit × 6,000 units sold). In Illustration 21.7, we demonstrate the effect of

ILLUSTRATION 21.7
The Cost-Volume-Profit Chart

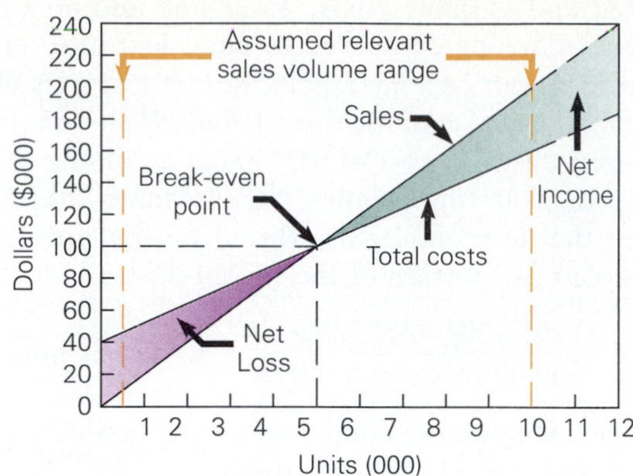

volume on revenue, costs, and net income, for a particular price, variable cost per unit, and fixed cost per period.

At each volume, one can estimate the company's profit or loss. For example, at a volume of 6,000 units, the profit is $8,000. We can find the net income either by constructing an income statement or using the profit equation. The income statement gives the following results (shown in the next table) for a volume of 6,000 units:

Revenue	$120,000
Less: variable costs	72,000
Contribution margin	$ 48,000
Less: Fixed costs	40,000
Net income	$ 8,000

We have introduced a new term in this income statement—*the contribution margin*. The **contribution margin** is the amount by which revenue exceeds the variable costs of producing that revenue. We can calculate it on a per unit or total sales volume basis. On a per unit basis, the contribution margin for Video Productions is $8 (the selling price of $20 minus the variable cost per unit of $12).

The contribution margin indicates the amount of money remaining after the company covers its variable costs. This remainder contributes to the coverage of fixed costs and to net income. In Video Production's income statement, the $48,000 contribution margin covers the $40,000 fixed costs and leaves $8,000 in net income.

PROFIT EQUATION The profit equation is just like the income statement, except it presents the analysis in a slightly different form. According to the **profit equation:**

$$\text{Net income} = \text{Revenue} - \text{Total variable costs} - \text{Fixed costs}$$

For Video Productions, the profit equation looks like this:

$$\text{Net income} = \$120{,}000 - \$72{,}000 - \$40{,}000$$
$$\text{Net income} = \$8{,}000$$

Illustration 21:7 shows cost data for Video Productions in a relevant range of output from 500 to 10,000 units. Recall the relevant range is the range of production or sales volume over which the basic cost behavior assumptions hold true. For volumes outside these ranges, costs behave differently and alter the assumed relationships. For example, if Video Productions produced and sold more than 10,000 units per month, it might be necessary to increase plant capacity (thus incurring additional fixed costs) or to work extra shifts (thus incurring overtime charges and other inefficiencies). In either case, the assumed cost relationships would no longer be valid.

Finding the Break-Even Point

Objective 4
Find the break-even point.

A company *breaks even* for a given period when sales revenue and costs charged to that period are equal. Thus, the **break-even point** is that level of operations at which a company realizes no net income or loss.

A company may express a break-even point in dollars of sales revenue or number of units produced or sold. No matter how a company expresses its break-even point, it is still the point of zero income or loss. To illustrate the calculation of a break-even point, recall that Video Productions produces videotapes selling for $20 per unit. Fixed costs per period total $40,000, while variable cost is $12 per unit.

Break-Even in Units We compute the break-even point in units by dividing total fixed costs by the contribution margin per unit. The contribution margin per unit is $8 ($20 selling price per unit − $12 variable cost per unit). In the following break-even equation, BE refers to the break-even piont:

$$BE_{\text{units}} = \frac{\text{Fixed costs}}{\text{Contribution margin per unit}}$$

$$BE_{\text{units}} = \frac{\$40{,}000}{\$8 \text{ per unit}}$$

$$BE_{\text{units}} = 5{,}000 \text{ units}$$

The result tells us that Video Productions breaks even at a volume of 5,000 units per month. We can prove that to be true by computing the revenue and total costs at a volume of 5,000 units. Revenue = 5,000 units × $20 sales price per unit = $100,000. Total costs = $100,000 = $40,000 fixed costs + $60,000 variable costs ($60,000 = $12 per unit × 5,000 units).

Look at Illustration 21.7 and note that the revenue and total cost lines cross at 5,000 units—the break-even point. Video Productions has net income at volumes greater than 5,000, but it has losses at volumes less than 5,000 units.

Break-Even in Sales Dollars Companies frequently think of volume in sales dollars instead of units. For a company such as General Motors that makes Cadillacs and spark plugs, it makes no sense to think of a break-even point in units. GM breaks even in sales dollars.

The formula to compute the break-even point in sales dollars looks a lot like the formula to compute the break-even in units, except we divide fixed costs by *the contribution margin ratio* instead of the contribution margin per unit.

$$BE_{\text{dollars}} = \frac{\text{Fixed costs}}{\text{Contribution margin ratio}}$$

The **contribution margin ratio** expresses the contribution margin as a percentage of sales. To calculate this ratio, divide the contribution margin per unit by the selling price per unit, or total contribution margin by total revenues. Video Production's contribution margin ratio is:

$$\text{Contribution margin ratio} = \frac{\text{Contribution margin per unit}}{\text{Selling price per unit}}$$

$$= \frac{\$20 - \$12}{\$20} = \frac{\$8}{\$20}$$

$$= 0.40$$

Or, referring to the income statement in which Video Productions had a total contribution margin of $48,000 on revenues of $120,000, we compute the contribution margin ratio as follows:

$$\text{Contribution margin ratio} = \frac{\text{Total contribution margin}}{\text{Total revenues}}$$

$$= \frac{\$48{,}000}{\$120{,}000}$$

$$= 0.40$$

That is, for each dollar of sales, there is a \$0.40 contribution to covering fixed costs and generating net income.

Using this ratio, we calculate Video Production's break-even point in sales dollars as:

$$BE_{dollars} = \frac{\text{Fixed costs}}{\text{Contribution margin ratio}}$$

$$BE_{dollars} = \frac{\$40{,}000}{0.40}$$

$$= \$100{,}000$$

The break-even volume of sales is \$100,000 (5,000 units at \$20 per unit). At this level of sales, fixed costs plus variable costs equal sales revenue, as shown here:

Revenues	\$100,000
Less: Variable costs	60,000
Contribution margin	\$ 40,000
Less; Fixed costs	40,000
Net income.	–0–

The cost-volume-profit chart in Illustration 21.7 shows that in a period of complete idleness, Video Productions would lose \$40,000 (the amount of fixed costs). However, when Video Productions has an output of 10,000 units, the company has net income of \$40,000. Other points on the graph show that sales of 7,500 units results in \$150,000 of revenue. At that point, Video Production's total costs amount to \$130,000, leaving net income of \$20,000.

Calculating Break-Even for a Multiproduct Company

Although you are likely to use cost-volume-profit analysis for a single product, you will more frequently use it in multiproduct situations. The easiest way to use cost-volume-profit analysis for a multiproduct company is to use dollars of sales as the volume measure. For CVP purposes, a multiproduct company must assume a given product mix. **Product mix** refers to the proportion of the company's total sales attributable to each type of product sold.

To illustrate the computation of the break-even point for Wonderfood, a multiproduct company that makes three types of cereal, assume the following historical data:

	Product							
	1		2		3		Total	
	Amount	Percent	Amount	Percent	Amount	Percent	Amount	Percent
Sales	\$60,000	100%	\$30,000	100%	\$10,000	100%	\$100,000	100%
Less: Variable costs	40,000	67	16,000	53	4,000	40	60,000	60
Contribution margin . . .	\$20,000	33%	\$14,000	47%	\$ 6,000	60%	\$ 40,000	40%

We use the data in the total columns to compute the break-even point. The contribution margin ratio is 40% (\$40,000/\$100,000). Assuming the product mix remains constant and fixed costs for the company are \$50,000, break-even sales are \$125,000, computed as follows:

$$BE_{dollars} = \frac{\text{Fixed costs}}{\text{Contribution margin ratio}}$$

$$BE_{dollars} = \frac{\$50,000}{0.40}$$

$$= \$125,000$$

[To check our answer: ($125,000 × 0.40) − $50,000 = $0.]

To find the three product sales totals, we multiply total sales dollars by the percent of product mix for each of the three products. The product mix for products 1, 2, and 3 is 60 : 30 : 10, respectively. That is, out of the $100,000 total sales, there were sales of $60,000 for product 1, $30,000 for product 2, and $10,000 for product 3. Therefore, the company has to sell $75,000 of product 1 (0.6 × $125,000), $37,500 of product 2 (0.3 × $125,000), and $12,500 of product 3 (0.1 × $125,000) to break even.

An Accounting Perspective

Business Insight The founder of Domino's Pizza, Inc., nearly went bankrupt several times before he finally made Domino's a financial success. One early problem was that the company was providing small pizzas that cost almost as much to make and just as much to deliver as larger pizzas. Because they were small, the company could not charge enough to cover its costs. At one point, the company's founder was so busy *producing* small pizzas that he did not have time to determine that the company was losing money on them.

Margin of Safety

Objective 5
Compute the margin of safety.

If a company's current sales are more than its break-even point, it has a margin of safety equal to current sales minus break-even sales. The **margin of safety** is the amount by which sales can decrease before the company incurs a loss. For example, assume Video Productions currently has sales of $120,000 and its break-even sales are $100,000. The margin of safety is $20,000, computed as follows:

$$\begin{aligned}\text{Margin of safety} &= \text{Current sales} - \text{Break-even sales}\\ &= \$120,000 - \$100,000\\ &= \$20,000\end{aligned}$$

Sometimes people express the margin of safety as a percentage, called the *margin of safety rate*. The **margin of safety rate** is equal to (Current sales − Break-even sales)/Current sales. Using the data just presented, we compute the margin of safety rate as follows:

$$\text{Margin of safety rate} = \frac{\text{Current sales} - \text{Break-even sales}}{\text{Current sales}}$$

$$= \frac{\$120,000 - \$100,000}{\$120,000}$$

$$= 16.67\%$$

This means that sales volume could drop by 16.67% before the company would incur a loss.

Cost-Volume-Profit Analysis Illustrated

Objective 6
Demonstrate applications of cost-volume-profit analysis.

CVP analysis has many applications. This section illustrates several applications using airline data.

Calculating the Break-Even Point

The management of a major airline wishes to know how many seats must be sold on Flight 529 to break even. To solve this problem, management must identify and separate costs into fixed and variable categories.

The fixed costs of Flight 529 are the same regardless of the number of seats filled. Fixed costs include the fuel required to fly the plane and crew (with no passengers) to its destination; depreciation on the plane used on the flight; and salaries of required crew members, gate attendants, and maintenance and refueling personnel.

The variable costs vary directly with the number of passengers. Variable costs include meals and beverages provided to passengers, baggage handling costs, and the cost of the additional fuel required to fly the plane with passengers to its destination. Management would express each variable cost on a per passenger basis.

Assume that after analyzing the various costs and separating them into fixed or variable categories, management finds the fixed costs for Flight 529 are $12,000 and variable costs are $25 per passenger. Tickets cost $125. Thus, the contribution margin ratio is 80% [($125 − $25)/$125].

We can express the break-even point either in sales dollars or in the number of passengers. The break-even point in sales dollars is:

$$BE_{\text{dollars}} = \frac{\text{Fixed costs}}{\text{Contribution margin ratio}}$$

$$= \frac{\$12,000}{0.80}$$

$$= \$15,000$$

We can find the break-even point in number of passengers (units) by dividing fixed costs by the contribution margin per unit:

$$BE_{\text{units}} = \frac{\text{Fixed costs}}{\text{Contribution margin per unit (or passenger)}}$$

$$= \frac{\$12,000}{\$125 - \$25}$$

$$= 120 \text{ passengers}$$

To check our answers: 120 passengers × $125 ticket price = $15,000.

Calculating Sales Volume Needed for Desired Net Income

With a simple adjustment in the break-even formulas, CVP analysis can also show the sales volume needed to generate some desired level of net income (ignore taxes). To make this adjustment, management adds the desired net income amount to the fixed costs that must be covered. From this, management can determine the necessary sales volume in dollars or units to provide the desired net income. For example, assume management wishes to earn $8,000 of net income on Flight 529.

How many passenger tickets must the airline sell to earn $8,000? Remember, the contribution margin per ticket is $100. We compute the number of tickets to be sold to earn $8,000 on a flight as follows:

$$\text{Number of units} = \frac{\text{Fixed costs} + \text{Desired net income}}{\text{Contribution margin per unit}}$$

$$= \frac{\$12,000 + \$8,000}{\$100}$$

$$= \frac{\$20,000}{\$100}$$

$$= 200 \text{ tickets}$$

The airline must sell 200 tickets to earn net income of \$8,000. To check our answer: (200 tickets × \$125 sales price per ticket) − (200 tickets × \$25 variable cost per ticket) − \$12,000 fixed costs = \$25,000 − \$5,000 − \$12,000 = \$8,000.

Calculating the Effect of Changing the Sales Price on Net Income

The airline management can also use cost-volume-profit analysis to determine the effect of changing the sales price. To illustrate, assume that Flight 529 normally carries 150 passengers (sales of \$18,750 and net income of \$3,000), and the airline decides to increase ticket prices by 5%. If variable and fixed costs remain constant and passenger load does not change, net income increases from \$3,000 to \$3,937.50 as follows:

$$\begin{aligned} \text{Revenue} - \text{Total variable costs} - \text{Fixed costs} &= \text{Net income} \\ [\$125(1.05) \times 150 \text{ passengers}] - (\$25 \times 150 \text{ passengers}) - \$12{,}000 &= \text{NI} \\ \$19{,}687.50 - \$3{,}750 - \$12{,}000 &= \text{NI} \\ \$19{,}687.50 - \$15{,}750 &= \text{NI} \\ \$3{,}937.50 &= \text{NI} \end{aligned}$$

Net income would rise by the entire amount of the price increase (\$19,687.50 − \$18,750 = \$937.50).

Calculating Sales Needed to Maintain Net Income When Costs Change

Management can use cost-volume-profit analysis to calculate the sales needed to maintain net income when costs change. For example, assume both fixed and variable costs would increase for the airline if the price of fuel rises. Assume that fixed costs increase by \$4,000 and variable costs increase by \$6.25 per passenger. Variable costs are now 25% (\$31.25/\$125) of the sales price. The contribution margin is now \$93.75 (\$125 − \$31.25) per passenger. The contribution margin ratio is now 75% (\$93.75/\$125).

To maintain the current net income of \$3,000, the airline needs to increase sales revenue to \$25,333:

$$\begin{aligned} \text{Revenue required} &= \frac{\text{Fixed costs} + \text{Desired net income}}{\text{Contribution margin ratio}} \\ &= \frac{\$16{,}000 + \$3{,}000}{0.75} \\ &= \$25{,}333 \end{aligned}$$

Other Uses of Cost-Volume-Profit Analysis

Management can also use its knowledge of cost-volume-profit relationships to determine whether to increase sales promotion costs in an effort to increase sales volume or to accept an order at a lower-than-usual price. In general, the careful study of cost behavior helps management plan future courses of action.

Assumptions Made in Cost-Volume-Profit Analysis

Objective 7
List the assumptions underlying cost-volume-profit analysis.

To summarize, the most important assumptions underlying CVP analysis are:

1. Selling price, variable cost per unit, and total fixed costs remain constant through the relevant range. This means that a company can sell more or fewer units at the same price and that the company has no change in technical efficiency as volume changes.
2. In multiproduct situations, the product mix is known in advance.
3. Costs can be accurately classified into their fixed and variable portions.

Critics may call these assumptions unrealistic in many situations, but they greatly simplify the analysis.

Using Computer Spreadsheets for CVP Analysis

Objective 8
Describe how computer spreadsheets expand your capability to use cost-volume-profit analysis.

Computer spreadsheet packages are well suited for CVP analysis because they enable managers to answer what-if questions. The cost and revenue items in CVP analysis are estimates, not actual results. Since they are used in planning and decision making, it is reasonable to ask whether plans or decisions would change if the estimates changed. The most important issue is whether the information is correct. The output is only as good as the information that goes in.

A Broader Perspective

Major Television Networks Are Finding It Harder to Break Even

With increasing competition from cable television, prerecorded videos, and independent stations, the three major television networks are facing smaller and smaller margins of safety. Most new shows do not break even. Many do not even cover their variable costs and are dropped during the first season.

As the networks find it more and more difficult to break even on their regular shows, they are expanding into cable, satellite, and pay-per-view television. For example, the National Broadcasting Company (NBC), a major television network owned by General Electric Company, is part owner of a national cable channel and a sports channel. The company has also invested in CNBC, a cable network that specializes in consumer and business issues.

Based on the authors' research.

Illustration 21.8
Spreadsheet Analysis of CVP Relationships

Fixed Cost	Ticket Price	Number of Passengers	Percent Contribution Margin to Revenue	Income
$200,000	$3,000	100	70%	$10,000
200,000	3,000	80	70	(32,000)
200,000	3,000	100	75	25,000
200,000	3,000	80	75	(20,000)
200,000	4,000	70	70	(4,000)
200,000	4,000	50	70	(60,000)
200,000	4,000	70	75	10,000
200,000	4,000	50	75	(50,000)

Consider the following example: The management of Prince Cruises wants to know what the income before taxes would be for a proposed product, a Caribbean cruise. The analyst prepared the following formulas for the spreadsheet:

- Revenue equals ticket price times number of passengers (amounts to be inserted for ticket price and number of passengers).
- Contribution margin equals (amount to be inserted)% of revenue.
- Fixed costs equal $200,000.
- Income equals revenue minus variable costs minus fixed costs.

Management then inserted various values for ticket price, number of passengers, the percent of variable cost to revenue, and fixed costs, all per cruise. Illustration 21.8 shows the results. Based on these results, management sees what combinations of ticket price, number of passengers, and contribution ratio are required for the cruise to be profitable.

We show only a few of the possible combinations in Illustration 21.8 to save space. Spreadsheets provide the advantage of a large number of possible combinations with minimal data entry.

An Accounting Perspective

Uses of Technology Cost-volume-profit analysis using a computer spreadsheet is becoming routine. In many business meetings, we find one or more people crunching cost-volume-profit numbers on their notebook or laptop computers.

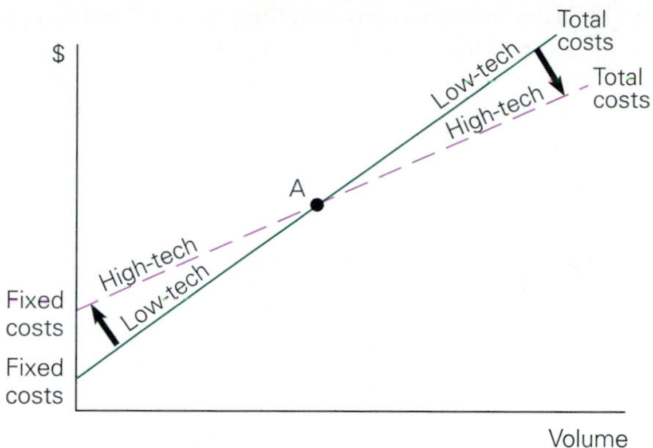

ILLUSTRATION 21.9
Effects of Automation

EFFECT OF AUTOMATION ON COST-VOLUME-PROFIT ANALYSIS

Objective 9
Describe the impact of automation on fixed-variable cost relationships.

Increasing automation does not affect the fundamental CVP model or the types of analysis we have discussed. However, it does affect the relative size of fixed and variable costs. As companies become more automated, they substitute machinery for labor. Companies that make this substitution often increase fixed costs and decrease variable costs. For example, when banks installed automated teller machines, their labor costs decreased but their fixed costs, including machine depreciation, increased.

When a company substitutes fixed costs for variable costs, the total cost line shifts up as shown in Illustration 21.9. At low levels of volume, becoming more automated increases total costs, but at high levels of volume it decreases them. What does this do to the company's break-even point? It depends on where the revenue line crosses the total cost line. If it crosses at low volumes, to the left of point A in Illustration 21.9, then increasing automation increases the company's break-even point. At high volumes, however, if increasing automation lowers total costs, it lowers the company's break-even point.

In this chapter we began studying short-run decisions based on cost-volume-profit analysis. In Chapter 22 we will apply differential analysis to short-term decisions.

UNDERSTANDING THE LEARNING OBJECTIVES

Objective 1
Explain and describe cost behavior patterns.

- **Fixed costs.** These costs remain constant over some relevant range of output and are often described as time-related costs. Depreciation and insurance are examples.
- **Variable costs.** These costs vary in total directly with changes in the volume of production or sales. Direct materials and sales commissions are examples.
- **Mixed costs.** These costs contain a fixed portion of cost incurred even when the plant is completely idle and a variable portion that increases directly with production volume. Electricity is an example of a mixed cost.
- **Step costs.** These costs remain constant at a certain fixed amount over a short range of output (or sales) but increase to higher amounts at certain points. The cost of supervisors' salaries is an example.

Objective 2
Separate mixed costs into fixed and variable components using the scatter diagram and high-low method.

- The scatter diagram shows plots of actual costs incurred for various levels of activity.
- The high-low method uses the highest and lowest points on a scatter diagram to fit a line to the data.

Objective 3
Explain the relationship among costs, volume, revenue, and profits.

- Cost-volume-profit analysis (sometimes called *break-even analysis*) can determine what effects any changes in a company's selling prices, costs, and/or volume will have on net income in the short run.

Objective 4
Find the break-even point.

- The break-even point is that level of operations at which a company realizes no income or loss.
- To compute the break-even point in sales dollars:

$$BE_{dollars} = \frac{\text{Fixed costs}}{\text{Contribution margin ratio}}$$

Or, to express the break-even point in units:

$$BE_{units} = \frac{\text{Fixed costs}}{\text{Contribution margin per unit}}$$

Objective 5
Compute the margin of safety.

- To compute the margin of safety:

$$\text{Margin of safety} = \text{Current sales} - \text{Break-even sales}$$

Objective 6
Demonstrate applications of cost-volume-profit analysis.

- Applications include calculation of the break-even point, calculation of the sales volume needed for a desired net income, calculation of the effect of changing price on net income, and calculation of the sales needed to maintain net income when costs change.

Objective 7
List the assumptions underlying cost-volume-profit analysis.

- Selling price, variable cost per unit, and total fixed costs remain constant through the relevant range.
- In multiproduct situations, the product mix is known in advance.
- Costs can be accurately classified into their fixed and variable portions.

Objective 8
Describe how computer spreadsheets expand your capability to use cost-volume-profit analysis.

- Computer spreadsheet packages are well suited for CVP analysis because they enable managers to answer what-if questions.

Objective 9
Describe the impact of automation on fixed-variable cost relationships.

- As companies become more automated, they substitute machinery for labor, which generally increases fixed costs and decreases variable costs.

Demonstration Problem 21–A

Davis Company has fixed costs of $625,000 per year and variable costs of $7.50 per unit. Its product sells for $12.50 per unit. Full capacity is 200,000 units. The contribution margin is $5 per unit ($12.50 − $7.50).

Required

a. Compute the break-even point in (1) sales dollars and (2) units.

b. Compute the number of units the company must sell if it wishes to have net income of $300,000.

SOLUTION TO DEMONSTRATION PROBLEM 21–A

a. (1) The contribution margin ratio is 0.40.

$$BE_{dollars} = \frac{\text{Fixed costs}}{\text{Contribution margin ratio}}$$

$$BE_{dollars} = \frac{\$625{,}000}{0.40} = \$1{,}562{,}500$$

(2)

$$BE_{units} = \frac{\text{Fixed costs}}{\text{Contribution margin per unit}}$$

$$BE_{units} = \frac{\$625{,}000}{\$5} = 125{,}000 \text{ units}$$

b.

$$\text{Number of units} = \frac{\text{Fixed cost + Desired net income}}{\text{Contribution margin per unit}}$$

$$= \frac{\$625{,}000 + \$300{,}000}{\$5}$$

$$= \frac{\$925{,}000}{\$5}$$

$$= 185{,}000 \text{ units}$$

DEMONSTRATION PROBLEM 21–B

At the beginning of this chapter, we presented a problem: A campus organization wants to show movies. Recall that the movie rental would be $1,000. Rent for an auditorium, salaries to the ticket takers and other personnel, and other fixed costs would be $800 for the weekend. The organization would sell tickets for $4 per person. In addition, profits from the sale of soft drinks, popcorn, and candy are estimated to be $1 per ticket holder. How many people have to buy tickets for the organization to break even?

SOLUTION TO DEMONSTRATION PROBLEM 21–B

$$\text{Number of ticket buyers to break even} = \frac{\$1{,}000 + \$800}{\$4 + \$1}$$

$$= \frac{\$1{,}800}{\$5}$$

$$= 360 \text{ ticket buyers}$$

NEW TERMS*

Break-even point That level of operations at which revenues for a period are equal to the costs assigned to that period so there is no net income or loss. *772*

Contribution margin The amount by which revenue exceeds the variable costs of producing that revenue. The contribution margin per unit is the selling price minus the variable cost per unit. *772*

Contribution margin ratio Contribution margin per unit divided by selling price per unit, or total contribution margin divided by total revenues. *773*

Cost-volume-profit (CVP) analysis An analysis of the effect that any changes in a company's selling prices, costs, and/or volume will have on income (profits) in the short run. Also called *break-even analysis*. *771*

Cost-volume-profit (CVP) chart A graph that shows the relationships among sales, volume, costs, and net income or loss. *771*

Fixed costs Costs that remain constant (in total) over some relevant range of output. *767*

High-low method A method used in dividing mixed costs into their fixed and variable portions. The high plot and low plot of actual costs are used to draw a line representing a total mixed cost. *771*

* Some terms listed in earlier chapters are repeated here for your convenience.

Margin of safety Amount by which sales can decrease before a loss is incurred. *775*

Margin of safety rate Margin of safety expressed as a percentage, which equals (Current sales − Break-even sales)/Current sales. *775*

Mixed cost Contains a fixed portion of cost incurred even when the plant is completely idle and a variable portion that increases directly with production volume. *768*

Product mix The proportion of the company's total sales attributable to each type of product sold. *774*

Profit equation The equation is Net income = Revenue − Total variable costs − Fixed costs. *772*

Relevant range The range of production or sales volume over which the assumptions about cost behavior are valid. *769*

Scatter diagram A diagram that shows plots of actual costs incurred for various levels of activity; it is used in dividing mixed costs into their fixed and variable portions. *770*

Short run The time during which a company's management cannot change the effects of certain past decisions; often determined to be one year or less. In the short run, many costs are assumed to be fixed and unchangeable. *767*

Step cost A cost that remains constant at a certain fixed amount over a range of output (or sales) but then keeps increasing to a higher amount at certain points. *768*

Variable costs Costs that vary (in total) directly with changes in the volume of production or sales. *768*

Self-Test

True-False

Indicate whether each of the following statements is true or false.

1. The scatter diagram method is less precise than the high-low method for evaluating costs.
2. A break-even point is expressed only in dollars of sales revenues.
3. Total contribution margin indicates the amount of money remaining after variable and fixed costs are covered.
4. The margin of safety is calculated using the following formula:

$$\text{Margin of safety} = \text{Break-even sales} - \text{Current sales}$$

5. Dollars of sales are used when computing the break-even point for a multiproduct company.

Multiple-Choice

Select the best answer for each of the following questions.

1. Under which of the following cost behavior patterns would electricity be categorized?
   - **a.** Variable cost.
   - **b.** Fixed cost.
   - **c.** Mixed cost.
   - **d.** Step cost.
2. Which of the following are characteristics of step costs?
   - **a.** Fixed and variable characteristics.
   - **b.** Can change directly in relation to production.
   - **c.** Can remain constant over some relevant range of output.
   - **d.** All of the above.
3. Using the following data, calculate the sales revenue needed to break even:

Selling price per unit	$ 10
Fixed costs	20,000
Variable cost per unit	6

   - **a.** $40,000.
   - **b.** $33,333.
   - **c.** $50,000.
   - **d.** $60,000.
4. Using the following data, calculate the contribution margin:

Selling price	$20
Fixed costs	4
Variable cost	6

   - **a.** $14.
   - **b.** $10.
   - **c.** $16.
   - **d.** $18.
5. Using the following data, calculate the break-even point in units:

Selling price per unit	$ 20
Fixed costs	28,000
Variable cost per unit	6

   - **a.** 1,400 units.
   - **b.** 2,800 units.
   - **c.** 2,275 units.
   - **d.** 2,000 units.
6. Which of the following best describes the underlying assumptions of cost-volume-profit analysis?
   - **a.** Selling price, variable cost per unit, and total fixed costs remain constant through the relevant range.
   - **b.** In multiproduct situations, the product mix is known in advance.
   - **c.** Costs can be accurately classified into their fixed and variable portions.
   - **d.** All of the above.

Now turn to page 790 to check your answers.

QUESTIONS

1. Name and describe four cost behavior patterns.
2. Describe two methods of determining the fixed and variable components of mixed costs.
3. What is meant by the term *break-even point*?
4. What are two ways in which the break-even point can be expressed?
5. What is the relevant range?
6. What is the formula for calculating the break-even point in sales revenue?
7. What formula is used to solve for the break-even point in units?
8. How can the break-even formula be altered to calculate the number of units that must be sold to achieve a desired level of income?
9. Why might a business wish to lower its break-even point? How would it go about lowering the break-even point?
10. What effect would you expect the mechanization and automation of production processes to have on the break-even point?

MAYTAG

11. **Real World Question** Refer to the 1993 income statement for Maytag Corporation in the annual report booklet. Consider only revenue, cost of sales, and selling and administrative expenses. Ignore taxes, interest, and other items on the income statement. Assume that for 1993, 90% of Maytag's selling and administrative expenses were fixed and 30% of cost of goods sold were fixed. The remainder of those costs were variable costs. At what level of revenues would Maytag break even in 1993?
12. **Real World Question** Refer to Question 11. What assumptions did you make to derive Maytag's break-even point?
13. **Real World Question** Assume your college is considering hiring a lecturer to teach a special class in communication skills. Identify at least two costs that college administrators might consider in deciding whether to hire the lecturer and add the class.
14. **Real World Question** Two enterprising students are considering renting space and opening a class videotape service. They would hire camera operators to videotape large introductory classes. The students taking the classes would be charged a fee to rent the tape or to view it on one of the service's television sets. Identify as many costs of this business as you can and indicate which would be variable and which would be fixed.

EXERCISES

Exercise 21–1
Match cost behavior types with diagrams (L.O. 1)

Name and match the types of cost behavior with the appropriate diagram below.

(a)
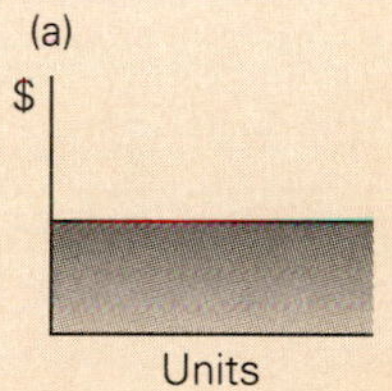

(b)
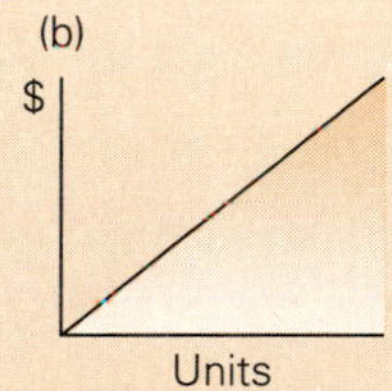

(c)
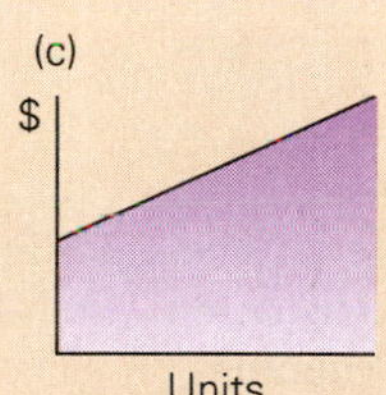

(d)
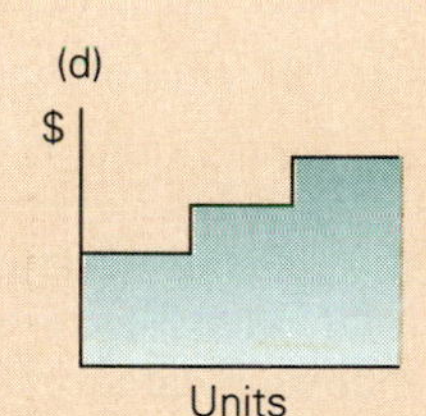

Exercise 21–2
Analyze mixed cost using high-low method (L.O. 2)

Accuracy, Inc., performs laboratory tests. Use the high-low method to determine the fixed and variable components of a mixed cost, given the following observations:

Volume (number of tests)	Total Cost
2,400	$6,000
9,600	9,600

Exercise 21–3
Compute break-even point in sales dollars (L.O. 4)

Compute the break-even point in sales dollars if fixed costs are $200,000 and the total contribution margin is 40% of revenue.

Exercise 21–4
Compute break-even point in units (L.O. 4)

Giants Company makes and sells stuffed animals. One product, Barry Bears, sells for $20 per bear. Barry Bears have fixed costs of $100,000 per month and a variable cost of $12 per bear. How many Barry Bears must be produced and sold each month to break even?

Exercise 21–5
Compute break-even point in sales dollars (L.O. 4)

Maria Ortiz is considering buying a company if it will break even or earn net income on revenues of $100,000 per month. The company that Ortiz is considering sells each unit it produces for $5. Use the following cost data to compute the variable cost per unit and the fixed cost for the period. Calculate the break-even point in sales dollars. Should Ortiz buy this company?

Volume (units)	Cost
8,000	$ 70,000
68,000	190,000

Exercise 21–6
Compute break-even point in sales dollars and units under varying assumptions; comment on results (L.O. 3, 4)

Speedster Delivery currently delivers packages for $18 each. The variable cost is $6 per package, and fixed costs are $120,000 per month. Compute the break-even point in both sales dollars and units under each of the following assumptions. Comment on why the break-even points are different.

a. The costs and selling price are as just given.
b. Fixed costs are increased to $150,000.
c. Selling price is increased by 10%.
d. Variable cost is increased to $9 per unit.

Exercise 21–7
Decide whether to increase advertising; compute margin of safety (L.O. 3, 5)

Motel 4 is a regional motel chain. Its rooms rent for $100 per night, on average. The variable cost is $40 a room per night. Fixed costs are $5,000,000 per year. The company currently rents 200,000 units per year, with each unit defined as one room for one night. Should this company undertake an advertising campaign resulting in a $500,000 increase in fixed costs per year, no change in variable cost per unit, and a 10% increase in revenue? What is the margin of safety before and after the campaign?

Exercise 21–8
Compute multiproduct break-even point and margin of safety (L.O. 4, 5)

Free-Fall Company sells three products. Last year's sales were $300,000 for parachutes, $400,000 for hang gliders, and $100,000 for bungee jumping harnesses. Variable costs were: parachutes, $200,000; hang gliders, $350,000; and bungee jumping harnesses, $50,000. Fixed costs were $120,000. Find (*a*) the break-even point in sales dollars and (*b*) the margin of safety.

Exercise 21–9
Compute break-even points to achieve a specified level of income (L.O. 6)

Developmental Day Care Center has fixed costs of $600,000 per year and variable costs of $10 per child per day. If it charges $25 a child per day, what will be its break-even point expressed in dollars of revenue? How much revenue would be required for Developmental Day Care to earn $100,000 net income per year?

PROBLEMS

Problem 21–1
Analyze mixed cost using high-low method and scatter diagram (L.O. 2)

Assume the local franchise of Domingo's Pizza Company assigns you the task of estimating total maintenance cost on its delivery vehicles. This cost is a mixed cost. You receive the following data from past months:

Month	Units	Costs
March.	4,000	$ 7,000
April	5,000	7,480
May	4,500	7,600
June	5,500	7,960
July.	5,000	7,960
August	6,500	8,440
September	7,000	9,040
October	9,000	9,640
November	10,000	10,600

Required

a. Using the high-low method, determine the total amount of fixed costs and the amount of variable cost per unit. Draw the cost line.
b. Prepare a scatter diagram, plot the actual costs, and visually fit a linear cost line to the points. Estimate the amount of total fixed costs and the amount of variable cost per unit.

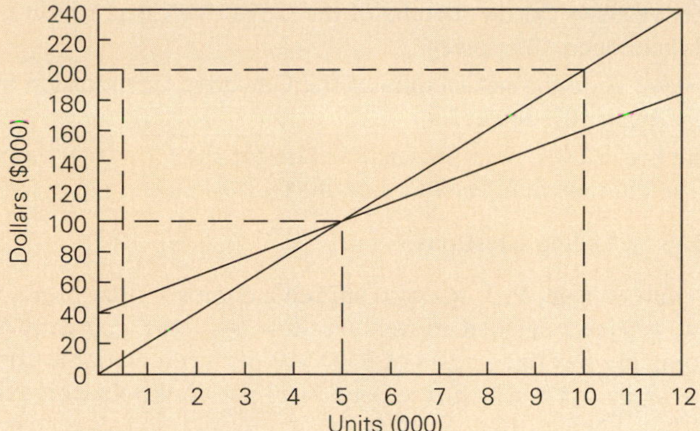

Problem 21–2
Identify points on a cost-volume-profit chart (L.O. 3)

Required

a. Using the preceding graph, label the relevant range, total costs, fixed costs, break-even point, and profit and loss areas.
b. At 8,000 units, what are the variable costs, fixed costs, sales, and contribution margin amounts in dollars?
c. At 8,000 units, is there net income or loss? How much?

Problem 21–3
Determine break-even point under varying assumptions (L.O. 3, 4)

The management of Sky High Company want to know the break-even point for its new line of hiking boots under each of the following independent assumptions. The selling price is $50 per pair of boots (unit) unless otherwise stated.

a. Fixed costs are $600,000; variable cost is $30 per unit.
b. Fixed costs are $600,000; variable cost is $20 per unit.
c. Fixed costs are $500,000; variable cost is $20 per unit.
d. Fixed costs are $500,000; selling price is $40; and variable cost is $30 per unit.

Required

Compute the break-even point in units and sales dollars for each of the four independent cases.

Problem 21–4
Determine the margin of safety (L.O. 5)

Refer to Problem 21–3. Sky High Company's sales are $2,200,000. Determine the margin of safety in dollars for cases (**a**) through (**d**).

Problem 21–5
Compute the level of sales needed to achieve a specified level of income (L.O. 6)

Using the data in Problem 21–3 (**a** through **d**), determine the level of sales required to achieve a net income of $250,000.

Problem 21–6
Compute multiproduct break-even point (L.O. 4)

Wheelrite, Inc., sells three types of bicycles. It has fixed costs of $500,000 per month. The sales and variable costs of these products for April follow:

	Bikes		
	Racing	**Mountain**	**Touring**
Sales	$1,000,000	$1,500,000	$2,500,000
Variable costs	700,000	900,000	1,250,000

Required

Compute the break-even point in sales dollars.

Problem 21–7
Applying cost-volume-profit analysis to various situations (L.O. 6)

a. Assume that fixed costs of Hawks Corporation are $180,000 per year, variable cost is $6 per unit, and selling price is $15 per unit. Determine the break-even point in sales dollars.
b. Celtics Company breaks even when its sales amount to $44,800,000. In 1993, its sales were $7,200,000, and its variable costs amounted to $2,880,000. Determine the amount of its fixed costs.
c. The sales of Cowboys Corporation last year amounted to $20,000,000, its variable costs were $6,000,000, and its fixed costs were $4,000,000. At what level of sales dollars would the Cowboys Corporation break even?
d. What would have been the net income of the Cowboys Corporation in Part (**c**), if sales volume had been 10% higher but selling prices had remained unchanged?

e. What would have been the net income of the Cowboys Corporation in Part (**c**), if variable costs had been 10% lower?

f. What would have been the net income of the Cowboys Corporation in Part (**c**), if fixed costs had been 10% lower?

g. Determine the break-even point in sales dollars for the Cowboys Corporation on the basis of the data given in (**e**) and then in (**f**).

Required Answer each of the preceding questions.

Problem 21–8
Compute break-even point and sales needed to achieve a specified level of income (L.O. 6)

After graduating from college, P. J. Masako started a company that produced cookbooks. After three years, Masako decided to analyze how well the company was doing. He discovered the company has fixed costs of $600,000 per year, variable cost of $14.40 per cookbook (on average), and a selling price of $26.90 per cookbook (on average).

Required How many units (that is, cookbooks) must be sold to break even? How many units will the company have to sell to earn $48,000?

Problem 21–9
Prepare cost-volume-profit chart; compute break-even point; prepare income statement for two companies (L.O. 3, 4, 6)

The operating results for two companies follow:

	Smokies	Rockies
Sales (20,000) units	$1,920,000	$1,920,000
Variable costs	480,000	1,056,000
Contribution margin	1,440,000	864,000
Fixed costs	960,000	384,000
Net income	480,000	480,000

Required

a. Prepare a cost-volume-profit chart for Smokies Company, indicating the break-even point, the contribution margin, and the areas of income and losses.

b. Compute the break-even point of both companies in sales dollars and units.

c. Assume that without changes in selling price, the sales of each company decline by 10%. Prepare income statements similar to the preceding statements for both companies.

Problem 21–10
Compute break-even point; compute expected net income; make leasing decision (L.O. 4, 6)

Noise 'R' Us Company, a leading manufacturer of electronic equipment, decided to analyze the profitability of its new portable compact disc (CD) players. On the CD player line, the company incurred $2,520,000 of fixed costs per month while selling 20,000 units at $300 each. Variable cost was $120 per unit.

Recently, a new machine used in the production of CD players has become available; it is more efficient than the machine currently being used. The new machine would reduce the company's variable costs by 20%, and leasing it would increase fixed costs by $96,000 per year.

Required

a. Compute the break-even point in units assuming use of the old machine.

b. Compute the break-even point in units assuming use of the new machine.

c. Assuming that total sales remain at $6,000,000 and that the new machine is leased, compute the expected net income.

d. Should the new machine be leased? Why?

Problem 21–11
Decide whether to undertake a sales promotion campaign (L.O. 6)

Starfire CD Company reports sales of $720,000, variable costs of $432,000, and fixed costs of $108,000. If the company spends $72,000 on a sales promotion campaign, it estimates that sales will be increased by $270,000.

Required Determine whether the sales promotion campaign should be undertaken. Provide calculations.

Alternate Problems

Problem 21–1A
Analyze a mixed cost using high-low method and scatter diagram (L.O. 2)

What Company has identified certain variable and fixed costs in its production of hearing aids. Management wants you to divide one of its mixed costs into its fixed and variable portions. Here are the data for this cost:

Month	Units	Costs
January	20,800	$57,600
February	20,000	54,000
March	22,000	58,500
April.	25,600	57,600
May.	28,400	58,500
June.	30,000	62,100
July	32,800	63,900
August.	35,600	68,400
September. . . .	37,600	72,000
October	40,000	77,400

Required

a. Using the high-low method, determine the total amount of fixed costs and the amount of variable cost per unit. Draw the cost line.

b. Prepare a scatter diagram, plot the actual costs, and visually fit a linear cost line to the points. Estimate the amount of total fixed costs and the variable cost per unit.

Problem 21–2A
Identify points on a cost-volume-profit chart (L.O. 3)

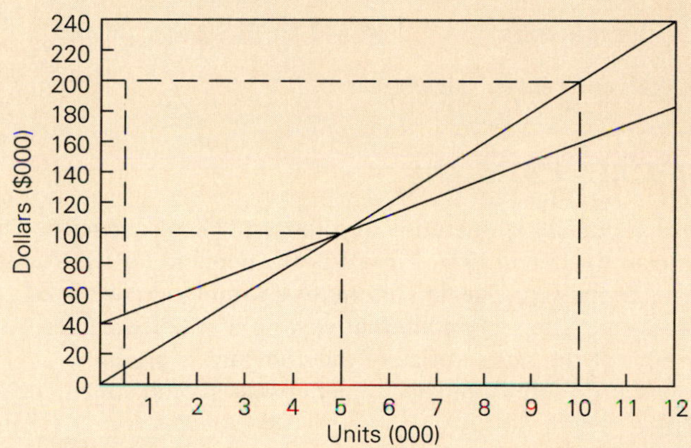

Required

a. Using the preceding graph, label the relevant range, total costs, fixed costs, break-even point, and profit and loss areas.

b. At 9,000 units, what would sales revenue, total costs, fixed and variable costs be?

c. At 9,000 units, would there be a profit or loss? How much?

Problem 21–3A
Compute level of sales needed to break even and earn a specified level of income (L.O. 4)

Hancock Company has a plant capacity of 100,000 units, at which level variable costs are $720,000. Fixed costs are expected to be $216,000. Each unit of product sells for $12.

Required

a. Determine the company's break-even point in sales dollars and units.

b. At what level of sales dollars would the company earn net income of $144,000?

c. If the selling price were raised to $14.40 per unit, at what level of sales dollars would the company earn $144,000?

Problem 21–4A
Determine break-even point under varying assumptions (L.O. 4)

a. Determine the break-even point in sales dollars and units for Longhorn Company that has fixed costs of $63,000, variable cost of $12.25 per unit, and a selling price of $17.50 per unit.

b. Hoosiers Company breaks even when sales are $280,000. In March, sales were $670,000, and variable costs were $536,000. Compute the amount of fixed costs.

c. Wildcats Company had sales in June of $84,000; variable costs of $46,200; and fixed costs of $25,200. At what level of sales, in dollars, did the company break even?

d. What would the break-even point in sales dollars have been in (**c**) if variable costs had been 10% higher?

e. What would the break-even point in sales dollars have been in (**c**) if fixed costs had been 10% higher?

f. Compute the break-even point in sales dollars for Wildcats Company in (**c**) under the assumptions of (**d**) and (**e**) together.

Required

Answer each of the preceding questions.

Problem 21–5A
Prepare cost-volume-profit chart; compute break-even sales and sales needed to achieve a specified level of income (L.O. 3, 4, 6)

U C Now Company makes contact lenses. The company has a plant capacity of 200,000 units. Variable costs are $4,000,000 at 100% capacity. Fixed costs are $2,000,000 per year, but this is true only between 50,000 and 200,000 units.

Required

a. Prepare a cost-volume-profit chart for U C Now Company assuming it sells its product for $40 each. Indicate on the chart the relevant range, break-even point, and the areas of net income and losses.

b. Compute the break-even point in units.

c. How many units would have to be sold to earn $200,000 per year?

Problem 21–6A
Compute break-even point in a multiproduct company (L.O. 4)

Sugar Lakes Corporation has fixed costs of $180,000 per year. It sells three types of cookies. The cost and revenue data for these products follow:

	Cookies		
	Cream Cake	Goo Fill	Sweet Tooth
Sales.	$64,000	$95,000	$131,000
Variable costs	38,400	55,100	66,000

Required Compute the break-even point in sales dollars.

BEYOND THE NUMBERS—CRITICAL THINKING

Business Decision Case 21–1
Compute break-even point and projected net income for two investment alternatives; determine best alternative (L.O. 5)

Carolina Furniture Company is operating at almost 100% of capacity. The company expects sales to increase by 25% in 1997. To satisfy the demand for its product, the company is considering two alternatives: The first alternative would increase fixed costs by 15% but not affect variable costs. The second alternative would not affect fixed costs but increase variable costs to 60% of the selling price of the company's product.

This is Carolina Furniture Company's condensed income statement for 1996:

Sales.		$3,600,000
Costs:		
Variable.	$1,620,000	
Fixed.	660,000	2,280,000
Income before taxes		$1,320,000

Required

a. Determine the break-even point in sales dollars for 1997 under each of the alternatives.

b. Determine projected income for 1997 under each of the alternatives.

c. Which alternative would you recommend? Why?

Business Decision Case 21–2
Compute break-even point; determine point at which factory should shut down rather than produce (L.O. 5)

When the Martin Company's plant is completely idle, fixed costs amount to $720,000. When the plant operates at levels of 50% of capacity or less, its fixed costs are $840,000; at levels more than 50% of capacity, its fixed costs are $1,200,000. The company's variable costs at full capacity (100,000 units) amount to $1,800,000.

Required

a. Assuming that the company's product sells for $60 per unit, what is the company's break-even point in sales dollars?

b. Using only the data given, at what level of sales would it be more economical to close the factory than to operate it? In other words, at what level would operating losses approximate the losses incurred if the factory closed down completely?

c. Assume that Martin Company is operating at half of its capacity and decides to reduce the selling price from $60 per unit to $36 per unit to increase sales. At what percentage of capacity must the company operate to break even at the reduced sales price?

Business Decision Case 21–3
Find variable cost and calculate cost to manufacture part; decide whether to buy a part (L.O. 5)

Hopkins Company has recently been awarded a contract to sell 25,000 units of its product to the federal government. Hopkins manufactures the components of the product rather than purchasing them. When the news of the contract was released to the public, President Bob Hopkins, received a call from the president of the McLean Corporation, Carl Cahn. Cahn offered to sell Hopkins 25,000 units of a needed component, Part J, for $15.00 each. After receiving the offer, Hopkins calls you into his office and asks you to recommend whether to accept or reject Cahn's offer.

You go to the company's records and obtain the following information concerning the production of Part J:

	Costs at Current Production Level (200,000 units)
Direct labor	$1,248,000
Direct materials	576,000
Manufacturing overhead	600,000
Total cost	$2,424,000

You calculate the unit cost of Part J to be $12.12 ($2,424,000 ÷ 200,000). But you suspect that this unit cost may not hold true at all production levels. To find out, you consult the production manager. She tells you that to meet the increased production needs, equipment would have to be rented and the production workers would work some overtime. She estimates the machine rental to be $60,000 and the total overtime premiums to be $108,000. She provides you with the following information:

	Costs at Projected Production Level (225,000 units)
Direct labor	$1,404,000
Direct materials	648,000
Manufacturing overhead (including equipmental rental and overtime premiums)	828,000
Total cost	$2,880,000

The production manager advises you to reject Cahn's offer, since the unit cost of Part J would rise to $12.80 ($2,880,000/225,000 units) with the additional costs of equipment rental and overtime premiums. This is much less than the $15.00 offered by Cahn. Undecided, you return to your office to consider the matter further.

Required

a. Using the high-low method, compute the variable cost portion of manufacturing overhead. (Remember that the costs of equipment rental and overtime premiums are included in manufacturing overhead. Subtract these amounts before performing the calculation).

b. Compute the total costs to manufacture the additional units of Part J. (Note: include overtime premiums as a part of direct labor.)

c. Compute the unit cost to manufacture the additional units of Part J.

d. Write a report recommending that Hopkins accept or reject Cahn's offer.

Business Decision Case 21–4
Writing Assignment

Refer to the "A Broader Perspective" discussion of cost-volume-profit analysis for television networks on page 778. Write a memo to your instructor describing how the networks reduce their break-even points.

Group Project 21–5
Develop a cost-volume-profit equation for a new business

In teams of two or three students, develop a cost-volume-profit equation for a new business that you might start. Examples of such businesses are a portable espresso bar, a pizza stand, a campus movie theater, a package delivery service, a campus-to-airport limousine service, and a T-shirt printing business.

Your equation should be in the form: Profits = (Price per unit × Volume) − (Variable cost per unit × Volume) − Fixed costs per period. Pick a period of time, say one month, and project the unit price, volume, unit variable cost, and fixed costs for the period. From this information, you will be able to estimate the profits—or losses—for the period. Select one spokesperson for your team to tell the class about your proposed business and its profits or losses. Good luck, and have fun.

Answers to Self-Test

True-False

1. **False.** The high-low method is less precise than the scatter diagram because it requires only two data points in the computation.
2. **False.** The break-even point can also be expressed in units produced or sold.
3. **False.** Total contribution margin is the amount by which revenue exceeds variable costs of producing that revenue.
4. **False.** Margin of safety = Current sales − Break-even sales.
5. **True.** Dollars of sales are used as the measure of volume when a company has many different products.

Multiple-Choice

1. **c.** Electricity is a mixed cost.
2. **d.** Step costs have all of these characteristics—a fixed component, changes in steps, and constancy over a relevant range for a step.
3. **c.**

$$BE_{dollars} = \frac{\text{Fixed costs}}{\text{Contribution margin ratio}}$$

$$\text{Contribution margin ratio} = (\$10 - \$6)/\$10 = 0.40$$

$$BE_{dollars} = \frac{\$20{,}000}{0.40} = \$50{,}000$$

4. **a.** Contribution margin = Selling price − Variable costs = $20 − $6 = $14
5. **d.**

$$BE_{units} = \frac{\text{Fixed costs}}{\text{Contribution margin per unit}}$$

$$BE_{units} = \frac{\$28{,}000}{\$14 \text{ per unit}}$$

$$= 2{,}000 \text{ units}$$

6. **d.** All of these are assumptions—prices and costs remain constant through the relevant range, product mix is known, and costs can be accurately classified into fixed and variable components.

22

Short-Term Decision Making

Differential Analysis

In this chapter, we will discuss how companies use financial information in making decisions. The framework for our discussion is differential analysis. We begin by presenting an alternative to the traditional income statement format. This alternative, the contribution margin income statement, generally is more useful for the managerial decisions we discuss in this chapter. Then we discuss differential analysis as a method of choosing the best solution to decision problems. We also present several applications of differential analysis to managerial problems that you will likely encounter.

Learning Objectives

After studying this chapter, you should be able to:

1. Compare and contrast contribution margin income statements to traditional income statements.
2. Explain differential analysis and describe its components.
3. Make pricing decisions using differential analysis.
4. Use differential analysis to decide whether to accept or reject special orders.

(continued)

Contribution Margin Income Statements

Both this and the previous chapter discuss the use of accounting for managerial decision making. We have introduced the concepts of *fixed* and *variable costs*, and shown how you can use these concepts in making decisions. However, income statements published for external use do not break costs down into fixed and variable components. We now present another income statement that not only breaks down costs into their fixed and variable components but also presents the total contribution margin. The contribution margin income statement subtracts variable costs from revenues to show the contribution margin, and then subtracts fixed costs to derive net income.

You can see the differences between the traditional and contribution margin income statements by contrasting two income statements based on the same data. Assume Bart Company had the following data relating to manufacturing and sales activities for May 1997:

BART COMPANY
May 1997

Variable manufacturing costs (per unit):	
Direct materials	$1
Direct labor	1
Overhead	1
Total	$3

(concluded)

5. Decide whether to eliminate or add product lines or segments of the business using differential analysis.

6. Use differential analysis to decide whether to sell joint products at the split-off point or process them further.

7. Decide whether to make or buy products using differential analysis.

8. Use differential analysis to decide whether to improve product quality.

Variable selling expenses (per unit)	$0.50
Fixed costs:	
Manufacturing overhead ($1.00 per unit for 9,000 units)	$ 9,000
Selling expenses	15,000
Administrative expenses	18,000
Selling price (per unit)	$9

Look at Illustration 22.1, where we compare the traditional and contribution margin methods. The contribution margin method shows managers the amount of variable costs, the amount of fixed costs, and the contribution the company is making toward covering fixed costs and earning net income. For example, suppose the managers of Bart Company asked, "What would be the impact on net income if we increase sales units by 10 percent without changing unit price or variable cost per unit or total fixed costs?" Looking at the contribution margin statement, we predict the following increases:

Revenue increase (10% of $81,000)		$8,100
Variable cost of goods sold increase (10% of $27,000)	$2,700	
Increase in total variable selling expense (10% of $4,500)	450	3,150
Increase in total contribution margin		$4,950

If we assume no increase in fixed costs, we expect Bart's net income to increase by $4,950.

Objective 1
Compare and contrast contribution margin income statements to traditional income statements.

The traditional statement does not break down costs into fixed and variable components, so we cannot answer the question posed by Bart's management. Most companies use the traditional approach for external financial statements, but they use the contribution margin format for internal purposes because it is more informative. Management often needs information on the contribution margin rather than the gross margin to calculate break-even points and make decisions regarding special-order pricing.

An Accounting Perspective

Use of Technology Generating multiple financial reports in different formats does not mean companies must keep several sets of books. After data are entered into the database, it is relatively simple for computer software to generate several sets of financial statements—a contribution margin income statement for managers, a traditional income statement for external financial reporting, and yet another report for tax purposes. Two problems remain: First, the reports are only as good as the quality of the data in the database. Second, people who read the financial statements must be sufficiently informed to understand the differences in the way the information is presented.

Differential Analysis

Objective 2
Explain differential analysis and describe its components.

Differential analysis involves analyzing the different costs and benefits that would arise from alternative solutions to a particular problem. **Relevant revenues or costs** in a given situation are future revenues or costs that differ depending on the alternative course of action selected. **Differential revenue** is the difference in revenues between two alternatives. **Differential cost or expense** is the difference between the amounts of relevant costs for two alternatives.[1]

Future costs that do not differ between alternatives are irrelevant and may be

[1] Some authors equate relevant cost and differential cost. This text uses the term *relevant* to identify which costs should be considered in a situation and the term *differential* to identify the amount by which these costs differ.

ILLUSTRATION 22.1
Comparative Income Statements

A. Traditional Method

BART COMPANY
Income Statement
For the Month Ending May 31, 1997

Revenue (9,000 units at $9 per unit)	$81,000
Less: Cost of goods sold (9,000 units at $4 manufacturing cost per unit: $3 variable + $1 fixed)	36,000
Gross margin	$45,000
Less: Selling and administrative expenses (9,000 units at $0.50 variable selling cost per unit, plus fixed costs of $15,000 for selling and $18,000 for administrative)	37,500
Net income before tax	$ 7,500

B. Contribution Margin Method

BART COMPANY
Income Statement
For the Month Ending May 31, 1997

Revenue (9,000 units at $9 per unit)		$81,000
Less: Variable cost of goods sold (9,000 units at $3 variable manufacturing cost per unit)	$27,000	
Variable selling expenses (9,000 units at $0.50 per unit)	4,500	31,500
Total contribution margin		$49,500
Less: Fixed manufacturing costs	$ 9,000	
Fixed selling expenses	15,000	
Fixed administrative expenses	18,000	42,000
Net income before tax		$ 7,500

ignored since they affect both alternatives similarly. Past costs, also known as **sunk costs,** are not relevant in decision making because they have already been incurred; therefore, these costs cannot be changed no matter which alternative is selected.

For certain decisions, revenues do not differ between alternatives. Under those circumstances, management should select the alternative with the least cost. In other situations, costs do not differ between alternatives. Accordingly, management should select the alternative that results in the largest revenue. Many times both future costs and revenues differ between alternatives. In these situations, the management should select the alternative that results in the greatest positive difference between future revenues and expenses (costs).

To illustrate relevant, differential, and sunk costs, assume that Joanna Bennett invested $400 in a tiller so she could till gardens to earn $1,500 during the summer. Not long afterward, Bennett was offered a job at a horse stable feeding horses and cleaning stalls for $1,200 for the summer. The costs that she would incur in tilling are $100 for transportation and $150 for supplies. The costs she would incur at the horse stable are $100 for transportation and $50 for supplies. If Bennett works at the stable, she would still have the tiller, which she could loan to her parents and friends at no charge.

The tiller cost of $400 is not relevant to the decision because it is a *sunk* cost. The transportation cost of $100 is also not relevant because it is the same for both alternatives. These costs and revenues are relevant:

	Performing Tilling Service	Working at Horse Stable	Differential
Revenues	$1,500	$1,200	$300
Costs	150	50	100
Net benefit in favor of tilling service			$200

Based on this differential analysis, Joanna Bennett should perform her tilling service rather than work at the stable. Of course, this analysis considers only cash flows; nonmonetary considerations, such as her love for horses, could sway the decision.

In many situations, total variable costs differ between alternatives while total fixed costs do not. For example, suppose you are deciding between taking the bus to work or driving your car on a particular day. The differential costs of driving a car to work or taking the bus would involve only the variable costs of driving the car versus the variable costs of taking the bus.

Suppose the decision is whether to drive your car to work every day for a year versus taking the bus for a year. If you bought a second car for commuting, certain costs such as insurance and an auto license that are fixed costs of owning a car would be differential costs for this particular decision.

Before studying the applications of differential analysis, you must realize that (1) two types of fixed costs exist and (2) opportunity costs are also relevant in choosing between alternatives. For this reason, we discuss committed fixed costs, discretionary fixed costs, and opportunity costs before concentrating on the applications of differential analysis.

Nature of Fixed Costs

Up to this point, we have treated fixed costs as if they were all alike. Now we describe two types of fixed costs—committed fixed costs and discretionary fixed costs.

Committed Fixed Costs **Committed fixed costs** relate to the basic facilities and organizational structure that a company must have to continue operations. These costs cannot be changed in the short run without seriously disrupting operations. Examples of committed fixed costs are leases on buildings and equipment and salaries of key executives. In the short run, these costs are not subject to the discretion or control of management. These costs result from past decisions that *committed* the company for several years. For instance, once a company constructs a building to house production operations, it is committed to use the building for many years. Thus, unlike some other types of fixed costs, the depreciation on that building is not as subject to management's control.

Discretionary Fixed Costs In contrast to committed fixed costs, management controls **discretionary fixed costs** from year to year. Each year management decides how much to spend on advertising, research and development, and employee training or development programs. Because it makes such decisions each year, these costs are under management's *discretion*. Management is not locked in or committed to a certain level of expense for longer than one budget period. In the next period, management may change the level of expense or eliminate the expense completely.

To some extent, management's philosophy can affect which fixed costs are committed and which are discretionary. For instance, some companies terminate people in the upper levels of management when they downsize, while other companies keep their management team intact. Thus, in some companies the salaries of top-level managers are discretionary while in other companies they are committed.

The discussion of committed fixed costs and discretionary fixed costs is relevant to CVP analysis. When almost all of a company's fixed costs are committed fixed costs, it has more difficulty reducing its break-even point for the next budget period than if most of its fixed costs are discretionary. A company with a large proportion of discretionary fixed costs may be able to reduce fixed costs dramatically in recessionary periods. By running lean, the company may show some income even when economic conditions are difficult. As a result, the company may enhance its chances of long-run survival.

Opportunity Costs

Another cost concept relevant to decision making is opportunity cost. An **opportunity cost** is the potential benefit that is forgone from *not* following the next best alternative course of action. For example, assume that the two best uses of a plot of land are as a mobile home park (annual income of $100,000) and as a golf driving range (annual income of $60,000). The opportunity cost of using the land as a mobile home park is $60,000, while the opportunity cost of using the land as a driving range is $100,000.

Companies do not record opportunity costs in the accounting records because they are the costs of not following a certain alternative. Thus, opportunity costs are not transactions that occurred but that did not occur. However, opportunity cost is a relevant cost in many decisions because it represents a real sacrifice when one alternative is chosen instead of another.

Applications of Differential Analysis

Objective 3
Make pricing decisions using differential analysis.

To illustrate the application of differential analysis to specific decision problems, we consider five decisions: (1) setting prices of products; (2) accepting or rejecting special orders; (3) adding or eliminating products, segments, or customers; (4) processing or selling joint products; and (5) deciding whether to make products or buy them. Although these five decisions are not the only applications of differential analysis, they represent typical short-term business decisions using differential analysis. Our discussion ignores income taxes.

Pricing Decisions

When applying differential analysis to pricing decisions, each possible price for a given product represents an alternative course of action. The sales revenues for each alternative and the costs that differ between alternatives are the relevant amounts in these decisions. Total fixed costs often remain the same between pricing alternatives and, if so, may be ignored. In selecting a price for a product, the goal is to select the price at which total future revenues exceed total future costs by the greatest amount, thus maximizing income.

A high price is not necessarily the price that maximizes income. The product may have many substitutes. If a company sets a high price, the number of units sold may decline substantially as customers switch to lower-priced competitive products. Thus, in the maximization of income, the expected volume of sales at each price is as important as the contribution margin per unit of product sold. In making any pricing decision, management should seek the combination of price and volume that produces the largest total contribution margin. This combination is often difficult to identify in an actual situation, because management may have to estimate the number of units that can be sold at each price.

For example, assume that a company selling fried chicken in the New York market estimates product demand for its large bucket of chicken for a particular period to be:

Choice	Demand
1	15,000 units at $6 per unit
2	12,000 units at $7 per unit
3	10,000 units at $8 per unit
4	7,000 units at $9 per unit

The company's fixed costs of $20,000 per year are not affected by the different volume alternatives. Variable costs are $5 per unit. What price should be set for the product? Based on the calculations shown in the table on the next page, the company should select a price of $8 per unit because choice (3) results in the greatest total contribution margin. In the short run, maximizing total contribution margin maximizes profits.

ILLUSTRATION 22.2
Rios Company before Special Order

RIOS COMPANY
Income Statement
For the Period Ending May 31, 1997

Revenue (5,000 units at $20)			$100,000
Variable costs:			
Direct materials cost	$20,000		
Labor	5,000		
Overhead	10,000		
Marketing and administrative costs	5,000		
Total variable costs		$ 40,000	
Fixed costs:			
Overhead	$28,000		
Marketing and administrative costs	20,000		
Total fixed costs		48,000	
Total costs			88,000
Net income			$ 12,000

Contribution Choice	Contribution Margin per Unit*	× Number of Units	= Total Margin	Fixed Costs	Net Income (loss)
1	$1	15,000	$15,000	$20,000	$(5,000)
2	2	12,000	24,000	20,000	4,000
3	3	10,000	30,000	20,000	10,000
4	4	7,000	28,000	20,000	8,000

* Sales price − Variable cost.

Accepting or Rejecting Special Orders: Providing Discounts

Objective 4
Use differential analysis to decide whether to accept or reject special orders.

Sometimes management has an opportunity to sell its product in two or more markets at two or more different prices. Movie theaters, for example, sell tickets at discount prices to particular groups of people—children, students, and senior citizens. Differential analysis can determine whether companies should sell their products at prices below regular levels.

Good business management requires keeping the cost of idleness at a minimum. When operating at less than full capacity, management should seek additional business. Management may decide to accept such additional business at prices lower than average unit costs if the differential revenues from the additional business exceed the differential costs. By accepting special orders at a discount, businesses can keep people employed that they would otherwise lay off.

To illustrate, assume Rios Company produces and sells a single product with a variable cost of $8 per unit. (See Illustration 22.2 for details.) Annual capacity is 10,000 units, and annual fixed costs total $48,000. The selling price is $20 per unit and production and sales are budgeted at 5,000 units. Thus, budgeted income before income taxes is $12,000, as shown in Illustration 22.2.

Assume the company receives an order from a foreign distributor for 3,000 units at $10 per unit. This $10 price is not only half of the regular selling price per unit, but also less than the $17.60 average cost per unit ($88,000/5,000 units). However, the $10 price offered exceeds the variable cost per unit by $2. If the company accepts the order, net income increases to $18,000.

As shown in the income statement in Illustration 22.3, revenue increases to $130,000 with the special order. Each of the variable costs increases in total by 60 percent because total volume increases by 60 percent (3,000 units in the special order/5,000 units regularly produced).

Note that the fixed costs do not increase with the special order. Because the special order does not increase the fixed costs, the special order's revenues need only cover its variable costs.

If Rios Company continues to operate at 50% capacity (producing 5,000 units) it would generate income of only $12,000. By accepting the special order, net income increases by $6,000.

ILLUSTRATION 22.3
Rios Company If Special Order Is Accepted

RIOS COMPANY
Income Statement
For the Period Ending May 31, 1997

Revenue (5,000 units at $20, 3,000 units at $10)			$130,000
Variable costs:			
Direct materials cost	$32,000		
Labor	8,000		
Overhead	16,000		
Marketing and adminstrative costs	8,000		
Total variable costs		$ 64,000	
Fixed costs:			
Manufacturing overhead	$28,000		
Marketing and administrative costs	20,000		
Total fixed costs		48,000	
Total costs			112,000
Net income			$ 18,000

Differential analysis would provide the following calculations:

	Accept Order	Reject Order	Differential
Revenues	$130,000	$100,000	$30,000
Costs	112,000	88,000	24,000
Net benefit of accepting order			$ 6,000

Variable costs set a floor for the selling price in special-order situations. Even if the price exceeds variable costs only slightly, the additional business increases net income, assuming fixed costs do not change. However, pricing just above variable costs of special-order business often brings only short-term increases in net income. In the long run, companies must cover all of their costs, not just the variable costs.

Adding or Eliminating Products, Segments, or Customers

Objective 5
Decide whether to eliminate or add product lines or segments of the business using differential analysis.

Periodically, management has to decide whether to add or eliminate certain products, segments, or customers. If you have watched a store or a plant open or close in your area, you have seen the results of these decisions. Differential analysis is useful in this decision making because a company's income statement does not automatically associate costs with certain products, segments, or customers. Thus, companies must reclassify costs as those that the action would change and those that it would not change.

If companies add or eliminate products, they usually increase or decrease variable costs. The fixed costs may change, but not in many cases. Management bases decisions to add or eliminate products only on the differential items; that is, the costs and revenues that change.

To illustrate, assume that the Campus Bookstore is considering eliminating its art supplies department. If the bookstore dropped the art supplies department, it would lose revenues of $100,000 annually. The bookstore's management assigns costs of $110,000 ($80,000 variable and $30,000 fixed) to the art supplies department. Therefore, art supplies has an apparent annual loss of $10,000 ($100,000 revenue minus $110,000 costs). But careful cost analysis reveals that if the art supplies department were dropped, the reduction in costs would be only $80,000. The $30,000 fixed costs were general bookstore fixed costs allocated to the art supplies department. These fixed costs would continue to be incurred and would not be saved by closing the art supplies department. Look at the differential analysis in Illustration 22.4. Note that the art supplies department has been con-

ILLUSTRATION 22.4
Differential Analysis: Decision Whether to Close a Department

	Art Supplies Department		
	Keep	**Close**	**Differential**
Revenues	$100,000	$ -0-	$100,000
Variable costs	80,000	-0-	80,000
Fixed costs	30,000	30,000	-0-
Net benefit of keeping art supplies department			$20,000

tributing $20,000 ($100,000 revenues − $80,000 variable costs) annually toward covering the fixed costs of the business. Consequently, its elimination could be a costly mistake unless there is a more profitable use for the vacated facilities.

If the company has a profitable alternative use for the vacated facilities, the potential income from that alternative represents an opportunity cost of retaining the product, segment, or customer. Assume, for example, that the bookstore could use the facilities currently occupied by the art supplies department to open a new department to display and sell personal computers, printers, and software. This new department would contribute $30,000 to the bookstore's income.

The relevant costs in the decision to retain the art supplies department are $110,000 ($80,000 of variable manufacturing costs and $30,000 of opportunity cost), while the relevant revenues are still $100,000. Therefore, the bookstore has a net disadvantage in keeping the art supplies department because it loses $10,000 compared to the computer department.

Processing or Selling Joint Products

Objective 6
Use differential analysis to decide whether to sell joint products at the split-off point or process them further.

ARCO
Atlantic-Richfield Company, also called ARCO, is a large oil company that produces oil and other petroleum products.

Sometimes two or more products result from a common raw material or production process; these products are called **joint products**. Companies can process these products further or sell them in their current condition. For instance, when Atlantic-Richfield Company refines crude oil, it produces a wide variety of fuels, solvents, lubricants, and residual petrochemicals.

Management can use differential analysis to decide whether to process a joint product further or to sell it in its present condition. **Joint costs** are those costs incurred up to the point where the joint products split off from each other. These costs are sunk costs and are not considered when deciding whether to process a joint product further before selling it or to sell it in its condition at the split-off point.

The following example illustrates the issue of whether to process or sell joint products. Assume that Pacific Paper, Inc., produces two paper products, A and B, from a common manufacturing process. Each of the products could either be sold in its present form or processed further and sold at a higher price. Data for both products follow:

Product	Selling Price per Unit at Split-Off Point	Cost per Unit of Further Processing	Selling Price per Unit after Further Processing
A	$10	$6	$21
B	12	7	18

The differential revenues and costs of further processing of the two products are as follows:

Product	Differential Revenue of Further Processing	Differential Cost of Further Processing	Net Advantage (Disadvantage) of Further Processing
A	$11	$6	$5
B	6	7	(1)

Based on this analysis, Pacific Paper should process product A further to increase income by $5 per unit sold. The company should not process product B further because that would decrease income by $1 per unit sold.

Companies use this same form of differential analysis to decide whether they should discard their by-products or process them further. **By-products** are additional products resulting from the production of a main product and generally have a small market value compared to the main product. Sometimes companies consider by-products to be waste materials. For example, the bark from trees cut into lumber is a by-product of lumber production. Although a by-product, companies convert this bark into fuel or landscaping material. When the differential revenue of further processing exceeds the differential cost, firms should do further processing. As concerns increase about the effects of waste on the environment, companies find more and more waste materials that can be converted into by-products.

Deciding to Make or Buy

Objective 7
Decide whether to make or buy products using differential analysis.

Managers also apply differential analysis to make-or-buy decisions. A **make-or-buy decision** occurs when management must decide whether to make or purchase a part or material used in manufacturing another product. Management must compare the price paid for a part with the *additional costs* incurred to manufacture the part. When most of the manufacturing costs are fixed and would exist in any case, it is likely to be more economical to make the part rather than buy it.

To illustrate the application of differential analysis to make-or-buy decisions, assume that Small Motor Company manufactures a part costing $6 for use in its toy automobile engines. Cost components are: materials, $3.00; labor, $1.50; fixed overhead costs, $1.05; and variable overhead costs, $0.45. Small could purchase the part for $5.25. Fixed overhead would presumably continue even if the part were purchased. The added costs of manufacturing amount to only $4.95 ($3.00 + $1.50 + $0.45). This amount is 30 cents per unit less than the purchase price of the part. Therefore, manufacturing the part should be continued as shown in the following analysis:

	Make	Buy	Differential
Costs	$4.95	$5.25	$0.30
Net advantage of making			$0.30

In make-or-buy decisions, management also should consider the opportunity cost of not utilizing the space for some other purpose. In the previous example, if the opportunity costs of not using this space in its best alternative use is more than 30 cents per unit times the number of units produced, the part should be purchased.

In some manufacturing situations, firms avoid a portion of fixed costs by buying from an outside source. For example, suppose eliminating a part would reduce production so that a supervisor's salary could be saved. In such a situation, firms should treat these fixed costs the same as variable costs in the analysis because they would be relevant costs.

Sometimes the cost to manufacture may be only slightly less than the cost of purchasing the part or material. Then management should place considerable weight on other factors such as the competency of existing personnel to undertake manufacturing the part or material, the availability of working capital, and the cost of any loans that may be necessary.

Applying Differential Analysis to Quality

Objective 8
Use differential analysis to decide whether to improve product quality.

High quality is essential to success in a competitive environment. Therefore, companies use differential analysis to make decisions about the quality of their products.

Assume Erie Waters produces bottled water. The variable cost of a case (12 one-liter bottles) is as follows:

Water and bottles	$2.00
Inspection and rework costs	1.00
All other variable costs	3.00
Total variable cost per case	$6.00

In addition, the company has $150,000 of fixed costs per year.

The company inspects the product at various stages. When inspectors find the water is below standard or the bottles have defects, production workers replace the water and/or the bottles. The cost of inspecting the product and replacing water and/or bottles averages $1.00 per case, and is shown as inspection and rework costs.

Management of Erie Waters is concerned about product quality. Despite the inspection just noted, management has learned that dissatisfied customers are switching to competitive products. Management is considering purchasing a high-quality water product. This product would increase water and bottle costs to $2.50 per case while decreasing inspection and rework costs to $.40 per case. All other variable costs would remain at $3.00 per case. Erie Waters would sell this water for $8.00 per case. If the high-quality water is purchased, Erie Waters expects to sell 100,000 cases of water this year at $8.00 per case. If Erie continues to use the current low-quality water, the company expects to sell 90,000 cases of water this year at $8.00 per case. Fixed costs are $150,000 per year whether the company buys high-quality water or low-quality water. Should Erie Waters buy the high-quality water? We compare the two alternatives in Illustration 22.5.

An Accounting Perspective

Business Insight The 1950s and 1960s were boom periods for manufacturing companies in the United States. As one of the few industrial countries left intact after World War II, the United States had little competition from manufacturers in other countries. By the 1970s, countries such as Japan had made a comeback and were making inroads in steel, automobiles, and electronics.

Hewlett-Packard Company is a leading manufacturer of electronic products and systems for customers all over the world. In the early 1980s, a Hewlett-Packard study stated that its lowest-quality Japanese supplier was better than its highest-quality U.S. supplier. By the end of the 1980s, U.S. industry realized that without a substantial improvement in quality, it could not compete in worldwide markets.

Illustration 22.5
Decision Whether to Improve Quality

	Low-Quality Water (90,000 Cases)	High-Quality Water (100,000 Cases)
Revenue at $8.00 per case	$720,000	$800,000
Water and bottles at $2.00 per case for low quality and $2.50 per case for high quality	(180,000)	(250,000)
Inspection and rework at $1.00 per case for low quality and $0.40 per case for high quality	(90,000)	(40,000)
All other variable costs at $3.00 per case	(270,000)	(300,000)
Fixed costs	(150,000)	(150,000)
Net income	$ 30,000	$ 60,000

A Broader Perspective

Differential Analysis in Sports

The Los Angeles Kings hockey club acquired Wayne Gretzky from the Edmonton Oilers in exchange for $15 million, a young star, and three future draft choices. Although the cost was high, the Kings needed a big attraction in the highly competitive Los Angeles sports market that includes the Lakers, Rams, Raiders, and two major college sports teams. The Kings' management believed acquiring Gretzky would be profitable for the club based on the differential revenues from increased attendance and media coverage compared to the differential costs caused by hiring Gretzky.

When the San Francisco Giants acquired Barry Bonds, many people in the baseball world wondered if it was a wise financial decision. The year after acquiring Bonds, the Giants became a pennant contender, and attendance at their games nearly doubled compared to the previous year. The differential costs of acquiring Bonds appear to have been justified.

Sports teams routinely face make-or-buy decisions concerning their players. Some teams, such as the New York Yankees, have extensive farm systems. They usually develop players by bringing them up through the system. Teams also buy players by waiting until young players have proven themselves with other teams, then acquiring them as the Giants did with Barry Bonds and the Los Angeles Kings did with Wayne Gretzky.

Erie Waters should purchase the high-quality water because it increases net income from $30,000 to $60,000 per year. In addition, a high-quality product improves the company's prospects for maintaining or even increasing its market share in years to come. Many companies have learned the hard way that letting quality slip creates a bad reputation that is hard to overcome.

The focus of this chapter has been short-term decision making. Part of decision making involves planning through the use of budgets. The topic of Chapter 23 is budgeting—an important tool of company management.

Understanding The Learning Objectives

Objective 1
Compare and contrast contribution margin income statements to traditional income statements.

- The contribution margin format separates fixed costs from variable costs; the traditional method does not.
- The contribution margin format reports contribution margin; the traditional method reports gross margin. In a manufacturing company:

  Contribution margin = Revenue − Variable manufacturing costs − Variable nonmanufacturing costs

  Gross margin = Revenue − Cost of goods sold (where cost of goods sold = Variable manufacturing cost of goods sold + Fixed manufacturing cost of goods sold)

Objective 2
Explain differential analysis and describe its components.

- Differential analysis involves analyzing the different costs and benefits that would arise from alternative solutions to a particular situation.
- The components are: (1) differential revenue, the difference in revenue between two alternatives; and (2) differential cost or expense, the difference between relevant costs for two alternatives.

Objective 3
Make pricing decisions using differential analysis.

- In selecting a price for a product, the goal is to select the price at which total future revenues exceed total future variable costs by the greatest amount or, in other words, the price that results in the greatest total contribution margin.

Objective 4
Use differential analysis to decide whether to accept or reject special orders.

- Variable costs set a floor for the selling price in cost analyses. Such pricing should be appraised concerning their long-range effects on company and industry price structures. In the long run, full costs must be covered.

Objective 5
Decide whether to eliminate or add product lines or segments of the business using differential analysis.

- Costs must be reclassified as those that would be changed by the elimination and those that would not. In effect, one must simply assume elimination and compare the reduction in revenues with the eliminated costs.

Objective 6
Use differential analysis to decide whether to sell joint products at the split-off point or process them further.

- Joint costs are those costs incurred up to the point where the joint products split off from each other. These costs are sunk costs in deciding whether to process a joint product further before selling it or to sell it in its condition at the split-off point.

Objective 7
Decide whether to make or buy products using differential analysis.

- A make-or-buy decision concerns whether to manufacture or purchase a part or material used in manufacturing another product. The price that would be paid for the part if it were purchased is compared with the additional costs that would be incurred if the part were manufactured.

Objective 8
Use differential analysis to decide whether to improve product quality.

- High quality is essential to success in a competitive environment. Therefore, companies use differential analysis to make decisions about the quality of their products.

Demonstration Problem

National Express, an international delivery service, is considering eliminating operations in Eastern Europe. If the company dropped the East European market, it would lose revenues of $1,000,000 annually. Management assigns costs of $1,200,000 ($800,000 variable and $400,000 fixed) to the East European market. Therefore, the East European market has an apparent annual loss of $200,000 per year ($1,000,000 revenue minus $1,200,000 costs). Careful cost analysis reveals that if East European operations were dropped, the reduction in costs would be only $800,000 of variable and $250,000 of fixed costs. The remaining $150,000 of fixed costs were general fixed costs the company allocated to the East European market. These costs would continue to be incurred and would not be saved by shutting down the East European market.

Solution to Demonstration Problem

The differential analysis for National Express's analysis of its East European operations is as follows:

	East European Operations		
	Keep	**Eliminate**	**Differential**
Revenues	$1,000,000	$ –0–	$1,000,000
Variable costs	800,000	–0–	800,000
Fixed costs	400,000	150,000	250,000
Benefit (loss) of keeping East European operations open			$ (50,000)

Elimination of the East European market is justified according to this analysis. National Express would lose $1,000,000 of revenues but would save $1,050,000 costs ($800,000 + $250,000), resulting in a $50,000 benefit of closing the operations (or a $50,000 differential loss by keeping the operations open).

New Terms

By-products Additional products resulting from the production of a main product. By-products generally have a small market value compared to the main product. *799*

Committed fixed costs Costs relating to the basic facilities and organizational structure that a company must have to continue operations. *794*

Differential analysis An analysis of the different costs and benefits that would arise from alternative solutions to a particular problem. *792*

Differential cost or expense The difference between the amounts of relevant costs for two alternatives. *792*

Differential revenue The difference between the amounts of relevant revenues for two alternatives. *792*

Discretionary fixed costs Fixed costs subject to management control from year to year; an example is advertising expense. *794*

Joint costs Those costs incurred up to the point where the joint products split off from each other. *798*

Joint products Two or more products resulting from a common raw material or production process. *798*

Make-or-buy decision A decision concerning whether to manufacture or purchase a part or material used in manufacturing another product. *799*

Opportunity cost The potential benefit that is forgone from not following the next best alternative course of action. *795*

Relevant revenues or costs Revenues or costs that will differ in the future depending on which alternative course of action is selected. *792*

Sunk cost Past costs that are not relevant in decision making because they have already been incurred. *793*

Self Test

True-False

Indicate whether each of the following statements is true or false.

1. Opportunity costs are recorded in the accounting records because they are the costs of not following a certain alternative.
2. Only variable costs can be differential costs.
3. Contribution margin is often more valuable to management than gross margin when making decisions.
4. It is important to estimate sunk costs for decision making.
5. The decision whether to sell at the split-off point or process further is one that a petroleum company might make.
6. A restaurant's chef must decide whether to make soup from dry soup mix purchased at a store or to make the soup from scratch using vegetables, meats, and pasta. This decision is an example of a make-or-buy decision.

Multiple Choice

Select the best answer for each of the following questions.

1. Differential analysis is best described by which of the following statements:
   - **a.** Determines the difference in revenues between two alternatives.
   - **b.** Analyzes opportunity costs.
   - **c.** Determines the difference between relevant costs for two alternatives.
   - **d.** Analyzes future revenues and costs that differ depending on the course of action selected.
2. In selecting a price for a product using differential analysis, which of the following decisions should be made?
   - **a.** The highest price should always be selected.
   - **b.** The price that will result in the greatest total contribution margin, assuming fixed costs are the same for each price-quantity combination, should be selected.
   - **c.** Total future revenues should exceed total future variable and fixed costs.
   - **d.** All of the above.
3. Which of the following decisions involve differential analysis?
   - **a.** The decision to close a segment of a business.
   - **b.** The decision by a record store to add videotapes to its product line.
   - **c.** The decision by a university to drop its intercollegiate football program.
   - **d.** All of the above.
4. Assume Mikey Shoe Company is considering making special shoes just for Olympic athletes. In making this decision, how would you categorize the salary of the president of Mikey?
   - **a.** Differential variable cost.
   - **b.** Differential revenue.
   - **c.** Discretionary fixed cost.
   - **d.** Committed fixed cost.

Now turn to page 810 to check your answers.

Questions

1. Identify types of decisions that can be made using differential analysis.
2. What is a committed fixed cost? Give some examples.
3. What is a discretionary fixed cost? Give some examples.
4. Give an example of a fixed cost that might be considered committed for one company and discretionary for another.
5. What is the disadvantage of a company having all committed fixed costs? Explain.
6. What is an opportunity cost? Give some examples.
7. What essential feature distinguishes the contribution margin income statement from the traditional income statement?
8. **Real World Question** Give an example of a make-or-buy decision that you have made or someone you know has made.
9. **Real World Question** Give an example in which your campus bookstore replaces one of its departments with another it currently does not have. (For example, it stops selling magazines and starts selling cameras.) What revenues and costs would be differential?
10. **Real World Question** Assume that McDonald's, of McDonald's fast-food restaurants, currently buys its french fries from agricultural growers and food processors. In doing so, McDonald's has decided to buy the materials for its french fries instead of "make" them. (Assume that making french fries includes growing the potatoes.) What factors would go into McDonald's decision to buy instead of make french fries?

The Coca-Cola Company

11. **Real World Question** Refer to The Coca-Cola Company's financial statements in the annual report booklet. Does Coca-Cola use the traditional or contribution margin format in its income statement?
12. **Real World Question** Suppose that Wal-Mart, one of the fastest growing companies in the world, were to close one of its stores. Which differential revenues and costs would be affected by that decision?

Exercises

Exercise 22–1
Prepare income statements using traditional and contribution margin formats (L.O. 1)

The following data are for Gore Company for the year ended December 31, 1996:

Costs:	
Direct materials	$180,000
Direct labor	260,000
Manufacturing overhead:	
Variable	90,000
Fixed	180,000
Sales commissions (variable)	50,000
Sales salaries (fixed)	40,000
Administrative expenses (fixed)	70,000
Selling price per unit	$20
Units produced and sold	60,000

Assume direct materials and direct labor are variable costs. Prepare a contribution margin income statement and a traditional income statement.

Exercises 22–2
Identify relevant and differential revenues and costs (L.O. 2)

Assume you had invested $500 in a lawn mower to set up a lawn mowing business for the summer. During the first week, you could choose either to mow the grounds at a housing development for $700 or to help paint a garage for $680. Each job would take one week. You cannot do both. You would incur additional costs of $80 for lawn mowing and $40 for garage painting. These costs include $30 under each alternative for transportation to the job. Prepare a schedule showing the net benefit or advantage of selecting one alternative over the other.

Exercises 22–3
Pricing decisions (L.O. 3)

The marketing department of Starburst Coffee Shoppe estimates the following monthly demand for espresso in these four price-quantity relationships:

	Demand
1	5,000 cups at $1 per cup
2	4,000 cups at $1.25 per cup
3	3,000 cups at $1.50 per cup
4	2,000 cups at $1.75 per cup

The fixed costs of $3,000 per month are not affected by the different price-volume alternatives. Variable costs are $0.25 per cup. What price should Starburst Coffee Shoppe set for espresso?

Exercise 22–4
Decide whether to accept or reject a special order (L.O. 4)

Raiders Corporation is operating at 80% of capacity, which means it produces 16,000 units. Variable cost is $100 per unit. Wholesaler A offers to buy 4,000 additional units at $120 per unit. Wholesaler B proposes to buy 3,000 additional units at $140 per unit. Which offer, if either, should Raiders Corporation accept?

Exercise 22–5
Decide whether to keep a product line (L.O. 5)

Analysis of Helene Company's citrus hair conditioner reveals that it is losing $10,000 annually. The company sells 5,000 units of citrus hair conditioner each year at $20 per unit. Variable costs are $12 per unit. None of the company's fixed costs would be saved if the citrus hair conditioner were eliminated. What would be the increase or decrease in company net income if citrus hair condition were eliminated?

Exercise 22–6
Decide whether to keep or eliminate a department (L.O. 5)

The luggage department of McMacy Company has revenues of $2,000,000; variable expenses of $500,000; direct fixed costs of $1,000,000; and allocated, indirect fixed costs of $600,000 in an average year. If the company eliminates this department, what would be the effect on net income?

Exercise 22–7
Decide whether to process joint products further (L.O. 6)

Viking Company manufactures two joint products. At the split-off point, they have sales values of:

Product 1	$9 per unit
Product 2	6 per unit

After further processing, the company can sell them for $18 and $8, respectively. Product 1 costs $6 per unit to process further and Product 2 costs $4 to process further. Should further processing be done on either or both of these products? Why or why not?

Exercise 22–8
Decide whether to make or buy a part (L.O. 7)

Ortez Corporation currently is manufacturing 80,000 units per year of a part used in its final product. The cost of producing this part is $50 per unit. The variable portion of this cost consists of direct materials of $30, direct labor of $15, and variable manufacturing overhead of $3. The company could earn $100,000 per year from the space now used to manufacture this part. Assuming equal quality and availability, what is the maximum price per unit that Ortez Corporation should pay to buy the part rather than make it? (The total fixed costs would not be affected by this decision.)

Exercise 22–9
Decide whether to purchase high-quality materials (L.O. 8)

Diego Company buys strawberries and produces strawberry jam. The variable cost of a case of strawberry jam is as follows:

Materials (strawberries and jars)	$ 5.00
Inspection and rework costs	2.00
All other variable costs	4.00
Total variable cost per case	$11.00

In addition, the company has $500,000 of fixed costs per year.

The company inspects the product at various stages. The cost of inspecting the product and replacing jam and/or jars averages $2.00 per case, shown as in the inspection and rework costs.

Management is considering purchasing high-quality strawberries. This would increase materials costs to $6.00 per case, while decreasing inspection and rework costs to $1.00 per case. All other costs would remain at $4.00 per case for variable costs and $500,000 for fixed costs whether or not the high-quality strawberries were purchased. Diego's jam sells for $20 per case. If the high-quality strawberries were purchased, the company could sell 100,000 cases of jam this year at $20 per case. If the company continued to use the current low-quality berries, it could sell 80,000 cases of jam this year at $20 per case.

Should Diego purchase the high-quality strawberries?

PROBLEMS

Problem 22–1
Prepare income statements using contribution margin and traditional formats; discuss differences (L.O. 1)

Gopherit Company has the following selected data for the current year:

Sales (10,000 units)	$180,000
Direct materials	60,000
Direct labor costs	20,000
Variable manufacturing overhead	7,000
Fixed manufacturing overhead	15,000
Variable selling and administrative expenses	5,000
Fixed selling and administrative expenses	30,000

The company produced and sold 10,000 units. Direct materials and direct labor are variable costs.

Required

a. Prepare an income statement for the current year using the contribution margin format.

b. Prepare an income statement for the current year using the traditional format.

c. What additional information do you learn from the contribution margin format?

Problem 22–2
Determine the most profitable price-quantity combination (L.O. 3)

A-Roma Company is introducing a new coffee in its stores and must decide what price to set for the coffee beans. An estimated demand schedule for the product follows:

Price	One-Pound Units Demanded
$ 5.	40,000
6.	36,000
7.	28,000
8.	24,000
9.	18,000
10.	15,000

Estimated costs follow:

Variable manufacturing costs	$2 per unit
Fixed manufacturing costs	$20,000 per year
Variable selling and administrative costs	$1 per unit
Fixed selling and administrative costs	$10,000 per year

Required

a. Prepare a schedule showing management the total revenue, total cost, and total profit or loss for each selling price.

b. Which price do you recommend to the management of A-Roma? Explain your answer.

Problem 22–3
Decide whether to accept or reject a special order (L.O. 4)

Sights 'R' Us operates tour boats. Its predicted operations for the year are as follows:

Sales (1,000 tours per year)	$400,000
Costs:	
Variable	$250 per tour
Fixed	$100,000 per year

The company has received a request to offer 100 tours for $300 each. Sights 'R' Us has plenty of capacity to do these tours in addition to its regular business. Doing these tours would not affect the company's regular sales or its fixed costs.

Required

a. Should the company do the special tours for $300 per tour?

b. What is the effect of the decision on the company's operating profit?

Problem 22–4
Decide whether to keep or eliminate a product line (L.O. 5)

Following are sales and other operating data for the three products made and sold by Hillary's Pharmaceuticals Company:

	Product			
	A	B	C	Total
Sales	$300,000	$150,000	$100,000	$550,000
Manufacturing costs:				
Fixed	$ 30,000	$ 10,000	$ 30,000	$ 70,000
Variable	140,000	110,000	50,000	300,000
Selling and administrative expenses:				
Fixed	10,000	10,000	6,000	26,000
Variable	20,000	10,000	15,000	45,000
Total costs	$200,000	$140,000	$101,000	$441,000
Net income (loss)	$100,000	$ 10,000	$ (1,000)	$109,000

In view of the net loss for product C, Hillary's management is considering dropping that product. All variable costs are direct costs and would be eliminated if product C were dropped. Fixed costs are indirect costs; no fixed costs would be eliminated. Assume that the space used to produce product C would be left idle.

Required Would you recommend the elimination of product C? Give supporting computations.

Problem 22–5
Decide whether to process further or sell joint products (L.O. 6)

Ecowise Timber Company produces lumber. The company has two grades of lumber at the split-off point, A and B. Grade A sells for $2 per board foot and Grade B sells for $1 per board foot. This lumber is suitable for framing and most exterior work but not for the interior of buildings. Either grade can be further processed to make it suitable for interior work at a cost of $0.60 per board foot. After this further processing, the firm can sell Grade A lumber for $2.75 per board foot and Grade B for $1.50 per board foot.

Required

Would you recommend the company sell the lumber at the split-off point or process it further to make it suitable for interior work? Explain and give supporting computations.

Problem 22–6
Decide whether to make or buy a product (L.O. 7)

Hit the Road Enterprises, a skateboard manufacturer, is currently operating at 70% capacity and producing about 10,000 units a year. To use more capacity, the manager has been considering the research and development department's suggestion that the company manufacture its own wheels.

Currently the company purchases wheels from a supplier at a unit price of $20. (Each unit is a set of wheels for a skateboard.) Estimates show the company can manufacture its own wheels at $10 for direct materials costs and $4 for direct labor cost per unit. The variable factory overhead is $1 per unit. The company's accountants would probably allocate another $6 per unit to the wheels.

Required

a. Should Hit the Road make or buy the wheels?

b. Suppose Hit the Road could rent out the factory space needed to make the wheels for $10,000 a month. How would this affect your decision in Part (**a**), if at all?

Problem 22–7
Decide whether to purchase high-quality materials (L.O. 8)

Tech-Now, Inc., purchases calculator components and assembles them into handheld calculators. The variable cost of one Model T–21 is as follows:

Materials	$20
Inspection and rework costs	4
All other variable costs	10
Total variable cost per case	$34

In addition, this product incurs $10,000,000 of fixed costs per year.

The company inspects the product at various stages. The cost of inspecting the product and replacing components averages $4 per calculator, shown as the inspection and rework costs.

Management is considering purchasing better components that would both increase quality and expand the calculator's capacity. These new components would increase materials costs to $25 per calculator, but would decrease inspection and rework costs to $3 per calculator. All other variables costs would remain at $10 per calculator. Fixed costs would remain at $10,000,000 per year.

Tech-Now currently sells each T–21 calculator for $50 at a volume of 1 million calculators per year. Management believes it can increase the price of the calculator (which would now be called the T–21 STAR) to $60 per calculator because of its increased capability. Sales volume would remain at 1 million calculators per year for the improved T–21 STAR. Should Tech-Now purchase the better components?

ALTERNATE PROBLEMS

Problem 22–1A
Compare contribution margin to traditional format income statements (L.O. 1)

The following data are for Havana Company for the current year:

Sales (20,000 units)	$375,000
Direct materials	135,000
Direct labor cost	45,000
Variable manufacturing overhead	13,500
Fixed manufacturing overhead	18,000
Variable selling and administrative expenses	22,500
Fixed selling and administrative expenses	75,000

The company produced and sold 20,000 units.

Required

a. Prepare an income statement for the current year using the contribution margin format.

b. Prepare an income statement for the current year using the traditional format.

c. What additional information does the contribution margin format provide compared to the traditional format?

Problem 22–2A
Determine the most profitable price-quantity combination (L.O. 3)

The Nets Company is introducing a new product and must decide its price. An estimated demand schedule for the product is as follows:

Price	Units Demanded
$ 5	20,000
6	18,000
7	14,000
8	12,000
9	9,000
10	8,000

Estimated costs are as follows:

Variable manufacturing costs	$2.20 per unit
Fixed manufacturing costs	$20,000 per year
Variable selling and administrative costs	$1.00 per unit
Fixed selling and administrative costs	$5,000 per year

Required

a. Prepare a schedule showing the total revenue, total cost, and total profit or loss for each selling price.

b. Which price should Nets select? Explain?

Problem 22–3A
Decide whether to keep or eliminate a product line (L.O. 5)

Following are sales and other operating data for the three products made and sold by Yuppie Enterprises:

	Product			
	A	B	C	Total
Sales	$300,000	$180,000	$480,000	$960,000
Manufacturing costs:				
Fixed	$ 30,000	$ 50,000	$ 60,000	$140,000
Variable	240,000	70,000	268,000	578,000
Selling and administrative expenses:				
Fixed	10,000	60,000	20,000	90,000
Variable	5,000	10,000	12,000	27,000
Total costs	$285,000	$190,000	$360,000	$835,000
Net income (loss)	$ 15,000	$ (10,000)	$120,000	$125,000

In view of the net loss shown for product B, company management is considering dropping that product. All variable costs are direct costs and would be eliminated if product B were dropped; all fixed costs are indirect costs and would not be eliminated. Assume that the space used to produce product B would be left idle.

Required Would you recommend the elimination of product B? Give supporting computations.

Problem 22–4A
Decide whether to make or buy a product (L.O. 7)

Surf Enterprises, a wind sailing board manufacturer, is currently operating at 70% capacity and producing about 20,000 units a year. To use more capacity, the manager has been considering the research and development department's suggestion that Surf Enterprises manufacture its own sails. Currently Surf purchases sails from a supplier at a unit price of $50. Estimates show that Surf Enterprises can manufacture its own sails for a $20 direct materials cost and a $16 direct labor cost per unit. The variable factory overhead is $4 per sail. The company's accountants would allocate fixed manufacturing overhead of $15 per sail to the sail production.

Required

a. Should Surf Enterprises make or buy the sails?

b. Suppose that Surf Enterprises could rent out the part of the factory that would otherwise be used for sail manufacturing for $4,000 a month. How would this affect the decision in Part (**a**)?

Problem 22–5A
Decide whether to purchase high-quality materials (L.O. 8)

On-Ice Company produces and sells ice cream for ice cream shops. Management is considering purchasing better ingredients. The variable cost of producing a gallon of ice cream is as follows:

Materials (cream, containers, etc.)	$1.40
Inspection and replacement costs	.40
All other variable costs	.70
Total variable cost per gallon	$2.50

In addition, the company has $1,000,000 of fixed costs per year.

The company inspects the product at various stages. The cost of inspecting the product and replacing ice cream averages $0.40 per gallon, shown as the inspection and replacement costs.

Management is considering purchasing high-quality ingredients, in particular, high-quality dairy products. These high-quality ingredients would increase materials costs to $1.80 per gallon, but would decrease inspection and replacement costs to $0.30 per gallon. All other costs would remain at $0.70 per gallon for variable costs and $1,000,000 for fixed costs whether or not the high-quality ingredients are purchased. Ice cream is sold for $4 per gallon. If the high-quality ingredients are purchased, the company expects to sell 1,200,000 gallons of ice cream this year at $4 per gallon. If the company continues to use the current low-quality ingredients, the company expects to sell 1,000,000 gallons of ice cream at $3.50 per gallon. Should On-Ice Company buy the high-quality ingredients for its ice cream?

BEYOND THE NUMBERS—CRITICAL THINKING

Business Decision Case 22–1
Determine whether a department should be closed (L.O. 5)

Prior to 1997, Kahn Wholesalers Company had not kept department income statements. To achieve better management control, the company decided to install department-by-department accounts. At the end of 1997, the new accounts showed that although as a whole the business was profitable, the dry goods department had a substantial loss. The following income statement for the dry goods department reports on operations for 1997:

KAHN WHOLESALERS COMPANY
Dry Goods Department
Partial Income Statement for 1997

Sales		$600,000
Cost of goods sold		400,000
Gross margin		$200,000
Costs:		
Payroll, direct labor, and supervision	$60,000	
Commissions of sales staff[a]	30,000	
Rent[b]	20,000	
Insurance on inventory	10,000	
Depreciation[c]	40,000	
Administration and general office[d]	40,000	
Interest for inventory carrying costs[e]	5,000	
Total costs		205,000
Net income (loss)		$ (5,000)

[a] All sales staff are compensated on straight commission, at a uniform 6% of all sales.
[b] Rent charged to departments on a square-foot basis. The company rents an entire building, and the dry goods department occupies 15% of the building.
[c] Depreciation is 8.5% of the cost of the departmental equipment.
[d] Allocated on basis of departmental sales as a fraction of total company sales.
[e] Based on average inventory quantity multiplied by the company's borrowing rate for three-month loans.

Analysis of these results has led management to suggest closing the dry goods department. Members of the management team agree that keeping the dry goods department is not essential to maintaining good customer relations and supporting the rest of the company's business. In other words, eliminating the dry goods department is expected to have no effect on the amount of business done by the other departments.

Required

Prepare a written report recommending whether or not Kahn should close the dry goods department. Explain why. State your assumptions.

Business Decision Case 22–2
Differential cost analysis in a service organization (L.O. 2–4)

After working for a software company for several years, Santi and Gary quit their jobs and set up their own consulting firm called Creative Software, Inc. Major customers include corporate, professional, and government organizations that are setting up information networks.

The cost per billable hour of service at the company's normal volume of 3,000 billable hours per month follows. (A billable hour is one hour billed to a client.)

Average cost per hour billed to client:		
Variable labor—consultants	$50	
Variable overhead, including supplies and clerical support	20	
Fixed overhead, including allowance for unbilled hours	80	
		$150
Marketing and administrative costs per billable hour (all fixed)		40
Total hourly cost		$190

Treat each of the following questions independently. Unless given otherwise, the regular fee per hour is $200.

Required

a. How many hours must the firm bill per month to break even? (You may need to refer to Chapter 21 to answer this question.)

b. Market research estimates that a fee increase to $250 per hour would decrease monthly volume to 2,000 hours. The accounting department estimates that fixed overhead costs would be $120 per hour, while variable cost per hour would remain unchanged. What effect would a fee increase have on profits?

c. Assume Creative Software is operating at its normal volume of 3,000 hours per month. It has received a special request from one of its long-time customers to provide services on a special-order basis. Because of the long-term nature of the contract (four months) and the magnitude (1,000 hours per month), the customer believes a fee reduction is in order. Creative Software has a capacity limitation of 4,000 hours per month. Fixed costs would not change if the firm accepts the special order. What is the lowest fee Creative Software would be willing to charge?

Business Decision Case 22–3
Writing Assignment

Refer to "A Broader Perspective" on page 801. In a memorandum to your instructor, identify which costs and revenues you think would be differential for a sports team acquiring a major star like Bonds or Gretzky. The heading of the memorandum should contain the date, to whom it is written, from whom, and the subject matter.

Group Project 22–4
Determine effects of closing a department

In teams of two or three students, visit a local department store and imagine the types of costs that it would save if it closed a significant department (for example, the housewares department). List the types of costs that would be saved, but do not attempt to assign numbers to those costs. For example, would rent be saved? Would security be saved? What about taxes on inventories? Consider the effects of closing the department on the people who work there. As a team, write a memorandum describing the costs saved and the effects of closing a department in a local department store. The heading of the memorandum should contain the date, to whom it is written, from whom, and the subject matter.

Answers to Self-Test

True-False

1. **False.** Opportunity costs are not recorded in the accounting records. However, opportunity costs are relevant costs in many decisions because they represent real sacrifices that come about because one alternative is chosen instead of another.
2. **False.** Fixed costs also can be differential costs. For example, the differential cost between operating at a production level of 40,000 units compared to 60,000 units might include increases in both variable and fixed costs.
3. **True.** The contribution margin is often more important to management because it is needed to calculate break-even points and make decisions.
4. **False.** Sunk costs are not relevant for decision making.
5. **True.** Petroleum companies make this decision; for example, they might decide whether to sell crude oil or refine it further into gasoline or other petroleum products.
6. **True.** A decision to make the soup from scratch is a make decision; deciding to make the soup from purchased mix is a buy decision.

MULTIPLE-CHOICE

1. **d.** Differential analysis estimates future revenues and costs that differ depending on the course of action.
2. **b.** This is the best answer. Assuming fixed costs remain the same for each price-quantity combination, maximizing the total contribution margin maximizes net income. We did not choose (**c**) because it does not result in net income maximization, merely that net income be greater than zero.
3. **d.** All of these decisions involve differential analysis.
4. **d.** The president's salary would be a committed fixed cost. (Those who believe the salary should be a discretionary fixed cost have a good point.)

VIII

Planning and Control

Part Outline

A Manager's Perspective

Jim Wardlaw

Regional Vice-President and

General Manager

Atlanta Region

The Coca-Cola Company

I began my career with The Coca-Cola Company as an account manager supplying product to local stores and restaurants in my territory. I then spent some time as Area Marketing Manager and Area Sales Development Manager before reaching my current position.

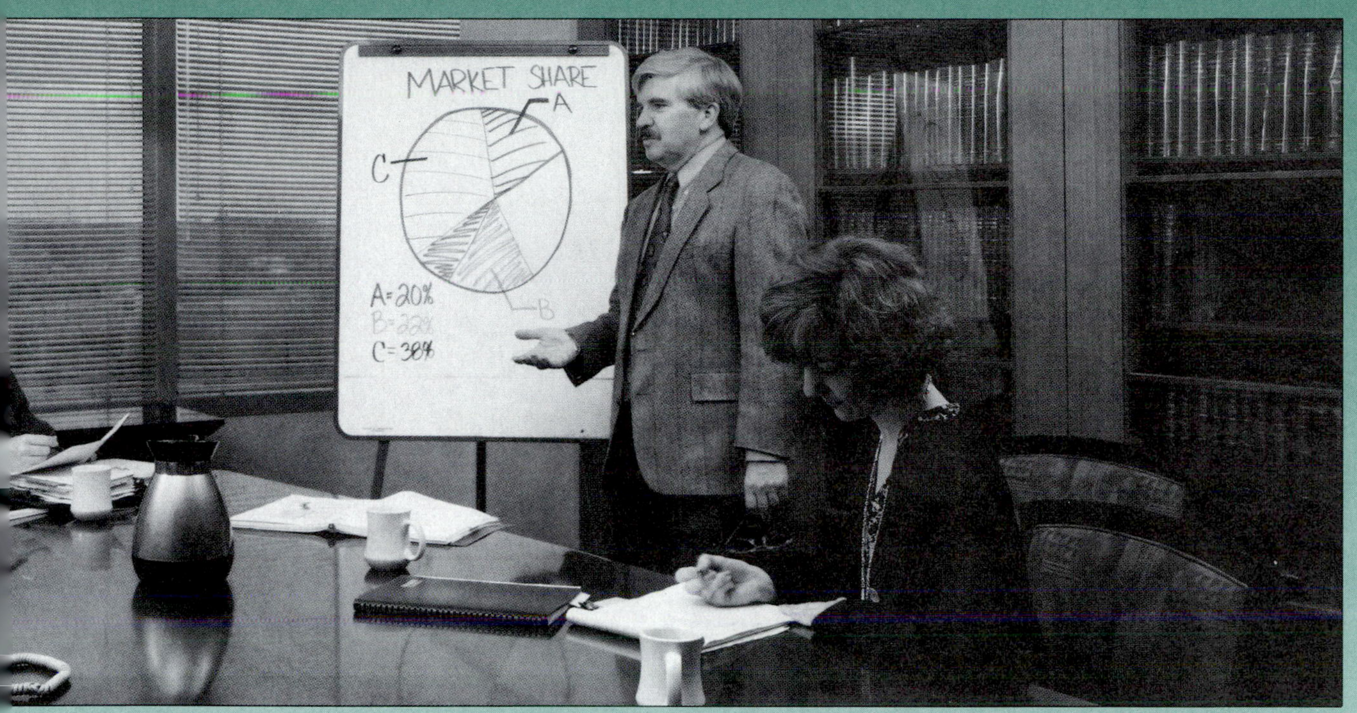

As Regional Vice President and General Manager, I oversee the administration and operations of a region spanning 150,000 square miles, and one of my primary objectives is to maintain a successful return on investment. I manage three division vice presidents and four regional vice presidents, and I try to spend about sixty percent of my time working with account managers who call on retail trade accounts.

In fact, a lot of my job is providing training and inspiration. We hold monthly meetings with each division to assess sales and provide motivation for the account managers. I also monitor daily key indicator reports to track sales performance in the region.

Behind increasing sales, a strong emphasis on training is one of my most important objectives. For example, Coca-Cola recently instituted a six-week training program for new account managers. The program brings new members of the sales team up to speed on the company and sales techniques, then puts them out in the field. Our sales base is constantly expanding, and we're starting to call on different buyers, so we need ongoing training to stay competitive.

All of this training helps the region achieve its number one objective—increasing sales and making the "bottom line." Sales for each division are closely monitored, and we measure employees' performances against the sales budget established for the region.

23

Budgeting for Planning and Control

In managing your personal finances, you may prepare a written plan of your anticipated cash inflows and outflows. In fact, financial advisors often recommend that we prepare a written plan of cash inflows and outflows, then—here is the hard part—follow it. Such a written plan is a budget.

Companies prepare budgets to plan for and then control their revenues (inflows) and expenses (outflows). Failure to prepare a budget could lead to significant cash flow problems or even financial disaster for a company. In fact, one of the leading causes of failure in small businesses is failing to plan and control operations through the use of budgets.

This chapter first provides a conceptual foundation for budgeting. Then we describe and illustrate a master budget. The chapter concludes with special topics relating to budgeting.

Learning Objectives

After studying this chapter, you should be able to:

1. Define a budget and name several kinds of budgets.
2. List several benefits of a budget.
3. List five general principles of budgeting.
4. Prepare a planned operating budget and its supporting budgets, such as the sales budget, production and purchases budgets, and other expense budgets.
5. Prepare flexible operating budgets.
6. Prepare a financial budget and its supporting budgets.

The Budget—For Planning and Control

Time and money are scarce resources to all individuals and organizations; the efficient and effective use of these resources requires planning. Planning alone, however, is insufficient. Control is also necessary to ensure that plans actually are carried out. A budget is a tool that managers use to plan and control the use of scarce resources. A **budget** is a plan showing the company's objectives and how management intends to acquire and use resources to attain those objectives.

Companies, nonprofit organizations, and governmental units use many different types of budgets. *Responsibility budgets*, discussed in Chapter 25, are designed to judge the performance of an individual segment or manager. *Capital budgets*, discussed in Chapter 26, evaluate long-term capital projects such as the addition of equipment or the relocation of a plant. This chapter examines the **master budget,** which consists of a planned operating budget and a financial budget. The **planned operating budget** helps to plan future earnings and results in a projected income statement. The **financial budget** helps management plan the financing of assets and results in a projected balance sheet.

Purposes of Budgets

Objective 1
Define a budget and name several kinds of budgets.

Objective 2
List several benefits of a budget.

The budgeting process involves planning for future profitability, because earning a reasonable return on resources used is a primary company objective. A company must devise some method to deal with the uncertainty of the future. A company that does no planning whatsoever chooses to deal with the future by default and can react to events only as they occur. Most businesses, however, devise a blueprint for the actions they will take given the foreseeable events that may occur.

A budget: (1) shows management's operating plans for the coming periods; (2) formalizes management's plans in quantitative terms; (3) forces all levels of management to think ahead, anticipate results, and take action to remedy possible poor results; and (4) may motivate individuals to strive to achieve stated goals.

Companies can use budget-to-actual comparisons to evaluate individual performance. For instance, the standard variable cost of producing a personal computer at IBM is a budget figure. This figure can be compared with the actual cost of producing personal computers to help evaluate the performance of the personal computer production managers and employees who produce personal computers. Chapter 24 illustrates this type of comparison.

Many other benefits result from the preparation and use of budgets. For example: (1) businesses can better coordinate their activities; (2) managers become aware of other managers' plans; (3) employees become more cost conscious and try to conserve resources; (4) the company reviews its organization plan and changes it when necessary; and (5) managers foster a vision that otherwise might not be developed.

The planning process that results in a formal budget provides an opportunity for various levels of management to think through and commit future plans to writing. In addition, a properly prepared budget allows management to follow the management-by-exception principle by devoting attention to results that deviate significantly from planned levels. For all these reasons, a budget must clearly reflect the expected results.

Considerations in Preparing a Budget

Failing to budget because of the uncertainty of the future is a poor excuse for not budgeting. In fact, the less stable the conditions, the more necessary and desirable is budgeting, although the process becomes more difficult. Obviously, stable operating conditions permit greater reliance on past experience as a basis for budgeting. Remember, however, that budgets involve more than a company's past results. Budgets also consider a company's future plans and express expected activities. As a result, budgeted performance is more useful than past performance as a basis for judging actual results.

A budget should describe management's assumptions relating to: (1) the state of the economy over the planning horizon; (2) plans for adding, deleting, or changing product lines; (3) the nature of the industry's competition; and (4) the effects of existing or possible government regulations. If these assumptions change during the budget period, management should analyze the effects of the changes and include this in an evaluation of performance based on actual results.

Budgets are quantitative plans for the future. However, they are based mainly on past experience adjusted for future expectations. Thus, accounting data related to the past play an important part in budget preparation. The accounting system and the budget are closely related. The details of the budget must agree with the company's ledger accounts. In turn, the accounts must be designed to provide the appropriate information for preparing the budget, financial statements, and interim financial reports to facilitate operational control.

Management should frequently compare accounting data with budgeted projections during the budget period and investigate any differences. Budgeting, however, is not a substitute for good management. Instead, the budget is an important tool of managerial control. Managers make decisions in budget preparation that serve as a plan of action.

The period covered by a budget varies according to the nature of the specific activity involved. Cash budgets may cover a week or a month; sales and production budgets may cover a month, a quarter, or a year; and the general operating budget may cover a quarter or a year.

Some General Principles of Budgeting

Objective 3
List five general principles of budgeting.

Budgeting involves the coordination of financial and nonfinancial planning to satisfy organizational goals and objectives. No foolproof method exists for preparing an effective budget. However, budget makers should carefully consider the conditions that follow:

Top Management Support All management levels must be aware of the budget's importance to the company and must know that the budget has top management's support. Top management, then, must clearly state long-range goals and broad objectives. These goals and objectives must be communicated throughout the organization. Long-range goals include the expected quality of products or services, growth rates in sales and earnings, and percentage-of-market targets. Overemphasis on the mechanics of the budgeting process should be avoided.

Participation in Goal Setting Management uses budgets to show how it intends to acquire and use resources to achieve the company's long-range goals. Employees are more likely to strive toward organizational goals if they participate in setting them and in preparing budgets. Often, employees have significant information that could help in preparing a meaningful budget. Also, employees may be motivated to perform their own functions within budget constraints if they are committed to achieving organizational goals.

Communicating Results People should be promptly and clearly informed of their progress. Effective communication implies (1) timeliness, (2) reasonable accuracy, and (3) improved understanding. Managers should effectively communicate results so employees can make any necessary adjustments in their performance.

Flexibility If significant basic assumptions underlying the budget change during the year, the planned operating budget should be restated. For control purposes, after the actual level of operations is known, the actual revenues and expenses can be compared to expected performance at that level of operations.

Follow-up Budget follow-up and data feedback are part of the control aspect of budgetary control. Since the budgets are dealing with projections and estimates for future operating results and financial positions, managers must continuously check their budgets and correct them if necessary. Often management uses performance reports as a follow-up tool to compare actual results with budgeted results.

Behavioral Implications of Budgets

The term *budget* has negative connotations for many employees. Often in the past, management has imposed a budget from the top without considering the opinions and feelings of the personnel affected. Such a dictatorial process may result in resistance to the budget. A number of reasons may underlie such resistance, including lack of understanding of the process, concern for status, and an expectation of increased pressure to perform. Employees may believe that the performance evaluation method is unfair or that the goals are unrealistic and unattainable. They may lack confidence in the way accounting figures are generated or may prefer a less formal communication and evaluation system. Often these fears are completely unfounded, but if employees believe these problems exist, it is difficult to accomplish the objectives of budgeting.

Problems encountered with such imposed budgets have led accountants and management to adopt participatory budgeting. **Participatory budgeting** means that

ILLUSTRATION 23.1
Flowchart of the Financial Planning Process

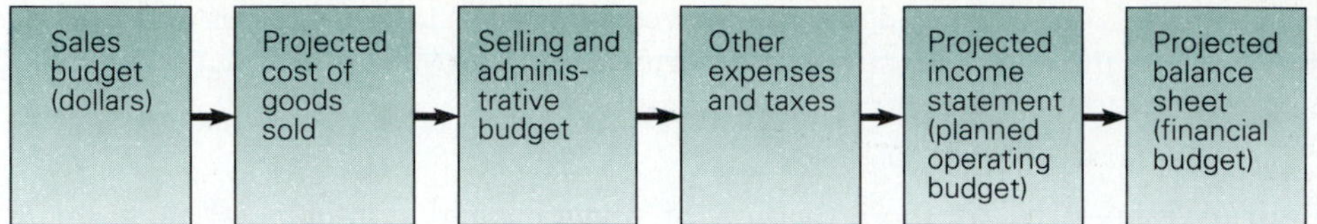

all levels of management responsible for actual performance actively participate in setting operating goals for the coming period. Managers and other employees are more likely to understand, accept, and pursue goals when they are involved in formulating them.

Within a participatory budgeting process, accountants should be compilers or coordinators of the budget, not preparers. They should be on hand during the preparation process to present and explain significant financial data. Accountants must identify the relevant cost data that enables management's objectives to be quantified in dollars. Accountants are responsible for designing meaningful budget reports. Also, accountants must continually strive to make the accounting system more responsive to managerial needs. That responsiveness, in turn, increases confidence in the accounting system.

Although many companies have used participatory budgeting successfully, it does not always work. Studies have shown that in many organizations, participation in the budget formulation failed to make employees more motivated to achieve budgeted goals. Whether or not participation works depends on management's leadership style, the attitudes of employees, and the organization's size and structure. Participation is not the answer to all the problems of budget preparation. However, it is one way to achieve better results in organizations that are receptive to the philosophy of participation.

The Master Budget Concept

A **master budget** consists of a projected income statement (planned operating budget) and a projected balance sheet (financial budget) showing the organization's objectives and proposed ways of attaining them. In Illustration 23.1, we depict a flowchart of the financial planning process that you can use as an overview of the elements in a master budget. The remainder of this chapter describes how a company prepares a master budget. We emphasize the master budget because of its prime importance to financial planning and control in a business entity.

The budgeting process starts with management's plans and objectives for the next period. These plans take into consideration various policy decisions concerning selling price, distribution network, advertising expenditures, and environmental influences from which the company forecasts its sales for the period (in units by product or product line). Managers arrive at the sales budget in dollars by multiplying sales units times sales price per unit. They use expected production, sales volume, and inventory policy to project cost of goods sold. Next, managers project operating expenses such as selling and administrative expenses.

This chapter cannot cover all areas of budgeting in detail—entire books have been written on budgeting. However, the following presentation provides an overview of a budgeting procedure that many successful companies have used. We begin by discussing the planned operating budget or projected income statement.

Preparing the Planned Operating Budget at the Expected Level of Operations

The projected balance sheet, or financial budget, depends on many items in the projected income statement. Thus, the logical starting point in preparing a master budget is the projected income statement, or planned operating budget. However, since the planned operating budget shows the net effect of many interrelated activities, management must prepare several supporting budgets (sales, production, and purchases, to name a few) before preparing the planned operating budget. The process begins with the sales budget.

Sales Budget The cornerstone of the budgeting process is the sales budget because the usefulness of the entire operating budget depends on it. The sales budget involves estimating or forecasting how much demand exists for a company's goods and then determining if a realistic, attainable profit can be achieved based on this demand. Sales forecasting can involve either formal or informal techniques, or both.

Formal sales forecasting techniques involve the use of statistical tools. For example, to predict sales for the coming period, management may use economic indicators (or variables) such as the gross national product or gross national personal income, and other variables such as population growth, per capita income, new construction, and population migration.

To use economic indicators to forecast sales, a relationship must exist between the indicators (called *independent variables*) and the sales that are being forecast (called the *dependent variable*). Then management can use statistical techniques to predict sales based on the economic indicators.

Management often supplements formal techniques with informal sales forecasting techniques such as intuition or judgment. In some instances, management modifies sales projections using formal techniques based on other changes in the environment. Examples include the effect on sales of any changes in the expected level of advertising expenditures, the entry of new competitors, and/or the addition or elimination of products or sales territories. In other instances, companies do not use any formal techniques. Instead, sales managers and salespersons estimate how much they can sell. Managers then add up the estimates to arrive at total estimated sales for the period.

Usually, the sales manager is responsible for the sales budget and prepares it in units and then in dollars by multiplying the units by their selling price. The sales budget in units is the basis of the remaining budgets that support the operating budget.

Production Budget The **production budget** considers the units in the sales budget and the company's inventory policy. Managers develop the production budget in units and then in dollars. Determining production volume is an important task. Companies should schedule production carefully to maintain certain minimum quantities of inventory while avoiding excessive inventory accumulation. The principal objective of the production budget is to coordinate the production and sale of goods in terms of time and quantity.

Companies using a just-in-time inventory system, which we discussed in Chapter 20, need to closely coordinate purchasing, sales, and production. In general, maintaining high inventory levels allows for more flexibility in coordinating purchases, sales, and production. However, businesses must compare the convenience of carrying inventory with the cost of carrying inventory; for example, they must consider storage costs and the opportunity cost of funds tied up in inventory.

Firms often subdivide the production budget into budgets for materials, labor, and manufacturing overhead. Usually materials, labor, and some elements of manufacturing overhead vary directly with production within a given relevant range of production. Fixed manufacturing overhead costs do not vary directly with production but are constant in total within a relevant range of production. For example, fixed manufacturing overhead costs may be $150,000 when production ranges from 60,000 to 80,000 units. However, when production is 80,001 to 95,000 units, the fixed manufacturing overhead costs might be $250,000. To determine fixed manufacturing overhead costs accurately, management must determine the relevant range for the expected level of operations.

Selling, Administrative, and Other Expense Budgets (Schedules) The costs of selling a product are closely related to the sales forecast. Generally, the higher the forecast, the higher the selling expenses. Administrative expenses are likely to be less dependent on the sales forecast because many of the items are fixed costs (e.g., salaries of administrative personnel and depreciation of administrative buildings and office equipment). Managers must also estimate other expenses such as interest expense, income tax expense, and research and development expenses. Once management has prepared the planned operating budget, the next task is to prepare the financial budget (or projected balance sheet).

Preparing the Financial Budget

Preparing a projected balance sheet, or financial budget, involves analyzing every balance sheet account. The beginning balance for each account is the amount on the balance sheet prepared at the end of the preceding period. Then, managers consider the effects of any planned activities on each account. Many accounts are affected by items appearing in the operating budget and by either cash inflows or outflows. Cash inflows and outflows usually appear in a cash budget discussed later in the chapter.

The complexities encountered in preparing the financial budget often require the preparation of detailed schedules. These schedules analyze such things as planned accounts receivable collections and balances, planned material purchases, planned inventories, changes in all accounts affected by operating costs, and the amount of federal income taxes payable. Dividend policy, inventory policy, financing policy and constraints, credit policy, and planned capital expenditures also affect the amounts in the financial budget.

An Accounting Perspective

Business Insight To a manager, a budget is like an architect's blueprints or a house builder's plans. Like the blueprints, a budget shows the details of each part of the plan and how the various parts fit together into the overall plan. Production people focus on production plans, salespeople focus on sales plans, and financial people focus on projected cash receipts and disbursements. The general manager, like the house builder, must be able to see the big picture and tie all of the pieces together.

The Master Budget Illustrated

Earlier this chapter discussed general concepts relating to the preparation of a master budget. This section illustrates the step-by-step preparation of a master budget for 1997 for Leed Company, which manufactures low-priced running shoes.

Preparing the Planned Operating Budget in Units for Leed Company

Objective 4
Prepare a planned operating budget and its supporting budgets, such as the sales budget, production and purchases budgets, and other expense budgets.

A company develops its planned operating budget in units rather than dollars. Because revenues and many expenses vary with volume, they can be forecasted more easily after the company estimates sales and production quantities.

To illustrate this step, assume that Leed's management forecasts sales for the year 1997 at 100,000 units (each pair of shoes is one unit). Quarterly sales are expected to be 20,000, 35,000, 20,000, and 25,000 units, reflecting higher demand for shoes in the late spring and again around Christmas.

Assuming the company's policy is to stabilize production, it would produce 100,000 units uniformly throughout the year. Therefore, production would be 25,000 units per quarter (100,000 units/four quarters). To simplify our example, assume the company has no beginning or ending work in process inventories (although it would be equivalent to assume that work in process inventories would remain at a constant amount throughout the year). Finished goods inventory on January 1, 1997, is 10,000 units. From these data, we can prepare the schedule of planned production and sales. Illustration 23.2 shows the first two quarters.

Notice that if Leed wants to maintain a stable production of running shoes, it must allow the ending inventory to fluctuate if sales vary. Thus, the finished goods inventory is affected by the difference between production and sales. When establishing inventory policy, Leed's management has decided that it is less costly to deal with fluctuating inventories than with fluctuating production.

LEED COMPANY
Planned Production and Sales (in units)

	Quarter Ending	
	March 31, 1997	**June 30, 1997**
Beginning finished goods inventory	10,000*	15,000
Add: Planned production	25,000	25,000
Units available for sale	35,000	40,000
Less: Sales forecast	20,000	35,000
Ending finished goods inventory	15,000	5,000

* Actual on January 1.

ILLUSTRATION 23.2
Leed Company: Planned Production and Sales (in units) for the First Two Quarters of 1997

LEED COMPANY
Budget Estimates of Selling Price and Costs
For Quarters Ending March 31 and June 30, 1997

Forecasted selling price	$ 20
Manufacturing costs:	
Variable (per unit manufactured):	
Direct materials	2
Direct labor	6
Manufacturing overhead	1
Fixed overhead (total each quarter)	75,000
Selling and administrative expenses:	
Variable (per unit sold)	2
Fixed (total each quarter)	100,000

ILLUSTRATION 23.3
Leed Company: Budget Estimate of Selling Price and Costs

Sometimes we receive sales and ending inventory data described as a certain percentage of the next period's sales, and we must calculate the required level of production. Assume Leed Company wishes to have ending inventory of 15,000 units. We could use the following format to calculate planned production:

Sales forecast (units)—current quarter	20,000
Add: Planned ending finished goods inventory	15,000
Total units required for the period	35,000
Deduct: Beginning finished goods inventory	10,000
Planned production (units)	25,000

Preparing the Planned Operating Budget in Dollars

Next, Leed's management must introduce dollars into the analysis. To do this, management forecasts the expected selling price and costs. Illustration 23.3 shows Leed's forecasted selling price and costs. Note that Leed's management classifies costs into variable or fixed categories and budgets accordingly. As noted earlier, **variable costs** vary in total directly with production or sales. **Fixed costs** are unaffected in total by the relative level of production or sales.

Management must now prepare a schedule to forecast cost of goods sold, the next major amount in the planned operating budget. Illustration 23.4 shows this schedule. Notice that the beginning finished goods inventory amount for the quarter ending March 31 is the amount shown on the December 31, 1996, year-end balance sheet (see Illustration 23.9 on page 827). From the data in Illustration 23.3, management calculates the cost of goods manufactured using the variable costs of production plus an allocated amount of fixed manufacturing overhead ($75,000/25,000 units). The amount of ending finished goods inventory is the number of units determined to be in ending inventory (from Illustration 23.2) times the cost per unit manufactured during the period.

ILLUSTRATION 23.4
Leed Company: Planned Cost of Goods Sold

LEED COMPANY
Planned Cost of Goods Sold

	Quarter Ending	
	March 31, 1997	**June 30, 1997**
Beginning finished goods inventory	$130,000*	$180,000
Cost of goods manufactured:		
Direct materials (25,000 × $2)	$ 50,000	$ 50,000
Direct labor (25,000 × $6)	150,000	150,000
Variable manufacturing overhead (25,000 × $1)	25,000	25,000
Fixed manufacturing overhead (per Illustration 23.3)	75,000	75,000
Cost of goods manufactured (25,000 units at $12)	$300,000	$300,000
Cost of goods available for sale	$430,000	$480,000
Ending finished goods inventory:		
(15,000 at $12)†	180,000	
(5,000 at $12)		60,000
Cost of goods sold	$250,000	$420,000

* Actual on January 1 (10,000 at $13); see balance sheet Illustration 23.9.
† First-in, first-out procedure assumed.

ILLUSTRATION 23.5
Leed Company: Planned Operating Budgets

LEED COMPANY
Planned Operating Budgets

	Quarter Ending	
	March 31, 1997	**June 30, 1997**
Forecasted sales (20,000 and 35,000 at $20, per Illustration 23.3)	$400,000	$700,000
Cost of goods sold (per Illustration 23.4)	250,000	420,000
Gross margin	$150,000	$280,000
Selling and administrative expenses:		
Variable (20,000 and 35,000 at $2, per Illustration 23.3)	$ 40,000	$ 70,000
Fixed (per Illustration 23.3)	100,000	100,000
Total selling and administrative expenses	$140,000	$170,000
Income before income taxes	$ 10,000	$110,000
Deduct: Estimated income taxes (assumed to be 40%)	4,000	44,000
Net income	$ 6,000	$ 66,000

After managers forecast cost of goods sold, they prepare a separate budget for all selling and administrative expenses. Several supporting schedules may be prepared for items such as advertising expense, office expense, and payroll department expense. Although we do not show the schedules to support budgeted selling and administrative expenses here, note the total selling and administrative expenses for each of the first two quarters in the planned operating budget in Illustration 23.5.

Planned Operating Budget Illustrated

Illustration 23.5 shows the operating budget for Leed Company. We have discussed and explained all of the items appearing in the planned operating budget except the income tax accrual. State and federal income taxes are budgeted for Leed Company at an assumed rate of 40% of income before income taxes.

If the planned operating budget does not show the desired net income, managers must formulate new operating plans and develop a new budget. The purpose of preparing a planned operating budget is to gain some knowledge of the results of a period's activities before they actually occur.

A Broader Perspective

Planning in a Changing Environment

Few industries have changed as much in the past decade as the telephone industry. The old-fashioned phone company monopoly is over; it now faces intense competition in many markets. Furthermore, the industry is characterized by scientific advances and rapidly changing technology.

Bell Atlantic Corporation provides telephone service in the mid-Atlantic region. Its old approach to planning and budgeting was not dynamic and creative enough to deal with the new competitive environment. To start thinking about planning in the new environment, 1,400 of Bell Atlantic's managers met to discuss the company's basic values. These managers developed such values as respect and trust in each other, excellence, profitable growth, individual fulfillment, and integrity as the foundation for the company's goals and plans. Management then established corporate goals along the lines of these values, such as profit growth goals, and goals for achieving excellence in customer service.

Employee participation in setting goals, planning, and budgeting has been key to Bell Atlantic's success in communicating corporate values and goals. To communicate the company's goals, top management wrote down the company's basic business problems and the steps they wanted to take to solve these problems. This action put Bell Atlantic's goals in terms that employees could understand. After this communication step, employees knew better how to relate their day-to-day work activities to the big picture, namely, ultimate corporate objectives.

Illustration 23.6
Leed Company: Flexible Budget for Manufacturing Overhead

LEED COMPANY
Flexible Budget for Manufacturing Overhead

Element of Manufacturing Overhead	Volume (percent of capacity)*				
	70%	**80%**	**90%**	**100%**	
Units	**17,500**	**20,000**	**22,500**	**25,000**	
Supplies	$ 1,400	$ 1,600	$ 1,800	$ 2,000	Variable portion is $25,000
Power	7,000	8,000	9,000	10,000	
Insurance	4,200	4,800	5,400	6,000	
Maintenance	4,900	5,600	6,300	7,000	
Depreciation	18,000	18,000	18,000	18,000	Fixed portion is $75,000
Supervision	57,000	57,000	57,000	57,000	
	$92,500	$95,000	$97,500	$100,000	

* Capacity is 25,000 units per three-month period.

A company seldom operates at the level of operations assumed in preparing the planned operating budget. After the company knows the results of actual operations, management compares actual expenses with budgeted expenses *at the actual level of operations*. To facilitate adjusting the budgeted items to the actual level of operations, management sometimes prepares in advance flexible budgets for the entire operating budget or for certain expenses. The next section discusses these flexible operating budgets and shows how companies prepare budget variances.

Flexible Operating Budgets

Objective 5
Prepare flexible operating budgets.

Early in the chapter, you learned that a budget should be adjusted for changes in assumptions or variations in the level of operations. Managers use a technique known as flexible budgeting to deal with budgetary adjustments. A **flexible operating budget** is a special kind of budget that provides detailed information about budgeted expenses (and revenues) at various levels of output.

Illustration 23.6 shows a flexible budget for Leed Company's manufacturing overhead costs at various levels of output. To keep the example simple, we assume that the first four costs are strictly variable, starting at zero. On the other hand, the last two costs, depreciation and supervision, are fixed costs in this example because they are assumed to be constant over the entire relevant range of activity.

Leed's management could prepare a similar flexible budget for selling and administrative expenses with supporting schedules for each expense item. Using flexible budgeting, a company calculates variable expenses for various levels of sales volume, while fixed costs remain constant within the relevant range.

Budget Variances When management uses a flexible budget to appraise a department's performance, it bases the evaluation on the amounts budgeted for the level of activity actually experienced. The difference between actual costs incurred and the flexible budget amount for that same level of operations is called a **budget variance.** Budget variances can indicate a department's or company's degree of efficiency, since they emerge from a comparison of what was with what should have been.

To illustrate the computation of budget variances, assume that Leed's management prepared an overhead budget based on an expected volume of 100%, or 25,000 units. At this level of production, the budgeted amount for supplies is $2,000. By the end of the period, Leed has used $1,900 of supplies. Our first impression is that a favorable variance of $100 exists.

However, if Leed's actual production for the period was only 22,500 units (90% of capacity), the company actually has an unfavorable variance of $100. Why? Because at 90% of capacity, according to the flexible operating budget, only $1,800 of supplies should have been used. Consequently, it appears that Leed used supplies inefficiently.

To give another example using the data in Illustration 23.6, Leed's management may have budgeted maintenance at $5,600 for a given period assuming the company planned to produce 20,000 units (80% of operating capacity). However, Leed's actual maintenance costs may have been $6,200 for the period. This result does not necessarily mean that Leed had an unfavorable variance of $600. The variance depends on actual production volume.

Assume once again that Leed actually produced 22,500 units during the period. The company had budgeted maintenance costs at $6,300 for *that* level of production. Therefore, there would actually be a favorable variance of $100 ($6,300 − $6,200).

Flexible budgets often show budgeted amounts for every 10% change in the level of operations, such as at the 70%, 80%, 90%, and 100% levels of capacity. However, actual production may fall between the levels shown in the flexible budget. If so, the company can find the budgeted amounts at that level of operations using the following formula:

$$\text{Budgeted amount} = \begin{matrix}\text{Budgeted}\\\text{fixed portion}\\\text{of costs}\end{matrix} + \left[\begin{matrix}\text{Budgeted}\\\text{variable portion}\\\text{of cost per unit}\end{matrix} \times \begin{matrix}\text{Actual}\\\text{units of}\\\text{output}\end{matrix}\right]$$

Flexible Operating Budget and Budget Variances Illustrated As stated earlier, a flexible operating budget provides detailed information about budgeted expenses at various levels of activity. The main advantage of using a flexible operating budget along with a planned operating budget is that management can appraise performance on two levels. First, management can compare the actual results with the planned operating budget, which enables management to analyze the deviation of actual output from expected output. Second, given the actual level of operations, management can compare actual costs at actual volume with budgeted costs at actual volume. The use of flexible operating budgets gives a valid basis for comparison when actual production or sales volume differs from expectations.

Using the data from Illustration 23.3, Illustrations 23.7 and 23.8 present Leed's detailed planned operating budget and flexible operating budget for the quarter ended March 31, 1997. The planned operating budget was based on a sales forecast of 20,000 units and a production forecast of 25,000 units. Illustrations 23.7 and 23.8 show actual sales of 19,000 units and actual production of 25,000 units.

ILLUSTRATION 23.7
Leed Company: Comparison of Planned Operating Budget and Actual Results

LEED COMPANY
Comparison of Planned Operating Budget and Actual Results
For Quarter Ended March 31, 1997

	Planned Budget	Actual
Sales (budgeted 20,000 units, actual 19,000 units)	$400,000	$380,000
Cost of goods sold:		
Beginning finished goods inventory	$130,000	$130,000
Cost of goods manufactured (25,000 units):		
Direct materials	$ 50,000	$ 62,500
Direct labor	150,000	143,750
Variable manufacturing overhead	25,000	31,250
Fixed manufacturing overhead	75,000	75,000
Cost of goods manufactured	$300,000	$312,500
Cost of goods available for sale	$430,000	$442,500
Ending finished goods inventory	180,000	200,000
Cost of goods sold	$250,000	$242,500
Gross margin	$150,000	$137,500
Selling and administrative expenses:		
Variable	$ 40,000	$ 28,500
Fixed	100,000	95,000
Total selling and administrative expenses	$140,000	$123,500
Income before income taxes	$ 10,000	$ 14,000
Deduct: Estimated income taxes (40%)	4,000	5,600
Net income	$ 6,000	$ 8,400

ILLUSTRATION 23.8
Leed Company: Comparison of Flexible Operating Budget and Actual Results

LEED COMPANY
Comparison of Flexible Operating Budget and Actual Results
For Quarter Ended March 31, 1997

	Flexible Budget	Actual	Budget Variance Over (Under)
Sales (19,000) units	$380,000	$380,000	$ –0–
Cost of goods sold:			
Beginning finished goods inventory	$130,000	$130,000	$ –0–
Cost of goods manufactured (25,000 units):			
Direct materials	$ 50,000	$ 62,500	$ 12,500
Direct labor	150,000	143,750	(6,250)
Variable manufacturing overhead	25,000	31,250	6,250
Fixed manufacturing overhead	75,000	75,000	–0–
Cost of goods manufactured	$300,000	$312,500	$ 12,500
Cost of goods available for sale	$430,000	$442,500	$ 12,500
Ending finished goods inventory	192,000	200,000	8,000
Cost of goods sold (19,000 units)	$238,000	$242,500	$ 4,500
Gross margin	$142,000	$137,500	$ (4,500)
Selling and administrative expenses:			
Variable	$ 38,000	$ 28,500	$ (9,500)
Fixed	100,000	95,000	(5,000)
Total selling and administrative expenses	$138,000	$123,500	$(14,500)
Income before income taxes	$ 4,000	$ 14,000	$ 10,000
Deduct: Estimated income taxes (40%)	1,600	5,600	4,000
Net income	$ 2,400	$ 8,400	$ 6,000

(As is typically the case, the budgeted and actual amounts are not equal.) The actual selling price was $20 per unit, the same price that management had forecast.

In Illustration 23.7 we compare the actual results with the planned operating budget. Comparison of actual results with the planned operating budget yields some useful information because it shows where actual performance deviated from planned performance. For example, sales were 1,000 units lower than expected, sales revenue was $20,000 less than expected, gross margin was $12,500 less than expected, and net income was $2,400 more than expected.

The comparison of actual results with the planned operating budget does not provide a basis for evaluating whether or not management performed efficiently at the actual level of operations. For example, in Illustration 23.7, the cost of goods sold was $7,500 less than expected. The meaning of this difference is not clear, however, because the actual cost of goods sold relates to the 19,000 units actually sold, while the planned cost of goods sold relates to the 20,000 units expected.

A company makes a valid analysis of expense controls by comparing actual results with a flexible operating budget based on the levels of sales and production that actually occurred. Illustration 23.8 shows the comparison of Leed's flexible operating budget with the actual results. Note that the flexible budget in Illustration 23.8 is made up of several pieces. The flexible budget amounts for sales revenue and selling and administrative expenses come from a flexible sales budget (not shown) for 19,000 units of sales.

In comparisons such as these, if the number of units produced is equal to the number sold, many companies do not show their beginning and ending inventories in their flexible operating budgets. Instead, the flexible operating budget may show the number of units actually sold multiplied by the budgeted unit cost of direct materials, direct labor, and manufacturing overhead. This budget also shows actual costs for direct materials, direct labor, and manufacturing overhead for the number of units sold.

The comparison of the actual results with the flexible operating budget (Illustration 23.8) reveals some inefficiencies for items in the cost of goods manufactured section. For instance, direct materials and variable overhead costs were considerably higher than expected. Direct labor costs, on the other hand, were somewhat lower than expected. Both variable and fixed selling and administrative expenses were lower than expected. Net income was $6,000 more than expected at a sales level of 19,000 units.

Now that Leed's management has prepared the operating budget (or projected income statement), it can prepare its financial budget. Remember that the financial budget is a projected balance sheet.

Preparing the Financial Budget for Leed Company

Objective 6
Prepare a financial budget and its supporting budgets.

To prepare a projected balance sheet, Leed's management must analyze each balance sheet account. Managers take the beginning balance from the balance sheet at the end of the preceding period. Look at Illustration 23.9, Leed Company's balance sheet as of December 31, 1996. Management must consider the effects of planned activities on these balances. Many accounts are affected by items in the planned operating budget, by cash inflows and outflows, and by policy decisions. Management uses the planned operating budget in Illustration 23.5 and the other illustrations previously given to prepare Leed Company's financial budget for the first two quarters of 1997.

Accounts Receivable Leed must prepare several new schedules to prepare a financial budget. The first of these schedules is the accounts receivable schedule in Illustration 23.10. Assume that Leed will collect 60% of the current quarter's sales in that quarter, and the remaining 40% will be collected in the following quarter. Thus, collections for the first quarter will be $440,000. The $440,000 equals 60% of budgeted sales of $400,000 for the first quarter plus the uncollected sales of the previous quarter [(0.6 × $400,000) + $200,000]. Second quarter collec-

ILLUSTRATION 23.9
Leed Company: Balance Sheet at Beginning of Period

LEED COMPANY
Balance Sheet
December 31, 1996

Assets		
Current assets:		
Cash		$ 130,000
Accounts receivable		200,000
Inventories:		
Materials	$ 40,000	
Finished goods	130,000	170,000
Prepaid expenses		20,000
Total current assets		$ 520,000
Property, plant, and equipment:		
Land		$ 60,000
Buildings	$1,000,000	
Less: Accumulated depreciation	400,000	600,000
Equipment	$ 600,000	
Less: Accumulated depreciation	180,000	420,000
Total property, plant, and equipment		$1,080,000
Total assets		$1,600,000
Liabilities and Stockholders' Equity		
Current liabilities:		
Accounts payable		$ 80,000
Accrued liabilities payable		160,000
Income taxes payable		100,000
Total current liabilities		$ 340,000
Stockholders' equity:		
Capital stock (100,000 shares of $10 par value)		$1,000,000
Retained earnings		260,000
Total stockholders' equity		$1,260,000
Total liabilities and stockholders' equity		$1,600,000

ILLUSTRATION 23.10
Leed Company: Planned Accounts Receivable Collections and Balances

LEED COMPANY
Planned Accounts Receivable Collections and Balances

	Quarter Ending	
	March 31, 1997	**June 30, 1997**
Planned balance at beginning of quarter	$200,000*	$160,000
Planned sales for period (per Illustration 23.5)	400,000	700,000
Total	$600,000	$860,000
Projected collections during quarter (per discussion in text)	440,000	580,000
Planned balance at end of quarter	$160,000	$280,000

* Actual on January 1.

tions would be $580,000 [(0.6 × $700,000) + $160,000]. We have simplified the illustration by assuming all sales are on credit, and that there are no sales returns or allowances, no discounts, and no uncollectible accounts.

INVENTORIES Leed's management must prepare a schedule of planned materials purchases and inventories. Planned usage and cost per unit of materials are from the planned cost of goods sold schedule (Illustration 23.4 on page 822). We assume no work in process inventories to simplify the illustration; there are only materials and finished goods inventories.

In Illustration 23.11, we show a schedule of planned purchases and inventories of materials for Leed Company. Leed normally maintains its Materials inven-

Illustration 23.11
Leed Company: Planned Materials Purchases and Inventories

LEED COMPANY
Planned Materials Purchases and Inventories

	Quarter Ending	
	March 31, 1997	**June 30, 1997**
Planned usage (25,000 × $2) (per Illustration 23.4)	$50,000	$50,000
Planned ending inventory (½ × 25,000 × $2) (per discussion in text)	25,000	25,000
Planned materials available for use	$75,000	$75,000
Inventory at beginning of quarter	40,000*	25,000
Planned purchases for the quarter	$35,000	$50,000

* Actual on January 1.

tory at a level of one half of next quarter's planned usage. The $40,000 beginning inventory was greater than normal because of a strike threat in the supplier company. This threat has now passed, and the materials inventory is reduced at the end of the first quarter to the normal planned level. In Illustration 23.4, we calculated the planned ending finished goods inventories.

Accounts Affected by Operating Costs Leed's management would prepare individual schedules for each of the accounts affected by operating costs. For illustrative purposes, however, we prepare a schedule that combines all the accounts affected by materials purchases or operating costs. We assume that:

1. All purchases of materials are made on account.
2. Direct labor incurred is credited to Accrued Liabilities Payable.
3. Manufacturing overhead incurred is credited to the following accounts:

	Quarter Ending	
	March 31	**June 30**
Accounts Payable	$ 16,000	$ 13,000
Accrued Liabilities Payable	60,000	64,000
Prepaid Expenses	6,000	5,000
Accumulated Depreciation—Building	5,000	5,000
Accumulated Depreciation—Equipment	13,000	13,000
Total	$100,000	$100,000

4. Selling and administrative expenses incurred are credited to the following accounts:

	Quarter Ending	
	March 31	**June 30**
Accounts Payable	$ 5,000	$ 10,000
Accrued Liabilities Payable	130,000	154,000
Prepaid Expenses	2,000	3,000
Accumulated Depreciation—Building	1,000	1,000
Accumulated Depreciation—Equipment	2,000	2,000
Total	$140,000	$170,000

5. Planned cash payments are as follows:

	Quarter Ending	
	March 31	**June 30**
Accounts Payable	$ 80,000	$ 56,000
Accrued Liabilities Payable	330,000	354,000
Prepaid Expenses	–0–	10,000
Total	$410,000	$420,000

ILLUSTRATION 23.12 Leed Company: Analyses of Accounts Credited for Materials Purchases and Operating Costs

LEED COMPANY
Analyses of Accounts Credited for Materials Purchases and Operating Costs
For Quarters Ending March 31 and June 30, 1997

	Total Debits	Accounts Payable	Accrued Liabilities Payable	Prepaid Expenses	Accumulated Depreciation — Building	Accumulated Depreciation — Equipment
Beginning balances, January 1 (per Illustration 23.9)		$ 80,000	$160,000	$20,000*	$400,000	$180,000
Purchases or operating costs, quarter ending March 31 (credits made to accounts shown at right):						
Direct materials (per Illustration 23.11)	$ 35,000*	$ 35,000				
Direct labor (per Illustration 23.4)	150,000*		$150,000			
Manufacturing overhead (per Illustration 23.4 and above schedules)	100,000*	16,000	60,000	$ 6,000	$ 5,000	$ 13,000
Selling and administrative expenses (per Illustration 23.5 and above schedules)	140,000*	5,000	130,000	2,000	1,000	2,000
Total	$425,000	$ 56,000	$340,000	$ 8,000	$ 6,000	$ 15,000
Total including January 1 balances		$136,000	$500,000	$12,000*	$406,000	$195,000
Planned cash payments (debits made to accounts shown)		80,000*	330,000*			
Planned balances, March 31		$ 56,000	$170,000	$12,000*	$406,000	$195,000
Purchases or operating costs, quarter ending June 30 (credits made to accounts shown at right):						
Direct materials (per Illustration 23.11)	$ 50,000*	$ 50,000				
Direct labor (per Illustration 23.4)	150,000*		$150,000			
Manufacturing overhead (per Illustration 23.4 and above schedules)	100,000*	13,000	64,000	$ 5,000	$ 5,000	$ 13,000
Selling and administrative expenses (per Illustration 23.5 and above schedules)	170,000*	10,000	154,000	3,000	1,000	2,000
Total	$470,000	$ 73,000	$368,000	$ 8,000	$ 6,000	$ 15,000
Total including March 31 balances		$129,000	$538,000	$ 4,000*	$412,000	$210,000
Planned cash payments (debits made to accounts shown)		56,000*	354,000*	10,000*		
Planned balances, June 30		$ 73,000	$184,000	$14,000*	$412,000	$210,000

* Debit balance or debit to account.

Illustration 23.12 shows analyses of the accounts credited as a result of these data. The illustration provides a considerable amount of information needed in constructing financial budgets for the quarters ended March 31, 1997, and June 30, 1997. The balances on both dates for Accounts Payable, Accrued Liabilities Payable, Prepaid Expenses (the only debit balance account shown), Accumulated Depreciation—Building, and Accumulated Depreciation—Equipment are computed in the schedule.

INCOME TAXES PAYABLE A separate schedule could be prepared showing the changes in the state and federal Income Taxes Payable account, but in this example, a brief discussion suffices. Balances reported in the financial budgets assume that Leed pays one half of the $100,000 liability in the December 31, 1996, balance sheet in each of the first two quarters of 1997 (shown in Illustration 23.15 on page 831). The accrual for the current quarter is added (Illustration 23.5). Thus, the balance on March 31, 1997, is $54,000, calculated as ($100,000 − $50,000 + $4,000). The balance on June 30, 1997, is $48,000, calculated as ($54,000 − $50,000 + $44,000). On June 30, the balance equals the accrual for the current year, $4,000 for the first quarter and $44,000 for the second quarter.

Illustration 23.13
Leed Company:
Planned Cash Receipts

LEED COMPANY
Planned Cash Receipts

	Quarter Ending	
	March 31, 1997	**June 30, 1997**
Collections on accounts receivable:		
From preceding quarter's sales	$200,000	$160,000 (0.4 × $400,000)
From current quarter's sales	240,000 (0.6 × $400,000)	420,000 (0.6 × $700,000)
Total cash receipts (per Illustration 23.10)	$440,000	$580,000

Illustration 23.14
Leed Company:
Planned Cash
Disbursements

LEED COMPANY
Planned Cash Disbursements

	Quarter Ending	
	March 31, 1997	**June 30, 1997**
Payment of accounts payable (per Illustration 23.12)	$ 80,000	$ 56,000
Payment of accrued liabilities payable (per Illustration 23.12)	330,000	354,000
Payment of income tax liability	50,000	50,000
Payment of dividends	20,000	40,000
Expenses prepaid (per Illustration 23.12)	–0–	10,000
Total cash disbursements	$480,000	$510,000

Cash Budget After the preceding analyses have been prepared, sufficient information is available to prepare the cash budget and compute the balance in the Cash account on March 31 and June 30, 1997. Preparing a **cash budget** requires information about cash receipts and cash disbursements.

Cash Receipts We can prepare the cash receipts schedule from the information used to compute the accounts receivable schedule (Illustration 23.10). In Illustration 23.13, we show the schedule of planned cash receipts for Leed Company.

Cash Disbursements Companies need cash to pay for purchases, wages, rent, interest, income taxes, cash dividends, and most other expenses. We can obtain the amount of each cash disbursement from other budgets or schedules. Look at Illustration 23.14, the cash disbursements schedule for Leed Company. You can see where the information came from, except for the payment of income taxes and dividends. Income taxes are assumed to be 40% of income before income taxes. We assume that $20,000 of dividends will be paid in the first quarter and $40,000 in the second quarter.

Once cash receipts and disbursements have been determined, we can prepare a cash budget for Leed Company, as shown in Illustration 23.15. The **cash budget** is a plan indicating expected inflows and outflows of cash.

This cash budget helps management to decide whether enough cash will be available for short-term needs. If a company's cash budget indicates a cash shortage at a certain date, the company may need to borrow money on a short-term basis. If the company's cash budget indicates a cash excess, the company may wish to invest the extra funds for short periods to earn interest rather than leave the cash idle. Knowing in advance that a possible cash shortage or excess may occur allows management sufficient time to plan for such occurrences and avoid a cash crisis.

The Financial Budget Illustrated

The preparation of Leed's financial budget for the quarters ending March 31 and June 30 (Illustration 23.16) completes the master budget. Management now has information to help appraise the policies it has adopted before implementing them.

ILLUSTRATION 23.15
Leed Company: Planned Cash Flows and Cash Balances

LEED COMPANY
Planned Cash Flows and Cash Balances

	Quarter Ending	
	March 31, 1997	**June 30, 1997**
Planned balance at beginning of quarter	$130,000*	$ 90,000
Planned cash receipts:		
Collections of accounts receivable (per Illustration 23.13)	440,000	580,000
	$570,000	$670,000
Planned cash disbursements:		
Payment of accounts payable (per Illustration 23.12)	$ 80,000	$ 56,000
Payment of accrued liabilities payable (per Illustration 23.12)	330,000	354,000
Payment of income tax liability	50,000	50,000
Payment of dividends	20,000	40,000
Expenses prepaid (per Illustration 23.12)	-0-	10,000
Total cash disbursements	$480,000	$510,000
Planned balance at end of quarter	$ 90,000	$160,000

* Actual on January 1.

ILLUSTRATION 23.16
Leed Company: Projected Balance Sheet

LEED COMPANY
Projected Balance Sheet
As of March 31 and June 30, 1997

	March 31, 1997	**June 30, 1997**
Assets		
Current assets:		
Cash (per Illustration 23.15)	$ 90,000	$ 160,000
Accounts receivable (per Illustration 23.10)	160,000	280,000
Inventories:		
Materials (per Illustration 23.11)	25,000	25,000
Finished goods (per Illustration 23.4)	180,000	60,000
Prepaid expenses (per Illustration 23.12)	12,000	14,000
Total current assets	$ 467,000	$ 539,000
Property, plant, and equipment:		
Land (per Illustration 23.9)	$ 60,000	$ 60,000
Buildings, net ($1,000,000 less accumulated depreciation of $406,000 and $412,000) (per Illustrations 23.9 and 23.12)	594,000	588,000
Equipment, net ($600,000 less accumulated depreciation of $195,000 and $210,000) (per Illustrations 23.9 and 23.12)	405,000	390,000
Total property, plant, and equipment	$1,059,000	$1,038,000
Total assets	$1,526,000	$1,577,000
Liabilities and Stockholders' Equity		
Current liabilities:		
Accounts payable (per Illustration 23.12)	$ 56,000	$ 73,000
Accrued liabilities payable (per Illustration 23.12)	170,000	184,000
Income taxes payable (per discussion in the text)	54,000	48,000
Total current liabilities	$ 280,000	$ 305,000
Stockholders' equity:		
Capital stock (100,000 shares of $10 par value) (per Illustration 23.9)	$1,000,000	$1,000,000
Retained earnings (see footnotes below)	246,000*	272,000†
Total stockholders' equity	$1,246,000	$1,272,000
Total liabilities and stockholders' equity	$1,526,000	$1,577,000

* $260,000 (per Illustration 23.9) + Income of $6,000 − Dividends of $20,000.
† $246,000 + Income of $66,000 − Dividends of $40,000.

If the master budget shows the results of these policies to be unsatisfactory, the company can change its policies before serious problems arise.

For example, Leed Company's management had a policy of stable production each period. The master budget shows that production can be stabilized even though sales fluctuate widely. However, the planned ending inventory at June 30 may be considered somewhat low in view of the fluctuations in sales. Management now knows this in advance and can take corrective action if necessary.

An Accounting Perspective

Uses of Technology Imagine the difficulty of coordinating budgets in companies having worldwide operations, companies such as PepsiCo and Amoco Corporation. Amoco has oil and gas exploration, production, and marketing facilities in various countries. The Amoco plant in Singapore, for example, has to transmit its budget information to corporate headquarters in Chicago, where managers coordinate the budgets of various operations worldwide, request additional information, require revisions in the budgets, and otherwise interact constantly with far-flung operations. Recent advances in electronic mail and data transmission have made this process much faster and easier. Managers in the Singapore plant of Amoco can get reactions from corporate headquarters almost immediately. Corporate headquarters can get answers to its questions fast and can coordinate the budgets from various worldwide operations quickly.

Budgeting in Merchandising Companies

Budget preparation for merchandising companies and service companies is similar to budgeting for manufacturing companies. This section discusses budgeting in merchandising companies.

Purchases Budget for a Merchandising Company

Throughout this chapter, we have focused on budgeting in a manufacturing company. Suppose managers in a retail merchandising business, such as a dress shop or a furniture store, prepare a budget. In this case, the company prepares a purchases budget instead of a production budget. To compute the purchases for each quarter, management must estimate the cost of the goods to be sold during the quarter and the inventory required at the end of the quarter.

Suppose Strobel Furniture Company prepared a sales budget like the one in Illustration 23.17. Assume the company maintains sufficient inventory to cover one half of the next quarter's sales. Cost of goods sold is 55% of sales. The ending inventory on December 31, 1996, was $8,250. The purchases budget can now be prepared, as shown in Illustration 23.18. For the first quarter of 1997, notice that the ending inventory is one half of the second quarter's cost of goods sold [$0.5 \times (0.55 \times \$80,000) = \$22,000$].

Strobel can now use the information in its purchases budget to prepare the cost of goods sold section of the operating budget, to prepare cash disbursements schedules, and to prepare the inventory and accounts payable amounts in the financial budget.

Budgeting in Service Companies

The concepts discussed in this chapter are equally applicable to service companies. Service firms have service revenues and operating expenses that must be budgeted. Projected income statements and balance sheets can be prepared for service companies using the techniques described in this chapter.

Additional Concepts Related to Budgeting

Two additional concepts that affect budgeting are sometimes used in industry. These concepts are just-in-time inventory systems and zero-base budgeting.

ILLUSTRATION 23.17
Strobel Furniture Company: Sales Budget

STROBEL FURNITURE COMPANY
Sales Budget
For Quarters Ending March 31, 1997, through March 31, 1998

March 31, 1997	June 30, 1997	September 30, 1997	December 31, 1997	March 31, 1998
$30,000	$80,000	$50,000	$90,000	$40,000

ILLUSTRATION 23.18
Strobel Furniture Company: Purchases Budget

STROBEL FURNITURE COMPANY
Purchases Budget
For Quarters Ending March 31 through December 31, 1997

	March 31, 1997	June 30, 1997	September 30, 1997	December 31, 1997
Ending inventory desired*	$22,000	$13,750	$24,750	$11,000
Cost of goods sold (55% of sales)	16,500	44,000	27,500	49,500
Total	$38,500	$57,750	$52,250	$60,500
Less: Beginning inventory	8,250	22,000	13,750	24,750
Purchases required	$30,250	$35,750	$38,500	$35,750

* Next period's sales × 55% × 50%.

Just-in-Time Inventory

Chapter 20 described just-in-time inventory. Recall that the **just-in-time inventory system** provides that materials are bought just in time to be put into the manufacturing process; small parts, or subparts, are purchased just in time to be assembled into a final product; and goods are produced and delivered just in time to be sold.

The overall purpose of the just-in-time inventory system is to decrease, or in some cases eliminate, inventories in a company. By eliminating inventory, companies reduce the buffer stock between purchasing, production, and sales. Consequently, companies using just-in-time inventory must budget purchasing, production, and sales so the goods are purchased just in time for production and produced just in time for sales.

Zero-Base Budgeting

Zero-base budgeting became popular in the 1970s, particularly when President Jimmy Carter supported it for state and federal governmental units. It has received less attention since then.

Under **zero-base budgeting,** managers in a company start each year with zero budget levels and must justify every dollar that appears in the budget. Managers do not assume any costs incurred in previous years should be incurred this year. Each manager prepares decision packages that describe the nature and cost of tasks that can be performed by that unit and the consequences of not performing each task. Top organization officials rank the decision packages and approve those that they believe are most worthy. A major drawback to the use of this concept is the massive amounts of paperwork and time needed to prepare and rank decision packages, especially in large organizations.

This chapter discussed the general concepts of budgeting. In Chapter 26, we will discuss another type of budgeting known as capital budgeting.

The next chapter discusses standard costs, which are used in budgeting and are important in controlling operations.

UNDERSTANDING THE LEARNING OBJECTIVES

Objective 1
Define a budget and name several kinds of budgets.

- A budget is a plan showing the company's objectives and how management intends to acquire and use resources to attain those objectives.
- Several kinds of budgets are responsibility, capital, master, planned operating, and financial budgets.

Objective 2
List several benefits of a budget.

- A budget: (1) shows management's operating plans for the coming periods; (2) formalizes management's plans in quantitative terms; (3) forces all levels of management to think ahead, anticipate results, and take action to remedy possible poor results; and (4) may motivate individuals to strive to achieve stated goals.
- Other benefits are: business activities are better coordinated; managers become aware of other managers' plans; employees may become cost conscious and try to conserve resources; the company reviews its organization plan and changes it when necessary; and managers foster a vision that might not otherwise be developed.

Objective 3
List five general principles of budgeting.

- Top management support: All management levels must be aware of the budget's importance to the company and must know that the budget has top management's support.
- Participation in goal setting: Employees are generally more likely to strive toward organizational goals if they participate in setting them.
- Communicating results: People should be promptly and clearly informed of their progress.
- Flexibility: The operating budget should be restated if the basic assumptions underlying the budget change during the year. For control purposes, after the actual level of operations is known, the actual revenues and expenses should be compared to the expected performance at that level of operations.
- Follow-up: Managers should check budgets continuously and correct them whenever necessary because budgets deal with projections and estimates of future operating results, cash flows, and financial position.

Objective 4
Prepare a planned operating budget and its supporting budgets, such as the sales budget, production and purchases budgets, and other expense budgets.

- Managers develop a planned operating budget in units rather than dollars. Managers forecast sales units for the year. Then, based on the sales forecast and the company's inventory policy, they forecast production requirements in units.
- Next, dollars must be introduced into the analysis. A forecast of expected selling prices must be made, and costs must be analyzed.
- Management then prepares a schedule to forecast cost of goods sold.
- After forecasting the cost of goods sold, management prepares a separate budget for all selling and administrative expenses. Several supporting schedules may be involved for other various expenses.
- The totals on the separate budgets are combined to form the planned operating budget, which shows the budgeted income after income taxes for a certain period.

Objective 5
Prepare flexible operating budgets.

- A flexible operating budget is a special kind of budget that provides detailed information about budgeted expenses (and revenues) at various levels of output.
- This budget shows the effect that different volume changes, in percents of capacity, have on the expenses of a company.

Objective 6
Prepare a financial budget and its supporting budgets.

- Preparing a financial budget involves analyzing every balance sheet account in light of the planned activities expressed in the income statement.
- Managers usually prepare a separate cash budget to show sources, uses, and net changes in cash for the period.
- Supporting budgets also may be developed for accounts receivable, inventories, accounts affected by operating costs, and federal income taxes payable.

Demonstration Problem

During January 1997, Ramos Company plans to sell 40,000 units of its product at a price of $30 per unit. The company estimates selling expenses to be $120,000 plus 2% of sales revenue. Administrative expenses are estimated to be $90,000 plus 1% of sales revenue. Federal income tax expense is estimated to be 40% of income before federal income taxes.

Ramos plans to produce 50,000 units during January with estimated variable costs per unit as follows: $3 for material, $7.50 for labor, and $4.50 for variable overhead. Estimated fixed overhead cost is $60,000 per month. The finished goods inventory at January 1, 1997, is 8,000 units with a cost per unit of $15. The company uses FIFO inventory procedure.

Required Prepare a projected income statement for January 1997.

Solution to Demonstration Problem

RAMOS COMPANY
Projected Income Statement
For January 1997

Sales (40,000 × $30)		$1,200,000
Cost of goods sold (see Planned Cost of Goods Sold)		638,400
Gross margin		$ 561,600
Selling expenses:		
Fixed	$120,000	
Variable (0.02 × $1,200,000)	24,000	
Administrative expenses:		
Fixed	90,000	
Variable (0.01 × $1,200,000)	12,000	246,000
Income before federal income taxes		$ 315,600
Deduct: Federal income tax expense (40%)		126,240
Net income		$ 189,360

RAMOS COMPANY
Planned Cost of Goods Sold

Beginning finished goods inventory (8,000 × $15)		$120,000
Cost of goods manufactured:		
Direct materials (50,000 × $3)	$150,000	
Direct labor (50,000 × $7.50)	375,000	
Variable manufacturing overhead (50,000 × $4.50)	225,000	
Fixed manufacturing overhead	60,000	
Cost of goods manufactured (50,000 × $16.20)		810,000
Cost of goods available for sale		$930,000
Ending finished goods inventory (18,000 × $16.20)		291,600
Cost of goods sold		$638,400

New Terms*

Budget A plan showing a company's objectives and proposed ways of attaining the objectives. Major types of budgets are (1) master budget, (2) responsibility budget, and (3) capital budget. *815*

Budgeting The coordination of financial and nonfinancial planning to satisfy an organization's goals. *817*

Budget variance The difference between an actual cost incurred (or revenue earned) at a certain level of operations and the budgeted amount for the same level of operations. *824*

Cash budget A plan indicating expected inflows (receipts) and outflows (disbursements) of cash; it helps management decide whether enough cash will be available for short-term needs. *830*

Financial budget The projected balance sheet portion of a master budget. *815*

Fixed costs Costs that are unaffected in total by the relative level of production or sales. *821*

Flexible operating budget A special budget that provides detailed information about budgeted expenses (and revenues) at various levels of output. *823*

Just-in-time inventory system Provides that goods are produced and delivered just in time to be sold. *833*

Master budget The projected income statement (planned operating budget) and projected balance sheet (financial budget) showing the organization's objectives and proposed ways of attaining them; includes supporting budgets for various items in the master budget; also called *master profit plan*. The master budget is the overall plan of the enterprise and ideally consists of all of the various segmental budgets. *815, 818*

Participatory budgeting A method of preparing the budget that includes the participation of all levels of management responsible for actual performance. *817*

Planned operating budget The projected income statement portion of a master budget. *815*

Production budget A budget that takes into account the units in the sales budget and the company's inventory policy. *819*

Variable costs Costs that vary in total directly with production or sales and are a constant dollar amount per unit of output over different levels of output or sales. *821*

Zero-base budgeting Managers in a company start each year with zero budget levels and must justify every dollar that will appear in the budget. *833*

* Some terms defined in earlier chapters are repeated here for your convenience.

SELF-TEST

TRUE-FALSE

Indicate whether each of the following statements is true or false.

1. Budgets are based on more than past results.
2. Cash budgets may cover a week or a month, sales and production budgets a month, a quarter, or a year, and general operating budgets may cover a quarter or a year.
3. The planned operating budget is developed first in units and then in dollars.
4. Planned operating budgets based on planned activity levels and flexible budgets are the same if planned activity levels and actual activity levels are not the same.

MULTIPLE-CHOICE

Select the best answer for each of the following questions.

1. Which of the following best describes some of the benefits related to the preparation and use of budgets:
   - **a.** Business activities are better coordinated.
   - **b.** Managers become aware of other managers' plans.
   - **c.** Employees may become cost conscious and try to conserve resources.
   - **d.** Managers may review the organizational plan and make necessary changes more often.
   - **e.** All of the above.
2. When preparing a projected income statement, which of the following budgets is prepared first?
   - **a.** Projected cost of goods sold budget.
   - **b.** Selling and administrative budget.
   - **c.** Sales budget.
   - **d.** Financial budget.
3. Fixed costs are $60,000, variable cost per unit is $1.20, and budgeted units of output are 200,000 units. Determine the budgeted production costs.
   - **a.** $300,000.
   - **b.** $360,000.
   - **c.** $240,000.
   - **d.** $276,000.
4. Production costs (including $30,000 of fixed costs) are budgeted at $150,000 for an expected output of 100,000 units. Actual output was 90,000 units, while actual costs were $142,500. What is the budget variance and is it favorable or unfavorable?
   - **a.** $5,500 unfavorable.
   - **b.** $6,500 favorable.
   - **c.** $6,500 unfavorable.
   - **d.** $4,500 unfavorable.

Now turn to page 845 to check your answers.

QUESTIONS

1. What are three purposes of budgeting?
2. What are the purposes of a master, planned operating, and financial budget?
3. How does the management by exception concept relate to budgeting?
4. What are five basic principles which, if followed, should improve the probability of preparing a meaningful budget? Why is each important?
5. What is the difference between an imposed budget and a participatory budget?
6. Define and explain a budget variance.
7. What are the two major budgets in the master budget? Which should be prepared first? Why?
8. Distinguish between a master budget and a responsibility budget.
9. The budget established at the beginning of a given period carried an item for supplies expense in the amount of $40,000. At the end of the period, the supplies used amounted to $44,000. Can it be concluded from these data that there was an inefficient use of supplies or that care was not exercised in purchasing the supplies?
10. Management must make certain assumptions about the business environment when preparing a budget. What areas should be considered?
11. Why is budgeted performance better than past performance as a basis for judging actual results?
12. Describe the concepts of just-in-time inventory systems and zero-base budgeting.

THE LIMITED, INC.

13. **Real World Question** Refer to the financial statements for The Limited in the annual report booklet. An industry analyst has asked you to forecast sales for each of the years 1994, 1995, 1996, 1997, and 1998. Assume sales increase each year by the same percentage. That is, the percentage increase from 1993 to 1994 is expected to be the same as it was between 1992 and 1993. What is your estimate of sales in each of the years 1994 through 1998?

THE LIMITED, INC.

14. **Real World Question** Refer to your forecasts of sales for The Limited in question 13. Evaluate the

simple forecasting method you were asked to use in that question. What additional factors should be used in forecasting sales?

15. **Real World Question** Do you think the sales for a particular grocery store in your neighborhood will go up, go down, or stay the same next year compared to this year? Give your answer in sales volume, then give it in sales dollars.

16. **Real World Question** The text refers to the benefits of participation in budgeting. Assume your college bookstore is preparing a budget for next year and wants to include employees in the budgeting process. Give examples of the people who should be included and state what information they could provide.

EXERCISES

Exercise 23–1
Prepare a schedule of planned sales and production (L.O. 4)

Oregon Outdoors Company has decided to produce 144,000 pairs of socks at a uniform rate throughout 1997. The sales department of Oregon Outdoors Company has estimated sales for 1997 according to the following schedule:

	Sales of Pairs of Socks
First quarter	38,400
Second quarter	31,200
Third quarter	36,000
Fourth quarter	50,400
Total for 1997	156,000

Assume the December 31, 1996, inventory is estimated to be 19,200 pairs of socks. Prepare a schedule of planned sales and production for the first two quarters of 1997.

Exercise 23–2
Compute budgeted income (L.O. 4)

Duke Company projects sales of 25,000 units during May at $3 per unit. Production costs are $0.90 per unit. Variable selling and administrative expenses are $0.30 per unit; fixed selling and administrative expenses are $30,000. Compute the budgeted income before income taxes.

Exercise 23–3
Prepare an operating budget (L.O. 4)

Freewheel Company plans to sell 45,000 skateboards next quarter at a price of $36 per unit. Production costs are $14.40 per unit. Selling and administrative expenses are: variable, $7.20 per unit; and fixed, $302,400 per quarter. What are the budgeted earnings for next quarter? (Do not consider federal income taxes.)

Exercise 23–4
Prepare a flexible production budget (L.O. 5)

Cowboys Corporation considers materials and labor to be completely variable costs. Expected production for the year is 100,000 units. At that level of production, direct materials cost is budgeted at $198,000, and direct labor cost is budgeted at $450,000. Prepare a flexible budget for materials and labor for possible production levels of 105,000, 120,000, and 135,000 units of product.

Exercise 23–5
Compute budget variances (L.O. 5)

Assume that in Exercise 23–4 actual production was 120,000 units, materials cost was $247,000, and labor cost was $510,000. What are the budget variances?

Exercise 23–6
Compute the budget variance for operations (L.O. 5)

Fixed production costs for Spenser Company are budgeted at $288,000, assuming 40,000 units of production. Actual sales for the period were 35,000 units, while actual production was 40,000 units. Actual fixed costs used in computing cost of goods sold amounted to $252,000. What is the budget variance?

Exercise 23–7
Prepare a purchases budget (L.O. 6)

The shoe department of Blazendale's Department Store has prepared a sales budget for April calling for a sales volume of $150,000. The department expects to begin in April with a $100,000 inventory and to end the month with an $85,000 inventory. Its cost of goods sold averages 70% of sales.

Prepare a purchases budget for the department showing the amount of goods to be purchased during April.

PROBLEMS

Problem 23–1
Determine budgeted cost of goods sold; prepare operating budgets (L.O. 4)

Francisco Corporation prepares monthly operating and financial budgets. The operating budgets for March and April are based on the following data:

	Units Produced	Units Sold
March	200,000	180,000
April.	180,000	200,000

All sales are at $60 per unit. Direct materials, direct labor, and variable manufacturing overhead are estimated at $6, $12, and $6 per unit, respectively. Total fixed manufacturing overhead is budgeted at $1,080,000 per month. Selling and administrative expenses are budgeted at $1,200,000 plus 10% of sales, while federal income taxes are budgeted at 40% of income before federal income taxes. The inventory at March 1 consists of 100,000 units with a cost of $34.20 each.

Required

a. Prepare monthly budget estimates of cost of goods sold assuming that FIFO inventory procedure is used.

b. Prepare planned operating budgets for March and April.

Problem 23–2
Prepare a flexible operating budget (L.O. 5)

The computation of operating income for Cougars Company for 1995 follows:

Sales		$3,600,000
Cost of goods manufactured and sold:		
Direct materials	$720,000	
Direct labor	480,000	
Variable manufacturing overhead	240,000	
Fixed manufacturing overhead.	480,000	1,920,000
Gross margin		$1,680,000
Selling expenses:		
Variable.	$264,000	
Fixed	336,000	600,000
		$1,080,000
Administrative expenses:		
Variable.	$312,000	
Fixed	384,000	696,000
Net operating income		$ 384,000

An operating budget is prepared for 1996 with sales forecasted at a 25% increase in volume. Direct materials, direct labor, and all costs labeled as variable are completely variable. Fixed costs are expected to continue except for a $48,000 increase in fixed administrative costs. Actual operating data for 1996 are:

Sales	$4,320,000
Direct materials	888,000
Direct labor	576,000
Variable manufacturing overhead	297,600
Fixed manufacturing overhead	492,000
Variable selling expenses	372,000
Fixed selling expenses	314,400
Variable administrative expenses	396,000
Fixed administrative expenses	436,400

Required

a. Prepare a budget report comparing the 1996 planned operating budget with actual 1996 data.

b. Prepare a budget report that would be useful in appraising the performance of the various persons charged with responsibility to provide satisfactory income. (Hint: Prepare budget data on a flexible basis and use the percentage by which sales were actually experienced.)

c. Comment on the differences revealed by the two reports.

Problem 23–3
Prepare a planned operating budget and a flexible operating budget
(L.O. 4, 5)

a. Use the following data to prepare a planned operating budget for Kim Company for the year ending December 31, 1996:

Plant capacity	100,000 units
Expected sales volume	90,000 units
Expected production	90,000 units
Actual production	90,000 units
Forecasted selling price	$12.00 per unit
Actual selling price	$13.50 per unit
Manufacturing costs:	
Variable (per unit):	
Direct materials	$3.60
Direct labor	$1.50
Manufacturing overhead	$2.25
Fixed manufacturing overhead	$108,000
Selling and administrative expenses:	
Variable (per unit)	$1.20
Fixed	$60,000

Assume no beginning or ending inventory. Federal income taxes are budgeted at 40% of income before federal income taxes.

b. The actual operating data for the year ending December 31, 1996, follow:

Sales		$1,080,000
Cost of goods sold:		
Direct materials	$337,500	
Direct labor	135,000	
Variable manufacturing overhead	202,500	
Fixed manufacturing overhead	108,000	
Total	$783,000	
Less: Ending inventory ($783,000 × 10/90)	87,000	696,000
Gross margin		$ 384,000
Selling expenses:		
Variable	$102,000	
Fixed	72,000	174,000
Income before federal income taxes		$ 210,000
Deduct: Federal income taxes at 40%		84,000
Net income		$ 126,000

Required

a. Prepare a planned operating budget for the year ended December 31, 1996, for part (**a**).

b. Using a flexible operating budget, analyze the efficiency of operations and comment on the company's sales policy for part (**b**).

Problem 23–4
Prepare a flexible budget for selling and administrative expenses
(L.O. 5)

Hi-Lo Company wants you to prepare a flexible budget for selling and administrative expenses. The general manager and the sales manager have met with all the department heads, who provided the following information regarding selling and administrative expenses:

1. The company presently employs 30 full-time salespersons with a base of $1,800 each per month plus commissions and 10 full-time salespersons with a salary of $3,000 each per month plus commissions. In addition, the company employs nine regional sales managers with a salary of $10,800 per month, none of whom is entitled to any commissions.
2. If sales volume exceeds $40 million per year, the company must hire four more salespersons, each at a salary of $1,800 per month plus commissions.
3. Sales commissions are either 10% or 5% of the selling price, depending on the product sold. Typically, a 10% commission applies on 60% of sales, and a 5% commission applies on the remaining 40% of sales.
4. Salespersons' travel allowances average $750 per month per salesperson (excluding managers).
5. Advertising expenses average $75,000 per month plus 3% of sales.
6. Selling supplies expense is estimated at 1% of sales.

7. Administrative salaries are $150,000 per month.
8. Other administrative expenses include the following:

   Rent—$24,000 per month
   Office supplies—2% of sales
   Other administrative expenses (telephone, etc.)—$6,000 per month

Required Prepare a flexible budget for selling and administrative expenses for sales volume of $18 million, $24 million, and $30 million per year.

Problem 23–5
Prepare a cash receipts schedule and a purchases budget (L.O. 6)

Classic Lumination Company manufactures and sells lighting fixtures. Estimated sales for the next three months are

September	$ 700,000
October	1,000,000
November	800,000

Sales for August were $800,000. All sales are on account. Classic Lumination Company estimates that 60% of the accounts receivable are collected in the month of sale with the remaining 40% collected the following month. The units sell for $30 each. The cash balance for September 1 is $200,000.

Generally, 60% of purchases are due and payable in the month of purchase with the remainder due the following month. Purchase cost per unit for materials is $18. The company maintains an end-of-the-month inventory of 2,000 units plus 10% of next month's unit sales.

Required Prepare a cash receipts schedule for September and October and a purchases budget for August, September, and October.

Problem 23–6
Prepare a cash budget (L.O. 6)

Refer to Problem 23–5. In addition to the information given, selling and administrative expenses paid in cash are $240,000 per month.

Required Prepare a monthly cash budget for September and October for Classic Lumination Company.

Alternate Problems

Problem 23–1A
Prepare schedules showing budgeted production and budgeted cost of goods sold (L.O. 4)

Joyce Company prepares monthly operating and financial budgets. Estimates of sales in units are made for each month. Production is scheduled at a level high enough to take care of current needs and to carry into each month one half of the next month's unit sales. Direct materials, direct labor, and variable manufacturing overhead are estimated at $6, $3, and $2 per unit, respectively. Total fixed manufacturing overhead is budgeted at $240,000 per month. Sales for April, May, June, and July 1996 are estimated at 100,000, 120,000, 160,000, and 120,000 units. The inventory at April 1, 1996, consists of 50,000 units with a cost of $14.40 per unit.

Required

a. Prepare a schedule showing the budgeted production in units for April, May, and June 1996.
b. Prepare a schedule showing the budgeted cost of goods sold for the same three months assuming that the FIFO method is used for inventories.

Problem 23–2A
Prepare a flexible operating budget (L.O. 5)

Following is a summary of operating data of Andrea Company for the year 1995:

Sales		$7,000,000
Cost of goods manufactured and sold:		
Direct materials	$1,200,000	
Direct labor	1,100,000	
Variable manufacturing overhead	300,000	
Fixed manufacturing overhead	800,000	3,400,000
Gross margin		$3,600,000
Selling expenses:		
Variable	$ 300,000	
Fixed	400,000	700,000
		$2,900,000
General and administrative expenses:		
Variable	$ 100,000	
Fixed	1,200,000	1,300,000
Net operating income		$1,600,000

Sales volume for 1996 is budgeted at 90% of 1995 sales volume. Prices are not expected to change. The 1996 budget amounts for the various other costs and expenses differ from those reported in 1995 only for the expected volume change in the variable items. Actual operating data for 1996 follow:

Sales	$5,800,000
Direct materials	1,300,000
Direct labor	1,100,000
Variable manufacturing overhead	300,000
Fixed manufacturing overhead	780,000
Variable selling expenses	270,000
Fixed selling expenses	290,000
Variable administrative expenses	110,000
Fixed administrative expenses	1,100,000

Required

a. Prepare a budget report comparing the planned operating budget for 1996 with the actual results for that year.

b. Prepare a budget report that would be useful in pinpointing responsibility for the poor showing in 1996. (Hint: Prepare a flexible operating budget.)

Problem 23–3A
Prepare a planned operating budget and a flexible operating budget
(L.O. 4, 5)

a. Use the following data for Bugs Company in preparing its 1996 operating budget:

Plant capacity	500,000 units
Expected sales volume	450,000 units
Expected production	500,000 units
Forecasted selling price	$36.00 per unit
Variable manufacturing costs per unit:	
Direct materials	$13.50
Direct labor	4.50
Manufacturing overhead	3.00
Fixed manufacturing overhead per period	$450,000
Selling and administrative expenses:	
Variable (per unit)	$1.50
Fixed (per period)	$375,000

Assume no beginning inventory. Federal income taxes are budgeted at 40% of income before income taxes.

b. The actual results for Bugs Company for the year ended December 31, 1996, follow. (Note: The actual sales price was $40 per unit. Actual unit production was equal to actual unit sales.)

Sales (500,000 units @ $40 per unit)		$20,000,000
Cost of goods sold:		
Direct materials	$6,000,000	
Direct labor	2,200,000	
Variable manufacturing overhead	2,000,000	
Fixed manufacturing overhead	500,000	10,700,000
Gross margin		$ 9,300,000
Selling and administrative expenses:		
Variable	$ 700,000	
Fixed	400,000	1,100,000
Income before federal income taxes		$8,200,000
Deduct: Federal income taxes at 40%		3,280,000
Net income		$ 4,920,000

Required

a. Prepare a planned operating budget for the year ended December 31, 1996, for part (**a**).

b. Using a flexible operating budget, analyze the efficiency of operations. Comment on the results of 1996 and on the company's sales policy in part (**b**).

Problem 23–4A
Prepare a cash budget
(L.O. 6)

Durango Company gathered the following budget information for the quarter ending September 30, 1996:

Sales	$270,000
Purchases	225,000
Salaries and wages	97,000
Rent	5,000
Supplies	4,000
Insurance	1,000
Other cash expenses	6,000

A cash balance of $18,000 is planned for July 1. Accounts receivable are expected to be $30,000 on July 1. All but one half of 1% of the July 1 Accounts Receivable balance will be collected in the quarter ending September 30. The company's sales collection pattern is 95% in the quarter of sale and 5% in the quarter after sale. Accounts payable will be $15,000 on July 1 and will be paid during the coming quarter. The company's purchases payment pattern is 75% in the quarter of purchase and 25% in the quarter after purchase. Expenses are paid in the quarter in which they are incurred.

Required Prepare a cash budget for the quarter ending September 30, 1996.

Beyond the Numbers—Critical Thinking

Business Decision Case 23–1
Prepare a cash budget
(L.O. 6)

Wisconsin Company has applied at a local bank for a short-term loan of $300,000 starting on October 1, 1996. The bank's loan officer has requested a cash budget from the company for the quarter ending December 31, 1996. The following information is needed to prepare the cash budget:

Sales	$1,200,000
Purchases	700,000
Salaries and wages to be paid	250,000
Rent payments	14,000
Supplies (payments for)	9,000
Insurance payments	3,000
Other cash payments	44,000

A cash balance of $48,000 is planned for October 1. Accounts receivable are expected to be $96,000 on October 1. All of these accounts will be collected in the quarter ending December 31. In general, sales are collected as follows: 90% in the quarter of sale, and 10% in the quarter after sale. Accounts payable will be $960,000 on October 1 and will be paid during the quarter ending December 31. All purchases are paid in the quarter after purchase.

Required

a. Prepare a cash budget for the quarter ending December 31, 1996. Assume that the $300,000 loan will be made on October 1 and will be repaid with interest at 10% on December 31.

b. Will the company be able to repay the loan on December 31? If the company desires a minimum cash balance of $36,000, will the company be able to repay the loan as planned?

Ethics Case—Writing Experience 23–2

The state of California faced large budget deficits. Meanwhile, officials in a particular community college district were looking for ways to spend the money that had been budgeted for the district. The community college was entering the last three months of the fiscal year with excess funds because the area had experienced a mild winter resulting in lower than usual utilities and maintenance costs.

At a budget meeting, one official commented, "You know what will happen if we don't spend all of our budget. The state will claim we don't need as much money next year. What happens if we have a hard winter next year? We'll need every cent we can get!"

The community college's accounting manager commented, "We are legally entitled to spend all of the money this year that has been budgeted to us. I am concerned about the memorandum that we received requesting that we cut expenditures wherever possible to help reduce the state's deficit."

The first official responded, "That deficit is the state's problem, not ours. We wouldn't have a deficit in the first place if the state administrators were able to estimate taxes and do a better job of budgeting. Let's deal with our problems and let them deal with theirs!"

Required

Write a response from the point of view of the taxpayers of the state of California. Should the community college spend all of the money that had been budgeted for it?

Broader Perspective—Writing Assignment 23–3

Refer to the Broader Perspective, "Planning in a Changing Environment," on page 823. Describe and evaluate Bell Atlantic's new approach to planning. How would you advise company management to communicate the company's values and plans to employees?

Group Project 23–4
Developing a budget

In groups of three, develop a budget for an organization that publishes financial statements, such as The Coca-Cola Company or Maytag Corporation. Your budget should include three different types of projected income statements for the coming month, quarter, or year. These three income statements should be for optimistic, pessimistic, and expected scenarios. Collect or develop as much information as possible to prepare the budget. For example, to prepare a budgeted income statement for a publicly traded company such as Coca-Cola, look at previous annual reports and collect whatever additional information you can from news reports. Be sure to state the assumptions used in preparing the budget in a memorandum you write as a team. The heading of the memorandum should contain the date, to whom it is written, from whom, and the subject matter. Don't forget to include the three different projected income statements.

Comprehensive Problems

Comprehensive Problem 23–1
Prepare a master budget
(L.O. 6)

Barney Corporation prepares annual budgets by quarters. The company's post-closing trial balance as of December 31, 1997, is as follows:

	Debits	Credits
Cash	$138,000	
Accounts Receivable	360,000	
Allowance for Uncollectible Accounts		$ 12,000
Inventories	156,000	
Prepaid Expenses	12,000	
Furniture and Equipment	180,000	
Accumulated Depreciation—Furniture and Equipment		12,000
Accounts Payable		120,000
Accrued Liabilities Payable		36,000
Notes Payable, 5% (due 1998)		480,000
Capital Stock		300,000
Retained Earnings (deficit)	114,000	
	$960,000	$960,000

All of the capital stock of Barney Corporation was recently acquired by Juan Jackson. After the purchase, Jackson loaned substantial sums of money to the corporation, which still owes him $480,000 on a 5% note. There are no accrued federal income taxes payable, but future earnings will be subject to income taxation.

Jackson is anxious to withdraw $120,000 from the corporation (as a payment on the note payable to him) but will not do so if it reduces the corporation's cash balance below $120,000. Thus, he is quite interested in the budgets for the quarter ending March 31, 1998.

Additional data

1. Sales for the coming quarter ending March 31, 1998, are forecasted at $1,200,000; for the following quarter they are forecasted at $1,500,000. All sales are priced to yield a gross margin of 40%. Inventory is to be maintained on hand at the end of any quarter in an amount equal to 20% of the goods to be sold in the next quarter. All sales are on account, and 95% of the December 31, 1997, receivables plus 70% of the current quarter's sales will be collected during the quarter ending March 31, 1998.
2. Selling expenses are budgeted at $48,000 plus 6% of sales; $24,000 will be incurred on account, $66,000 accrued, $27,000 from expiration of prepaid rent and prepaid insurance, and $3,000 from allocated depreciation.
3. Purchasing expenses are budgeted at $34,800 plus 5% of purchases for the quarter; $9,000 will be incurred on account, $48,000 accrued, $13,800 from expired prepaid expenses, and $1,200 from allocated depreciation.

4. Administrative expenses are budgeted at $42,000 plus 2% of sales; $3,000 will be incurred on account, $36,000 accrued, $13,200 from expired prepayments, and $1,800 from allocated depreciation. Uncollectible accounts are estimated at 1% of sales.
5. Interest accrues at 5% annually on the notes payable and is credited to Accrued Liabilities Payable.
6. All of the beginning balances in Accounts Payable and Accrued Liabilities Payable, plus 80% of the current credits to Accounts Payable, and all but $30,000 of the current accrued liabilities will be paid during the quarter. An $18,000 insurance premium is to be paid prior to March 31, and a full year's rent of $144,000 is due on January 2.
7. Federal income taxes are budgeted at 40% of the income before federal income taxes. The taxes should be accrued, and no payments are due in the first quarter.

Required

a. Prepare a planned operating budget for the quarter ending March 31, 1998, including supporting schedules for planned purchases and operating expenses.
b. Prepare a financial budget for March 31, 1998. Supporting schedules should be included that (1) analyze accounts credited for purchases and operating expenses, (2) show planned accounts receivable collections and balance, and (3) show planned cash flows and cash balance.
c. Will Jackson be able to collect the $120,000 on his note?

Comprehensive Problem 23–2
Prepare a master budget
(L.O. 6)

Lindbaugh Corporation is a rapidly expanding company. The company's post-closing balance as of December 31, 1997, is as follows:

LINDBAUGH CORPORATION
Post-Closing Trial Balance
December 31, 1997

	Debits	Credits
Cash	$ 240,000	
Accounts Receivable	480,000	
Allowance for Uncollectible Accounts		$ 36,000
Inventories	600,000	
Prepaid Expenses	72,000	
Land	600,000	
Buildings and Equipment	1,800,000	
Accumulated Depreciation—Buildings and Equipment		240,000
Accounts Payable		360,000
Accrued Liabilities Payable (including income taxes)		240,000
Capital Stock		2,400,000
Retained Earnings		516,000
	$3,792,000	$3,792,000

Sales in the last quarter of 1997 amounted to $2,400,000 and are projected at $3,000,000 and $4,800,000 for the first two quarters of 1998. This expansion has created a need for cash. Management is especially concerned about the probable cash balance of March 31, 1998, since a payment of $360,000 for some new equipment must be made on delivery on April 2. The current cash balance of $240,000 is considered to be the minimum workable balance.

Additional data

1. Purchases, all on account, are to be scheduled so that the inventory at the end of any quarter is equal to one third of the goods expected to be sold in the coming quarter. Cost of goods sold averages 60% of sales.
2. Selling expenses are budgeted at $120,000 plus 8% of sales; $24,000 is expected to be incurred on account, $288,000 accrued, $33,600 from expired prepayments, and $14,400 from allocated depreciation.
3. Purchasing expenses are budgeted at $84,000 plus 5% of purchases; $12,000 will be incurred on account, $156,000 accrued, $13,200 from expired prepayments, and $10,800 from allocated depreciation.
4. Administrative expenses are budgeted at $150,000 plus 3% of sales; $24,000 will be incurred on account, $132,000 accrued, $13,200 from expired prepayments, and $10,800 from allocated depreciation.

5. Federal income taxes are budgeted at 40% of income before federal income taxes and are recorded as accrued liabilities. Payments on these taxes are included in the payments on accrued liabilities discussed in item **8**.
6. All December 31, 1997, accounts payable plus 80% of current credits to this account will be paid in the first quarter. All of the December 31, 1997, accrued liabilities payable (except for $72,000) will be paid in the first quarter. Of the current quarter's accrued liabilities, all but $288,000 will be paid during the first quarter.
7. Cash outlays for various expenses normally prepaid will amount to $96,000 during the quarter.
8. All sales are made on account; 80% of the sales are collected in the quarter in which made, and all of the remaining sales are collected in the following quarter, except for 2% which is never collected. The Allowance for Uncollectible Accounts account shows the estimated amount of accounts receivable at December 31, 1997, arising from 1997 sales that will not be collected.

Required

a. Prepare an operating budget for the quarter ending March 31, 1998. Supporting schedules for planned purchases and operating expenses should be included.
b. Prepare a financial budget for March 31, 1998. Include supporting schedules that (1) analyze accounts credited for purchases and expenses, (2) show planned cash flows and cash balance, and (3) show planned collections of accounts receivable and the accounts receivable balance.
c. Will sufficient cash be on hand April 2 to pay for the new equipment?

Answers to Self-Test

True-False

1. **True.** Budgets are estimates of the future and should consider future plans and conditions.
2. **True.** Cash budgets may cover a week or a month; sales and production budgets a month, a quarter, or a year; and general operating budgets may cover a quarter or a year.
3. **True.** The planned operating budget is developed first in units, then in dollars.
4. **False.** Flexible budgets are based on actual activity and planned operating budgets are based on planned activity. Planned operating budgets based on planned activity levels and flexible budgets are *not* the same if planned activity levels and actual activity levels are not the same.

Multiple-Choice

1. **e.** The benefits of budgeting include **a** through **d**.
2. **c.** The sales budget is first. We need to know sales before we predict cost of goods sold, selling and administrative expenses, and the financial budget.
3. **a.**

$$\text{Budgeted amount} = \text{Fixed costs} + \left(\text{Variable cost per unit} \times \text{Units of output}\right)$$
$$= \$60{,}000 + (\$1.20 \times 200{,}000)$$
$$= \$60{,}000 + \$240{,}000$$
$$= \$300{,}000 \text{ budgeted amount}$$

4. **d.**

$150,000 − $30,000 = $120,000 variable cost
$120,000/100,000 units = $1.20 per unit variable cost

Budgeted costs at 90,000 units:	
90,000 × $1.20	$108,000
Fixed costs	30,000
	$138,000
Actual costs	142,500
Unfavorable budget variance	$ 4,500

24

CONTROL THROUGH STANDARD COSTS

This chapter discusses the uses of standard costs, the advantages and disadvantages of using standard costs, and how to compute the difference, or *variance*, between an actual cost and a standard cost. We discuss how managers can improve efficiency by investigating variances and taking corrective action.

LEARNING OBJECTIVES

After studying this chapter, you should be able to:

1. Discuss the nature of standard costs, including how standards are set.
2. Define budgets and discuss how budgets are used in a standard cost system.
3. Discuss the advantages and disadvantages of using standard costs.
4. Calculate the six variances from standard and determine if the variance is favorable or unfavorable.

(continued)

USES OF STANDARD COSTS

Whenever you have set goals that you have sought to achieve, these goals could have been called *standards*. Periodically, you might measure your actual performance against these standards and analyze the differences to see how close you are to your goal. Similarly, management sets goals, such as standard costs, and compares actual costs with these goals to identify possible problems.

This section begins with a discussion of the nature of standard costs. Next, we explain how managers use standard costs to establish budgets. Then we describe how management uses the concept of **management by exception** to investigate variances from standards. We also explain setting standards and how management decides whether to use ideal or practical standards. The section closes with a discussion of the other uses of standard costs.

Nature of Standard Costs

A **standard cost** is a carefully predetermined measure of what a cost should be under stated conditions. Standard costs are not only estimates of what costs will be but also goals to be achieved. When standards are properly set, their achievement represents a reasonably efficient level of performance.

Usually, effective standards are the result of engineering studies and of time and motion studies undertaken to determine the amounts of materials, labor, and other services required to produce a product. Also considered in setting standards are general economic conditions because these conditions affect the cost of materials and other services that must be purchased by a manufacturing company.

(concluded)

5. Discuss what each of the six variances shows and prepare journal entries to record the variance.
6. Discuss the three selection guidelines used to investigate variances from standard.
7. Discuss theoretical and practical methods for disposing of variances from standard.

Manufacturing companies determine the standard cost of each unit of product by establishing the standard cost of direct materials, direct labor, and manufacturing overhead necessary to produce that unit. Determining the standard cost of direct materials and direct labor is less complicated than determining the standard cost of manufacturing overhead.

The standard direct materials cost per unit of a product consists of the standard amount of material required to produce the unit multiplied by the standard price of the material. You must distinguish between the terms *standard price* and *standard cost*. Standard price usually refers to the price per unit of inputs into the production process, such as the price per pound of raw materials.

Standard cost, however, is the standard quantity of an input required per unit of output times the standard price per unit of that input. For example, if the standard price of cloth is $3 per yard and the standard quantity of material required to produce a dress is 3 yards, the standard direct materials cost of the dress is 3 yards × $3 per yard = $9. Similarly, a company computes the standard direct labor cost per unit for a product as the standard number of hours needed to produce one unit multiplied by the standard labor or wage rate per hour.

Objective 1
Discuss the nature of standard costs, including how standards are set.

Standard Manufacturing Overhead Cost To find the standard manufacturing overhead cost of a unit, use the following steps. First, determine the expected level of output for the year. This level of output is called the **standard level of output**. Second, determine the total budgeted manufacturing overhead cost at the standard level of output. The total budgeted overhead cost includes both fixed and variable components. Total fixed cost is the same at every level of output within a relevant range. Variable overhead varies in direct proportion to the number of units produced. Third, compute the standard manufacturing overhead cost per unit by dividing the total budgeted manufacturing overhead cost at the standard level of output by the standard level of output. The result is standard overhead cost (or rate) per unit of output.

The formula to compute the standard overhead cost per unit is:

$$\text{Standard overhead cost (or rate) per unit} = \frac{\text{Total budgeted overhead cost at the standard level of output}}{\text{Standard level of output}}$$

Sometimes accountants find the standard overhead rate per unit of input, such as direct labor-hour instead of per unit. To find the standard overhead cost per unit, multiply the direct labor-hours per unit times the standard overhead cost per direct labor-hour. For instance, if the standard overhead costs per direct labor-hour is $5 and the standard number of direct labor-hours is two hours per unit, the standard overhead cost per unit is $5 × 2 hours = $10.

Use of Standard Costs in Developing Budgets

As discussed in Chapter 23, **budgets** are formal written plans that represent management's planned actions in the future and the impacts of these actions on the business. As a business incurs actual expenses and revenues, management compares them with the budgeted amounts. To control operations, management investigates any differences between the actual and budgeted amounts and takes corrective action.

Management by Exception

When management compares actual expenses and revenues with budgeted expenses and revenues, differences—called *variances*—are likely to occur. The responsibility of management is to investigate significant variances. Obviously, management must determine when a variance is significant. This process of focusing on only the most significant variances is known as **management by exception**. The process of management by exception enables management to concentrate its efforts on those variances that could have a big effect on the company, ignoring those variances that are not significant.

Ideal versus Practical Standards

In developing standards, management must consider the assumed conditions under which these standards can be met. Standards generally fall into two groups—ideal and practical.

Objective 2
Define budgets and discuss how budgets are used in a standard cost system.

A company attains **ideal standards** under the best circumstances—with no machinery problems or worker problems. The company can attain these unrealistic standards only when it has highly efficient, skilled workers who are working at their best effort throughout the entire period needed to complete the job.

Practical standards are strict but attainable standards that have allowances made for machinery problems and rest periods for workers. Companies can meet these standards if average workers are efficient at their work. These standards are generally used in planning.

Generally, management does not use ideal standards because ideal standards do not allow for normal repairs to machinery or rest periods for workers. A company rarely runs its operations under ideal conditions. Since planning under ideal standards is unrealistic, managers rarely use ideal standards in budgeting. Instead, management uses practical standards in planning because these standards are more realistic, allowing for machinery repairs and rest periods for workers. Any variances that result when practical standards are used indicate abnormal or unusual problems.

Other Uses of Standard Costs

In addition to developing budgets, companies use standard costs in evaluating management's performance, evaluating workers' performance, and setting appropriate selling prices.

Firms evaluate management's and workers' performances through the use of a budget. When management compares actual results with budgeted amounts, it can see how well it is performing its own duties and managing its employees. Management also can evaluate workers based on how well they performed relative to the budgeted amounts pertaining to the activities they performed.

Standard costs are useful in setting selling prices. The budget shows the expected expenses incurred by the business. By considering these expenses, management can determine how much to charge for a product so that it can produce the desired net income. As the business actually incurs these expenses, management determines if the selling prices set are still reasonable and, when necessary, considers some price adjustments after taking competition into account.

Advantages and Disadvantages of Using Standard Costs

Advantages of Using Standard Costs

Objective 3
Discuss the advantages and disadvantages of using standard costs.

Five of the benefits that result from a business using a standard cost system are:

1. Improved cost control.
2. More useful information for managerial planning and decision making.
3. More reasonable and easier inventory measurements.
4. Cost savings in record-keeping.
5. Possible reductions in production costs incurred.

Improved Cost Control Companies can gain greater cost control by setting standards for each type of cost incurred and then highlighting exceptions or variances—instances where things did not go as planned. Variances provide a starting point for judging the effectiveness of managers in controlling the costs for which they are held responsible.

Assume, for example, that in a production center, actual direct materials costs of $52,015 exceeded standard costs by $6,015. Knowing that actual direct materials costs exceeded standard costs by $6,015 is more useful than merely knowing the actual direct materials costs amounted to $52,015. Now the firm can investigate the cause of the excess of actual costs over standard costs and take action.

Further investigation should reveal whether the exception or variance was caused by the inefficient use of materials or resulted from higher prices due to inflation or inefficient purchasing. In either case, the standard cost system acts as an early warning system by highlighting a potential hazard for management.

More Useful Information for Managerial Planning and Decision Making When management develops appropriate cost standards and succeeds in controlling production costs, future actual costs should be close to the standard. As a result, management can use standard costs in preparing more accurate budgets and in estimating costs for bidding on jobs. A standard cost system can be valuable for top management in planning and decision making.

More Reasonable and Easier Inventory Measurements A standard cost system provides easier inventory valuation than an actual cost system. Under an actual cost system, unit costs for batches of identical products may differ widely. For example, this variation can occur because of a machine malfunction during the production of a given batch that increases the labor and overhead charged to that batch. Under a standard cost system, the company would not include such unusual costs in inventory. Rather, it would charge these excess costs to variance accounts after comparing actual costs to standard costs.

Thus, in a standard cost system, a company assumes that all units of a given product produced during a particular time period have the same unit cost. Logically, identical physical units produced in a given time period should be recorded at the same cost.

Cost Savings in Record-Keeping Although a standard cost system may seem to require more detailed record-keeping during the accounting period than an actual cost system, the reverse is true. For example, a system that accumulates only actual costs shows cost flows between inventory accounts and eventually into costs of goods sold. It records these varying amounts of actual unit costs that must be calculated during the period. In a standard cost system, a company shows the cost flows between inventory accounts and into cost of goods sold at consistent standard amounts during the period. It needs no special calculations to determine actual unit costs during the period. Instead, companies may print standard cost sheets in advance showing standard quantities and standard unit costs for the materials, labor, and overhead needed to produce a certain product.

Possible Reductions in Production Costs Incurred A standard cost system may lead to cost savings. The use of standard costs may cause employees to become more cost conscious and to seek improved methods of completing their tasks. Only when employees become active in reducing costs can companies really become successful in cost control.

Disadvantages of Using Standard Costs

Three of the disadvantages that result from a business using standard costs are:

1. Controversial materiality limits for variances.
2. Nonreporting of certain variances.
3. Low morale for some workers.

Controversial Materiality Limits for Variances Determining the materiality limits of the variances may be controversial. The management of each business has the responsibility for determining what constitutes a material or unusual variance. Because materiality involves individual judgment, many problems or conflicts may arise in setting materiality limits.

Nonreporting of Certain Variances Workers do not always report all exceptions or variances. If management only investigates unusual variances, workers may not report negative exceptions to the budget or may try to minimize these exceptions to conceal inefficiency. Workers who succeed in hiding variances diminish the effectiveness of budgeting.

Low Morale for Some Workers The management by exception technique focuses on the unusual variances. The purpose of this technique is to investigate significant differences. Thus, workers who stay within the budget's contraints may be overlooked and not praised for their efforts. As a result, the morale of these workers may suffer.

An Accounting Perspective

Business Insight Workers Develop Their Own Standards at the Toyota-GM Joint Venture

The Toyota-General Motors joint venture in Fremont, California, known as New United Motor Manufacturing, Inc. (NUMMI), produces the Toyota Corolla and Geo Prizm small cars. NUMMI has succeeded in allowing employees to set their own work standards. In the old days, industrial engineers would shut themselves in a room and ponder how to set standards. The industrial engineers ignored the workers, who in turn ignored the standards. Now, workers themselves hold the stopwatches and set the standards. Worker team members time each other, looking for the most efficient and safest way to do the work. They standardize each task so everyone in the team does it the same way. The workers are more informed about how to do the work right than industrial engineers, and they are more motivated to meet the standards they set.

Source: Based on Paul S. Adler, "Time-and-Motion Regained," *Harvard Business Review*, January–February 1993, pp. 97–108.

Computing Variances

Objective 4
Calculate the six variances from standard and determine if the variance is favorable or unfavorable.

As stated earlier, standard costs represent goals. Standard cost is the amount a cost should be under a given set of circumstances. The accounting records also contain information about actual costs.

The amount by which actual cost differs from standard cost is called a **variance.** When actual costs are less than the standard cost, a cost variance is favorable. When actual costs exceed the standard costs, a cost variance is unfavorable. Do not automatically equate favorable and unfavorable variances with good and bad. You must base such an appraisal on the causes of the variance.

Objective 5
Discuss what each of the six variances shows and prepare journal entries to record the variance.

The following section explains how to compute the dollar amount of variances, a process called *isolating variances*, using data for Beta Company. Beta manufactures and sells a single product, each unit of which has the following standard costs:

Materials—5 sheets at $6	$30
Direct labor—2 hours at $10	20
Manufacturing overhead—2 direct labor-hours at $5	10
Total standard cost per unit	$60

We present additional data regarding the production activities of the company as needed.

Materials Variances

The standard materials cost of any product is simply the standard quantity of materials that should be used multiplied by the standard price that should be paid for those materials. Actual costs may differ from standard costs for materials because the price paid for the materials and/or the quantity of materials used varied from the standard amounts management had set. These two factors are accounted for by isolating two variances for materials—a price variance and a usage variance.

Accountants isolate these two materials variances for three reasons. First, different individuals may be responsible for each variance—a purchasing agent for the price variance and a production manager for the usage variance. Second, materials might not be purchased and used in the same period. The variance associated with the purchase should be isolated in the period of purchase, and the variance associated with usage should be isolated in the period of use. As a general rule, the sooner a variance can be isolated, the greater its value in cost control. Third, it is unlikely that a single materials variance—the difference between the standard cost and the actual cost of the materials used—would be of any real value to management for effective cost control. A single variance would not show management what caused the difference, or one variance might simply offset another and make the total difference appear to be immaterial.

Materials Price Variance In a manufacturing company, the purchasing and accounting departments usually set a standard price for materials meeting certain engineering specifications. They consider factors such as market conditions, vendors' quoted prices, and the optimum size of a purchase order when setting a standard price. A **materials price variance (MPV)** occurs when a company pays a higher or lower price than the standard price set for materials. Materials price variance (MPV) is the difference between actual price paid (AP) and standard price allowed (SP) multiplied by the actual quantity of materials purchased (AQ). In equation form, the materials price variance is:

$$\text{Materials price variance} = \left(\begin{matrix}\text{Actual}\\ \text{price}\end{matrix} - \begin{matrix}\text{Standard}\\ \text{price}\end{matrix}\right) \times \begin{matrix}\text{Actual quantity}\\ \text{purchased}\end{matrix}$$

To illustrate, assume that a new supplier entered the market enabling Beta Company to purchase 60,000 sheets of material at a price of \$5.90 each. Since the standard price set by management is \$6 per sheet, the materials price variance is computed as:

$$\begin{aligned}\text{Materials price variance} &= \left(\begin{matrix}\text{Actual}\\ \text{price}\end{matrix} - \begin{matrix}\text{Standard}\\ \text{price}\end{matrix}\right) \times \begin{matrix}\text{Actual quantity}\\ \text{purchased}\end{matrix}\\ &= (\$5.90 - \$6.00) \times 60{,}000\\ &= \$-0.10 \times 60{,}000\\ &= \$-6{,}000 \text{ (favorable)}\end{aligned}$$

The materials price variance of \$6,000 is considered favorable since the materials were acquired for a price less than the standard price. If the actual price had exceeded the standard price, the variance would be unfavorable because the costs incurred would have exceeded the standard price. The journal entry to record the purchase of materials is:

		Debit	Credit
(*a*)	Materials Inventory	360,000	
	Materials Price Variance		6,000
	Accounts Payable		354,000
	To record the purchase of materials at less than standard cost.		

Note that the Accounts Payable account shows the actual debt owed to suppliers, while the Materials Inventory account shows the standard price of the actual quantity of materials purchased. The Materials Price Variance account shows the difference between the actual price and standard price multiplied by the actual quantity purchased.

Materials Usage Variance Because the standard quantity of materials used in making a product is largely a matter of physical requirements or product specifications, usually the engineering department sets it. But if the quality of materials used varies with price, the accounting and purchasing departments may perform special studies to find the right quality.

The **materials usage variance (MUV)** occurs when more or less than the standard amount of materials is used to produce a product or complete a process. The variance shows only differences from the standard quantity caused by the quantity of materials used; it does not include any effect of variances in price.

Thus, the materials usage variance (MUV) is equal to actual quantity used (AQ) minus standard quantity allowed (SQ) multiplied by standard price (SP):

$$\text{Materials usage variance} = \left(\begin{array}{c}\text{Actual quantity}\\ \text{used}\end{array} - \begin{array}{c}\text{Standard}\\ \text{quantity}\\ \text{allowed}\end{array}\right) \times \begin{array}{c}\text{Standard}\\ \text{price}\end{array}$$

To illustrate, assume that Beta Company used 55,500 sheets of material to produce 11,000 units of a product for which the standard quantity allowed is 55,000 sheets (5 sheets per unit allowed × 11,000 units actually produced). Since the standard price of the material is $6 per sheet, the materials usage variance of $3,000 would be computed as follows:

$$\begin{aligned}\text{Materials usage variance} &= \left(\begin{array}{c}\text{Actual quantity}\\ \text{used}\end{array} - \begin{array}{c}\text{Standard}\\ \text{quantity}\\ \text{allowed}\end{array}\right) \times \begin{array}{c}\text{Standard}\\ \text{price}\end{array}\\ &= (55{,}500 - 55{,}000) \times \$6\\ &= 500 \times \$6\\ &= \$3{,}000 \text{ (unfavorable)}\end{aligned}$$

The variance is unfavorable because more materials were used than the standard quantity allowed to complete the job. If the standard quantity allowed had exceeded the quantity actually used, the materials usage variance would have been favorable.

The journal entry to record the use of the materials is:

		Debit	Credit
(*b*)	Work in Process Inventory	330,000	
	Materials Usage Variance	3,000	
	Materials Inventory		333,000
	To record the use of materials and to establish the materials usage variance.		

The Materials Usage Variance account shows the standard cost of the excess materials used. Note also that the Work in Process Inventory account contains both standard quantity and standard prices.

In the equations for both the materials variances, positive amounts were unfavorable variances and negative amounts were favorable variances. Unfavorable variances are debits in variance accounts because they add to the costs incurred, which are recorded as debits. Similarly, favorable variances are shown as negative amounts because they are reductions in costs. Thus, favorable variances are recorded in variance accounts as credits. We use this format in this text, but a word of caution is in order. Far greater understanding is achieved if you determine whether a variance is favorable or unfavorable by reliance on reason or logic. If more materials were used than the standard quantity, or if a price greater than the standard price was paid, the variance is unfavorable. If the reverse is true, the variance is favorable.

Illustration 24.1 shows the relationship between standard and actual materials cost and the computation of the materials variances; it is based on the following data relating to Beta Company:

Standard price per sheet of material	$6.00
Actual price per sheet of material	$5.90
Number of sheets of material purchased	60,000
Standard number of sheets of material per unit of product	5
Units of product produced in period	11,000
Actual number of sheets of material used	55,500

Labor Variances

The standard labor cost of any product is equal to the standard quantity of labor time allowed multiplied by the wage rate that should be paid for this time. Here again, it follows that the actual labor cost may differ from standard labor cost because of the wages paid for labor, the quantity of labor used, or both. Thus, two labor variances exist—a rate variance and an efficiency variance.

Illustration 24.1
Materials Price and Usage Variances

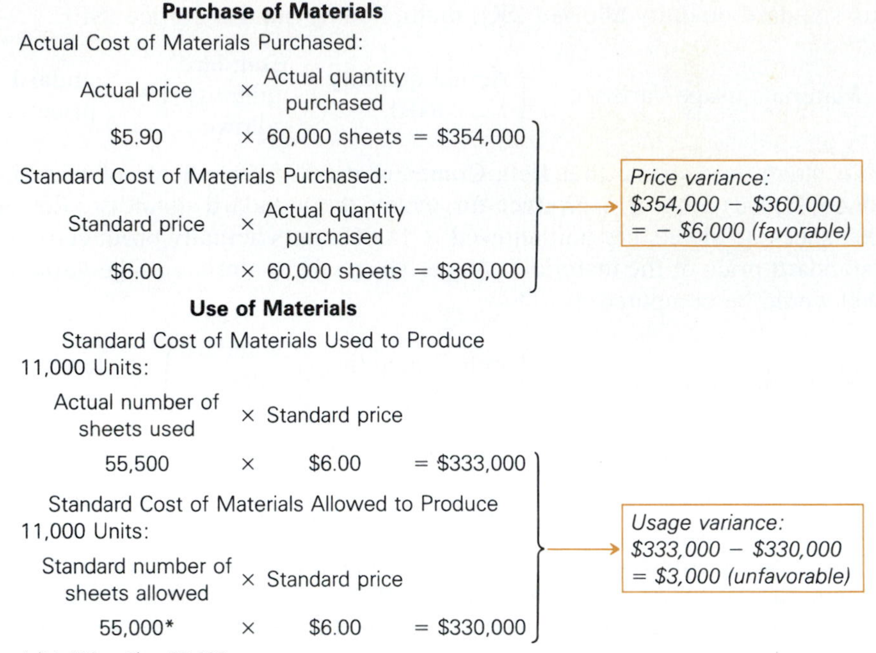

Purchase of Materials
Actual Cost of Materials Purchased:
Actual price × Actual quantity purchased
$5.90 × 60,000 sheets = $354,000
Standard Cost of Materials Purchased:
Standard price × Actual quantity purchased
$6.00 × 60,000 sheets = $360,000
Price variance:
$354,000 − $360,000
= − $6,000 (favorable)
Use of Materials
Standard Cost of Materials Used to Produce 11,000 Units:
Actual number of sheets used × Standard price
55,500 × $6.00 = $333,000
Standard Cost of Materials Allowed to Produce 11,000 Units:
Standard number of sheets allowed × Standard price
55,000* × $6.00 = $330,000
Usage variance:
$333,000 − $330,000
= $3,000 (unfavorable)
* (11,000 × 5) = 55,000.

Labor Rate Variance The **labor rate variance (LRV)** occurs when the average rate of pay is higher or lower than the standard cost to produce a product or complete a process. The labor rate variance is similar to the materials price variance.

To compute the labor rate variance (LRV), multiply the difference between the actual direct labor-hour rate paid (AR) and the standard direct labor-hour rate allowed (SR) by the actual hours of direct labor services worked (AH):

$$\text{Labor rate variance} = \left(\begin{matrix}\text{Actual}\\\text{rate}\end{matrix} - \begin{matrix}\text{Standard}\\\text{rate}\end{matrix}\right) \times \begin{matrix}\text{Actual hours}\\\text{worked}\end{matrix}$$

To continue the Beta example, assume that the direct labor payroll of the company consisted of 22,200 hours at a total cost of $233,100 (an average actual hourly rate of $10.50). Because management has set a standard direct labor-hour rate of $10 per hour, the labor rate variance is:

$$\begin{aligned}\text{Labor rate variance} &= \left(\begin{matrix}\text{Actual}\\\text{rate}\end{matrix} - \begin{matrix}\text{Standard}\\\text{rate}\end{matrix}\right) \times \begin{matrix}\text{Actual hours}\\\text{worked}\end{matrix}\\ &= (\$10.50 - \$10.00) \times 22{,}200\\ &= \$0.50 \times 22{,}200\\ &= \$11{,}100 \text{ (unfavorable)}\end{aligned}$$

The variance is positive and unfavorable because the actual rate paid exceeded the standard rate allowed. If the reverse were true, the variance would be favorable.

Labor Efficiency Variance Usually, the company's engineering department sets the standard amount of direct labor-hours needed to complete a product. Engineers may base the direct labor-hours standard on time and motion studies or on bargaining with the employees' union. The **labor efficiency variance (LEV)** occurs when employees use more or less than the standard amount of direct labor-hours to produce a product or complete a process. The labor efficiency variance is similar to the materials usage variance.

To compute the labor efficiency variance (LEV), multiply the difference between the actual direct labor-hours worked (AH) and the standard direct labor-hours allowed (SH) by the standard direct labor-hour rate per hour (SR):

$$\text{Labor efficiency variance} = \left(\begin{matrix}\text{Actual hours}\\\text{worked}\end{matrix} - \begin{matrix}\text{Standard hours}\\\text{allowed}\end{matrix}\right) \times \begin{matrix}\text{Standard}\\\text{rate}\end{matrix}$$

To illustrate, assume that the 22,200 hours of direct labor-hours worked by Beta Company employees resulted in 11,000 units of production. Assume these 11,000 units have a standard direct labor-hours of 22,000 hours (11,000 units at 2 hours per unit). Since the standard direct labor rate is $10 per hour, the labor efficiency variance is $2,000, computed as follows:

$$\begin{aligned}\text{Labor efficiency variance} &= \left(\begin{matrix}\text{Actual hours}\\\text{worked}\end{matrix} - \begin{matrix}\text{Standard hours}\\\text{allowed}\end{matrix}\right) \times \begin{matrix}\text{Standard}\\\text{rate}\end{matrix}\\ &= (22{,}200 - 22{,}000) \times \$10\\ &= 200 \times \$10\\ &= \$2{,}000 \text{ (unfavorable)}\end{aligned}$$

The variance is unfavorable since more hours than the standard number of hours were required to complete the period's production. If the reverse were true, the variance would be favorable.

The standard direct labor-hours allowed for the period's output is 22,000 hours (11,000 units at 2 hours per unit). The standard direct labor cost is $10 per hour; therefore, the standard direct labor cost for the output achieved is assigned to inventory, regardless of the actual direct labor cost.

The journal entry to charge the direct labor cost to Work in Process Inventory is:

		Debit	Credit
(c)	Work in Process Inventory	220,000	
	Labor Rate Variance	11,100	
	Labor Efficiency Variance	2,000	
	Payroll Summary		233,100
	To charge work in process with direct labor and to establish the two labor variances.		

With this entry, gross wages earned by direct-production employees ($233,100) are distributed as follows: $220,000 (the standard labor cost of production) to Work in Process Inventory and the balance to the two labor variance accounts. The unfavorable labor rate variance is not necessarily caused by paying employees more wages than they are entitled to receive. More probable reasons are either that more highly skilled employees with higher wage rates worked on production than originally anticipated, or that employee wage rates increased after the standard was developed and the standard was not revised. Favorable rate variances, on the other hand, could be caused by using less-skilled, cheaper labor in the production process. Typically, the hours of labor employed are more likely to be under management's control than the rates that are paid. For this reason, labor efficiency variances are generally watched more closely than labor rate variances.

In Illustration 24.2, we show the relationship between standard and actual direct labor cost and the computation of the labor variances. The illustration is based on the following data relating to Beta Company:

Standard direct labor-hours per unit	2 hours
Equivalent units produced in period	11,000 units
Standard labor rate per direct labor-hour	$10
Total direct labor wages paid (at actual rate of $10.50 per hour)	$233,100
Actual direct labor-hours worked	22,200 hours

Summary of Labor Variances The accuracy of the two labor variances can be checked by comparing their sum with the difference between actual and standard labor cost for a period. In the Beta Company illustration, this difference was:

Actual labor cost incurred (22,200 hours × $10.50)	$233,100
Standard labor cost allowed (22,000 hours × $10)	220,000
Total labor variance (unfavorable)	$ 13,100

ILLUSTRATION 24.2
Labor Rate and Efficiency Variances

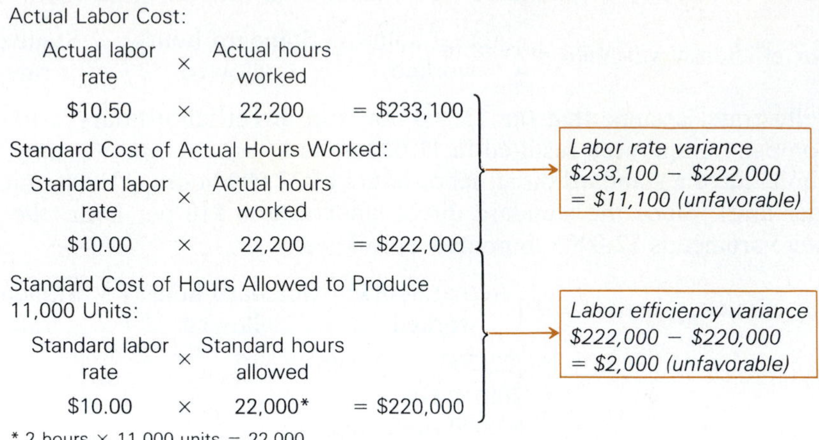

This $13,100 is made up of two labor variances, both unfavorable:

Labor rate variance (22,200 × $0.50)	$11,100
Labor efficiency variance (200 × $10)	2,000
Total labor variance (unfavorable)	$13,100

Labor Variances in Nonmanufacturing Organizations

Labor costs are typically a major cost in service organizations. Banks, public accounting firms, law firms, hospitals, and parking enforcement agencies are just a few organizations that monitor labor costs closely. University officials developed the following standards for a university's parking enforcement people. (The university's officials explained that they do not have ticket quotas, but they expect their parking ticket writers "to be enforcing parking laws, not hanging out at the coffee house."

Assume the university officials developed the following standard costs:

Standard direct labor time per ticket	12 minutes
Number of tickets written in March.	2,000 tickets
Standard labor rate per hour	$14
Total labor costs for ticket writing (at an average rate of $13.50 per hour).	$5,670
Actual ticket writing hours worked	420 hours

The university has calculated labor rate and efficiency variances as follows:

$$\text{Labor rate variance} = \left(\begin{matrix}\text{Actual}\\\text{rate}\end{matrix} - \begin{matrix}\text{Standard}\\\text{rate}\end{matrix}\right) \times \begin{matrix}\text{Actual}\\\text{hours}\end{matrix}$$
$$= (\$13.50 - \$14.00) \times 420 \text{ hours}$$
$$= \$-0.50 \times 420 \text{ hours}$$
$$= \$-210 \text{ (favorable)}$$

$$\text{Labor efficiency variance} = \left(\begin{matrix}\text{Actual}\\\text{hours}\end{matrix} - \begin{matrix}\text{Standard}\\\text{hours}\end{matrix}\right) \times \begin{matrix}\text{Standard}\\\text{rate}\end{matrix}$$

$$\text{Standard hours} = 12 \text{ minutes}/60 \text{ minutes} \times 2{,}000 \text{ tickets}$$
$$= 0.2 \text{ hours} \times 2{,}000 \text{ tickets}$$
$$= 400 \text{ hours}$$

$$\text{Labor efficiency variance} = (420 \text{ hours} - 400 \text{ hours}) \times \$14$$
$$= 20 \text{ hours} \times \$14$$
$$= \$280 \text{ (unfavorable)}$$

Overhead Variances

In a standard cost system, accountants apply the manufacturing overhead to the goods produced using a standard overhead rate. They set the rate prior to the start of the period by dividing the budgeted manufacturing overhead cost by a standard

ILLUSTRATION 24.3
Flexible Manufacturing Overhead Budget

BETA COMPANY
Flexible Manufacturing Overhead Budget

Machine-hours	18,000	20,000	22,000
Units of output	9,000	10,000	11,000
Variable overhead:			
Indirect materials	$ 7,200	$ 8,000	$ 8,800
Power	9,000	10,000	11,000
Royalties	1,800	2,000	2,200
Other	18,000	20,000	22,000
Total variable overhead	$36,000	$ 40,000	$ 44,000
Fixed overhead:			
Insurance	$ 4,000	$ 4,000	$ 4,000
Property taxes	6,000	6,000	6,000
Depreciation	20,000	20,000	20,000
Other	30,000	30,000	30,000
Total fixed overhead	$60,000	$ 60,000	$ 60,000
Total manufacturing overhead	$96,000	$100,000	$104,000
Standard overhead rate ($100,000 ÷ 20,000 hours)		$5	

level of output or activity. Total budgeted manufacturing overhead varies at different levels of standard output, but since some overhead costs are fixed, total budgeted manufacturing overhead does not vary in direct proportion with output.

Managers use a **flexible budget** to isolate overhead variances and to set the standard overhead rate. Flexible budgets show the budgeted amount of manufacturing overhead for various levels of output.

Look at Beta Company's flexible budget for the period in Illustration 24.3. Note that Beta's flexible budget shows the variable and fixed manufacturing overhead costs expected to be incurred at three levels of activity: 9,000 units, 10,000 units, and 11,000 units. For product costing purposes, Beta must estimate the expected level of activity in advance and set a rate based on that level. The level chosen is called the standard volume of output. This standard volume of output (or activity) may be expressed in terms of any of the activity bases used in setting standard overhead rates. These activity bases include percentage of capacity, units of output machine-hours, and direct labor-hours, among others. In our example, standard volume is assumed to be 10,000 units produced. Management expects to use 20,000 machine-hours of services.

Assume that Beta applies manufacturing overhead using a rate based on machine-hours. According to the flexible manufacturing overhead budget, the expected manufacturing overhead cost at the standard volume (20,000 machine-hours) is $100,000, so the standard overhead rate is $5 per machine-hour ($100,000 ÷ 20,000 machine-hours).

Knowing the separate rates for variable and fixed overhead is useful for decision making, as discussed in Chapters 21 and 22. The variable overhead rate is $2 ($40,000 ÷ 20,000 hours) per hour, and the fixed overhead rate is $3 ($60,000 ÷ 20,000 hours) per hour. If the expected volume had been 18,000 machine-hours, the standard overhead rate would have been $5.33 ($96,000 ÷ 18,000 hours). If the standard volume had been 22,000 machine-hours, the standard overhead rate would have been $4.73 ($104,000 ÷ 22,000 hours).

Note that the difference in rates is due solely to dividing fixed overhead by a different number of machine-hours. That is, the variable overhead cost per unit stays constant ($2 per machine-hour) regardless of the number of units expected to be produced, and only the fixed overhead cost per unit changes.

Continuing with the Beta Company illustration, assume that the company incurred $108,000 of actual manufacturing overhead costs in a period during which 11,000 units of product were produced. The actual costs would be debited to Manufacturing Overhead and credited to a variety of accounts such as Accounts

Payable, Accumulated Depreciation, Prepaid Insurance, Property Taxes Payable, and so on. According to the flexible budget, the standard number of machine-hours allowed for 11,000 units of production is 22,000 hours. Therefore, $110,000 of manufacturing overhead is applied to production ($5 per machine-hour times 22,000 hours) by debiting Work in Process Inventory and crediting Manufacturing Overhead for $110,000. The journal entry to apply manufacturing overhead to production would be:

Work in Process Inventory	110,000	
Manufacturing Overhead		110,000
To apply manufacturing overhead to production (22,000 hours at $5 per hour).		

These accounts show that manufacturing overhead has been overapplied to production by the $2,000 credit balance in the Manufacturing Overhead account. Because of its fixed component, manufacturing overhead tends to be overapplied when actual production is greater than standard production.

Although various complex computations can be made for overhead variances, we use a simple approach in this text. In this approach, known as the *two-variance approach to overhead variances,* we calculate only two variances—an overhead budget variance and an overhead volume variance.

Overhead Budget Variance The **overhead budget variance (OBV)** shows in one amount how economically overhead services were purchased and how efficiently they were used. This overhead variance is similar to a combined price and usage variance for materials or labor. The overhead budget variance (OBV) is equal to the difference between total actual overhead costs (actual OH) and total budgeted overhead costs (BOH) for the actual output attained.

To calculate the total budgeted overhead costs, multiply the variable overhead rate times the standard machine-hours allowed for production achieved, plus the constant amount of fixed overhead. For Beta Company, this would be $2 variable overhead times 22,000 hours, or $44,000 variable overhead, plus $60,000 of fixed overhead—a total of $104,000. Since the total actual overhead was $108,000 and the total budgeted overhead was $104,000, the overhead budget variance is computed as follows:

$$\text{Overhead budget variance} = \begin{matrix}\text{Actual}\\ \text{overhead}\end{matrix} - \begin{matrix}\text{Budgeted overhead at actual}\\ \text{production volume level}\end{matrix}$$
$$= \$108{,}000 - \$104{,}000$$
$$= \$4{,}000 \text{ (unfavorable)}$$

The variance is unfavorable because actual overhead costs were $108,000, while according to the flexible budget, they should have been $104,000.

Overhead Volume Variance The **overhead volume variance (OVV)** is caused by producing at a level other than that used in setting the standard overhead application rate. The OVV shows whether plant assets produced more or fewer units than expected. Because fixed overhead is not constant on a per unit basis, any deviation from planned production causes the overhead application rate to be incorrect. The OVV is the difference between the budgeted amount of overhead for the actual volume achieved (BOH) and the applied overhead (Applied OH):

$$\text{Overhead volume variance} = \text{Budgeted overhead} - \text{Applied overhead}$$

In the Beta Company illustration, the 11,000 units produced in the period have a standard allowance of 22,000 machine-hours. We calculated budgeted overhead when computing the overhead budget variance. The flexible budget in Illustration 24.3 shows that the budgeted overhead for 22,000 machine-hours is $104,000. Overhead is applied to work in process on the basis of standard hours allowed for a particular amount of production; in this case, 22,000 hours at $5 per hour. The overhead volume variance then is:

$$\text{Overhead volume variance} = \frac{\text{Budgeted}}{\text{overhead}} - \frac{\text{Applied}}{\text{overhead}}$$
$$= \$104{,}000 - \$110{,}000$$
$$= \$-6{,}000 \text{ (favorable)}$$

Note that the amount of the overhead volume variance is related solely to fixed overhead. As we show in Illustration 24.3, fixed overhead at all levels of activity is $60,000. Since Beta Company used 20,000 machine-hours as its standard, the fixed overhead rate is $3 per machine-hour. Beta worked 2,000 more standard hours (22,000 − 20,000) than was expected. Beta also can calculate the overhead volume variance as follows:

$$\left(\begin{array}{c}\text{Number of hours}\\ \text{used in setting}\\ \text{predetermined}\\ \text{overhead rates}\end{array} - \begin{array}{c}\text{Number of standard}\\ \text{hours allowed}\\ \text{for production}\\ \text{level achieved}\end{array}\right) \times \begin{array}{c}\text{Fixed overhead}\\ \text{rate per hour}\end{array} = \begin{array}{c}\text{Overhead}\\ \text{volume}\\ \text{variance}\end{array}$$
$$(20{,}000 - 22{,}000) \times \$3 = \$-6{,}000 \text{ (favorable)}$$

The variance is favorable because the company achieved a higher level of production than was expected.

Recording Overhead Variances These journal entries are related to overhead:

		Debit	Credit
(*d*)	Work in Process	110,000	
	Manufacturing Overhead		110,000
	To record the application of manufacturing overhead to work in process.		
(*e*)	Manufacturing Overhead	108,000	
	Various accounts		108,000
	To record actual manufacturing overhead.		
(*f*)	Manufacturing Overhead	2,000	
	Overhead Budget Variance	4,000	
	Overhead Volume Variance		6,000
	To record the variances related to overhead and close the Manufacturing Overhead account.		

The first entry applies manufacturing overhead to Work in Process at the rate of $5 per standard machine-hour. The second entry records the actual manufacturing overhead costs incurred during the period by Beta Company. The final entry reduces the Manufacturing Overhead account balance to zero and sets up the two variances calculated for overhead; these two variance accounts reveal the causes of the overapplied manufacturing overhead for the period.

Summary of Overhead Variances To easily determine the accuracy of the two overhead variances Beta would compare the sum of the budget and volume variances with the difference between the costs of actual manufacturing overhead and applied manufacturing overhead (the amount of over or underapplied overhead). For Beta Company, the difference between actual and applied manufacturing overhead was:

Actual manufacturing overhead incurred	$108,000
Applied manufacturing overhead allowed (22,000 machine-hours × $5 per hour)	110,000
Total overhead variance (favorable)	$ −2,000

ILLUSTRATION 24.4
Summary of Variances from Standard

Materials price variance = (Actual price − Standard price) × Actual quantity purchased
Materials usage variance = (Actual quantity used − Standard quantity allowed) × Standard price
Labor rate variance = (Actual rate − Standard rate) × Actual hours worked
Labor efficiency variance = (Actual hours worked − Standard hours allowed) × Standard rate
Overhead budget variance = Actual overhead − Budgeted overhead
Overhead volume variance = Budgeted overhead − Applied overhead

This difference is made up of the two overhead variances:

Overhead budget variance—unfavorable ($108,000 − $104,000)	$ 4,000
Overhead volume variance—favorable [$104,000 − (22,000 × $5)]	−6,000
Total overhead variance (favorable)	$−2,000

For a summary of the six variances from standard discussed in this chapter, see Illustration 24.4.

AN ACCOUNTING PERSPECTIVE

USES OF TECHNOLOGY Although standard costing often appears more difficult than actual costing to students, standard costing is generally easier in the real world. The key to this simplicity is the computer's capability to store, retrieve, and update standards. Once a firm sets standards for a product, it is relatively simple to update these standards for changes in labor rates, product prices, and efficiency improvements.

GOODS COMPLETED AND SOLD

To complete the standard cost system example, assume Beta Company completed and transferred 11,000 units to finished goods and sold on account 10,000 units at a price equal to 160% of standard cost. Also, there were no beginning or ending work in process inventories, and no beginning finished goods inventory. Journal entry (*g*) transfers the standard cost of the units completed, 11,000 × $60 = $660,000, from Work in Process Inventory to Finished Goods Inventory. Entry (*h*) records the sales for the period, 160% × $60 × 10,000 = $960,000. Entry (*i*) records the cost of goods sold, 10,000 × $60 = $600,000.

		Debit	Credit
(*g*)	Finished Goods Inventory	660,000	
	Work in Process Inventory		660,000
	To record the transfer of completed units to finished goods inventory.		
(*h*)	Accounts Receivable	960,000	
	Sales		960,000
	To record sales for the period.		
(*i*)	Cost of Goods Sold	600,000	
	Finished Goods Inventory		600,000
	To record cost of goods sold for the period.		

Beta debits the Work in Process Inventory with the standard cost of materials, labor, and manufacturing overhead for units put into production. Therefore, the entry recording the transfer of the standard cost of the completed units, 11,000 × $60 = $660,000, reduces Work in Process Inventory to a zero balance.

Sales for the period amount to 10,000 units at $96 each (160% of $60). It is fairly common practice to base selling prices at least partially on standard costs. Note that Beta debited Finished Goods Inventory with the standard cost of goods completed and credited it with the standard cost of goods sold. Thus, the ending Finished Goods Inventory consists of the units actually on hand (1,000) at their standard cost of $60 each, or $60,000.

Investigating Variances from Standard

Objective 6
Discuss the three selection guidelines used to investigate variances from standard.

Once all variances have been computed, management must decide which variances should be investigated further. Because numerous variances occur, managers cannot investigate all of them. Management needs some selection guidelines. Possible guidelines include the (1) amount of the variance; (2) size of the variance relative to the cost incurred; and (3) controllability of the cost associated with the variance—that is, whether it is considered controllable or noncontrollable. Managers also may use statistical analysis in deciding which variances to investigate. For instance, they could determine the average value of actual costs for a period so that only those variances deviating from the average by more than a certain percentage would be investigated. To decide which selection guidelines are most useful, management should seek the opinions of knowledgeable operating personnel.

Any analysis of variances is likely to disclose some variances that are controllable within the company and others that are not. For instance, quantities used are generally controllable internally. Prices paid for materials purchased may or may not be controllable. Management may discover that the purchasing agent is not getting competitive bids; therefore, the price paid for materials would have been more controllable had the agents sought competitive bids. On the other hand, a raw materials shortage may exist that drives the price upward, and the price paid may be beyond the buyer's control.

Another point to remember about the analysis of variances is that separate variances are not necessarily independent. For example, an unfavorable labor rate variance may result from using higher paid employees in a certain task. However, higher paid employees may be more productive, resulting in a favorable labor efficiency variance. These employees also may be more highly skilled and may waste fewer materials, resulting in a favorable materials usage variance. Therefore, significant variances, both favorable and unfavorable, should be investigated.

Performance Reports

At the end of a month or quarter, management may develop performance reports that compare the actual results and costs with the budgeted results and costs. These reports enable management to determine how well they and their workers were able to perform within the budget. At the bottom of the performance report, the supervisor or manager responsible for the elements mentioned in the report gives reasons for any variances. Management then investigates any variance not supported by an acceptable reason.

Disposing of Variances from Standard

Objective 7
Discuss theoretical and practical methods for disposing of variances from standard.

At the end of the year, variances from standard must be disposed of in the accounting records. The variances may be (1) viewed as losses due to inefficiency and closed to the Income Summary; (2) allocated as adjustments to the recorded cost of Work in Process Inventory, Finished Goods Inventory, and Cost of Goods Sold; or (3) closed to Cost of Goods Sold. Theoretically, the alternative chosen should depend on whether the standards set were reasonably attainable and whether the variances were controllable by company employees. For instance, a firm may consider an unfavorable materials usage or labor efficiency variance caused by carelessness or inefficiency a loss and close it to the Income Summary because the standard was attainable and the variance was controllable. The business may consider an unfavorable materials price variance caused by an unexpected price change an added cost and allocate it to the inventory accounts and Cost of Goods Sold because the standard was unattainable and the variance was uncontrollable. As a practical matter, companies usually close small variances to the Cost of Goods Sold account rather than allocate them to the inventory accounts and to cost of goods sold.

A Broader Perspective

Quality Management and the Baldrige Award

Many of the methods successfully used in the Japanese quality movement originated in the United States. The use of statistical controls in assessing processes originated in the United States, but Japanese managers applied the concept and had much greater employee involvement in quality improvement than U.S. companies. Although lagging in implementing quality management programs, many U.S. companies have jumped on the quality management bandwagon.

In 1987, the U.S. Congress created the Malcolm Baldrige National Quality Award in honor of the former secretary of commerce. This award is given to businesses that excel in major aspects of quality, such as quality planning, human resource development, and customer focus. Companies that have won this award include well-known manufacturing companies such as Motorola, Westinghouse (Commercial Nuclear Fuel Division), IBM, Texas Instruments (Defense Systems and Electronics Group), and General Motors (Cadillac Division). The award has also been given to large service organizations—Ritz-Carlton Hotels, Federal Express, and AT&T (Network Systems Group)—and to small businesses such as Granite Rock Co. in Watsonville, California, and Globe Metallurgical in Cleveland. The Baldrige Award promotes sharing of information about effective quality management programs and identifies companies with role-model quality management systems.

Source: Based on George S. Easton, "The 1993 State of U.S. Total Quality Management: A Baldrige Examiner's Perspective," *California Management Review* 35, no. 3 (Spring 1993), pp. 32–54.

Entry *(j)* reflects this practical disposition of Beta Company's variances by closing them to Cost of Goods Sold:

		Debit	Credit
(*j*)	Materials Price Variance	6,000	
	Overhead Volume Variance	6,000	
	Cost of Goods Sold	8,100	
	Materials Usage Variance		3,000
	Labor Rate Variance		11,100
	Labor Efficiency Variance		2,000
	Overhead Budget Variance		4,000
	To close the variance accounts.		

Companies do not report variances separately in financial statements released to the public but simply include them in the reported cost of goods sold amount. Reports prepared for internal use may list the variances separately after the cost of goods sold is shown at standard cost.

Nonfinancial Performance Measures

Although variances provide important measures of performance, nonfinancial performance measures are also important. Nonfinancial performance measures are particularly important for evaluating quality and customer service. Chapter 20 discussed various nonfinancial measures of performance.

Businesses measure quality by the number and type of customer complaints or by the number of product defects. If they reduce the number of product defects, firms are likely to reduce the number of customer complaints. The objective is to increase customer satisfaction with their products, increase repeat sales, reduce the costs of dealing with customer complaints, and reduce the costs of repairing products.

Managers can reduce materials waste by improving the quality of raw materials so there is less waste from defective materials. Managers also can increase employee training so workers make fewer mistakes and improve the production process. Materials waste may show up in the materials efficiency variance. Workers are generally motivated to find ways to reduce waste if companies keep track of materials waste every day. While reporting variances from standard costs is important to department heads and plant managers, workers are more likely to be motivated by immediate feedback in nonfinancial language.

Activity-Based Costing, Standards, and Variances

Activity-based costing is commonly used with standard costing. Hewlett-Packard, a pioneer in the development of activity-based costing, uses it to develop standard costs. In our example, we applied overhead using just one cost driver—machine-hours. Using activity-based costing, a company uses multiple activity-bases, or cost drivers, as discussed in Chapter 20.

An Accounting Perspective

Business Insight Managers of many companies criticize standard costing because they believe it keeps workers from continuous improvement. These managers argue that workers who achieve standards do not try to improve beyond those standards. We believe workers can beat the standards and strive for continuous improvement if they are properly motivated.

By striving to meet standards, management assumes responsibility for reducing the production costs of its products. In Chapter 25, you will learn about responsibility accounting in a broader sense. Many successful companies rely on responsibility accounting to make their business operations profitable.

Understanding the Learning Objectives

Objective 1
Discuss the nature of standard costs, including how standards are set.

- A standard cost is a carefully predetermined measure of what a cost should be under stated conditions.
- Engineering studies and time and motion studies are undertaken to determine the amounts of materials, labor, and other services required to produce a product.

Objective 2
Define budgets and discuss how budgets are used in a standard cost system.

- Budgets are formal written plans that represent management's planned actions in the future and the impacts of these actions on the business.
- Comparison of actual amounts to the budgeted amounts allows management to evaluate their own performance and that of their workers.

Objective 3
Discuss the advantages and disadvantages of using standard costs.

- Advantages of using standard costs include improved cost control, more useful information for managerial planning and decision making, more reasonable inventory measurements, cost savings in record-keeping, and possible reductions in production costs incurred.
- Disadvantages of using standard costs include controversial materiality limits for variances, nonreporting of certain variances, and low morale for some workers.

Objective 4
Calculate the six variances from standard and determine if the variance is favorable or unfavorable.

- **Materials price variance:**
  (Actual price − Standard price) × Actual quantity purchased.
- **Materials usage variance:**
  (Actual quantity used − Standard quantity allowed) × Standard price.
- **Labor rate variance:**
  (Actual rate − Standard rate) × Actual hours worked.
- **Labor efficiency variance:**
  (Actual hours worked − Standard hours allowed) × Standard rate.
- **Overhead budget variance:**
  Actual overhead − Budgeted overhead.
- **Overhead volume variance:**
  Budgeted overhead − Applied overhead.

Objective 5
Discuss what each of the six variance accounts shows and prepare journal entries to record the variance.

- The **materials price variance** shows whether the price paid for materials purchased was higher or lower than the standard price. This journal entry records the purchase of materials:

  Materials Inventory (debit)
  Materials Price Variance (debit or credit)
  Accounts Payable (credit)

  The Materials Price Variance account is debited if the variance is unfavorable and credited if the variance is favorable.
- The **materials usage variance** shows whether the actual quantity of materials used was higher or lower than the standard quantity. The journal entry to record materials usage is:

  Work in Process Inventory (debit)
  Materials Usage Variance (debit or credit)
  Materials Inventory (credit)

  The Materials Usage Variance account is debited if unfavorable and credited if favorable.
- The **labor rate variance** shows whether the actual direct labor-hour rate paid is higher or lower than the standard rate.
- The **labor efficiency variance** shows whether the actual direct labor-hours worked were greater or less than the standard hours. This journal entry charges the direct labor cost to Work in Process Inventory:

  Work in Process Inventory (debit)
  Labor Rate Variance (debit or credit)
  Labor Efficiency Variance (debit or credit)
  Payroll Summary (credit)

  The Labor Rate Variance account is debited if the variance is unfavorable and credited if the variance is favorable. The Labor Efficiency Variance account is debited if the variance is unfavorable and credited if the variance is favorable.
- The **overhead budget variance** shows the difference between total actual overhead costs and total budgeted overhead costs.
- The **overhead volume variance** shows the difference between the budgeted amount of overhead for the actual volume achieved and the applied overhead. This journal entry records the overhead variance:

  Manufacturing Overhead (debit or credit)
  Overhead Budget Variance (debit or credit)
  Overhead Volume Variance (debit or credit)

  The debit or credit to Manufacturing Overhead closes that account. The Overhead Budget Variance account is debited if the variance is unfavorable and credited if the variance is favorable. The Overhead Volume Variance account is credited if the variance is favorable and debited if the variance is unfavorable.

Objective 6
Discuss the three selection guidelines used to investigate variances from standard.

- Three possible selection guidelines are (1) amount of variance, (2) size of the variance relative to cost incurred, and (3) controllability of the cost associated with the variance.
- Significant variances, both favorable and unfavorable, should be investigated.

Objective 7
Discuss theoretical and practical methods for disposing of variances from standard.

- Variances may be viewed as losses due to inefficiency and closed to the Income Summary account; allocated as adjustments to the recorded cost of Work in Process Inventory, Finished Goods Inventory, and Cost of Goods Sold; or closed to Cost of Goods Sold.
- Practically, variances are usually closed to Cost of Goods Sold.

Demonstration Problem

Gleim Company manufactures children's toys that are identical. The standard cost of each toy is:

Direct materials:	
Three blocks of wood at $0.24	$0.72
Direct labor (1 hour at $6)	6.00
Overhead:	
Fixed ($21,600 ÷ 60,000 units)	0.36
Variable	0.48
	$7.56

Gleim bases the standard overhead rate on a volume of 60,000 units per month. In May, it manufactured 50,000 units. Using the following detailed data relative to production, compute the six variances from standard for the month.

Materials purchased:	
160,000 blocks of wood at	$0.26
Materials used:	
152,000 blocks of wood	
Direct labor: 49,000 hours at	$6.12
Fixed manufacturing overhead	$21,840
Variable manufacturing overhead	$24,420

Solution to Demonstration Problem

Materials price variance:	
($0.26 − $0.24) × 160,000	$3,200 (unfavorable)
Materials usage variance:	
(152,000 − 150,000*) × $0.24	480 (unfavorable)
Total materials variance	$3,680 (unfavorable)
Labor rate variance:	
($6.12 − $6.00) × 49,000	$5,880 (unfavorable)
Labor efficiency variance:	
(49,000 − 50,000) × $6.00	−6,000 (favorable)
Net labor variance	$−120 (favorable)

* 50,000 units × 3 blocks per unit.

Overhead budget variance:	
Actual ($21,840 + $24,420)	$46,260
Budgeted [$21,600 + (50,000 × $0.48)]	45,600
Overhead budget variance	$ 660 (unfavorable)
Overhead volume variance:	
Budget − Applied [$45,600 − (50,000 × $0.84)]	$ 3,600 (unfavorable)
Total overhead variance	$ 4,260 (unfavorable)
Total variance for month	$ 7,820 (unfavorable)

New Terms

Budgets Formal written plans that represent management's planned actions in the future and the impacts of these actions on the business. *848*

Flexible budget A budget that shows the budgeted amount of manufacturing overhead for various levels of output; used in isolating overhead variances and setting standard overhead rates. *857*

Ideal standards Standards that can be attained under the best circumstances—that is, with no machinery problems or worker problems. These unrealistic standards can only be met when the company has highly efficient, skilled workers who are working at their best effort throughout the entire period needed to complete the job. *849*

Labor efficiency variance (LEV) A variance from standard caused by using more or less than the standard amount of direct labor-hours to produce a product or complete a process; computed as (Actual hours worked − Standard hours allowed) × Standard rate per hour. *854*

Labor rate variance (LRV) A variance from standard caused by paying a higher or lower average rate of pay than the standard cost to produce a product or complete a process; computed as (Actual rate − Standard rate) × Actual hours worked. *854*

Management by exception The process where management only investigates those variances that are unusually favorable or unfavorable or that have a material effect on the company. *847, 848*

Materials price variance (MPV) A variance from standard caused by paying a higher or lower price than the standard for materials purchased; computed as (Actual price − Standard price) × Actual quantity purchased. *852*

Materials usage variance (MUV) A variance from standard caused by using more or less than the standard amount of materials to produce a product or complete a process; computed as (Actual quantity used − Standard quantity allowed) × Standard price. *852*

Overhead budget variance (OBV) A variance from standard caused by incurring more or less than the standard manufacturing overhead for the actual production volume achieved, as shown by a flexible budget; computed as Actual overhead − Budgeted overhead at the actual production volume level. *858*

Overhead volume variance (OVV) A variance from standard caused by producing at a level other than that used in setting the standard overhead application rates; computed as Budgeted overhead − Applied overhead. *858*

Practical standards Standards that are strict but attainable. Allowances are made for machinery problems and rest periods for workers. These standards are generally used in planning. *849*

Standard cost A carefully predetermined measure of what a cost should be under stated conditions. *847*

Standard level of output A carefully predetermined measure of what the expected level of output should be for a specified period of time, usually one year. *848*

Variance A deviation of actual costs from standard costs; may be favorable or unfavorable. That is, actual costs may be less than or more than standard costs. Variances may relate to materials, labor, or manufacturing overhead. *851*

SELF-TEST

TRUE-FALSE

Indicate whether each of the following statements is true or false.

1. Standard cost usually refers to the standard price per unit of inputs into the production process.
2. Standard costs are useful in evaluating management's and workers' performance.
3. Under a standard cost system, all units of a given product produced during a particular period are typically in inventory at the same unit cost.
4. This journal entry records the use of materials and establishes a Materials Usage Variance account: debit Accounts Payable and Materials Usage Variance; credit Materials Inventory.
5. Favorable variances are credits in variance accounts.

MULTIPLE-CHOICE

Select the best answer for each of the following questions.

1. Which of the following best explains why accountants separate materials variances into a purchase price variance and a usage variance?
   - **a.** Different individuals may be responsible for each variance.
   - **b.** Materials might not be purchased and used in the same period.
   - **c.** These two variances are likely to be more informative to top management than one overall materials variance.
   - **d.** All of the above.

2. Determine the materials usage variance and materials price variance from the following data:

Materials purchased	30,000 units
Price per unit purchased	$3.00
Standard price per unit	$3.10
Materials used	25,000 units
Standard quantity allowed	22,000 units

   - **a.** 9,300 favorable (MUV)
3,000 unfavorable (MPV).
   - **b.** 9,300 unfavorable (MUV)
3,000 favorable (MPV).
   - **c.** 9,000 unfavorable (MUV)
2,200 favorable (MPV).
   - **d.** 9,000 favorable (MUV)
2,500 unfavorable (MPV).

3. To which account would an unfavorable materials usage or labor efficiency variance caused by carelessness or inefficiency be closed?
   - **a.** Materials Inventory.
   - **b.** Income Summary.
   - **c.** Work in Process.
   - **d.** Finished Goods Inventory.

4. Which of the following journal entries is correct for closing out the variance accounts?
   - **a.** Sales
Materials Usage Variance
Labor Rate Variance
    Materials Price Variance
    Overhead Volume Variance
    Labor Efficiency Variance
    Overhead Budget Variance
   - **b.** Materials Price Variance
Overhead Volume Variance
Accounts Payable
    Materials Usage Variance
    Labor Rate Variance
    Labor Efficiency Variance
    Overhead Budget Variance
   - **c.** Materials Price Variance
Overhead Volume Variance
Accounts Receivable
    Materials Usage Variance
    Labor Rate Variance
    Labor Efficiency Variance
    Overhead Budget Variance

d. Materials Price Variance
Overhead Budget Variance
Accounts Receivable
    Materials Usage Variance

Overhead Volume Variance
Labor Efficiency Variance
Labor Rate Variance

Now turn to page 871 to check your answers.

QUESTIONS

1. Is a standard cost an estimated cost? What is the primary objective of employing standard costs in a cost system?
2. What is a budget?
3. What is the difference between ideal and practical standards? Which standard generally is used in planning?
4. What is meant by the term *management by exception*?
5. What are some advantages of using standard costs? What are some disadvantages?
6. Describe how the materials price and usage variances would be computed from the following data:

   Standard—1 unit of material at $20 per unit.
   Purchased—1,200 units of material at $20.30; used—990 units.
   Production—1,000 units of finished goods.

7. When might a given company have a substantial favorable materials price variance and a substantial unfavorable materials usage variance?
8. What is the usual cause of a favorable or unfavorable labor rate variance? What other labor variance is isolated in a standard cost system? Of the two variances, which is more likely to be under the control of management? Explain.
9. Identify the type of variance indicated by each of the following situations and indicate whether it is favorable or unfavorable:
   a. The cutting department of a company during the week ending July 15 cut 12 size-S cogged wheels out of three sheets of 12-inch high-tempered steel. Usually three wheels of such size are cut out of each sheet.
   b. A company purchased and installed an expensive new cutting machine to handle expanding orders. This purchase and the related depreciation had not been anticipated when the overhead was budgeted.
   c. Edwards, the band saw operator, was on vacation last week. Lands took her place for the normal 40-hour week. Edwards' wage rate is $12 per hour, while Lands' is $10 per hour. Production was at capacity last week and the week before.
10. Theoretically, how would an accountant dispose of variances from standard? How does an accountant typically dispose of variances?
11. Why are variances typically isolated as soon as possible?
12. Is it correct to consider favorable variances as always being desirable? Explain.
13. How do the use of standard costs permit the application of the principle of management by exception?
14. How do standards help in controlling production costs?
15. **Real World Question** Refer to the discussion of employees setting standards in "An Accounting Perspective" on page 851. What are the advantages and disadvantages of having employees set their own standards?
16. **Real World Question** Imagine you are making and selling pizzas for Domino's Pizza. How would you set standards for one pizza to be made and delivered?

EXERCISES

Exercise 24–1
Compute materials variances (L.O. 4)

During July, the cutting department completed 4,000 units of a product that had a standard materials cost of 2 square feet per unit at $2.40 per square foot. The actual materials purchased consisted of 8,200 square feet at $2.20 per square foot, for a total cost of $18,040. The actual material used this period was 8,080 square feet. Compute the materials price and usage variances. Indicate whether each is favorable or unfavorable.

Exercise 24–2
Compute materials variances; comment on purchase decisions (L.O. 4)

Blackman Company produces a product that has the following standard costs:

Direct materials—4 pounds at $10 per pound	$ 40
Direct labor—3 hours at $12 per hour	36
Manufacturing overhead—150% of direct labor	54
	$130

Blackman's purchasing agent took advantage of a special offer from one of its suppliers to purchase 44,000 pounds of material at $8.20 per pound. Assume 5,500 units were produced and 34,100 pounds of material were used. Compute the variances for materials. Comment on the purchasing agent's decision to take the special offer.

Exercise 24–3
Compute labor variances (L.O. 4)

Compute the labor variances in the following situation:

Actual direct labor payroll (25,800 hours at $18)	$464,400
Standard direct labor allowed per unit, 4.20 hours at $19.20	$ 80.64
Production for month (in units)	5,000

Exercise 24–4
Compute labor variances; evaluate labor (L.O. 4)

Whitewater Company manufactures a product that has a standard direct labor cost of four hours per unit at $12 per hour. In producing 6,000 units, the foreman used a different crew than usual, which resulted in a total labor cost of $13 per hour for 22,000 hours. Compute the labor variances and comment on the foreman's decision to use a different crew.

Exercise 24–5
Compute overhead volume and budget variances (L.O. 4)

The following data relate to the manufacturing activities of Levi Company for the first quarter of the current year:

Standard activity (in units)	30,000
Actual production (units)	24,000
Budgeted fixed manufacturing overhead	$36,000
Variable overhead rate (per unit)	$ 4.00
Actual fixed manufacturing overhead	$37,200
Actual variable manufacturing overhead	$88,800

Compute the overhead budget variance and the overhead volume variance.

Exercise 24–6
Compute overhead volume variance (L.O. 4)

Assume that the actual production in Exercise 24–5 was 26,000 units rather than 24,000. What was the overhead volume variance?

Exercise 24–7
Close all variance accounts (L.O. 5)

The standard cost variance accounts of Timberwolves Company at the end of its fiscal year had the following balances:

Materials price variance (unfavorable)	$ 9,000
Materials usage variance (unfavorable)	7,200
Labor rate variance (favorable)	5,400
Labor efficiency variance (unfavorable)	19,800
Overhead budget variance (favorable)	1,000
Overhead volume variance (unfavorable)	10,800

Prepare one journal entry to record the closing of the variance accounts to Cost of Goods Sold.

PROBLEMS

Problem 24–1
Compute materials variances (L.O. 4)

A product has a standard materials usage and cost of 2 pounds per unit at $7.00 per pound. During the month, 1,200 pounds of materials were purchased at $7.30 per pound. Production for the month totaled 550 units requiring 1,050 pounds of materials.

Required Compute the materials variances.

Problem 24–2
Prepare journal entries for materials variances (L.O. 5)

During October, a department completed 2,500 units of a product that has a standard materials usage and cost of 1.2 square feet per unit at $0.24 per square foot. The actual material used consisted of 3,050 square feet at an actual cost of $1,332.24. The actual purchase of this material amounted to 4,500 square feet at a total cost of $1,965.60.

Required Prepare journal entries (*a*) for the purchase of the materials and (*b*) for the issuance of materials to production.

Problem 24–3
Compute labor variances (L.O. 4)

Dave Company makes plastic garbage bags. One box of bags requires two hours of direct labor at an hourly rate of $6. The company produced 200,000 boxes of bags using 416,000 hours of direct labor at a total cost of $2,288,000.

Required Compute the labor variances.

Problem 24–4
Compute labor variances; prepare journal entries (L.O. 4, 5)

The finishing department of Martin Company produced 25,000 units during November. The standard number of direct labor-hours per unit is two hours. The standard rate per hour is $18.90. During the month, 51,250 direct labor-hours were worked at a cost of $871,250.

Required

a. Compute labor variances. Record the labor data in a journal entry.

b. Record the journal entry to dispose of any variances (close to Cost of Goods Sold).

Problem 24–5
Compute overhead variances under two assumptions (L.O. 4)

The standard amount of output for the Chicago plant of Sisterhood Company is 50,000 units per month. Overhead is applied based on units produced. The flexible budget of the month for manufacturing overhead allows $180,000 for fixed overhead and $4.80 per unit of output for variable overhead. Actual overhead for the month consisted of $181,440 of fixed overhead; the actual variable overhead follows.

Required

Compute the overhead budget variance and the overhead volume variance assuming the following actual production in units and actual variable overhead in dollars:

a. 37,500 and $182,400.

b. 55,000 and $270,480.

Problem 24–6
Compute materials, labor, and overhead variances (L.O. 4)

Based on a standard volume of output of 96,000 units per month, the standard cost of the product manufactured by Learn 'R Else Company consists of:

Direct materials (0.25 pounds)	$2.00	($8 per pound)
Direct labor (0.5 hours)	3.80	($7.60 per hour)
Variable manufacturing overhead	2.50	
Fixed manufacturing overhead ($144,000)	1.50	
Total	$9.80	

A total of 25,200 pounds of materials was purchased at $8.40 per pound. During May, 98,400 units were produced with the following costs:

Direct materials used (24,000 pounds at $8.40)	$201,600
Direct labor (50,000 hours at $7.80)	390,000
Variable manufacturing overhead	249,000
Fixed manufacturing overhead	145,000

Required

Compute the materials price and usage variances, the labor rate and efficiency variances, and the overhead budget and volume variances. (Overhead is applied based on units produced.)

Alternate Problems

Problem 24–1A
Compute materials and labor variances; prepare journal entries (L.O. 4, 5)

The following data apply to Shakespeare Company for June, when 2,500 finished units were produced:

Materials used: 8,000 pounds
Standard materials per finished unit: 3 pounds at $5 per pound
Materials purchased: 12,000 pounds at $4.80 per pound
Direct labor: 5,800 hours at a total cost of $69,600
Standard labor per finished unit: 2 hours at $11 per hour.

Required

a. Compute the materials and labor variances.

b. Prepare journal entries to record the transactions involving these variances.

Problem 24–2A
Compute materials variances (L.O. 4)

During December, Roseanne Company produced 15,000 units of a product called Creative. Creative has a standard materials cost of two pieces per unit at $4 per piece. The actual materials used consisted of 30,000 pieces at a cost of $115,000. Actual purchases of the materials amounted to 40,000 pieces at a cost of $150,000.

Required

Compute the two materials variances.

Problem 24–3A
Calculate actual labor rate given standards and rate variance (L.O. 4)

Some of the records of Worldworth Company's repair and maintenance division were accidentally shredded. Salvaged records indicate that actual direct labor-hours for the period were 7,000 hours and the standard direct labor-hours were 8,000. The total labor variance was $6,000, favorable. The standard labor rate was $7 per direct labor-hour, and the labor rate variance was $2,000, unfavorable.

Required Compute the actual direct labor rate per hour and prepare the journal entry to record the labor rate and the labor efficiency variances.

Problem 24–4A
Compute overhead volume variances for two levels of volume (L.O. 4)

All Fixed Overhead Company computes its overhead rate based on a standard level of output of 40,000 units. Fixed manufacturing overhead for the current year is budgeted at $30,000. Actual fixed manufacturing overhead for the current year was $31,000. Overhead is applied based on units produced.

Required Compute the amount of overhead volume variance for the year under each of the following assumptions regarding actual output:

a. 25,000 units.

b. 45,000 units.

Beyond the Numbers—Critical Thinking

Business Decision Case 24–1
Discuss possible causes for variances (L.O. 6)

Turn to Exercise 24–7 in this chapter. For each of the variances listed, give a possible reason for its existence.

Business Decision Case 24–2
Analyze situation where actual costs differ from standard costs; evaluate the two managers involved (L.O. 2, 3)

Penny Rios, the president of the Newlight Company, has a problem that does not involve substantial dollar amounts but does involve the important question of responsibility for variances from standard costs. She has just received the following report:

Standard materials at standard price for the actual production in May	$ 9,000
Unfavorable materials price variance ($3.60 − $3.00) × 3,450 pounds	2,070
Unfavorable materials usage variance (3,450 − 3,000 pounds) × $3	1,350
Total actual materials cost for the month of May (3,450 pounds at $3.60 per pound)	$12,420

Rios has discussed the unfavorable price variance with Heather Hart, the purchasing officer. Hart agrees that under the circumstances she should be held responsible for most of the materials price variance. But she objects to the inclusion of $270 (450 pounds of excess materials used at $0.60 per pound). This, she argues, is the responsibility of the production department. If the production department had not been so inefficient in the use of materials, she would not have had to purchase the extra 450 pounds.

On the other hand, David Goodman, the production manager, agrees that he is basically responsible for the excess quantity of materials used. But, he does not agree that the materials usage variance should be revised to include the $270 of unfavorable price variance on the excess materials used. "That's Heather's responsibility," he says.

Rios now turns to you for help. Specifically, she wants you to tell her:

a. Who is responsible for the $270 in dispute?

b. If responsibility cannot be clearly assigned, how should the accounting department categorize the variance (price or usage)? Why?

c. Are there likely to be other circumstances where materials variances cannot be considered the responsibility of the manager most closely involved with them? Explain.

Required Prepare written answers to the three questions Rios asked.

A Broader Perspective—Writing Experience 24–3

Refer to "A Broader Perspective" on page 862. The Baldrige Award has been criticized for fostering a winner-versus-loser mentality, instead of encouraging every organization to improve its quality. Further, the award has been criticized for grading on the curve by awarding companies that are the best in U.S. industry but still do not compete well against foreign competition.

Required Write a response to each of these criticisms of the Baldrige Award.

Group Project 24–4

Many workers hate standards. Some people claim standards reduce morale and productivity. Others believe standards are necessary to motivate people. Based on your own experience in school or on a job, what do you think?

In groups of three, choose an organization or business to use as an example. List all the possible standards you could set for this organization or business. Then decide whether your group favors setting standards. If the group does, decide who should set each of the standards on your list. If the group does not favor standards, discuss your reasons. Choose one member to report for your group to the class.

Answers to Self-Test

True-False

1. **False.** Standard cost is the standard quantity of an input required per unit of output times the standard price per unit of that input. **Standard price** refers to the price per unit of inputs into the production process.
2. **True.** Standard costs are useful in evaluating the performance of management and workers.
3. **True.** Under a standard cost system all units of a given product are carried in inventory at the same unit cost.
4. **False.** The general journal entry to record the use of materials and establish the materials usage variance debits Work in Process Inventory (not Accounts Payable) and Materials Usage Variance and credits Materials Inventory.
5. **True.** Favorable variances are shown as credits.

Multiple-Choice

1. **d.** All of these answers are correct. Different people are often responsible for the two variances, materials are sometimes purchased and used in different accounting periods, and the two separate variances are likely to provide more information to top management than just one materials variance.
2. **b.**

$$\text{Materials usage variance} = \left(\text{Actual quantity used} - \text{Standard quantity allowed}\right) \times \text{Standard price}$$
$$= (25{,}000 - 22{,}000) \times \$3.10$$
$$= 3{,}000 \times \$3.10$$
$$= \$9{,}300 \text{ (unfavorable)}$$

$$\text{Materials price variance} = \left(\text{Actual price} - \text{Standard price}\right) \times \text{Actual quantity purchased}$$
$$= (\$3.00 - \$3.10) \times 30{,}000$$
$$= -\$0.10 \times 30{,}000$$
$$= -\$3{,}000 \text{ (favorable)}$$

3. **b.** An unfavorable materials usage or labor efficiency variance caused by carelessness or inefficiency may be considered a loss and closed to Income Summary because the standard was attainable and the variance was controllable.
4. **c.** The other answers incorrectly close the variance accounts.

25

Responsibility Accounting

Segmental Analysis

Learning Objectives

After studying this chapter, you should be able to:

1. Explain responsibility accounting and its use in a business entity.
2. Prepare responsibility accounting reports.
3. Prepare a segmental income statement using the contribution margin format.
4. Calculate return on investment, margin, and turnover for a segment.
5. Calculate the residual income of a segment.
6. Allocate costs from service departments to operating departments (Appendix).

When a business is small, the owner usually supervises many different activities in the business. As a business grows, responsibility for some of these activities must be given to other persons. Obviously, the success of a business depends to a great extent on the persons responsible for these activities.

In this chapter, you learn about delegating authority to lower-level managers for managing various business activities and holding these lower-level managers responsible for the activities under their control. You also learn how to assess the performance of these managers. A company's activities are grouped into responsibility centers. The company measures the performance of each center manager in terms of the items of revenue and expense over which that manager has control.

Responsibility Accounting

The term **responsibility accounting** refers to an accounting system that collects, summarizes, and reports accounting data relating to the responsibilities of individual managers. A responsibility accounting system provides information to evaluate each manager on the revenue and expense items over which that manager has primary control (authority to influence).

A responsibility accounting report contains those items controllable by the responsible manager. When both controllable and uncontrollable items are included in the report, accountants should clearly separate the categories. The identification of controllable items is a fundamental task in responsibility accounting and reporting.

To implement responsibility accounting in a company, the business entity must be organized so that responsibility is assignable to individual managers. The various company managers and their lines of authority (and the resulting levels of responsibility) should be fully defined. The organization chart in Illustration 25.1 demonstrates lines of authority and responsibility that could be used as a basis for responsibility reporting.

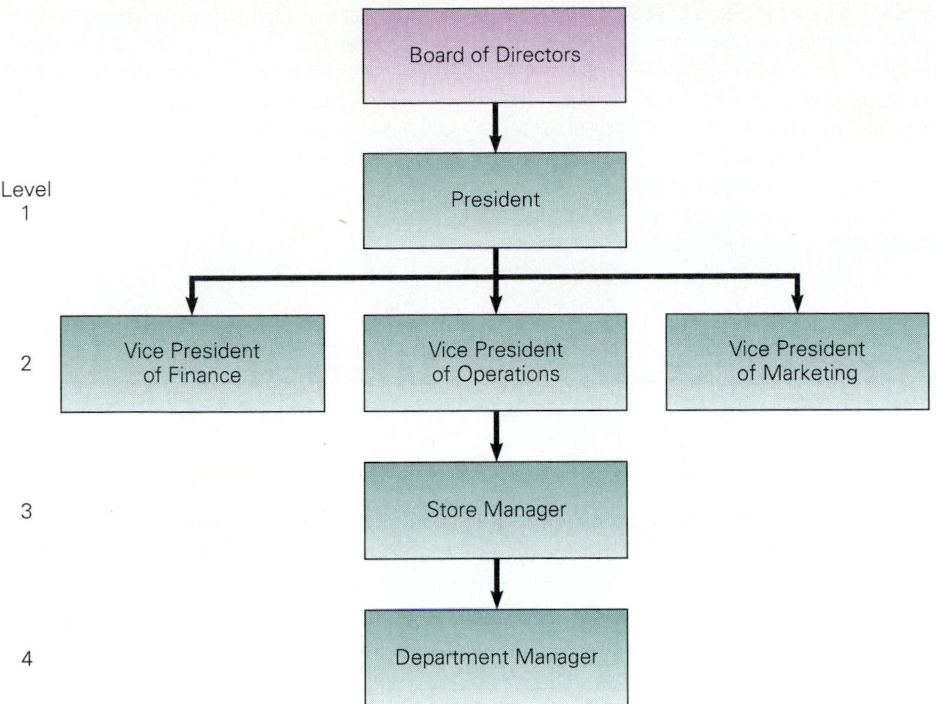

ILLUSTRATION 25.1
A Corporate Functional Organization Chart including Four Levels of Management

Objective 1
Explain responsibility accounting and its use in a business entity.

To identify the items over which each manager has control, the lines of authority should follow a specified path. For example, in Illustration 25.1, we show that a department store supervisor may report to a store manager, who reports to the vice president of operations, who reports to the president. The president is ultimately responsible to stockholders or their elected representatives, the board of directors. In a sense, the president is responsible for all revenue and expense items of the company, since at the presidential level all items are controllable over some period. The president usually delegates authority to lower-level managers since one person cannot keep fully informed of the day-to-day operating details of all areas of the business.

The manager's level in the organization also affects those items over which that manager has control. The president is usually considered a first-level manager. Managers (usually vice presidents) who report directly to the president are second-level managers. Notice on the organization chart in Illustration 25.1 that individuals at a specific management level are on a horizontal line across the chart. Not all managers at that level, however, necessarily have equal authority and responsibility. The degree of a manager's authority varies from company to company.

While the president may delegate much decision-making power, some revenue and expense items remain exclusively under the president's control. For example, in some companies, large capital (plant and equipment) expenditures may be approved only by the president. Therefore, depreciation, property taxes, and other related expenses should not be designated as a store manager's responsibility since these costs are not primarily under that manager's control.

The controllability criterion is crucial to the content of performance reports for each manager. For example, at the department supervisor level, perhaps only direct materials and direct labor cost control are appropriate for measuring performance. A plant manager, however, has the authority to make decisions regarding many other costs not controllable at the supervisory level, such as the salaries of department supervisors. These other costs would be included in the performance evaluation of the store manager, not the supervisor.

A Broader Perspective

Employee Buyouts

Traditional organization lines of responsibility have workers reporting to supervisors or department managers, who in turn report to higher managers, who report to even higher managers, and so forth on up the organization. Top management is accountable to stockholders.

What happens when those stockholders are also employees, as in the case of many employee buyouts (such as United Airlines)? Now, employees report to managers who are accountable back to the employees in their role as stockholders. Employees wear two hats: They own the company and they work for the company. In some sense, this makes each employee like a proprietor of a business. Presumably, after employees buy their company, they have greater incentives to make the company successful.

Source: Based on the authors' research.

Responsibility Reports

Objective 2
Prepare responsibility accounting reports.

Responsibility accounting provides reports to different levels of management. The amount of detail varies depending on the manager's level in the organization. A performance report to a department manager of a retail store would include actual and budgeted dollar amounts of all revenue and expense items under that supervisor's control. The report issued to the store manager would show only totals from all the department supervisors' performance reports and any additional items under the store manager's control, such as the store's administrative expenses. The report to the company's president includes summary totals of all the stores' performance levels plus any additional items under the president's control. In effect, the president's report should include all revenue and expense items in summary form because the president is responsible for controlling the profitability of the entire company.

Management by exception is the principle that upper-level management does not need to examine operating details at lower levels unless there appears to be a problem. As businesses become increasingly complex, accountants have found it necessary to filter and condense accounting data so that these data may be analyzed quickly. Most executives do not have time to study detailed accounting reports and search for problem areas. Reporting only summary totals highlights any areas needing attention and makes the most efficient use of the executive's time.

The condensation of data in successive levels of management reports is justified on the basis that the appropriate manager will take the necessary correct action. Thus, specific performance details need not be reported to superiors.

For example, if sales personnel costs have been excessively high in a particular department, that departmental manager should find and correct the cause of the problem. When the store manager questions the unfavorable budget variance of the department, the departmental supervisor can inform the store manager that corrective action was taken. Hence, it is not necessary to report to any higher authority that a particular department within one of the stores is not operating satisfactorily because the matter has already been resolved. Alternatively, if a manager's entire store has been performing poorly, summary totals reported to the vice president of operations discloses this situation, and an investigation of the store manager's problems may be indicated.

In preparing responsibility accounting reports, companies use two basic methods to handle revenue or expense items. In the first approach, only those items over which a manager has direct control are included in the responsibility report for that management level. Any revenue and expense items that cannot be directly controlled are not included. The second approach is to include all revenue and expense items that can be traced directly or allocated indirectly to a particular manager, whether or not they are controllable. This second method represents a full-cost approach, which means all costs of a given area are disclosed in a single report. When this approach is used, care must be taken to separate controllable from noncontrollable items to differentiate those items for which a manager can and should be held responsible.

Features of Responsibility Reports

For accounting reports to be of maximum benefit, they must be timely. That is, accountants should prepare reports as soon as possible after the end of the performance measurement period. Timely reporting allows prompt corrective action to be taken. When reports are delayed excessively, they lose their effectiveness as control devices. For example, a report on the previous month's operations that is not received until the end of the current month is virtually useless for analyzing poor performance areas and taking corrective action.

Companies also should issue reports regularly so that managers can spot trends. Then, appropriate management action can be initiated before major problems occur. Regular reporting allows managers to rely on reports and become familiar with their contents.

Firms should make the format of their responsibility reports relatively simple and easy to read. Confusing terminology should be avoided. Where appropriate, expressing results in physical units may be more familiar and understandable to some managers. To assist management in quickly spotting budget variances, companies can report both budgeted (expected) and actual amounts. A **budget variance** is the difference between the budgeted and actual amounts of an item. Because variances highlight problem areas (exceptions), they are helpful in applying the management-by-exception principle. To help management evaluate performance to date, responsibility reports often include both a current period and year-to-date analysis.

Responsibility Reports—An Illustration

Illustration 25.2 shows how Macy's Corporation could relate its responsibility accounting reports. Assume Macy's has four management levels—the president, vice president of operations, store manager, and department manager. In Illustration 25.3, we show that a responsibility report would be prepared for each management level.

Note in Illustration 25.4 the detailed information included in the responsibility reports for each manager. Only the individual manager's controllable expenses are contained in these reports. For example, the store manager's report includes only totals from the Men's Clothing Department manager's report. In turn, the report to the vice president includes only totals from the store manager's report, and so on. Detailed data from the lower levels are summarized or condensed and reported at the next higher level.

You can see that at each level, more and more costs become controllable. Also, the company introduces controllable costs not included on lower-level reports into the reports for levels 3, 2, and 1. The only store cost not included at the store manager's level is the store manager's salary, because it is noncontrollable by that store manager. It is, however, controllable by the store manager's supervisor, the vice president of operations.

Based on an analysis of these reports, the Men's Clothing Department manager probably would take immediate action to see why supplies and overtime were significantly over budget this month. The store manager may ask the department manager what the problems were and whether they are now under control. The vice president may ask the same question of the store manager. The president may ask each vice president why the budget was exceeded this month and what corrective action has been taken.

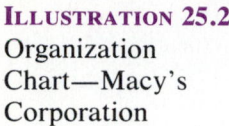

Illustration 25.2
Organization Chart—Macy's Corporation

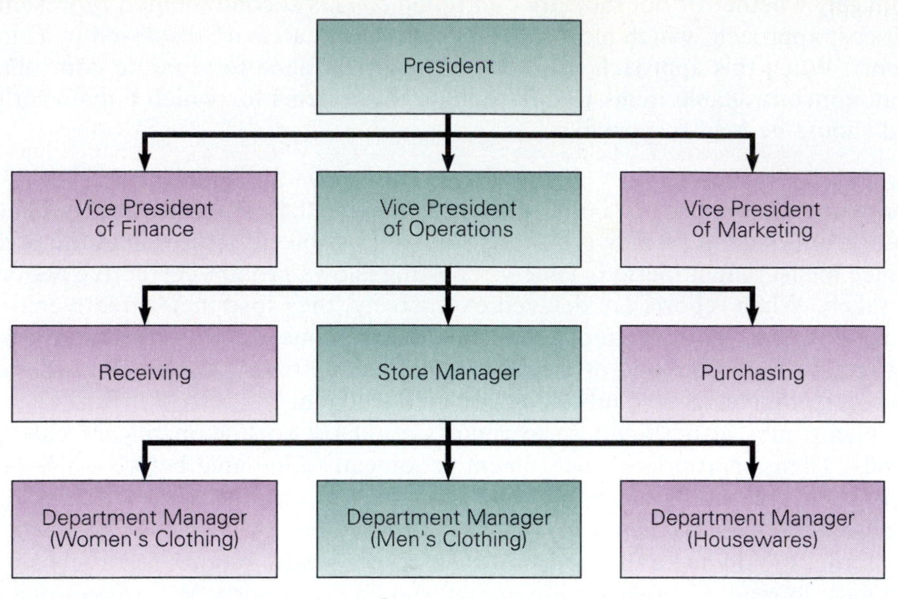

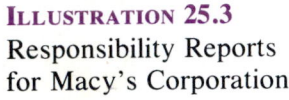

Illustration 25.3
Responsibility Reports for Macy's Corporation

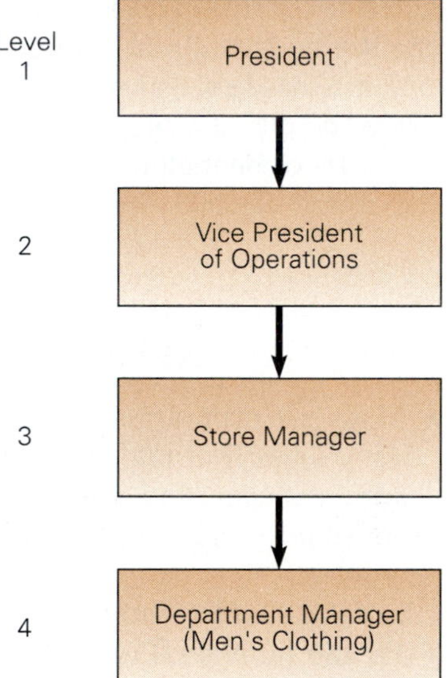

Responsibility Centers

A **segment** is a fairly autonomous unit or division of a company defined according to function or product line. Traditionally, owners have organized their companies along functional lines. The segments or departments organized along functional lines perform a specified function such as marketing, finance, purchasing, production, or shipping. Recently, large companies have tended to organize segments according to product lines such as an electrical products division, shoe department, or food division.

A **responsibility center** is a segment of an organization for which a particular executive is responsible. There are three types of responsibility centers—expense (or cost) centers, profit centers, and investment centers. In designing a responsibility accounting system, management must examine the characteristics of each

ILLUSTRATION 25.4
Responsibility Reports for Macy's Corporation

First Level

MACY'S CORPORATION
President

Controllable Expenses	Amount This Month	Amount Year to Date	Over or (Under) Budget This Month	Over or (Under) Budget Year to Date
President's office expense	$ 11,000	$ 55,000	$ 1,000	$ 2,000
Vice president of operations	128,720	700,000	6,000	8,000
Vice president of marketing	18,700	119,000	4,000	8,000
Vice president of finance	14,000	115,000	8,000	9,000
Vice presidents' salaries	29,000	145,000	-0-	-0-
Total	$201,420	$1,134,000	$19,000	$27,000

Second Level

MACY'S CORPORATION
Vice President of Operations

Controllable Expenses	Amount This Month	Amount Year to Date	Over or (Under) Budget This Month	Over or (Under) Budget Year to Date
Vice president's office expense	$ 2,840	$ 9,500	$ (500)	$(8,000)
Store manager	88,800	490,000	2,500	5,000
Purchasing	5,380	32,500	1,000	2,000
Receiving	4,700	33,000	3,000	9,000
Salaries of store managers and heads of purchasing and receiving	27,000	135,000	-0-	-0-
Total (include in report for next higher level)	$128,720	$700,000	$6,000	$ 8,000

Third Level

MACY'S CORPORATION
Store Manager

Controllable Expenses	Amount This Month	Amount Year to Date	Over or (Under) Budget This Month	Over or (Under) Budget Year to Date
Store manager's office expense	$ 8,000	$ 91,000	$ (500)	$(1,000)
Men's clothing department	16,800	86,000	1,600	2,300
Housewares department	10,000	50,000	800	1,300
Women's clothing department	4,000	13,000	600	2,400
Salaries of department managers	50,000	250,000	-0-	-0-
Total (include in report for next higher level)	$88,800	$490,000	$2,500	$ 5,000

Fourth Level

MACY'S CORPORATION
Manager, Men's Clothing Department

Controllable Expenses	Amount This Month	Amount Year to Date	Over or (Under) Budget This Month	Over or (Under) Budget Year to Date
Inventory losses	$ 2,000	$10,000	$ 100	$ 400
Supplies	1,800	8,500	800	950
Salaries	11,000	53,000	(100)	810
Overtime	2,000	14,500	800	140
Total (include in report for next higher level)	$16,800	$86,000	$1,600	$2,300

segment and the extent of the responsible manager's authority. Care must be taken to ensure that the basis for evaluating the performance of an expense center, profit center, or investment center matches the characteristics of the segment and the authority of the segment's manager. The following sections of the chapter discuss the characteristics of each of these centers and the appropriate bases for evaluating the performance of each type.

Expense Centers

An **expense center** is a responsibility center incurring only expense items and producing no direct revenue from the sale of goods or services. Examples of expense centers are service centers (e.g., the maintenance department or accounting department) or intermediate production facilities that produce parts for assembly into a finished product. Managers of expense centers are held responsible only for specified expense items.

The appropriate goal of an expense center is the long-run minimization of expenses. Short-run minimization of expenses may not be appropriate. For example, a production supervisor could eliminate maintenance costs for a short time, but in the long run, total costs might be higher due to more frequent machine breakdowns.

Profit Centers

A **profit center** is a responsibility center having both revenues and expenses. Because segmental earnings equal segmental revenues minus related expenses, the manager must be able to control both of these categories. The manager must have the authority to control selling price, sales volume, and all reported expense items. To properly evaluate performance, the manager must have authority over all of these measured items. **Controllable profits of a segment** result from deducting the expenses under a manager's control from revenues under that manager's control.

Investment Centers

Closely related to the profit center concept is an investment center. An **investment center** is a responsibility center having revenues, expenses, and an appropriate investment base. When a firm evaluates an investment center, it looks at the rate of return it can earn on its investment base. Accountants compute the **return on investment (ROI),** also called the *rate of return*, by dividing segmental income by the appropriate investment base. For example, a segment that earns $500,000 on an investment base of $5,000,000 has an ROI of 10%.

Determining the investment base to be used in the ROI calculation is a tricky matter. Normally, the assets available for use by the division make up its investment base. But accountants disagree on whether depreciable assets should be included in the ROI calculation at original cost, original cost less accumulated depreciation, or current replacement cost. **Original cost** is the price paid to acquire the assets. **Original cost less accumulated depreciation** is the book value of the assets—the amount paid less total depreciation taken. **Current replacement cost** is the cost of replacing the present assets with similar assets in the same condition as those now in use. A different rate of return results from each of these measures. Therefore, management must select and agree on an appropriate measure of investment base prior to making ROI calculations or interdivision comparisons.

Even after the investment base is defined, problems may still remain because many segment managers have limited control over some of the items included in the investment base of their segment. For instance, top-level management often makes capital expenditure decisions for major store assets rather than allowing the segment managers to do so. Therefore, the segment manager may have little control over the store assets used by the segment. Another problem area may be the company's centralized credit and collection department. The segment manager may have little or no control over the amount of accounts receivable included as segment assets since the manager cannot change the credit-granting or collection policies of the company.

Usually these problems are overcome when managers realize that if all segments are treated in the same manner, the inclusion of noncontrollable items in the investment base may have negligible effects. Then, comparisons of the ROI for all segments are based on a consistent treatment of items. To avoid adverse reactions or decreased motivation, segment managers must agree to this treatment.

Companies prefer to evaluate segments as investment centers because the ROI criterion facilitates performance comparisons between segments. Segments with more resources should produce more profits than segments with fewer resources, so it is difficult to compare the performance of segments of different sizes on the basis of profits alone. However, when ROI is a performance measure, performance comparisons take into account the differences in the sizes of the segments. The segment with the highest percentage ROI is presumably the most effective in using whatever resources it has.

Typical investment centers are large, autonomous segments of large companies. The centers are often separated from one another by location, types of products, functions, and/or necessary management skills. Segments such as these often seem to be separate companies to an outside observer. But the investment center concept can be applied even in relatively small companies in which the segment managers have control over the revenues, expenses, and assets of their segments.

Transfer Prices

Profit centers and investment centers inside companies often exchange products with each other. The Pontiac, Buick, and other divisions of General Motors buy and sell automobile parts from each other, for example. No market exchange takes place, so the company sets transfer prices that represent revenue to the selling division and costs to the buying division.

A **transfer price** is an artificial price used when goods or services are transferred from one segment to another segment within the same company. Accountants record the transfer price as a revenue of the producing segment and as a cost, or expense, of the receiving segment. Usually no cash actually changes hands between the segments. Instead, the transfer price is an internal accounting transaction.

Segments are generally evaluated based on some measure of profitability. The transfer price is important because it affects the profitability of the buying and selling segments. The higher the transfer price, the better for the seller. The lower the transfer price, the better for the buyer.

Ideally, a transfer price provides incentives for segment managers to make decisions not only in their best interests but also in the interests of the entire company. For example, if the selling segment can sell everything it produces for $100 per unit, the buying segment should pay the market price of $100 per unit. A seller with excess capacity, however, should be willing to transfer a product to the buying segment for any price at or above the differential cost of producing and transferring the product to the buying segment.

In practice, companies mostly base transfer prices on (1) the market price of the product, (2) the cost of the product, or (3) some amount negotiated by the buying and selling segment managers.

Use of Segmental Analysis

So far we have described only the fundamentals of responsibility accounting. In this section we focus specifically on segmental analysis.

Decentralization is the dispersion of decision-making authority among individuals at lower levels of the organization. In other words, the extent of decentralization refers to the degree of control that segment managers have over the revenues, expenses, and assets of their segments. When a segment manager has control over these elements, the investment center concept can be applied to the segment. Thus, the more decentralized the decision making is in an organization, the more applicable is the investment center concept to the segments of the company. The more centralized the decision making is, the more likely responsibility centers are to be established as expense centers.

Some advantages of decentralized decision making are:

1. Managing segments trains managers for high-level positions in the company. The added authority and responsibility also represent *job enlargement* and often increase job satisfaction and motivation.
2. Top management can be more removed from day-to-day decision making at lower levels of the company and can manage by exception. When top management is not involved with routine problem solving, it can devote more time to long-range planning and to the company's most significant problem areas.
3. Decisions can be made at the point where problems arise. It is often difficult for top managers to make appropriate decisions on a timely basis when they are not intimately involved with the problem they are trying to solve.
4. Since decentralization permits the use of the investment center concept, performance evaluation criteria such as ROI and residual income (to be explained later) can be used.

Concepts Used in Segmental Analysis

To understand segmental analysis, you need to know about the concepts of variable cost, fixed cost, direct cost, indirect cost, net income of a segment, and contribution to indirect expenses. Next, we describe each concept.

Direct Cost and Indirect Cost

Costs may be either directly or indirectly related to a particular cost objective. A **cost objective** is a segment, product, or other item for which costs may be accumulated. In other words, a cost is not *direct* or *indirect* in and of itself. It is only direct or indirect in relation to a given cost objective.

A **direct cost (expense)** is specifically traceable to a given cost objective. An **indirect cost (expense)** is not traceable to a given cost objective but has been allocated to it. Accountants can designate a particular cost (expense) as direct or indirect by reference to a given cost objective. Thus, a cost that is direct to one cost objective may be indirect to another. For instance, the salary of a segment manager may be a direct cost of a given manufacturing segment but an indirect cost of one of the products manufactured by that segment. In this example, the segment and the product are two distinct cost objectives.

Because a direct cost is traceable to a cost objective, the cost is likely to be eliminated if the cost objective is eliminated. For instance, if the plastics segment of a business closes down, the salary of the manager of that segment probably is eliminated. Sometimes a direct cost would remain even if the cost objective were eliminated, but this is the exception rather than the rule.

An indirect cost is not traceable to a particular cost objective; therefore, it only becomes an expense of the cost objective through an allocation process. For example, consider the depreciation expense on the company headquarters building that is allocated to each segment of the company. The depreciation expense is a direct cost for the company headquarters, but it is an indirect cost to each segment. If a segment of the company is eliminated, the indirect cost for depreciation assigned to that segment does not disappear; the cost is simply allocated among the remaining segments. In a given situation, it may be possible to identify an indirect cost that would be eliminated if the cost objective were eliminated, but this would be the exception to the general rule.

Because the direct costs of a segment are clearly identified with that segment, these costs are often controllable by the segment manager. In contrast, indirect costs become segment costs only through allocation; therefore, most indirect

ILLUSTRATION 25.5
Contribution Margin Format Income Statement

A. All Expenses Allocated to Segments

	Segment A	Segment B	Total
Sales	$2,500,000	$1,500,000	$4,000,000
Less: Variable expenses (all of which are direct expenses)	700,000	650,000	1,350,000
Contribution margin	**$1,800,000**	**$ 850,000**	**$2,650,000**
Less: Direct fixed expenses	450,000	550,000	1,000,000
Contribution to indirect expenses	**$1,350,000**	**$ 300,000**	**$1,650,000**
Less: Indirect fixed expenses	270,000	330,000	600,000
Net income	**$1,080,000**	**$ (30,000)**	**$1,050,000**

B. Indirect Expenses Not Allocated to Segments

	Segment A	Segment B	Total
Sales	$2,500,000	$1,500,000	$4,000,000
Less: Variable expenses	700,000	650,000	1,350,000
Contribution margin	**$1,800,000**	**$ 850,000**	**$2,650,000**
Less: Direct fixed expenses	450,000	550,000	1,000,000
Contribution to indirect expenses	**$1,350,000**	**$ 300,000**	**$1,650,000**
Less: Indirect fixed expenses			600,000
Net income			**$1,050,000**

costs are noncontrollable by the segment manager. Be careful, however, not to equate direct costs with controllable costs. For example, the salary of a segment manager may be direct to that segment and yet is noncontrollable by that manager because managers cannot specify their own salaries.

Net Income of a Segment—Evaluation Criteria for a Profit Center

Objective 3
Prepare a segmental income statement using the contribution margin format.

When preparing internal reports on the performance of segments of a company, management often finds it is important to classify expenses as fixed or variable and as direct or indirect to the segment. These classifications may be more useful to management than the traditional classifications of cost of goods sold, operating expenses, and nonoperating expenses that are used for external reporting in the company's financial statements. As a result, many companies prepare an income statement for internal use with the format shown in Illustration 25.5(A).

This format is called the **contribution margin format** for an income statement because it shows the contribution margin. **Contribution margin** is defined as sales revenue less variable expenses. Notice in Illustration 25.5(A) that all variable expenses are direct expenses of the segment. The second subtotal in the contribution margin format income statement is the segment's contribution to indirect expenses. **Contribution to indirect expenses** is defined as sales revenue less all direct expenses of the segment (both variable direct expenses and fixed direct expenses). The final total in the income statement is **segmental net income,** defined as segmental revenues less all expenses (direct expenses and allocated indirect expenses).

Earlier we stated that the performance of a profit center is evaluated on the basis of the segment's profits. It is tempting to use segmental net income to make this evaluation since total net income is used to evaluate the performance of the entire company. The problem with using segmental net income to evaluate performance is that segmental net income includes certain indirect expenses that have been allocated to the segment but are not directly related to it or its operations. Because segmental contribution to indirect expenses includes only revenues and expenses directly related to the segment, this amount is often more appropriate for evaluation purposes.

Given the facts in Illustration 25.5(A), if management relied on segmental net income to judge segmental performance, management might conclude that Segment B should be eliminated since it shows a loss of $30,000. But this action would reduce overall company income by $300,000, as shown here:

Reduction in corporate revenues		$1,500,000
Reduction in corporate expenses:		
Variable expenses	$650,000	
Direct fixed expenses	550,000	1,200,000
Reduction in corporate income		$ 300,000

Notice that the elimination of Segment B would not eliminate the $330,000 of allocated fixed costs. These costs would need to be allocated to Segment A if Segment B no longer existed.

To stress the importance of a segment's contribution to indirect expenses, many companies prefer the contribution margin income statement format in Illustration 25.5(B), over that in Illustration 25.5(A). The difference is that indirect fixed costs are not allocated to individual segments in Illustration 25.5(B). Indirect fixed expenses appear only in the total column for the computation of net income for the entire company. The computation for each segment stops with the segment's contribution to indirect expenses; this is the appropriate figure to use for evaluating the earnings performance of a segment. Only for the company as a whole is net income (revenues minus all expenses) computed; this is, of course, the appropriate figure to use for evaluating the company as a whole.

Arbitrary Allocations of Indirect Fixed Expenses As stated earlier, indirect fixed expenses, such as depreciation on the corporate administration building or on the computer facility maintained at company headquarters, can only be allocated to segments on some arbitrary basis. The two basic guidelines for allocating indirect fixed expenses are by the benefit received and by the responsibility for the incurrence of the expense.

Accountants can make an allocation on the basis of benefit received for certain indirect expenses. For instance, assume the entire company used a corporate computer for a total of 10,000 hours. If it used 4,000 hours, Segment K could be charged (allocated) with 40% of the computer's depreciation for the period, since it received 40% of the total benefits for the period.

For certain other indirect expenses, accountants base allocation on responsibility for incurrence. For instance, assume that Segment M contracts with a magazine to run an advertisement benefiting Segment M and various other segments of the company. Some companies would allocate the entire cost of the advertisement to Segment M because it was responsible for incurring the advertising expense.

To further illustrate the allocation of indirect expenses based on a measure of benefit or responsibility for incurrence, assume that Daily Company operates two segments, X and Y. It allocates the following indirect expenses to its two segments using the designated allocation bases:

Expense	Allocation Base
Administrative office building occupancy expense, $50,000	Net sales
Insurance expense, $35,000	Cost of segmental plant assets
General administrative expenses, $40,000	Number of employees

The following additional data are provided:

	Segment X	Segment Y	Total
Net sales	$400,000	$500,000	$900,000
Segmental plant assets	$250,000	$400,000	$650,000
Number of employees	50	80	130

Illustration 25.6
Computation of Return on Investment (ROI)

		Segment A	Segment B	Segment C	Total
(a)	Income	$ 250,000	$1,000,000	$ 500,000	$1,750,000
(b)	Investment	2,500,000	5,000,000	2,000,000	9,500,000
	Return on investment *(a)* ÷ *(b)*	10%	20%	25%	18.42%

The following expense allocation schedule shows the allocation of indirect expenses:

	Segment X	Segment Y	Total
Administrative office building occupancy expense	$22,222[a]	$27,778[b]	$50,000
Insurance expense	13,462[c]	21,538[d]	35,000
General administrative expenses	15,385[e]	24,615[f]	40,000

[a] $\frac{\$400{,}000}{\$900{,}000} \times \$50{,}000 = \$22{,}222.$
[b] $\frac{\$500{,}000}{\$900{,}000} \times \$50{,}000 = \$27{,}778.$
[c] $\frac{\$250{,}000}{\$650{,}000} \times \$35{,}000 = \$13{,}462.$
[d] $\frac{\$400{,}000}{\$650{,}000} \times \$35{,}000 = \$21{,}538.$
[e] $\frac{50}{130} \times \$40{,}000 = \$15{,}385.$
[f] $\frac{80}{130} \times \$40{,}000 = \$24{,}615.$

When it uses neither benefit nor responsibility to allocate indirect fixed expenses, a company must find some other reasonable, but arbitrary, basis. Often, for lack of a better approach, a firm may allocate indirect expenses based on net sales. For instance, if Segment X's net sales were 60% of total company sales, then 60% of the indirect expenses would be allocated to Segment X. Allocating expenses based on sales is not recommended because it reduces the incentive of a segment manager to increase sales, since this would result in more indirect expenses being allocated to that segment.

Having covered some basic concepts essential to segmental analysis, next we present some specific procedures for performance evaluation.

Investment Center Analysis

Objective 4
Calculate return on investment, margin, and turnover for a segment.

To this point, the segmental analysis discussion has concentrated on the contribution to indirect expenses and segmental net income approaches. Now we introduce the investment base concept into the analysis. Two evaluation bases that include the concept of investment base in the analysis are ROI (return on investment) and RI (residual income).

Return on Investment (ROI)

A segment that has a large amount of assets usually earns more in an absolute sense than a segment that has a small amount of assets. Therefore, a firm cannot use absolute amounts of segmental income to compare the performance of different segments. To measure the relative effectiveness of segments, a company might use **return on investment (ROI),** which calculates the return (income) as a percentage of the assets employed (investment). The formula for ROI is:

$$\text{ROI} = \frac{\text{Income}}{\text{Investment}}$$

To illustrate the difference between using absolute amounts and using percentages in evaluating a segment's performance, consider the data in Illustration 25.6 for a company with three segments. When using absolute dollars of income to evaluate performance, Segment B appears to be doing twice as well as Segment C. However, using ROI to evaluate the segments indicates that Segment C is really performing the best (25%), Segment B is next (20%), and Segment A is performing the worst (10%). Therefore, ROI is a more useful indicator of the relative performance of segments than absolute income.

Although ROI appears to be a quite simple and straightforward computation, there are several alternative methods for making the calculation. These alternatives focus on what is meant by *income* and *investment*. Illustration 25.7 shows various definitions and applicable situations for each type of computation.

As discussed earlier in the chapter, alternative valuation bases include cost less accumulated depreciation, original cost, and current replacement cost. Each of the valuation bases has merits and drawbacks, as we discuss next. First, cost less accumulated depreciation is probably the most widely used valuation base and is easily determined. Because of the many types of depreciation methods,

ILLUSTRATION 25.7
Possible Definitions of Income and Investment

Situation	Definition of Income	Definition of Investment
1. Evaluation of the earning power of the company. Do not use for segments or segment managers due to inclusion of noncontrollable expenses.	Net income of the company.*	Total assets of the company.†
2. Evaluation of rate of income contribution of segment. Do not use for segment managers due to inclusion of noncontrollable expenses.	Contribution to indirect expenses.	Assets directly used by and identified with the segment.
3. Evaluation of income performance of segment manager.	*Controllable* income. Begin with contribution to indirect expenses and eliminate any revenues and direct expenses not under the control of the segment manager.	Assets under the control of the segment manager.

* Often *net operating income* is used; this term is defined as income before interest and taxes.

† *Operating assets* are often used in the calculation. This definition excludes assets not used in normal operations.

comparisons between segments or companies may be difficult. Also, as book value decreases, a constant income results in a steadily increasing ROI even though the segment's performance is unchanged. Second, the use of original cost eliminates the problem of decreasing book value but has its own drawback. The cost of old assets is much less than an investment in new assets, so a segment with old assets can earn less than a segment with new assets and realize a higher ROI. Third, current replacement cost is difficult to use because replacement cost figures often are not available, but this base does eliminate some of the problems caused by the other two methods. Whichever valuation basis is adopted, all ROI calculations that are to be used for comparative purposes should be made consistently.

AN ACCOUNTING PERSPECTIVE

BUSINESS INSIGHT Although financial performance measures such as ROI are important for providing incentives to perform well, so is the company's culture. For example, Johnson & Johnson has a culture emphasizing high ethical standards. The Johnson & Johnson Credo, published in its annual report and displayed throughout the company, is a famous example of this culture. Hewlett-Packard is known as a people-oriented company that emphasizes personal development and long-term employment.

To encourage long-term growth, 3M requires that at least 25% of each division's sales come from new products. This encourages constant innovation and new product development. In addition, the company allows employees to spend 15% of their time on innovative projects, encourages sharing of technology across divisions, and provides "seed" grants for employees to develop new products. With this corporate culture, 3M has a worldwide reputation for innovation.

EXPANDED FORM OF ROI COMPUTATION The ROI formula breaks into two component parts:

$$\text{ROI} = \frac{\text{Income}}{\text{Sales}} \times \frac{\text{Sales}}{\text{Investment}}$$

The first part of the formula, Income/Sales, is called *margin* or *return on sales*. The **margin** refers to the percentage relationship of income or profits to sales. This percentage shows the number of cents of profit generated by each dollar of sales. The second part of the formula, Sales/Investment, is called *turnover*. **Turnover** shows the number of dollars of sales generated by each dollar of investment. Turnover measures how effectively each dollar of assets was used.

A manager can increase ROI in the following three ways. In Illustration 25.8, note the possible outcomes of some of these strategies to increase ROI.

1. By concentrating on increasing the profit margin while holding turnover constant: Pursuing this strategy means keeping selling prices constant and making every effort to increase efficiency and thereby reduce expenses.
2. By concentrating on increasing turnover by reducing the investment in assets while holding income and sales constant: For example, working capital could be decreased, thereby reducing the investment in assets.
3. By taking actions that affect both margin and turnover: For example, disposing of nonproductive depreciable assets would decrease investment while also increasing income (through the reduction of depreciation expense). Thus, both margin and turnover would increase. An advertising campaign would probably increase sales and income. Turnover would increase, and margin might increase or decrease depending on the relative amounts of the increases in income and sales.

ILLUSTRATION 25.8
Strategies for Increasing Return on Investment (ROI)

Past year's return on investment:

$$\text{ROI} = \text{Margin} \times \text{Turnover}$$

$$\text{ROI} = \frac{\text{Income}}{\text{Sales}} \times \frac{\text{Sales}}{\text{Investment}}$$

$$\text{ROI} = \frac{\$100{,}000}{\$2{,}000{,}000} \times \frac{\$2{,}000{,}000}{\$1{,}000{,}000}$$

$$\text{ROI} = 5\% \times 2 \text{ times}$$

$$\text{ROI} = 10\%$$

1. Increase margin through reducing expenses by $40,000; no effect on sales or investment.

$$\text{ROI} = \frac{\$140{,}000}{\$2{,}000{,}000} \times \frac{\$2{,}000{,}000}{\$1{,}000{,}000}$$

$$\text{ROI} = 7\% \times 2 \text{ times}$$

$$\text{ROI} = 14\%$$

2. Increase turnover through reducing investment in assets by $200,000; no effect on sales or income.

$$\text{ROI} = \frac{\$100{,}000}{\$2{,}000{,}000} \times \frac{\$2{,}000{,}000}{\$800{,}000}$$

$$\text{ROI} = 5\% \times 2.5 \text{ times}$$

$$\text{ROI} = 12.5\%$$

3(a). Increase margin and turnover by disposing of nonproductive depreciable assets; income increased by $10,000; investment decreased by $200,000; no effect on sales.

$$\text{ROI} = \frac{\$110{,}000}{\$2{,}000{,}000} \times \frac{\$2{,}000{,}000}{\$800{,}000}$$

$$\text{ROI} = 5.5\% \times 2.5 \text{ times}$$

$$\text{ROI} = 13.75\%$$

3(b). Increase margin and turnover through increased advertising; sales increased by $500,000 and income by $50,000; no effect on investment.

$$\text{ROI} = \frac{\$150{,}000}{\$2{,}500{,}000} \times \frac{\$2{,}500{,}000}{\$1{,}000{,}000}$$

$$\text{ROI} = 6\% \times 2.5 \text{ times}$$

$$\text{ROI} = 15\%$$

3(c). Increase turnover through increased advertising; sales increased by $500,000 and income by $12,500; no effect on investment.

$$\text{ROI} = \frac{\$112{,}500}{\$2{,}500{,}000} \times \frac{\$2{,}500{,}000}{\$1{,}000{,}000}$$

$$\text{ROI} = 4.5\% \times 2.5 \text{ times}$$

$$\text{ROI} = 11.25\%$$

Residual Income

Objective 5
Calculate the residual income of a segment.

When a company uses ROI to evaluate performance, managers have incentives to focus on the average returns from their segments' assets. However, the company's best interest is served if managers also focus on the marginal returns.

To illustrate, assume the manager of Segment 3 in Illustration 25.9 has an opportunity to take on a project involving an investment of $100,000 that is estimated to return $22,000, or 22%, on the investment. Since the segment's ROI is currently 25%, the manager may decide to reject the project because accepting the project will cause the segment's ROI to decline. Suppose however, from the company's point of view, all projects earning greater than a 10% return should be accepted, even if they are lower than a particular segment's ROI.

The rejection by a segment manager of a project that exceeds the 10% desired minimum return is an example of *suboptimization*. **Suboptimization** occurs when a segment manager takes an action that is in the segment's best interest but is not in the best interest of the company as a whole.

To deal with this type of suboptimization, companies sometimes use the concept of *residual income*. **Residual income (RI)** is defined as the amount of income a segment has in excess of a desired minimum ROI. Each company sets its minimum ROI based on many factors, including expected growth rate, debt coverage, industry technology, and desired returns to stockholders. The formula for residual income (RI) is:

$$\text{RI} = \text{Income} - (\text{Investment} \times \text{Minimum ROI})$$

When a company uses RI to evaluate performance, the segment rated as the best is the segment with the greatest amount of RI rather than the one with the highest ROI.

Returning to our example, the project opportunity for Segment 3 could earn in excess of the desired minimum ROI of 10%. In fact, Segment 3 has RI of $12,000, calculated as ($22,000 − [10% × $100,000]). If RI were applied as the basis for evaluating segmental performance, the manager of Segment 3 would accept the project because doing so would improve the segment's performance. That choice would also be beneficial to the entire company.

Critics of the RI method complain that larger segments are likely to have the highest RI. In a given situation, it may be advisable to look at both ROI and RI in assessing performance.

Illustration 25.9
Computation of Residual Income (RI)

Before acceptance of the project by Segment 3, the amounts are as follows:

	Segment 1	Segment 2	Segment 3	Total Company
a. Income	$ 100,000	$ 500,000	$ 250,000	$ 850,000
b. Investment	1,000,000	2,500,000	1,000,000	4,500,000
c. Rate of return on investment (ROI)	10%	20%	25%	18.89%
d. Desired minimum ROI (10%)	$ 100,000	$ 250,000	$ 100,000	*
e. Residual income (RI)	–0–	250,000	150,000	*

With acceptance of the project by Segment 3, the amounts would be as follows:

	Segment 1	Segment 2	Segment 3	Total Company
a. Income	$ 100,000	$ 500,000	$ 272,000†	$ 872,000
b. Investment	1,000,000	2,500,000	1,100,000‡	4,600,000
c. Rate of return on investment (ROI)	10%	20%	24.7%	18.96%
d. Desired minimum ROI (10%)	$ 100,000	$ 250,000	$ 110,000	*
e. Residual income (RI)	–0–	250,000	162,000	*

* The RI concept is generally not used for evaluating an entire company, since the problem of suboptimization, by definition, does not exist for the company as a whole.

† $250,000 + (22% of $100,000).

‡ $1,000,000 original investment + $100,000 new investment.

A manager tends to make choices that improve the segment's performance. The challenge is to select evaluation bases for segments that result in managers making choices that benefit the entire company. When performance is evaluated using RI, choices that improve a segment's performance are more likely also to improve the entire company's performance.

When calculating RI for a **segment,** the income and investment definitions are contribution to indirect expenses and assets directly used by and identified with the segment. When calculating RI for a **manager** of a segment, the income and investment definitions should be income controllable by the manager and assets under the control of the segment manager.

Using Judgment in Performance Evaluation

In evaluating the performance of a segment or a segment manager, comparisons should be made with (1) the current budget, (2) other segments or managers within the company, (3) past performance of that segment or manager, and (4) similar segments or managers in other companies. Consideration must be given to factors such as general economic conditions and market conditions for the product being produced. A superior segment in Company A may be considered superior because it is earning a return of 12%, which is above similar segments in other companies but below other segments in Company A. However, segments in Company A may be more profitable because of market conditions and the nature of the company's products rather than because of the performance of the segment managers. Top management must use careful judgment whenever performance is evaluated.

Segmental Reporting in External Financial Statements

Formerly, segmental information was reported only to management for internal decision-making purposes. In December 1976, the Financial Accounting Standards Board issued *Statement of Financial Accounting Standards No. 14,* "Financial Reporting for Segments of a Business Enterprise." This statement requires publicly held companies to publish certain segmental information in their annual financial statements. Thus, external users of financial statements now have segmental information to aid them in their decisions regarding these companies. However, these external statements present fewer details than reports intended for management.

In this chapter you learned about responsibility accounting and segmental analysis. Chapter 26 discusses capital budgeting and long-term planning.

Understanding the Learning Objectives

Objective 1
Explain responsibility accounting and its use in a business entity.

- Responsibility accounting refers to an accounting system that collects, summarizes, and reports accounting data relating to the responsibilities of individual managers.

Objective 2
Prepare responsibility accounting reports.

- Although the amount of detail varies, reports issued under a responsibility accounting system are interrelated. Totals from the report on one level of management are carried forward in the report to the management level immediately above.

Objective 3
Prepare a segmental income statement using the contribution margin format.

- The contribution margin format for the income statement shows the contribution margin for the company.
- Contribution to indirect expenses is defined as sales revenue less all direct expenses of the segment.
- The final total in the income statement is segmental net income, defined as segmental revenues less all expenses (direct expenses and allocated indirect expenses).

Objective 4
Calculate return on investment, margin, and turnover for a segment.

- Return on investment measures the relative effectiveness of segments. The formula for return on investment is:

$$\text{Return on investment} = \frac{\text{Income}}{\text{Investment}}$$

- Alternatively, the formula for return on investment can be broken into two components:

$$\text{Return on investment} = \frac{\text{Income}}{\text{Sales}} \times \frac{\text{Sales}}{\text{Investment}}$$

- Margin refers to the percentage relationship of income or profits to sales. This percentage shows the number of cents of profit generated by each dollar of sales. The formula for margin can be expressed as:

$$\text{Margin} = \frac{\text{Income}}{\text{Sales}}$$

- Turnover shows the number of dollars of sales generated by each dollar of investment. Turnover measures how effectively each dollar of assets was used. The formula for turnover can be expressed as:

$$\text{Turnover} = \frac{\text{Sales}}{\text{Investment}}$$

Objective 5
Calculate the residual income of a segment.

- Residual income is defined as the amount of income a segment has in excess of a desired minimum return on investment.
- Each company sets its minimum return on investment based on many factors, including expected growth rate, debt coverage, industry technology, and desired returns to stockholders.
- The formula for residual income is:

$$\text{RI} = \text{Income} - (\text{Investment} \times \text{Minimum ROI})$$

Objective 6
Allocate costs from service departments to operating departments. (Appendix)

- Two basic methods exist for allocating service department costs: (1) the direct method and (2) the step method.

Appendix

Allocation of Service Department Costs

Objective 6
Allocate costs from service departments to operating departments.

Throughout this text, we have emphasized cost allocations only in the operating departments of a company. These operating departments perform the primary purpose of the company—to produce goods and services for consumers. Examples of operating departments are the assembly departments of manufacturing firms and the departments in hotels that take and confirm reservations.

The costs of service departments are allocated to the operating departments because they exist to support the operating departments. Examples of service departments are maintenance, administration, cafeterias, laundries, and receiving. Service departments aid multiple production departments at the same time, and accountants must allocate and account for all of these costs. It is crucial that these service department costs be allocated to the operating departments so that the costs of conducting business in the operating departments are clearly and accurately reflected.

Accountants allocate service department costs using some type of base. When the companies' managers choose bases to use, they consider such criteria as the types of services provided, the benefits received, and the fairness of the allocation method. Examples of bases used to allocate service department costs are number of employees, machine-hours, direct labor-hours, square footage, and electricity usage.

Two basic methods exist for allocating service department costs. The first method, the direct method, is the simplest of the two. The direct method allocates costs of each of the service departments to each operating department based on each department's share of the allocation base. Services used by other service departments are ignored. For example, if

Service Department A uses some of Service Department B's services, these services would be ignored in the cost allocation process. Because these services are not allocated to other service departments, some accountants believe the direct method is not accurate.

The second method of allocating service department costs is the step method. This method allocates service costs to the operating departments and other service departments in a sequential process. The sequence of allocation generally starts with the service department that has incurred the greatest costs. After this department's costs have been allocated, the service department with the next highest costs has its costs allocated, and so forth until the service department with the lowest costs has had its costs allocated. Costs are not allocated back to a department that has already had all of its costs allocated.

To illustrate the direct method and the step method, we use the following data:

	Service Departments		Operating Departments	
	Maintenance	**Administration**	**1**	**2**
Costs	$8,000	$4,000	$32,000	$36,000
Machine-hours used	1,000	2,000	1,500	2,500
Number of employees	100	200	250	150

The costs of the maintenance department are allocated based on the machine-hours used. For the administration department, the cost allocation is based on the number of employees.

Direct Method

Using the preceding data, an example of the direct method follows:

	Service Departments		Operating Departments	
	Maintenance	**Administration**	**1**	**2**
Costs	$ 8,000	$ 4,000	$32,000	$36,000
Allocation of maintenance department's costs*	(8,000)		3,000	5,000
	$ -0-			
Allocation of administration department's costs†		(4,000)	2,500	1,500
		$ -0-	$37,500	$42,500

* Department 1's fraction is 1,500/4,000; Department 2's fraction is 2,500/4,000.

† Department 1's fraction is: 250/400; Department 2's fraction is 150/400.

Step Method

Using the same data, an example of the step method follows:

	Service Departments		Operating Departments	
	Maintenance	**Administration**	**1**	**2**
Costs	$ 8,000	$ 4,000	$32,000	$36,000
Allocation of maintenance department's costs*	(8,000)	2,667	2,000	3,333
	$ -0-			
Allocation of administration department's costs†		(6,667)	4,167	2,500
		$ -0-	$38,167	$41,833

* Administration's fraction: 2,000/6,000; Department 1's fraction: 1,500/6,000; Department 2's fraction: 2,500/6,000.

† Department 1's fraction: 250/400; Department 2's fraction: 150/400.

Note in the preceding examples that the maintenance department costs were not allocated to the administration department under the direct method but were allocated under the step method. Also, to eliminate the administration department's costs, under the step method those costs allocated to the administration department from the maintenance department must be allocated to the operating departments as part of the total administration department's cost.

Demonstration Problem

The results of operations for Alan Company's two segments in 1996 follow:

	Segment 1	Segment 2	Total
Sales	$90,000	$135,000	$225,000
Variable expenses	63,000	81,000	144,000
Fixed expenses:			
Direct	9,000	25,200	34,200
Indirect			12,600

The company has total operating assets of $315,000, $288,000 of these assets are identified with particular segments as follows:

	Segment 1	Segment 2
Assets directly used by and identified with the segment	$108,000	$180,000

Required

a. Prepare a statement showing the contribution margin, contribution to indirect expenses for each segment, and the total income for Alan Company.

b. Determine the return on investment for each segment and then for the entire company.

c. Comment on the results of (**a**) and (**b**).

Solution to Demonstration Problem

a.

ALAN COMPANY
Income Statement Showing Segmental Contribution to Indirect Expenses
For the Year Ended December 31, 1996

	Segment 1	Segment 2	Total
Sales	$90,000	$135,000	$225,000
Less: Variable expenses	63,000	81,000	144,000
Contribution margin	$27,000	$ 54,000	$ 81,000
Less: Direct fixed expenses	9,000	25,200	34,200
Contribution to indirect expenses	$18,000	$ 28,800	$ 46,800
Less: Indirect fixed expenses			12,600
Net income			$ 34,200

b. **1.**

$$\text{ROI} = \frac{\text{Contribution to indirect expenses}}{\text{Assets directly used by and identified with the segment}}$$

Segment 1

$$\text{ROI} = \frac{\$18{,}000}{\$108{,}000} = 16.67\%$$

Segment 2

$$\text{ROI} = \frac{\$28{,}800}{\$180{,}000} = 16\%$$

2.

$$\text{ROI} = \frac{\text{Net operating income}}{\text{Operating assets}} = \frac{\$34{,}200}{\$315{,}000} = 10.9\%$$

c. In Part (**a**), Segment 2 showed a higher contribution to indirect expenses. But in (**b**), Segment 1 showed a higher return on investment. The difference between these calculations shows that when a segment is evaluated as a profit center, the center with the highest investment base usually shows the best results. But when the segment is evaluated as an investment center, the segment with the highest investment base does not necessarily show the highest return. The computations in (**b**) also demonstrate that the return on investment for the company as a whole will be lower than that of each segment because of the increased investment base.

New Terms*

Budget variance The difference between the budgeted and actual amounts of an item. *875*

Contribution margin Sales revenues less variable expenses. *881*

Contribution margin format An income statement format that shows the contribution margin (Sales − Variable expenses) for a segment. *881*

Contribution to indirect expenses Sales revenue less all direct expenses of the segment. *881*

Controllable profits of a segment Profit of a segment when expenses under a manager's control are deducted from revenues under that manager's control. *878*

Cost objective A segment, product, or other item for which costs may be accumulated. *880*

Current replacement cost The cost of replacing the present assets with similar assets in the same condition as those now in use. *878*

Decentralization The dispersion of decision-making authority among individuals at lower levels of the organization. *879*

Direct cost (expense) A cost that is specifically traceable to a given cost objective. *880*

Expense center A responsibility center incurring only expense items and producing no direct revenue from the sale of goods or services. Examples include the accounting department and the maintenance department. *878*

Indirect cost (expense) A cost that is not traceable to a given cost objective but has been allocated to it. *880*

Investment center A responsibility center having revenues, expenses, and an appropriate investment base. *878*

Management by exception The principle that upper-level management does not need to examine operating details at lower levels unless there appears to be a problem (an exception). *874*

Margin (as used in ROI) The percentage relationship of income (or profits) to sales. *884*

$$\text{Margin} = \frac{\text{Income}}{\text{Sales}}$$

* Some terms listed in earlier chapters are repeated here for your convenience.

Original cost The price paid to acquire an asset. *878*

Original cost less accumulated depreciation The book value of an asset—the amount paid less total depreciation taken. *878*

Profit center A responsibility center having both revenues and expenses. *878*

Residual income (RI) The amount of income a segment has in excess of a desired minimum ROI. Residual income is equal to Income − (Investment × Minimum ROI). *886*

Responsibility accounting Refers to an accounting system that collects, summarizes, and reports accounting data relating to the responsibility of the individual managers. A responsibility accounting system provides information to evaluate each manager on revenue and expense items over which that manager has primary control. *872*

Responsibility center A segment of an organization for which a particular executive is responsible. *876*

Return on investment (ROI) Calculates the return (income) as a percentage of the assets employed (investment). *878, 883*

$$\text{Return on investment} = \frac{\text{Income}}{\text{Investment}} \text{ or } \frac{\text{Income}}{\text{Sales}} \times \frac{\text{Sales}}{\text{Investment}}$$

Segment A fairly autonomous unit or division of a company defined according to function or product line. *876*

Segmental net income The final total in the income statement; segmental revenues less all expenses (direct expenses and allocated indirect expenses). *881*

Suboptimization A situation when a segment manager takes an action in the segment's best interest but not in the best interest of the company as a whole. *886*

Transfer price An artificial price used when goods or services are transferred from one segment to another segment within the same company. *879*

Turnover (as used in ROI) The number of dollars of sales generated by each dollar of investment. *884*

$$\text{Turnover} = \frac{\text{Sales}}{\text{Investment}}$$

Self-Test

True-False

Indicate whether each of the following statements is true or false.

1. Items that a manager has direct control over are included in responsibility accounting reports for that management level.
2. An appropriate goal of an expense center is the long-run minimization of expenses.
3. The salary of a segment manager would be considered a direct cost as well as an uncontrollable cost to that segment.
4. Segmental net income is the most appropriate figure to use when evaluating the performance of a segment.
5. When calculating RI for a segment, the income and investment definitions are income controlled by a manager, and assets directly used by and identified with the segment.

MULTIPLE-CHOICE

Select the best answer for each of the following questions.

1. The investment base used when determining the ROI calculation could be which of the following?
   a. Current replacement cost.
   b. Original cost.
   c. Original cost less accumulated depreciation.
   d. Any of the above.
2. Which of the following actions would increase ROI?
   a. Reduce operating expenses with no effect on sales or assets.
   b. Increase investment in assets, with no change in income.
   c. Increase sales with no change in income or assets.
   d. None of the above.
3. Calculate ROI using the expanded form (margin times turnover) from the following data:

Sales	$1,000,000
Investment	500,000
Income	50,000

   a. 20%. c. 15%.
   b. 10%. d. None of the above.
4. In evaluating the performance of a segment or manager, comparisons should be made with:
   a. Other segments and managers within the company and in other companies.
   b. Past performance of the segment manager.
   c. The current budget.
   d. All of the above.
5. Calculate the ROI and RI for each of the following segments and determine if a segment should be dropped based on RI.

	Segment 1	Segment 2	Segment 3
Income	$ 180,000	$1,000,000	$ 500,000
Investment. . . .	2,000,000	5,000,000	2,000,000
ROI	?	?	?
Desired minimum ROI (10%) . . .	200,000	500,000	200,000
RI	?	?	?

   a. 9%, 20%, 20%
   $0, $500,000, $200,000
   Consider dropping Segment 1.
   b. 20%, 20%, 20%
   $200,000, $500,000, $200,000
   Do not drop any segment.
   c. 9%, 20%, 25%
   $(20,000), $500,000, $300,000
   Consider dropping Segment 1.
   d. 20%, 20%, 25%
   $200,000, $500,000, $300,000
   Do not drop any segment.

Now turn to page 901 to check your answers.

QUESTIONS

1. What is the fundamental principle of responsibility accounting?
2. List five important factors that should be considered in designing reports for a responsibility accounting system.
3. How soon should accounting reports be prepared after the end of the performance measurement period? Explain.
4. Name and describe three types of responsibility centers.
5. Describe a segment of a business enterprise that is best treated as an expense center. List four indirect expenses that may be allocated to such an expense center.
6. Compare and contrast an expense center and an investment center.
7. What purpose is served by setting transfer prices?
8. What is the advantage of using investment centers as a basis for performance evaluation?
9. Which categories of items must a segment manager have control over for the investment center concept to be applicable?
10. What is the connection between the extent of decentralization and the investment center concept?
11. Give some of the advantages of decentralization.
12. Differentiate between a direct cost and an indirect cost of a segment. What happens to these categories if the segment to which they are related is eliminated?
13. Is it possible for a cost to be direct to one cost objective and indirect to another cost objective? Explain.
14. Describe some of the methods by which indirect expenses are allocated to a segment.
15. Give the general formula for return on investment (ROI). What are its two components?
16. Give the three sets of definitions for income and investment that can be used in ROI calculations, and explain when each set is applicable.
17. Give the various valuation bases that can be used for plant assets in investment center calculations. Discuss some of the advantages and disadvantages of these methods.
18. In what way is the use of the residual income (RI) concept superior to the use of ROI?
19. How is residual income (RI) determined?
20. If the RI for segment manager A is $50,000 while the RI for segment manager B is $100,000, does this necessarily mean that B is a better manager than A? Explain.

The Coca-Cola Company

21. **Real World Question** Refer to the annual report booklet. Compare the performance of The Coca-Cola Company's three lines of business: (1) Soft Drinks—USA, (2) Soft Drinks—International, and (3) Foods. (See footnote 19 called "Lines of Business.") Which business line had the most profits? Which business performed better in 1993 using ROI, profit margin, and asset turnover as the performance measures? Use end-of-year identifiable operating amounts to measure assets, operating income amounts to measure profits, and net operating revenues to measure sales.

The Coca-Cola Company

22. **Real World Question** Refer to the annual report booklet. Which of Coca-Cola's geographic areas had the highest ROI in 1993? To compute the answer, use "Operating Income" for the profit measure and end-of-year "Identifiable Operating Assets" for the measure of assets. (See footnote 19 of Coca-Cola's annual report.)
23. (Based on Appendix) Briefly discuss the two methods of allocating service department costs.

EXERCISES

Exercise 25–1
Prepare a responsibility report for a given management level (L.O. 2)

The following information refers to the inspection department of a soft drink bottling plant for May:

	Amount	Over or (Under) Budget
Supplies	$ 36,000	$ (7,200)
Repairs and maintenance	180,000	14,400
Overtime paid to inspectors	72,000	7,200
Salary of inspection department manager	21,600	(3,600)
Salary of plant manager	28,800	–0–
Allocation of company accounting costs	21,600	7,200
Allocation of building depreciation to the inspection department	14,400	(3,600)

Using this information, prepare a responsibility report for the manager of the inspection department for May. Include those items for which you think the inspection department manager would be held responsible.

Exercise 25–2
Prepare an income statement for a segment using the contribution margin format (L.O. 3)

Present the following information for the Sharks Division of Hockey, Inc., using the contribution margin format, excluding indirect fixed expenses:

Sales	$2,800,000
Variable selling and administrative expenses	200,000
Fixed direct manufacturing expenses	70,000
Fixed indirect manufacturing expenses	112,000
Variable manufacturing expenses	800,000
Fixed direct selling and administrative expenses	350,000
Fixed indirect selling and administrative expenses	56,000

Exercise 25–3
Prepare an income statement for a segment using the contribution margin format; determine effect of elimination of segment on company income (L.O. 3)

Given the following data, prepare a schedule that shows contribution margin, contribution to indirect expenses, and net income of the Hardware Division of ABC Computer Company:

Direct fixed expenses	$108,000
Indirect fixed expenses	86,400
Sales	700,000
Variable expenses	500,000

What would be the effect on the company income if the segment were eliminated?

Exercise 25–4
Allocate expenses to various segments using a specified allocation base (L.O. 3)

Three segments (A, B, and C) of Tramp Enterprises have net sales of $600,000, $300,000, and $100,000, respectively. A decision is made to allocate the pool of $50,000 of administrative overhead expenses of the home office to the segments, using net sales as the basis for allocation.

a. How much of the $50,000 should be allocated to each segment?
b. If Segment C is eliminated, how much of the $50,000 will be allocated to A and B?

Exercise 25–5
Calculate return on investment, margin, and turnover for a segment (L.O. 4)

Two segments (hardware and software) showed the following data for the most recent year:

	Software	Hardware
Contribution to indirect expenses	$1,680,000	$ 1,008,000
Assets directly used by and identified with the segment	5,040,000	4,368,000
Sales	6,720,000	13,440,000

a. Calculate return on investment for each segment in the most direct manner.

b. Calculate return on investment using the margin and turnover components.

Exercise 25–6
Determine the effect on margin, turnover, and return on investment when the variables are altered (L.O. 4)

Calculate the new margin, turnover, and return on investment of the software segment in Exercise 25–5 for each of the following changes. Consider each change independently of the others.

a. Direct variable expenses were reduced by $67,200. Sales and assets were unaffected.

b. Assets used by the segment were reduced by $1,080,000, while income and sales were unaffected.

c. An advertising campaign increased sales by $672,000 and income by $100,000. Assets directly used by the segment were unaffected.

Exercise 25–7
Calculate the return on investment in evaluating the income performance of a segment manager and the rate of income contribution of a segment (L.O. 4)

The following data are available for the travel segment of Exquisite Voyages, Inc.:

Net income of the segment	$ 48,000
Contribution to indirect expenses	60,000
Controllable income by manager	72,000
Assets directly used by the segment	360,000
Assets under the control of the segment manager	240,000

Determine the return on investment for evaluating (**a**) the income performance of the manager of the travel segment and (**b**) the rate of income contribution of the segment.

Exercise 25–8
Determine residual income in evaluating segments (L.O. 5)

Heidel Company has three segments: P, Q, and R. Data concerning income and investment follow:

	Segment P	Segment Q	Segment R
Contribution to indirect expenses	$ 86,400	$ 172,800	$ 230,400
Assets directly used by and identified with the segment	576,000	1,152,000	2,592,000

Assuming that the minimum desired return on investment is 10%, calculate the residual income of each of the segments. Do the results indicate that any of the segments should be eliminated?

Exercise 25–9
Calculate return on investment and residual income in evaluating a manager (L.O. 4, 5)

Assume that for Segment P in Exercise 25–8, $28,800 of the direct expenses and $72,000 of the segmental assets are not under the control of the segment manager. Top management wishes to evaluate the segment manager's income performance. Calculate the manager's return on investment and residual income. (Because certain expenses and assets are not controllable by the segment manager, the minimum desired return on investment is 15%.)

PROBLEMS

Problem 25–1
Prepare responsibility reports for various levels of management (L.O. 2)

You are given the following information for Territory Printers Company for the year ended December 31, 1996. The company is organized according to functions:

Controllable Expenses	Plant Manager		Vice President of Manufacturing		President	
	Budget	Actual	Budget	Actual	Budget	Actual
Office expense	$ 7,200	$ 9,600	$12,000	$16,800	$ 24,000	$ 16,800
Printing	19,200	16,800				
Paging	2,400	2,160				
Binding	4,800	4,800				
Purchasing			24,000	26,400		
Receiving			12,000	14,400		
Inspection			19,200	16,800		
Vice president of marketing					192,000	168,000
Controller					144,000	120,000
Treasurer					96,000	72,000
Vice president of personnel					48,000	72,000

Required

Prepare the responsibility accounting reports for the three levels of management—plant manager, vice president of manufacturing, and president.

Problem 25–2
Evaluate responsibility centers as profit centers and investment centers (L.O. 2)

Farflung Corporation has production plants in Boston, Chicago, and Atlanta. Following is a summary of the results for 1996:

Plant	Revenues	Expenses	Investment Base (gross assets)
Boston	$ 900,000	$450,000	$ 9,000,000
Chicago	900,000	360,000	6,750,000
Atlanta	1,350,000	495,000	14,400,000

Required

a. If the plants are treated as profit centers, which plant manager appears to have done the best job?

b. If the plants are treated as investment centers, which plant manager appears to have done the best job? (Assume the plant managers are evaluated by return on investment on gross assets.)

c. Do the results of profit center analysis and investment center analysis give different findings? If so, why?

Problem 25–3
Allocate indirect expense to illustrate the arbitrary nature of expense allocation (L.O. 3)

Joey Bauer Company allocates all of its home office expenses to its two segments, X and Y. Allocations are based on the following selected expense account balances and additional data:

Expenses (allocation bases)	
Home office building expense (net sales)	$38,400
Buying expense (net purchases)	33,600
Uncollectible accounts (net sales)	4,000
Depreciation of home office equipment (net sales)	10,560
Advertising expense (indirect, allocated on basis of relative amounts of direct advertising)	43,200
Insurance expense (relative amounts of equipment plus average inventory in department)	11,520

Additional data

	Segment X	Segment Y	Total
Purchases (net)	$121,600	$38,400	$160,000
Sales (net)	256,000	64,000	320,000
Equipment (cost)	48,000	32,000	80,000
Advertising (cost)	12,800	6,400	19,200
Average inventory	80,000	32,000	112,000

Required

a. Prepare a schedule showing the amounts of each type of expense allocable to Segments X and Y using these data and bases of allocation.

b. Evaluate and criticize these allocation bases.

Problem 25–4
Prepare a schedule showing contribution margin and contribution to indirect expenses using contribution margin format; prepare segmental income statements
(L.O. 3)

Quinn, Inc., is a company with two segments, 1 and 2. Its revenues and expenses for 1996 follow:

	Segment 1	Segment 2	Total
Net sales	$192,000	$288,000	$480,000
Direct expenses:*			
Cost of goods sold	90,000	198,000	288,000
Selling	27,360	14,400	41,760
Administrative:			
Uncollectible accounts	6,000	3,600	9,600
Insurance	4,800	2,400	7,200
Interest	960	480	1,440
Indirect expenses (all fixed):			
Selling			36,000
Administrative			50,400

* All the direct expenses are variable except insurance and interest, which are fixed.

Required

a. Prepare a schedule showing the contribution margin, the contribution to indirect expenses of each segment, and net income for the company as a whole. Do not allocate indirect expenses to the segments.

b. Assume that indirect selling expenses are to be allocated on the basis of net sales and that indirect administrative expenses are to be allocated on the basis of direct administrative expenses. Prepare a statement (starting with the contribution to indirect expenses) that shows the net income of each segment.

c. Comment on the appropriateness of the income amounts shown in Parts (**a**) and (**b**) for determining the income contribution of the segments.

Problem 25–5
Prepare an income statement for two segments using the contribution margin format; calculate the return on investment for (1) the entire company, (2) each segment, and (3) each manager (L.O. 3)

The following data pertain to the operating revenues and expenses for Lonestar Company for 1996:

	Dallas Segment	Austin Segment	Total
Sales	$360,000	$720,000	$1,080,000
Variable expenses	192,000	480,000	672,000
Direct fixed expenses	48,000	60,000	108,000
Indirect fixed expenses			144,000

Of the direct fixed expenses, $12,000 of those for the Austin segment and $10,800 of those for the Dallas segment were not under the control of that segment's manager.

Regarding the company's total operating assets of $1,800,000, the following facts exist:

	Dallas Segment	Austin Segment
Assets directly used by and identified with the segment	$360,000	$720,000
Assets under the control of the segment manager	300,000	600,000

Required

a. Prepare a statement showing the contribution margin of each segment, the contribution to indirect expenses of each segment, and the total income of Lonestar Company.

b. Determine the return on investment for evaluating (1) the earning power of the entire company, (2) the performance of each segment, and (3) the performance of each segment manager.

c. Comment on the results of Part (**b**).

Problem 25–6
Calculate return on investment and residual income for each segment and segment manager
(L.O. 4, 5)

Winston Company operates with three segments, E, F, and G. Data regarding these segments follow:

	Segment E	Segment F	Segment G
Contribution to indirect expenses	$ 324,000	$ 180,000	$144,000
Income controllable by the manager	450,000	270,000	230,400
Assets directly used by and identified with the segment	1,800,000	1,440,000	720,000
Assets under the control of the segment manager	1,584,000	1,278,000	648,000

Required

a. Calculate the return on investment for each segment and each segment manager. Rank them from highest to lowest.

b. Assume the minimum desired rates of return are 12% for a segment and 20% for a segment manager. Calculate residual income for each manager. Rank them from highest to lowest.

c. Repeat (**b**), but assume the desired minimum rates of return are 17% for a segment and 25% for a segment manager. Rank them from highest to lowest.

d. Comment on the rankings achieved.

Problem 25–7
Determine margin, turnover, and return on investment for a segment and the effect on each when the variables are changed (L.O. 4)

The manager of the Shaq Company faced the following data for the year 1996:

Contribution to indirect expenses	$ 1,800,000
Assets directly used by and identified with the segment	22,500,000
Sales	36,000,000

Required

a. Determine the margin, turnover, and return on investment for the segment in 1996.

b. Determine the effect on margin, turnover, and return on investment of the segment in 1997 if each of the following changes were to occur. Consider each change separately and assume that any items not specifically mentioned remain the same as in 1996:

1. A campaign to control costs resulted in $360,000 of reduced expenses.
2. Certain nonproductive assets were eliminated. As a result, investment decreased by $1,800,000, and expenses decreased by $144,000.
3. An advertising campaign resulted in increasing sales by $7,200,000, cost of goods sold by $5,400,000, and advertising expense by $1,080,000.
4. An investment was made in productive assets costing $1,800,000. As a result, sales increased by $720,000, and expenses increased by $108,000.

Problem 25–8
Evaluate the desirability of adopting a new project using return on investment, margin, and turnover (L.O. 4)

For the year ended December 31, 1996, Eagle Company reported the following information for the company as a whole and for the sports segment of Eagle Corporation:

	Eagle Company	Sports Segment		
		Golf Project	Tennis Project	Total
Sales	$6,000,000	$675,000	$300,000	$ 975,000
Income	1,125,000	300,000	37,500	337,500
Investment	4,500,000	900,000	105,000	1,005,000

Eagle Company anticipates that these relationships (return on investment, margin, and turnover) will hold true for the upcoming year. The sports segment is faced with the possibility of adding a new project in 1997, with the following projected data:

	Softball Project
Sales	$225,000
Income	52,500
Investment	187,500

Required

a. Determine the return on investment for Eagle Company, for the sports segment, and for the golf and tennis projects separately for the year ended December 31, 1996.

b. Using this information, determine the effect of adding the softball project on the sports segment's return on investment. What problem may be encountered?

Problem 25–9
Evaluate the desirability of adopting a new project using residual income (L.O. 5)

Using the data provided in Problem 25–8, determine the residual income (1) for all three projects and (2) for the sports segment with and without the softball project, if the desired return on investment is 25% (the return on investment for the company as a whole). What is the effect on the sport segment's residual income if the softball project is added? How does this result compare with your answer to Problem 25–8?

Alternate Problems

Problem 25–1A
Evaluate responsibility centers as profit centers and investment centers (L.O. 2)

Kason Corporation has three production plants (M, N, and O). Following is a summary of the results for January 1996:

Plant	Revenues	Expenses	Investment Base (gross assets)
M	$ 360,000	$ 300,000	$ 1,440,000
N	480,000	180,000	1,920,000
O	2,520,000	1,920,000	13,200,000

Required

a. If the plants are treated as profit centers, which plant manager appears to have done the best job?

b. If the plants are treated as investment centers, which plant manager appears to have done the best job? (Assume the plant managers are evaluated by return on investment.)

c. Do the results of profit center analysis and investment center analysis give different findings? If so, why?

Problem 25–2A
Allocate indirect expenses to illustrate arbitrary nature of expense allocation (L.O. 2)

Rao, Inc., allocates expenses and revenues to the two segments that it operates. Rao extends credit to customers under a revolving charge plan whereby all account balances not paid within 30 days are charged interest at the rate of 1½% per month.

Following are selected revenue and expense accounts and some additional data needed to complete the allocation of the one revenue amount and the expenses.

Revenue and Expenses (allocation bases)

Revolving charge service revenue (net sales)	$30,000
Home office building occupancy expense (net sales)	22,500
Buying expenses (net purchases)	75,000
General administrative expenses (number of employees in department)	37,500
Insurance expense (relative average inventory plus cost of equipment and fixtures in each department)	9,000
Depreciation expense on home office equipment (net sales)	15,000

Additional data

	Segment D	Segment E	Total
Number of employees	3	7	10
Net sales	$150,000	$300,000	$450,000
Net purchases	120,000	180,000	300,000
Average inventory	30,000	60,000	90,000
Cost of equipment and fixtures	45,000	90,000	135,000

Required

a. Prepare a schedule showing allocation of these items to segments D and E.

b. Criticize some of these allocation bases.

Problem 25–3A
Prepare a schedule showing contribution margin and contribution to indirect expenses using contribution margin format; prepare segmental income statements (L.O. 3)

Babbitt, Inc., operates two segments, interior and exterior. The revenue and expense data for 1996 follow:

	Interior	Exterior	Total
Net sales	$671,400	$1,107,600	$1,779,000
Direct expenses:*			
Cost of goods sold	372,000	564,000	936,000
Selling	63,600	54,000	117,600
Administrative	18,000	12,000	30,000
Uncollectible accounts	4,800	13,200	18,000
Indirect expenses (all fixed):			
Selling			252,000
Administrative			312,000

* All the direct expenses are variable except administrative expense, which is fixed.

Required

a. Prepare a schedule showing the contribution margin, the contribution to indirect expenses of each segment, and net income for the company as a whole. Do not allocate indirect expenses to the segments.

b. Assume that indirect selling expenses are to be allocated to segments on the basis of net sales (round to the nearest percent) and that indirect administrative expenses are to be allocated on the basis of direct administrative expenses. Prepare a statement (starting with the contribution to indirect expenses) which shows the net income of each segment.

c. Comment on the appropriateness of the income amounts shown in Parts (**a**) and (**b**) for determining the income contribution of the segments.

Problem 25–4A
Determine the contribution margin using the contribution margin format; calculate return on investment for (1) the entire company, (2) each segment, and (3) each manager (L.O. 3)

Goodwin Corporation has three segments. Following are the results of operations for 1996:

	Segment 1	Segment 2	Segment 3	Total
Sales	$18,000,000	$10,800,000	$7,200,000	$36,000,000
Variable expenses	12,960,000	6,120,000	4,860,000	23,940,000
Fixed expenses:				
Direct	2,520,000	900,000	360,000	3,780,000
Indirect.				1,800,000

Of the direct fixed expenses, $180,000 of those shown for Segment 1, $126,000 of those shown for Segment 2, and $180,000 of those shown for Segment 3 were not under the control of that segment's manager.

For the company's total operating assets of $50,400,000, the following facts exist:

	Segment 1	Segment 2	Segment 3
Assets directly used by and identified with the segment	$25,200,000	$14,400,000	$7,200,000
Assets under the control of the segment manager . .	21,600,000	11,520,000	5,760,000

Required

a. Prepare a statement (in thousands of dollars) showing the contribution margin, the contribution to indirect expenses for each segment, and the total income of the Goodwin Corporation.

b. Determine the return on investment for evaluating (1) the earning power of the entire company, (2) the rate of income contribution of each segment, and (3) the income performance of each segment manager.

c. Comment on the results of Part (**a**).

Problem 25–5A
Calculate return on investment and residual income for each segment and segment manager (L.O. 4, 5)

Elliott Company has three segments, R, S, and T. Data regarding these segments follow:

	Segment R	Segment S	Segment T
Contribution to indirect expenses	$ 432,000	$ 208,800	$ 72,000
Income controllable by the manager	475,200	226,800	86,400
Assets directly used by and identified with the segment.	3,600,000	1,440,000	360,000
Assets under the control of the segment manager. . .	3,456,000	1,368,000	324,000

Required

a. Calculate the return on investment for each segment and each segment manager. Rank them from highest to lowest.

b. Assume the minimum desired rates of return are 10% for a segment and 12% for a segment manager. Calculate the residual income for each manager. Rank them from highest to lowest.

c. Repeat (**b**), but assume the desired minimum rates of return are 14% for a segment and 16% for a segment manager. Rank them from highest to lowest.

d. Comment on the rankings achieved.

BEYOND THE NUMBERS—CRITICAL THINKING

Business Decision Case 25–1
Allocate unusual expenses to departments; determine controllable and noncontrollable expenses (L.O. 2)

Pero Company manufactures skateboards. Because the company's business is seasonal, between August and December skilled manufacturing employees are laid off. To improve morale, the financial vice president suggested that 10 employees not be laid off in the future. Instead, she suggested that they work in general labor from August to December but still be paid their manufacturing wages of $10 per hour. General labor personnel earn $6.60 per hour. What are the implications of this plan for the assignment of costs to the various segments of the business?

Business Decision Case 25–2
Assign responsibility (L.O. 2)

Texas Company builds new homes. Sarah Richards is in charge of the construction department. Among other responsibilities, Sarah hires and supervises the carpenters and other workers who build the homes. Texas Company does not do its own foundation work. The construction of foundations is done by subcontractors hired by Leslie Larue of the procurement department.

To start the development of a 500-home community, Larue hired Dire Company to build the foundations for the homes. On the day construction was to begin, Dire Company went out of business. Consequently, construction was delayed six weeks while Larue hired a new subcontractor. Which department should be charged with the cost of the delay in construction? Why?

Business Decision Case 25–3
Assign responsibility
(L.O. 2)

Peter Clark is the supervisor of Department 21 of Alabama Company. The annual budget for Clark's department is as follows:

Annual Budget for Department 21

Small tools	$ 6,750
Set up	7,500
Direct labor	8,250
Direct materials	15,000
Supplies	3,750
Supervision	22,500
Property taxes	3,750
Property insurance	750
Depreciation, machinery	1,500
Depreciation, building	1,500
Total	$71,250

Clark's salary of $15,000 is included in supervision. The remaining $7,500 in supervision is the salary of the assistant supervisor directly responsible to Clark. Identify the budget items that Clark controls.

Broader Perspective—Writing Experience 25–4
Employee buyouts and motivation

Refer to "A Broader Perspective" on page 874. Write a brief report explaining the effects of employee buyouts on employee motivation.

Group Project 25–5*
Respond to ethics situation

Macrofast Software, Inc., faces stiff competition in selling its products. Macrofast's top management feels considerable pressure from the company's stockholders to increase earnings.

Mac Washington, the vice president of marketing at the company's Production Software Division, received a memorandum from top management that said, in effect, "Increase your division's earnings or look for a new job."

Washington could think of only one way to increase earnings by the end of the year. The Production Software Division had several installations that should be completed early the following year, probably in February or March. For each of those jobs, he asked the customers to sign a Completed Installation document stating the job was completed to the customer's satisfaction. He did this because Macrofast's accounting department would record the revenue from the job when it received the Completed Installation document.

Several customers signed Completed Installation documents even though the jobs were not complete because Washington gave them a personally signed letter stating the Completion Installation document was not legally binding.

The scheme initially worked. Revenues were prematurely recorded for these jobs, sales and earnings for the year were up, Macrofast's top management was delighted with the results, and Washington was rewarded with a large bonus and a promotion to a vice presidency at corporate headquarters.

The following June, a staff accountant discovered the scheme when a customer called to complain that he was being billed for a job that was not yet completed. When the accountant produced the customer's Completed Installation document, the customer produced Washington's letter saying the document was not binding. The accountant did some detective work and unearthed the scheme. When she presented the results to her supervisor, the supervisor said, "This practice is unfortunate and is against company policy. But what's done is done. Don't worry about last year's financial statements. Just be sure it doesn't happen again."

* Source: Based on events at a real software company. The name of the company was changed for this example.

Required

a. In teams of four, discuss what the staff accountant should do.
b. Then, decide how your solution would change if all jobs had been completed to the customers' satisfaction.
c. As a team, write a memorandum to your instructor describing your solutions. The heading of the memo should contain the date, to whom it is written, from whom, and the subject matter.

Answers to Self-Test

True-False

1. **True.** Those items that a manager has direct control over are included in responsibility reports for that management level.
2. **True.** An appropriate goal of an expense center is the long-run minimization of expenses.
3. **True.** The manager's salary would be a direct cost of the segment but not controllable at that level. (The salary would be controllable by someone higher in the organization.)
4. **False.** Segments should be evaluated using their revenues and direct expenses.
5. **False.** The income and investment definitions when calculating RI for a segment are contribution to indirect expenses and assets directly used by and identified with the segment.

Multiple-Choice

1. **d.** Any of these bases—current replacement cost, original cost, and original cost less accumulated depreciation—could be used.
2. **a.** ROI would increase if operating expenses were reduced, all other things remaining constant.
3. **b.**

$$\text{ROI} = \frac{\text{Income}}{\text{Sales}} \times \frac{\text{Sales}}{\text{Investment}}$$

$$\text{ROI} = 50{,}000/1{,}000{,}000 \times 1{,}000{,}000/500{,}000$$

$$\text{ROI} = .05 \times 2$$

$$\text{ROI} = 10\%$$

4. **d.** All of these should be used to evaluate managerial performance.
5. **c.**

	Segment 1	Segment 2	Segment 3
Income	$ 180,000	$1,000,000	$ 500,000
Investment	2,000,000	5,000,000	2,000,000
ROI	9%	20%	25%
Desired minimum ROI (10%)	200,000	500,000	200,000
RI	$ (20,000)	$ 500,000	$ 300,000

Consider dropping Segment 1.

26

CAPITAL BUDGETING
LONG-RANGE PLANNING

LEARNING OBJECTIVES

After studying this chapter, you should be able to:

1. Define capital budgeting and explain the effects of making poor capital budgeting decisions.
2. Determine the net cash inflows, after taxes, for both an asset addition and an asset replacement.
3. Evaluate projects using the payback period.
4. Evaluate projects using the unadjusted rate of return.
5. Evaluate projects using the net present value.
6. Evaluate projects using the profitability index.

(continued)

In your personal life, you make many short-run decisions, such as where to go on vacation this year, and many long-run decisions, such as whether to buy a home. The quality of these decisions determines, to a large extent, the success of your life. Businesses also face short-run and long-run decisions.

In previous chapters, you studied how accountants help management make short-run decisions, such as what prices to charge for their products this year. Accountants also play an important role in advising management on long-range decisions that will benefit the company for many years, such as investing in new buildings and equipment. Long-run decisions have a great impact on the long-run success of a company. Incorrect long-run decisions can threaten the survival of a company.

Whereas short-run decisions involve items such as selling prices, costs, volume, and profits in the current year, long-run decisions involve investments in capital assets, such as buildings and equipment, affecting the current year and many future years. Planning for these investments is referred to as capital budgeting.

This chapter introduces the general concepts behind capital budgeting. Then, it discusses and illustrates four methods for selecting the best alternatives among capital projects. Two of these methods involve the use of present value concepts. Finally, the chapter stresses the importance of the postaudit review of capital project decisions.

CAPITAL BUDGETING DEFINED

Capital budgeting is the process of considering alternative capital projects and selecting those alternatives that provide the most profitable return on available funds, within the framework of company goals and objectives. A **capital project** is any available alternative to purchase, build, lease, or renovate buildings, equipment, or other long-range major items of property. The alternative selected usually involves large sums of money and brings about a large increase in fixed costs for a number of years in the future. Once a company builds a plant or undertakes some other capital expenditure, its future plans are less flexible.

Poor capital-budgeting decisions can be costly because of the large sums of money and relatively long periods involved. If a poor capital budgeting decision is implemented, the company can lose all or part of the funds originally invested in the project and not realize the expected benefits. In addition, other actions taken within the company regarding the project, such as finding suppliers of raw materials, are wasted if the capital-budgeting decision must be revoked. Poor capital-budgeting decisions may also harm the company's competitive position because the company does not have the most efficient productive assets needed to compete in world markets.

(concluded)

7. Evaluate projects using the time-adjusted rate of return.
8. Determine, for project evaluation, the effect of an investment in working capital.

Investment of funds in a poor alternative can create other problems as well. Workers hired for the project might be laid off if the project fails, creating morale and unemployment problems. Many of the fixed costs still remain even if a plant is closed or not producing. For instance, advertising efforts would be wasted, and stock prices could be affected by the decline in income.

Objective 1
Define capital budgeting and explain the effects of making poor capital budgeting decisions.

On the other hand, failure to invest enough funds in a good project also can be costly. Ford's Mustang is an excellent example of this problem. At the time of the original capital-budgeting decision, if Ford had correctly estimated the Mustang's popularity, the company would have expended more funds on the project. Because of an undercommitment of funds, Ford found itself short on production capacity, which caused lost and postponed sales of the automobile.

Finally, the amount of funds available for investment is limited. Thus, once a company makes a capital investment decision, alternative investment opportunities are normally lost. The benefits or returns lost by rejecting the best alternative investment are the **opportunity cost** of a given project.

For all these reasons, companies must be very careful in their analysis of capital projects. Capital expenditures do not occur as often as ordinary expenditures such as payroll or inventory purchases but involve substantial sums of money that are then committed for a long period. Therefore, the means by which companies evaluate capital expenditure decisions should be much more formal and detailed than would be necessary for ordinary purchase decisions.

PROJECT SELECTION: A GENERAL VIEW

Making capital-budgeting decisions involves analyzing cash inflows and outflows. This section shows you how to calculate the benefits and costs used in capital-budgeting decisions. Because money has a time value, these benefits and costs are adjusted for time under the last two methods covered in the chapter.

Time Value of Money

Money received today is worth more than the same amount of money received at a future date, such as a year from now. This principle is known as the *time value of money*. Money has time value because of investment opportunities, not because of inflation. For example, $100 today is worth more than $100 to be received one year from today because the $100 received today, once invested, grows to some amount greater than $100 in one year. Future value and present value concepts are extremely important in assessing the desirability of long-term investments (capital budgeting). If you need to review these concepts, refer back to the appendix to Chapter 15, which covers these concepts.

Net Cash Inflow

The **net cash inflow** (as used in capital budgeting) is the net cash benefit expected from a project in a period. The net cash inflow is the difference between the periodic cash inflows and the periodic cash outflows for a proposed project.

Objective 2
Determine the net cash inflows, after taxes, for both an asset addition and an asset replacement.

ASSET ACQUISITION Assume, for example, that a company is considering the purchase of new equipment for $120,000. The equipment is expected (1) to have a useful life of 15 years and no salvage value, and (2) to produce cash inflows (revenue) of $75,000 per year and cash outflows (costs) of $50,000 per year. Ignoring depreciation and taxes, the annual net cash inflow is computed as follows:

Cash inflows	$75,000
Cash outflows	50,000
Net cash inflow	$25,000

DEPRECIATION AND TAXES The computation of the net cash inflow usually includes the effects of depreciation and taxes. Although depreciation does not involve a cash outflow, it is deductible in arriving at federal taxable income. Thus, depreciation reduces the amount of cash outflow for federal income taxes. This reduction is a tax savings made possible by a depreciation tax shield. A **tax shield** is the total amount by which taxable income is reduced due to the deductability of an item. For example, if depreciation is $8,000, the tax shield is $8,000. To simplify the illustration, we assume the use of the straight-line depreciation for tax purposes throughout the chapter. Straight-line depreciation can be elected for tax purposes, even under the new tax law.

The tax shield results in a tax savings. The amount of the tax savings can be found by multiplying the tax rate by the amount of the depreciation tax shield. The formula is:

$$\text{Tax rate} \times \text{Depreciation tax shield} = \text{Tax savings}$$

Using the data in the previous example and assuming straight-line depreciation of $8,000 per year and a 40% tax rate, the amount of the tax savings is $3,200 (40% × $8,000 depreciation tax shield). Now, considering taxes and depreciation, we compute the annual net cash inflow from the $120,000 of equipment as follows:

	Change in Net Income	Change in Cash Flow
Cash inflows.	$75,000	$75,000
Cash outflows	50,000	50,000
Net cash inflow before taxes	$25,000	$25,000
Depreciation.	8,000	
Income before income taxes	$17,000	
Deduct: Income tax at 40%	6,800	6,800
Net income after taxes	$10,200	
Net cash inflow (after taxes).		$18,200

If there were no depreciation tax shield, federal income tax expense would have been $10,000 ($25,000 × 40%), and the net after-tax cash inflow from the investment would have been $15,000 ($25,000 − $10,000), or [$25,000 × (1 − 40%)]. The depreciation tax shield, however, reduces federal income tax expense by $3,200 ($8,000 × 40%) and increases the investment's after-tax net cash inflow by the same amount. Therefore, the following formula also can be used to determine the after-tax net cash inflow from an investment:

$$\text{Net cash inflow after taxes} = \underbrace{\left[\text{Net cash inflow before taxes} \times \left(1 - \text{Tax rate}\right)\right]}_{\text{Net cash inflow after taxes (ignoring depreciation)}} + \underbrace{\left[\text{Depreciation expense} \times \text{Tax rate}\right]}_{\text{Tax savings attributable to depreciation tax shield}}$$

$$= [\$25{,}000 \times (1 - .4)] + [\$8{,}000 \times .4] = \$18{,}200$$

ASSET REPLACEMENT Sometimes a company must decide whether or not it should replace existing plant assets. Such replacement decisions often occur when faster and more efficient machinery and equipment appear on the market.

The computation of the net cash inflow is more complex for a replacement decision than for an acquisition decision because cash inflows and outflows for two items (the asset being replaced and the new asset) must be considered. To illustrate, assume that a company operates two machines purchased four years ago at a cost of $18,000 each. The estimated useful life of each machine is 12 years (with no salvage value). Each machine will produce 40,000 units of product per year. The annual cash operating expenses (labor, repairs, etc.) for the two machines together total $14,000. After the old machines have been used for four years, a new machine becomes available. The new machine can be acquired for $28,000 and has an estimated useful life of eight years (with no salvage value). The new machine produces 60,000 units annually and entails annual cash operating expenses of $10,000. The $4,000 reduction in operating expenses ($14,000 − $10,000) is a $4,000 increase in net cash inflow (savings) before taxes.

The firm pays $28,000 in the first year to acquire the new machine. In addition to this initial outlay, the annual net cash inflow from replacement is computed as follows:

$$\begin{matrix}\text{Net cash inflow}\\ \text{after taxes}\end{matrix} = \left[\begin{matrix}\text{Annual net cash}\\ \text{inflows (savings)}\\ \text{before taxes}\end{matrix} \times \left(1 - \begin{matrix}\text{Tax}\\ \text{rate}\end{matrix}\right)\right] + \left[\begin{matrix}\text{Additional}\\ \text{annual}\\ \text{depreciation}\\ \text{expense}\end{matrix} \times \begin{matrix}\text{Tax}\\ \text{rate}\end{matrix}\right]$$

Using these data, the following display shows how you can use this formula to find the net cash flow after taxes:

Annual cash operating expenses:		
Old machines		$14,000
New machine		10,000
Annual net cash inflow (savings) before taxes		$ 4,000
1 − Tax rate		×60%
Annual net cash inflow (savings)* after taxes ignoring depreciation (1)		$ 2,400
Annual depreciation expense:		
Old machines	$3,000	
New machine	3,500	
Additional annual depreciation expense	$ 500	
Tax rate	×40%	
Tax savings from additional depreciation (2)		200
Net cash inflow after taxes (1) + (2)		$ 2,600

* Cash savings are considered to be cash inflows.

In formula format, the calculation is:

$$\begin{matrix}\text{Net cash inflow}\\ \text{after taxes}\end{matrix} = [\$4{,}000 \times (1 - .4)] + [\$500 \times .4] = \$2{,}600$$

Notice that these figures concentrated only on the differences in costs for each of the two alternatives. Two other items also are relevant to the decision. First, the purchase of the new machine creates a $28,000 cash outflow immediately after acquisition. Second, the two old machines can probably be sold, and the selling price or salvage value of the old machines creates a cash inflow in the period of disposal. Also, the previous example used straight-line depreciation. If the modified Accelerated Cost Recovery System (modified ACRS) had been used, the tax shield would have been larger in the early years and smaller in the later years of the asset's life.

Out-of-Pocket and Sunk Costs A distinction between out-of-pocket costs and sunk costs needs to be made for capital budgeting decisions. An **out-of-pocket cost** is a cost requiring a future outlay of resources, usually cash. Out-of-pocket costs can be avoided or changed in amount. Future labor and repair costs are examples of out-of-pocket costs.

Sunk costs are costs already incurred. Nothing can be done about sunk costs at the present time; they cannot be avoided or changed in amount. The price paid for a machine becomes a sunk cost the minute the purchase has been made (before that moment it was an out-of-pocket cost). The amount of that past outlay cannot be changed, regardless of whether the machine is scrapped or used. Thus, depreciation is a sunk cost because it represents a past cash outlay. Depletion and amortization of assets, such as ore deposits and patents, are also sunk costs.

A sunk cost is a past cost, while an out-of-pocket cost is a future cost. Only the out-of-pocket costs (the future cash outlays) are relevant to capital budgeting decisions. Sunk costs are not relevant, except for any effect they have on the cash outflow for taxes.

Initial Cost and Salvage Value Any cash outflows necessary to acquire an asset and place it in a position and condition for its intended use are part of the **initial cost of the asset.** If an investment has a salvage value, that value is a cash inflow in the year of the asset's disposal.

The Cost of Capital The cost of capital is important in project selection. Certainly, any acceptable proposal should offer a return that exceeds the cost of the funds used to finance it. **Cost of capital,** usually expressed as a rate, is the cost of all sources of capital (debt and equity) employed by a company. For convenience, most current liabilities, such as accounts payable and federal income taxes payable, are treated as being without cost. Every other item on the right (equity) side of the balance sheet has a cost. The subject of determining the cost of capital is a controversial topic in the literature of accounting and finance and is not discussed here. We give the assumed rates for the cost of capital in this book. Next, we describe several techniques for deciding whether to invest in capital projects.

Project Selection: Payback Period

Objective 3
Evaluate projects using the payback period.

The **payback period** is the time it takes for the cumulative sum of the annual net cash inflows from a project to equal the initial net cash outlay. In effect, the payback period answers the question: How long will it take the capital project to recover, or pay back, the initial investment? If the net cash inflows each year are a constant amount, the formula for the payback period is:

$$\text{Payback period} = \frac{\text{Initial cash outlay}}{\text{Annual net cash inflow (or benefit)}}$$

For the two assets discussed in the previous section, you can compute the payback period as follows. The purchase of the \$120,000 equipment creates an annual net cash inflow after taxes of \$18,200, so the payback period is 6.6 years, computed as follows:

$$\text{Payback period} = \frac{\$120{,}000}{\$18{,}200} = 6.6 \text{ years}$$

The payback period for the replacement machine with a \$28,000 cash outflow in the first year and an annual net cash inflow of \$2,600, is 10.8 years, computed as follows:

$$\text{Payback period} = \frac{\$28{,}000}{\$2{,}600} = 10.8 \text{ years}$$

Remember that the payback period indicates how long it will take the machine to pay for itself. The replacement machine being considered has a payback period of 10.8 years, but a useful life of only 8 years. Therefore, because the investment cannot pay for itself within its useful life, the company should not purchase a new machine to replace the two old machines.

In each of the previous examples, the projected net cash inflow per year was uniform. When the annual returns are uneven, companies use a cumulative calculation to determine the payback period, as shown in the following situation.

Neil Company is considering a capital investment project that costs $40,000 and is expected to last 10 years. The projected annual net cash inflows are:

Year	Investment	Annual Net Cash Inflow	Cumulative Net Cash Inflows
0	$40,000	—	—
1	—	$8,000	$ 8,000
2	—	6,000	14,000
3	—	7,000	21,000
4	—	5,000	26,000
5	—	8,000	34,000
6	—	6,000	**40,000**
7	—	3,000	43,000
8	—	2,000	45,000
9	—	3,000	48,000
10	—	1,000	49,000

The payback period in this example is six years—the time it takes to recover the $40,000 original investment.

When using payback period analysis to evaluate investment proposals, management may choose one of these rules to decide on project selection:

1. Select the investments with the shortest payback periods.
2. Select only those investments that have a payback period of less than a specified number of years.

Both decision rules focus on the rapid return of invested capital. If capital can be recovered rapidly, a firm can invest it in other projects, thereby generating more cash inflows or profits.

Some managers use payback period analysis in capital budgeting decisions due to its simplicity. However, this type of analysis has two important limitations:

1. Payback period analysis ignores the time period beyond the payback period. For example, assume Allen Company is considering two alternative investments; each requires an initial outlay of $30,000. Proposal Y returns $6,000 per year for five years, while proposal Z returns $5,000 per year for eight years. The payback period for Y is five years ($30,000/$6,000) and for Z is six years ($30,000/$5,000). But, if the goal is to maximize income, proposal Z should be selected rather than proposal Y, even though Z has a longer payback period. This is because Z returns a total of $40,000, while Y simply recovers the initial $30,000 outlay.

2. Payback analysis also ignores the time value of money. For example, assume the following net cash inflows are expected in the first three years from two capital projects:

	Net Cash Inflows	
	Project A	Project B
First year	$15,000	$ 9,000
Second year	12,000	12,000
Third year	9,000	15,000
Total	$36,000	$36,000

Assume that both projects have the same net cash inflow each year beyond the third year. If the cost of each project is $36,000, each has a payback period of three years. But common sense indicates that the projects are not equal because money has time value and can be reinvested to increase income. Because larger amounts of cash are received earlier under project A, it is the preferable project.

Project Selection: Unadjusted Rate of Return

Objective 4
Evaluate projects using the unadjusted rate of return.

Another method of evaluating investment projects that you are likely to encounter in practice is the **unadjusted rate of return** method. To compute the unadjusted rate of return, divide the average annual income after taxes by the average amount of investment in the project. The *average investment* is the (Beginning balance + Ending balance)/2. If the ending balance is zero (as we assume), the average investment equals the original cash investment divided by 2. The formula for the unadjusted rate of return is:

$$\text{Unadjusted rate of return} = \frac{\text{Average annual income after taxes}}{\text{Average amount of investment}}$$

Notice that this calculation uses annual income rather than net cash inflow.[1]

To illustrate the use of the unadjusted rate of return, assume Thomas Company is considering two capital project proposals, each having a useful life of three years. The company does not have enough funds to undertake both projects. Information relating to the projects follows:

Proposal	Initial Cost	Salvage Value	Average Annual Before-Tax Net Cash Inflow	Average Annual Depreciation
1 . .	$76,000	$4,000	$45,000	$24,000
2 . .	95,000	5,000	55,000	30,000

Assuming a 40% tax rate, Thomas Company can determine the unadjusted rate of return for each project as follows:

	Proposal 1	Proposal 2
Average investment:		
(original outlay + salvage value) ÷ 2 . . . .(1)	$40,000	$50,000
Annual net cash inflow (before income taxes)	$45,000	$55,000
Annual depreciation	24,000	30,000
Annual income (before income taxes)	$21,000	$25,000
Deduct: Income taxes at 40%	8,400	10,000
Average annual net income from investment. . . . . . .(2)	$12,600	$15,000
Rate of return (2) ÷ (1).	31.5%	30%

From these calculations, if Thomas Company makes an investment decision solely on the basis of the unadjusted rate of return, it would select proposal 1 since it has a higher rate.

Also, the company could compute the unadjusted rate of return with the following formula:

$$\text{Rate of return} = \frac{\left(\text{Average annual before-tax net cash inflow} - \text{Average annual depreciation}\right) \times \left(1 - \text{Tax rate}\right)}{\text{Average investment}}$$

[1] Some formulas use the initial investment in the denominator instead of the average investment. We prefer the average investment because it approximates the use of assets throughout the year not just at the beginning of the year.

For proposal 1, the computation is as follows:

$$\text{Rate of return} = \frac{(\$45{,}000 - \$24{,}000) \times (1 - 0.4)}{[(\$76{,}000 + \$4{,}000)/2]} = \frac{(\$21{,}000) \times (0.6)}{\$40{,}000}$$

$$= \frac{\$12{,}600}{\$40{,}000} = 31.5\%$$

For proposal 2, the computation is as follows:

$$\text{Rate of return} = \frac{(\$55{,}000 - \$30{,}000) \times (1 - 0.4)}{[(\$95{,}000 + \$5{,}000)/2]} = \frac{(\$25{,}000) \times (0.6)}{\$50{,}000}$$

$$= \frac{\$15{,}000}{\$50{,}000} = 30\%$$

Sometimes companies receive information on the average annual after-tax net cash inflow. Average annual after-tax net cash inflow is equal to annual before-tax cash inflow minus taxes. Given this information, the firms could deduct the depreciation to arrive at average net income. For instance, for proposal 2, Thomas Company would compute average net income as follows:

After-tax net cash inflow ($55,000 − $10,000)	$45,000
Less: Depreciation	30,000
Average net income	$15,000

The unadjusted rate of return, like payback period analysis, has several limitations:

1. The length of time over which the return is earned is not considered.
2. The rate allows a sunk cost, depreciation, to enter into the calculation. Since depreciation can be calculated in so many different ways, the rate of return can be manipulated by simply changing the method of depreciation used for the project.
3. The timing of cash flows is not considered. Thus, the time value of money is ignored.

Unlike the two project selection methods just illustrated, the remaining two methods—net present value and time-adjusted rate of return—take into account the time value of money in the analysis. In both of these methods, we assume that all net cash inflows occur at the end of the year. Often used in capital budgeting analysis, this assumption makes the calculation of present values less complicated than if we assume the cash flows occurred at some other time.

Project Selection: Net Present Value Method

Objective 5
Evaluate projects using the net present value.

In this section, you learn to calculate the net present value of capital projects. Then you learn how to use the profitability index to evaluate projects costing different amounts. The profitability index is a refinement of the net present value method.

The **net present value** method uses the company's required minimum rate of return as a discount rate and discounts all expected after-tax cash inflows and outflows from the proposed investment back to their present values. The net present value of the proposed investment is the difference between the present value of the annual net cash inflows and the present value of the required cash outflows.

In many projects, the only cash outflow is the initial investment, and since it occurs immediately, the initial investment does not need to be discounted. Therefore, in such projects, a company may compute the net present value of the proposed project as the present value of the annual net cash inflows minus the initial investment. Other types of projects require that additional investments, such as a major repair, be made at later dates in the life of the project. In those cases, the company must discount the cash outflows to their present value before comparing them to the present value of the net cash inflows.

A major issue in acknowledging the time value of money in the net present value method is determining an appropriate discount rate to use in computing the present value of cash flows. Management requires some minimum rate of return on its investments. This rate should be the company's cost of capital, but that rate is difficult to determine. Therefore, under the net present value method, management often selects a target rate that it believes to be at or above the company's cost of capital, and then uses that rate as a basis for present value calculations.

To illustrate the net present value method, assume Morris Company is considering a capital investment project that will cost $25,000. Morris expects net cash inflows after taxes for the next four years to be $8,000, $7,500, $8,000, and $7,500, respectively. Management requires a minimum rate of return of 14% and wants to know if the project is acceptable. The following analysis uses the tables in the Appendix at the end of this text:

	Annual Net Cash Inflow (after taxes)	Present Value of $1 at 14% (from Table 3)	Total Present Value
First year	$8,000	0.87719	$ 7,018
Second year	7,500	0.76947	5,771
Third year	8,000	0.67497	5,400
Fourth year	7,500	0.59208	4,441
Present value of net cash inflows			$22,630
Cost of investment			25,000
Net present value			$ (2,370)

Because the present value of the net cash inflows, $22,630, is less than the initial outlay of $25,000, the project is not acceptable. The net present value for the project is equal to the present value of its net cash inflows less the present value of its cost (the investment amount), which in this instance is −$2,370, calculated as ($22,630 − $25,000).

When a company uses the net present value method to screen alternative projects, it considers the project with the higher net present value to be more desirable. In general, a proposed capital investment is acceptable if it has a positive net present value. In the previous example, if the expected net cash inflows from the investment had been $10,000 per year for four years, the present value of the benefits would have been (from Table 4 in the Appendix):

$$\$10{,}000 \times 2.91371 = \$29{,}137$$

This calculation yields a net present value of $4,137, or $29,137 − $25,000. Since the net present value is positive, the investment proposal is acceptable. However, a competing project may have an even higher net present value.

When comparing investment projects costing different amounts, the net present value method does not provide a valid means by which to rank the projects in order of desirability assuming limited financial resources. A profitability index provides this additional information to management.

PROFITABILITY INDEX

Objective 6
Evaluate projects using the profitability index.

A **profitability index** is the ratio of the present value of the expected net cash inflows (after taxes) divided by the initial cash outlay (or present value of cash outlays if future outlays are required). The profitability index formula is:

$$\text{Profitability index} = \frac{\text{Present value of net cash inflows}}{\text{Initial cash outlay (or present value of cash outlays if future outlays are required)}}$$

Management should consider only those proposals having a profitability index greater than or equal to 1.00. Proposals with a profitability index of less than 1.00 cannot yield the minimum rate of return because the present value of the projected cash inflows is less than the initial cost.

To illustrate use of the profitability index, assume that a company is considering two alternative capital outlay proposals that have the following initial costs and expected net cash inflows after taxes:

	Proposal X	Proposal Y
Initial outlay	$7,000	$9,500
Expected net cash inflow (after taxes):		
Year 1	$5,000	$9,000
Year 2	4,000	6,000
Year 3	6,000	3,000

Management's minimum desired rate of return is 20%.

The net present values and profitability indexes can be computed as follows, using Table 3 in the Appendix at the end of this book:

	Present Value	
	Proposal X	Proposal Y
Year 1 (net cash inflow in year 1 × 0.83333)	$ 4,167	$ 7,500
Year 2 (net cash inflow in year 2 × 0.69444)	2,778	4,167
Year 3 (net cash inflow in year 3 × 0.57870)	3,472	1,736
Present value of net cash inflows	$10,417	$13,403
Initial outlay	7,000	9,500
Net present value	$ 3,417	$ 3,903

	Proposal X	Proposal Y
Profitability index	$\frac{\$10,417}{\$7,000} = 1.49$	$\frac{\$13,403}{\$9,500} = 1.41$

When the net present values are compared, proposal Y appears to be more favorable than proposal X because its net present value is higher. However, the profitability indexes indicate proposal X is the more desirable investment because it has the higher profitability index. The higher the profitability index, the more profitable the project per dollar of investment. Proposal X earns a higher rate of return on a smaller investment than proposal Y.

Another technique for evaluating capital projects that accounts for the time value of money is the time-adjusted rate of return method. The next section discusses this method.

An Accounting Perspective

Business Insight Like U.S. managers, Japanese managers incorporate the cost of capital into their capital investment decisions. However, Japanese managers tend to rely more on consensus decision making, less on the numbers. Discount rates in Japan are generally lower than in the United States. Typical U.S. discount rates range from 10% to 25% depending on the riskiness of the project and the rate of inflation. In Japan, the discount rates tend to be around 10%, even lower in some cases.

Project Selection: The Time-Adjusted Rate of Return (or Internal Rate of Return)

Objective 7
Evaluate projects using the time-adjusted rate of return.

The **time-adjusted rate of return,** also called the *internal rate of return*, equates the present value of expected after-tax net cash inflows from an investment with the cost of the investment. It does this by finding the rate at which the net present value of the project is zero. If the time-adjusted rate of return equals or exceeds the cost of capital or target rate of return, a firm should consider the investment further. If the proposal's time-adjusted rate of return is less than the minimum rate, the firm should reject the proposal. Ignoring other considerations, the higher the time-adjusted rate of return, the more desirable the project.

Calculators and computer software with time-adjusted rate of return functions are readily available. Present value tables also can approximate the time-adjusted rate of return. To illustrate, assume Young Company is considering a $90,000 investment expected to last 25 years with no salvage value. The investment yields a $15,000 annual after-tax net cash inflow. This $15,000 is referred to as an **annuity,** which is a series of equal cash inflows.

The first step in computing the rate of return is to determine the payback period. In this case, the payback period is six years ($90,000 ÷ $15,000). The second step is to examine Table 4 in the Appendix (present value of an annuity) to find the present value factor that is nearest in amount to the payback period of 6. Since the investment is expected to yield returns for 25 years, look at that row in the table. In that row, the factor nearest to 6 is 5.92745, which appears under the 16.5% interest column. The third step is to multiply the annual return of $15,000 by the 5.92745 factor; the result is $88,912, which is just below the $90,000 cost of the project. Thus, the actual rate of return is slightly less than 16.5%. The rate of return is less than 16.5% but more than 16% because as interest rates increase, present values decrease because less investment is needed to generate the same income.

The preceding example involves uniform net cash inflows from year to year. But what happens when net cash inflows are not uniform? In such instances, a trial and error procedure is necessary if present value tables are used. For example, assume that Young Company is considering a $200,000 project that will last four years and yield the following returns:

Year	Net Cash Inflow (after taxes)
1	$ 20,000
2	40,000
3	80,000
4	150,000
Total	$290,000

The average annual cash inflow is $290,000 ÷ 4 = $72,500. Based on this average net cash inflow, the payback period is $200,000 ÷ $72,500 = 2.76 years. Looking in the four-year row of Table 4 in the Appendix, we find that the factor 2.77048 is nearest to the payback period of 2.76. In this case, however, cash flows are not uniform. The largest returns occur in the later years of the asset's life. Since the early returns have the largest present value, the rate of return is likely to be less than the 16.5% rate that corresponds to the present value factor 2.77048. If the returns had been greater during the earlier years of the asset's life, the correct rate of return would have been higher than 16.5%. To find the specific discount rate that yields a present value closest to the initial outlay of $200,000, we try out several interest rates less than 16%. The rate of return is found by trial and error. The following computation reveals the rate to be slightly higher than 12%:

Year	Return	Present Value Factor at 12%	Present Value of Net Cash Inflows
1	$ 20,000	0.89286	$ 17,857
2	40,000	0.79719	31,888
3	80,000	0.71178	56,942
4	150,000	0.63553	95,330
			$202,017

Since the cost of capital is not a precise percentage, some financial theorists argue that the time-adjusted rate of return method is preferable to the net present

A Broader Perspective
Caterpillar, Inc.

Caterpillar, Inc., invested $1.5 billion in a worldwide factory modernization program. Caterpillar's management realized it must continually monitor the performance of this modernization if the project was to realize its potential.

At Caterpillar, the projects are grouped into "bundles" of related projects. For example, all of the new assets used for a new product would be bundled together. "Each bundle is monitored every six months at Caterpillar, although a few key characteristics of some bundles are monitored monthly" [p. 32]. Characteristics used in monitoring performance include the amount of money projected versus the amount actually spent on the projects, the number of people expected to be used on the projects versus the number actually used, and the estimated reduction in product cost versus the reduction in product cost actually achieved.

Many firms believe their evaluation of project performance leaves much to be desired. Caterpillar's idea of "bundling" similar projects should be helpful to other firms making significant changes in their production processes and product lines.

Source: Based on the article by James A. Hendricks, Robert C. Bastian, and Thomas L. Sexton, "Bundle Monitoring of Strategic Projects," *Management Accounting,* February 1992, pp. 31–35.

value method. Under the time-adjusted rate of return method, the cost of capital is used only as a cutoff point in deciding which projects are acceptable and should be given more consideration.

No matter which time value of money concept is considered better, these methods are both theoretically superior to the payback period and the unadjusted rate of return methods. However, the time value of money methods are more difficult to compute unless you use a business calculator or a microcomputer spreadsheet program. In reality, no single method should be used by itself to make capital-budgeting decisions. Managers should consider all aspects of the investment, including such nonquantitative factors as employee morale (layoff of workers due to higher efficiency of a new machine) and company flexibility (versatility of production of one machine over another). The company commits itself to its investment in a capital project for a long time and should use the best selection techniques and judgment available.

Too often, in capital project selection decisions, investments in working capital are ignored. The next section shows how to incorporate this factor into the analysis.

An Accounting Perspective

Use of Technology People use computer spreadsheets extensively in evaluating capital projects. Decisions about investing in capital projects require a lot of thinking about the future. Because no one can predict the future with certainty, people often make numerous estimates of future cash flows—some optimistic, some pessimistic, and some simply best guesses. Computer spreadsheets make the preparation of numerous forecasts feasible, and even fun.

Investments in Working Capital

Objective 8
Determine, for project evaluation, the effect of an investment in working capital.

An investment in a capital asset usually must be supported by an investment in working capital, such as accounts receivable and inventory. For example, companies often invest in a capital project expecting to increase sales. Increased sales usually bring about an increase in accounts receivable from customers and an increase in inventory to support the higher sales level. The increases in current assets—accounts receivable and inventory—are investments in working capital that usually are recovered in full at the end of a capital project's life. Such working capital investments should be considered in capital-budgeting decisions.

To illustrate, assume that a company is considering a capital project involving a $50,000 investment in machinery and a $40,000 investment in working capital. The machine, which will produce a new product, has an estimated useful life of eight years and no salvage value. The annual cash inflows (before taxes) are estimated at $25,000, with annual cash outflows (before taxes) of $5,000. The annual net cash inflow from the project is computed as follows (assuming straight-line depreciation and a 40% tax rate):

Cash inflows	$25,000
Cash outflows	5,000
Net cash inflow before taxes	$20,000
1 − Tax rate	×60%
Net cash inflow after taxes (ignoring depreciation) (1)	$12,000
Depreciation tax shield ($50,000 ÷ 8 years)	$6,250
Income tax rate	×40%
Depreciation tax savings (2)	$ 2,500
Annual net cash inflow, years 1–8 (1) + (2)	$14,500

The annual net cash inflow from the machine is $14,500 each year for eight years. However, the working capital investment must be considered. The investment of $40,000 in working capital at the start of the project is an additional outlay that must be made when the project is started. The $40,000 would be tied up every year until the project is finished, or in this case, until the end of the life of the machine. At that point, the working capital would be released, and the $40,000 could be used for other investments. Therefore, the $40,000 is a cash outlay at the start of the project and a cash inflow at the end of the project.

The net present value of the project is computed as follows (assuming a 14% minimum desired rate of return):

Net cash inflow, years 1–8 ($14,500 × 4.63886)	$67,263
Recovery of investment in working capital ($40,000 × 0.35056)	14,022
Present value of net cash inflows	$81,285
Initial cash outlay ($50,000 + $40,000)	90,000
Net present value	$ (8,715)

The discount factor for the cash inflows, 4.63886, comes from Table 4 in the Appendix at the end of the book, because the cash inflows in this example are a series of equal payments—an annuity. The recovery of the investment in working capital is assumed to represent a single lump sum received at the end of the project's life. As such, it is discounted using a factor (0.35056) that comes from Table 3 in the Appendix.

The investment is not acceptable because it has a negative net present value. If the working capital investment had been ignored, the proposal would have had a rather large positive net present value of $17,263 ($67,263 − $50,000). Thus, it should be obvious that investments in working capital must be considered if correct capital-budgeting decisions are to be made.

The next topic discussed in the chapter is the postaudit. This important step improves the chances that future capital project selection decisions are based on realistic projections of benefits and costs.

The Postaudit

The last step in the capital-budgeting process is a postaudit review that should be performed by a person not involved in the capital-budgeting decision-making process. Such a person can provide an impartial judgment on the project's worthiness. This step should be performed early in the project's life, but enough time should have passed for any operational bugs to have been worked out. Actual operating costs and revenues should be determined and compared with those estimated when the project was originally reviewed and accepted. The postaudit review performs these functions:

1. Lets management know if the projections were accurate and if the particular project is performing as expected regarding cash inflows and outflows.

2. May identify additional factors for management to consider in upcoming capital-budgeting decisions, such as cash outflows that were forgotten in a particular project.
3. Provides a review of the capital-budgeting process to determine how effectively and efficiently it is working. The postaudit provides information that allows management to compare the actual results of decisions with the expectations it had during the planning and selection phases of the capital-budgeting process.

Investing in High Technology Projects

Many companies have found it hard to justify high technology investments. A U.S. auto manufacturer, for example, found it difficult to justify investing in a new computer-based flexible manufacturing system because its cost savings occurred so far in the future. When discounted, the present value of these savings did not justify the initial outlay. The president of the company was convinced, however, that the new system had benefits not quantified in the cash flow estimates, so he approved the investment even though it had a negative net present value.

Companies have difficulty in justifying an investment in high technology projects for several reasons. First, often several years pass before companies see the cash inflows from the investment. Even if the cash inflows are high, their net present value is low if they come several years in the future.

Second, management has difficulty identifying and measuring all of the benefits of new technology. When personal computers replaced typewriters, for example, people learned many new ways of creating and storing documents by using the computer. These benefits occurred because people used computers and experimented with them. These benefits would have been difficult to predict, much less measure, back when companies were trying to justify investment in personal computers. Managers believe that sometimes they just have to have faith that the investment is a good one, even though they cannot justify it on quantifiable economic grounds.

Capital Budgeting in Not-for-Profit Organizations

The concepts discussed in this chapter also apply to not-for-profit organizations, such as universities, school districts, cities, and not-for-profit hospitals. Since these organizations are not subject to as many taxes as profit-making organizations, the cash flows related to taxes are usually zero or near zero.

Epilogue

You have now completed the last chapter in this text. Thank you for using our textbook. The knowledge you have gained will serve you well in any career you choose. Good luck!

Understanding the Learning Objectives

Objective 1
Define capital budgeting and explain the effects of making poor capital budgeting decisions.

- Capital budgeting is the process of considering alternative capital projects and selecting those alternatives that provide the most profitable return on available funds, within the framework of company goals and objectives.
- Poor capital budgeting decisions can cause a company to lose all or part of the funds originally invested in a project and can harm the company's competitive position in world markets.

Objective 2
Determine the net cash inflows, after taxes, for both an asset addition and an asset replacement.

- Asset addition:

$$\begin{array}{c}\text{Net cash}\\ \text{inflow}\\ \text{after taxes}\end{array} = \left[\begin{array}{c}\text{Net cash}\\ \text{inflow}\\ \text{before taxes}\end{array} \times \left(1 - \begin{array}{c}\text{Tax}\\ \text{rate}\end{array}\right)\right] + \left[\begin{array}{c}\text{Depreciation}\\ \text{expense}\end{array} \times \begin{array}{c}\text{Tax}\\ \text{rate}\end{array}\right]$$

- Asset replacement:

$$\text{Net cash inflow after taxes} = \left[\text{Annual net cash inflows (savings) before taxes} \times \left(1 - \text{Tax rate}\right)\right] + \left[\text{Additional annual depreciation expense} \times \text{Tax rate}\right]$$

Objective 3
Evaluate projects using the payback period.

- $$\text{Payback period} = \frac{\text{Initial cash outlay}}{\text{Annual net cash inflows (or benefits)}}$$

Objective 4
Evaluate projects using the unadjusted rate of return.

- $$\text{Unadjusted rate of return} = \frac{\text{Average annual income after taxes}}{\text{Average amount of investment}}$$

Objective 5
Evaluate projects using the net present value.

- All expected after-tax cash inflows and outflows from the proposed investment are discounted to their present values using the company's required minimum rate of return as a discount rate. The net present value of the proposed investment is the difference between the present value of the annual net cash inflows and the present value of the required cash outflows.

Objective 6
Evaluate projects using the profitability index.

- $$\text{Profitability index} = \frac{\text{Present value of net cash inflows}}{\text{Initial cash outlay (or present value of cash outlays if future outlays are required)}}$$

Objective 7
Evaluate projects using the time-adjusted rate of return.

- The time-adjusted rate of return equates the present value of expected after-tax net cash inflows from an investment with the cost of the investment by finding the rate at which the net present value of the project is zero. If the time-adjusted rate of return equals or exceeds the cost of capital or the target rate of return, the project should be considered. If the rate is less than the minimum rate, the project should be rejected.

Objective 8
Determine, for project evaluation, the effect of an investment in working capital.

- The investment in working capital causes the net present value to be lower than it would be if the working capital investment is ignored. Therefore, the required return of a project must be higher to account for the investment in working capital.

Demonstration Problem

Barkley Company is considering three different investments; the following data relate to these investments:

Investment	Initial Cash Outlay	Expected Before-Tax Net Cash Inflow per Year	Expected After-Tax Net Cash Inflow per Year	Expected Life of Proposals* (years)
A.	$50,000	$13,333	$10,000	10
B.	60,000	12,000	8,800	15
C.	75,000	15,000	10,500	20

* No estimated salvage value. Use straight-line depreciation.

The income tax rate is 40%. The salvage value of each investment is zero. Management requires a minimum return on investments of 14%.

Required Rank these proposals using the following selection techniques:

a. Payback period.
b. Unadjusted rate of return.
c. Profitability index.
d. Time-adjusted rate of return.

Solution to Demonstration Problem

a. Payback period:

Proposal	(a) Investment	(b) Annual After-Tax Cash Inflow	(a) ÷ (b) Payback Period (years)
A	$50,000	$10,000	5.00
B	60,000	8,800	6.82
C	75,000	10,500	7.14

b. Unadjusted rate of return:

Proposal	(a) Average Investment	(b) Average Annual Before-Tax Net Cash Inflow	(c) Average Depreciation	(d) = [(b − c) × (1 − .4)] Average Annual Income	(d) ÷ (a) Rate of Return
A . .	$25,000	$13,333	$5,000	$5,000	20%
B . .	30,000	12,000	4,000	4,800	16
C . .	37,500	15,000	3,750	6,750	18

The proposals in order of desirability are A, C, and B.

c. Profitability index:

Proposal	(a) Annual After-Tax Net Cash Inflow	(b) Present Value Factor at 14%	(c) = (a) × (b) Present Value of Annual Net Cash Inflow	(d) Initial Cash Outlay	(c) ÷ (d) Profitability Index
A	$10,000*	5.21612	$52,161	$50,000	1.04
B	8,800	6.14217	54,051	60,000	0.90
C	10,500	6.62313	69,543	75,000	0.93

* This amount was given. However, the amount can also be calculated as follows:

Expected before-tax net cash inflow	$13,333
Less depreciation	5,000
Taxable income	$ 8,333
1 − Tax rate	× 60%
After-tax annual income	$ 5,000
Add back depreciation	5,000
Annual after-tax net cash inflow	$10,000

The proposals in order of desirability are A, C, and B. (But neither B nor C should be considered acceptable since each has a profitability index of less than one.)

d. Time-adjusted rate of return:

Proposal	Rate	How Found
A.	15% (slightly above)	($50,000/$10,000) = Factor of 5 in 10 period row
B.	12 (slightly below)	($60,000/$8,800) = Factor of 6.82 in 15 period row
C.	13 (slightly below)	($75,000/$10,500) = Factor of 7.14 in 20 period row

The proposals in order of desirability are A, C, and B. (But neither B nor C earns the minimum rate of return.)

New Terms*

Annuity A series of equal cash inflows. *912*

Capital budgeting The process of considering alternative capital projects and selecting those alternatives that provide the most profitable return on available funds, within the framework of company goals and objectives. *902*

Capital project Any available alternative to purchase, build, lease, or renovate equipment, buildings, property, or other long-term assets. *902*

Cost of capital The cost of all sources of capital (debt and equity) employed by a company. *906*

Initial cost of an asset Any cash outflows necessary to acquire an asset and place it in a position and condition for its intended use. *906*

Net cash inflow The periodic cash inflows from a project less the periodic cash outflows related to the project. *903*

Net present value A project selection technique that discounts all expected after-tax cash inflows and outflows from the proposed investment to their present values using the company's minimum rate of return as a discount rate. If the amount obtained by this process exceeds or equals the investment amount, the proposal is considered acceptable for further consideration. *909*

Opportunity cost The benefits or returns lost by rejecting the best alternative investment. *903*

Out-of-pocket cost A cost requiring a future outlay of resources, usually cash. *906*

Payback period The period of time it takes for the cumulative sum of the annual net cash inflows from a project to equal the initial net cash outlay. *906*

Profitability index The ratio of the present value of the expected net cash inflows (after taxes) divided by the initial cash outlay (or present value of cash outlays if future outlays are required). *910*

Sunk costs Costs that have already been incurred. Nothing can be done about sunk costs at the present time; they cannot be avoided or changed in amount. *906*

Tax shield The total amount by which taxable income is reduced due to the deductability of an item. *904*

Time-adjusted rate of return A project selection technique that finds a rate of return that will equate the present value of future expected net cash inflows (after taxes) from an investment with the cost of the investment; also called *internal rate of return*. *911*

Unadjusted rate of return The rate of return computed by dividing average annual income after taxes from a project by the average amount of the investment. *908*

Self-Test

True-False

Indicate whether each of the following is true or false.

1. Depreciation does not involve a cash outflow; it is deductible in arriving at federal taxable income.
2. The price a company is going to pay for a machine is an out-of-pocket cost.
3. Sunk costs and out-of-pocket costs are relevant to capital-budgeting decisions.
4. A formula for unadjusted rate of return is as follows:

$$\text{Unadjusted rate of return} = \frac{\text{Average annual income after taxes}}{\text{Average amount of investment}}$$

5. When investment projects costing different amounts are being compared, the net present value does not provide a valid means by which to rank projects in order of contribution to income or desirability assuming limited financial resources.

Multiple-Choice

Choose the best answer for each of the following questions.

1. Which of the following is incorrect regarding the payback period method?
   - **a.** The payback period ignores the time period beyond the payback period.
   - **b.** When using payback analysis for investment decisions, one rule is to select the shortest payback period investment.
   - **c.** The formula for the payback period is:

     $$\text{Payback period} = \frac{\text{Initial cash outlay}}{\text{Annual amount of investment}}$$

   - **d.** Payback analysis ignores the time value of money.
2. When using time value of money concepts, all aspects of the investment should be considered including which of the following?
   - **a.** Employee morale.
   - **b.** No single time value of money method should be used by itself to make capital budgeting decisions.
   - **c.** Company flexibility.
   - **d.** All of the above.
3. Which of the following best describes the limitations when using the unadjusted rate of return.
   - **a.** Timing of cash flows is not considered.
   - **b.** It allows a sunk cost, depreciation, to enter into the calculation.

* Some terms listed in earlier chapters are repeated here for your convenience.

   c. The length of time over which the return will be earned is not considered.
   d. All of the above.
4. Which of the following statements is (are) true regarding the profitability index?
   a. Only proposals with profitability indexes greater than 1.00 should be considered.
   b. Only proposals with profitability indexes less than 1.00 should be considered.
   c. The profitability index is the ratio of the initial cash outlay divided by the present value of cash benefits (before taxes).
   d. **b** and **c**.
5. Which of the following statements is (are) true regarding net present value?
   a. When determining an appropriate discount rate, management uses net cash outflow.
   b. With projects that require an investment at a later date, management must discount the cash outflow to its present value before it is compared to the present value of cash inflows.
   c. When using the net present value to screen alternative projects, as long as the project's net present value is equal to the investment the project is desirable.
   d. **b** and **c**.
6. Which of the following statements is (are) true regarding the time-adjusted rate of return?
   a. The first step in computing the rate of return is determining the payback period.
   b. The annual after-tax net cash inflow also is called an annuity.
   c. The cost of capital is used only as a cutoff point in deciding which projects should be considered further.
   d. All of the above.

Now turn to page 926 to check your answers.

Questions

1. How do capital expenditures differ from ordinary expenditures?
2. What effects can capital-budgeting decisions have on a company?
3. What effect does depreciation have on cash flow?
4. Give an example of an out-of-pocket cost and a sunk cost by describing a situation in which both are encountered.
5. A machine is being considered for purchase. The salesperson attempting to sell the machine says that it will pay for itself in five years. What is meant by this statement?
6. Discuss the limitations of the payback period method.
7. What is the profitability index, and of what value is it?
8. What is the time-adjusted rate of return on a capital investment?
9. What role does the cost of capital play in the time-adjusted rate of return method and in the net present value method?
10. What is the purpose of a postaudit? When should a postaudit be performed?
11. A friend who knows nothing about the concepts in this chapter is considering purchasing a house for rental to students. In just a few words, what would you tell your friend to think about in making this decision?

Exercises

Exercise 26–1
Determine estimated income and net cash inflow for an asset addition (L.O. 2)

Zen Manufacturing Company is considering investing $300,000 in new equipment with an estimated useful life of 10 years and no salvage value. The equipment is expected to produce $120,000 in cash inflows and $80,000 in cash outflows annually. The company uses straight-line depreciation, and has a 40% tax rate. Determine the annual estimated net income and net cash inflow.

Exercise 26–2
Determine additional cash inflow for an asset replacement (L.O. 2)

Get-Fit Athletic Club is considering replacing a four-year-old weight machine with a new, advanced model. The old machine was purchased for $30,000, has an estimated useful life of 10 years with no salvage value, and has annual maintenance costs of $7,500. The new machine would cost $22,500, but annual maintenance costs would be only $3,000. The new machine would have an estimated useful life of 10 years with no salvage value. Using straight-line depreciation and an assumed 40% tax rate, compute the additional annual cash inflow if the old machine is replaced.

Exercise 26–3
Compute payback period for a new machine (L.O. 3)

Given the following annual costs, compute the payback period for the new machine if its initial cost is $840,000.

	Old Machine	New Machine
Depreciation	$ 36,000	$ 84,000
Labor	144,000	126,000
Repairs	42,000	9,000
Other costs	24,000	7,200
	$246,000	$226,200

Exercise 26–4
Compute unadjusted rate of return for a new machine (L.O. 4)

Diana Company is considering investing $16,500 in a new machine. The machine is expected to last five years and to have a salvage value of $4,000. Annual before-tax net cash inflow from the machine is expected to be $3,500. Calculate the unadjusted rate of return. The income tax rate is 40%.

Exercise 26–5
Compute the profitability index for two projects and rank projects (L.O. 6)

Compute the profitability index for each of the following two proposals assuming the desired minimum rate of return is 20%. Based on the profitability indexes, which proposal is better?

	Proposal A	Proposal B
Initial cash outlay	$32,000	$20,600
Net cash inflow (after taxes):		
First year	20,000	12,000
Second year	18,000	12,000
Third year	12,000	8,000
Fourth year	–0–	5,000

Exercise 26–6
Rank projects using the payback period (L.O. 3)

Jefferson Company is considering three alternative investment proposals. Using the following information, rank the proposals in order of desirability using the payback period method.

	Proposal		
	D	E	F
Initial outlay	$720,000	$ 720,000	$ 720,000
Net cash inflow (after taxes):			
First year	$ –0–	$ 180,000	$ 180,000
Second year	360,000	540,000	360,000
Third year	360,000	180,000	540,000
Fourth year	180,000	360,000	900,000
	$900,000	$1,260,000	$1,980,000

Exercise 26–7
Determine acceptability of a project using net present value (L.O. 5)

Ross Company is considering the purchase of a new machine costing $45,000. It is expected to save $9,000 cash per year for 10 years, has an estimated useful life of 10 years, and no salvage value. Management will not make any investment unless at least an 18% rate of return can be earned. Using the net present value method, determine if the proposal is acceptable. Assume all tax effects are included in these numbers.

Exercise 26–8
Compute time-adjusted rate of return (L.O. 7)

Refer to the data in Exercise 26–7. Calculate the time-adjusted rate of return.

Exercise 26–9
Rank projects using the payback period, net present value, and time-adjusted rate of return (L.O. 3, 5, 7)

Rank the following investments for Simone Company in order of their desirability using the (*a*) payback period method, (*b*) net present value method, and (*c*) time-adjusted rate of return method. Management requires a minimum rate of return of 14%.

Investment	Initial Cash Outlay	Expected After-Tax Net Cash Inflow per Year	Expected Life of Proposal (years)
A	$120,000	$15,000	8
B	150,000	26,000	20
C	240,000	48,000	10

PROBLEMS

Problem 26–1
Determine net cash inflow and payback period for an asset addition (L.O. 2, 3)

Graham Company is considering the purchase of a new machine that would cost $200,000 and would have an estimated useful life of 10 years with no salvage value. The new machine is expected to have annual before-tax cash inflows of $100,000 and annual before-tax cash outflows of $40,000. The company will depreciate the machine using straight-line depreciation, and the assumed tax rate is 40%.

Required

a. Determine the net after-tax cash inflow for the new machine.

b. Determine the payback period for the new machine.

Problem 26–2
Determine additional cash inflow for an asset replacement (L.O. 2)

Hamlet Company currently uses four machines to produce 400,000 units annually. The machines were bought three years ago for $50,000 each and have an expected useful life of 10 years with no salvage value. These machines cost a total of $28,000 per year to repair and maintain.

The company is considering replacing the four machines with one technologically superior machine capable of producing 400,000 units annually by itself. The machine would cost $140,000 and have an estimated useful life of seven years with no salvage value. Annual repair and maintenance costs are estimated at $14,000.

Required

Assuming straight-line depreciation and a 40% tax rate, determine the annual additional after-tax net cash inflow if the new machine is acquired.

Problem 26–3
Evaluate asset replacement using payback and net present value (L.O. 3, 5)

Span Company owns five machines that it uses in its manufacturing operations. Each of the machines was purchased four years ago at a cost of $120,000. Each machine has an estimated life of 10 years with no expected salvage value. A new machine has become available. One new machine has the same productive capacity as the five old machines combined; it can produce 800,000 units each year. The new machine will cost $648,000, is estimated to last six years, and will have a salvage value of $72,000. A trade-in allowance of $24,000 is available for each of the old machines. These are the operating costs per unit:

	Five Old Machines	New Machine
Repairs	$0.6796	$0.0856
Depreciation	0.1500	0.2400
Power	0.1890	0.1036
Other operating costs	0.1620	0.0496
Operating costs per unit	$1.1806	$0.4788

Required

Ignore federal income taxes. Use the payback period method for **(a)** and **(b)**.

a. Do you recommend replacing the old machines? Support your answer with computations. Disregard all factors except those reflected in the data just given.

b. If the old machines were already fully depreciated, would your answer be different? Why?

c. Using the net present value method with a discount rate of 20%, present a schedule showing whether or not the new machine should be acquired.

Problem 26–4
Calculate time-adjusted rate of return for new equipment; determine effect of altering useful life and net cash inflows (L.O. 7)

Newman's Veggie Company has used a particular canning machine for several years. The machine has a zero salvage value. The company is considering buying a technologically improved machine at a cost of $232,000. The new machine will save $50,000 per year after taxes in cash operating costs. If the company decides not to buy the new machine, it can use the old machine for an indefinite time by incurring heavy repair costs. The new machine would have an estimated useful life of eight years.

Required

a. Compute the time-adjusted rate of return for the new machine.

b. Management thinks the estimated useful life of the new machine may be more or less than eight years. Compute the time-adjusted rate of return for the new machine if its useful life is (1) 5 years and (2) 12 years, instead of 8 years.

c. Suppose the new machine's useful life is eight years, but the annual after-tax cost savings are only $40,000. Compute the time-adjusted rate of return.

d. Assume the annual after-tax cost savings from the new machine will be $44,000 and its useful life will be 10 years. Compute the time-adjusted rate of return.

Problem 26–5
Rank proposals using the payback period, unadjusted rate of return, profitability index, and time-adjusted rate of return (L.O. 3, 4, 6, 7)

Macro, Inc., is considering three different investments involving depreciable assets with no salvage value. The following data relate to these investments:

Investment	Initial Cash Outlay	Expected Before-Tax Net Cash Inflow per Year	Expected After-Tax Net Cash Inflow per Year	Expected Life of Proposal (years)
1	$140,000	$37,333	$28,000	10
2	240,000	72,000	48,000	20
3	360,000	89,333	68,000	10

The income tax rate is 40%. Management requires a minimum return on investment of 12%.

Required Rank these proposals using the following selection techniques:

a. Payback period.
b. Unadjusted rate of return.
c. Profitability index.
d. Time-adjusted rate of return.

Problem 26–6
Make capital-budgeting decision using net present value (L.O. 5)

Van Gogh Company has decided to computerize its accounting system. The company has two alternatives—it can lease a computer under a three-year contract or purchase a computer outright.

If the computer is leased, the lease payment will be $4,500 each year. The first lease payment will be due on the day the lease contract is signed. The other two payments will be due at the end of the first and second years. The lessor will provide all repairs and maintenance.

If the company purchases the computer outright, it will incur the following costs:

Acquisition cost	$10,500
Repairs and maintenance:	
First year	300
Second year	250
Third year	350

The computer is expected to have only a three-year useful life because of obsolescence and technological advancements. The computer will have no salvage value and be depreciated on a double-declining-balance basis. Van Gogh Company's cost of capital is 16%.

Required

a. Calculate the net present value of out-of-pocket costs for the lease alternative.
b. Calculate the net present value of out-of-pocket costs for the purchase alternative.
c. Do you recommend that the company purchase or lease the machine?

Problem 26–7
Make capital-budgeting decision using the net present value (L.O. 5)

Young Sports Company is trying to decide whether to add tennis equipment to its existing line of football, baseball, and basketball equipment. Market research studies and cost analyses have provided the following information:

1. Young will need additional machinery and equipment to manufacture the tennis equipment. The machines and equipment will cost $450,000, have an estimated 10-year useful life, and have a $10,000 salvage value.
2. Sales of tennis equipment for the next 10 years have been projected as follows:

Years	Sales in Dollars
1.	$ 75,000
2.	112,500
3.	168,750
4.	187,500
5.	206,250
6–10 (each year)	225,000

3. Variable costs are 60% of selling price, and fixed costs (including straight-line depreciation) will total $88,500 per year.
4. The company must advertise its new product line to gain rapid entry into the market. Its advertising campaign costs will be:

Years	Annual Advertising Cost
1–3.	$75,000
4–10	37,500

5. The company requires a 14% minimum rate of return on investments.

Required Using the net present value method, decide whether or not Young Sports Company should add the tennis equipment to its line of products. (Ignore federal income taxes.) Round to the nearest dollar.

Problem 26–8
Evaluate investment proposal using net present value (L.O. 5)

Shaq Company is considering purchasing new equipment costing $1,800,000. Shaq estimates that the useful life of the equipment will be five years and that it will have a salvage value of $600,000. The company uses straight-line depreciation. The new equipment is expected to have a net cash inflow (before taxes) of $258,000 annually. Assume that the tax rate is 40% and that management requires a minimum return of 14%.

Required

Using the net present value method, determine whether the equipment is an acceptable investment.

Problem 26–9
Make capital-budgeting decision using net present value (L.O. 5)

Governors Company has an opportunity to sell some equipment for $40,000. Such a sale will result in a tax-deductible loss of $4,000. If the equipment is not sold, it is expected to produce net cash inflows after taxes of $12,000 for the next 10 years. After 10 years, the equipment can be sold for its book value of $4,000. Assume a 40% federal income tax rate.

Required

Management currently has other opportunities that will yield 18%. Using the net present value method, show whether the company should sell the equipment. Prepare a schedule to support your conclusion.

Alternate Problems

Problem 26–1A
Determine increase of cash inflow for machine replacement (L.O. 2)

Kevin's Manufacturing Company is currently using three machines that it bought seven years ago to manufacture its product. Each machine produces 10,000 units annually. Each machine originally cost $25,500 and has an estimated useful life of 17 years with no salvage value.

The new assistant manager of Kevin's Manufacturing Company suggests that the company replace the three old machines with two technically superior machines for $22,500 each. Each new machine would produce 15,000 units annually and would have an estimated useful life of 10 years with no salvage value.

The new assistant manager points out that the cost of maintaining the new machines would be much lower. Each old machine costs $2,500 per year to maintain; each new machine would cost only $1,000 a year to maintain.

Required

Compute the increase in after-tax annual net cash inflow that would result from replacing the old machines; use straight-line depreciation and an assumed tax rate of 40%.

Problem 26–2A
Determine desirability of asset replacement using payback; develop schedule to aid in project evaluation (L.O. 3)

United Express Company is considering replacing 10 of its delivery vans that originally cost $30,000 each; depreciation of $18,750 has already been taken on each van. The vans were originally estimated to have useful lives of eight years and no salvage value. Each van travels an average of 150,000 miles per year. The 10 new vans, if purchased, will cost $36,000 each. Each van will be driven 150,000 miles per year and will have no salvage value at the end of its three-year estimated useful life. A trade-in allowance of $3,000 is available for each of the old vans. Following is a comparison of costs of operation per mile:

	Old Vans	New Vans
Fuel, lubricants, etc.	$0.152	$0.119
Tires	0.067	0.067
Repairs	0.110	0.087
Depreciation	0.025	0.080
Other operating costs	0.051	0.043
Operating costs per mile	$0.405	$0.396

Required

Use the payback period method for Parts (**a**) and (**b**).

a. Do you recommend replacing the old vans? Support your answer with computations and disregard all factors not related to the preceding data.

b. If the old vans were already fully depreciated, would your answer be different? Why?

c. Assume that all cost flows for operating costs fall at the end of each year and that 18% is an appropriate rate for discounting purposes. Using the net present value method, present a schedule showing whether or not the new vans should be acquired.

Problem 26–3A
Compute time-adjusted rate of return for asset replacement and effect of altering useful life and cash flows in calculations (L.O. 7)

Ohio Canal Company has been using an old-fashioned computer for many years. The computer has no salvage value. The company is considering buying a computer system at a cost of $35,000. The new computer system will save $7,000 per year after taxes in cash (including tax effects of depreciation). If the company decides not to buy the new computer system, it can use the old one for an indefinite time. The new computer system will have an estimated useful life of 10 years.

Required

a. Compute the time-adjusted rate of return for the new computer system.

b. The company is uncertain about the new computer system's 10-year useful life. Compute the time-adjusted rate of return for the new computer system if its useful life is (1) 6 years and (2) 15 years, instead of 10 years.

c. Suppose the computer system has a useful life of 10 years, but the annual after-tax cost savings are only $6,000. Compute the time-adjusted rate of return.

d. Assume the annual after-tax cost savings will be $8,000 and the useful life will be eight years. Compute the time-adjusted rate of return.

Problem 26–4A
Evaluate asset replacement using net present value (L.O. 5)

Lloyd's Landscaping Company has always purchased its trucks outright and sold them after three years. The company is ready to sell its present fleet of trucks and is trying to decide whether it should continue to purchase trucks or whether it should lease trucks. If the trucks are purchased, the company will incur the following costs:

	Costs per Fleet
Acquisition cost	$312,000
Repairs:	
First year	3,600
Second year.	6,600
Third year	9,000
Other annual costs	9,600

At the end of three years, the trucks could be sold for a total of $96,000. Another fleet of trucks would then be purchased. The costs just listed, including the same acquisition cost, also would be incurred with respect to the second fleet of trucks. The second fleet also could be sold for $96,000 at the end of three years.

If the company leases the trucks, the lease contract will run for six years. One fleet of trucks will be provided immediately, and a second fleet of trucks will be provided at the end of three years. The company will pay $126,000 per year under the lease contract. The first lease payment will be due on the day the lease contract is signed. The lessor bears the cost of all repairs.

Required Using the net present value method, determine if the comapny should buy or lease the trucks. Assume the company's cost of capital is 18%. (Ignore federal income taxes.)

BEYOND THE NUMBERS—CRITICAL THINKING

Business Decision Case 26–1
Compute net present value of several proposals; rank proposals in order of acceptability (L.O. 5)

Slickers Company wishes to invest $750,000 in capital projects that have a minimum expected rate of return of 14%. The company is evaluating five proposals. Acceptance of one proposal does not preclude acceptance of any of the other proposals. The company's criterion is to select proposals that meet its 14% minimum required rate of return. The relevant information related to the five proposals is as follows:

Investment	Initial Cash Outlay	Expected After-Tax Net Cash Inflow per Year	Expected Life of Proposal (years)
A	$150,000	$45,000	5
B	300,000	60,000	8
C	375,000	82,500	10
D	450,000	78,000	12
E	150,000	31,500	10

Required

a. Compute the net present value of each of the five proposals.

b. Which projects should be undertaken? Why? Rank them in order of desirability.

Business Decision Case 26–2
Evaluate computation of a project's net present value; determine acceptability of project (L.O. 5)

Sun Company is considering a capital project involving a $225,000 investment in machinery and a $45,000 investment in working capital. The machine has an expected useful life of 10 years and no salvage value. The annual cash inflows (before taxes) are estimated at $90,000 with annual cash outflows (before taxes) of $30,000. The company uses straight-line depreciation. Assume the federal income tax rate is 40%.

The company's new accountant computed the net present value of the project using a minimum required rate of return of 16% (the company's cost of capital). The accountant's computations follow:

Cash inflows	$ 90,000
Cash outflows	30,000
Net cash inflow	$ 60,000
Present value factor at 16%	×4.833
Present value of net cash inflow	$289,980
Initial cash outlay	225,000
Net present value	$ 64,980

Required

a. Are the accountant's computations correct? If not, compute the correct net present value.

b. Is this capital project acceptable to the company? Why or why not?

An Accounting Perspective—Writing Experience 26–3
Compare Japanese and U.S. measures of cost of capital

Refer to "An Accounting Perspective" on page 911. Write a brief paper explaining why managers in Japan might use lower measures of the cost of capital than U.S. managers.

Ethics Case—Writing Experience 26–4

Rebecca Peters just learned that First Bank's investment review committee rejected her pet project, a new computerized method of storing data that would enable customers to have instant access to their bank records. Peters' software consulting firm specializes in working with financial institutions. This project for First Bank was her first as project manager.

Following up, Peters learned that First Bank's investment review committee liked the idea but were not convinced that the new software's financial benefits would justify the cost of the software. When she told a colleague about the rejection at First Bank, the colleague said, "Why don't you tell the committee this software will increase the bank's profits? After we installed the software in the bank in Indianapolis, their profits increased substantially. We even have data from that bank that you could present."

Peters thought about the suggestion. She knew First Bank would be pleased with the software if they installed it, and she wanted to make the sale. She also knew that the situation in Indianapolis was different; profits there had increased primarily because of other software that had reduced the bank's operating costs.

Required

What should Rebecca Peters do? Write her a letter telling what you would do.

Group Assignment 26–5
Discuss a new business idea

For summer employment, a friend is considering investing in a coffee stand on a busy street near office buildings. Being unfamiliar with the concepts in this chapter, your friend doesn't know how to make the decision. In teams of four, help your friend get started by providing a framework and questions that your friend should answer. (For example, how much will the investment be? How much are the estimated cash flows from sales, etc.) Prepare a memorandum from the group to your instructor; list your questions and suggestions for your friend. In the heading, include the date, to whom it is written, from whom, and the subject matter.

Answers to Self-Test

True-False

1. **True.** Depreciation does not involve a cash outflow; it is deductible in arriving at federal taxable income.
2. **True.** The price paid for a machine becomes a sunk cost the minute the purchase has been made.
3. **False.** Only the out-of-pocket costs (the future cash outlays) are relevant to capital-budgeting decisions.
4. **True.**

$$\text{Unadjusted rate of return} = \frac{\text{Average annual income after taxes}}{\text{Average amount of investment}}$$

5. **True.** The profitability index should be used to rank these projects.

Multiple-Choice

1. **c.** The correct formula is:

$$\text{Payback period} = \frac{\text{Initial cash outlay}}{\text{Annual net cash inflow (or benefit)}}$$

2. **d.** All of the above choices are correct answers.
3. **d.** All of the above choices are correct answers.
4. **a.** A profitability index is the ratio of the present value of the expected net cash inflows (after taxes) divided by the initial cash outlay (or present value of cash outlays if future outlays are required).
5. **b.** With projects that require an investment at a later date, management must discount the cash outflow to its present value before it is compared to the present value of cash inflows.
6. **d.** All of the choices are correct answers.

APPENDIX

COMPOUND INTEREST AND ANNUITY TABLES

APPENDIX OUTLINE

The following tables are included in this Appendix:

TABLE A.1 Future Value of $1 at Compound Interest: 1%–20% $F_{in} = (1 + i)^n$

Period	1%	2%	3%	4%	5%	6%	7%	8%	9%	10%
1	1.01000	1.02000	1.03000	1.04000	1.05000	1.06000	1.07000	1.08000	1.09000	1.10000
2	1.02010	1.04040	1.06090	1.08160	1.10250	1.12360	1.14490	1.16640	1.18810	1.21000
3	1.03030	1.06121	1.09273	1.12486	1.15762	1.19102	1.22504	1.25971	1.29503	1.33100
4	1.04060	1.08243	1.12551	1.16986	1.21551	1.26248	1.31080	1.36049	1.41158	1.46410
5	1.05101	1.10408	1.15927	1.21665	1.27628	1.33823	1.40255	1.46933	1.53862	1.61051
6	1.06152	1.12616	1.19405	1.26532	1.34010	1.41852	1.50073	1.58687	1.67710	1.77156
7	1.07214	1.14869	1.22987	1.31593	1.40710	1.50363	1.60578	1.71382	1.82804	1.94872
8	1.08286	1.17166	1.26677	1.36857	1.47746	1.59385	1.71819	1.85093	1.99256	2.14359
9	1.09369	1.19509	1.30477	1.42331	1.55133	1.68948	1.83846	1.99900	2.17189	2.35795
10	1.10462	1.21899	1.34392	1.48024	1.62889	1.79085	1.96715	2.15892	2.36736	2.59374
11	1.11567	1.24337	1.38423	1.53945	1.71034	1.89830	2.10485	2.33164	2.58043	2.85312
12	1.12683	1.26824	1.42576	1.60103	1.79586	2.01220	2.25219	2.51817	2.81266	3.13843
13	1.13809	1.29361	1.46853	1.66507	1.88565	2.13293	2.40985	2.71962	3.06580	3.45227
14	1.14947	1.31948	1.51259	1.73168	1.97993	2.26090	2.57853	2.93719	3.34173	3.79750
15	1.16097	1.34587	1.55797	1.80094	2.07893	2.39656	2.75903	3.17217	3.64248	4.17725
16	1.17258	1.37279	1.60471	1.87298	2.18287	2.54035	2.95216	3.42594	3.97031	4.59497
17	1.18430	1.40024	1.65285	1.94790	2.29202	2.69277	3.15882	3.70002	4.32763	5.05447
18	1.19615	1.42825	1.70243	2.02582	2.40662	2.85434	3.37993	3.99602	4.71712	5.55992
19	1.20811	1.45681	1.75351	2.10685	2.52695	3.02560	3.61653	4.31570	5.14166	6.11591
20	1.22019	1.48595	1.80611	2.19112	2.65330	3.20714	3.86968	4.66096	5.60441	6.72750
21	1.23239	1.51567	1.86029	2.27877	2.78596	3.39956	4.14056	5.03383	6.10881	7.40025
22	1.24472	1.54598	1.91610	2.36992	2.92526	3.60354	4.43040	5.43654	6.65860	8.14027
23	1.25716	1.57690	1.97359	2.46472	3.07152	3.81975	4.74053	5.87146	7.25787	8.95430
24	1.26973	1.60844	2.03279	2.56330	3.22510	4.04893	5.07237	6.34118	7.91108	9.84973
25	1.28243	1.64061	2.09378	2.66584	3.38635	4.29187	5.42743	6.84848	8.62308	10.83471
26	1.29526	1.67342	2.15659	2.77247	3.55567	4.54938	5.80735	7.39635	9.39916	11.91818
27	1.30821	1.70689	2.22129	2.88337	3.73346	4.82235	6.21387	7.98806	10.24508	13.10999
28	1.32129	1.74102	2.28793	2.99870	3.92013	5.11169	6.64884	8.62711	11.16714	14.42099
29	1.33450	1.77584	2.35657	3.11865	4.11614	5.41839	7.11426	9.31727	12.17218	15.86309
30	1.34785	1.81136	2.42726	3.24340	4.32194	5.74349	7.61226	10.06266	13.26768	17.44940

Period	11%	12%	13%	14%	15%	16%	17%	18%	19%	20%
1	1.11000	1.12000	1.13000	1.14000	1.15000	1.16000	1.17000	1.18000	1.19000	1.20000
2	1.23210	1.25440	1.27690	1.29960	1.32250	1.34560	1.36890	1.39240	1.41610	1.44000
3	1.36763	1.40493	1.44290	1.48154	1.52088	1.56090	1.60161	1.64303	1.68516	1.72800
4	1.51807	1.57352	1.63047	1.68896	1.74901	1.81064	1.87389	1.93878	2.00534	2.07360
5	1.68506	1.76234	1.84244	1.92541	2.01136	2.10034	2.19245	2.28776	2.38635	2.48832
6	1.87041	1.97382	2.08195	2.19497	2.31306	2.43640	2.56516	2.69955	2.83976	2.98598
7	2.07616	2.21068	2.35261	2.50227	2.66002	2.82622	3.00124	3.18547	3.37932	3.58318
8	2.30454	2.47596	2.65844	2.85259	3.05902	3.27841	3.51145	3.75886	4.02139	4.29982
9	2.55804	2.77308	3.00404	3.25195	3.51788	3.80296	4.10840	4.43545	4.78545	5.15978
10	2.83942	3.10585	3.39457	3.70722	4.04556	4.41144	4.80683	5.23384	5.69468	6.19174
11	3.15176	3.47855	3.83586	4.22623	4.65239	5.11726	5.62399	6.17593	6.77667	7.43008
12	3.49845	3.89598	4.33452	4.81790	5.35025	5.93603	6.58007	7.28759	8.06424	8.91610
13	3.88328	4.36349	4.89801	5.49241	6.15279	6.88579	7.69868	8.59936	9.59645	10.69932
14	4.31044	4.88711	5.53475	6.26135	7.07571	7.98752	9.00745	10.14724	11.41977	12.83918
15	4.78459	5.47357	6.25427	7.13794	8.13706	9.26552	10.53872	11.97375	13.58953	15.40702
16	5.31089	6.13039	7.06733	8.13725	9.35762	10.74800	12.33030	14.12902	16.17154	18.48843
17	5.89509	6.86604	7.98608	9.27646	10.76126	12.46768	14.42646	16.67225	19.24413	22.18611
18	6.54355	7.68997	9.02427	10.57517	12.37545	14.46251	16.87895	19.67325	22.90052	26.62333
19	7.26334	8.61276	10.19742	12.05569	14.23177	16.77652	19.74838	23.21444	27.25162	31.94800
20	8.06231	9.64629	11.52309	13.74349	16.36654	19.46076	23.10560	27.39303	32.42942	38.33760
21	8.94917	10.80385	13.02109	15.66758	18.82152	22.57448	27.03355	32.32378	38.59101	46.00512
22	9.93357	12.10031	14.71383	17.86104	21.64475	26.18640	31.62925	38.14206	45.92331	55.20614
23	11.02627	13.55235	16.62663	20.36158	24.89146	30.37622	37.00623	45.00763	54.64873	66.24737
24	12.23916	15.17863	18.78809	23.21221	28.62518	35.23642	43.29729	53.10901	65.03199	79.49685
25	13.58546	17.00006	21.23054	26.46192	32.91895	40.87424	50.65783	62.66863	77.38807	95.39622
26	15.07986	19.04007	23.99051	30.16658	37.85680	47.41412	59.26966	73.94898	92.09181	114.47546
27	16.73865	21.32488	27.10928	34.38991	43.53531	55.00038	69.34550	87.25980	109.58925	137.37055
28	18.57990	23.88387	30.63349	39.20449	50.06561	63.80044	81.13423	102.96656	130.41121	164.84466
29	20.62369	26.74993	34.61584	44.69312	57.57545	74.00851	94.92705	121.50054	155.18934	197.81359
30	22.89230	29.95992	39.11590	50.95016	66.21177	85.84988	111.06465	143.37064	184.67531	237.37631

Table A.2 Future Value of an Ordinary Annuity of $1 per Period: 1%–20% $F_{A_{in}} = \dfrac{(1+i)^n - 1}{i}$

Period	1%	2%	3%	4%	5%	6%	7%	8%	9%	10%
1	1.00000	1.00000	1.00000	1.00000	1.00000	1.00000	1.00000	1.00000	1.00000	1.00000
2	2.01000	2.02000	2.03000	2.04000	2.05000	2.06000	2.07000	2.08000	2.09000	2.10000
3	3.03010	3.06040	3.09090	3.12160	3.15250	3.18360	3.21490	3.24640	3.27810	3.31000
4	4.06040	4.12161	4.18363	4.24646	4.31012	4.37462	4.43994	4.50611	4.57313	4.64100
5	5.10101	5.20404	5.30914	5.41632	5.52563	5.63709	5.75074	5.86660	5.98471	6.10510
6	6.15202	6.30812	6.46841	6.63298	6.80191	6.97532	7.15329	7.33593	7.52333	7.71561
7	7.21354	7.43428	7.66246	7.89829	8.14201	8.39384	8.65402	8.92280	9.20043	9.48717
8	8.28567	8.58297	8.89234	9.21423	9.54911	9.89747	10.25980	10.63663	11.02847	11.43589
9	9.36853	9.75463	10.15911	10.58280	11.02656	11.49132	11.97799	12.48756	13.02104	13.57948
10	10.46221	10.94972	11.46388	12.00611	12.57789	13.18079	13.81645	14.48656	15.19293	15.93742
11	11.56683	12.16872	12.80780	13.48635	14.20679	14.97164	15.78360	16.64549	17.56029	18.53117
12	12.68250	13.41209	14.19203	15.02581	15.91713	16.86994	17.88845	18.97713	20.14072	21.38428
13	13.80933	14.68033	15.61779	16.62684	17.71298	18.88214	20.14064	21.49530	22.95338	24.52271
14	14.94742	15.97394	17.08632	18.29191	19.59863	21.01507	22.55049	24.21492	26.01919	27.97498
15	16.09690	17.29342	18.59891	20.02359	21.57856	23.27597	25.12902	27.15211	29.36092	31.77248
16	17.25786	18.63929	20.15688	21.82453	23.65749	25.67253	27.88805	30.32428	33.00340	35.94973
17	18.43044	20.01207	21.76159	23.69751	25.84037	28.21288	30.84022	33.75023	36.97370	40.54470
18	19.61475	21.41231	23.41444	25.64541	28.13238	30.90565	33.99903	37.45024	41.30134	45.59917
19	20.81090	22.84056	25.11687	27.67123	30.53900	33.75999	37.37896	41.44626	46.01846	51.15909
20	22.01900	24.29737	26.87037	29.77808	33.06595	36.78559	40.99549	45.76196	51.16012	57.27500
21	23.23919	25.78332	28.67649	31.96920	35.71925	39.99273	44.86518	50.42292	56.76453	64.00250
22	24.47159	27.29898	30.53678	34.24797	38.50521	43.39229	49.00574	55.45676	62.87334	71.40275
23	25.71630	28.84496	32.45288	36.61789	41.43048	46.99583	53.43614	60.89330	69.53194	79.54302
24	26.97346	30.42186	34.42647	39.08260	44.50200	50.81558	58.17667	66.76476	76.78981	88.49733
25	28.24320	32.03030	36.45926	41.64591	47.72710	54.86451	63.24904	73.10594	84.70090	98.34706
26	29.52563	33.67091	38.55304	44.31174	51.11345	59.15638	68.67647	79.95442	93.32398	109.18177
27	30.82089	35.34432	40.70963	47.08421	54.66913	63.70577	74.48382	87.35077	102.72313	121.09994
28	32.12910	37.05121	42.93092	49.96758	58.40258	68.52811	80.69769	95.33883	112.96822	134.20994
29	33.45039	38.79223	45.21885	52.96629	62.32271	73.63980	87.34653	103.96594	124.13536	148.63093
30	34.78489	40.56808	47.57542	56.08494	66.43885	79.05819	94.46079	113.28321	136.30754	164.49402

Period	11%	12%	13%	14%	15%	16%	17%	18%	19%	20%
1	1.00000	1.00000	1.00000	1.00000	1.00000	1.00000	1.00000	1.00000	1.00000	1.00000
2	2.11000	2.12000	2.13000	2.14000	2.15000	2.16000	2.17000	2.18000	2.19000	2.20000
3	3.34210	3.37440	3.40690	3.43960	3.47250	3.50560	3.53890	3.57240	3.60610	3.64000
4	4.70973	4.77933	4.84980	4.92114	4.99337	5.06650	5.14051	5.21543	5.29126	5.36800
5	6.22780	6.35285	6.48027	6.61010	6.74238	6.87714	7.01440	7.15421	7.29660	7.44160
6	7.91286	8.11519	8.32271	8.53552	8.75374	8.97748	9.20685	9.44197	9.68295	9.92992
7	9.78327	10.08901	10.40466	10.73049	11.06680	11.41387	11.77201	12.14152	12.52271	12.91590
8	11.85943	12.29969	12.75726	13.23276	13.72682	14.24009	14.77325	15.32700	15.90203	16.49908
9	14.16397	14.77566	15.41571	16.08535	16.78584	17.51851	18.28471	19.08585	19.92341	20.79890
10	16.72201	17.54874	18.41975	19.33730	20.30372	21.32147	22.39311	23.52131	24.70886	25.95868
11	19.56143	20.65458	21.81432	23.04452	24.34928	25.73290	27.19994	28.75514	30.40355	32.15042
12	22.71319	24.13313	25.65018	27.27075	29.00167	30.85017	32.82393	34.93107	37.18022	39.58050
13	26.21164	28.02911	29.98470	32.08865	34.35192	36.78620	39.40399	42.21866	45.24446	48.49660
14	30.09492	32.39260	34.88271	37.58107	40.50471	43.67199	47.10267	50.81802	54.84091	59.19592
15	34.40536	37.27971	40.41746	43.84241	47.58041	51.65951	56.11013	60.96527	66.26068	72.03511
16	39.18995	42.75328	46.67173	50.98035	55.71747	60.92503	66.64885	72.93901	79.85021	87.44213
17	44.50084	48.88367	53.73906	59.11760	65.07509	71.67303	78.97915	87.06804	96.02175	105.93056
18	50.39594	55.74971	61.72514	68.39407	75.83636	84.14072	93.40561	103.74028	115.26588	128.11667
19	56.93949	63.43968	70.74941	78.96923	88.21181	98.60323	110.28456	123.41353	138.16640	154.74000
20	64.20283	72.05244	80.94683	91.02493	102.44358	115.37975	130.03294	146.62797	165.41802	186.68800
21	72.26514	81.69874	92.46992	104.76842	118.81012	134.84051	153.13854	174.02100	197.84744	225.02560
22	81.21431	92.50258	105.49101	120.43600	137.63164	157.41499	180.17209	206.34479	236.43846	271.03072
23	91.14788	104.60289	120.20484	138.29704	159.27638	183.60138	211.80134	244.48685	282.36176	326.23686
24	102.17415	118.15524	136.83147	158.65862	184.16784	213.97761	248.80757	289.49448	337.01050	392.48424
25	114.41331	133.33387	155.61956	181.87083	212.79302	249.21402	292.10486	342.60349	402.04249	471.98108
26	127.99877	150.33393	176.85010	208.33274	245.71197	290.08827	342.76268	405.27211	479.43056	567.37730
27	143.07864	169.37401	200.84061	238.49933	283.56877	337.50239	402.03234	479.22109	571.52237	681.85276
28	159.81729	190.69889	227.94989	272.88923	327.10408	392.50277	471.37783	566.48089	681.11162	819.22331
29	178.39719	214.58275	258.58338	312.09373	377.16969	456.30322	552.51207	669.44745	811.52283	984.06797
30	199.02088	241.33268	293.19922	356.78685	434.74515	530.31173	647.43912	790.94799	966.71217	1181.88157

TABLE A.3 Present Value of $1 at Compound Interest: 1%–20% $P_{i,n} = \frac{1}{(1+i)^n}$

Period	1%	2%	3%	4%	5%	6%	7%	8%	9%	10%
1.	0.99010	0.98039	0.97087	0.96154	0.95238	0.94340	0.93458	0.92593	0.91743	0.90909
2.	0.98030	0.96117	0.94260	0.92456	0.90703	0.89000	0.87344	0.85734	0.84168	0.82645
3.	0.97059	0.94232	0.91514	0.88900	0.86384	0.83962	0.81630	0.79383	0.77218	0.75131
4.	0.96098	0.92385	0.88849	0.85480	0.82270	0.79209	0.76290	0.73503	0.70843	0.68301
5.	0.95147	0.90573	0.86261	0.82193	0.78353	0.74726	0.71299	0.68058	0.64993	0.62092
6.	0.94205	0.88797	0.83748	0.79031	0.74622	0.70496	0.66634	0.63017	0.59627	0.56447
7.	0.93272	0.87056	0.81309	0.75992	0.71068	0.66506	0.62275	0.58349	0.54703	0.51316
8.	0.92348	0.85349	0.78941	0.73069	0.67684	0.62741	0.58201	0.54027	0.50187	0.46651
9.	0.91434	0.83676	0.76642	0.70259	0.64461	0.59190	0.54393	0.50025	0.46043	0.42410
10.	0.90529	0.82035	0.74409	0.67556	0.61391	0.55839	0.50835	0.46319	0.42241	0.38554
11.	0.89632	0.80426	0.72242	0.64958	0.58468	0.52679	0.47509	0.42888	0.38753	0.35049
12.	0.88745	0.78849	0.70138	0.62460	0.55684	0.49697	0.44401	0.39711	0.35553	0.31863
13.	0.87866	0.77303	0.68095	0.60057	0.53032	0.46884	0.41496	0.36770	0.32618	0.28966
14.	0.86996	0.75788	0.66112	0.57748	0.50507	0.44230	0.38782	0.34046	0.29925	0.26333
15.	0.86135	0.74301	0.64186	0.55526	0.48102	0.41727	0.36245	0.31524	0.27454	0.23939
16.	0.85282	0.72845	0.62317	0.53391	0.45811	0.39365	0.33873	0.29189	0.25187	0.21763
17.	0.84438	0.71416	0.60502	0.51337	0.43630	0.37136	0.31657	0.27027	0.23107	0.19784
18.	0.83602	0.70016	0.58739	0.49363	0.41552	0.35034	0.29586	0.25025	0.21199	0.17986
19.	0.82774	0.68643	0.57029	0.47464	0.39573	0.33051	0.27651	0.23171	0.19449	0.16351
20.	0.81954	0.67297	0.55368	0.45639	0.37689	0.31180	0.25842	0.21455	0.17843	0.14864
21.	0.81143	0.65978	0.53755	0.43883	0.35894	0.29416	0.24151	0.19866	0.16370	0.13513
22.	0.80340	0.64684	0.52189	0.42196	0.34185	0.27751	0.22571	0.18394	0.15018	0.12285
23.	0.79544	0.63416	0.50669	0.40573	0.32557	0.26180	0.21095	0.17032	0.13778	0.11168
24.	0.78757	0.62172	0.49193	0.39012	0.31007	0.24698	0.19715	0.15770	0.12640	0.10153
25.	0.77977	0.60953	0.47761	0.37512	0.29530	0.23300	0.18425	0.14602	0.11597	0.09230
26.	0.77205	0.59758	0.46369	0.36069	0.28124	0.21981	0.17220	0.13520	0.10639	0.08391
27.	0.76440	0.58586	0.45019	0.34682	0.26785	0.20737	0.16093	0.12519	0.09761	0.07628
28.	0.75684	0.57437	0.43708	0.33348	0.25509	0.19563	0.15040	0.11591	0.08955	0.06934
29.	0.74934	0.56311	0.42435	0.32065	0.24295	0.18456	0.14056	0.10733	0.08215	0.06304
30.	0.74192	0.55207	0.41199	0.30832	0.23138	0.17411	0.13137	0.09938	0.07537	0.05731
31.	0.73458	0.54125	0.39999	0.29646	0.22036	0.16425	0.12277	0.09202	0.06915	0.05210
32.	0.72730	0.53063	0.38834	0.28506	0.20987	0.15496	0.11474	0.08520	0.06344	0.04736
33.	0.72010	0.52023	0.37703	0.27409	0.19987	0.14619	0.10723	0.07889	0.05820	0.04306
34.	0.71297	0.51003	0.36604	0.26355	0.19035	0.13791	0.10022	0.07305	0.05339	0.03914
35.	0.70591	0.50003	0.35538	0.25342	0.18129	0.13011	0.09366	0.06763	0.04899	0.03558
36.	0.69892	0.49022	0.34503	0.24367	0.17266	0.12274	0.08754	0.06262	0.04494	0.03235
37.	0.69200	0.48061	0.33498	0.23430	0.16444	0.11579	0.08181	0.05799	0.04123	0.02941
38.	0.68515	0.47119	0.32523	0.22529	0.15661	0.10924	0.07646	0.05369	0.03783	0.02673
39.	0.67837	0.46195	0.31575	0.21662	0.14915	0.10306	0.07146	0.04971	0.03470	0.02430
40.	0.67165	0.45289	0.30656	0.20829	0.14205	0.09722	0.06678	0.04603	0.03184	0.02209

Period	11%	12%	13%	14%	15%	16%	17%	18%	19%	20%
1.	0.90090	0.89286	0.88496	0.87719	0.86957	0.86207	0.85470	0.84746	0.84034	0.83333
2.	0.81162	0.79719	0.78315	0.76947	0.75614	0.74316	0.73051	0.71818	0.70616	0.69444
3.	0.73119	0.71178	0.69305	0.67497	0.65752	0.64066	0.62437	0.60863	0.59342	0.57870
4.	0.65873	0.63553	0.61332	0.59208	0.57175	0.55229	0.53365	0.51579	0.49867	0.48225
5.	0.59345	0.56743	0.54276	0.51937	0.49718	0.47611	0.45611	0.43711	0.41905	0.40188
6.	0.53464	0.50663	0.48032	0.45559	0.43233	0.41044	0.38984	0.37043	0.35214	0.33490
7.	0.48166	0.45235	0.42506	0.39964	0.37594	0.35383	0.33320	0.31393	0.29592	0.27908
8.	0.43393	0.40388	0.37616	0.35056	0.32690	0.30503	0.28478	0.26604	0.24867	0.23257
9.	0.39092	0.36061	0.33288	0.30751	0.28426	0.26295	0.24340	0.22546	0.20897	0.19381
10.	0.35218	0.32197	0.29459	0.26974	0.24718	0.22668	0.20804	0.19106	0.17560	0.16151
11.	0.31728	0.28748	0.26070	0.23662	0.21494	0.19542	0.17781	0.16192	0.14757	0.13459
12.	0.28584	0.25668	0.23071	0.20756	0.18691	0.16846	0.15197	0.13722	0.12400	0.11216
13.	0.25751	0.22917	0.20416	0.18207	0.16253	0.14523	0.12989	0.11629	0.10421	0.09346
14.	0.23199	0.20462	0.18068	0.15971	0.14133	0.12520	0.11102	0.09855	0.08757	0.07789
15.	0.20900	0.18270	0.15989	0.14010	0.12289	0.10793	0.09489	0.08352	0.07359	0.06491
16.	0.18829	0.16312	0.14150	0.12289	0.10686	0.09304	0.08110	0.07078	0.06184	0.05409
17.	0.16963	0.14564	0.12522	0.10780	0.09293	0.08021	0.06932	0.05998	0.05196	0.04507
18.	0.15282	0.13004	0.11081	0.09456	0.04081	0.06914	0.05925	0.05083	0.04367	0.03756
19.	0.13768	0.11611	0.09806	0.08295	0.07027	0.05961	0.05064	0.04308	0.03670	0.03130
20.	0.12403	0.10367	0.08678	0.07276	0.06110	0.05139	0.04328	0.03651	0.03084	0.02608
21.	0.11174	0.09256	0.07680	0.06383	0.05313	0.04430	0.03699	0.03094	0.02591	0.02174
22.	0.10067	0.08264	0.06796	0.05599	0.04620	0.03819	0.03162	0.02622	0.02178	0.01811
23.	0.09069	0.07379	0.06014	0.04911	0.04017	0.03292	0.02702	0.02222	0.01830	0.01509
24.	0.08170	0.06588	0.05323	0.04308	0.03493	0.02838	0.02310	0.01883	0.01538	0.01258
25.	0.07361	0.05882	0.04710	0.03779	0.03038	0.02447	0.01974	0.01596	0.01292	0.01048
26.	0.06631	0.05252	0.04168	0.03315	0.02642	0.02109	0.01687	0.01352	0.01086	0.00874
27.	0.05974	0.04689	0.03689	0.02908	0.02297	0.01818	0.01442	0.01146	0.00912	0.00728
28.	0.05382	0.04187	0.03264	0.02551	0.01997	0.01567	0.01233	0.00971	0.00767	0.00607
29.	0.04849	0.03738	0.02889	0.02237	0.01737	0.01351	0.01053	0.00823	0.00644	0.00506
30.	0.04368	0.03338	0.02557	0.01963	0.01510	0.01165	0.00900	0.00697	0.00541	0.00421
31.	0.03935	0.02980	0.02262	0.01722	0.01313	0.01004	0.00770	0.00591	0.00455	0.00351
32.	0.03545	0.02661	0.02002	0.01510	0.01142	0.00866	0.00658	0.00501	0.00382	0.00293
33.	0.03194	0.02376	0.01772	0.01325	0.00993	0.00746	0.00562	0.00425	0.00321	0.00244
34.	0.02878	0.02121	0.01568	0.01162	0.00864	0.00643	0.00480	0.00360	0.00270	0.00203
35.	0.02592	0.01894	0.01388	0.01019	0.00751	0.00555	0.00411	0.00305	0.00227	0.00169
36.	0.02335	0.01691	0.01228	0.00894	0.00653	0.00478	0.00351	0.00258	0.00191	0.00141
37.	0.02104	0.01510	0.01087	0.00784	0.00568	0.00412	0.00300	0.00219	0.00160	0.00118
38.	0.01896	0.01348	0.00962	0.00688	0.00494	0.00355	0.00256	0.00186	0.00135	0.00098
39.	0.01708	0.01204	0.00851	0.00604	0.00429	0.00306	0.00219	0.00157	0.00113	0.00082
40.	0.01538	0.01075	0.00753	0.00529	0.00373	0.00264	0.00187	0.00133	0.00095	0.00068

TABLE A.4 Present Value of an Ordinary Annuity of $1 per Period: 1%–20% $P_{A_{i,n}} = \dfrac{1 - \dfrac{1}{(1+i)^n}}{i}$

Period	1%	2%	3%	4%	5%	6%	7%	8%	9%	10%
1. . .	0.99010	0.98039	0.97087	0.96154	0.95238	0.94340	0.93458	0.92593	0.91743	0.90909
2. . .	1.97040	1.94156	1.91347	1.88609	1.85941	1.83339	1.80802	1.78326	1.75911	1.73554
3. . .	2.94099	2.88388	2.82861	2.77509	2.72325	2.67301	2.62432	2.57710	2.53129	2.48685
4. . .	3.90197	3.80773	3.71710	3.62990	3.54595	3.46511	3.38721	3.31213	3.23972	3.16987
5. . .	4.85343	4.71346	4.57971	4.45182	4.32948	4.21236	4.10020	3.99271	3.88965	3.79079
6. . .	5.79548	5.60143	5.41719	5.24214	5.07569	4.91732	4.76654	4.62288	4.48592	4.35526
7. . .	6.72819	6.47199	6.23028	6.00205	5.78637	5.58238	5.38929	5.20637	5.03295	4.86842
8. . .	7.65168	7.32548	7.01969	6.73274	6.46321	6.20979	5.97130	5.74664	5.53482	5.33493
9. . .	8.56602	8.16224	7.78611	7.43533	7.10782	6.80169	6.51523	6.24689	5.99525	5.75902
10. . .	9.47130	8.98259	8.53020	8.11090	7.72173	7.36009	7.02358	6.71008	6.41766	6.14457
11. . .	10.36763	9.78685	9.25262	8.76048	8.30641	7.88687	7.49867	7.13896	6.80519	6.49506
12. . .	11.25508	10.57534	9.95400	9.38507	8.86325	8.38384	7.94269	7.53608	7.16073	6.81369
13. . .	12.13374	11.34837	10.63496	9.98565	9.39357	8.85268	8.35765	7.90378	7.48690	7.10336
14. . .	13.00370	12.10625	11.29607	10.56312	9.89864	9.29498	8.74547	8.24424	7.78615	7.36669
15. . .	13.86505	12.84926	11.93794	11.11839	10.37966	9.71225	9.10791	8.55948	8.06069	7.60608
16. . .	14.71787	13.57771	12.56110	11.65230	10.83777	10.10590	9.44665	8.85137	8.31256	7.82371
17. . .	15.56225	14.29187	13.16612	12.16567	11.27407	10.47726	9.76322	9.12164	8.54363	8.02155
18. . .	16.39827	14.99203	13.75351	12.65930	11.68959	10.82760	10.05909	9.37189	8.75563	8.20141
19. . .	17.22601	15.67846	14.32380	13.13394	12.08532	11.15812	10.33560	9.60360	8.95011	8.36492
20. . .	18.04555	16.35143	14.87747	13.59033	12.46221	11.46992	10.59401	9.81815	9.12855	8.51356
21. . .	18.85698	17.01121	15.41502	14.02916	12.82115	11.76408	10.83553	10.01680	9.29224	8.64869
22. . .	19.66038	17.65805	15.93692	14.45112	13.16300	12.04158	11.06124	10.20074	9.44243	8.77154
23. . .	20.45582	18.29220	16.44361	14.85684	13.48857	12.30338	11.27219	10.37106	9.58021	8.88322
24. . .	21.24339	18.91393	16.93554	15.24696	13.79864	12.55036	11.46933	10.52876	9.70661	8.98474
25. . .	22.02316	19.52346	17.41315	15.62208	14.09394	12.78336	11.65358	10.67478	9.82258	9.07704
26. . .	22.79520	20.12104	17.87684	15.98277	14.37519	13.00317	11.82578	10.80998	9.92897	9.16095
27. . .	23.55961	20.70690	18.32703	16.32959	14.64303	13.21053	11.98671	10.93516	10.02658	9.23722
28. . .	24.31644	21.28127	18.76411	16.66306	14.89813	13.40616	12.13711	11.05108	10.11613	9.30657
29. . .	25.06579	21.84438	19.18845	16.98371	15.14107	13.59072	12.27767	11.15841	10.19828	9.36961
30. . .	25.80771	22.39646	19.60044	17.29203	15.37245	13.76483	12.40904	11.25778	10.27365	9.42691
31. . .	26.54229	22.93770	20.00043	17.58849	15.59281	13.92909	12.53181	11.34980	10.34280	9.47901
32. . .	27.26959	23.46833	20.38877	17.87355	15.80268	14.08404	12.64656	11.43500	10.40624	9.52638
33. . .	27.98969	23.98856	20.76579	18.14765	16.00255	14.23023	12.75379	11.51389	10.46444	9.56943
34. . .	28.70267	24.49589	21.13184	18.41120	16.19290	14.36814	12.85401	11.58693	10.51784	9.60857
35. . .	29.40858	24.99862	21.48722	18.66461	16.37419	14.49825	12.94767	11.65457	10.56682	9.64416
36. . .	30.10751	25.48884	21.83225	18.90828	16.54685	14.62099	13.03521	11.71719	10.61176	9.67651
37. . .	30.79951	25.96945	22.16724	19.14258	16.71129	14.73678	13.11702	11.77518	10.65299	9.70592
38. . .	31.48466	26.44064	22.49246	19.36786	16.86789	14.84602	13.19347	11.82887	10.69082	9.73265
39. . .	32.16303	26.90259	22.80822	19.58448	17.01704	14.94907	13.26493	11.87858	10.72552	9.75696
40. . .	32.83469	27.35548	23.11477	19.79277	17.15909	15.04630	13.33171	11.92461	10.75736	9.77905

Period	11%	12%	13%	14%	15%	16%	17%	18%	19%	20%
1.	0.90090	0.89286	0.88496	0.87719	0.86957	0.86207	0.85470	0.84746	0.84034	0.83333
2.	1.71252	1.69005	1.66810	1.64666	1.62571	1.60523	1.58521	1.56564	1.54650	1.52778
3.	2.44371	2.40183	2.36115	2.32163	2.28323	2.24589	2.20958	2.17427	2.13992	2.10648
4.	3.10245	3.03735	2.97447	2.91371	2.85498	2.79818	2.74324	2.69006	2.63859	2.58873
5.	3.69590	3.60478	3.51723	3.43308	3.35216	3.27429	3.19935	3.12717	3.05763	2.99061
6.	4.23054	4.11141	3.99755	3.88867	3.78448	3.68474	3.58918	3.49760	3.40978	3.32551
7.	4.71220	4.56376	4.42261	4.28830	4.16042	4.03857	3.92238	3.81153	3.70570	3.60459
8.	5.14612	4.96764	4.79877	4.63886	4.48732	4.34359	4.20716	4.07757	3.95437	3.83716
9.	5.53705	5.32825	5.13166	4.94637	4.77158	4.60654	4.45057	3.30302	4.16333	4.03097
10.	5.88923	5.65022	5.42624	5.21612	5.01877	4.83323	4.65860	4.49409	4.33893	4.19247
11.	6.20652	5.93770	5.68694	5.45273	5.23371	5.02864	4.83641	4.65601	4.48650	4.32706
12.	6.49236	6.19437	5.91765	5.66029	5.42062	5.19711	4.98839	4.79322	4.61050	4.43922
13.	6.74987	6.42355	6.12181	5.84236	5.58315	5.34233	5.11828	4.90951	4.71471	4.53268
14.	6.98187	6.62817	6.30249	6.00207	5.72448	5.46753	5.22930	5.00806	4.80228	4.61057
15.	7.19087	6.81086	6.46238	6.14217	5.84737	5.57546	5.32419	5.09158	4.87586	4.67547
16.	7.37916	6.97399	6.60388	6.26506	5.95423	5.66850	5.40529	5.16235	4.39770	4.72956
17.	7.54879	7.11963	6.72909	6.37286	6.04716	5.74870	5.47461	5.22233	4.98966	4.77463
18.	7.70162	7.24967	6.83991	6.46742	6.12797	5.81785	5.53385	5.27316	5.03333	4.81219
19.	7.83929	7.36578	6.93797	6.55037	6.19823	5.87746	5.58449	5.31624	5.07003	4.84350
20.	7.96333	7.46944	7.02475	6.62313	6.25933	5.92884	5.62777	5.35275	5.10086	4.86958
21.	8.07507	7.56200	7.10155	6.68696	6.31246	5.97314	5.66476	5.38368	5.12677	4.89132
22.	8.17574	7.64465	7.16951	6.74294	6.35866	6.01133	5.69637	5.40990	5.14855	4.90943
23.	8.26643	7.71843	7.22966	6.79206	6.39884	6.04425	5.72340	5.43212	5.16685	4.92453
24.	8.34814	7.78432	7.28288	6.83514	6.43377	6.07263	5.74649	5.45095	5.18223	4.93710
25.	8.42174	7.84314	7.32998	6.87293	6.46415	6.09709	5.76623	5.46691	5.19515	4.94759
26.	8.48806	7.89566	7.37167	6.90608	6.49056	6.11818	5.78311	5.48043	5.20601	4.95632
27.	8.54780	7.94255	7.40856	6.93515	6.51353	6.13636	5.79753	5.49189	5.21513	4.96360
28.	8.60162	7.98442	7.44120	6.96066	6.53351	6.15204	5.80985	5.50160	5.22280	4.96967
29.	8.65011	8.02181	7.47009	6.98304	6.55088	6.16555	5.82039	5.50983	5.22924	4.97472
30.	8.69379	8.05518	7.49565	7.00266	6.56598	6.17720	5.82939	5.51681	5.23466	4.97894
31.	8.73315	8.08499	7.51828	7.01988	6.57911	6.18724	5.83709	5.52272	5.23921	4.98245
32.	8.76860	8.11159	7.53830	7.03498	6.59053	6.19590	5.84366	5.52773	5.24303	4.98537
33.	8.80054	8.13535	7.55602	7.04823	6.60046	6.20336	5.84928	5.53197	5.24625	4.98781
34.	8.82932	8.15656	7.57170	7.05985	6.60910	6.20979	5.85409	5.53557	5.24895	4.98984
35.	8.85524	8.17550	7.58557	7.07005	6.61661	6.21534	5.85820	5.53862	5.25122	4.99154
36.	8.87859	8.19241	7.59785	7.07899	6.62314	6.22012	5.86171	5.54120	5.25312	4.99295
37.	8.89963	8.20751	7.60872	7.08683	6.62881	6.22424	5.86471	5.54339	5.25472	4.99412
38.	8.91859	8.22099	7.61833	7.09371	6.63375	6.22779	5.86727	5.54525	5.25607	4.99510
39.	8.93567	8.23303	7.62684	7.09975	6.63805	6.23086	5.86946	5.54682	5.25720	4.99592
40.	8.95105	8.24378	7.63438	7.10504	6.64178	6.23350	5.87133	5.54815	5.25815	4.99660

Real World Companies Index

New Terms Index

Subject Index

CHART OF ACCOUNTS FOR CHAPTERS 1–11

Account Number	Account Title
Asset Accounts	
100	Cash
101	Petty Cash
103	Accounts Receivable
104	Allowance for Uncollectible Accounts
105	Merchandise Inventory
106	Repair Parts Inventory
107	Supplies on Hand
108	Prepaid Insurance
109	Store Supplies on Hand
110	Prepaid Advertising
111	Prepaid Printing Expense
112	Prepaid Rent
113	Receivable from Employees
114	Receivable from Insurance Company
115	Rent Receivable
120	Notes Receivable
121	Interest Receivable
125	Salvaged Materials
130	Land
140	Buildings
141	Accumulated Depreciation–Buildings
150	Trucks
151	Accumulated Depreciation–Trucks
152	Automobiles
153	Accumulated Depreciation–Automobiles
160	Office Furniture
161	Accumulated Depreciation–Office Furniture
165	Furniture and Fixtures
166	Accumulated Depreciation–Furniture and Fixtures
170	Equipment
171	Accumulated Depreciation–Equipment
172	Office Equipment
173	Accumulated Depreciation–Office Equipment
174	Store Fixtures
175	Accumulated Depreciation–Store Fixtures
180	Machinery
181	Accumulated Depreciation–Machinery
185	Other Assets
190	Ore Deposits
191	Accumulated Depletion–Ore Deposits
192	Land Improvements
193	Accumulated Depreciation–Land Improvements
194	Leasehold
195	Leasehold Improvements

Number Account	Title
Asset Accounts (continued)	
196	Franchises
197	Patents
198	Copyrights
199	Goodwill
Liability Accounts	
200	Accounts Payable
201	Notes Payable
202	Discount on Notes Payable
203	Loan Payable
204	Interest Payable
205	Vouchers Payable
206	Salaries Payable (or Wages Payable)
207	Sales Salaries Payable
208	Office Salaries Payable
209	Officers' Salaries Payable
210	Unearned Delivery Fees
211	Unearned Subscriptions
212	Unearned Ticket Fees
213	Unearned Laundry Fees
214	Unearned Management Fees
215	Unearned Rent
216	Unearned Service Fees
217	Unearned Commissions
218	Mortgage Note Payment
219	Travel Expenses Payable
220	Employees' Federal Income Taxes Payable
221	FICA Taxes Payable
222	Medical Insurance Premiums Payable
223	Employees' State Income Taxes Payable
224	Federal Unemployment Taxes Payable
225	State Unemployment Taxes Payable
226	Sales Tax Payable
227	Federal Excise Tax Payable
230	Estimated Product Warranty Payable
232	Estimated Property Taxes Payable
235	Other Liabilities
240	Commissions Payable
Stockholder's Equity Accounts	
300	Capital Stock
310	Retained Earnings
320	Dividends